C000007480

Microsoft®

MCSE
Training Kit

Microsoft®
Windows® 2000
Accelerated

PUBLISHED BY
Microsoft Press
A Division of Microsoft Corporation
One Microsoft Way
Redmond, Washington 98052-6399

Copyright © 2000 by Microsoft Corporation

All rights reserved. No part of the contents of this book may be reproduced or transmitted in any form or by any means without the written permission of the publisher.

Library of Congress Cataloging-in-Publication Data
MCSE Training Kit. Microsoft Windows 2000 Accelerated / Microsoft Corporation.
     p. cm.
   Includes index.
   ISBN 0-7356-1249-8
   1. Microsoft Windows (Computer file) 2. Operating Systems (Computers). I. Title:
Microsoft Windows 2000 accelerated. II. Microsoft Corporation.
QA76.76.O63 M426 2000
005.4'4769--dc21   00-045264

Printed and bound in the United States of America.

1 2 3 4 5 6 7 8 9   QWT   5 4 3 2 1 0

Distributed in Canada by Penguin Books Canada Limited.

A CIP catalogue record for this book is available from the British Library.

Microsoft Press books are available through booksellers and distributors worldwide. For further information about international editions, contact your local Microsoft Corporation office or contact Microsoft Press International directly at fax (425) 936-7329. Visit our Web site at mspress.microsoft.com. Send comments to *tkinput@microsoft.com.*

Active Directory, BackOffice, FrontPage, Microsoft, Microsoft Press, MS-DOS, MSDN, Visual Basic, Visual C++, Windows, and Windows NT are either registered trademarks or trademarks of Microsoft Corporation in the United States and/or other countries. Other product and company names mentioned herein may be the trademarks of their respective owners.

Unless otherwise noted, the example companies, organizations, products, people, and events depicted herein are fictitious. No association with any real company, organization, product, person, or event is intended or should be inferred.

Acquisitions Editor: Thomas Pohlmann
Project Editor: Lynn Finnel
Author: Jeff Madden
Technical Editor: Nick Cavalancia
Copy Editor: Uma Kukathas
Desktop Publisher: Design Laboratory, Inc.

Contents

About This Book

Welcome to *MCSE Training Kit—Microsoft Windows 2000 Accelerated*. This kit presents information about the Microsoft Windows 2000 family of products and prepares you to install, configure, administer, and support Microsoft Windows 2000 Professional and Microsoft Windows 2000 Server. This kit introduces the various tools for administering and configuring Windows 2000 including the Microsoft Management Console, Task Scheduler, Active Directory service, network protocols, and many other topics.

However, this kit does assume you meet certain minimum prerequisites. This book is designed for use by seasoned Microsoft Windows NT 4 professionals. As such, certain topics; like NTFS permissions, domains, trust relationships, and so on are not covered in any detail. What is covered is the knowledge and skills a Windows NT 4 professional needs to implement and support a computer network for an enterprise-size company.

This book is divided into parts that loosely relate to the four parts of the 70-240, Microsoft Windows 2000 Accelerated Exam for MCPs Certified on Microsoft Windows NT 4 certification exam. However, while this training kit is organized around the exam objectives, there is no guarantee that the exam will present questions in this sequence. In fact, the questions for the exam will be displayed randomly from across all four sections.

The parts are divided into chapters. Each chapter in this book is divided into lessons. Some of the lessons include hands-on procedures that allow you to practice or demonstrate a particular concept or skill. Each lesson ends with a short summary and each chapter ends with a set of review questions to test your knowledge of the chapter material.

The "Getting Started" section of this chapter provides important setup instructions that describe the hardware and software requirements to complete the procedures in this course. It also provides information about the networking configuration necessary to complete some of the hands-on procedures. Read through this section thoroughly before you start the lessons.

Intended Audience

While anyone who wants to learn more about Windows 2000 Professional and Windows 2000 Server will find this book useful, this book was developed for seasoned information technology (IT) professionals who wish to learn about Windows 2000 without receiving redundant information.

Note For more information on becoming a Microsoft Certified Systems Engineer, see the section, "The Microsoft Certified Professional Program," later in this chapter.

Prerequisites

This book is designed for seasoned Windows NT 4 professionals who want to prepare for the 70-240, Microsoft Windows 2000 Accelerated Exam for MCPs Certified on Microsoft Windows NT 4 certification exam. Before you can attempt the 70-240 exam, you must have already passed three Windows NT 4 certification exams (70-067, 70-068, and 70-073). This book assumes that you have the skills and knowledge listed in the following objectives and therefore content may not be presented on these skills. For example, NTFS permissions are basically the same in Windows 2000 as they were in Windows NT 4. For that reason, this book will not fully explain NTFS permissions. NTFS information is limited to what makes sense for the flow and presentation of content in the appropriate chapters. There are other content areas, such as domains, trust relationships, and so on, that will not be covered because they will be assumed as prerequisite knowledge for anyone qualified to take the 70-240 exam.

The following objectives list the skills and knowledge you must have before attempting to prepare for the 70-240 exam.

Skills Being Measured on Exam 70-067

This certification exam measures your ability to implement, administer, and troubleshoot information systems that incorporate Windows NT Server version 4.0 in a simple computing environment. A simple computing environment is typically a homogeneous LAN. It might include one or more servers, a single domain, and a single location; and it might have file-sharing and print-sharing capabilities. Before taking the exam, you should be proficient in the following job skills.

Planning

Plan the disk drive configuration for various requirements. Requirements include:

- Choosing a file system
- Choosing a fault-tolerance method

Choose a protocol for various situations. Protocols include:

- TCP/IP
- NWLink IPX/SPX Compatible Transport
- NetBEUI

Installation and Configuration

Install Windows NT Server on Intel-based platforms.

Install Windows NT Server to perform various server roles. Server roles include:

- Primary domain controller
- Backup domain controller
- Member server

Install Windows NT Server by using various methods. Installation methods include:

- CD-ROM
- Over-the-network
- Network Client Administrator
- Express versus custom

Configure protocols and protocol bindings. Protocols include:

- TCP/IP
- NWLink IPX/SPX Compatible Transport
- NetBEUI

Configure network adapters. Considerations include:

- Changing IRQ, IObase, and memory addresses
- Configuring multiple adapters

Configure Windows NT Server core services. Services include:

- Directory Replicator
- License Manager
- Other services

Configure peripherals and devices. Peripherals and devices include:

- Communication devices
- SCSI devices
- Tape device drivers
- UPS devices and UPS service
- Mouse drivers, display drivers, and keyboard drivers

Configure hard disks to meet various requirements. Requirements include:

- Allocating disk space capacity
- Providing redundancy
- Improving performance
- Providing security
- Formatting

Configure printers. Tasks include:

- Adding and configuring a printer
- Implementing a printer pool
- Setting print priorities

Configure a Windows NT Server computer for various types of client computers. Client computer types include:

- Windows NT Workstation
- Microsoft Windows 95
- Microsoft MS-DOS-based

Managing Resources

Manage user and group accounts. Considerations include:

- Managing Windows NT groups
- Managing Windows NT user rights
- Managing Windows NT groups
- Administering account policies
- Auditing changes to the user account database

Create and manage policies and profiles for various situations. Policies and profiles include:

- Local user profiles
- Roaming user profiles
- System policies

Administer remote servers from various types of client computers. Client computer types include:

- Windows 95
- Windows NT Workstation

Manage disk resources. Tasks include:

- Copying and moving files between file systems
- Creating and sharing resources
- Implementing permissions and security
- Establishing file auditing

Connectivity

Configure Windows NT Server for interoperability with NetWare servers by using various tools. Tools include:

- Gateway Service for NetWare
- Migration Tool for NetWare

Install and configure Remote Access Service (RAS). Configuration options include:

- Configuring RAS communications
- Configuring RAS protocols
- Configuring RAS security
- Configuring Dial-Up Networking clients

Monitoring and Optimization

Monitor performance of various functions by using Performance Monitor. Functions include:

- Processor
- Memory
- Disk
- Network

Identify performance bottlenecks.

Troubleshooting

Choose the appropriate course of action to take to resolve installation failures.

Choose the appropriate course of action to take to resolve boot failures.

Choose the appropriate course of action to take to resolve configuration errors.

Choose the appropriate course of action to take to resolve printer problems.

Choose the appropriate course of action to take to resolve RAS problems.

Choose the appropriate course of action to take to resolve connectivity problems.

Choose the appropriate course of action to take to resolve resource access problems and permission problems.

Choose the appropriate course of action to take to resolve fault-tolerance failures. Fault-tolerance methods include:

- Tape backup
- Mirroring
- Stripe set with parity
- Disk duplexing

Skills Being Measured on Exam 70-068

This certification exam measures your ability to implement, administer, and troubleshoot information systems that incorporate Windows NT Server version 4.0 in an enterprise computing environment. An enterprise computing environment is typically a heterogeneous WAN. It might include multiple servers and multiple domains, and it might run sophisticated server applications. Before taking the exam, you should be proficient in the following job skills.

Planning

Plan the implementation of a directory services architecture. Considerations include:

- Selecting the appropriate domain model
- Supporting a single logon account
- Allowing users to access resources in different domains

Plan the disk drive configuration for various requirements. Requirements include choosing a fault-tolerance method.

Choose a protocol for various situations. Protocols include:

- TCP/IP
- TCP/IP with DHCP and WINS
- NWLink IPX/SPX Compatible Transport Protocol
- Data Link Control (DLC)
- AppleTalk

Installation and Configuration

Install Windows NT Server to perform various server roles. Server roles include:

- Primary domain controller
- Backup domain controller
- Member server

Configure protocols and protocol bindings. Protocols include:

- TCP/IP
- TCP/IP with DHCP and WINS

- NWLink IPX/SPX Compatible Transport Protocol
- DLC
- AppleTalk

Configure Windows NT Server core services. Services include:

- Directory Replicator
- Computer Browser

Configure hard disks to meet various requirements. Requirements include:

- Providing redundancy
- Improving performance

Configure printers. Tasks include:

- Adding and configuring a printer
- Implementing a printer pool
- Setting print priorities

Configure a Windows NT Server computer for various types of client computers. Client computer types include:

- Windows NT Workstation
- Windows 95
- Macintosh

Managing Resources

Manage user and group accounts. Considerations include:

- Managing Windows NT user accounts
- Managing Windows NT user rights
- Managing Windows NT groups
- Administering account policies
- Auditing changes to the user account database

Create and manage policies and profiles for various situations. Policies and profiles include:

- Local user profiles
- Roaming user profiles
- System policies

Administer remote servers from various types of client computers. Client computer types include:

- Windows 95
- Windows NT Workstation

Manage disk resources. Tasks include:

- Creating and sharing resources
- Implementing permissions and security
- Establishing file auditing

Connectivity

Configure Windows NT Server for interoperability with NetWare servers by using various tools. Tools include:

- Gateway Service for NetWare
- Migration Tool for NetWare

Install and configure multiprotocol routing to serve various functions. Functions include:

- Internet router
- BOOTP/DHCP Relay Agent
- IPX router

Install and configure Internet Information Server.

Install and configure Internet services. Services include:

- World Wide Web
- DNS
- Intranet

Install and configure Remote Access Service (RAS). Configuration options include:

- Configuring RAS communications
- Configuring RAS protocols
- Configuring RAS security

Monitoring and Optimization

Establish a baseline for measuring system performance. Tasks include creating a database of measurement data.

Monitor performance of various functions by using Performance Monitor. Functions include:

- Processor
- Memory
- Disk
- Network

Monitor network traffic by using Network Monitor. Tasks include:

- Collecting data
- Presenting data
- Filtering data

Identify performance bottlenecks.

Optimize performance for various results. Results include:

- Controlling network traffic
- Controlling server load

Troubleshooting

Choose the appropriate course of action to take to resolve installation failures.

Choose the appropriate course of action to take to resolve boot failures.

Choose the appropriate course of action to take to resolve configuration errors. Tasks include:

- Backing up and restoring the registry
- Editing the registry

Choose the appropriate course of action to take to resolve printer problems.

Choose the appropriate course of action to take to resolve RAS problems.

Choose the appropriate course of action to take to resolve connectivity problems.

Choose the appropriate course of action to take to resolve resource access and permission problems.

Choose the appropriate course of action to take to resolve fault-tolerance failures. Fault-tolerance methods include:

- Tape backup
- Mirroring
- Stripe set with parity

Perform advanced problem resolution. Tasks include:

- Diagnosing and interpreting a blue screen
- Configuring a memory dump
- Using the Event Log service

Skills Being Measured on Exam 70-073

This certification exam measures your ability to implement, administer, and troubleshoot information systems that incorporate Windows NT Workstation version 4.0. Before taking the exam, you should be proficient in the following job skills.

Planning

Create unattended installation files.

Plan strategies for sharing and securing resources.

Choose the appropriate file system to use in a given situation. File systems and situations include:

- NTFS
- FAT
- HPFS
- Security
- Dual-boot systems

Installation and Configuration

Install Windows NT Workstation on an Intel platform in a given situation.

Set up a dual-boot system in a given situation.

Remove Windows NT Workstation in a given situation.

Install, configure, and remove hardware components for a given situation. Hardware components include:

- Network adapter drivers
- SCSI device drivers
- Tape device drivers
- UPS
- Multimedia devices
- Display drivers
- Keyboard drivers
- Mouse drivers

Use Control Panel applications to configure a Windows NT Workstation computer in a given situation.

Upgrade to Windows NT Workstation 4.0 in a given situation.

Configure server-based installation for wide-scale deployment in a given situation.

Managing Resources

Create and manage local user accounts and local group accounts to meet given requirements.

Set up and modify user profiles.

Set up shared folders and permissions.

Set permissions on NTFS partitions, folders, and files.

Install and configure printers in a given environment.

Connectivity

Add and configure the network components of Windows NT Workstation.

Use various methods to access network resources.

Implement Windows NT Workstation as a client in a NetWare environment.

Use various configurations to install Windows NT Workstation as a TCP/IP client.

Configure and install Dial-Up Networking in a given situation.

Configure Microsoft Peer Web Services in a given situation.

Running Applications

Start applications on Intel and RISC platforms in various operating system environments.

Start applications at various priorities.

Monitoring and Optimization

Monitor system performance by using various tools.

Identify and resolve a given performance problem.

Optimize system performance in various areas.

Troubleshooting

Choose the appropriate course of action to take when the boot process fails.

Choose the appropriate course of action to take when a print job fails.

Choose the appropriate course of action to take when the installation process fails.

Choose the appropriate course of action to take when an application fails.

Choose the appropriate course of action to take when a user cannot access a resource.

Modify the registry using the appropriate tool in a given situation.

Implement advanced techniques to resolve various problems. .

Reference Materials

You might find the following reference materials useful:

- Windows 2000 white papers and case studies, available online at *http://www.microsoft.com/windows/server*

- Windows 2000 Server Help, available on the Start menu when Windows 2000 Server is installed

- Windows 2000 Support Tools Help, available on the Start, Programs, Windows 2000 Support Tools menu when Windows 2000 Support Tools are installed

- *Microsoft Windows 2000 Server Resource Kit*, in print format or on CD-ROM

- *MCP Magazine Online*. Available online at *http://www.mcpmag.com*.

- Microsoft Web site (*http://www.microsoft.com*) and *Microsoft TechNet Technical Plus*, available monthly on CD-ROM and on the Microsoft Web site.

- *MCSE Training Kit–Microsoft Windows 2000 Professional*. Microsoft Press, 2000.

- *MCSE Training Kit–Networking Essentials Plus*, 3rd ed. Microsoft Press, 1999.

- Silberschatz A and P. Galvin. *Operating System Concepts*, 5th ed. Addison-Wesley Publishing Company, 1998. This is just one of many good text books that explores operating systems fundamentals.

- *Windows 2000 Magazine*. This online magazine can be found at *http://www.winntmag.com* and is published by Duke Communications.

- Sysinternals Freeware Web site: *http://www.sysinternals.com*.

About the CD-ROM

The Supplemental Course Materials CD-ROM contains files used in hands-on exercises. These files can be used directly from the CD-ROM or copied onto your hard drive. For more information regarding the contents and use of the Supplemental Course Materials CD-ROM, see the ReadMe.txt on the CD.

Features of This Book

Each chapter opens with a "Before You Begin" section, which prepares you for completing the chapter.

The chapters are then broken into lessons. Whenever possible, lessons contain practices that give you an opportunity to use the skills being presented or explore the part of the application being described. All practices offer step-by-step procedures that are identified with a bullet symbol like the one to the left of this paragraph.

The "Review" section at the end of the chapter allows you to test what you have learned in the chapter's lessons. Appendix A, "Questions and Answers," contains all of the book's questions and corresponding answers.

Notes

Several types of notes appear throughout the lessons.

- Notes marked **Tip** contain explanations of possible results or alternative methods.

- Notes marked **Important** contain information that is essential to completing a task.

- Notes marked **Note** contain supplemental information.

- Notes marked **Caution** contain warnings about possible loss of data.

Conventions

The following conventions are used throughout this book.

Notational Conventions

- Characters or commands that you type appear in **bold** type.

- *Italic* in syntax statements indicates placeholders for variable information. *Italic* is also used for book titles.

- Names of files and folders appear in Title Caps, except when you are to type them directly. Unless otherwise indicated, you can use all lowercase letters when you type a filename in a dialog box or at a command prompt.

- Filename extensions appear in all lowercase.

- Acronyms appear in all uppercase.

- Monospace type represents code samples, examples of screen text, or entries that you might type at a command prompt or in initialization files.

- Square brackets [ ] are used in syntax statements to enclose optional items. For example, [*filename*] in command syntax indicates that you can choose to type a filename with the command. Type only the information within the brackets, not the brackets themselves.

- Braces { } are used in syntax statements to enclose required items. Type only the information within the braces, not the braces themselves.

- Icons represent specific sections in the book as follows:

Icon	Represents
	A file contained on the CD-ROM. Some files are needed to complete a hands-on practice. The purpose of the file and its location are described in the accompanying text.
	A multimedia presentation. You will find the applicable multimedia presentation on the course compact disc.
	A hands-on practice. You should perform the practice to give yourself an opportunity to use the skills being presented in the lesson.
	Chapter review questions. These questions at the end of each chapter allow you to test what you have learned in the lessons. You will find the answers to the review questions in the Questions and Answers section at the end of the book.

Keyboard Conventions

- A plus sign (+) between two key names means that you must press those keys at the same time. For example, "Press Alt+Tab" means that you hold down Alt while you press Tab.

- A comma (,) between two or more key names means that you must press each of the keys consecutively, not together. For example, "Press Alt, F, X" means that you press and release each key in sequence. "Press Alt+W, L" means that you first press Alt and W together, and then release them and press L.

- You can choose menu commands with the keyboard. Press the Alt key to activate the menu bar, and then sequentially press the keys that correspond to the highlighted or underlined letter of the menu name and the command name. For some commands, you can also press a key combination listed on the menu.

- You can select or clear check boxes or option buttons in dialog boxes with the keyboard. Press the Alt key, and then press the key that corresponds to the underlined letter of the option name. Or you can press Tab until the option is highlighted, and then press the spacebar to select or clear the check box or option button.

- You can cancel the display of a dialog box by pressing the Esc key.

Chapter and Appendix Overview

This self-paced training course combines notes, hands-on procedures, and review questions to teach you how to install, configure, administer, and support Windows 2000 Professional. It is designed to be completed from beginning to end, but you can choose a customized track and complete only the sections that interest you. (See the next section, "Finding the Best Starting Point for You," for more information.) If you choose the customized track option, see the "Before You Begin" section in each chapter. Any hands-on procedures that require preliminary work from preceding chapters refer to the appropriate chapters.

The book is divided into the following Sections and Chapters:

- The "About This Book" section contains a self-paced training overview and introduces the components of this training. Read this section thoroughly to get the greatest educational value from this self-paced training and to plan which lessons you will complete.

- The "Introduction to Windows 2000" chapter presents an overview of the Windows 2000 operating system and the four products that make up this family. It introduces some of the new features and benefits of Windows 2000 and explains why Windows 2000 is easier to use and manage and provides greater compatibility, file management capabilities, and security than previous versions of Windows. This chapter also provides an introduction to workgroups and domains.

- Part 1: "Microsoft Windows 2000 Professional." This part contains most of the information that relates to the Windows 2000 Professional portion of the 70-240 exam. The chapters in Part 1 primarily use Windows 2000 Professional during the various hands-on practices and exercises. However, much of the information presented here is also applicable to Windows 2000 Server.

- Chapter 1, "Installing Windows 2000 Professional," steps you through the process of installing from a CD-ROM, and as a hands-on exercise, has you install Windows 2000 Professional on your computer. The chapter then discusses installing Windows 2000 over the network and how to troubleshoot installation problems. Once the basic installation methods are covered, the chapter moves into more advanced installation techniques such as automating the installation, using disk duplication to deploy and performing remote installations. The chapter describes what to expect when upgrading from prior versions of Windows and concludes with a discussion on installing Service Packs.

- Chapter 2: "Managing Hardware Devices and Drivers," gives you an overview of installing, configuring, and managing hardware devices and drivers. Microsoft Management Console (MMC) is introduced and used throughout this chapter. The chapter covers installing hardware (both Plug and Play and non-Plug and Play devices), disk management, disk quotas, power management, multiple processors, and monitoring system performance.

- Chapter 3, "Managing Resources," covers using NTFS permissions to manage files and folders. This includes sharing, compression, and determining access. In addition, this chapter explains how to setup and manager printers in a Windows 2000 environment.

- Chapter 4, "Managing User Accounts," explains how you can use user accounts to create consistent user environments across multiple systems. This chapter covers planning, creating, configuring, and troubleshooting user accounts.

- Chapter 5, "Managing Network Protocols and Services," presents the information necessary to configure TCP/IP and to install other network protocols, including NWLink, NetBIOS Enhanced User Interface (NetBEUI), and Data Link Control (DLC). The chapter also discusses the process for configuring *network bindings,* which are links that enable communication between network adapter cards, protocols, and services.

- Chapter 6, "Monitoring and Optimizing System Performance," discusses the various tools that you can use to monitor and then optimize the performance of your system. This includes tools like Task Scheduler, Backup Wizard, control sets, recovery console and more.

- Chapter 7, "Managing Security," discusses several methods to enhance security for Windows 2000. This includes using groups, policies, auditing, and the Encrypting File System (EFS).

- Part 2: "Network Infrastructure." This part contains most of the information that relates to the Network Infrastructure portion of the 70-240 exam. This includes various network protocols and services. The chapters in this part primarily use Windows 2000 Server during the various hands-on practices and exercises, which is why the first chapter in this section installs Windows 2000 Server. However, much of the information presented here is also applicable to Windows 2000 Professional.

- Chapter 8, "Installing Windows 2000 Server," explains the process of installing Windows 2000 Server. It outlines the type of information you should gather to prepare for your installation and describes the steps you should take before you begin. The chapter includes the phases of a normal installation and a discussion of upgrading to Windows 2000 Server. In addition, there is information on troubleshooting installation problems and automating the installation.

- Chapter 9, "Managing Network Protocols," reviews the common network protocols (TCP/IP, NWLink) and then discusses IPSec in detail. IPSec is a new protocol. It has built-in security features that may make it the protocol of the future for Internet applications.

- Chapter 10, "Managing Domain Name System," explains how DNS is used to resolve host names on your network and across the public Internet. Microsoft Windows 2000 includes an enhanced version of DNS. This chapter also explains how to work with DNS zones. This includes implementing a delegated zone, and configuring zones for dynamic updates.

- Chapter 11, "Managing DHCP," explains how DHCP is used to manage and configure client computers on your network from a central Windows 2000 server. You will learn how to identify the primary components of DHCP, install and configure DHCP on both a client and server, and troubleshoot DHCP.

- Chapter 12, "Managing Remote Access," explains how to implement Remote Access Services to provide your clients the ability to access network resources from the road or their home. You will learn how to implement secure connections with techniques such as VPNs.

- Chapter 13, "Managing Windows Internet Name Service (WINS)," explains how WINS is used to resolve host names on your network. You will also learn how to identify the primary components of WINS, install and configure WINS, and troubleshoot WINS on Windows 2000.

- Chapter 14, "Managing Network Address Translation (NAT)," describes the network address translation (NAT) protocol, which allows a network with private addresses to access information on the Internet through an IP translation process. You will learn how to configure your home network or small office network to share a single connection to the Internet with NAT.

- Chapter 15, "Managing Microsoft Certificate Services," explains the concepts of certificates, which are fundamental elements of the Microsoft Public Key Infrastructure (PKI). You will learn how to install and configure certificates.

- Part 3: "Active Directory Directory Service." This part contains most of the information that relates to the Active Directory service portion of the 70-240 exam. This includes installing and configuring, managing network protocols, configuring desktops, and maintaining security. The chapters in this section primarily use Windows 2000 Server during the various hands-on practices and exercises. However, much of the information presented here is also applicable to Windows 2000 Professional.

- Chapter 16, "Introduction to Active Directory Directory Service," provides you with an overview of Active Directory, its components, and administration tasks.

- Chapter 17, "Installing and Configuring Active Directory Directory Service," walks you through the steps of installing Active Directory using the Active Directory Installation wizard, and shows you how to implement an Organizational Unit (OU) structure and provides procedures for setting OU properties. This chapter also introduces you to configuring site settings and inter-site replication, and discusses the tasks necessary for configuring server settings.

- Chapter 18, "Managing Domain Name System for Active Directory," explores the benefits of using Active Directory–integrated zones and provides practice in configuring zones. It also discusses zone replication and transfer and provides information on troubleshooting an Active Directory DNS configuration.

- Chapter 19, "Managing Active Directory Components," goes beyond setup and configuration. It includes locating objects, assigning permissions to objects, publishing resources, moving objects within and between domains, delegating administrative control to organizational units (OUs), backing up and restoring, troubleshooting, monitoring performance, and diagnosing Active Directoryproblems. This chapter details Active Directory administrative tasks, including how to use performance monitoring tools, diagnostic tools, and shared folder monitoring.

- Chapter 20, "Managing Desktop Configurations Using Group Policies and Remote Installation Services," explains the use of both group policies and Remote Installation Services (RIS) to maintain a consistent desktop configuration across a corporation. Group policies can be used to manage desktop configurations for groups of computers and users. Group policy is very flexible and includes options for registry-based policy settings, security settings, application management, scripts, computer startup and shutdown, logon and logoff, and folder redirection. RIS can be used to set up new client computers remotely without the need to physically visit each client machine.

- Chapter 21, "Managing Active Directory Security Solutions, " discusses the use of security settings to determine a system's security configuration, including auditing, using security logs, user rights, using security templates, and the Security Configuration and Analysis tool. The chapter concludes with information on troubleshooting a security configuration.

- Part 4: "Microsoft Windows 2000 Server." This part contains information that relates to the Windows 2000 Server portion of the 70-240 exam. However, because a lot of the objectives for this portion of the exam are redundant with objectives from the Windows 2000 Professional portion of the exam, the redundant information is not included (except where necessary for content and presentation flow). This section concentrates on the unique aspects of Windows 2000 Server. The chapters in this section primarily use Windows 2000 Server during the various hands-on practices and exercises.

- Chapter 22, "Managing Windows 2000 Terminal Service," explains Terminal Services, what tools are included, and how to install Terminal Services. An important aspect of Terminal Services is managing the appropriate software licensing, which is discussed in this chapter. There is also a discussion on deploying Terminal Services to client computers.

- Chapter 23, "Internet Services," focuses on various Internet services supported by Windows 2000 Server. This includes Internet Information Services (IIS), Web site management, and Telnet services. The chapter also provides the information necessary to implement each of these services into a Windows 2000 environment and administer that service once it is implemented

- Chapter 24, "Advanced File Systems," explores the Distributed File System and the File Replication Service. Dfs allows system administrators to make it easier for users to access and manage files that are physically distributed across a network. With Dfs, you can make files distributed across multiple servers appear to users as if they reside in one place on the network. Users no longer need to know and specify the actual physical location of files in order to access them. Dfs uses FRS to automatically synchronize content between assigned replicas. The Microsoft Active Directory Sites And Services snap-in uses FRS to replicate topology and global catalog information across domain controllers.

- Chapter 25, "Disaster Planning and Recovery," focuses on planning and implementing disaster protection. In addition, the chapter reviews several approaches to disaster recovery, should your system fail.

- Chapter 26, "Windows 2000 Server Network Management and Monitoring," discusses using Simple Network Management Protocol (SNMP) and network monitor to monitor and communicate the status of the network

- Chapter 27, "Microsoft Windows 2000 Security," explores public key infrastructure (PKI), public key technologies, and Kerberos in Windows 2000. The chapter also covers security configuration tools and implementing auditing in Windows 2000.

- Appendix A, "Questions and Answers," lists all of the practice questions and review questions from the book, showing the chapter and section where the question appears, and the suggested answer.

- Appendix B, "Microsoft Services for UNIX" (presented only in the e-book version, located on the Supplemental Materials CD-ROM) provides you with an overview of Services for UNIX (SFU) version 2, and how you can use it to securely share data in a heterogeneous environment (Windows 2000 and UNIX). Information provided in this chapter is taken from the following sources:

  - Microsoft white papers: "User Name Mapping Service," "Password Synchronization in Windows Services for UNIX," "Server for NIS Overview," "Services for UNIX Component Summary," and "Windows Services for UNIX version 2."

  - "Windows 2000 Professional in a UNIX Environment, Scenario Guide and Walkthrough." This white paper was written by Charlie Russel, author of *Microsoft Windows 2000 Server Administrator's Companion* (Microsoft Press 2000).

  - Microsoft Corporation. *Windows 2000 Professional Resource Kit*. Chapter 25, "Interoperability with UNIX" (Microsoft Press 2000).

- The glossary (presented only in the e-book version, located on the Supplemental Materials CD-ROM) provides definitions for many of the key words and concepts presented in the course. It also contains some basic networking terminology.

Finding the Best Starting Point for You

Because this book is self-paced, you can skip some lessons and revisit them later. But note that you must complete the procedures in Chapter 1, "Installing Windows 2000 Professional," before you can perform procedures in the other chapters. Use the following table to find the best starting point for you:

If you	Follow this learning path
Are preparing to take the Microsoft Certified Professional exam 70-240, Microsoft Windows 2000 Accelerated Exam for MCPs Certified on Microsoft Windows NT 4.	Read the "Getting Started" and "Introduction" sections. Then work through Chapter 1. Work through the remaining chapters in any order, though you should complete Chapter 8 before working on chapters 9–27.
Are reviewing information about specific topics from the exam	Use the "Where to Find Specific Skills in This Book" section that follows this table.

Where to Find Specific Skills in This Book

The following tables provide a list of the skills measured on certification exam 70-240: Microsoft Windows 2000 Accelerated Exam for MCPs Certified on Microsoft Windows NT 4.0 The table provides the skill, and where in this book you will find the lesson relating to that skill.

Note Exam skills are subject to change without prior notice and at the sole discretion of Microsoft.

Part 1: Microsoft Windows 2000 Professional (Exam 70-210: Installing, Configuring and Administering Microsoft Windows 2000 Professional)

Installing Windows 2000 Professional

Skill Being Measured	Location in Book
Perform an attended installation of Windows 2000 Professional	Chapter 1, Lessons 1 and 2
Perform an unattended installation of Windows 2000 Professional	Chapter 1, Lessons 4, 5, and 6
• Install Windows 2000 Professional by using Windows 2000 Server Remote Installation Services (RIS)	Chapter 1, Lesson 6
• Install Windows 2000 Professional by using the System Preparation Tool	Chapter 1, Lesson 5
• Create unattended answer files by using Setup Manager to automate the installation of Windows 2000 Professional.	Chapter 1, Lesson 4
Upgrade from a previous version of Windows to Windows 2000 Professional	Chapter 1, Lessons 7
• Apply update packs to installed software applications	Chapter 1, Lesson 7
• Prepare a computer to meet upgrade requirements	Chapter 1, Lessons 7 and 8
Deploy service packs	Chapter 1, Lesson 8
Troubleshoot failed installations	Chapter 1, Lesson 3

Implementing and Conducting Administration of Resources

Skill Being Measured	Location in Book
Monitor, manage, and troubleshoot access to files and folders	Chapter 3, Lessons 1, 2, 3, 4, and 5
• Configure, manage, and troubleshoot file compression	Chapter 3, Lesson 4
• Control access to files and folders by using permissions.	Chapter 3, Lessons 1 and 2
• Optimize access to files and folders.	Chapter 3, Lesson 5
Manage and troubleshoot access to shared folders	Chapter 3, Lessons 3 and 5
• Create and remove shared folders.	Chapter 3, Lesson 5
• Control access to shared folders by using permissions	Chapter 3, Lesson 5
• Manage and troubleshoot Web server resources.	Chapter 3, Lesson 5
Connect to local and network print devices	Chapter 3, Lesson 6, 7, and 8
• Manage printers and print jobs.	Chapter 3, Lesson 10 and 11
• Control access to printers by using permissions.	Chapter 3, Lessons 10, 11
• Connect to an Internet printer.	Chapter 3, Lesson 12
• Connect to a local print device.	Chapter 3, Lesson 6
Configure and manage file systems	Chapter 3, Lesson
• Convert from one file system to another file system.	Chapter 3, Lesson 1, 2 and 3
• Configure file systems by using NTFS, FAT32, or FAT.	Chapter 3, Lesson 1

Implementing, Managing, and Troubleshooting Hardware Devices and Drivers

Skill Being Measured	Location in Book
Implement, manage, and troubleshoot disk devices	Chapter 2, Lessons 1, 2, 4, 7, 8, 9
▪ Install, configure, and manage DVD and CD-ROM devices.	Chapter 2, Lesson 1, 2, and 11
▪ Monitor and configure disks.	Chapter 2, Lesson 1 and 2
▪ Monitor, configure, and troubleshoot volumes.	Chapter 2, Lesson 8
▪ Monitor and configure removable media, such as tape devices.	Chapter 2, Lessons 1, 2, and 11
Implement, manage, and troubleshoot display devices	Chapter 2, Lessons 3
▪ Configure multiple-display support	Chapter 2, Lesson 3
▪ Install, configure, and troubleshoot a video adapter	Chapter 2, Lesson 3
Implement, manage, and mobile computer hardware	Chapter 2, Lesson 10
▪ Configure Advanced Power Management (APM).	Chapter 2, Lesson 10
▪ Configure and manage card services	Chapter 2, Lesson 4
Implement, manage, and troubleshoot input and output devices	Chapter 2, Lessons 1, 2, 6, 7, 8
▪ Monitor, configure, and troubleshoot I/O devices, such as printers, scanners, multimedia devices, mouse, keyboard, and smart card reader.	Chapter 2, Lesson 4
▪ Monitor, configure, and troubleshoot multimedia hardware, such as cameras.	Chapter 2, Lesson 4
▪ Install, configure, and manage modems.	Chapter 2, Lesson 2, 4, and 11
▪ Install, configure, and manage Infrared Data Association (IrDA) devices.	Chapter 2, Lesson 4
▪ Install, configure, and manage wireless devices.	Chapter 2, Lesson 4
▪ Install, configure, and manage USB devices.	Chapter 2, Lesson 4

Configuring and Troubleshooting the Desktop Environment

Skill Being Measured	Location in Book
Configure and manage user profiles.	Chapter 4, Lesson 1
Configure support for multiple languages or multiple locations.	Chapter 4, Lesson 2
▪ Enable multiple-language support	Chapter 4, Lesson 2
▪ Configure multiple-language support for users.	Chapter 4, Lesson 2
▪ Configure local settings.	Chapter 4, Lesson 2
▪ Configure Windows 2000 Professional for multiple locations.	Chapter 4, Lesson 2
Install applications by using Windows Installer packages.	Chapter 20, Lesson 2
Configure and troubleshoot desktop settings.	Chapter 4, Lesson 2
Configure and troubleshoot fax support	Chapter 2, Lesson 4
Configure and troubleshoot accessibility services	Chapter 4, Lesson 2

Implementing, Managing, and Troubleshooting Network Protocols and Services

Skill Being Measured	Location in Book
Configure and troubleshoot the TCP/IP protocol.	Chapter 5, Lesson 1
Connect to computers by using dial-up networking	Chapter 5, Lesson 2
▪ Connect to computers by using a virtual private network (VPN) connection	Chapter 5, Lesson 3
▪ Create a dial-up connection to connect to a remote access server	Chapter 12, Lesson 2
▪ Connect to the Internet by using dial-up networking	Chapter 5, Lesson 2–3
▪ Configure and troubleshoot Internet Connection Sharing	Chapter 5, Lesson 2–3
▪ Connect to shared resources on a Microsoft network.	Chapter 3, Lessons 2, 5, and 7

Monitoring and Optimizing System Performance and Reliability

Skill Being Measured	Location in Book
Manage and troubleshoot driver signing	Chapter 6, Lesson 3
Configure, manage, and troubleshoot Task Scheduler	Chapter 6, Lesson 1
Manage and troubleshoot the use and synchronization of offline files	Chapter 6, Lesson 2
Optimize and troubleshoot performance of the Windows 2000 Professional desktop	Chapter 2, Lesson 12
▪ Optimize and troubleshoot memory performance	Chapter 2, Lesson 12
▪ Optimize and troubleshoot processor utilization	Chapter 2, Lesson 12
▪ Optimize and troubleshoot disk performance	Chapter 2, Lessons 8 and 9
▪ Optimize and troubleshoot network performance	Chapter 9, Lessons 2, 7 and 8
▪ Optimize and troubleshoot application performance Windows NT 4 experience	Chapter 20, Lesson 2
Manage hardware profiles	Chapter 2, Lessons 5 and 6
Recover systems and user data	Chapter 6, Lesson 2
▪ Recover systems and user data by using Windows Backup	Chapter 6, Lesson 2
▪ Troubleshoot system restoration by using Safe Mode	Chapter 6, Lesson 4
▪ Recover systems and user data by using the Recovery Console	Chapter 6, Lesson 5

Implementing, Monitoring, and Troubleshooting Security

Skill Being Measured	Location in Book
Encrypt data on a hard disk by using Encrypting File System (EFS).	Chapter 7, Lesson 4
Implement, configure, manage, and troubleshoot local Group Policy	Chapter 7, Lesson 1
Implement, configure, manage, and troubleshoot local user accounts	Chapter 4, Lessons 1, 2, 3, 4
■ Implement, configure, manage, and troubleshoot auditing.	Chapter 7, Lesson 5
■ Implement, configure, manage, and troubleshoot account settings.	Chapter 4, Lesson 4 Chapter 7, Lesson 3
■ Implement, configure, manage, and troubleshoot account policy	Chapter 4, Lesson 4
■ Create and manage local users and groups.	Chapter 4, Lesson 3 Chapter 7, Lesson 1
■ Implement, configure, manage, and troubleshoot user rights.	Chapter 4, Lessons 3 and 5 Chapter 7, Lesson 3
Implement, configure, manage, and troubleshoot local user authentication	Chapter 7, Lesson 6
■ Configure and troubleshoot local user accounts	Chapter 4, Lesson 3
■ Configure and troubleshoot domain user accounts	Chapter 4, Lesson 4 and 5; Chapter 20, Lesson 4
Implement, configure, manage, and troubleshoot a security configuration	Chapter 7, Lesson 1, 3, and 6

Part 2: Network Infrastructure (Exam 70-216: Implementing and Administering a Microsoft Windows 2000 Network Infrastructure)

Installing, Configuring, Managing, Monitoring, and Troubleshooting DNS in a Windows 2000 Network Infrastructure

Skill Being Measured	Location in Book
Install, configure, and troubleshoot DNS	Chapter 9, Lessons 1–5
▪ Install the DNS Server service	Chapter 10, Lesson 2
▪ Configure a root name server	Chapter 10, Lesson 3
▪ Configure zones	Chapter 10, Lesson 4
▪ Configure a caching-only server	Chapter 10, Lesson 5
▪ Configure a DNS client	Chapter 10, Lesson 5
▪ Configure zones for dynamic updates	Chapter 10, Lesson 4
▪ Test the DNS Server Service	Chapter 10, Lesson 5
▪ Implement a delegated zone for DNS	Chapter 10, Lesson 4
▪ Manually create DNS resource records	Chapter 10, Lesson 3
Manage and monitor DNS	Chapter 10, Lessons 3 and 5

Installing, Configuring, Managing, Monitoring, and Troubleshooting DHCP in a Windows 2000 Network Infrastructure

Skill Being Measured	Location in Book
Install, configure, and troubleshoot DHCP	Chapter 11, Lessons 1–4
▪ Install the DHCP Server service	Chapter 11, Lesson 1
▪ Create and manage DHCP scopes, superscopes, and multicast scopes	Chapter 11, Lesson 2
▪ Configure DHCP for DNS integration	Chapter 11, Lesson 3
▪ Authorize a DHCP server in Active Directory	Chapter 11, Lesson 4
Manage and monitor DHCP	Chapter 11, Lesson 5

Configuring, Managing, Monitoring, and Troubleshooting Remote Access in a Windows 2000 Network Infrastructure

Skill Being Measured	Location in Book
Configure and troubleshoot remote access	Chapter 12, Lessons 2, 4, 5, and 6
▪ Configure inbound connections	Chapter 12, Lesson 2
▪ Create a remote access policy	Chapter 12, Lesson 2
▪ Configure a remote access profile	Chapter 12, Lesson 2
▪ Configure a VPN	Chapter 12, Lesson 4
▪ Configure multilink connections	Chapter 12, Lesson 5
▪ Configure Routing and Remote Access for DHCP integration	Chapter 12, Lesson 6
Manage and monitor remote access	Chapter 12, Lesson 7; Chapter 14, Lesson 1
Configure remote access security	Chapter 4, Lesson 3; Chapter 12, Lesson 2; Chapter 14, Lesson 2
▪ Configure authentication protocols	Chapter 14, Lesson 2
▪ Configure encryption protocols	Chapter 4, Lesson 3; Chapter 14, Lesson 2
▪ Create a remote access policy	Chapter 12, Lesson 2; Chapter 14, Lesson 2

Installing, Configuring, Managing, Monitoring, and Troubleshooting Network Protocols in a Windows 2000 Network Infrastructure

Skill Being Measured	Location in Book
Install, configure, and troubleshoot network protocols	Chapter 9, Lessons 1–4, 6 and 7
▪ Install and configure TCP/IP	Chapter 9, Lesson 1
▪ Install the NWLink protocol	Chapter 9, Lesson 2
▪ Configure network bindings	Chapter 9, Lesson 2
Configure TCP/IP packet filters	Chapter 9, Lesson 1
Configure and troubleshoot network protocol security	Chapter 9, Lesson 6 and 7
Manage and monitor network traffic	Chapter 9, Lesson 7
Configure and troubleshoot IPSec	Chapter 9, Lessons 3–6
▪ Enable IPSec	Chapter 9, Lessons 3
▪ Configure IPSec for transport mode	Chapter 9, Lesson 4
▪ Configure IPSec for tunnel mode	Chapter 9, Lesson 3
▪ Customize IPSec policies and rules	Chapter 9, Lesson 5
▪ Manage and monitor IPSec	Chapter 9, Lesson 6 and 7

Installing, Configuring, Managing, Monitoring, and Troubleshooting WINS in a Windows 2000 Network Infrastructure

Skill Being Measured	Location in Book
Install, configure, and troubleshoot WINS	Chapter 13, Lessons 1–4
Configure WINS replication	Chapter 13, Lesson 4
Configure NetBIOS name resolution	Chapter 13, Lesson 1; Chapter 13, Lesson 2
Manage and monitor WINS	Chapter 13, Lesson 3; Chapter 13, Lesson 4

Installing, Configuring, Managing, Monitoring, and Troubleshooting IP Routing in a Windows 2000 Network Infrastructure

Skill Being Measured	Location in Book
Install, configure, and troubleshoot IP routing protocols	Chapter 9, Lesson 1; Chapter 12, Lessons 2 and 3
• Update a Windows 2000-based routing table by means of static routes	Chapter 9, Lesson 1; Chapter 12, Lesson 3
• Implement demand-dial routing	Chapter 12, Lesson 2
Manage and monitor IP routing	Chapter 9, Lesson 1; Chapter 12, Lessons 1, 5 and 6
• Manage and monitor border routing	Chapter 9, Lesson 1; Chapter 12, Lesson 1 and 6
• Manage and monitor internal routing	Chapter 9, Lesson 1; Chapter 12, Lesson 5
• Manage and monitor IP routing protocols	Chapter 9, Lesson 1; Chapter 12, Lesson 1 and 6

Installing, Configuring, and Troubleshooting NAT

Skill Being Measured	Location in Book
Install Internet Connection Sharing	Chapter 14, Lesson 2
Install NAT	Chapter 14, Lessons 2 and 3
Configure NAT properties	Chapter 14, Lesson 3
Configure NAT interfaces	Chapter 14, Lesson 3

Installing, Configuring, Managing, Monitoring, and Troubleshooting Certificate Services

Skill Being Measured	Location in Book
Install and configure Certificate Authority (CA)	Chapter 15, Lesson 2
Create certificates	Chapter 15, Lesson 2
Issue certificates	Chapter 15, Lesson 2
Revoke certificates	Chapter 15, Lesson 3
Remove the Encrypting File System (EFS) recovery keys	Chapter 15, Lesson 3

Part 3: Active Directory Directory Service (Exam 70-217: Implementing and Administering a Microsoft Windows 2000 Directory Services Infrastructure)

Installing, Configuring, and Troubleshooting Active Directory

Skill Being Measured	Location in Book
Install Active Directory	Chapter 17, Lesson 1
Create sites	Chapter 17, Lesson 4
Create subnets	Chapter 17, Lesson 4
Create site links	Chapter 17, Lesson 4
Create site link bridges	Chapter 17, Lesson 5
Create connection objects	Chapter 17, Lesson 5
Create global catalog servers	Chapter 17, Lesson 6
Move server objects between sites	Chapter 17, Lesson 6
Transfer Operations Master roles	Chapter 17, Lesson 2
Verify Active Directory installation	Chapter 17, Lesson 1
Implement an OU structure	Chapter 17, Lesson 3
Back Up and Restore Active Directory	
Perform an authoritative restore of Active Directory	Chapter 11, Lesson 6
Recover from a system failure	Chapter 11, Lesson 7

Installing, Configuring, Managing, Monitoring, and Troubleshooting DNS for Active Directory

Skill Being Measured	Location in Book
Install, Configure, and Troubleshoot DNS for Active Directory	
▪ Integrate an Active Directory DNS with a non-ActiveDirectory DNS	Chapter 18, Lessons 1 and 2
▪ Configure zones for dynamic updates	Chapter 10, Lesson 4
Manage, Monitor, and Troubleshoot DNS	
▪ Manage replication of DNS data	Chapter 18, Lesson 2

Installing, Configuring, Managing, Monitoring, Optimizing, and Troubleshooting Change and Configuration Management

Skill Being Measured	Location in Book
Implement and Troubleshoot Group Policy	
Create a group policy object (GPO)	Chapter 20, Lessons 1 and 4
Link an existing GPO	Chapter 20, Lesson 1
Delegate administrative control of group policy	Chapter 20, Lesson 1
Modify group policy inheritance	Chapter 20, Lesson 1
Filter group policy settings by associating security groups to GPOs	Chapter 20, Lessons 1 and 4
Modify group policy	Chapter 20, Lessons 1 and 4
Manage and Troubleshoot User Environments by Using Group Policy	
Control user environments by using Administrative Templates	Chapter 20, Lessons 1 and 4
Assign script policies to users and computers	Chapter 20, Lessons 1 and 4
Manage and Troubleshoot Software by Using Group Policy	
Deploy software by using group policy	Chapter 20, Lesson 2
Maintain software by using group policy	Chapter 20, Lesson 2

continues

Skill Being Measured	Location in Book
Configure deployment options	Chapter 20, Lesson 2
Troubleshoot common problems that occur during software deployment	Chapter 20, Lesson 4
Manage Network Configuration by Using Group Policy	Chapter 20, Lesson 3
Deploy Windows 2000 by Using RIS	
Install an image on an RIS client computer	Chapter 20, Lesson 6
Create an RIS boot disk	Chapter 1, Lesson 6; Chapter 20, Lesson 6
Configure remote installation options	Chapter 1, Lesson 6; Chapter 20, Lesson 6
Troubleshoot RIS problems	Chapter 20, Lesson 8
Manage images for performing remote installations	Chapter 20, Lesson 7
Configure RIS Security	
Authorize an RIS server	Chapter 20, Lesson 7
Grant computer account creation rights	Chapter 20, Lesson 7
Prestage RIS client computers for added security and load balancing	Chapter 20, Lesson 7

Managing, Monitoring, and Optimizing the Components of Active Directory

Skill Being Measured	Location in Book
Manage Active Directory Objects	
Move Active Directory objects	Chapter 19, Lesson 4
Publish resources in Active Directory	Chapter 19, Lesson 3
Locate objects in Active Directory	Chapter 19, Lesson 1
Create and manage accounts manually or by scripting and 5 Chapter 8, Lessons 4, and 5	Chapter 1, Lesson 4
Control access to Active Directory objects	Chapter 19, Lesson 2
Delegate administrative control of objects in Active Directory	Chapter 19, Lesson 5

Skill Being Measured	Location in Book
Manage Active Directory Performance	
Monitor, maintain, and troubleshoot domain controller performance	Chapter 19, Lessons 6, 7, and 8
Monitor, maintain, and troubleshoot Active Directory components	Chapter 19, Lessons 6, 7, and 8
Manage and Troubleshoot Active Directory Replication	
Manage inter-site replication	Chapter 17, Lesson 5 and 6
Manage intra-site replication	Chapter 17, Lesson 6

Configuring, Managing, Monitoring, and Troubleshooting Active Directory Security Solutions

Skill Being Measured	Location in Book
Configure and Troubleshoot Security in a Directory Services Infrastructure	
Apply security policies by using group policy	Chapter 21, Lessons 1, 3, 4, and 7
Create, analyze, and modify security configurations by using Security Configuration and Analysis and Security Templates	Chapter 21, Lessons 5, 6, and 7
Implement an audit policy	Chapter 7, Lesson 5; Chapter 21, Lessons 2 and 7
Monitor and Analyze Security Events	Chapter 21, Lesson 3

Part 4: Microsoft Windows 2000 Server (Exam 70-215: Installing, Configuring and Administering Microsoft Windows 2000 Server)

Installing Windows 2000 Server

Skills Being Measured	Location in Book
Perform an attended installation of Windows 2000 Server.	Chapter 8, Lesson 1–2
Perform an unattended installation of Windows 2000 Server	Chapter 8, Lesson 4
▪ Create unattended answer files by using Setup Manager to automate the installation of Windows 2000 Server.	Chapter 8, Lesson 4
▪ Create and configure automated methods for installation of Windows 2000.	Chapter 8, Lesson 4–5
Upgrade a server from Microsoft Windows NT 4.0.	Chapter 8, Lesson 2
Deploy service packs.	Chapter 1,
Troubleshoot failed installations.	Chapter 8, Lesson 3

Installing, Configuring, and Troubleshooting Access to Resources

Skills Being Measured	Location in Book
Install and configure network services for interoperability.	Chapter 9, Lesson 2–4; Chapter 11, Lesson 1-2
Monitor, configure, troubleshoot, and control access to printers.	Chapter 3, Lesson 8–10
Monitor, configure, troubleshoot, and control access to files, folders, and shared folders.	Chapter 3, Lesson 2, 3, 5
Configure, manage, and troubleshoot a stand-alone Distributed file system (Dfs).	Chapter 4, Lesson 1
Configure, manage, and troubleshoot a domain-based Distributed file system (Dfs).	Chapter 2 and 4, Lesson 1
Monitor, configure, troubleshoot, and control local security on files and folders.	Chapter 8, Lesson 1–23
Monitor, configure, troubleshoot, and control access to files and folders in a shared folder.	Chapter 3, Lesson 2, 3, and 5

Skills Being Measured	Location in Book
Monitor, configure, troubleshoot, and control access to files and folders via Web services.	Chapter 23, Lesson 2
Monitor, configure, troubleshoot, and control access to Web sites	Chapter 23, Lesson 1–3

Configuring and Troubleshooting Hardware Devices and Drivers

Skills Being Measured	Location in Book
Configure hardware devices.	Chapter 2, Lesson 1–5
Configure driver signing options.	Chapter 2, Lesson 11; Chapter 6, Lesson 4
Update device drivers.	Chapter 1, Lesson 8; Chapter 2, Lesson 1–2
Troubleshoot problems with hardware.	Chapter 2, Lesson 4

Managing, Monitoring, and Optimizing System Performance, Reliability, and Availability

Skills Being Measured	Location in Book
Monitor and optimize usage of system resources.	Chapter 2, Lesson 2
Manage processes.	Chapter 2, Lesson 2
Optimize disk performance.	Chapter 2, Lesson 7–9
Manage and optimize availability of system state data and user data.	Chapter 2, Lesson 2, 11, 12
Recover systems and user data.	Chapter 6, Lesson 2, 5, 6; Chapter 25, Lesson 2
▪ Recover systems and user data by using Windows Backup	Chapter 6, Lesson 2; Chapter 25, Lesson 2
▪ Troubleshoot system restoration by using Safe Mode	Chapter 6, Lesson 5; Chapter 25, Lesson 2
▪ Recover systems and user data by using the Recovery Console.	Chapter 6, Lesson 6; Chapter 25, Lesson 2

Managing, Configuring, and Troubleshooting Storage Use

Skills Being Measured	Location in Book
Configure and manage user profiles.	Chapter 4, Lesson 1–4
Monitor, configure, and troubleshoot disks and volumes.	Chapter 2, Lesson 7–9
Configure data compression.	Chapter 3, Lesson 4
Monitor and configure disk quotas.	Chapter 2, Lesson 9
Recover from disk failures.	Chapter 2, Lesson 8; Chapter 25, Lesson 1, 2

Configuring and Troubleshooting Windows 2000 Network Connections

Skills Being Measured	Location in Book
Install, configure, and troubleshoot shared access.	Chapter 5, Lesson 1–3
Install, configure, and troubleshoot a virtual private	Chapter 12, Lesson 3
Install, configure, and troubleshoot network protocols.	Chapter 9, Lesson 2, 3, 4
Install and configure network services.	Chapter 5, Lesson 1; Chapter 26, Lesson 1
Configure, monitor, and troubleshoot remote access.	Chapter 12, Lesson 1–9
▪ Configure inbound connections.	Chapter 5, Lesson 2, 8
▪ Create a remote access policy.	Chapter 12, Lesson 2, 8
▪ Configure a remote access profile.	Chapter 12, Lesson 2
Install, configure, monitor, and troubleshoot Terminal Services.	Chapter 22
▪ Remotely administer servers by using Terminal Services.	Chapter 22, Lesson 3–4
▪ Configure Terminal Services for application sharing.	Chapter 22, Lesson 2–4
▪ Configure applications for use with Terminal Services.	Chapter 22, Lesson 2–4
Configure the properties of a connection. Chapter 23, Lesson 1	Chapter 5, Lesson 2, 3;
Install, configure, and troubleshoot network adapters	Chapter 1, Lesson 1; Chapter 2, Lesson 1, 2

Implementing, Monitoring, and Troubleshooting Security

BookSkills Being Measured	Location in
Encrypt data on a hard disk by using Encrypting File System (EFS).	Chapter 27, Lesson 2
• Implement, configure, manage, and troubleshoot policies in a Windows 2000 environment.	Chapter 20, Lesson 6; Chapter 27, Lesson 4–5
• Implement, configure, manage, and troubleshoot Local Policy in a Windows 2000 environment.	Chapter 7, Lesson 3; Chapter 20, Lesson 1–4; Chapter 27, Lesson 5
• Implement, configure, manage, and troubleshoot System Policy in a Windows 2000 environment.	Chapter 27, Lesson 5
Implement, configure, manage, and troubleshoot auditing.	Chapter 7, Lesson 8; Chapter 27, Lesson 5
Implement, configure, manage, and troubleshoot local accounts.	Chapter 7, Lesson 1–3
Implement, configure, manage, and troubleshoot Account Policy.	Chapter 7, Lesson 3
Implement, configure, manage, and troubleshoot security by using the Security Configuration Tool Set.	Chapter 27, Lesson 4

Getting Started

This self-paced training kit contains hands-on practices to help you learn about Windows 2000 Professional. Because this kit covers networking information, a minimum of two computers are required to complete all the exercises in this kit. These should be computers that do not contain useful data as you will be reformatting both computers multiple times throughout the exercises in this training kit. If the computers do contain data that you do not wish deleted, make sure you back up important data so you can restore it once you have completed the exercises.

Hardware Requirements

Each computer must have the following minimum configuration. All hardware should be on the Microsoft Windows 2000 Hardware Compatibility List.

Hardware	Minimum requirements
Processor	One Intel Pentium processor, 133 MHz or higher or Pentium II, 233 or higher (up to four processors are supported)
Memory	128 MB (256 MB recommended)
Hard disk	One or more hard drives with a minimum of 2.5 GB between the drives. One drive should have at least 1 GB of free space on the boot partition.
Video	VGA or higher video card and monitor
Other components	CD-ROM installation: CD-ROM or DVD-ROM drive
Networking	Network interface card and related cables
Accessories	Keyboard and mouse or other pointing device. To make full use of the multimedia presentations, a sound card and speakers or headphones should be available.

Caution Several exercises may require you to make changes to your servers. This may have undesirable results if you are connected to a larger network. Check with your network administrator before attempting these exercises.

Software Requirements

The following software is required to complete the procedures in this course: Microsoft Windows 2000 Professional, Microsoft Windows 2000 Server

- An evaluation copy of Windows 2000 Server software is included with this training kit. You can also check the Microsoft Web site for the availability of a downloadable evaluation copy of the Windows 2000 Server software at the following address:

    http://microsoft.com/windows2000/default.asp

This site includes directions on how to download this evaluation version of the software for free.

Setup Instructions

Set up your computer according to the manufacturer's instructions.

Instructions on installing Microsoft Windows 2000 Professional and Microsoft Windows 2000 Server are covered in Chapter 1 and Chapter 8, respectively, in this training kit.

The Microsoft Certified Professional Program

The Microsoft Certified Professional (MCP) program is the best way to show your command of current Microsoft products and technologies. Microsoft, an industry leader in certification, is on the forefront of testing methodology. Our exams and corresponding certifications are developed to validate your mastery of critical competencies as you design and develop, or implement and support, solutions with Microsoft products and technologies. Computer professionals who become Microsoft certified are recognized as experts and are sought after industry-wide.

The Microsoft Certified Professional program offers eight certifications, based on specific areas of technical expertise:

- *Microsoft Certified Professional (MCP).* Demonstrated in-depth knowledge of at least one Microsoft operating system. Candidates may pass additional Microsoft certification exams to further qualify their skills with Microsoft BackOffice products, development tools, or desktop programs.

- *Microsoft Certified Professional + Internet.* MCPs with a specialty in the Internet are qualified to plan security, install and configure server products, manage server resources, extend servers to run scripts, monitor and analyze performance, and troubleshoot problems.

- *Microsoft Certified Professional + Site Building.* Demonstrated what it takes to plan, build, maintain, and manage Web sites using Microsoft technologies and products.

- *Microsoft Certified Systems Engineer (MCSE).* Qualified to effectively plan, implement, maintain, and support information systems in a wide range of computing environments with Microsoft Windows NT Server and the Microsoft BackOffice integrated family of server software.

- *Microsoft Certified Systems Engineer + Internet.* MCSEs with an advanced qualification to enhance, deploy, and manage sophisticated intranet and Internet solutions that include a browser, proxy server, host servers, database, and messaging and commerce components. In addition, an MCSE + Internet–certified professional is able to manage and analyze Web sites.

- *Microsoft Certified Database Administrator (MCDBA)*. Individuals who derive physical database designs, develop logical data models, create physical databases, create data services by using Transact-SQL, manage and maintain databases, configure and manage security, monitor and optimize databases, and install and configure Microsoft SQL Server.

- *Microsoft Certified Solution Developer (MCSD)*. Qualified to design and develop custom business solutions with Microsoft development tools, technologies, and platforms, including Microsoft Office and Microsoft BackOffice.

- *Microsoft Certified Trainer (MCT)*. Instructionally and technically qualified to deliver Microsoft Official Curriculum through a Microsoft Certified Technical Education Center (CTEC).

Microsoft Certification Benefits

Microsoft certification, one of the most comprehensive certification programs available for assessing and maintaining software-related skills, is a valuable measure of an individual's knowledge and expertise. Microsoft certification is awarded to individuals who have successfully demonstrated their ability to perform specific tasks and implement solutions with Microsoft products. Not only does this provide an objective measure for employers to consider, it also provides guidance for what an individual should know to be proficient. And as with any skills-assessment and benchmarking measure, certification brings a variety of benefits to the individual and to employers and organizations.

Microsoft Certification Benefits for Individuals

As a Microsoft Certified Professional, you receive many benefits:

- Industry recognition of your knowledge and proficiency with Microsoft products and technologies.

- Access to technical and product information directly from Microsoft through a secured area of the MCP Web site.

- MSDN Online Certified Membership that helps you tap into the best technical resources, connect to the MCP community, and gain access to valuable resources and services. (Some MSDN Online benefits might be available only in English or might not be available in all countries.) See the MSDN Web site for a growing list of certified member benefits.

- Logos to enable you to identify your Microsoft Certified Professional status to colleagues or clients.

- Invitations to Microsoft conferences, technical training sessions, and special events.

- A Microsoft Certified Professional certificate.

- Subscription to *Microsoft Certified Professional Magazine* (North America only), a career and professional development magazine.

Additional benefits, depending on your certification and geography, include

- A complimentary one-year subscription to the *Microsoft TechNet Technical Plus*, providing valuable information on monthly CD-ROMs.

- A one-year subscription to the Microsoft Beta Evaluation program. This benefit provides you with up to 12 free monthly CD-ROMs containing beta software (English only) for many of Microsoft's newest software products.

Microsoft Certification Benefits for Employers and Organizations

Through certification, computer professionals can maximize the return on investment in Microsoft technology. Research shows that Microsoft certification provides organizations with

- Excellent return on training and certification investments by providing a standard method of determining training needs and measuring results.

- Increased customer satisfaction and decreased support costs through improved service, increased productivity, and greater technical self- sufficiency.

- A reliable benchmark for hiring, promoting, and career planning.

- Recognition and rewards for productive employees by validating their expertise.

- Retraining options for existing employees so they can work effectively with new technologies.

- Assurance of quality when outsourcing computer services.

To learn more about how certification can help your company, see the backgrounders, white papers, and case studies that are available on *http://www.microsoft.com/mcp/mktg/bus_bene.htm*:

- Financial Benefits to Supporters of Microsoft Professional Certification, IDC white paper (1998wpidc.doc 1,608K)

- Prudential Case Study (prudentl.exe 70K self-extracting file)

- The Microsoft Certified Professional Program Corporate Backgrounder (mcpback.exe 50K)

- A white paper (mcsdwp.doc 158K) that evaluates the Microsoft Certified Solution Developer certification

- A white paper (mcsestud.doc 161K) that evaluates the Microsoft Certified Systems Engineer certification

- Jackson Hole High School Case Study (jhhs.doc 180K)

- Lyondel Case Study (lyondel.doc 21K)

- Stellcom Case Study (stellcom.doc 132K)

Requirements for Becoming a Microsoft Certified Professional

The certification requirements differ for each certification and are specific to the products and job functions addressed by the certification.

To become a Microsoft Certified Professional, you must pass rigorous certification exams that provide a valid and reliable measure of technical proficiency and expertise. These exams are designed to test your expertise and ability to perform a role or task with a product, and are developed with the input of professionals in the industry. Questions in the exams reflect how Microsoft products are used in actual organizations, giving them real-world relevance.

Microsoft Certified Product Specialists are required to pass one operating system exam. Candidates can pass additional Microsoft certification exams to further qualify their skills with Microsoft BackOffice products, development tools, or desktop applications.

Microsoft Certified Professional + Internet specialists are required to pass the prescribed Microsoft Windows NT Server 4, TCP/IP, and Microsoft Internet Information System exam series.

Microsoft Certified Professionals with a specialty in site building are required to pass two exams covering Microsoft FrontPage, Microsoft Site Server, and Microsoft Visual InterDev technologies to provide a valid and reliable measure of technical proficiency and expertise.

Microsoft Certified Systems Engineers are required to pass a series of core Microsoft Windows operating system and networking exams, and BackOffice technology elective exams.

Microsoft Certified Systems Engineers + Internet specialists are required to pass seven operating system exams and two elective exams that provide a valid and reliable measure of technical proficiency and expertise.

Microsoft Certified Database Administrators are required to pass three core exams and one elective exam that provide a valid and reliable measure of technical proficiency and expertise.

Microsoft Certified Solution Developers are required to pass two core Microsoft Windows operating system technology exams and two BackOffice technology elective exams.

Microsoft Certified Trainers are required to meet instructional and technical requirements specific to each Microsoft Official Curriculum course they are certified to deliver. In the United States and Canada, call Microsoft at (800) 636-7544 for more information on becoming a Microsoft Certified Trainer, or visit *http://www.microsoft.com/train_cert/mct/*. Outside the United States and Canada, contact your local Microsoft subsidiary.

Technical Training for Computer Professionals

Technical training is available in a variety of ways, with instructor-led classes, online instruction, or self-paced training available at thousands of locations worldwide.

Self-Paced Training

For motivated learners who are ready for the challenge, self-paced instruction is the most flexible, cost-effective way to increase your knowledge and skills.

A full line of self-paced print and computer-based training materials is available direct from the source—Microsoft Press. Microsoft Official Curriculum courseware kits from Microsoft Press designed for advanced computer system professionals are available from Microsoft Press and the Microsoft Developer Division. Self-paced training kits from Microsoft Press feature print-based instructional materials, along with CD-ROM-based product software, multimedia presentations, lab exercises, and practice files. The Mastering Series provides in-depth, interactive training on CD-ROM for experienced developers. They're both great ways to prepare for Microsoft Certified Professional (MCP) exams.

Online Training

For a more flexible alternative to instructor-led classes, turn to online instruction. It's as near as the Internet and it's ready whenever you are. Learn at your own pace and on your own schedule in a virtual classroom, often with easy access to an online instructor. Without ever leaving your desk, you can gain the expertise you need. Online instruction covers a variety of Microsoft products and technologies. It includes options ranging from Microsoft Official Curriculum to choices available nowhere else. It's training on demand, with access to learning resources 24 hours a day. Online training is available through Microsoft Certified Technical Education Centers.

Microsoft Certified Technical Education Centers

Microsoft Certified Technical Education Centers (CTECs) are the best source for instructor-led training that can help you prepare to become a Microsoft Certified Professional. The Microsoft CTEC program is a worldwide network of qualified technical training organizations that provide authorized delivery of Microsoft Official Curriculum courses by Microsoft Certified Trainers to computer professionals.

For a listing of CTEC locations in the United States and Canada, visit *http://www.microsoft.com/CTEC/default.htm*.

Technical Support

Every effort has been made to ensure the accuracy of this book. If you have comments, questions, or ideas regarding this book, please send them to Microsoft Press using either of the following methods:

E-mail:

TKINPUT@MICROSOFT.COM

Postal Mail:

Microsoft Press
Attn: *MCSE Training Kit—Microsoft Windows 2000 Accelerated* Editor
One Microsoft Way
Redmond, WA 98052-6399

Microsoft Press provides corrections for books through the World Wide Web at the following address:

> *http://mspress.microsoft.com/support/*

Please note that product support is not offered through the above mail addresses. For further information regarding Microsoft software support options, please connect to *http://www.microsoft.com/support/* or call Microsoft Support Network Sales at (800) 936-3500.

For information about ordering the full version of any Microsoft software, please call Microsoft Sales at (800) 426-9400 or visit *www.microsoft.com*.

Introduction to Microsoft Windows 2000

About This Chapter

This chapter introduces the Microsoft Windows 2000 operating system. It includes an overview of the products that comprise the Windows 2000 operating system, the roles they play, and a description of the administrative differences between them in a workgroup and a domain. Overviews of the Microsoft Windows 2000 architecture and Windows 2000 Directory Services are also provided. Hands-on practices guide you through the basic procedures of logging on and performing key tasks from the Windows Security dialog box.

Before You Begin

To complete the lessons in this chapter, you must have completed the Setup procedures located in "About This Book."

Lesson 1: Windows 2000 Overview

This lesson introduces you to the Windows 2000 family of products, including their features and benefits. It explains the key administrative differences between these products and the environment for which each product is designed.

After this lesson, you will be able to

- Describe Windows 2000

- Explain the key differences between Microsoft Windows 2000 Professional and Windows 2000 Server

- Describe the features and benefits of Windows 2000

- Describe the difference between a workgroup model and a domain model in a network environment

Estimated lesson time: 15 minutes

Overview of Windows 2000

Windows 2000 is a multipurpose operating system with integrated support for client/server and peer-to-peer networks. It incorporates technologies that reduce the total cost of ownership and provides for scalability from a small network to a large enterprise network. *Total cost of ownership (TCO)* is the total amount of money and time associated with purchasing computer hardware and software and deploying, configuring, and maintaining the hardware and software. TCO includes hardware and software updates, training, maintenance and administration, and technical support. One other major factor in TCO is lost productivity. Lost productivity can occur because of user errors, hardware problems, or software upgrades and retraining.

This training kit focuses on the following two versions of the Windows 2000 operating system:

- **Windows 2000 Professional.** This product is a high-performance, secure network client computer and corporate desktop operating system that includes the best features of Microsoft Windows 98 and significantly extends the manageability, reliability, security, and performance of Microsoft Windows NT Workstation 4.0. Windows 2000 Professional can be used alone as a desktop operating system, networked in a peer-to-peer workgroup environment, or used as a workstation in a Windows 2000 Server or Windows NT domain environment. Windows 2000 Professional can be used with the Microsoft BackOffice family of products to access resources from all the BackOffice products. This product is the main Microsoft desktop operating system for businesses of all sizes.

- **Windows 2000 Server.** This product is a file, print, terminal, and applications server, as well as a Web-server platform that contains all of the features of Windows 2000 Professional plus many new server-specific functions. This product is ideal for small- to medium-sized enterprise application deployments, Web servers, workgroups, and branch offices.

The Windows 2000 family also includes the following two products:

- **Windows 2000 Advanced Server.** This product is a powerful depart-mental and application server and provides rich network operations system (NOS) and Internet services. Advanced Server supports large physical memories, clustering, and load balancing. This product is beyond the scope of this training kit; features unique to Advanced Server will not be covered in this kit.

- **Windows 2000 Datacenter Server.** This product is the most powerful and functional server operating system in the Windows 2000 family. It is optimized for large data warehouses, econometric analysis, large-scale simulations in science and engineering, and server consolidation projects. This product is beyond the scope of this training kit; features unique to Datacenter Server will not be covered in this kit.

The following table describes the new features included in Windows 2000.

New Features Included in Windows 2000

Feature	Description
Active Directory directory service	Active Directory directory service is an enterprise-class directory service that is scalable, built from the ground up using Internet-standard technologies, and fully integrated at the operating-system level. Active Directory simplifies administration and makes it easier for users to find resources. Active Directory provides a wide range of features and capabilities, including group policy, scalability without complexity, support for multiple authentication protocols, and the use of Internet standards.
Active Directory Service Interfaces (ADSI)	ADSI is a directory service model and a set of Component Object Model (COM) interfaces. It enables Windows 95, Windows 98, Windows NT, and Windows 2000 applications to access several network directory services, including Active Directory. It is supplied as a Software Development Kit (SDK).
Asynchronous Transfer Mode (ATM)	ATM is a high-speed, connection-oriented protocol designed to transport multiple types of traffic across a network. It is applicable to both local area networks (LANs) and wide area networks (WANs). Using ATM, your network can simultaneously transport a wide variety of network traffic: voice, data, image, and video.
Certificate Services	Using Certificate Services and the certificate management tools in Windows 2000, you can deploy your own public key infrastructure. With a public key infrastructure, you can implement standards-based technologies such as smart card logon capabilities, client authentication (through Secure Sockets Layer and Transport Layer Security), secure e-mail, digital signatures, and secure connectivity (using Internet Protocol Security).
Component Services	Component Services is a set of services based on extensions of the COM and on Microsoft Transaction Server (an earlier release of a component-based transaction processing system). Component Services provides improved threading and security, transaction management, object pooling, queued components, and application administration and packaging.
Disk quota support	You can use disk quotas on volumes formatted with the NTFS file system to monitor and limit the amount of disk space available to individual users. You can define the responses that result when users exceed your specified thresholds.

Feature	Description
Dynamic Host Configuration Protocol (DHCP) with Domain Name System (DNS) and Active Directory	DHCP works with DNS and Active Directory on Internet Protocol (IP) networks, freeing you from assigning and tracking static IP addresses. DHCP dynamically assigns IP addresses to computers or other resources connected to an IP network.
Encrypting File System (EFS)	The EFS in Windows 2000 complements existing access controls and adds a new level of protection for your data. The Encrypting File System runs as an integrated system service, making it easy to manage, difficult to attack, and transparent to the user.
Graphical Disk Management	Disk Management is a graphical tool for managing disk storage that includes many new features, such as support for new dynamic volumes, online disk management, local and remote drive management, and Volume Mount Points.
Group Policy (part of Active Directory)	Policies can define the allowed actions and the settings for users and computers. In contrast with local policy, you can use group policy to set policies that apply across a given site, domain, or organizational unit in Active Directory. Policy-based management simplifies such tasks as operating system updates, application installation, user profiles, and desktop-system lock down.
Indexing Service	Indexing Service provides a fast, easy, and secure way for users to search for information locally or on the network. Users can use powerful queries to search in files in different formats and languages, either through the Start menu Search command or through Hypertext Markup Language (HTML) pages that they view in a browser.
IntelliMirror	IntelliMirror provides high levels of control on client systems running Windows 2000 Professional. You can use IntelliMirror to define policies based on the respective user's business roles, group memberships, and locations. Using these policies, Windows 2000 Professional desktops are automatically reconfigured to meet a specific user's requirements each time that user logs on to the network, no matter where the user logs on.
Internet Authentication Service (IAS)	IAS provides you with a central point for managing authentication, authorization, accounting, and auditing of dial-up or Virtual Private Network users. IAS uses the Internet Engineering Task Force (IETF) protocol called Remote Authentication Dial-In User Service (RADIUS).

continues

New Features Included in Windows 2000 *(continued)*

Feature	Description
Internet Connection Sharing	With the Internet connection sharing feature of Network and Dial-Up Connections, you can use Windows 2000 to connect your home network or small office network to the Internet. For example, you might have a home network that connects to the Internet by using a dial-up connection. By enabling Internet connection sharing on the computer that uses the dial-up connection, you are providing network address translation, addressing, and name resolution services for all computers on your network.
Internet Information Services (IIS) 5.0	The powerful features in Internet Information Services (IIS), a part of Microsoft Windows 2000 Server, make it easy to share documents and information across a company intranet or the Internet. Using IIS, you can deploy scalable and reliable Web-based applications, and you can bring existing data and applications to the Web. IIS includes Active Server Pages and other features.
Internet Security (IPSec) support	Use IPSec to secure communications within an intranet and to create secure Virtual Private Network solutions across the Internet. IPSec was designed by the IETF and is an industry standard for encrypting Transmission Control Protocol/ Internet Protocol (TCP/IP) traffic.
Kerberos v5 Protocol support	Kerberos v5 is a mature, industry-standard network authentication protocol. With Kerberos v5 support, a fast, single logon process gives users the access they need to Windows 2000 Server-based enterprise resources, as well as to other environments that support this protocol. Support for Kerberos v5 includes additional benefits such as mutual authentication (client and server must both provide authentication) and delegated authentication (the user's credential is tracked end-to-end).
Layer 2 Tunneling Protocol (L2TP) support	L2TP is a more secure version of Point-to-Point Tunneling Protocol (PPTP) and is used for tunneling, address assignment, and authentication.
Lightweight Directory Access Protocol (LDAP) support	LDAP, an industry standard, is the primary access protocol for Active Directory. LDAP version 3 was defined by the IETF.
Message queuing	Integrated message-queuing functionality in Windows 2000 helps developers build and deploy applications that run more reliably over networks, including the Internet. These applications can interoperate with applications running on different platforms such as mainframes and UNIX-based systems.

Feature	Description
Microsoft Management Console (MMC)	Use MMC to arrange the administrative tools and processes you need within a single interface. You can also delegate tasks to specific users by creating preconfigured MMC consoles for them. The console will provide the user with the tools you select.
Network Address Translation (NAT)	NAT hides internally managed IP addresses from external networks by translating private internal addresses to public external addresses. This reduces IP address registration costs by letting you use unregistered IP addresses internally, with translation to a small number of registered IP addresses externally. It also hides the internal network structure, reducing the risk of attacks against internal systems.
Operating system migration, support, and integration	Windows 2000 integrates seamlessly with existing systems and contains support for earlier Windows operating systems, as well as new features for supporting other popular operating systems. Windows 2000 offers: Interoperability with Windows NT Server 3.51 and 4.0; support for clients running a variety of operating systems including Windows 3.x, Windows 95, Windows 98, and Windows NT Workstation 4.0; mainframe and midrange connectivity, using S/390 and AS/ 400 transaction and queuing gateways through Systems Network Architecture (SNA) Server; File Server for Macintosh, allowing Macintosh clients to use the TCP/IP protocol (AppleTalk File Protocol (AFP) over IP) to share files and to access shares on a Windows 2000 server.
Plug and Play	With Plug and Play, a combination of hardware and software support, the server can recognize and adapt to hardware configuration changes automatically, without your intervention and without restarting.
Public key infrastructure (PKI) and smart card infrastructure	Using Certificate Services and the certificate management tools in Windows 2000, you can deploy your own public key infrastructure. With a public key infrastructure, you can implement standards-based technologies such as smart card logon capabilities, client authentication (through Secure Sockets Layer and Transport Layer Security), secure e-mail, digital signatures, and secure connectivity (using Internet Protocol Security). Using Certificate Services, you can setup and manage certification authorities that issue and revoke X.509 v3 certificates. This means that you don't have to depend on commercial client authentication services, although you can integrate commercial client authentication into your public key infrastructure if you choose.

continues

New Features Included in Windows 2000 *(continued)*

Feature	Description
Quality of Service (QoS)	Using QoS, you can control how applications are allotted network bandwidth. You can give important applications more bandwidth and less important applications less bandwidth. QoS-based services and protocols provide a guaranteed, end-to-end, express delivery system for information across the network.
Remote Installation Services (RIS)	With Remote Installation Services, you can install Windows 2000 Professional remotely, without the need to visit each client. The target clients must either support remote booting with the Pre-Boot eXecution Environment (PXE) ROM, or else must be started with a remote-startup floppy disk. Installation of multiple clients becomes much simpler.
Removable Storage and Remote Storage	Removable Storage makes it easy to track your removable storage media (tapes and optical discs) and to manage the hardware libraries, such as changers and jukeboxes, that contain them. Remote Storage uses criteria you specify to automatically copy little-used files to removable media. If hard-disk space drops below specified levels, Remote Storage removes the (cached) file content from the disk. If the file is needed later, the content is automatically recalled from storage. Since removable optical discs and tapes are less expensive per mega-byte (MB) than hard disks, Removable Storage and Remote Storage can decrease your costs.
Routing and Remote Access service	Routing and Remote Access service is a single integrated service that terminates connections from either dial-up or Virtual Private Network (VPN) clients, or provides routing (IP, IPX, and AppleTalk), or both. With Routing and Remote Access, your Windows 2000 server can function as a remote access server, a VPN server, a gateway, or a branch-office router.
Safe mode startup	With safe mode, you can start Windows 2000 with a minimal set of drivers and services, and then view a log showing the sequence of events at startup. Using safe mode, you can diagnose problems with drivers and other components that might be preventing normal startup.
Smart card infrastructure	Using Certificate Services and the certificate management tools in Windows 2000, you can deploy your own public key infrastructure. With a public key infrastructure, you can implement standards-based technologies such as smart card logon capabilities, client authentication (through Secure Sockets Layer and Transport Layer Security), secure e-mail, digital signatures, and secure connectivity (using Internet Protocol Security).

Feature	Description
TAPI 3.0	TAPI 3.0 unifies IP and traditional telephony to enable developers to create a new generation of powerful computer telephony applications that work as effectively over the Internet or an intranet as over the traditional telephone network.
Terminal Services	The Windows 2000 Server family offers the only server operating systems that integrate terminal emulation services. Using Terminal Services, a user can access programs running on the server from a variety of older devices. For example, a user could access a virtual Windows 2000 Professional desktop and 32-bit Windows-based applications from hardware that couldn't run the software locally. Terminal Services provides this capability for both Windows and non-Windows-based client devices. (Non-Windows devices require add-on software by Citrix Systems.)
Virtual Private Network (VPN)	You can allow users ready access to the network even when they're out of the office, and reduce the cost of this access, by implementing a VPN. Using VPNs, users can easily and securely connect to the corporate network. The connection is through a local Internet Service Provider (ISP), which reduces connect-time charges. With Windows 2000 Server, you can use several new, more secure protocols for creating Virtual Private Networks, including: L2TP, a more secure version of PPTP (L2TP is used for tunneling, address assignment, and authentication) and IPSec, a standard-based protocol that provides the highest levels of VPN security. Using IPSec, virtually everything above the networking layer can be encrypted.
Windows Media Services	Using Windows Media Services, you can deliver high-quality streaming multimedia to users on the Internet and intranets.
Windows Script Host (WSH)	Using WSH, you can automate actions such as creating a shortcut and connecting to and disconnecting from a network server. WSH is language-independent. You can write scripts in common scripting languages such as VBScript and JScript.

Windows 2000 Network Environments

A Windows 2000–based network environment can be set up using either a workgroup model or a domain model. Both Windows 2000 Professional and Windows 2000 Server can participate in either of these two models. The administrative differences between the two products depend on the network environmental model.

Windows 2000 Workgroup Model

A Windows 2000 *workgroup* is a logical grouping of networked computers that share resources, such as files and printers. A workgroup is referred to as a *peer-to-peer* network because all computers in the workgroup can share resources as equals, or as peers, without a dedicated server. Each computer in the workgroup, running either Windows 2000 Server or Windows 2000 Professional, maintains a local security database, as shown in the figure below. A *local security database* is a list of user accounts and resource security information for the computer on which it resides. Therefore, the administration of user accounts and resource security in a workgroup is decentralized.

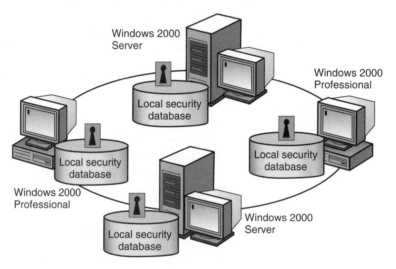

An example of a Windows 2000 workgroup

The following are disadvantages of using workgroup mode:

- A user must have a user account on each computer to which he or she wants to gain access.

- Any changes to user accounts, such as changing a user's password or adding a new user account, must be made on each computer in the workgroup. If you forget to add a new user account to a computer in your workgroup, the new user will not be able to log on to that computer and will be unable to access resources on it.

- Device and file sharing is handled by individual computers, and only for the users that have accounts on each individual computer.

A Windows 2000 workgroup provides the following advantages:

- A workgroup does not require a computer running Windows 2000 Server to hold centralized security information.

- A workgroup is simple to design and implement. A workgroup does not require the extensive planning and administration that a domain requires.

- A workgroup is convenient for a limited number of computers in close proximity. (A workgroup becomes impractical in environments with more than 10 computers.)

Note In a workgroup, a computer running Windows 2000 Server that is not a member of a Windows 2000 domain is called a *stand-alone server*.

Windows 2000 Domain Model

A Windows 2000 *domain* is a logical grouping of network computers that share a central directory database. A *directory database* contains user accounts and security information for the domain. This directory database is known as the directory and is the database portion of Active Directory, which is the Windows 2000 directory service. Active Directory replaces all previous "domain" information storage containers, including multiple domains. Active Directory also contains information about services and other resources, organizations, and more.

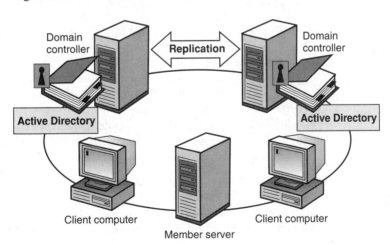

An example of a Windows 2000 domain

In a domain, the directory resides on computers that are configured as domain controllers. A *domain controller* is a server that manages all security-related aspects of user-domain interactions. Security and administration are centralized. Only computers running Windows 2000 Server may be designated as domain controllers.

A domain does not refer to a single location or specific type of network configuration. The computers in a domain can share physical proximity on a small LAN or can be located in different corners of the world, communicating over any number of physical connections, including dial-up lines, Integrated Services Digital Network (ISDN) lines, fiber lines, Ethernet lines, token ring connections, frame relay connections, satellite connections, and leased lines. The benefits of a Windows 2000 domain are as follows:

- A domain allows centralized administration because all user information is stored centrally. If a user changes his or her password, the change is automatically replicated throughout the domain.

- A domain provides a single logon process for users to gain access to network resources, such as file, print, and application resources for which they have permissions. In other words, a user can log on to one computer and use resources on another computer in the network as long as he or she has appropriate privileges to the resource.

- A domain provides scalability so that an administrator can create very large networks.

A typical Windows 2000 domain will have the following types of computers:

- **Domain controllers running Windows 2000 Server.** Each domain controller stores and maintains a copy of the directory. In a domain, you create a user account once, which Windows 2000 records in the directory. When a user logs on to a computer in the domain, a domain controller checks the directory for the user name, password, and logon restrictions to authenticate the user. When there are multiple domain controllers, they periodically replicate their directory information.

- **Member servers running Windows 2000 Server.** A *member server* is a server that is not configured as a domain controller. A member server does not store directory information and cannot authenticate domain users. Member servers provide shared resources such as shared folders or printers.

- **Client computers running Windows 2000 Professional.** Client computers run a user's desktop environment and allow the user to gain access to resources in the domain.

Lesson Summary

In this lesson you learned that Windows 2000 is a multipurpose operating system with integrated support for client/server and peer-to-peer networks. Windows 2000 consists of a family of four products: Windows 2000 Professional, Windows 2000 Server, Windows 2000 Advanced Server, and Windows 2000 Datacenter Server. Windows 2000 Professional is optimized for use alone as a desktop operating system, as a networked computer in a peer-to-peer workgroup environment, or as a workstation in a Windows 2000 Server domain environment. Windows 2000 Server is optimized for use as a file, print, and application server, as well as a Web-server platform.

A Windows 2000 workgroup is a logical grouping of networked computers that share resources, such as files and printers. A workgroup does not have a Windows 2000 Server domain controller. Security and administration for Windows 2000 Professional and Windows 2000 Server member servers are not centralized in a workgroup because each computer maintains a list of user accounts and resource security information for that computer.

A Windows 2000 domain is a logical grouping of networked computers that share a central directory database containing security and user account information. This directory database is known as the directory and is the database portion of Active Directory, the Windows 2000 directory service. In a domain, security and administration are centralized because the directory resides on domain controllers, which manage all security-related aspects of user-domain interactions.

Lesson 2: Windows 2000 Architecture Overview

Windows 2000 is a modular operating system—a collection of small, self-contained software components that work together to perform operating system tasks. Each component provides a set of functions that act as an interface to the rest of the system.

After this lesson, you will be able to

- Identify the layers and layer components in the Windows 2000 operating system architecture

Estimated lesson time: 15 minutes

Windows 2000 Layers, Subsystems, and Managers

The Windows 2000 architecture contains two major layers: user mode and kernel mode, as illustrated below. This lesson provides an overview of the Windows 2000 architecture layers and their respective components.

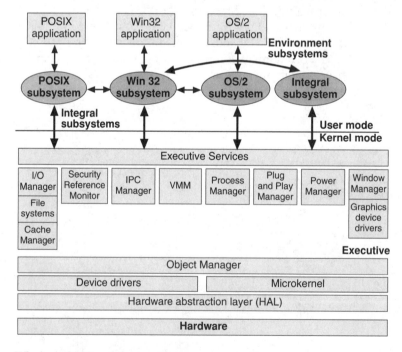

Windows 2000 architecture layers

User Mode

Windows 2000 has two different types of user mode components: *environ-ment subsystems* and *integral subsystems*.

Environment Subsystems

One of the features of Windows 2000 is the ability to run applications written for different operating systems. Windows 2000 accomplishes this through the use of environment subsystems. *Environment subsystems* emulate different operating systems by presenting the application programming interfaces (APIs) that the applications expect to be available. The environment sub-systems accept the API calls made by the application, convert the API calls into a format understood by Windows 2000, and then pass the converted API to the Executive Services for processing.

The following table lists the environment subsystems included with Windows 2000.

Environment Subsystems Included with Windows 2000

Environment subsystem	Function
Windows 2000 32-bit Windows-based subsystem (Win32)	Responsible for controlling Win32-based applications, as well as for providing an environment for Win16 and Microsoft MS-DOS-based applications. Controls all screen-oriented input/output (I/O) between subsystems. This ensures a consistent user interface, regardless of the application a user runs.
OS/2 subsystem	Provides a set of APIs for 16-bit, character mode OS/2 applications.
Portable Operating System Interface for UNIX (POSIX) subsystem	Provides APIs for POSIX-based applications.

The environment subsystems and the applications that run within them are subject to the following limitations and restrictions:

- They have no direct access to hardware.

- They have no direct access to device drivers.

- They have no access to the certain Clipboard API operations.

- They have no access to certain Microsoft CD-ROM Extensions (MSCDEX).

- They have no access to task-switching APIs.

- They are limited to an assigned address space.

- They are forced to use hard disk space as virtual random access memory (RAM) whenever the system needs memory.

- They run at a lower priority level than kernel mode processes.

- Because they run at a lower priority level than the kernel mode processes, they have less access to central processing unit (CPU) cycles than processes that run in kernel mode.

Integral Subsystems

Many different integral subsystems perform essential operating system functions. In the previous figure, there is a generic subsystem on the far right of the figure labeled *integral subsystem*. This integral subsystem represents any of the various integral subsystems. To introduce you to some of the more important integral subsystems, the following table lists some examples.

Windows 2000 Integral Subsystems

Integral subsystem	Function
Security subsystem	Tracks rights and permissions associated with user accounts. Tracks which system resources are audited. Accepts user logon requests. Initiates logon authentication.
Workstation service	Networking integral subsystem that provides an API to access the network redirector. Allows a user running Windows 2000 to access the network.
Server service	Networking integral subsystem that provides an API to access the network server. Allows a computer running Windows 2000 to provide network resources.

Kernel Mode

The kernel mode layer has access to system data and hardware. Kernel mode provides direct access to memory and executes in an isolated memory area. Kernel mode consists of four components: Windows 2000 Executive, Device Drivers, the Microkernel, and the Hardware Abstraction Layer (HAL).

Windows 2000 Executive

This component performs most of the I/O and object management, including security. It does not perform screen and keyboard I/O; the Microsoft Win32 subsystem performs these functions. The Windows 2000 Executive contains the Windows 2000 kernel mode components. Each of these components provides the following two distinct sets of services and routines:

- **System services** are available to both the user mode subsystems and to other Executive components.

- **Internal routines** are available only to other components within the Executive.

The Executive consists of the kernel mode components listed in the following table.

Windows 2000 Executive Components

Component	Function
I/O Manager	Manages input from and the delivery of output to different devices. The components that make up the I/O Manager include the following: *File systems* accept the oriented I/O requests and translate these requests into device-specific calls. The network redirector and the network server are both implemented as file system drivers. *Device drivers* are low-level drivers that directly manipulate hardware to accept input or to write output. *Cache Manager* improves disk I/O by storing disk reads in system memory. Cache Manager also improves write performance by caching write requests and writes to disk in the background.
Security Reference Monitor	Enforces security policies on the local computer.
Interprocess Communication (IPC) Manager	Manages communications between clients and servers, for example, between an environment subsystem (which would be acting like a client requesting information) and an Executive Services component (which would be acting like a server and satisfying the request for information). The IPC Manager consists of the following two components: *Local procedure call (LPC) facility* manages communications when clients and servers exist on the same computer. *Remote procedure call (RPC) facility* manages communications when clients and servers exist on separate computers.

continues

Windows 2000 Executive Components *(continued)*

Component	Function
Virtual Memory Manager (VMM)	Implements and controls *virtual memory*, a memory management system that provides and protects the private address space for each process. The VMM also controls demand paging. *Demand paging* allows the use of disk space as a storage area to move code and data in and out of physical RAM.
Process Manager	Creates and terminates processes and threads. (A *process* is a program or part of a program. A *thread* is a specific set of commands within a program.)
Plug and Play	Maintains central control of the Plug and Play process. Communicates with device drivers, directing the drivers to add and start devices.
Power Manager	Controls power management APIs, coordinates power events, and generates power management requests.
Window Manager and Graphical Device Interface (GDI)	These two components, implemented as a single device driver named Win32k.sys, manage the display system. They perform the following functions: *Window Manager* controls window displays and manages screen output. This component is also responsible for receiving input from devices such as the keyboard and the mouse and then passing the input messages to applications. *GDI* contains the functions that are required for drawing and manipulating graphics.
Object Manager	Creates, manages, and deletes objects that represent operating system resources, such as processes, threads, and data structures.

Device Drivers

This component translates driver calls into hardware manipulation.

Microkernel

This component manages the microprocessor only. The kernel coordinates all I/O functions and synchronizes the activities of the Executive Services.

Hardware Abstraction Layer (HAL)

This component virtualizes, or hides, the hardware interface details, making Windows 2000 more portable across different hardware architectures. The HAL contains the hardware-specific code that handles I/O interfaces, interrupt controllers, and multiprocessor communication mechanisms. This layer allows Windows 2000 to run on both Intel-based and Alpha-based systems without having to maintain two separate versions of Windows 2000 Executive.

Lesson Summary

This lesson introduced you to the Windows 2000 architecture. The Windows 2000 architecture contains two major layers: user mode and kernel mode. User mode has two different types of components: environment subsystems, which allow Windows 2000 to run applications written for different operating systems, and integral subsystems, which perform essential operating system functions. The kernel mode layer has access to system data and hardware, provides direct access to memory, and executes in an isolated memory area.

Lesson 3: Windows 2000 Directory Services Overview

You use a directory service to uniquely identify users and resources on a network. Windows 2000 uses Active Directory to provide directory services. It is important to understand the overall purpose of Active Directory and the key features it provides. Understanding the interactions of Active Directory architectural components provides the basis for understanding how Active Directory stores and retrieves data. This lesson introduces you to Active Directory functions, features, and architecture.

After this lesson, you will be able to

- Explain the function of a directory service
- Explain the purpose of Active Directory
- Identify the features of Active Directory
- Identify the layers in the Active Directory architecture

Estimated lesson time: 20 minutes

What Is a Directory Service?

A *directory* is a stored collection of information about objects that are related to one another in some way. For example, a telephone directory stores names of entities and their corresponding telephone numbers. The telephone directory listing may also contain an address or other information about the entity.

In a distributed computing system or a public computer network such as the Internet, there are many objects, such as file servers, printers, fax servers, applications, databases, and users. Users must be able to locate and use these objects. Administrators must be able to manage how these objects are used. A directory service stores all the information needed to use and manage these objects in a centralized location, simplifying the process of locating and managing these resources.

In this course, the terms *directory* and *directory service* refer to the directories found in public and private networks. A *directory* provides a means of storing information related to the network resources to facilitate locating and managing these resources. A *directory service* is a network service that identifies all resources on a network and makes them accessible to users and applications. A directory service differs from a directory in that it is both the source of the information and the services making the information available to the users.

A directory service acts as the main switchboard of the network operating system. It is the central authority that manages the identities and brokers the relationships between distributed resources, enabling them to work together. Because a directory service supplies these fundamental operating system functions, it must be tightly coupled with the management and security mechanisms of the operating system to ensure the integrity and privacy of the network. It also plays a critical role in an organization's ability to define and maintain the network infrastructure, perform system administration, and control the overall user experience of a company's information systems.

Why Have a Directory Service?

A directory service provides the means to organize and simplify access to resources of a networked computer system. Users and administrators may not know the exact name of the objects they need. However, they may know one or more attributes of the objects in question. As illustrated in the figure below, they can use a directory service to query the directory for a list of objects that match known attributes. For example, "Find all color printers on the third floor" queries the directory for all color printer objects with the attributes of color and third floor (or maybe a location attribute that has been set to "third floor"). A directory service makes it possible to find an object based on one or more of its attributes.

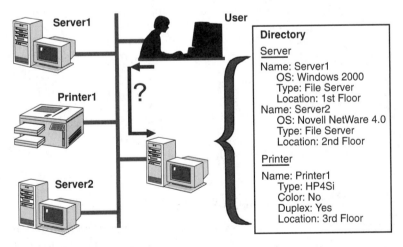

Using a directory service

Other functions of the directory service are:

- Enforcing security to protect the objects in its database from outside intruders or from internal users who do not have permission to access those objects.

- Distributing a directory across many computers in a network.

- Replicating a directory to make it available to more users and resistant to failure.

- Partitioning a directory into multiple stores that are located on different computers across the network. This makes more space available to the directory as a whole and allows the storage of a large number of objects.

A directory service is both an administration tool and an end user tool. As a network becomes larger, more resource objects must be managed and the directory service becomes a necessity.

Windows 2000 Directory Services

Active Directory is the directory service included in Windows 2000 Server. Active Directory includes the directory, which stores information about network resources, as well as all the services that make the information available and useful. The resources stored in the directory, such as user data, printers, servers, databases, groups, services, computers, and security policies, are known as *objects*.

Active Directory is integrated within Windows 2000 Server and offers:

- Simplified administration
- Scalability
- Open standards support
- Support for standard name formats

Simplified Administration

Active Directory organizes resources hierarchically in domains. A *domain* is a logical grouping of servers and other network resources under a single domain name. The domain is the basic unit of replication and security in a Windows 2000 network.

Each domain includes one or more domain controllers. A *domain controller* is a computer running Windows 2000 Server that manages user access to a network, which includes logging on, authentication, and access to the directory and shared resources. To simplify administration, all domain controllers in the domain are equal. You can make changes to any domain controller, and the updates are replicated to all other domain controllers in the domain.

Active Directory further simplifies administration by providing a single point of administration for all objects on the network. Because Active Directory provides a single point of logon for all network resources, an administrator can log on to one computer and administer objects on any computer in the network.

Scalability

In Active Directory, the directory stores information by organizing the directory into sections that permit storage for a very large number of objects. As a result, the directory can expand as an organization grows, allowing users to scale from a small installation with a few hundred objects to a large installation with millions of objects.

Note You can distribute directory information across several computers in a network.

Open Standards Support

Active Directory integrates the Internet concept of a name space with the Windows 2000 directory services. This allows you to unify and manage the multiple name spaces that now exist in the heterogeneous software and hardware environments of corporate networks. Active Directory uses DNS for its name system and can exchange information with any application or directory that uses LDAP or Hypertext Transfer Protocol (HTTP).

Important Active Directory also shares information with other directory services that support LDAP version 2 and version 3, such as Novell Directory Services (NDS).

DNS

Because Active Directory uses DNS as its domain naming and location service, Windows 2000 domain names are also DNS names. Windows 2000 Server uses Dynamic DNS (DDNS), which enables clients with dynamically assigned addresses to register directly with a server running the DNS service and update the DNS table dynamically. DDNS eliminates the need for other Internet naming services, such as Windows Internet Name Service (WINS), in a homogeneous environment.

Important For Active Directory and associated client software to function correctly, you must have installed and configured the DNS service.

Support for LDAP and HTTP

Active Directory further embraces Internet standards by directly supporting LDAP and HTTP. LDAP is a version of the X.500 directory access protocol, which was developed as a simpler alternative to the Directory Access Protocol (DAP). Active Directory supports both LDAP version 2 and version 3. HTTP is the standard protocol for displaying pages on the World Wide Web. A user can display every object in Active Directory as an HTML page in a Web browser. Thus, users receive the benefit of the familiar Web browsing model when querying and viewing objects in Active Directory.

Note Active Directory uses LDAP to exchange information between directories and applications.

More Info For more information about LDAP, use your Web browser to search for **RFC 1777** and retrieve the text of this Request for Comment.

Support for Standard Name Formats

Active Directory supports several common name formats. Consequently, users and applications can access Active Directory using the format with which they are most familiar. The following table describes some standard name formats supported by Active Directory.

Standard Name Formats Supported by Active Directory

Format	Description
RFC 822	Takes the form of *someone@domain* and is familiar to most users as an Internet e-mail address.
HTTP Uniform Resource Locator (URL)	Takes the form of *http://domain/path-to-page* and is familiar to users with Web browsers.
Universal Naming Convention (UNC)	Takes the form of *\\microsoft.com\xl\BUDGET.XLS* and is used in Windows 2000 Server-based networks to refer to shared volumes, printers, and files.
LDAP URL	Active Directory supports a draft to RFC 1779 and uses the attributes in the following example: LDAP:// someserver.microsoft.com/CN=FirstnameLastname, OU=sys, OU=product, OU=division, DC=devel Where CN represents Common Name OU represents Organizational Unit Name DC represents Domain Component Name An LDAP URL specifies the server on which the Active Directory services reside and the attributed name of the object.

Active Directory in the Windows 2000 Architecture

As you learned in the previous lesson, Windows 2000 uses modules and modes that combine to provide operating system services to applications. Two processor access modes, *kernel* and *user*, divide the low-level, platform-specific processes from the upper level processes, respectively, to shield applications from platform differences and to prevent direct access to system code and data by applications. Each application, including service applications, runs in a separate *module* in user mode, from which it requests system services through an API that gains limited access to system data. An application process begins in user mode and is transferred to kernel mode, where the actual service is provided in a protected environment. The process is then transferred back to user mode. Active Directory runs in the security subsystem in user mode. The *security reference monitor*, which runs in kernel mode, is the primary authority for enforcing the security rules of the security subsystem. The following figure shows the location of Active Directory within Windows 2000.

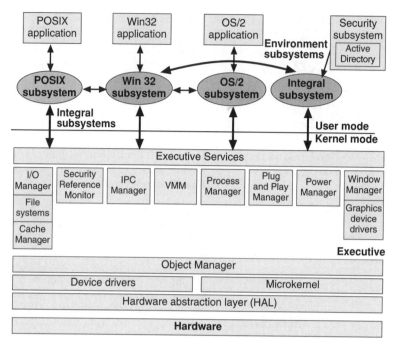

Location of Active Directory within Windows 2000

The tight integration of the directory service and security subsystem services is key to the implementation of Windows 2000 distributed systems. Access to all directory objects first requires proof of identity (authentication), which is performed by components of the security subsystem, and then validation of access permissions (authorization), which is performed by the security subsystem in conjunction with the security reference monitor. The security reference monitor enforces the access control applied to Active Directory objects.

Active Directory Architecture

Active Directory functionality can be illustrated as a layered architecture in which the layers represent the server processes that provide directory services to client applications. Active Directory consists of three service layers and several interfaces and protocols that work together to provide directory services. The three service layers accommodate the different types of information required to locate records in the directory database. Above the service layers in this architecture are the protocols and APIs that enable communication between clients and directory services.

The following figure shows the Active Directory service layers and their respective interfaces and protocols. The direction of the arrows indicates how different clients gain access to Active Directory through the interfaces.

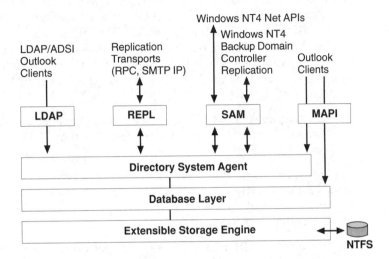

Active Directory architecture

The key service components include the following:

- **Directory System Agent (DSA)** builds a hierarchy from the parent-child relationships stored in the directory. Provides APIs for directory access calls.

- **Database Layer** provides an abstraction layer between applications and the database. Calls from applications are never made directly to the database; they go through the database layer.

- **Extensible Storage Engine** communicates directly with individual records in the directory data store on the basis of the object's relative distinguished name attribute.

- **Data store (the database file NTDS.DIT)** is manipulated only by the Extensible Storage Engine database engine, stored in the \Winnt\NTDS folder on the domain controller. You can administer the file by using the NTDSUTIL tool, located in the \Winnt\system32 folder on the domain controller.

Clients obtain access to Active Directory by using one of the following mechanisms that is supported by the DSA:

- **LDAP/ADSI.** Clients that support LDAP use it to connect to the DSA. Active Directory supports LDAP version 3 (defined by RFC 2251) and LDAP version 2 (defined by RFC 1777). Windows 2000 clients, as well as Windows 98 and Windows 95 clients that have the Active Directory client components installed, use LDAP version 3 to connect to the DSA. ADSI is a means of abstracting LDAP API; however, Active Directory uses only LDAP.

- **Messaging API (MAPI).** Legacy MAPI clients, such as Microsoft Outlook, connect to the DSA by using the MAPI RPC address book provider interface.

- **Security Accounts Manager (SAM).** Windows clients that use Windows NT 4.0 or earlier use the SAM interface to connect to the DSA. Replication from backup domain controllers in a mixed-mode domain goes through the SAM interface as well.

- **Replication (REPL).** When they are performing directory replication, Active Directory DSAs connect to each other by using a proprietary RPC interface.

Lesson Summary

In this lesson, you learned that a directory service is a network service that identifies all resources on a network and makes them accessible to users and applications. A directory service differs from a directory in that it is both the source of the information and the services making the information available to the users.

You also learned that Active Directory is the directory service included in Windows 2000 Server. Active Directory includes the directory, which stores information about network resources such as user data, printers, servers, databases, groups, computers, and security policies. The directory can scale from a small installation with a few hundred objects to a large installation with millions of objects. Active Directory offers simplified administration, scalability, open standards support, and support for standard name formats.

Finally, you learned that Active Directory runs in the security subsystem in the user mode in the Windows 2000 architecture. The security reference monitor, which runs in kernel mode, is the primary authority for enforcing the security rules of the security subsystem. Active Directory functionality can be illustrated as a layered architecture in which the layers represent the server processes that provide directory services to client applications. Active Directory consists of three service layers and several interfaces and protocols that work together to provide directory services.

Lesson 4: Logging On to Windows 2000

This lesson explains the process of logging on to the domain or local computer using the Log On To Windows dialog box. It also explains how Windows 2000 authenticates a user during the logon process to verify the identity of the user. This mandatory process ensures that only valid users can gain access to resources and data on a computer or the network.

After this lesson, you will be able to

- Identify the features of the Log On To Windows dialog box
- Identify how Windows 2000 authenticates a user when the user logs on to a domain or logs on locally
- Log on to a stand-alone server

Estimated lesson time: 10 minutes

Logging On to a Domain

To log on to a computer running Windows 2000, you must provide a user name and password. Windows 2000 authenticates the user during the logon process to verify the user identity. Only valid users can gain access to resources and data on a computer or the network. Windows 2000 authenticates users who log on to either the domain or a local computer.

When you start a computer running Windows 2000, the Welcome To Windows window prompts you to press Ctrl+Alt+Delete to log on (see the figure below). By pressing Ctrl+Alt+Delete you guarantee that you are providing your user name and password to only the Windows 2000 operating system. Windows 2000 then displays the Log On To Windows dialog box.

The Welcome To Windows window and the Log On To Windows dialog box

The following table describes the default options on the Log On To Windows dialog box.

Log On To Windows Dialog Box Options

Option	Description
User Name box	A unique user logon name that is assigned by an administrator. To log on to a domain with the user name, the user account must reside in the directory.
Password box	Passwords are case-sensitive. The password components appear on the screen as asterisks (*) to maintain privacy. To prevent unauthorized access to resources and data, you must keep passwords secret.
Log On To list	Select the domain that contains your user account. This list contains all of the domains in a domain tree.
Log On Using Dial-Up Connection check box	Permits a user to connect to a domain server by using dial-up networking, which allows a user to log on and perform work from a remote location.
Shutdown button	Closes all files, saves all operating system data, and prepares the computer so that a user can safely turn it off. On a computer running Windows 2000 Server, the Shutdown button is unavailable by default. This prevents an unauthorized person from using this dialog box to shut down the server. To shut down a server, a user must be able to log on to it.
Options button	Toggles on and off the Log On To list and the Log On Using Dial-Up Connection check box.

Important A user cannot log on to either the domain or the local computer from any computer running Windows 2000 Server unless that user is assigned the Log On Locally user right by an administrator or has administrative privileges for the server. This feature helps to secure the server.

Logging On to a Local Computer

A user can log on locally to either of the following:

- A computer that is a member of a workgroup.

- A computer that is a member of a domain but is not a domain controller. The user selects the computer name in the Log On To list in the Log On To Windows dialog box.

Note Domain controllers do not maintain a local security database. Therefore, local user accounts are not available on domain controllers, and a user cannot log on locally to a domain controller.

Windows 2000 Authentication Process

To gain access to a computer running Windows 2000 or to any resource on that computer, a user must provide a user name and password. The way Windows 2000 authenticates a user varies based on whether the user is logging on to a domain or logging on locally to a computer.

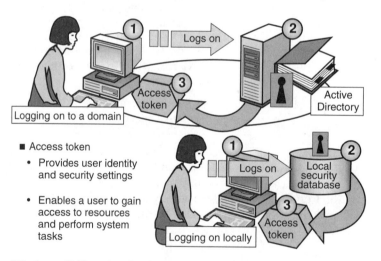

- Access token
  - Provides user identity and security settings
  - Enables a user to gain access to resources and perform system tasks

Windows 2000 authentication process at logon

▶   **The steps in the authentication process are as follows:**

1. The user logs on by providing logon information, including user name and password.

   ▪ If the user is logging on to a domain, Windows 2000 forwards this information to a domain controller.

   ▪ If the user is logging on locally, Windows 2000 forwards this information to the security subsystem of that local computer.

2. Windows 2000 compares the logon information with the user information that is stored in the appropriate database.

   ▪ If the user is logging on to a domain, the domain controller contains a copy of the directory that Windows 2000 uses to validate the logon information.

   ▪ If the user is logging on locally, the security subsystem of the local computer contains the local security database that Windows 2000 uses to validate the logon information.

3. If the information matches and the user account is enabled, Windows 2000 creates an access token for the user. An *access token* is the user's identification for the computers in the domain or for that local computer, and it contains the user's security settings, including the user's security ID (SID). These security settings allow the user to gain access to the appropriate resources and to perform specific system tasks. The SID is a unique number that identifies user, group, and computer accounts.

4. If the logon information does not match or the user account is not validated, access to the domain or local computer is denied.

Note In addition to the logon process, any time a user makes a connection to a computer or to other resources, that computer or resource authenticates the user and returns an access token. This authentication process is invisible to the user.

Practice: Logging On to a Standalone Server

In this practice, you will use the Log On To Windows dialog box to log on to a stand-alone server in a workgroup.

1. Press Ctrl+Alt+Delete.

   The Log On To Windows dialog box appears.

2. In the User Name box, type **administrator** (the administrator account you configured during Setup described in "About This Book"). By default, the account name that was last used to log on appears in this box. If this is the first time logging on, the default administrator account appears in this box.

3. In the Password box, type **password** (the password you assigned to the administrator account during Setup). Keep in mind that passwords are case-sensitive, and note that for security reasons, the password appears as asterisks to shield the password from onlookers.

4. Click OK.

Lesson Summary

In this lesson, you learned that when a user starts a computer running Windows 2000, the user is prompted to press Ctrl+Alt+Delete to log on. Windows 2000 then displays the Log On To Windows dialog box, and the user must enter a valid user name and password to log on. You also learned about the various options available in the Log On To Windows dialog box. In the practice portion of this lesson, you logged on to a stand-alone server in a workgroup.

When a user logs on, he or she can log on to the local computer or, if the computer is a member of a domain, the user can log on to the domain. If a user supplies a valid domain user account, the directory in the domain controller validates the user name and password. If a user supplies a valid local user account, the user name and password are validated by the security database in the local computer.

Lesson 5: The Windows Security Dialog Box

This lesson explains the options and functionality of the Windows Security dialog box.

After this lesson, you will be able to

- Use the functions of the Windows Security dialog box

Estimated lesson time: 20 minutes

Using the Windows Security Dialog Box

The Windows Security dialog box provides easy access to important security functions. You will need to educate your users about these functions.

The Windows Security dialog box displays the user account currently logged on, the domain or computer to which the user is logged on, and the date and time at which the user logged on. This information is important for users with multiple user accounts, such as an individual who has a regular user account as well as a user account with administrative privileges. You access the Windows Security dialog box by pressing Ctrl+Alt+Delete.

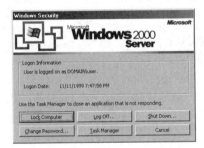

Windows Security dialog box

The following table describes the Windows Security dialog box buttons.

Buttons on the Windows Security Dialog Box

Button	Description
Lock Computer	Allows you to secure the computer without logging off. All programs remain running. You should lock your computer if you leave it for a short period of time. The user who locks the computer can unlock it by pressing Ctrl+Alt+Delete and entering the valid password. An administrator can also unlock a locked computer by logging off the current user; however, this is a forced logoff and data may be lost.
Log Off	Allows you to log off as the current user and close all running programs, but leaves Windows 2000 running.
Shut Down	Allows you to close all files, save all operating system data, and prepare the computer so that you can safely turn it off.
Change Password	Allows you to change your user account password. You must know the old password to create a new one. This is the only way you can change your own password. Administrators should require users to change their passwords regularly and should set password restrictions as part of account policy.
Task Manager	Provides a list of the current programs that are running, a summary of overall CPU and memory usage, and a quick view of how each program, program component, or system process is using the CPU and memory resources. You can also use Task Manager to switch between programs and to stop a program that is not responding.
Cancel	Closes the Windows Security dialog box.

Practice: Using the Windows Security Dialog Box

In this practice, you'll use the Windows Security dialog box to perform various security functions.

Exercise 1: Locking a Computer

1. Press Ctrl+Alt+Delete.

   The Windows Security dialog box appears.

2. Click Lock Computer.

   The Computer Locked window appears, indicating that the computer is in use, but locked, and can only be opened by an administrator or by the authenticated user.

3. Press Ctrl+Alt+Delete.

   The Unlock Computer dialog box appears.

4. In the Password box, enter your password, and then click OK to unlock your computer.

Exercise 2: Changing Your Password

1. Press Ctrl+Alt+Delete.

   The Windows Security dialog box appears.

2. Click Change Password.

   The Change Password dialog box appears. Notice that the User Name box and the Log On To list show the current user account and domain or computer name.

3. In the Old Password box, enter the current password.

4. In the New Password and Confirm New Password boxes, enter the new password, and then click OK.

   Your password change is confirmed.

5. Click OK to return to the Windows Security dialog box.

6. Click Cancel.

Exercise 3: Closing a Program Using Task Manager

In this procedure, you open WordPad and then close it using Task Manager. Use this procedure when a program has stopped responding and you need to close it.

1. Click the Start button, point to Programs, point to Accessories, and then click WordPad.

   WordPad opens.

2. Type in a few miscellaneous letters or words.

3. Press Ctrl+Alt+Delete.

   The Windows Security dialog box appears.

4. Click Task Manager.

   The Windows Task Manager dialog box appears.

5. Click the Applications tab if it is not already the default.

   A list of open programs appears.

6. Under Task, click WordPad, and then click End Task.

   When WordPad has stopped responding, the following message appears.

End Program message

Note If a program stops responding on its own (without invoking End Task), the Wait button appears, allowing you to wait for the application to respond.

If you want to return to WordPad to save changes made to a document before WordPad stops responding, click Cancel. If you want to end WordPad without saving changes, click End Now to end the WordPad session.

Note When Task Manager closes a program, all unsaved data is lost.

---

7. Exit Task Manager.

Exercise 4: Logging Off

1. Press Ctrl+Alt+Delete.

   The Windows Security dialog box appears.

2. Click Log Off.

   A message appears, asking if you're sure you want to log off.

3. Click Yes.

Note Another method to log off is to click the Start button, click Shut Down, and then select Log Off Administrator.

Exercise 5: Shutting Down Your Computer

To shut down your computer

1. Press Ctrl+Alt+Delete.

   The Windows Security dialog box appears.

2. Click Shut Down.

   The Shut Down Windows dialog box appears. The default is Shut Down.

3. Click OK to shut down or click Cancel to return to the Windows Security dialog box.

Note Another method to shut down the computer is to click the Start button, click Shut Down, and then select Shut Down.

Lesson Summary

In this lesson, you learned that you access the Windows Security dialog box by pressing Ctrl+Alt+Delete and that this dialog box provides information such as the user account currently logged on and the domain or computer to which the user is logged on. In the practice portion of this lesson, you used the Windows Security dialog box to lock your computer, to change your password, to access Task Manager, to log off your computer while leaving Windows 2000 running, and to shut down your computer.

Review

The following questions are intended to reinforce key information presented in the chapter. If you are unable to answer a question, review the appropriate lesson and then try the question again. Answers to the questions can be found in Appendix A, "Questions and Answers."

1. What is the primary difference between Windows 2000 Professional and Windows 2000 Server?

2. What is the major difference between a workgroup and a domain?

3. Which of the integral subsystems is responsible for running Active Directory?

4. What is the purpose of Active Directory?

5. What happens when a user logs on to a domain?

6. How would you use the Windows Security dialog box?

PART 1

Microsoft Windows 2000 Professional

Part 1 contains most of the information that relates to the Windows 2000 Professional portion of the 70-240 exam. The chapters in this part primarily use Windows 2000 Professional during the various hands-on practices and exercises. However, much of the information presented here is also applicable to Windows 2000 Server.

This part covers installing Windows 2000 Professional, configuring hardware (such as disk drives, printers, etc.), managing resources (such as files, folders, and such), and provides an overview of network protocols. It also covers monitoring and securing the system. Much of this information will be familiar to a Windows NT 4.0 professional, but it lays a groundwork for the rest of the training kit.

C H A P T E R   1

Installing Microsoft Windows 2000 Professional

About This Chapter

As with most versions of Microsoft Windows, there are a variety of ways to install Microsoft Windows 2000 Professional. Which method you use depends on the configuration of your environment and your goals for setup. The methods in this chapter are presented from the simplest configuration (a standalone workstation installing from the CD-ROM) to more complex environments (Windows 2000 Professsional being installed remotely on multiple computers) with other configurations also being addressed.

This chapter starts with installing Windows 2000 Professional from a CD-ROM and then moves into installation from the network. Troubleshooting setup is then discussed before moving into automating the installation.

Automating setup makes installing Windows 2000 Professional on a large number of computers much easier. The chapter introduces the various methods of automating the installation of Microsoft Windows 2000 Professional, such as using the Setup Manager or using disk duplication. It introduces the Windows 2000 System Preparation tool and Remote Installation Services (RIS). It also addresses the issues involved in upgrading previous versions of Windows to Windows 2000 Professional and installing service packs.

Before You Begin

To complete the exercises in this chapter, you must have the following:

- A computer that meets or exceeds the minimum hardware requirements listed in the section "Hardware Requirements" in "About This Book"

- The Microsoft Windows 2000 Professional CD-ROM or, if your computer is connected to a network, access to a distribution server containing the Windows 2000 Professional installation files

- Four 3.5-inch floppy disks to create the Setup disks, if your computer is not configured with an El Torito–compatible CD-ROM drive, which allows you to boot off your Windows 2000 Professional CD-ROM

- A blank, formatted 3.5-inch floppy disk

Lesson 1: Installing Windows 2000 Professional from a CD-ROM

This lesson teaches you how to install Windows 2000 Professional from a Microsoft CD-ROM. There are four stages in the installation process (see Figure 1.1).

1. Running the Setup program

2. Running the Setup wizard

3. Installing Windows networking

4. Completing the installation

These stages are described in detail in this lesson. After you learn about these four stages, you will install Windows 2000 Professional on your computer.

After this lesson, you will be able to

- Install Windows 2000 Professional from a CD-ROM

Estimated lesson time: 90 minutes

The Windows 2000 Professional Installation Process

Installing Windows 2000 Professional to a clean hard disk is a four-stage process (see Figure 1.1) where files are copied, information is gathered (either by you or automatically), and the system is installed.

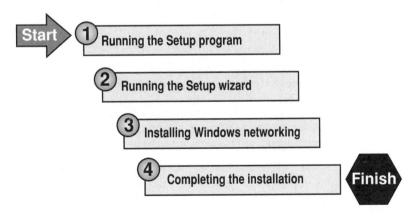

Figure 1.1 Windows 2000 installation steps

Installing Windows 2000 from a CD-ROM to a clean hard disk consists of these four stages:

1. Running the Setup program

   The Setup program prepares the hard disk for later stages of the installation and copies the necessary files to the hard disk to run the Setup wizard. This is the Text-mode portion of setup.

2. Running the Setup wizard

   The Setup wizard requests setup information about the computer, which includes names, passwords, and regional settings. This is the Graphics-mode portion of the setup.

3. Installing Windows networking

   After gathering information about the computer, the Setup wizard prompts you for networking information. After it has recorded the relevant information, it installs the networking components so that the computer can communicate with other computers on the network.

4. Completing the installation

   To complete the installation, Setup copies files to the hard disk, registers components, and configures the computer. The system restarts after installation is complete.

Running the Setup Program

To start Setup, use the Setup boot disks. Insert the disk labeled Setup Boot Disk (Disk 1) into drive A, and then turn on, or restart, the computer. If your computer supports booting from a CD-ROM drive, you can also start the installation by using the Windows 2000 Professional CD-ROM.

▶ **Follow these steps to run the Setup program on a clean disk drive (see Figure 1.2).**

1. After the computer starts, a minimal version of Windows 2000 is copied into memory. This version of Windows 2000 starts the Setup program.

2. Setup starts the text-based version of the Setup program. This version of Setup prompts you to read and accept a licensing agreement.

3. Setup prompts you to select the partition on which to install Windows 2000 Professional. You can select an existing partition or create a new partition by using unpartitioned space on the hard disk. You can even delete a partition, if necessary, to reconfigure the hard disk's partitions.

4. After you create the installation partition, Setup prompts you to select a file system for the new partition. Then Setup formats the partition with the selected file system.

5. After formatting the Windows 2000 partition, Setup copies files to the hard disk and saves configuration information.

6. Setup restarts the computer and then starts the Windows 2000 Setup wizard. By default, the Windows 2000 operating system files are installed in the C:\Winnt folder.

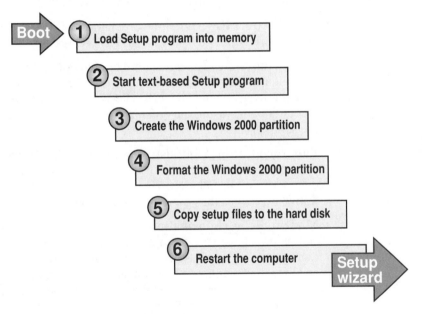

Figure 1.2 Steps in the Setup program

Running the Setup Wizard

The graphical user interface (GUI)–based Windows 2000 Setup wizard leads you through the next stage of the installation process. It gathers information about you, your organization, and your computer.

After installing Windows 2000 Professional security features and installing and configuring devices, the Windows 2000 Setup wizard prompts you to provide the following information:

- **Regional settings.** Configure this information to customize language, locale, and keyboard settings as appropriate. You can configure Windows 2000 Professional to use multiple languages and regional settings.

- **Name and organization.** Enter the name of the person to whom and the organization to which this copy of Windows 2000 Professional is licensed.

- **Your Product Key.** Enter the 25-character Product Key that is on the sticker affixed to the back of your CD-ROM case.

- **Computer name.** Enter a computer name of up to 15 characters. The computer name must be different from other computer, workgroup, or domain names on the network. The Windows 2000 Setup wizard displays a default name, using the organization name that you entered earlier in the setup process.

- **Password for the Administrator account.** Specify a password for the Administrator user account, which the Windows 2000 Setup wizard creates during installation. The Administrator account provides administrative privileges that are required to manage the computer.

- **Modem dialing information.** Select the country or region where the computer is located. Often this will have already been done when the regional settings were selected. You also must enter the area (or city) code for the computer's location as well as the number for obtaining an outside line, if necessary. Finally, select whether your telephone system is tone dialing or pulse dialing.

Note You won't be prompted to enter modem dialing information during installation if no modem is attached to the computer on which you are installing Windows 2000 Professional.

- **Date and time settings.** If necessary, set the current date and time and select the correct time zone for your computer's location. These settings will most likely already be set correctly. You can also select whether to have Windows 2000 Professional automatically adjust the computer's clock setting for daylight savings changes.

After you complete this stage in the installation, the Windows 2000 Setup wizard starts to install the Windows networking components.

Installing Windows Networking Components

After gathering information about your computer, the Windows 2000 Setup program automatically installs the network software.

The following list describes the installation of networking components:

1. **Detects network adapter cards.** The Windows 2000 Setup wizard detects and configures any network adapter cards that are installed on the computer.

2. **Copies and configures networking components.** Windows 2000 Professional installs (copies) files that allow your computer to connect to other computers, networks, and the Internet. Then the Setup program prompts you to choose whether to use typical settings or customized settings to configure the following networking components:

   - **Client for Microsoft Networks.** This component allows your computer to gain access to network resources on Microsoft networks.

   - **File and Printer Sharing for Microsoft Networks.** This component allows other computers to gain access to file and print resources on your computer.

   - **TCP/IP.** This is the default networking protocol that allows your computer to communicate over local area networks (LANs) and wide area networks (WANs).

   You can install other clients, services, and network protocols (such as NetBIOS Enhanced User Interface [NetBEUI], AppleTalk, and NWLink IPX/SPX/NetBIOS–compatible transport) at any time after you install Windows 2000 Professional.

3. **Joins a workgroup or domain.** If you create a computer account in the domain for your computer during the installation, the Windows 2000 Setup wizard prompts you for the name and password of an account on the domain that has the authority to create computer accounts.

4. **Installs components.** The Windows 2000 Setup wizard installs and configures the Windows networking components that you selected.

Completing the Installation

After installing the networking components, the Windows 2000 Setup wizard copies additional files to the hard drive to configure Windows 2000 Professional. Then the Setup program automatically starts the fourth step in the installation process to perform a set of final tasks (see Figure 1.3).

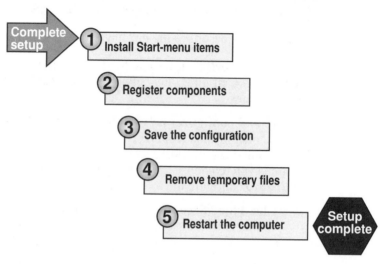

Figure 1.3 The final steps in completing the installation

The following list describes the tasks that Setup performs to complete the installation:

1. Installs Start-menu items

   The Setup program sets up shortcuts that will appear on the Start menu.

2. Registers components

   Setup applies the configuration settings that you specified in the Windows 2000 Setup wizard.

3. Saves the configuration

   Setup saves your configuration settings to the local hard disk. The computer will automatically use this configuration the next time you start Windows 2000 Professional.

4. Removes temporary files

   To save hard disk space, Setup deletes any files that it installed for use only during installation.

5. Restarts the computer

   After completing the preceding steps, Setup restarts the computer. This completes the installation of Windows 2000 Professional on a client or standalone system from a CD-ROM.

Practice: Installing Windows 2000 Professional from a CD-ROM

In this practice, you install Windows 2000 Professional from a CD-ROM.

Exercise 1: Running the Setup Program

1. Insert the Windows 2000 Professional CD-ROM into the CD-ROM drive.

   Note If your computer is configured with an El Torito–compatible CD-ROM drive, you can install Windows 2000 Professional without using the Setup disks. You can run the Setup program by restarting the computer with the CD-ROM inserted into the CD-ROM drive and then skip to step 4 in this practice. If you need to create the Setup disks, see Appendix B, "Creating Setup Boot Disks."

2. Insert the disk labeled Setup Boot Disk into drive A, and then turn on, or restart, the computer.

3. When prompted, insert Setup Disk 2 into drive A and proceed as directed for Setup Disks 3 and 4.

4. When Setup displays the Setup Notification message on the Windows 2000 Professional Setup screen, read it and then press Enter to continue.

   Setup displays the Welcome To Setup screen. Notice that, in addition to using it for installation, you can use Windows 2000 Setup to repair a damaged Windows 2000 Professional installation.

   Note Notice at this point that if you want to quit Setup for any reason, you can press F3 to exit.

5. Read the Welcome To Setup screen and press Enter to continue.

   Setup displays the Windows 2000 Licensing Agreement screen.

6. Read the licensing agreement, and then press F8 to agree to the licensing terms.

   Setup prompts you to select an area of free space or an existing partition on which to install Windows 2000 Professional. You may also create and delete partitions on your hard disk at this time if necessary.

7. Press Enter to select the default C: partition.

   Note If you already have an operating system installed on the C: partition, you can choose another partition. If you do, remember during the rest of the book to replace C: with the appropriate location for your Windows 2000 Professional installation.

   If you have a version of Windows 2000 Professional already installed and you want to replace it with a fresh installation, press Esc. When prompted, select the appropriate partition on which you will install Windows 2000 Professional, press Enter, and follow the directions on the screen.

   Setup displays a list of file system choices.

8. Ensure that the Format The Partition Using The NTFS File System option is highlighted, and press Enter.

   Note If you decide to format the partition with the FAT file system, you can use the Convert command provided in Windows 2000 Professional to convert a partition to NT file system (NTFS) without having to reformat the partition and lose all the information contained on the partition.

   Warning Reformatting the hard drive will delete any existing information on the computer. Be sure that the computers you use for all exercises in this book are ones that do not contain important data and can be reformatted.

   Setup formats the hard disk, examines it, and then copies files to the Windows 2000 Professional installation folders. This might take several minutes. Setup then initializes Windows 2000 Professional.

   Note If the partition is already formatted, Setup displays a Caution message indicating that formatting this drive will delete all files on it. If you see this message, and this is the partition on which you want to install Windows 2000 Professional, ensure that this partition option is selected and press Enter to format the drive.

9. When Setup prompts you to restart the computer, remove all the disks from the disk drives, and then press Enter.

Important If your computer supports booting from the CD-ROM drive and you do not remove the Windows 2000 Professional CD-ROM before Setup restarts the computer, the computer might reboot from the Windows 2000 Professional CD-ROM. This will cause Setup to begin the installation process from the start. If this happens, remove the CD-ROM and then restart the computer.

The computer restarts, and a message box appears prompting you to insert the CD-ROM labeled Windows 2000 Professional into your CD-ROM drive.

Exercise 2: Running the Setup Wizard, Installing Network Components and Completing the Installation

1. Insert the CD-ROM labeled Windows 2000 Professional into your CD-ROM drive, and then click OK.

   The Windows 2000 Professional Setup wizard appears.

2. If necessary, click Next to continue.

   Setup detects and installs devices. This might take several minutes. Setup configures NTFS folder and file permissions for the operating system files, detects the hardware devices in the computer, and then installs and configures device drivers to support the detected hardware. This process takes several minutes.

   Setup then prompts you to customize Windows 2000 Professional for different regions and languages.

3. Select the appropriate system locale, user locale, and keyboard layout, or ensure that they are correct for your language and location, and then click Next to continue.

   Note You can modify regional settings after you install Windows 2000 Professional by using Regional Settings in Control Panel.

   Setup displays the Personalize Your Software page, prompting you for your name and organization name. Setup uses your organization name to generate the default computer name. Many applications that you install later will use this information for product registration and document identification.

4. In the Name box, type your name; in the Organization box, type the name of your organization. Click Next.

   Setup displays the Your Product Key page, prompting you for the 25-character Product Key that appears on the sticker affixed to your CD-ROM case.

5. Type the 25-character Product Key that appears on the back of your CD case in the five Product Key boxes, and then click Next.

   Setup displays the Computer Name And Administrator Password page.

6. Type **Pro1** in the Computer Name box.

   Note that Windows 2000 Professional displays the computer name entirely in capital letters, no matter how you type it.

   Important If your computer is on a network, check with the network administrator before assigning a name to your computer. Throughout the rest of this chapter, the practice sections will refer to Pro1. If you don't name your computer Pro1, you will have to substitute the name of your computer whenever the book refers to Pro1.

   ---

7. In the Administrator Password box and in the Confirm Password box, type **password**, and then click Next.

   Important For the practice sections in this self-paced training kit, you will use *password* as the Administrator account password. However, you should always use a complex password for the Administrator account (one that others cannot easily guess). Microsoft recommends mixing uppercase and lowercase letters, numbers, and symbols (for example, Lp6*g9).

   If a modem is connected to the computer to which you are installing Windows 2000 Professional, Setup displays the Modem Dialing Information page; otherwise, Setup displays the Date And Time Settings page. If your computer does not have a modem, go to step 12.

8. Ensure that the correct country and region is selected.

9. Type in the correct area code or city code.

10. If you dial a number to get an outside line, type in the correct number.

11. Ensure that the correct telephone system is selected, and then click Next.

    Setup displays the Date And Time Settings page.

12. On the Date And Time Settings page, confirm that the Date & Time setting and the Time Zone setting are correct for your location.

13. Select the Automatically Adjust Clock For Daylight Saving Changes check box if you want Windows 2000 Professional to automatically change the time on your computer for daylight saving time changes, and then click Next.

> **Note** If you have configured your computer for dual booting with another operating system that can also adjust your clock for daylight saving time changes, enable this feature for only one operating system. Enable this feature on the operating system you use most frequently so that the daylight saving adjustment will occur only once.

Setup displays the Network Settings page and automatically installs network software so that you can connect to other networks and to the Internet. This will take a few moments. After the files are copied, the Setup program prompts you to choose whether to use typical or custom settings for configuring network components.

14. Ensure that the Typical Settings option is selected, and click Next.

Setup displays the Workgroup Or Computer Domain page.

15. Select the option No, This Computer Is Not On A Network, Or Is On A Network Without A Domain. Ensure that WORKGROUP appears in the Workgroup Or Computer Domain box, and click Next.

Setup displays the Installing Components page, displaying the status as Setup copies files to install and configure Windows 2000 Professional components. This process takes several minutes.

Setup then displays the Performing Final Tasks page and displays the status as Setup installs Start menu items, registers components, saves settings, and removes any temporary files. This process also takes several minutes.

The Completing The Windows 2000 Setup Wizard page appears.

16. Remove the CD-ROM from the CD-ROM drive, and then click Finish to continue setting up Windows 2000 Professional.

The computer restarts, and the Welcome To The Network Identification wizard appears.

Exercise 3: Configuring Networking Identification

1. To use the Welcome To The Network Identification Wizard, click Next.

   The Users Of This Computer page appears.

2. Select Users Must Enter A User Name And Password To Use This Computer, and then click Next.

   The Completing The Network Identification Wizard page appears.

3. Click Finish.

Exercise 4: Testing your installation

1. In the Log On To Windows dialog box, ensure that Administrator appears in the User Name box, and in the Password box, type **password**.

2. Click OK.

Note If the Found New Hardware wizard appears, read the information displayed, and then click Finish.

The Getting Started With Windows 2000 Professional dialog box appears.

3. Clear the Show This Screen At Startup check box, and then click Exit to close the Getting Started With Windows 2000 Professional dialog box.

Lesson Summary

In this lesson, you learned that installing Windows 2000 Professional is a four-stage process. You learned the tasks involved with each of these four stages, and you installed Windows 2000 Professional from a CD-ROM. During installation, you formatted your installation partition as NTFS and had the computer join the default workgroup.

Lesson 2: Installing Windows 2000 Professional over the Network

In addition to being installed from a CD-ROM, Windows 2000 Professional can be installed over the network. This lesson demonstrates the similarities and differences between installing from a CD-ROM and installing over the network. The major difference is the location of the source files needed to install Windows 2000 Professional. This lesson also describes the requirements for a network installation.

After this lesson, you will be able to

- Identify the steps for completing a network installation of Windows 2000 Professional

Estimated lesson time: 10 minutes

Preparing for an Over-the-Network Installation

In a network installation, the Windows 2000 Professional installation files reside in a shared location on a network file server, which is called a *distribution server*. From the computer on which you want to install Windows 2000 Professional (the target computer), you connect to the distribution server and then run the Setup program.

The basic environment requirement for a network installation is shown in Figure 1.4. You need to prepare this environment before starting the installation.

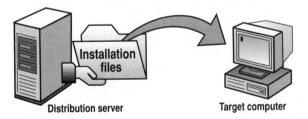

Distribution server   Target computer

Requirements for a network installation:

- Distribution server
- FAT partition on the target computer
- Network client

Figure 1.4 A network installation's basic environment

The following list describes what you need to do to prepare your environment for a successful network installation.

- **Locate a distribution server.** The distribution server contains the installation files from the i386 folder on the Windows 2000 Professional CD-ROM. These files must reside in a common network location in a shared folder. The computers on the network can gain access to the installation files because they are in a shared folder. Contact a network administrator to obtain the path to the installation files on the distribution server.

Note Once you have created or located a distribution server, you can use the over-the-network installation method to concurrently install Windows 2000 Professional on multiple computers.

- **Create a FAT partition on the target computer.** The target computer requires a formatted partition on which to copy the installation files. Create a 650-MB (1GB or larger recommended) partition and format it with the FAT file system.

- **Install a network client.** A network client is software that allows the target computer to connect to the distribution server. On a computer without an operating system, you must boot from a client disk that includes a network client that enables the target computer to connect to the distribution server.

Creating a Distribution Server

A distribution server stores the distribution folder structure. The distribution folder structure contains the files necessary to install Windows 2000 Professional over the network. If you have many computers on which to install Windows 2000 Professional, or if you will be doing multiple Windows 2000 Professional installations simultaneously, create more than one set of distribution folders. Having distribution folders set up on several computers will make the file copying during the Windows 2000 Setup faster. Even if you have several different types of hardware configurations on which to install Windows 2000 Professional, you need create only one set of distribution folders and use them with different answer files to install to all the different hardware types. Later in this chapter you will learn how to use scripts and answer files to automate installation.

Note If you are installing Windows 2000 Professional on a computer running Windows 95, Windows 98, Windows NT, or an earlier version of Windows 2000, the Winnt32.exe program allows you to specify up to eight locations on which to store the distribution folders.

▶   **To create a distribution server, follow these steps:**

1. Log on to the server as Administrator or connect to the server on which you want to create a distribution file structure.

2. Create a folder on the server named W2000P.

   Note The name W2000P is for a distribution folder structure containing the source files for Windows 2000 Professional. You can use W2000S for Windows 2000 Server and W2000AS for Windows 2000 Advanced Server. If you are creating distribution folder structures on more than one server, you can name them W2000P1, W2000P2, W2000P3, W2000P4, and so on.

3. Copy the contents of the i386 folder from the Windows 2000 Professional CD-ROM to the folder you created on the distribution server.

4. In the W2000P folder you created, create an OEM subfolder.

   Note The OEM subfolder is used to hold applications, drivers, or utilities you want Setup to copy to the target computer.

If Setup finds the OEM folder in the root of the distribution folder, it copies all of the files found in this directory to the temporary directory created during the text-mode portion of Setup.

Note The OEMFILESPATH key in the answer file allows you to create the OEM subfolder outside of the distribution folder.

Performing an Installation over the Network

The Windows 2000 Professional Setup program copies the installation files to the target computer. After copying the installation files, Setup restarts the target computer. From this point on, you install Windows 2000 Professional in the same way that you install from a CD-ROM.

▶ **The steps for installing Windows 2000 Professional over the network are as follows (see Figure 1.5):**

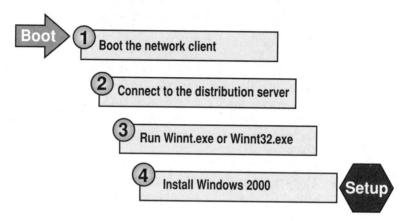

Figure 1.5 Installing Windows 2000 over the network

1. On the target computer, boot from the network client.

2. Connect to the distribution server. After you start the network client on the target computer, connect to the shared folder on the distribution server that contains the Windows 2000 Professional installation files.

3. Run Winnt.exe or Winnt32.exe to start the Setup program. Use Winnet.exe for an installation using Windows 3.*x* on the source system, and use Winnet32.exe for an installation using Windows 95, 98, NT 4.0 (or NT 3.5), or 2000 on the source system. Winnt.exe and Winnt32.exe reside in the shared folder on the distribution server. When you run Winnt.exe from the shared folder, it does the following:

   - Creates the Win_nt.~ls temporary folder on the target computer

   - Copies the Windows 2000 Professional installation files from the shared folder on the distribution server to the Win_nt.~ls folder on the target computer

4. Install Windows 2000 Professional. Setup restarts the target computer and begins installing Windows 2000 Professional.

Modifying the Setup Process

You can modify a server-based installation by changing how setup is executed using Winnt.exe. Table 1.1 describes the switches that you can use with Winnt.exe to control the setup process.

Table 1.1 Available Switches for Winnt.exe

Switch	Description
/a	Enables accessibility options.
/e[:*command*]	Specifies a command to be executed at the end of Setup's GUI mode.
/r[:*folder*]	Specifies an optional folder to be installed. The folder is retained after installation.
/rx[:*folder*]	Specifies an optional folder to be copied. Setup deletes the folder after installation.
/s[:*sourcepath*]	Specifies the source location of Windows 2000 Professional files. The location must be a full path of the form x:\ [path] or \\server\share\ [path]. The default location is the current folder.
/t[:*tempdrive*]	Specifies a drive to contain temporary setup files. If not specified, Setup attempts to locate a drive for you.
/u[:*answer file*]	Performs an unattended setup using an answer file. The answer file provides answers to some or all of the prompts that you normally respond to during Setup. (This switch also requires the use of the /s switch.)
/udf:*id*[,*UDF_file*]	Establishes an identifier (ID) that Setup uses to specify how a Uniqueness Database File (UDF) modifies an answer file. This switch overrides answer file values, and the identifier determines the values in the UDB file that are used. If you don't specify a UDB file, Setup prompts for the disk containing the $Unique$.udb file.

Modifying the Setup Process Using Winnt32.exe

You can modify a server-based installation by changing how setup is executed using Winnt32.exe. Table 1.2 describes the switches that you can use with Winnt32.exe to control the setup process.

Table 1.2 Available Switches for Winnt32.exe

Switch	Description
/checkupgradeonly	Checks the computer for upgrade compatibility with Windows 2000 Professional; for upgrade installations, it creates a report.
/copydir:*folder_name*	Creates an additional folder within the *systemroot* folder (the folder that contains the Windows 2000 Professional system files). For example, if your source folder contains a folder called My_drivers, type **/copydir:My_drivers** to copy the My_drivers folder to your system folder. You can use the /copydir switch to create as many additional folders as you like.
/copysource:*folder_name*	Creates an additional folder within the *systemroot* folder. Setup deletes files created with /copysource after installation completes.
/cmd: *command_line*	Executes a command before the final phase of Setup.
/cmdcons	Adds a Recovery Console option to the operating system selection screen.
/debug[*level*] [:*file_name*]	Creates a debug log at the specified level. By default, it creates C:\Winnt32.log at level 2 (the warning level).
/m:*folder_name*	Forces Setup to copy replacement files from another location and to look in that location first. If files are present, this switch tells Setup to use those files instead of files from the default location.
/makelocalsource	Forces Setup to copy all installation files to the local hard disk. Use this switch when installing Windows 2000 Professional from a CD-ROM if you want to access installation files when the CD-ROM drive isn't available later in the installation.
/noreboot	Forces Setup to not restart the computer following the file copy phase, which enables a command to be entered by the user prior to completing setup.

Switch	Description
/s:*source_path*	Specifies the source location of Windows 2000 Professional installation files. To simultaneously copy files from multiple paths, use a separate /s switch for each source path.
/syspart:*drive_letter*	Copies Setup startup files to a hard disk and marks the drive as active. You can then install the drive on another computer. When you start that computer, Setup starts at the next phase. Use of /syspart requires use of the /tempdrive switch.
/tempdrive:*drive_letter*	Places temporary files on the specified drive and installs Windows 2000 Professional on that drive.
/unattend [number] [:*answer_file*]	Performs an unattended installation. The answer file provides your custom specifications to Setup. If you don't specify an answer file, all user settings are taken from the previous installation. You can specify the number of seconds between the time that Setup finishes copying the files and when it restarts. You can specify the number of seconds only on a computer running Windows 2000 Professional that is upgrading to a later version of Windows 2000 Professional.
/udf:id[,*udf_file*]	Indicates an identifier (ID) that Setup uses to specify how a Uniqueness Database File (UDF) modifies an answer file. The .UDF file overrides values in the answer file, and the identifier determines which values in the .UDF file are used. For example, /udf:RAS_user, Our_company.udf overrides settings that are specified for the RAS_user identifier in the Our_company.udf file. If you don't specify a .UDF file, Setup prompts the user to insert a disk that contains the $Unique$.udf file.

Lesson Summary

In this lesson, you learned that the main difference between an over-the-network installation and an installation from a CD-ROM is the location of the source files. Once you connect to the shared folder containing the source files and start Winnt.exe or Winnt32.exe, the installation proceeds like an installation from a CD-ROM. Several switches are available for Winnt.exe and for Winnt32.exe to modify the installation process.

Lesson 3: Troubleshooting Windows 2000 Professional Setup

Your installation of Windows 2000 Professional should complete without any difficulty. However, there are some common problems that you might encounter during installation. They are discussed in this lesson.

After this lesson, you will be able to

- Troubleshoot problems encountered during the setup of Windows 2000 Professional

Estimated lesson time: 5 minutes

Resolving Common Problems

Table 1.3 lists some common installation problems and offers solutions to resolve them.

Table 1.3 Troubleshooting Tips

Problem	Solution
Media errors	If you are installing from a CD-ROM, use a different CD-ROM. To request a replacement CD-ROM, contact Microsoft or your vendor.
Nonsupported CD-ROM drive	Replace the CD-ROM drive with one that is supported, or if that isn't possible, try another method of installing, such as installing over the network. Then, after you have completed the installation, you can add the adapter card driver for the CD-ROM drive if it is available.
Insufficient disk space	Use the Setup program to create a partition by using existing free space on the hard disk; or, delete and create partitions as needed to create a partition that is large enough for installation; or, reformat an existing partition to create more space.
Failure of dependency service to start	In the Windows 2000 Setup wizard, return to the Network Settings dialog box and verify that you installed the correct protocol and network adapter. Verify that the network adapter has the proper configuration settings, such as transceiver type, and that the local computer name is unique on the network.

Problem	Solution
Failure to connect to the domain controller	Verify that the server running the DNS Service and the domain controller are both running and online. If you can't locate a domain controller, install in a workgroup and then join the domain after installation.
	Verify that the domain name is correct.
	Verify that the network adapter card and protocol settings are set correctly.
	If you are reinstalling Windows 2000 Professional and using the same computer name, delete and then recreate the computer account.
Failure of Windows 2000 Professional to install or start	Verify that Windows 2000 Professional is detecting all of the hardware and that all of the hardware is on the hardware compatibility list (HCL).

Setup Logs

During setup, Windows 2000 Professional generates a number of log files. These logs contain information about the installation process that can help you resolve any problems that occur after the Setup program has finished running. Two of the logs are especially useful for troubleshooting. These are the action log and the error log.

Using the Action Log

The action log provides a description of the actions that Setup performs. These actions are recorded in chronological order, and they include such actions as copying files and creating registry entries. The action log also includes any entries that are written to the error log. The action log is stored in the file named Setupact.log.

Using the Error Log

The error log contains a description of any errors that occur during setup, along with an indication of the severity of each error. If errors occur, the log viewer shows the user the error log at the end of setup. The error log is stored in the file Setuperr.log.

Additional Logs

A number of additional logs are created during setup. These logs include the following:

- *windir***comsetup.log.** This log outlines installation for Optional Component Manager and Com+ components.

- *windir***mmdet.log.** As a detection log for multimedia devices, this log details port ranges for each device.

- *windir***setupapi.log.** An entry is logged each time a line from an .INF file is implemented. If for some reason an error occurs, information is logged here to indicate the failure.

- *windir***debug\NetSetup.log.** Activity for joining a domain or workgroup is logged here.

Lesson Summary

In this lesson, you learned about some common problems that you might encounter when installing Windows 2000 Professional. For example, bad media can cause installation problems, in which case you will have to get a new CD-ROM to be able to perform the installation. You might also encounter problems with your installation if your hardware isn't on the hardware compatibility list (HCL). If your CD-ROM drive isn't listed on the HCL, you can swap it out for a supported drive or install over the network and add the driver to support the CD-ROM drive if it's available.

If you failed to complete your preinstallation tasks and none of the partitions have enough room to install Windows 2000 Professional, you can create a new partition from unused space on the hard disk if the space is available; you can delete some existing partitions so that you can create one large enough to install Windows 2000 Professional; or you can format an existing partition to provide enough space to install Windows 2000 Professional.

You also learned some tips to try in case you can't connect to the domain controller. If you can't connect to the domain controller, you can complete the installation by joining the computer to a workgroup. After you have completed the installation and determined what is preventing you from connecting to the domain controller, you can join the computer to the domain.

Lesson 4: Automating Installations

The previously discussed installation methods required that someone be physically present to respond to system prompts during installation. That is not a convenient situation when multiple systems are being installed.

This lesson presents methods that will help you to automate Windows 2000 Professional installations. When you must install Windows 2000 Professional on computers with varying configurations, scripting provides automation with increased flexibility. You will learn how the improved Setup Manager makes it easy to create the Unattend.txt files that are necessary for scripted installations.

After this lesson, you will be able to

- Automate installations of Windows 2000 Professional by using the Windows 2000 Setup Manager wizard

- Apply application update packs while upgrading previous versions of Windows

Estimated lesson time: 45 minutes

Automating Installations by Using the Windows 2000 Setup Manager

The computers in most networks are not identical, but they still have many similarities. You can use installation scripts to specify the variations in the hardware configurations of the computers that are to be installed with Windows 2000 Professional.

One of the most significant improvements in Windows 2000 Professional is the ease and flexibility of scripting installations. The new Windows 2000 Setup Manager wizard allows you to quickly create a script for a customized installation of Windows 2000 Professional. Knowing how to use Setup Manager enables you to perform customized installations on workstations and servers that meet the specific hardware and network requirements of your organization.

You can create or modify an answer file by using Setup Manager (see Figure 1.6). Although you can still use Unattend.txt files created with a simple text editor, such as Notepad, using Setup Manager will reduce errors in syntax. You can copy Setup Manager to your hard disk by extracting the files in the Deploy.cab file located on your Windows 2000 Professional CD-ROM in the Support\Tools folder. To extract the files, double-click the .CAB file to display the files, select the files you want to extract, right-click the files, and then click Extract on the menu that appears.

Note For detailed steps on how to install Setup Manager, see the next Practice, "Installing the Windows 2000 Professional Installation Deployment Tools," in this chapter.

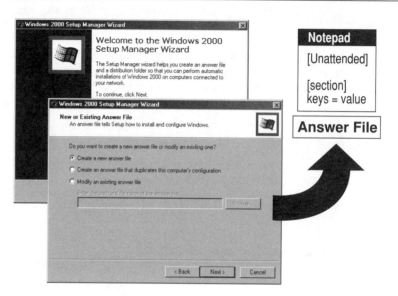

Figure 1.6 Windows Setup Manager

Setup Manager does the following:

- Provides a graphical interface with which you can create and modify answer files and UDFs
- Allows you to specify computer-specific or user-specific information
- Allows you to include application setup scripts in the answer file
- Creates the distribution folder that you use for the installation files

When you start Setup Manager, you will be presented with the following three options:

- Create A New Answer File
- Create An Answer File That Duplicates This Computer's Configuration
- Modify An Existing Answer File

If you select the Create A New Answer File option, you then need to choose the type of answer file you want to create. Setup Manager can create the following types of answer files:

- Windows 2000 Professional unattended installation

- Sysprep installation

- Remote Installation Services (RIS)

> **Note** Remote Installation Services will be discussed in Lesson 6 of this chapter, "Performing Remote Installations."

The remaining options in the Setup Manager wizard allow you to specify the level of user interaction with the Setup program and to enter all the information required to complete Setup.

Practice: Installing the Windows 2000 Professional Installation Deployment Tools

In this practice, you extract the Windows 2000 Professional installation deployment tools from the Windows 2000 Professional CD-ROM you used to install Windows 2000 Professional. You then use System Manager to create an unattended setup script.

Exercise 1: Extracting the Windows 2000 Professional Installation Deployment Tools

In this exercise, you extract the Windows 2000 Professional installation deployment tools from the CD-ROM you used to install Windows 2000 Professional and copy them to your hard disk.

1. Log on as Administrator and insert the Windows 2000 Professional CD-ROM in the CD-ROM drive.

2. Start Windows Explorer and create the folder Deploy in the root folder of drive C: (or in the root folder of your system drive).

   The Deploy folder will be used to store the files extracted from the Deploy.cab file on the Windows 2000 Professional CD-ROM.

3. Double-click the Deploy file in the Support\Tools folder on drive D.

> **Note** If D isn't the correct drive letter for your CD-ROM drive, replace the D in these instructions with the letter representing your CD-ROM drive.

Windows 2000 Professional displays the contents of the Deploy.cab file.

4. Select all of the files listed in the Deploy.cab file.

> **Tip** To select all the files in the Deploy.cab file, hold down the Ctrl key, and then click each of the files listed. If your file icons are listed in one column, you can also select the files by clicking the first file in the list, holding down the Shift key, and then clicking the last file in the list.

5. Right-click any of the selected files and click Extract on the menu that appears.

   The Browse For Folder dialog box appears.

6. Select the Deploy folder on drive C (or your system drive, if it is a drive other than C), and then click OK.

   The Copying dialog box appears briefly as the files are extracted and copied to the Deploy folder.

7. In Windows Explorer, click the Deploy folder to view its contents.

   You should see the seven files from the Deploy.cab file listed. These files have been extracted from the .CAB file and are now ready to use.

8. Double-click Readme.txt.

9. Take a moment to view the topics covered in the Readme.txt file, and then close Notepad.

Exercise 2: Using Setup Manager to Create an Unattended Setup Script

In this exercise, you use the Windows 2000 Setup Manager to create an unattended setup script. At the same time, the Setup Manager wizard creates a distribution folder and a .UDF file.

▶ **To create an unattended setup script using the Setup Manager wizard**

1. In Windows Explorer, double-click the Setupmgr.exe file.

   The Windows 2000 Setup Manager wizard appears.

2. Click Next.

   The New Or Existing Answer File page appears.

3. Ensure that the Create A New Answer File option is selected, and then click Next.

   The Product To Install page appears. Notice that you have three choices: Windows 2000 Unattended Installation, Sysprep Install, and Remote Installation Services.

4. Ensure that Windows 2000 Unattended Installation is selected, and then Click Next.

   The Platform page appears. Notice you have two choices: Windows 2000 Professional or Windows 2000 Server.

5. Ensure that Windows 2000 Professional is selected, and then click Next.

   The User Interaction Level page appears. Notice that you have five choices:

   - **Provide Defaults.** The answers you provide in the answer file are the default answers that the user sees. The user can accept the default answers or change any of the answers supplied by the script.

   - **Fully Automated.** The installation is fully automated. The user doesn't have the chance to review or change the answers supplied by the script.

   - **Hide Pages.** The answers provided by the script are supplied during the installation. Any page for which the script supplies all answers is hidden from the user so that the user can't review or change the answers supplied by the script.

   - **Read Only.** The script provides the answers, and the user can view the answers on any page that is not hidden, but the user can't change the answers.

   - **GUI Attended.** The Text-mode portion of the installation is automated, but the user must supply the answers for the GUI-mode (or Graphics-mode) portion of the installation.

6. Select Fully Automated, and then click Next.

   The License Agreement page appears.

   Note If you had chosen any option other than Fully Automated, this page would not have displayed.

7. Click I Accept The Terms Of The License Agreement, and then click Next.

   The Customize The Software page appears.

8. Enter your name in the Name box and your organization in the Organization box, and then Click Next.

   The Computer Names page appears. Notice that you have three choices:

   - Type in a series of names to be used during the various iterations of the script.

   - Provide the name of a text file to import that has one computer name per line listed. (Setup imports and uses these names as the computer names in the various iterations of the script.)

   - Select Automatically Generate Computer Names Based On Organization Name to allow the system to automatically generate the computer names to be used.

9. Type **PRO2** and then click Add. Repeat this step to add PRO3 and PRO4 to the list of names.

   Notice that the names PRO2, PRO3, and PRO4 appear in the Computers To Be Installed box.

10. Click Next.

   The Administrator Password page appears. Notice that you have two choices: Prompt The User For An Administrator Password and Use The Following Administrator Password (127 Characters Maximum).

   Note On the User Interaction Level page, you selected Fully Automated, so the Prompt The User For An Administrator Password option is not available.

   Notice that you can also have the administrator log on automatically, and you can set the number of times you want the administrator to log on automatically when the computer is restarted.

11. Ensure that Use The Following Administrator Password (127 Characters Maximum) is selected, and type **password** in the Password box and the Confirm Password box. Then click Next.

   The Display Settings page appears. Notice that you can adjust the Colors, Screen Area, and Refresh Frequency settings for the display. You can also choose Custom to create your own settings rather than picking from the selections listed under each of the three fields.

12. Click Next to accept the default settings.

    The Network Settings page appears. Notice that you can choose Typical Settings—which installs TCP/IP, enables DHCP, and installs the Client For Microsoft Networks protocol for each destination computer—or you can choose Custom Settings.

13. Select Custom Settings, and then click Next.

    The Number Of Network Adapters page appears.

14. Ensure that the default option, One Network Adapter, is selected and then click Next.

    The Networking Components page appears. Notice that the Client For Microsoft Networks, File And Printer Sharing For Microsoft Networks, and Internet Protocol (TCP/IP) components are installed by default.

15. Select Internet Protocol (TCP/IP), and then click Properties.

    The General tab of the Internet Protocol (TCP/IP) Properties dialog box appears. Notice that it is identical to configuring TCP/IP through Network and Dial-up Connections.

16. Click Cancel, and then click Next to accept the default settings for networking components.

    The Workgroup Or Domain page appears.

17. Click Next to accept the default option, Workgroup, and the workgroup name WORKGROUP.

    The Time Zone page appears.

18. Select the appropriate time zone, and then click Next.

    The Additional Settings page appears.

19. Ensure that the default option, Yes, Edit The Additional Settings is selected, and then click Next.

    The Telephony page appears.

20. Select the appropriate setting for What Country/Region Are You In?

21. Type the appropriate numbers for What Area (Or City) Code Are You In?

22. Type the appropriate number(s) for If You Dial A Number To Access An Outside Line, What Is It?

23. Select the appropriate setting for The Phone System At This Location Uses, and then click Next.

    The Regional Settings page appears. The default selection is Use The Default Regional Settings For The Windows Version You Are Installing.

24. Click Next to accept the default.

    The Languages page appears; it allows you to add support for additional languages.

25. Click Next to accept the default.

    The Browser And Shell Settings page appears. Notice that you can choose from the following three settings: Use Default Internet Explorer Settings, Use An Autoconfiguration Script Created By The Internet Explorer Administration Kit To Configure Your Browser, and Individually Specify Proxy And Default Home Page Settings.

26. Click Next to accept the default option, Use Default Internet Explorer Settings.

    The Installation Folder page appears. Notice that you can select from three choices: A Folder Named Winnt, A Uniquely Named Folder Generated By Setup, and This Folder.

27. Select This Folder, and in the This Folder box, type **W2000Pro** and then click Next.

    The Install Printers page appears.

28. Click Next to continue without having the script install any network printers.

    The Run Once page appears. This page allows you to configure Windows to run one or more commands the first time a user logs on.

29. Click Next to continue without having the script run any additional commands.

    The Distribution Folder page appears. This page allows you to have the Setup Manager wizard create a distribution folder on your computer or network with the required installation files. You can add additional files to this distribution folder.

Note If you were upgrading systems to Windows 2000 Professional, you could add any application update packs to the distribution folder and enter the commands to apply the update packs to the application as part of the upgrade.

---

30. Ensure that the default option, Yes, Create Or Modify A Distribution Folder, is selected, and then click Next.

Note The other selection is No, This Answer File Will Be Used To Install From A CD. If you are going to be doing a large number of installations, you don't want to try to simultaneously install the operating system on multiple computers from a CD-ROM. You should create one or more distribution folders.

The Distribution Folder Name page appears.

31. Click Next to accept the default option, Create A New Distribution Folder.

The Additional Mass Storage Drivers page appears.

32. Click Next to continue without adding any additional drivers.

The Hardware Abstraction Layer page appears. This page allows you to replace the default hardware abstraction layer (HAL).

33. Click Next to use the default HAL.

The Additional Commands page appears. This page allows you to specify additional commands to be run at the end of the unattended setup.

34. Click Next to continue without running any additional commands.

The OEM Branding page appears. This page allows you to customize Windows Setup by adding your customer OEM branding. You can specify both a logo bitmap and a background bitmap.

35. Click Next to continue without specifying any OEM branding.

The Additional Files Or Folders page appears. This page allows you to specify additional files or folders to be copied to the destination computers.

36. Click Next to continue without specifying any additional files or folders to copy.

The Answer File Name page appears.

37. Type the path **C:\Deploy\Unattend.txt** in the Location And File Name box, and then click Next.

The Location Of Setup Files page appears. The files can be copied from the CD-ROM or you can specify a network location.

38. Click Next to accept the default option, Copy The Files From CD.

   The Copying Files page appears while the Setup Manager wizard copies the distribution files. This will take a few minutes. An indicator shows you the progress of the copy operation.

   The Completing The Windows 2000 Setup Manager wizard appears.

39. Click Finish.

   Notice that three new files were created in C:\Deploy: They are Unattend.bat, Unattend.txt, and Unattend.udf. Notice also that a C:\Win2000dist folder was also created and shared.

▶ **To verify the existence of the distribution files**

   1. Click C:\Win2000dist to view the distribution files.

   2. Close Windows Explorer.

Lesson Summary

In this lesson, you learned that the Windows 2000 Professional Setup Manager wizard makes it easy to create the Unattend.txt files that are necessary for scripted installations. Setup Manager provides an easy-to-use graphical interface with which you can create and modify answer files and UDFs.

You also learned that before you can use the Setup Manager wizard, you must copy the Windows 2000 Professional deployment tools, including Setup Manager, by extracting the files located in the Deploy.cab file on the Windows 2000 Professional CD-ROM. The Setup Manager wizard makes it easy to specify computer-specific or user-specific information, and to include application setup scripts in the answer file. The Setup Manager wizard also creates the distribution folder that you use for the installation files.

Lesson 5: Using Disk Duplication to Deploy Windows 2000 Professional

When you install Windows 2000 Professional on several computers with identical hardware configurations, the most efficient installation method to use is disk duplication. By creating a disk image of a Windows 2000 Professional installation and copying that image to multiple destination computers, you save time in the mass installation of Windows 2000 Professional. This method also creates a convenient reference image that you can easily copy again to a computer that is experiencing significant problems.

Disk imaging and duplication technologies have been improved in Windows 2000 Professional over previous versions of Windows. One of the tools that you will use for disk duplication is the improved System Preparation tool (Sysprep.exe) that now ships with Windows 2000 Professional. Knowing how to use this tool can help support professionals prepare master disk images for efficient mass installations. You can use a number of third-party disk-imaging tools to copy the image to other computers. This lesson explains how to use the System Preparation tool to prepare the master image.

After this lesson, you will be able to

- Install and use the Windows 2000 System Preparation tool to deploy Windows 2000 Professional

Estimated lesson time: 25 minutes

Examining the Disk Duplication Process

To install Windows 2000 Professional by using disk duplication, you first need to install and configure Windows 2000 Professional on a test computer. After you have done this, you need to install and configure any applications and application update packs on the test computer. Then you run Sysprep.exe on the test computer to prepare the computer for duplication.

Extracting the Windows 2000 Professional System Preparation Tool

Before you can use the Windows 2000 Professional System Preparation tool, you must copy the necessary files onto the computer you are using to create the master image. To copy the System Preparation tool, you must extract the files from the Deploy.cab file in the Support\Tools folder on the Windows 2000 Professional CD-ROM. For the steps to do this, see Exercise 1, "Extracting the Windows 2000 Professional Installation Deployment Tools," in Lesson 4 of this chapter.

Using the System Preparation Tool to Prepare the Master Image

The System Preparation tool was developed to eliminate several problems you might encounter when copying disks. First of all, every computer must have a unique security ID (SID). If you copied an existing disk image to other computers, every computer on which the image was copied would have the same SID. To prevent this problem, the System Preparation tool adds a system service to the master image that will create a unique local domain SID the first time the computer to which the master image is copied is started.

The System Preparation tool also adds a Mini-Setup wizard to the master copy. The Mini-Setup wizard runs the first time the computer to which the master image is copied is started. The Mini-Setup wizard guides the user through the process of entering such user-specific information as the following:

- End-user license agreement
- Product ID
- Regional settings
- User name
- Company name
- Network configuration
- Whether the computer is joining a workgroup or domain
- Time zone selection

Note The Mini-Setup wizard can be scripted using the Setup Manager wizard so that this user-specific information can be entered automatically.

The System Preparation tool causes the master image to force the computer on which the master image is copied to run a full Plug and Play device detection. The hard disk controller device driver and the HAL on the computer on which the disk image was generated and on the computer to which the disk image was copied must be identical. The other peripherals, such as the network adapter, the video adapter, and sound cards on the computer on which the disk image was copied, need not be identical to the ones on the computer on which the image was generated.

The System Preparation tool can also be customized; Table 1.4 describes the switches that you can use to customize Sysprep.exe.

Table 1.4 Available Switches for Sysprep.exe

Switch	Description
/quiet	Runs with no user interaction
/pnp	Forces Setup to detect Plug and Play devices on the destination computers
/reboot	Restarts the source computer
/nosidgen	Doesn't regenerate SIDs on the destination computers

Practice: Using the System Preparation Tool to Create a Master Disk Image

In this practice, you will use the Windows 2000 System Preparation tool to prepare a master image for disk duplication.

Note You must complete Exercise 1 of Lesson 4 in this chapter and extract the System Preparation tool from the Windows 2000 Professional CD-ROM before you can complete the following exercise.

Caution If you complete the following exercise, you will have to reinstall Windows 2000 Professional on your computer.

Exercise 1: Using the System Preparation Tool

1. Log on as Administrator.

2. In Windows Explorer, double-click the Sysprep.exe file in the Deploy folder.

   A Windows 2000 Professional System Preparation Tool message box appears, warning you that running Sysprep might modify some of the security parameters of this system.

   Caution If you run Sysprep on your computer, you will lose some of the security parameters on your computer.

3. If you are certain that you don't mind having to reinstall Windows 2000 Professional, click OK to continue.

4. Your computer shuts down and prompts you to turn it off.

5. Turn off your computer.

Note You can run the Setup Manager wizard to create a Sysprep.inf file. Sysprep.inf provides answers to the Mini-Setup wizard on the destination computers. You can also use this file to specify customized drivers. The Setup Manager wizard creates a Sysprep folder at the root of the drive image and places Sysprep.inf in this folder. The Mini-Setup wizard checks for Sysprep.inf in the Sysprep folder at the root of the drive in which Windows 2000 Professional is being installed.

Installing Windows 2000 Professional from a Master Disk Image

After running Sysprep on your test computer, you are ready to run a third-party disk image copying tool to create a master disk image. Save the new disk image on a shared folder or CD-ROM. Copy this image to the multiple destination computers.

End users can then start the destination computers. The Mini-Setup wizard will prompt the user for computer-specific variables, such as the administrator password for the computer and the computer name. If a Sysprep.inf file was provided, the Mini-Setup wizard will be bypassed and the system will load Windows 2000 Professional without user intervention. You can also automate the completion of the Mini-Setup wizard further by creating a Sysprep.inf file.

Note When you use disk duplication, the mass storage controllers and HALs for the test computer and all destination computers must be identical.

Practice: Using the System Preparation Tool to Install Windows 2000 Professional

In this practice, you use a master disk image to install Windows 2000 Professional. You have just created a master disk image. Normally you would use a third-party tool to copy this disk image to another computer. For the purposes of this practice, you reinstall Windows 2000 Professional using the master disk image as if it were a computer that had the disk image copied to it.

Exercise 1: Installing Windows 2000 from a Master Image

1. Turn on your computer.

    After a few minutes, the Welcome To The Windows 2000 Setup wizard appears.

2. Click Next.

    The License Agreement page appears.

3. Read through the license agreement, click I Accept This Agreement, and then click Next.

    The Regional Settings page appears.

4. Ensure that the System Locale, the User Locale, and the Keyboard Layout are correct, and then click Next.

    The Personalize Your Software page appears.

5. In the Name box, type your name; in the Organization box, type your organization name, and then click Next.

    The Your Product Key page appears.

6. Enter your product key, and then click Next.

    The Computer Name And Administrator Password page appears.

7. In the Computer Name box, type **PRO1** (or type the name of your computer, if you are using another valid name for your network).

8. In the Password and Confirm Password boxes, type **password** and then click Next.

    The Modem Dialing Information page appears.

9. Select the appropriate setting for the What Country/Region Are You In Now? option.

10. Type the appropriate code for the What Area Code (Or City Code) Are You In Now? setting.

11. Type the appropriate number for the If You Dial A Number To Get An Outside Line, What Is It? setting.

12. Select the appropriate option for The Phone System At This Location Uses, and then click Next.

    The Date And Time Settings page appears.

13. Ensure that the Date, Time, and Time Zone settings are correct and that the Automatically Adjust Clock For Daylight Saving Changes check box is selected, if you want Windows 2000 Professional to adjust the clock. Then click Next.

    The Networking Settings page appears. This might take a few minutes.

14. Ensure that the default option, Typical Settings, is selected, and then click Next.

    The Workgroup Or Computer Domain page appears.

15. Ensure that the No, This Computer Is Not On A Network Or Is On A Network Without A Domain option is selected.

16. Ensure that WORKGROUP appears in the Workgroup Or Computer Domain box, and then click Next.

    The Performing Final Tasks page appears briefly, and then the Completing The Windows 2000 Setup Wizard page appears. This might take a few minutes while Setup completes.

17. Click Finish.

    The computer restarts, and the Welcome To The Network Identification wizard appears.

18. Click Next.

    The Users Of This Computer page appears.

19. Click Users Must Enter A User Name And Password To Use This Computer, and then click Next.

    The Completing The Network Identification wizard appears.

20. Click Finish.

21. Log on as Administrator with a password of **password**.

Lesson Summary

The System Preparation tool (Sysprep.exe) described in this lesson prepares the master computer to be duplicated. One of the primary functions of the System Preparation tool is to delete SIDs and all other user-specific or computer-specific information. You can use four switches to customize Sysprep.exe.

This lesson also showed you that after you run Sysprep.exe on the master computer, you can use a third-party tool to capture the image and copy it to the destination computers. When the user restarts the destination computer, the Mini-Setup wizard appears. You can also automate the completion of the Mini-Setup wizard further by creating a Sysprep.inf file.

Lesson 6: Performing Remote Installations

When you are deploying Windows 2000 Professional over a very large or geographically disparate set of systems, one of the most efficient methods is to use remote installation. You can perform remote installations of Windows 2000 Professional if you have a Windows 2000 Server infrastructure in place and the computers in your network support remote boot.

Note For more information about installing and configuring Windows 2000 Server, see Section II, Chapter 8, "Installing Microsoft Windows 2000 Server" in this book.

After this lesson, you will be able to

- Describe how to deploy Windows 2000 Professional using Remote Installation Services (RIS)

- Install RIS

- Create a boot floppy

Estimated lesson time: 40 minutes

Note To be able to install RIS and to create a boot floppy for network interface cards that are not equipped with a Pre-Boot Execution Environment (PXE) boot ROM, or for systems with BIOSs that don't support starting from the PXE boot ROM, you must have a computer running one of the Windows 2000 Server family of products. You must also have either the CD-ROM or access to a network source of files used to install the Server product. For more information, see the section "Examining the Prerequisites," on page 45.

Understanding Remote Installation

Remote installation is the process of connecting to a server running Remote Installation Services, called the RIS server, and then starting an automated installation of Windows 2000 Professional on a local computer. Remote installation enables administrators to install Windows 2000 Professional on client computers throughout a network from a central location. This reduces the time administrators spend visiting all the computers in a network, thereby reducing the cost of deploying Windows 2000 Professional.

RIS provides the following benefits:

- Enables remote installation of Windows 2000 Professional
- Simplifies server image management by eliminating hardware-specific images and by detecting Plug and Play hardware during setup
- Supports recovery of the operating system and computer in the event of computer failure
- Retains security settings after restarting the destination computer
- Reduces the total cost of operations by allowing either users or technical staff to install the operating system on individual computers

Installing and Configuring Remote Installation Services

Before beginning a mass installation of Windows 2000 Professional using RIS, become familiar with the prerequisites for the service and install the service using the Remote Installation Services Setup wizard.

Examining the Prerequisites

RIS is available only on computers running one of the Windows 2000 Server family of products. The RIS server can be a domain controller or a member server. Table 1.5 lists the network services required for RIS and their RIS function. These network services don't have to be installed on the same computer as RIS, but they must be available somewhere on the network.

Table 1.5 Network Services Required for RIS

Network service	RIS function
DNS Service	RIS relies on the DNS server for locating both the directory service and client computer accounts.
DHCP Service	Client computers that can perform a network boot receive an IP address from the DHCP server.
Active Directory directory services	RIS relies on the directory services based on Active Directory technology in Windows 2000 for locating existing client computers as well as existing RIS servers.

Remote installation requires that RIS (included on the Windows 2000 Server CD-ROM) be installed on a volume that is shared over the network. This shared volume must meet the following criteria:

- The shared volume can't be on the same drive that is running Windows 2000 Server;

- The shared volume must be large enough to hold the RIS software and the various Windows 2000 Professional images; and

- The shared volume must be formatted with the Microsoft Windows 2000 File System (NTFS).

Using the Remote Installation Services Setup Wizard

When your network meets the prerequisites for RIS, you can run the Remote Installation Services Setup wizard, which does the following:

- Installs the RIS software

- Creates the remote installation folder and copies the Windows 2000 Professional installation files to the server

- Adds .SIF files, which are a variation of an Unattend.txt file

- Configures the Client Installation Wizard screens that will appear during a remote installation

- Updates the registry

- Starts RIS

When installation of RIS is complete, you can configure it using the server's computer object in the Active Directory Users And Computers snap-in.

The RIS server stores the RIS images used to automatically install Windows 2000 Professional on client computers that are enabled for remote boot. The RIS server can be a domain controller or a standalone server that is a member of a domain containing Active Directory directory services.

Practice: Installing RIS

In this practice, you install Windows 2000 Remote Installation Services from a Windows 2000 Server CD-ROM.

Note To complete this exercise, you must have a Windows 2000 Professional CD-ROM or access to a shared folder that contains the Windows 2000 Professional installation files. You must also have a drive on the computer running one of the Windows 2000 Server family of products on which you installed RIS that is formatted with NTFS version 5 or later and that contains enough room to hold the Windows 2000 Professional installation files. You must have available on your network a DHCP server, a DNS server, and a domain.

Exercise 1: Installing Remote Installation Services

In this exercise, you install Remote Installation Services on a computer running Windows 2000 Server.

1. Log on as Administrator, and insert the Windows 2000 Server CD-ROM into your CD-ROM drive.

2. Open Control Panel, and double-click Add/Remove Programs.

   The Add/Remove Programs window appears.

3. Click Add/Remove Windows Components.

   The Windows Components page of the Windows Components wizard appears.

4. Select the Remote Installation Services check box in the Components box, and then click Next.

   Setup installs and configures RIS.

   The Completing The Windows Components Wizard page appears.

5. Click Finish.

   The System Settings Change dialog box appears, indicating that you must reboot before the new settings will take effect.

6. Remove the Windows 2000 Server CD-ROM from your CD-ROM drive and click Yes.

Exercise 2: Configuring Remote Installation Services

1. Log on as Administrator.

   The Microsoft Windows 2000 Configure Your Server screen appears, indicating that you have selected components that require additional configuration.

   Note If the Microsoft Windows 2000 Configure Your Server screen doesn't appear after you restart and log on as Administrator, open Control Panel, double-click Add/Remove Programs, and click Add/Remove Windows Components. Under Set Up Services, you should see the Configure Remote Installation Services item with an associated Configure button. Skip step 2 that follows and proceed with step 3.

   ---

2. Click Finish Setup.

   The Add/Remove Programs window appears, indicating that you now need to configure Remote Installation Services.

3. Click Configure.

   The Remote Installation Services Setup wizard appears.

4. Insert the Windows 2000 Professional CD-ROM in the CD-ROM drive of the server. If the Microsoft Windows 2000 CD dialog box appears, click Exit.

5. Read the information on the welcome screen and then click Next.

   The Remote Installation Folder Location page appears.

   Notice that the drive on which you create the Remote Installation folder can't be the system drive and must be formatted with NTFS version 5 or later.

6. Type **E:\RemoteInst** in the Path box, and click Next.

   Note Enter a path that is appropriate for your system. The folder should not exist; it will be created as part of the configuration process. Remember that the drive must be on the computer on which you installed RIS, must be formatted with NTFS version 5 or later, and must have about 300 MB of space available to hold the Windows 2000 Professional installation files.

   The Initial Settings page appears.

   Note By default, the RIS server doesn't support client computers until you configure it to do so.

7. Select the Respond To Client Computers Requesting Service check box and then click Next.

   The Installation Source Files Location page appears.

8. Enter the path to the installation source files and then click Next.

   Note If you were using a Windows 2000 Professional CD-ROM in the CD-ROM drive of the server on which you were configuring RIS, you would enter *x:***i386**, where *x* is the drive letter for the CD-ROM drive.

   The Windows Installation Image Folder Name page appears.

9. Click Next to accept the default name of Win2000.pro.

   The Friendly Description And Help Text page appears.

10. Click Next to accept the default friendly description and help text.

   The Review Settings page appears.

   Note The default description is "Microsoft Windows 2000 Professional." The help text is "Automatically installs Windows Professional without prompting the user for input."

11. Review the information, and then click Finish.

It will take several minutes for the following tasks to be completed:

- The remote installation folder is created.
- The files needed by the services are copied.
- The Windows installation files are copied.
- The Client Installation Wizard screen files are updated.
- A new unattended Setup answer file is created.
- RIS is created.
- The registry is updated.
- The required remote installation services are started.

12. When all the tasks are completed, click Done and close any open windows.

Understanding Client Requirements for Remote Installation

Client computers that support remote installation must have one of the following configurations:

- A configuration meeting the Net PC specification
- A network interface card with a PXE boot ROM and BIOS support for starting from the PXE boot ROM
- A supported network interface card and a remote installation boot disk

Net PCs

The Net PC is a highly manageable platform that can perform a network boot and manage upgrades and prevents users from changing the hardware or operating system configuration. Additional requirements for the Net PC are the following:

- The network adapter must be set as the primary boot device within the system BIOS.

- The user account that will be used to perform the installation must be assigned the user right "Log on as a batch job."

Note   The Administrator group doesn't have the right to log on to a batch job by default and thus needs to be assigned this right before attempting a remote installation.

- Users must be assigned permission to create computer accounts in the domain that they are joining. The domain is specified in the advanced settings on the RIS server.

Computers Not Meeting the Net PC Specification

Computers that don't directly meet the Net PC specification can still interact with the RIS server. You can enable remote installation on a computer that doesn't meet the Net PC specification by doing the following:

1. Install a network interface card with a PXE boot ROM.

2. Set the BIOS to start from the PXE boot ROM.

3. Assign the user right "Log on as a batch job" to the user account that will be used to perform the installation.

4. Assign users permission to create computer accounts in the domain that they are joining. You specify the domain in the advanced settings on the RIS server.

Creating Boot Floppies

If the network interface card in a client isn't equipped with a PXE boot ROM or the BIOS doesn't allow starting from the network interface card, create a remote installation boot disk. The boot disk simulates the PXE boot process. Windows 2000 Professional ships with the Windows 2000 Remote Boot Disk Generator that allows you to easily create a boot disk (see Figure 1.7).

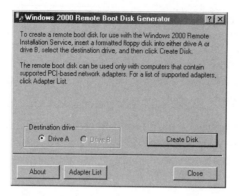

Figure 1.7 The Windows 2000 Remote Boot Disk Generator dialog box

Start the Windows 2000 Remote Boot Disk Generator by running Rbfg.exe. The Rbfg.exe file is located in the RemoteInstall\admin\i386 folder on the Remote Installation Server. These boot floppies support only the PCI-based network adapters listed in the Adapter List. To see the list of the supported network adapters, click the Adapter List button shown in Figure 1.7. A partial listing of the supported network adapter cards is shown in Figure 1.8.

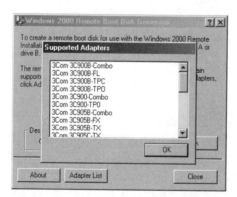

Figure 1.8 Network adapters supported by boot floppies

Practice: Creating a Remote Boot Disk

In this practice, you create a remote boot disk.

1. Log on as Administrator.

2. Click Start and then click Run.

    The Run dialog box appears.

3. Type **E:\RemoteInstall\Admin\i386\rbfg** in the Open box (where E: is your CD-ROM drive).

Note Your path to Rbfg.exe might vary. See step 6 in Exercise 2, "Configuring Remote Installation Services," in the previous practice.

4. Click OK.

The Windows 2000 Remote Boot Disk Generator dialog box appears.

5. Read the information in the Windows 2000 Remote Boot Disk Generator dialog box and then click Adapter List.

6. Scroll through the list of supported adapters, and then click OK to return to the Windows 2000 Remote Boot Disk Generator dialog box.

7. Insert a formatted 3.5-inch floppy into your floppy disk drive.

Note If your computer has more than one floppy disk drive, make sure you select the appropriate floppy disk drive you will be using when you are choosing the drive in the Windows 2000 Remote Boot Disk Generator dialog box.

8. Click Create Disk.

A Windows 2000 Remote Boot Disk Generator dialog box appears, prompting you to create another boot floppy.

9. Click No.

10. Click Close to close the Windows 2000 Remote Boot Disk Generator dialog box.

Lesson Summary

In this lesson, you learned that if you have a Windows 2000 Server infrastructure in place, and the computers in your network support remote boot, the most efficient method of deploying Windows 2000 Professional is to use remote installation. Remote installation is the process of connecting to an RIS server and then starting an automated installation of Windows 2000 Professional on a local computer. Remote installation enables administrators to install Windows 2000 Professional on client computers throughout a network from a central location. This reduces the time that administrators spend visiting all the computers in a network, thereby reducing the cost of deploying Windows 2000 Professional.

You also learned that client computers that support remote installation must have one of the three following configurations: a configuration meeting the Net PC specification, for which the network interface card must be set as the primary boot device within the system BIOS; a network interface card with a PXE boot ROM and BIOS support for starting from the PXE boot ROM; or a supported network interface card and a remote installation boot disk.

Finally, you saw that the user account that is to be used to perform the installation must be assigned the user right "Log on as a batch job," and users must be assigned permission to create computer accounts in the domain that they are joining. The domain is specified in the advanced settings on the RIS server.

Lesson 7: Upgrading Previous Versions of Windows to Windows 2000 Professional

In most cases, you will be upgrading a previous version of Windows to Windows 2000 Professional. You can upgrade most previous versions of Windows operating systems directly to Windows 2000 to take advantage of the new features offered in the Windows 2000 Professional operating system. However, before upgrading to Windows 2000 Professional, ensure that the computer hardware meets the minimum Windows 2000 hardware requirements. You must also check the HCL or test the computers for hardware compatibility using the Windows 2000 Compatibility tool. You want to ensure that the hardware is compatible with Windows 2000 to avoid surprises when you start the upgrade on a large number of client computers.

Computers running previous versions of Windows that use compatible hardware can be upgraded directly to Windows 2000. If Windows 95 and Windows 98 client systems are using incompatible or insufficient hardware, you can still take advantage of the functionality of Active Directory directory services provided by a Windows 2000 domain by installing the Windows 2000 Directory Service Client on these systems.

After this lesson, you will be able to

- Explain how to upgrade older Windows client operating systems to Windows 2000

Estimated lesson time: 25 minutes

Identifying Client Upgrade Paths

You can upgrade most client computers running older versions of Windows directly to Windows 2000. However, computers running Windows NT 3.1 or 3.5 require an additional step. Table 1.6 lists the Windows 2000 Professional upgrade paths for client operating systems.

Table 1.6 Windows 2000 Professional Upgrade Paths for Client OSs

Upgrade from	Upgrade to
Windows 95 and Windows 98	Windows 2000 Professional
Windows NT 3.51 and Windows NT 4.0 Workstation	Windows 2000 Professional
Windows NT 3.1 or 3.5	Windows NT 3.51 or Windows NT 4.0 Workstation first, then upgrade to Windows 2000 Professional

Note Windows 2000 Professional also upgrades all released service packs for Windows NT 3.51 and Windows NT 4.0 Workstation.

Identifying Hardware Requirements and Compatibility

Before you upgrade a client computer to Windows 2000 Professional, make sure that it meets the minimum hardware requirements. Table 1.7 describes these hardware requirements.

Table 1.7 Windows 2000 Professional Minimum Hardware Requirements

Hardware	Minimum requirements
Processor	One processor, Intel Pentium 133 MHz or higher (dual CPU systems are supported)
Memory	Pentium-based: 64 MB
Hard disk	2 GB drive with at least 650 MB of free space on the boot partition
Video	VGA or higher video card and monitor
Other components	CD-ROM installation: CD-ROM or DVD-ROM drive
Networking	Network interface card and related cables
Accessories	Keyboard and mouse or other pointing device

Most hardware devices that functioned properly in Windows NT 4.0 Workstation will also function properly in Windows 2000 Professional. However, you might have to replace some third-party drivers with new drivers designed for Windows 2000. You can obtain these new drivers from the manufacturer of the specific device.

Generating a Hardware Compatibility Report

You generate a hardware and software compatibility report using the Windows 2000 Compatibility tool. This tool runs automatically during system upgrades, but Microsoft recommends that you run it before beginning the upgrade to identify any hardware and software problems. This is especially important when upgrading many computers with similar hardware, so compatibility problems can be fixed before the upgrade begins.

Generating the Report

You can generate a compatibility report using the Windows 2000 Compatibility tool in two ways:

- Run Winnt32/checkupgradeonly.

  Using the /checkupgradeonly switch with the Winn32 command launches the first part of the Windows 2000 Setup program. Instead of running the entire setup process, it checks only for compatible hardware and software. This generates a report that you can analyze to determine which system components are Windows 2000–compatible.

- Run the Chkupgrd.exe utility.

  This immediately generates the compatibility report. You can download this utility from *http://www.microsoft.com/windows/downloads/default.asp*.

Reviewing the Report

Both Winnt32 /checkupgradeonly and the Chkupgrd.exe utility generate the same report. This report appears as a text document; you can view it in the utility's window or save it as a text file.

The report documents the system hardware and software that is incompatible with Windows 2000. It also identifies whether you need to obtain an upgrade pack for software installed on the system, and any additional changes or modifications you must make to the system to maintain functionality in Windows 2000.

Identifying Software Compatibility

Most applications that run in either Windows NT 4.0 Workstation or Windows NT 3.51 will run in Windows 2000 Professional. However, some applications will be incompatible. You should remove the following software applications before you upgrade to Windows 2000 Professional:

- Any third-party networking protocols and any third-party client software that doesn't have an update in the i386\Winntupg folder on the Windows 2000 CD-ROM

- All antivirus applications and disk quota software because of the changes in the NTFS file system from version 4, which was used in Windows NT 4.0 Workstation, to version 5, which is used in Windows 2000 Professional

- Any custom power management software or tools because they are replaced by Windows 2000's support of Advanced Configuration and Power Interface (ACPI) and Advanced Power Management (APM)

Upgrading Compatible Windows 95 and Windows 98 Computers

For client systems that test as compatible with Windows 2000, you run the Windows 2000 Setup program (winnt32.exe) to complete the upgrade process by completing the following steps:

1. Run the winnt32.exe command.

2. Accept the license agreement.

3. If the computer you are upgrading is already a member of a domain, you must create a computer account in that domain. Windows 95 and Windows 98 clients don't require a computer account, but Windows 2000 Professional clients do.

4. You are asked to provide upgrade packs for any applications that might need them. Upgrade packs update software so it works with Windows 2000. Upgrade packs are available from the software vendor.

5. You are prompted to upgrade to NTFS. Select the upgrade if you don't plan to set up the client computer to dual boot operating systems.

6. The Windows 2000 Compatibility tool runs, generating a report. If the report shows the computer as Windows 2000 compatible, continue with the upgrade. If the report shows the computer to be incompatible with Windows 2000, terminate the upgrade.

7. The upgrade is completed without further user intervention. After the upgrade is complete, you must enter the password for the local computer's Administrator account.

If your computer is Windows 2000 compatible, it is now upgraded and is a member of your domain. If your computer is not Windows 2000 compatible, you must upgrade your hardware, if possible, or you can install the Windows 2000 Directory Service Client.

Installing the Directory Service Client

Windows 95 or Windows 98 computers that don't meet the hardware compatibility requirements can still take advantage of Active Directory directory services by using Directory Service Client. Directory Service Client upgrades Windows 95 and Windows 98 systems so that they support Active Directory features, and can do the following:

- Use fault-tolerant Dfs

- Search Active Directory directory services

- Change your password on any domain controller

Note Before installing Directory Service Client on a computer running Windows 95, you must install Internet Explorer 4.01 or later and enable the Active Desktop component. Otherwise, the Directory Service Client Setup wizard won't run.

You can complete the following steps to install Directory Service Client on a non-Windows 2000-compatible computer:

1. In the Clients\Win9*x* folder on the Windows 2000 Server or Advanced Server CD-ROM, run the Dsclient.exe command.

   The Directory Service Client Setup wizard starts.

2. Click Next.

   The Ready To Install page appears.

3. Click Next.

   The Setup wizard copies files and displays a progress indicator. When copying is complete, the Installation Completed page appears.

4. Click Finish to complete the installation.

   A Systems Settings Change message box appears, advising you that your computer must restart before the new settings will take effect.

5. Click Yes to restart the computer.

Upgrading Windows NT 3.51 and 4 Clients

The upgrade process for computers running Windows NT 3.51 and Windows NT Workstation 4.0 is similar to the upgrade process for computers running Windows 95 and Windows 98.

Verifying Compatibility

Before you perform the upgrade, you must verify that the systems are compatible with Windows 2000. Use the Windows 2000 Compatibility tool to identify any potential problems before you start the upgrade.

Upgrading Compatible Systems

Computers running Windows NT Workstation 3.51 and Windows NT Workstation 4.0 that meet the hardware compatibility requirements can upgrade directly to Windows 2000. You can start the upgrade process by completing the following procedure:

1. Insert the Windows 2000 CD-ROM in the CD-ROM drive.

2. Click Start, and then click Run.

3. In the Run box, type *d*:\i386\winnt32 (where *d* is the drive letter for your CD-ROM), and then press Enter.

    The Welcome To The Windows 2000 Setup wizard appears.

4. Select Upgrade To Windows 2000 (Recommended), and then click Next.

    The License Agreement page appears.

5. Read the license agreement and then click I Accept This Agreement.

6. Click Next.

    The Upgrading To The Windows 2000 NTFS File System page appears.

7. Click Yes, Upgrade My Drive, and then click Next.

    The Copying Installation Files page appears.

    The Restarting The Computer page appears and the computer will now restart.

The upgrade finishes without further user intervention.

Using Incompatible Systems

Computers running Windows NT 3.51 or Windows NT 4.0 Workstation that do not meet the hardware compatibility requirements can still log on to a Windows 2000 network, but they won't be able to take advantage of many Windows 2000 features. No Directory Service Client is available for computers running Windows NT 3.51 or Windows NT 4.0 Workstation.

Lesson Summary

In this lesson, you learned that you can upgrade most client computers running older versions of Windows directly to Windows 2000. However, you must first upgrade computers running Windows NT 3.1 or Windows NT 3.5 to Windows NT 3.51 or Windows NT 4.0 Workstation, and then you can upgrade them to Windows 2000 Professional.

You also learned that before you upgrade a client computer to Windows 2000 Professional, you must make sure that it meets the minimum hardware requirements. You can generate a hardware and software compatibility report using the Windows 2000 Compatibility tool. This tool runs automatically during system upgrades, but Microsoft recommends that you run this tool before beginning the upgrade to identify any hardware and software problems. This is especially important when upgrading many computers with similar hardware, so compatibility problems can be fixed before the upgrade begins.

Finally, you learned that for client systems that test as being compatible with Windows 2000, you run the Windows 2000 Setup program (Winnt32.exe) to complete the upgrade process. If your computer isn't Windows 2000 compatible, you must upgrade your hardware, if possible, or you can install Directory Service Client. Computers running Windows 95 or Windows 98 that don't meet the hardware compatibility requirements can still take advantage of Active Directory directory services by using Directory Service Client. Directory Service Client upgrades Windows 95 and 98 systems so that they support Active Directory features and are able to use fault-tolerant Dfs, search Active Directory directory services, and change your password on any domain controller.

Lesson 8: Installing Service Packs

With previous versions of Windows, you were required to install the Windows operating system and then apply each required service pack separately. Also, in the earlier versions of Windows, when components were installed or removed, the service pack had to be reapplied. For example, if you were to add remote access services to a computer running Windows NT 4.0 Workstation with service pack 4, you would have to reapply service pack 4 in order to make the installed component compliant with service pack 4.

Windows 2000 Professional eliminates the need to reapply a service pack after installing new components and allows you to apply a service pack at the same time that you install Windows 2000. This lesson describes this process.

After this lesson, you will be able to

- Deploy service packs

Estimated lesson time: 5 minutes

Slipstreaming Service Packs

Windows 2000 Professional supports service-pack slipstreaming, so service packs can be integrated with the Windows 2000 Professional installation files. This allows you to keep one master image of the operating system. When Windows 2000 Professional is installed from this master source, the appropriate files from the service pack are also installed. This saves you having to manually apply service packs after each Windows 2000 installation.

To apply a new service pack, run Update.exe with the /slip switch. This replaces the existing Windows 2000 files with the appropriate files from the service pack. Some of the key Windows 2000 files that are replaced when you apply a service pack include the following: Layout.inf, Dosnet.inf, Txtsetup.sif, and if any drivers have changed, a new Driver.cab file.

Deploying Service Packs After Installing Windows 2000

To apply a service pack to a computer running Windows 2000, run Update.exe. Running Update.exe replaces the existing Windows 2000 files with the appropriate new files from the service pack.

Unlike earlier versions of Windows, where each time you changed the system by adding or removing services, you had to reapply any service packs, Windows 2000 automatically recognizes that a service pack has been applied to the system and which files have been replaced or updated. Whenever you add or remove services from a computer running Windows 2000, the system copies the required files from either the Windows 2000 installation files or from the service pack install location, so you don't have to reapply the service pack.

Lesson Summary

Windows 2000 Professional simplifies the installation and maintenance of service packs and supports service-pack slipstreaming, so service packs can be integrated with the Windows 2000 installation files. As you install Windows 2000, the appropriate files from the service pack(s) are automatically applied during the installation.

This lesson also explained that when you apply a service pack to a computer running Windows 2000, and you later decide to add or remove services, you don't need to reapply the service pack. Windows 2000 automatically recognizes that a service pack has been applied to the system and copies the required files from either the Windows 2000 installation files or from the service pack installation location. This frees you from having to reapply the service pack every time services are added or removed from a computer.

Review

The following questions will help you determine whether you have learned enough to move on to the next chapter. If you have difficulty answering these questions, please go back and review the material in this chapter before beginning the next chapter. See Appendix A, "Questions and Answers," for the answers to these questions.

1. How do you install the Windows 2000 deployment tools, such as the Setup Manager wizard and the System Preparation tool?

2. Which five resources must you have to use Remote Installation Services to install Windows 2000 Professional?

3. What utility is provided in Windows 2000 to create boot floppies and how do you access it?

4. You are planning on installing 45 computers with Windows 2000 Professional. You have determined that these 45 computers have seven different network adapter cards. How do you determine whether these seven different types of network adapter cards are supported by the boot floppies you created?

5. You have a portable computer running Windows 95 and you want to upgrade it to Windows 2000. The computer has 16 MB of RAM, and this can be upgraded to 24 MB. Can you upgrade this computer to Windows 2000? If not, how would you make it so this computer was able to access Active Directory directory services?

6. Name at least two problems the System Preparation tool resolves when creating and copying a master disk image to other computers.

7. Your company has decided to install Windows 2000 Professional on all new computers that are purchased for desktop users. What should you do before you purchase new computers to ensure that Windows 2000 can be installed and run without difficulty?

8. You are attempting to install Windows 2000 Professional from a CD-ROM. However, you have discovered that your computer doesn't support booting from the CD-ROM drive. How can you install Windows 2000?

9. You are installing Windows 2000 Server on a computer that will be a client in an existing Windows 2000 domain. You want to add the computer to the domain during installation. What information do you need, and which computers must be available on the network before you run the Setup program?

10. You are using a CD-ROM to install Windows 2000 Professional on a computer that was previously running another operating system. How should you configure the hard disk to simplify the installation process?

11. You are installing Windows 2000 Professional over the network. Before you install to a client computer, what must you do?

C H A P T E R   2

Managing Hardware Devices and Drivers

About This Chapter

With Microsoft Windows 2000 Professional, all aspects of installing, configuring, and managing hardware devices and their associated drivers are improved over previous versions of Windows. Plug and Play hardware is supported and non–Plug and Play devices can be easily installed and configured.

As the various devices are installed and configured, Microsoft Windows 2000 Professional stores this information in two locations: the registry and the directory services based on Active Directory technology. Modifications to the registry or Active Directory directory services change the configuration of the Windows 2000 environment. You use the following tools to modify the registry or Active Directory directory services:

- Microsoft Management Console
- Device Manager
- Control Panel
- Registry Editor

As a Windows NT 4 professional, you should already be familiar with using the Control Panel and Registry Editor. This chapter begins with a discussion of the Microsoft Management Console (MMC) and how it is used to manage and monitor hardware. You will have the opportunity to use the MMC in the various exercises presented throughout this chapter The hardware topics discussed include:

- Disk management
- Power management
- Monitoring hardware performance

The chapter concludes with an overview of using the Performance Console to monitor system performance.

Before You Begin

To complete this chapter, you must have

- A computer that meets the minimum hardware requirements listed in "Hardware Requirements," in "About This Book."
- The Windows 2000 Professional software installed on the computer

Lesson 1: Installing Hardware Automatically

Windows 2000 Professional supports both Plug and Play and non–Plug and Play hardware. This lesson introduces you to the automatic hardware installation features of Windows 2000 Professional.

After this lesson, you will be able to

- Describe how to install hardware automatically

Estimated lesson time: 15 minutes

Installing Plug and Play Hardware

With most Plug and Play hardware, you simply connect the device to the computer, and Windows 2000 Professional automatically configures the new settings. However, you might occasionally need to initiate automatic installation for some Plug and Play hardware. You do this with the Add/Remove Hardware wizard.

Installing Non–Plug and Play Hardware

For non–Plug and Play hardware, Windows 2000 Professional often identifies the hardware and automatically installs and configures it. For non–Plug and Play hardware that Windows 2000 Professional doesn't identify, install, and configure, you initiate the automatic installation of the hardware with the Add/Remove Hardware wizard.

▶   **Follow these steps for automatic hardware installations:**

1. Initiate automatic hardware installation by starting the Add/Remove Hardware wizard.

   Windows 2000 Professional queries the hardware about the hardware resources that it requires and the settings needed for those resources. A hardware resource allows a hardware device to communicate directly with the operating system. Windows 2000 Professional can resolve conflicts between different Plug and Play hardware devices for hardware resources.

2. Confirm the automatic hardware installation.

   Once Windows 2000 Professional finishes the installation, verify correct installation and configure the hardware.

Using the Add/Remove Hardware Wizard

You use the Add/Remove Hardware wizard to initiate automatic hardware installation and to troubleshoot devices. You also use the wizard to install undetected hardware devices—both Plug and Play devices and non–Plug and Play devices.

▶ **Follow these steps to begin installing new hardware using the Add/Remove Hardware wizard:**

1. In Control Panel, double-click Add/Remove Hardware Wizard.

2. Click Next to close the welcome page.

3. Select Add/Troubleshoot A Device, and then click Next.

   Windows searches for new devices.

After the Add/Remove Hardware wizard starts, it searches for new Plug and Play hardware and then proceeds to install any devices it finds. If the wizard finds no new devices, it displays the Choose A Hardware Device page, shown in Figure 2.1. If no new hardware devices are detected, Windows 2000 Professional prompts you to select one of the installed devices to troubleshoot it.

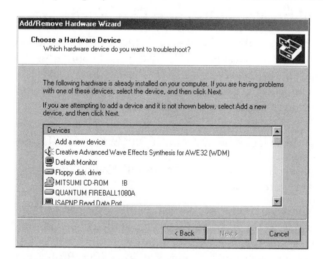

Figure 2.1 Troubleshooting with the Add/Remove Hardware wizard

Confirming Hardware Installation

▶   **After installing hardware, follow these steps to confirm the installation using Device Manager:**

1. Double-click the System icon in Control Panel.

2. Click the Hardware tab, and then click Device Manager.

    This allows you to view the installed hardware, as shown in Figure 2.2.

Windows 2000 Professional uses icons in the right pane of the Computer Management window to identify each installed hardware device. If Windows 2000 Professional doesn't have an icon for the device type, it displays a question mark.

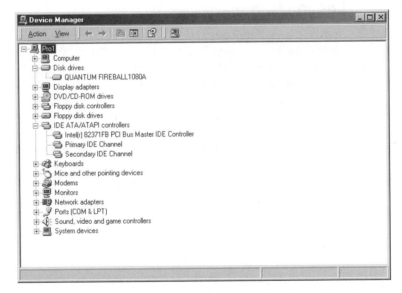

Figure 2.2 The Device Manager window showing devices listed by type

Expand the device tree to locate the newly installed hardware device. The device icon indicates whether the hardware device is operating properly. You can use the information in Table 2.1 to determine the hardware status.

Table 2.1 Device Manager Hardware Status

Icon	Hardware status
Normal icon	Hardware is operating properly.
Stop sign on icon	Windows 2000 Professional disabled the hardware device because of hardware conflicts. To correct this, right-click the device icon, and then click Properties. Set the hardware resources manually according to what is available on the system.
Exclamation point on icon	The hardware device is incorrectly configured or its drivers are missing.

Lesson Summary

In this lesson, you learned that Windows 2000 Professional supports both Plug and Play and non–Plug and Play hardware. With most Plug and Play hardware, you connect the device to the computer, and Windows 2000 Professional automatically configures the new settings. For non–Plug and Play hardware, Windows 2000 Professional often identifies the hardware and automatically installs and configures it. For Plug and Play hardware devices and non–Plug and Play hardware that Windows 2000 Professional doesn't identify, install, and configure, you must initiate automatic hardware installation with the Add/Remove Hardware wizard.

Lesson 2: Installing Hardware Manually

Occasionally, Windows 2000 Professional fails to automatically detect a hardware device. When this occurs, you must manually install the hardware device. You might also have to manually install a hardware device if the device requires a specific hardware resource. You manually install these devices to ensure that they have the necessary resources.

To manually install hardware, you must do the following:

- Determine which hardware resource the hardware device requires.
- Determine the available hardware resources.
- Change hardware resource assignments.

After this lesson, you will be able to

- Install hardware manually
- Determine hardware resource need and availability
- Reassign hardware resources

Estimated lesson time: 10 minutes

Determining Which Hardware Resources Are Required

When installing new hardware, you need to know which available resources in Windows 2000 Professional the hardware can use. You can refer to the product documentation to determine what resources a hardware device requires. Table 2.2 describes the resources that hardware devices use to communicate with an operating system.

Table 2.2 Hardware Device Resources

Resource	Description
Interrupts	Hardware devices use interrupts to send messages. The microprocessor knows this as an interrupt request (IRQ). The microprocessor uses this information to determine which device needs its attention and the type of attention that it needs. Windows 2000 Professional provides 16 IRQs, numbered 0 to 15, which are assigned to devices; for example, Windows 2000 Professional assigns IRQ 1 to the keyboard.
Input/output (I/O) ports	I/O ports are a section of memory that a hardware device uses to communicate with the operating system. When a microprocessor receives an IRQ, the operating system checks the I/O port address to retrieve additional information about what the hardware device wants it to do. An I/O port is represented as a hexadecimal number.
Direct memory access (DMA) channels	DMA channels allow a hardware device, such as a floppy disk drive, to access memory directly, without interrupting the microprocessor. DMA channels speed up access to memory. Windows 2000 Professional has eight DMA channels, numbered 0 to 7.
Memory	Many hardware devices, such as a network adapter card (NAC), use onboard memory or reserve system memory. This reserved memory is unavailable for use by other devices or Windows 2000 Professional.

Determining Available Hardware Resources

After you determine which resources a hardware device requires, you can look for an available resource. Device Manager provides a list of all hardware resources and their availability, as shown in Figure 2.3.

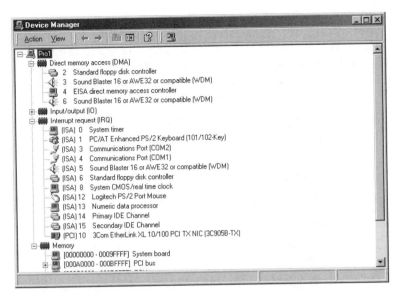

Figure 2.3 The Device Manager window showing resources listed by connection

▶ **Follow these steps to view the hardware resources lists:**

1. From the System Properties dialog box, click the Hardware tab, and then click Device Manager.

2. On the View menu, click Resources By Connection.

   Device Manager displays the resources that are currently in use (for example, IRQs).

3. To view a list of resources for another type of hardware resource, on the View menu, click the type of hardware resource that you want to see.

Once you know which hardware resources are available, you can install the hardware manually with the Add/Remove Hardware wizard.

Note If you select a hardware resource during manual installation, you might need to configure the hardware device so that it can use the resource. For example, for a network adapter to use IRQ 5, you might have to set a jumper on the adapter and configure Windows 2000 Professional so that it recognizes that the adapter now uses IRQ 5.

Changing Hardware Resource Assignments

You might need to change hardware resource assignments. For example, a hardware device might require a specific resource presently in use by another device. You might also encounter a conflict that is the result of two hardware devices requesting the same hardware resource.

To change a resource setting, use the Resources tab in the device's Properties dialog box.

▶   **Follow these steps to access the Resources tab:**

1. From the Hardware tab of the System Properties dialog box, click Device Manager.

2. Expand the device list, right-click the specific device, and then click Properties.

3. In the Properties dialog box for the device, click the Resources tab.

Tip When you change a hardware resource, print the content of Device Manager. This will provide you with a record of the hardware configuration. If you encounter problems, you can use the printout to verify the hardware resource assignments.

From this point on, follow the same procedures that you used to choose a hardware resource during a manual installation.

Note Changing the resource assignments for non–Plug and Play devices in Device Manager doesn't change the resources used by that device. You use Device Manager only to set device configuration for the operating system. To change the resources used by a non–Plug and Play device, consult the device documentation to see whether switches or jumpers must be configured on the device.

Lesson Summary

In this lesson, you learned about installing hardware manually. If Windows 2000 Professional fails to automatically detect a hardware device, or if a hardware device requires a specific hardware resource, you might have to manually install these devices. When you manually install hardware, you must determine any resources required by that hardware device. Hardware resources include interrupts, I/O ports, and memory. Refer to the product documentation to determine what resources a device requires. You also must determine which of the appropriate hardware resources are available on Windows 2000 Professional. The Device Manager snap-in provides a list of all hardware resources and their availability on Windows 2000 Professional.

You also learned that you might need to change hardware resource assignments. For example, a hardware device might require a specific resource presently in use by another device. You saw that to change a hardware resource, you also use Device Manager.

Lesson 3: Configuring the Display

One of the more common tasks of hardware configuration is setting the display properties to meet the desires of the users. Users with permission to load and unload device drivers can also install and test video drivers. Windows 2000 Professional can change video resolutions dynamically without restarting the system.

After this lesson, you will be able to

- Use Control Panel to configure the display

Estimated lesson time: 25 minutes

Setting Display Properties

To view or modify the display properties, in Control Panel, double-click the Display icon, and then click the Settings tab (see Figure 2.4). Alternatively, right-click your desktop and select Properties from the shortcut menu. Configurable display options include the number of colors, video resolution, font size, and refresh frequency.

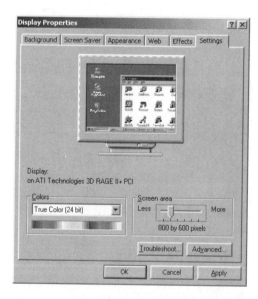

Figure 2.4 The Settings tab of the Display Properties dialog box

Table 2.3 describes the options available on the Settings tab for configuring the display settings.

Table 2.3 Settings Tab Options for Configuring the Display

Option	Description
Colors	Lists color depths for the display adapter
Screen Area	Allows you to set the resolution for the display adapter
Troubleshoot	Opens the Display Troubleshooter to aid in diagnosing display problems
Advanced	Opens the Properties dialog box for the display adapter, as described in Table 2.4.

If the basic settings are not sufficient to configure your monitor, you can used the more detailed settings under the Advanced tab. Table 2.4 describes the display adapter options.

Table 2.4 Display Adapter Advanced Options

Tab	Option group	Description
General	Display	Provides the Small Font, Large Font, and Other options.
		The Other option allows you to choose any font size.
	Compatibility	Lets you choose what Windows 2000 Professional should do when you change display settings. After you change the color settings, you must choose one of the following options:
		▪ Restart The Computer Before Applying The New Display Settings
		▪ Apply The New Display Settings Without Restarting
		▪ Ask Me Before Applying The New Display Settings

continues

Table 2.4 Display Adapter Advanced Options *(continued)*

Tab	Option group	Description
Adapter	Adapter Type	Provides the manufacturer and model number of the installed adapter. The Properties button provides additional information, including device status, resource settings, and whether there are any conflicting devices.
	Adapter Information	Provides additional information about the display adapter, such as video chip type, digital-to-analog converter (DAC) type, memory size, and BIOS.
	List All Modes	Displays all compatible modes for your display adapter and lets you select resolution, color depth, and refresh frequency in one step.
Monitor	Monitor Type	Provides the manufacturer and model number of the monitor currently installed. The Properties button provides additional information and allows you access to the Display Troubleshooter to help in resolving problems with this device.
	Monitor Settings	Allows you to configure the refresh rate frequency. This option applies only to high-resolution drivers. Don't select a refresh rate/screen resolution combination that is unsupported by the monitor. If you are unsure, refer to your monitor documentation, or select the lowest refresh rate option.
Troubleshooting	Hardware Acceleration	Lets you progressively decrease your display hardware's acceleration features to help you isolate and eliminate display problems.
Color Management		Lets you choose the color profile for your monitor.

Using Multiple Displays

Windows 2000 Professional adds support for multiple display configurations. Multiple displays allow you to extend your desktop across more than one monitor, as shown in Figure 2.5. Windows 2000 supports extending your display across a maximum of 10 monitors.

- Use of multiple displays extends the desktop across a maximum of 10 monitors.
- Multiple displays must use Peripheral Component Interconnect (PCI) or Accelerated Graphics Port (AGP) devices.
- Hardware requirements for primary (main) and secondary displays differ.

Figure 2.5 Multiple displays

Important You must use Peripheral Component Interconnect (PCI) or Accelerated Graphics Port (AGP) devices when configuring multiple displays.

If one of the display adapters is built into the motherboard, note these additional considerations:

- The motherboard adapter always becomes the secondary adapter. It must be multiple-display compatible.

- You must set up Windows 2000 before installing another adapter. Windows 2000 Setup will disable the motherboard adapter if it detects another adapter. Some systems completely disable the onboard adapter upon detecting an add-in adapter. If you are unable to override this detection in the basic input/output system (BIOS), you will not be able to use the motherboard adapter with multiple displays.

Typically, the system BIOS selects the primary display based on PCI slot order. However, on some computers, the BIOS allows the user to select the primary display device.

You can't stop the primary display. This consideration is important for portable computers with docking stations. For example, some docking stations contain a display adapter; these often disable, or turn off, a portable computer's built-in display. Multiple display support will not function on these configurations unless you attach multiple adapters to the docking station.

Configuring Multiple Displays

You must configure each display in a multiple-display environment.

▶ **Follow these steps to configure your display in a multiple-display environment:**

1. In Control Panel, double-click Display.

2. In the Display Properties dialog box, click the Settings tab.

3. Click the monitor number for the primary display device.

4. Select the display adapter for the primary display, and then select the color depth and resolution.

5. Click the monitor number for the secondary display device.

6. Select the display adapter for the secondary display, and then select the Extend My Windows Desktop Onto This Monitor check box.

7. Select the color depth and resolution for the secondary display.

8. Repeat steps 5 to 7 for each additional display.

Windows 2000 uses the virtual desktop concept to determine the relationship of each display. The virtual desktop represents the entire viewable area of all displays combined. The virtual desktop uses coordinates to track the position of each individual display desktop.

The coordinates of the upper-left corner of the primary display are always 0,0. Windows 2000 sets secondary display coordinates so that all the displays adjoin each other on the virtual desktop. This allows the system to maintain the illusion of a single, large desktop, where users can cross from one monitor to another without losing track of the mouse's position on the virtual desktop, as well as on which display it should appear.

To change the display positions on the virtual desktop, on the Settings tab, click Identify, and drag the display representations to the desired position. The positions of the icons dictate the coordinates and the relative positions of the displays to one another.

Troubleshooting Multiple Displays

If you encounter difficulties with multiple displays, use the troubleshooting guidelines in Table 2.5 to help resolve those problems.

Table 2.5 Troubleshooting Tips for Multiple Displays

Problem	Solution
You can't see any output on the secondary displays.	Activate the device in the Display Properties dialog box.
	Confirm that you chose the correct video driver.
	Restart the computer to confirm that the secondary display is initialized. If not, check the status of the video adapter in Device Manager.
	Switch the order of the adapters in the slots. (The primary adapter must qualify as a secondary adapter.)
The Extend My Windows Desktop Onto This Monitor check box is unavailable.	Select the secondary display rather than the primary one in the Display Properties dialog box.
	Confirm that the secondary display adapter is supported.
	Confirm that Windows 2000 can detect the secondary display.
An application fails to display on the secondary display.	Run the application on the primary display.
	Run the application in full-screen mode (Microsoft MS-DOS) or maximized (Microsoft Windows).
	Disable the secondary display to determine whether the problem is specific to multiple display support.

Lesson Summary

In this lesson, you learned that users with permission to load and unload device drivers can also install and test video drivers. With Windows 2000, you can change video resolutions dynamically without restarting the system.

You also learned that you use the Display icon in Control Panel to view or modify display properties, such as the number of colors, video resolution, font size, and refresh frequency. You too learned that Windows 2000 supports multiple displays, with up to a maximum of 10 additional monitors, and that you must configure each display. This lesson concluded with a section on troubleshooting multiple displays.

Lesson 4: Installing, Managing, and Troubleshooting Other Devices

This lesson explains how to install, configure, and troubleshoot miscellaneous devices, including fax and mouse support.

After this lesson, you will be able to

- Configure and troubleshoot a fax device

- Manage and troubleshoot I/O devices

Estimated lesson time: 15 minutes

Configuring and Troubleshooting Fax Support

If you have a fax device, such as a fax modem installed, then Control Panel will have a Fax icon. You can use the Fax icon to add, monitor, and trouble-shoot fax devices, including fax modems and fax printers. Double-click the Fax icon, and then select the Advanced Options tab.

Note The Advanced Options tab appears only if you are logged on as Administrator or have administrator privileges.

The following three options are available on the Advanced Options page:

- **Open Fax Service Management Console.** This option allows you to view any fax devices you have installed and to change properties for these devices.

- **Open Fax Services Management Help.** This option allows you to start a Help session for the Open Fax Services Management Console.

- **Add A Fax Printer.** This option allows you to install a fax printer.

Using the Fax Service Management Console

Using the Fax Service Management window, you can administer fax support on your local computer or on other computers on your network. According to your default settings, you are set up to send faxes, not to receive them. The Fax Service Management is used for the folowing tasks:

- Setting up your fax devices to receive faxes

- Changing security permissions for users

- Changing the number of rings before a fax device answers a fax receive

- Configuring the number of retries before a fax terminates a fax send

- Configuring where to store sent and received faxes

The Open Fax Services Management Help option provides Help for the Fax Service Management console. You can use the third option, Add A Fax Printer, to install a fax printer. The newly installed fax printer is added to the Printers folder.

Faxing a Document

You can use any Windows-based application that contains a Print command to fax a document. Click File and then click Print to open the Print dialog box. Select the fax printer, and then click Print to open the Send Fax wizard. The wizard guides you through configuration and help you send the fax.

Monitoring a Fax

Open Fax in Control Panel and select the Status Monitor tab. Ensure that Display The Status Monitor is selected, and then click OK. With this option selected, the Fax Monitor dialog box will automatically be displayed when a fax is sent or a call is received. The Fax Monitor dialog box allows you to view details of the fax being sent—for example, you can see if the fax is actually being sent or if the system is still dialing and trying to establish a connection. The Fax dialog box also allows you to easily end a fax call.

Managing and Troubleshooting Input/Output Devices

The list of devices that you can install is too long to include in this training kit. This section includes some of the more common devices you can install and explains how they are installed, configured, and managed.

Scanners and Cameras

Most scanners and cameras are Plug and Play devices, and Windows 2000 installs them automatically when you connect them to your computer. If they are not installed automatically when you connect your computer, or if they are not Plug and Play compatible, use the Scanner And Camera Installation wizard. To open this wizard, double-click Scanners And Cameras in Control Panel, and then click Add.

To configure a scanner or a camera, double-click Scanners And Cameras in Control Panel to open the Scanners And Cameras Properties dialog box, select the appropriate device, and then click Properties. For example, you can configure an alternate color profile for a device. The standard color profile for Integrated Color Management (ICM 2) is RGB, but you can add, remove, or select an alternate color profile. To change the color profile for a device, click the Color Management tab. If you are having problems with your scanner or camera, click Troubleshoot in the Scanners And Cameras Properties dialog box.

Mouse Devices

Double-click the Mouse icon in Control Panel to open the Mouse Properties dialog box, which you can use to configure and troubleshoot your mouse. The Buttons tab allows you to configure your Mouse for a left-handed or right-handed user. It also allows you to configure your mouse so that a single mouse click either selects or opens an item. You can also use this tab to control the double-click speed of your mouse.

From the Pointers tab, you can select or create a custom scheme for your pointer. From the Motion tab you can adjust the speed and acceleration of your pointer and to set Snap To Default, which moves the pointer automatically to the default button in dialog boxes. From the Hardware tab you can access the troubleshooter and advanced configuration for your mouse's port. Options for advanced configuration include uninstalling or updating your driver, viewing or changing the resources allocated to your mouse, and increasing or decreasing the sensitivity of your mouse by varying the sample rate, which changes how often Windows 2000 determines the position of your mouse.

Modems

To install or configure a modem, double-click Phone And Modem Options in Control Panel, and select the Modems tab. To configure an installed modem, select the modem from the list of installed modems and click Properties. Select the appropriate tab or check box according to what changes you want to make. For example, select the General tab if you want to set the maximum port speed, and select the Wait For Dial Tone Before Dialing check box if you want the modem to wait for a dial tone before dialing in to another computer. You can get help troubleshooting the modem from the Diagnostics tab. If you want to add a modem, click Add to start the Add/Remove Hardware wizard, which will step you through the process of installing a modem.

Universal Serial Bus Devices

To install a Universal Serial Bus Device (USB), for example, a USB game controller, attach the USB game controller to a USB port. If a USB device doesn't install properly, in Device Manager, look under Human Interface Devices. If the controller isn't listed, check to make sure that USB is enabled in BIOS. When prompted during system startup, enter BIOS setup and enable USB. If USB is enabled in BIOS, contact the maker or vendor of your computer and obtain the current version of BIOS.

To configure the controller, in Device Manager right-click the appropriate controller and then select Properties. In Device Status, a message will describe any problems and suggest what action you can take. You might also need to check the USB port entry in Device Manager. Click Universal Serial Bus Controllers, right-click USB Hub, and then click Properties.

IrDA Devices and Wireless Devices

Most Internal Infrared Data Association (IrDA) devices should be installed by Windows 2000 Setup, or once you start Windows 2000 after adding one of these devices. If you attach an IrDA transceiver to a serial port, you must install it using the Add/Remove Hardware wizard.

To configure an IrDA device, in Control Panel, click Wireless Link. On the Hardware tab, click the device you want to configure, and then click Properties.

Keyboards

To configure your keyboard, double-click Keyboards in Control Panel. From the Input Locales tab, you can add and remove locales and control the hot keys to switch between locales.

Note What icons appear in Control Panel depend on what devices you have installed.

Lesson Summary

In this lesson you learned that you can use the Fax program in Control Panel, to add, monitor, and troubleshoot fax devices you have installed, including fax modems and fax printers. As a default, you are set up to send faxes, but not to receive them.

You also learned that you can use the Fax Service Management window to administer fax support on your local computer or on other computers on your network, including setting up fax devices to receive faxes, changing security permissions for users, configuring where to store sent and received faxes, and other settings. You also learned that you can use any Windows-based application that contains a Print command to fax a document. Generally, this involves using a Send Fax wizard that guides you through any configuration settings and helps you send the fax.

Finally, you learned how to install, configure, and manage some of the more common devices that may be connected to your system, including scanners and cameras, mouse devices, modems, USB devices, IrDA devices, wireless devices, and keyboards.

Lesson 5: Introducing the Microsoft Management Console

This lesson introduces the MMC and defines consoles, console trees, details panes, snap-ins, and extensions. The lesson also explains the differences between Author mode and User mode. You also learn that the .MSC file extension is assigned to the consoles you create and the My Administrative Tools folder where the consoles you create are stored as files. The My Administrative Tools folder is accessible from the Programs menu and offers easy access to the consoles that you create.

After this lesson, you will be able to

- Describe the function and components of the Microsoft Management Console, including snap-ins, console options, and modes

Estimated lesson time: 20 minutes

Microsoft Management Consoles

One of the primary administrative tools that that is available for managing Windows 2000 is the Microsoft Management Console. The MMC provides a standardized method to create, save, and open administrative tools, which are called *consoles*. The MMC does not itself provide management functions; it's the program that hosts management applications, called *snap-ins,* which you use to perform administrative tasks. The MMC allows you to do the following:

- **Administer tasks and troubleshoot problems.** You can perform most of your administrative tasks and troubleshoot many problems using only the MMC. Being able to use one interface intead of many saves time.

- **Centralize administration.** You can use consoles to perform the majority of your administrative tasks from one computer.

- **Administer tasks and troubleshoot problems remotely.** You can use most snap-ins for remote administration and troubleshooting. Not all snap-ins are available for you to use on remote computers, so Windows 2000 prompts you with a dialog box to tell you if you can use the snap-in remotely.

Note Third-party vendors can design their administrative tools as snap-ins for use in the MMC.

Consoles contain one or more snap-ins. They are saved as files with an .msc extension. All the settings for the snap-ins contained in the console are saved and are restored when the file is opened, even if the console file is opened on a different computer or network.

You configure consoles to hold snap-ins to perform specific tasks. You determine how a console operates by configuring console options. By using console options, you can create consoles for other administrators to use from their own computers to perform specific tasks.

Console Tree and Details Pane

Every console has a console tree. A *console tree* displays the hierarchical organization of the snap-ins that are contained within that console. As illustrated in Figure 2.6, this console contains the Disk Defragmenter snap-in and the Device Manager On Local Computer snap-in.

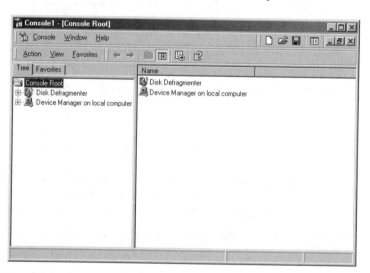

Figure 2.6 The MMC window

The console tree organizes snap-ins that are a part of a console. This allows you to easily locate a specific snap-in. Items that you add to the console tree appear under the console root. The *details pane* lists the contents of the active snap-in.

Every console contains an Action menu and a View menu. The contents of these menus vary, depending on the current selection of snap-ins in the console tree.

Administrative Tools

By default, Windows 2000 saves custom console files (with an .MSC extension) in the Administrative Tools folder. If your Windows 2000 Professional operating system is on drive C: and you are logged on as Administrator, the path to these files should be C:\Documents and Settings\Administrator\ Start Menu\Programs\Administrative Tools. The folder structure below C:\Documents and Settings doesn't exist until a user logs on for the first time.

Even after the folder structure is created for a new user who logs on for the first time, the Administrative Tools folder might not appear on the Programs menu if its display is turned off, which it is by default when Windows 2000 Professional is first installed. (To turn on the Administrative Tool folder display without using MMC, click Start, point to Settings, click Taskbar & Start Menu, and select the Display Administrative Tools check box on the Advanced tab of the Taskbar And Start Menu Properties dialog box.) When you run MMC and save a custom console, Windows 2000 turns on the display of the Administrative Tools folder for each user.

Note In Windows 2000 Server, the private folder containing the consoles you create are in the My Administrative Tools folder. There is an Administrative Tools folder, but it holds some preconfigured consoles for use with the MMC.

Snap-Ins

Snap-ins are applications that are designed to work in the MMC. You use snap-ins to perform administrative tasks. There are two types of snap-ins: standalone snap-ins and extension snap-ins.

Standalone Snap-Ins

Standalone snap-ins are usually referred to simply as snap-ins. Use standalone snap-ins to perform Windows 2000 administrative tasks. Each snap-in serves one function or a related set of functions. Windows 2000 Server comes with standard snap-ins. Windows 2000 Professional includes a smaller set of standard snap-ins.

Extension Snap-Ins

Extension snap-ins are usually referred to as *extensions*. They are snap-ins that provide additional administrative functionality to another snap-in. The following are characteristics of extensions:

- Extensions are designed to work with one or more standalone snap-ins, based on the function of the standalone snap-in.

- When you add an extension, Windows 2000 displays only extensions that are compatible with the standalone snap-in. Windows 2000 places the extensions in the appropriate location within the standalone snap-in.

- When you add a snap-in to a console, MMC adds all available extensions by default. You can remove any extension from the snap-in.

- You can add an extension to multiple snap-ins.

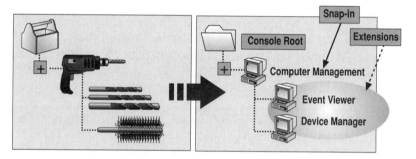

- Snap-ins are administrative tools.
- Extensions provide additional functionality to snap-ins.
  - Extensions are preassigned to snap-ins.
  - Multiple snap-ins may use the same extensions.

Figure 2.7 Snap-ins and extensions

Figure 2.7 illustrates the function of snap-ins and extensions. You can think of snap-ins and extensions as bits of a drill. You can use a drill with its standard drill bit, or you can use different drill bits to perform additional functions. The same is true for snap-ins and extensions.

Console Options

Some standalone snap-ins can use extensions that provide additional functionality. Computer Management is one such snap-in. Some snap-ins, like Event Viewer, can act as either a snap-in or an extension.

Use console options to determine how each console operates by selecting the appropriate *console mode*. The console mode determines the console functionality for the person who is using a saved console. The two available console modes are *Author mode* and *User mode*.

Author Mode

When you save a console in Author mode, you allow any user full access to all MMC functionality. This includes allowing users to modify the console. Save the console using Author mode to allow those using it to do the following:

- Add or remove snap-ins
- Create new windows
- View all portions of the console tree
- Save consoles

Note By default, all new consoles are saved in Author mode.

User Mode

If you plan to distribute a console to other administrators, you should save the console in User mode. When you set a console to User mode, users can't add snap-ins to, remove snap-ins from, or save the console. The three types of User modes that exist allow different levels of access and functionality. Table 2.6 describes when to use each User mode.

Table 2.6 Console User Modes

Use	When
Full Access	You want to be able to have all MMC functionality. This includes allowing them to add or remove snap-ins, to create new windows, to create task pad views and tasks, and to gain access to all portions of the console tree.
Delegated Access, Multiple Windows	You don't want to allow users to open new windows or gain access to a portion of the console tree. You do want to allow users to view multiple windows in the console.
Delegated Access, Single Window	You don't want to allow users to open new windows or gain access to a portion of the console tree. You do want to allow users to view only one window in the console.

Lesson Summary

In this lesson, you learned that one of the primary administrative tools that you use to manage Windows 2000 is the MMC. The MMC enables you to create, save, and open administrative tools, which are called consoles, using a standardized method and from a single, central location. Consoles hold one or more applications called snap-ins, which you use to perform administrative tasks and troubleshoot problems locally and on remote computers. By default, Windows 2000 saves custom console files in the Administrative Tools folder of the user who created it.

You also learned that every console has a console tree. The console tree displays the hierarchical organization of the snap-ins that are contained within that console. This allows you to easily locate a specific snap-in. The details pane lists the contents of the active snap-in. You also learned about the two types of snap-ins: standalone snap-ins and extension snap-ins. A standalone snap-in is usually referred to simply as a snap-in and provides one function or a related set of functions. An extension snap-in is usually referred to as an extension, and it provides additional administrative functionality to a snap-in. An extension is designed to work with one or more standalone snap-ins, based on the function of the standalone snap-in.

Finally, in this lesson you learned about console options. You use console options to determine how each console operates by selecting the appropriate console mode. The two available console modes are Author mode and User mode. When you save a console in Author mode, you enable full access to all MMC functionality, which includes modifying the console. You save the console using Author mode to allow those using it to add or remove snap-ins, create new windows, view all portions of the console tree, and save consoles. If you plan to distribute a console to other administrators, you should save the console in User mode. When you set a console to User mode, users can't add snap-ins to, remove snap-ins from, or save the console.

Lesson 6: Using Consoles

This lesson explains how to create, use, and modify consoles. This lesson also explains how to use consoles for remote administration.

After this lesson, you will be able to

- Create and use consoles
- Create custom consoles for remote administration

Estimated lesson time: 40 minutes

Creating Consoles

You can create your own custom consoles by combining multiple preconfigured snap-ins with third-party snap-ins, which are provided by independent software vendors (ISVs) to perform related tasks. You can then do the following:

- Save the custom consoles so you can use them again.
- Distribute the custom consoles to other administrators.
- Use the custom consoles from any computer to centralize and unify administrative tasks.

Creating custom consoles allows you to combine snap-ins that you use to perform common administrative tasks. When you have created a custom console, you don't have to switch between different programs because all of the snap-ins that you need to perform your job are located in that one console. You start MMC with an empty console.

▶   **Follow these steps to start the MMC:**

1. Click the Start button.
2. Click Run.

3. Type **mmc** in the Open box, and then click OK.

A console window titled Console1 opens; it contains a window titled Console Root. This is an empty console that is ready for you to customize. Use the Console menu to create, open, save, and customize a console. The following table describes the different commands on the Console menu.

Console Menu Commands

Command	Purpose
New	To create a new custom console
Open	To open and use a saved console
Save or Save As	To save the console and use it later
Add/Remove Snap-In	To add or remove one or more snap-ins and their associated extensions to or from a console
Options	To configure the console mode and create a custom console

4. Close the MMC window.

Using Consoles for Remote Administration

When you create custom consoles, you can set up a snap-in for remote administration. Remote administration allows you to perform administrative tasks from any location. For example, you can use a computer running Windows 2000 Professional to perform administrative tasks on a computer running Windows 2000 Server. You can't use all snap-ins for remote administration; the design of each snap-in dictates whether you can use it for remote administration.

To perform remote administration, you can use snap-ins from computers running either Windows 2000 Professional or Windows 2000 Server. You must use specific snap-ins that are designed for remote administration. If the snap-in is available for remote administration, Windows 2000 prompts you to choose the target computer to administer.

Practice: Creating a Customized Microsoft Management Console

In this practice, you create a customized console. You use this console to confirm when your computer was last started. You also add a snap-in with extensions.

Exercise 1: Creating and Confirming a Customized Console

▶ **To create a customized console**

1. Click the Start button, and then click Run.

2. In the Open box, type **mmc** and then click OK.

   MMC starts and displays an empty console.

3. Maximize the Console1 window by clicking its Maximize button.

4. Maximize the Console Root window by clicking its Maximize button.

5. To view the currently configured options, click Options on the Console menu.

   Notice that the default console mode is Author mode. Remember that Author mode grants users full access to all MMC functionality.

6. In the Console Mode box, make sure that Author Mode is selected, and then click OK.

7. On the Console menu, click Add/Remove Snap-In.

   MMC displays the Add/Remove Snap-In dialog box.

8. Click Add.

   MMC displays the Add Standalone Snap-In dialog box, as shown in Figure 2.8.

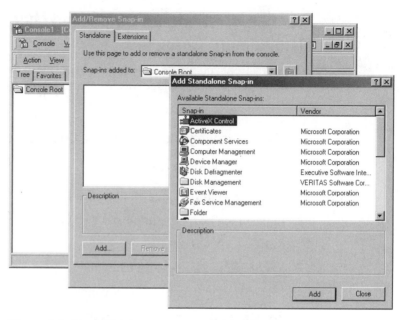

Figure 2.8 The Add Standalone Snap-In dialog box

Notice the available snap-ins. MMC allows you to add one or more snap-ins to a console, enabling you to create your own customized management tools.

9. Select Computer Management and then click Add.

   The Computer Management dialog box displays.

10. Ensure that Local Computer: (The Computer This Console Is Running On) is selected, and then click Finish.

   Notice that Computer Management (Local) appears in the Add/Remove Snap-In dialog box.

11. Click Close to close the Add Standalone Snap-In dialog box.

12. Click OK to close the Add/Remove Snap-In dialog box.

13. On the Console menu, click Save As.

   MMC displays the Save As dialog box.

14. In the File Name box, type **All Events** and then click Save.

   The name of your console appears on the MMC title bar.

   Next you should confirm that the console was saved in the Administrative Tools folder by closing and then reopening the console.

▶   **To confirm the location of a customized console**

1. On the Console menu, click Exit.

   You have now created and saved a customized console named All Events.

2. Click the Start button, click Run, type **mmc** and then click OK.

3. On the Console menu, click Open.

   MMC displays the Open dialog box. Notice that the console you created (All Events.MSC) is in the Administrative Tools folder.

4. Click the All Events file and then click Open.

   Windows 2000 opens the All Events console that you saved previously.

Exercise 2: Configuring and Using Event Viewer

▶   **To add the Event Viewer snap-in to a console**

1. On the Console menu, click Add/Remove Snap-In.

   MMC displays the Add/Remove Snap-In dialog box with the Standalone tab showing. Notice that Computer Management is the only loaded snap-in. You will add a snap-in to the console root.

2. In the Add/Remove Snap-In dialog box, click Add.

   MMC displays the Add Standalone Snap-In dialog box.

3. In the Add/Remove Snap-In dialog box, select Event Viewer, and then click Add.

   MMC displays the Select Computer dialog box, allowing you to specify which computer you want to administer.

   Notice that you can add Event Viewer for the local computer on which you are working. If your local computer is part of a network, you can also add Event Viewer for a remote computer.

   To add Event Viewer for a remote computer, you would select the Another Computer option, and then click Browse. In the Select Computer dialog box, you would click the remote computer for which you would like to add Event Viewer, and then click OK.

4. To add Event Viewer for your computer, the local computer, in the Select Computer dialog box, make sure that Local Computer is selected, and then click Finish.

5. In the Add Standalone Snap-In dialog box, click Close. In the Add/ Remove Snap-In dialog box, click OK.

    Event Viewer (Local) now appears in the console tree along with Computer Management (Local).

Tip To see the entire folder name, drag the border between the console and details panes to the right.

▶   **To determine when your computer was last started**

1. In the console tree of the All Events console, expand the Event Viewer (Local) folder, and then click System.

    MMC displays the most recent system events in the details pane.

2. In the details pane, double-click the most recent Information event listed as Eventlog in the Source column. If the Description box doesn't say "The Event Log Service Was Started," click the up arrow until you find this description.

    The Event log service starts as part of your system startup. The date and time represents the approximate time that your system was started. Make a note of the date and time.

3. To close the Event Properties dialog box, click OK.

4. On the Console menu, click Exit to close the All Events console.

    A Microsoft Management Console dialog box appears, asking whether you want to save the console settings to All Events.

5. Click No.

Exercise 3: Configuring a Snap-In

1. Click the Start button, and then click Run.

2. In the Open box, type **mmc** if necessary, and then click OK.

    MMC displays an empty console.

3. Maximize the Console1 and Console Root windows, if necessary.

4. On the Console menu, click Add/Remove Snap-In.

    MMC displays the Add/Remove Snap-In dialog box with the Standalone tab showing. You will add a snap-in to the console root.

5. Click Add.

   All snap-ins that are listed here are standalone snap-ins.

6. In the Add Standalone Snap-In dialog box, in the Available Standalone Snap-Ins box, click Computer Management, and then click Add.

   MMC displays the Select Computer dialog box, allowing you to specify which computer you want to administer. Add the Computer Management snap-in for your own computer.

7. Verify that Local Computer is selected, and then click Finish.

8. Click Close.

   Computer Management appears in the list of snap-ins that have been added.

9. In the Add/Remove Snap-In dialog box, click OK.

   MMC displays the Computer Management snap-in in the console tree below Console Root. Console Root acts as a container for several categories of administrative functions.

10. Expand Computer Management and review the available functions, and then expand System Tools.

   Note Do not use any of the tools at this point.

   Notice that several extensions are available, including Event Viewer, System Information, and Device Manager. You can restrict the functionality of a snap-in by removing extensions.

11. On the Console menu, click Add/Remove Snap-In.

   The MMC displays the Add/Remove Snap-In dialog box with the Standalone tab active.

12. Click Computer Management (Local), and then click the Extensions tab.

   The MMC displays a list of available extensions for the Computer Management snap-in.

   What option determines which extensions MMC displays in the Available Extensions list in this dialog box?

13. Clear the Add All Extensions check box, and then in the Available Extensions box, clear the Device Manager Extension check box and the System Information Extension check box.

14. Click OK.

15. Expand Computer Management and then expand System Tools to confirm that Device Manager and System Information have been removed.

Note Do not use any of the tools at this point.

---

16. Close the console.

    MMC displays a message, prompting for confirmation to save console settings.

17. Click No.

Lesson Summary

In this lesson, you learned how to create custom consoles to perform a unique set of administrative tasks. Once you create customized consoles, you can access them by using the Run command on the Start menu.

In the practice portion of this lesson, you created two customized consoles. The first console contained the Computer Management snap-in. You added the Event Viewer snap-in to the console. You used the Event Viewer snap-in to determine when your computer was last started. The second custom console you created contained the Computer Management snap-in. After you created the second customized console, you learned how to restrict the functionality of a console by removing two of the extensions normally available with the Computer Management snap-in.

Lesson 7: Introducing Disk Management

Another important hardware issue for administrators is disk storage space and management. In this lesson, you learn about disk management. You learn, for example, that if you have free space on your hard disk, you need to partition and format it so that you can store data on that part of the disk. In addition, if you have more than one hard disk, each disk must be partitioned and formatted so that you can store data on it.

After this lesson, you will be able to

- Describe disk management concepts
- Describe the difference between basic and dynamic storage
- Describe both primary and extended partitions

Estimated lesson time: 25 minutes

Tasks for Setting Up a Hard Disk

Whether you are setting up the remaining free space on a hard disk on which you installed Windows 2000 or are setting up a new hard disk, you need to be aware of the tasks that are involved. Before you can store data on a new hard disk, you must perform the following tasks to prepare the disk:

1. Initialize the disk and specify a storage type. Initialization defines the fundamental structure of a hard disk.

   Windows 2000 supports basic storage and dynamic storage.

2. Create partitions on a basic disk or create volumes on a dynamic disk.

3. Format the disk. After you create a partition or volume, you must format it with a specific file system—NTFS file system, FAT, or FAT32.

   The file system that you choose affects disk operations. This includes how you control user access to data, how data is stored, hard disk capacity, and which operating systems can gain access to the data on the hard disk.

Before you can decide how to perform the tasks of setting up a hard disk, you must understand the storage types, partition types, and volume types available in Windows 2000 Professional.

Storage Types

As mentioned earlier, Windows 2000 supports two types of disk storage: basic storage and dynamic storage. A physical disk must be either basic or dynamic; you can't use both storage types on one disk. You can, however, use both types of disk storage in a multidisk system.

Basic Storage

The traditional industry standard for disk storage is *basic storage*. It dictates the division of a hard disk into partitions (see Figure 2.9). A *partition* is a portion of the disk that functions as a physically separate unit of storage. Windows 2000 recognizes primary and extended partitions. A disk that is initialized for basic storage is called a *basic disk*. A basic disk can contain primary partitions, extended partitions, and logical drives. New disks added to a computer running Windows 2000 are basic disks.

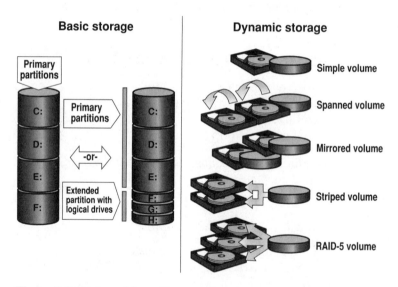

Figure 2.9 Basic and dynamic storage types

Because basic storage is the traditional industry standard, all versions of Microsoft Windows, MS-DOS, Windows NT, and Windows 2000 support basic storage. For Windows 2000, basic storage is the default, so all disks are basic disks until you convert them to dynamic storage disks.

Dynamic Storage

Only Windows 2000 supports *dynamic storage,* which is a standard that creates a single partition that includes the entire disk. A disk that you initialize for dynamic storage is a *dynamic disk.*

You divide dynamic disks into *volumes,* which can consist of a portion, or portions, of one or more physical disks. On a dynamic disk, you can create simple volumes, spanned volumes, and striped volumes, as described later in this chapter. You create a dynamic disk by upgrading a basic disk.

Dynamic storage doesn't have the restrictions of basic storage; for example, you can size and resize a dynamic disk without restarting Windows 2000.

Note Removable storage devices contain primary partitions only. You can't create extended partitions, logical drives, or dynamic volumes on removable storage devices. You can't mark a primary partition on a removable storage device (with the intent of booting the computer from the device) as active.

Partition Types (Basic Disks)

You can divide a basic disk into primary and extended partitions. *Partitions* function as physically separate storage units. This allows you to separate different types of information, such as user data on one partition and applications on another. A basic disk can contain up to four primary partitions, or up to three primary partitions and one extended partition, for a maximum of four partitions. Only one partition can be an extended partition, as shown in Figure 2.10.

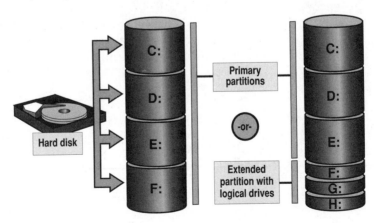

Figure 2.10 Partition types

Primary Partitions

Windows 2000 can use a part of a disk called a *primary partition* to start the computer. Only a primary partition can be marked as the active partition. The active partition is where the hardware looks for the boot files to start the operating system. Only one partition on a single hard disk can be active at a time. Multiple primary partitions allow you to isolate different operating systems or types of data.

To dual boot Windows 2000 with Microsoft Windows 95 or MS-DOS, the active partition must be formatted as FAT because Windows 95 can't read a partition formatted as FAT32 or NTFS. To dual boot with Microsoft Windows 95 OSR2 (a later release of Windows 95 that contained enhancements to Windows 95, such as the ability to read partitions formatted with FAT32) or Windows 98, the active partition must be formatted as FAT or FAT32.

Extended Partitions

An *extended partition* is created from free space. There can be only one extended partition on a hard disk, so you should include all remaining free space in the extended partition. Unlike primary partitions, extended partitions are not formatted or assigned drive letters. You divide extended partitions into segments. Each segment is a logical drive. You assign a drive letter to each logical drive and format it with a file system.

Note The Windows 2000 *system partition* is the active partition that contains the hardware-specific files required to load the operating system. The Windows 2000 *boot partition* is the primary partition or logical drive where the operating system files are installed. The boot partition and the system partition can be the same partition. However, the system partition must be on the active partition, typically drive C, while the boot partition could be on another primary partition or on an extended partition.

Volume Types (Dynamic Disks)

You can convert basic disks to dynamic storage and then create Windows 2000 volumes. Consider which volume type best suits your needs for efficient use of disk space and performance.

- A *simple volume* contains disk space from a single disk and is not fault tolerant.

- A *spanned volume* includes disk space from multiple disks (up to 32). Windows 2000 writes data to a spanned volume on the first disk, completely filling the space, and continues in this manner for each disk that you include in the spanned volume. A spanned volume is not fault tolerant. If any disk in a spanned volume fails, the data in the entire volume is lost.

- A *striped volume* combines areas of free space from multiple hard disks (up to 32) into one logical volume. In a striped volume, Windows 2000 optimizes performance by adding data to all disks at the same rate. If a disk in a striped volume fails, the data in the entire volume is lost.

Note The Windows 2000 Server products provide fault tolerance on dynamic disks. *Fault tolerance* is the capability of a computer or operating system to respond to a catastrophic event without loss of data. The Windows 2000 Server products provide mirrored volumes and RAID-5 volumes that are fault tolerant. Windows 2000 Professional does not provide fault tolerance to a computer.

Creating multiple partitions or volumes on a single hard disk allows you to efficiently organize data for tasks such as backing up data. For example, partition one-third of a hard disk for the operating system, one-third for applications, and one-third for data. Then, when you back up your data, you can back up the entire partition instead of just a specific folder.

File Systems

Windows 2000 supports the NTFS, FAT, and FAT32 file systems. Use NTFS when you need a partition to have file- and folder-level security, disk compression, disk quotas, or encryption. Only Windows 2000 and Windows NT 4.0 Workstation can access data on a local hard disk that is formatted as NTFS. If you plan to promote a server to a domain controller, format the installation partition with NTFS.

FAT and FAT32 allow access by, and compatibility with, other operating systems. To dual boot Windows 2000 and another operating system, format the system partition with either FAT or FAT32. FAT and FAT32 don't offer many of the features that NTFS supports such as file-level security. Therefore, in most situations, you should format the hard disk with NTFS. The only reason to use FAT or FAT32 is for dual booting.

If you have a volume that is formatted with FAT or FAT32, you can use the Convert command provided by Windows 2000 Professional to convert your volume from FAT or FAT32 to NTFS without having to reformat. To do this you type the following command in a command prompt window:

```
Convert volume /FS:NTFS /V
```

Note that you should replace *volume* with the appropriate drive letter followed by a colon. The /V indicates the command should be run in verbose mode. For example, if you wanted to convert drive C from FAT to NTFS you would type the following command:

```
Convert C: /FS:NTFS /V
```

The Disk Management Snap-In

Use the Disk Management snap-in to configure and manage your network storage space. The Disk Management snap-in can display your storage system in either a graphical view or a list view. You can modify the display to suit your preferences by using the commands on the View menu.

Lesson Summary

In this lesson, you learned that before you can store data on a new hard disk, you must initialize the disk by specifying a storage type using the Disk Management snap-in. Windows 2000 supports basic storage and dynamic storage. A basic disk can contain primary partitions, extended partitions, and logical drives. All versions of Microsoft Windows, MS-DOS, and Windows 2000 support basic storage. Windows 2000 Professional has basic storage as its default, so all disks are basic disks until you convert them to dynamic storage.

You also learned that dynamic storage creates a single partition that covers the entire disk. You divide dynamic disks into volumes, which can consist of a portion, or portions, of one or more physical disks. A dynamic disk can contain simple volumes, spanned volumes, and striped volumes. Dynamic storage doesn't have the restrictions of basic storage; for example, you can size and resize a dynamic disk without restarting Windows 2000.

Finally, in this lesson you learned that after you create partitions on a basic disk or create volumes on a dynamic disk, you must format the partition or volume with a specific file system such as NTFS, FAT, or FAT32. Which file system you choose affects disk operations, such as how you control user access to data, how data is stored, how much hard disk capacity you have, and which operating systems can gain access to the data on the hard disk. You use the Disk Management snap-in to configure and manage your network storage space.

Lesson 8: Common Disk Management Tasks

Windows 2000 includes a tool that allows you to use a central location to be used for monitoring and managing disk information. The Disk Management snap-in allows you to perform such tasks as creating and deleting partitions and volumes. With the proper permissions, you can manage disks locally and on remote computers. Other disk management tasks you can perform using the Disk Management snap-in include adding and removing hard disks and changing the disk storage type.

This lesson introduces the following disk management tasks:

- Working with simple volumes
- Working with spanned volumes
- Working with striped volumes
- Adding disks
- Changing storage types
- Viewing and updating information
- Managing disks on a remote computer

After this lesson, you will be able to

- Identify common disk management tasks
- Create and configure a dynamic disk

Estimated lesson time: 50 minutes

Working with Simple Volumes

A *simple volume* contains disk space from a single disk. You can extend a simple volume to include unallocated space on the same disk.

You can create a simple volume and format it with NTFS, FAT, or FAT32 using the Create Volume wizard (see Figure 2.11). However, you can extend a simple volume only if it is formatted with NTFS.

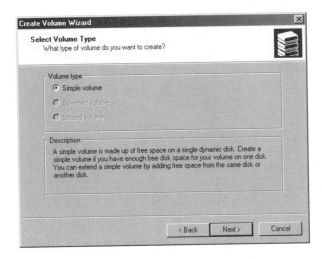

Figure 2.11 Creating a simple volume

▶ **Follow these steps to create a simple volume:**

1. Select Disk Management in the Storage section of the Computer Management snap-in.

2. On the dynamic disk where you want to create the volume, right-click the unallocated space, and then click Create Volume.

   This launches the Create Volume wizard.

3. In the Create Volume wizard, click Next.

4. Click Simple Volume, and then follow the instructions on your screen.

To extend an NTFS simple volume, right-click the simple volume that you want to extend, click Extend Volume, and then follow the instructions on your screen. When you extend a simple volume to another disk, it becomes a spanned volume.

Working with Spanned Volumes

A *spanned volume* consists of disk space from multiple disks. Spanned volumes enable you to use the total available free space on multiple disks more effectively. You can create spanned volumes only on dynamic disks, and you need at least two dynamic disks to create a spanned volume. Spanned volumes can't be part of a striped volume and are not fault tolerant. Figure 2.12 introduces some of the important concepts for combining free space to create spanned volumes, to extend spanned volumes, and to delete spanned volumes.

- **Combining free space**
  - Spanned volumes combine space from 2 – 32 disks
  - Data is written to one disk until full
- **Extending and deleting**
  - Only NTFS-spanned volumes can be extended
  - Deleting any part of a spanned volume deletes the entire volume

Figure 2.12 Creating, extending, and deleting spanned volumes

Combining Free Space to Create a Spanned Volume

You create spanned volumes by combining areas of free space of various sizes (from 2 to 32 disks) into one large logical volume. The areas of free space that make up a spanned volume can be different sizes. Windows 2000 organizes spanned volumes so that data is stored in the free space on one disk until it is full, and then, starting at the beginning of the next disk, data is stored in the free space on the second disk. Windows 2000 continues this process in the same way on each subsequent disk for up to a maximum of 32 disks.

By deleting smaller volumes and combining them into a single spanned volume, you can free drive letters for other uses and create a large volume for file system use.

Extending and Deleting Spanned Volumes

You can extend existing spanned volumes formatted with NTFS by adding free space. Disk Management formats the new area without affecting any existing files on the original volume. You can't extend volumes formatted with FAT or FAT32.

You can extend spanned volumes on dynamic disks onto a maximum of 32 dynamic disks. After a volume is extended onto multiple disks (spanned), it can't be part of a striped volume. After a spanned volume is extended, no portion of it can be deleted without deleting the entire spanned volume. You can't extend a system volume or a boot volume.

Working with Striped Volumes

Striped volumes offer the best performance of all the Windows 2000 disk management techniques. In a striped volume, data is written evenly across all physical disks in 64-KB units, as shown in Figure 2.13. Because all the hard disks that belong to the striped volume perform the same functions as a single hard disk, Windows 2000 can issue and process concurrent I/O commands simultaneously on all hard disks. In this way, striped volumes can increase the speed of system I/O.

You create striped volumes by combining areas of free space from multiple disks (from 2 to 32) into one logical volume. With a striped volume, Windows 2000 writes data to multiple disks, much as it does with spanned volumes. However, on a striped volume, Windows 2000 writes files across all disks so that data is added to all disks at the same rate. Like spanned volumes, striped volumes don't provide fault tolerance to a computer. If a disk in a striped volume fails, the data in the entire volume is lost.

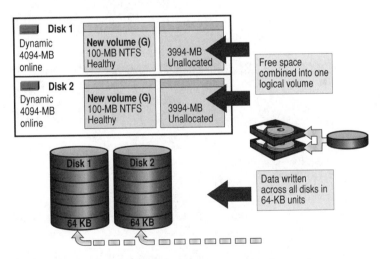

Figure 2.13 Benefits of working with striped volumes

You need at least two dynamic disks to create a striped volume. You can create a striped volume onto a maximum of 32 disks. You can't extend striped volumes.

▶   **Follow these steps to create a striped volume:**

1. In Disk Management, on the dynamic disk where you want to create the striped volume, right-click the unallocated space, and then click Create Volume. This launches the Create Volume wizard.

2. In the Create Volume wizard, click Next, click Striped Volume, and then follow the instructions on your screen.

Adding Disks

When you install new disks in a computer running Windows 2000, they are added as basic storage.

Adding New Disks

To add a new disk, install or attach the new physical disk (or disks), and then click Rescan Disks on the Action menu of the Disk Management snap-in, as shown in Figure 2.14. You must use Rescan Disks every time you remove or add disks to a computer.

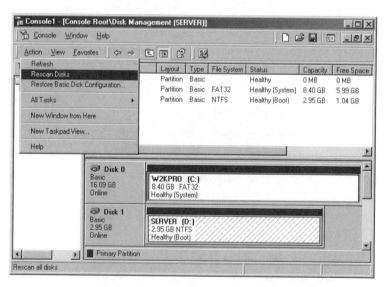

Figure 2.14 Adding disks using the Disk Management snap-in

You shouldn't need to restart the computer when you add a new disk to your computer. However, you might need to restart the computer if Disk Management doesn't detect the new disk after you run Rescan Disks.

Adding Disks That You Removed from Another Computer

If you want to uninstall or remove a disk from one computer and then install the disk in a different computer, the process is different.

▶ **Follow these steps to add a disk that has been removed from another computer by doing the following:**

1. Remove the disk from the original computer and install the disk in the new computer.

2. Open Disk Management.

   Disk Management displays the new disk labeled as Foreign.

3. Right-click the new disk, and then click Import Foreign Disk. A wizard provides onscreen instructions.

Adding Multiple Disks That You Removed from Another Computer

If you want to uninstall or remove multiple disks from one computer and then install the disks in a different computer, the process is much the same as doing so for a single disk.

▶ **Follow these steps to add multiple inherited disks:**

1. Remove the disks from the original computer and install them in the new computer.

2. Open Disk Management.

3. Right-click any of the new disks, and then click Add Disk. The disks appear as a group.

4. To specify which disks from the group you want to add, click Select Disk. Note that if you don't have any dynamic disks installed, all of the disks are added regardless of the disks that you select.

When you move a dynamic disk to your computer from another computer running Windows 2000, you can see and use any existing volumes on that disk. However, if a volume on a foreign disk extends to multiple disks and you don't move all the disks for that volume, Disk Management will not show the portion of the volume that resides on the foreign disk.

Changing Storage Type

You can upgrade a disk from basic storage to dynamic storage at any time, with no loss of data. When you upgrade a basic disk to a dynamic disk, any existing partitions on the basic disk become simple volumes. Any existing striped or spanned volume sets created with Windows NT 4.0 Workstation become dynamic striped or spanned volumes, respectively.

Any disks to be upgraded must contain at least 1 MB of unallocated space for the upgrade to succeed. Before you upgrade disks, close any programs that are running on those disks.

Table 2.7 shows the results of converting a disk from basic storage to dynamic storage.

Table 2.7 Basic Disk and Dynamic Disk Organization

Basic disk organization	Dynamic disk organization
System partition	Simple volume
Boot partition	Simple volume
Primary partition	Simple volume
Extended partition	Simple volume for each logical drive and any remaining unallocated space
Logical drive	Simple volume
Volume set	Spanned volume
Stripe set	Striped volume

Important Always back up the data on the disk to be converted before converting the storage type.

Upgrading Basic Disks to Dynamic Disks

To upgrade a basic disk to a dynamic disk, in the Disk Management snap-in, right-click the basic disk that you want to upgrade, and then click Upgrade To Dynamic Disk. A wizard provides onscreen instructions. The upgrade process requires that you restart your computer.

After you upgrade a basic disk to a dynamic disk, you can create volumes with improved capabilities on the disk. After you upgrade a disk to dynamic storage, it can't contain partitions or logical drives. Only Windows 2000 can access dynamic disks.

Reverting to a Basic Disk from a Dynamic Disk

You must remove all volumes from the dynamic disk before you can convert it back to a basic disk. To convert a dynamic disk back to a basic disk, right-click the dynamic disk that you want to convert back to a basic disk, and then click Revert To Basic Disk.

Caution Converting a dynamic disk to a basic disk causes all data to be lost.

Viewing and Updating Information

The Properties dialog box for a selected disk or volume provides a concise view of all of the pertinent properties of that disk or volume.

Disk Properties

To view disk properties in Disk Management, right-click the name of a disk in the Graphical View window (don't click any of its volumes), and then click Properties. Table 2.8 describes the information displayed in the Properties dialog box for a disk.

Table 2.8 The Properties Dialog Box for a Disk

Category	Description
Disk	The number for the disk in the system, for example, Disk 0, Disk 1, Disk 2, and so on
Type	The type of storage (basic, dynamic, or removable)
Status	The current status of the disk (online, offline, foreign, or unknown)
Capacity	The total capacity for the disk
Unallocated Space	The amount of available free space
Device Type	The type of devices—Integrated Device Electronics (IDE), Small Computer System Interface (SCSI), or Enhanced IDE (EIDE)—as well as the IDE channel (primary or secondary) on which the disk resides
Hardware Vendor	The hardware vendor for the disk and the disk type
Adapter Name	The type of controller to which the disk is attached
Volumes Contained On This Disk	The volumes that exist on the disk and their total capacity

Volume Properties

To view volume properties in Disk Management, right-click a volume in the Graphical View window or in the Volume List window, and then click Properties. Table 2.9 describes the tabs in the Properties dialog box for a volume.

Table 2.9 Properties Dialog Box for a Volume

Tab	Description
General	Lists the volume label, type, file system, and used free space. Click Disk Cleanup to delete unnecessary files. NTFS volumes list two options: Compress Drive To Save Disk Space, and Index Drive For Fast File Searching.
Tools	Provides a single location from which you can perform volume error-checking, backup, and defragmentation tasks.
Hardware	Checks properties of and troubleshoots the physical disks installed on the system.
Sharing	Sets network-shared volume parameters and permissions.
Security	Sets NTFS access permissions. This tab is available only for NTFS version 4 and 5 volumes. (Windows 2000 uses NTFS version 5.0.)
Quota	Sets user quotas for NTFS 5 volumes.

Refresh and Rescan

When you are working with Disk Management, you might need to update the information in the display. The two commands for updating the display are Refresh and Rescan Disks.

Refresh updates drive letter, file system, volume, and removable media information, and determines whether unreadable volumes are now readable. To update drive letter, file system, and volume information, click Action and then click Refresh.

Rescan Disks updates hardware information. When Disk Management rescans disks, it scans all attached disks for disk configuration changes. It also updates information on removable media, CD-ROM drives, basic volumes, file systems, and drive letters. Rescanning disks can take several minutes, depending on the number of hardware devices installed. To update disk information, click Action, and then click Rescan Disks.

Managing Disks on a Remote Computer

As a member of the Administrators group or the Server Operators group, you can manage disks on a computer running Windows 2000 that is a member of your domain or a trusting domain from any other computer running Windows 2000 on the network.

Note A domain will only exist if you have at least one computer running one of the Windows 2000 Server products, configured as a domain controller, on your network.

If you are in a workgroup, you can also manage disks on a remote computer running Windows 2000 Professional, if you have the same account with the exact same password set up on both the local and remote computers. The passwords must match or the service will fail and you will not be able to manage disks on a remote computer. In a workgroup, each computer has its own local security database.

To manage one computer from another computer—to perform *remote management*—create a custom console that is focused on the remote computer.

▶ **Follow these steps to create a custom console to manage disks on a remote computer:**

1. Click Start, click Run, type **mmc** and then click OK.

2. On the Console menu, click Add/Remove Snap-In.

3. Click Add.

4. Click Disk Management, and then click Add.

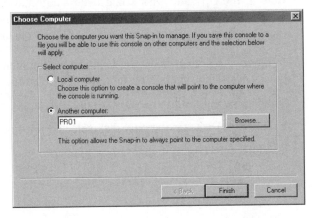

Figure 2.15 Creating a custom console to manage disks on a remote computer

5. In the Choose Computer dialog box illustrated in Figure 2.15, click Another Computer, and then type the name of the computer.

6. Click Finish.

Practice: Working with Dynamic Storage

After completing this practice, you will be able to

- Upgrade a basic disk to a dynamic disk
- Create a new volume
- Mount a simple volume

Exercise 1: Upgrading a Disk

In this exercise, you use Disk Management to upgrade a basic disk to a dynamic disk.

▶ **To upgrade a basic disk**

1. Ensure that you are logged on as Administrator.

2. Right-click My Computer, and then click Manage.

   The Computer Management window appears.

3. In the console tree, if necessary, double-click Storage to expand it, and then click Disk Management.

   Notice that Disk 0's storage type is Basic.

   Note If the Upgrade Disk wizard starts automatically, click Cancel. This might occur if your computer contains a disk configured for basic storage that doesn't contain the Windows 2000 boot partition.
   ---

4. In the lower-right pane of the Computer Management window, right-click Disk 0, and then click Upgrade To Dynamic Disk.

   The Upgrade To Dynamic Disk dialog box appears.

5. Ensure that Disk 0 is the only disk selected for upgrade, and then click OK.

   The Disks To Upgrade dialog box appears.

6. Click Upgrade.

A Disk Management dialog box appears, warning that, after this upgrade, you will not be able to boot previous versions of Windows from any volumes on this disk.

Caution If you are dual booting with another operating system, for example Windows 95 or Windows 98 loaded on drive C, these operating systems will no longer run. Only Windows 2000 can access a dynamic drive.

7. Click Yes.

An Upgrade Disks dialog box appears notifying you that file systems on any of the disks to be upgraded will be forcibly dismounted.

8. Click Yes.

A Confirm message box appears notifying you that a reboot will take place to complete the upgrade process.

Note The reboot only occurs when the disk contains either the system or boot partitions. Disks without these partitions will not require a reboot.

9. Click OK.

Your computer restarts.

▶   **To confirm the upgrade**

1. Log on as Administrator.

Note If the System Settings Change dialog box appears, prompting you to restart your computer, click Yes. If, after the computer restarts and you log on as Administrator, you see this same System Settings Change message box again prompting you to restart your computer, click No. Restarting the computer again is not necessary.

2. Right-click My Computer, and then click Manage.

The Computer Management window appears.

3. In the console tree, if necessary, double-click Storage to expand it, and then click Disk Management.

Note If your computer has more than one disk, the Upgrade Disk wizard might appear. If it does, click Cancel to close it.

Notice that the storage type of Disk 0 is Dynamic.

4. Minimize the Computer Management window.

Exercise 2: Extending a Volume

In this exercise, you use Disk Management to create a new simple volume. You then mount the new volume onto an existing folder on another volume. If drive C is formatted as NTFS, you create a folder named Mount under the root folder of drive C. If drive C isn't formatted as NTFS, you create the folder named Mount on the volume that is formatted as NTFS and contains the Windows 2000 files.

▶   **To create a folder for mounting the new volume**

1. Right-click My Computer.

2. Click Explore.

3. Click Local Disk C if it is formatted as NTFS; otherwise, click the disk that is formatted as NTFS and contains your Windows 2000 files.

4. On the File menu, click New, and then click Folder.

5. Type **Mount** and then press Enter.

▶   **To create a new simple volume**

1. Restore the Computer Management window.

2. Right-click the remaining unallocated space on Disk 0 in the lower-right pane, and then click Create Volume.

    The Create Volume wizard appears.

3. Click Next.

    The Select Volume Type page appears.

    Notice that Simple Volume is the only available option.

4. Click Next.

    The Select Disks page appears. The value in the For Selected Disks box represents the remaining free space on Drive 0.

5. Set the volume size to an appropriate size based on the amount of space available (25 MB is plenty), and then click Next.

    The Assign Drive Letter Or Path page appears.

6. Click Mount This Volume At An Empty Folder That Supports Drive Paths, and then type **x:\mount** where x is the letter of the drive containing the Mount folder.

7. Click Next.

   The Format Volume page appears.

8. Ensure that Format This Volume As Follows is selected and that File System To Use is set to NTFS.

9. Type **Mounted Vol** in the Volume Label box.

10. Click Perform A Quick Format, and then click Next.

11. Read the information on the Completing The Create Volume Wizard page, and then click Finish.

    The new volume is created, formatted, and mounted on the C:\Mount folder; or if C is not formatted as NTFS, it is mounted where you created the Mount folder.

12. Leave the Computer Management window open.

▶ **To examine the new volume**

1. Open Microsoft Windows Explorer.

2. Click Local Disk (C:), if necessary, to display the Local Disk (C:) window.

   Important If you mounted your volume on a drive other than drive C, click that drive instead.

   ---

3. Right-click the Mount folder, and then click Properties.

   The Mount Properties dialog box appears.

   Notice that x:\Mount (where x is the drive on which you mounted the volume) is a mounted volume.

4. Click OK.

5. Create a new text document in the x:\Mount folder.

6. Close Windows Explorer.

7. Open a command prompt.

8. Change the working directory to the root directory of drive C (if necessary) or to the root directory of the drive where you mounted your volume, type **dir** and then press Enter.

How much free space does the Dir command report?

Why is there a difference between the free space reported for drive C and the free space reported for C:\Mount?

9. Close the command prompt.

10. Close the Computer Management window.

Lesson Summary

In this lesson, you learned that the Disk Management snap-in provides a central location for monitoring disk information and managing tasks such as creating and deleting partitions and volumes. With the proper permissions, you can manage disks locally and on remote computers. Other disk management tasks that you might need to perform include adding and removing hard disks and changing the disk storage type.

This lesson also introduced you to working with simple volumes, spanned volumes, and striped volumes. It also discussed adding disks, changing the storage type, viewing and updating information, and managing disks on a remote computer.

Lesson 9: Managing Disk Quotas

While it may sound like a fine idea to allow users to have all the storage space they desire, this practice can start increasing the total cost of ownership (TCO) of your computer systems. In large distributed environments in particular it may become important to manage the amount of disk storage users can utilize.

When you must manage storage growth in distributed environments, you use disk quotas. *Disk quotas* allow you to allocate disk space usage based on the files and folders that users own. You can set disk quotas, quota thresholds, and quota limits for all users and for individual users. You can also monitor the amount of hard disk space that users have and the amount that they have left against their quota.

After this lesson, you will be able to

- Configure and manage disk quotas

Estimated lesson time: 20 minutes

Understanding Windows 2000 Disk Quota Management

Windows 2000 disk quotas track and control disk usage on a per-user, per-volume basis. Windows 2000 tracks disk quotas for each volume, even if the volumes are on the same hard disk. Because quotas are tracked on a per-user basis, every user's disk space is tracked regardless of the folder in which the user stores files. Table 2.10 describes the characteristics of Windows 2000 Professional disk quotas.

Table 2.10 Disk Quota Characteristics and Descriptions

Characteristic	Description
Disk usage is based on file and folder ownership.	Windows 2000 Professional calculates disk space usage based on the files and folders that users own. When a user copies or saves a new file to an NTFS volume or takes ownership of a file on an NTFS volume, Windows 2000 charges the disk space for the file against the user's quota limit.
Disk quotas do not use compression.	Windows 2000 Professional ignores compression when it calculates hard disk space usage. Usage totals are based on uncompressed file sizes, regardless of how much hard disk space is actually used. This is done partially because file compression produces different degrees of compression for different types of files. Different uncompressed file types that are the same size might end up to be different sizes when they are compressed.
Free space for applications is based on quota limit.	When you enable disk quotas, the free space that Windows 2000 Professional reports to applications for the volume is the amount of space remaining within the user's disk quota limit.

Note Disk quotas can be applied only to Windows 2000 NTFS volumes.

You use disk quotas to monitor and control hard disk space usage. System administrators can do the following:

- Set a disk quota limit to specify the amount of disk space for each user.

- Set a disk quota warning to specify when Windows 2000 should log an event, indicating that the user is nearing his or her limit.

- Enforce disk quota limits and deny users access if they exceed their limit, or allow them continued access.

- Log an event when a user exceeds a specified disk space threshold. The threshold could be when users exceed their quota limit, or when they exceed their warning level.

After you enable disk quotas for a volume, Windows 2000 collects disk usage data for all users who own files and folders on the volume. This allows you to monitor volume usage on a per-user basis. By default, only members of the Administrators group can view and change quota settings. However, you can allow users to view quota settings.

Setting Disk Quotas

You can enable disk quotas and enforce disk quota warnings and limits for all users or for individual users.

If you want to enable disk quotas, open the Properties dialog box for a disk, click the Quota tab, and configure the options that are described in Table 2.11 and displayed in Figure 2.16.

Table 2.11 Quota Tab Options

Option	Description
Enable Quota Management	Select this check box to enable disk quota management.
Deny Disk Space To Users Exceeding Quota Limit	Select this check box so that when users exceed their hard disk space allocation, they receive an "out of disk space" message and cannot write to the volume.
Do Not Limit Disk Usage	Click this option when you don't want to limit the amount of hard disk space for users.
Limit Disk Space To	Configure the amount of disk space that users can have.
Set Warning Level To	Configure the amount of disk space that users can fill before Windows 2000 logs an event indicating that a user is nearing his or her limit.
Quota Entries	Click this button to open the Quota Entries For dialog box, where you can add a new entry, delete an entry, and view the per-user quota information.

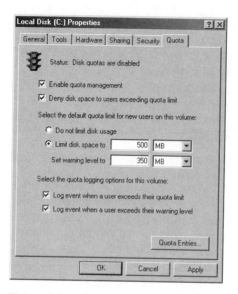

Figure 2.16 The Quota tab of the Properties dialog box for a disk

▶ **You can enforce identical quota limits for all users as follows:**

1. In the Limit Disk Space To box and the Set Warning Level To box, enter the values for the limit and warning level that you want to set.

2. Select the Deny Disk Space To Users Exceeding Quota Limit check box.

Windows 2000 will monitor usage and will not allow users to create files or folders on the volume when they exceed the limit.

Determining the Status of Disk Quotas

You can determine the status of disk quotas in the Properties dialog box for a disk by checking the traffic light icon and by reading the status message to its right (see Figure 2.16).

- A red traffic light indicates that disk quotas are disabled.

- A yellow traffic light indicates that Windows 2000 is rebuilding disk quota information.

- A green traffic light indicates that the disk quota system is active.

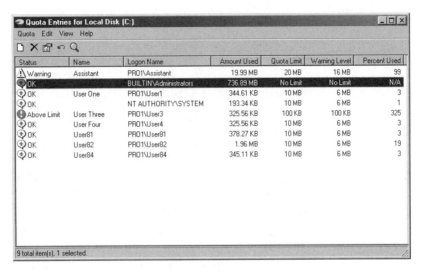

Figure 2.17 The Quota Entries for Local Disk window

▶ **You can enforce different quota limits for one or more specific users, as follows:**

1. Open the Properties dialog box for a disk, click the Quota tab, and then click the Quota Entries button.

2. In the Quota Entries For window, shown in Figure 2.17, double-click the user account for which you want to set a disk quota limit, or create an entry (in which you will establish a disk quota for a particular user) by clicking New Quota Entry on the Quota menu.

3. Configure the disk space limit and the warning level for the user. Do the same for other users according to the individual warning levels you want to assign to them.

Monitoring Disk Quotas

You use the Quota Entries For window to monitor usage for all users who have copied, saved, or taken ownership of files and folders on the volume. Windows 2000 will scan the volume and monitor the amount of disk space that each user occupies. Use the Quota Entries For window to view the following:

- The amount of hard disk space that each user occupies

- Users who are over their quota-warning threshold, which is signified by a yellow triangle

- Users who are over their quota limit, which is signified by a red circle

- The warning threshold and the disk quota limit for each user

Determining Best Uses of Disk Quotas

The following are general guidelines for using disk quotas:

- If you enable disk quota settings on the volume where Windows 2000 is installed and your user account has a disk quota limit, log on as Administrator to install additional Windows 2000 components and applications. This way, Windows 2000 won't count the disk space that you use to install applications against the disk quota allowance for your user account.

- You can monitor hard disk usage and generate hard disk usage information without preventing users from saving data. To do so, clear the Deny Disk Space To Users Exceeding Quota Limit check box when you enable disk quotas.

- Set more restrictive default limits for all user accounts, and then modify the limits to allow more disk space to users who work with large files.

- If computers running Windows 2000 Professional are shared by more than one user, set disk quota limits on computer volumes so that disk space is shared by all users who share the computer.

- Generally, you should set disk quotas on shared volumes to limit storage for users. Set disk quotas on public folders and network servers to ensure that users share hard disk space appropriately. When storage resources are scarce, you might want to set disk quotas on all shared hard disk space.

- Delete disk quota entries for a user who no longer stores files on a volume. You can delete quota entries for a user account only after all files that the user owns have been removed from the volume or another user has taken ownership of the files.

- Before you can delete a quota entry for a user account, you or the user must remove all files that the user owns from the volume, or another user must take ownership of the files.

Practice: Enabling and Disabling Disk Quotas

In this practice, you configure default quota management settings to limit the amount of data that users can store on drive C (their hard disk drive). Next, you configure a custom quota setting for a user account. You increase the amount of data the user can store on drive C to 20 MB with a warning level set to 16. Finally, you turn off quota management for drive C.

Note If you didn't install Windows 2000 Professional on drive C, substitute the NTFS partition on which you did install Windows 2000 Professional whenever drive C is referred to in this practice.

Exercise 1: Configuring Quota Management Settings

In this exercise, you configure the quota management settings for drive C to limit the data that users can store on the volume. You can then configure custom quota settings for a user account.

▶ **To configure default quota management settings**

1. Log on as Administrator and create a user account, User5. Assign the password of *password* to the account, and clear the User Must Change Password At Next Logon check box.

2. In Windows Explorer, right-click drive C, and then click Properties.

   Windows 2000 displays the Local Disk (C:) Properties dialog box with the General tab active.

3. Click the Quota tab.

   Notice that disk quotas are disabled by default.

4. On the Quota tab, click the Enable Quota Management check box.

5. Select Deny Disk Space To Users Exceeding Quota Limit.

6. Click Limit Disk Space To.

7. Type **10** in the Limit Disk Space To box and then type **6** in the Set Warning Level To box.

   Notice the default unit size is KB.

8. Change the unit sizes to MB, and then click Apply.

   Windows 2000 displays the Disk Quota message box, warning you that the volume will be rescanned to update disk usage statistics if you enable quotas.

9. Click OK to enable disk quotas.

▶   **To configure quota management settings for a user**

1. On the Quota tab of the Local Disk (C:) Properties dialog box, click the Quota Entries button.

   Windows 2000 displays the Quota Entries For Local Disk (C:) window.

   Are any user accounts listed? Why or why not?

2. On the Quota menu, click New Quota Entry.

   Windows 2000 displays the Select Users dialog box.

3. In the Look In box, select PRO1.

   Note If you didn't name your computer PRO1 or if your computer is part of a domain, select the appropriate computer or domain name.
   ---

4. At the top of the dialog box, under Name, select User5, and then click Add.

   The user name appears in the Name list at the bottom of the dialog box.

5. Click OK.

   Windows 2000 displays the Add New Quota Entry dialog box.

   What are the default settings for the user you just set a quota limit for?

6. Increase the amount of data that User5 can store on drive C: by changing the Limit Disk Space To option to 20 MB and the Set Warning Level To option to 16 MB.

7. Click OK to return to the Quota Entries window.

8. Close the Quota Entries window.

9. Click OK to close the Local Disk (C:) Properties dialog box.

10. Log off.

▶   **To test quota management settings**

1. Log on as User5 with a password of *password*.

2. Start Windows Explorer and create a User5 folder on drive C.

3. Insert into your CD-ROM drive the CD-ROM you used to install Windows 2000 Professional.

4. If a dialog box appears as a result of inserting the CD-ROM, close it.

5. Copy the i386 folder from your CD-ROM to the User5 folder.

    Windows 2000 Professional begins copying files from the i386 folder on the CD-ROM to a new i386 folder in the User5 folder on drive C. After copying several files, however, Windows 2000 displays the Error Copying File Or Folder dialog box, indicating that there isn't enough room on the disk.

    Why did you get this error message?

6. Click OK to close the dialog box.

7. Right-click the User5 folder and then click Properties.

    Notice that the Size On Disk value is slightly less than your quota limit of 20 MB.

8. Close all open windows and log off.

Exercise 2: Disabling Quota Management

In this exercise, you disable quota management settings for drive C.

1. Log on as Administrator and start Windows Explorer.

2. Delete the User5 folder.

3. Right-click drive C, and then click Properties.

   Windows 2000 displays the Local Disk (C:) Properties dialog box with the General tab active.

4. Click the Quota tab.

5. On the Quota tab, clear the Enable Quota Management check box.

   Notice that all quota settings for drive C are no longer available.

6. Click Apply.

   Windows 2000 displays the Disk Quota message box, warning you that if you disable quotas, the volume will be rescanned if you enable them later.

7. Click OK to close the Disk Quota message box.

8. Click OK to close the Local Disk (C:) Properties dialog box.

9. Close all applications.

Lesson Summary

In this lesson, you learned that you use disk quotas to allocate disk space usage. You can set disk quotas, quota thresholds, and quota limits for all users and for individual users. You can also monitor the amount of hard disk space that users have and the amount that they have left against their quota. You also learned that Windows 2000 ignores compression when it calculates hard disk space usage and that you can apply disk quotas only to Windows 2000 NTFS volumes.

Windows 2000 disk quotas track and control disk usage on a per-user, per-volume basis. Windows 2000 tracks disk quotas for each volume, even if the volumes are on the same hard disk. Because quotas are tracked on a per-user basis, every user's disk space is tracked regardless of the folder in which the user stores files.

Lesson 10: Configuring Power Options

Controlling energy usage is becoming more and more of an issue with computer users. If a computer only uses power when it is actively being used (instead of the entire time it is powered on) a company or user can realize significant energy savings. This is especially important for portable computer and other mobile computer users. A mobile computer should only be using power when it is in use, as this could extend battery time.

The Power Options program in Control Panel in Windows 2000 Professional allows you to configure power schemes, Hibernation mode, and the Advanced Power Mangement (APM) specification. These utilities help you control energy use and hopefully extend your overall battery use time. This lesson discusses these utilities and how they are configured.

After this lesson, you will be able to

- Configure power schemes
- Enable Hibernate mode
- Enable Advanced Power Management

Estimated lesson time: 15 minutes

Configuring Power Schemes

Power schemes allow you to configure Windows 2000 to turn off the power to your monitor and your hard disk, which conserves energy when you aren't actively using your computer. To configure power schemes, you use the Power Options program in Control Panel. Your hardware must support turning off the monitor and hard disk for you to be able to configure power schemes.

Using Hibernate Mode

When your computer hibernates, it saves the current system state to your hard disk, and then your computer shuts down. When you restart the computer after it has been hibernating, it returns to its previous state. Returning to the previous state includes automatically restarting any programs that were running when it went into Hibernate mode and even restoring any network connections that were active at the time. To configure your computer to use Hibernate mode, you use the Power Options program in Control Panel. Select the Hibernate tab in the Power Options Properties dialog box, and then select the Enable Hibernate Support check box.

Caution Many commercial airlines require you to turn off portable computers during certain portions of your flight. Hibernate mode might make your computer appear to be turned off, but it is not. You must shut down your computer to comply with these airline regulations.

Configuring Advanced Power Management

Windows 2000 supports the APM 1.2 specification. Using APM helps reduce the power consumption of your system. To configure your computer to use APM, you use the Power Options program in Control Panel. Select the APM tab in the Power Options Properties dialog box, and then select the Enable Advanced Power Management Support check box. You must be logged on as a member of the Administrators group to configure APM.

Note APM is available only in Windows 2000 Professional. It is not available in Windows 2000 Server, Windows 2000 Advanced Server, or Windows 2000 Datacenter.

If your computer doesn't have an APM-BIOS installed, then Windows 2000 will not install APM, and the Power Options Properties dialog box will not have an APM tab. However, your computer can still function as an Advanced Configuration and Power Interface (ACPI computer if it has an ACPI-based BIOS. The ACPI-based BIOS takes over system configuration and power management from the Plug and Play BIOS.

If your portable computer has an ACPI-based BIOS, you can insert and remove PC cards on the fly and Windows 2000 will automatically detect and configure them without requiring you to restart your machine. This is known as *dynamic configuration of PC cards*. Two other similar features rely on dynamic Plug and Play and are important to mobile computers: Hot and Warm Docking/Undocking and Hot Swapping of IDE and floppy devices.

With *Hot and Warm Docking/Undocking* you can dock and undock from the Windows 2000 Start button without turning off your computer. Windows 2000 automatically creates two hardware profiles for portable computers, one for the docked state and one for the undocked state.

With Hot Swapping of IDE and floppy devices you can remove devices such as floppy drives, DVD/CD drives, and hard disks; you can swap devices; or you can do both, without shutting down your system or restarting it. Windows 2000 Professional automatically detects and configures these devices.

Practice: Configuring Power Options

In this practice, you use Control Panel to configure power options.

Exercise 1: Configuring Power Options

1. Ensure that you are logged on as Administrator.

2. Click Start, point to Settings, and then click Control Panel.

   Control Panel appears.

3. Double-click Power Options.

   The Power Options Properties dialog box appears with the Power Schemes tab active. In the Power Schemes box, you can select one of the preconfigured power schemes or you can create your own.

4. In the Power Schemes box, select Portable/Laptop.

5. In the Turn Off Monitor drop-down list, select After 10 Minutes.

6. In the Turn Off Hard Disks drop-down list, select After 20 Minutes.

7. Click Save As, and then in the Save Scheme box, type **Airplane** and then click OK.

8. Click Apply.

9. Click the Power Scheme drop-down list arrow to verify that you just created your own power scheme. You should see Airplane listed.

   From now on, whenever you want to use this power scheme, you would select it here and then click Apply.

10. Select the Hibernate tab.

11. Select the Enable Hibernate Support check box, and then click Apply.

    By selecting the Enable Hibernate Support check box and clicking Apply, you enable Hibernate mode on your computer.

12. Select the APM tab.

   Note If you don't have an APM tab because your system doesn't have an APM-BIOS installed, skip this step and go to step 14.

13. Select the Enable Advanced Power Management Support check box, and then click Apply.

By selecting the Enable Advanced Power Management Support check box and clicking Apply, you enable APM support on your computer.

14. Click OK to close the Power Options Properties dialog box.

Lesson Summary

In this lesson, you learned that the Power Options program in Control Panel allows you to configure power schemes, Hibernation mode, and the APM specification. You learned how each of these is configured. Power schemes allow you to configure Windows 2000 to turn off the power to your monitor and your hard disk, which conserves energy when you aren't actively using your computer.

When your computer hibernates, it saves the current system state to your hard disk before shutting down, and then when you restart the computer after it has been hibernating, it will return to its previous state. Returning to the previous state includes automatically restarting any programs that were running when it went into Hibernate mode and even restoring any network connections that were active at the time.

Finally, you learned that Windows 2000 supports the APM 1.2 specification. Using APM helps reduce the power consumption of your system. You must be logged on as a member of the Administrators group to configure APM. If your computer doesn't have an APM-BIOS installed, then Windows 2000 won't install APM, and the Power Options Properties dialog box won't have an APM tab. However, your computer can still function as an ACPI computer if it has an ACPI-based BIOS.

Lesson 11: Using Device Manager and System Information

One of the primary tools for implementing, managing and troubleshooting hardware devices and drives is Device Manager, a snap-in you will find in Computer Management. This lesson introduces Device Manager and explains how you use it to manage and troubleshoot devices. This lesson also introduces the System Information snap-in, discusses how to use it, and explains how it helps you manage your system.

After this lesson, you will be able to

- Use Device Manager to configure and troubleshoot devices
- Use System Information to manage devices

Estimated lesson time: 30 minutes

Introducing Device Manager

Device Manager is one of the snap-ins located under System Tools in Computer Management. Device Manager provides you with a graphical view of the hardware installed on your computer (see Figure 2.18) and helps you manage and troubleshoot that hardware. You use Device Manager to disable, uninstall, and update device drivers.

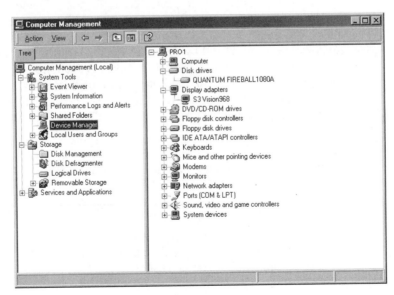

Figure 2.18 The Device Manager snap-in

Note Device Manager works with Plug and Play devices and legacy devices supported in Windows NT 4.0 Workstation.

Device Manager helps you to determine whether the hardware on your computer is working properly. It lists devices with problems, and each device that is flagged is displayed with the corresponding status information. Windows 2000 also provides hardware troubleshooters in Help to troubleshoot hardware problems.

Installing Devices

Windows 2000 Professional supports Plug and Play hardware. For most devices that are Plug and Play compliant, as long as the appropriate driver is available and the BIOS on the computer is a Plug and Play BIOS or an ACPI BIOS, Windows 2000 automatically detects, installs, and configures the device.

For the occasional Plug and Play device that is not automatically detected, installed, and configured by Windows 2000, and for non–Plug and Play hardware that Windows 2000 doesn't identify, install, and configure, you initiate the installation of the hardware with the Add/Remove Hardware wizard.

Configuring and Troubleshooting Devices

When you manually change device configurations, Device Manager can help you to avoid problems. Device Manager allows you to identify free resources and assign a device to those resources, disable devices to free resources, and reallocate resources used by devices to free a required resource. You must be logged on as a member of the Administrators group to change resource settings. Even if you are logged on as Administrator, if your computer is connected to a network, policy settings on the network might prevent you from changing resources.

Caution Improperly changing resource settings on devices can disable your hardware and cause your computer to no longer work.

Windows 2000 automatically identifies Plug and Play devices and arbitrates their resource requests. However, the resource allocation among Plug and Play devices isn't permanent. If another Plug and Play device requests a resource that has already been allocated, Windows 2000 again arbitrates the requests to satisfy all resource requests.

You should not manually change resource settings for a Plug and Play device because Windows 2000 won't be able to arbitrate the assigned resources if requested by another Plug and Play device. In Device Manager, Plug and Play devices have a Resources tab on their Properties dialog box. To free the resource settings you manually assigned and allow Windows 2000 to again arbitrate the resources, select the Use Automatic Settings check box on the Resources tab.

Note Devices that Windows NT 4.0 Workstation support have fixed resource settings. These resource settings are usually defined during an upgrade from Windows NT 4.0 Workstation to Windows 2000 Professional, but you can also define them by using the Add New Hardware wizard in Control Panel.

▶ **You can use Device Manager to configure or troubleshoot a device as follows:**

1. Right-click My Computer, and then click Manage.

   The Computer Management window opens.

2. Under System Tools, click Device Manager.

3. In the Details pane, double-click the device type, and then double-click the device you want to configure.

   The *Device* Properties dialog box appears (where *Device* is a specific device).

   The tabs available on the Properties page for the device will vary depending on the device selected but might include some of those listed in Table 2.12.

4. To configure a device, choose the appropriate tab. To troubleshoot, on the General tab, click Troubleshooter.

Table 2.12 Properties Dialog Box Tabs for Selected Devices

Tab	Function
Advanced or Advanced Properties	The properties listed in this tab will vary depending on the device selected.
General	This tab displays the device type, manufacturer, and location. It also displays the device status and provides a troubleshooter to help you solve any problems you are having with the device. The troubleshooter guides you through a series of questions to determine the problem and provide a solution.

continues

Table 2.12 Properties Dialog Box Tabs for Selected Devices *(continued)*

Tab	Function
Device Properties	The properties listed in this tab will vary depending on what device is selected.
Driver	This tab displays the driver provider, driver date, driver version, and digital signer. This tab also provides the following three additional buttons: Driver Details, Uninstall, and Driver Update. These buttons allow you to get additional information on the driver, uninstall the driver, or update the driver with a newer version.
Port Settings	In a communications port (COM1) Properties dialog box, this tab displays and allows you to configure bits per second, data bits, parity, stop bits, and flow control.
Properties	This tab displays options that determine how Windows uses the device. For example, on the CD-ROM, the properties could include Volume and Digital CD Playback, which allows you to enable digital instead of analog playback. These settings determine how Windows uses the CD-ROM for playing music from a CD.
Resources	This tab displays the resource type and setting, whether there are any resource conflicts, and whether you can change the resource settings.

Using the System Information Snap-In

System Information is a snap-in that you can add to a custom console (by using the MMC) so that you can manage devices by collecting and viewing configuration information about your system. To use System Information, use the MMC to create a custom console and add the System Information snap-in to it (see Figure 2.19). When you add the snap-in to a custom console, you can focus it on the local machine or on a remote machine. The System Information snap-in also helps you to troubleshoot problems.

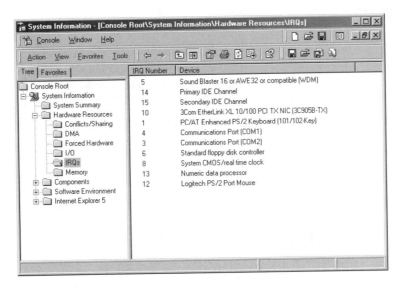

Figure 2.19 The System Information snap-in

Table 2.13 describes the nodes of the System Information snap-in.

Table 2.13 System Information Nodes

Node	Description
System Summary	This node displays information such as the operating system, the version number of the operating system, and the manufacturer of the operating system. It displays the NetBIOS computer name, the computer manufacturer, model number, and type, as well as information about the processor and the BIOS. It also lists the installation folder, locale, and time zone information. Finally, it lists the total and available physical memory, the total and available virtual memory, and the page file size.
Hardware Resources	This node displays hardware resource settings such as any conflicts or resource sharing, DMA, IRQs, I/O addresses, and memory addresses.
Components	This node displays information about the configuration and status of devices including the following categories: multimedia, display, infrared, input, modems, network, ports, storage, printing, problem devices, and USB.

continues

Table 2.13 System Information Nodes *(continued)*

Node	Description
Software Environment	This node displays what is loaded into memory at a particular instant. The display includes the drivers, environment variables, network connections, tasks, and services loaded into memory.
Internet Explorer 5	This node displays configuration settings for Microsoft Internet Explorer. The summary displays the version, build, product ID, install location, language, and cipher strength. It also displays a list of associated files and version numbers, settings for connectivity, file caching, and security.

Practice: Using Device Manager and System Information

In this practice, you will use Device Manager and System Information to monitor and review your system configuration. You will also use trouble-shooters to simulate solving a problem with a disk drive.

Exercise 1: Using Device Manager to Review Devices and to Troubleshoot a Device

In this exercise, you practice using Device Manager to review the devices on your system and to determine their status. You will also use Device Manager to simulate troubleshooting an unterminated SCSI chain.

1. Right-click My Computer, and then click Manage.

   The Computer Management window opens.

2. Under System Tools, click Device Manager.

3. In the Details pane, double-click Disk Drives, and then double-click one of the drives listed.

   The Properties page appears and the General tab shows a Device Status that indicates if any problems exist with the drive.

4. Click Troubleshooter. (Normally you would do this only if a problem was indicated with this device.)

   Notice that online Help starts with the Drives Troubleshooter displayed. Troubleshooter steps you through a series of questions to help you resolve your problem.

5. Click I'm Having A Problem With My Hard Drive Or Floppy Disk Drive, and then click Next.

6. Click Yes, I'm Having A Problem With A SCSI Device, and then click Next.

   You are asked, "Does Your Device Work When You Terminate The SCSI Chain?"

7. Click Yes, My Device Works, and then click Next.

   If an unterminated SCSI chain was the problem you were trying to solve, you would have just fixed the problem.

8. Close online Help, close the Properties dialog box for the selected disk drive, and close the Computer Management window.

Exercise 2: Using System Information

In this exercise, you practice using System Information to view configuration information about your computer.

1. Use the MMC to create a custom console and add the System Information snap-in to it, with the focus directed on the local computer.

2. Double-click System Information in the console tree.

   Notice that a Refreshing System Information message appears in the details pane while System Information takes a snapshot of the current system configuration.

3. Review the information displayed in the details pane.

4. In the details pane, double-click Hardware Resources, and then double-click IRQs.

   Are there any IRQs being shared?

5. In the details pane, double-click Software Environment, and then double-click Services.

6. Review which services are running and which services are stopped.

7. Save the custom console containing the System Information snap-in as System Information, and then close System Information.

Lesson Summary

In this lesson, you learned about two of the Windows 2000 snap-ins: Device Manager and System Information. You learned how to use Device Manager to configure and troubleshoot devices. You also learned how to use System Information quickly to gather and display your system configuration and to help you manage and troubleshoot your computer.

Lesson 12: Monitoring System Performance

The Performance console contains many indicators to help you determine how efficiently your system is operating. This lesson introduces Performance Console and explains how to use it to monitor system performance.

After this lesson, you will be able to

- Use Performance Console to monitor your system

Estimated lesson time: 10 minutes

Using Performance Console to Monitor System Performance

You can monitor the activity of your symmetric multiprocessing (SMP) system by using Performance Console and its counters. Performance Console helps you to gauge a computer's efficiency and locate and resolve current or potential problems. In Performance Console, a set of counters exists for each object. Table 2.14 describes a few of the available objects.

Table 2.14 Performance Console Objects

Object	Description
Cache	Monitors the file system cache that is used to buffer physical device data
Memory	Monitors the physical and virtual memory on the computer
PhysicalDisk	Monitors a hard disk as a whole
Processor	Monitors CPUs

Adding Counters

Adding counters to an object, such as the ones described in Table 2.14, allows you to track certain aspects of the objects. You can use the following steps to add counters to an object in Performance Console.

1. Click Start, point to Settings, Taskbar and Start Menu, and click the Advanced tab.

2. On the Advanced tab, check Display Administrative Tools, then click OK.

3. Click Start, point to Programs, point to Administrative Tools, and then click Performance.

   Performance Console starts.

4. At the bottom right of the console, right-click Counter and click Add Counters.

   The Add Counters dialog box appears.

5. In the Performance Object box, select the object for which you want to add counters.

6. Ensure that Select Counters From List is selected.

   You can add all counters, but that usually provides more information than you need or can interpret.

7. Select a counter from the list and click Add.

   For an explanation of a counter, select it and then click Explain.

Note If you want to add several counters at the same time, you can hold the Ctrl key down and select the individual counters of your choice from the list. If you want to select several counters in a row, hold down the Shift key and click the first in the list that you want and then click the last in the list that you want to select. All counters listed between the first and last you clicked will automatically be selected.

---

8. When you have completed your selection of objects and counters, click Close to return to Performance Console.

Table 2.15 describes a few of the counters you might find useful in evaluating your system's performance.

Table 2.15 Performance Counters

Counter	Description
Under Processor, choose % Processor Time	This counter shows the percentage of time that the processor spends executing a non-idle thread. This counter is an indicator of percentage of time that the processor is active. During some operations, this can reach 100 percent. These periods of 100-percent activity should occur only occasionally and should not reflect the normal amount of activity for the processor.
Under Processor, choose % DPC Time	This counter determines how much time the processor is spending processing deferred procedure calls (DPCs). *DPCs are software interrupts or tasks that require immediate processing, causing other tasks to be handled at a lower priority. DPCs represent further processing of client requests.*
Under Processor, choose \Interrupts/Sec	This counter determines the average number of hardware interrupts the processor is receiving and servicing in each second. It doesn't include DPCs. This counter value is an indicator of the activity of devices that generate interrupts, such as the system clock, mouse, network adapter cards, and other peripheral devices. If the processor time value is more than 90 percent and the Interrupts/Sec value is greater than 15 percent, this processor probably needs assistance to handle the interrupt load.
Under System, choose Processor Queue Length	This counter determines how many threads there are in the processor queue. There is a single queue for processor time, even on computers with multiple processors. A sustained processor queue of greater than two threads usually indicates that the processor is causing a problem to the overall system performance.

Lesson Summary

In this lesson you learned that you can use Performance Console and its counters to monitor the activity of your SMP system. Performance Console helps you to gauge a computer's efficiency and locate and resolve current or potential problems. Adding counters to an object allows you to track certain aspects of the objects.

Review

The following questions will help you determine whether you have learned enough to move on to the next chapter. If you have difficulty answering these questions, please go back and review the material in this chapter before beginning the next chapter. See Appendix A, "Questions and Answers," for the answers to these questions.

1. What should you do if you can't see any output on the secondary display?

2. You have configured recovery options on a computer running Windows 2000 Professional to write debugging information to a file if a system failure occurs. You notice, however, that the file isn't being created. What could be causing this problem?

3. You installed a new network interface card (NIC) in your computer, but it doesn't seem to be working. Describe how you would troubleshoot this problem.

4. You install a new 10-GB disk drive that you want to divide into five equal 2-GB sections. What are your options?

5. You are trying to create a striped volume on your Windows NT Server to improve performance. You confirm that you have enough unallocated disk space on two disks in your computer, but when you right-click an area of unallocated space on a disk, a dialog box appears indicating that your only option is to create a partition. What is the problem and how would you resolve it?

6. You add a new disk to your computer and attempt to extend an existing volume to include the unallocated space on the new disk, but the option to extend the volume isn't available. What is the problem and how would you resolve it?

7. You dual boot your computer with Windows 98 and Windows 2000 Professional. You upgrade a second drive—which you are using to archive files—from basic storage to dynamic storage. The next time you try to access your archived files from Windows 98, you are unable to read the files. Why?

8. You are the administrator for a computer running Windows 2000 Professional. You want to restrict users to 25 MB of available storage space. How do you configure the volumes on the computer?

9. The Sales department archives old sales data on a network computer running Windows 2000 Professional. Several other departments share the server. You have begun to receive complaints from users in other departments that the server has little remaining disk space. What can you do to alleviate the problem?

10. A friend of yours just installed Windows 2000 Professional on his home computer. He called you to help him configure Advanced Power Management (APM), and when you told him to double-click Power Options in Control Panel and click on the APM tab, he told you he did not have an APM tab. What is the most likely reason there is no APM tab?

11. Many commercial airlines require you to turn off portable computers during certain portions of a flight. Does placing your computer in Hibernate mode comply with these airline regulations? Why or why not?

12. Your boss has started to manually assign resource settings to all devices, including Plug and Play devices, and wants you to finish the job. What should you do?

13. You receive a call at the Help desk from a user who is trying to configure her fax settings, and she tells you that she does not have an Advanced Options tab. What could the problem be?

CHAPTER 3

Managing Resources

About This Chapter

As an experienced Windows NT 4.0 professional, you should already be familiar with managing files, folders, and printers. This chapter presents an overview of Microsoft Windows 2000's New Technology File System (NTFS) folder and file permissions and how it is used in a Windows 2000 Professional environment.

In this chapter you learn how to assign NTFS folder and file permissions to user accounts and groups, and you will see how moving or copying files and folders affects NTFS file and folder permissions. The chapter also discusses how to troubleshoot common resource access problems.

The chapter then explains how to use NTFS compressions to better manage the space on a computer.

Once you understand how to manage permissions, you are introduced to sharing folders and using both shared folder and NTFS permissions to control access to folders.

The chapter then moves onto a discussion of another common shared resource: the printer. You are introduced to setting up and configuring printers so users can print over a network. You then are shown how to manage printers and documents from a remote location and how to administer a printer using a web browser.

Before You Begin

To complete this chapter, you must have

- A computer that meets the minimum hardware requirements listed in "Hardware Requirements" in "About This Book"

- Microsoft Windows 2000 Professional installed on the computer

Note You do *not* need a printer to complete the exercises in this chapter.

Lesson 1: NTFS Permissions

After this lesson, you will be able to

- Define the standard NTFS folder and file permissions
- Describe the results of combining user account and group permissions
- Describe the results of assigning permissions for folders that are different from those of the files in the folder
- Assign NTFS folder and file permissions to user accounts and groups

Estimated lesson time: 15 minutes

File Systems

After you create the installation partition, Setup prompts you to select the file system with which to format the partition. Windows 2000 supports three file systems: Windows 2000 file system (NTFS), file allocation table (FAT), and FAT32.

The Table 3.1 lists the features of the various file systems.

Table 3.1   File System Features

File system	Feature
NTFS	File and Folder level security
	Disk Compression
	Disk Quota management
	Encryption
	Remote Storage
	Dynamic Volume
	Mounting of Volumes to Folders
	Permission settings
FAT and FAT32	Dual Booting No File-level security

Unless you require dual booting, NTFS is the file system to use.

File and Folder Permissions

NTFS also allows you to specify which users and groups can gain access to files and folders and what they can do with the contents of the file or folder. NTFS permissions are available only on NTFS volumes. NTFS permissions are *not* available on volumes that are formatted with FAT or FAT32 file systems. NTFS security is effective whether a user gains access to the file or folder locally or from the network. The permissions you assign for folders are different from the permissions you assign for files.

NTFS Folder Permissions

You assign folder permissions to control the access that users have to folders and to the files and subfolders contained within the folder.

Table 3.2 lists the standard NTFS folder permissions that you can assign and the type of access that each provides to users.

Table 3.2 NTFS Folder Permissions

NTFS folder permission	Allows the user to
Read	See files and subfolders in the folder and view folder ownership, permissions, and attributes (such as Read-Only, Hidden, Archive, and System)
Write	Create new files and subfolders within the folder; change folder attributes; view details of folder ownership and permissions
List Folder Contents	See the names of files and subfolders in the folder
Read & Execute	Move through folders to reach other files and folders, even if the users don't have permission for those folders; perform actions permitted by the Read permission and the List Folder Contents permission
Modify	Delete the folder; perform actions permitted by the Write permission and the Read & Execute permission
Full Control	Change permissions, take ownership, and delete subfolders and files; perform actions permitted by all other NTFS folder permissions

As an administrator, you can deny permission to any user account or group. To deny all access to a user account or group for a folder, deny the Full Control permission.

NTFS File Permissions

You assign file permissions to control the access that users have to files. Table 3.3 lists the standard NTFS file permissions that you can assign and the type of access that each permission provides.

Table 3.3 NTFS File Permissions

NTFS file permission	Allows the user to
Read	Read the file view file attributes, ownership, and permissions
Write	Overwrite the file; change file attributes; view file ownership and permissions
Read & Execute	Run applications; perform the actions permitted by the Read permission
Modify	Modify and delete the file; perform the actions permitted by the Write permission and the Read & Execute permission
Full Control	Change permissions and take ownership; perform the actions permitted by all other NTFS file permissions

Applying NTFS Permissions

Administrators, the owners of files or folders, and users with Full Control permission can assign NTFS permissions to users and groups to control access to files and folders.

Access Control List

NTFS stores an access control list (ACL) with every file and folder on an NTFS volume. The ACL contains a list of all user accounts and groups that have been granted access for the file or folder, as well as the type of access that they have been granted. If a user attempts to gain access to a resource, the ACL must contain an entry called an access control entry (ACE) for the user account or a group to which the user belongs. The entry must allow the type of access that is requested (for example, Read access) for the user to gain access. If no ACE exists in the ACL, the user can't gain access to the resource.

Multiple NTFS Permissions

You can assign multiple permissions to a user account and to each group in which the user is a member. To assign permissions, you must understand the rules and priorities regarding how NTFS assigns and combines multiple permissions and NTFS permission inheritance.

Cumulative Permissions

A user's effective permissions for a resource are the sum of the NTFS permissions that you assign to the individual user account and to all of the groups to which the user belongs. If a user has Read permission for a folder and is a member of a group with Write permission for the same folder, the user has both Read and Write permission for that folder.

Overriding Folder Permissions with File Permissions

NTFS file permissions take priority over NTFS folder permissions. A user with access to a file will be able to gain access to the file even if he or she doesn't have access to the folder containing the file. A user can gain access to the files for which he or she has permissions by using the full universal naming convention (UNC) or local path to open the file from its respective application, even though the folder in which it resides will be invisible if the user has no corresponding folder permission. In other words, if you don't have permission to access the folder containing the file you want to access, you will have to know the full path to the file to access it. Without permission to access the folder, you can't see the folder, so you can't browse for the file you want to access.

Overriding Other Permissions with Deny

You can deny permission to a user account or group for a specific file, although this is not the recommended way to control access to resources. Denying a permission overrides all instances where that permission is allowed. Even if a user has permission to gain access to the file or folder as a member of a group, denying permission to the user blocks that and any other permission the user might have (see Figure 3.1).

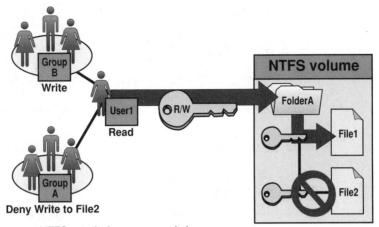

- NTFS permissions are cumulative.
- File permissions override folder permissions.
- Deny overrides other permissions.

Figure 3.1 Multiple NTFS permissions

In Figure 3.1, User1 has Read permission for FolderA and is a member of Group A and Group B. Group B has Write permission for FolderA. Group A has been denied Write permission for File2.

Because of the read and write permissions User1 has to FolderA, User1 can read and write to File1. The user can also read File2 because of the folder permissions, but she cannot write to File2 because she is a member of Group A, which has been denied Write permission for File2.

NTFS Permissions Inheritance

By default, permissions that you assign to the parent folder are inherited by and propagated to the subfolders and files that are contained in the parent folder. However, you can prevent permissions inheritance, as shown in Figure 3.2.

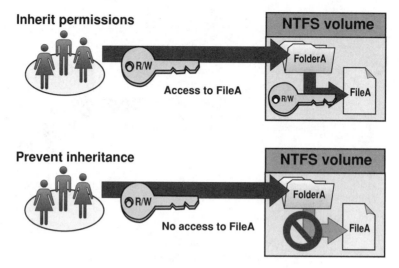

Figure 3.2 Inheritance

You can prevent permissions assigned to a parent folder from being inherited by subfolders and files that are contained within the folder. That is, the subfolders and files will not inherit permissions that have been assigned to the parent folder containing them.

The folder for which you prevent permissions inheritance becomes the new parent folder, and permissions that are assigned to this folder will be inherited by the subfolders and files that are contained within it.

Planning NTFS Permissions

You should follow certain guidelines for assigning NTFS permissions. Assign permissions according to group and user needs, which includes allowing or preventing permissions inheritance from parent folders to subfolders and files that are contained in the parent folder.

If you take the time to plan your NTFS permissions and follow a few guide-lines, you will find that NTFS permissions are easy to manage. Use the following guidelines when you assign NTFS permissions:

- To simplify administration, group files into application, data, and home folders. Centralize home and public folders on a volume that is separate from applications and the operating system. Doing so has the following benefits:

  - You assign permissions only to folders, not to individual files.

  - Backup is less complex because you don't need to back up application files, and all home and public folders are in one location.

- Allow users only the level of access that they require. If a user only needs to read a file, assign the Read permission to his or her user account for the file. This reduces the possibility of users accidentally modifying or deleting important documents and application files.

- Create groups according to the access that the group members require for resources, and then assign the appropriate permissions to the group. Assign permissions to individual user accounts only when necessary.

- When you assign permissions for working with data or application folders, assign the Read & Execute permission to the Users group and the Administrators group. This prevents application files from being accidentally deleted or damaged by users or viruses.

- When you assign permissions for public data folders, assign the Read & Execute permission and the Write permission to the Users group and the Full Control permission to the CREATOR OWNER user. By default, the user who creates a file is also the owner of the file. After you create a file, you can grant another user permission to take ownership of the file. The person who takes ownership then becomes the owner of the file. If you assign the Read & Execute permission and the Write permission to the Users group and the Full Control permission to the CREATOR OWNER user, users can read and modify documents that other users create and they are able to read, modify, and delete the files and folders that they create.

- Deny permissions only when it is essential to deny specific access to a specific user account or group.

- Encourage users to assign permissions to the files and folders they create and educate users about how to do so.

Setting NTFS Permissions

By default, when you format a volume with NTFS, the Full Control permission is assigned to the Everyone group. You should change this default permission and assign other appropriate NTFS permissions to control the access that users have to resources.

Assigning or Modifying Permissions

Administrators, users with the Full Control permission, and the owners of files and folders (CREATOR OWNER) can assign permissions to user accounts and groups.

To assign or modify NTFS permissions for a file or a folder, on the Security tab of the Properties dialog box for the file or folder, configure the options that are shown in Figure 3.3 and described in Table 3.4.

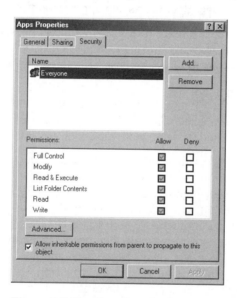

Figure 3.3 The Security tab of the Apps Properties dialog box for a folder

Table 3.4 Security Tab Options

Option	Description
Name	Allows you to select the user account or group for which you want to change permissions or that you want to remove from the list
Permissions	Allows you to select the Allow check box to allow a permission
	Allows you to select the Deny check box to deny a permission
Add	Allows you to open the Select Users, Computers, Or Groups dialog box, which you use to select user accounts and groups to add to the Name list
Remove	Allows you to remove the selected user account or group and the associated permissions for the file or folder
Advanced	Allows you to open the Access Control Settings for the selected folder so that you can grant or deny additional permissions

Preventing Permissions Inheritance

By default, subfolders and files inherit permissions that you assign to their parent folder. This is indicated on the Security tab in the Properties dialog box by a check mark in the Allow Inheritable Permissions From Parent To Propagate To This Object check box. To prevent a subfolder or file from inheriting permissions from a parent folder, clear the Allow Inheritable Permissions From Parent To Propagate To This Object check box. If you clear this check box, you are prompted to select one of the options described in Table 3.5.

Table 3.5 Preventing Permissions Inheritance Options

Option	Description
Copy	Allows you to copy the permissions from the parent folder to the current folder and then deny subsequent permissions inheritance from the parent folder
Remove	Allows you to remove the permissions that are inherited from the parent folder and retain only the permissions that you explicitly assign to the file or folder
Cancel	Allows you to cancel the dialog box and restore the check mark in the Allow Inheritable Permissions From Parent To Propagate To This Object check box

Lesson Summary

In this lesson, you learned that, by default, when you format a volume with NTFS, the Full Control permission is assigned to the Everyone group. You should change this default permission and assign other appropriate NTFS permissions to control the access that users have to resources. To assign or modify NTFS permissions for a file or a folder, you use the Security tab of the Properties dialog box for the file or folder.

You also learned that, by default, subfolders and files inherit permissions that you assign to their parent folder. You can disable this feature so that subfolders and files don't inherit the permissions assigned to their parents.

Lesson 2: Assigning Special Access Permissions

The standard NTFS permissions generally provide all of the access control that you need to secure your resources. However, sometimes the standard NTFS permissions don't provide the specific level of access that you might want to assign to users. To create a specific level of access, you assign NTFS special access permissions.

After this lesson, you will be able to

- Allow users to change permissions on files or folders
- Allow users to take ownership of files and folders

Estimated lesson time: 5 minutes

Using Special Access Permissions

There are 14 special access permissions. Two of them are particularly useful for controlling access to resources. These are Change Permissions and Take Ownership.

When you assign special access permissions to folders, you can choose where to apply the permissions down the tree to subfolders and files.

Changing Permissions

You can enable other administrators and users to change permissions for a file or folder without giving them the Full Control permission over the file or folder. In this way, the administrator or user can't delete or write to the file or folder but can assign permissions to the file or folder.

To enable administrators to change permissions, assign Change Permissions to the Administrators group for the file or folder.

Taking Ownership

You can transfer ownership of files and folders from one user account or group to another user account or group. You enable someone to take ownership and, as an administrator, you can take ownership of a file or folder.

The following rules apply for taking ownership of a file or folder:

- The current owner or any user with Full Control permission can assign the Full Control standard permission or the Take Ownership special access permission to another user account or group, allowing the user account or a member of the group to take ownership.

- An administrator can take ownership of a folder or file, regardless of assigned permissions. If an administrator takes ownership, the Administrators group becomes the owner, and any member of the Administrators group can change the permissions for the file or folder and assign the Take Ownership permission to another user account or group.

  For example, if an employee leaves the company, an administrator can take ownership of the employee's files, assign the Take Ownership permission to another employee, and then that employee can take ownership of the former employee's files.

Note You cannot *assign* anyone ownership of a file or folder. The owner of a file, an administrator, or anyone with Full Control permission can assign Take Ownership permission to a user account or group, allowing them to take ownership. To become the owner of a file or folder, a user or group member with Take Ownership permission must explicitly take ownership of the file or folder, as explained later in this chapter.

Setting Special Access Permissions

▶ **Follow these steps to assign special access permissions to enable users to change permissions and take ownership of files and folders:**

1. In the Access Control Settings dialog box for a file or folder, on the Permissions tab, select the user account or group for which you want to apply NTFS special access permissions.

2. Click View/Edit to open the Permissions Entry dialog box (see Figure 3.4).

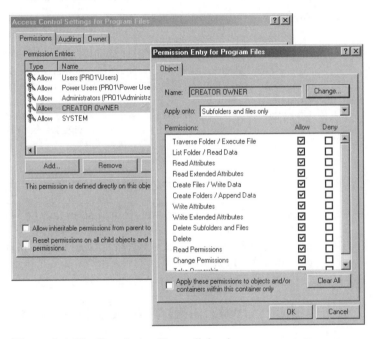

Figure 3.4 The Permission Entry dialog box

The options in the Permissions Entry dialog box are described in Table 3.6.

Table 3.6   Options in the Permissions Entry Dialog Box

Option	Description
Name	The user account or group name. To select a different user account or group, click Change.
Apply Onto	The level of the folder hierarchy at which the special NTFS permissions are inherited. The default is This Folder, Subfolders And Files.
Permissions	The special access permissions. To allow the Change Permissions permission or Take Ownership permission, select the Allow check box.
Apply These Permissions To Objects And/Or Containers Within This Container Only	Specify whether subfolders and files within a folder inherit the special access permissions from the folder. Select this check box to propagate the special access permissions to files and subfolders. Clear this check box to prevent permissions inheritance.
Clear All	Click this button to clear all selected permissions.

Note You can view the permissions that are applied to the file or folder, the owner, and where the permissions apply in the Access Control Settings dialog box, on the Permissions tab. When special access permissions have been assigned, Windows 2000 displays Special under Permissions.

Taking Ownership of a File or Folder

▶ **Follow these steps to take ownership of a file or folder. The user or a group member with Take Ownership permission must explicitly take ownership of the file or folder.**

   1. In the Access Control Settings dialog box, on the Owner tab, in the Change Owner To list, select your name.

   2. Select the Replace Owner On Subcontainers And Objects check box to take ownership of all subfolders and files that are contained within the folder.

Lesson Summary

In this lesson, you learned that there are 14 special access permissions, and two of them are especially useful. These are Change Permissions and Take Ownership. You can enable administrators and other users to change permissions for a file or folder without giving them the Full Control permission over the file or folder. This prevents the administrator or user from deleting or writing to the file or folder, but it still allows them to assign permissions to the file or folder.

You also learned that you can transfer ownership of files and folders from one user account or group to another user account or group. The current owner or any user with Full Control permission can assign the Full Control standard permission or the Take Ownership special access permission to another user account or group, allowing the user account or a member of the group to take ownership. An administrator can take ownership of a folder or file, regardless of assigned permissions. When an administrator takes ownership of a file or folder, the Administrators group becomes the owner, and any member of the Administrators group can change the permissions for the file or folder and assign the Take Ownership permission to another user account or group.

Lesson 3: Solving Permissions Problems

When you assign or modify NTFS permissions to files and folders, problems might arise. Troubleshooting these problems is important to keep resources available to users.

After this lesson, you will be able to

- Troubleshoot resource access problems

Estimated lesson time: 5 minutes

Troubleshooting Permissions Problems

Table 3.7 describes some common permissions problems that you might encounter and the solutions you can use to try to resolve them.

Table 3.7 Permissions Problems and Troubleshooting Solutions

Problem	Solution
A user can't gain access to a file or folder.	If the file or folder was copied, or if it was moved to another NTFS volume, the permissions might have changed.
	Check the permissions that are assigned to the user account and to groups of which the user is a member. The user might not have permission or might be denied access either individually or as a member of a group.
You add a user account to a group to give that user access to a file or folder, but the user still can't gain access.	For access permissions to be updated to include the new group to which you have added the user account, the user must either log off and then log on again, or close all network connections to the computer on which the file or folder resides and then make new connections.
A user with Full Control permission to a folder deletes a file in the folder, although that user doesn't have permission to delete the file itself. You want to stop the user from being able to delete more files.	You must clear the special access permission—the Delete Subfolders And Files check box—on the folder to prevent users with Full Control of the folder from being able to delete files in the folder.

Note Windows 2000 supports POSIX applications that are designed to run on UNIX. On UNIX systems, Full Control permission allows you to delete files in a folder. In Windows 2000, the Full Control permission includes the Delete Subfolders And Files special access permission, which also allows you to delete files in that folder regardless of the permissions that you have for the files in the folder.

Avoiding Permissions Problems

The following is a list of best practices for implementing NTFS permissions. These guidelines will help you avoid permission problems.

- Assign the most restrictive NTFS permissions that still enable users and groups to accomplish necessary tasks.

- Assign all permissions at the folder level, not at the file level. Group files in a separate folder for which you want to restrict user access, and then assign that folder restricted access.

- For all application-executable files, assign Read & Execute and Change Permissions to the Administrators group, and assign Read & Execute to the Users group. Damage to application files is usually the result of accidents and viruses. By assigning Read & Execute to users and Read & Execute and Change Permissions to administrators, you can prevent users or viruses from modifying or deleting executable files. To update files, members of the Administrators group can assign Full Control to their user account to make changes and then reassign Read & Execute and Change Permissions to their user account.

- Assign Full Control to the CREATOR OWNER group for public data folders so that users can delete and modify files and folders that they create. Doing so gives the user who creates the file or folder (CREATOR OWNER) full access to only the files or folders that he or she creates in the public data folder.

- For public folders, assign Full Control to the CREATOR OWNER group and Read and Write to the Everyone group. This gives users full access to the files that they create, but members of the Everyone group can only read files in the folder and add files to the folder.

- Use long, descriptive names if the resource will be accessed only at the computer. If a folder will eventually be shared, use folder and filenames that are accessible to all client computers.

- Allow permissions rather than deny permissions. If you don't want a user or group to gain access to a particular folder or file, don't assign permissions. Denying permissions should be an exception, not a common practice.

Lesson Summary

When you assign or modify NTFS permissions for files and folders, problems might arise. Troubleshooting these problems is important to keep resources available to users. In this lesson, you learned about some common permissions problems and some possible solutions to resolve these problems.

Lesson 4: Managing NTFS Compression

NTFS compression enables you to compress files and folders. Compressed files and folders occupy less space on an NTFS-formatted volume than do regular files and folders, which means you can store more data on them. Each file and folder on an NTFS volume has a *compression state* of either *compressed* or *uncompressed*.

After this lesson, you will be able to

- Manage disk compression
- Compress and uncompress files and folders

Estimated lesson time: 10 minutes

Using Compressed Files and Folders

Compressed files can be read by and written to any Microsoft Windows–based or MS-DOS-based application without first being uncompressed by another program. When an application, such as Microsoft Word for Windows, or an operating system command, such as Copy, requests access to a compressed file, NTFS automatically uncompresses the file before making it available. When you close or explicitly save a file, NTFS compresses it again.

NTFS allocates disk space based on the uncompressed file size. If you copy a compressed file to an NTFS volume with enough space for the compressed file but not enough space for the uncompressed file, you might get an error message stating that there is not enough disk space for the file. The file will not be copied to the volume.

Compressing Files and Folders

You can set the compression state of folders and files, and you can change the color that is used to display compressed files and folders in Windows Explorer.

If you want to set the compression state of a folder or file, right-click the folder or file in Windows Explorer, click Properties, and then click the Advanced button. In the Advanced Attributes dialog box, select the Compress Contents To Save Disk Space check box, as shown in Figure 3.5. Click OK, and then click Apply in the Properties dialog box.

Note NTFS encryption and compression are mutually exclusive. Therefore, if you select the Encrypt Contents To Secure Data check box, you can't compress the folder or file.

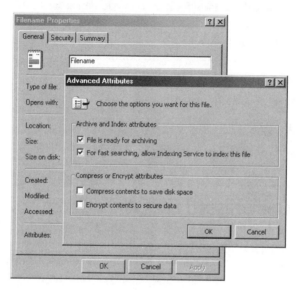

Figure 3.5 The Advanced Attributes dialog box

Important To change the compression state for a file or folder, you must have Write permission for that file or folder.

The compression state for a folder doesn't reflect the compression state of the files and subfolders in that folder. A folder can be compressed, yet all of the files in that folder can be uncompressed. Alternatively, an uncompressed folder can contain compressed files. When you compress a folder, Windows 2000 displays the Confirm Attribute Changes dialog box, which has the two options that are described in Table 3.8.

Table 3.8 Confirm Attribute Changes Dialog Box Options

Option	Description
Apply Changes To This Folder Only	Compresses only the folder that you have selected
Apply Changes To This Folder, Subfolder, And Files	Compresses the folder and all subfolders and files contained in it now as well as any others that might be added to it in the future

Note Windows 2000 doesn't support NTFS compression for cluster sizes larger than 4 KB because compression on large clusters causes performance degradation. If you select a larger cluster size when you format an NTFS volume, compression isn't available for that volume.

Selecting an Alternate Display Color for Compressed Files and Folders

Windows Explorer makes it easy for you to determine quickly whether a file or folder is compressed by allowing you to select a different display color for compressed files and folders. This allows you to distinguish them from uncompressed files and folders.

▶ **Follow these steps to set an alternative display color for compressed files and folders:**

1. In Windows Explorer, on the Tools menu, click Folder Options.

2. On the View tab, select the Display Compressed Files And Folders With Alternate Color check box.

Copying and Moving Compressed Files and Folders

Specific rules determine whether the compression state of files and folders is retained when you copy or move them within and between NTFS and FAT volumes.

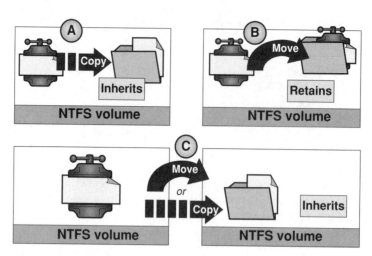

Figure 3.6 The effects of copying and moving compressed folders and files

The following list describes how Windows 2000 treats the compression state of a file or folder when you copy or move a compressed file or folder within or between NTFS volumes or between NTFS and FAT volumes.

- Copying a file within an NTFS volume. When you copy a file within an NTFS volume (shown as A in Figure 3.6), the file inherits the compression state of the target folder. For example, if you copy a compressed file to an uncompressed folder, the file is automatically uncompressed.

- Moving a file or folder within an NTFS volume. When you move a file or folder within an NTFS volume (shown as B in Figure 3.6), the file or folder retains its original compression state. For example, if you move a compressed file to an uncompressed folder, the file remains compressed.

- Copying a file or folder between NTFS volumes. When you copy a file or folder between NTFS volumes (shown as C in Figure 3.6), the file or folder inherits the compression state of the target folder.

- Moving a file or folder between NTFS volumes. When you move a file or folder between NTFS volumes (shown as C in Figure 3.6), the file or folder inherits the compression state of the target folder. Because Windows 2000 treats a move as a copy and then a delete, the files inherit the compression state of the target folder.

- Moving or copying a file or folder to a FAT volume. Windows 2000 supports compression only for NTFS files. Because of this, when you move or copy a compressed NTFS file or folder to a FAT volume, Windows 2000 automatically uncompresses the file or folder.

- Moving or copying a compressed file or folder to a floppy disk. When you move or copy a compressed NTFS file or folder to a floppy disk, Windows 2000 automatically uncompresses the file or folder.

Note When you copy a compressed NTFS file, Windows 2000 uncompresses the file, copies the file, and then compresses the file again as a new file. This might cause system performance degradation.

Using NTFS Compression

The following is a list of best practices for using compression on NTFS volumes:

- Because some file types compress more than others, select file types to compress based on the anticipated resulting file size. For example, because Windows bitmap files contain more redundant data than application executable files, this file type compresses to a smaller size. Bitmaps often compress to less than 50 percent of the original file size, whereas application files rarely compress to less than 75 percent of the original size.

- Do not store compressed files, such as PKZIP files, in a compressed folder. Windows 2000 will attempt to compress these files, wasting system time and yielding no additional disk space.

- To make it easier to locate compressed data, use a different display color for compressed folders and files.

- Compress static data rather than data that changes frequently. Compressing and uncompressing files incurs some system overhead. By choosing to compress files that are infrequently accessed, you minimize the amount of system time that is dedicated to compression and uncompression activities.

Lesson Summary

In this lesson, you learned how to compress and uncompress files and folders on an NTFS volume. You learned that compressed files can be read by and written to any Microsoft Windows–based or MS-DOS-based application without first being uncompressed by another program. The Windows NTFS file system automatically uncompresses the file before making it available, and when you close or explicitly save a file, NTFS compresses it again.

You also learned how to change the color used to display compressed files and folders in Windows Explorer to distinguish them from uncompressed files and folders. You learned too that NTFS encryption and compression are mutually exclusive.

Finally, you learned about copying and moving compressed files. When you copy a file within an NTFS volume, the file inherits the compression state of the target folder. When you move a file or folder within an NTFS volume, the file or folder retains its original compression state. When you copy or move a file or folder between NTFS volumes, the file or folder inherits the compression state of the target folder. Finally, when you move or copy a compressed NTFS file or folder to a FAT volume or a floppy disk, Windows 2000 automatically uncompresses the file or folder.

Lesson 5: Sharing Folders

You can make resources available to others by sharing folders containing those resources. To share a folder, you must be a member of one of several groups, depending on the role of the computer where the shared folder resides. When you share a folder, you can control access to the folder by limiting the number of users who can simultaneously gain access to it, and you can also control access to the folder and its contents by assigning permissions to selected users and groups. Once you have shared a folder, users must connect to the shared folder and must have the appropriate permissions to gain access to it. After you have shared a folder, you might want to modify it. You can stop sharing it, change its share name, and change user and group permissions to gain access to it.

After this lesson, you will be able to

- Create and modify shared folders
- Make a connection to a shared folder
- Combine shared folder permissions and NTFS permissions

Estimated lesson time: 35 minutes

Requirements for Sharing Folders

In Windows 2000 Professional, members of the built-in Administrators and Power Users groups are able to share folders. Which groups can share folders and on which computers they can share them depends on what type of computer the shared folder resides, and whether it resides on a workgroup or a domain. The following list describes which group can share folders when they are in a domain or workgroup.

- In a Windows 2000 domain, the Administrators and Server Operators groups can share folders residing on any machines in the domain. The Power Users group is a local group and can share folders residing only on the standalone server or computer running Windows 2000 Professional where the group is located.

- In a Windows 2000 workgroup, the Administrators and Power Users groups on a Windows 2000 Server standalone server or on a computer running Windows 2000 Professional can share folders on those individual computers.

Note If the folder to be shared resides on an NTFS volume, users must also have at least the Read permission for that folder to be able to share it.

Administrative Shared Folders

By default, Windows 2000 shares certain folders for administrative purposes. The share names of these folders consist of the folder name appended with dollar signs ($), which hide the shared folders from users who browse the computer. The root of each volume, the system root folder, and the location of the printer drivers are all hidden shared folders that you can gain access to across the network.

Table 3.9 describes the purpose of the administrative shared folders that Windows 2000 provides by default.

Table 3.9 Windows 2000 Administrative Shared Folders

Share	Purpose
C$, D$, E$, and so on	The administrative shares are used to remotely connect to the computer to perform administrative tasks. Windows 2000 assigns the Full Control permission to the Administrators group. The root of each volume on a hard disk shared by default, and the share name is the drive letter appended with a dollar sign ($). When you connect to this shared folder, you have access to the entire volume.
	CD-ROM drives are also shared by default and their share names are created by appending the dollar sign to the CD-ROM drive letter.
Admin$	The system root folder, which is C:\Winnt by default, is shared as Admin$. Only members of the Administrators group have access to this share. Windows 2000 assigns the Full Control permission to the Administrators group. Administrators can gain access to this shared folder to administer Windows 2000 without knowing which folder it is installed in.
Print$	When you install the first shared printer, the *systemroot*\System32\Spool\Drivers folder is shared as Print$. This folder provides access to printer driver files for clients. Only members of the Administrators, Server Operators, and Print Operators groups have the Full Control permission. The Everyone group has the Read permission.

Hidden shared folders aren't limited to those that the system creates by default. You can create additional hidden shares by appending a dollar sign to the end of the share name. Then only users who know the folder name can gain access to it, if they also have the appropriate permissions.

Sharing a Folder

When you share a folder, you can give it a share name, create comments to describe the folder and its content, limit the number of users who have access to the folder, assign permissions, and share the same folder multiple times.

▶ **Follow these steps to share a folder:**

1. Log on with a user account that is a member of a group that is able to share folders.

2. Right-click the folder that you want to share, and then click Sharing.

3. On the Sharing tab select Share This Folder and configure the options shown in Figure 3.7 and described in Table 3.10.

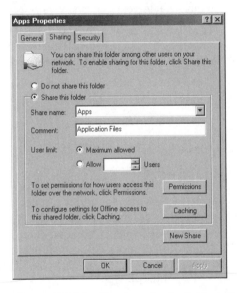

Figure 3.7 The Sharing tab of a folder's Properties dialog box

Table 3.10 Sharing Tab Options

Option	Description
Share Name	The name that users from remote locations use to make a connection to the shared folder. You must enter a share name.
Comment	An optional description for the share name. The comment appears in addition to the share name when users at client computers browse the server for shared folders. This comment can be used to identify contents of the shared folder.
User Limit	The number of users who can concurrently connect to the shared folder. If you click Maximum Allowed as the user limit, Windows 2000 Professional will support 10 connections. Windows 2000 Server can support an unlimited number of connections, but the number of Client Access Licenses (CALs) that you purchased limits the number of connections you can make.
Permissions	The shared folder permissions that apply *only* when the folder is accessed over the network. By default, the Everyone group is assigned Full Control for all new shared folders.
Caching	The settings to configure offline access to this shared folder.

Caching

Copies of the files are stored in a reserved portion of disk space on your computer called a *cache,* which makes shared folders available offline. Since the cache is on your hard disk, the computer can access this cache regardless of whether it is connected to the network. By default, the cache size is set to 10 percent of the available disk space. You can change the size of the cache on the Offline Files tab of the Folder Options dialog box. You can also see how much space the cache is using by opening the Offline Files folder and clicking Properties on the File menu.

Note Shared network files are stored in the root folder of your hard disk. If you want to change the location of the cache you can do so using, the Offline Files Mover (Cachemov.exe), which is available on the Windows 2000 Professional Resource Kit, to change the cache location.

When you share a folder, you can allow others to make the shared folder available offline by clicking Caching in the folder's Properties dialog box. In the Caching Settings dialog box (see Figure 3.8), the Allow Caching Of Files In This Shared Folder check box allows you to turn caching on and off.

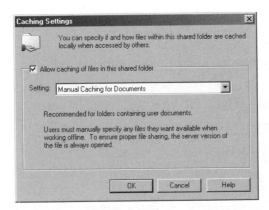

Figure 3.8 The Caching Settings dialog box

The Caching Settings dialog box contains the following three caching options:

- **Manual Caching For Documents.** The files that someone using your shared folder specifically (or manually) identifies are the only ones available offline. This caching option is recommended for a shared network folder containing files that are to be accessed and modified by several people. This option is the default.

- **Automatic Caching For Documents.** Makes every file that someone opens from your shared folder available to him or her offline. Files that aren't opened are not available offline.

- **Automatic Caching For Programs.** Provides offline access to shared folders containing files that are read, referenced, or run, but that are not changed in the process. This setting reduces network traffic because offline files are opened directly without accessing the network versions in any way, and generally start and run faster than the network versions.

Assigning Shared Folder Permissions

After you have shared a folder, the next step is to specify which users have access to the shared folder by assigning shared folder permissions to selected user accounts and groups.

▶ **Follow these steps to assign permissions to user accounts and groups for a shared folder:**

1. On the Sharing tab of the Properties dialog box, click Permissions.

2. In the Permissions dialog box, ensure that the Everyone group is selected and then click Remove.

3. In the Permissions dialog box, click Add (see Figure 3.9).

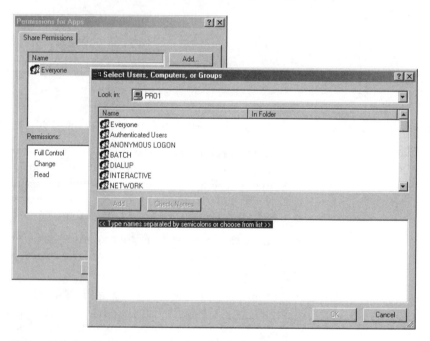

Figure 3.9 Setting permissions for a shared folder

4. In the Select Users, Computers, Or Groups dialog box, click the user accounts and groups to which you want to assign permissions.

5. Click Add to add the user account or group to the shared folder. Repeat this step for all user accounts and groups to which you want to assign permissions.

6. Click OK.

7. In the Permissions dialog box for the shared folder, click the user account or group, and then, under Permissions, select the Allow check box or the Deny check box for the appropriate permissions for the user account or group.

Modifying Shared Folders

You can modify shared folders, stop sharing a folder, modify the share name, and modify shared folder permissions.

▶ **Follow these steps to modify a shared folder:**

1. Click the Sharing tab in the Properties dialog box of the shared folder.

2. To complete the appropriate task, use the steps listed for each task in the following table.

Modifying a Shared Folder

To	Do this
Stop sharing a folder	Click Do Not Share This Folder.
Modify the share name	Click Do Not Share This Folder to stop sharing the folder; click Apply to apply the change; click Share This Folder, and then enter the new share name in the Share Name box.
Modify shared folder permissions	Click Permissions. In the Permissions dialog box, click Add or Remove. In the Select Users, Computers, Or Groups dialog box, click the user account or group whose permissions you want to modify.
Share folder multiple times	Click New Share to share a folder with an additional shared folder name. Do so to consolidate multiple shared folders into one while allowing users to continue to use the same shared folder name that they used before you consolidated the folders.
Remove a share name	Click Remove Share. This option appears only after the folder has been shared more than once.

Note If you stop sharing a folder while a user has a file open, the user might lose data. If you click Do Not Share This Folder and a user has a connection to the shared folder, Windows 2000 displays a dialog box notifying you that a user has a connection to the shared folder.

Strategies for Combining Shared Folder Permissions and NTFS Permissions

You share folders to provide network users with access to resources. If you are using a FAT volume, the shared folder permissions are the only resource available to provide security for the folders you have shared and the folders and files they contain. If you are using an NTFS volume, you can assign NTFS permissions to individual users and groups to better control access to the files and subfolders in the shared folders. When you combine shared folder permissions and NTFS permissions, the more restrictive permission is always the overriding permission.

One strategy for providing access to resources on an NTFS volume is to share folders with the default shared folder permissions and then control access by assigning NTFS permissions. When you share a folder on an NTFS volume, both shared folder permissions and NTFS permissions combine to secure file resources.

Shared folder permissions provide limited security for resources. You gain the greatest flexibility by using NTFS permissions to control access to shared folders. Also, NTFS permissions apply whether the resource is accessed locally or over the network.

When you use shared folder permissions on an NTFS volume, the following rules apply:

- You can apply NTFS permissions to files and subfolders in the shared folder. You can apply different NTFS permissions to each file and subfolder that a shared folder contains.

- In addition to having shared folder permissions, users must have NTFS permissions for the files and subfolders that shared folders contain to gain access to those files and subfolders. In contrast, on FAT volumes, which have no file level security, permissions for a shared folder are the only permissions protecting files and subfolders in the shared folder.

- When you combine shared folder permissions and NTFS permissions, the more restrictive permission is always the overriding permission.

In Figure 3.10, the Users group has the shared folder Full Control permission for the Public folder and the NTFS Read permission for FileA. The Users group's effective permission for FileA is Read because Read is the more restrictive permission. The effective permission for FileB is Full Control because both the shared folder permission and the NTFS permission allow this level of access.

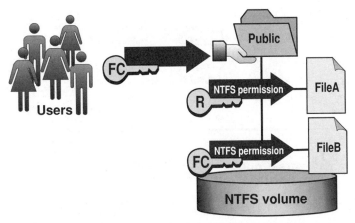

- NTFS permissions are required on NTFS volumes.
- Apply NTFS permissions to files and subfolders.
- The most restrictive permission is the effective permission.

Figure 3.10 Combining shared folder permissions and NTFS permissions

Practice: Managing Shared Folders

In this practice, you determine users' effective permissions, plan shared folders, plan permissions, share a folder, assign shared folder permissions, connect to a shared folder, stop sharing a folder, and test the combined effects of shared folder permissions and NTFS permissions.

Exercise 1: Combining Permissions

Figure 3.11 shows examples of shared folders on NTFS volumes. These shared folders contain subfolders that have also been assigned NTFS permissions. In this exercise, you determine a user's effective permissions for each example.

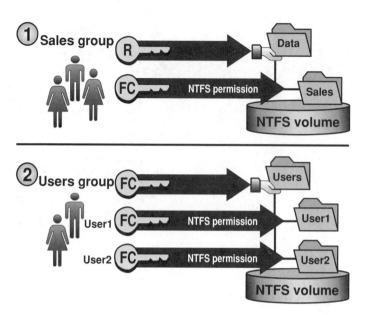

Figure 3.11 Combined permissions

1. In the first example, the Data folder is shared. The Sales group has the shared folder Read permission for the Data folder and the NTFS Full Control permission for the Sales subfolder.

   What are the Sales group's effective permissions for the Sales subfolder when they gain access to the Sales subfolder by making a connection to the Data shared folder?

2. In the second example, the Users folder contains user home folders. Each user home folder contains data that is accessible only to the user for whom the folder is named. The Users folder has been shared, and the Users group has the shared folder Full Control permission for the Users folder. User1 and User2 have the NTFS Full Control permission for *only* their home folder and no NTFS permissions for other folders. These users are all members of the Users group.

   What permissions does User1 have when he or she accesses the User1 subfolder by making a connection to the Users shared folder? What are User1's permissions for the User2 subfolder?

Exercise 2: Planning Shared Folders

In this exercise, you plan how to share resources on servers in the main office of a manufacturing company. Record your decisions in the table at the end of this exercise.

Figure 3.12 illustrates a partial folder structure for the servers at the manufacturing company.

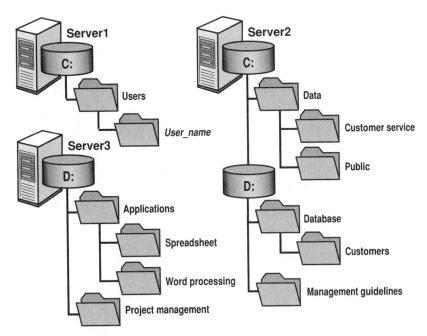

Figure 3.12 A partial folder structure for the servers at a manufacturing company

You need to make resources on these servers available to network users. To do this, determine which folders to share and which permissions to assign to groups, including the appropriate built-in groups.

Base your planning decisions on the following criteria:

- Members of the Managers group need to read and revise documents in the Management Guidelines folder. Nobody else should have access to this folder.

- Administrators need complete access to all shared folders, except for Management Guidelines.

- The customer service department requires its own network location to store working files. All customer service representatives are members of the Customer Service group.

- All employees need a network location to share information with each other.

- All employees need to use the spreadsheet, database, and word processing software.

- Only members of the Managers group should have access to the project management software.

- Members of the CustomerDBFull group need to read and update the customer database.

- Members of the CustomerDBRead group need to read only the customer database.

- Each user needs a private network location to store files. This location must be accessible only by that user.

- Share names must be accessible from Windows 2000, Windows NT, Windows 98, Windows 95, and non-Windows-NT-based platforms.

Record your answers in the following table.

Folder name and location	Shared name	Groups and permissions
Example:		
Management Guidelines	MgmtGd	Managers: Full Control

Lesson Summary

In this lesson, you learned that you share folders to provide network users with access to resources. On a FAT volume, the shared folder permissions are all that is available to provide security for the folders you have shared and for the folders and files they contain. On an NTFS volume, you can assign NTFS permissions to individual users and groups to better control access to the files and subfolders in the shared folders. When you combine shared folder permissions and NTFS permissions, the more restrictive permission is always the overriding permission.

Lesson 6: Setting Up Network Printers

The printer is another commonly shared resource. Setting up and sharing a network printer makes it possible for multiple users to print to single printer, eliminating the need for every user to have his or her own printer.

You can set up a printer for a local print device that is connected directly to the print server, or you can set up a printer for a network-interface print device that is connected to the print server over the network. In larger organizations, most printers connect to network-interface print devices.

After this lesson, you will be able to

- Identify the requirements for setting up a network printer and network printing resources
- Add and share a new printer for a local print device or a network-interface print device
- Set up client computers

Estimated lesson time: 15 minutes

Adding and Sharing a Printer for a Local Print Device

The steps for adding a printer for a local print device or for a network-interface print device are similar.

▶   **Follow these steps to add a printer for a local print device:**

1. Log on as Administrator on the print server.

2. Click Start, point to Settings, and then click Printers.

   You add and share a printer by using the Add Printer wizard in the Printers folder.

3. Double-click Add Printer to launch the Add Printer wizard.

   The Add Printer wizard starts with the Welcome To The Add Printer Wizard page displayed.

4. Click Next, and the Add Printer wizard displays the Local Or Network Printer page (see Figure 3.13).

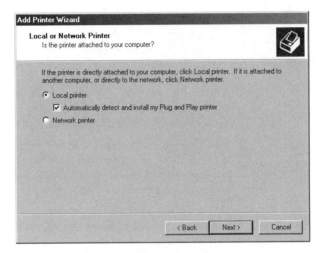

Figure 3.13 The Local Or Network Printer page

The Add Printer wizard guides you through the steps to add a printer for a print device that is connected to the print server. The number of local print devices that you can connect to a print server through physical ports depends on your hardware configuration.

Table 3.11 describes the Add Printer wizard options for adding a printer for a local print device.

Table 3.11   The Add Printer Wizard Options for a Local Print Device

Option	Description
Local Printer	This check box indicates that you are adding a printer to the computer at which you are sitting, which is the print server.
	The Automatically Detect And Install My Plug And Play Printer check box allows you to enable Windows 2000 to automatically detect and install a Plug and Play printer.
Use The Following Port	The port on the print server to which you attached the print device.
	You can also create a new port. Creating a port allows you to print to nonstandard hardware ports, such as a network-interface connection.
Manufacturers	The correct printer driver for the local print device. Select the manufacturer of your print device.

continues

Table 3.11 The Add Printer Wizard Options for a Local Print Device *(continued)*

Option	Description
Printers	A list of printer models available for use as your print device. You should select the appropriate printer model for your print device. If your print device isn't on the list, you must provide a printer driver from the manufacturer or select a model that is similar enough that the print device can use it.
Printer Name	The name that will identify the printer to the users. Use a name that is intuitive and descriptive of the print device. Some applications might not support more than 31 characters in the server and printer name combinations.
	If your computer running Windows 2000 Professional is part of a domain, this name also appears in the result of an Active Directory search.
Default Printer	The default printer for all Windows-based applications. Select the Yes button for the Do You Want Your Windows-Based Programs To Use This Printer As The Default Printer? option so that users don't have to set a printer for each application. The first time that you add a printer to the print server, this option doesn't appear because the printer is automatically selected as the default printer.
Share As	A share name that users (with the appropriate permission) can use to make a connection to the printer over the network. This name appears when users browse for a printer or supply a path to a printer.
	Ensure that the share name is compatible with the naming conventions for all client computers on the network. By default, the share name is the printer name truncated to an 8.3-character filename. If you use a share name that is longer than an 8.3-character filename, some client computers might not be able to connect.
Location	Information about the print device's location. You should provide information that helps users determine whether the print device fits their needs.

Option	Description
Comment	General information about the print device, such as its capabilities (color, duplex, etc.), physical access (secured, in public space, etc.), or other useful information about the print device. Users can search Active Directory directory services for the information that you enter here or in the Location box. You should standardize the type of information that you enter so that users can compare printers in search results.
Do You Want To Print A Test Page?	Verification that you have installed the printer correctly. Select the Yes option button to print a test page.

Adding and Sharing a Printer for a Network-Interface Print Device

In larger companies, most print devices are network-interface print devices. These print devices offer several advantages. You don't need to locate print devices with the print server. In addition, network connections transfer data more quickly than printer cable connections.

You add a printer for a network-interface print device by using the Add Printer wizard. The main differences between adding a printer for a local print device and adding a printer for a network-interface print device is that for a typical network-interface print device, you provide additional port and network protocol information.

The default network protocol for Windows 2000 is TCP/IP, which is used by many network-interface print devices. For TCP/IP, you provide additional port information in the Add Standard TCP/IP Printer Port wizard.

Figure 3.14 shows the Select The Printer Port page of the Add Printer wizard, and Table 3.12 describes the options on the Select The Printer Port page that pertain to adding a network-interface print device.

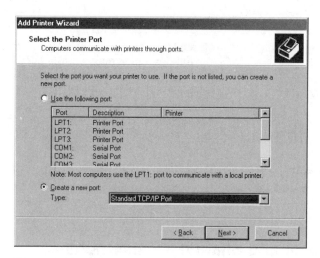

Figure 3.14 The Select The Printer Port page of the Add Printer wizard

**Table 3.12   Select the Printer Port Page Options
that Affect Adding a Network-Interface Print Device**

Option	Description
Create A New Port	Allows you to start the process of creating a new port for the print server to which the network-interface print device is connected. In this case, the new port points to the network connection of the print device.
Type	Allows you to determine which network protocol to use for the connection. If you select Standard TCP/IP Port, it will start the Add Standard TCP/IP Printer Port wizard.

Figure 3.15 shows the Add Port page of the Add Standard TCP/IP Printer Port wizard, and Table 3.13 describes the options on the Add Port page of the Add Standard TCP/IP Printer Port wizard.

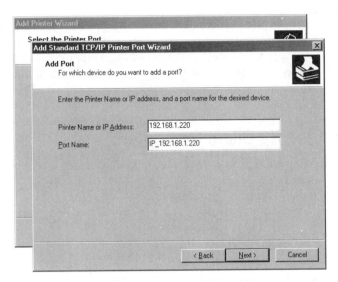

Figure 3.15 The Add Port page of the Add Standard TCP/IP Printer Port wizard

**Table 3.13 Select the Printer Port Page Options
that Affect Adding a Network-Interface Print Device**

Option	Description
Printer Name Or IP Address	The network location of the print device. You must enter either the IP address or a DNS name of the network-interface print device.
	If you provide an IP address, Windows 2000 automatically supplies a suggested port name for the print device in the form IP_*IPaddress*.
	If Windows 2000 can't connect to and identify the network-interface print device, you must supply additional information about the type of print device. To enable automatic identification, make sure that the print device is switched on and connected to the network.
Port Name	The name that Windows 2000 assigns to the port that you created and defined. You can assign a different name.
	After you create the port, Windows 2000 displays it on the Select The Printer Port page of the Add Printer wizard. You don't have to redefine the port if you point additional printers to the same print device.

Note If your print device uses a network protocol other than TCP/IP, you must install the network protocol before you can add a printer for this device. After you install the protocol, you can add other ports that use the protocol. What tasks and setup information are required to configure a printer port depend on the network protocol.

Setting Up Client Computers

After you add and share a printer, you need to set up client computers so that users can print. Although the steps needed to set up client computers vary depending on which operating systems are running on the client computers, all client computers require that a printer driver be installed.

The following lists key points regarding the installation of printer drivers according to the computer's operating system:

- Windows 2000 automatically downloads the printer drivers for client computers running Windows 2000, Windows NT version 4 and earlier, Windows 98, or Windows 95.

- Client computers running other Microsoft operating systems require installation of printer drivers.

- Client computers running non-Microsoft operating systems require installation of both printer drivers and the print service on the print server.

Client Computers Running Windows 2000, Windows NT, Windows 98, or Windows 95

Users of client computers running Windows 2000, Windows NT, Windows 98, and Windows 95 need to make a connection only to the shared printer. The client computer automatically downloads the appropriate printer driver, as long as a copy of it resides on the print server.

If your client computer is running Windows 2000 and you want to make a connection to the shared printer, on the client computer, start the Add Printer wizard. On the Local Or Network Printer page, select Network Printer, and then click Next. The Locate Your Printer page appears (see Figure 3.16).

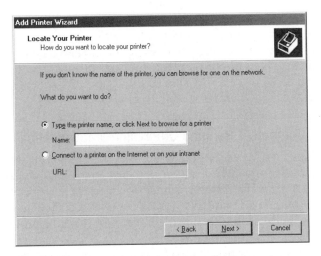

Figure 3.16 The Locate Your Printer page

If you aren't sure what the name of the shared printer is, you can browse for it by leaving the Name box blank and clicking Next. The Browse For Printer page appears (see Figure 3.17).

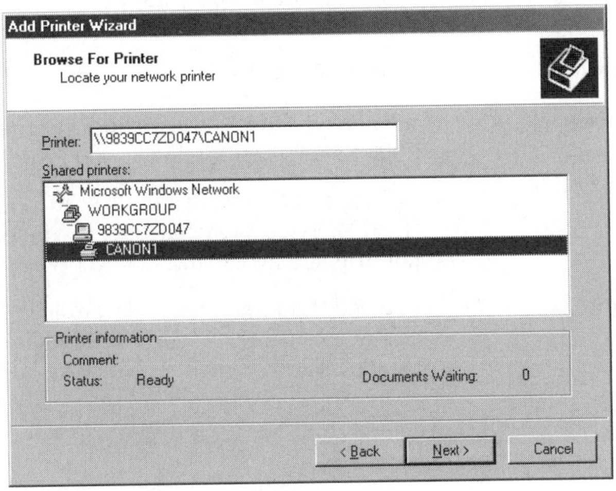

Figure 3.17 The Browse For Printer page

Once you have located the shared printer and selected it, click Next and you will be asked whether it should be the default printer. If you want it to be the default printer, click Yes; otherwise, click No and then click Next. The Completing The Add Printer Wizard page appears. Check over the information and then click Finish. You have successfully made a connection from your client computer to the shared printer.

Client Computers Running Other Microsoft Operating Systems

For client computers running other Microsoft operating systems (such as Windows 3.x or MS-DOS) to print to a shared Windows 2000–based printer, you must manually install a printer driver on the client computer. You can get the appropriate printer driver for a Windows-based client computer from the installation disks for that client computer or from the printer manufacturer.

Client Computers Running Non-Microsoft Operating Systems

To enable users of client computers running non-Microsoft operating systems to print, the print server must have additional services installed on it. Table 3.14 lists services that are required for Macintosh and UNIX client computers or computers running a NetWare client.

Table 3.14 Services Required for Client Computers Running Non-Microsoft Operating Systems

Client computer	Required services
Macintosh	Services for Macintosh are included only with Windows 2000 Server, not Windows 2000 Professional.
UNIX	TCP/IP Printing, which is also called Line Printer Daemon (LPD) Service, is included with Windows 2000 Server but is not installed by default.
NetWare	File and Print Services for NetWare (FPNW), an optional add-on service for Windows 2000 Server, isn't included with Windows 2000 Server or Windows 2000 Professional.

Practice: Installing and Sharing a Printer

As an experienced Windows NT 4.0 professional, you have probably installed many printers. As you know, a physical printer does not have to be attached to your system for you to install a printer. In this practice, you will use the Add Printer wizard to install and share a local printer. You use this printer in other exercises throughout this book. By sharing the printer, you make it available to other users on the network. You also take the printer offline and then print a document. Printing a document with the printer offline loads the document into the print queue.

Exercise 1: Adding and Sharing a Printer

In this exercise, you use the Add Printer wizard to add a local printer to your computer and share it.

▶ **To add a local printer**

1. Log on as Administrator.

2. Click the Start button, point to Settings, and then click Printers.

   Windows 2000 displays the Printers window. If you added a fax modem, a Fax icon appears in the Printers system folder.

3. Double-click Add Printer.

4. In the Add Printer Wizard, click Next.

   The Add Printer wizard prompts you for the location of the printer. Because you are creating the printer on the computer at which you are sitting and not on a different computer, this printer is referred to as a local printer.

5. Click Local Printer, ensure that the Automatically Detect And Install My Plug And Play Printer check box is not selected, and then click Next.

   What port types are available depends on the installed network protocols. For this exercise, assume that the print device that you are adding is directly attached to your computer and using the LPT1 port.

   Note If the print device is connected to a port that is not listed, click Other, and then enter the port type.

6. Verify that the Use The Following Port option is selected, and then under Use The Following Port, select LPT1.

7. Click Next.

   The wizard prompts you for the printer manufacturer and model. You will add an HP LaserJet 5Si printer.

8. Under Manufacturers, click HP; under Printers, click HP LaserJet 5Si; and then click Next.

   The wizard displays the Name Your Printer page. In the Printer Name box, Windows 2000 automatically defaults to the printer name HP LaserJet 5Si. For this exercise, do not change this name.

9. If other printers are already installed, the wizard will also ask whether you want to make this the default printer. If the wizard displays the message, Do You Want Your Windows-Based Programs To Use This Printer As The Default Printer?, click Yes.

10. To accept the default printer name, click Next.

    The Printer Sharing page appears, prompting you for printer sharing information.

▶ **To share a printer**

1. In the Add Printer Wizard, on the Printer Sharing page, select the Share As option.

   Notice that you can assign a shared printer name, even though you already supplied a printer name. The shared printer name is used to identify a printer on the network and must conform to a naming convention. This shared name is different from the printer name that you entered ealier. The printer name is a description that will appear with the printer's icon in the Printers system folder and in Active Directory directory services.

2. In the Share As box, type **Printer1** and then click Next.

   The Location And Comment page appears.

   Note If your computer running Windows 2000 Professional is part of a domain, Windows 2000 displays the values that you enter for Location and Comment when a user searches Active Directory directory services for a printer. Entering this information is optional, but it can help users locate the printer more easily.

   ---

3. In the Location box, type **Third Floor East** and in the Comment box, type **Mail Room**, click option, and click Next.

The Print Test Page page appears, asking you whether you want to print a test page.

4. Click No and then click Next.

The wizard displays the Completing The Add Printer Wizard page and provides a summary of your installation choices.

Note As you review the summary, you might notice an error in the information you entered. To modify these settings, click Back.

5. Confirm the summary of your installation choices, and then click Finish.

Windows 2000 will either copy files from the *systemroot* folder or display the Files Needed dialog box, prompting you for the location of the Windows 2000 Professional distribution files. If the Files Needed dialog box appears, continue with step 6; otherwise, Windows 2000 creates the shared printer and displays an icon for the HP LaserJet 5Si printer in the Printers window. In this case, you can skip steps 6 to 8.

6. Insert the Windows 2000 Professional CD-ROM, and wait for about 10 seconds.

7. If Windows displays the Windows 2000 CD-ROM window, close it.

8. Click OK to close the Insert Disk dialog box.

Windows 2000 copies the printer files and creates the shared printer. An icon for the HP LaserJet 5Si printer appears in the Printers window.

Notice that Windows 2000 displays an open hand under the printer icon. This indicates that the printer is shared. Notice also the check mark just above the printer, which indicates that the printer is the default printer.

Lesson Summary

In this lesson, you learned that to set up and share a printer for a local print device or for a network-interface print device, you use the Add Printer wizard in the Printers folder. Sharing a local printer makes it possible for multiple users on the network to print to it.

You also learned that users of client computers running Windows 2000, Windows NT, Windows 98, or Windows 95 need to make a connection only to the shared printer to be able to print. The client computer automatically downloads the appropriate printer driver, as long as a copy of it exists on the print server. To enable client computers running other Microsoft operating systems (such as Windows 3.x or MS-DOS) to print to a shared Windows 2000–based printer, you must manually install a printer driver on the client computer. You can get the appropriate printer driver for a Windows-based client computer from the installation disks for that client computer or from the printer manufacturer. To enable users of client computers running non-Microsoft operating systems to print, the print server must have additional services installed on it.

Lesson 7: Connecting to Network Printers

After you have set up the print server with all required printer drivers for the shared printers, users on client computers running Windows 2000, Windows NT, Windows 98, and Windows 95 can easily make a connection and start printing. For most Windows-based client computers, if the appropriate printer drivers are on the print server, the client computer automatically downloads the printer when the user makes a connection to the printer.

When you add and share a printer, by default, all users can make a connection to that printer and print documents. What method you use to make a connection to a printer depends on the client computer. Client computers running Windows 2000, Windows NT, Windows 98, or Windows 95 can use the Add Printer wizard, although the Add Printer wizard in Windows 2000 provides more features than in the earlier versions. Client computers running Windows 2000 can also use a Web browser to make a connection to the printer.

After this lesson, you will be able to

- Make a connection to a network printer by using the Add Printer wizard or a Web browser

Estimated lesson time: 10 minutes

Using the Add Printer Wizard

Client computers running Windows 2000, Windows NT, Windows 98, or Windows 95 can use the Add Printer wizard to connect to a printer. This is the same wizard that you use to add and share a printer. What options are available in the Add Printer wizard that allow you to locate and connect to a printer vary depending on the operating system that the client computer is running (see Figure 3.18).

Client Computers Running Windows 2000

When you use the Add Printer wizard on client computers running Windows 2000, you can make a connection to a printer using the following methods:

- **Use the UNC name.** You can use the UNC name (*print_server*\\ *printer_name*) to make connections by selecting Type The Printer Name Or Click Next To Browse For A Printer on the Locate Your Printer page of the Add Printer wizard. If you know the UNC name, this can be an efficient method to use.

- **Browse the network.** You can also browse the network for the printer by selecting Type The Printer Name Or Click Next To Browse For A Printer on the Locate Your Printer page of the Add Printer wizard, leaving the Name box blank, and clicking Next.

- **Use the URL name.** You can also connect to a printer on the Internet or your intranet by selecting Connect To A Printer On The Internet Or On Your Intranet on the Locate Your Printer page of the Add Printer wizard.

- **Search Active Directory directory service.** If your computer running Windows 2000 Professional is a member of a domain, you can find the printer by using Active Directory directory service's search capabilities. You can search either the entire directory or just a portion of it. You can also narrow the search by providing features of the printer, such as color printing.

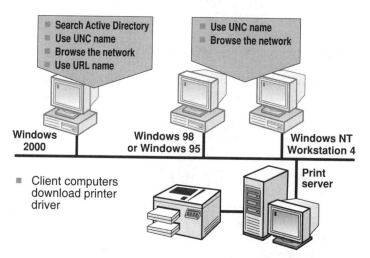

Figure 3.18 Using the Add Printer wizard to locate and connect to a network printer

Client Computers Running Windows NT 4, Windows 98, or Windows 95

On client computers running Windows NT 4, Windows 98, or Windows 95, the Add Printer wizard allows you only to enter a UNC name or to browse Network Neighborhood to locate the printer.

Note You can also make a connection to a printer by using the Run command on the Start menu. Type the UNC name of the printer in the Open box, and click OK.

Client Computers Running Other Microsoft Operating Systems

Users at client computers running Windows 3.x and Windows for Workgroups use Print Manager instead of the Add Printer wizard to make a connection to a printer.

Users at any Windows-based client computer can make a connection to a network printer by using the command

```
net use lptx: \\server_name\share_name
```

where x is the number of the printer port.

The Net Use command is also the only method that is available for making a connection to a network printer from client computers running MS-DOS or OS/2 with Microsoft LAN Manager client software installed.

Using a Web Browser

If you're using a client computer running Windows 2000, you can make a connection to a printer through your corporate intranet. You can type an URL in your Web browser, and you don't have to use the Add Printer wizard. After you make a connection, Windows 2000 automatically copies the correct printer drivers to the client computer.

A Web designer can customize this Web page, and can, for example, display a floor plan that shows the location of print devices to which users can connect. There are two ways to make a connection to a printer by using a Web browser:

- http://*server_name*/printers

  This Web page lists all of the shared printers on the print server that you have permission to use. The page contains information about the printers, including the printer name, status of print jobs, location, model, and any comments that were entered when the printer was installed. This information helps you select the correct printer for your needs. You must have permission to use the printer.

- http://*server_name*/*printer_share_name*

  You provide the intranet path for a specific printer. You must have permission to use the printer.

Downloading Printer Drivers

When users at client computers running Windows 2000, Windows NT, Windows 98, or Windows 95 make the first connection to a printer on the print server, the client computer automatically downloads the printer driver. The print server must have a copy of the printer driver.

Thereafter, client computers running Windows 2000 and Windows NT verify that they have the current printer driver each time that they print. If not, they download the new printer driver. For these client computers, you need to update printer drivers only on the print server. Client computers running Windows 98 or Windows 95 don't check for updated printer drivers. You must manually install updated printer drivers.

Lesson Summary

In this lesson, you learned that client computers running Windows 2000, Windows NT, Windows 98, or Windows 95 can use the Add Printer wizard to connect to a printer. On client computers running Windows 2000, you can make a connection to a printer by using Active Directory directory services' search capabilities, or you can select Connect To The Printer Using A Network Name on the Locate Your Printers page of the Add Printer wizard. If you know the UNC name, you can use it, or you can browse the network for the printer.

You also learned that on client computers running Windows NT 4.0 Workstation, Windows 98, or Windows 95, the Add Printer wizard only allows you to enter a UNC name or to browse Network Neighborhood to locate the printer. Users at client computers running Windows 3.x and Windows for Workgroups use Print Manager to make a connection to a printer.

Finally, in this lesson you learned that users at any Windows-based client computer can make a connection to a network printer by using the Net Use command. The Net Use command is also the only method that is available for making a connection to a network printer from client computers running MS-DOS or OS/2 with Microsoft LAN Manager client software installed.

Lesson 8: Configuring Network Printers

After you have set up and shared network printers, you might need to configure printer settings so that your printing resources better fit the needs of your company and the users it will be serving.

The following are three common configuration changes you can make:

- You can share an existing nonshared printer if your printing load increases.

- You can create a printer pool so that the printer automatically distributes print jobs to the first available print device. Then users don't have to search for an available printer.

- You can set priorities between printers so that critical documents always print before noncritical documents.

After this lesson, you will be able to

- Share an existing printer

- Create a printer pool

- Set priorities between printers

Estimated lesson time: 15 minutes

Sharing an Existing Printer

If the printing demands on your network increase and your network has an existing, nonshared printer for a print device, you can share it so that users can print to the print device.

When you share a printer, keep in mind the following:

- You need to assign the printer a share name, which appears in My Network Places. Use an intuitive name to help users when they are browsing for a printer.

- You can add printer drivers for all versions of Windows NT, for Windows 95 and Windows 98, and for Windows 2000 and Windows NT running on different hardware platforms.

To share an existing printer, use the Sharing tab, in the Properties dialog box for the printer (see Figure 3.19).

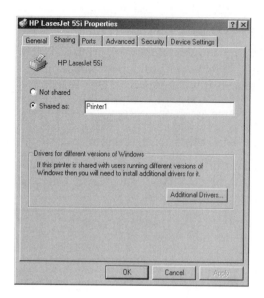

Figure 3.19 The Sharing tab in the Properties dialog box for a printer

▶ **Follow these steps to access the Sharing tab in a printer's Properties dialog box:**

1. In the Printers folder, click the icon for the printer that you want to share.

2. On the File menu, click Properties.

3. In the Properties dialog box for the printer, click the Sharing tab.

After you have shared the printer, Windows 2000 puts an open hand under the printer icon, indicating that the printer has been shared.

Setting Up a Printer Pool

A *printer pool* is one printer that is connected to multiple print devices through multiple ports on a print server. The print devices can be local or network-interface print devices. Print devices should be identical; however, you can use print devices that are not identical but that use the same printer driver (see Figure 3.20).

When you create a printer pool, users can print documents without having to find out which print device is available—the printer checks for an available port.

Note When you set up a printer pool, place the print devices in the same physical area so that users can easily locate their documents.

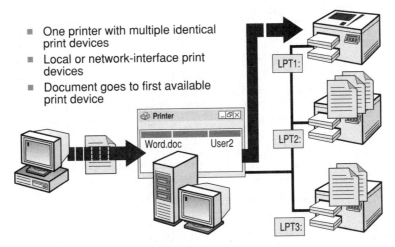

- One printer with multiple identical print devices
- Local or network-interface print devices
- Document goes to first available print device

Figure 3.20 A printer pool

A printer pool has the following advantages:

- In a network with a high volume of printing, it decreases the time that documents wait on the print server.

- It simplifies administration because you can administer multiple print devices from a single printer.

Before you create a printer pool, make sure that you connect the print devices to the print server.

▶ **Follow these steps to create a printer pool:**

1. In the Properties dialog box for the printer, click the Ports tab.

2. Select the Enable Printer Pooling check box.

3. Select the check box for each port to which a print device that you want to add to the pool is connected, and then click OK.

Setting Priorities Between Printers

If you have two or more printers pointing to the same print device, you may want to establish a priority for each printer. Setting priorities between printers makes it possible to establish which printer's queued documents should print first, which allows users to send critical documents to a high-priority printer and noncritical documents to a lower-priority printer. The critical documents always print first. Consider the following two methods to set priorities between printers:

- Point two or more printers to the same print device—that is, the same port. The port can be either a physical port on the print server or a port that points to a network-interface print device.

- Set a different priority for each printer that is connected to the print device, and then have different groups of users print to different printers, or have users send different types of documents to different printers.

For an example, see Figure 3.21. User1 sends documents to a printer with the lowest priority of 1, while User2 sends documents to a printer with the highest priority of 99. In this example, User2's documents always print before User1's.

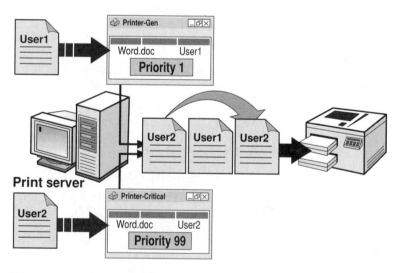

Figure 3.21 A printer pool with different priorities set

► **Follow these steps to set the priority for a printer:**

1. In the Properties dialog box for the printer, click the Advanced tab.

2. In the Priority box, select the appropriate priority, and then click OK.

   Windows 2000 sets the priority for the printer.

Lesson Summary

In this lesson, you learned that to share an existing printer, you use the Sharing tab in the Properties dialog box for the printer and select Shared As. After you have shared the printer, Windows 2000 puts an open hand under the printer icon, indicating that the printer is shared.

You also learned that a printer pool is one printer that is connected to multiple print devices through multiple ports on a print server. The print devices in a printer pool should be identical; however, you can use print devices that aren't identical if all the print devices use the same printer driver. A printer pool can cut down the time that documents wait on the print server, and it simplifies administration because you can administer multiple print devices from a single printer. To create a printer pool, in the Properties dialog box for the printer, use the Ports tab to select the Enable Printer Pooling check box.

Setting priorities between printers makes it possible to set priorities between groups of documents that all print on the same print device. Multiple printers may point to the same print device, which allows users to send critical documents to a high-priority printer and noncritical documents to a lower-priority printer. This way, the critical documents always print first.

Lesson 9: Printer Administration

After your printing network is set up, you are responsible for its administration. You can administer network printers at the print server or remotely over the network. In this lesson, you learn about the four major types of tasks that are involved with administering network printers: managing printers, managing documents, troubleshooting printers, and performing tasks that require the Manage Printers permission. In this lesson, you also learn that before you can administer printers, you must know how to access them and control access to them.

After this lesson, you will be able to

- Identify the tasks and requirements for administering a printer
- Gain access to printers for administration
- Assign printer permissions to user accounts and groups

Estimated lesson time: 20 minutes

Managing Printers

One of the most important aspects of printer administration is managing printers. Managing printers includes the following tasks:

- Assigning forms to paper trays
- Setting a separator page
- Pausing, resuming, and canceling printing of documents
- Redirecting documents
- Taking ownership of a printer

Managing Documents

A second major aspect of printer administration is managing documents. Managing documents includes the following tasks:

- Pausing and resuming printing of a document
- Setting notification, priority, and printing time
- Deleting a document

Troubleshooting Printers

A third major aspect of printer administration is troubleshooting printers. Troubleshooting printers means identifying and resolving all printer problems. The types of problems you need to troubleshoot include the following:

- Printers are off or offline
- Printers are out of paper, ink, or toner
- Users documents cannot print or print correctly
- Printer can't be accessed by a user

Performing Tasks That Require the Manage Printers Permission

The following tasks involved with administering printers require the Manage Printers permission:

- Adding and removing printers
- Sharing printers
- Taking ownership of a printer
- Changing printer properties or permissions

By default, members of the Administrators and Power Users groups have the Manage Printers permission for all printers.

Accessing Printers

You can gain access to printers for administration by using the Printers window (shown in Figure 3.22), which you open by selecting the Start button, pointing to Settings, and clicking the Printers system folder.

▶ **Follow these steps to perform all administrative tasks by gaining access to the printer from the Printers window:**

1. Click the Start button, point to Settings, and then click Printers.

2. In the Printers window, select the appropriate printer icon.

3. On the File menu,

   - Click Open to open the printer's window to perform print document tasks.

   - Click Properties to open the Properties dialog box to change printer permissions or to edit Active Directory information about the printer.

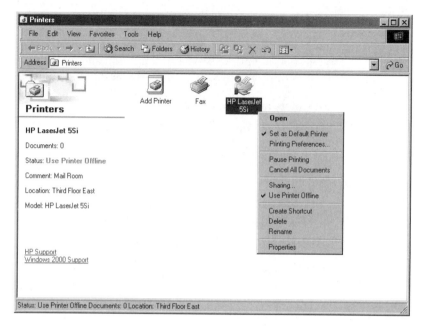

Figure 3.22 Accessing printers using the Printers window

Setting Printer Permissions to Control Access

Windows 2000 allows you to control printer use and administration by assigning permissions. By using printer permissions, you control who can use a printer. You can also assign printer permissions to control who can administer a printer and the level of administration, which includes who manages printers and documents.

For security reasons, you might need to limit user access to certain printers. You can also use printer permissions to delegate responsibilities for specific printers to users who are not administrators. Windows 2000 provides three levels of printer permissions: Print, Manage Documents, and Manage Printers. Table 3.16 lists the capabilities that are available at each level of permission.

Table 3.15 Printing Capabilities of Windows 2000 Printer Permissions

Capabilities	Permissions		
	Print	**Manage Documents**	**Manage Printers**
Print documents	✔	✔	✔
Pause, resume, restart, and cancel the user's own document	✔	✔	✔
Connect to a printer	✔	✔	✔
Control job settings for all documents		✔	✔
Pause, resume, restart, and cancel all other users' documents		✔	✔
Cancel all documents			✔
Share a printer			✔
Change printer properties			✔
Delete a printer			✔
Change printer permissions			✔

You can allow or deny printer permissions. Denied permissions always override allowed permissions. For example, if you select the Deny check box next to Manage Documents for the Everyone group, no one can manage documents, even if you granted this permission to another user account or group. This is because all user accounts are members of the Everyone group.

Assigning Printer Permissions

By default, Windows 2000 assigns the Print permission for each printer to the built-in Everyone group, allowing all users to send documents to the printer.

▶ **Follow these steps to assign printer permissions to users or groups:**

1. Open the Properties dialog box for the printer, click the Security tab, and then click Add.

2. In the Select Users, Computers, Or Groups dialog box, select the appropriate user account or group, and then click Add. Repeat this step for all users or groups that you are adding.

3. Click OK.

4. On the Security tab, shown in Figure 3.23, select a user account or group, and then do one of the following:

   - Click the permissions in the bottom part of the dialog box that you want to assign.

   - Click Advanced, assign additional printer permissions that don't fit into the predefined permissions on the Security tab, and then click OK.

   The bottom part of the dialog box shows the permissions granted to the user or group selected in the upper part.

5. Click OK to close the Properties dialog box.

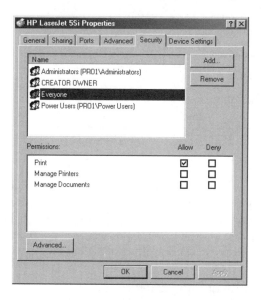

Figure 3.23 Assigning printer permissions

Modifying Printer Permissions

You can change the default printer permissions that Windows 2000 assigned, or that you previously assigned for any user or group, by simply accessing the Sercurity tab of the printers property dialog box. On this tab you can select the appropriate user or group and change permissions as necessary.

Lesson Summary

In this lesson, you learned that administering printers involves four major types of tasks: managing printers, managing documents, troubleshooting printers, and performing tasks that require the Manage Printers permission. You gain access to printers for administration by selecting the Start button, pointing to settings, and selecting the Printers system folder.

You also learned that Windows 2000 allows you to control printer use and administration by assigning permissions. You might need to limit access to certain printers—for example, a printer used to print checks. You can also use printer permissions to delegate responsibilities for specific printers to users who are not administrators.

Lesson 10: Managing Printers

Tasks involved in managing printers include assigning forms to paper trays; setting up separator pages; and pausing, resuming, and canceling documents if a problem occurs on a print device. If a print device is faulty or you add print devices to your network, you might need to redirect documents to a different printer. In addition, you might need to change who has administrative responsibility for printers, which involves changing ownership.

After this lesson, you will be able to

- Assign forms to paper trays
- Set up a separator page
- Pause, resume, and cancel documents on a printer
- Redirect documents to a different printer
- Take ownership of a printer

Estimated lesson time: 30 minutes

Assigning Forms to Paper Trays

If a print device has multiple trays that regularly hold different paper sizes, you can assign a form to a specific tray. A *form* refers to a particular paper size. Users can then select the paper size from within their applications. When the user prints, Windows 2000 automatically routes the print job to the paper tray that holds the correct form. Examples of forms include the following: Legal, A4, Envelope #10, and Letter Small.

▶   **Follow these steps to assign a form to a paper tray:**

1. Right-click the icon of the appropriate printing device, and then click Properties.

2. In the Properties dialog box for the printer, click the Device Settings tab.

3. In the drop-down list box next to each paper tray, click the form for the tray's paper type, as shown in Figure 3.24.

4. Click OK.

After you have set up a paper tray, users specify the paper size from within applications. Windows 2000 knows in which paper tray the form is located.

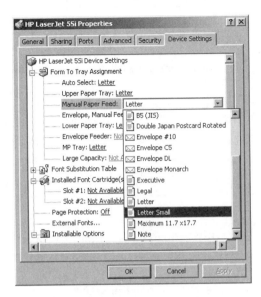

Figure 3.24 Setting forms for a printer

Setting a Separator Page

A *separator page* is a file that contains print device commands. Separator pages have two functions:

- To identify and separate printed documents.

- To switch print devices between Print modes. Some print devices can switch between Print modes that take advantage of different device features. You can use separator pages to specify the correct page description language. For example, you can specify PostScript or Printer Control Language (PCL) for a print device that can switch between different print modes but cannot automatically detect which language a print job uses.

Windows 2000 includes four separator page files. They are located in the *systemroot*\System32 folder. Table 3.16 lists the filename and describes the function for each of the included separator page files.

Table 3.16 Separator Page Files

Filename	Function
Sysprint.sep	Prints a page before each document. Compatible with PostScript print devices.
Pcl.sep	Switches the print mode to PCL for HP-series print devices and prints a page before each document.
Pscript.sep	Switches the print mode to PostScript for HP-series print devices but doesn't print a page before each document.
Sysprtj.sep	A version of Sysprint.sep that uses Japanese characters.

Once you have decided to use a separator page and have chosen an appropriate one, you use the Advanced tab in the printer's Properties dialog box to have the separator page printed at the beginning of each print job.

▶ **Follow these steps to set up a separator page:**

1. On the Advanced tab in the Properties dialog box for the printer, click Separator Page.

2. In the Separator Page box, type the name of the separator page file. You can also browse for the file.

3. Click OK, and then click OK again.

Pausing, Resuming, and Canceling Documents

Pausing and resuming a printer or canceling all documents on a printer might be necessary if a printing problem occurs.

To pause or cancel all documents, right-click a printing device in the Printers folder, and then click the appropriate command. To resume printing, right-click the printer, and click Pause Printer to deselect it.

Redirecting Documents to a Different Printer

You can redirect documents to a different printer. For example, if a printer is connected to a faulty print device, redirect the documents so that users don't need to resubmit them. You can redirect all print jobs for a printer, but you can't redirect specific documents. The new printer must use the same printer driver as the current printer.

▶ **Follow these steps to redirect documents to a different printer:**

1. Open the Printers window, right-click the printer, and then click Properties.

2. In the Properties dialog box, click the Ports tab.

3. Click Add Port.

4. In the Available Port Types list, click Local Port, and then click the New Port button.

5. In the Port Name dialog box, in the Enter A Port Name box, type the UNC name for the printer to which you are redirecting documents (for example, \\prntsrv6\HPLaser5), as shown in Figure 3.25.

6. Click OK to close the Port Name dialog box.

7. Click Close to close the Printer Ports dialog box.

8. Click Close to close the printer's Properties dialog box.

If another print device is available for the current print server, you can continue to use the same printer and configure the printer to use the other print device. To configure a printer to use another local or network print device that uses the same printer driver, select the appropriate port on the print server and cancel the selection of the current port.

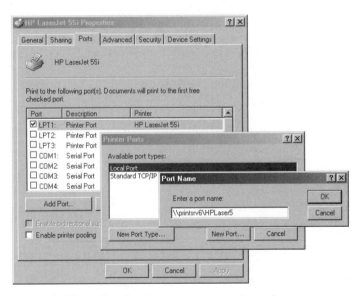

Figure 3.25 Redirecting documents to another printer

Taking Ownership of a Printer

Sometimes the owner of a printer can no longer manage that printer and you need to take ownership. Taking ownership of a printer enables you to change administrative responsibility for a printer. By default, the user who installed the printer owns it. If that user can no longer administer the printer, you should take ownership of it—for example, if the current owner leaves the company.

The following users can take ownership of a printer:

- A user or a member of a group who has the Manage Printers permission for the printer
- Members of the Administrators and Power Users groups (By default, these groups have the Manage Printers permission, which allows them to take ownership.)

▶ **Follow these steps to take ownership of a printer:**

1. In the Properties dialog box for the printer, click the Security tab, and then click Advanced.

2. In the Access Control Settings dialog box, click the Owner tab, and then click your user account under Change Owner To, as shown in Figure 3.26.

   Note If you are a member of the Administrators group and you want the Administrators group to take ownership of the printer, click the Administrators group.

3. Click OK, and then click Close.

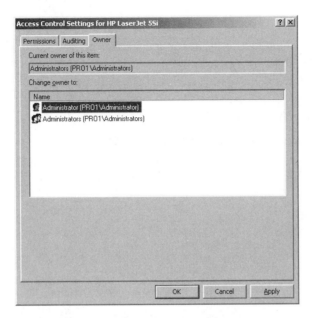

Figure 3.26 Taking ownership of a printer

Practice: Performing Printer Management

In this practice, you perform three tasks that are part of managing printers. In the first exercise, you assign forms to paper trays. In the second exercise, you set up a separator page. In the third exercise, you learn how to take ownership of a printer.

Exercise 1: Assigning Forms to Paper Trays

In this exercise, you assign a paper type (form) to a paper tray so that when users print to a specified form, the print job is automatically routed to and adjusted for the correct tray.

1. Click Start, point to Settings, and select Printers.

2. Right-click the icon for your printer, and then click Properties.

3. In the Properties dialog box, click the Device Settings tab.

   Notice that there are multiple selections under Form To Tray Assignment. Some of the selections are labeled Not Available because they depend on options that aren't installed.

4. Click Lower Paper Tray, and then select Legal.

   Whenever a user prints on legal size paper, Windows 2000 will instruct the printer to use paper from the lower paper tray.

5. Click Apply and leave the Properties dialog box open for the next exercise.

Exercise 2: Setting Up Separator Pages

In this exercise, you set up a separator page to print between documents. This separator page includes the user's name and the date and time that the document was printed.

1. Click the Advanced tab of the Properties dialog box.

2. Click Separator Page.

   The Separator Page dialog box appears.

3. In the Separator Page dialog box, click Browse.

   Windows 2000 displays another Separator Page dialog box.

4. Select Sysprint.sep, and then click Open.

   The selected separator page file's path appears in the first Separator Page dialog box.

5. Click OK.

   Windows 2000 will now print a separator page between print jobs.

6. Leave the Properties dialog box open for the next exercise.

Exercise 3: Taking Ownership of a Printer

In this exercise, you practice taking ownership of a printer.

To take ownership of a printer

1. Click the Security tab of the Properties dialog box.

2. On the Security tab, click Advanced, and then click the Owner tab.

   Who currently owns the printer?

3. To take ownership of the printer, select another user in the Name box.

4. If you actually wanted to take ownership, you would click Apply now, but click Cancel instead to leave the ownership unchanged.

5. Click OK to close the Properties dialog box, close the Printers window, and then log off Windows 2000.

Lesson Summary

In this lesson, you learned that managing printers includes assigning forms to paper trays; setting up a separator page; pausing, resuming, and canceling documents on a printer; redirecting documents to a different printer; and taking ownership of a printer. In the practice portion of this lesson, you assigned a form to a paper tray and set up a separator page. In addition, you learned how to change who has administrative responsibility for printers, which involves changing ownership.

Lesson 11: Managing Documents

In addition to managing printers, Windows 2000 allows you to manage individual documents. Managing documents includes pausing, resuming, restarting, and canceling a document if a printing problem occurs. In addition, you can set someone to notify when a print job is finished, set the priority to allow a critical document to print before other documents, and set a specific time for a document to print.

After this lesson, you will be able to

- Pause, resume, restart, and cancel the printing of a document
- Set a notification, priority, and printing time
- Delete a document from the print queue

Estimated lesson time: 20 minutes

Pausing, Restarting, and Canceling a Document

If a printing problem occurs with a specific document, you can pause and resume printing of the document. You can also restart or cancel printing of a document. You must have the Manage Documents permission for the appropriate printer to perform these actions. Because the creator of a document has the default permissions to manage that document, users can perform any of these actions on their own documents.

To manage a document, right-click the printing device for the document and click Open. Select the appropriate document(s), click the Document menu, and then click the appropriate command to pause, resume, start from the beginning, or cancel a document.

Setting Notification, Priority, and Printing Time

You can control print jobs by setting the notification, priority, and printing time. To perform these document management tasks, you must have the Manage Documents permission for the appropriate printer.

You set the notification, priority, and printing time for a document on the General tab of the Properties dialog box for the document, as shown in Figure 3.27. To open the Properties dialog box for one or more documents, first select the documents in the printer's window, click the Document menu, and then click Properties.

Table 3.17 describes the tasks that you might perform when you control print jobs, how to perform the tasks, and examples of situations in which you might perform these tasks.

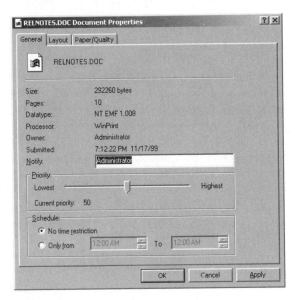

Figure 3.27 Setting notification, priority, and printing time for a document

Table 3.17 Setting a Notification, Changing Priority, and Scheduling Print Times

Task	Action	Example
Setting a notification	In the Notify box, type the logon name of the user who should receive the notification. By default, Windows 2000 enters the name of the user who printed the document.	Change the print notification when someone other than the user who printed the document needs to retrieve it.
Changing a document priority	Move the Priority slider to the priority that you want. The highest priority is 99 and the lowest is 1.	Change a priority so that a critical document prints before other documents.
Scheduling print times	To restrict print times, click Only From in the Schedule section, and then set the hours between which you want the document to print.	Set the print time for a large document so that it will print during off hours, such as late at night.

Practice: Managing Documents

In this practice, you manage documents by printing a document, setting a notification for a document, changing the priority for a document, and then canceling a document.

Exercise 1: Managing Documents

▶ **To verify that a printer is offline**

1. Log on as Administrator.
2. Click the Start button, point to Settings, and then click Printers.
3. In the Printers window, click the printer's icon.
4. Do one of the following to verify that the printer is offline:
   - On the File menu, verify that Use Printer Offline is selected.
   - Right-click the printer icon and verify that Use Printer Offline is selected.
   - If the Printers window is displayed in Web view, verify that Use Printer Offline is displayed in the left portion of the folder window.
5. On the File menu (or by right-clicking the printer's icon), verify that Set As Default Printer is selected.

   The printer's icon will display a check mark to show that it is the default. If necessary, press F5 to update the display.
6. Minimize the Printers window.

Note Keep the printer offline to prevent it from trying to communicate with a nonexistent print device. This will eliminate error messages in later exercises when documents are spooled.

▶ **To print a document**

1. Insert the Windows 2000 Professional CD-ROM into the CD-ROM drive.
2. When the Microsoft Windows 2000 CD dialog box appears, click Browse This CD.
3. Double-click Readme.doc.

   WordPad starts and displays the Readme.doc file.

4. Click File and click Print.

   The Print dialog box appears. Notice that the file will be printed on the HP Laserjet 5SI printer.

5. Click Print, and then close WordPad.

▶   **To set a notification**

1. Restore the Printers window.

2. Double-click HP LaserJet 5Si.

3. In the printer's window, select README.txt, and then click Properties on the Document menu.

   Windows 2000 displays the README.txt Document Properties dialog box with the General tab active.

   Which user is specified in the Notify box? Why?

Note   To change the person to be notified, you would type in the name of the user in the Notify box and click apply.

▶   **To increase the priority of a document**

1. In the README.txt Document Properties dialog box, on the General tab, notice the default priority.

   What is the current priority? Is it the lowest or highest priority?

2. In the Priority box, move the slider to the right to increase the priority of the document, and then click OK.

   Nothing changes visibly in the HP LaserJet 5Si - Use Printer Offline window.

3. On the Printer menu, click Use Printer Offline to remove the check mark, and then immediately click Use Printer Offline again.

Note If Windows 2000 displays a Printers Folder dialog box with an error message informing you that the printer port is unavailable, finish the following procedure, and then, in the dialog box, click Cancel.

4. Check the status of README.txt to confirm that Windows 2000 has started to print this document.

▶ **To cancel printing of a document**

1. Select README.txt in the document list in the printer's window.

2. On the Document menu, click Cancel.

Notice that the Status column changes to Deleting. Then README.txt is removed from the document list.

Tip You can also cancel a document by pressing the Delete key.

3. Close the printer's window, and then close the Printers window.

Lesson Summary

In this lesson, you learned that managing documents includes pausing, resuming, restarting, and canceling a document; setting who is notified when a print job is finished; setting the document priority to allow a critical document to print before other documents; and setting a specific time for a document to print. You must have the Manage Documents permission for the appropriate printer to perform these actions. The creator of a document has the default permissions to manage that document, so users can perform any of these actions on their own documents.

Lesson 12: Administering Printers Using a Web Browser

Windows 2000 enables you to manage printers from any computer running a Web browser, regardless of whether the computer is running Windows 2000 or has the correct printer driver installed. You can perform the same management tasks using a Web browser as you do by using Windows 2000 management tools. The difference in administering with a Web browser is the interface, which is a Web-based interface. To gain access to a printer by using a Web browser, the print server on which the printer resides must have Internet Information Server (IIS) installed.

After this lesson, you will be able to

- Describe the advantages of administering printers using a Web browser
- Describe how to administer printers using a Web browser

Estimated lesson time: 5 minutes

Understanding Web Servers

A Web server is a computer that responds to requests from a user's browser. Shortcuts or links to a resource on a Web server from a user's computer are known as Web folders or HTTP folders. For a Web server to provide Web folders, the Web server must support one of the following protocols or extensions: the Web Extension Client (WEC) protocol, FrontPage extensions, or the Web Distributed Authoring and Versioning (WebDAV) protocol and IIS.

Using a Web Browser to Manage Printers

The following are the advantages of using a Web browser to manage printers:

- It allows you to administer printers from any computer running a Web browser, regardless of whether the computer is running Windows 2000 or has the correct printer driver installed.
- It allows you to customize the interface. For example, you can create your own Web page containing a floor plan with the locations of the printers and the links to the printers.
- It provides a summary page listing the status of all printers on a print server.
- It can report real-time print device data, such as whether the print device is in power-saving mode, if the printer driver makes such information available. This information isn't available from the Printers window.

Accessing Printers Using a Web Browser

If you want to gain access to all printers on a print server by using a Web browser, open the Web browser, and then in the Address box, type

```
http://print_server_name/printers
```

If you want to gain access to a specific printer by using a Web browser, open the Web browser, and then in the Address box, type

```
http://server_name/printer_share_name
```

Lesson Summary

This lesson showed you one benefit of using a Web browser to administer printers: it allows you to administer printers from any computer running a Web browser, regardless of whether the computer is running Windows 2000 or has the correct printer driver installed.

Review

The following questions will help you determine whether you have learned enough to move on to the next chapter. If you have difficulty answering these questions, please go back and review the material in this chapter before beginning the next chapter. See Appendix A, "Questions and Answers," for the answers to these questions.

1. A print server can connect to two different types of print devices. What are these two types of print devices, and what are the differences?

2. You have added and shared a printer. What must you do to set up client computers running Windows 2000 so that users can print, and why?

3. What advantages does connecting to a printer by using http://*server_name*/ printers provide for users?

4. Why would you connect multiple printers to one print device?

5. Why would you create a printer pool?

6. Which printer permission does a user need to change the priority on another user's document?

7. In an environment where many users print to the same print device, how can you help reduce the likelihood of users picking up the wrong documents?

8. Can you redirect a single document?

9. A user needs to print a large document. How can the user print the job after hours, without being present while the document prints?

10. What are the advantages of using a Web browser to administer printing?

11. What is the default permission when a volume is formatted with NTFS? Who has access to the volume?

12. If a user has Write permission for a folder and is also a member of a group with Read permission for the folder, what are the user's effective permissions for the folder?

13. If you assign the Modify permission to a user account for a folder and the Read permission for a file, and then you copy the file to that folder, which permission does the user have for the file?

14. What happens to permissions that are assigned to a file when the file is moved from one folder to another folder on the same NTFS volume? What happens when the file is moved to a folder on another NTFS volume?

15. If an employee leaves the company, what must you do to transfer ownership of his or her files and folders to another employee?

16. What three details should you check when a user can't gain access to a resource?

17. The Sales department archives existing sales data on a network computer running Windows 2000 Professional. Several other departments share the server. You have begun to receive complaints from users in other departments that the server has little remaining disk space. What can you do to alleviate the problem?

18. When a folder is shared on a FAT volume, what does a user with the Full Control shared folder permissions for the folder have access to?

19. What are the shared folder permissions?

20. By default, what are the permissions that are assigned to a shared folder?

21. When a folder is shared on an NTFS volume, what does a user with the Full Control shared folder permissions for the folder have access to?

22. When you share a public folder, why should you use centralized data folders?

23. What is the best way to secure files and folders that you share on NTFS partitions?

C H A P T E R   4

Managing User Accounts

About This Chapter

A user account is a record that of all the information that defines a user to Microsoft Windows 2000. This includes the user name and password required for the user to log on, the groups in which the user account has membership, and the rights and permissions the user has for using the computer and network and accessing their resources. User accounts help you create consistent user environments across your entire system.

This chapter introduces you to user accounts and to how to plan them. It also explains how to create and configure the properties for local user accounts. This chapter concludes with discussion on using user accounts to troubleshoot issues with desktop settings.

Before You Begin

To complete this chapter, you must have

- A computer that meets the minimum hardware requirements listed in "Hardware Requirements" in "About This Book"
- Windows 2000 Professional installed on the computer
- The Windows 2000 Professional CD-ROM

Lesson 1: Understanding User Accounts

Microsoft Windows 2000 supports three different types of user accounts: local user accounts, domain user accounts, and built-in user accounts. A *local user account* allows a user to log on to a specific computer to gain access to resources on that computer. A *domain user account* allows a user to log on to the domain to gain access to network resources. A *built-in user account* allows a user to perform administrative tasks or to gain access to local or network resources.

After this lesson, you will be able to

- Describe the role and purpose of user accounts

Estimated lesson time: 10 minutes

Local User Accounts

Local user accounts allow users to log on at and gain access to resources only on the computer on which the local user account has been created. When you create a local user account, Windows 2000 creates the account *only* in that computer's security database, which is called the *local security database,* as shown in Figure 4.1. Windows 2000 doesn't replicate local user account information to any other computer. After the local user account has been created, the computer uses its local security database to authenticate the local user account, which allows the user to log on to that computer.

Local user

Local user accounts

- Provide access to resources on the local computer
- Are created only on computers that are not in a domain
- Are created in the local security database

Figure 4.1 Characteristics of local user accounts

If you have a workgroup that consists of five computers running Windows 2000 Professional and you create a local user account—for example, User1 on Computer1—you can log on to Computer1 only with the User1 account. If you need to be able to log on to all five of the computers in the workgroup as User1, you must create a local user account, User1, on each of the five computers. Furthermore, if you decide to change the password for User1, you must change the password for User1 on each of the five computers because each of these computers maintains its own local security database.

Note Do not create local user accounts on computers running Windows 2000 that are part of a domain because the domain doesn't recognize local user accounts. The user would be unable to gain access to resources in the domain and the domain administrator would be unable to administer the local user account properties or assign access permissions for domain resources.

Domain User Accounts

Domain user accounts allow users to log on to the domain and gain access to resources anywhere on the network. The user provides his or her password and user name at logon. Windows 2000 authenticates the user and then builds an access token that contains information about the user and security settings. The access token identifies the user to computers that are part of the Windows 2000 domain on which the user tries to gain access to resources. Windows 2000 provides the access token for the duration of the logon session.

Note You can have domain user accounts only if you have a domain. You can have a domain only if you have at least one computer running one of the Windows 2000 Server products that is configured as a domain controller, which has the directory services based on Active Directory technology installed.

You create a domain user account in the copy of the Active Directory database (the Directory) on a domain controller, as shown in Figure 4.2. The domain controller replicates the new user account information to all domain controllers in the domain. After Windows 2000 replicates the new user account information, all of the domain controllers in the domain tree can authenticate the user at logon.

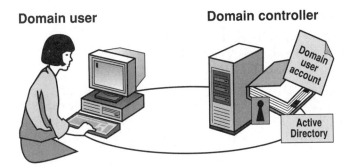

Domain user accounts

■ Provide access to network resources

■ Provide the access token for authentication

■ Are created in Active Directory directory services
  on a domain controller

Figure 4.2 Characteristics of domain user accounts

Built-In User Accounts

Windows 2000 automatically creates accounts called *built-in accounts*. Two commonly used built-in accounts are Administrator and Guest accounts.

Administrator

Use the built-in Administrator account to manage the overall computer network. If your computer is part of a domain, use the built-in Administrator account to manage the domain configuration. Tasks done using the Administrator account include creating and modifying user accounts and groups, managing security policies, creating printers, and assigning permissions and rights to user accounts to gain access to resources.

If you are the administrator, you should create a user account that you use to perform nonadministrative tasks. Log on by using the Administrator account only when you perform administrative tasks.

Note You can't delete the Administrator account. You should always rename the built-in Administrator account to provide a greater degree of security. Use a name that doesn't identify it as the Administrator account. This makes it difficult for unauthorized users to break into the Administrator account because they don't know which user account it is.

Guest

Use the built-in Guest account to allow occasional users to log on and gain access to resources. For example, an employee who needs access to resources for a short time could use the Guest account.

Note The Guest account is disabled by default. Enable the Guest account only in low-security networks and always assign it a password. You can rename the Guest account, but you can't delete it.

Lesson Summary

In this lesson, you learned that Microsoft Windows 2000 supports local user accounts, domain user accounts, and built-in user accounts. With a local user account, a user logs on to a specific computer to gain access to resources on that computer. With a domain user account, a user can log on to the domain to gain access to network resources. With built-in user accounts, you can perform administrative tasks or gain access to resources.

When you create a local user account, Windows 2000 creates the account only in that computer's security database, which is called the local security database. If you need to have access to multiple computers in your workgroup, you must create an account on each of the computers in the workgroup. You don't create built-in user accounts; Windows 2000 creates them automatically.

You also learned that if your computer is part of a domain, Windows 2000 provides domain user accounts. And built-in user accounts exist that are domain user accounts. These are used to perform administrative tasks or gain access to network resources. When you create a domain user account, Windows 2000 creates the account in the copy of the Active Directory database (the Directory) on a domain controller. The domain controller then replicates the new user account information to all domain controllers in the domain, simplifying user account administration.

Lesson 2: Planning New User Accounts

You can streamline the process of creating user accounts by planning and organizing the information for the user accounts. Your account planning should include the following issues:

- Naming conventions for user accounts
- Requirements for passwords

After this lesson, you will be able to

- Plan a strategy for creating new user accounts

Estimated lesson time: 5 minutes

Naming Conventions

The naming convention establishes how users are identified in the domain. A consistent naming convention helps you and your users to remember user logon names and locate them in lists. Table 4.1 explains how to determine a naming convention for your organization based on various considerations.

Table 4.1 Naming Convention Considerations

Consideration	Explanation
User logon names must be unique.	Local user account names must be unique on the computer on which the local user account is created. User logon names for domain user accounts must be unique to the Directory.
Use 20 characters maximum.	User logon names can contain up to 20 uppercase or lowercase characters; the field accepts more than 20 characters, but Windows 2000 recognizes only the first 20.
Avoid invalid characters.	The following characters are invalid: " $/ \setminus [\;] : ; | = , + * ? < >$
User logon names are not case sensitive.	You can use a combination of special and alphanumeric characters to help uniquely identify user accounts. User logon names are *not* case sensitive, but Windows 2000 preserves the case.

continues

Table 4.1 Naming Convention Considerations *(continued)*

Consideration	Explanation
Accommodate employees with duplicate names.	If two users have the same name, you can use the first name and the last initial and then add letters from the last name to differentiate the duplicate names. If, for example, two users are named John Doe, one user account logon name could be Johnd and the other Johndo. Another possibility would be to number each user logon name—for example, Johnd1 and Johnd2.
Identify the type of employee.	In some organizations, it is useful to identify temporary employees by their user accounts. To identify temporary employees, you can use a T and a dash in front of the user's logon name—for example, T-Johnd. Alternatively, use parentheses in the name—for example, John Doe (Temp).

Password Requirements

To protect access to individual computers, every user account should have a password. The following are guidelines for passwords:

- Always assign a password for the Administrator account to prevent unauthorized access to the account.

- Determine whether the Administrator or the users will control passwords. You can assign unique passwords for the user accounts and prevent users from changing them, or you can allow users to create their own passwords the first time they log on. In most cases, users should control their passwords.

- Use passwords that are hard to guess. For example, avoid using passwords with an obvious association, such as a family member's name.

- Passwords can be up to 128 characters; a minimum length of eight characters is recommended.

- Use both uppercase and lowercase letters, numerals, and valid nonalphanumeric characters.

Lesson Summary

In this lesson, you learned that in planning user accounts, you should determine naming conventions for user accounts and requirements for passwords. You learned that domain user accounts can be up to 20 characters long and must be unique within the directory where you create the domain user account. Local user account names can also be up to 20 characters long and must be unique on the computer where you create the local user account.

You also learned about passwords and were given some advice on keeping passwords secure.

Making these decisions before you start creating user accounts will reduce the amount of time it takes to create the needed user accounts and will simplify managing these accounts.

Lesson 3: Creating User Accounts

Use the Computer Management snap-in to create a new local user account. When you create a local user account, it is always created in the local security database of that computer.

After this lesson, you will be able to

- Create a local user account

Estimated lesson time: 10 minutes

The Computer Management Snap-in

The Computer Management snap-in (illustrated in Figure 4.3) is the tool you use to create local user accounts.

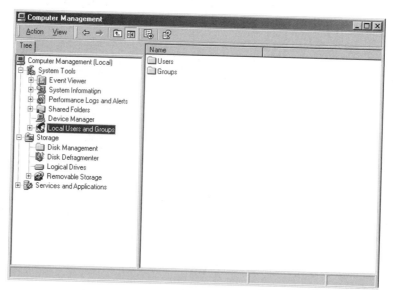

Figure 4.3 The Computer Management snap-in

▶ **Follow these steps to create local user accounts:**

1. Click the Start button, point to Programs, point to Administrative Tools, and then click Computer Management.

2. In the Computer Management window, in the console pane, click Local Users And Groups.

3. In the details pane, right-click Users, and then click New User.

4. Fill in the appropriate fields in the New User dialog box (see Figure 4.4), and then click Create.

Table 4.2 describes the local user account options shown in Figure 4.4.

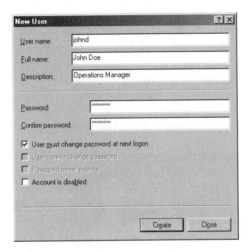

Figure 4.4 The New User dialog box

Table 4.2 Local User Account Options

Option	Description
User Name	The user's logon name. This field is required.
Full Name	The user's full name. This includes the user's first and last names but can also include the middle name or initial.
Description	An optional field that allows you to type descriptive text about the user account or the user.
Password	The password that is used to authenticate the user. For greater security, *always* assign a password. Notice that you don't see the password. It is represented as a series of asterisks when you type the password, regardless of the length of the password.
Confirm Password	Confirm the password by typing it a second time to make sure that you typed the password correctly. This is required if you assign a password.

continues

Table 4.2 Local User Account Options *(continued)*

Option	Description
User Must Change Password At Next Logon	Select this check box if you want the user to change his or her password the first time that he or she logs on. This ensures that the user is the only person who knows the password. By default, this check box is selected.
User Cannot Change Password	Select this check box if you have more than one person using the same user account (such as Guest) or to maintain control over user account passwords. This allows only administrators to control passwords. When the User Must Change Password At Next Logon check box is selected, the User Cannot Change Password check box isn't available.
Password Never Expires	Select this check box if you never want the password to change—for example, for a user account that will be used by a program or a Windows 2000 service. The User Must Change Password At Next Logon check box overrides the Password Never Expires check box. When the User Must Change Password At Next Logon check box is selected, the Password Never Expires check box isn't available.
Account Is Disabled	Select this check box to prevent use of this user account—for example, for a new employee who has not yet begun working at the organization.

Note Always require new users to change their passwords the first time they log on. This forces them to use passwords that only they know.

Tip For added security on networks, create random initial passwords for all new user accounts by using a combination of letters and numbers. Creating a random initial password will help keep the user account secure.

Practice: Creating Local User Accounts

In this practice, you create the user accounts whose details are shown in the following table. Then you will test the logon procedure with one of the users you created.

User name	Full name	Password	Change password
User1	User One	(blank)	Must
User2	User Two	(blank)	(blank)
User3	User Three	User3	Must
User4	User Four	User4	(blank)

Exercise 1: Create and Test a Local User Account

This exercise leads you through the steps that are required to create the first user account by using the Computer Management snap-in. After you have created the first user account, follow the same steps to create the remaining user accounts and use the information in the table to set them up.

▶   **To create a local user account**

1. Log on as Administrator.

2. Click the Start button, point to Programs, point to Administrative Tools, and then click Computer Management.

   Windows 2000 displays the Computer Management snap-in.

3. Click Local Users And Groups.

4. Right-click Users, and then click New User.

   Windows 2000 displays the New User dialog box.

5. Type **User1** in the User Name box.

6. Type **User One** in the Full Name box.

7. In the Password box and the Confirm Password box, type the password or leave these boxes blank if you aren't assigning a password.

   If you type in a password, notice that the password is displayed as a series of asterisks as you type. This prevents onlookers from viewing the password as it is entered.

   In high-security environments, assign initial passwords to user accounts and then require users to change their password the next time that they log on. This prevents a user account from existing without a password and ensures that, once the user logs on and changes his or her password, only the user knows the password.

8. Specify whether or not the user can change his or her password.

9. After you have selected the appropriate password options, click Create.

The New User dialog box clears and remains displayed so that you can create another user account.

10. Complete steps 5 to 10 for the remaining user accounts.

11. When you finishing creating users, click Close to close the New User dialog box.

12. Close the Computer Management window.

▶ **To test a local user account**

1. Log off as Administrator.

2. Log on as User1 with no password.

3. When prompted to change User1's password, leave the Old Password box empty, type **password** in the Password and Confirm Password boxes, and then click OK.

A Change Password dialog box appears.

4. Click OK.

Lesson Summary

In this lesson, you learned how to use the Computer Management snap-in to create a new local user account. When you create a local user account, it is only created in the local security database of that computer. You can configure options for the accounts you create, including a user name, a full name, and a description. You can also configure password options such as whether users must change their passwords at the next logon, whether users can ever change their passwords, and whether the passwords expire. In the practice portion of this lesson, you created four local user accounts.

Lesson 4: Setting Properties for User Accounts

A set of default properties is associated with each local user account that you create. After you create a local user account, you can configure these account properties. A user's Properties dialog box has three tabs that contain information about each user account: the General tab, the Member Of tab, and the Profile tab.

After this lesson, you will be able to

- Set properties for user accounts

Estimated lesson time: 15 minutes

The General Tab in a User Account's Properties

The General tab in the Properties dialog box for a user account (see Figure 4.5) allows you to set or edit all the fields from the New User dialog box, except for User Name, Password, and Confirm Password. It also provides one additional check box: Account Is Locked Out.

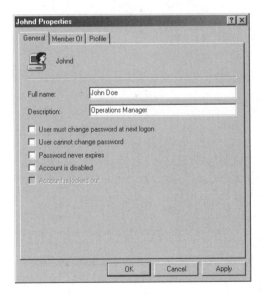

Figure 4.5 The General tab of a user's Properties dialog box

You can't select the Account Is Locked Out check box because it is unavailable when the account is active and not locked out of the system. The system locks out a user if he or she exceeds the limit set on the number of failed logon attempts. This is a security feature to make it more difficult for an unauthorized user to break into the system. If an account has been locked out by the system, the Account Is Locked Out check box becomes available and an administrator can clear the check box to allow the user access to the system.

The Member Of Tab in a User Account's Properties

The Member Of tab in the Properties dialog box for a user account allows you to add the user account to or remove the user account from a group.

The Profile Tab in a User Account's Properties

The Profile tab in the Properties dialog box for a user account allows you to set a path for the user profile, logon script, and home folder (see Figure 4.6).

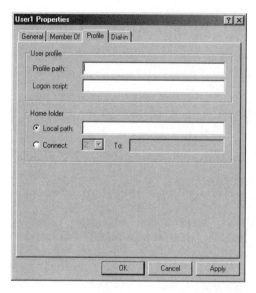

Figure 4.6 The Profile tab of a user's Properties dialog box

User Profile

A *user profile* is a collection of folders and files that stores the user's current desktop environment, application settings, and personal data. A user profile also contains all of the network connections that are established when a user logs on to a computer, such as Start menu items and mapped drives to network servers. User profiles maintain consistency for users in their desktop environments by providing each user the same desktop environment he or she had the last time that he or she logged on to the computer.

Windows 2000 creates a user profile the first time a user logs on at a computer. After the user logs on for the first time, Windows 2000 stores the user profile on that computer. This user profile is also known as a *local user profile*.

User profiles operate in the following manner:

- When a user logs on to a client computer running Windows 2000, the user always receives his or her individual desktop settings and connections, regardless of how many users share the same client computer.

- The first time a user logs on to a client computer running Windows 2000, Windows 2000 creates a default user profile for the user and stores it in the *system partition root*Documents and Settings*user_logon_name* folder (typically C:\\Documents and Settings*user_logon_name*), where *user_logon_name* is the name the user types in when logging on to the system.

- A user profile contains the My Documents folder, which provides a place for users to store personal files. My Documents is the default location for the File Open and Save As commands. By default, Windows 2000 creates a My Documents icon on the user's desktop. This makes it easy for users to locate their personal documents.

- A user can change his or her user profile by changing desktop settings. For example, a user makes a new network connection or adds a file to My Documents. Then, when the user logs off, Windows 2000 incorporates the changes into the user profile. The next time the user logs on, the new network connection and the file are present.

Note You should have users store their documents in My Documents rather than in home directories. Home directories are covered later in this chapter. Windows 2000 automatically sets up My Documents, which is the default location for storing data for Microsoft applications.

By opening the System program in Control Panel and clicking the User Profiles tab, an administrator can easily copy, delete, or change the type of a user profile. Changing the type for user profiles means changing it from a local user profile, which sets up the user's desktop environment on a specific computer, to a roaming user profile. A *roaming user profile* is especially helpful in a domain environment, because it follows the user around, setting up the same desktop environment for the user no matter what computer the user logs on to in the domain.

There is a third type of user profile, the mandatory user profile, which is a read-only roaming user profile. When the user logs off, Windows 2000 does not save any changes made during the session, so the next time the user logs on the profile is exactly the same as the last time the user logged on. You can create a mandatory user profile for a specific user or for a group of users.

Note A hidden file called Ntuser.dat contains the section of the Windows 2000 system settings that applies to the individual user account and contains the user environment settings. This file can be used to create a profile for a mandatory roaming user. To create a profile for a mandatory roaming user, you create a user account that you can use to create user profiles. Log on as the user for the account you created, and configure all the desktop environment settings you want. Log on as administrator and locate the Ntuser.dat file in C:\Documents and Settings*user_logon_name*. Change the name of the Ntuser.dat file to Ntuser.man. You can then copy this file to apply the mandatory user profile to any other user or group.

Logon Script

A logon script is a file you can create and assign to a user account to configure the user's working environment. For example, a login script can be used to establish network connections or start applications. Each time a user logs on, the assigned logon script is run.

Home Folder

In addition to the My Documents folder, Windows 2000 provides you with the means to create another location for users to store their personal documents. This additional location is the user's home folder. You can store a home folder on a client computer or in a shared folder on a file server. In fact, you can locate all users' home folders in a central location on a network server.

Storing all home folders on a file server has the following advantages:

- Users can gain access to their home folders from any client computer on the network.

- Backing up and administrating user documents is centralized.

- The home folders are accessible from a client computer running any Microsoft operating system (including MS-DOS, Windows 95, Windows 98, and Windows 2000).

Note Store home folders on an NTFS file system volume so that you can use NTFS permissions to secure user documents. If you store home folders on a FAT volume, you can restrict home folder access only by using shared folder permissions.

To create a home folder on a network file server, you must perform the following three tasks:

- Create and share a folder in which to store all home folders on a network server. The home folder for each user will reside in this shared folder.

- For the shared folder, remove the default Full Control permission from the Everyone group and assign Full Control to the Users group. This ensures that only users with domain user accounts can gain access to the shared folder.

- Provide the path to the user's home folder in the shared home directory folder on the Profile tab of the Properties dialog box for the user account. Since the home folder is on a network server, click Connect and specify a drive letter to use to connect. In the To box, you would specify a UNC name—for example, *server_name**shared_folder_name*\ *user_logon_name*. Type the *username* variable as the user's logon name to automatically give each user's home folder the user logon name (for example, type ***server_name****Users****%username%**).

  If you use the *username* variable to name a folder on an NTFS volume, the user is assigned the NTFS Full Control permission, and all other permissions are removed for the folder, including those for the Administrator account.

▶ **Follow these steps to set User Account Properties:**

1. On the Administrative Tools menu, click Computer Management.

2. Right-click the appropriate local user account, and then click Properties.

3. Click the appropriate tab for the properties that you want to type in or change, and then type in values for each property.

Practice: Modifying User Account Properties

In this practice, you modify user account properties and then test them.

Exercise 1: Testing Account Properties

In this exercise, you again test the User Must Change Password At Next Logon property of the users you created in the previous Practice. You then set the User Cannot Change Password Account property on User1 and the Account Is Disabled property on User2. Finally, you test these account properties.

1. If a user is currently logged on to your computer, log that user off.

2. Log on to the system as User3. Remember to use this user's password: User3.

   Windows 2000 displays a Logon Message dialog box indicating that you are required to change your password at first logon.

3. Click OK.

   Windows 2000 displays a Change Password dialog box. Notice that the password you just typed is in the Old Password box.

4. Type **password** in both the New Password box and in the Confirm New Password box.

5. Click OK.

   Windows 2000 displays a Change Password dialog box indicating that your password has been changed.

6. Click OK.

Exercise 2: Setting User Account Properties

In this exercise, you set and then test the User Cannot Change Password property.

▶ **To set the User Cannot Change Password property**

1. Log off as User3.

2. Log on as Administrator.

3. Start Computer Management from the Administrative Tools menu.

4. Expand Local Users And Groups, and then click Users.

   Windows 2000 displays the users in the details pane.

5. Right-click User1, and then click Properties.

The User1 Properties dialog box appears.

6. Select User Cannot Change Password.

The User Cannot Change Password check box should contain a check mark indicating that it is selected. Notice that the User Must Change Password At Next Logon check box is now unavailable.

7. Click OK to close the User1 Properties dialog box.

8. Right-click User2, and then select Properties.

The User2 Properties dialog box appears.

9. Select Account Is Disabled.

The Account Is Disabled check box should contain a check mark indicating that it is selected.

10. Click OK to close the User2 Properties dialog box, close Computer Management, and then log off the computer.

▶   **To test user account properties**

1. Log on as User1 with a password of password.

2. Press Ctrl+Alt+Delete.

Windows 2000 displays the Windows Security dialog box.

3. Click Change Password.

The Change Password dialog box appears.

4. Type **password** in the Old Password box, and then type **User1** in the New Password and the Confirm New Password boxes.

5. Click OK.

A Change Password dialog box appears indicating that you do not have permission to change your password.

6. Click OK.

7. Click Cancel to close the Change Password dialog box.

8. Log off as User1 and then log on as User2 with no password.

A Logon Message dialog box appears, indicating that your account has been disabled.

9. Click OK to close the Logon Message dialog box.

Lesson Summary

In this lesson, you learned that a set of default properties is associated with each local user account that you create. These properties include whether users can change their own passwords, whether users are required to change their passwords at the next logon, and whether an account is disabled. The Computer Management snap-in allows you to configure or modify these account properties easily.

In the practice portion of this lesson, you configured account properties, which included those that prohibit users from changing their passwords and disabled a user account. Finally, you tested these properties to verify that they worked as expected.

Lesson 5: Configuring and Troubleshooting the Desktop Environment

Windows 2000 provides great flexibility in configuring the desktop. You can configure your computer for multiple languages and multiple locations. This is especially important for employees of international companies that do business with customers in more than one country or who live in a country where more than one language is spoken. Windows 2000 also provides accessibility options that allow you to make Windows 2000 easier to use. All of the desktop settings available through Control Panel are as easy to configure as those discussed in detail in this lesson.

After this lesson, you will be able to

- Configure and troubleshoot multiple language settings
- Configure and troubleshoot multiple locale settings
- Configure and troubleshoot accessibility options
- Configure and troubleshoot desktop settings

Estimated lesson time: 25 minutes

Configuring Language and Location Settings

Through the Regional Options program in Control Panel, you can configure your computer for multiple languages and multiple locations. You can select multiple languages on the General tab of the Regional Options dialog box by clicking the check box in front of each language that you want your computer to support. Regional Options also allows you to configure your computer to use multiple locations or locales. The General tab shows you the current locale setting, and the Input Locale tab allows you to add locales.

There are additional tabs in the Regional Options dialog box that allow you to configure items that vary from language to language, such as currency, how dates and time are displayed, etc. The Numbers tab allows you to configure the appearance of numbers, including the following: the decimal symbol; the number of places after a decimal; the digital grouping symbol, such as the comma in 1,246; and the measurement symbol. The Currency tab, Time tab, and Date tab also allow you to configure the way money, the time, and the date are displayed.

If there are any problems with the way the support for your multiple languages or locales is working, you may want to double-check your settings. You can also try uninstalling the multiple language support or multiple locales support. Make sure that everything is working correctly with only one language or locale, and then reconfigure and reinstall the multiple language or multiple locale support.

Practice: Using Control Panel to Configure a Computer for Multiple Languages and Multiple Locations

In this practice, you use the Regional Options program in Control Panel to configure multiple languages and multiple locations.

Exercise 1: Configuring for Multiple Languages

In this exercise, you use Control Panel to configure your system to support an additional language.

1. Log on as Administrator.

2. In Control Panel, double-click the Regional Options icon.

   The Regional Options dialog box appears.

3. On the General tab, scroll through the items in the box labeled Your System Is Configured To Read And Write Documents In Multiple Languages to determine the current default language and some of the available languages.

   Note If you want to have your system use multiple languages, click the check box in front of each language you want to support.

4. Click Advanced.

   The Advanced Regional Options dialog box appears.

5. Click to select 1147 (IBM EBCDIC – France (20297 + Euro)), and then click OK.

6. When prompted, insert the Windows 2000 Professional CD-ROM into your CD-ROM drive.

   When the files have finished copying, your system is configured for multiple languages.

Note If you were only configuring for multiple languages, you would click OK to close the Regional Options dialog box. You would leave the Regional Options dialog box open for the next procedure.

Exercise 2: Configuring for Multiple Locales

In this exercise, you walk through the process of using the Control Panel to configure your system to support additional locations. You should not make any actual changes. You should cancel the operation at the end of the exercise.

1. On the General tab, note the default locale in the Your Locale (Location) box, and scroll through some of the choices.

Note Do not change your default locale.

---

2. Click the Input Locales tab.

Note The Installed Input Locales box shows which locales are currently installed on your computer and the current keyboard layout. For example, if you are in the United States, you will probably see the following: EN English Language **US**

---

3. Click Properties.

   The Input Locale Properties dialog box appears.

4. Click the down arrow for the Keyboard Layout/IME drop-down list to view the other keyboard layout options you could select.

Note Be careful not to change your keyboard layout.

---

5. Click Cancel.

   The Regional Options dialog box is again active.

6. Click Add.

The Add Input Locale dialog box appears.

Note This is the dialog box that allows you to configure for multiple locales.

7. Click Cancel.

Configuring and Troubleshooting Accessibility Options

Windows 2000 allows you to configure accessibility options through the Accessibility Options program in Control Panel. The five options that you can configure in Accessibility Options are controlled by the Keyboard, Sound, Display, Mouse, and General tabs.

Configuring Keyboard Options

The Keyboard tab allows you to configure StickyKeys. Turning on StickyKeys allows you to press a multiple key combination, such as Ctrl+Alt+Delete, one key at a time. This is useful for people who have difficulty pushing more than one key at a time. This is a check box selection, so it is either on or off.

The Keyboard tab also allows you to configure FilterKeys. Turning on FilterKeys causes the keyboard to ignore brief or repeated keystrokes. This option also allows you to configure the keyboard repeat rate, or the rate at which a key continuously held down repeats the keystroke. This is a check box selection, so it too is either on or off.

The Keyboard tab allows you to configure ToggleKeys. Turning on ToggleKeys causes the computer to make a high-pitched sound each time the Caps Lock, Num Lock, or Scroll Lock keys are switched on. Turning on ToggleKeys also causes the computer to make a low-pitched sound each time these three keys are turned off.

Configuring Sound Options

The Sound tab allows you to configure Windows 2000 to use SoundSentry. SoundSentry generates visual warnings when your computer makes a sound. The Sound tab also allows you to configure ShowSounds, which displays captions for the speech and sounds programs make. These two features are toggled on or off by selecting the respective check boxes.

Configuring Display Options

The Display tab contains a check box that allows you to configure Windows 2000 to use color and fonts designed for easy reading.

Configuring Mouse Options

The Mouse tab contains a check box that allows you to configure Windows 2000 to allow you to control the pointer with the numeric keypad.

Configuring General Tab Options

The General tab allows you to configure Automatic Reset, which turns off all the accessibility features, except the SerialKeys devices, after the computer has been idle for a specified amount of time. The General tab also allows you to activate the SerialKeys devices feature, which configures Windows 2000 to support an alternative input device (also called an augmentative communication device) connected to your computer's serial port.

Other options on the General tab include the Notification feature and the Administrative Options feature. The Notification feature allows you to configure Windows 2000 to display a warning message when a feature is activated and to make a sound when turning a feature on or off. The Administrative Options feature contains two check boxes that allow you to configure Windows 2000 to apply all configured accessibility options to this user at logon and to apply all configured accessibility options to all new users.

Configuring and Troubleshooting Additional Desktop Settings

There are many configurable desktop settings in Windows 2000 that are configured through Control Panel programs. Some of these programs include Fax Services, Internet Options, and Phone And Modem Options. To configure any of the settings these programs control, double-click the appropriate icon, click the appropriate tab, and provide the requested information.

Configuration Management

The configuration management capabilities in Windows 2000 create a consistent environment for the end user and help ensure that users have the data, applications, and operating system settings that they need.

Windows 2000 includes the following configuration management enhancements:

- **Add/Remove Programs wizard.** This wizard simplifies the process of installing and removing programs. Users can install applications by pointing directly to a location on the corporate network or Internet. The user interface provides additional feedback and sort options for viewing installed or available applications by size, frequency of use, and time of last use.

- **Windows Installer service.** This service manages application installation, modification, repairs, and removal. It provides a standard format for managing the components of a software package and an API for managing applications and tools.

Troubleshooting Tools

Windows 2000 Professional includes diagnostic and troubleshooting tools that make it easier to support the operating system. Troubleshooting tools in Windows 2000 Professional include the following:

- **Compatibility tool.** This tool detects and warns the user about whether certain installed applications or components will cause an upgrade to fail, or whether the components won't work after an upgrade is complete. The compatibility tool can be run by using the /checkupgradeonly switch with the command to start Setup. This generates the Report System Compatibility screen that lists any items that are incompatible with Windows 2000. For more information on the compatibility tool, see Chapter 1, "Installing Windows 2000 Professional."

- **Troubleshooters.** These tools included in Windows 2000 online Help as troubleshooting wizards can be used to solve many common computer problems.

Lesson Summary

In this lesson you learned how to use the Regional Options program in Control Panel to configure Windows 2000 Professional for multiple languages and multiple locales. You also learned how to change your keyboard layout and how to configure currency, date, and time settings.

You also learned how to use the Accessibility Options program in Control Panel to make Windows 2000 Professional easier to use. All of the configurable settings for the desktop that are set through Control Panel are easy to configure and troubleshoot. To configure or troubleshoot them, simply double-click the appropriate icon and provide the appropriate information.

Review

The following questions will help you determine whether you have learned enough to move on to the next chapter. If you have difficulty answering these questions, please go back and review the material in this chapter before beginning the next chapter. See Appendix A, "Questions and Answers," for the answers to these questions.

1. What information is required to create a local user account?

2. What are built-in user accounts and what are they used for?

C H A P T E R   5

Managing Network Protocols and Services

About This Chapter

A *protocol* is a set of rules and conventions for sending information over a network. The network protocol Microsoft Windows 2000 relies on most commonly is TCP/IP. TCP/IP is an industry-standard suite of protocols that enables enterprise networking and connectivity on Windows 2000–based computers. TCP/IP is used for logon, file and print services, replication of information between one domain controller and another, and other common functions.

This chapter presents the skills and knowledge necessary to configure and install TCP/IP (these are the same skills used to to install other network protocols, including NWLink, NetBIOS Enhanced User Interface (NetBEUI), and Data Link Control (DLC). The chapter then moves into a discussion of configuring inbound and outbound connections using either dial-up or virtual private network connections.

Before You Begin

To complete this chapter, you must have

- A computer that meets the minimum hardware requirements listed in "Hardware Requirements" in "About This Book"
- Windows 2000 Professional installed on the computer

Lesson 1: TCP/IP

TCP/IP allows you to communicate across networks of computers using various hardware architectures and operating systems. Microsoft's implementation of TCP/IP enables enterprise networking and connectivity between computers running Windows 2000.

After this lesson, you will be able to

- Describe the TCP/IP protocol suite and the TCP/IP utilities included with Windows 2000
- Configure TCP/IP

Estimated lesson time: 65 minutes

Understanding the TCP/IP Protocol Suite

Adding TCP/IP to a Windows 2000 configuration offers the following advantages:

- A routable networking protocol supported by most operating systems. Most large networks rely on TCP/IP.
- A technology for connecting dissimilar systems. You can use many standard connectivity utilities to access and transfer data between dissimilar systems. Windows 2000 includes several of these standard utilities.
- A robust, scalable, cross-platform client/server framework. TCP/IP supports the Microsoft Windows Sockets (winsock) interface, which is ideal for developing client/server applications for WinSock-compliant stacks.
- A method of gaining access to Internet resources.

The TCP/IP suite of protocols provides a set of standards for how computers communicate and how networks are interconnected. The TCP/IP suite of protocols maps to a four-layer conceptual model that helps to understand the tasks for which each protocol in the suite is responsible: network interface, Internet, transport, and application. These layers are illustrated in Figure 5.1.

The Network Interface Layer

At the base of the model is the network interface layer. This layer puts frames on the wire and pulls frames off the wire. There are no protocols in the TCP/IP suite that correspond to this layer of the model.

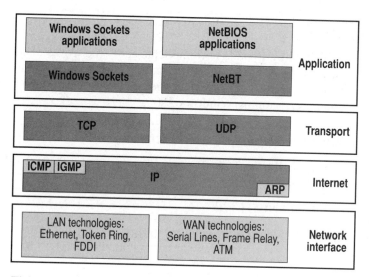

Figure 5.1 The TCP/IP suite of protocols within four layers

The Internet Layer

Internet layer protocols encapsulate packets into Internet datagrams and run all the necessary routing algorithms. The four Internet layer protocols are Internet Protocol (IP), Address Resolution Protocol (ARP), Internet Control Message Protocol (ICMP), and Internet Group Management Protocol (IGMP). Table 5.1 describes these four Internet layer protocols.

Table 5.1 Protocols Included in the Internet Layer

Protocol	Description
IP	Provides connectionless packet delivery for all other protocols in the suite. Doesn't guarantee packet arrival or correct packet sequence.
ARP	Provides IP address mapping to the media access control (MAC) sublayer address to acquire the physical MAC control address of the destination. IP broadcasts a special ARP inquiry packet containing the IP address of the destination system. The system that owns the IP address replies by sending its physical address to the requester. The MAC sublayer communicates directly with the network adapter card and is responsible for delivering error-free data between two computers on a network.

Protocol	Description
ICMP	Provides special communication between hosts, allowing them to share status and error information. Higher-level protocols use this information to recover from transmission problems. Network administrators use this information to detect network trouble. The ping utility uses ICMP packets to determine whether a particular IP device on a network is functional.
IGMP	Provides multicasting, which is a limited form of broadcasting, to communicate and manage information between all member devices in a multicast group. IGMP informs neighboring multicast routers of the host group memberships present on a particular network. Windows 2000 supports multicast capabilities that allow developers to create multicast programs, such as Windows 2000 Server NetShow Services.

The Transport Layer

Transport layer protocols provide communication sessions between computers. The desired method of data delivery determines what transport protocol will be used. The two transport layer protocols are Transmission Control Protocol (TCP) and User Datagram Protocol (UDP). Table 5.2 describes the two protocols included in the transport layer.

Table 5.2 Protocols Included in the Transport Layer

Protocol	Description
TCP	Provides connection-oriented, reliable communications for applications that typically transfer large amounts of data at one time or that require an acknowledgment for data received. TCP guarantees the delivery of packets, ensures proper sequencing of the data, and provides a checksum feature that validates both the packet header and its data for accuracy.
UDP	Provides connectionless communications and doesn't guarantee that packets will be delivered. Applications that use UDP typically transfer small amounts of data at one time. Reliable delivery is the responsibility of the application.

The Application Layer

At the top of the model is the application layer, in which applications gain access to the network. Many standard TCP/IP utilities and services reside in the application layer. These include File Transport Protocol (FTP), Telnet, Simple Network Management Protocol (SNMP), Domain Name System (DNS), and so on.

TCP/IP provides two interfaces for network applications to use the services of the TCP/IP protocol stack: Winsock and the NetBIOS over TCP/IP (NetBT) interface. Table 5.3 describes these two interfaces.

Table 5.3 Interfaces That Applications Use for TCP/IP Services

Interface	Description
Winsock	Serves as the standard interface between socket-based applications and TCP/IP protocols.
NetBT	Serves as the standard interface for NetBIOS services, including name, datagram, and session services. NetBT also provides a standard interface between NetBIOS-based applications and TCP/IP protocols.

Configuring TCP/IP to Use a Static IP Address

By default, client computers running Windows 2000, Windows 95, or Windows 98 obtain TCP/IP configuration information automatically from the Dynamic Host Configuration Protocol (DHCP) Service. However, even in a DHCP-enabled environment, you should assign a static IP address to selected network computers. For example, the computer running the DHCP Service can't be a DHCP client, so it must have a static IP address. If the DHCP Service isn't available, you must also configure TCP/IP to use a static IP address. For each network adapter card that uses TCP/IP in a computer, you can configure an IP address, subnet mask, and default gateway, as shown in Figure 5.2.

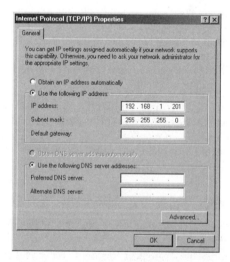

Figure 5.2 Configuring a static TCP/IP address

Table 5.4 describes options that can be used when configuring a static TCP/IP address.

Table 5.4 Options for Configuring a Static TCP/IP Address

Option	Description
IP address	A logical 32-bit address that identifies a TCP/IP host. Each network adapter card in a computer running TCP/IP requires a unique IP address. Each address has two parts: a network ID, which identifies all hosts on the same physical network, and a host ID, which identifies a host on the network. For the unique IP address 192.168.1.108, for example, the network ID is 192.168.1, and the host ID is 108.
Subnet mask	A network in a multiple-network environment that uses IP addresses derived from a single network ID. Subnets divide a large network into multiple physical networks connected with routers. A subnet mask blocks out part of the IP address so that TCP/IP can distinguish the network ID from the host ID. When TCP/IP hosts try to communicate, the subnet mask determines whether the destination host is on a local or remote network. To communicate on a network, computers must have the same subnet mask.
Default gateway	The intermediate device on a local network that stores network IDs of other networks in the enterprise or Internet. To communicate with a host on another network, configure an IP address for the default gateway. TCP/IP sends packets for remote networks to the default gateway (if no other route is configured), which forwards the packets to other gateways until the packet is delivered to a gateway connected to the specified destination.

▶ **Follow these steps to configure TCP/IP to use a static IP address:**

1. Right-click My Network Places, and then click Properties.

2. In the Network And Dial-Up Connections window, right-click Local Area Connection, and then click Properties.

3. In the Local Area Connection Properties dialog box, click Internet Protocol (TCP/IP), verify that the check box to its left is selected, and then click Properties.

4. In the Internet Protocol (TCP/IP) Properties dialog box, on the General tab, click Use The Following IP Address, type the TCP/IP configuration parameters, and then click OK.

5. Click OK to close the Local Area Connection Properties dialog box, and then close the Network And Dial-Up Connections window.

Caution IP communications can fail if duplicate IP addresses exist on a network. Therefore, you should always check with the network administrator to obtain a valid static IP address.

Configuring TCP/IP to Obtain an IP Address Automatically

If a server running the DHCP Service is available on the network, it can automatically assign TCP/IP configuration information to the DHCP client, as shown in Figure 5.3. You can then configure any clients running Windows 2000, Windows 95, and Windows 98 to obtain TCP/IP configuration information automatically from the DHCP Service. Using DHCP to configure TCP/IP automatically on client computers simplifies administration and ensures correct configuration information.

Note Windows 2000 Professional doesn't include the DHCP Service. Only the Windows 2000 Server products provide the DHCP Service.

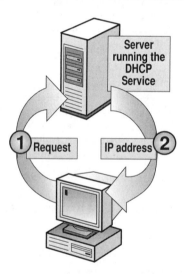

Figure 5.3 A server running the DHCP Service assigns TCP/IP addresses

Note Windows 2000 Professional also includes an Automatic Private IP Addressing feature that provides DHCP clients with limited network functionality if a DHCP server is unavailable during startup.

You can use the DHCP Service to provide clients with TCP/IP configuration information automatically. However, you must configure a computer as a DHCP client before it can interact with the DHCP Service.

▶   **Follow these steps to configure a DHCP client:**

1. Right-click My Network Places, and then click Properties.

2. In the Network And Dial-Up Connections window, right-click Local Area Connection, and then click Properties.

3. In the Local Area Connection Properties dialog box, click Internet Protocol (TCP/IP), verify that the check box to its left is selected, and then click Properties.

4. In the Internet Protocol (TCP/IP) Properties dialog box, on the General tab, click Obtain An IP Address Automatically.

5. Click OK to close the Local Area Connection Properties dialog box, and then close the Network And Dial-Up Connections window.

Using Automatic Private IP Addressing

The Windows 2000 implementation of TCP/IP supports a new mechanism for automatic address assignment of IP addresses for simple LAN-based network configurations. This addressing mechanism is an extension of dynamic IP address assignment for LAN adapters. It enables configuration of IP addresses without using static IP address assignment or installing the DHCP Service.

For the Automatic Private IP Addressing feature to function properly on a computer running Windows 2000, you must configure a network LAN adapter for TCP/IP and click Obtain An IP Address Automatically in the Internet Protocol (TCP/IP) Properties dialog box.

The process that causes Windows 2000 to utilize the Automatic Private IP Addressing feature, as shown in Figure 5.4, is explained in the following steps:

1. Windows 2000 TCP/IP attempts to find a DHCP server on the attached network to obtain a dynamically assigned IP address.

2. In the absence of a DHCP server during startup—for example, the server is down for maintenance or repairs—the client cannot obtain an IP address.

3. Automatic Private IP Addressing generates an IP address in the form of 169.254.$x.y$ (where $x.y$ is the client's unique identifier) and a subnet mask of 255.255.0.0.

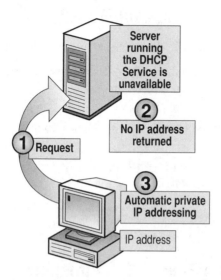

Figure 5.4 The Automatic Private IP Addressing feature

Note The Internet Assigned Numbers Authority (IANA) has reserved 169.254.0.0 to 169.254.255.255 for Automatic Private IP Addressing. As a result, Automatic Private IP Addressing provides addresses that are guaranteed not to conflict with routable addresses.

After the computer generates the address, it broadcasts to this address and then assigns the address to itself, if no other computer responds. The computer continues to use this address until it detects and receives configuration information from a DHCP server. This allows two computers that are plugged into a LAN hub to restart without any IP address configuration and to use TCP/IP for local network access.

Note Windows 98 also supports Automatic Private IP Addressing.

Automatic Private IP Addressing can assign a TCP/IP address to DHCP clients automatically. However, Automatic Private IP Addressing doesn't generate all the information that typically is provided by the DHCP service, such as the address of a default gateway.

Consequently, computers enabled with Automatic Private IP Addressing can communicate only with computers on the same subnet that also have addresses of the form 169.254.*x*.*y*.

Disabling Automatic Private IP Addressing

By default, the Automatic Private IP Addressing feature is enabled. However, you can disable this feature by adding the IPAutoconfigurationEnabled value to the HKEY_LOCAL_MACHINE\SYSTEM\CurrentControlSet\Services\ Tcpip\Parameters\Interfaces\Adapter subkey of the registry and setting its value to 0.

Note This subkey includes the globally unique identifier (GUID) for the computer's LAN adapter.

The IPAutoconfigurationEnabled entry uses a REG_DWORD data type. A value of 0 disables Automatic Private IP Addressing, and the default value of 1 enables Automatic Private IP Addressing.

Using TCP/IP Utilities

Windows 2000 includes several utilities that you can use to troubleshoot TCP/IP and test connectivity, which are illustrated in Figure 5.5.

Utilities for troubleshooting TCP/IP

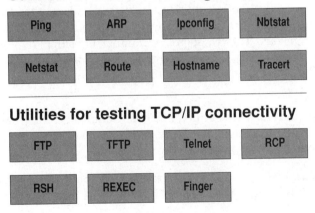

Utilities for testing TCP/IP connectivity

Figure 5.5 TCP/IP utilities included with Windows 2000

Troubleshooting TCP/IP

Table 5.5 describes the Windows 2000 utilities that you can use to trouble-shoot TCP/IP.

Table 5.5 Utilities Used to Troubleshoot TCP/IP

Option	Description
Ping	Verifies configurations and tests connections
ARP	Displays locally resolved IP addresses as physical addresses
Ipconfig	Displays the current TCP/IP configuration
Nbtstat	Displays statistics and connections using NetBIOS over TCP/IP
Netstat	Displays TCP/IP protocol statistics and connections
Route	Displays or modifies the local routing table
Hostname	Returns the local computer's host name for authentication by the Remote Copy Protocol (RCP), remote shell (RSH), and remote execution (REXEC) utilities
Tracert	Checks the route to a remote system

These troubleshooting utilities are all executed from the Command Prompt window. For information on how to use all of these commands, except Hostname and Tracert, open the Command Prompt window, type the command followed by /? and then press Enter. For example, for information on the Ping command, open the Command Prompt window, type **Ping** /? and then press Enter.

To use the Hostname utility, open the Command Prompt window, type **Hostname** and then press Enter. Hostname will return the name of the local computer.

For information on how to use the Tracert command, open a Command Prompt window, type **Tracert** and then press Enter.

Testing TCP/IP Connectivity

Windows 2000 also provides utilities for testing TCP/IP connectivity. Table 5.6 describes these utilities.

Table 5.6 Utilities Used to Test TCP/IP Connectivity

Option	Description
FTP	Provides bidirectional file transfer between a computer running Windows 2000 and any TCP/IP host running FTP. Windows 2000 Server can serve as an FTP client or server.
Trivial File Transfer Protocol (TFTP)	Provides bidirectional file transfer between a computer running Windows 2000 and a TCP/IP host running TFTP.
Telnet	Provides terminal emulation to a TCP/IP host running Telnet. Windows 2000 Server can serve as a Telnet client.
Remote Copy Protocol (RCP)	Copies files between a client and a host that support RCP, such as a computer running Windows 2000 and a UNIX host.
Remote shell (RSH)	Runs commands on a UNIX host.
Remote execution (REXEC)	Runs a process on a remote computer.
Finger	Retrieves system information from a remote computer that supports TCP/IP and the finger utility.

Testing a TCP/IP Configuration

After configuring TCP/IP and restarting the computer, you should use the ipconfig and ping command-prompt utilities to test the configuration and connections to other TCP/IP hosts and networks. Such testing helps to ensure that TCP/IP is functioning properly.

Using Ipconfig

You use the ipconfig utility to verify the TCP/IP configuration parameters on a host. This helps to determine whether the configuration is initialized, or whether a duplicate IP address exists. Use the ipconfig command with the /all switch to verify configuration information.

Tip Type **ipconfig /all | more** to prevent the ipconfig output from scrolling off the screen; to scroll down and view additional output, press the Spacebar.

The result of using the ipconfig /all command is as follows:

- If a configuration has initialized, the ipconfig utility displays the IP address and subnet mask. If it is assigned, the ipconfig utility displays the default gateway.

- If a duplicate IP address exists, the ipconfig utility indicates that the IP address is configured; however, the subnet mask is 0.0.0.0.

- If the computer is unable to obtain an IP address from a server running the DHCP Service on the network, the ipconfig utility displays the IP address as the address provided by Automatic Private IP Addressing.

Using Ping

After you have verified the TCP/IP configuration, use the ping utility to test connectivity. The *ping utility* is a diagnostic tool that you can use to test TCP/IP configurations and diagnose connection failures. Use the ping utility to determine whether a particular TCP/IP host is available and functional. To test connectivity, use the Ping command with the following syntax:

```
ping IP_address
```

Using Ipconfig and Ping

Figure 5.6 illustrates the steps for verifying a computer's configuration and for testing router connections.

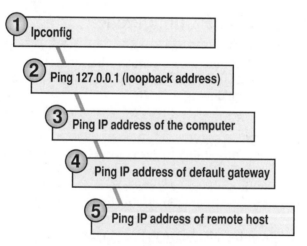

Figure 5.6 Using ipconfig and ping

The following are the steps illustrated in Figure 5.6:

1. Use the ipconfig command to verify that the TCP/IP configuration has been initialized.

2. Use the ping command with the loopback address (ping 127.0.0.1) to verify that TCP/IP is correctly installed and bound to your network adapter card.

3. Use the ping command with the IP address of the computer to verify that your computer is not a duplicate of another IP address on the network.

4. Use the ping command with the IP address of the default gateway to verify that the default gateway is operational and that your computer can communicate with the local network.

5. Use the ping command with the IP address of a remote host to verify that the computer can communicate through a router.

Note Typically, if you ping the remote host (step 5) and the ping command is successfully executed, steps 1 through 4, if ran, would also be successful by default. If the ping command isn't successfully executed, ping the IP address of another remote host before completing the entire diagnostic process because the current host might be turned off.

By default, the following message appears four times in response to a successfully executed ping command:

```
Reply from IP_address
```

Practice: Installing and Configuring TCP/IP

In this practice, you use two TCP/IP utilities to verify your computer's configuration. You then configure your computer to use a static IP address and verify your computer's new configuration. Next you configure your computer to use a DHCP server to automatically assign an IP address to your computer, whether or not a DHCP server is available on your network. Finally you test the Automatic Private IP Addressing feature in Windows 2000 by disabling the DHCP server, if one exists on your network.

To complete this practice, you will need

- TCP/IP as the only installed protocol
- A server running the DHCP Service to provide IP addresses (optional)

If you are working on a computer that isn't part of a network and a server isn't running the DHCP service, you won't be able to do certain procedures in this practice.

In the following table, record the IP address, subnet mask, and default gateway that your network administrator provides for you to use during this practice. Also, ask your network administrator whether you can use another computer to test your computer's connectivity, and record the IP address of that computer as well. If you are not on a network, you can use the suggested values.

Variable value	Suggested value	Your value
Static IP address	192.168.1.201	
Subnet mask	255.255.255.0	
Default gateway (if required)	None	
Computer to test connectivity	N/A	

Exercise 1: Verifying a Computer's TCP/IP Configuration

In this exercise, you use two TCP/IP utilities, ipconfig and ping, to verify your computer's configuration.

Note To do the exercises in this practice, you use the Command Prompt and Network Connections windows frequently. For the sake of efficiency, open the windows once and then minimize and restore them as necessary.

1. Open the Command Prompt window.

2. At the command prompt, type **ipconfig /all | more** and then press Enter.

    The Windows 2000 IP Configuration utility displays the TCP/IP configuration of the physical and logical adapters configured on your computer.

3. Press Spacebar as necessary to display the heading Local Area Connection. Use the information displayed in this section to complete as much of the following table as possible. Press Spacebar to display additional information, as necessary, and to return to the command prompt.

Setting	Value
Host name	
Description	
Physical address	
DHCP enabled	
Autoconfiguration enabled	
IP address	
Subnet mask	
Default gateway	
DNS servers	

4. Press Spacebar as necessary to scroll through the configuration information and return to the command prompt.

5. To verify that the IP address is working and configured for your adapter, type **ping 127.0.0.1** and then press Enter.

   A response similar to the following indicates a successful ping:

   ```
   Pinging 127.0.0.1 with 32 bytes of data:
   Reply from 127.0.0.1: bytes=32 time<10ms TTL=128
   Reply from 127.0.0.1: bytes=32 time<10ms TTL=128
   Reply from 127.0.0.1: bytes=32 time<10ms TTL=128
   Reply from 127.0.0.1: bytes=32 time<10ms TTL=128
   Ping statistics for 127.0.0.1:
       Packets: Sent = 4, Received = 4, Lost = 0 <0% loss>,
   Approximate round trip times in milliseconds:
       Minimum = 0ms, Maximum = 0ms, Average = 0ms
   ```

6. Minimize the Command Prompt window.

Exercise 2: Configuring TCP/IP to Use a Static IP Address

In this exercise, you configure TCP/IP to use a static IP address.

▶ **To configure TCP/IP to use a static IP address**

1. Right-click My Network Places, and then click Properties.

   The Network And Dial-Up Connections window appears.

2. Right-click Local Area Connection, and then click Properties.

   The Local Area Connection Properties dialog box appears, displaying the network adapter in use and the network components used in this connection.

3. Click Internet Protocol (TCP/IP), and then verify that the check box to the left of the entry is selected.

4. Click Properties.

   The Internet Protocol (TCP/IP) Properties dialog box appears.

5. Click Use The Following IP Address.

6. In the IP Address box, the Subnet Mask box, and the Default Gateway box (if required), type the values that you typed in the table before you started Exercise 1, or the suggested values listed in that table.

   Important Be careful when manually entering IP configuration settings, especially numeric addresses. The most frequent cause of TCP/IP connection problems is incorrectly entered IP address information.
   ---

7. Click OK.

   You are returned to the Local Area Connection Properties dialog box.

8. Click OK to close the Local Area Connection Properties dialog box.

9. Minimize the Network And Dial-Up Connections window.

▶ **To test the static TCP/IP configuration**

1. Restore the Command Prompt.

2. At the command prompt, type **ipconfig /all | more** and then press Enter.

   The Windows 2000 IP Configuration utility displays the physical and logical adapters configured on your computer.

3. Press Spacebar as needed to scroll through the configuration information and locate the local area connection information.

4. Record the current TCP/IP configuration settings for your local area connection in the following table.

Setting	Value
IP address	
Subnet mask	
Default gateway	

5. Press Spacebar as necessary to scroll through the configuration information and return to the command prompt.

6. To verify that the IP address is working and configured for your adapter, type **ping 127.0.0.1** and then press Enter.

   What happens?

7. If you have a computer that you are using to test connectivity, type **ping** *ip_address* (where *ip_address* is the IP address of the computer you are using to test connectivity), and then press Enter. If you don't have a computer to test connectivity, skip this step and proceed to step 8.

   What happens?

8. Minimize the command prompt.

Exercise 3: Configuring TCP/IP to Automatically Obtain an IP Address

In this exercise, you configure TCP/IP to automatically obtain an IP address. Then you test the configuration to verify that the DHCP Service has provided the appropriate IP addressing information. Be sure to perform the first part of this exercise even if you have no DHCP Service server because you will also use these settings in Exercise 4.

▶ **To configure TCP/IP to automatically obtain an IP address**

1. Restore the Network And Dial-Up Connections window, right-click Local Area Connection, and then click Properties.

   The Local Area Connection dialog box appears.

2. Click Internet Protocol (TCP/IP), and then verify that the check box to the left of the entry is selected.

3. Click Properties.

   The Internet Protocol (TCP/IP) Properties dialog box appears.

4. Click Obtain An IP Address Automatically.

Which IP address settings will the DHCP Service configure for your computer?

5. Click OK to close the Internet Protocol (TCP/IP) Properties dialog box.

6. Click OK to close the Local Area Connection Properties dialog box.

7. Minimize the Network And Dial-Up Connections window.

▶ **To test the TCP/IP configuration**

Note If a server running the DHCP Service isn't available to provide an IP address, skip this procedure and proceed to Exercise 4.

1. Restore the command prompt, type **ipconfig /release** and then press Enter.

2. At the command prompt, type **ipconfig /renew** and then press Enter.

3. At the command prompt, type **ipconfig | more** and then press Enter.

4. Pressing Spacebar as necessary, record the current TCP/IP configuration settings for your local area connection in the following table.

Setting	Value
IP address	
Subnet mask	
Default gateway	

5. To test that TCP/IP is working and bound to your adapter, type **ping 127.0.0.1** and then press Enter.

The internal loopback test displays four replies if TCP/IP is bound to the adapter.

Exercise 4: Obtaining an IP Address
by using Automatic Private IP Addressing

For this exercise, if you have a server running the DHCP Service, you must disable it on that server so that a DHCP server will not be available to provide an IP address for your computer. Without a DHCP server available to provide an IP address, the Windows 2000 Automatic Private IP Addressing feature provides unique IP addresses for your computer. If the DHCP Service can't be disabled, simply disconnect your network adapter cable.

▶ **To obtain an IP address by using Automatic Private IP Addressing**

1. At the command prompt, type **ipconfig /release** and then press Enter.

2. At the command prompt, type **ipconfig /renew** and then press Enter.

   There will be a pause while Windows 2000 attempts to locate a DHCP server on the network.

   What message appears, and what does it indicate?

▶ **To test the TCP/IP configuration**

1. At the command prompt, type **ipconfig | more** and then press Enter.

2. Pressing Spacebar as necessary, record the current TCP/IP settings for your local area connection in the following table.

Setting	Value
IP address	
Subnet mask	
Default gateway	

   Is this the same IP address that was assigned to your computer in Exercise 3? Why or why not?

3. Press Spacebar to finish scrolling through the configuration information, as necessary.

4. To verify that TCP/IP is working and bound to your adapter, type **ping 127.0.0.1** and then press Enter.

   The internal loopback test displays four replies if TCP/IP is bound to the adapter.

5. If you have a computer to test TCP/IP connectivity with your computer, type **ping *ip_address*** (where *ip_address* is the IP address of the computer that you are using to test connectivity), and then press Enter. If you don't have a computer to test connectivity, skip this step and proceed to Exercise 5.

   Were you successful? Why or why not?

Exercise 5: Obtaining an IP Address by using DHCP

In this exercise, you enable the DHCP Service running on the computer that is acting as a DHCP server (or you reconnect your network cable if you disconnected it in Exercise 4). Your computer will obtain IP addressing information from the DHCP server.

Note If a server running the DHCP Service isn't available to provide an IP address, skip this exercise.

---

1. At the command prompt, type **ipconfig /release** and then press Enter.

2. At the command prompt, type **ipconfig /renew** and then press Enter.

   After a short wait, a message indicates the adapter's local area connection.

3. At the command prompt, type **ipconfig /all | more** and then press Enter.

4. Verify that the DHCP server has assigned an IP address to your computer.

5. Close the Command Prompt window.

Lesson Summary

In this lesson, you learned that TCP/IP enables enterprise networking and connectivity on computers running Windows 2000. It provides a robust, scalable, cross-platform client/server framework that is supported by most large networks, including the Internet. You learned that the TCP/IP suite of protocols maps to a four-layer conceptual model: network interface, Internet, transport, and application.

By default, client computers running Windows 2000 obtain TCP/IP configuration information automatically from the DHCP Service. However, even in a DHCP-enabled environment, some computers, such as the computer running the DHCP Service, require a static IP address. For each network adapter card that uses TCP/IP in a computer, you can configure an IP address, a subnet mask, and a default gateway.

You also learned that Windows 2000 includes utilities that you can use to troubleshoot TCP/IP and test connectivity. Ping and ipconfig are two common troubleshooting utilities, and FTP and telnet are two connectivity utilities.

Finally, in this lesson you learned that the Windows 2000 implementation of TCP/IP supports automatic private IP addressing. Automatic private IP addressing is a new mechanism for automatic address assignment of IP addresses for simple LAN-based network configurations. It is an extension of dynamic IP address assignment for LAN adapters and enables configuration of IP addresses without using static IP address assignments or installing the DHCP Service. By default, the Automatic Private IP Addressing feature is enabled. However, you can disable this feature by adding IPAutoconfigurationEnabled to the registry.

Lesson 2: Configuring Inbound Connections

In Windows 2000 Professional, all of the processes for creating network connections are consolidated in the Network Connection wizard. An inbound connection is one type of network connection that you can create using the Network Connection wizard.

After this lesson, you will be able to

- Configure inbound connections in Windows 2000
- Configure remote access to allow incoming virtual private network (VPN) connections

Estimated lesson time: 20 minutes

Allowing Inbound Dial-up Connections

To configure and administer inbound connections on a computer running Windows 2000 Professional, you use the Network Connection wizard.

1. To access the Network Connection wizard, click Start.
2. Point to Settings, click Network Connections.
3. Double-click Make New Connection.

   The Welcome to the Network Connection wizard appears.
4. Click Next to continue, and the Network Connection Type page appears.
5. Select Accept Incoming Connections (see Figure 5.7).

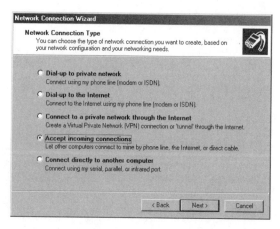

Figure 5.7 The Network Connection Type page

Configuring Devices for Incoming Connections

Once you have selected Accept Incoming Connections, click Next. The Devices For Incoming Connections page appears, so you can choose one of the available devices on your computer to accept incoming calls. If the device you select is configurable, click the Properties button to configure it. For example, if you have selected a modem, possible options to configure include port speed, compression, and the type of flow control (see Figure 5.8). The Advanced tab contains additional configurable options that might include the number of data bits, parity, and number of stop bits.

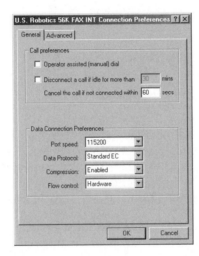

Figure 5.8 Configuring a device for inbound connections

Allowing Virtual Private Connections

When you have finished configuring the device, click OK to close the Properties dialog box and then click Next on the Devices For Incoming Connection page. The Incoming Virtual Private Connection page appears. Select the appropriate check box either to allow or not allow virtual private connections, and then click Next.

Specifying Users and Callback Options

You must specify which users can access this inbound connection on the Allowed Users page, as shown in Figure 5.9.

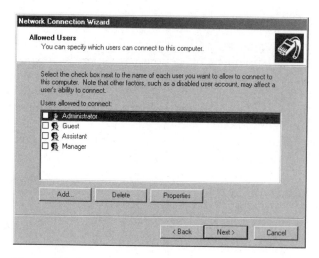

Figure 5.9 Specifying the users who can access this inbound connection

After you select a user, click Properties and click the Callback tab to set the callback options. You can select Do Not Allow Callback, Allow The Caller To Set The Callback Number, or Always Use The Following Callback Number. Enabling callback causes the remote server, in this case your computer, to disconnect from the client calling in, and then to call the client computer back.

By using callback, you can have the bill for the telephone call charged to your telephone number rather than to the telephone number of the user who called in. You can also use callback to increase security. If you specify the callback number, you don't have to worry about someone trying to break in. Even if an unauthorized user calls in, the system calls back at the number you specified, not the number of the unauthorized user.

Selecting Networking Components

After you specify the callback options you can select the appropriate network components.

Click Next, and the Networking Components page appears. You can choose the networking components you want to enable for incoming connections. You can also install additional networking components by clicking Install.

▶ **For example, follow these steps to install NWLink IPX/SPX/NetBIOS
  Compatible Transport Protocol:**

1. Click Install.

2. Select Protocol.

3. Click Add.

4. On the Select Network Protocol page, select NWLink IPX/SPX/
   NetBIOS Compatible Transport Protocol.

5. Insert the Windows 2000 Professional CD-ROM in the CD-ROM drive,

6. Click OK.

   Windows 2000 installs the protocol.

After the protocol is installed, you are returned to the Networking Components page. When you click Next, you are prompted to type a name for the
connection. You should then click Finish. If you would like a shortcut to
appear on your desktop, select the Add A Shortcut To My Desktop check box.
Click Finish to create the connection.

Practice: Configuring an Inbound Connection

In this practice, you configure an inbound connection.

Exercise 1: Configure an Inbound Connection

1. Log on as Administrator with a password of *password*.

2. On the Start menu, point to Settings, and click Network And Dial-Up
   Connections.

   The Network And Dial-Up Connections window appears.

3. Double-click Make New Connection.

4. The Network Connection wizard appears. Click Next.

   The Network Connection Type page appears.

5. Select Accept Incoming Connections, and then click Next.

   The Devices For Incoming Connections page appears.

6. Select the modem device option for your computer in the Connection
   Devices list, and then click Next.

   The Incoming Virtual Private Connection page appears.

7. Select Allow Virtual Private Connections, and then click Next.

   The Allowed Users page appears.

8. Select Administrator, and then click Properties.

   The Administrator Properties dialog box appears.

9. Click the Callback tab.

10. Review the Callback tab's options, leave the default Do Not Allow Callback option selected, and then click OK.

11. Click Next.

   The Networking Components page appears.

12. Review the available networking components, click Internet Protocol TCP/IP, and then click Properties.

   The Incoming TCP/IP Properties dialog box appears.

13. Select Specify TCP/IP addresses.

14. In the From box, type **192.168.1.201**, and in the To box, type **192.168.1.205**. Click OK.

Note If your computer is on a network and there is a valid address that you can use to test your inbound connection, use a range of IP addresses that includes that address.

---

15. Click Next.

16. Click Finish to accept the default Incoming Connections in The Connection Will Be Named box.

Lesson Summary

In this lesson, you learned that you configure inbound connections in Windows 2000 Professional by using the Network Connection wizard. You can choose which of the available devices on your computer to have accept incoming calls. If these devices are configurable, you can click the Properties button to configure them. You must also specify which user accounts can use inbound connections. For each user account, you can specify whether to allow callback and, if allowed, whether you or the caller should specify the callback number.

Lesson 3: Configuring Outbound Connections

You can configure all outbound connections in Windows 2000 with the Network Connection wizard. Much of the work of configuring protocols and services is automated when you use this tool. Understanding the options available in the wizard will help you to configure connections efficiently.

There are three basic types of outbound connections:

- Dial-up connections
- Connections to a VPN
- Direct connections to another computer through a cable

After this lesson, you will be able to

- Configure outbound connections to a private network
- Configure outbound connections to an Internet service provider
- Configure outbound connections to a virtual private network
- Configure outbound connections directly to another computer

Estimated lesson time: 25 minutes

Dial-Up Connections

Dial-up connections are outbound dial-up connections to either private networks or to Internet service providers (ISPs). To create and configure an outbound dial-up connection, use the Network Connection wizard. On the Network Connection Type page, select Dial-Up To Private Network to create a connection to a private network, or select Dial-Up To The Internet to create a connection to an ISP.

The Dial-Up To A Private Network Option

If you select the Dial-Up To A Private Network option and click Next, you are prompted to type the telephone number of the computer or network to which you want to connect; this can be an ISP for an Internet connection or the modems for your private network. Enter the telephone number, click Next, and you are prompted to specify who can use this connection. If you want this connection to be made available to all users of this computer, click For All Users, and then click Next. If you want to reserve the connection for yourself, click Only For Myself. When you click Next, you will be prompted to type a name for the connection. If you would like a shortcut to appear on your desktop, select the Add A Shortcut To My Desktop check box. Click Finish to create the connection.

The Dial-Up To The Internet Option

If you have selected the Dial-Up To The Internet option and then you click Next, the Welcome To The Internet Connection Wizard starts (see Figure 5.10). The wizard presents the following three options:

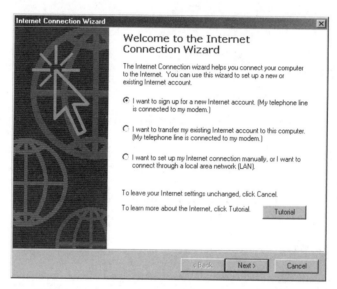

Figure 5.10 The Welcome To The Internet Connection Wizard page

- **I Want To Sign Up For A New Internet Account.** If you select this option, the wizard presents a three-step procedure for choosing an ISP, specifying your address and billing information, and setting up your e-mail account.

- **I Want To Transfer My Existing Internet Account To This Computer.** If you already have an account with an ISP and have obtained all the necessary connection information, you can select this option to connect to your account using your telephone line. If you select this option and click Next, you are prompted to enter the telephone number you dial to connect to your ISP or the modem for your private network. To complete the wizard, you are prompted for the user name and password that you use to log on to your ISP, and you will be prompted to type a name for the dial-up connection.

- **I Want To Set Up My Internet Account Manually, Or I Want To Connect Through A Local Area Network (LAN).** If you select this option, you have a choice of specifying that you connect to the Internet through a telephone line and modem or through a LAN. You are then prompted for a proxy server and other settings.

Note To configure Internet connection sharing, ensure that Enable Internet Connection Sharing For This Connection is selected on the Sharing tab of the connection's properties dialog box.

Connections to a VPN

A VPN is a network that is created by using tunneling protocols such as PPTP or L2TP to create secure connections across an untrusted network. To create a new VPN connection, you also use the Network Connection wizard. On the Network Connection Type page, click Connect To A Private Network Through The Internet, click Next, and then do one of the following:

- If you need to establish a connection with your ISP or some other network before connecting to the VPN, click Automatically Dial This Initial Connection, select a connection on the list, and then click Next.

- If you don't want to automatically establish an initial connection, click Do Not Dial The Initial Connection, and then click Next.

You are then prompted to type the host name or IP address of the computer or network to which you are connecting. Type in the name or address and then click Next. If you want this connection to be made available to all users of this computer, click For All Users, and then click Next. If you want to reserve the connection for yourself, click Only For Myself. When you click Next, you will be prompted to type a name for the connection. Type in the name and then click Finish. If you would like a shortcut to appear on your desktop, select the Add A Shortcut To My Desktop check box. Click Finish to create the connection.

Direct Connections to Another Computer Through a Cable

You can also use the Network Connection wizard to create a direct cable connection to another computer. On the Network Connection Type page, click Connect Directly To Another Computer, click Next, and then do one of the following:

- If your computer will be the host for the connection, click Host, and then click Next.

- If your computer will be the guest for the connection, click Guest, and then click Next.

After specifying Host or Guest, you select the port that is connected to the other computer and then click Next. You must specify which users can access this connection and then click Next. You will be prompted to type a name for the connection. If you would like a shortcut to appear on your desktop, select the Add A Shortcut To My Desktop check box. Click Finish to create the connection.

Practice: Configuring an Outbound Connection

In this practice, you configure an outbound connection.

Exercise 1: Configure an Outbound Connection

1. Log on as Administrator with a password of *password*.

2. On the Start menu, point to Settings, and click Network And Dial-Up Connections.

   The Network And Dial-Up Connections window appears.

3. Double-click Make New Connection.

   The Network Connection wizard appears.

4. Click Next.

5. On the Network Connection Type page, select Connect To A Private Network Through The Internet, and then click Next.

6. On the Public Network page, select Do Not Dial The Initial Connection, and then click Next.

7. On the Destination Address page, type **192.168.1.202** and then click Next.

Note If your computer is on a network and there is a valid address that you can use to test your outbound connection, use that address instead of 192.168.1.202.

8. On the Connection Availability page, select Only For Myself, and click Next.

9. Click Finish.

   The Connect Virtual Private Connection dialog box appears.

10. Ensure that the user name is set to Administrator, and type **password** for the password.

Note If your computer is on a network and you entered a valid address in step 7, enter a valid user name and password in step 10.

11. Click Connect.

Note If your computer is a standalone computer, this operation will fail. If your computer is on a network and you entered a valid address to a computer accepting virtual private connections in step 7 and a valid user name and password in step 10, a message will be displayed stating that Virtual Private Connection is now connected.

12. If your connection failed, click Cancel. If you connected successfully to another computer, double-click the connection icon in the system tray, click Disconnect, and then click Yes.

    The Network And Dial-Up Connections window is again visible. Notice the Virtual Private Connection icon for the outbound connection you just created.

13. Close all windows and log off.

Lesson Summary

In this lesson, you learned that you can configure all outbound connections in Windows 2000 using the Network Connection wizard. Using the Network Connection wizard automates much of the work of configuring protocols and services. Understanding the options found in the wizard helps you to configure the three basic types of outbound connections efficiently. The three types of outbound connections are dial-up connections, connections to a VPN, and direct connections to another computer through a cable.

Review

The following questions will help you determine whether you have learned enough to move on to the next chapter. If you have difficulty answering these questions, please go back and review the material in this chapter before beginning the next chapter. See Appendix A, "Questions and Answers," for the answers to these questions.

1. Your computer running Windows 2000 Client for Microsoft Networks was configured manually for TCP/IP. You can connect to any host on your own subnet, but you can't connect to or even ping any host on a remote subnet. What is the likely cause of the problem and how would you fix it?

2. While you're using the Network Connection wizard, you must configure two new settings regarding sharing the connection. Describe the difference between these two settings.

3. What is callback and when might you want to enable it?

C H A P T E R   6

Monitoring and Optimizing System Performance

About This Chapter

While most systems perform quite well in their default configuration, in some cases changes to the basic configuration result in a more efficient system. Since every situation is unique, you need to know what type of changes you should make to increase efficiency. You do this by monitoring system performance before and after you make changes.

Windows 2000 Professional provides you with a variety of tools that can be used to monitor and optimize system performance. These include:

- **Task Scheduler.** Allows you to schedule routine maintenance when the system is not being fully utilized.

- **Backup wizard.** Allows you to easily back up data on a regular basis.

- **Offline Folders and Files.** Help users keep their data synchronized.

- **Signed Drivers.** Make sure that the correct drivers used are used for a specific system configuration.

- **Control Sets.** Assist in recovering from inappropriate changes to the system configuration.

- **Recovery Console.** Allows you to recover your system if a failure occurs.

This chapter discusses these features and explains how they can be used to optimize your system.

Before You Begin

To complete this chapter, you must have

- A computer that meets the minimum hardware requirements listed in "Hardware Requirements" in "About This Book"

- A blank, high-density floppy disk, which you will use to create a Windows 2000 Professional boot disk

- Microsoft Windows 2000 Professional software installed on the computer

Lesson 1: Using Task Scheduler

Task Scheduler is used to schedule programs and batch files to run once, at regular intervals, or at specific times. You can also use Task Scheduler to schedule any script, program, or document to start at a specified time and interval or when certain operating system events occur. You can use Task Scheduler to automate many administrative tasks.

After this lesson, you will be able to

- Use Task Scheduler to schedule tasks

Estimated lesson time: 25 minutes

Introduction to Task Scheduler

Windows 2000 saves scheduled tasks in the Scheduled Tasks folder, which is in Control Panel in My Computer. You can also access Scheduled Tasks on another computer by browsing that computer's resources using My Network Places. This allows you to move tasks from one computer to another. For example, you can create task files for maintenance and then add them to a user's computer as needed.

Task Scheduler may be used to accomplish the following:

- Run maintenance utilities at specific intervals
- Run programs when less demand exists for computer resources

Options

To schedule a task, you use the Scheduled Task wizard. You access the wizard in the Scheduled Tasks folder by double-clicking Add Scheduled Task. Table 6.1 describes the options that you can configure using the Scheduled Task wizard.

Table 6.1 Scheduled Task Wizard Options

Option	Description
Application	A list of the applications that are to be scheduled. Select the applications to schedule from a list of applications that are registered with Windows 2000, or click Browse to specify any program or batch file.
Task Name	A descriptive name for the task.

continues

Table 6.1 Scheduled Task Wizard Options *(continued)*

Option	Description
Frequency	The number of times Windows 2000 will perform the task. You can choose to have the task performed daily, weekly, monthly, one time only, when the computer starts, or when you log on.
Time And Date	The start time and start date for the task to occur. If applicable, you can enter the days on which to repeat the task.
Name And Password	A user name and password. You can enter your user name and password or another user name and password to have the application run under the security settings for that user account. If the user account that you used to log on doesn't have the rights that are required by the scheduled task, you can use another user account that does have the required rights. For example, you can run a scheduled backup by using a user account that has the required rights to back up data but doesn't have other administrative privileges.
Advanced Properties	A check box that you can select if you want the wizard to display the Advanced Properties dialog box so that you can configure additional properties after you click Finish.

Advanced Properties

There are several other options for tasks in addition to the options that are available in the Scheduled Task wizard. You can change options that you set with the Scheduled Task wizard or set additional advanced options by configuring advanced properties for the task.

Table 6.2 describes the tabs in the Advanced Properties dialog box for the scheduled task.

Table 6.2 Scheduled Task Wizard Advanced Options

Tab	Description
Task	Changes the scheduled task or the user account that is used to run the task. You can also turn the task on and off.
Schedule	Sets and displays multiple schedules for the same task. You can set the date, time, and number of repeat occurrences for the task. For example, you can set up a task to run every Friday at 10:00 P.M.

Tab	Description
Settings	Set options that affect when a task starts or stops, such as how long a backup can take, whether the computer can be in use, or whether the computer can be running on batteries when it runs the task.
Security	Changes the list of users and groups that have permission to perform the task, or changes the permissions for a specific user or group.

Practice: Using Task Scheduler

In this practice, you schedule Word Pad to start at a predetermined time. You can use this as a reminder to review address information. You also configure Task Scheduler options.

Exercise 1: Scheduling a Task

▶ **To schedule a task to start automatically**

1. Double-click My Computer, double-click Control Panel, and then double-click Scheduled Tasks.

   Windows 2000 opens the Scheduled Tasks window. Because no tasks are currently scheduled, only the Add Scheduled Task icon appears.

2. Double-click Add Scheduled Task.

   The Scheduled Task wizard appears.

3. Click Next.

   Windows 2000 displays a list of currently installed programs. To schedule a program that isn't registered with Windows 2000, you click the Browse button to locate the program.

4. Click Browse.

   The Select Program To Schedule dialog box appears.

5. Double-click Program Files, and then double-click Windows NT.

6. Double-click Accessories, and then double-click WordPad.

7. In the Name box, type **Launch WordPad** as shown in Figure 6.1.

   The Name box allows you to enter a description that is more intuitive than the program name. Windows 2000 displays this name in the Scheduled Tasks folder when you finish using the wizard.

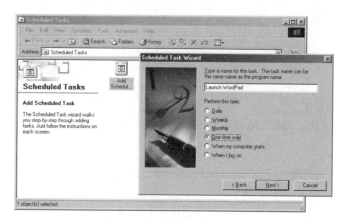

Figure 6.1 Using the Scheduled Task wizard

8. Click One Time Only, and then click Next.

9. In the Start Time box, set the time to 4 minutes after the current system time and make a note of this time.

   To confirm the current system time, look at the taskbar. Don't change the entry in the Start Date box.

10. Click Next.

    The wizard requires that you enter the name and password of a user account. When Task Scheduler runs the scheduled task, the program receives all of the rights and permissions of the user account that you enter here. The program is also bound by any restrictions on the user account. Notice that your user name, Pro1\Administrator, is already filled in as the default. (If your computer name isn't Pro1, Pro1 will be replaced by your computer's name.) You must type the correct password for the user account in both password boxes before you can continue.

    You will schedule the console to run with your administrative privileges.

11. In both the Enter The Password box and the Confirm Password box, type **password**.

12. Click Next.

    Don't select the check box to open the Advanced Properties dialog box for this task. You will review these properties in the next procedure.

13. Click Finish.

Notice that the wizard added the task to the list of scheduled tasks.

14. To confirm that you scheduled the task successfully, wait for the time that you configured in step 9. WordPad starts.

15. Close WordPad.

▶ **To configure advanced Task Scheduler options**

1. In the Scheduled Tasks window, double-click Launch WordPad.

Windows 2000 displays the Launch WordPad dialog box. Review the options on the tabs. These are the same options that are available if you select the check box for setting advanced options on the last page of the Scheduled Task wizard. Don't change any of the settings.

2. Click the Settings tab.

Review the options that are available on the Settings tab.

3. Select the Delete The Task If It Is Not Scheduled To Run Again check box.

4. Click the Schedule tab, and then set the start time for 2 minutes after the current system time.

Make a note of this time.

5. Click OK.

To confirm that you scheduled the task successfully, wait for the amount of time that you set in step 4 of this procedure. WordPad will start.

6. Close WordPad.

Notice that the scheduled event is no longer in the Scheduled Tasks folder. The option to automatically delete a task after it finishes is useful for cleaning up after tasks that need to run only once.

7. Close the Scheduled Tasks window.

8. Log off Windows 2000.

Lesson Summary

In this lesson, you learned that you can use Task Scheduler to schedule programs and batch files to run once, at regular intervals, at specific times, or when certain operating system events occur. Windows 2000 saves scheduled tasks in the Scheduled Tasks folder, which is in Control Panel in My Computer. Once you have scheduled a task to run, you can modify any of the options or advanced features for the task, including the program to be run.

You also learned that you can access Scheduled Tasks on another computer by browsing that computer's resources using My Network Places. This allows you to move tasks from one computer to another. For example, you can create task files for maintenance and then add them to a user's computer as needed. In the practice portion of this lesson, you used the Scheduled Task wizard to schedule WordPad to launch at a specified time.

Lesson 2: Backing Up Data

Backing up data is probably one of the most important tasks you can perform. You never know when some disaster may occur that will cause a hard disk to fail, potentially losing important data. However, backing up data manually can be a tiresome and boring task.

Windows 2000 provides the Backup wizard to automate the task of backing up data. You can even use Task Scheduler to automate the process so you don't even have to be present.

After this lesson, you will be able to

- Identify the user rights and permissions that are necessary to back up and restore data

- Identify the different backup types

- Back up data at a computer and over the network

- Schedule a backup job

- Set backup options for the Backup wizard

- Restore data, whether an entire volume or a single file

- Configure and use offline folders and files

Estimated lesson time: 40 minutes

Windows 2000 contains the Windows 2000 Backup And Recovery Tools, which are shown in Figure 6.2. These tools includes the Backup wizard, a tool that allows you to easily back up and restore data.

You can use Backup to back up data manually or to schedule unattended backup jobs regularly. You can back up data to a file or to a tape. Files can be stored on hard disks, removable disks (such as Iomega Zip and Jaz drives), and recordable compact discs and optical drives.

To launch Backup, on the Start menu, point to Programs, point to Accessories, point to System Tools, and then click Backup. Or, on the Start menu, click Run, type **ntbackup** and then click OK.

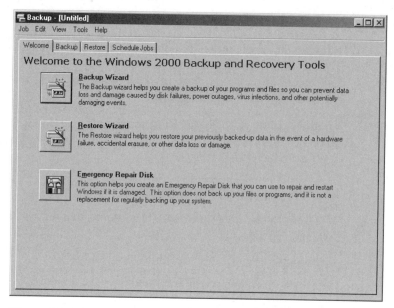

Figure 6.2 The Windows 2000 Backup And Recovery Tools

To successfully back up and restore data on a computer running Windows 2000 Professional, you must have the appropriate permissions and user rights, as described in the following list:

- All users can back up their own files and folders. They can also back up files for which they have the Read, Read & Execute, Modify, or Full Control permission.

- All users can restore files and folders for which they have the Write, Modify, or Full Control permission.

- Members of the Administrators and Backup Operators groups can back up and restore all files (regardless of the assigned permissions). By default, members of these groups have the Backup Files and Directories, and the Restore Files and Directories user rights.

Backup Types

There are a variety of ways you can use the Backup wizard, depending on your needs. For example you may want to backup all the files on a daily basis or you may want to back up just the files that have changed since the last backup. The Backup wizard lets you select from five different types of backup operations (see Figure 6.3).

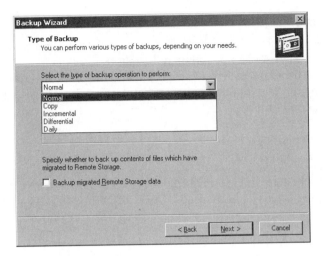

Figure 6.3 Selecting the backup type

Some backup types use backup *markers,* also known as archive attributes, which mark files as having changed. When a file changes, an attribute is set on the file that indicates that the file has changed since the last backup. When you back up the file, this clears or resets the attribute.

Normal

During a *normal* backup, all selected files and folders are backed up. A normal backup doesn't rely on markers to determine which files to back up. During a normal backup, any existing marks are cleared and each file is marked as having been backed up. Normal backups speed up the restore process because all of the backup files are marked as the most current and you don't need to restore multiple backup jobs with different dates to get all the data restored.

Copy

During a *copy* backup, all selected files and folders are backed up. The Backup wizard neither looks for nor clears markers. Because other backup methods use the markers to determine which files should be backed up, use a copy backup if you don't want to clear markers and affect the other backup methods. For example, use a copy backup between a normal and an incremental backup to create an archival snapshot of network data.

Incremental

During an *incremental* backup, only selected files and folders that have a marker are backed up, and then the markers are cleared. Because an incremental backup clears markers, if incremental backups were performed in a row on a file and nothing changed in the file, the file would not be backed up the second time.

Differential

During a *differential* backup, only selected files and folders that have markers are backed up, but the backup doesn't clear markers. Because a differential backup doesn't clear markers, if two differential backups were performed in a row on a file and nothing changed in the file, the entire file would be backed up each time.

Daily

During a *daily* backup, all selected files and folders that have changed during the day are backed up. The Backup wizard neither looks for nor clears markers. If you want to back up all files and folders that change during the day, use a daily backup.

Combining Backup Methods

An effective backup strategy will likely use a combination of different backup methods. Some backup methods require more time to back up data but less time to restore data. Conversely, other backup methods require less time to back up data but more time to restore data. If you combine backup methods, markers are critical. Incremental and differential backup methods check for and rely on the markers.

The following are some examples of ways to combine backup methods:

- **Normal and differential backups.** On Monday a normal backup is performed, and on Tuesday through Friday differential backups are performed. Differential backups don't clear markers, which means that each backup includes all changes made since Monday. If data becomes corrupt on Friday, you need to restore only the normal backup from Monday and the differential backup from Thursday. This strategy takes more time for backup but less time to restore.

- **Normal and incremental backups.** On Monday a normal backup is performed, and on Tuesday through Friday incremental backups are performed. Incremental backups clear markers, which means that each backup includes only the files that have changed since the previous backup. If data becomes corrupt on Friday, you must restore the normal backup from Monday and all incremental backups from Tuesday through Friday. This strategy takes less time for backup but more time to restore.

- **Normal, differential, and copy backups.** This strategy is the same as the first example that used normal and incremental backups, except that on Wednesday, you perform a copy backup. Copy backups include all selected files and do not clear markers or interrupt the usual backup schedule. Therefore, each differential backup includes all changes made since Monday. The copy backup done on Wednesday is not part of the Friday restore. Copy backups are helpful when you need to create a snapshot of your data.

Performing Preliminary Tasks

An important part of each backup job is performing the necessary preliminary tasks. One task that you must do is ensure that the files that you want to back up are closed. You should notify users to close files before you begin backing up data. The Backup wizard doesn't back up files that are locked open by applications. You can use e-mail or the Send Console Message dialog box in the Computer Management snap-in to send administrative messages to users.

▶ **Follow these steps to send a console message:**

1. On the Start menu, point to Programs, point to Administrative tools, and click Computer Management.

2. On the Action menu, click All Tasks, and then click Send Console Message.

   The Send Console Message dialog box appears. See Figure 6.4.

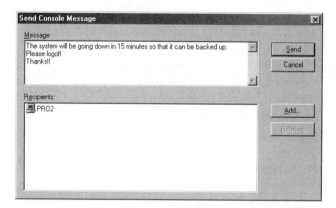

Figure 6.4 The Send Console Message dialog box

3. Type the desired message in the Message box. Note the recipients in the Recipients box. You can add or remove recipients.

4. Click Send to send the message to the listed recipients.

If you use a removable media device, make sure that the following preliminary issues are addressed:

- The backup device is attached to a computer on the network and is turned on. If you are backing up to tape, you must attach the tape device to the computer on which you run the Backup wizard.

- The media device is listed on the Windows 2000 Hardware Compatibility List (HCL).

- The media is loaded in the media device. For example, if you are using a tape drive, ensure that a tape is loaded in the tape drive.

Selecting Files and Folders to Back Up

After you have completed the preliminary tasks, you can perform the backup. Use the Backup Wizard button shown in Figure 6.5 to start the Backup wizard. To start the Backup wizard, click Start, point to Accessories, point to System Tools, click Backup, and then click Backup Wizard; or you can use the Run command on the Start menu to run Ntbackup, and then click Backup Wizard. Click Next to close the Welcome tab and display the What To Back Up page.

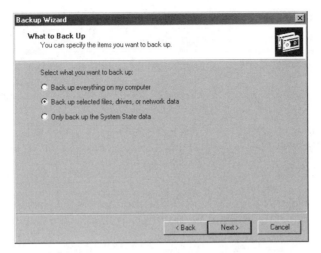

Figure 6.5 The What To Back Up page of the Backup wizard

The first phase of backup is to specify what to back up by choosing one of the following options:

- **Back Up Everything On My Computer.** Backs up all files on the computer on which you are running Backup wizard, except those files that Backup wizard excludes by default, such as certain power management files.

- **Back Up Selected Files, Drives, Or Network Data.** Backs up selected files and folders. This includes files and folders on the computer on which you run Backup wizard and any shared file or folder on the network. When you click this option, the Backup wizard provides a hierarchical view of the computer and the network (through My Network Places).

- **Only Back Up The System State Data.** Backs up important system components, such as the Registry and the boot files for the computer on which you are running Backup wizard.

Specifying Backup Destination and Media Settings

After you select what you want to back up, you need to provide information about backup media. Table 6.3 describes the information that you must provide on the Where To Store The Backup page.

Table 6.3 Where To Store The Backup Page Options

Option	Description
Backup Media Type	The target medium to use, such as a tape or file. A file can be located on any disk-based media, including a hard disk, a shared network folder, or a removable disk, such as an Iomega Zip drive.
Backup Media Or File Name	The location where Windows Backup stores the data. For a tape, enter the tape name. For a file, enter the path for the backup file.

After you have provided the media information, the Backup wizard displays the Completing The Backup Wizard page. You may then do either of the following:

- **Start the backup.** If you click Finish, during the backup process the Backup wizard displays status information about the backup job in the Backup Progress dialog box.

- **Specify advanced backup options.** If you click Advanced, the Backup wizard allows you to select the advanced backup settings described in Table 6.4.

Table 6.4 Advanced Backup Settings

Advanced option	Description
Select The Type Of Backup Operation To Perform	Allows you to choose the backup type that is used for this normal, copy, incremental, differential, or daily.
Backup Migrated Remote	Backs up the contents of files that have been migrated to remote storage. Windows 2000 Server automatically moves files that are rarely used to remote storage.
Verify Data After Backup	Confirms that files are correctly backed up. The Backup wizard compares the backup data and the source data to verify that they are the same. *Microsoft recommends that you select this option.*
Use Hardware Compression, If Available	Enables hardware compression for tape devices that support it. If your tape device doesn't support hardware compression, this option is unavailable.

Advanced option	Description
If The Archive Media Already Contains Backups:	
Append This Backup To The Media	Choose Append This Backup To The Media to store multiple backup jobs on a storage device.
Or	
Replace The Data On The Media With This Backup	Choose Replace The Data On The Media With This Backup if you don't need to save previous backup jobs and you want to save only the most recent backup data.
Allow Only The Owner And The Administrator Access To The Backup Data And To Any Backups Appended To This Media	Allows you to restrict who can gain access to the completed backup file or tape. This option is available only if you choose to replace an existing backup on a backup medium, rather than appending to the backup medium. If you back up the registry or Active Directory directory services, click this option to prevent others from getting copies of the backup job.
Backup Label	Allows you to specify a name and description for the backup job. The name and description appear in the backup log. The default is Set Created *date* At *time*. You can change the name and description to a more intuitive name (for example, Sales-normal backup September 14, 2000).
Media Label	Allows you to specify the name of the backup media (for example, the tape name). The default name is Media Created *date* At *time,* where *date* is the current date and *time* is the current time. The first time you back up to a new medium or overwrite an existing backup job, you can specify the name, such as Active Directory backup.
When To Back Up	Allows you to specify Now or Later. If you choose Later, you specify the job name and the start date. You can also set the schedule.

Note When the backup process is complete, you can choose to review the backup report, which is the backup log. A *backup log* is a text file that records backup operations and is stored on the hard disk of the computer on which you are running the Backup wizard.

Specifying Advanced Backup Settings

When you specify advanced backup settings, you are changing the default backup settings for only the current backup job. The advanced settings cover the backup media and characteristics of the backup job.

Depending on whether you chose to back up now or later, Backup wizard provides you with the opportunity to do either of the following:

- If you chose to finish the backup process, the Backup wizard displays the Completing The Backup Wizard settings and then presents the option to finish and immediately start the backup. During the backup, the wizard displays status information about the backup job.

- If you chose to back up later, you are shown additional dialog boxes to schedule the backup process to occur later, as described in the next section.

Scheduling Backup Jobs

Scheduling a backup job means you can have an unattended backup job take place when users aren't at work and files are closed. You can also schedule backup jobs to occur at regular intervals. To make this possible, Windows 2000 integrates the Backup wizard with the Task Scheduler service.

▶   **Follow these steps to schedule a backup:**

1. Click Later on the When To Back Up page of the Backup wizard.

   Task Scheduler presents the Set Account Information dialog box, prompting you for your password. The user account must have the appropriate user rights and permissions to perform backup jobs.

   Note If the Task Scheduler service isn't running or isn't set to start automatically, Windows 2000 displays a dialog box prompting you to start the service. Click OK, and the Set Account Information dialog box appears.

2. Enter your password in the Password box and Confirm Password box, and then click OK.

   The When To Back Up page appears. You must provide a name for the backup job, and by default, the wizard displays the present date and time for the start date.

3. Type the appropriate name in the Job Name box.

4. Click Set Schedule to set a different start date and time. This selection causes Task Scheduler to display the Schedule Job dialog box.

In the Schedule Job dialog box, you can set the date, time, and number of occurrences for the backup job to repeat, such as every Friday at 10:00 P.M. You can also display all of the scheduled tasks for the computer by selecting the Show Multiple Schedules check box. This helps you avoid scheduling multiple tasks on the same computer at the same time.

You can click the Advanced button to schedule how long the backup can last and for how many days, weeks, months, or years you want this schedule to continue.

After you schedule the backup job and the Backup wizard finishes, Windows Backup places the backup job on the calendar on the Schedule Jobs tab in Windows Backup. The backup job automatically starts at the time you specified.

Restoring Data

The first step in restoring data is selecting the data to restore. You can select individual files and folders, an entire backup job, or a backup set. A *backup set* is a collection of files or folders from one volume that you back up during a backup job. If you back up two volumes on a hard disk during a backup job, the job has two backup sets.

▶ **Follow these steps to restore data using the Restore wizard:**

1. In the Restore wizard, expand the media type that contains the data you want to restore. This can be either tape or file media.

2. Expand the appropriate media set until the data you want to restore is visible. You can restore a backup set or specific files and folders.

3. Select the data you want to restore, and then click Next.

The Restore wizard displays the settings for the restore.

4. Do one of the following:

- Finish the restore process. If you choose to finish the restore job, during the restore The Restore wizard requests verification for the source of the restore media and then performs the restore. During the restore, the Restore wizard displays status information about the restore.

- Specify advanced restore options.

Specifying Advanced Restore Settings

The advanced settings in the Restore wizard vary, depending on the type of backup media from which you are restoring, such as a tape device or an Iomega Zip drive. Table 6.5 describes the advanced restore options.

Table 6.5   Advanced Restore Settings

Option	Description
Restore Files To	The target location for the data you are restoring. The choices are:
	Original Location. Replaces corrupted or lost data.
	Alternate Location. Restores an older version of a file or does a practice restore.
	Single Folder. Consolidates the files from a tree structure into a single folder. Use this option if, for example, you want copies of specific files but don't want to restore the hierarchical structure of the files.
	If you select either an alternate location or a single directory, you must provide the path.
When Restoring Files That Already Exist (Click Options on the Tools menu to access these options.)	Use this option to choose whether you want to overwrite existing files. The choices are:-
	Do Not Replace The File On My Disk (Recommended). Prevents accidental overwriting of existing data. (This is the default.)
	Replace The File On Disk Only If It Is Older Than The Backup Copy. Verifies that the most recent copy exists on the computer.
	Always Replace The File On Disk. The Restore wizard doesn't provide a confirmation message if it encounters a duplicate filename during the restore operation.

Option	Description
Select The Special Restore Options You Want To Use (Click the Start Restore button to access these options.)	Use this option to choose whether you want to restore security or special system files. The choices are:
	Restore Security. Applies the original permissions to files you are restoring to a Windows 2000 NTFS volume. Security settings include access permissions, audit entries, and ownership. This option is available only if you have backed up data from an NTFS volume and are restoring to an NTFS volume.
	Restore Removable Storage Database. Restores the configuration database for removable storage devices and the media pool settings. The database is located in *systemroot*\system32\remotestorage.
	Restore Junction Points, Not The Folders And File Data They Reference. Restores junction points on your hard disk as well as the data that the junction points refer to. If you have any mounted drives, and you want to restore the data that mounted drives point to, select this check box. If you don't select this check box, the junction point will be restored but the data your junction point refers to might not be accessible.
	When Restoring Replicated Data Sets, Make The Restored Data As The Primary Data For All Replicas. Restores the data for all replicated data sets.

After you have finished using the Restore wizard, Windows Backup does the following:

- Prompts you to verify your selection of the source media to use to restore data. After the verification, Windows Backup starts the restore process.

- Displays status information about the restore process. As with a backup process, you can choose to view the report (restore log) of the restore. It contains information about the restore, such as the number of files that have been restored and the duration of the restore process.

Lesson Summary

In this lesson, you learned that after you have planned your backup, the next step is to prepare to back up your data. An important part of each backup job is performing certain preliminary tasks. One task is to ensure that the files you want to back up are closed, because Windows Backup doesn't back up files that are locked open by applications. Next you perform the backup.

You also learned that in the Backup wizard, the first phase is to specify what to back up. You can choose from three options: back up everything on the computer; back up selected files, drives, or network data; or back up only the system state data. After you have selected what you want to back up, you must provide the target destination and the backup media or filename. Then you can finish the backup or you can specify any advanced backup options. This lesson concluded with an explanation of using the Restore wizard to restore the backed up files.

Lesson 3: Using Offline Folders and Files

Sharing files and folders on the network is a very efficient way for a group to work. Centralized data can be maintained and everyone who needs to can follow the progress of changes and updates to the data. However, there may be times when the network is unavailable.

When the network is down, or when you are on the road and your portable computer is undocked, offline folders and files allow you to continue working on files that are stored on shared folders on the network. These network files are cached on your local disk so they are available even if the network is not. When the network is back up or when you dock your portable computer, your connection to the network is reestablished. Offline files synchronize the cached files and folders on your local disk with those stored on the network.

After this lesson, you will be able to

- Configure and use offline folders and files

Estimated lesson time: 30 minutes

Configuring Your Computer to Use Offline Folders and Files

Before you can use offline folders and files, you must configure the server or network share and your portable computer. You configure offline folders and files on the Offline Files tab in the Folder Options dialog box, which you can access through the Tools menu in the My Computer window or the Windows Explorer window. You must select the Enable Offline Files and the Synchronize All Offline Files Before Logging Off check boxes to use offline files (see Figure 6.6).

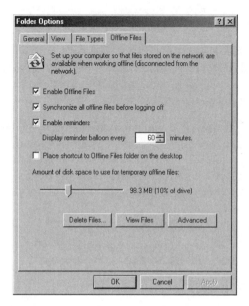

Figure 6.6 The Offline Files tab in the Folder Options dialog box

On the Offline Files tab, you can use the Delete Files button to delete the locally cached copy of a network file. The View Files button shows you the files stored in the Offline Files folder; these are the locally cached files that you have stored on your system. From the Advanced button you can configure how your computer responds when a network connection is lost. For example, when a network connection is lost, you can configure your computer to notify you and allow you to begin working offline.

Practice: Configuring Offline Folders

In this practice, you configure your computer running Windows 2000 Professional just as you would if it were a portable computer running Windows 2000 Professional so you can use offline folders and files.

Exercise 1: Configure Offline Folders and Files

1. Log on as Administrator.

2. Right-click My Computer and then click Open.

3. On the Tools menu, click Folder Options.

   The Folder Options dialog box appears.

4. Click the Offline Files tab.

5. Ensure that the Enable Offline Files and the Synchronize All Offline Files Before Logging Off check boxes are selected, and then click OK.

Note By default, the Enable Offline Files check box and the Synchronize All Offline Files Before Logging Off check box are selected in Windows 2000 Professional, but they aren't selected in Windows 2000 Server.

---

6. Close the My Computer window.

Configuring Your Computer to Provide Offline Folders and Files

Before other users on the network can use offline folders and files on your computer, you must configure the resource to allow caching for offline use. You configure offline folders and files through the Windows Explorer, My Computer, or Internet Explorer window. Figure 6.7 shows the Allow Caching Of Files In This Shared Folder check box in the Caching Settings dialog box.

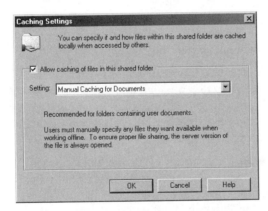

Figure 6.7 The Allow Caching Of Files In This Shared Folder check box

Practice: Configuring Offline Folders

In this practice, you configure a network share on a computer running Windows 2000 Professional so that users can access the files in the share and use them offline.

Exercise 1: Enabling a Network Share

1. Ensure that you are still logged on as Administrator, and start Windows Explorer.

2. Create a folder named C:\Offline.

3. Right-click Offline and then click Sharing.

   The Offline Properties dialog box appears with the Sharing tab active.

4. Click Share This Folder, and then click Caching.

   The Caching Settings dialog box appears.

5. Click the Setting drop-down list arrow.

   Notice that caching has the following three settings:

   - **Manual Caching For Documents.** This is the default setting. Users must manually specify which documents that they want to have available when they are working offline.

   - **Automatic Caching For Documents.** Every file a user opens is automatically downloaded and cached on the user's hard disk so that it will be available offline. If an older version of a file is already loaded on the user's hard disk, it is automatically replaced with a newer version.

   - **Automatic Caching For Programs.** Opened files are automatically downloaded and cached on the user's hard disk so that they will be available offline. If an older version of a file is already loaded on the user's hard disk, it is automatically replaced with a newer version.

6. Ensure that Manual Caching For Documents is selected and then click OK.

7. Click OK to close the Offline Properties dialog box.

   Leave the Windows Explorer window open.

Synchronizing Files

File synchronization is straightforward if the copy of the file on the network doesn't change while you are editing a cached version of the file. Your edits are incorporated into the copy on the network. However, it is possible that another user could edit the network version of the file while you are working offline. If both of your cached offline copies of the file and the network copy of the file are edited, you are given a choice of retaining your edited version and not updating the network copy with your edits, of overwriting your cached version with the version on the network, or of keeping a copy of both versions of the file. In the last case, you must rename your version of the file, and both copies will exist on your hard disk and on the network.

Configuring Synchronization Manager

To configure Synchronization Manager, open Windows Explorer, click the Tools menu, and then click Synchronize. Notice that you can manually synchronize your offline files with those on the network by clicking the Synchronize button. You can also configure Synchronization Manager by clicking the Setup button.

You have three sets of options for configuring synchronization using Synchronization Manager. The first set of options is accessed through the Logon/ Logoff tab (see Figure 6.8). You can configure synchronization to occur when you log on, when you log off, or at both times. You can also specify that you want to be asked before synchronization occurs. You can specify the items to be synchronized at logon, at logoff, or at both times, and you can specify which network connection.

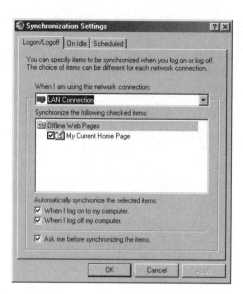

Figure 6.8 The Logon/Logoff tab in the Synchronization Settings dialog box

The second set of options you can use to configure Synchronization Manager is available on the On Idle tab. The configurable items are similar to those that are configurable on the Logon/Logoff tab. The following configurable settings are available on the On Idle tab:

- **When I Am Using This Network Connection.** This option allows you to specify which network connection.

- **Synchronize The Following Checked Items.** This option allows you to specify which items you want to synchronize.

- **Synchronize The Selected Items While My Computer Is Idle.** This option allows you to turn synchronization off or on during idle time.

The Advanced button on the On Idle tab lets you configure the following options: Automatically Synchronize The Specified Items After My Computer Has Been Idle For X minutes; While My Computer Remains Idle, Repeat Synchronization Every X minutes; and Prevent Synchronization When My Computer Is Running On Battery Power.

The third set of options for scheduling synchronization is located on the Scheduled tab. You can click Add to start the Scheduled Synchronization Wizard to do the following: specify the connection; specify the items; decide whether you want the computer to connect automatically; determine whether you are not connected when the scheduled time for synchronization arrives; specify the starting time for the synchronization; specify the frequency of the synchronization, which you can set for every day, every weekday, or every X days; and specify the starting date for the synchronization to begin.

Practice: Configuring Synchronization Manager

In this practice, you configure Synchronization Manager.

Exercise 1: Configure Synchronization Manager

1. Ensure that you are still logged on as Administrator.

   Windows Explorer should be open from the last practice.

2. Click Tools and then click Synchronize.

   The Items To Synchronize dialog box appears. This allows you to specify which folders you want to synchronize.

3. If nothing is selected, click My Current Home Page, and then click Setup.

   The Synchronization Settings dialog box appears with the Logon/Logoff tab selected.

4. Review the options on the Logon/Logoff tab, and then review the options on the On Idle tab and the Scheduled tab.

5. On the Logon/Logoff tab, select My Current Home Page.

6. Ensure that the check boxes When I Log On To My Computer and When I Log Off My Computer are both selected.

7. Select the Ask Me Before Synchronizing The Items check box, and then click OK.

8. Click Close to close the Items To Synchronize dialog box, and then close the Windows Explorer window.

Lesson Summary

Windows 2000 makes it easy to work offline, as you learned in this lesson. Working with offline folders and using Synchronization Manager makes it easy to synchronize different versions of files that are cached on local computers, network servers, or shares. Before you can use offline folders and files, you must configure the server or network share and your portable computer. This lesson also explained how to configure Synchronization Manager and the various sets of options available for synchronizing files.

Lesson 4: Configuring, Monitoring, and Troubleshooting Driver Signing

The source of many system problems can be traced to inappropriate drivers being installed. To reduce the occurrence of such problems, Windows 2000 drivers and operating system files have been digitally signed by Microsoft to ensure their quality. In Device Manager, you can look at the Driver tab to verify that the digital signer of the installed driver is correct. Some applications overwrite existing operating files as part of their installation process. These files can cause system errors that are difficult to troubleshoot. Microsoft has greatly simplified the tracking and troubleshooting of altered files by signing the original operating system files and allowing you to easily verify these signatures.

After this lesson, you will be able to

- Configure driver signing
- Describe the System File Checker (SFC) utility and how to use it to verify and troubleshoot driver signing
- Use the Windows Signature Verification utility (sigverif) to monitor and troubleshoot driver signing

Estimated lesson time: 20 minutes

Configuring Driver Signing

You can configure how the system responds to unsigned files by opening System in Control Panel and clicking the Hardware tab. On the Hardware tab, in the Device Manager box, click Driver Signing to display the Driver Signing Options dialog box (see Figure 6.9).

Figure 6.9 Configuring driver signing

The following three settings are available to configure driver signing:

- **Ignore.** This option allows any files to be installed regardless of their digital signature or the lack thereof.

- **Warn.** This option displays a warning message before allowing the installation of an unsigned file. This is the default option.

- **Block.** This option prevents the installation of unsigned files.

If you are logged on as Administrator or as a member of the Administrators group, you can select Apply Setting As System Default to apply the driver signing configuration you set up to all users who log on to this computer.

Monitoring and Troubleshooting Driver Signing

You can use Device Manager to track the digital signature of files. Windows 2000 also provides System File Checker (SFC), a command-line utility you can use to check the digital signature of files. The syntax of the SFC utility is as follows:

```
Sfc [/scannow] [/scanonce] [/scanboot] [/cancel] [/quiet]
[/enable] [/purgecache] [/cachesize=x]
```

Table 6.6 describes System File Checker's optional parameters.

Table 6.6 SFC's Parameters

Parameter	Description
/scannow	Causes the SFC utility to scan all protected system files immediately
/scanonce	Causes the SFC utility to scan all protected system files at the next system restart
/scanboot	Causes the SFC utility to scan all protected system files every time the system restarts
/cancel	Cancels all pending scans of protected system files
/quiet	Replaces all incorrect system file versions without prompting the user
/enable	Returns Windows File Protection to default operation, prompting the user to restore protected system files when files with incorrect versions are detected
/purgecache	Purges the file cache and scans all protected system files immediately
/cachesize=x	Sets the file cache size

Using the File Signature Verification Utility

Windows 2000 also provides a File Signature Verification utility. To use this utility, click Start, point to Run, type **sigverif** and press Enter. Once the File Signature Verification utility starts, you can click the Advanced button to configure it. The File Signature Verification utility allows you to view the file's name, its location, its modification date, its type, and its version number.

Practice: Using the Windows Signature Verification Utility

In this practice, you use the File Signature Verification utility (sigverif) to monitor and troubleshoot driver signing on your system.

Exercise 1: Using the Signature Verification Utility

1. Click Start, point to Run, type **sigverif** and then press Enter.

   The File Signature Verification dialog box appears.

2. Click Advanced.

   The Advanced File Signature Verification Settings dialog box appears with the Search tab active. Notice that, by default, you are notified if any system files are not signed. Notice also that you can select Look For Other Files That Are Not Digitally Signed. This setting has the File Signature Verification utility verify nonsystem files to see whether they are digitally signed. If you select this option, you can specify the search parameters for the files you want checked.

3. Leave the default setting Notify Me If Any System Files Are Not Signed selected, and then click the Logging tab.

   Notice that, by default, the File Signature Verification utility saves the file signature verification to a log file, named Sigverif.txt.

4. Leave the default settings and click OK to close the Advanced File Signature Verification Settings dialog box.

5. Click Start.

   When the File Signature Verification utility completes its check, a Signature Verification Results window appears if there are files that are not signed. Otherwise you see a message box telling you that your files have been scanned and verified as being digitally signed.

6. If you get a Signature Verification Results window, review the results and then click Close to close the Signature Verification Results window. Otherwise, click OK to close the message box.

7. Click Close to exit the File Signature Verification utility.

Lesson Summary

In this lesson, you learned about the two utilities that verify the digital signatures of system files. One is a command-line utility, System File Checker (SFC). It has a number of optional parameters that let you control how and when it will run. The second utility is a Windows utility, File Signature Verification (sigverif). You practiced monitoring and troubleshooting digital signatures using the sigverif utility.

Lesson 5: Control Sets in the Registry

A *control set* contains configuration data used to control the system, such as a list of which device drivers and services to load and start. Control sets are modified whenever you change the configuration of your computer. However, old versions of the control sets are not deleted. This lesson discusses the Windows 2000 control sets and how they are used with the Last Known Good Process when you have problems restarting your computer due to inappropriate changes in your configuration.

After this lesson, you will be able to

- Explain Windows 2000 control sets

Estimated lesson time: 15 minutes

Windows 2000 Control Sets

Control sets are stored as subkeys of the registry key HKEY_LOCAL_MACHINE\ SYSTEM. The registry might contain several control sets depending on how often you change or have problems with system settings. A typical Windows 2000 installation contains the following control set subkeys: Clone, ControlSet001, ControlSet002, and CurrentControlSet.

The CurrentControlSet subkey is a pointer to one of the ControlSet00x keys. The Clone control set is a clone of the control set used to initialize the computer (either Default or LastKnownGood), and is created by the kernel initialization process each time you start your computer. The Clone control set isn't available after you log on.

To better understand control sets, you should know about the registry subkey HKEY_LOCAL_MACHINE\ SYSTEM\Select. The entries contained in this subkey include Current, Default, Failed, and LastKnownGood.

- **Current.** Identifies which control set is the CurrentControlSet. When you use Control Panel options or Registry Editor to change the registry, you modify information in the CurrentControlSet.

- **Default.** Identifies the control set to use the next time that Windows 2000 starts, unless you select the LastKnownGood control set. Default and Current typically contain the same control set number.

- **Failed.** Identifies the control set that was designated as failed the last time that the computer was started using the LastKnownGood control set.

- **LastKnownGood.** Identifies a copy of the control set that was used the last time that the computer started Windows 2000 successfully. After a successful logon, the Clone control set is copied to the LastKnownGood control set.

Each of these entries in HKEY_LOCAL_MACHINE\SYSTEM\Select takes a REG_DWORD data type, and the value for each entry refers to a specific control set. For example, if the value for the Current entry is set to 0x1, the CurrentControlSet points to ControlSet001. Similarly, if the value for the LastKnownGood entry is set to 0x2, the LastKnownGood control set points to ControlSet002.

The Last Known Good Process

If you change the Windows 2000 configuration to load a driver and have problems rebooting, you can use the last known good process to recover your working configuration. The last known good process uses the LastKnownGood control set, stored in the registry, to boot Windows 2000.

Windows 2000 provides two configurations for starting a computer, Default and LastKnownGood. The upper portion of Figure 6.10 shows the events that occur when you make configuration changes to your system. Any configuration changes (for example, adding or removing drivers) are saved in the Current control set.

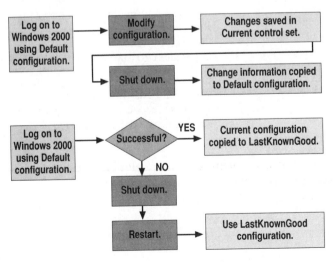

Figure 6.10 Using the Default and LastKnownGood configurations

After you reboot the computer, the kernel copies the information in the Current control set to the Clone control set during the kernel initialization phase. When you successfully log on to Windows 2000, the information in the Clone control set is copied to the LastKnownGood control set, as shown in the lower part of Figure 6.10.

If you experience startup problems that you think might relate to Windows 2000 configuration changes, shut down the computer *without* logging on, and then restart it. When you are prompted to select the operating system to start from a list of the operating systems specified in the Boot.ini file, press F8 to open the Windows 2000 Advanced Options Menu screen. Then select the Last Known Good Configuration option, or after you select Windows 2000 on the Please Select The Operating System To Start screen, you can press Spacebar to open the Hardware Profile/Configuration Recovery Menu screen, and then press L to select Last Known Good Configuration.

The next time you log on, the Current configuration is copied to the Default configuration. If your configuration changes work correctly, the next time you log on, the Current configuration is copied to the Default configuration. If your configuration changes don't work, you can restart and use the Last Known Good Configuration option to log on.

Table 6.7 describes the purposes of the Default and LastKnownGood configuration control sets.

Table 6.7 Default and LastKnownGood Configurations Control Sets

Configuration	Description
Default	Contains information that the system saves when a computer shuts down. To start a computer using the default configuration, select Windows 2000 on the Please Select The Operating System To Start menu that the Boot.ini file presents.
LastKnownGood	Contains information that the system saves after a successful logon. The LastKnownGood control set loads only if the system is recovering from a severe or critical device driver loading error or if it is selected during the boot process.

Table 6.8 lists problems and their solutions provided in the Last Known Good Configuration option.

Table 6.8 Situations for Using the Last Known Good Configuration Option

Problem	Solution
After a new device driver is installed, Windows 2000 restarts, but the system stops responding.	Use the Last Known Good Configuration option to start Windows 2000 because the LastKnownGood control set doesn't contain any reference to the new, and possibly faulty, driver.
You accidentally disable a critical device driver (such as the ScsiPort driver).	Some critical drivers are written to keep users from making the mistake of disabling them. With these drivers, the system automatically reverts to the LastKnownGood control set if a user disables the driver. If the driver doesn't automatically cause the system to revert to the LastKnownGood control set, you must manually select the Last Known Good Configuration option.

Using the LastKnownGood control set does *not* help in the following situations:

- When the problem isn't related to Windows 2000 configuration changes. Such a problem might arise from incorrectly configured user profiles or incorrect file permissions.

- After you log on. The system updates the LastKnownGood control set with Windows 2000 configuration changes after a successful logon.

- When startup failures relate to hardware failures or missing or corrupted files.

Important Starting Windows 2000 using the LastKnownGood control set overwrites any changes made since the last successful boot of Windows 2000.

Lesson Summary

In this lesson, you learned that a control set contains configuration data used to control the system, such as a list of which device drivers and services to load and which to start. Control sets are stored as subkeys of the registry key HKEY_LOCAL_MACHINE\SYSTEM, and a typical Windows 2000 installation contains the following control sets: Clone, ControlSet001, ControlSet002, and CurrentControlSet. The registry might contain several other control sets, depending on how often you have changed or had problems with system settings.

You also learned that if you make incorrect changes to a computer's configuration, you might have problems restarting your computer. If you can't restart your computer because of a configuration change, Windows 2000 provides the Last Known Good Process so that you don't have to reinstall your Windows 2000 software to restart your computer. You can boot your computer using the LastKnownGood control set. The LastKnownGood control set contains the configuration settings from the last successful restart and logon to your computer. After restarting your computer using the LastKnownGood control set, you can reconfigure the computer. The last known good process uses the LastKnownGood control set, which is stored in the registry, to restart Windows 2000.

Lesson 6: Using the Recovery Console

If changes to the system have resulted in the system not operating properly, and you have tried the Last Known Good configuration but still have problems, you may still be able to solve the problem by using the Windows 2000 Recovery Console. The Windows 2000 Recovery Console is a command-line interface you can use to perform a variety of troubleshooting and recovery tasks, including:

- Starting and stopping services

- Reading and writing data on a local drive (including drives that are formatted with the NTFS file system)

- Formatting hard disks

After this lesson, you will be able to

- Install and use the Recovery Console

Estimated lesson time: 20 minutes

Installing and Starting the Recovery Console

To install the Recovery Console, insert the Microsoft Windows 2000 Professional CD-ROM into your CD-ROM drive, and close the Microsoft Windows 2000 CD dialog box, if it opens. Open the Run dialog box or a Command Prompt window in Windows 2000, change to the i386 folder on the Windows 2000 CD-ROM, and then run the winnt32 command with the /cmdcons switch. After you install the Recovery Console, you can access it from the Please Select Operating System To Start menu. You can also use the Windows 2000 Setup disks or the Windows 2000 Professional CD-ROM to start your computer and then select the Recovery Console option, when you are prompted to choose repair options, to access the Recovery Console.

After you start the Recovery Console, you must specify which installation of Windows 2000 you want to log on to (if you have a dual boot or multiple boot configuration), and then you must log on as Administrator.

Using the Windows 2000 Recovery Console

You can also run the Recovery Console from the Windows 2000 installation CD-ROM. The Recovery Console provides you with a limited set of administrative commands that you can use to repair your Windows 2000 installation.

▶ **Follow these steps to start the Recovery Console from a Windows 2000 Professional CD-ROM:**

1. Insert the Windows 2000 Professional CD-ROM into the CD-ROM drive and restart the computer. If your computer or the workstation you want to repair does not have a bootable CD-ROM drive, you will need to insert your Windows 2000 Setup Boot disk into your floppy disk drive, and then insert the additional Windows 2000 Setup disks when you are prompted to do so.

2. When Setup displays the Setup Notification message, read it, and then press Enter to continue.

   Setup displays the Welcome To Setup screen. Notice that, in addition to the initial installation of Windows 2000, you can use Windows 2000 Setup to repair or recover a damaged Windows 2000 installation.

3. Press R to repair a Windows 2000 installation.

   The Windows 2000 Repair Options screen appears. Notice that you can repair a Windows 2000 installation using the Recovery Console or the Emergency Repair Process.

4. Press C to start the Recovery Console.

   If you have more than one installation of Windows 2000 on the computer, you will be prompted to select which installation you want to repair.

5. Type **1** and then press Enter.

   You are prompted to enter the Administrator's password.

6. Type the Administrator password and then press Enter.

   A command prompt appears.

7. Type **Help** and press Enter for a list of the commands available.

8. When you have completed the repair process, type **exit** and press Enter.

   The computer will restart.

Understanding the Recovery Console Commands

There are a number of commands available in the Recovery Console. Table 6.9 describes some of these commands.

Table 6.9 Recovery Console Commands

Command	Description
Chdir (cd)	Displays the name of the current folder or changes the current folder
Chkdsk	Checks a disk and displays a status report
Cls	Clears the screen
Copy	Copies a single file to another location
Delete (del)	Deletes one or more files
Dir	Displays a list of files and subfolders in a folder
Disable	Disables a system service or a device driver
Enable	Starts or enables a system service or a device driver
Exit	Exits the Recovery Console and restarts your computer
Fdisk	Manages partitions on your hard disks
Fixboot	Writes a new partition boot sector onto the system partition
Fixmbr	Repairs the master boot record of the partition boot sector
Format	Formats a disk
Help	Lists the commands that you can use in the Recovery Console
Logon	Logs on to a Windows 2000 installation
Map	Displays the drive letter mappings
Mkdir (md)	Creates a folder
More	Displays a text file
Rmdir (rd)	Deletes a folder
Rename (ren)	Renames a single file
Systemroot	Sets the current folder to the systemroot folder of the system that you are currently logged on to
Type	Displays a text file

Practice: Troubleshooting with the Windows 2000 Recovery Console

In this practice you use the Windows 2000 Recovery Console to troubleshoot a Windows 2000 installation that will not boot. You also install and start the Recovery Console, and you will look at Help to determine the commands available in the Recovery Console. You also use the Listsvc command to view the services and then use the Disable command to disable the Alerter service.

Exercise 1: Troubleshooting a Windows 2000 Installation

In this exercise you troubleshoot a Windows 2000 installation and repair it by using the Recovery Console.

▶ **To create a system boot failure**

1. Rename the file Ntldr as Oldntldr.

2. Restart the computer.

   What error do you receive when attempting to restart the computer?

▶ **To use the Recovery Console to repair the installation**

1. Insert the Windows 2000 installation CD-ROM into the CD-ROM drive and restart the computer.

   Note If your computer is not equipped with a CD-ROM drive that is capable of booting from a CD-ROM, you can insert your Windows 2000 Setup Boot disk into your floppy disk drive for step 3. Insert the other three Windows 2000 Setup disks when you are prompted to do so.

2. When Setup displays the Setup Notification message, read it, and then press Enter to continue.

   Setup displays the Welcome To Setup screen.

3. Press R to repair a Windows 2000 installation.

   The Windows 2000 Repair Options screen appears.

4. Press C to start the Recovery Console.

5. Type **1** and then press Enter.

   You are prompted to enter the Administrator's password.

6. Type **password** and then press Enter.

   A C:\Winnt command prompt appears.

7. Type **cd ..** and press Enter to change to the root folder (C:\). Be sure to include a space between the "cd" and the ".." characters in the command.

8. Type **copy oldntldr ntldr** and press Enter.

9. If there is a disk in your floppy drive, remove it. If your computer is capable of booting from the CD-ROM drive, remove the Windows 2000 Professional CD-ROM from your CD-ROM drive.

10. Type **exit** and press Enter.

   The computer reboots and should start normally.

Exercise 2: Installing the Windows 2000 Recovery Console

In this exercise, you install the Recovery Console.

1. Log on as Administrator.

2. Insert the Windows 2000 Professional CD into the CD-ROM drive.

3. When the Microsoft Windows 2000 CD window appears, close it.

4. In the Run dialog box, type **<cd_drive>:\i386\winnt32 /cmdcons** (where *<cd_drive>* represents the letter assigned to your CD-ROM drive), and then click OK.

   The Windows 2000 Setup message box appears.

5. Click Yes to install the Windows 2000 Recovery Console.

   Windows 2000 Setup installs the Windows 2000 Recovery Console to your hard disk.

6. Click OK to close the Microsoft Windows 2000 Professional Setup dialog box.

Exercise 3: Using the Windows 2000 Recovery Console

In this exercise you use the Help command to view the available commands. You then use the available Listsvc and Disable commands.

1. Restart your computer.

2. Select Microsoft Windows 2000 Command Console from the boot loader menu.

   The Windows 2000 Recovery Console starts up and prompts you to select which Windows 2000 installation you would like to log on to. If you had more than one Windows 2000 installation on this computer, they would be listed here.

3. Type **1** and then press Enter.

4. Type **password** when prompted for the Administrator password, and then press Enter.

5. Type **help** and then press Enter to see the list of available commands.

   Notice the Listsvc command. You can use this command to view all available services.

6. Type **listsvc** and press Enter, and then scroll through the list of available services.

7. Press Esc to stop.

8. Type **disable /?** and then press Enter.

   The Disable command allows you to disable a Windows system service or driver.

9. Type **disable alerter** and then press Enter.

   Recovery Console displays several lines of text describing how the registry entry for the Alerter service has been modified. The Alerter service is now disabled.

10. Type **exit** and then press Enter to restart your computer.

Exercise 4: Restarting the Alerter service

In this exercise you confirm that the Alerter service is disabled and then restart it.

1. Log on as Administrator.

2. Open the Computer Management window, expand Services And Applications, and then click Services.

   Notice that the Startup Type value for the Alerter service is Disabled.

3. Double-click Alerter, change the Startup Type option to Automatic, and then click OK.

4. Right-click Alerter, and then click Start.

5. Close the Computer Management window.

Lesson Summary

The Windows 2000 Recovery Console is a command-line interface that you can use to perform a variety of troubleshooting and recovery tasks, including starting and stopping services, reading and writing data on a local drive, and formatting hard disks.

You install the Recovery Console by starting a command prompt, changing to the i386 folder on the Windows 2000 CD-ROM, and running the winnt32 command with the /cmdcons switch. After you install the Recovery Console, you can access it from the Startup menu or by using the Windows 2000 Setup disks or the Windows 2000 CD to start your computer, and then selecting the Recovery Console option when you are prompted to choose repair options.

Review

The following questions will help you determine whether you have learned enough to move on to the next chapter. If you have difficulty answering these questions, please go back and review the material in this chapter before beginning the next chapter. See Appendix A, "Questions and Answers," for the answers to these questions.

1. What benefits do you gain by Microsoft digitally signing all system files?

2. What are three tools/utilities Microsoft has provided to help you make sure the files on your system have the correct digital signature?

3. You need to schedule a maintenance utility to automatically run once a week on your computer, which is running Windows 2000 Professional. How do you accomplish this?

4. You need to create a custom console for an administrator who needs to use only the Computer Management and Active Directory Manager snap-ins. The administrator

   a. Must not be able to add any additional snap-ins.

   b. Needs full access to all snap-ins.

   c. Must be able to navigate between snap-ins.

   Which console mode would you use to configure the custom console?

5. A user calls the help desk in a panic. She spent 15 hours editing a proposal as an offline file at her house. Over the weekend, her boss came into the office and spent about 4 hours editing the same proposal. She needs to synchronize the files, but she doesn't want to lose her edits or those made by her boss. What can she do?

6. You install a new device driver for a SCSI adapter in your computer. When you restart the computer, however, Windows 2000 stops responding after the kernel load phase. How can you get Windows 2000 to restart successfully?

C H A P T E R   7

Managing Security

About This Chapter

There are several methods you can use to enhance security when using Microsoft Windows 2000 Professional. You can either set policies for individuals or set policies for groups. The latter is a more efficient method when dealing with a large number of users.

Windows 2000 includes tools that allow you to encrypt and decrypt folders and files. There are additional functions (such as restricting how the computer can be shut down and displaying the user name in the logon screen) that help make the system more secure.

These tools, along with an appropriate auditing policy, can greatly enhance the security of your system. This chapter explains these various features and tools and allows you to implement them on your system.

Before You Begin

To complete this chapter, you must have

- A computer that meets the minimum hardware requirements listed in "Hardware Requirements" in "About This Book"

- Microsoft Windows 2000 Professional installed on the computer (PRO1)

Lesson 1: Implementing Local Groups

A local group is a collection of user accounts on a computer. You can use local groups to assign permissions to resources residing on the computer on which the local group is created. Windows 2000 creates local groups in the local security database. In this lesson, you learn what groups are and how you can use them to simplify user account administration.

After this lesson, you will be able to

- Describe the key features of groups
- Describe local groups
- Create and delete local groups
- Add members to local groups
- Remove members from local groups

Estimated lesson time: 30 minutes

Understanding Groups

A *group* is a collection of user accounts. Administration is simplified when you assign permissions and rights to a group of users rather than to each individual user account (see Figure 7.1).

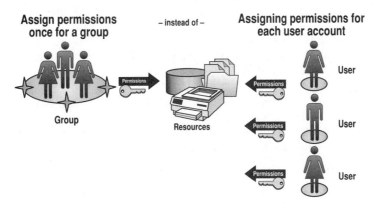

- Groups are a collection of user accounts.
- Members receive permissions given to groups.
- Users can be members of multiple groups.
- Groups can be members of other groups.

Figure 7.1 Simplified administration using groups

Permissions control what users can do with a resource, such as a folder, file, or printer. When you assign permissions, you give users the capability to gain access to a resource, and you define the type of access they have. For example, if several users need to read the same file, you would add their user accounts to a group. You would then give the group permission to read the file. Rights allow users to perform system tasks such as changing the time on a computer, backing up or restoring files, or logging on locally.

Users can be members of multiple groups. A group contains a list of members with references to the actual individual user account.

Preparing to Use Local Groups

The following are guidelines for using local groups:

- Use local groups on computers that don't belong to a domain.

  You can use local groups only on the computer on which you create the local groups. Although local groups are available on member servers and domain computers running Windows 2000 Professional, don't use local groups on computers that are part of a domain. Using local groups on domain computers prevents you from centralizing group administration. Local groups don't appear in directory services based on Active Directory technology, and you have to administer local groups separately for each computer.

- Assign permissions to local groups for access only to the resources on the computer on which you create the local groups.

Note You can't create local groups on domain controllers because domain controllers cannot have a security database that is independent of the database in Active Directory directory service.

Membership rules for local groups include the following:

- Local groups can contain local user accounts from the computer on which you create the local groups.

- Local groups can't be a member of any other group.

Creating Local Groups

Use the Computer Management snap-in to create local groups, as shown in Figure 7.2. You create local groups in the Groups folder.

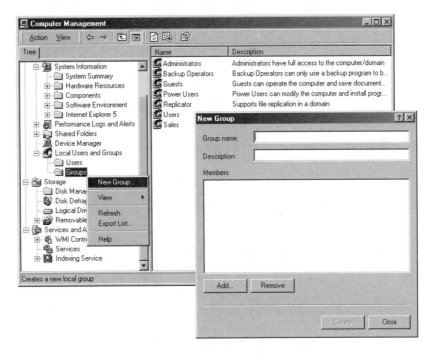

Figure 7.2   The Computer Management snap-in

▶ **Follow these steps to create a local group:**

1. In Computer Management, expand Local Users And Groups and click the Groups folder.

2. Right-click Groups, and then click New Group.

   Table 7.1 describes the options available in the New Group dialog box.

3. Enter the appropriate information and then click Create.

Table 7.1   New Local Group Options

Option	Description
Group Name	A unique name for the local group. This is the only required entry. Use any character except for the backslash (\). The name can contain up to 256 characters; however, very long names might not be displayed completely in some windows.
Description	Describes the group.
Add	Adds a user to the list of members.
Remove	Removes a user from the list of members.
Create	Creates the group.
Close	Closes the New Group dialog box.

You can add members to a local group when you create the group by using the Add button, but you can also add users to a local group after you create it.

Deleting Local Groups

Use the Computer Management snap-in to delete local groups. Each group that you create has a unique identifier. Windows 2000 uses this value to identify the group and the permissions that are assigned to it. When you delete a group, Windows 2000 doesn't use the identifier again, even if you create a new group with the same name as the group that you deleted. Therefore, you cannot restore access to resources by recreating the group.

When you delete a group, you delete only the group and remove the permissions and rights that are associated with it. Deleting a group doesn't delete the user accounts that are members of the group. To delete a group, right-click the group, and then click Delete.

Adding Members to a Group

To add members to a group that has already been created, start the Computer Management snap-in and expand Local Users And Groups. Click Groups, and then in the details pane, right-click the appropriate group and click Properties. In the Properties dialog box, click Add. The Select Users Or Groups dialog box appears, as shown in Figure 7.3.

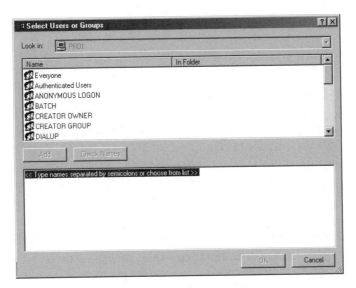

Figure 7.3 The Select Users Or Groups dialog box

In the Look In list, ensure that the computer on which you created the group is selected. In the Name box, select the user account that you want to add to the group, and then click Add.

Note If you want to add multiple user accounts, you can repeat the process of selecting them one at a time and then click Add, or you can hold down the Shift or Ctrl key to select multiple user accounts at once. With the Shift key down you can select a consecutive range of accounts; with the Ctrl key down you can pick some accounts and skip others. Click Add when you have selected all the accounts that you want to add.

Clicking Add lists the accounts you have selected. Review the accounts to make sure that they are the accounts you want to add to the group, and click OK to add the members.

Note You can also add a user account to a group from the Member Of tab in the Properties dialog box for that user account. Use the Member Of tab to quickly add the same user account to multiple groups.

Practice: Creating and Managing Local Groups

In this practice, you create two local groups. You add members to the local groups when you create them and then add another member to one of the groups after the groups have been created. You delete a member from one of the groups, and then you delete one of the local groups that you created.

Note This practice requires user accounts that you created when you complete the practice "Creating Local User Accounts" in Chapter 4, "Managing User Accounts." If you didn't set up the user accounts as described in Chapter 4, go back and do the practice in that chapter to set up the user accounts you will work with in this practice.

Exercise 1: Creating Local Groups and Adding and Removing Members

In this exercise, you create two local groups, Sales and Testing. You add members to both groups when you create them. You add a member to an existing group by adding an additional member to the Testing group, and then you remove a member from the Testing group.

▶ **To create a local group**

1. Log on to your computer as Administrator.

2. Click the Start button, point to Programs, point to Administrative Tools, and then click Computer Management.

3. Expand Local Users And Groups, and then click Groups.

    In the details pane, Computer Management displays a list of current and built-in local groups.

4. To create a new group, right-click Groups, and then click New Group.

    Computer Management displays the New Group dialog box.

5. Type **Sales** in the Group Name box, and type **Access to Customer Files** in the Description box.

6. Click Add.

    The Select Users Or Groups dialog box appears.

7. Hold the Ctrl key down and select User1 and User3.

8. Click Add.

   PRO1\User1 and PRO1\User3 should be listed in the box below the Add button.

   Note If you didn't name your computer PRO1, then PRO1 will be replaced by the name of your computer.

   ---

9. Click OK.

   In the New Group dialog box, notice that User1 and User3 are listed in the Members box.

10. Click Create.

    Windows 2000 creates the group and adds it to the list of users and groups. Note the New Group dialog box is still open and might block your view of the list of users and groups.

11. Repeat steps 5 to 10 to create a group named Testing. Type **Access to Troubleshooting Tips File** in the Description box, and make User2 and User4 members of the Testing group.

12. When you have created both the Sales and the Testing groups, click Close to close the New Group dialog box.

    Notice that the Sales and Testing groups are listed in the details pane.

▶   **To add members to and remove members from a local group**

1. In the details pane of Computer Management, double-click Testing.

   The Testing Properties dialog box displays the properties of the group. Notice that User2 and User4 are listed in the Members box.

2. To add a member to the group, click Add.

   The Select Users Or Groups dialog box appears.

3. In the Name box, select User3, click Add, and then click OK.

   The Testing Properties dialog box displays User2, User3, and User4 listed in the Members box.

4. Select User4 and then click Remove.

   Notice that User4 is no longer listed in the Members box. User4 still exists as a local user account, but it is no longer a member of the Testing group.

5. Click OK.

Exercise 2: Deleting a Local Group

In this exercise, you delete the Testing local group.

1. Right-click Testing in the Computer Management details pane, and then click Delete.

    A Local Users And Groups dialog box appears, asking whether you are sure that you want to delete the group.

2. Click Yes.

    Notice that Testing is no longer listed in the Computer Management window. The members of the group were not deleted. User2 and User3 are still local user accounts on PRO1.

3. Close Computer Management.

Lesson Summary

In this lesson, you learned that a group is a collection of user accounts. Administration is simplified when you assign permissions and rights to a group of users rather than to each individual user account.

You also learned that when naming a group you should make the name intuitive. You use the Computer Management snap-in to create groups, to add members to a group, to remove members from a group, and to delete groups. In the practice portion of this lesson, you created two local groups and added members to the groups as you created the local groups. You then added another member to one of the local groups. You deleted a member from one of the local groups, and then you deleted one of the local groups.

Lesson 2: Implementing Built-In Local Groups

Windows 2000 has two categories of built-in groups: local and system. Built-in groups have a predetermined set of user rights or group membership. Windows 2000 creates these groups for you so you don't have to create groups and assign rights and permissions for commonly used functions.

After this lesson, you will be able to

- Describe the Microsoft Windows 2000 built-in groups

Estimated lesson time: 10 minutes

Built-In Local Groups

All standalone servers, member servers, and computers running Windows 2000 Professional have built-in local groups. *Built-in local groups* give rights to perform system tasks on a single computer, such as backing up and restoring files, changing the system time, and administering system resources. Windows 2000 places the built-in local groups into the Groups folder in Computer Management.

Table 7.2 describes the capabilities that members of the most commonly used built-in local groups have. Except where noted, there are no initial members in these groups.

Table 7.2   Built-In Local Groups

Local group	Description
Administrators	Members can perform all administrative tasks on the computer. By default, the built-in Administrator user account for the computer is a member.
	When a member server or a computer running Client for Microsoft Networks joins a domain, Windows 2000 adds the Domain Admins group to the local Administrators group.
Backup Operators	Members can use Windows Backup to back up and restore the computer.

continues

Table 7.2   Built-In Local Groups *(continued)*

Local group	Description
Guests	Members can perform only tasks for which you have specifically granted rights and can gain access only to resources for which you have assigned permissions; members can't make permanent changes to their desktop environment. By default, the built-in Guest account for the computer is a member.
	When a member server or a computer running Client for Microsoft Networks joins a domain, Windows 2000 adds the Domain Guests group to the local Guests group.
Power Users	Members can create and modify local user accounts on the computer and share resources.
Replicator	Members support file replication in a domain.
Users	Members can perform only tasks for which you have specifically granted rights and can gain access only to resources for which you have assigned permissions. By default, Windows 2000 adds local user accounts that you create on the computer to the Users group. When a member server or a computer running Windows 2000 Professional joins a domain, Windows 2000 adds the Domain Users group to the local Users group.

Built-In System Groups

Built-in system groups exist on all computers running Windows 2000. *System groups* don't have specific memberships that you can modify, but they can represent different users at different times, depending on how a user gains access to a computer or resource. You don't see system groups when you administer groups, but they are available for use when you assign rights and permissions to resources. Windows 2000 bases system group membership on how the computer is accessed, not on who uses the computer. Table 7.3 describes the most commonly used built-in system groups.

Table 7.3   Commonly Used Built-In System Groups

System group	Description
Everyone	Includes all users who access the computer. Be careful if you assign permissions to the Everyone group and enable the Guest account. Windows 2000 authenticates a user who does not have a valid user account as Guest. The user automatically gets all rights and permissions that you have assigned to the Everyone group.
Authenticated Users	Includes all users with valid user accounts on the computer (or if your computer is part of a domain, it includes all users in Active Directory directory services). Use the Authenticated Users group instead of the Everyone group to prevent anonymous access to a resource.
Creator Owner	Includes the user account for the user who created or took ownership of a resource. If a member of the Administrators group creates a resource, the Administrators group is owner of the resource.
Network	Includes any user with a current connection from another computer on the network to a shared resource on the computer.
Interactive	Includes the user account for the user who is logged on at the computer. Members of the Interactive group gain access to resources on the computer at which they are physically located. They log on and gain access to resources by "interacting" with the computer.
Anonymous Logon	Includes any user account that Windows 2000 didn't authenticate.
Dialup	Includes any user who currently has a dial-up connection.

Lesson Summary

In this lesson, you learned that Windows 2000 has two categories of built-in groups: local and system. You also learned that built-in groups have a predetermined set of user rights or group membership. Windows 2000 creates these groups for you so you don't have to create groups and assign rights and permissions for commonly used functions.

Lesson 3: Configuring Account Policies

In Chapter 4, "Managing User Accounts," you learned about assigning user account passwords and how to unlock an account that was locked by the system. In this lesson, you learn how to improve the security of users' passwords and how to control when the system locks out a user account.

After this lesson, you will be able to

- Configure Account Policies

Estimated lesson time: 35 minutes

Configuring Password Policy

Password Policy allows you to improve security on your computer by controlling how passwords are created and managed. You can specify the maximum length of time a password can be used before the user must change it. Changing passwords decreases the chances of an unauthorized person breaking into your computer. If a hacker has discovered a user account and password combination for your computer, forcing users to change their passwords regularly will cause the user account and password combination to fail and lock the hacker out of the system.

Other settings are available in Password Policy that you can use to improve your computer's security. For example, you can specify a minimum password length. The longer the password, the more difficult it is to discover. You can also maintain a history of the passwords used and block users from reusing their most recently used passwords. This prevents a user from having only a few passwords and alternating between them.

You can configure Password Policy on a computer running Windows 2000 Professional by using Group Policy or Local Security Policy.

▶ **Follow these steps to configure Password Policy using Group Policy:**

1. Use the MMC to create a custom console, add the Group Policy snap-in, and save it with the name Group Policy.

2. Expand Local Computer Policy. Then, under Computer Configuration, expand Windows Settings, expand Security Settings, expand Account Policies, and then click on Password Policy.

3. Select the setting you want to configure, and then, on the Action menu, click Security.

The console displays the current Password Policy settings in the details pane, as shown in Figure 7.4.

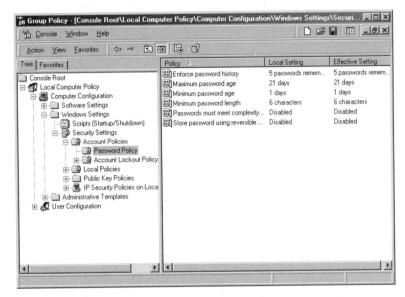

Figure 7.4 Current Password Policy settings using Group Policy

Table 7.4 describes the settings available in Password Policy.

Table 7.4 Password Policy Settings

Setting	Description
Enforce Password History	The value you enter in this setting indicates the number of passwords to be kept in a password history.
	A value of 0 indicates that no password history is being kept. This is the default.
	You can set the value from 0 to 24, indicating the number of passwords to be kept in password history. This value indicates the number of new passwords that a user must access before he or she can reuse an old password.
Maximum Password Age	The value you enter in this setting is the number of days a user can access a password before he or she is required to change it.
	A value of 0 indicates that the password will not expire.
	The default value is 42 days. You can set the range of values from 0 to 999 days.

continues

Table 7.4 Password Policy Settings *(continued)*

Setting	Description
Minimum Password Age	The value you enter in this setting is the number of days a user must keep a password before he or she can change it.
	A value of 0 indicates that the password can be changed immediately. This is the default. If you are enforcing password history, you should not set this value to 0.
	You can set the range of values from 0 to 999 days. This value indicates how long the user must wait before changing his or her password again. Use this value to prevent a user who was forced by the system to change his or her password from immediately changing it back to the old password.
	The minimum password age must be less than the maximum password age.
Minimum Password Length	The value you enter in this setting is the minimum number of characters required in a password. The value can range from 0 up to 14 characters inclusive.
	A value of 0 indicates that no password is required. This is the default value.
Passwords Must Meet Complexity Requirements	The options are Enabled or Disabled.
	The default is Disabled.
	If enabled, all passwords must meet or exceed the specified minimum password length; must comply with the password history settings; must contain capitals, numerals or punctuation; and cannot contain the user's account or full name.
Store Password Using Reversible Encryption For All Users In The Domain	The options are Enabled or Disabled. The default is Disabled. This enables Windows 2000 to store a reversibly encrypted password for all users in the domain—for example to be used with the Challenge Handshake Authentication Protocol (CHAP). This option is only applicable if your computer running Windows 2000 Professional is in a domain.

The Local Security Policy Setting dialog box appears for the selected policy. Figure 7.5 shows the Local Security Policy Setting dialog box for the Maximum Password Age policy.

Figure 7.5 The Local Security Policy Setting dialog box for the Maximum Password Age policy

By carefully planning and configuring your Password Policy options, you can improve the security of your computer by decreasing the chances of an unauthorized user gaining access to it.

Configuring Account Lockout Policy

The Account Lockout Policy settings also allow you to improve the security on your computer. If no account lockout policy is in place, an unauthorized user can repeatedly try to break into your computer. If, however, you have set an account lockout policy, the system will lock out the user account under the conditions you specify in Account Lockout Policy.

You access Account Lockout Policy using either the Group Policy snap-in or the Local Security Settings window, just as you did to configure Password Policy. The Group Policy console displaying the current Account Lockout Policy settings in the details pane is shown in Figure 7.6.

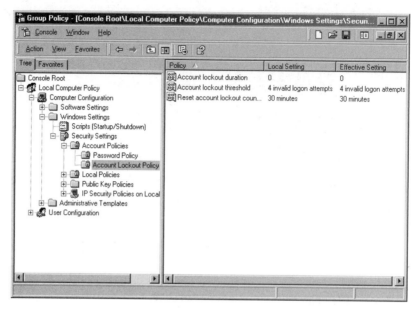

Figure 7.6 Current Account Lockout Policy settings using Group Policy

Table 7.5 explains the settings available in Account Lockout Policy.

Table 7.5 Account Lockout Policy Settings

Setting	Description
Account Lockout Duration	This value indicates the number of minutes that the account is locked out. A value of 0 indicates that the user account is locked out indefinitely until the Administrator unlocks the user account. You can set the value from 0 to 99999 minutes. (The maximum value of 99999 minutes is approximately 69.4 days.)
Account Lockout Threshold	The value you enter in this setting is the number of invalid logon attempts it takes before the user account is locked out from logging on to the computer.
	A value of 0 indicates that the account will not be locked out, no matter how many invalid logon attempts are made.
	You can set the range of values from 0 to 999 attempts.
Reset Account Lockout Counter After	The value you enter in this setting is the number of minutes to wait before resetting the account lockout counter.
	You can set the range of values from 1 to 99999 minutes.

Practice: Configuring Account Policies

In this practice, you configure the account policies for your computer and then test your Account Policy to make sure it is correctly configured.

Exercise 1: Configuring Minimum Password Length

In this exercise, you configure a Password Policy setting, Minimum Password Length, for your computer. You then test the password length you configured to confirm that it was set.

▶ **To configure the Minimum Password Length setting**

1. Log on to your computer as Administrator.

2. Use the MMC to create a custom console containing the Group Policy snap-in.

3. In the Group Policy console, expand Local Group Policy, expand Computer Configuration, expand Windows Settings, expand Security Settings, and then expand Account Policies.

4. Click Password Policy in the console tree.

5. In the details pane, right-click Minimum Password Length and then click Security.

6. Type **6** in the Characters box, and then click OK.

7. Close the Local Security Settings window.

▶ **To test the Minimum Password Length setting**

1. Press Ctrl+Alt+Delete, and in the Windows Security dialog box, click Change Password.

2. In the Old Password box, type **password** and type **water** in the New Password and Confirm Password boxes.

3. Click OK.

    A Change Password message box appears indicating that your new password must be at least six characters long. This means the Minimum Password Length setting in Password Policy is working.

4. Click OK, and then click Cancel.

5. Click Cancel to close the Windows Security dialog box.

Exercise 2: Configuring and Testing Additional Account Policies Settings

In this exercise, you configure and test additional Account Policies settings.

▶   **To configure Account Policies settings**

1. Use the Group Policy snap-in to configure the following Account Policies settings:

    ▪ A user should have at least five different passwords before he or she accesses a previously used password.

    ▪ After changing a password, a user must wait 24 hours before changing it again.

    ▪ A user should change his or her password every three weeks.

    Which settings did you use for each of the three listed items?

2. Close the Group Policy snap-in.

▶   **To test Account Policies settings**

1. Log on as User4 with a password of *User4*.

    Note If you get a Logon Message dialog box indicating that your password will expire in a specified number of days and asking whether you want to change it now, click No.
    ---

2. Change your password to *waters*.

    Were you successful? Why or why not?

3. Change your password to *papers*.

Were you successful? Why or why not?

4. Close all windows and log off.

Exercise 3: Configuring Account Lockout Policy

In this exercise, you configure the Account Lockout Policy settings, and you then test them to make sure they're set up correctly.

▶   **To configure the Account Lockout Policy settings**

1. Log on to your computer as Administrator.

2. Click Start, point to Programs, point to Administrative Tools, and then click Group Policy.

3. In the Group Policy console tree, if necessary, double-click Local Computer Policy, then Computer Configuration, then Windows Settings, then Security Settings, and then Account Policies.

4. Click Account Lockout Policy.

5. Use Account Lockout Policy settings to do the following:

   - Lock out a user account after four failed logon attempts.

   - Lock out user accounts until the administrator unlocks the user account.

   Which Account Lockout Policy settings did you use for each of the two conditions?

6. Log off as Administrator.

▶   **To test the Account Lockout Policy settings**

1. Try to log on as User4 with a password of *papers*. Try this four times.

2. Try to log on as User4 with a password of *papers* for the fifth time.

   A message box appears, indicating that the account is locked out.

3. Click OK and then log on as Administrator.

Lesson Summary

In this lesson, you learned that the Windows 2000 Local Security Settings window allows you to improve the security on your computer by making it more difficult for an unauthorized user to gain access to it. Using the Password Policy settings is one method you can use to improve the security on your computer. Setting Password Policy allows you to manage the passwords used on your computer. For example, Password Policy includes settings that allow you to force users to change their passwords regularly and to control the minimum length of a password.

You also learned about using another method of improving security on your computer: Account Lockout Policy. If no Account Lockout Policy settings are in place, an unauthorized user can repeatedly try to break into your computer. Using Account Lockout Policy, you can determine how many invalid logon attempts must be made before a user account is locked out of the computer. Account Lockout Policy also allows you to determine how long the account will be locked out; you can even set Account Lockout Policy to require that an administrator manually unlock the user account. In the practice portion of the lesson, you set and tested various account settings.

Lesson 4: Increasing Security with EFS

The Microsoft Encrypting File System (EFS) provides encryption for data in NTFS files stored on disk. EFS encryption is public key–based and runs as an integrated-system service, making it easy to manage, difficult to attack, and transparent to the file owner. If a user who attempts to access an encrypted NTFS file has the private key to that file, the file can be decrypted so that the user can open the file and work with it transparently as a normal document. A user without the private key is denied access.

Windows 2000 includes the Cipher command-line utility, which enables you to encrypt and decrypt files and folders from a command prompt. Windows 2000 also provides a recovery agent utility so that if the owner loses the private key, the recovery agent can still recover the encrypted file.

After this lesson, you will be able to

- Encrypt folders and files

Estimated lesson time: 30 minutes

Understanding EFS

EFS allows users to encrypt NTFS files by using a strong public key–based cryptographic scheme that encrypts all files in a folder. Users with roaming profiles can use the same key with trusted remote systems. No administrative effort is needed, and most operations are transparent. Backups and copies of encrypted files are also encrypted if they are in NTFS volumes. Files remain encrypted if you move or rename them, and encryption isn't defeated by temporary files created during editing and left unencrypted in the paging file or in a temporary file.

You can set policies to recover EFS-encrypted data when necessary. The recovery policy is integrated into the overall Windows 2000 security policy. Control of this policy can be delegated to individuals with recovery authority, and different recovery policies can be configured for different parts of the enterprise. Data recovery discloses only the recovered data, not the key that was used to encrypt the file. Several protections are in place to ensure that data recovery is possible and that no data is lost in the event of a total system failure.

EFS is implemented either from Windows Explorer or from the command line. It can be enabled or disabled for a computer, domain, or organizational unit by resetting recovery policy in the Group Policy console in the MMC.

Note To set group policy for the domain or for an organizational unit, your computer must be part of a Windows 2000 domain.

You can use EFS to encrypt and decrypt files on remote file servers but not to encrypt data that is transferred over the network. Windows 2000 provides network protocols, such as Secure Sockets Layer (SSL) authentication, to encrypt data over the network.

Table 7.6 describes the key features provided by Windows 2000 EFS.

Table 7.6   EFS Features

Feature	Description
Transparent encryption	In EFS, file encryption doesn't require the file owner to decrypt and re-encrypt the file on each use. Decryption and encryption happen transparently on file reads and writes to disk.
Strong protection of encryption keys	Public key encryption resists all but the most sophisticated methods of attack. Therefore, in EFS, the file encryption keys that are used to encrypt the file are encrypted by using a public key from the user's certificate. (Note: Windows 2000 uses X.509 v3 certificates.) The list of encrypted file-encryption keys is stored with the encrypted file and is unique to it. To decrypt the file-encryption keys, the file owner supplies a private key, which only the file owner has.
Integral data recovery	If the owner's private key is unavailable, the recovery system agent can open the file using his or her own private key. There can be more than one recovery agent, each with a different public key, but at least one public recovery key must be present on the system to encrypt a file.
Secure temporary and paging files	Many applications create temporary files while you edit a document, and these temporary files can be left unencrypted on the disk. On computers running Windows 2000, EFS is implemented at the folder level, so any temporary copies of an encrypted file are also encrypted, provided that all files are on NTFS volumes. EFS resides in the Windows operating system kernel and uses the nonpaged pool to store file encryption keys, ensuring that they are never copied to the paging file.

Encrypting

The recommended method to encrypt files is to create an NTFS folder and then "encrypt" the folder. To encrypt a folder, in the Properties dialog box for the folder, click the General tab. On the General tab, click the Advanced button, and then select the Encrypt Contents To Secure Data check box. All files placed in the folder will be encrypted. The folder is now marked for encryption. Folders that are marked for encryption aren't actually encrypted; only the files within the folder are encrypted.

Note Compressed files can't be encrypted, and encrypted files can't be compressed.

After you encrypt the folder, when you save a file in that folder, the file is encrypted by using *file encryption keys,* which are fast symmetric keys designed for bulk encryption. The file is encrypted in blocks, with a different file encryption key assigned to each block. All of the file encryption keys are stored and encrypted in the Data Decryption Field (DDF) and the Data Recovery Field (DRF) in the file header.

Note By default, encryption provided by EFS is standard 56-bit encryption. For additional security, North American users can obtain 128-bit encryption by ordering the Enhanced CryptoPAK from Microsoft. Files encrypted by the CryptoPAK cannot be decrypted, accessed, or recovered on a system that supports only 56-bit encryption.

You use a file that you encrypted just as you would use any other file. Encryption is transparent. You don't need to decrypt a file you encrypted before you can use it. When you open an encrypted file, your private key is applied to the DDF to unlock the list of file-encryption keys, allowing the file contents to appear in plain text. EFS automatically detects an encrypted file and locates a user certificate and associated private key. You open the file, make changes to it, and save it as you would any other file. However, if someone else tries to open your encrypted file, he or she will be unable to access the file and will receive an "access denied" message.

Note Encrypted files can't be shared.

Decrypting

Decrypting a folder or file refers to clearing the Encrypt Contents To Secure Data check box in a folder's or file's Advanced Attributes dialog box, which you access from the Properties dialog box for the folder or file. Once decrypted, the file remains decrypted until you select the Encrypt Contents To Secure Data check box. The only reason you might want to decrypt a file is if other people needed access to the folder or file; for example, if you want to share the folder or make the file available across the network.

Using the Cipher Command

Windows 2000 also includes command-line utilities for the richer functionality that is required for some administrative operations. The Cipher command-line utility allows you to encrypt and decrypt files and folders from a command prompt.

The following syntax example shows the available options for the Cipher command. Table 7.7 describes these options.

```
cipher [/e | /d] [/s:folder_name] [/a] [/i] [/f] [/q] [/h]
[/k] [file_name [...]]
```

Table 7.7   Cipher Command Options and Descriptions

Option	Description
/e	Encrypts the specified folders. Folders are marked so that files that are added later will be encrypted.
/d	Decrypts the specified folders. Folders are marked so that files that are added later will not be encrypted.
/s	Performs the specified operation on folders in the given folder and all subfolders.
/a	Performs the specified operation on files as well as folders. Encrypted files could be decrypted when modified, if the parent folder is not encrypted. To avoid this, encrypt the file and the parent folder.
/i	Continues performing the specified operation even after errors have occurred. By default, Cipher stops when an error is encountered.
/f	Forces the encryption operation on all specified files, even those that are already encrypted. Files that are already encrypted are skipped by default.
/q	Reports only the most essential information.

Option	Description
/h	Displays files with the hidden or system attributes, which are not shown by default.
/k	Creates a new file encryption key for the user running the Cipher command. Using this option causes the Cipher command to ignore all other options.
file_name	Specifies a pattern, file, or folder.

If you run the Cipher command without parameters, it displays the encryption state of the current folder and any files that it contains. You can specify multiple filenames and use wildcards. You must put spaces between multiple parameters.

Using the Recovery Agent

If the owner's private key is unavailable, a person designated as the recovery agent can open the file using his or her own private key, which is applied to the DRF to unlock the list of file-encryption keys. If the recovery agent is on another computer in the network, send the file to the recovery agent. The recovery agent can bring his or her private key to the owner's computer, but it is never a good security practice to copy a private key onto another computer.

Note The default recovery agent is the administrator of the local computer unless the computer is part of a domain. In a domain, the domain administrator is the default recovery agent.

It is a good security practice to rotate recovery agents. However, if the agent designation changes, access to the file is denied. Therefore, Microsoft recommends that you keep recovery certificates and private keys until you have updated all files that are encrypted with them.

The person designated as the recovery agent has a special certificate and associated private key that allow data recovery. To recover an encrypted file, the recovery agent would do the following:

1. Use Backup or another backup tool to restore a user's backup version of the encrypted file or folder to the computer on which his or her file recovery certificate is located.

2. In Windows Explorer, open the Properties dialog box for the file or folder, and on the General tab, click the Advanced button.

3. Clear the Encrypt Contents To Secure Data check box.

4. Make a backup version of the decrypted file or folder and return the backup version to the user.

Practice: Encrypting and Decrypting Files

In this practice, you encrypt a folder and its files.

Exercise 1: Encrypting Files

▶ **To encrypt a file**

1. Ensure you are logged on as Administrator and in Windows Explorer, on the root of drive C, create the folder Secret and in the folder Secret, create the file File1.txt. Then right-click File1 and click Properties.

   Windows 2000 displays the Properties dialog box with the General tab active.

2. Click Advanced.

   The Advance Attributes dialog box appears.

3. Click the Encrypt Contents To Secure Data check box and then click OK.

4. Click OK to close the File1 Properties dialog box.

   An Encryption Warning dialog box informs you that you are about to encrypt a file that isn't in an encrypted folder. The default is to encrypt the folder and file, but you can also choose to encrypt only the file.

5. Click Cancel, and then click Cancel again to close the Owner Properties dialog box.

6. In Windows Explorer, right-click the Secret folder and then click Properties.

7. Click Advanced.

   The Advance Attributes dialog box appears.

8. Click the Encrypt Contents To Secure Data check box and then click OK.

9. Click OK to close the Secret Properties dialog box.

   The Confirm Attribute Changes dialog box informs you that you are about to encrypt a folder. You have two choices: you can encrypt only this folder, or you can encrypt the folder and all subfolders and files in the folder.

10. Select the Apply Changes To This Folder, Subfolders And Files option, and then click OK.

▶ **To verify that the folder's content is encrypted**

1. In the Secret folder, right-click File1 and then click Properties.

   The File1 Properties dialog box appears.

2. Click Advanced.

   The Advanced Attributes dialog box appears. Notice that the Encrypt Contents To Secure Data check box is selected.

3. Close the Advanced Attributes dialog box.

4. Close the Properties dialog box.

5. Close all windows and log off.

Exercise 2: Testing the Encrypted Files

In this exercise, you log on using the User3 account and then attempt to open an encrypted file. You then try to disable encryption on the encrypted files.

▶ **To test an encrypted file**

1. Log on as User3 with a password of *password*.

2. Start Windows Explorer and open the file File1.txt in the Secret folder.

   What happens?

3. Close Notepad.

▶ **To attempt to disable the encryption**

1. Right-click File1.txt and then click Properties.

2. Click Advanced.

3. Clear the Encrypt Contents To Secure Data check box and then click OK.

4. Click OK to close the File1 Properties dialog box.

   The Error Applying Attributes dialog box appears and informs you that access to the file is denied.

5. Click Cancel.

6. Close all open windows and dialog boxes.

7. Log off as User3 and log on as Administrator.

Exercise 3: Decrypting Folders and Files

In this exercise, you decrypt the folder and file that you previously encrypted.

1. Start Windows Explorer.

2. Right-click File1.txt, and then click Properties.

3. Click Advanced.

4. Clear the Encrypt Contents To Secure Data check box and then click OK.

5. Click OK to close the File1 Properties dialog box.

6. Close Windows Explorer and log off.

Lesson Summary

In this lesson, you learned that EFS provides the core file-encryption technology for storage of NTFS files on disk. EFS allows users to encrypt NTFS files by using a strong public key–based cryptographic scheme that encrypts all files in a folder. Users with roaming profiles can use the same key with trusted remote systems. Backups and copies of encrypted files are also encrypted if they are in NTFS volumes. Files remain encrypted if you move or rename them, and encryption is not defeated by leakage to paging files. Windows 2000 also provides a recovery agent utility. If an owner loses the private key, the recovery agent can still recover the encrypted file.

You also learned that EFS is implemented either from Windows Explorer or from the command line, using commands such as Cipher. EFS can be enabled or disabled for a computer, domain, or organizational unit by resetting recovery policy in the Group Policy console in the MMC.

Finally, you learned that you can use EFS to encrypt and decrypt files on remote computers, but you can't use it to encrypt data that is transferred over the network. Windows 2000 provides network protocols, such as SSL, to encrypt data over the network.

Lesson 5: Implementing an Audit Policy

Auditing is a powerful capability used for tracking events on computers. To implement auditing, you need to meet the auditing requirements and set the audit policy. After you set an audit policy on a computer, you can implement auditing on files, folders, and printers.

After this lesson, you will be able to

- Set up auditing on files and folders
- Set up auditing on printers

Estimated lesson time: 25 minutes

Configuring Auditing

For computers running Windows 2000 Professional, you set up an audit policy for each individual computer.

Auditing Requirements

The following are the requirements to set up and administer auditing:

- You must have the Manage Auditing And Security Log user right for the computer on which you want to configure an audit policy or review an audit log. By default, Windows 2000 grants these rights to the Administrators group.
- The files and folders to be audited must be on Microsoft Windows 2000 File System (NTFS) volumes.

Setting Up Auditing

Setting up auditing is a two-part process:

1. Set the audit policy. The audit policy enables auditing of objects but doesn't activate auditing of specific objects.
2. Enable auditing of specific resources. You specify the specific events to audit for files, folders, printers, and Active Directory objects. Windows 2000 then tracks and logs the specified events.

Setting an Audit Policy

The first step in implementing an audit policy is selecting the types of events that Windows 2000 audits. For each event that you can audit, the configuration settings indicate whether to track successful or failed attempts. You set audit policies in the Local Security Settings window, which you open by selecting Local Security Policy on the Administrative Tools menu.

Table 7.8 describes the types of events that Windows 2000 can audit.

Table 7.8   Types of Events Audited by Windows 2000

Event	Description
Account Logon Events	A domain controller received a request to validate a user account. (This is applicable only if your computer running Windows 2000 Professional joins a Windows 2000 domain.)
Account Management	An administrator created, changed, or deleted a user account or group. A user account was renamed, disabled, or enabled, or a password was set or changed.
Directory Service Access	A user gained access to an Active Directory object. You must configure specific Active Directory objects for auditing to log this type of event. (Active Directory directory services are available only if your computer running Windows 2000 Professional joins a Windows 2000 domain.)
Logon Events	A user logged on or logged off, or a user made or canceled a network connection to the computer.
Object Access	A user gained access to a file, folder, or printer. You must configure specific files, folders, or printers for auditing. Object access is auditing a user's access to files, folders, and printers.
Policy Change	A change was made to the user security options, user rights, or audit policies.
Privilege Use	A user exercised a right, such as changing the system time. (This doesn't include rights that are related to logging on and logging off.)
Process Tracking	A program performed an action. This information is generally useful only for programmers who want to track details of program execution.
System Events	A user restarted or shut down the computer, or an event occurred that affects Windows 2000 security or the security log. (For example, the audit log is full and Windows 2000 starts discarding entries.)

▶ **Follow these steps to set an audit policy on a computer that is running Windows 2000 Professional:**

1. Click Start, point to Programs, point to Administrative Tools, and then click Local Security Policy.

2. In the Local Security Settings window's console tree, double-click Local Policies, and then click Audit Policy.

The console displays the current audit policy settings in the details pane, as shown in Figure 7.7.

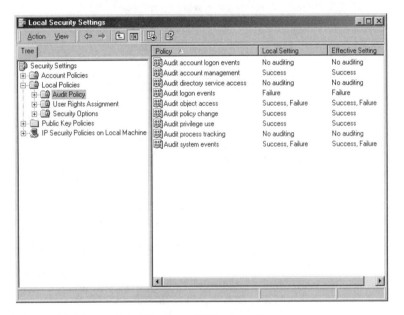

Figure 7.7 Events that Windows 2000 can audit

3. Select the type of event to audit, and then, on the Action menu, click Security.

The Local Security Policy Setting dialog box appears for the selected event. Figure 7.8 shows the Local Security Policy Setting dialog box for Audit Logon Events, and Table 7.9 defines the fields available in the Local Security Policy Setting dialog box.

4. Select the Success check box, the Failure check box, or both.

5. Click OK.

6. Restart your computer.

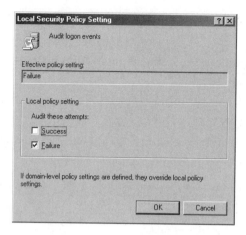

Figure 7.8 The Local Security Policy Setting dialog box for Audit Logon Events

Table 7.9   Local Security Policy Setting Dialog Box Fields

Field	Description
Effective Policy Setting	Indicates whether or not auditing is turned on. No auditing indicates it is auditing this event. Failure indicates it is auditing failed attempts. Success indicates it is auditing successful attempts. Success, Failure indicates it is auditing all attempts.
Local Policy Setting	A check mark in the Success check box indicates that auditing is in effect for successful attempts. A check mark in the Failure check box indicates that auditing is in effect for failed attempts.

Once you have set the audit policy, remember that the changes that you make to your computer's audit policy don't take effect until you restart your computer.

Auditing Access to Files and Folders

If security breaches are an issue for your organization, you can set up auditing for files and folders on NTFS partitions. To audit user access to files and folders, you must first set your audit policy to audit access to objects, which includes files and folders.

Once you have set your audit policy to audit access to objects, you enable auditing for specific files and folders and specify which types of access, by which users or groups, to audit.

▶ **Follow these steps to enable auditing for specific files and folders:**

1. On the Security tab in the Properties dialog box for a file or folder, click Advanced.

2. On the Auditing tab, click Add, select the users for whom you want to audit file and folder access, and then click OK.

3. In the Auditing Entry dialog box, select the Successful check box or the Failed check box for the events that you want to audit. For a list of the events, see Figure 7.9.

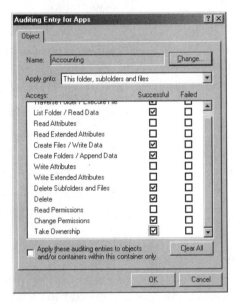

Figure 7.9 Events that can be audited for files and folders

Table 7.10 describes when to audit these events.

4. Click OK to return to the Access Control Settings dialog box.

   By default, any auditing changes that you make to a parent folder also apply to all child folders and all files in the parent and child folders.

5. To prevent changes that are made to a parent folder from applying to the currently selected file or folder, clear the Allow Inheritable Auditing Entries From Parent To Propagate To This Object check box.

6. Click OK.

Table 7.10   User Events and What Triggers Them

Event	User activity that triggers the event
Traverse Folder/Execute File	Running a program or gaining access to a folder to change directories
List Folder/Read Data	Displaying the contents of a file or folder
Read Attributes Read Extended Attributes	Displaying the attributes of a file or folder
Create Files/Write Data	Changing the contents of a file or creating new files in a folder
Create Folders/Append Data	Creating folders in the folder
Write Attributes Write Extended Attributes	Changing attributes of a file or folder
Delete Subfolders And Files	Deleting a file or subfolder in a folder
Delete	Deleting a file or folder
Read Permissions	Viewing permissions or the file owner for a file or folder
Change Permissions	Changing permissions for a file or folder
Take Ownership	Taking ownership of a file or folder

Auditing Access to Printers

Audit access to printers to track access to sensitive printers. To audit access to printers, set your audit policy to audit access to objects, which include printers. Then enable auditing for specific printers and specify which types of access to audit and which users will have access. After you select the printer, you use the same steps that you use to set up auditing on files and folders.

▶   **Follow these steps to set up auditing on a printer:**

1. In the Properties dialog box for the printer, click the Security tab, and then click Advanced.

2. On the Auditing tab, click Add, select the appropriate users or groups for whom you want to audit printer access, and then click OK.

3. In the Apply Onto box in the Auditing Entry dialog box, select resource where the auditing setting applies.

4. Under Access, select the Successful check box or the Failed check box for the events that you want to audit (see Figure 7.10).

5. Click OK in the appropriate dialog boxes to exit.

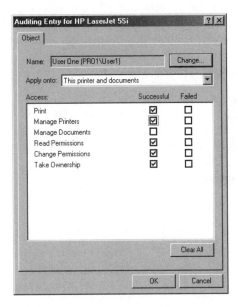

Figure 7.10 Printer events that can be audited

Table 7.11 describes what user activities trigger events for printers.

Table 7.11   Printer Events and What Triggers Them

Event	User activity that triggers the event
Print	Printing a file
Manage Printers	Changing printer settings, pausing a printer, sharing a printer, or removing a printer
Manage Documents	Changing job settings; pausing, restarting, moving, or deleting documents; sharing a printer; or changing printer properties
Read Permissions	Viewing printer permissions
Change Permissions	Changing printer permissions
Take Ownership	Taking printer ownership

Lesson Summary

In this lesson, you learned that the first step in implementing an audit policy is selecting the types of events that Windows 2000 audits. You can select the events to audit for files and folders, and you can select the events you want to audit for printers. For each event that you can audit, the configuration settings indicate whether to track successful attempts, failed attempts, or both. You use the Local Security Settings window to set audit policies, and then you restart your computer to enable auditing.

You also learned that you can set up auditing for access to files, folders, and printers on NTFS partitions. To do so, you must first set your audit policy to audit access to objects, which includes files, folders, and printers. Once you have set your audit policy to audit object access, you enable auditing for specific files, folders, and printers and specify which types of access, by which users or groups, to audit.

Lesson 6: Configuring Security Options

The Security Options node lives under the Local Policies node. Close to 40 additional security options are available here that allow you to increase the effective security on your computer. In this lesson, you learn about a few of these available options.

After this lesson, you will be able to

- Configure Security Options

Estimated lesson time: 15 minutes

Shutting Down the Computer Without Logging On

By default, Windows 2000 Professional doesn't require a user to be logged on to the computer before it can be shut down. Security Options allow you to disable this feature and force users to log on to the computer before it can be shut down. You access Security Options using the Group Policy snap-in, just as you did to configure the Account Policies settings. Once you open the Group Policy snap-in, expand Local Computer Policy, expand Computer Configuration, expand Windows Settings, expand Security Settings, expand Local Policies, and then select Security Options.

Figure 7.11 shows the Local Security Policy Setting dialog box for the Allow System To Be Shut Down Without Having To Log On option. This option is either enabled, which is the default, or disabled.

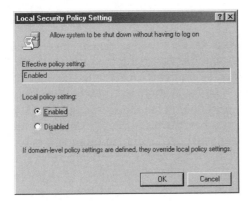

Figure 7.11 Setting the Allow System To Be Shut Down Without Having To Log On option

Clear Virtual Memory Pagefile When System Shuts Down

By default, Windows 2000 Professional doesn't clear the virtual memory pagefile when the system is shut down. In some organizations, this is considered a breach of security because the data in the pagefile might be accessible to users who aren't authorized to have access to that information. To enable this feature and clear the pagefile each time the system is shut down, open the Group Policy snap-in, expand Local Computer Policy, expand Computer Configuration, expand Windows Settings, expand Security Settings, expand Local Policies, and then select Security Options. Right-click Clear Virtual Memory Pagefile When System Shuts Down and then click Security (see Figure 7.12). This feature is either enabled or disabled.

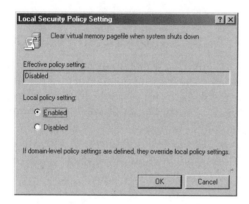

Figure 7.12 Setting the Clear Virtual Memory Pagefile When System Shuts Down option

Disable Ctrl+Alt+Del Requirement For Logon

By default, Windows 2000 Professional doesn't require users to press Ctrl+Alt+Del to log on to the computer. To increase security on your computers, you can disable this feature. By forcing users to press Ctrl+Alt+Del, you are using a key combination recognized only by Windows to ensure that you are giving the password only to Windows and not to a Trojan horse program waiting to capture your password. You set this option using the Group Policy snap-in. You should disable this option and force users to use Ctrl+Alt+Del (see Figure 7.13).

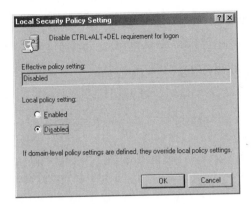

Figure 7.13 Setting the Disable Ctrl+Alt+Del Requirement For Logon option

Do Not Display Last User Name In Logon Screen

By default, Windows 2000 Professional displays the last user name to log on to the computer in the Windows Security or Log On To Windows dialog box. In some situations, this is considered a security risk because an authorized user can see a valid user account displayed on the screen, making it much easier to break into the computer.

To prevent the last user name from being displayed, in the Group Policy snap-in, expand Local Computer Policy, expand Computer Configuration, expand Windows Settings, expand Security Settings, expand Local Policies in the console tree, and then click Security Options. In the details pane, right-click Do Not Display Last User Name In Logon Screen, click Security, and then disable this feature. This feature is either enabled or disabled (see Figure 7.14).

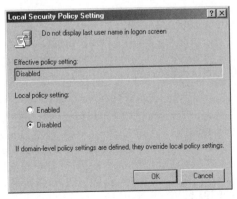

Figure 7.14 Disabling the Do Not Display Last User Name In Logon Screen option

Practice: Configuring Security Settings

In this practice, you configure Security Options on your computer.

Exercise 1: Configuring Security Settings

1. Log on to your computer as Administrator.

2. Click Start, point to Programs, point to Administrative Tools, and then click Group Policy.

3. In the Group snap-in's console tree, double-click Local Computer Policy, expand Computer Configuration, expand Windows Settings, expand Security Settings, expand Local Policies, and then click Security Options.

4. Configure your computer so that the following conditions apply:

   - Users must log on to shut down the computer.

   - Users must press Ctrl+Alt+Del to log on to the computer.

   - Windows 2000 will not display the user account last logged on the computer in the Windows Security dialog box.

5. Log off.

   Notice that you are prompted to press Ctrl+Alt+Del to log on.

6. Press Ctrl+Alt+Del.

   Notice that the Log On To Windows dialog box appears with the User Name box blank and the Shutdown options dimmed. (Click Options if you cannot see the Shutdown button.)

Lesson Summary

Some computers require more security than others. In this lesson, you learned that Security Options in the Group Policy Local Security Policy snap-ins allow you to improve the effective security on any of your computers that require more security. For example, you can prevent an unauthorized user from shutting down your computer by forcing users to log on before they can shut down the computer.

You also learned that you can prevent a Trojan horse application from stealing user passwords by forcing users to press Ctrl+Alt+Del before they can log on. Windows recognizes the Ctrl+Alt+Del key combination, so only Windows picks up the keystrokes entered in for user name and password. You can also increase security by not displaying a valid user name, the last user account that logged on, in the Windows Security or Log On To Windows dialog box. These options and the other Security Options available help you to increase security on your network.

Review

The following questions will help you determine whether you have learned enough to move on to the next chapter. If you have difficulty answering these questions, please go back and review the material in this chapter before beginning the next chapter. See Appendix A, "Questions and Answers," for the answers to these questions.

1. Why should you use groups?

2. How do you create a local group?

3. Are there any consequences to deleting a group?

4. What's the difference between built-in local groups and local groups?

5. What two tasks must you perform to audit access to a file?

6. Who can set up auditing for a computer?

7. Why would you want to force users to change passwords?

8. Why would you want to control the length of the passwords used on your computers?

9. Why would you want to lock out a user account?

10. Why would you want to force users to press Ctrl+Alt+Del before they can log on to your computers?

11. How do you prevent the last user name from being displayed in the Windows Security or Log On To Windows dialog box?

PART 2

Network Infrastructure

Part 2 contains most of the information that relates to the Windows 2000 Network Infrastructure portion of the 70-240 exam. This includes various network protocols and services. The chapters in this part primarily use Windows 2000 Server during the various hands-on practices and exercises, which is why the first chapter in this part installs Windows 2000 Server. However, much of the information presented here is also applicable to Windows 2000 Professional.

Because Windows 2000 Server is used throughout this part and the remainder of this training kit, this part starts with a chapter on installing Windows 2000 Server. It then continues with information about various network protocols and services. Some of this information will be familiar to Windows NT professionals (such as Domain Name System [DNS], Dynamic Host Configuration Protocol [DHCP], and Windows Internet Naming Service [WINS]); however, there are enough new features that each chapter deserves a decent review from even the most seasoned Windows NT 4 professional. New information, such as Virtual Private Networks (VPN), Network Address Translations (NAT), and other features should be reviewed in detail.

C H A P T E R   8

Installing Microsoft Windows 2000 Server

About This Chapter

This chapter discusses the Microsoft Windows 2000 Server installation process. It outlines the type of information you should gather to prepare for your installation and describes the steps you should take before you begin. The chapter then takes you through the phases of a normal installation and continues with a discussion of upgrading to Windows 2000 Server. This is followed by a lesson on troubleshooting installation problems.

The chapter concludes with a discussion of the various ways you can automate the installation process.

Before You Begin

To complete all of the exercises in this chapter, you must have

- Two computers that meet the minimum hardware requirements listed in "Hardware Requirements." One of them (Server01) should be a "clean" computer that has no operating system installed, the hard disk is not partitioned, and bootable CD-ROM support, if available, is disabled. The other (Computer 2) may be the computer you installed Windows 2000 Professional on in Chapter 1.

  - Server01 will be running Microsoft Windows 2000 Server as a domain controller. (This will be accomplished during the exercises in this chapter.)

  - Computer 2 will be networked to Server01 and running either Windows 95 or Windows 98, Windows NT 3.51 or 4.0 Workstation, or Windows 2000 Professional. This can be the computer you installed Windows 2000 Professional on in Chapter 1 of this book.

- A copy of the Windows 2000 Server installation CD-ROM (a 120-day evaluation version is included with this book).

- Four blank, formatted 3.5-inch floppy disks.

Lesson 1: Installing Windows 2000 Server

Before you can begin to install Windows 2000 Server, you must prepare for the installation by gathering information and making decisions about how you want to install the software. Once you have performed all the necessary steps to prepare for a Windows 2000 Server installation, you are ready to begin the Windows 2000 setup process. This lesson focuses on gathering the information and performing a new installation of Windows 2000 Server.

After this lesson, you will be able to

- Prepare to install Windows 2000 Server by completing preinstallation tasks such as identifying hardware requirements and gathering the necessary installation information

- Determine which setup program you should use to install Windows 2000 Server

- Describe the three stages of the installation process

- Perform a new installation of Windows 2000 Server

Estimated lesson time: 90 minutes

Preparing for Installation

During installation, the Windows 2000 Setup program asks you to provide information about how to install and configure Windows 2000. You should gather all the necessary information. Good preparation helps you avoid problems during and after the installation.

Before you begin your Windows 2000 installation, review the list of tasks outlined in Table 8.1. Each task is discussed in greater detail in the sections that follow. For now, you need only complete the first two tasks listed in the table: verifying that your computer meets the minimum hardware requirements and checking hardware compatibility. The remaining tasks are completed during the actual installation of Windows 2000 Server, which you will perform in the exercises later in this chapter. The information in this table is meant only to prepare you so you know what to expect and can install Windows 2000 Server later without any unnecessary delays.

Table 8.1 Pre-installation Checklist

Task	
Verify that your computer meets the minimum hardware requirements. For example, your hard disk should meet the minimum space requirements and preferably have a minimum of 2 gigabytes (GB) of free disk space.	☐
Check all hardware (network adapters, video drivers, sound cards, CD-ROM drives, PC cards, and so on) for compatibility by checking them against the Windows 2000 Hardware Compatibility List (HCL).	☐
Identify how you want to partition the hard disk drive on which you are going to install Windows 2000 Server.	☐
Choose a file system that meets your requirements and provides the services you need. Choose NTFS unless you need to run more than one operating system on your computer.	☐
Select a licensing mode. You can switch to Per Seat from Per Server mode after installation, but not to Per Server from Per Seat mode.	☐
Choose the type of network group (workgroup or domain) your computer will join. If you will be joining a domain, you need additional information such as the domain name and the computer account name created for you. With an administrator account and password in the domain, you can create a computer account in the domain.	☐
Determine whether to perform a new installation or upgrade an existing version of Windows NT Server. Windows NT 4.0 Workstation, Windows 95 and Windows 98 cannot be upgraded to Windows 2000 Server.	☐
Select an installation method: using Setup disks, from a CD-ROM, or from over the network.	☐
Choose which components you need to install, such as Networking Services or Microsoft Indexing Service.	☐

In addition to the tasks in the checklist, there is more information you need to know that will help you prepare for installation and eliminate potential problems. This includes:

- Working with Domain Name System (DNS)
- Recording Information
- Backing Up Files
- Uncompressing the Drive
- Disabling Disk Mirroring

- Disconnecting UPS Devices
- Reviewing Applications
- Checking the Boot Sector for Viruses
- Gathering Information

Working with Domain Name System (DNS)

When you create a Windows 2000 domain, the DNS service must be running and configured. If you are joining a domain, you must know the DNS name of the domain that your computer is joining. If DNS is not running, it is installed automatically when you create a domain controller or when you promote a server to a domain controller.

Recording Information

You should write down the following information: previous operating system (if any), name of the computer (if on a network), name of the workgroup or domain (if on a network), and the IP address (if there is no DHCP server or an existing DHCP server will not be used for dynamic IP addressing).

Backing Up Files

Before you install Windows 2000 Server, you should back up the files that you want to preserve. You can back up files to a disk, a tape drive, or another computer on the network.

Uncompressing the Drive

Uncompress any DriveSpace or DoubleSpace volumes before installing Windows 2000. You should not install Windows 2000 on a compressed drive unless the drive was compressed with the NTFS compression utility. DriveSpace or DoubleSpace volumes are created in Windows 95 and Windows 98. Windows 95 and Windows 98 cannot be upgraded to Windows 2000 Server but can coexist on the same computer running Windows 2000 Server.

Disabling Disk Mirroring

If you are installing a clean copy of Windows 2000 and you have Windows NT disk mirroring installed on your target computer, disable it before running Setup. You can re-enable disk mirroring after completing the installation. If you are upgrading to Windows 2000, you can leave Windows NT mirroring enabled during setup.

Note It is not necessary to disable hardware level disk mirroring to complete a new installation of Windows 2000 is not necessary since the operating system is unaware of redundant array of inexpensive disks (RAID) implemented in hardware.

Disconnecting UPS Devices

If you have uninterruptible power supply (UPS) equipment connected to your target computer, disconnect the connecting serial cable before running Setup. Windows 2000 Setup attempts to automatically detect devices connected to serial ports, and UPS equipment can cause problems with detection.

Reviewing Applications

Before starting the Windows 2000 Server Setup program, be sure to read Readme.doc (in the root directory of the Windows 2000 Server installation CD-ROM) for information regarding applications that need to be disabled or removed before running Setup. You may need to remove virus-scanning software, third-party network services, or client software before performing your Windows 2000 Server installation.

Checking the Boot Sector for Viruses

A boot sector virus will cause the installation of Windows 2000 to fail. To verify that the boot sector is not infected with a virus, run the Makedisk.bat file in the \Valueadd\3rdparty\CA_antiv directory on the Windows 2000 Server installation CD-ROM. The Makedisk.bat utility creates a floppy disk that is used to check the boot sector. After creating this floppy disk, boot the computer with the floppy disk inserted. This will run a boot sector virus check. After the utility has run, remove the diskette and proceed to the next preinstallation step.

Gathering Information

▶ **Follow these steps to prepare for the Windows 2000 installation:**

1. Read any documentation pertaining to installing Windows 2000 for updated installation information. Review the pertinent .txt and .doc files located on the Windows 2000 Server installation CD-ROM.

2. Make sure you have all device driver disks and configuration settings for third-party hardware, including any third-party device driver disks and documentation.

3. Have the Windows 2000 Server installation CD-ROM or a network share with the Windows 2000 Server files available.

4. Format three 3.5-inch 1.44 MB floppy disks (if creating optional Setup boot disks).

Important Windows NT 4.0 Setup disks are not compatible with Windows 2000.

Minimum Hardware Requirements

You should be familiar with the minimum hardware requirements necessary to install and operate Windows 2000 Server so that you can determine whether your system meets these requirements. The minimum installation requirements for Windows 2000 are listed in Table 8.2.

Table 8.2 Minimum Hardware Requirements for Windows 2000 Server

Component	Minimum requirement
Processor	32-bit Pentium 133 MHz
Free hard disk space	One or more hard disks where %systemroot% (C:\WINNT by default) is located on a partition with at least 671 MB of free space (2 GB recommended)
Memory	128 MB for networking with one to five client computers; 256 MB minimum is recommended for most network environments
Display	VGA monitor capable of 640 x 480 (1024 x 768 recommended)
CD-ROM drive	12x or faster recommended; not required for network installations
Additional drives	High-density 3.5-inch disk drive, unless your CD-ROM is bootable and supports starting the Setup program from a CD-ROM
Optional components	Mouse or other pointing device
	For network installation: a network adapter and an MS-DOS–based network operating system that permits connection to a server containing the Windows 2000 Setup files

Hardware Compatibility

Windows 2000 Setup automatically checks your hardware and software and reports any potential conflicts. However, to ensure a successful installation, you should make sure that your computer hardware is compatible with Windows 2000 Server before starting the setup process. To do this, verify that your hardware is on the HCL. The HCL is included on your Windows 2000 Server installation CD-ROM in the \Support folder in Hcl.txt. The HCL lists each hardware model that has passed the Hardware Compatibility Tests (HCTs). The list also indicates which devices Windows 2000 Server supports. Testing is conducted by Windows Hardware Quality Labs (WHQL) and by some hardware vendors. Installing Windows 2000 Server on a computer that does not have hardware listed in the HCL might not be successful.

Note Microsoft regularly releases an updated HCL. Review the most up-to-date list of supported hardware at the Microsoft WHQL Web site, *http://www.microsoft.com/hcl/default.asp*. If this URL fails, try *http://www.microsoft.com/isapi/redir.dll?prd=Win2000HCL&pver=1*. This URL should direct you to the WHQL Web site. If it doesn't display the WHQL Web site, search *http://www.microsoft.com* using the keyword "HCL."

A hardware model is "supported" if it is listed on the HCL and you are using a Microsoft-supplied driver to control that hardware. The term "unsupported" does not imply anything about the relative quality of hardware or of third-party drivers. Many unsupported computers and devices work correctly with Windows 2000. However, the Windows 2000 support staff at Microsoft does not offer a full range of support services for problems specific to unsupported hardware or drivers.

Microsoft supports only those devices on the HCL. If one of the computer's devices is not on the HCL, contact the device manufacturer to request a Windows 2000 driver, if it exists.

Disk Partitions

The Windows 2000 Server Setup program allows you to install Windows 2000 Server onto an existing partition or to create a partition and then install Windows 2000 onto the new one. During installation, the Setup program examines the hard disk. Depending on the state of the disk, you will be provided with some or all of the following partitioning choices during the installation:

- If the entire hard disk is unpartitioned, you must create and size the installation partition.

- If the disk has partitions, but there is enough unpartitioned disk space, you can create and size the installation partition by using that unpartitioned space.

- If there is an existing partition that is large enough, you can install Windows 2000 Server onto that partition.

- If the hard disk has an existing partition, you can delete it to create more unpartitioned disk space and then use that unpartitioned space to create the Windows 2000 partition.

- If you specify any action that will cause information to be erased, you will be prompted to confirm your choice. If you delete an existing partition, you will cause any data on that partition to be erased. Performing a new installation of Windows 2000 on a partition that contains another operating system will cause that operating system to be overwritten.

Although you can use the Windows 2000 Setup program to create other partitions, you should create and size only the installation partition. After Windows 2000 is installed, use the Disk Management tool to partition any remaining unpartitioned space on the hard disk.

Sizing the Installation Partition

The Windows 2000 Server Setup program requires a boot partition of at least 671 MB of free space to install all Windows 2000 operating system files. However, it is recommended that you create a boot partition of at least 2 GB to allow for future installations of files and programs, such as the Windows 2000 paging file, operating system tools, and operating system updates. The boot partition holds the core operating system files.

The system partition is the partition that holds the files needed to begin the initial installation of Windows 2000. On an *x*86-based computer, the operating system starts from the system partition. This means that Windows 2000 looks for certain files, such as Ntldr, Ntdetect.com, and Boot.ini in the root directory, usually the C: drive (Disk 0) when the computer is started. The operating system cannot start unless the system partition is marked active.

Windows 2000 Server is installed on the boot partition. It contains the operating system parent directory (Winnt, by default), the \System32 subdirectory, the Windows 2000 kernel, and all other files required to run the operating system. If Windows 2000 Server is installed on the active partition, it is both the boot and system partition.

The disk partition where you store Windows 2000 files must be on a permanent hard disk and must have enough unused disk space to hold all the files. This partition must be formatted either with the NTFS (NTFS 4.0 or NTFS 5.0) or with the FAT16 or FAT32 file systems. However, you cannot install Windows 2000 to a FAT16 or FAT32 partition that has implemented disk compression, such as Microsoft DriveSpace.

Note In Windows 2000, if you choose to format NTFS during the installation, the partition will be formatted directly to NTFS. In previous versions, the partition was formatted to FAT and then converted to NTFS. This new process allows you to create partitions larger than 4 GB, although a limit of 7.8 GB still exists on the PC architecture.

Winnt.exe and Winnt32.exe, the Setup executable files, report an error if they are unable to find a drive with enough free disk space available (greater than 671 MB), or if the drive specified with the /t: or /tempdrive: switch has insufficient free disk space. If such an error occurs, you must free some disk space and then run Winnt or Winnt32 again.

Windows 2000 looks for certain files in the root directory of the active partition when you start your computer; however, the Windows 2000 operating system may be installed on another drive, such as drive D, as long as the drive is configured with a supported file system. If you want to dual boot your computer to operating systems that do not support NTFS, such as Windows 98, drive C must be formatted either with FAT16 or FAT32.

If a system's hard disk contains basic input/output system (BIOS) controlled partitions, other file systems such as network file system (NFS), stripe sets, volume sets, or mirrors, those elements appear on the Setup screen as partitions of an unknown type. To avoid deleting elements inadvertently, do not use Setup to delete partitions that are displayed as unknown.

If you are installing a new copy of Windows 2000 on a partition mirrored in software, you must disable mirroring before running Setup and then reestablish mirroring after installation is complete. However, if you are upgrading Windows NT Server versions 3.51 or 4.0 or Windows 2000 Server, you can leave mirroring enabled during setup.

Do not install Windows 2000 or upgrade to Windows 2000 on a compressed drive unless the drive was compressed with the NTFS file system compression utility. Uncompress a Windows 95 or Windows 98 DriveSpace or DoubleSpace volume before running Windows 2000 Setup on it.

If you are setting up a dual-boot configuration of Windows 2000 with another operating system such as MS-DOS, Windows 3.0, Windows 95, Windows 98, or Windows NT, install Windows 2000 onto its own partition. Although it is possible to install Windows 2000 onto the same partition as an existing operating system, it is highly recommended that you install Windows 2000 onto a separate partition, because the Windows 2000 Setup program can overwrite files in the Program Files folder installed by other operating systems.

File Systems

When you install Windows 2000 Setup onto unpartitioned disk space, you are prompted to select the file system that should be used to format the partition. You should decide which file system to use before installing Windows 2000 Server. Windows 2000 supports NTFS and the FAT16 and FAT32 file systems.

Table 8.3 compares the different features of the three file systems supported by Windows 2000.

Table 8.3 Operating System Feature Comparison

Operating system	FAT16	FAT32	NTFS
Overall compatibility	Recognized by MS-DOS, Windows 3.*x*, Windows 95, Windows 98, Windows NT, Windows 2000, and OS/2.	Recognized by Windows 95 OSR2, Windows 98, Windows NT and Windows 2000.	Recognized by Windows NT and Windows 2000. When the computer is running another operating system (such as MS-DOS, Windows 95, Windows 98, or OS/2), that operating system cannot gain access to files on an NTFS volume on the same computer.
Supported by MS-DOS and Windows 3.*x*	Yes	No	No
Supported by Windows 95 pre-OSR2 releases	Yes	No	No
Supported by Windows 95 OSR2 and Windows 98	Yes	Yes	No
Supported by Windows NT 3.51	Yes	No	Yes, but Windows NT 3.51 does not support NTFS version 5.0.
Supported by Windows NT 4.0	Yes	No	Yes. Windows NT 4.0 supports NTFS version 5.0 with Service Pack 4 or later installed.
Supported by Windows 2000	Yes	Yes	Yes

Licensing

Windows 2000 Server supports two licensing modes: Per Server and Per Seat. In Per Server mode, Client Access Licenses (CALs) are assigned to a server. In Per Seat mode, each computer that accesses the Windows 2000 Server computer requires a separate CAL.

Workgroups and Domains

During installation, you must choose the type of network you want the computer to join. A computer running Windows 2000 can join one of two types of networks: workgroup or domain.

Joining a Workgroup

When joining a workgroup, assign a workgroup name to the computer. The workgroup name assigned can be the name of an existing workgroup or the name of a workgroup created during installation. In either case, the computer appears as a member of that workgroup when other computer users in the network browse for network resources.

A domain and a workgroup can share a name. However, consider the following:

- The workgroup computers are not members of the domain and are not included in domain administration.

- The workgroup computers appear with the domain computers in Windows 2000 Explorer.

Joining a Domain

When joining a domain, the Windows 2000 Setup wizard prompts you to provide the DNS name of an existing domain.

Before a computer running Windows NT or Windows 2000 can join a domain, a computer account must be created in or added to the domain database. Only users who have the Join A Computer To The Domain permission can create a computer account. Members of the Administrators, Domain Administrators, or Account Operators groups have this user right by default.

When joining a domain, create a computer account for that computer in advance, or create it during installation by selecting the Create A Computer Account In The Domain check box. Next, supply a user account and password that have the authority to add computer accounts in the domain. By default, this must be an Administrator account.

> **Note** When joining a domain, even if the computer account has been previously created, domain credentials must be supplied.

At least one domain controller and one DNS server must be online when you install a computer in the domain. If you install Windows 2000 Server as a standalone server without joining a domain, you can join a domain later by using the Network Identification tab in the System Properties dialog box, as shown in Figure 8.1.

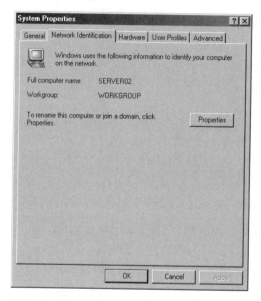

Figure 8.1 The Network Identification tab in the System Properties dialog box

Upgrade or New Installation

Before running Windows 2000 Server Setup, you must determine whether to upgrade your existing installation of Windows NT or to perform a new installation. See Table 8.4 for a list of possible upgrades.

Upgrading is the process of installing Windows 2000 Server in a directory that currently contains certain versions of Windows NT.

Table 8.4 Upgrade Choices

If your current Windows operating system is:	You can upgrade to:
A version earlier than Windows NT 3.51 Server	Windows NT 3.51 Server or Windows NT 4.0 Server
Windows NT 3.51 Server	Windows 2000 Server
Windows NT 4.0 Server	Windows 2000 Server
Windows NT Terminal Server	Windows 2000 Server
Windows NT 4.0 Server Enterprise	Windows 2000 Advanced Server

An upgrade automatically installs Windows 2000 Server into the same directory as the currently installed operating system.

Installing, in contrast to upgrading, is the process of placing the operating system in a new directory, wiping out the previous operating system at setup, or installing Windows 2000 Server on a disk or disk partition that previously contained no operating system.

If you want to perform a new installation on a disk partition that contains applications you want to retain, you must back them up and reinstall them after installing Windows 2000 Server.

If you want to perform a new installation of Windows 2000 Server on a partition that previously contained Windows 2000 Server, and you have documents under My Documents that you want to save, back up the documents in the Documents and Settings directory and copy the documents back into the folder after completing the installation. My Documents points to subdirectories below the Documents and Settings directory.

Installation Methods

Just as with Windows 2000 Professional, there are three different ways to access the installation files to install Windows 2000 Server on the Intel platform:

- Using Setup disks
- From a CD-ROM
- From over the network

Setup Disks

Windows 2000 Server is distributed on a CD-ROM and includes four setup floppy disks. These Setup disks are required if you are installing Windows 2000 Server on an *x*86-based computer that is not running MS-DOS or a Windows operating system and does not support the bootable CD-ROM format. These disks also let you start Windows 2000 at times when it might not be able to start on its own because of a computer error, and to initiate an emergency repair.

You can create a set of Setup disks by running Makeboot.exe or Makebt32.exe from the \Bootdisk directory on the Windows 2000 Server installation CD-ROM. Makeboot.exe is a 16-bit DOS application that runs on MS-DOS, 16-bit operating systems like Windows 3.11, Windows 95, and Windows 98. Makebt32.exe is a 32-bit application that runs on Windows NT and Windows 2000.

After the initial phase of installation, Windows 2000 starts and the remainder of Setup runs under Windows 2000, which is helpful for troubleshooting. For example, the install process displays a standard Windows 2000 error check code if an error occurs during setup.

To start an installation of Windows 2000 Server by using the Setup disks, you should first turn off the computer, insert the disk labeled Windows 2000 Setup Boot Disk into drive A, and then turn on your computer. Setup starts automatically.

Note If you are installing Windows 2000 Server on a computer that previously contained no operating system, and you are using an MS-DOS boot floppy disk (performing an over-the-network setup), you have to format the drive first. However, if you are using the Windows 2000 Setup disks to start Setup, you can format the drive during setup.

During installation from the Setup disks, the bar at the bottom of the screen displays the Windows 2000 components being loaded. These components are described in Table 8.5.

Table 8.5 Components Loaded from Each Setup Boot Disk

Setup disk	What gets loaded...
Disk One	The Setupldr.bin file starts the setup. The computer is inspected and machine identification data is collected. If a driver is not found for the fixed disk that contains the boot partition, you might need to load a third-party driver. The text-mode portion of Windows 2000 Setup is installed. The Ntkrnlmp.exe file loads the Windows 2000 Executive.
Disk Two	This disk loads the HAL, configuration tools, fonts, locale-specific data, drivers, and controllers.
Disk Three	This disk loads the Compaq drive array and disk controller drivers. During this process, Setup detects the appropriate drivers for the system and loads the dynamic volume support (dmboot1).
Disk Four	This disk loads the floppy disk drivers; SCSI CD-ROM, floppy, and fixed drive drivers; and file system drivers (FAT, NTFS, and CDFS). Windows 2000 is loaded and takes over the setup process. At this point, the CD-ROM drive is accessed. After the files are copied, the system reboots. Remove any floppy disks before the reboot.

After Disk Four

After the system reboots, Windows 2000 Setup starts in graphical user interface (GUI) mode. CD-ROM files continue to be copied to the hard disk. Setup detects and installs devices and then prompts you for user information. You must then choose which components to install. From there, choose the type of network installation (typical or custom) and the type of network (workgroup or domain) to join. Setup builds the file list and installs and configures the components.

Bootable CD-ROM

If your Windows 2000 Server installation files are on compact disc and your computer's BIOS supports the bootable CD-ROM (No-emulation mode) format, insert the Windows 2000 Server CD-ROM into the CD-ROM drive and then turn off your computer. When you turn your computer back on, Setup starts automatically.

When Setup requests that you remove the CD-ROM from the CD-ROM drive, do so on bootable CD-ROM systems. Otherwise, Setup starts all over again on the following boot.

Important Although your system might support bootable CD-ROMs, you might have to modify your system BIOS to boot to the CD-ROM.

If your computer is running an operating system such as Windows 95, Windows 98, or Windows NT and you insert the Windows 2000 installation CD-ROM while the computer is running, the Windows 2000 Setup Wizard dialog box appears (provided you haven't turned off AutoPlay).

Over-the-Network (Server-Based)

The Windows 2000 Server system files must be available over the network. Copy the Windows 2000 installation CD-ROM, or at a minimum, the source directory (\I386), to a directory on the hard disk of a network server and share the directory.

Upgrading Windows 95, Windows 98, or Windows NT 4.0 Workstation

As mentioned earlier, you cannot upgrade to Windows 2000 Server from Windows 95, Windows 98, or Windows NT 4.0 Workstation. You can only install a new copy of Windows 2000 Server over these operating systems. Upgrading to Windows 2000 Server retains most system settings, preferences, and application installations. If you prefer a dual-boot configuration, choose the Install Windows 2000 Server option. Press Enter or click Next to continue.

Performing a New Installation

If you do not have Windows 95, Windows 98, or Windows NT installed, you must run MS-DOS and an MS-DOS network client to establish your connection to the shared network folder containing the Setup files.

Running the MS-DOS network client, connect to the system files over the network and run Winnt.exe, which is located on the network share.

The MS-DOS computer needs 500 KB of free conventional memory to run the setup routine successfully. Make sure you have loaded Emm386.exe and are loading all device drivers high.

Tip To free some memory, run LoadHigh Winnt.exe to load portions of Winnt.exe high.

You should run Smartdrv.exe or your installation will be slow, taking from 4 to 12 hours.

Choosing Which Components to Install

Windows 2000 Server includes a wide variety of core components from which to choose, including a number of administrative tools that are automatically installed by Setup. In addition, you can choose from a number of components that extend the functionality of Windows 2000 Server. These components can be installed during setup or added afterward (through the Add/Remove Windows Components option within Control Panel's Add/Remove Programs application).

These components provide more capabilities on the server. However, you should choose only the components you need, since each component requires additional disk space. Table 8.6 will help you choose the components you need in your installation.

Table 8.6 Server function components

Possible server function	Optional components to consider installing
DHCP, DNS, or WINS server (in a TCP/IP network)	Dynamic Host Configuration Protocol (DHCP), DNS, or Windows Internet Name Service (WINS)—all part of Networking Services
Centralized administration of networks	Management and Monitoring Tools
	Remote Installation Services
Authentication and secure communication	Internet Authentication Services (part of Networking Services)
	Certificate Services
File access	Microsoft Indexing Service
	Remote Storage
	Other Network File and Print Services (support for NetWare, Macintosh, and UNIX). NetWare client computers are supported through Gateway Services for NetWare (GSNW). The Directory Service Migration Tool installs GSNW if NetWare Directory Service (NDS) is not installed.

continues

Table 8.6 Server Function Components *(continued)*

Possible server function	Optional components to consider installing
Print access	Other Network File and Print Services (support for NetWare, Macintosh, and UNIX)
Terminal services	Terminal Services
	Terminal Services Licensing
Application support	Message Queuing Services
	Quality of Service (QoS) Admission Control Service (part of Networking Services)
Internet (Web) infrastructure	Internet Information Services (IIS)
	Site Server and Lightweight Directory Access Protocol (LDAP; part of Networking Services)
Phone and fax support	Connection Manager Administration Kit and Connection Point Services (part of Management and Monitoring Tools)
Multimedia communications	Windows Media Services
Support for a variety of client operating systems	Other Network File and Print Services (support for NetWare, Macintosh, and UNIX)

Table 8.7 describes each of the optional components. Use this table in conjunction with Table 8.6 to choose appropriate components to install.

Table 8.7 Optional Components

Optional component	Description
Certificate Services	Provides authentication support, including secure e-mail, Web-based authentication, and smart card authentication.
Internet Information Services (IIS)	Provides support for Web site creation, configuration, and management, along with Network News Transfer Protocol (NNTP), FTP, and Simple Mail Transfer Protocol (SMTP).

Optional component	Description
Management and Monitoring Tools	Provides tools for network management and monitoring, specifically Network Monitoring Tools Monitor, a packet analyzer. Also includes the Simple Network Management Protocol (SNMP).
	Other management tools include support for client dialing and updating client telephone books, and a utility for migrating from NDS to the Windows 2000 Active Directory services.
Message Queuing Services	Provides services that support the messaging needed by distributed applications, allowing these applications to function reliably in heterogeneous networks or when a computer is temporarily offline.
Microsoft Indexing Service	Provides indexing functions for documents stored on disk, allowing users to search for specific document text or properties.
Microsoft Script Debugger	Provides support for script development.
Networking Services	Provides important support for networking, including the following:
	COM Internet Services Proxy Supports distributed applications that use HTTP to communicate through IIS.
	Domain Name System (DNS) Provides name resolution for clients running Windows 2000. With name resolution, users can access servers by name, instead of having to use IP addresses that are difficult to recognize and remember.
	Dynamic Host Configuration Protocol (DHCP) Enables a server to provide IP addresses dynamically to other servers on the network. With DHCP, you do not need to set and maintain static IP addresses on any intranet servers except for those providing DHCP, DNS, or WINS.
	Internet Authentication Service Provides authentication for dial-in users.
	QoS Admission Control Service Allows you to control how applications are allotted network bandwidth. Important applications can be given more bandwidth and less important applications less bandwidth.

continues

Table 8.7 Optional Components *(continued)*

Optional component	Description
Networking Services, *continued*	**Simple TCP/IP Services** Supports Character Generator, Daytime Discard, Echo, and Quote of the Day.
	Site Server ILS Service Supports telephony applications, which help users access features such as caller ID, conference calls, video conferencing, and faxing. This support depends on IIS.
	Windows Internet Naming Service Provides NetBIOS over TCP/IP name resolution for clients running Windows NT and earlier versions of Microsoft operating systems. With name resolution, users can access servers by name instead of having to use IP addresses that are difficult to recognize and remember.
	Note The Clients directory on the Windows 2000 Server installation CD-ROM contains two sub-directories. The WIN9X directory contains the directory service client for Windows 95 and Windows 98 clients. The WIN9XIPP.CLI directory contains the Internet Printing client for Windows 95 and Windows 98. These services remove the WINS requirement from Windows 95 and Windows 98 client computers.
Other Network File and Print Services	Provides file and print services for Macintosh, as well as print services for UNIX.
Remote Installation Services (RIS)	Provides services that allow you to set up new client computers remotely without having to visit each client. The target clients must support remote booting. On the server, a separate partition will be needed for RIS.
Remote Storage	Provides an extension to your disk space by making removable media, such as tapes, more accessible. Infrequently used data can automatically be transferred to tape and retrieved when needed.

Optional component	Description
Terminal Services	Enables you to run client applications on the server so that client computers can function as terminals rather than independent systems. The server provides a multisession environment and runs the Windows-based programs being used on the clients. If you install Terminal Services, you must also install Terminal Services Licensing (to license Terminal Services' clients). However, temporary licenses can be issued for clients that allow you to use Terminal servers for up to 90 days.
Terminal Services Licensing	Allows you to register and track licenses for Terminal Services Licensing clients. If you install Terminal Services, you must also install Terminal Services Licensing (to license Terminal Services' clients). However, temporary licenses can be issued for clients that allow you to use Terminal servers for up to 90 days.
Windows Media Services	Provides multimedia support, allowing you to deliver content using Advanced Streaming Format over an intranet or the Internet.

Windows 2000 Server Setup Programs

Regardless of which method you use to install Windows 2000 Server, you must execute either Winnt.exe or Winnt32.exe. You can use the Setup.exe program to launch Winnt.exe or Winnt32.exe, or you can execute Winnt32.exe or Winnt.exe directly. For a clean installation on a computer running MS-DOS or Windows 3.x, run Winnt.exe from the MS-DOS command line. For a clean installation from Windows 95, Windows 98, or Windows NT Workstation, run Winnt32.exe. For a clean installation or upgrade from Windows NT Server 3.51 or 4.0, run Winnt32.exe. Several switches can be used with Winnt.exe and Winnt32.exe to customize how Windows 2000 Server is installed on your computer.

Windows 2000 Setup Program

The Windows 2000 Setup program, Setup.exe, is located in the root directory of the Windows 2000 Server installation CD-ROM. When you execute Setup.exe, the Microsoft Windows 2000 CD screen appears. From there, you can choose to install Windows 2000 Server, install add-on components, browse the CD, or exit the Setup program. If you select the Install Windows 2000 option, either the Winnt.exe or the Winnt32.exe program runs, depending on which operating system you are currently using.

If Autorun is enabled on your system, the Windows 2000 CD screen appears when you insert the Windows 2000 Server installation CD-ROM into your CD-ROM drive. Autorun calls Setup.exe, which checks the operating system. If Setup determines that the computer is running Windows NT Server 3.51, Windows NT Server 4.0, or an earlier version of Windows 2000 Server, you are prompted either to upgrade or install Windows 2000. If a newer version of Windows 2000 Server is installed on the computer, Setup.exe will not allow the installation of Windows 2000 Server to continue.

Winnt.exe Setup Program

Winnt.exe is commonly used for over-the-network installations that use an MS-DOS network client. Winnt.exe does the following:

1. Creates a WIN_NT.~BT temporary directory on the system partition and copies Setup boot files into this directory.

2. Creates a WIN_NT.~LS temporary directory and copies the Windows 2000 files from the server into this directory.

3. Prompts users to restart their systems. After the computer restarts, the boot menu appears and installation continues.

Winnt.exe installs Windows 2000 Server and can be executed from an MS-DOS or a Windows 16-bit operating system command prompt.

Winnt.exe Switches

You can use the following switches to modify the behavior of the Winnt.exe Setup program:

```
WINNT [/s[:sourcepath]] [/t[:tempdrive]] [/u[:answer_file]]
[/udf:id[,UDF_file]][/r:folder] [/rx:folder] [/e:command] [/a]
```

These switches are described in detail in Table 8.8.

Table 8.8 Winnt.exe Switches

Switch	Description
/s[:*sourcepath*]	Specifies the source location of the Windows 2000 files. The location must be a full path of the form *x*:[*path*] or a valid UNC.
/t[:*tempdrive*]	Directs Setup to place temporary files on the specified drive and to install Windows 2000 on that drive. If you do not specify a location, Setup attempts to locate a drive for you.

Switch	Description
/u[:*answer_file*]	Performs an unattended setup using an answer file (requires /s). The answer file automatically provides answers to some or all of the prompts that the end user normally responds to during setup.
/udf:*id*[,*UDF_file*]	Indicates an identifier (*id*) that Setup uses to specify how a Uniqueness Database File (UDF) modifies an answer file (see /u [:*answer_file*]). The /udf parameter overrides values in the answer file, and the identifier determines which values in the UDF file are used. If no UDF_file is specified, Setup prompts you to insert a disk that contains the $Unique$.udb file.
/r[:*folder*]	Specifies an optional folder to be installed. The folder remains on the computer after setup is complete.
/rx[:*folder*]	Specifies an optional folder to be copied. The folder is deleted after setup is complete.
/e[:*command*]	Specifies a command to be executed at the end of GUI-mode Setup.
/a	Enables accessibility options.

Winnt32.exe Setup Program

Winnt32.exe is used to install Windows 2000 Server from computers with Windows 95, Windows 98, or Windows NT 4.0 Workstation already installed. It can be executed by double-clicking Winnt32.exe in the root of the source folder (such as \I386) on the Windows 2000 Server installation CD-ROM or in a network share location for over-the-network installations. You can also execute Winnt32.exe by using the run command from the Start Menu, which allows switches to be specified. In addition, the Winnt32 command can be run from the Windows 95, Windows 98, or Windows NT (all Windows 32-bit operating systems) command prompts.

If the Windows 2000 Server installation is initiated over the network, Winnt32.exe creates a WIN_NT.~LS temporary directory and copies the Windows 2000 Server files from the server into this directory. The temporary directory is created on the first partition that is large enough, unless otherwise specified by the /t switch. This is known as the Pre-Copy Phase.

WINNT32.EXE Switches

You can use the following switches to modify the behavior of the
Winnt32.exe Setup program:

```
winnt32 [/s:sourcepath] [/tempdrive:drive_letter]
[/unattend[num]:
[answer_file]] [/copydir:folder_name]
[/copysource:folder_name]
[/cmd:command_line] [/debug[level]:[filename]]
[/udf:id[,UDF_file]]
[/syspart:drive_letter] [/checkupgradeonly] [/cmdcons]
[/m:folder_name]
[/makelocalsource] [/noreboot]
```

These switches are described in detail in Table 8.9.

Table 8.9 Winnt32.Exe Switches

Switch	Description
/s:*sourcepath*	Specifies the source location of the Windows 2000 files. To simultaneously copy files from multiple servers, specify multiple /s sources. If you use multiple /s switches, the first specified server must be available or setup will fail.
/tempdrive:*drive_letter*	Directs Setup to place temporary files on the specified partition and to install Windows 2000 on that partition.
/Unattend or /u	Upgrades your previous version of Windows 2000 in Unattended Setup mode. All user settings are taken from the previous installation, so no user intervention is required during setup.
	Using the /unattend switch to automate setup affirms that you have read and accepted the End-User License Agreement (EULA) for Windows 2000. Before using this switch to install Windows 2000 on behalf of an organization other than your own, you must confirm that the end user has received, read, and accepted the terms of the Windows 2000 EULA. Original equipment manufacturers (OEMs) may not use this switch on computers being sold to end users.

Switch	Description
/unattend[*num*][:*answer_file*]	Performs a fresh installation in Unattended Setup mode. The answer file provides Setup with your custom specifications. *Num* is the number of seconds between the time that Setup finishes copying the files and when it restarts your computer. You can use num on any computer running Windows NT or Windows 2000. The *answer_file* placeholder is the name of the answer file.
/copydir:*folder_name*	Creates an additional folder within the folder in which the Windows 2000 files are installed. For example, if the source folder contains a folder called Private_drivers that has modifications just for your site, you can type **/copydir:Private_drivers** to have Setup copy that folder to your installed Windows 2000 folder. The new folder location would then be %systemroot%\Private_drivers. You can use /copydir to create as many additional folders as you want.
/copysource:*folder_name*	Creates a temporary additional folder within the folder in which the Windows 2000 files are installed. For example, if the source folder contains a folder called Private_drivers that has modifications just for your site, you can type **/copysource:Private_drivers** to have Setup copy that folder to your installed Windows 2000 folder and use its files during setup. The temporary folder location would then be %systemroot%\Private_drivers. Unlike the folders /copydir creates, /copysource folders are deleted after setup is complete.
/cmd:*command_line*	Instructs Setup to carry out a specific command before the final phase of setup. This occurs after your computer has restarted twice and after Setup has collected the necessary configuration information, but before setup is complete.
/debug[*level*][:*filename*]	Creates a debug log at the level specified, for example, /debug4:C:\ Win2000.log. The default log file is %systemroot%\Winnt32.log, with the debug level set to 2. The log levels are as follows: 0-severe errors, 1-errors, 2-warnings, 3-information, and 4-detailed information for debugging. Each level includes the levels below it.

continues

Table 8.9 Winnt32.Exe Switches *(continued)*

Switch	Description
/udf:*id*[,*UDF_file*]	Indicates an identifier (*id*) that Setup uses to specify how a Uniqueness Database File (UDF) modifies an answer file (see the /unattend entry). The UDF overrides values in the answer file, and the identifier determines which values in the UDF are used. For example, /udf:RAS_user, Our_company.udb overrides settings specified for the identifier RAS_user in the Our_company.udb file. If no UDF is specified, Setup prompts the user to insert a disk that contains the $Unique$.udb file.
/syspart:*drive_letter*	Specifies that you can copy Setup startup files to a hard disk, mark the disk as active, and then install the disk into another computer. When you start that computer, it automatically starts with the next phase of setup. You must always use the /tempdrive parameter with the /syspart parameter.
	The /syspart switch for Winnt32.exe runs only from a computer that already has Windows NT 3.51, Windows NT 4.0, or Windows 2000 installed on it. It cannot be run from Windows 95 or Windows 98.
/checkupgradeonly	Checks your computer for upgrade compatibility with Windows 2000. For Windows 95 or Windows 98 upgrades, Setup creates a report named Upgrade.txt in the Windows installation folder. For Windows NT 3.51 or 4.0 upgrades, it saves the report to the Winnt32.log in the installation folder.
/cmdcons	Adds a Recovery Console option to the operating system selection screen for repairing a failed installation. It is only used post-setup.
/m:*folder_name*	Specifies that Setup copies replacement files from an alternate location. Instructs Setup to look in the alternate location first and if files are present, use them instead of the files from the default location.

Switch	Description
/makelocalsource	Instructs Setup to copy all installation source files to your local hard disk. Use /makelocalsource when installing from a CD-ROM to provide installation files when the CD-ROM is not available later in the installation.
/noreboot	Instructs Setup not to restart the computer after the file copy phase of winnt32 is completed so that you can execute another command.

The Installation Process

Windows 2000 Server uses the same four-stage installation process that Windows 2000 Professional uses:

- **Running the Setup program.** The Setup program prepares the hard disk for later stages of the installation and copies the necessary files to run the Setup wizard. This is the text-mode portion of setup.

- **Running the Setup wizard.** The Setup wizard requests setup information about the computer, which includes names, passwords, regional settings, and so on. This is the graphics-mode portion of setup.

- **Installing Windows Networking.** After gathering information about the computer, the Setup wizard prompts you for networking information and then installs the networking components so that the computer can communicate with other computers on the network.

- **Completing the Installation.** To complete the installation, Setup copies files to the hard disk, registers components, and configures the computer. The system restarts after installation is complete.

Running the Setup Program

When you run the Setup program, you specify which components will be installed. Setup will copy all of the files needed for the installation to temporary directories on the local hard drive. When you use the Winnt.exe or Winnt32.exe command to initiate an installation over the network, all the files needed to complete the installation are copied over the network to a temporary directory named WIN_NT.~LS. Setup then continues as it would if you were performing the installation from a local drive.

You can choose not to create the boot floppies by selecting the check box Copy All Setup Files From The Setup CD To The Hard Drive check box. The check box is under the Advanced Options button. When you select this option, a WIN_NT.~BT directory is created on the disk. This directory contains the files that would have been on the four boot floppies.

While the files are being copied into the WIN_NT.~LS directory, Windows 95, Windows 98, or Windows NT is still running. This means there is less down time during the upgrade.

In the next section of setup you are prompted for information needed to complete the installation. After you accept the license agreement, you specify or create an installation partition and choose a file system. All files required for installation are copied from the temporary directory (or the CD-ROM) into the installation directory on the hard disk of the target computer.

Existing Installations

If Setup detects any existing Windows 2000 installations, it displays them in a list. You can select an installation and press R to repair it, or press Esc to continue.

Partitions

Setup displays all existing partitions and free space on the system. Using the Up and Down arrow keys you can select where you want to install Windows 2000 Server. You can also create and delete partitions. Press Enter to continue.

File Systems

Setup gives you the option of keeping the current file system intact or converting it to NTFS. If you do not want to change it, select the Leave Current File System Intact option, which is the default, and press Enter to continue.

Setup examines your hard disks and copies the files it needs for installation from the temporary directory to the installation directory. (Winnt is the default directory.)

After the files are copied, the computer restarts and the Setup wizard begins. During this phase, Setup gathers information about your computer and allows you to select which optional components to install and allows you to select the administrator password.

The Setup wizard presents a series of dialog boxes through which Windows 2000 collects configuration information for setting up your system. During this stage, Windows 2000 security features are installed and devices are installed and configured.

Regional Settings

Windows 2000 displays the current (default) regional settings. You can add support for additional languages, change your location settings for the system, and configure the user account default settings.

Personalize Your Software

When configuring your system, you must type in the name of the person to whom 2000 Server is registered to. You can also add the name of the organization, although this is optional.

Licensing Mode

You must select the Per Server or Per Seat licensing method. If you select Per Server, you must type in the number of Per Server licenses.

Computer Name and Administrator Password

You must type in a computer name (NetBIOS name of up to 15 characters) when you install Windows 2000. Note that the autogenerated name is 15 characters long. The name you type in must be different from other computer, workgroup, or domain names on the network. A default computer name is displayed. You can use the default name or type in a new computer name.

You can also type in an Administrator password for the local Administrator user account. This password can be up to 127 characters long. You may also leave the Password field blank.

Optional Component Manager

The Optional Component Manager allows you to add or remove components during and after installation.

Date and Time Settings

During installation, you must select the appropriate time zone and adjust the date and time settings, if necessary. You should also make adjustments for daylight savings time.

Installing Windows 2000 Server Networking

When the Setup wizard has gathered the necessary information, the Setup program examines the computer to detect installed network adapters. This can take several minutes.

Networking Settings

The Windows 2000 networking setup begins with a dialog box that offers a choice between Typical settings (default) or Custom settings. Typical settings configure the system with all the defaults: Client for Microsoft Networks, File and Print Sharing for Microsoft Networks, and Internet Protocol (TCP/IP) configured as a DHCP client.

Custom settings allows you to configure the following items:

- **Clients.** The default client is Client For Microsoft Networks. You can add Gateway (and Client) Services for NetWare.

- **Services.** The default service is File and Printer Sharing for Microsoft Networks. You can add SAP Agent and QoS Packet Scheduler. You can modify the settings for File and Printer Sharing for Microsoft Networks by highlighting the service and clicking Properties. This allows you to optimize server service settings and provide server service compatibility for LAN Manager 2.*x* clients.

- **Protocols.** The default protocol is Internet Protocol (TCP/IP). You can add other protocols, including NWLink IPX/SPX, NetBEUI, DLC, AppleTalk, and Network Monitor Driver. You can also modify the settings for a protocol (if applicable) by highlighting the protocol and clicking Properties.

Completing the Installation

The Completing the Installation stage performs the following actions and requires no user interaction. Table 8.10 describes the tasks performed by Setup during this stage.

Table 8.10 Tasks Performed during Installation Completion

Task	Description
Copying files	Setup copies any remaining files that are necessary for installation, such as accessories and bitmaps, to the installation directory.
Configuring the computer	Setup creates your start menu and program groups and sets up the print spooler, printers, services, the administrator account, fonts, the Pagefile, and the registration of many dynamic-link libraries (DLLs).

Task	Description
Saving the configuration	Setup saves your configuration to the registry, creates the repair directory, and resets the Boot.ini.
Removing temporary files	Setup removes the temporary files and directories created and used during installation, such as the WIN_NT.~LS directory, and also compacts the system hives in the registry.

Practice: Installing Windows 2000 Server

In this practice, you install Windows 2000 Server on a computer with no formatted partitions. During installation, you use the Windows 2000 Server Setup program to create a partition on your hard disk, on which you install Windows 2000 Server as a standalone server in a workgroup.

Exercise 1: Creating Windows 2000 Server Setup Disks

Complete this exercise on a computer running MS-DOS or any version of Windows with access to the Bootdisk directory on the Windows 2000 Server installation CD-ROM.

If your computer is configured with a bootable CD-ROM drive, you can install Windows 2000 without using the Setup disks. To complete this exercise as outlined, bootable CD-ROM support must be disabled in the BIOS.

Important This exercise requires four formatted 1.44-MB disks. If you use diskettes that contain data, the data will be overwritten without warning.

---

1. Label the four blank, formatted 1.44-MB diskettes as follows:

   Windows 2000 Server Setup Disk #1

   Windows 2000 Server Setup Disk #2

   Windows 2000 Server Setup Disk #3

   Windows 2000 Server Setup Disk #4

2. Insert the Microsoft Windows 2000 Server CD-ROM into the CD-ROM drive.

3. If the Windows 2000 CD-ROM dialog box appears prompting you to install or upgrade to Windows 2000, click Exit.

4. Open a command prompt.

5. At the command prompt, change to your CD-ROM drive. For example, if your CD-ROM drive name is E, type **E:** and press Enter.

6. At the command prompt, change to the Bootdisk directory by typing **cd bootdisk** and pressing Enter.

7. If you are creating the Setup boot disks from a computer running MS-DOS, a Windows 16-bit operating system, Windows 95, or Windows 98, type **makeboot a:** (where a: is the name of your floppy disk drive) and then press Enter. If you are creating Setup boot disks from a computer running Windows NT or Windows 2000, type **makebt32 a:** (where a: is the name of your floppy disk drive) and then press Enter.

   Windows 2000 displays a message indicating that this program creates the four setup disks for installing Windows 2000. It also indicates that four blank, formatted high-density floppy disks are required.

8. Press any key to continue.

   Windows 2000 displays a message prompting you to insert the disk that will become the Windows 2000 Setup disk.

9. Insert the blank, formatted disk labeled Windows 2000 Server Setup Disk #1 into the floppy disk drive, and then press any key to continue.

   After Windows 2000 creates the disk image, it displays a message prompting you to insert the disk labeled Windows 2000 Server Setup Disk #2.

10. Remove Disk #1, insert the blank formatted disk labeled Windows 2000 Server Setup Disk #2 into the floppy disk drive, and then press any key to continue.

    After Windows 2000 creates the disk image, it displays a message prompting you to insert the disk labeled Windows 2000 Server Setup Disk #3.

11. Remove Disk #2, insert the blank formatted disk labeled Windows 2000 Server Setup Disk #3 into the floppy disk drive, and then press any key to continue.

    After Windows 2000 creates the disk image, it displays a message prompting you to insert the disk labeled Disk #4.

12. Remove Disk #3, insert the blank formatted disk labeled Windows 2000 Server Setup Disk #4 into the floppy disk drive, and then press any key to continue.

   After Windows 2000 creates the disk image, it displays a message indicating that the imaging process is done.

13. At the command prompt, type **exit** and then press Enter.

14. Remove the disk from the floppy disk drive and the CD-ROM from the CD-ROM drive.

Exercise 2: Running the Setup Program

This exercise is completed on Computer 1. It is assumed for this exercise that Computer 1 has no operating system installed, the disk is not partitioned, and bootable CD-ROM support, if available, is disabled. To verify that Computer 1 meets all pre-installation requirements, please review "About This Book." Computer 1 should be your second computer, not the computer where you installed Windows 2000 Professional (PRO1) earlier in this book.

1. Insert the disk labeled Windows 2000 Server Setup Disk #1 into the floppy disk drive, insert the Windows 2000 Server CD-ROM into the CD-ROM drive, and restart Computer 1.

   After the computer starts, Windows 2000 Setup displays a brief message that your system configuration is being checked, and then the Windows 2000 Setup screen appears.

   Notice that the gray bar at the bottom of the screen indicates that the computer is being inspected and that the Windows 2000 Executive, which is a minimal version of the Windows 2000 kernel, is loading.

2. When prompted, insert Setup Disk #2 into the floppy disk drive, and then press Enter.

   Notice that Setup indicates that it is loading the HAL, fonts, local specific data, bus drivers, and other software components to support your computer's motherboard, bus, and other hardware. Setup also loads the Windows 2000 Setup program files.

3. When prompted, insert Setup Disk #3 into the floppy disk drive, and then press Enter.

   Notice that Setup indicates that it is loading disk drive controller drivers. After the drive controllers load, the Setup program initializes drivers appropriate to support access to your disk drives. Setup might pause several times during this process.

4. When prompted, insert Setup Disk #4 into the floppy disk drive, and then press Enter.

   Setup loads peripheral support drivers, like the floppy disk driver and file systems. It then initializes the Windows 2000 Executive and loads the rest of the Windows 2000 Setup program.

   If you are installing the evaluation version of Windows 2000, a Setup notification screen appears informing you that you are about to install an evaluation version of Windows 2000.

5. Read the Setup Notification message, and then press Enter to continue.

   Setup displays the Welcome To Setup screen.

   Notice that, in addition to the initial installation of Windows 2000, you can use Windows 2000 Setup to repair or recover a damaged Windows 2000 installation.

6. Read the Welcome To Setup message, and then press Enter to begin the installation phase of Windows 2000 Setup.

   Setup displays the License Agreement screen.

7. Read the license agreement, pressing Page Down to scroll to the bottom of the screen.

8. Select I Accept The Agreement by pressing F8.

   Setup displays the Windows 2000 Server Setup screen, prompting you to select an area of free space or an existing partition on which to install Windows 2000. At this stage of setup you can create and delete partitions on your hard disk.

   If Computer 1 does not contain any disk partitions (as required for this exercise), you will notice that the hard disk listed on the screen contains an existing unformatted partition.

9. Make sure that the Unpartitioned space partition is highlighted, and then type **C**.

   Setup displays the Windows 2000 Setup screen, confirming that you've chosen to create a new partition in the unpartitioned space and informing you of the minimum and maximum sizes of the partition you can create.

10. Specify the size of the partition you want to create (2048 MB), and then press Enter to continue.

Note Although you can create additional partitions from the remaining unpartitioned space during setup, it is recommended that you perform additional partitioning tasks after you install Windows 2000. To partition hard disks after installation, use the Disk Management snap-in.

Setup displays the Windows 2000 Setup screen, showing the new partition as C: New (Unformatted).

11. Make sure the new partition is highlighted, and press Enter.

You are prompted to select a file system for the partition.

12. Use the arrow keys to select Format The Partition Using The NTFS File System, and then press Enter.

The Setup program formats the partition with NTFS. After it formats the partition, Setup examines the hard disk for physical errors that might cause Setup to fail and then copies files to the hard disk. This process takes several minutes.

Eventually, Setup displays the Windows 2000 Server Setup screen. A red status bar counts down for 15 seconds before Setup restarts the computer.

13. Remove the Setup disk from the floppy disk drive.

Important If your computer supports booting from the CD-ROM drive, and this feature was not disabled in the BIOS, the computer will boot from the Windows 2000 Server installation CD-ROM after Windows 2000 Setup restarts. This will cause Setup to run from the beginning. If this happens, remove the CD-ROM and restart the computer.

---

14. Setup copies additional files and then restarts your computer and loads the Windows 2000 Setup wizard.

Exercise 3: Running the Setup Wizard and Information-Gathering Phase of Windows 2000 Server Setup

1. On the Welcome to the Windows 2000 Setup Wizard screen, click Next to begin gathering information about your computer.

Setup configures NTFS folder and file permissions for the operating system files, detects the hardware devices in the computer, and then installs and configures device drivers to support the detected hardware. This process takes several minutes.

2. On the Regional Settings page, make sure that the system locale, user locale, and keyboard layout are correct for your language and location, and then click Next.

Note You can modify regional settings after you install Windows 2000 by using Regional Options in Control Panel.

Setup displays the Personalize Your Software page, prompting you for your name and organization name. Setup uses your organization name to generate the default computer name. Many applications that you install later will use this information for product registration and document identification.

3. In the Name field, type your name. In the Organization field, type the name of an organization. Click Next.

Note If the Your Product Key screen appears, type in the product key provided with Windows 2000 Server and then click Next.

Setup displays the Licensing Modes screen, prompting you to select a licensing mode. By default, the Per Server licensing mode is selected. Setup prompts you to type in the number of licenses you have purchased for this server.

4. Select the Per Server radio button, type **5** for the number of concurrent connections, and then click Next.

Important Using the Per Server Number Of Concurrent Connections option and choosing 5 concurrent connections are only suggested values to be used for this exercise. You should use a legal number of concurrent connections based on the actual licenses you own. You can also choose to use Per Seat instead of Per Server.

Setup displays the Computer Name And Administrator Password screen.

Notice that Setup uses your organization name to generate a suggested name for the computer.

5. In the Computer Name field, type **Server01**.

Windows 2000 displays the computer name in all capital letters regardless of how it was typed in.

Warning To complete this exercise, your computer cannot be connected to a network.

6. In the Administrator Password field and the Confirm Password field, type **password** (all lowercase) and then click Next. Passwords are case sensitive, so make sure you type password in all lowercase letters.

Note For the exercises in this self-paced training kit, you will use the password value of "password" for the Administrator account. In a production environment, you should always use a complex password for the Administrator account (one that others cannot easily guess). Microsoft recommends mixing uppercase and lowercase letters, numbers, and symbols (for example, Lp6*g9).

Setup displays the Windows 2000 Components screen that indicates which Windows 2000 system components Setup will install.

You can install additional components after you install Windows 2000 by using Add/Remove Programs in Control Panel. Make sure you install only the components selected by default during setup. Later in this training guide, you will learn how to install additional components.

7. Click Next.

If a modem is detected in the computer during setup, Setup displays the Modem Dialing Information page.

8. If the Modem Dialing Information screen appears, type in an area code or city code and click Next.

The Date and Time Settings screen appears.

Important Windows 2000 services perform many tasks whose successful completion depends on the computer's time and date settings. Be sure to select the correct time zone for your location to avoid problems in later exercises.

---

9. Enter the correct date and time and time zone settings, and then click Next.

The Network Settings screen appears and Setup installs networking components.

Exercise 4: Completing the Installing Windows Networking Components Phase of Windows 2000 Server Setup

Networking is an integral part of Windows 2000 Server. Networking can be configured in many ways. In this exercise, basic networking is configured. In a later practice, you will install additional network components.

1. On the Networking Settings screen, make sure that Typical Settings is selected, and then click Next to begin installing Windows networking components.

   This setting installs networking components that are used to gain access to and share resources on a network. It also configures TCP/IP to automatically obtain an IP address from a DHCP server on the network.

   Setup displays the Workgroup Or Computer Domain screen, which prompts you to join either a workgroup or a domain.

2. On the Workgroup Or Computer Domain screen, make sure that the No, This Computer Is Not On A Network Or Is On A Network Without A Domain radio button is selected, and that the workgroup name is WORKGROUP. Then click Next.

   Setup displays the Installing Components screen, displaying the status as Setup installs and configures the remaining operating system components according to the options you specified. This will take several minutes.

   Setup then displays the Performing Final Tasks screen, which shows the status as Setup finishes copying files, makes and saves configuration changes, and deletes temporary files. Computers that do not exceed the minimum hardware requirements might take 30 minutes or more to complete this phase of installation.

   Setup then displays the Completing The Windows 2000 Setup Wizard screen.

3. Remove the Windows 2000 Server CD-ROM from the CD-ROM drive, and click Finish.

Important If your computer supports booting from the CD-ROM drive and you did not remove the installation CD-ROM, and if you disable this feature in the BIOS, the computer will run Setup again soon after Setup restarts the computer. If this happens, remove the CD-ROM and then restart the computer.

Windows 2000 restarts and runs the newly installed version of Windows 2000 Server.

Exercise 5: Completing the Hardware Installation Phase of Windows 2000 Server Setup

During this final phase of installation, any Plug and Play hardware not detected in the previous phases of setup will be detected.

1. At the completion of the startup phase, log on by pressing Ctrl+Alt+Delete.

2. In the Enter Password dialog box, type **Administrator** in the User Name field and type **password** in the Password field.

3. Click OK.

   If Windows 2000 detects hardware that was not detected during setup, the Found New Hardware Wizard screen appears, indicating that Windows 2000 is installing the appropriate drivers.

4. If the Found New Hardware Wizard screen appears, verify that the Restart The Computer When I Click Finish check box is cleared and then click Finish to complete the Found New Hardware wizard.

   Windows 2000 displays the Microsoft Windows 2000 Configure Your Server dialog box. From this dialog box, you can configure a variety of advanced options and services.

5. Select the I Will Configure This Server Later radio button, and click Next.

6. From the next screen that appears, clear the Show This Screen At Startup check box.

7. Close the Configure Your Server screen.

Exercise 6: Adjusting the Display Settings

Setup selects a default resolution that is compatible with the video adapter that Setup has detected. You can change the default settings now or at any time after you install Windows 2000.

Warning If you do not know the refresh frequency that your monitor supports with the color palette and screen area you selected, do not change the default setting. Setting the refresh frequency too high might damage your monitor.

---

1. If you wish to adjust your display settings to show more colors or a higher screen resolution, open Control Panel and select Display.

   The Display Properties dialog box appears.

2. From the Settings tab, adjust your screen area and colors, and click OK.

   A Display Properties message box appears warning you that your settings will be applied and that if you don't respond to the message box that appears after the display settings are adjusted, the original display settings will be restored.

3. Click OK.

   If the display settings are valid, a Monitor Settings message box will appear.

4. Click Yes to make the changes permanent.

   You have now completed the Windows 2000 Server installation and are logged on as Administrator.

5. Close Control Panel.

Note To properly shut down Windows 2000 Server, click the Start button, choose Shut Down, and then follow the directions that appear.

Lesson Summary

To install Windows 2000 Server, you must run either Winnt.exe or Winnt32.exe. Winnt.exe is used on computers running MS-DOS or Windows 16-bit operating systems. Winnt32.exe is used on computers running Windows 32-bit operating systems (Windows 95, Windows 98, Windows NT, or Windows 2000). You can use a number of parameters with Winnt.exe and Winnt32.exe to customize how Windows 2000 Server is installed on your computer. Once one of the Setup files is launched, the Windows 2000 Server installation begins. This process takes place in four phases:

1. Starting the Setup program is when you specify the components to install.

2. Running the Setup wizard which prompts you to provide the various information that setup cannot automatically determine.

3. Installing Windows Networking is when the setup program detects the installed network adapters.

4. Completing the Installation is when the setup program uses the information gathered in the prior steps to copy files, configure the computer and clean up the files as the installation is completed.

Lesson 2: Upgrading to Windows 2000 Server

The process for upgrading existing servers from Windows NT Server to Windows 2000 Server is mostly automated. During the upgrade, Windows 2000 Setup migrates the old operating system settings, requiring little administrator input during the process. This lesson discusses upgrading to the Windows 2000 Server operating system, upgrading Windows NT domains, and consolidating domains.

After this lesson, you will be able to

- Upgrade a Windows NT computer to Windows 2000 Server

Estimated lesson time: 30 minutes

Upgrading to Windows 2000 Server

There is only one basic process for upgrading a member server. Once you begin the installation process, the Setup wizard guides you through the upgrade. When prompted, select the Upgrade To Windows 2000 option. During the final stages of installation, Windows 2000 Server Setup gathers information, using preexisting settings from the previous operating system.

There are several reasons to choose to upgrade, assuming that your previous operating system is a version that allows upgrading. Configuration is simpler; your existing users, settings, groups, rights, and permissions are retained; and files and applications do not need to be recopied to the disk after installation. (As with any major changes to the hard disk, however, you should plan on backing up the disk before running Setup.)

If you want to upgrade and then use the same applications as you did with your old operating system, review the Windows 2000 Compatibility Guide at *http://www.microsoft.com* and read the Read1st.txt file and the Relnotes.doc file (in the root directory of the Windows 2000 Server installation CD-ROM). You can also install the Windows 2000 Support Tools, which are located in the \Support\Tools directory of the Windows 2000 Server installation CD-ROM. The Support Tools include the Windows 2000 Server Resource Kit Deployment Planning Guide. Review the "Testing Applications for Compatibility with Microsoft Windows 2000" chapter for information about using your old applications.

When you upgrade, you must consider whether to convert the file system on any FAT16 or FAT32 partitions that you might have to the NTFS file system. It is possible to install Windows 2000 Server and also allow the computer to sometimes run another operating system by setting up the computer as a dual-boot system. Using dual booting, however, presents complexities because of file system issues.

Upgrading Servers

Windows 2000 Server supports upgrades from Windows NT 3.51 Server, Windows NT Server 4.0, and earlier versions of Windows 2000 Server. If a computer is running versions of Windows NT older than Windows NT 3.51, upgrade to Windows NT Server 4.0 before upgrading to Windows 2000 Server.

Note Windows 2000 supports all service packs for Windows NT 3.51 and Windows NT 4.0. The upgrade of installed applications varies with the system.

Upgrade Methods

The easiest way to upgrade Windows NT Server is to insert the Windows 2000 Server installation CD-ROM into the computer's CD-ROM drive. You can also run Winnt32 from the CD-ROM.

Setup cannot upgrade the operating system from the boot floppies or from booting the CD-ROM. Winnt32 or Autorun must be used to upgrade Windows NT Server. You can also upgrade your system by running Winnt32.exe over the network.

Finding Windows NT Installations to Upgrade

To find Windows NT Server installations on the system, the C:\Boot.ini file is examined on *x*86-based systems.

Note Windows 2000 does not support RISC-based systems.

The Setup program attempts to access the partition indicated by the Advanced RISC Computing (ARC) path in *<active partition>*:\Boot.ini for each installation it finds. The active partition is usually C:, so references to the drive containing Boot.ini will be C:. If Setup can access the partition, it then examines the root directory by searching for the following items:

- **Directories.** The Setup program searches for System32, System32\Drivers, and System32\Config subfolders.

- **Files.** Under the System32 subfolders, Setup searches for Ntoskrnl.exe and Ntdll.dll.

After searching for directories and files, Setup attempts to load portions of the registry to determine whether an attempt to upgrade this installation has failed. Setup also determines the type of the current Windows NT installation and finds the edition (Server or Workstation), version number of the Windows NT installation (either 3.1, 3.5, 3.51, or 4.0), and build number.

The system's current version and build number must be less than or equal to the version number to which the system will be upgraded. Also, the edition of the installation must be Server. Therefore, the Windows 2000 Server upgrade process upgrades only Windows NT Server 3.51 and Windows NT Server 4.0 systems.

Once each installation in C:\Boot.ini has been found and each entry has met the above criteria for version, build, and edition, Setup presents a menu that lists the installations on the system that can be upgraded.

If a Windows NT Server installation does not appear in the list of possible installations to upgrade, it probably did not meet one of the above criteria. At this point, you can press F3 to exit from the upgrade and still boot into any version of Windows NT installed on the system to ensure that the installation meets the criteria.

Note If there are multiple C:\Boot.ini entries that point to the same Windows NT installation, the installation is listed in the upgrade selection menu only once.

Upgrading a Windows NT Domain

A critical task in upgrading your network to Windows 2000 Server is upgrading the Windows NT Server domain. Domains are an important feature of both Windows NT Server and Windows 2000 Server. A domain is a grouping of accounts and network resources under a single domain name and security boundary. It is necessary to have one or more domains if you want to use domain-based user accounts and other domain security features in Windows 2000 Server. (This was true for Windows NT Server as well.)

With Windows 2000, servers can play one of three roles in relation to domains. Servers can be domain controllers, which contain matching copies of the user accounts and other Active Directory services data in a given domain. They can also be member servers, which belong to a domain but do not contain a copy of Active Directory services data. Third, servers can be standalone servers, which do not belong to a domain but belong to a workgroup. A domain must have at least one domain controller, and it should generally have multiple domain controllers, each one backing up the user accounts and other Active Directory services data for the others and helping provide logon support to users.

You should plan the roles that your servers will play within domains in Windows 2000 before running Setup; however, if adjustments are necessary to these roles, they can still be made after setup.

There are several important points to remember about upgrading an existing Windows NT domain to Windows 2000 domain:

- You must use the NTFS file system on domain controllers.

- Any servers that have any partition formatted with FAT16 or FAT32 will lack local security. On FAT16 or FAT32 partitions, shared folders can be protected only with permissions set on the directories, not on individual files, and there is no access protection against local access to the partition.

- When upgrading the domain controllers in a Windows NT domain to Windows 2000, you must upgrade the primary domain controllers (PDCs) first.

The roles of the servers in a domain are named somewhat differently in Windows 2000 Server compared to Windows NT Server. With Windows NT Server, the possible roles were PDC (limited to one per domain), backup domain controller (BDC), member server, or standalone server. Windows 2000 has only one kind of domain controller (without a "primary" or "backup" designation) and also includes the roles of member server and standalone server. Table 8.11 shows what server roles Windows 2000 Setup assigns when you upgrade.

Table 8.11 Comparison of Server Roles

Role in Windows NT domain	Role in Windows 2000 domain
Primary domain controller	Domain controller
Backup domain controller	Your choice of domain controller or member server
Member server	Your choice of member server or standalone server
Standalone server	Your choice of member server (if a Windows 2000 domain exists) or standalone server

Upgrading a Windows NT domain takes place over the following five stages:

1. Planning for a Windows NT domain upgrade

2. Preparing for a Windows NT domain upgrade

3. Upgrading the PDC

4. Upgrading the BDCs

5. Upgrading member servers

Planning for a Windows NT Domain Upgrade

The following are the main considerations when planning a Windows 2000 upgrade :

- **DNS domain name organization.** Develop DNS structure for the root domain of an enterprise tree or multiple trees in a forest of disjointed DNS domain names. Once the root DNS domain is created, other subdomains can be added to build the tree. For example, microsoft.com is a root domain, and dev.microsoft.com and mktg.microsoft.com are subdomains.

- **Name space organization within large account domains.** Determine how to use organizational units to structure the employees and project resources.

- **Domain consolidation.** Rebalance administration and control of centrally managed and distributed network services by merging resource domains into a smaller number of Windows 2000 domains.

- **New computer accounts added for long-term organization.** Determine the location of computer accounts in Windows 2000 organizational units. This is an important part of deploying Windows 2000 computer security policies.

- **Deployment of advanced technologies.** Deploy new advanced technologies such as PKI security for smart card logon and remote access authentication or IP security for secure data transfer over private intranet and public Internet communications.

Note For more information, see the *Windows 2000 Support Tools' Deployment and Planning Guide*. The installation program for this guide and other support tools is located in the \Support\Tools directory on the Windows 2000 Server installation CD-ROM.

Preparing for a Windows NT Domain Upgrade

Whenever you make any major changes to the contents of the hard disks on your servers, you should back up the hard disks before upgrading any of them. Before upgrading, you should also consider disconnecting the network cable of a BDC in your existing Windows NT network. After upgrading your PDC to Windows 2000 Server, this disconnected system is available for promotion to a Windows NT PDC if needed. (In the course of an uneventful upgrade, you would not promote the Windows NT BDC to PDC, but instead continue the upgrade process, eventually reconnecting the disconnected server and upgrading it.)

In addition, for any computer that will be a domain controller in the Windows 2000 domain, you should make sure there is plenty of room on the disk, beyond the space needed for the operating system itself. When the user accounts database is upgraded to the format used by Windows 2000 Server, it can expand significantly.

Preparing to Upgrade the Domain Controller

Before upgrading a domain controller, there are a number of tasks that must be completed:

- Disable WINS by using the Services option in Control Panel in Windows NT Server 4.0 so that the WINS database can be converted during the upgrade process.

- Disable DHCP by using the Services option in Control Panel in Windows NT Server 4.0 so that the DHCP database can be converted during the upgrade.

- Set up a test environment by creating test user accounts so that you can test the upgrade once it is complete. Create users and groups that are consistent with your implementation of Windows NT Server 4.0.

Table 8.12 lists items you might want to include in a test environment and explains how to implement them.

Table 8.12 Items to Include During Testing

Item	Implementation
User and Group policies	Include both user and group policies that are easy to verify after the upgrade. For example, remove the Run command from the Start menu.
User profiles	Set up individual user profiles for the test users that are obvious and easy to verify, such as different background wallpaper.
Logon scripts	Use logon script commands that are easy to verify after the upgrade, such as mapping network drives with the net use command.

Note It is always a good idea to test any upgrade in a lab environment before implementing it in a production environment. To that end you may remove a BDC from the network and promote it to be a PDC in a private network. Then you can upgrade the PDC to Windows 2000 Server. If that is successful, you can bring that computer back to the production environment.

Upgrading the Primary Domain Controller

The first domain controller to be upgraded in a Windows NT domain must be the PDC. As you upgrade this server, you are given the choices of creating a new domain or a child domain and of creating a new forest or a domain tree in an existing forest. For upgrading a domain of three to five servers, create a new domain and a new forest. You should also define the domain name space to set up the top-level name space for the organization. Other domains can be added to the tree as child domains.

During the upgrade, you can choose the location of three important files: the database containing user accounts and other Active Directory data, the log file, and the system volume file (SYSVOL). The database and the log file can be on any type of partition (FAT16, FAT32, or NTFS); the previous SAM database can expand significantly from the size it had with Windows NT Server, so you should allow plenty of room for it. (Initially, the log file will take up very little space.) The system volume file must be on an NTFS partition.

After the first server is upgraded to a Windows 2000 domain controller, it will be fully backward compatible. This means that in a multiple-server environment the domain controller appears as a Windows 2000 domain controller to Windows 2000 servers and clients but emulates a Windows NT 4.0 PDC to other servers and clients.

Upgrading the Backup Domain Controllers

After upgrading your PDC and ensuring that it is functioning to your satisfaction, you next upgrade any BDCs. (If possible, it is best to begin the next upgrades soon after the PDC upgrade, rather than allowing a long delay.) Be sure that the first server upgraded (the former PDC) is running and available on the network when you upgrade other domain controllers. This server is used as a template for the other domain controllers to copy as they are upgraded.

Upgrade the BDCs one at a time, and ensure that each is backed up before upgrading. Start and test each server on the network to ensure that it is functioning to your satisfaction before upgrading another BDC.

When you have completely upgraded all servers to Windows 2000 domain controllers, you can change the domain from Mixed mode (where Windows NT domain controllers can exist in the domain) to Native mode (where only Windows 2000 domain controllers can exist in the domain). You cannot revert to Mixed mode after changing to Native mode, so it is important that you think carefully about changing the domain. Figure 8.2 shows the transition from a Windows NT domain to a Windows 2000 Native mode domain.

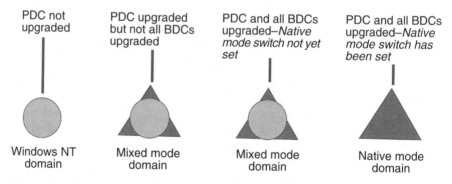

Figure 8.2 Transition from Windows NT domain to Windows 2000 Native mode domain

Mixed Mode

Mixed mode refers to a domain that contains both Windows 2000 and Windows NT 3.51/4.0 domain controllers. In Mixed mode the PDC is upgraded to Windows 2000 Server and one or more BDCs remain at version Windows NT Server 3.51/4.0. The Windows 2000 domain controller that was the PDC uses the Active Directory store to save objects. It is still fully backward compatible because it exposes the data as a native NT 4 domain flat store to down-level computers.

The PDC appears as a Windows 2000 domain controller to other Windows 2000 computers, and as a Windows NT 3.51/4.0 domain controller to computers that are not yet upgraded.

The domain still uses a single master replication with a Windows 2000 PDC; it is recognized as the domain master by the Windows NT Server 3.51/4.0 BDCs.

In Mixed mode the domain is limited by the functionality of the Windows NT 4.0 domain controllers. The limitations on Windows 2000 operating in Mixed mode include the following:

- No group nesting is available.
- Non–Windows 2000 clients cannot benefit from transitive trust; they are limited to the limitations of pre–Windows 2000 trust relationships for access to resources.

Mixed mode is the default mode and is generally an interim step in the implementation of Windows 2000.

Native Mode

Once all domain controllers in a domain are upgraded, the domain can be moved from Mixed mode to Native mode. In Native mode all clients make use of Windows 2000 transitive trust. This means that a user can connect to any resource in the enterprise. Native mode also allows group nesting.

Note Moving to Native mode is a one-way move; once in Native mode, it is not possible to move the domain back to Mixed mode.

Upgrading Member Servers

Upgrade the NT 4 member servers to Windows 2000. Member servers in the domain can be upgraded in any order.

Domain Consolidation

Domain consolidation is a planning process for organizing domain resources to take advantage of new advanced features of the Windows 2000 Active Directory services. Domain reconfiguration is optional; it is not a requirement for installing Windows 2000. Domain reconfiguration can take place over time as individual computers are upgraded and moved to different domains. Reconfiguration is also a fairly intensive and time-consuming administrator operation, as computers are moved to new domains and access control is verified or updated as needed.

There are two general ways to consolidate domains:

- Move user accounts from one domain to another to form a single larger domain.

- Move server computers from one resource domain into the organizational unit of another domain.

One advantage of domain consolidation is that the number of master account domains can be reduced because each domain can be scaled to handle a much larger number of user, group, and computer accounts. Combining master account domains can reduce the number of server computers and interdomain trust accounts. However, moving users from one domain to another requires the creation of a new temporary password for the user account in the new domain. User passwords are not preserved when a user account is moved from one domain to another, although the security identifier (SID) for the user is.

Another advantage to domain consolidation is that the number of resource domains can be reduced by moving servers from many small domains into a combined resource domain. The domain controllers of the resource domains become member servers in the larger combined domain. This reduces the number of interdomain trust relationships between resource domains and account domains, saving system resources on domain controllers. Domain consolidation also makes it easier to redeploy server computers from one project or department to another.

Windows 2000 includes the following features that enable domain reconfiguration:

- Users and groups can be moved across domain boundaries and preserve security identity. The SID history is kept with the user account, and access tokens will contain both the new and the old SID to preserve access rights.

- Domain controllers can be demoted to a member server and moved to another domain.

- Security policies can be defined centrally and applied to many systems. These policies can grow in scope and change over time. They are used to deploy new technology, such as public key security and IP security. As new computers join a domain, they can automatically pick up the security policy in effect for the new domain.

- Computers can be moved to different domains by using remote administration tools.

- Access rights can be updated to reflect changes in an organization's structure or philosophy.

Lesson Summary

The upgrade from Windows NT Server to Windows 2000 Server is, for the most part, an automated process. The easiest way to upgrade Windows NT Server is to use the Windows 2000 Server installation CD-ROM in the computer's CD-ROM drive. The Setup wizard then guides you through the upgrade. An important aspect of upgrading to Windows 2000 is upgrading the domain, which involves a number of stages. First you must plan how you will upgrade the domain. This includes determining a domain name organization and deploying new technologies. Next you must prepare for that upgrade by completing such tasks as backing up files and disconnecting network cables. In addition, you must prepare to upgrade the domain controllers. The next step in upgrading the domain is to upgrade the PDC. This is followed by upgrading the BDCs and the member servers. When you have completed these steps, you should consider consolidating your domain to take advantage of the new advanced features of the Windows 2000 Active Directory services.

Lesson 3: Troubleshooting a Windows 2000 Server Installation

Your installation of Windows 2000 Server should run to completion without any problems. However, you might encounter some difficulties during installation. This lesson covers some common issues involved in Windows 2000 Server installation.

After this lesson, you will be able to

- Troubleshoot Windows 2000 installations

Estimated lesson time: 15 minutes

Troubleshooting Windows 2000 Server

When installing Windows 2000 Server, you might encounter problems caused by such things as bad media or incompatible hardware. Table 8.13 lists some of these common installation problems and offers solutions to resolve them.

Table 8.13 Common Installation Problems

Problem	Solution
Media errors	If you are installing from a CD-ROM, use a different CD-ROM drive. If you still receive media errors, request a replacement CD-ROM by contacting Microsoft or your vendor.
Unsupported	Replace the CD-ROM drive with one that is supported, or if that is not possible, try another method of installation, such as installing over the network. After you have completed the installation, you can add the driver for the CD-ROM drive if it is available.
Insufficient disk space	Use the Setup program to create a partition by using existing free space on the hard disk.
	Delete and create partitions as needed to create a partition that is large enough for installation.
	Reformat an existing partition to create more space.
Failure of dependency service to start	Use the Windows 2000 Setup wizard, and return to the Network Settings dialog box and verify that you installed the correct protocol and network adapter. Verify that the network adapter has the proper configuration settings, such as transceiver type, and that the local computer name is unique on the network.

Problem	Solution
Failure to connect to the domain controller	Verify that the domain name is correct.
	Verify that the server running the DNS service and the domain controller are both running and online. If you cannot locate a domain controller, install into a workgroup and then join the domain after installation.
	Verify that the network adapter card and protocol settings are set correctly.
	If you are reinstalling Windows 2000 and using the same computer name, delete and then recreate the computer account.
Failure of Windows 2000 Server to install or start	Verify that Windows 2000 is detecting all of the hardware and that all of the hardware is on the HCL.

Lesson Summary

This lesson provides an overview of some of the common problems that can be encountered when installing Windows 2000 Server. Installation problems can be caused by bad media or incompatible hardware. In addition, there may not be enough room on any of the partitions to install Windows 2000 Server because you did not complete the preinstallation tasks. Other problems that might arise are the failure to connect to the domain controller or failure of Windows 2000 Server to install or start.

Lesson 4: Preparing for an Unattended Installation of Windows 2000 Server

When you perform an unattended installation of Windows 2000 Server, you create an answer file that supplies information to the setup routine. In addition, if you are going to install Windows 2000 Server on multiple computers over a network, you must create at least one set of distribution folders. This lesson describes the process of creating an answer file and setting up the distribution files necessary for a network installation.

After this lesson, you will be able to

- Create a customized answer file for an unattended installation

- Set up your distribution directory for a network installation of Windows 2000 Server

Estimated lesson time: 45 minutes

Creating the Answer File

The answer file is a customized script (usually saved as a .txt file) that allows you to run an unattended installation of Windows 2000 Server. The file, sometimes called the unattend file or the unattend script file, answers the questions that Setup normally prompts you for during installation. The \i386 directory of the Windows 2000 Server installation CD-ROM contains a sample answer file, Unattend.txt, which you can edit and use in your unattended installation. You can leave the name of the answer file as is, or you can change it according to the needs of your organization. For example, Comp1.txt, Install.txt, and Setup.txt are all valid names for an answer file, as long as those names are correctly specified in the Setup command. Being able to use different names allows you to build and use multiple answer files if you need to maintain different scripted installations for different parts of your organization.

Note that other programs, such as the Sysprep tool, which is used to facilitate the creation of a disk image of your Windows 2000 Server installation, also use answer files. Table 8.14 describes how the answer file can be named and when it is used.

Table 8.14 Appropriate Names for Answer File

Filename	When the file is used
<filename>.txt	When performing an unattended installation. You can use any name for the .txt file. Unattend.txt is the name of the sample answer file included with Windows 2000 Server.
Winnt.sif	When installing Windows 2000 Server from a bootable CD-ROM drive.
Sysprep.inf	When using the Sysprep tool to create a disk image of your Windows 2000 Server installation.

The same format that is used in Unattend.txt is used for the answer files listed in Table 8.14. The answer file contains multiple optional sections that you modify to supply information about your installation requirements. The file supplies Setup with answers to all the questions you are asked when you install Windows 2000 Server manually. In addition, the answer file tells Setup how to interact with the distribution folders and files that you have created. For example, in the [Unattended] section there is an OEM Preinstall entry that tells Setup whether to copy the OEM subfolders from the distribution folders to the target computer.

Answer File Format

An answer file consists of section headers, keys, and the values for each key. Most of the section headers are predefined, but some can be user defined. The following information is included in the Unattend.txt file. You can copy this file from the CD-ROM to writeable media, like a fixed disk, and then edit the file as necessary to meet the needs of your unattended installation. You can also rename the file.

```
Microsoft Windows 2000 Professional, Server, Advanced Server
and Datacenter
 (c) 1994 - 1999 Microsoft Corporation. All rights reserved.

Sample Unattended Setup Answer File

This file contains information about how to automate the
installation
or upgrade of Windows 2000 Professional and Windows 2000
Server so the
Setup program runs without requiring user input.


 [Unattended]
Unattendmode = FullUnattended
OemPreinstall = NO
```

```
TargetPath = WINNT
Filesystem = LeaveAlone

[UserData]
FullName = "Your User Name"
OrgName = "Your Organization Name"
ComputerName = "COMPUTER_NAME"

[GuiUnattended]
Sets the Timezone to the Pacific Northwest
Sets the Admin Password to NULL
Turn AutoLogon ON and login once
TimeZone = "004"
AdminPassword = *
AutoLogon = Yes
AutoLogonCount = 1

For Server installs
[LicenseFilePrintData]
AutoMode = "PerServer"
AutoUsers = "5"

[GuiRunOnce]
List the programs that you want to launch when the machine
is logged on to for the first time

[Display]
BitsPerPel = 8
XResolution = 800
YResolution = 600
VRefresh = 70

[Networking]
When set to YES, setup will install default networking
components. The components to be set are
TCP/IP, File and Print Sharing, and the Client for Microsoft
Networks.
InstallDefaultComponents = YES

[Identification]
JoinWorkgroup = Workgroup
```

You do not need to specify all the possible keys in an answer file if the installation does not require them. Invalid key values generate errors or can cause incorrect behavior after setup.

The answer file is broken into sections. A section name is enclosed in brackets, as in the following example:

```
[UserData]
```

Sections contain keys and the corresponding values for those keys. Each key and value are separated by a space, an equal sign, and a space:

```
BitsPerPel = 8
```

Values that have spaces in them require double quotes around them:

```
OrgName = "Microsoft Corporation"
```

Some sections have no keys and merely contain a list of values:

```
[OEMBootFiles]
Txtsetup.oem
```

Comment lines start with a semicolon:

```
;Setup program runs without requiring user input.
```

Answer File Keys and Values

Every key in an answer file must have a value assigned to it; however, some keys are optional, and some keys have default values that are used if the key is omitted. Key values are strings of text, unless a numeric string is specified. If a numeric string is specified, the value is decimal unless otherwise noted.

Note Keys are not case sensitive; they can be uppercase or lowercase.

The Unattend.doc file has detailed information about the answer file keys and values. You can find Unattend.doc in the Deploy.cab file on the Windows 2000 Server installation CD-ROM, under the \Support\Tools folder. To extract or view the contents of the Deploy.cab file, use Windows Explorer. For more details about opening the Unattend.doc file, see the Sreadme.doc file on the Windows 2000 Server installation CD-ROM.

Important Running Setup.exe or 2000rkst.msi from the \Support\Tools folder installs the Windows 2000 Support Tools in Support.cab, but it does not extract the Unattend.doc file or any of the other compressed files in Deploy.cab.

Methods for Creating an Answer File

You can create an answer file by using Setup Manager or by creating the file manually.

Creating the Answer File by Using Setup Manager

To help you create or modify the answer file, an application called Setup Manager is available on the Windows 2000 Server installation CD-ROM in the Support\Tools\Deploy.cab file.

You can use Setup Manager to perform the following tasks:

- Specify the platform for the answer file (Windows 2000 Professional, Windows 2000 Server, Remote Operating System Installation, or Sysprep)

- Specify the level of automation for Unattended Setup mode (Provide Defaults, Fully Automated, Hide Pages, Read Only, and GUI mode attended Setup)

- Specify default user name and organization information

- Define one computer name or many computer names to support multiple unattended installations

- Configure up to 99 automatic administrator logons to complete setup

- Configure display settings

- Configure network settings

- Configure joining a workgroup or domain and automatically add a computer account to the domain

- Create distribution folders

- Add a custom logo and background files

- Add files to the distribution folders

- Add commands to the [GuiRunOnce] section of the answer file

- Create Cmdlines.txt files

- Specify code pages and other language-specific settings

- Specify regional settings

- Specify a time zone

- Specify Telephony Application Programming Interface (TAPI) information

- Customize browser and shell settings

- Define the installation folder name. The boot partition (the partition containing the operating system files) is specified with the /t: or /tempdrive: switch

- Add printers

- Add mass storage device drivers and a custom HAL to be used during an unattended installation

- Create a distribution folder and share for the distribution or specify that the unattended installation will run from the Windows 2000 Server CD-ROM

With Setup Manager, you can add consistency to the process of creating or updating the answer file. However, you cannot use Setup Manager to specify all answer file settings, optional components, create Txtsetup.oem files, or create subfolders in the distribution folder.

After you use Setup Manager to create an answer file, add more settings by using a text editor. Refer to Unattend.doc and Readme.txt included in the Deploy.cab for a comprehensive list of available settings.

Table 8.15 describes the most commonly used Setup Manager specifications.

Table 8.15 Common Setup Manager Specifications

Parameter	Purpose
Upgrade option	Specifies whether to install Windows 2000 Professional or Windows 2000 Server
Target computer name	Specifies the user name, organization name, and computer names to apply to the target computers
Product ID	Specifies the product license number obtained from the product documentation
Workgroup or domain	Specifies the name of the workgroup or domain to which the computer should be added
Time zone	Specifies the time zone for the computer
Network configuration information	Specifies the network adapter type and configuration information, including network protocols

Creating the Answer File Manually

To create the answer file manually, you can use a text editor such as Notepad. In general, an answer file consists of section headers, parameters, and values for those parameters. Although most of the section headers are predefined, you can also define additional section headers. Note that it is not necessary to specify all the possible parameters in the answer file if the installation does not require them.

Creating the Distribution Folders

To install Windows 2000 Server on multiple computers over a network, you must create at least one set of distribution folders. The distribution folders typically reside on a server to which the destination computers can connect. This allows users to install Windows 2000 Server by running Winnt.exe or Winnt32.exe on those computers. You can use one set of distribution folders and multiple answer files for different system implementations. Even if you intend to use disk imaging as your installation method, starting with distribution folders helps to provide consistent implementations for a variety of system types. In addition, distribution folders allow you to update future images by editing the files in the distribution folders to generate updated images without having to start from the beginning.

To help load balance the servers and to make the file-copy process of Windows 2000 Setup faster, you can create distribution folders on multiple servers to support the installation process on computers that are running Windows 95, Windows 98, Windows NT, or Windows 2000. You can run Winnt32.exe with up to eight sets of distribution folders. Each set of distribution folders contains the Windows 2000 Server installation files as well as any device drivers and other files needed for installation.

To create a distribution folder manually, connect to the network server on which you want to create the distribution folder, and create a \W2kdist folder on the network share. To help differentiate between multiple distribution shares for the different editions of Windows 2000 (Windows 2000 Professional, Windows 2000 Server, and Windows 2000 Advanced Server), choose different names for each folder. If you need localized language versions of Windows 2000 to meet requirements for international branches of your organization, you can create separate distribution shares for each localized version. For each edition of Windows 2000, copy the contents of the \i386 folder to the distribution share created for it. For instance, if you are preparing a distribution for Windows 2000 Server, create and share a folder named \W2kdists and copy the \i386 directory on the Windows 2000 Server installation CD-ROM to the folder.

Note The distribution share to support a default installation of Windows 2000 Server requires approximately 313 megabytes (MB) of disk space.

You can also use Setup Manager to automatically create and share a distribution folder.

Structuring the Distribution Folder

The distribution folder (usually called i386 for Intel systems) consists of various folders and subfolders of information used during the installation of Windows 2000 Server. This folder needs to be organized in the appropriate order. Figure 8.3 illustrates how these folders should be structured.

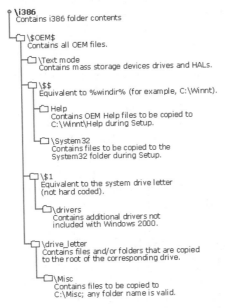

Figure 8.3 Example of a structure for the distribution folders

\i386 (On Windows 2000 Installation CD-ROM Copied to Distribution Share)

This is the primary distribution folder. It contains all the files required to install Windows 2000 Server. You copy the contents of this folder from the Windows 2000 Server installation CD-ROM to the root of the distribution share.

\OEM (On Distribution Share and Copied to WIN_NT.~LS)

The \$OEM$ subfolder is located directly beneath the primary distribution folder. During Setup you can automatically copy directories, standard Microsoft format 8.3 files, and any tools needed for your automated installation process to \$OEM$. Note that if you use the OEMFILESPATH key in the answer file, you can create the \$OEM$ subfolder outside of the distribution folder.

\$OEM\$ provides the necessary folder structure for supplemental files to be copied to the target computer during setup. These files include drivers, utilities, applications, and any other files required to deploy Windows 2000 Server within your organization.

\$OEM\$ can contain the optional file Cmdlines.txt, which contains a list of commands to be run during the Setup wizard of setup. These commands can be used to install optional components, such as tools and utilities. Commands contained in Cmdlines.txt are run before the computer is logged on to the network.

As long as Setup finds \$OEM\$ in the root of the distribution point, it copies all the files found in this directory to the \$WIN_NT\$.~LS temporary directory created during the completing phase of setup. During completing phase, subfolders of \$OEM\$ are copied to the corresponding location on the target computer. At setup completion, \$OEM\$ and all subfolders are deleted along with \$WIN_NT\$.~LS.

Note All folders described next are located on the distribution share below \$OEM\$ and are copied to various locations on the computer running Setup.

\$OEM\$\textmode (Copied to \$WIN_NT\$.~BT)

The \$OEM\$\textmode subfolder contains new or updated files for installing mass storage device drivers and HALs. These files can include OEM HALs, drivers for SCSI devices, and the Txtsetup.oem file, which directs the loading and installing of these components.

All files placed in the \$OEM\$\textmode subfolder (HALs and drivers) must be listed in the [OEMBootFiles] section of the answer file.

\$OEM\$\\$\$ (Copied to %windir% and Subfolders of %windir%)

The \$OEM\$\\$\$ subfolder corresponds to the contents of the %windir% environment variable. The subfolder contains the operating system files (either new files or replacements for retail files) that are copied to the various subfolders when Windows 2000 is installed. The structure of this subfolder must match the structure of a standard Windows 2000 installation, where \$OEM\$\\$\$ matches %windir%, \$OEM\$\\$\$\System32 matches %windir%\System32, and so on. Each subfolder must contain the files that will be copied to the corresponding operating system folder on the target computer.

Note In Windows 2000, %systemroot% is equivalent to %windir%.

\$OEM\$\\$1 (Copied to $systemdrive$)

The \$OEM\$\\$1 subfolder, which is new for Windows 2000, corresponds to the drive on which Windows 2000 is installed. $1 is equivalent to the %systemdrive% environment variable. For example, if you are installing Windows 2000 on the D: drive, \$OEM\$\\$1 corresponds to the D: drive. This makes it possible to install Windows 2000 to drives other than the C: drive.

\$OEM\$\\$1\Drivers (Copied to $systemdrive$\Drivers and Subfolders of $systemdrive$\Drivers)

The \$OEM\$\\$1\Drivers subfolder, which is new for Windows 2000, allows you to place new or updated Plug and Play device drivers and their supporting files (catalog files and .inf installation files) in and below the Drivers subfolder. These folders and their contents are copied to the %systemdrive%\ Drivers folder on the target computer. Adding the OemPnPDriversPath parameter to your answer file will tell Windows 2000 where to look for the new or updated Plug and Play drivers. When searching for appropriate Plug and Play device drivers to install during setup or afterward, Windows 2000 looks at the files in the folders you created as well as those originally included with the system. Note that you can replace Drivers with a name of your own choosing that follows the 8.3 MS-DOS naming convention.

Note The \$OEM\$\\$1\Drivers subfolder replaces the \Display and \Net subfolders used in Windows NT installation.

\$OEM\$\\$1\Sysprep (Copied to %systemdrive%\Sysprep)

The \$OEM\$\\$1\Sysprep subfolder contains the files needed to run the Sysprep utility. Sysprep.exe and Sysprepcl.exe must be in %systemdrive%\Sysprep folder for Sysprep to function properly.

Tip Add Sysprep.inf (created by Setup Manager or written manually) to the \$OEM\$\\$1\Sysprep directory on the distribution share. Otherwise, a floppy disk containing the Sysprep.inf file is necessary to complete a Sysprep setup.

\$OEM\$*drive_letter*

During the Text-mode portion of setup, the structure of each \$OEM\$*drive_letter* subfolder is copied to the root of the corresponding drive in the target computer. For example, files that you place in the \$OEM\$\D subfolder are copied to the root of the D: drive. You can also create subfolders within these subfolders. For example, \$OEM\$\E\Misc causes Setup to create a \Misc subfolder on the E: drive.

Files that have to be renamed must be listed in the $$Rename.txt file. Note that the files in the distribution folders must have short file names (format 8.3).

Practice: Preparing and Running an Automated Installation

In this exercise, you create and run an automated installation of Windows 2000 Server on Computer 2. To prepare for the automated installation, you use the Windows 2000 Server Setup Manager to create an answer file and a distribution share on Server01.

Warning Do not customize the desktop or any of the Windows 2000 applications on Server01. If you do, the steps in this exercise may not work. For example, this exercise is designed for the double-click behavior of the default desktop, so you must not have customized your desktop settings to alter this.

Exercise 1: Running Setup Manager

Complete this exercise on a Server01 with the Windows 2000 Server installation CD-ROM inserted.

1. Create a folder named Deploy underneath C:\Program Files.

2. Using Windows Explorer, locate the \Support\Tools folder on the Windows 2000 Server installation CD-ROM.

3. Select the TOOLS folder in the Folders pane and then double-click the DEPLOY file in the right pane.

   The contents of the Deploy.cab file appears.

4. From the Edit menu, choose Select All.

5. From the File menu, choose Extract.

   A Browse For Folder window appears.

6. Click on the + sign to the left of Local Disk (C:) to expand the C: drive.

7. Click on the + sign to the left of Program Files to expand the Program Files folder.

8. Click on the Deploy folder.

   The Deploy folder opens.

9. Click OK.

   A Copying message box appears momentarily as the files in the Deploy.cab file are extracted to C:\Program Files\Deploy.

10. From the C:\Program Files\Deploy folder, double-click setupmgr.

    Setup Manager starts, and the Windows 2000 Setup Manager wizard appears.

11. Read the descriptive text, and then click Next.

    The New Or Existing Answer File screen appears, and the Create A New Answer File radio button is selected.

12. Click Next.

    The Product To Install screen appears, and the Windows 2000 Unattended Installation radio button is selected.

13. Click Next.

    The Platform screen appears, and the Windows 2000 Professional radio button is selected.

14. Select the Windows 2000 Server radio button, and click Next.

    The User Interaction Level screen appears, and the Provide Defaults radio button is selected.

15. Select the Fully Automated radio button, read the Description text, and then click Next.

    The License Agreement screen appears.

16. Read the text on this screen, select the I Accept The Terms Of The License Agreement check box, and then click Next.

    The Customize The Software screen appears.

17. In the Name text box, type your name and press the Tab key.

18. In the Organization text box, type your organization name or **MSPress Self-Study** and click Next.

    The Licensing Mode screen appears, and the Per Server radio button is selected.

19. Select the Per Seat radio button, and click Next.

    The Computer Names screen appears.

20. Insert the Windows 2000 Training Supplemental CD-ROM into Server01, and click Import.

    The Open window appears.

21. In the File Name drop-down list box, type *<cd-rom_drive:>***\chapt03\ex1\ computer names.txt** and then click Open.

The Computer Names screen appears showing a list of computers to be installed.

22. Click Next.

The Administrator Password screen appears.

23. In the password text boxes, type **password**, and select the check box named When The Computer Starts, Automatically Log On As Administrator.

The Number of times to Auto Logon is set to 1.

24. Click Next.

The Display Settings screen appears.

25. Leave all text box values set to Use Windows Default, and click Next.

The Network Settings screen appears, and the Typical Settings radio button is selected.

26. Click Next.

The Workgroup Or Domain screen appears and the Workgroup radio button is selected.

Server01 is currently configured as a member of a workgroup named WORKGROUP. Do not change the values appearing on the Workgroup Or Domain screen. When the automated installation is run on Computer 2, it will become a member of the same workgroup. Later in this self-paced study, Server01 will become a domain controller and the computer you are preparing an answer file for will join that domain.

Note The answer file you are preparing now can be modified later to automatically join a domain and create computer accounts in the domain. These modifications are made by using either Setup Manager or a text editor.

---

27. Click Next.

The Time Zone screen appears.

28. From the Time Zone drop-down list box, select your time zone and click Next.

The Additional Settings screen appears, and the Yes, Edit The Additional Settings radio button is selected.

29. Click Next.

The Telephony screen appears.

30. You may type in your country/region area code or city code, and any other settings you require to dial out. If Computer 2 does not have dial-out access, you can ignore this screen and continue.

31. Click Next.

   The Regional Settings screen appears, and the Use The Default Regional Settings For The Windows Version You Are Installing radio button is selected.

32. Click Next.

   The Languages screen appears.

33. Select any additional language support you want to have available for the operation of Windows 2000 Server, and then click Next.

   The Browser And Shell Settings screen appears, and the Use Default Internet Explorer Settings radio button is selected.

34. Click Next.

   The Installation Folder screen appears, and the A Folder Named Winnt radio button is selected.

35. Click Next.

   The Install Printers screen appears.

36. Click Next.

   The Run Once screen appears.

37. In the Command To Run text box, type **Notepad.exe** and click Add.

   Typically, the Command To Run text box contains a script or other executable program to further configure the user's environment. For the purpose of training, running Notepad is sufficient for configuration.

   Notice that if you added a printer on the previous screen, the AddPrinter command runs to add your printer to the list of installed printers.

38. Click Next.

   The Distribution Folder screen appears.

39. Select the Yes, Create Or Modify A Distribution Folder radio button, and click Next.

   The Distribution Folder Name screen appears, and the Create A New Distribution Folder radio button is selected.

   The Distribution folder text box contains C:\win2000dist, and the Share As Text box contains win2000dist.

40. Click Next.

    The Additional Mass Storage Drivers screen appears.

41. Read the screen, and click Next.

    The Hardware Abstraction Layer screen appears.

42. Read the screen, and click Next.

    The Additional Commands screen appears.

43. Read the screen, and click Next.

    Commands entered here are written to Cmdlines.txt. This file is created under the distribution folder in the OEM subfolder.

    The OEM Branding screen appears.

44. Click Next.

    The Additional Files Or Folders screen appears.

45. Browse the folders by clicking on them and reading the information that appears under Description.

    Click Next.

    The Answer File Name screen appears showing a path and file name located on the CD-ROM in the Location And File Name text box.

46. Verify the path and file name to **C:\Win2000dist\Unattend.txt** and click Next.

    The Location Of Setup Files screen appears, and the Copy The Files From CD radio button is selected.

47. Remove the Windows 2000 Server Training Supplemental CD-ROM, and insert the Windows 2000 Server installation CD-ROM.

    After the Windows 2000 Server installation CD-ROM is read, the Microsoft Windows 2000 CD screen appears.

48. Close the Microsoft Windows 2000 CD screen.

49. Click Next on the Location Of Setup Files screen.

    The Copying Files screen appears as the files are copied from the \i386 directory on the installation CD-ROM to C:\Win2000Dist.

50. Allow the file copy to complete before continuing to the next exercise.

    At the completion of Setup Manager's tasks, a Completing The Windows 2000 Setup Manager Wizard screen appears.

51. Read what appears on the screen, and then click Finish.

Exercise 2: Inspecting the Distribution Folder Created by Setup Manager

In this exercise you inspect the folder structure created by Setup Manager, an answer file (Unattend.txt), a UDF file (Unattend.udf), and a batch file (Unattend.bat).

1. Click Start and then Run.

   The Run dialog box appears.

2. In the Open text box, type **C:\Win2000dist** and click OK.

   The Win2000dist window appears.

3. Open another window to the following directory on the Windows 2000 installation CD-ROM: *<cd-rom drive:>*\i386.

   The i386 window appears.

4. Arrange the windows so that you can see both the Win2000dist window and the i386 window.

   What folder appears directly under the Win2000dist folder that does not appear in the i386 folder?

5. Examine the directory structure below OEM, and review Figure 8.3. You will be asked a question about this structure in the "Review" section of this chapter.

6. Return to the Win2000dist folder, and locate the three Unattend files.

   Notice that two of the Unattend files do not appear with extensions.

7. To show file extensions for all files, select Tools and choose Folder Options.

   The Folder Options dialog box appears.

8. Click the View tab.

9. From the Advanced Settings box, clear the Hide File Extensions For Known File Types check box, and click OK.

10. Locate the Unattend files again.

    The Unattend files appear with their file extensions showing.

    Select Unattend.txt, and from the File menu, choose Open.

    Unattend.txt appears in Notepad.

11. Locate the `[User Data]` section and add an additional line named ProductID+<*your_product_key*>. For the value of ProductID, type the Product Key provided with your copy of Windows 2000 Server.

12. Save and close Unattend.txt.

13. For an explanation of any sections in this file, refer to Unattend.doc located in the C:\Program Files\Deploy folder you created at the start of this exercise. Unattend.doc can be opened in Microsoft Wordpad, Microsoft Word, or any word processor capable of reading Microsoft Word files.

14. Close Unattend.doc.

15. From the Win2000dist window, select Unattend.udf; and from the File menu choose Open With.

    The Open With dialog box appears.

16. Select Notepad from the Choose The Program You Want To Use box, and click OK.

    Notice that the 12 computer names imported during the operation of Setup Manager appear here.

    What is the purpose of the UDF file?

17. Close the UDF file.

18. From the Win2000dist window, select Unattend.bat; and from the File menu, choose Edit.

    The contents of the batch file appear in Notepad.

19. Notice that the batch file sets variables, and then the variables are used to run Winnt32 with switches. Notice also that you must specify the computer name when calling the batch file since a UDF file is involved in the setup routine.

20. Close the Unattend.bat window.

Exercise 3: Running an Unattended Setup of Windows 2000 Server from Computer 2

Computer 2 must already be running a Windows 32-bit operating system, such as Windows 95 or Windows NT. In addition, Server01 must be connected to the same network as Computer 2. All requirements for the exercises are outlined in "About This Book."

Caution If Computer 2 is running Windows NT, the boot partition is C:\ and the operating system directory is Winnt, change the name of the installation directory in Unattend.txt. The directory name listed in Unattend.txt is found under the Unattended section, and the valuename is TargetPath. For example, change the value so that TargetPath=\WIN2000S.

1. From Computer 2, connect a drive letter (H: will be used throughout this exercise), to \\Server01\Win2000dist. You can connect to Server01 by using the Administrator username and the password of "password."

   Note If you are running Windows 95 or Windows 98 and are having trouble connecting to Server01, make sure the computer is a member of WORKGROUP and logon as Administrator with a password of "password."

2. Open a command prompt and type **cdh:**.

   Caution If you have upgraded from Windows 95 or Windows 98, you might find that Setup can't find the .udf file. If this happens, open Unattend.txt on Server01 and specify the full path to the .udf file.

3. From the command prompt, type **H:\Unattend Server02**.

4. The Copying Installation Files screen appears as Windows 2000 Server runs an automated installation over the network.

   At the conclusion of this phase, a warning screen will inform you that the computer will be restarted.

   Note This pre-Text-mode phase of setup can be completed using the \syspart switch with Winnt32.exe.

5. Allow the computer to restart.

Upon reboot, the Windows 2000 boot menu appears and Microsoft Windows 2000 Server Setup continues to Text mode.

The computer reboots again, and the boot menu appears showing Windows 2000 Server.

Windows 2000 installation continues the Graphics-mode portion of setup. The Installing Devices And Installing Components screens take time to complete. The Performing Final Tasks screen appears as Windows 2000 Server completes the setup routine. When setup is completed, the Windows 2000 Setup screen announces that the computer will restart.

6. After the computer restarts, notice that it automatically logs on as Administrator as specified in Setup Manager. The printer is installed and Notepad.exe runs.

7. Close Notepad.

The Windows 2000 Configure Your Server screen appears.

8. Select the I Will Configure This Server Later radio button, and click Next.

The Configure Your Server screen appears.

9. Clear the Show This Screen At Startup check box, and close the screen.

Caution If you are upgrading from Windows 95 or Windows 98, check to see if your partition is NTFS. If not, you must convert it. You can do this by typing **convert c: /fs:ntfs** at the command prompt.

Lesson Summary

Before you can perform an unattended installation of Windows 2000 Server, you must create an answer file, which is a customized script file that contains multiple optional sections that you modify to supply information about your installation requirements. The file supplies Setup with answers to all the questions you are asked when you install Windows 2000 Server manually. In addition, the answer file tells Setup how to interact with the distribution folders and files that you have created. You must create at least one set of distribution folders to install Windows 2000 Server over a network. Use Setup Manager to create a distribution folder and an answer file manually or automatically. To further customize the answer file, refer to the Unattend.doc file located on the Windows 2000 Server installation CD-ROM.

Lesson 5: Automating the Installation of Windows 2000 Server

Automated installations of Windows 2000 Server involve running Setup with an answer file. You can perform automated installations on multiple computers so that Setup can take place in an unattended fashion. The following types of software can have their installations automated:

- The core Windows 2000 Server operating system

- Any application that does not run as a service

- Additional language support for Windows 2000 Server through the installation of various language packs

- Service packs for Windows 2000 Server

After this lesson, you will be able to

- Perform an unattended installation of the Windows 2000 Server operating system

Estimated lesson time: 45 minutes

Performing an Unattended Installation

To perform an unattended installation of Windows 2000 Server, you must specify the answer file when you run Setup. There are three basic types of unattended installations that you can use to set up Windows 2000 Server: the bootable CD-ROM method, the Winnt.exe method, or the Winnt32.exe method.

Bootable CD-ROM

To start Windows 2000 Setup in Unattended mode from the Windows 2000 Server installation CD-ROM, the following conditions must be met:

- The computer must support the El Torito–bootable CD-ROM (No-emulation mode) format to boot from the CD-ROM drive.

- The answer file must be named Winnt.sif and be placed on a floppy disk to be inserted into the floppy drive as soon as the computer boots from the CD-ROM.

- The answer file must contain a [Data] section with the required keys specified.

Winnt.exe or Winnt32.exe

The following Winnt.exe command provides an example for implementing an unattended installation:

```
Winnt /s:Z:\i386 /u:Z:\unattend.txt /t:c
```

Note the use of the /u: command-line switch, which indicates an unattended installation. The /t: switch indicates which drive Setup will copy the source files to continue the installation. Z:\i386 is the network location containing the Windows 2000 installation source files. The command line example assumes the local computer has mapped the Z: drive to the network share containing the i386 subfolder.

The following Winnt32.exe command provides an example similar to the previous Winnt example for implementing an unattended installation:

```
Winnt32 /s:Z:\i386 /unattend 10:Z:\unattend.txt /tempdrive:C
```

Winnt32.exe uses /unattend: rather then /u: for running an unattended setup. The number following the /unattend: switch indicates to the setup routine how long it should wait after copying files to automatically reboot the computer and continue setup. The num command works on Windows NT or Windows 2000 but is ignored on computers running Windows 95 or Windows 98.

Figure 8.4 illustrates the steps necessary to run the sample unattended installation commands discussed earlier.

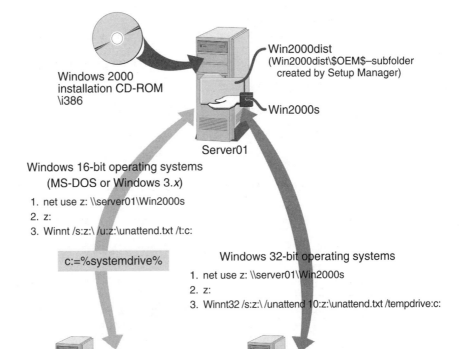

Figure 8.4 Initiating an unattended installation on computers running 16-bit and 32-bit operating systems

Automating the Installation of Windows 2000 Server

Several methods are available for creating an automated installation of Windows 2000 Server. The method you choose depends on the desired outcome. In certain situations, installation methods can be combined. For example, Syspart and Sysprep can be used together in certain setup installation scenarios.

In addition to the basic installation methods described above, you can use the following methods to perform automated installations of Windows 2000 Server:

- The Winnt32.exe Setup program along with the /syspart parameter
- The System Preparation Tool (Sysprep)
- Systems Management Server (SMS)
- Bootable CD-ROM
- Remote Installation Service (RIS)

These methods either build on or replace the over-the-network unattended installation method described above. Table 8.16 provides details about when to use each installation method.

Table 8.16 When to Use the Various Installation Methods

Installation method	Use	Upgrade	Clean installation
Syspart	Use Syspart for clean installations to computers that have dissimilar hardware.	No	Yes
Sysprep	Use Sysprep when the master computer and the target computers have identical or nearly identical hardware, including the HAL and mass storage devices.	No	Yes
SMS	Use SMS to perform managed upgrades of Windows 2000 Server to multiple systems, especially those that are geographically dispersed.	Yes	Yes
Bootable CD-ROM	Use the bootable CD-ROM method with a computer whose BIOS allows it to boot from the CD-ROM.	No	Yes

Installation method	Use	Upgrade	Clean installation
RIS (Remote Installation Service)	Use RIS with a computer that supports PXE or a bootable RIS floppy disk. Either method allows the computer to connect to a networked RIS Server during the initial boot process and receive an installation of Windows 2000 Professional. Pre-Boot Execution Environment (PXE) allows a computer that contains a PXE ROM to boot to the network server. The PXE ROM is either coded into the system BIOS or is located on a NIC as an optional ROM.	No for Server	No for Server

Note RIS can roll out automated installations of Windows 2000 Professional only. It does not support automated installations of Windows 2000 Server. Future enhancement to RIS might allow roll-outs of Windows 2000 Server and other operating systems.

Table 8.16 also shows which installation methods can be used to perform upgrades or clean installations. Before you can automate the installation of Windows 2000 Server, you must decide if the installation will be an upgrade from Windows NT Server or a clean installation.

If you do perform a clean installation, note that because an automated installation is unattended, a clean installation can replace existing partitions or files on existing partitions. Application files and data files can still remain on partitions, although applications should be reinstalled in order to be reregistered with the new operating system installation.

Using Syspart

Syspart is executed by including it as a parameter of the Winnt32.exe Setup program. Winnt32 with the Syspart switch is run on a reference computer to complete the first phase of installation. If the reference computer and the computers on which you will complete the installation of Windows 2000 Server do not have similar hardware, you can use the Syspart method. This method reduces deployment time by completing the file-copy phase of setup on the reference computer, thereby eliminating this step on the computers targeted for installation.

Syspart requires that you use two physical disks, with a primary partition on the target hard disk. However, the target hard disk does not need to be located in the master computer. It can be in another computer on a network, as long as it is a clean disk with no operating systems installed.

If you require a similar installation and operating system configuration on hardware types in which the HALs or mass storage controllers differ, you can use Syspart to create a master set of files with the necessary configuration information and driver support. This file set can then be used on dissimilar systems to properly detect the hardware and consistently configure the base operating system.

After the reference computer is running, connect to the distribution folder and run Setup by executing the Winnt32.exe program from the command prompt:

```
winnt32 /unattend:unattend.txt /s:install_source /
syspart:install_target /tempdrive:install_target /noreboot
```

After running the previous command where *install_target* equals D, the structure shown in Figure 8.5 is created on the D: drive.

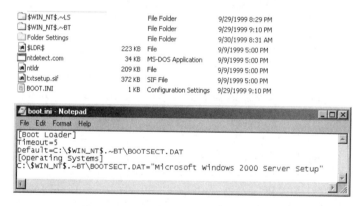

Figure 8.5 The contents of the target computer's D: drive and Boot.ini after running Syspart

There are several parameters and values you can use with the Win32.exe setup program. Using these allow you to customize the setup to your specific environment.

- The Unattend.txt value is the answer file used for an unattended setup. It provides answers to some or all of the prompts the end user normally responds to during Setup. Using an answer file is optional when creating the master file set.

- The *install_source* value is the location of the Windows 2000 Server files. Specify multiple /s command-line switches if you want to install from multiple sources simultaneously. Figure 8.6 shows a file copy occurring from two sources. The first source is a network drive, the second source is a local CD-ROM drive. As the figure shows, up to eight installation sources can be specified.

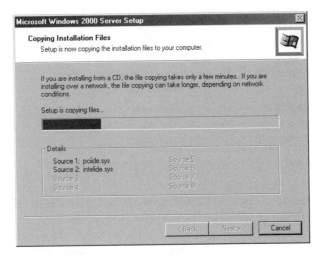

Figure 8.6 The Copy Installation Files screen showing two sources for file copy

- The /syspart and /tempdrive parameters must point to the same partition of a secondary hard disk. The Windows 2000 Server installation must take place on a primary partition of that secondary hard disk. Syspart sets the partition to active so that it is bootable.

- The /tempdrive parameter must be used for the Syspart installation to be successful. When you use the /tempdrive command-line switch, make sure you have sufficient free disk space on your second partition to install both Windows 2000 Server and the installation files it places in WIN_NT.~LS.

- The *install_drive* value is the partition that contains the preinstallation of Windows 2000 Server. The files on this drive are shown in Figure 8.5.

Note Syspart will automatically mark the drive as active in preparation for moving it to the target computer.

Using Sysprep

Sysprep is a tool that facilitates creating a disk image of your Windows 2000 Server installation. Disk duplication is a good choice if you need to install an identical configuration on multiple computers. To use the Sysprep tool, you should install Windows 2000 Server on a reference computer. You should also install any other applications on the reference computer that you want installed on the target computers. Then run Sysprep followed by a third-party disk-imaging utility. Sysprep prepares the hard disk on the master computer so that the disk imaging utility can transfer an image of the hard disk to the other computers. This method decreases deployment time dramatically compared to standard or scripted installations.

Tip Create a CD-ROM containing the disk image or move the image to a network location so that the image can be used to rapidly set up many identical or nearly identical computers.

To use Sysprep, the master computer and target computers must have identical HALs, Advanced Configuration and Power Interface (ACPI) support, and mass storage devices. Windows 2000 automatically detects Plug and Play devices, and Sysprep redetects and re-enumerates the devices on the system when the computer is turned on after Sysprep has run. This means the Plug and Play devices, such as network cards, modems, video adapters, and sound cards, do not have to be the same on the master and target computers. The major advantage of Sysprep installation is speed. The image can be packaged and compressed and only the files required for the given configuration are created as part of the image. Additional Plug and Play drivers that might be needed on other systems are also created. The image can also be copied to a CD-ROM to be distributed to remote sites that have slow links.

Note Because the master and target computers must have identical HALs, ACPI support, and mass storage devices, you might need to maintain multiple images for your environment.

Sysprep allows you to configure a master image containing the necessary components for a member server and then later configure the server and optionally promote it to a domain controller. This can be done manually or by running the commands in the [GuiRunOnce] section of the Sysprep.inf file.

If your environment includes multiple types of hardware-dependent systems, you can use Syspart in conjunction with Sysprep to create a master for each type. To do this, you install Windows 2000 on one computer of each type, and then use the Sysprep utility to help create images to be used on the remaining computers of each type. For more information about Sysprep, see "Using Sysprep to Extend Disk Partitions," later in this lesson.

Before you begin, choose a computer to use as a reference computer. The reference computer must have Windows NT Server or Windows 2000 Server installed.

Note Sysprep can also be used to create installations of Windows 2000 Professional.

The Sysprep Process

The following is an overview of building a source computer to use for Sysprep duplication.

- **Install Windows 2000.** Windows 2000 Server should be installed on a computer with hardware similar to the intended target computers. The computer should not be joined to a domain while it is being built. In addition, the local administrator password should be kept blank.

- **Configure the computer.** You should be logged on as the administrator when you install and customize Windows 2000 Server and the associated applications. You might include IIS or install and configure other services.

- **Validate the image.** You should run a client audit, based on your criteria, to verify that the image configuration is correct. Remove residual information, including anything left behind from audit and event logs.

- **Prepare the image for duplication.** Once you are confident the computer is configured exactly the way you want, the system can be prepared for duplication. This is accomplished by running Sysprep with the optional Sysprep.inf file, which is described later in this section. When Sysprep has completed running, the computer shuts down automatically or indicates that it is safe to be shut down.

- **Duplicate the installation.** At this point, the computer hard disk is prepared to run Plug and Play detection, create a unique SID, and run the Mini-Setup wizard the next time the system is started. Before continuing the next stage of installation, the system is duplicated by using a third-party imaging utility such as Norton Utilities Ghost or PowerQuest Drive Image Pro 3.0. The next time Windows 2000 Server is booted from this hard disk, or from any duplicated hard disk created from this image, the system will detect and re-enumerate the Plug and Play devices, create a unique SID, and run the Mini-Setup wizard to complete the installation and configuration on the target computer.

Warning Components that depend on the Active Directory services cannot be duplicated. Local users and groups should not be created on the member server because new SIDs will not be assigned to these user and group accounts.

Sysprep Files

There are three sysprep files: Sysprep.exe, Sysprep.inf , and Setupcl.exe. To use Sysprep, run Sysprep.exe manually or configure Setup to run Sysprep.exe automatically by using the [GuiRunOnce] section of the answer file. To run Sysprep, the files Sysprep.exe and Setupcl.exe must be located in a Sysprep folder at the root of the system drive (%systemdrive%\Sysprep\). To place the files in the correct location through Setup, you must add these files to your distribution folders under the OEM\$1\Sysprep\ subfolder.

The Sysprep files prepare the operating system for cloning and start the Mini-Setup wizard. An optional answer file, Sysprep.inf, can be included in the Sysprep folder. Sysprep.inf contains default parameters that can be used to provide consistent responses where appropriate. This limits the requirement for user input, thereby reducing potential user errors. Sysprep.inf can also be placed on a floppy disk to be placed in the floppy drive after the boot loader dialog appears. This provides more customized responses and further reduces the initial boot requirement for the end user. When the Mini-Setup wizard has successfully completed its tasks, the system reboots one last time, the Sysprep folder and all its contents are deleted, and the system is ready for the user to log on.

Sysprep.exe has three optional parameters, which are described in Table 8.17.

Table 8.17 Sysprep.exe Optional Parameters

Parameter	Description
-quiet	Runs Sysprep without displaying onscreen messages.
-nosidgen	Runs Sysprep without regenerating SIDs that are already on the system. This is useful if you do not intend to clone the computer on which you are running Sysprep.
-reboot	Automatically reboots the computer after Sysprep shuts it down, eliminating the need for you to manually turn the computer back on. In addition, the -reboot parameter forces a system reboot after disk duplication is completed so that Mini-Setup (the version of Setup that runs when there is a duplicated image on the hard disk) runs automatically. The only time you want to use this switch is if you are auditing the Sysprep process and want to make sure the Mini-Setup wizard is working properly.

The Sysprep.inf file is an answer file used during the cloning process to provide unique configuration information for each of the target computers. It uses the same .ini-like file syntax and key names (for supported keys) as the Setup answer file (unattend.txt). Sysprep.inf needs to be placed in the %systemdrive%\Sysprep\ folder or on a floppy disk. If you use a floppy disk, immediately after the system boots and the boot loader appears, place the floppy disk in the drive; the system will look for an updated Sysprep.inf on a floppy disk drive. Note that if you do not include Sysprep.inf when running Sysprep, the Mini-Setup wizard displays all the available dialogs, which are listed in the Mini-Setup wizard section later in this lesson.

If you use Sysprep.inf when creating the master computer and when running Sysprep, use the floppy disk method to provide an alternate Sysprep.inf. Locations specified for system files needed during Mini-Setup, such as OEMPnPDriversPath and InstallFilesPath, must remain the same for Sysprep.inf in the distribution folder and for Sysprep.inf on the floppy disk.

The following script is a sample of a Sysprep.inf file:

```
[Unattended]
;Prompt the user to accept the End Use License Agreement
(EULA).
OemSkipEula=No
;Use Sysprep's default and regenerate the page file for the
system
;to accommodate potential differences in available RAM.
KeepPageFile=0
;Provide the location for additional language support files
that
;may be needed in a global organization.
InstallFilesPath=%systemroot%\Sysprep\i386

[GuiUnattended]
;Specify a non-null administrator password.
;Any password supplied here will take effect only if the
original source
;for the image (master computer) specified a non-null pass-
word.
;Otherwise, the password used on the master computer will be
;the password used on this computer. This can be changed
only by
;logging on as Local Administrator and manually changing the
password.
AdminPassword=password
;Set the time zone
TimeZone=20
;Skip the Welcome screen when the system boots
OemSkipWelcome=1
;Do not skip the regional options dialog so that the user
can indicate
;which regional options apply to her or him.
OemSkipRegional=No

[UserData]
;Prepopulate user information for the system
```

```
FullName="Authorized User"
OrgName="Organization Name"
ComputerName=XYZ_Computer1

[GUIRunOnce]
;Promote this computer to a Domain Controller on reboot
DCPromo

[Identification]
;Join the computer to the domain ITDOMAIN
JoinDomain=ITDOMAIN

 [Networking]
;Bind the default protocols and services to the network
card(s) used
;in this computer.
InstallDefaultComponents=Yes
```

You can change the administrative password by using Sysprep.inf only if the existing administrative password is null. This is also true if you want to change the administrator password through the Sysprep GUI.

The Setupcl.exe file processes Sysprep.inf to determine pages for the Mini-Setup wizard and starts the Mini-Setup wizard.

Note The combination of Sysprep.exe and Setupcl.exe can be used to replace the Rollback.exe tool used in previous versions of Windows NT.

Mini-Setup Wizard

The Mini-Setup wizard starts the first time a computer boots from a disk that has been duplicated using the Sysprep tool. The wizard gathers any information needed to further customize the target computer. If you do not use Sysprep.inf or if you leave some sections of the file blank, the Mini-Setup wizard will display screens for which no answers were provided in Sysprep.inf.

The screens that the Mini-Setup wizard can display include the following:

- EULA
- Regional options
- User name and company
- Computer name and administrator password
- Network settings

- Server licensing

- Time zone selection

- Finish/Restart

If you want to bypass these screens, you can specify certain parameters within the Sysprep.inf file. These parameters and their values are listed in Table 8.18.

Table 8.18 Sysprep.inf Parameters

Parameter	Value
EULA	[Unattended]
	OemSkipEula=Yes
Regional options	[RegionalSettings]
	LanguageGroup=1
	Language=00000409
User name and company	[UserData]
	FullName="User Name"
	OrgName="Organization Name"
Computer name and administrator password	[UserData]
	ComputerName=W2B32054
	[GuiUnattended]
	AdminPassword="password"
Network settings	[Networking]
	InstallDefaultComponents=Yes
TAPI settings	[TapiLocation]
	AreaCode=425
Time zone selection	OEMSkipRegional=1
	TimeZone=20
Finish/Restart	NA

Because Setup detects optimal settings for display devices, Display Settings is no longer a screen seen during Setup or during the Mini-Setup wizard. You can specify display settings either in the answer file used to create the master computer or in the Sysprep.inf file used on the target computer. If the display settings are in the answer file used on the master computer, Sysprep retains those settings unless Sysprep.inf contains different settings or a different video adapter or monitor type is detected that requires different settings from the master computer.

By using OemSkipEula=Yes, you are accepting the responsibility for agreeing to all licensing stipulations within the EULA on behalf of the user.

If you run Setup from the network and intend to use Sysprep, you need to configure your network adapters differently than how it is done by the InstallDefaultComponents option. You must provide the specific networking information in Sysprep.inf. If enabling DHCP on all adapters is sufficient and installing Microsoft Client for Microsoft Networks, TCP/IP, and File and Print Sharing for Microsoft Networks on all adapters is sufficient, there is nothing additional you need to specify in Sysprep.inf.

Running Sysprep

There are two ways to run the Sysprep utility: manually or automatically.

Running Sysprep Manually

After you install Windows 2000 Server, you can use Sysprep to prepare the system for transfer to other similarly configured computers. To run Sysprep manually, you must first install Windows 2000 Server, configure the system, and install the applications. Then run Sysprep without the -reboot command-line switch. After the system shuts down, clone the image of the drive to the similarly configured computers.

Note You can find the Sysprep utility in Deploy.cab, which is located in the \Support\Tools directory of the Windows 2000 Server installation CD-ROM.

When users start up their cloned computers for the first time, the Mini-Setup wizard runs, allowing users to customize their systems. You can also preassign all or part of the Sysprep configuration parameters by using Sysprep.inf. The Sysprep folder (which contains Sysprep.exe and Setupcl.exe) is automatically deleted after Sysprep Mini-Setup completes.

The following is an overview of preparing a Windows 2000 Server installation for duplication.

- **Prepare the Sysprep folder.** A Sysprep folder must be created at the root of the drive. The Sysprep.exe, the Setupcl.exe, and if applicable, the Sysprep.inf files should be copied to the Sysprep folder.

- **Run the Sysprep utility.** The Sysprep utility should be run from a command prompt within the Sysprep folder. One of the following commands should be used:

```
Sysprep
Sysprep -reboot
Sysprep /<optional parameter>
Sysprep /<optional parameter> -reboot
Sysprep /<optional parameter 1>.../<optional parameter X>
Sysprep /<optional parameter 1>.../<optional parameter X>
-reboot
```

- **Run Sysprep without the -reboot switch.** When a message appears saying that the computer should be shut down, select the Shut Down command from the Start menu. A third-party disk-imaging utility can now be used to create an image of the installation.

- **Run Sysprep with the -reboot switch.** The computer reboots automatically and the Mini-Setup wizard runs. The wizard's prompts should be verified. In addition, the system and other applications can be audited. When auditing is completed, Sysprep should be run again, without the -reboot command-line switch. When a message appears saying that the computer should be shut down, select the Shut Down command from the Start menu. A third-party disk-imaging utility can now be used to create an image of the installation.

Note You can add a Cmdlines.txt file to the Sysprep folder to be processed by Setup. This file runs post-Setup commands, including those required for application installation.

Running Sysprep Automatically

The [GuiRunOnce] section of the answer file contains commands to be executed after Setup completes. You can use the [GuiRunOnce] section to create an installation that completes Setup, automatically logs on to the computer, runs Sysprep in quiet mode, and then shuts down the computer.

To run Sysprep automatically, the Sysprep files should be added to the distribution folders under OEM\$1\Sysprep\. This ensures that the files are copied to the correct location on the system drive. In addition, the last command in the [GuiRunOnce] section of the answer file should be as follows:

```
%systemdrive%\Sysprep\Sysprep.exe -quiet
```

If multiple reboots are required, this command should be added as the last item run in the last [GuiRunOnce] section used.

If the computer has Advanced Power Management (APM) or ACPI support, Sysprep automatically shuts down the computer once this process has completed.

Using Sysprep to Extend Disk Partitions

Windows 2000 is designed to extend a partition in GUI mode. This new functionality allows you to create images that can be extended to take full advantage of hard disks that might have more space than the original hard disk on the master computer. In addition, it provides a way to reduce the image size needed by not requiring that the image take up a full hard disk. This maximizes the amount of hard disk space that can be used. Because Sysprep uses GUI mode, it can take advantage of this functionality.

If your imaging tools allow you to edit the image, you can delete the Pagefile.sys, Setupapi.log, and the Hyberfil.sys (if applicable) because these files will be re-created when the Mini-Setup wizard runs on the target computer. You must *not* delete these files on an active system because doing so can cause the system to function improperly. These files should be deleted, if desired, from the image only.

To extend a hard disk partition when using a third-party imaging product that supports NTFS, you should first configure the partition on the master computer hard disk to the minimum size required to install Windows 2000 Server with all the desired components and applications. This helps to reduce your overall image size requirements. You must also modify the answer file used to create the master image by including the FileSystem = ConvertNTFS option in the [Unattended] section. You should not include ExtendOemPartition here because you want to maintain the smallest possible image size. Then you can install Windows 2000 Server to the master computer and create an image of the drive. From there, you should place the image on the target computer where the target computer has the same size system partition as the master computer. After you reboot the target computer, the Mini-Setup wizard begins and the partition is extended almost instantaneously.

Using Systems Management Server

You can use Systems Management Server (SMS) to perform managed upgrades of Windows 2000 Server to multiple systems, especially those that are geographically dispersed. Note that SMS is used only for installations to computers that contain a previously installed operating system and are running the SMS client agent responsible for receiving software installation instructions. Before you use SMS to perform an upgrade, you should assess your existing network infrastructure, including bandwidth, hardware, and geographical constraints. The primary advantage of using SMS to upgrade is that you can maintain centralized control of the upgrade process. For example, you can control when upgrades take place (such as during or after training, after hardware verification, and after user data is backed up), which computers will be upgraded, and how you will apply network constraints.

SMS 2.0 contains package definition files (with an .sms extension) that allow you to import Windows 2000 Server installation routines into SMS 2.0 Package and Program settings. After importing the package definition, provide SMS with a data source for the Windows 2000 Server installation CD-ROM or an accessible network location containing the Windows 2000 Server distribution files.

Using a Bootable CD-ROM

You can use the bootable CD-ROM method to install Windows 2000 Server on a computer whose BIOS allows it to boot from a CD-ROM. This method is useful for computers at remote sites with slow links and no local information technology (IT) department. The bootable CD-ROM method runs Winnt32.exe, which allows for a fast installation.

Note You can use the bootable CD-ROM method only for clean installations. To perform upgrades, you must run Winnt32.exe from within the existing operating system.

To ensure maximum flexibility for setting up Windows 2000 Server, set the boot order in the BIOS as follows:

1. Network Adapter for PXE-compliant read-only memory (ROM), this option can be used to support operating system installation from a RIS server.

2. CD-ROM for bootable CD-ROM operating system installation.

3. Hard Disk for Sysprep or Syspart prepared local disk-based operating system installation.

4. Floppy Disk for floppy disk based operating system installation.

To use a bootable CD-ROM for a fully automated operating system installation, the following criteria must be met:

- Your computer's BIOS must support the El Torito–bootable CD-ROM (No-emulation mode) format.

- The answer file must contain a [Data] section with the required keys.

- The answer file must be called Winnt.sif and be located on a floppy disk.

▶   **To install Windows 2000 Server by using a bootable CD-ROM drive, complete the following steps:**

1. **Boot the system.** After the Windows 2000 Server CD has been inserted into the CD-ROM drive, the system should be rebooted.

2. **Load the Winnt.sif file.** After the system reboots, the blue screen for Windows 2000 Setup appears. The floppy disk that contains the Winnt.sif file should be inserted into the floppy drive. Once the computer reads the floppy drive, the floppy disk should be removed. Setup will now run from the CD-ROM drive as specified by the Winnt.sif file.

Note The bootable CD-ROM method requires that all necessary files be on the CD-ROM. UDFs cannot be used with this method. UDFs are not usable because a unique identifier is called for each installation when specifying a UDF file from Winnt.exe or Winnt32.exe.

Lesson Summary

There are four methods available for automating the installation of Windows 2000 Server. The first method is to run the Winnt32.exe command along with the Syspart parameter. This is the method you should use if the hardware on the target computers is not similar to the hardware on the master computer. If the hardware is similar, you can use the Sysprep utility to perform an unattended installation. Sysprep is a tool that facilitates creating a disk image of your Windows 2000 Server installation. A third option for automating installations is to use SMS to perform managed upgrades of Windows 2000 Server to multiple systems, especially those that are geographically dispersed. SMS is used only for installations to computers that contain a previously installed operating system and the appropriate SMS agent. Finally, one other method available for automated installations is the bootable CD-ROM. This method is useful for computers at remote sites with slow links and no local IT department.

Review

The following questions will help you determine whether you have learned enough to move on to the next chapter. If you have difficulty answering these questions, please go back and review the material in this chapter before beginning the next chapter. See Appendix A, "Questions and Answers," for the answers to these questions.

1. If you are installing Microsoft Windows NT in a dual-boot configuration on the same computer, which file system should you choose? Why?

2. Which licensing mode should you select if users in your organization require frequent access to multiple servers? Why?

3. You are installing Windows 2000 Server on a computer that will be a member server in an existing Windows 2000 domain. You want to add the computer to the domain during installation. What information do you need, and what computers must be available on the network, before you run the Setup program?

4. You are using a CD-ROM to install Windows 2000 Server on a computer that was previously running another operating system. There is not enough space on the hard disk to run both operating systems, so you have decided to repartition the hard disk and install a clean copy of Windows 2000 Server. Name two methods for repartitioning the hard disk.

5. You are installing Windows 2000 over the network. Before you install to a client computer, what must you do?

6. A client is running Windows NT 3.5 Server and is interested in upgrading to Windows 2000. From the list of choices, choose all possible upgrade paths:

   a. Upgrade to Windows NT 3.51 Workstation and then to Windows 2000 Server.

   b. Upgrade to Windows NT 4.0 Server and then to Windows 2000 Server.

   c. Upgrade directly to Windows 2000 Server.

   d. Run Convert.exe to modify any NTFS partitions for file system compatibility with Windows 2000, and then upgrade to Windows 2000 Server.

   e. Upgrade to Windows NT 3.51 Server and then to Windows 2000 Server.

7. In your current network environment, user disk space utilization has been a major issue. Describe three services in Windows 2000 Server to help you manage this issue.

8. What is the purpose of using the /tempdrive: or /t: installation switches with Winnt32.exe or Winnt.exe, respectively?

9. You are asked to develop a strategy for rapidly installing Windows 2000 Server for one of your clients. You have assessed their environment and have determined that the following three sets of computers require Windows 2000 Server:

- There are 30 unidentical computer configurations currently running Windows NT Server 4.0 that need to be upgraded to Windows 2000 Server.

- There are 20 identical computers that need a new installation of Windows 2000 Server.

- Remote sites will run a clean installation of Windows 2000 Server. You want to make sure that they install a standard image of Windows 2000 Server that is consistent with your local configuration of the operating system. You will provide them with hard disks that they will install in their servers.

What are the steps for your installation strategy?

10. What is the purpose of the OEM folder and the subfolders created beneath it by Setup Manager?

11. How does Cmdlines.txt differ from `[GuiRunOnce]`?

12. How does Syspart differ from Sysprep?

C H A P T E R   9

Managing Network Protocols

About This Chapter

Network protocols allow various computers to communicate with each other on a specified network. There are many different network protocols supported by Windows 2000. This chapter starts with an overview of Internet Protocol (IP) routing, and then looks at the three most common protocols: Transmission Control Protocol/Internet Protocol (TCP/IP), IPX/SPX/NetBIOS Compatible Transport Protocol (NWLink), and Internet Protocol Security (IPSec). TCP/IP is currently the most common protocol used. It is the default protocol for virtually any internet application. It is also the default protocol supported by Windows 2000 Server. NWLink allows computers to communicate on a network requiring an IPX/SPX-compatible protocol. IPX/SPX is typically used on a Novell NetWare local area network (LAN). NWLink allows you to interoperate with NetWare networks. IPSec is a new protocol. It has built-in security features that may make it the protocol of the future for internet applications.

As a Windows NT 4.0 Workstation professional, you should be familiar with TCP/IP and NWLink. This chapter reviews these protocols and then discusses IPSec in depth. The chapter concludes with a discussion on how to monitor network security.

Before You Begin

To complete this chapter, you must have

- Two computers (named Pro1 and Server01) that meet the specifications listed in "Hardware Requirements" in "About This Book"

- Installed Microsoft Windows 2000 Server on at least one of two computers (Server01)

- Windows 2000 Professional, Windows 98, or Windows 95 running on one computer (Pro1)

Lesson 1: Basic Concepts of IP Routing

Routing is the process of choosing a path over which to send packets, which is a primary function of the internet protocol (IP). A router (commonly referred to as a gateway) is a device that forwards packets from one physical network to another. When a router receives a packet, the network adapter forwards the datagrams to the IP layer. IP examines the destination address on the datagram and then compares it to an IP routing table. A decision is then made as to where the packet is to be forwarded. This lesson explains basic IP routing concepts.

After this lesson, you will be able to

- Update a Windows 2000–based routing table by means of static routes

- Manage and monitor internal routing

- Manage and monitor border routing

Estimated lesson time: 40 minutes

Overview of Routing

A router helps local area networks (LANs) and wide area networks (WANs) to achieve interoperability and connectivity, and can link LANs that have different network topologies, such as Ethernet and Token Ring. Each packet sent over a LAN has a packet header that contains source and destination address fields. Routers match packet headers to a LAN segment and choose the best path for the packet, optimizing network performance. As each route is found, the packet is sent to the next router, called a *hop*, until finally delivered to the destination host. If a route is not found, an error message is sent to the source host. For example, if a packet is sent from Computer A to Computer C, as illustrated in Figure 9.1, the best route uses only one hop. If Router 1 is the default router for Computer A, the packet will be rerouted through Router 2. Computer A will be notified of the better route by which to send packets to Computer C.

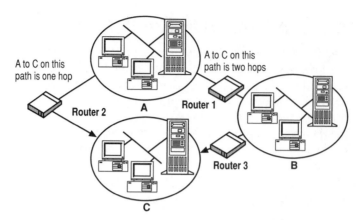

Figure 9.1 Packet routed from Computer A to Computer C

To make routing decisions, the IP layer consults a routing table that is stored in memory, as illustrated in Figure 9.2.

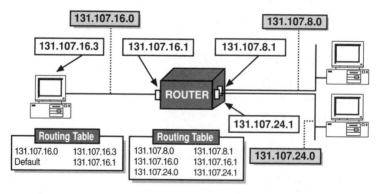

Figure 9.2 IP layer consulting a routing table

A routing table contains entries with the IP addresses of router interfaces to other networks that it can communicate with. A routing table is a series of entries, called *routes*, that contain information about where the network IDs of the internetwork are located. A routing table in a computer that is running Windows 2000 is built automatically, based on its TCP/IP configuration. You can view a routing table by typing **route print** at a command prompt, as illustrated in Figure 9.3.

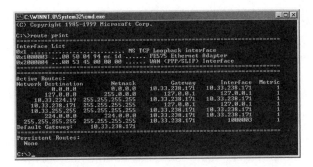

Figure 9.3 Displaying a routing table using a command prompt

Note The routing table is not exclusive to a router. A host also has a routing table that is used to determine the optimal route.

Static and Dynamic IP Routing

Routers use different processes to obtain routing information depending on whether the router performs static or dynamic IP routing. Static routing is a function of IP that limits you to fixed routing tables. Static routing requires that routing tables are built and updated manually. You use the Route command to add static entries to the routing table (see Table 9.1).

Table 9.1 Route Commands

To add or modify a static route, type the following:	Purpose
route add [*network*] **mask** [*netmask*] [*gateway*]	Adds a route
route -p add [*network*] **mask** [*netmask*] [*gateway*]	Adds a persistent route
route delete [*network*] [*gateway*]	Deletes a route
route change [*network*] [*gateway*]	Modifies a route
route print	Displays the routing table
route -f	Clears all routes

Practice: Updating a Windows 2000–Based Routing Table

In this practice, you update a Windows 2000–based routing table by means of static routers.

Exercise 1: Updating a Routing Table

1. On Pro1, open a command prompt.

2. At the command prompt, type **route add *IP_ address* mask *net_mask gateway*** to add a route to enable communications with a network from a host on another network.

   For example, to add a route to enable communications with network 10.107.24.0 from a host on network 10.107.16.0, you would type **route add 10.107.24.0 mask 255.255.255.0 10.107.16.2**, as illustrated in Figure 9.4.

3. At the command prompt, type **route print** to see the addition of the route in your routing table.

4. At the command prompt, type **route del *IP_address*** (the same IP address you used in step 2) to delete the route you just added.

5. Verify the route has been removed from the routing table by typing **route print** again.

Figure 9.4 Adding a static route to a routing table

Using Dynamic Routing

If a route changes, static routers do not inform each other of the change. Neither do static routers exchange routes with dynamic routers. In contrast, dynamic routing automatically updates the routing tables, reducing administrative overhead. However, dynamic routing increases traffic in large networks.

Routing Protocols

Dynamic routing is a function of routing protocols, such as the Routing Information Protocol (RIP) and Open Shortest Path First (OSPF). Routing protocols periodically exchange routes to known networks among dynamic routers. If a route changes, other routers are automatically informed of the change. You must have multiple network adapters (one per network) on a Windows 2000 Server or Windows 2000 Advanced Server. In addition, you must install and configure Routing and Remote Access because dynamic routing protocols are not installed by default when you install Windows 2000.

Windows 2000 offers two primary IP routing protocols: The Routing Information Protocol (RIP) and the Open Shortest Path First (OPFS) protocol. You can choose one or the other depending on such factors as network size and topology. These routing protocols are explained in the next two sections.

Routing Information Protocol (RIP)

RIP is a routing protocol provided for backwards compatibility with existing RIP networks. RIP allows a router to exchange routing information with other RIP routers to make them aware of any change in the internetwork layout. RIP broadcasts the information to neighboring routers, and sends periodic RIP broadcast packets containing all routing information known to the router. These broadcasts keep all internetwork routers synchronized.

Open Shortest Path First (OSPF)

OSPF is a routing protocol that enables routers to exchange routing information and create a map of the network that calculates the best possible path to each network. Upon receiving changes to this map (actually a database, called the link-state database), the routing table is recalculated. As the size of the link-state database increases, memory requirements and route computation times increase. To address this scaling problem, OSPF divides the internetwork into collections of contiguous networks called areas. Areas are connected to each other through a backbone area. A backbone router in OSPF is a router that is connected to the backbone area. Backbone routers include routers that are connected to more than one area. However, backbone routers do not have to be Area Border Routers (ABRs). Routers that have all networks connected to the backbone are internal routers.

Each router only keeps a link-state database for those areas that are connected to the router. ABRs connect the backbone area to other areas, as illustrated in Figure 9.5.

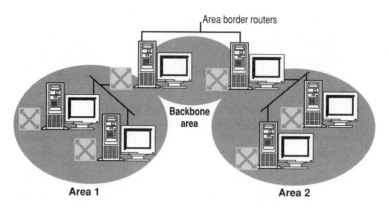

Figure 9.5 A basic OSPF area design

An OSPF-routed environment is best suited to a large to very large, multipath, dynamic IP internetwork such as a corporate or institutional campus or worldwide corporate or institutional internetwork.

The following are guidelines for managing your internal and border routers.

- Ensure that the ABRs for the area are configured with the proper pairs (Destination, Network Mask) that summarize that area's routes.

- Ensure that the source and route filtering configured on the ABR is not too restrictive, thus preventing proper routes from being propagated to the OSPF autonomous system. External source and route filtering is configured on the External Routing tab in the OSPF Routing Protocol Properties dialog box.

- Ensure that all ABRs are either physically connected to the backbone or logically connected to the backbone by using a virtual link. There should not be backdoor routers, which are routers that connect two areas without going through the backbone.

▶ **Follow these steps on Server01 (the Windows 2000 Server) to administer a router:**

1. Click Start, point to Programs, point to Administrative Tools, and then click Routing And Remote Access.

2. In the console tree, right-click Server Status, then click Add Server.

3. In the Add Server dialog box, do one of the following:

- Click The Following Computer, and type the computer name or IP address of the server.

- Click All Routing And Remote Access Servers In The Domain, and then type the name of the domain containing the server you want to administer. Click OK, and then select the server.

- Click Browse The Active Directory, click Next, and in the Find Routers Or Remote Access Servers dialog box, select the check boxes next to the types of servers that you want to search for. Click OK, and then select the server.

You can administer a remote server once it appears as an item in the console tree.

Lesson Summary

Routers forward packets from one physical network to another. The IP layer consults a routing table that is stored in memory. A routing table contains entries with the IP addresses of router interfaces to other networks. Static routers require that routing tables be built and updated manually. With dynamic routing, if a route changes, other routers are automatically informed of the change.

Lesson 2: Microsoft TCP/IP Configuration

This lesson describes the procedure for configuring Microsoft TCP/IP. Follow this procedure if you have not previously installed the TCP/IP network protocol on the computer(s) you are using to perform the practice procedures for this course.

After this lesson, you will be able to

- Set TCP/IP configuration parameters

- Identify some common TCP/IP utilities

- Describe packet filtering

Estimated lesson time: 15 minutes

Configuring TCP/IP

If you are implementing TCP/IP for the first time on your network, you should construct a detailed plan for IP addressing on your network. Your TCP/IP network addressing scheme can include either public or private addresses. You can use either public or private addresses if your network is not connected to the Internet. However, you will most likely implement some public IP addresses for Internet interconnectivity support. This is because devices connected directly to the Internet require a public IP address. InterNIC assigns public addresses to Internet service providers (ISPs). ISPs, in turn, assign IP addresses to organizations when network connectivity is purchased. IP addresses assigned this way are guaranteed to be unique and are programmed into Internet routers in order for traffic to reach the destination host.

Furthermore, you can implement a private addressing scheme to shield your internal addresses from the rest of the Internet by configuring private addresses on all the computers on your private network (or intranet). Private addresses are not reachable on the Internet because they are separate from public addresses, and they do not overlap.

Note Before you continue with the lesson, run the Ch09A.exe demonstration file located in the Media folder on the *Supplemental Course Materials* CD-ROM that accompanies this book. The file provides an overview of installing the TCP/IP protocol.

You can assign IP addresses in Windows 2000 dynamically using Dynamic Host Configuration Protocol (DHCP), as well as Automatic Private IP Addressing (see Chapter 5, "Managing Network Protocols and Services" for more details). You can also configure TCP/IP manually. You configure TCP/IP on a particular computer based on that computer's function. For example, servers in a client/server relationship within an organization should be assigned an IP address manually. However, you can configure TCP/IP dynamically through a DHCP server for the majority of clients on a network.

Dynamic Configuration

Windows 2000 computers attempt to obtain the TCP/IP configuration from a DHCP server on your network by default, as illustrated in Figure 9.7. If a static TCP/IP configuration is currently implemented on a computer, you can implement a dynamic TCP/IP configuration.

▶ **Follow these steps to implement a dynamic TCP/IP configuration:**

1. Click Start, point to Settings, and then click Network And Dial-Up Connections.

2. Right-click the Local Area Connection, and then click Properties.

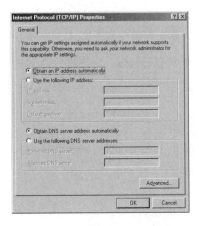

Figure 9.7 Configuring your computer to obtain TCP/IP settings automatically

3. On the General tab, click Internet Protocol (TCP/IP), and then click Properties.

    For other types of connections, click the Networking tab.

4. Click Obtain An IP Address Automatically, and then click OK.

Manual Configuration

Some servers, such as DHCP, DNS, and WINS servers, should be assigned an IP address manually. If you do not have a DHCP server on your network, you must configure TCP/IP computers manually to use a static IP address.

▶ **Follow these steps to configure a TCP/IP computer to use static addressing:**

1. Click Start, point to Settings, and then click Network And Dial-Up Connections.

2. Right-click Local Area Connection, and then click Properties.

3. On the General tab, click Internet Protocol (TCP/IP), and then click Properties.

4. Select Use The Following IP Address.

You will then have to type in an IP, subnet mask, and default gateway address. If your network has a DNS server, you can set up your computer to use DNS.

▶ **Follow these steps to set up your computer to use DNS:**

1. Select Use The Following DNS Server Addresses.

2. In Preferred DNS Server and Alternate DNS Server, type the primary and secondary DNS server addresses, as illustrated in Figure 9.8.

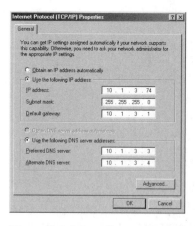

Figure 9.8 Manually configuring TCP/IP settings on your computer

You can also configure additional IP addresses and default gateways by performing the following procedure.

▶ **Follow these steps to configure additional IP addresses and default gateways:**

1. In the Internet Protocol (TCP/IP) Properties dialog box, click Advanced.

2. On the IP Settings tab, in IP Addresses, click Add.

3. In IP Address And Subnet Mask, type an IP address and subnet mask, and then click Add.

4. Repeat steps 2 and 3 for each IP address you want to add, and then click OK.

5. On the IP Settings tab, in Default Gateways, click Add.

6. In Gateway And Metric, type the IP address of the default gateway and the metric, and then click Add.

   You can also type a metric value in Interface Metric to configure a custom metric for this connection.

7. Repeat steps 5 and 6 for each IP address you want to add, and then click OK.

Automatic Private IP Address Assignment

Another TCP/IP address configuration option is to use Automatic Private IP Addressing when DHCP is not available. In previous versions of Windows, IP address configuration could be performed either manually or dynamically through DHCP. If a client was not able to obtain an IP address from a DHCP server, network services for the client were unavailable. The Automatic Private IP Addressing feature of Windows 2000 automates the process of assigning an unused IP address in the event that DHCP is not available.

The Automatic Private IP Addressing address is selected from the Microsoft-reserved address block 169.254.0.0, with the subnet mask 255.255.0.0. When the Automatic Private IP Addressing feature of Windows 2000 is used, an address in the Microsoft-reserved IP addressing range from 169.254.0.1 through 169.254.255.254 is assigned to the client. The assigned IP address is used until a DHCP server is located. The subnet mask 255.255.0.0 is automatically used.

Testing TCP/IP with Ipconfig and Ping

You should always verify and test your TCP/IP configuration to make sure your computer can connect to other TCP/IP hosts and networks. You can perform basic TCP/IP configuration testing using Ipconfig and ping utilities.

With Ipconfig, you verify the TCP/IP configuration parameters on a host, including the IP address, subnet mask, and default gateway, from a command prompt. This is useful in determining whether the configuration is initialized, or if a duplicate IP address is configured.

▶ **Follow these steps to use Ipconfig from a command prompt:**

1. Open a command prompt.

2. When the command prompt is displayed, type **Ipconfig** and then press Enter.

   TCP/IP configuration information is displayed, as illustrated in Figure 9.9.

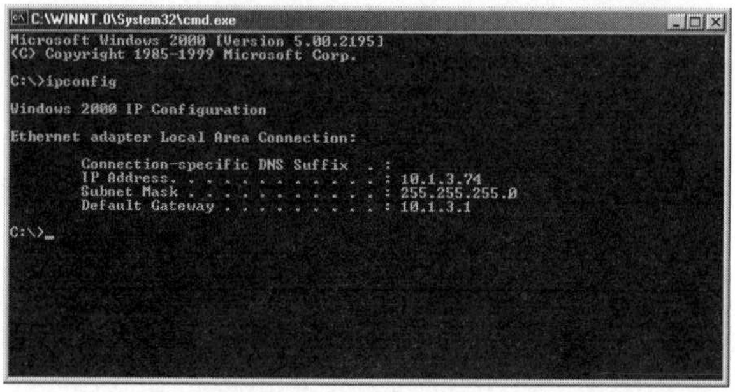

Figure 9.9 Using Ipconfig to display TCP/IP configuration information

After you verify the configuration with the Ipconfig utility, you can use the ping utility to test connectivity. The ping utility is a diagnostic tool that tests TCP/IP configurations and diagnoses connection failures. Ping uses the Internet Control Message Protocol (ICMP) Echo Request and Echo Reply messages to determine whether a particular TCP/IP host is available and functional. Like the Ipconfig utility, the ping utility is executed at the command prompt. The command syntax is:

```
Ping IP_Address
```

If ping is successful, a message appears that is similar to that shown in Figure 9.10.

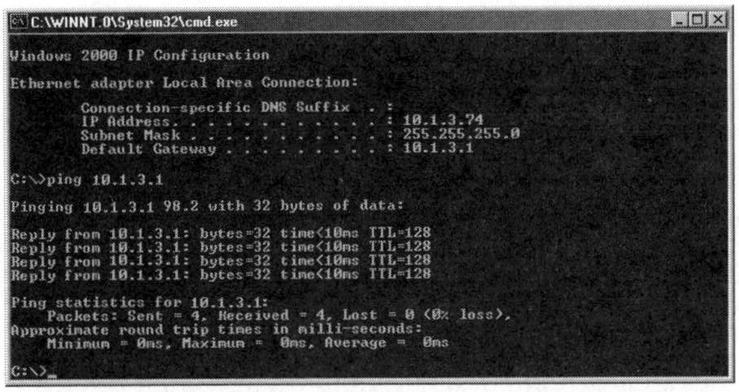

Figure 9.10 Reply messages displayed by the ping utility

Configuring Packet Filters

You can use IP packet filtering to trigger security negotiations for a communication based on the source, destination, and type of IP traffic. This allows you to define which specific IP and IPX traffic triggers will be secured, blocked, or allowed to pass through a network unfiltered.

For example, you can limit the type of access allowed to and from the network to restrict traffic to desired systems. You should make sure that you do not configure packet filters that are too restrictive, impairing the functionality of useful protocols on the computer. For example, if a computer running Windows 2000 is also running Internet Information Services (IIS) as a Web server, and packet filters are defined so that only Web-based traffic is allowed, you cannot use ping (which uses ICMP Echo Requests and Echo Replies) to perform basic IP troubleshooting.

You can configure the TCP/IP protocol to filter IP packets based on the following:

- TCP port number
- UDP port number
- IP protocol number

Practice: Implementing IP Packet Filters

In this practice, you implement TCP/IP packet filtering on a Windows 2000 Server computer for a LAN connection.

Exercise 1: Implementing TCP/IP Packet Filtering

1. On Server01, Click Start, point to Settings, and then click Network And Dial-Up Connections.

2. Right-click Local Area Connection and then click Properties. The Local Area Connection Properties dialog box appears.

3. Select Internet Protocol (TCP/IP), then click Properties. The Internet Protocol (TCP/IP) Properties dialog box appears.

4. Click Advanced.

   The Advanced TCP/IP Settings dialog box appears.

5. Click the Options tab, select TCP/IP Filtering, and then click Properties.

   The TCP/IP Filtering dialog box appears, as illustrated in Figure 9.11.

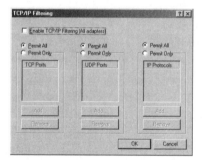

Figure 9.11 Setting TCP/IP packet filters in the TCP/IP Filtering dialog box

6. Click Enable TCP/IP Filtering (All Adapters).

You can now add TCP, UDP, and IP protocol filtering by clicking the Permit Only option and then clicking Add below the TCP, UDP, or IP Protocols list.

Some TCP/IP filtering implementations you can use include:

- Enabling only TCP port 23, which filters all traffic except Telnet traffic
- Enabling only TCP port 80 on a dedicated Web server to process only Web-based TCP traffic

Caution By enabling only TCP port 80, all network communications outside of port 80 will be disabled.

7. Click OK repeatedly to close all open dialog boxes.

Lesson Summary

By default, Windows 2000 installs the TCP/IP protocol if Setup detects a network adapter. You can also manually install TCP/IP. After you install TCP/IP on a computer, you can either configure it to obtain an IP address automatically or set configuration properties manually. You can also implement packet filters to limit the type of access allowed to and from the network to restrict traffic to desired systems.

Lesson 3: Installing and Configuring NWLink

In this lesson, you learn how to install NWLink, which is included in all varieties of Windows 2000 to support connectivity to computers running NetWare and other compatible systems.

After this lesson, you will be able to

- Install the NWLink protocol in Windows 2000
- Configure the NWLink protocol in Windows 2000
- Identify the purpose of a frame type and network number

Estimated lesson time: 30 minutes

Windows 2000 Professional and NetWare Connectivity

Windows 2000 Professional uses Client Service for NetWare and the NWLink protocol to provide connectivity between Windows 2000 Professional and servers running Novell NDS or NetWare bindery–based servers. NWLink is the Windows component that includes the IPX/SPX protocol.

With Windows 2000 Professional, you can leave the Novell Client 32 on the operating system while upgrading from Windows 95, Windows 98, or Windows NT 4.0 Workstation. Windows 2000 Professional upgrades computers running versions of Novell Client 32 earlier than 4.7. During the upgrade to Windows 2000 Professional, Novell Client 32 version 4.51 is installed. This process allows for a seamless upgrade of Novell Client 32 with no loss in functionality. To obtain a full version of Novell Client for Windows 2000, contact Novell directly.

Configuring Client Service for NetWare

When you install Client Service for NetWare on Windows 2000 Professional, the NWLink IPX/SPX/NetBIOS Compatible Transport Protocol (NWLink) is automatically installed.

▶ **Follow these steps to install Client Service for NetWare:**

1. Open the Network And Dial-Up Connections Control Panel applet.
2. Right-click the local area connection for which you want to install Client Service for NetWare, and then click Properties.
3. In the General tab, click Install.

4. In the Select Network Component Type dialog box, click Client, and then click Add.

5. In the Select Network Client dialog box, click Client Service For NetWare, and then click OK.

Note To install Client Service for NetWare, you need Administrator rights to the computer running Windows 2000 Professional.

Installing NWLink

Unlike TCP/IP, the NWLink protocol is not installed by default during Windows 2000 setup. However, you have the option of installing NWLink during Setup, along with other protocols, or you can install it later.

▶ **Follow these steps to install NWLink:**

1. Open the Network And Dial-Up Connections Control Panel applet.

2. Right-click a local area connection, then click Properties.

3. In the General tab, click Install.

4. In the Select Network Component Type dialog box, click Protocol, and then click Add.

5. In the Select Network Protocol dialog box, click NWLink IPX/SPX/ NetBIOS Compatible Transport Protocol, then click OK.

   To confirm that NWLink is working properly, at a command prompt, type **ipxroute config**. You will see a table with information about the bindings for which NWLink is configured, as illustrated in Figure 9.12.

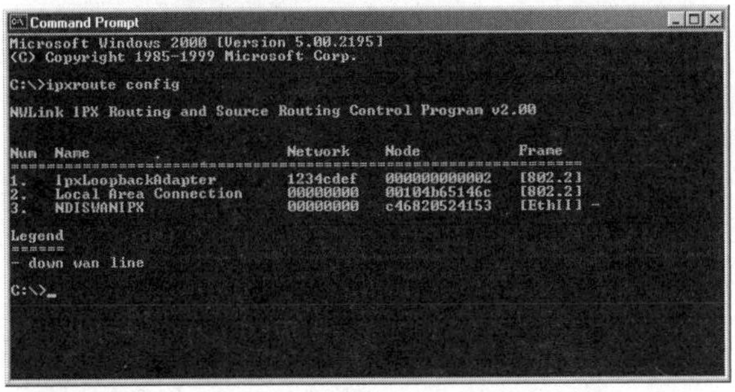

Figure 9.12 NWLink binding information

Internal Network Number

An internal network number is used for internal routing purposes when a computer running Windows 2000 also hosts IPX services. When calculating the best possible route for transmitting packets to a specified computer, multiple routes with the same route metrics can present ambiguity to computer hosts. When you specify a unique internal network number, you create a virtual network inside the computer. This allows for a singular optimum path to be calculated from the network to the services running on the computer.

▶ **Follow these steps to change the internal network number:**

1. In Control Panel, double-click Network And Dial-Up Connections.

2. Right-click a local area connection, then click Properties.

3. In the General tab, click NWLink IPX/SPX/NetBIOS Compatible Transport Protocol, then click Properties.

4. Type a value in the Internal Network Number box, which is illustrated in Figure 9.13, and then click OK.

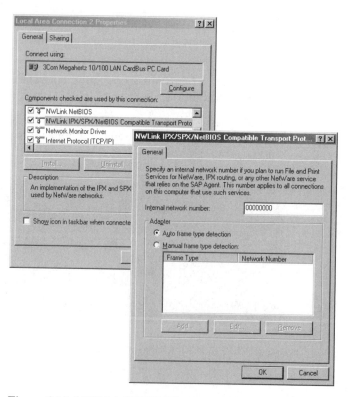

Figure 9.13 NWLink IPX/SPX/NetBIOS Compatible Transport Protocol dialog box

Frame Type and Network Number

A frame type defines the way in which a network adapter in a computer running Windows 2000 formats data to be sent over a network (specifically the header and footer formats used by the different data-link layer protocols). For example, to communicate between a computer running Windows 2000 and NetWare servers, you need to configure NWLink on the computer running Windows 2000 with the same frame type as that used by the NetWare servers. Table 9.2 lists the topologies and frame types supported by NWLink.

Table 9.2 NWLink Frame Types

Network type	Supported frame types
Ethernet	Ethernet II, 802.2, 802.3, 802.2 Subnetwork Access Protocol (SNAP)
Token Ring	802.5 and 802.5 SNAP
Fiber Distributed Data Interface	802.2 and SNAP

NWLink will try to automatically identify the frame type. During this auto detect process, NWLink tries each available frame type in the list for the associated medium access type. For example, on an Ethernet network, Ethernet 802.2, Ethernet 802.3, Ethernet II, and Ethernet Subnetwork Access Protocol (SNAP) are tested to see which frame types NWLink can communicate with. When NWLink receives a response from a NetWare server with one of the frame types, it also receives the network number associated with the frame type for the network segment where the client resides. NWLink then rebinds using the frame type(s) from which it received responses.

The external network number is a unique number that represents a specific network segment and associated frame type. All computers on the same network segment that use a given frame type must have the same external network number, which must be unique for each network segment.

The IPX frame type and network number are set during the initial NetWare server configuration. The Windows 2000 NWLink Auto Detect feature then detects the frame type and network number that were configured on the NetWare server(s). NWLink Auto Detect is the recommended option for configuring both the network number and the frame type.

Occasionally, Auto Detect selects an inappropriate network number and frame type combination for the adapter. Because Auto Detect uses the responses it receives from computers on the same network segment, Auto Detect might select an incorrect frame type and network number if computers respond with incorrect values. This is usually caused by an incorrect manual setting on another computer in the network. If the Auto Detect feature selects an inappropriate frame type and network number for a particular adapter, you can manually reset an NWLink frame type or network number for that given adapter. The frame type and network number on Windows 2000 Professional need to match the frame type and network number configured on the NetWare server. You can specify a frame type and network number of 00000000 to have the network number of the network segment automatically detected.

▶ **Follow these steps to change the network number and frame type:**

1. Open the Network And Dial-Up Connections Control Panel applet.

2. Right-click a local area connection, and click Properties.

3. In the General tab, click NWLink IPX/SPX/NetBIOS Compatible Transport Protocol, then click Properties.

4. In the Frame Type drop-down list box, select a frame type.

5. In the Network Number text box, type a network number, and then click OK.

Caution In most cases, you should not need to change the network number and frame type, because Auto Detect should correctly detect the frame type and network number. If you choose an incorrect setting, the client cannot connect to NetWare servers.

Configuring NWLink

To configure NWLink, you must first install the NWLink IPX/SPX/NetBIOS Compatible Transport Protocol and be a member of the Administrators group. You can use the following procedure if you want to bind NWLink to a different network adapter or to manually change the frame type.

▶ **Follow these steps to configure NWLink:**

1. Open the Network And Dial-Up Connections Control Panel applet.

2. Right-click a local area connection, then click Properties.

3. In the General tab, click NWLink IPX/SPX/NetBIOS Compatible Transport Protocol, and then click Properties.

4. In the General tab, type a value for Internal Network Number or leave this setting at the default value of 00000000.

5. If you want Windows 2000 to automatically select the frame type, click Auto Frame Type Detection, and then click OK. Skip Steps 6 through 10.

   By default, NWLink automatically detects the frame type used by the network adapter to which it is bound. If NWLink detects no network traffic or if multiple frame types are detected in addition to the 802.2 frame type, NWLink sets the frame type to 802.2.

6. To manually set the frame type, click Manual Frame Type Detection.

7. Click Add.

8. In the Manual Frame Detection dialog box, in Frame Type, click a frame type.

   You can determine which external network number, frame type, and internal network number your routers are using by typing **ipxroute config** at a command prompt.

9. In Network Number, type a network number, and then click Add.

10. Repeat these steps for each frame type you want to include, and then click OK.

Practice: Installing and Configuring NWLink

In this practice, you install and configure the NWLink IPX/SPX/NetBIOS Compatible Transport Protocol. You will also change the binding order of the NWLink protocol.

Exercise 1: Installing and Configuring NWLink

In this exercise, you will install NWLink and configure the appropriate frame detection.

1. On Pro1, Open the Network And Dial-Up Connections Control Panel applet.

2. Right-click a local area connection, and then click Properties.

   The Local Area Connection Properties dialog box appears.

3. Click Add.

   The Select Network Component Type dialog box appears.

4. Click Protocol, and then click Add.

5. Select NWLink IPX/SPX/NetBIOS Compatible Transport Protocol, and then click OK.

   The Local Area Connection Properties dialog box appears.

6. Select NWLink IPX/SPX/NetBIOS Compatible Transport Protocol, and then click Properties. At this point, you can select either auto or manual frame type detection.

Exercise 2: Modifying the NWLink Protocol Bindings Order

In this exercise, you will move the NWLink binding down in the protocol binding order list.

1. On Pro1, open the Network And Dial-Up Connections Control Panel applet.

2. Click the connection you want to modify and, on the Advanced menu, click Advanced Settings.

3. In the Adapters And Bindings tab, in Bindings For Adapter Name, click the NWLink protocol and move it down in the list by clicking the Down

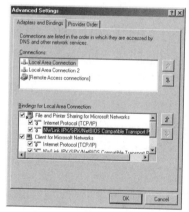

button, as illustrated in Figure 9.14.

Figure 9.14 The Advanced Settings dialog box

Lesson Summary

IPX/SPX is a protocol stack that is used in Novell networks. The NWLink IPX/SPX/NetBIOS Compatible Transport Protocol (NW Link) allows Windows 2000–based computers to communicate with Novell networks. When you install Client Service for NetWare on Windows 2000, NWLink is automatically installed.

To configure NWLink, you must first install NWLink and be a member of the Administrators group. The internal network number is used for internal routing purposes when the computer running Windows 2000 is also hosting IPX services. The frame type defines the way in which the network adapter, in a computer running Windows 2000, formats data to be sent over a network. The external network number is a unique number that represents a specific network segment and associated frame type. All computers on the same network segment that use a given frame type must have the same external network number, which must be unique for each network segment.

Lesson 4: Introducing and Enabling IPSec

Using Internet Protocol Security (IPSec) is the long-term solution for secure networking. More and more corporations are starting to use IPSec. It provides a key line of defense against private network and Internet attacks, balancing ease of use with security. This lesson discusses the technologies collectively referred to as IPSec.

After this lesson, you will be able to

- Explain the benefits of IPSec
- Describe the architecture of IPSec

Estimated lesson time: 15 minutes

Internet Protocol Security

As the Internet and intranets have evolved, the need for security has increased. Users are mainly concerned that that network traffic is safe from the following:

- Data modification while en route
- Interception
- Viewing or copying when intercepted
- Being accessed by unauthenticated parties

IPSec is a framework of open standards for ensuring private, secure communications over IP networks through the use of cryptographic security services. The Microsoft Windows 2000 implementation of IPSec is based on standards developed by the Internet Engineering Task Force (IETF) IPSec working group. IPSec has two goals:

1. To protect IP packets
2. To provide a defense against network attacks

Both goals are met through the use of cryptography-based protection services, security protocols, and dynamic key management. Starting with these two goals provides both the strength and flexibility to protect communications among computers on a private network, in remote sites connected by the Internet, and by dial-up clients. It can even be used to filter data packets on a network.

IPSec is based on an end-to-end security model, meaning that the only computers that must know about IPSec are the sending and receiving computers. Each handles security at its respective end, with the assumption that the medium over which the communication takes place is not secure. Routers that forward packets between the source and destination are not required to support IPSec. This model allows IPSec to be successfully deployed for these enterprise scenarios:

- Local area network (LAN) – client/server, peer-to-peer networks

- Wide area network (WAN) – router-to-router networks

- Remote access – access by dial-up clients, Internet access from private networks

IPSec Architecture

IPSec implementation in Windows 2000 consists of several components:

- IPSec policy agent
- ISAKMP/Oakley Key Management Service (IKE)
- IPSec driver
- IPSec model

IPSec Policy Agent Service

The policy agent is an IPSec mechanism residing on each Windows 2000 computer. The policy agent starts automatically when the computer is started. The policy agent performs the following tasks at the interval specified in the IPSec policy, as illustrated in Figure 9.15:

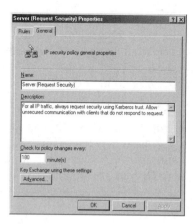

Figure 9.15 Specifying the IP security policy change interval

1. The policy agent retrieves the computer's assigned IPSec policy from Windows 2000 Active Directory directory services.

2. If there are no IPSec policies in the directory service or if the policy agent cannot connect to the directory service, it attempts to read the policy from the computer's registry. The policy agent service stops if there are no IPSec policies in the directory service or registry.

3. If there are policies in the directory service, the data transfer of policy information from the directory service to the computer is protected with data integrity and encryption services.

4. The policy agent sends the policy information to the IPSec driver, the IKE, and the computer's registry.

ISAKMP/Oakley Key Management Service (IKE)

This service is an IPSec mechanism residing on each computer running Windows 2000. Before IP datagrams can be transmitted from one computer to another, a security association must be established between the two computers. A security association is a set of parameters that defines the common security services and mechanisms used to protect the communication, such as keys and security properties.

The IKE centralizes security association management, reducing connection time. The Oakley protocol generates the actual keys that will be used to encrypt and decrypt the transferred data. IKE performs a two-phase operation:

1. It establishes a secure channel between the two computers for the communication. To achieve this, it authenticates computer identities and exchanges keying data to establish the shared, secret key the computers will use to encrypt and decrypt the data.

2. It establishes a security association between the two computers, which is passed to the IPSec driver, along with the shared key, on both the sending and receiving computers.

The policy agent automatically starts the IKE. This service does not start automatically or manually unless the policy agent service is running. If a security association cannot be established, the IPSec policy can be configured to either block communication or accept unsecured communication.

IPSec Driver

The IPSec driver (IPSEC.SYS) resides on each computer running Windows 2000. The driver watches all IP datagrams for a match with a filter list in the computer's security policy. The filter list defines which computers and networks require secure communications. If a filter match is found, the IPSec driver on the sending computer uses the SA and shared key to encrypt the data and sends it to the receiving computer. The IPSec driver on the receiving computer decrypts the transferred data and passes it to the receiving application.

Note The policy agent automatically starts the IPSec driver.

The IPSec Model

Figure 9.16 shows two users on intranet computers running Windows 2000 Server. Both Computer A and Computer B have an active IPSec policy. Alice is using Computer A and needs to send some information to Bob, who is using Computer B.

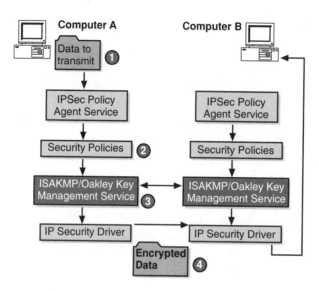

Figure 9.16 IPSec policy flow to encrypt data between two computers

1. Alice launches the File Transfer Protocol (FTP) application from Host A and sends data to Bob.

2. The IPSec driver on Host A notifies the IKE service that IPSec is needed for this communication by using the policies in the registry written by the policy agent.

3. The IKE services on Host A and Host B establish a shared key and SA.

4. The IPSec drivers on Host A and Host B each receive the key and SA.

5. The IPSec driver on Host A uses the key to encrypt the data and sends the data to Host B.

6. Host B's IPSec driver decrypts the data and passes it to the receiving application, where Bob retrieves the data.

Note Any routers or switches that are in the path between the communicating computers should only participate in forwarding the encrypted IP datagrams to their destination. However, if a firewall or other security gateway is between the communicating computers, IP forwarding must be enabled or special filtering must be created to permit forwarding of encrypted IP datagrams.

Considerations for IPSec

IPSec provides encryption of outgoing packets, but at a cost in performance. IPSec implements symmetric encryption of network data that is very efficient. However, for servers supporting many simultaneous network connections, the additional cost of encryption is significant, so you need to test IPSec using simulated network traffic before deploying it. Testing is also important if you are using a third-party hardware or software product to provide IP security. You can define IPSec policies for each domain. You can configure IPSec policies to do the following:

- Specify the types of authentication and the levels of confidentiality required between IPSec clients

- Specify the lowest security level at which communications are allowed to occur between IPSec-aware clients

- Allow or prevent communications with non-IPSec-aware clients

- Require all communications to be encrypted for confidentiality, or allow communications to be carried out in plaintext

Consider using IPSec to provide security for the following applications:

- Peer-to-peer communications over your organization's intranet, such as legal-department or executive-committee communications

- Client/server communications to protect sensitive (confidential) information stored on servers

- Remote access (dial-up or virtual private network [VPN]) communications (For VPNs using IPSec with Layer Two Tunneling Protocol [L2TP], remember to set up Group Policy to permit auto enrollment for IPSec certificates. For detailed information about machine certificates for L2TP over IPSec VPN connections, see Windows 2000 Help.)

- Secure router-to-router WAN communications

Consider the following strategies for IPSec in your network security deployment plan:

- Identify clients and servers to use IPSec communications

- Identify whether client authentication is based on Kerberos trust or digital certificates

- Describe each IPSec policy, including rules and filter lists

- Describe certificate services needed to support client authentication by digital certificates

- Describe enrollment processes and strategies to enroll users for IPSec certificates

Lesson Summary

IPSec is a framework of open standards for ensuring private, secure communications over IP networks through the use of cryptographic security services. IPSec is transparent to the user and provides a high level of secure communications with a low cost of use.

The architecture of IPSec is comprised of four major components: IPSec policy agent, IKE Service, IPSec driver, and IPSec model.

Lesson 5: Configuring IPSec

The Microsoft Management Console (MMC) can be used to create and configure IPSec policies. It can be configured to centrally manage policy (for Active Directory services), manage policy locally, or manage policy remotely for a computer. In this lesson you explore various screens used to configure IPSec. You also create a test IP Security policy.

After this lesson, you will be able to

- Describe how to implement IPSec
- Configure IPSec policies
- Describe the various property sheets of an IPSec policy, Authentication Method, IP Packet Filtering, Filter Actions, and additional IPSec tasks

Estimated lesson time: 30 minutes

Prerequisites for Implementing IPSec

The computers in your network need to have an IPSec policy defined that is appropriate for your network security strategy. Computers in the same domain might be organized into groups with IPSec policy applied to the groups. Computers in different domains might have complementary IPSec policies to support secure network communications.

How to Implement IPSec

You can view the default IP Security policies in the Group Policy MMC snap-in. The policies are listed under IP Security Policies on Active Directory: Group Policy Object\Computer Configuration\Windows Settings\Security Settings\IP Security Policies.

You can also view IPSec policies by using the IP Security Policy Management snap-in of the MMC. Each IPSec policy is governed by rules that determine when and how the policy is applied. Right-click a policy and select Properties. The Rules tab lists the policy rules. Rules can be further subdivided into filter lists, filter actions, and additional properties. The default snap-in is started from the Administrative Tools menu; this allows configuration of the local computer only. To centrally manage policy for multiple computers, add the IP Security Management snap-in to an MMC.

Configuring IPSec Policies

The initial window displays three predefined policy entries: Client (Respond Only), Secure Server (Require Security), and Server (Request Security). By default, none of these policies is enabled. These policies are shown in Figure 9.17.

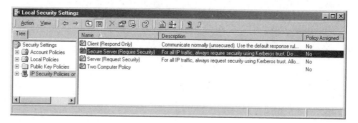

Figure 9.17 MMC of a Windows 2000 member server

These defaults are the same whether the IPSec policy is local or stored in Active Directory directory services as part of a group policy. In the example shown in Figure 9.17, the policy is local to a member server.

- The Client (Respond Only) policy allows communications in plaintext but will respond to IPSec requests and attempts to negotiate security. This policy effectively allows clear-text communication but attempts to negotiate security if a security request is made. Uses Kerberos v5 for authentication.

- The Server (Request Security) policy causes the server to attempt to initiate secure communications for every session. If a client who is not IPSec-aware initiates a session, the session is allowed.

- The Secure Server (Require Security) policy requires Kerberos trust for all IP packets sent from this computer, with the exception of broadcast, multicast, Resource Reservation Setup Protocol (RSVP), and IKE packets. This policy does not allow unsecured communications with clients. Therefore, any clients who connect to a server with this policy must be IPSec-aware.

To edit policies, right-click on the policy and select Properties.

Note Only one policy can be assigned at a time. If an IPSec policy is configured in several overlapping group policies, the normal group policy hierarchy applies.

Connection Types

The Connection Type tab can be chosen from the Edit Rule Properties dialog box (see Figure 9.18). It is also displayed as part of the Rule Creation wizard.

Note All policy settings can be configured through wizards. Use of the wizards is turned on by default, but can be turned off by deselecting the Use Add Wizard check box.

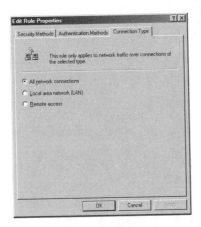

Figure 9.18 Edit Rule Properties dialog box

Designating a connection type for each rule determines which computer connections (network adapters or modems) will be affected by an IPSec policy. Each rule has a connection property that designates whether the rule applies to LAN connections, remote access connections, or all network connections.

Authentication Method

The authentication method defines how each user is going to be assured that the other computers or users really are who they say they are. As illustrated in Figure 9.19, each authentication method provides the necessary pieces to assure identity. Windows 2000 supports three authentication methods: the Kerberos protocol, using certificates, and using a preshared key.

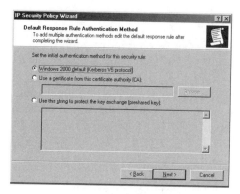

Figure 9.19 Default Response Rule Authentication Method dialog box

- **Kerberos protocol.** The Kerberos v5 security protocol is the default authentication technology. The Kerberos protocol issues tickets, or virtual proof-of-identity cards, when a computer logs on to a trusted domain. This method can be used for any clients running the Kerberos v5 protocol (whether or not they are Windows-based clients) who are members of a trusted domain.

- **Certificates.** Using certificates requires that at least one trusted certificate authority (CA) has been configured. Windows 2000 supports X.509 version 3 certificates, including CA certificates generated by commercial certifying authorities. A rule may specify multiple authentication methods. This ensures that a common method can be found when negotiating with a peer.

- **Preshared Key.** Users can also used a shared key that is secret and has been previously agreed upon. Using a preshared key is efficient and does not require the client to run the Kerberos protocol or have a public-key certificate. Both parties must manually configure IPSec to use this preshared key. This is a simple method for authenticating non-Windows-based hosts and standalone hosts.

Note The key derived from the authentication is for authentication *only*; it is *not* the key used to encrypt or authenticate the data.

Each rule may be configured with one or more authentication methods. Each configured authentication method appears in a list in the order of preference. If the first authentication method cannot be used, then the next will be attempted.

IP Packet Filtering

IP Security is applied to packets as they are sent and received. Packets are matched against filters when being sent (outbound) to see if they should be secured, blocked, or passed through as clear text. Packets are also matched when received (inbound) to see if security should be negotiated, or if the packets should be blocked or passed through and permitted into the system.

Individual filter specifications are grouped into a filter list to enable complex patterns of traffic to be grouped and managed as one named filter list, such as Building 7 File Servers, or All Blocked Traffic. Filter lists can be shared as necessary between different IPSec rules in the same policy or in different IPSec policies. Filter specifications should be set for incoming and outgoing traffic. Two types of filters may be specified. They are input filters and output filters, which correspond to incoming and outgoing traffic respectively.

- Input filters, which apply to traffic received, allow the receiving computer to match the traffic with the IP filter list, respond to requests for secure communication, or match the traffic with an existing SA and decrypt the secured packets.

- Output filters, which apply to traffic leaving a computer toward a destination, trigger a security negotiation that must take place before traffic is sent.

Important Although input and output filters are defined and used in the filter list, it is unclear in the user interface as to which filter is being created. The source and destination addresses determine whether the filter is inbound or outbound.

There must be a filter to cover any traffic scenarios to which the associated rule applies. A filter contains the following parameters: the source and destination address of the IP packet; the protocol over which the packet is being transferred; and the source and destination port of the protocol for TCP and UDP.

1. **Source and destination address of the IP packet.** As illustrated in Figure 9.20, the following address options can be chosen when creating or editing the filter:

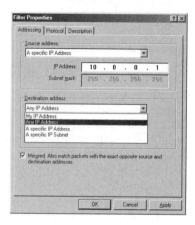

Figure 9.20 IP packet Filter Properties dialog box

- My IP Address – the IP address of the local machine
- Any IP Address – unicast addresses only (IPSec does not support multicast or broadcast addresses.)
- A Specific IP Address – refers to a specific IP address on the local network or on the Internet
- A Specific IP Subnet – includes any IP address on a specified IP subnet

Note IPSec populates My IP Address with the first bound IP address only. If the computer is multihomed, IPSec uses only one of the IP addresses, not both. Routing and Remote Access clients are considered to be multi-homed, and therefore IPSec may not populate the IP address properly.

2. **Protocol over which the packet is being transferred.** This automatically defaults to cover all IP client protocols in the TCP/IP suite.

Table 9.3 provides a list of the protocol types available in the Protocol tab in the Filter Properties dialog box, which is illustrated in Figure 9.21.

Table 9.3 Protocol Filtering

Protocol type	Description
ANY	Any Protocol
EGP	Exterior Gateway Protocol
HMP	Host Monitoring Protocol
ICMP	Internet Control Message Protocol
Other	Unspecified protocol based on IP protocol number
RAW	Raw data on top of IP
RDP	Reliable Datagram Protocol
RVD	MIT Remote Virtual Disk
TCP	Transmission Control Protocol
UDP	User Datagram Protocol
XNS-IDP	Xerox NS IDP

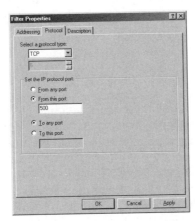

Figure 9.21 Protocol settings in the Filter Properties dialog box

3. **Source and destination port of the protocol for TCP and UDP.**
   This also defaults to cover all ports, but can be configured to apply
   only to packets sent or received on a specific port.

Select the filter properties when editing or creating a filter. Filters can be
managed globally by right-clicking on the managed computer in the left pane.
They can also be managed within each of the policies' Rule Properties pages.
The Filter Creation wizard allows these properties to be configured.

Mirroring

Mirroring allows a filter to match packets with the exact opposite source and destination addresses. An outbound filter specifying the IP address as the source address and the second computer as the destination address, for example, will automatically create an inbound filter specifying the second computer as the source address and the initiating computer's IP address as the destination.

Note The mirrored filter does not actually show in the filter list. Instead, the Mirrored check box will be checked in the Filter Properties dialog box.

Host A must do the following in order to always exchange data securely with Host B:

- To send secured data to Host B, Host A's IPSec policy must have a filter specification for any outbound packets going to Host B.

- To receive secured data from Host A, Host B's IPSec policy must have a filter specification for any inbound packets from Host A, or must have a policy with the default-response rule set to active.

- Mirroring would allow each host to send or receive from the other host without creating another filter to do so.

Filter Actions

The filter action specifies what security action to take once a filter has been triggered. The action specifies whether to block the traffic, permit the traffic, or negotiate the security for the given connection. The negotiation consists of support for *only* authenticity and integrity using the authentication header (AH) protocol, or for integrity and confidentiality using the Encapsulating Security Payload (ESP) protocol. Each filter action can be customized, allowing the administrator to choose which protocols require authenticity and which protocols require confidentiality.

One or more negotiated filter actions may be specified. As illustrated in Figure 9.22, the filter actions appear as a list with the first method listed taking precedence over the actions lower in the list. If that filter action cannot be negotiated, the next filter action is attempted.

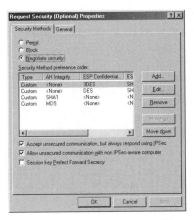

Figure 9.22 Secure Initiator Negotiation policy properties

It is also possible to choose either high or medium security rather than specifying a custom method. High security both encrypts and provides data integrity. Medium security only provides data integrity.

Additional IPSec Tasks

The administrator can perform several other tasks that are accessed by right-clicking on the IP Security Policy icon in the left window. These tasks include:

- **Managing IP Filter Lists and Filter Actions.** This allows the administrator to configure filters and filter actions separate from individual rules. Once a rule is created, the filters or filter actions may be activated, as illustrated in Figure 9.23.

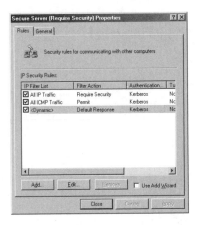

Figure 9.23 The Rules tab of the Secure Server Properties dialog box

- **Checking Policy Integrity.** Because Active Directory services takes the last information saved as current, if multiple administrators are editing a policy, the links between policy components could be broken. For example:

  Policy A uses Filter A.

  Policy B uses Filter B.

  This means that Filter A has a link to Policy A, and Filter B links to Policy B.

  Suppose Bob edits Policy A and adds a rule that uses Filter C.

  At the same time, Alice edits Policy B from a different location, and adds a rule that also uses Filter C.

  If both save the changes simultaneously, Filter C could link to both Policy A and Policy B. However, it is unlikely that they will save changes simultaneously. It is more likely that, for example, Policy A is saved last. If this it the case, it will overwrite the link from Filter C to Policy B. Filter C will link only to Policy A. This will cause problems in the future when Filter C is modified, because Policy A users will pick up the new changes, but Policy B users will not.

The policy integrity check eliminates this problem by verifying the links in all IPSec policies. It is a good idea to run the integrity check after modifications to a policy. The administrator can perform several other tasks that are accessed by right-clicking on the IP Security Policy icon in the left window. These tasks are :

- **Restoring Default Policies.** A predefined policy may be restored to its original configuration.

- **Importing Policies.** Policies are imported from another host on the network.

- **Exporting Policies.** A policy may be exported to another host on the network.

Practice: Testing IPSec

In this practice, you activate a built-in IPSec policy to see that it blocks communications if traffic cannot be secured. If both computers are running Windows 2000 Server and are members of the same or trusted Windows 2000 Server secure domains, the built-in IPSec policies can be used to establish secure communications easily. Otherwise, you will need to configure your own IPSec policy for testing on each computer with the steps provided in later sections.

Note Before you continue with the lesson, run the Ch09B.exe demonstration file located in the Media folder on the *Supplemental Course Materials* CD-ROM that accompanies this book. The file provides an overview of testing IPSec.

Exercise 1: Adding IPSec to the MMC

1. Verify that you can communicate with the other computer by pinging the other computer's IP address.

    You should receive four replies to the ping.

2. Using the Administrative Tools on the Start menu, run the Local Security Policy MMC plug-in.

3. Select IP Security Policies On Local Machine in the left pane.

4. In the right pane, right-click on Secure Server (Require Security), and then click Properties.

5. In the Secure Server (Require Security) Properties dialog box, click Add. The Security Rule wizard appears.

6. At the Welcome screen, click Next.

7. At the Tunnel Endpoint screen, click Next.

8. At the Network Type screen, click Next.

9. At the Authentication Method screen, click the Use This String To Protect The Key Exchange (Preshared Key) radio button. Type **MSPRESS** in the scroll box, then click Next.

10. Click All IP Traffic, and then click Next at the IP Filter List screen.

11. Click Require Security, and then click Next at the Filter Action screen.

12. Click Finish to close the wizard.

13. Now that you have added a restrictive filter list, deselect all default filter lists.

14. Close the Secure Server (Require Security) Properties dialog box.

15. Right-click on Secure Server (Require Security), and click Assign from the pop-up menu.

16. Ping your partner host.

    Notice that the ping was unsuccessful.

17. To let yourself communicate on the network again, unassign the Secure Server (Require Security) policy using the pop-up menu.

Lesson Summary

Before you can implement IPSec, you need to have an appropriate security policy defined. Three predefined policy entries—Client (Respond Only), Secure Server (Require Security), and Server (Request Security)—come with Windows 2000. These can be modified or removed at any time. Additionally, MMC can be used to add customized policies. The custom policies may address connections types, authentication methods, IP Filtering and other security issues.

Using IPSec, Windows 2000 can support various host authentication methods and provide IP packet filtering, thus allowing computers to communicate or denying communication based on a wide variety of rules and filters.

Lesson 6: Customizing IPSec Policies and Rules

IPSec is easily customizable with policies and rules. In this lesson you will explore how to secure a network using these various methods, taking into consideration such things as proxies, network address translation (NAT), Simple Network Management Protocol (SNMP), Dynamic Host Configuration Protocol (DHCP), Domain Name System (DNS), Windows Internet Name Service (WINS), and domain controllers.

After this lesson, you will be able to

- Explain IPSec policies and rules
- Describe how to configure IPSec for use with firewalls, NAT, and proxies
- Describe how to use IPSec to secure a network with SNMP, DHCP, DNS, WINS, or domain controllers

Estimated lesson time: 40 minutes

Policy-Based Security

Strong, cryptographic security methods have become necessary to protect communications, but they can also increase administrative overhead. IPSec reduces this by providing policy-based administration. Your network security administrator can configure IPSec policies to meet the security requirements of a user, group, application, domain, site, or global enterprise. Windows 2000 provides an administrative interface, called IPSec Policy Management, to define IPSec policies for individual computers or groups of computers within Active Directory.

IPSec Policies

An IPSec policy is a named collection of rules and key exchange settings. The policy may be assigned as a domain security policy or an individual computer's security policy. A domain computer automatically inherits the IPSec policy assigned to the domain security policy when it logs on to the domain. If a computer is not connected to a domain (for example, a roving portable computer or a standalone server), IPSec policies are stored in and retrieved from the computer registry.

This allows great flexibility in configuring security policies for groups of similar computers or individual computers with special requirements. For example, one security policy can be created for all users on the same network or all users in a particular department. IPSec policies are created with the IPSec Management snap-in for a Windows 2000 member server, as illustrated in Figure 9.24.

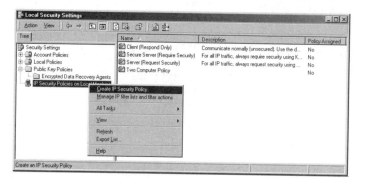

Figure 9.24 MMC of a Windows 2000 member server

Rules

Rules govern how and when IPSec is used. A rule contains a list of IP filters and specifies the security actions that take place upon a filter match. A rule is a collection of

- IP filters
- Negotiation policies
- Authentication methods
- IP tunneling attributes
- Adapter types

Each security policy may contain multiple rules. This provides the flexibility of assigning one IPSec policy to multiple computers with different communication scenarios. For example, one policy may cover all users in a department or network, but multiple rules may be required: one for intranet communications and another for Internet communications.

IP Filters and Filter Specifications

All rules are based on packets matching an IP filter. Each rule may only have a single IP filter active. The IPSec driver watches each IP datagram for a match with the active IP filter. If a match occurs, the action specified in the associated rule is implemented for that communication.

Filter Specifications

IP datagrams are checked for a match against each filter specification. Filter specifications contain the following properties:

- The source and destination address of an IP datagram, based on IP address, DNS name, or by a specific subnet or network

- The protocol, TCP, or UDP

- The specific source and destination protocol port numbers for either TCP or UDP

Security Methods and Negotiation Policies

The level of security used for a communication is determined by the security methods and the negotiation policy.

Security Methods

Each security method specifies a unique level of security to be used for the communication. Multiple security methods can be part of a single negotiation policy to increase the ability of two computers finding a common security method. The IKE service on each computer traverses the list of security methods in descending order until a common method is found. You can choose between preconfigured security methods of High or Medium or configure your own custom method.

- **High.** The IP ESP provides confidentiality, integrity, authentication, and antireplay protection services.

- **Medium.** The IP AH security protocol provides integrity, authentication, and antireplay protection services. Confidentiality is not a part of AH.

- **Custom.** In addition to choosing between ESP and AH, expert users can specify the algorithms for authentication, integrity, and confidentiality.

Negotiation Policies

A negotiation policy is a named collection of security methods. Each rule can have a single negotiation policy specified as currently active. If a common security method cannot be established between two computers, the negotiation policy can be configured to refuse communication with that computer or to send the data in clear text (without encryption).

Because IPSec does not disturb the original IP header, it is considered normal IP traffic and is routed as such.

ESP and Routers

The Encapsulating Security Payload (ESP) neither encrypts nor authenticates the IP header, leaving it undisturbed. Even in Tunnel mode, where the original IP header is encrypted, routing does not pose a problem. The new tunnel IP header (left undisturbed) is used to route between the tunnel endpoints. Once the packet reaches the tunnel destination endpoint, it is authenticated and decrypted. The original IP packet is forwarded without IPSec authentication or encryption to the final destination.

AH and Routers

The authentication header (AH) protocol uses all fields in the IP header to create the Integrity Check Value (ICV). Because routers modify fields in the IP header as they forward packets, this could cause problems; however, the fields that may be modified are set to zero for ICV calculation. Therefore, routers can change the mutable fields (Time to Live [TTL], checksum, and so on) without affecting the ICV calculation. At the receiving end, IPSec once again sets the mutable fields to zero for ICV calculation.

The same is true for Tunnel mode, where the new tunnel IP header would be used to calculate the ICV, but the mutable fields would be set to zero. At the tunnel destination endpoint, the hash is verified and the original IP packet forwarded without further authentication.

IPSec through Firewalls

Any routers or switches in the data path between the communicating hosts simply forwards the encrypted and/or authenticated IP packets to their destination. However, if there is a firewall or filtering router, IP forwarding must be enabled for the following IP protocols and UDP port:

- **IP Protocol ID of 51.** Both inbound and outbound filters should be set to pass AH traffic.

- **IP Protocol ID of 50.** Both inbound and outbound filters should be set to pass ESP traffic.

- **UDP Port 500.** Both inbound and outbound filters should be set to pass IKE traffic.

Be aware that these settings are used to allow IPSec traffic to pass through the firewall only when using Transport mode, or if the firewall is on the public side of the tunnel server. IPSec cannot be used in such a way that the firewall would implement IPSec on all incoming or outgoing packets. The router would have to create and maintain all the SAs associated with each connection.

Note Traditional firewall filtering (filtering on TCP or UDP ports) cannot be done to ESP traffic, as the port numbers are encrypted.

IPSec Not Possible through NAT and Proxies

It is not possible to use IPSec through a NAT or application proxy. Even though the IP header is left intact, the encryption and authentication do not allow for other fields in the packet to be changed.

This is a problem for NAT because it would require the security parameters index to change, which cannot be allowed as this would invalidate the ICV field. Also, NAT cannot update the UDP and TCP headers because they are within the encrypted portion of the ESP or have been used in the ICV calculation.

Application proxies pose another problem for IPSec. Because application proxies operate at the application layer they would need to be IPSec-aware and have a security association for each IPSec client. This is obviously unreasonable and not provided by application proxies.

Securing SNMP

All SNMP-enabled systems must be configured to use IPSec, or at a minimum, the IPSec policies must be configured to allow unsecured communications if all the SNMP-enabled hosts *cannot also* be IPSec-enabled. Otherwise, secured communication will fail and SNMP messages will not be exchanged.

IPSec does not automatically encrypt the SNMP protocol. The only exceptions are the predefined polices Secure Initiator and Lockdown, which have been configured to secure SNMP traffic as well. To secure SNMP, add two pairs of filter specifications to a new or existing policy on the SNMP-enabled host.

The first pair of filter specifications would be for typical SNMP traffic (SNMP messages) and would consist of one inbound and one outbound filter specification. The following steps explain how to set filter specifications for the first pair.

1. In the Addressing page of the IP Filter dialog box, set the Source address to the IP address of the SNMP management system.

2. Set the Destination address to My IP Address, which will translate to the IP address of the host to which the policy is assigned (an SNMP agent).

3. Enable Mirrored to automatically create the outbound filter specification.

4. In the Protocol page of the IP Filter List dialog box, set the Protocol Type to TCP or UDP (if both are required, create an additional filter specification).

5. Set From This Port and To This Port to 161.

The second set of filter specifications would be for SNMP trap messages and would also consist of one inbound and one outbound filter specification. The following steps explain how to set filter specifications for the second pair.

1. In the Addressing page of the IP Filter List dialog box set the Source address to the IP address of the SNMP management system.

2. Set the Destination address to My IP Address, which will translate to the IP address of the host to which the policy is assigned (an SNMP agent).

3. Enable Mirrored to automatically create the outbound filter specification.

4. In the Protocol page of the IP Filter List dialog box, set the Protocol Type to TCP or UDP (if both are required, create an additional filter specification).

5. Set From This Port and To This Port to 162.

The SNMP management system or console must also be IPSec-enabled. The SNMP service in Windows 2000 supports SNMP management software, but does not include SNMP management software. To secure SNMP traffic with IPSec, the third-party management software must be IPSec-capable.

DHCP, DNS, WINS Servers, or Domain Controllers

If enabling IPSec for any servers running these services, consider whether or not all their clients are IPSec-capable. Ensure that the policies, especially the authentication and negotiation settings, are compatible. Otherwise, secure negotiation might erroneously fail, and clients will not be able to access network resources.

When DNS Is Not IPSec-Enabled

To specify a host's DNS name in an IP Filter List specification (rather than the IP address) if DNS servers are not IPSec-enabled, a special policy setting is required. Otherwise, IPSec will not be able to successfully resolve the DNS host name to a valid IP address. The setting consists of a filter specification to exempt traffic between the host and the DNS server from requiring IPSec.

▶ **Follow these steps to add a filter specification to the applicable policy and rule:**

1. From the Addressing page of the IP Filter List dialog box, set the Source address to My IP Address. Set the Destination address to the IP address of the DNS server.

2. Enable Mirrored to automatically create the outbound filter specification.

3. In the Protocol page of the IP Filter List dialog box, set From This Port and To This Port to 53.

   This is the common port used by most DNS servers for communication; set this to whatever port the DNS service has been configured for traffic use.

Additionally, the negotiation policy for this rule must be set to Do Not Allow Secure Communication: No security methods should be configured. This will ensure that DNS traffic is never secured with IPSec.

TCP/IP Properties

If a computer that is a member of a domain is disconnected from its domain, a copy of the domain IPSec properties will be retrieved from the computer's registry. If the computer is not a member of a domain, a local IPSec policy will be stored in the registry. The TCP/IP properties allow the nondomain computer to always use IPSec, use IPSec only if possible, or never use IPSec.

Note If the computer is connected to a domain, TCP/IP properties will not be configurable.

Practice: Building a Custom IPSec Policy

Several built-in policies have been defined to permit you to examine and investigate their behavior and configuration. However, most installations of IPSec require custom policies to be built. In this practice, you will build and test your own IPSec policy. You should perform this practice on both computers.

Exercise 1: Building your own IPSec policy

In this exercise, you will use the MMC and the Add Wizard to create a custom IPSec security policy.

1. Using the Administrative Tools on the Start menu, run the Local Security Policy MMC plug-in.

2. In the left pane, right-click IP Security Policy On Local Machine.

3. From the pop-up menu, choose Create IP Security Policy.

4. When the wizard appears, click Next to continue.

5. Type the policy name **Two Computer Policy**, and then click Next.

6. Accept the default for the Requests For Secure Connection screen by leaving the Default Response Rule check box checked, and then click Next.

7. Accept the default response rule for Kerberos Authentication, and then click Next.

8. Be sure to leave the Edit Properties check box checked.

9. Click Finish to complete the initial setup.

10. The Properties box appears. *Do not close it.*

At this point, you still have not configured your custom rule. Only the default response rule properties have been configured.

What is the purpose of the default response rule?

Exercise 2: Adding a New Rule

In this exercise, you will add a new rule to the IPSec policy you just created without using the Add Wizard. The rule will be configured manually using the appropriate dialog boxes and property tabs.

1. At the bottom of the Properties dialog box, deactivate the Use Add Wizard check box.

2. In the Rules tab of the Property screen, click Add.

3. The New Rule Properties screen appears.

Exercise 3: Adding a New Filter

In this exercise, you will be configuring filters between your computer (Server01) and your second computer (Pro1). You will need to configure an outbound filter specifying your IP address as the source address and your second computer's IP as the destination address. The mirror processing then automatically configures an inbound filter specifying your second computer as the source address and your computer as the destination address.

1. Click the Add button.

The IP Filter List appears.

2. In the Name box, type the filter name **Host A–Host B Filter**.

3. Deactivate the Use Add Wizard check box.

4. Click the Add button in the IP Filter List tab.

5. The Filter Properties box appears.

6. Change Source Address to a specific IP address.

7. Add your IP (*w.x.y.z*) address.

8. Change the Destination Address to a specific IP address.

9. Add your second computer's IP (*w.x.y.z*) address.

10. Click OK and verify that your filter has been added in the Filters box of the IP Filter List dialog box.

11. Click Close.

12. From the IP Filter List tab, activate your filter by clicking the radio button next to the filter list you just added.

Exercise 4: Specifying a Filter Action

In the preceding exercise, you configured input and output filters for matching communication packets. In this exercise you configure the actions to take on the filtered packets.

1. Click the Filter Action tab and deactivate the Use Add Wizard check box.

2. Click the Add button to create a filter action.

3. In the Security Methods tab, ensure Negotiate Security is selected.

4. Verify that Allow Unsecured Communication With Non IPSEC Aware Computer is not selected.

5. Click Add to choose a security method.

6. Select Medium (AH) and click OK.

7. Click OK to close the New Filter Action Properties dialog box.

8. Click the radio button next to the filter you just created to activate it.

Exercise 5: Setting an Authentication Method

In this exercise, you specify how the two computers will trust each other by specifying the authentication method to use when attempting to establish an SA. You use a preshared key, which is a word or phrase that both computers must know to be trusted by one another. Both sides of the IPSec communication must know this value. It is not used to encrypt application data. Rather, it is used during negotiation to establish whether or not the two computers will trust one another.

1. Click the Authentication Methods tab.

2. Click Add.

3. Click the Pre-Shared Key radio button.

4. Type a preshared key or password in the text box and click OK.

5. Choose Pre-Shared Key in the list and click Move Up so it appears first in the list.

Exercise 6: Verifying Settings and Complete Rule Creation

All of the changes to your IPSec configuration are now complete, however they have not been implemented. In this exercise, you take the final steps to verify that the settings are correct and complete creating the rule.

1. Click the Tunnel Setting tab.

   Verify that This Rule Does Not Specify An IPSEC Tunnel is selected.

2. Click the Connection Type tab.

   Verify that All Network Connections is selected.

3. Click Close to return to Policy Properties and complete the creation of this rule.

   Verify that This New Rule is selected in the list box.

4. Close Policy Properties.

   Your new IPSec policy is now ready to be activated.

Exercise 7: Activating the New Policy

Now that you have configured your new IPSec policy, in this exercise, you activate the new policy and then test the IPSec configuration.

1. In the right pane of the MMC, right-click the Two Computer Policy you just created.

2. Click Assign.

   The Policy Assigned column value should now be Yes.

3. Enable the policy on your computer and your second computer.

4. Ping your second computer.

   The first ping after enabling the policy will usually fail due to the time it takes to negotiate policy.

   With matching policies active on both computers, future pings will work.

5. Alternatively, enable and disable the policy on your computer and your second computer to see the effects of nonmatching policy settings.

Lesson Summary

IPSec allows you to use policies, rules, filters, and other methods to create a secure network. Policy-based administration helps reduce the administrative overhead of implementing security. Using rules and filters you can create custom policies to meet specific needs. In this lesson, you learned how to secure a network using these various methods and taking into consideration such things as proxies, NAT, SNMP, DHCP, DNS, WINS, and domain controllers.

Lesson 7: Monitoring IPSec

To view how your IPSec policies and rules are being used in your network, you may want to monitor IPSec. In this lesson, you use several tools to do just that. You focus on IPSec monitoring tools like IPSECMON.EXE, Event Viewer, Performance Monitor, and Network Monitor. These tools help you to maintain a secure, IPSec-rich network.

After this lesson, you will be able to

- Troubleshoot IPSec with IPSECMON.EXE

- Troubleshoot IPSec with Event Viewer

- Troubleshoot IPSec with Network Monitor

- Describe troubleshooting with an IPSECPA.LOG or OAKLEY.LOG file

Estimated lesson time: 20 minutes

IPSec Management and Troubleshooting Tools

Windows 2000 provides tools that you can use to manage, monitor, and troubleshoot IPSec. This section provides an overview of these tools.

Management Tools

- The IP Security Policy Management snap-in creates and edits policies (the Group Policy Editor can also be used).

- The IP Security Management tool is also on the default Start/Programs/ Administrative Tools menu.

Monitoring and Troubleshooting Tools

IP Security Monitor (IPSECMON.EXE), illustrated in Figure 9.25, is started at a command prompt. This tool monitors IP SAs, rekeys, negotiation errors, and other IP Security statistics.

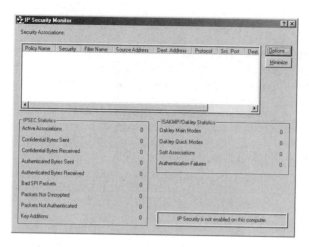

Figure 9.25 IP Security Monitor

IPSec Statistics

The following IPSec statistics can be measured using IP Security Monitor.

- **Active Associations.** Count the number of active SAs.

- **Confidential Bytes Sent/Received.** Total of bytes sent and received using the ESP protocol.

- **Authenticated Bytes Sent/Received.** Total of bytes sent and received using the AH protocol.

- **Bad SPI Packets.** Total number of packets for which the security parameters index (SPI) was wrong. The SPI is used in conjunction with the destination IP address in the standard IP header and IPSec header to identify an IPSec SA. If the SPI is bad, it may mean that the inbound SA has expired but that a packet using the old SPI has just arrived. This number is likely to increase if rekey intervals are short and there are a large number of SAs. Because SAs expire normally, a bad SPI packet does not necessarily indicate that IPSec is failing.

- **Packets Not Decrypted.** Total number of packets that failed decryption. As with bad SPI packets, this failure may indicate that a packet arrived for which the SA had expired. If the SA expires, the session key used to decrypt the packet dies, too. This does not necessarily indicate that IPSec is failing.

- **Packets Not Authenticated.** Similar to Bad SPI Packets and Packets Not Decrypted, this is the total number of packets containing data that could not be verified. The most likely cause is an expired SA.

- **Key Additions.** The total number of keys that IKE has sent to the IPSec driver. This indicates the total number of successful Phase 2 negotiations.

ISAKMP/Oakley (IKE) Statistics

The following IKE statistics can be measured using IP Security Monitor:

- **Oakley Main Modes.** Total number of successful IKE SAs created during Phase 1 negotiations.

- **Oakley Quick Modes.** Total number of successful IPSec SAs created during Phase 2 negotiations. Because these SAs may expire at different rates, this number will not necessarily match the Main Modes number.

- **Soft Associations.** Total number of Phase 2 negotiations that resulted in agreements to send using clear text. This typically reflects the number of associations formed with non-IPSec-aware computers.

- **Authentication Failures.** Total number of identity authentication failures (Kerberos, user certificate, manually configured passwords). This is not the same statistic as Packets Not Authenticated (message authentication through hashing).

Note To reset the statistics in IP Security Monitor, restart the IP Security Policy Agent.

Performance Monitor includes the following IPSec objects and counters that can be examined:

- Policy agent and IPSec driver events in the system log

- Oakley events in the application log

- IKE events (SA details) in the security log (if logon auditing is enabled)

These related events can also be recorded and then later analyzed in Event Viewer.

Using Network Monitor

Network Monitor version 2.0 is a useful troubleshooting tool that is included with IPSec. Both the limited version included with Windows 2000 Server and the full version included with Microsoft Systems Management Server version 2.0 feature parsers for IKE, AH, and ESP. Network Monitor captures all information transferred over a network interface at any given time.

Network Monitor version 2.0 contains parsers for IPSec packets. If IPSec is encrypting the packets, the contents are not visible, but the packet itself is. If only authentication is being used, the entire packet, including its contents, will be visible. ESP is displayed as IP protocol number 50 (decimal) and AH IS displayed as 51 (decimal). ISAKMP/Oakley is displayed as UDP port number 500 (decimal).

Note The ESP data itself is not readable because of the encryption.

Practice: Using Network Monitor to View Clear Text Traffic

Using the Network Monitor To View Clear Text Traffic tool, you capture and view data being sent across the wire between your computer and your second computer. Network Monitor version 2.0 contains parsers for IPSec and IKE packets. Network Monitor gets the packet after IPSec, so if IPSec encrypts the packet, the contents will not be visible.

Note Do the entire practice on both computers. This exercise is done one computer at a time.

Exercise 1: Viewing IPSec Integrity Packets (AH Format)

1. Start Network Monitor and set the capture network to the media access control (MAC) address of the network card that connects to the second system.

   Note You can run Ipconfig with the /all parameter to find the MAC address of your network interface card.

2. In the Local Security Settings MMC interface, assign the Two Computer Policy (from the practice in Lesson 5).

3. Start capturing packets with Network Monitor.

4. Run the Ipsecmon utility.

5. Ping your second computer's IP address.

6. You may have to repeat this step, as ping has a very short time-out, and there is some delay in establishing the IPSec association between the two computers.

7. Stop and view the Network Monitor trace.

8. View Ipsecmon.

9. Double-click the first Internet Control Message Protocol (ICMP) packet.

10. Notice that you see lines indicating headers for frame, Ethernet, IP, and AH.

11. From the details pane, expand the IP entry.

12. Record the IP Protocol number.

   Scroll to the bottom of the IP details and click on IP Data: Number Of Data Bytes Remaining = 64 (0x0040). Notice the IP payload is in clear text. The data in a ping is abcdefghij...

IPSec has created an ICV from the IP, ICMP, and Data fields of the frame. By doing this, IPSec prevents someone from capturing the data, altering it, and resending the bad data. When you look at the Hex pane you can still see the 32 characters sent in the ping. By configuring the AH security method, you ensure authentication but do not encrypt the data in the packet. AH just makes sure that the packet data, as well as most parts of the IP header, such as source and destination IP addresses, are not modified. Next you will look at packets using the ESP security method that will encrypt the data part of the IP packet.

Practice: Using Network Monitor to View Encrypted Traffic

In this practice, you use Network Monitor to set ESP encryption and view encrypted packets.

Exercise 1: Setting ESP encryption

Before you can view the encrypted packets (not the content itself), you need to set the ESP encryption.

1. Unassign the Two Computer Policy.

2. Edit the Two Computer Policy by right-clicking on it, then click Properties.

3. Click the Filter Action tab.

4. Edit the active New Filter Action.

5. Click Edit to modify the Security Method.

6. Change Medium to High (ESP).

7. Close all dialog boxes.

8. Assign the Two Computer Policy.

Exercise 2: Viewing ESP Packets

Once ESP encryption is enabled, you can use Network Monitor to capture and view the ESP packets.

1. Begin capturing packets with Network Monitor.

2. Run the Ipsecmon utility.

3. Ping the second computer's IP Address.

4. You may have to repeat this step as ping has a very short time-out and there is some delay in establishing the IPSec association between the two computers.

5. Stop and view the Netmon trace.

6. View Ipsecmon.

7. Double-click the first ESP frame.

8. This time you will see four entries in the details pane: Frame, Ethernet, IP, and ESP. IPSec has created a hash of the ICMP and Data fields of the frame.

9. Expand the IP section and record the IP Protocol.

10. Scroll to the bottom of the IP details and double-click the IP: Data: Number Of Data Bytes Remaining = 76 (0x004C) line. Look at the Hex pane; you will see the data has been encrypted.

Practice: Using Diagnostic Aids

In this practice, you use the IPSec Monitor diagnostic aid to verify that IPSec is active and to view the active SAs.

Using IPSec Monitor

Windows 2000 Server contains a monitoring tool for IPSec called IPSecmon. Run this tool to see active security associations, "soft" or "hard," on the local or remote machines. It does not show failed SAs or other filters.

Click Start, point to Run, then type **ipsecmon** [*computer name*]. For each soft or hard SA, you see one line in the white box. The column on the left titled Policy Name is the name of the policy that had been assigned and enforced on the computer. The Negotiation Policy column is actually the specific security method that was agreed to during the negotiation. An attempt is made to resolve the IP addresses for source and destination to DNS names.

There are a number of global statistics to note that have accumulated since the computer was last started:

- ISAKMP/Oakley Main Mode and Quick Mode - Successful IPSec SAs will initially cause one ISAKMP/Oakley Main Mode and one Quick Mode. Key renewal operations are generally reflected as additional quick modes.

- The total number of confidential (ESP) or authenticated (ESP and AH) bytes sent or received for all "hard" SAs is shown on the left. Because ESP provides both confidentiality and authenticity, both counters are incremented. Because AH provides only authenticity and not confidentiality, only the authenticated-bytes-sent counter is incremented.

- The total number of soft associations is shown on the right.

Exercise 1: Verifying that IPSec is Active and Viewing the Active SAs

1. Open Network And Dial-Up Connections from Control Panel.

2. Right-click on Local Area Connection, and then click Properties.

3. Select Internet Protocol (TCP/IP), and then click Properties.

4. Click Advanced.

5. Click the Options tab, select IP Security, and then click Properties.

   If the computer is using local policy, the name of the local policy is shown under Use This IP Security Policy. If you are using policy assigned through the Group Policy mechanisms in Active Directory services, the dialog is grayed out and the name of the assigned policy is shown in the same box.

Lesson Summary

Windows 2000 Server has several tools that can be used to manage and troubleshoot IPSec. There is an IPSec Security Policy Management snap-in for MMC that allows you to create and edit policies. IPSec Security Monitor allows you measure a variety of IPSec statistics which can be used to determine the efficiency and security of your network. And Network Monitor can be used to view encrypted packets. These tools allow you to monitor and troubleshoot IPSec communications on your network.

Lesson 8: Monitoring Network Security Events

Administrative policies for a security plan should include policies for delegation of administrative tasks and monitoring of audit logs to detect suspicious activity. In this lesson, you learn how to monitor network security events in Windows 2000 to prevent attacks and intrusion on your network.

After this lesson, you will be able to

- Manage and monitor network traffic

- Manage and monitor remote access

Estimated lesson time: 45 minutes

Monitoring Your Network Security

The network security technologies you implement, such as Microsoft Proxy Server, can meet your security goals only if you plan and configure them carefully. With thorough preparation, this work can be done very successfully. However, anticipating all possible risks can be very difficult because

- New risks develop.

- Systems can break down and the environment in which your systems are placed changes over time.

By continually reviewing your network security strategies, you can minimize security risks. However, you also need to watch the actual network security activity to spot weaknesses before they are exploited, and to stop attempts to break security before they are effective.

To watch your network security activity, you need tools to capture the details about the activities and to analyze the data. For example, Microsoft Proxy Server includes logging at two levels: normal and verbose. Windows 2000 also has event logging, which can be enhanced by enabling security auditing. IAS, discussed later in this chapter, has extensive activity reporting options. Third-party products are also available that can help with monitoring servers and applications, including security servers and applications.

Note When using security servers and applications, be sure to review the documentation for the systems you use and select the logging options that best meet your requirements.

Using Event Viewer to Monitor Security

Event Viewer allows you to monitor events in your system. It maintains logs about program, security, and system events on your computer. You can use Event Viewer to view and manage the event logs, gather information about hardware and software problems, and monitor Windows 2000 security events. The Event Log service starts automatically when you start Windows 2000. All users can view application and system logs. You can also set up the Windows operating system to audit accesses on specific resources and to have them recorded in the Security Log. Table 9.4 lists various events that you can audit and the specific security monitored by particular audit event monitors.

Table 9.4 Threats Detected with Auditing

Audit event	Threat detected
Failure audit for logon/logoff	Random password hack
Success audit for logon/logoff	Stolen password break-in
Success audit for user rights, user and group management, security change policies, restart, shutdown, and system events	Misuse of privileges
Success and failure audit for file-access and object-access events. File Manager success and failure audit of read/write access by suspect users or groups for the sensitive files	Improper access to sensitive files
Success and failure audit for file-access printers and object-access events. Print Manager success and failure audit of print access by suspect users or groups for the printers	Improper access to printers
Success and failure write access auditing for program files (.exe and .dll extensions). Success and failure auditing for process tracking. (Run suspect programs; examine security log for unexpected attempts to modify program files or create unexpected processes. Run only when actively monitoring the system log.)	Virus outbreak

Practice: Recording Failed Logon Attempts

Security auditing is not enabled by default. You have to activate the types of auditing you require by using the Group Policy snap-in to Microsoft Management Console (MMC). You also must enable auditing for the general areas or specific items you want to track. Perform the next two exercises on the same computer.

Exercise 1: Activating Security Auditing for Failed Logon Attempts

1. Click Start, click Run, type **mmc**, and then click OK.

2. On the Console menu, click Add/Remove Snap-In, then click Add.

   The Add/Remove Snap-In dialog box appears.

3. Click Add.

   The Add Standalone Snap-In dialog box appears.

4. Select Group Policy, and then click Add.

   The Select Group Policy dialog box appears.

5. Click Finish to add the local computer.

   You can also click Browse and then select another computer on your network.

6. In the Add Standalone Snap-In dialog box, click Close.

7. In the Add/Remove Snap-In dialog box, click OK.

8. Under Local Computer Policy\Computer Configuration\Windows Settings\Security Settings\Local Policies, click Audit Policy, as illustrated in Figure 9.26.

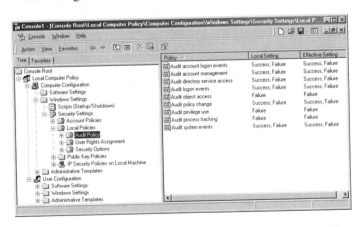

Figure 9.26 Selecting audit policy for the local computer policy

9. In the details pane, right-click the Audit Logon Events attribute, then right-click Security.

The Local Security Policy Setting dialog box appears.

10. Under Audit These Attempts, select Failure, and then click OK.

Viewing the Security Event Log

You can specify that an audit entry be written to the security event log whenever certain actions are performed or files are accessed. The audit entry shows the action performed, the user who performed it, and the date and time of the action. You can audit both successful and failed attempts at actions, so the audit trail can show who performed actions on the network and who tried to perform actions that are not permitted. You can view the security log in the Event Viewer.

Recording security events is a form of intrusion detection through auditing. Auditing and security logging of network activity are important safeguards. Windows 2000 enables you to monitor a wide variety of events that can be used to track the activities of an intruder.

The security log records security events, such as valid and invalid logon attempts, and events related to resource use, such as creating, opening, or deleting files or other objects. The security log helps track changes to the security system and identifies any possible breaches of security. For example, attempts to log on to the system might be recorded in the security log, if logon and logoff auditing are enabled. If the security log is examined regularly, it makes it possible to detect some types of attacks, such as password attacks, before they succeed. After a break-in, the security log can help you determine how the intruder entered and what he or she did. The log file entries can serve as legal evidence after the intruder has been identified.

Note For the highest level of security, monitor the log files constantly.

Practice: Viewing the Security Log

Event logs consist of a header, a description of the event (based on the event type), and, optionally, additional data that you may want recorded about a specific event. Most security log entries consist of the header and a description. Event Viewer displays events from each log separately. Each line shows information about a single event, including date, time, source, event type, category, event ID, user account, and computer name. In this practice, will view the security event log to detect attempted unauthorized network access. To complete this practice, you must have performed the steps in the Exercise of the previous practice, "Recording Failed Logon Attempts."

Exercise 1: Viewing the Security Event Log

1. Attempt to log on to the Windows 2000 computer on which you activated security auditing for failed logon attempts using an invalid user name and password.

2. After failing to log on, use a valid user name and password to log on to Windows 2000.

3. Click Start, point to Programs, point to Administrative Tools, then click Event Viewer.

   Event Viewer opens.

4. Click Security Log in the left pane.

   Notice that the failed logon attempt is shown in the right pane of the Event Viewer, as illustrated in Figure 9.27.

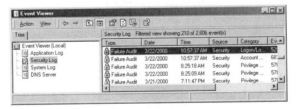

Figure 9.27 Invalid logon entry made in the security event log

5. Double-click the Failure Audit item in the event view to open the Event Properties window.

   Notice that the description section tells you the reason for the failure and the user name entered, but not the password entered.

6. Click OK to close the Event Properties window.

System Monitor

System Monitor is a tool that can be used to track system resources usage. System Monitor can be used to test an application's usage of system resources. Common objects that a user can log are memory, CPU, network, and disk activity. Some additional counters, although not performance related, provide useful information about server security. These include

- Server\Errors Access Permissions
- Server\Errors Granted Access
- Server\Errors Logon
- IIS Security

▶ **Follow these steps to monitor security events using System Monitor:**

1. Click Start, point to Programs, point to Administrative Tools, and then click Performance.

   System Monitor opens in the MMC.

2. In the right pane, click Add.

   The Add Counters dialog box appears, as illustrated in Figure 9.28.

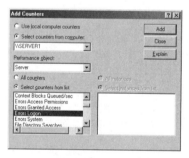

Figure 9.28 Adding the Error Logon counter

3. In the Performance Object drop-down list box, select Server.

4. Click Select Counters From List.

5. In the Counters list, select a counter, and then click Add.

6. Click Close to close the Add Counters dialog box.

Monitoring Security Overhead

Security is achieved only at some cost in performance. Measuring the performance overhead of a security strategy is not simply a matter of monitoring a separate process or thread. The features of the Windows 2000 security model and other security services are integrated into several different operating system services. You cannot monitor security features separately from other aspects of the services. Instead, the most common way to measure security overhead is to run tests comparing server performance with and without a security feature. The tests should be run with fixed workloads and a fixed server configuration so that the security feature is the only variable. During the tests, you should measure

- Processor activity and the processor queue
- Physical memory used
- Network traffic
- Latency and delays

Lesson Summary

You should monitor network security activity to identify weaknesses before they are exploited. You can use Event Viewer to view and manage Windows 2000 security events. The audit entry shows the action performed, the user who performed it, and the date and time of the action. Both System Monitor and Network Monitor can provide useful information about server security. The IPSec Monitor can confirm whether your secured communications are successful. In addition, you can use Routing and Remote Access to monitor remote access traffic in Windows 2000, and enable logging to review this data.

Review

The following questions will help you determine whether you have learned enough to move on to the next chapter. If you have difficulty answering these questions, please go back and review the material in this chapter before beginning the next chapter. See Appendix A, "Questions and Answers," for the answers to these questions.

1. What is the purpose of a subnet mask?

2. What is the minimum number of areas in an OSPF internetwork?

3. What is the NWLink Auto Detect feature?

4. By what standards group is IPSec defined?

5. Define the difference between secret- and public-key cryptography.

6. What functionality does ISAKMP/Oakley provide?

7. What are rules comprised of?

8. What is an IP filter used for?

9. How do System Monitor and Network Monitor allow you to monitor security on your network?

10. How is Event Viewer used to monitor security?

11. How do you enable remote access logging in Windows 2000?

C H A P T E R   1 0

Managing Domain Name System

About This Chapter

This chapter discusses how to use Domain Name System (DNS) on your local area network (LAN) and across the public Internet. Microsoft Windows 2000 includes an enhanced version of DNS. This chapter provides you with an overview of DNS and how to implement the service on Windows 2000. It explains how to implement a delegated zone and how to configure zones for dynamic updates. You will also learn how to configure a DNS server to work as a caching-only server and how to monitor DNS server performance. By the end of this chapter, you will be able to identify the primary components of DNS, install and configure DNS, and troubleshoot the DNS service on Windows 2000.

Before You Begin

To complete this chapter, you must have

- Installed Microsoft Windows 2000 Server with Transmission Control Protocol/Internet Protocol (TCP/IP) and DNS services on a computer

Lesson 1: Name Resolution and DNS Files

There are three types of queries that a client (resolver) can make to a DNS server: recursive, iterative, and inverse. Servers store their DNS information in four possible files: database, reverse lookup, cache, and boot.

After this lesson, you will be able to

- Explain how recursive, iterative, and inverse queries work
- Explain how queries are placed in a cache for future requests

Estimated lesson time: 10 minutes

Recursive Queries

In a recursive query, a client requests the DNS server for one of the following:

- Data of some sort
- An error stating that data of the requested type does not exist
- A response stating that the domain name specified does not exist

In a recursive query, the name server cannot refer the request to a different DNS server (sometimes called a *name server*).

Iterative Queries

In an iterative query, the queried name server gives the best answer it currently has to the requester. This answer may be the resolved name or a referral to another name server that may be able to answer the client's original request.

Figure 10.1 shows recursive and iterative queries. In this example, a client within a corporation is querying its DNS server for the IP address for *www.microsoft.com*.

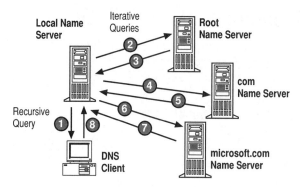

Figure 10.1 Recursive and iterative queries

1. The resolver sends a recursive DNS query to its local DNS server asking for the IP address of *www.microsoft.com*. The local name server is responsible for resolving the name and cannot refer the resolver to another name server.

2. The local name server checks its zones and finds no zones corresponding to the requested domain name. It then sends an iterative query for *www.microsoft.com* to a root name server.

3. The root name server has authority for the root domain and replies with the IP address of a name server for the .com top-level domain.

4. The local name server sends an iterative query for *www.microsoft.com* to the com name server.

5. The com name server replies with the IP address of the name server servicing the *microsoft.com* domain.

6. The local name server sends an iterative query for *www.microsoft.com* to the *microsoft.com* name server.

7. The microsoft.com name server replies with the IP address corresponding to *www.microsoft.com*.

8. The local name server sends the IP address of *www.microsoft.com* back to the original resolver.

Inverse Queries

In an inverse query, the resolver sends a request to a name server to resolve the host name associated with a known IP address. There is no correlation between host names and IP addresses in the DNS name space. Therefore, only a thorough search of all domains guarantees a correct answer.

To prevent an exhaustive search of all domains for an inverse query, a special domain called in-addr.arpa was created. Nodes in the in-addr.arpa domain are named after the numbers in the dotted-decimal representation of IP addresses. Because IP addresses get more specific from left to right and domain names get less specific from left to right, the order of IP address octets must be reversed when building the in-addr.arpa domain. With this arrangement, administration of lower levels of the in-addr.arpa domain can be delegated to organizations as they are assigned their class A, B, or C IP addresses.

Once the in-addr.arpa domain is built, special resource records called pointer (PTR) records are added to associate the IP addresses and the corresponding host name. For example, to find a host name for the IP address 157.55.200.51, the resolver queries the DNS server for a PTR record for 51.200.55.157.in-addr.arpa. The PTR record found contains the host name and corresponding IP address 157.55.200.51. This information is sent back to the resolver. Part of the administration of a DNS name server is ensuring that PTR records are created for hosts.

Caching and Time to Live

When a name server is processing a recursive query, it may be required to send out several queries to find the answer. The name server caches all of the information it receives during this process for a time that is specified in the returned data. This amount of time is referred to as the Time to Live (TTL). The name server administrator of the zone that contains the data decides on the TTL for the data. Smaller TTL values help ensure that data about the domain is more consistent across the network if this data changes often. However, this also increases the load on name servers.

Once data is cached by a DNS server, it must start decreasing the TTL from its original value so that it will know when to flush the data from its cache. If a query comes in that can be satisfied by this cached data, the TTL that is returned with the data is the current amount of time left before the data is flushed from the DNS server cache. Client resolvers also have data caches and honor the TTL value so that they know when to expire the data.

DNS Configuration Files

The DNS is a hierarchical, distributed database. The database itself consists of resource records, which primarily consist of a DNS name, a record type, and data values that are associated with that record type. For example, the most common records in the DNS database are address records, where the name of an address record is the name of a computer, and the data in the record is the TCP/IP address of that computer.

In a Domain Name System (DNS) database, a zone is a subtree of the DNS database that is administered as a single separate entity, a DNS server. This administrative unit can consist of a single domain or a domain with subdomains. A DNS zone administrator sets up one or more name servers for the zone.

To resolve names, servers consult their zones (also called DNS database files, or simply db files). The zones contain resource records (RRs) that make up the resource information associated with the DNS domain. For example, some RRs map friendly names to IP addresses, and others map IP addresses to friendly names.

Start of Authority Record

The first record in any database file must be the start of authority (SOA) record. The SOA defines the general parameters for the DNS zone. The following is an example of an SOA record:

```
@  IN  SOA      nameserver.example.microsoft.com.
postmaster.example.microsoft.com. (
                          1              ; serial number
                          3600           ; refresh    [1h]
                          600            ; retry      [10m]
                          86400          ; expire     [1d]
                          3600 )         ; min TTL    [1h]
```

The following rules apply to all SOA records:

- The at symbol (@) in a database file indicates "this server."

- IN indicates an Internet record.

- Any host name that does not end with a period (.) is appended with the root domain.

- The @ symbol is replaced by a period (.) in the e-mail address of the administrator.

- Parentheses (()) must enclose line breaks that span more than one line.

Name Server Record

The name server (NS) record lists the additional name servers. A database file may contain more than one NS record. The following is an example of an NS record:

```
@ IN NS nameserver2.microsoft.com
```

Host Record

A host address (A) resource record statically associates a host name to its IP address. Host records comprises most of the database file and list all hosts within the zone. The following are examples of host records:

```
rhino IN A 157.55.200.143
localhost    IN A 127.0.0.1
```

CNAME Record

A canonical name (CNAME) record enables you to associate more than one host name with an IP address. This is sometimes referred to as aliasing. The following is an example of a CNAME record:

```
FileServer1  CNAME rhino
www    CNAME rhino
ftp    CNAME rhino
```

The Reverse Lookup File

The reverse lookup file (*z.y.x.w*.in-addr.arpa) allows a resolver to provide an IP address and request a matching host name. A reverse lookup file is named like a zone file according to the in-addr.arpa zone for which it provides reverse lookups. For example, to provide reverse lookups for the IP network 157.57.28.0, a reverse lookup file is created with a file name 57.157.in-addr.arpa. This file contains SOA and NS records similar to other DNS database zone files, as well as PTR records.

This DNS reverse lookup capability is important because some applications provide the capabilities to implement security based on the connecting host names. For instance, if a browser sends a request to an Internet Information Server (IIS) Web server with this security arrangement, the Web server would contact the DNS server and do a reverse name lookup on the client's IP address. If the host name returned by the DNS server is not in the access list for the Web site or if the host name was not found by DNS, the request would be denied.

Note Windows 2000 does not require reverse lookup zones to be configured. However, reverse lookup zones might be necessary for some applications that are installed later or for administrative convenience.

The PTR Record

PTR records provide address-to-name mapping within a reverse lookup zone. IP numbers are written in backward order and "in-addr.arpa" is appended to the end to create this PTR record. As an example, looking up the name for 157.55.200.51 requires a PTR query for the name 51.200.55.157.in-addr.arpa. An example might read

```
51.200.55.157.in-addr.arpa. IN PTR
mailserver1.microsoft.com.
```

The Cache File

The CACHE.DNS file contains the records of the root domain servers. The cache file is essentially the same on all name servers and must be present. When the name server receives a query outside its zone, it starts resolution with these root domain servers. An example entry might read

```
.       3600000         IN    NS    A.ROOT-SERVERS.NET.
A.ROOT-SERVERS.NET. 3600000       A           198.41.0.4
```

The cache file contains host information that is needed to resolve names outside of authoritative domains, and also contains names and addresses of root name servers. The default file provided with the Windows 2000 DNS Server has the current records for all of the root servers on the Internet, and is stored in the %systemroot%\System32\Dns folder. For installations not connected to the Internet, the file should be replaced to contain the name server's authoritative domains for the root of the private network.

The Boot File

The boot file is the startup configuration file on the Berkeley Internet Name Daemon–specific implementation of DNS. This file contains host information needed to resolve names outside of authoritative domains. The file is not defined in a Request for Comments (RFC) and is not needed to be RFC-compliant. It is supported by Windows 2000 to improve compatibility with traditional, UNIX-based DNS services. The Berkeley Internet Name Daemon boot file controls the startup behavior of the DNS server. Commands must start at the beginning of a line and no spaces can precede commands. Table 10.1 provides descriptions of some of the boot file commands supported by Windows 2000.

Table 10.1 Windows 2000 Boot File Commands

Command	Description
Directory command	Specifies a directory where other files referred to in the boot file can be found.
Cache command	Specifies a file used to help the DNS service contact name servers for the root domain. This command and the file it refers to must be present. A cache file suitable for use on the Internet is provided with Windows 2000.
Primary command	Specifies a domain for which this name server is authoritative and a database file that contains the resource records for that domain (that is, the zone file). Multiple primary command records can exist in the boot file.
Secondary command	Specifies a domain for which this name server is authoritative and a list of master server IP addresses from which to attempt to download the zone information, rather than reading it from a file. It also defines the name of the local file for caching this zone. Multiple secondary command records could exist in the boot file.

Table 10.2 shows examples of the commands in a boot file.

Table 10.2 Examples of Boot File Commands

Syntax	Example
directory [*directory*]	directory c:\winnt\system32\dns
cache.[*file_name*]	cache.cache
primary [*domain*] [*file_name*]	primary microsoft.com.microsoft.dns primary dev.microsoft.com dev.dns
secondary [*domain*] [*hostlist*] [*local_file_name*]	secondary test.microsoft.com 157.55.200.100 test.dns

Lesson Summary

When clients need to resolve a host name or IP address, they can make one of three queries to DNS servers: recursive, iterative, or inverse. A DNS server only returns the information it has in cache. It may return information about the potential of an error when a client makes a recursive query. A more typical query is an iterative query. When a client makes an iterative query, the DNS server returns the requested information or provides the client with an alternative DNS server that provides the correct information. An inverse query requests reverse lookup information. If a DNS client needs a host name resolved from a known IP address, an inverse query is sent to the DNS server.

DNS servers store their name and configuration information in four files: database, reverse lookup, cache, and boot files.

Lesson 2: Installing DNS

Microsoft DNS is an RFC-compliant DNS server. As a result, it creates and uses standard DNS zone files and supports all standard resource record types. It is interoperable with other DNS servers and includes the DNS diagnostic utility NSLOOKUP. Microsoft DNS is tightly integrated with Windows Internet Name Service (WINS) and is administered through the graphical administration utility called DNS Manager. In this lesson, you install the DNS service on Windows 2000.

After this lesson, you will be able to

- Install the Microsoft DNS Server service
- Troubleshoot DNS with NSLOOKUP

Estimated lesson time: 45 minutes

Before installing the Microsoft Windows 2000 DNS Server service, it is important that the Windows 2000 server's TCP/IP protocol be configured correctly. The DNS Server service obtains the default settings for the host name and domain name through the Microsoft TCP/IP Properties dialog box. The DNS Server service creates default SOA, host, and NS records based on the specified domain name and host name. If the host name and domain name are not specified, only the SOA record is created.

Practice: Installing the DNS Server Service

In this practice, you install the Microsoft DNS Server service. You will configure DNS in a later lesson.

Note Before you continue with the lesson, run the Ch10A.exe demonstration file located in the Media folder on the *Supplemental Course Materials* CD-ROM that accompanies this book. The file provides an overview of installing the DNS Server service.

Note Complete this procedure from the computer you designate as the DNS server.

Exercise 1: Verifying DNS Client Settings

Before you install DNS, you need to verify that the client computer has the appropriate settings and specify what DNS server to use.

1. Right-click My Network Places, and then click Properties.

   The Network And Dial-Up Connections dialog box appears.

2. Right-click the connection (typically the Local Area Network properties) for which you want to configure the DNS server, and then click Properties.

   The Connection Properties dialog box appears.

3. Click Internet Protocol (TCP/IP), then click Properties.

   The Internet Protocol (TCP/IP) Properties dialog box appears.

4. On the Internet Protocol (TCP/IP) Properties page, type in the IP address of the existing DNS server in the Preferred DNS Server field.

   You can also add the IP address of an alternate DNS server in the Alternate DNS Server field.

5. If you need to specify more than one alternate DNS server, click Advanced, click the DNS tab, and then enter the servers in the DNS Server Addresses box.

6. Click OK to close the TCP/IP Properties dialog box.

7. Click OK to close the Connection Properties dialog box.

Exercise 2: Installing the DNS Server Service

Once the client is properly configured, you can install DNS Server service.

1. In Control Panel, double-click Add/Remove Programs, and then click Add/Remove Windows Components.

   The Windows Components wizard appears.

2. Click Networking Services, and then click Details.

   The Networking Services dialog box appears.

3. If it is not already selected, select the check box next to Domain Name System (DNS), as illustrated in Figure 10.2, and then click OK.

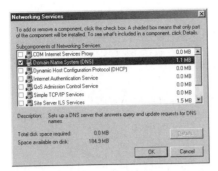

Figure 10.2 Domain Name System (DNS) check box in Networking Services

4. Click Next.

Windows 2000 installs DNS.

5. Click Finish.

Troubleshooting DNS with NSLOOKUP

NSLOOKUP is a useful tool for troubleshooting DNS problems such as host name resolution. When you start NSLOOKUP, it shows the host name and IP address of the DNS server that is configured for the local system, and then displays a command prompt for further queries. If you type a question mark (?), NSLOOKUP shows all available commands. You can exit the program by typing **exit**. To look up a host's IP address using DNS, type the host name and press Enter. NSLOOKUP defaults to using the DNS server configured for the computer on which it is running, but you can focus it on a different DNS server by typing **server <*name*>** (where <name> is the host name of the server you want to use for future lookups). Once another server is specified, anything entered after that point is interpreted as a host name.

NSLOOKUP Modes

NSLOOKUP has two modes: Interactive and Noninteractive. If a single piece of data is needed, use Noninteractive or Command-line mode. If more than one piece of data is needed, Interactive mode can be used.

NSLOOKUP Syntax

NSLOOKUP.EXE is a command-line administrative tool for testing and troubleshooting DNS servers. The following syntax is used to run the NSLOOKUP utility:

nslookup [–option ...] [computer-to-find | – [server]]

Syntax	Description
–option ...	Specifies one or more NSLOOKUP commands. For a list of commands, use the help option inside NSLOOKUP.
computer-to-find	If *computer-to-find* is an IP address and the query type is host or PTR, the name of the computer is returned. If *computer-to-find* is a name and does not have a trailing period, the default DNS domain name is appended to the name. To look up a computer outside the current DNS domain, append a period to the name. If a hyphen (–) is typed instead of *computer-to-find*, the command prompt changes to NSLOOKUP Interactive mode.
server	Use this server as the DNS name server. If the server is omitted, the currently configured default DNS server is used.

▶ **Follow these steps to use NSLOOKUP in Command-line mode:**

1. At a command prompt, modify the properties so that the command prompt window has a screen buffer size of 50.

    As illustrated in Figure 10.3, use the Layout property page to do this. When prompted, you should apply this change to all future instances of the command-prompt window; this will be needed in later lessons.

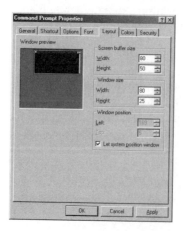

Figure 10.3 Command Prompt Properties dialog box

2. Type the following command:

```
nslookup hostx
```

where hostx is a host in your domain.

3. NSLOOKUP returns the IP address of the computer hostx because the information is stored in the DNS database.

4. Exit the command prompt.

▶ **Follow these steps to use NSLOOKUP in Interactive mode:**

1. At a command prompt, type **nslookup** and then press Enter.

The > prompt appears.

2. Type **set all** at the > prompt.

This command lists all of the current values of the NSLOOKUP options.

3. Use the following set commands to change the timeout value to 1 second and the number of retries to 7, as illustrated in Figure 10.4.

```
Set ti=1
Set ret=7
```

Figure 10.4 Setting the timeout and retry values in NSLOOKUP

4. Use Set All to verify that the defaults were changed.

5. Type the names of the other computers, one at a time, at the > prompt. Press Enter after each name.

6. Exit the command prompt.

Lesson Summary

Microsoft DNS is interoperable with other DNS servers. Before installing the DNS Server service, you should make sure that the Windows 2000 server's TCP/IP protocol is configured correctly.

The NSLOOKUP utility is the primary diagnostic tool for DNS. It allows you to display resource records on DNS servers.

Lesson 3: Configuring DNS

There are two ways to manage the Microsoft DNS server. Use the DNS Manager or manually edit the DNS configuration files. This lesson reviews the tools used to administer a DNS server.

After this lesson, you will be able to

- Administer a DNS server
- Create a zone file and populate it with resource records

Estimated lesson time: 60 minutes

Configuring DNS Server Properties

The primary tool that you use to manage a Windows 2000 DNS server is the DNS console, which is illustrated in Figure 10.5. Because the DNS server has no initial information about a user's network, the DNS server installs as a caching-only name server for the Internet. This means that the DNS server contains only information on the Internet root servers. For most DNS server configurations, additional information must be supplied to obtain the preferred operation.

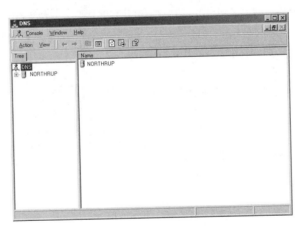

Figure 10.5 DNS settings in Microsoft Management Console (MMC)

▶   **Follow these steps to configure a new DNS server:**

1. Click Start, point to Programs, point to Administrative Tools, and then click DNS.

2. Highlight your server. On the Action menu, click Configure The Server.

3. Follow the instructions in the Configure DNS Server Wizard.

   In the Configure DNS Server Wizard, you can create one or more forward lookup zones. The following are types of zones you can create:

   - **Active Directory–integrated.** Active Directory–integrated DNS enables Active Directory storage and replication of DNS zone databases. Zone data is stored as an Active Directory object and is replicated as part of domain replication.

   - **Standard primary.** Standard primary zones are required to create and manage zones in your DNS name space if you are not using Active Directory services.

   - **Standard secondary.** Standard secondary zones help balance the processing load of primary servers and provide fault tolerance.

4. The next step in the New Zone Wizard is to create a forward or reverse lookup zone. If you select Forward lookup zone, you must provide a name for the new zone and then specify a zone file. If you select Reverse lookup zone, you must provide the network ID or zone name, and then specify a zone file.

5. Click Finish to close the wizard.

Manually Configuring DNS

The DNS server may be configured manually by editing files in the default installation path \\%systemroot%\\System32\\Dns. Administration is identical to traditional DNS administration. The files can be modified using a text editor, as illustrated in Figure 10.6. The DNS service must then be stopped and restarted.

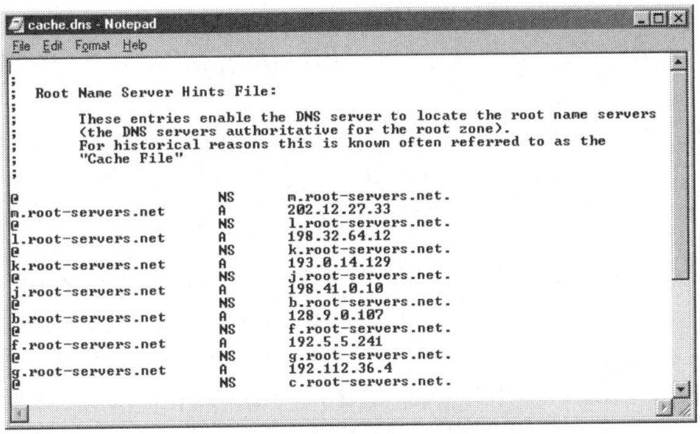

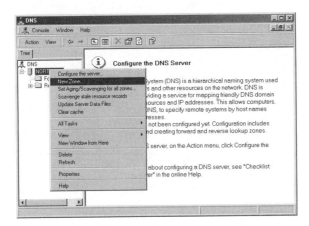

Figure 10.6   Editing the Cache.dns file

Adding DNS Domains and Zones

The first step in configuring the DNS server is to determine the hierarchy for your DNS domains and zones. Once the domain and zone information has been determined, this information must be entered into the DNS configuration using the DNS console.

Adding Primary or Secondary Zones

You add primary and secondary zones through the DNS console, as illustrated in Figure 10.7. After you enter your zone information, DNS Manager constructs a default zone file name. If the zone file already exists in the DNS directory, DNS console automatically imports these records.

Figure 10.7   Creating a new zone with the DNS console

A primary zone stores name-to-address mappings locally. When you configure a primary zone, you need no information other than the zone name.

Secondary zones obtain name-to-address mappings from a master server by zone transfer. When you configure a secondary zone, you must supply the names for the zone and master name server.

Once all zones have been added to the server, subdomains under the zones can be added. If multiple levels of subdomains are needed, create each successive subdomain. There is a key written to the DNS registry entry for each zone for which the DNS will be authoritative. The keys are located under HKEY_LOCAL_MACHINE\SYSTEM\CurrentControlSet\Services\DNS\Zones.

Each zone has its own key that contains the name of the database file, which indicates whether the DNS server is a primary or secondary name server. For example, for the zone dev.volcano.com, there is the following registry entry: HKEY_LOCAL_MACHINE\SYSTEM\CurrentControlSet\Services\DNS\Zones\dev.volcano.com.

Configuring Zone Properties

After you have successfully added a zone, you can configure and modify the zone properties, which are described in Table 10.3.

Table 10.3   Zone Properties

Property	Description
General	Configures the zone file in which the resource records are stored and specifies whether this is a primary or secondary name server.
SOA record	Configures zone transfer information and the name server administrator mailbox.
Notify	Specifies the secondary servers to be alerted when the primary server database changes. Also, additional security can be applied to the name server by specifying that only the listed secondary servers can contact this server.
WINS lookup	Enables the name server to query WINS to resolve names. A list of WINS servers can be configured in this dialog. The WINS servers can be set on a per-name-server basis by selecting the Settings Only Affect Local Server check box. If this is not selected, secondary servers will also use the configured WINS servers.

Practice: Configuring a DNS Server

In this practice, you configure the DNS server by adding a primary zone. Complete this practice from the DNS server computer.

Note Before you continue with the lesson, run the Ch10b.exe demonstration file located in the Media folder on the *Supplemental Course Materials* CD-ROM that accompanies this book. The file provides an overview of configuring the DNS Server service.

Exercise 1: Adding a Zone to a Server

1. Right-click your computer name, and then click New Zone. The New Zone wizard appears.

2. Click Next, select Standard Primary, and then click Next.

3. Select Forward Lookup Zone, and then click Next.

4. In the Name box, type **zone1.org** (where zone1.org is your zone name).

5. Click Create A New File With This File Name, and then click Next.

   Zone1.org.dns will be the file name (where zone1.org is your zone name).

6. Click Finish to create the new zone.

   The Forward Lookup Zones folder now contains your new zone, as illustrated in Figure 10.8.

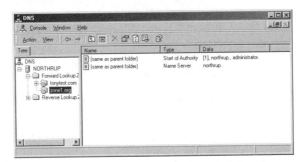

Figure 10.8 Zone added to the Forward Lookup Zones folder

Adding Resource Records

Once the zones and subdomains are configured, resource records can be added. To create a new host, right-click a zone or subdomain and then click New Host, as illustrated in Figure 10.9. Simply type the host name and click Add Host, and the host record is created.

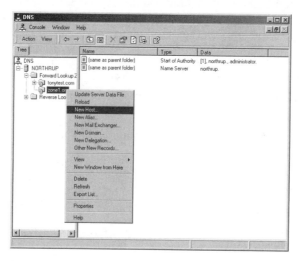

Figure 10.9 Adding a new host

To create a record of a different type, right-click a zone or subdomain and then click Other New Records. Next, select which resource record type to create. A dialog box displays various fields specific to record type, as illustrated in Figure 10.10.

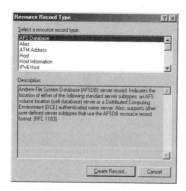

Figure 10.10 Selecting a type of record to create

Configuring Reverse Lookup

If you just have the host's IP address, and you want to be able to find the host's name, you need to use a reverse lookup zone. Like all zones, you must create the reverse lookup zone before it can be used.

You create a reverse lookup zone for each subnet on which the hosts in the DNS database reside. Adding a reverse lookup zone is procedurally identical to adding any other type of zone, except for the zone name which is reversed. For example, if a host has an address of 198.231.25.89, it would be represented in the in-addr.arpa domain as 89.25.231.198.in-addr.arpa. To enable this host to appear to a client who has the host's IP address, a zone would need to be added to the DNS for 25.231.198.in-addr.arpa. All PTR records for the network 198.231.25.0 would be added to this reverse lookup zone.

Lesson Summary

The first step in configuring Windows 2000 DNS server is to determine the hierarchy for your DNS domains and zones. Using MMC, you can create Active Directory–integrated zones, standard primary zones, and standard secondary zones. Once the zones and subdomains are configured, resource records can be added.

If you want the ability to find a host name using only the host IP address, you need to create a reverse lookup zone for each subnet on which hosts in the DNS database reside.

Lesson 4: Working with Zones

Servers refer to their zones (also called DNS database files or db files) to resolve names. The zones contain resource records that comprise the resource information associated with the DNS domain. For example, some resource records map friendly names to Internet Protocol (IP) addresses, and others map IP addresses to friendly names. Some resource records not only include information about servers in the DNS domain, they serve to define the domain by specifying which servers are authoritative for which zones. In this lesson, you learn how to configure DNS zones in Windows 2000.

After this lesson, you will be able to

- Implement a delegated zone for DNS

- Configure zones for dynamic updates

Estimated lesson time: 20 minutes

Delegating Zones

A DNS database can be partitioned into multiple zones. A zone is a portion of the DNS database that contains the resource records with the owner names that belong to the contiguous portion of the DNS name space. Zone files are maintained on DNS servers. A single DNS server can be configured to host zero, one, or multiple zones. Each zone is anchored at a specific domain name referred to as the zone's root domain. A zone contains information about all names that end with the zone's root domain name. A DNS server is considered authoritative for a name if it loads the zone containing that name. The first record in any zone file is a start of authority (SOA) resource record. The SOA resource record identifies a primary DNS name server for the zone as the best source of information for the data within that zone and as an entity processing the updates for the zone.

Names within a zone can also be delegated to other zones. Delegation is a process of assigning responsibility for a portion of a DNS name space to a separate entity. This separate entity could be another organization, department, or workgroup within your company. In technical terms, delegating means assigning authority over portions of your DNS name space to other zones. The name server record that specifies the delegated zone and the DNS name of the server authoritative for that zone represents such delegation. Delegating across multiple zones was part of the original design goal of DNS. The following are the main reasons for the delegation of a DNS name space:

- To delegate management of a DNS domain to a number of organizations or departments within an organization

- To distribute the load of maintaining one large DNS database among multiple name servers to improve the name resolution performance as well as create a DNS fault-tolerant environment

- To allow for hosts' organizational affiliations by including them in appropriate domains

The name server's resource records facilitate delegation by identifying DNS servers for each zone. They appear in all forward and reverse lookup zones. Whenever a DNS server needs to cross a delegation, it refers to the name server's resource records for DNS servers in the target zone. In Figure 10.11, the management of the microsoft.com domain is delegated across two zones: microsoft.com and mydomain.microsoft.com.

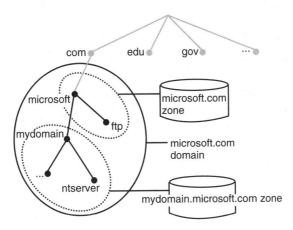

Figure 10.11 The microsoft.com domain delegated across two zones

Understanding DNS Zones and Domains

Domain name servers store information about part of the domain name space called a zone. The name server is authoritative for a particular zone. A single name server can be authoritative for many zones. Understanding the difference between a zone and a domain is sometimes confusing.

A zone is simply a portion of a domain. For example, the domain microsoft.com may contain all of the data for microsoft.com, marketing.microsoft.com, and development.microsoft.com. However, the zone microsoft.com contains only information for microsoft.com and references to the authoritative name servers for the subdomains. The zone microsoft.com can contain the data for subdomains of microsoft.com if they have not been delegated to another server. For example, marketing.microsoft.com may manage its own delegated zone. The parent, microsoft.com, may manage development.microsoft.com. If there are no subdomains, then the zone and domain are essentially the same. In this case the zone contains all data for the domain.

Note All domains (or subdomains) that appear as part of the applicable zone delegation must be created in the current zone prior to performing a zone delegation as described next. As necessary, use the DNS console to first add domains to the zone before completing the procedure that follows.

▶   **Follow these steps to create a zone delegation:**

1. Click Start, point to Programs, point to Administrative Tools, then click DNS.

2. In the console tree, right-click your subdomain and then click New Delegation, as illustrated in Figure 10.12.

   The New Delegation wizard appears.

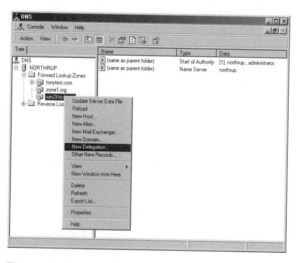

Figure 10.12 Adding a new delegation server

3. Click Next.

4. In the Delegated Domain Name dialog box, type a delegated domain name, then click Next.

5. In the Name Servers dialog box, click Add to specify names and IP addresses of DNS servers you want to have host the delegated zone.

   The New Resource Record dialog box appears, allowing you to specify DNS servers.

6. Type the DNS server name, click Add, and then click OK.

7. In the Name Servers dialog box, click Next.

8. Click Finish to close the New Delegation wizard.

Configuring Zones for Dynamic Update

DNS was originally designed to support only static changes to a zone database. Because of the design limitations of static DNS, adding, removing, or modifying resource records could only be done manually by a DNS system administrator. For example, a DNS system administrator would edit records on a zone's primary server and the revised zone database would then be propagated to secondary servers during zone transfer. This design is workable when the number of changes is small and updates occur infrequently, but is otherwise quite inefficient.

Windows 2000 provides client and server support for the use of dynamic updates. Dynamic updates enable DNS client computers to register and dynamically update their resource records with a DNS server whenever changes occur. This reduces the need for manual administration of zone records, especially for clients that frequently move or change locations and use DHCP to obtain an IP address.

By default, computers that run Windows 2000 and are statically configured for TCP/IP attempt to dynamically register host and pointer resource records for IP addresses that are configured and used by their installed network connections. Dynamic updates can be sent for any of the following reasons or events:

- An IP address is added, removed, or modified in the TCP/IP properties configuration for any one of the installed network connections.

- An IP address lease changes or renews with the DHCP server any one of the installed network connections; for example, when the computer is started or if the ipconfig /renew command is used.

- The ipconfig /registerdns command is used to manually force a refresh of the client name registration in DNS.

- The computer is turned on.

Dynamic Update Requirements

For DNS servers, the DNS service allows dynamic update to be enabled or disabled on a per-zone basis at each server configured to load either a standard primary or directory-integrated zone. By default, client computers running any version of Windows 2000 dynamically update their host resource records in DNS when configured for TCP/IP. When DNS zones are stored in Active Directory database, DNS is configured by default to accept dynamic updates.

Note Windows 2000 DNS servers support dynamic updates. The DNS server provided with Windows NT Server 4.0 does not.

For a request for a dynamic update to be performed, several prerequisite conditions can be configured. Each prerequisite must be satisfied for an update to occur. After all prerequisites are met, the zone's primary server can proceed with an update of its local zones. Some examples of prerequisites that can be set are:

- A required resource record or resource record set already exists or is in use prior to an update.

- A required resource record or resource record set does not exist or is not in use prior to an update.

- A requester is permitted to initiate an update of a specified resource record or resource record set.

For client computers to be registered and updated dynamically with a DNS server, you must do one of the following:

- Install or upgrade client computers to Windows 2000.

- Install and use a Windows 2000 DHCP server on your network to lease client computers.

Practice: Enabling Dynamic Updates

In this practice, you make it possible for DNS client computers to register and dynamically update their resource records with a DNS server whenever changes occur by enabling dynamic updates for a DNS zone.

Exercise 1: Allowing Dynamic Updates

1. Click Start, point to Programs, point to Administrative Tools, and then click DNS.

   The DNS administrative console appears.

2. In the console tree, right-click your zone, and then click Properties.
    The Zone Properties dialog box appears, as illustrated in Figure 10.13.

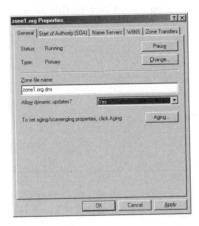

Figure 10.13 Zone Properties dialog box

3. In the Allow Dynamic Updates list box, click Yes.
4. Click OK to close the Zone Properties dialog box.
5. Close the DNS administrative console.

Lesson Summary

Delegation is a process of assigning responsibility for a portion of a DNS name space to a separate entity. The names server's resource records facilitate delegation by identifying DNS servers for each zone. They appear in all forward and reverse lookup zones. Windows 2000 provides client and server support for the use of dynamic updates. Dynamic updates enable DNS client computers to register and dynamically update their resource records with a DNS server whenever changes occur.

Lesson 5: Working with Servers

Because DNS servers are of critical importance in most environments, it is important to continually monitor them. In this lesson, you learn how to manage and monitor your DNS servers. In addition, you learn how to implement a caching-only server.

After this lesson, you will be able to

- Configure a caching-only server

- Manage and monitor DNS servers

Estimated lesson time: 15 minutes

Overview of DNS Servers and Caching

As DNS servers process client queries using recursion or iteration, they discover and acquire a significant store of information about the DNS name space. The server then caches this information. Caching provides a way to speed the performance of DNS resolution for subsequent queries of popular names while substantially reducing DNS-related query traffic on the network.

As DNS servers make recursive queries on behalf of clients, they temporarily cache resource records. Cached resource records contain information obtained from DNS servers during interative queries. Later, when other clients place new queries that request resource record information matching cached resource records, the DNS server can use the cached resource record information to answer them.

When information is cached, a Time to Live (TTL) value applies to all cached resource records. As long as the TTL for a cached resource record does not expire, a DNS server can continue to cache and use the resource record again when answering queries by its clients that match these resource records. Caching TTL values used by resource records in most zone configurations are assigned the minimum (default) TTL, which is set in the zone's SOA resource record. By default, the minimum TTL is 3600 seconds (1 hour), but can be adjusted. Or, if necessary, individual caching TTLs can be set at each resource record.

Implementing a Caching-Only Server

Although all DNS name servers cache queries that they have resolved, caching-only servers are DNS name servers that only perform queries, cache the answers, and return the results. They are not authoritative for any domains and the information that they contain is limited to what has been cached while resolving queries. The benefit of caching-only servers is that they do not generate zone transfer network traffic because they do not contain any zones. However, there is one disadvantage: When the server is initially started, it has no cached information and must build up this information over time as it services requests.

▶ **Follow these steps to install a caching-only DNS server:**

1. Install the DNS Server service on the computer.

    It is strongly recommended that, when operating the computer as a DNS server, you manually configure TCP/IP and use a static IP address.

2. Do not configure the DNS server to load any zones.

    A caching-only DNS server can be valuable at a site where DNS functionality is needed locally but it is not administratively desirable to create a separate domain or zone for that location. Caching-only DNS servers do not host any zones and are not authoritative for a particular domain. They are DNS servers that build a local server cache of names learned while performing recursive queries on behalf of their clients. This information is then available from its cache when answering subsequent client queries.

3. Verify that server root hints are configured or updated correctly.

When a DNS server starts, it needs a list of root server "hints." These hints are name server (NS) and address (A) records for the root servers, which are stored in what has historically been called the cache file.

You can configure root hints by clicking the Root Hints tab in the Properties dialog box for the DNS server in the DNS administrative console. The Root Hints tab is illustrated in Figure 10.14.

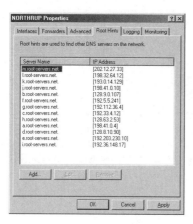

Figure 10.14 Root Hints tab on the DNS server's Properties dialog box

Monitoring DNS Server Performance

Because DNS servers are of critical importance in most environments, monitoring their performance can be useful for predicting, estimating, and optimizing DNS server performance. In addition, you can quickly identify degraded server performance either over time or during periods of peak activity. Windows 2000 Server provides a set of DNS server performance counters that can be used with System Monitor to measure and monitor various aspects of server activity.

Practice: Testing a Simple Query on a DNS Server

In this practice, you use the DNS administrative console to test a query on your DNS server.

Exercise 1: Testing a Query on your DNS Server

1. Click Start, point to Programs, point to Administrative Tools, and then click DNS.

2. In the console tree, right-click the DNS server, and then click Properties.

3. Click the Monitoring tab, illustrated in Figure 10.15.

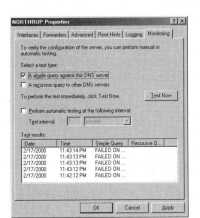

Figure 10.15 The Monitoring tab in the DNS server's Properties dialog box

4. Select the A Simple Query Against This DNS Server check box.

5. Click Test Now.

   The results of the query test appear in Test Results.

6. Click OK to close the DNS server's Properties dialog box.

DNS Server Performance Counters

Windows 2000 Server provides a set of DNS server performance counters that can be used to measure and monitor various aspects of server activity, such as the following:

- Overall DNS server performance statistics, such as the number of overall queries and responses processed by a DNS server

- User Datagram Protocol (UDP) or Transmission Control Protocol (TCP) counters, which measure DNS queries and responses that are processed using either of these transport protocols, respectively

- Dynamic update and secure dynamic update counters, which measure registration and update activity generated by dynamic clients

- Memory usage counters, which measure system memory usage and memory allocation patterns created by operating the server computer as a Windows 2000 DNS server

- Recursive lookup counters, which measure queries and responses when the DNS Server service uses recursion to look up and fully resolve DNS names on behalf of requesting clients

- Windows Internet Name Service (WINS) lookup counters, which measure queries and responses made to WINS servers when the WINS lookup integration features of the DNS Server service are used

- Zone transfer counters, including specific counters for measuring all-zone transfer (AXFR), incremental zone transfer (IXFR), and DNS zone update notification activity

Managing DNS Servers Remotely

DNS is an Internet and TCP/IP standard name service that enables a server running the DNS service to enable client computers on your network to register and resolve DNS domain names. These names can be used to find and access resources offered by other computers on the Internet. With Windows 2000 Administration Tools, which is included on the Windows 2000 Server and Windows 2000 Advanced Server compact disc sets, you can manage a server remotely from any computer that is running Windows 2000.

Windows 2000 Administration Tools contains Microsoft Management Console (MMC) snap-ins and other administrative tools that are used to manage computers running Windows 2000 Server and that are not provided with Windows 2000 Professional. Once Windows 2000 Administration Tools is installed on a computer, an administrator can open the server administrative tools and begin managing a remote server from that computer.

Lesson Summary

All DNS name servers cache queries that they have resolved, but caching-only servers are special DNS name servers that only perform queries, cache the answers, and return the results. The benefit provided by caching-only servers is that they do not generate zone transfer network traffic because they do not contain any zones. Windows 2000 Server provides a set of DNS server performance counters that can be used with System Monitor to measure and monitor various aspects of server activity. You can perform tests on the DNS server from the Monitoring tab in the DNS server's Properties dialog box in the DNS administrative console too. You can also use the Windows 2000 Administration Tools to manage a server remotely from any computer that is running Windows 2000.

Review

The following questions will help you determine whether you have learned enough to move on to the next chapter. If you have difficulty answering these questions, please go back and review the material in this chapter before beginning the next chapter. See Appendix A, "Questions and Answers," for the answers to these questions.

1. Describe the differences between primary, secondary, and master name servers.

2. Describe the difference between a domain and a zone.

3. Describe the difference between recursive and iterative queries.

4. List the files required for a Windows 2000 DNS implementation.

5. Describe the purpose of the boot file.

6. How many zones can a single DNS server host?

7. What benefits do DNS clients obtain from the dynamic update feature of Windows 2000?

8. Name one benefit and one disadvantage of a caching-only server.

9. List and describe three DNS performance counters.

C H A P T E R   1 1

Managing DHCP

About This Chapter

In this chapter, you learn how to use the Dynamic Host Configuration Protocol (DHCP) to automatically configure Transmission Control Protocol/Internet Protocol (TCP/IP) and eliminate some common configuration problems. During the lessons, you install and configure a DHCP server, test the DHCP configuration, and then obtain an Internet Protocol (IP) address from a DHCP server.

Before You Begin

To complete the lessons in this chapter, you must have

- Installed Microsoft Windows 2000 Server with TCP/IP on Server01

Lesson 1: Introducing and Installing DHCP

DHCP automatically assigns IP addresses to computers. DHCP overcomes the limitations of configuring TCP/IP manually. This lesson gives you an overview of DHCP and how it works.

After this lesson, you will be able to

- Describe the difference between manual and automatic configuration of TCP/IP
- Identify TCP/IP configuration parameters that can be assigned by a DHCP server
- Describe IP Lease Requests and Offers
- Install DHCP in Windows 2000

Estimated lesson time: 20 minutes

DHCP Overview

DHCP is an extension of the Boot Protocol (BOOTP). BOOTP enables clients without disks to start up and automatically configure TCP/IP. DHCP centralizes and manages the allocation of TCP/IP configuration information by automatically assigning IP addresses to computers configured to use DHCP. Implementing DHCP eliminates some of the configuration problems associated with manually configuring TCP/IP.

As illustrated in Figure 11.1, each time a DHCP client starts, it requests IP addressing information from a DHCP server, including the IP address, the subnet mask, and optional values. The optional values may include a default gateway address, Domain Name System (DNS) address, and Windows Internet Name Service (WINS) server address.

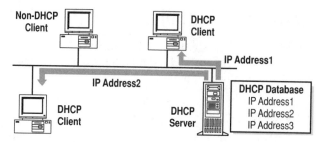

Figure 11.1 How a DHCP client interacts with a DHCP server

When a DHCP server receives a request, it selects IP addressing information from a pool of addresses defined in its database and offers it to the DHCP client. If the client accepts the offer, the IP addressing information is leased to the client for a specified period of time. If there is no available IP addressing information in the pool to lease to a client, the client cannot initialize TCP/IP.

Manual vs. Automatic Configuration

To understand why DHCP is beneficial in configuring TCP/IP on client computers, it is useful to contrast the manual method of configuring TCP/IP with the automatic method using DHCP.

Configuring TCP/IP Manually

Configuring TCP/IP manually means that users can easily pick a random IP address instead of getting a valid IP address from the network administrator. However, using incorrect addresses can lead to network problems that can be very difficult to trace to the source.

In addition, typing the IP address, subnet mask, or default gateway can lead to problems ranging from trouble communicating if the default gateway or subnet mask is wrong to problems associated with a duplicate IP address.

Another limitation of configuring TCP/IP manually is the administrative overhead on internetworks where computers are frequently moved from one subnet to another. For example, when a workstation is moved to a different subnet, the IP address and default gateway address must be changed for the workstation to communicate from its new location.

Configuring TCP/IP Using DHCP

Using DHCP to automatically configure IP addressing information means that users no longer need to acquire IP addressing information from an administrator to configure TCP/IP. The DHCP server supplies all of the necessary configuration information to all of the DHCP clients. Using DHCP eliminates many difficult-to-trace network problems.

TCP/IP configuration parameters that can be assigned by the DHCP server include

- IP addresses for each network adapter in a client computer

- Subnet masks that are used to identify the IP network portion from the host portion of the IP address

- Default gateways (routers) that are used to connect a single network segment to others

- Additional configuration parameters that can optionally be assigned to DHCP clients (such as IP addresses for DNS or WINS servers a client may use)

How DHCP Works

DHCP uses a four-phase process to configure a DHCP client, as shown in Table 11.1. If a computer has multiple network adapters, the DHCP process occurs separately over each adapter. A unique IP address is assigned to each adapter in the computer. All DHCP communication is done over User Datagram Protocol (UDP) ports 67 and 68.

Most DHCP messages are sent by broadcast. For DHCP clients to communicate with a DHCP server on a remote network, the IP routers must support forwarding DHCP broadcasts. DHCP configuration phases are shown in Table 11.1.

Table 11.1 Four Phases of DHCP Client Configuration

Phase	Description
IP lease discover	The client initializes a limited version of TCP/IP and broadcasts a request for the location of a DHCP server and IP addressing information.
IP lease offer	All DHCP servers that have valid IP addressing information available send an offer to the client.

continues

Table 11.1 Four Phases of DHCP Client Configuration *(continued)*

Phase	Description
IP lease request	The client selects the IP addressing information from the first offer it receives and broadcasts a message requesting to lease the IP addressing information in the offer.
IP lease acknowledgment	The DHCP server that made the offer responds to the message, and all other DHCP servers withdraw their offers. The IP addressing information is assigned to the client and an acknowledgment is sent. The client finishes initializing and binding the TCP/IP protocol. Once the automatic configuration process is complete, the client can use all TCP/IP services and utilities for normal network communications and connectivity to other IP hosts.

IP Lease Discover and Offer

As illustrated in Figure 11.2, in the first two phases of DHCP client configuration, the client broadcasts for a DHCP server and a DHCP server offers an IP address to the client.

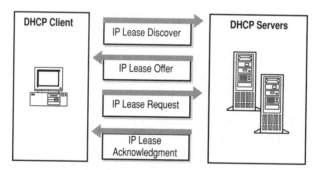

Figure 11.2 IP lease discover and offer

IP Lease Discover

During its boot process, a client requests to lease an IP address by broadcasting a request to all DHCP servers. Because the client does not have an IP address or know the IP address of a DHCP server, it uses 0.0.0.0 as the source address and 255.255.255.255 as the destination address.

The request for a lease is sent in a DHCPDISCOVER message. This message also contains the client's hardware address and computer name so that DHCP servers know which client sent the request.

The IP lease process is used when one of the following events occurs:

- TCP/IP is initialized for the first time as a DHCP client.

- The client requests a specific IP address and is denied, possibly because the DHCP server dropped the lease.

- The client previously leased an IP address but has released the lease and now requires a new lease.

IP Lease Offer

All DHCP servers that receive the request and have a valid configuration for the client broadcast an offer with the following information:

- The client's hardware address

- An offered IP address

- Subnet mask

- Length of the lease

- A server identifier (the IP address of the offering DHCP server)

A broadcast is used because the client does not yet have an IP address. As illustrated in Figure 11.3, the offer is sent as a DHCPOFFER message. The DHCP server reserves the IP address so that it will not be offered to another DHCP client. The DHCP client selects the IP address from the first offer it receives.

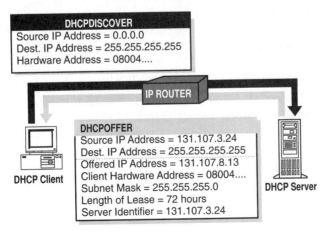

Figure 11.3 Sending a DHCPOFFER message

When No DHCP Servers Are Online

The DHCP client waits 1 second for an offer. If an offer is not received, the client is not able to initialize and it rebroadcasts the request three times (at 9-, 13-, and 16-second intervals, plus a random length of time between 0 and 1000 milliseconds). If an offer is not received after four requests, the client retries every 5 minutes.

Windows 2000–based clients can automatically configure an IP address and subnet mask if a DHCP server is unavailable at system start time. This is a new feature of Windows 2000 called Automatic Private IP Addressing (APIPA). This is useful for clients on small private networks, such as small business offices, home offices, or remote access clients. The Windows 2000 DHCP client service uses the following process to autoconfigure the client:

1. The DHCP client attempts to locate a DHCP server and obtain an address and configuration.

2. If a DHCP server cannot be found or does not respond, the DHCP client autoconfigures its IP address and subnet mask using a selected address from the Microsoft-reserved Class B network, 169.254.0.0, with the subnet mask 255.255.0.0.

   The DHCP client tests for an address conflict to make sure that the IP address it has chosen is not already in use on the network. If a conflict is found, the client selects another IP address. The client retries autoconfiguration for up to 10 addresses.

3. Once the DHCP client succeeds in self-selecting an address, it configures its network interface with the IP address. The client then continues, in the background, to check for a DHCP server every 5 minutes. If a DHCP server is found later, the client abandons its autoconfigured information. The DHCP client then uses an address offered by the DHCP server (and any other provided DHCP option information) to update its IP configuration settings.

IP Lease Request and Acknowledgment

In the last two phases of DHCP client configuration, the client selects an offer and the DHCP server acknowledges the lease.

IP Lease Request

After the client receives an offer from at least one DHCP server, it broadcasts to all DHCP servers that it has made a selection by accepting an offer.

The broadcast is sent in a DHCPREQUEST message and includes the server identifier (IP address) of the server whose offer was accepted. All other DHCP servers then retract their offers so that their IP addresses are available for the next IP lease request.

IP Lease Acknowledgment (Successful)

The DHCP server with the accepted offer broadcasts a successful acknowledgment to the client in the form of a DHCPACK message. This message contains a valid lease for an IP address and possibly other configuration information. When the DHCP client receives the acknowledgment, TCP/IP is completely initialized and is considered a bound DHCP client. Once bound, the client can use TCP/IP to communicate on the internetwork.

IP Lease Acknowledgment (Unsuccessful)

An unsuccessful acknowledgment in the form of a DHCPNACK message is broadcast if the client is trying to lease its previous IP address and the IP address is no longer available. It is also broadcast if the IP address is invalid because the client has been physically moved to a different subnet. When the client receives an unsuccessful acknowledgment, it returns to the process of requesting an IP lease.

Installing a DHCP Server

Before you install a DHCP server, you should identify the following:

- The hardware and storage requirements for the DHCP server

- Which computers you can immediately configure as DHCP clients for dynamic TCP/IP configuration and which computers you should manually configure with static TCP/IP configuration parameters, including static IP addresses

- The DHCP option types and their values to be predefined for DHCP clients

Before you install DHCP, answer the following questions:

- **Will all of the computers become DHCP clients?** If not, consider that non-DHCP clients have static IP addresses, and static IP addresses must be excluded from the DHCP server configuration. If a client requires a specific address, the IP address needs to be reserved.

- **Will a DHCP server supply IP addresses to multiple subnets?** If so, consider that any routers connecting subnets act as DHCP relay agents. If your routers are not acting as DHCP relay agents, at least one DHCP server is required on each subnet that has DHCP clients. The DHCP server could be a DHCP relay agent or a router that has BOOTP enabled.

- **How many DHCP servers are required?** Consider that a DHCP server does not share information with other DHCP servers. Therefore, it is necessary to create unique IP addresses for each server to assign to clients.

- **What IP addressing options will clients obtain from a DHCP server?** The IP addressing options determine how to configure the DHCP server, and whether the options should be created for all of the clients in the internetwork, clients on a specific subnet, or individual clients. The IP addressing options might be:

  - Default gateway

  - DNS server

  - NetBIOS over TCP/IP name resolution

  - WINS server

  - NetBIOS scope ID

▶ **Follow these steps to install a DHCP server:**

1. Open the Windows Components wizard by clicking Start, pointing to Settings, and clicking Control Panel.

   When Control Panel opens, double-click Add/Remove Programs, and then click Add/Remove Windows Components.

2. Under Components, scroll to and click Networking Services.

3. Click Details.

4. Under Subcomponents Of Networking Services, select Dynamic Host Configuration Protocol (DHCP), click OK, and then click Next.

If prompted, type the full path to the Windows 2000 distribution files and click Continue. Required files will be copied to your hard disk.

5. Click Finish to close the Windows Components wizard.

Note It is strongly recommended that you manually configure the DHCP server computer to use a static IP address. The DHCP server cannot be a DHCP client. It must have a static IP address, subnet mask, and default gateway address.

Ipconfig

Ipconfig is a command-line tool that displays the current configuration of the installed IP stack on a networked computer. It can display a detailed configuration report for all interfaces, including any configured wide area network (WAN) miniports, such as those used for remote access or virtual private network (VPN) connections. A sample report is illustrated in Figure 11.4.

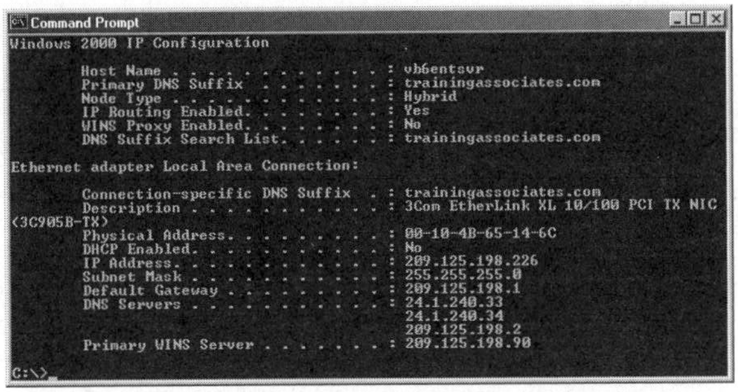

Figure 11.4 Report displayed for Ipconfig /all

Ipconfig Switches

The Ipconfig command is of particular use on systems running DHCP, as it allows users to determine which TCP/IP configuration values have been configured by DHCP. Table 11.2 explains the switches used with the Ipconfig command.

Table 11.2 Ipconfig Command-Line Switches

Switch	Effect
/all	Produces a detailed configuration report for all interfaces
/flushdns	Removes all entries from the DNS name cache
/registerdns	The DNS domain name for client resolutions
/displaydns	Displays the contents of the DNS resolver cache
/release *<adapter>*	Releases the IP address for a specified interface
/renew *<adapter>*	Renews the IP address for a specified interface
/showclassid *<adapter>*	Displays all the DHCP class IDs allowed for the adapter specified
/setclassid *<adapter>* *<classID to set>*	Changes the DHCP class ID for the adapter specified
/?	Displays the items in this table

Note Output can be redirected to a file and pasted into other documents.

▶ **Follow these steps to verify, release, or renew a client address lease:**

1. On a DHCP-enabled client computer running Windows 2000, open a command prompt.

2. Use the Ipconfig command-line utility to verify, release, or renew the lease of the client with a DHCP server, as follows:

   - To verify the current DHCP and TCP/IP configuration, type **ipconfig /all**.

   - To release a DHCP client lease, type **ipconfig /release**

   - To renew a DHCP client lease, type **ipconfig /renew**.

The Ipconfig utility is also supported for use in Windows NT 4.0 Server. For Windows 95 and Windows 98 clients, use Winipcfg, which is the Windows IP configuration program, to perform these tasks. To run Winipcfg on supporting clients, type **winipcfg** at either an MS-DOS command prompt or in the Run command window. When using Winipcfg to release or renew leases, click Release or Renew to perform these respective tasks.

DHCP Relay Agent

A relay agent is a small program that relays DHCP/BOOTP messages between clients and servers on different subnets. The DHCP Relay Agent component provided with the Windows 2000 router is a BOOTP relay agent that relays DHCP messages between DHCP clients and DHCP servers on different IP networks. For each IP network segment that contains DHCP clients, either a DHCP server or a computer acting as a DHCP relay agent is required.

▶ **Follow these steps to add the DHCP Relay Agent:**

1. Click Start, point to Programs, point to Administrative Tools, and then click Routing And Remote Access.

2. In the console tree, click Server Name\IP Routing\General.

3. Right-click General, and then click New Routing Protocol.

4. In the Select Routing Protocol dialog box, click DHCP Relay Agent, and then click OK.

Lesson Summary

DHCP was developed to solve configuration problems by centralizing IP configuration information for allocation to clients. DHCP uses a four-phase process to configure a DHCP client. The phases are: lease discover, lease offer, lease request, and lease acknowledgment. In addition to verifying a computer's IP configuration, you can use the Ipconfig utility to renew options, lease time, and relinquish a lease.

Lesson 2: Configuring DHCP

Once you have installed DHCP on a server, you will need to configure the server to meet specific needs. This lesson will show you have how DHCP is used on a network (by the clients and server) and explain how DHCP can be configured. Configuring includes setting the appropriate authorization and scope for the server.

After this lesson, you will be able to

- Identify the benefits of using DHCP on a network
- Configure a DHCP server and clients

Estimated lesson time: 10 minutes

Using DHCP on a Network

Configuring DHCP servers for a network provides the following benefits:

- The administrator can assign and specify global and subnet-specific TCP/IP parameters centrally for use throughout the entire network.
- Client computers do not require manual TCP/IP configuration.

  When a client computer moves between subnets, its old IP address is freed for reuse. The client reconfigures its TCP/IP settings automatically when the computer is restarted in its new location.

- Most routers can forward DHCP and BOOTP configuration requests, so DHCP servers are not required on every subnet in the network.

How Clients Use DHCP Servers

A computer running Windows 2000 becomes a DHCP client if Obtain An IP Address is selected in its TCP/IP properties, as illustrated in Figure 11.5.

When a client computer is set to use DHCP, it accepts a lease offer and can receive the following benefits from the server:

- Temporary use of an IP address known to be valid for the network it is joining
- Additional TCP/IP configuration parameters for the client to use in the form of options data

In addition, if conflict detection is configured, the DHCP server attempts to ping each available address in the scope prior to presenting the address in a lease offer to a client. This ensures that each IP address offered to clients is not already in use by another non-DHCP computer that uses manual TCP/IP configuration. Scopes are discussed in more detail later in this lesson.

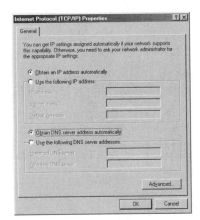

Figure 11.5 Setting a client to obtain an IP address from a DHCP server

How DHCP Servers Provide Optional Data

In addition to an IP address, DHCP servers can be configured to provide optional data to fully configure TCP/IP for clients. Some of the most common DHCP option types configured and distributed by the DHCP server during leases include:

- Default gateways (routers), which are used to connect a network segment to other network segments

- Other optional configuration parameters to assign to DHCP clients, such as IP addresses for the DNS servers or WINS servers that the client can use in resolving network host names

Installing and Configuring a DHCP Server

The DHCP Server service must be running in order to communicate with DHCP clients. Once DHCP Server is installed and started, several options must be configured. The following are the general steps for installing and configuring DHCP:

1. Install the Microsoft DHCP Server service.

2. Authorize the DHCP server.

3. Configure a scope or pool of valid IP addresses. This must be done before a DHCP server can lease IP addresses to DHCP clients.

4. Configure global scope and client scope options for a particular DHCP client.

5. Configure the DHCP server to always assign the same IP address to the same DHCP client.

Authorizing a DHCP Server

When configured correctly and authorized for use on a network, DHCP servers provide a useful administrative service. However, when a misconfigured or unauthorized DHCP server is introduced into a network, it can cause problems. For example, if an unauthorized DHCP server starts, it might begin either leasing incorrect IP addresses to clients or negatively acknowledging DHCP clients, thus attempting to renew current address leases. Either of these configurations can produce further problems for DHCP-enabled clients. For example, clients that obtain a configuration lease from the unauthorized server can fail to locate valid domain controllers, which prevents clients from successfully logging on to the network.

To avoid these problems in Windows 2000, servers are verified as legal in the network before they can service clients. This avoids most of the accidental damage caused by running DHCP servers with incorrect configurations or correct configurations on the wrong network.

How DHCP Servers Are Authorized

The process of authorizing DHCP servers is useful or in some cases necessary for DHCP servers running Windows 2000 Server. For the directory authorization process to work properly, it is assumed and necessary that the first DHCP server introduced onto your network participate in the Active Directory service. This requires that the server be installed as either a domain controller or a member server. When you are either planning for or actively deploying Active Directory service, it is important that you do not elect to install your first DHCP server computer as a standalone server. Windows 2000 Server provides some integrated security support for networks that use Active Directory. This avoids most of the accidental damage caused by running DHCP servers with wrong configurations or on the wrong networks.

The authorization process for DHCP server computers in Active Directory depends on the installed role of the server on your network. For Windows 2000 Server (as in earlier versions), there are three possible roles or server types for each server:

1. **Domain controller.** The computer keeps and maintains a copy of the Active Directory service database and provides secure account management for domain member users and computers.

2. **Member server.** The computer is not operating as a domain controller but has joined a domain in which it has a membership account in the Active Directory service database.

3. **Standalone server.** The computer is not operating as a domain controller or a member server in a domain. Instead, the server computer is made known to the network through a specified workgroup name, which can be shared by other computers, but is used only for browsing purposes and not to provide secured logon access to shared domain resources.

If you deploy Active Directory, all computers operating as DHCP servers must be either domain controllers or domain member servers before they can be authorized in the directory service and provide DHCP service to clients.

▶ **Follow these steps to authorize a computer as a DHCP server in Active Directory:**

1. Log on to the network using either an account that has enterprise administrative privileges or one that has been delegated authority to authorize DHCP servers for your enterprise.

   In most cases, it is simplest to log on to the network from the computer from which you want to authorize the new DHCP server. This ensures that other TCP/IP configuration of the authorized computer has been set up correctly prior to authorization. Typically, you can use an account that has membership in the Enterprise Administrators group. The account you use must allow you to have Full Control rights to the NetServices container object as it is stored in the enterprise root of the Active Directory service.

2. Install the DHCP service on this computer if necessary.

3. Click Start, point to Programs, point to Administrative Tools, then click DHCP.

4. On the Action menu, click Manage Authorized Servers, as illustrated in Figure 11.6.

   The Manage Authorized Servers dialog box appears.

5. Click Authorize.

6. When prompted, type the name or IP address of the DHCP server to be authorized, and then click OK.

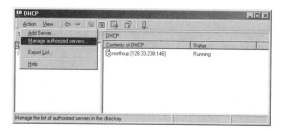

Figure 11.6 Authorizing a DHCP server

Protecting Against Unauthorized DHCP Servers

Active Directory is now used to store records of authorized DHCP servers. When a DHCP server comes up, the directory can be used to verify the status of that server. If that server is unauthorized, no response is returned to DHCP requests. A network manager with the proper access rights must respond. The domain administrator can assign access to the DHCP folder holding configuration data to allow only authorized personnel to add DHCP servers to the approved list.

The list of authorized servers can be created in Active Directory through the DHCP snap-in. When it first comes up, the DHCP server tries to find out if it is part of the directory domain. If it is, it tries to contact the directory to see if it is in the list of authorized servers. If it succeeds, it sends out DHCPINFORM to find out if there are other directory services running and makes sure that it is valid in others as well. If it cannot connect to the directory, it assumes that it is not authorized and does not respond to client requests. Likewise, if it does reach the directory but does not find itself in the authorized list, it does not respond to clients. If it does find itself in the authorized list, it starts to service client requests.

Creating a DHCP Scope

Before a DHCP server can lease an address to DHCP clients, you must create a scope. A scope is a pool of valid IP addresses available for lease to DHCP clients. After you have installed the DHCP service and it is running, the next step is to create a scope.

When creating a DHCP scope, consider the following points:

- You must create at least one scope for every DHCP server.

- You must exclude static IP addresses from the scope.

- You can create multiple scopes on a DHCP server to centralize administration and to assign IP addresses specific to a subnet. You can assign only one scope to a specific subnet.

- DHCP servers do not share scope information. As a result, when you create scopes on multiple DHCP servers, ensure that the same IP addresses do not exist in more than one scope to prevent duplicate IP addressing.

- Before you create a scope, determine starting and ending IP addresses to be used within it.

    Depending on the starting and ending IP addresses for your scope, the DHCP console suggests a default subnet mask useful for most networks. If you know a different subnet mask is required for your network, you can modify the value as needed.

▶   **Follow these steps to create a new scope:**

1. Click Start, point to Programs, point to Administrative Tools, and then click DHCP.

2. In the console tree, click the applicable DHCP server.

3. On the Action menu, click New Scope.

4. Follow the instructions in the New Scope wizard.

    When you finish creating a new scope, you might need to complete additional tasks, such as activating the scope for use or assigning scope options.

After Scopes Are Added

After you define a scope, you can configure the scope by performing the following tasks:

- **Set additional exclusion ranges.** You can exclude any other IP addresses that must not be leased to DHCP clients. You should use exclusions for all devices that must be statically configured. The excluded ranges should include all IP addresses that you assigned manually to other DHCP servers, non-DHCP clients, workstations without disks, or Routing and Remote Access and Point-to-Point (PPP) clients.

- **Create reservations.** You can choose to reserve some IP addresses for permanent lease assignment to specified computers or devices on your network. You should make reservations only for devices that are DHCP-enabled and that must be reserved for specific purposes on your network (such as print servers).

  If you are reserving an IP address for a new client or an address that is different from its current one, you should verify that the address has not already been leased by the DHCP server. Reserving an IP address in a scope does not automatically force a client currently using that address to stop using it. If the address is already in use, the client using the address must first release it by issuing a DHCP release message. To make this happen on a system running Windows 2000, at the command prompt type **ipconfig /release**. Reserving an IP address at the DHCP server also does not force the new client for which the reservation is made to immediately move to that address. In this case, too, the client must first issue a DHCP request message. To make this happen on a system running Windows 2000, at the command prompt type **ipconfig /renew**.

- **Adjust the length of lease durations.** You can modify the lease duration to be used for assigning IP address leases. The default lease duration is eight days. For most local area networks (LANs), the default value is acceptable but can be further increased if computers seldom move or change locations. Infinite lease times can also be set, but should be used with caution. For information about circumstances under which modifying this setting is most useful, see "Managing Leases."

- **Configure options and classes to be used with the scope.** To provide full configuration for clients, DHCP options need to be configured and enabled for the scope. For more advanced discrete management of scope clients, you can add or enable user- or vendor-defined option classes.

Table 11.3 describes some of the available options in the Configure DHCP Options: Scope Properties dialog box and includes all of the options supported by Microsoft DHCP clients.

Table 11.3 DHCP Scope Configuration Options

Option	Description
003 Router	Specifies the IP address of a router, such as the default gateway address. If the client has a locally defined default gateway, that configuration takes precedence over the DHCP option.
006 DNS servers	Specifies the IP address of a DNS server.
015 DNS Domain Name	The DNS domain name for client resolutions.
044 WINS/NBNS servers	The IP address of a WINS server available to clients. If a WINS server address is configured manually on a client, that configuration overrides the values configured for this option.
046 WINS/NBT node type	Specifies the type of NetBIOS over TCP/IP name resolution to be used by the client. Options are: 1 = B-node (broadcast); 2 = P-node (peer); 4 = M-node (mixed); 8 = H-node (hybrid)
044 WINS/NBNS servers	Specifies the IP address of a WINS server available to clients. If a WINS server address is manually configured on a client, that configuration overrides the values configured for this option.
047 NetBIOS Scope ID	Specifies the local NetBIOS scope ID. NetBIOS over TCP/IP will communicate only with other NetBIOS hosts using the same scope ID.

Implementing Multiple DHCP Servers

If your internetwork requires multiple DHCP servers, it is necessary to create a unique scope for each subnet. To ensure that clients can lease IP addresses in the event of a server failure, it is important to have multiple scopes for each subnet distributed among the DHCP servers in the internetwork. For example:

- Each DHCP server should have a scope containing approximately 75 percent of the available IP addresses for the local subnet.

- Each DHCP server should have a scope for each remote subnet containing approximately 25 percent of the available IP addresses for a subnet.

When a client's DHCP server is unavailable, the client can still receive an address lease from another DHCP server on a different subnet, assuming the router is a DHCP relay agent.

As illustrated in Figure 11.7, Server A has a scope for the local subnet with an IP address range of 131.107.4.20 through 131.107.4.150, and Server B has a scope with an IP address range of 131.107.3.20 through 131.107.3.150. Each server can lease IP addresses to clients on its own subnet.

Additionally, each server has a scope containing a small range of IP addresses for the remote subnet. For example, Server A has a scope for Subnet 2 with the IP address range of 131.107.3.151 through 131.107.3.200. Server B has a scope for Subnet 1 with the IP address range of 131.107.4.151 through 131.107.4.200. When a client on Subnet 1 is unable to lease an address from Server A, it can lease an address for its subnet from Server B, and vice versa.

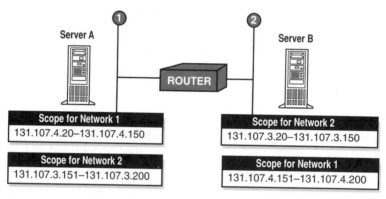

Figure 11.7 Scope and IP address ranges for Server A and Server B

Lesson Summary

A scope is a range of IP addresses that are available to be leased or assigned to clients. Multiple scopes and separate scopes for each subnet can be created to allow DHCP clients to obtain a valid IP address from any DHCP server. To implement DHCP, software is required on both the client and the server. Every DHCP server requires at least one scope.

Lesson 3: Integrating DHCP with Naming Services

With Windows 2000, a DHCP server can enable dynamic updates in the DNS name space for any of its clients that support these updates. Scope clients can then use DNS dynamic update protocol to update their host name-to-address mapping information (which is stored in zones on the DNS server) whenever changes occur to their DHCP-assigned address. In this lesson, you learn how to integrate DHCP with DNS.

After this lesson, you will be able to

- Integrate DNS and DHCP
- Describe how Dynamic DNS updates work
- Identify how DHCP client updates are typically handled

Estimated lesson time: 25 minutes

DNS and DHCP

Although DHCP provides a powerful mechanism for automatically configuring client IP addresses, until recently DHCP did not notify the DNS service to update the DNS records on the client—specifically, to update the client name to an IP address and the IP address-to-name mappings maintained by a DNS server. Without a way for DHCP to interact with DNS, the information maintained by DNS for a DHCP client may be incorrect. For example, a client may acquire its IP address from a DHCP server, but the DNS records do not reflect the IP address acquired or provide a mapping from the new IP address to the computer name (fully qualified domain name [FQDN]).

Registering for Dynamic DNS Updates

In Windows 2000, DHCP servers and clients can register with DNS if the server supports Dynamic DNS updates. The Windows 2000 DNS service supports dynamic updates. A Windows 2000 DHCP server can register with a DNS server and update pointer (PTR) and address (A) resource records on behalf of its DHCP-enabled clients using the Dynamic DNS update protocol. The ability to register both A- and PTR-type records lets a DHCP server act as a proxy for clients using Windows 95 and Windows NT 4.0 for the purpose of DNS registration. DHCP servers can differentiate between Windows 2000 and other clients. An additional DHCP option code (Option Code 81) enables the return of a client's FQDN to the DHCP server. If implemented, the DHCP server can dynamically update DNS to modify an individual computer's resource records with a DNS server using the dynamic update protocol. DHCP Servers that use Option Code 81 in their request message may have the following interactions when processing the DNS information.

- The DHCP server always registers the DHCP client for both the forward (A-type records) and reverse lookups (PTR-type records) with DNS.

- The DHCP server never registers the name-to-address (A-type records) mapping information for DHCP clients.

- The DHCP server registers the DHCP client for both forward (A-type records) and reverse lookups (PTR-type records) only when requested to by the client.

DHCP and static DNS service are not compatible for keeping name-to-address mapping information synchronized. This might cause problems with using DHCP and DNS together on a network if you are using older, static DNS servers, which are incapable of interacting dynamically when DHCP client configurations change.

▶ **Follow these steps to avoid failed DNS lookups for DHCP-registered clients when static DNS service is in effect:**

1. If WINS servers are used on the network, enable WINS lookup for DHCP clients that use NetBIOS.

2. Assign IP address reservations with an infinite lease duration for DHCP clients that use DNS only and do not support NetBIOS.

3. Wherever possible, upgrade or replace older, static-based DNS servers with DNS servers supporting updates. Dynamic updates are supported by the Microsoft DNS, which is included in Windows 2000.

Additional Recommendations

When using DNS and WINS together, consider the following options for interoperation:

- If a large percentage of clients use NetBIOS and you are using DNS, consider using WINS lookup on your DNS servers. If WINS lookup is enabled on the Microsoft DNS service, WINS is used for final resolution of any names that are not found using DNS resolution. The WINS forward lookup and WINS-R reverse lookup records are supported only by DNS. If you use servers on your network that do not support DNS, use DNS Manager to ensure that these WINS records are not propagated to DNS servers that do not support WINS lookup.

- If you have a large percentage of computers running Windows 2000 on your network, consider creating a pure DNS environment. This involves developing a migration plan to upgrade older WINS clients to Windows 2000. Support issues involving network name service are simplified by using a single naming and resource locator service (such as WINS and DNS) on your network.

Windows DHCP Clients and DNS Dynamic Update Protocol

In Windows 2000 Server, the DHCP Server service provides default support to register and update information for earlier DHCP clients in DNS zones. Earlier clients typically include other Microsoft TCP/IP client computers that were released prior to Windows 2000. The DNS/DHCP integration provided in Windows 2000 Server enables a DHCP client that is unable to dynamically update DNS resource records directly to have this information updated in DNS forward and reverse lookup zones by the DHCP server.

▶ **Follow these steps to allow dynamic updates for DHCP clients that do not support Dynamic DNS updates:**

1. Click Start, point to Programs, point to Administrative Tools, and then click DNS.

2. In the console tree, click the applicable zone.

3. On the Action menu, click Properties.

4. In the DNS Property tab, select Enable Updates For DNS Clients That Do Not Support Dynamic Update.

5. Select Only Secure Updates If Your Zone Type Is Active Directory-Integrated.

DHCP clients running Windows 2000 and earlier versions of Windows interact differently when performing the DHCP/DNS interactions previously described. The following sections explain how this process varies in different cases.

DHCP/DNS Update Interaction for Windows 2000 DHCP Clients

Windows 2000 DHCP clients interact with DNS dynamic update protocol as follows:

1. The client initiates a DHCP request message (DHCPREQUEST) to the server.

2. The server returns a DHCP acknowledgment message (DHCPACK) to the client, granting an IP address lease.

3. By default, the client sends a DNS update request to the DNS server for its own forward lookup record, a host (A) resource record.

Alternatively, the server can perform this update to the DNS server on behalf of the client if both the client and its configuration are modified accordingly.

4. The server sends updates for the DHCP client's reverse lookup record—a PTR resource record—using the process defined by the DNS dynamic update protocol.

This process is illustrated in Figure 11.8.

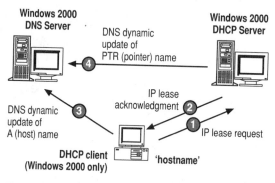

Figure 11.8 A DHCP client interacting with the DNS dynamic update protocol

DHCP/DNS Update Interaction for DHCP Clients Prior to Windows 2000

Earlier versions of Windows DHCP clients do not support the DNS dynamic update process directly and therefore cannot directly interact with the DNS server. For these DHCP clients, updates are typically handled as follows:

1. The client initiates a DHCP request message (DHCPREQUEST) to the server.

2. The server returns a DHCP acknowledgment message (DHCPACK) to the client, granting an IP address lease.

3. The server then sends updates to the DNS server for the client's forward lookup record, which is a host (A) resource record.

4. The server also sends updates for the client's reverse lookup record, which is a PTR resource record.

This process is illustrated in Figure 11.9.

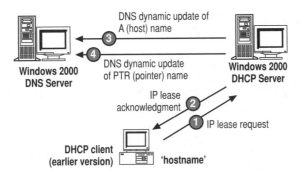

Figure 11.9 DHCP/DNS interaction with older Windows clients

Lesson Summary

With Windows 2000, a DHCP server can enable dynamic updates in the DNS name space for any of its clients that support these updates. With dynamic update, the primary server for a zone can also be configured to support updates that are initiated by another computer or device that supports dynamic update. For example, it can receive updates from workstations registering A and PTR resource records, or from DHCP servers.

Lesson 4: Using DHCP with Active Directory Directory Service

Microsoft DHCP provides integration with the Active Directory directory service and DNS service, enhanced monitoring and statistical reporting for DHCP servers, vendor-specific options and user-class support, multicast address allocation, and rogue DHCP server detection. This lesson will explain these new features and explain how DHCP is used with Active Directory directory services.

After this lesson, you will be able to

- Describe how IP address and naming management is managed through DHCP and Active Directory integration
- Describe how DHCP servers are authorized

Estimated lesson time: 15 minutes

Windows 2000 Integrated IP Management

Windows 2000 Server naming and address services offer the flexibility to manage networks more easily and to interoperate with other address and naming systems. As with Windows NT Server 4.0, Windows 2000 Server provides DHCP, DNS, and WINS services to continue to simplify address assignment and name resolution. New with Windows 2000 Server is support for Dynamic DNS, Active Directory integration of DHCP and DNS, and a DHCP relay agent.

Address Assignment and Naming Services

IP address and naming management is simplified through Active Directory integration. Customers can choose to use Active Directory to replicate and synchronize DNS naming throughout the corporate network. This eliminates the need to maintain a separate replication service for DNS. Integrated DHCP and Dynamic DNS services then utilize this directory-registered information to provide address assignment and naming services. As DHCP allocates addresses, DNS and Active Directory are dynamically updated. This lets administrators reassign IP addresses for end systems, and name resolution is updated automatically so they can be located easily.

Support for Legacy Servers

Interoperability with other DHCP and DNS services helps preserve investment in existing services. Customers have the option to use legacy IP address and naming management systems using the Windows 2000 Server DHCP, DHCP relay agent, and/or the DNS service. Standard zone transfer and referral support ensures that the Windows 2000 Server DNS interoperates with other DNS servers for enterprise and Internet address resolution. This lets customers use Active Directory integrated services for their network while maintaining interoperability with Internet and other corporate DNS systems. For example, a company can deploy Active Directory–integrated DNS and DHCP in a core part of its network while interoperating with existing DNS servers. Over time, the Active Directory–based IP management infrastructure can be expanded while interoperability with external DNS services is preserved.

Windows 2000 DHCP is also dynamically integrated with Windows 2000 DNS in support of Active Directory. Earlier versions of DNS do not offer this support, and you should consider upgrading if you plan to deploy Active Directory or want to use network load balancing.

Rogue DHCP Server Detection Feature

The Windows 2000 DHCP service provides a rogue DHCP server detection feature. This prevents rogue (unauthorized) DHCP servers from joining an existing DHCP network in which Windows 2000 Server and Active Directory are deployed. A DHCP server object is created in Active Directory, which lists the IP addresses of servers that are authorized to provide DHCP services to the network. When a DHCP server attempts to start on the network, Active Directory is queried and the server computer's IP address is compared to the list of authorized DHCP servers. If a match is found, the server computer is authorized as a DHCP server and is allowed to complete the system startup. If a match is not found, the server is identified as rogue, and the DHCP service is automatically shut down.

Lesson Summary

IP address and naming management is simplified through Active Directory integration. As DHCP allocates addresses, DNS and Active Directory are dynamically updated. Interoperability with other DHCP and DNS services helps preserve investment in existing services because you can use legacy IP address and naming management systems with Windows 2000 Server DHCP servers. The authorization process for DHCP server computers in Active Directory depends on whether the server is a domain controller, member server, or standalone server. In addition, Active Directory is now used to store records of authorized DHCP servers to protect against unauthorized DHCP servers. The list of authorized servers can be created in the Active Directory through the DHCP snap-in.

Lesson 5: Troubleshooting DHCP

The most common DHCP client problem is a failure to obtain an IP address or other configuration parameters from the DHCP server during startup. The most common DHCP server problems are the inability to start the server on the network in a Windows 2000 or Active Directory domain environment and the failure of clients to obtain configuration from a working server. In this lesson, you will learn how to troubleshoot DHCP clients and DHCP servers.

After this lesson, you will be able to

- Identify and solve DHCP client problems
- Identify and solve DHCP server problems

Estimated lesson time: 35 minutes

Preventing DHCP Problems

Many DHCP problems involve incorrect or missing configuration details. To help prevent the most common types of problems, you should do the following:

- **Use the 75/25 design rule for balancing scope distribution of addresses where multiple DHCP servers are deployed to service the same scope.** Using more than one DHCP server on the same subnet provides increased fault tolerance for servicing DHCP clients located on it. With two DHCP servers, if one server is unavailable, the other server can take its place and continue to lease new addresses or renew existing clients.

- **Use superscopes for multiple DHCP servers on each subnet in a LAN environment.** A superscope allows a DHCP server to provide leases from more than one scope to clients on a single physical network. When started, each DHCP client broadcasts a DHCP discover message (DHCPDISCOVER) to its local subnet to attempt to find a DHCP server. Because DHCP clients use broadcasts during their initial startup, you cannot predict which server will respond to a client's DHCP discover request if more than one DHCP server is active on the same subnet.

- **Deactivate scopes only when removing a scope permanently from service.** Once you activate a scope, it should not be deactivated until you are ready to retire the scope and its included range of addresses from use on your network. Once a scope is deactivated, the DHCP server no longer accepts those scope addresses as valid addresses.

- **Use server-side conflict detection on DHCP servers only when it is needed.** Conflict detection can be used by either DHCP servers or clients to determine whether an IP address is already in use on the network before leasing or using the address.

- **Reservations should be created on all DHCP servers that can potentially service the reserved client.** You can use a client reservation to ensure that a DHCP client computer always receives lease of the same IP address at its startup. If you have more than one DHCP server reachable by a reserved client, add the reservation at each of your other DHCP servers.

- **For server performance, remember that DHCP is disk-intensive and purchase hardware with optimal disk performance characteristics.** DHCP causes frequent and intensive activity on server hard disks. To provide the best performance, consider RAID 0 or RAID 5 solutions when purchasing hardware for your server computer.

- **Keep audit logging enabled for use in troubleshooting.** By default, the DHCP service enables audit logging of service-related events. With Windows 2000 Server, audit logging provides for a long-term service monitoring tool that makes limited and safe use of server disk resources.

- **Integrate DHCP with other services, such as WINS and DNS.** WINS and DNS can both be used for registering dynamic name-to-address mappings on your network. To provide name resolution services, you must plan for interoperability of DHCP with these services. Most network administrators implementing DHCP also plan a strategy for implementing DNS and WINS servers.

- **Use the appropriate number of DHCP servers for the number of DHCP-enabled clients on your network.** In a small LAN (for example, one physical subnet not using routers), a single DHCP server can serve all DHCP-enabled clients. For routed networks, the number of servers needed increases, depending on several factors, including the number of DHCP-enabled clients, the transmission speed between network segments, the speed of network links, the IP address class of the network, and whether DHCP service is used throughout the enterprise network or only on selected physical networks.

Troubleshooting DHCP Clients

Most DHCP-related problems start as failed IP configuration at a client, so it is a good practice when troubleshooting to start there. After you have determined that a DHCP-related problem does not originate at the client, check the system event log and DHCP server audit logs for possible clues. When the

DHCP service does not start, these logs generally explain the source of the service failure or shutdown. Furthermore, you can use the Ipconfig TCP/IP utility at the command prompt to get information about the configured TCP/IP parameters on local or remote computers on the network.

The following sections describe common symptoms for DHCP client problems. When a client fails to obtain configuration, you can use this information to quickly identify the source of the problem.

Invalid IP Address Configuration

If a DHCP client does not have an IP address configured or has an IP address configured as 168.254.*x.x*, that means that the client was not able to contact a DHCP server and obtain an IP address lease. This is either because of a network hardware failure or because the DHCP server is unavailable. If this occurs, you should verify that the client computer has a valid, functioning network connection. First, check that related client hardware devices (cables and network adapters) are working properly at the client.

Autoconfiguration Problems on the Current Network

If a DHCP client has an autoconfigured IP address that is incorrect for its current network, this means that the Windows 2000 or Windows 98 DHCP client could not find a DHCP server and has used the APIPA feature to configure its IP address. In some larger networks, disabling this feature is desirable for network administration. APIPA generates an IP address in the form of 169.254.*x.y* (where x.y is a unique identifier on the network that the client generates) and a subnet mask of 255.255.0.0. Note that Microsoft has reserved IP addresses from 169.254.0.1 through 169.254.255.254 and uses this range to support APIPA.

▶ **Follow these steps to fix an invalid autoconfigured IP address for your network:**

1. First, use the ping command to test connectivity from the client to the server. Next, verify or manually attempt to renew the client lease. Depending on your network requirements, it might be necessary to disable APIPA at the client.

2. If the client hardware appears to be functioning properly, check that the DHCP server is available on the network by pinging it from another computer on the same network as the affected DHCP client. Furthermore, you can try releasing or renewing the client's address lease, and check the TCP/IP configuration settings on automatic addressing.

Missing Configuration Details

If a DHCP client is missing configuration details, the client might be missing DHCP options in its leased configuration, either because the DHCP server is not configured to distribute them or the client does not support the options distributed by the server. If this occurs on Microsoft DHCP clients, verify that the most commonly used and supported options have been configured at either the server, scope, client, or class level of option assignment. Check the DHCP option settings.

Sometimes a client has the full and correct set of DHCP options assigned but its network configuration does not appear to be working correctly. If the DHCP server is configured with an incorrect DHCP router option (Option Code 3) for the Windows 98 or earlier client's default gateway address, you can do the following:

1. Change the IP address list for the router (default gateway) option at the applicable DHCP scope and server.

2. Set the correct value in the Scope Options tab of the Scope Properties dialog box.

   In rare instances, you might have to configure the DHCP client to use a specialized list of routers different from other scope clients. In such cases, you can add a reservation and configure the router option list specifically for the reserved client.

Clients running Windows NT 4.0 Server or Windows 2000 do not use the incorrect address because they support the dead gateway detection feature. This feature of the Windows 2000 TCP/IP protocol changes the default gateway to the next default gateway in the list of configured default gateways when a specific number of connections retransmits segments.

DHCP Servers Do Not Provide IP Addresses

If DHCP clients are unable to get IP addresses from the server, one of the following situations can cause this problem:

- **The IP address of the DHCP server was changed and now DHCP clients cannot get IP addresses.** A DHCP server can only service requests for a scope that has a network ID that is the same as the network ID of its IP address. Make sure that the DHCP server IP address falls in the same network range as the scope it is servicing. For example, a server with an IP address in the 192.168.0.0 network cannot assign addresses from scope 10.0.0.0 unless superscopes are used.

- **The DHCP clients are located across a router from the subnet where the DHCP server resides, and are unable to receive an address from the server.** A DHCP server can provide IP addresses to client computers on remote multiple subnets only if the router that separates them can act as a DHCP relay agent. Completing the following steps might correct this problem:

  1. Configure a BOOTP/DHCP relay agent on the client subnet (that is, the same physical network segment). The relay agent can be located on the router itself or on a Windows 2000 Server computer running the DHCP Relay service component.

  2. At the DHCP server, configure a scope to match the network address on the other side of the router where the affected clients are located.

  3. In the scope, make sure that the subnet mask is correct for the remote subnet.

  4. Do not include this scope (that is, the one for the remote subnet) in superscopes configured for use on the same local subnet or segment where the DHCP server resides.

- **Multiple DHCP servers exist on the same LAN.** Make sure that you do not configure multiple DHCP servers on the same LAN with overlapping scopes. You might want to rule out the possibility that one of the DHCP servers in question is a Small Business Server (SBS) computer. By design, the DHCP service, when running under SBS, automatically stops when it detects another DHCP server on the LAN.

Troubleshooting DHCP Servers

When a server fails to provide leases to its clients, the failure most often is discovered by clients when they experience one of three symptoms:

1. The client might be configured to use an IP address not provided by the server.

2. The server sends a negative response back to the client, and the client displays an error message or popup indicating that a DHCP server could not be found.

3. The server leases the client an address but the client appears to have other network configuration–based problems, such as the inability to register or resolve DNS or NetBIOS names, or to perceive computers beyond its subnet.

The first troubleshooting task is to make sure that the DHCP services are running. This can be verified by opening the DHCP service console to view service status, or by opening Services And Applications under Computer Manager. If the appropriate service is not started, start the service. In rare circumstances, a DHCP server cannot start, or a Stop error might occur.

▶ **Follow these steps to restart a DHCP server that is stopped:**

1. Start Windows 2000 Server, and log on as an administrator.

2. At the command prompt, type **net start dhcpserver**, and then press Enter.

Note Use Event Viewer in Administrative Tools to find the possible source of problems with DHCP services.

DHCP Relay Agent Service Is Installed but Not Working

The DHCP Relay Agent service is running on the same computer as the DHCP service. Because both services listen for and respond to BOOTP and DHCP messages sent using UDP ports 67 and 68, neither service works reliably if both are installed on the same computer. To solve this problem, install the DHCP service and the DHCP Relay Agent component on separate computers.

DHCP Console Incorrectly Reports Lease Expirations

When the DHCP console displays the lease expiration time for reserved clients for a scope, it indicates one of the following:

- If the scope lease time is set to an infinite lease time, the reserved client's lease is also shown as infinite.

- If the scope lease time is set to a finite length of time (such as eight days), the reserved client's lease uses this same lease time.

The lease term of a DHCP reserved client is determined by the lease assigned to the reservation. To create reserved clients with unlimited lease durations, create a scope with an unlimited lease duration and add reservations to that scope.

DHCP Server Uses Broadcast to Respond to All Client Messages

The DHCP server uses broadcast to respond to all client configuration request messages, regardless of how each DHCP client has set the broadcast bit flag. DHCP clients can set the broadcast flag (the first bit in the 16-bit flags field in the DHCP message header) when sending DHCPDISCOVER messages to indicate to the DHCP server that broadcast to the limited broadcast address

(255.255.255.255) should be used when replying to the client with a DHCPOFFER response.

By default, the DHCP server in Windows NT Server 3.51 and earlier versions ignored the broadcast flag in DHCPDISCOVER messages and broadcasted only DHCPOFFER replies. This behavior is implemented on the server to avoid problems that can result from clients not being able to receive or process a unicast response prior to being configured for TCP/IP.

Starting with Windows NT Server 4.0, the DHCP service still attempts to send all DHCP responses as IP broadcasts to the limited broadcast address, unless support for unicast responses is enabled by setting the value of the IgnoreBroadcastFlag registry entry to 1. The entry is located in: HKEY_LOCAL_MACHINE\System\CurrentControlSet\Services\DHCPServer\ Parameters\IgnoreBroadcastFlag. When set to 1, the broadcast flag in client requests is ignored, and all DHCPOFFER responses are broadcast from the server. When it is set to 0, the server transmission behavior (whether to broadcast or not) is determined by the setting of the broadcast bit flag in the client DHCPDISCOVER request. If this flag is set in the request, the server broadcasts its response to the limited local broadcast address. If this flag is not set in the request, the server unicasts its response directly to the client.

DHCP Server Fails to Issue Address Leases for a New Scope

You might find that a new scope has been added at the DHCP server for the purpose of renumbering the existing network but DHCP clients do not obtain leases from the newly defined scope. This situation is most common when you are attempting to renumber an existing IP network. For example, you might have obtained a registered class of IP addresses for your network, or you might be changing the address class to accommodate more computers or networks. In these situations, you want clients to obtain leases in the new scope instead of using the old scope to obtain or renew their leases. Once all clients are actively obtaining leases in the new scope, you intend to remove the existing scope.

When superscopes are not available or used, only a single DHCP scope can be active on the network at a given time. If more than one scope is defined and activated on the DHCP server, only one scope is used to provide leases to clients. The active scope used for distributing leases is determined by whether the scope range of addresses contains the first IP address that is bound and assigned to the DHCP server's network adapter hardware. When additional secondary IP addresses are configured on a server using the Advanced TCP/IP Properties tab, these addresses have no effect on the DHCP server in determining scope selection or responding to configuration requests from DHCP clients on the network.

This problem can be solved in the following ways:

- Configure the DHCP server to use a superscope that includes the old scope and the new scope.

- Change the primary IP address (the address assigned in the TCP/IP Properties tab) on the DHCP server's network adapter to an IP address that is part of the same network as the new scope.

For Windows NT Server 3.51, support for superscopes is not available. In this case, you must change the first IP address configured for the DHCP server's network adapter to an address in the new scope range of addresses. If necessary, you can still maintain the prior address that was first assigned as an active IP address for the server computer by moving it to the list of multiple IP addresses maintained in the Advanced TCP/IP Properties tab.

Monitoring Server Performance

Because DHCP servers are of critical importance in most environments, monitoring the performance of servers can help in troubleshooting cases where server performance degradation occurs. For Windows 2000 Server, the DHCP service includes a set of performance counters that can be used to monitor various types of server activity. By default, these counters are available after the DHCP service is installed. To access these counters, you must use System Monitor (formerly Performance Monitor). The DHCP server counters can monitor the following:

- All types of DHCP messages sent and received by the DHCP service

- The average amount of processing time spent by the DHCP server per message packet sent and received

- The number of message packets dropped because of internal delays on the DHCP server computer

Moving the DHCP Server Database

You may need to move a DHCP database to another computer.

▶ **Follow these steps to move a DHCP database:**

1. Stop the Microsoft DHCP service on the current computer.

2. Copy the \System32\Dhcp directory to the new computer that has been configured as a DHCP server.

   Make sure the new directory is under exactly the same drive letter and path as on the old computer. If you must copy the files to a different directory, copy DHCP.MDB, but do not copy the .log or .chk files.

3. Start the Microsoft DHCP service on the new computer. The service automatically starts using the .mdb and .log files copied from the old computer.

When you check DHCP Manager, the scope still exists because the registry holds the information on the address range of the scope, including a bitmap of the addresses in use. You need to reconcile the DHCP database to add database entries for the existing leases in the address bitmask. As clients renew, they are matched with these leases, and eventually the database is again complete.

▶ **Follow these steps to reconcile the DHCP database:**

1. In DHCP Manager, on the Scope menu, click Active Leases.

2. In the Active Leases dialog box, click Reconcile.

Although it is not required, you can force DHCP clients to renew their leases in order to update the DHCP database as quickly as possible. To do so, type **ipconfig /renew** at the command prompt.

Lesson Summary

The most common DHCP client problem is a failure to obtain an IP address or other configuration parameters from the DHCP server during startup. The most common DHCP server problem is the inability to start the server on the network in a Windows 2000 or Active Directory domain environment. Most DHCP-related problems start as failed IP configuration at a client, so it is a good practice when troubleshooting to start there.

Review

Answering the following questions will reinforce key information presented in this chapter. If you are unable to answer a question, review the appropriate lesson and then try the question again. Answers to the questions can be found in Appendix A, "Questions and Answers."

1. What is DHCP?

2. Describe the integration of DHCP with DNS.

3. What is a DHCP client?

4. What is IP autoconfiguration in Windows 2000?

5. Why is it important to plan an implementation of DHCP for a network?

6. What tool do you use to manage DHCP servers in Windows 2000?

7. What is the source of most DHCP-related problems?

C H A P T E R   1 2

Managing Remote Access

About This Chapter

Microsoft Windows 2000 remote access has been improved. This chapter presents an overview of the new protocols for use with remote access. It explains the new options and interfaces in Windows 2000 that are used to connect computers and configure protocols correctly to meet all your remote access requirements. The chapter starts out with a review of Internet Protocol (IP) routing and explains how information is actually transmitted across the Internet. It concludes with a look at the various security methods you can use to keep your network secure.

Before You Begin

To complete this chapter, you must have

- Two Microsoft Windows 2000 servers with local area network (LAN) connectivity

- Installed Windows 2000 Server on one of the two computers (Server01 would be preferred)

Lesson 1: Introducing Remote Access

The remote access feature of Microsoft Windows 2000 Server enables remote or mobile workers who use dial-up communication links to access corporate networks as if they were directly connected. Windows 2000 Server remote access also provides virtual private networking services so that users can access corporate networks over the Internet.

After this lesson, you will be able to

- Explain the features of Routing and Remote Access service
- Install Routing and Remote Access service
- Describe the difference between remote access and remote control
- Explain the effect of an upgrade on Routing and Remote Access service

Estimated lesson time: 25 minutes

Overview of Remote Access

Windows 2000 Server remote access, which is part of the integrated Routing and Remote Access service, connects remote or mobile workers to corporate networks. Remote users can work as if their computers were physically connected to the network. Users (or clients) run remote access software to initiate a connection to the remote access server. The remote access server, which is a computer running Windows 2000 Server with the Routing and Remote Access service enabled, authenticates users and services sessions until terminated. All services typically available to a user connected to a local area network (LAN), including file and print sharing, Web server access, and messaging, are enabled by means of the remote access connection.

Remote Access clients use standard tools to access network resources. For example, on a computer running Windows 2000, clients can use Microsoft Windows Explorer to map network drives and connect to printers. Connections are persistent, so users do not need to reconnect to network resources during their remote sessions. Because drive letters and universal naming convention (UNC) names are fully supported by remote access, most commercial and custom applications work without modification. A remote access server running Windows 2000 provides two different types of remote access connectivity:

- **Dial-up networking.** Dial-up networking is used when a remote access client makes a nonpermanent, dial-up connection to a physical port on a remote access server by using the service of a telecommunications provider such as analog telephone, Integrated Services Digital Network (ISDN), or X.25. The best example of dial-up networking is that of a dial-up networking client who dials the telephone number of one of the ports of a remote access server.

  Dial-up networking over an analog telephone or ISDN is a direct physical connection between the dial-up networking client and the dial-up networking server. You can encrypt data sent over the connection, but it is not required.

- **Virtual private networking.** Virtual private networking is the creation of secured, point-to-point connections across a private network or a public network such as the Internet. A virtual private networking client uses special Transmission Control Protocol/Internet Protocol (TCP/IP)-based protocols called tunneling protocols to make a call to a port on a virtual private network (VPN) server. The most practical example of a VPN is a dial-up user connecting across the Internet to a server on the corporate network. The remote access server answers the virtual call, authenticates the caller, and transfers data between the virtual private networking client and the corporate network.

  In contrast to dial-up networking, virtual private networking is a logical (rather than physical) connection between the VPN client and server. To ensure privacy, you must encrypt data sent over the connection.

Routing and Remote Access Features

The Windows Routing and Remote Access feature set provides Network Address Translation (NAT), multiprotocol routing, Layer Two Tunneling Protocol (L2TP), Internet Authentication Service (IAS), and Remote Access Policies (RAP). The lesson concludes with information about demand-dial filters, dial-out hours, dial-in user properties, remote access use of name servers and DHCP, Bandwidth Allocation Protocol (BAP), and monitoring remote access.

Router Discovery

Windows 2000 has a new feature called router discovery, which is specified in Request for Comments (RFC) 1256. Router discovery provides an improved method of configuring and detecting default gateways. When using DHCP or manual default gateway configuration, there is no way to adjust to network changes. Using router discovery, clients dynamically discover routers and can switch to backup routers if a network failure or administrative change is needed. Router discovery is made up of two types of packets:

- **Router solicitations.** When a host that supports RFC 1256 needs to be configured with a default gateway, it sends out a router solicitation using an Internet Control Message Protocol (ICMP) message. The router solicitation can be sent to the all-routers Internet Protocol (IP) multicast address of 224.0.0.2, the local Internet Protocol (IP) broadcast address, or the limited broadcast address (255.255.255.255). In practice, hosts send router solicitation messages to the multicast address. Routers on the host's network that support RFC 1256 immediately respond with a router advertisement, and the host chooses the router with the highest preference level as its default gateway.

- **Router advertisements.** Router advertisements are explicit notifications to the hosts on the network that the router is still available. A router sends out a periodic router advertisement using an ICMP message. The router advertisement can be sent to the all-hosts local IP broadcast address or the limited broadcast address. Like router solicitations, the router advertisement is sent to the multicast address in practice.

Note Microsoft Windows 2000 supports router discovery as a host and router.

Network Address Translator

NAT is a standard defined in RFC 1631. A NAT is a router that translates IP addresses of an intranet or home LAN to valid Internet addresses. A NAT allows Internet connectivity for a private network with private addresses through a single Internet IP address. Windows 2000 Server includes a full-featured NAT implementation called Connection Sharing and a configuration-free version called Shared Access.

Multicast Routing

Windows 2000 Server implements a limited form of multicast routing using a multicast proxy. This proxy can be used to extend multicast support beyond a true multicast router. The multicast proxy is best used to provide multicast for remote access users or a single LAN network connected to the Internet. On one or more interfaces Windows 2000 acts like a multicast router, communicating with local clients about their multicast needs. On an interface that has direct access to a true multicast router, Windows acts as a multicast client, forwarding multicast traffic on behalf of the local clients.

Layer Two Tunneling Protocol

L2TP can be thought of as the next version of Point-to-Point Tunneling Protocol (PPTP). It works much like PPTP but is now a combined development effort with Cisco. L2TP combines Cisco's Layer 2 Forwarding (L2F) and PPTP technologies (created by Microsoft, Ascend, 3Com, U.S. Robotics, and ECI-Telematics). L2TP is currently an RFC draft, soon to be an industry standard. L2TP is an Open Systems Interconnection (OSI) layer 2 (Data-link layer) protocol used to create VPNs.

Internet Authentication Service

IAS is a Remote Authentication Dial-In User Service (RADIUS) server. RADIUS is a network protocol that enables remote authentication, authorization, and accounting of users who are connecting to a network access server (NAS). A network access server such as Windows Routing and Remote Access can be a RADIUS client or RADIUS server.

Note Microsoft released a limited version of RADIUS server in the Windows NT 4.0 Option pack. A RADIUS server—IAS—is now available in Windows 2000.

Remote Access Policies

In Windows NT 3.5 and later versions, remote access was granted based on a simple Grant Dial-In Permission To User option in User Manager or the Remote Access Admin utility. Callback options were also granted on a per-user basis.

In Windows 2000, remote access connections are granted based on the dial-in properties of a user object and remote access policies (RAPs). A RAPs is a set of conditions and connection parameters that allows network administrators more flexibility in granting remote access permissions and usage. Some examples of conditions include time of day, group, and type of connection (VPN or dial-up). Some examples of connection parameters are authentication and encryption requirements, use of Multilink, and length of session. One benefit of this added control is requiring strong encryption on VPN connections and allowing no encryption on modem connections where it may not be needed.

RAPs are stored on the local computer and are shared between Windows 2000 Routing and Remote Access and Windows 2000 IAS. RAP is configured from the Internet Authentication Service Manager or from the Routing and Remote Access Manager.

Enabling Routing and Remote Access Service

Now that you have an understanding of Routing and Remote Access, you will enable the service. Before you enable this service, the Routing and Remote Access Manager will look like the illustration in Figure 12.1.

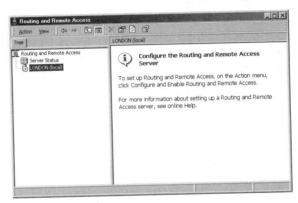

Figure 12.1 The Routing and Remote Access Manager before installation

Practice: Installing a Routing and Remote Access Server

In this practice, you install a Routing and Remote Access server using the Routing and Remote Access Manager.

Note Before you continue with the lesson, run the Ch12.exe demonstration file located in the Media folder on the *Supplemental Course Materials* CD-ROM that accompanies this book. The file provides an overview of installing a Routing and Remote Access server.

Exercise 1: Installing a Routing and Remote Access Server

1. Open the Routing and Remote Access Manager from within the Administrative Tools menu.

2. Right-click your computer name and choose Configure And Enable Routing And Remote Access.

3. In the Routing And Remote Access Server Setup wizard, click Next.

4. On the Common Configurations page, select the Remote Access Server button, and then click Next.

5. On the Remote Client Protocols page, under Protocols, make sure that TCP/IP is listed. Verify that Yes, All The Required Protocols Are On This List is selected, and then click Next.

6. On the IP Address Assignment page, make sure From A Specified Range Of Addresses is selected, and then click Next.

7. On the Address Range Assignment page, click New. Next to Starting Address type **10.0.0.10** (for computer 1, and 10.0.0.20 for computer 2). Under End Of IP Address type **10.0.0.19** (for computer 1, and 10.0.0.29 for computer 2). Under Number Of Addresses, verify that 10 is the number. Click OK to close the Edit Address Range window. Click Next.

8. On the Managing Multiple Remote Access Servers page, verify that No, I Don't Want To Set This Server Up To Use RADIUS Now is selected, and then click Next.

9. Click Finish.

10. Click OK to any warning messages that pop up.

The Routing and Remote Access Manager will look like the illustration in Figure 12.2.

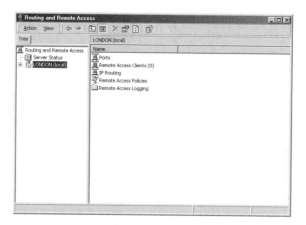

Figure 12.2 The Routing and Remote Access Manager after installation

Exercise 2: Enabling Dial-in Permissions for the Administrator Account

1. Open Active Directory Users And Computers (if in a domain) or Computer Management (if in a workgroup).

2. Open the User Properties For Administrator, go to the Dial-In tab, and select Allow Access.

Remote Access Versus Remote Control

The distinctions between remote access and remote control solutions are the following:

- The remote access server is a software-based multiprotocol router; remote control solutions work by sharing screen, keyboard, and mouse over the remote link. In remote access, the applications are run on the remote access client computer.

- In a remote control solution, users share a central processing unit (CPU) or multiple CPUs on the server. In remote control, the applications are run on the server. The remote access server's CPU is dedicated to facilitating communications between remote access clients and network resources, not to running applications.

The Effect of a Windows Upgrade on Routing and Remote Access

A system upgraded from Windows NT 4.0 Remote Access Service (RAS)/ Routing and Remote Access service (RRAS) to Windows 2000 has one minor problem. Windows NT 4.0 uses the LocalSystem account. When any service logs on as LocalSystem, it logs on with NULL credentials, meaning that the service does not provide a user name or password.

Active Directory directory service, by default, does not accept querying of object attributes through NULL sessions. Therefore, in a mixed environment, planning is necessary to allow Windows NT 4.0 Remote Access Service/ Routing and Remote Access Service servers to retrieve user dial-in properties from Active Directory directory service. Remote Access Service/Routing and Remote Access Service servers require this access to determine whether the user has been granted dial-in permissions and whether any other dial-in settings, such as callback telephone numbers, have been configured.

Note Using NULL credentials prevents an account from being able to access network resources relying on Windows NT LAN Manager (NTLM) authentication (unless the remote computer specifically allows NULL sessions).

Remote Access Server Upgrade Considerations

For a Windows NT 4.0 Remote Access Service/Routing and Remote Access Service server to retrieve user properties from Active Directory, you must meet one of the following conditions:

- You have a domain in Mixed mode and the Windows NT 4.0 Remote Access Service/Routing and Remote Access Service server is also a Windows NT 4.0 backup domain controller. In this case, Remote Access Service/Routing and Remote Access Service has access to the local Security Accounts Manager (SAM) database.

- You have a domain in Mixed mode and the Windows NT 4.0 Remote Access Service/Routing and Remote Access service server contacts a Windows NT 4.0 backup domain controller to determine user dial-in properties. This also will allow access to the local SAM database.

- The domain is in Mixed or Native mode and Active Directory security has been loosened to grant the built-in user Everyone permissions to read any property on any user object. This is configured with the Active Directory Installation wizard (DCPROMO.EXE) by selecting Permission Compatible With Pre–Windows 2000 Server.

Note Unless Active Directory security has been loosened or the Remote Access Service/Routing and Remote Access Service server is installed on a backup domain controller, dial-in connectivity success could be intermittent. Even if your domain runs in Mixed mode, it is impossible to configure the Remote Access Service/Routing and Remote Access Service server to contact a Windows NT 4.0 backup domain controller only for authentication. If a Windows 2000 domain controller authenticates the user, dial-in will fail.

The Permission Compatible With Pre-Windows 2000 Servers option places the Everyone group in the Pre-Windows 2000 Compatible Access Local group. You can strengthen permissions by deleting the Everyone group from this group's membership list after all remote access servers have been upgraded to Windows 2000. This Everyone group workaround should be used only after understanding its impact on Active Directory security. If it conflicts with your security requirements, it is recommended that you upgrade the Windows NT 4.0 Remote Access Service/Routing and Remote Access Service server to Windows 2000 and make it a member of a Windows 2000 mixed or native domain. This will help prevent inconsistent dial-in access while the domain is in Mixed mode.

If you would like to loosen security to allow Windows NT 4.0 Remote Access Service/Routing and Remote Access Service servers to function after running the Active Directory Installation wizard, you can add the Everyone group to the Pre-Windows 2000 Compatible Access group by typing the command **net localgroup "Pre-Windows 2000 Compatible Access" Everyone /add**.

Lesson Summary

This lesson provided a basic overview of remote access features. These include router discovery, NAT, multicast routing, L2TP, IAS, and RAPs. Installing and configuring Routing and Remote Access was also introduced.

Lesson 2: Configuring a Routing and Remote Access Server

Once Routing and Remote Access is installed, you can configure it for inbound connections, lock it down with Remote Access Policies (RAPs), add remote access profiles for security, and control access with Bandwidth Allocation Protocol (BAP). In this lesson, you explore these configurable options.

After this lesson, you will be able to

- Explain how to allow inbound connections
- Create a RAP
- Describe how to configure a remote access profile
- Describe how to configure BAP

Estimated lesson time: 45 minutes

Allowing Inbound Connections

When Routing and Remote Access is started for the first time, Windows 2000 automatically creates five PPTP and five L2TP ports, as illustrated in Figure 12.3. The number of VPN ports that are available to any remote access server is not limited by the hardware and can be configured. You can configure VPN ports under Ports in the console tree of Routing and Remote Access.

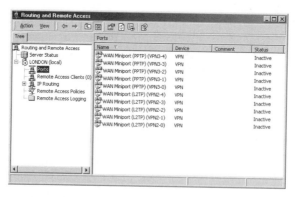

Figure 12.3 Routing and Remote Access ports

Creating a Remote Access Policy (RAP)

You can also add a parallel port by configuring Ports. Serial communication ports shows up only after a modem is installed for the Routing and Remote Access computer. Both types of ports can be configured for inbound and outbound connections.

RAPs are a named set of conditions, as illustrated in Figure 12.4, that are used to define who has remote access to the network and what the characteristics of that connection will be. Conditions for accepting or rejecting connections can be based on many different criteria, such as day and time, group membership, type of service, and so forth. Characteristics of the connection could be configured, for example, as an ISDN connection that can last only 30 minutes and that will not allow Hypertext Transfer Protocol (HTTP) packets.

Note RAPs are shared between routing and remote access and IAS. They can be configured from either tool.

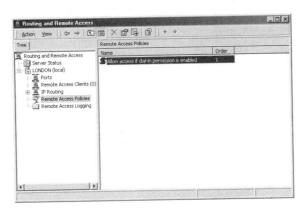

Figure 12.4 Routing and Remote Access policies

RAPs can be created, deleted, renamed, and reordered from the IAS administration tool or the Routing and Remote Access Manager. Note that there is no Save option, so it is not possible to save a copy to floppy disk. The order of policies is significant because the first matching policy will be used to accept or reject the connection.

Note Remote Access Policies are not stored in Active Directory; they are stored locally in the IAS.MDB file. Policies need to be created manually on each server. Remote Access Policies are applied to users in a Mixed-mode domain, even though the user's dial-in permission can only be set to Allow Access or Deny Access, as illustrated in Figure 12.5 (Control Access Through Remote Access Policy is not available on Mixed-mode domain controllers). If the user's permission is Allow Access, the user still must meet the conditions set forth in a policy before being allowed to connect.

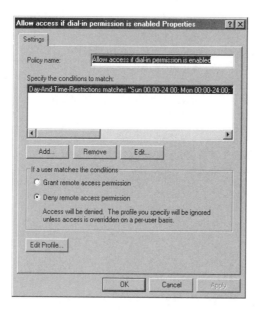

Figure 12.5 Configuring Remote Access policies

Conditions

Conditions can be added to a RAP in order for the system to grant or deny remote access permission. This works in conjunction with the dial-in permission associated with the user to determine whether the user is given access. The flowchart in Figure 12.6 shows the logic used to decide whether the connection request is granted or denied.

Note If no Remote Access Policy exists (if the default policy is deleted, for example), users will not be able to access the network, regardless of their individual Routing and Remote Access permission settings.

By using this flowchart, one can predict the outcome of a connection request for any situation. For example, a user's dial-in property is set to Control Access Through Remote Access Policy and the RAP is the default Allow Access If Dial-In Permission Is Enabled (the policy is to deny access, and the condition is to permit any day, any time). By following the flowchart, it can be seen that the user connection attempt will be rejected.

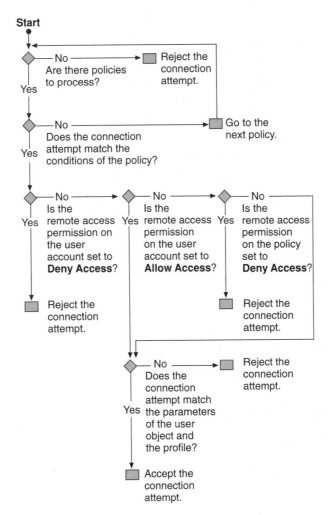

Start

◆ — No ——→ ▣ Reject the connection attempt.
Are there policies to process?
Yes

◆ — No ———————————→ ▣ Go to the next policy.
Does the connection attempt match the conditions of the policy?
Yes

◆ — No ——→ ◆ — No ——→ ◆ — No —
Is the | Is the | Is the
Yes remote access Yes remote access Yes remote access
permission on | permission | permission
the user | on the user | on the policy
account set to | account set to | set to
Deny Access? | **Allow Access**? | **Deny Access**?

▣ Reject the connection attempt.   ▣ Reject the connection attempt.

◆ — No ——→ ▣ Reject the connection attempt.
Does the connection attempt match
Yes the parameters of the user object and the profile?

▣ Accept the connection attempt.

Figure 12.6 Flowchart of Remote Access Policy

However, if the user's dial-in property (illustrated in Figure 12.7) is set to Allow Access and the default policy mentioned earlier is used, the user connection attempt will be accepted.

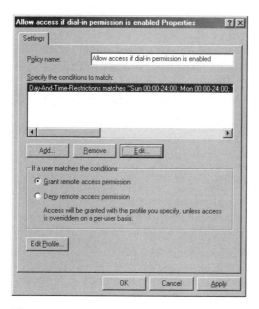

Figure 12.7 Setting dial-in properties to grant access

Grant or Deny Access

Policies can be configured to either grant or deny access. This works in conjunction with the user object's dial-in permission to decide whether or not a user is given access, by means of the logic shown in Figure 12.11.

Caller ID

Caller ID verifies that the caller is calling from the telephone number specified. If caller ID is configured, support for the passing of caller ID information all the way from the caller to Routing and Remote Access is required, or the connection attempt will be denied.

Note For backwards compatibility with previous versions of Windows NT, RAP, Caller ID, Apply Static Routes, and Assign A Static IP Address are not available in Mixed mode.

Practice: Creating a New Remote Access Policy

In this practice, you create a new policy that allows remote access based on the user's group membership.

Exercise 1: Creating a New Remote Access Policy

1. Using the Routing And Remote Access Administration tool, right-click Remote Access Policies and select New Remote Access Policy.

2. Add a friendly name of "Allow Domain Users," and then click Next.

3. Click Add to add a condition.

4. Select Windows-Groups, and then click Add.

5. Click Add, select Domain Users, and then click Add. Click OK.

6. Click OK to exit the Groups dialog.

7. Click Next, and then select Grant Remote Access Permission.

8. Click Next, and then click Finish.

Configuring a Remote Access Profile

The profile specifies what kind of access the user will be given if the conditions match. There are six different tabs that can be used to configure a profile.

Dial-In Constraints

Constraints on the actual connection are configured in the Edit Dial-In Profile dialog box, on the Constraints tab, as shown in Figure 12.8. Possible settings include idle time disconnect, maximum session time, day and time, telephone number, and media type (ISDN, tunnel, async, and so forth).

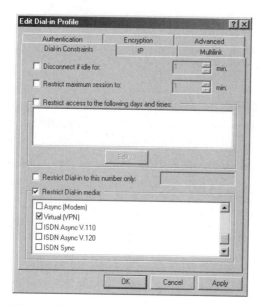

Figure 12.8 The Edit Dial-In Profile dialog box

IP

Configuration for client IP address assignment and IP packet filtering is set on this tab. Packet filters can be set for either inbound or outbound and can be configured for protocol and port.

Multilink

Set Multilink and BAP options here. A line can be dropped if bandwidth drops below a certain level for a given length of time.

Authentication

Authentication protocols such as Password Authentication Protocol (PAP), Challenge Handshake Authentication Protocol (CHAP), and Extensible Authentication Protocol (EAP) are set here.

Encryption

Encryption settings for Microsoft Routing and Remote Access servers are configured here. Options are to prohibit encryption, allow it, or require it.

Advanced

The Advanced tab allows for the configuration of additional network parameters that do not apply to Microsoft Routing and Remote Access servers. Included are standard RADIUS and Ascend attributes, which may apply to other manufacturers' NAS equipment.

Practice: Creating a Policy Filter

In this exercise, you edit the profile of the Allow Access If Dial-In Permission Enabled policy so that users who gain access through that policy cannot ping the Routing and Remote Access server's network, whereas users who are granted access via the Allow Domain Users policy can ping the Routing and Remote Access server.

Exercise 1: Create an ICMP Echo Filter in the Allow Access If Dial-In Permission Is Enabled Policy

1. Right-click the Allow Access If Dial-In Permission Enabled policy and select Properties.

2. Click the Edit Profile button.

3. Select the IP tab.

4. Click the From Client IP Packet filter.

5. Click Add.

6. Click the Destination Network box.

7. For the IP address, type the network number and netmask of the Routing and Remote Access server.

8. For the protocol, select ICMP.

9. Enter **8** for ICMP type, and enter **0** for ICMP code. (ICMP type 8 designates an Echo request.)

10. Click OK to exit the Add/Edit IP filter, and OK to exit the IP Packet Filters Configuration dialog box. Click OK again to exit the dialog box.

Configuring Bandwidth Allocation Protocol (BAP)

BAP and Bandwidth Allocation Control Protocol (BACP) enhance Multilink by dynamically adding or dropping links on demand. BAP and BACP are sometimes used interchangeably to refer to the same bandwidth-on-demand functionality. Both protocols are Point-to-Point (PPP) control protocols and work together to provide bandwidth on demand.

BAP functionality is implemented through a new Link Control Protocol (LCP) option, BACP, and BAP, as described in the following list:

- **Link Discriminator.** A new LCP option used as a unique identifier for each link of a Multilink bundle.

- **BACP.** BACP uses LCP negotiations to elect a "favored peer." The favored peer is used to determine which peer is favored if the peers simultaneously transmit the same BAP request.

- **BAP.** BAP provides a mechanism for link and bandwidth management. Link management allows you to add and drop links. This includes providing telephone numbers as well as type of hardware (modem or ISDN) of the additional available links. Bandwidth management decides when to add and drop links based on link utilization.

BAP and BACP are encapsulated in PPP Data-link layer frames with the following protocol field (in hex). This information may be useful when reading PPP logs. As illustrated in Figure 12.9, you can enable BAP and BACP bandwidth control using the PPP tab on the Connection Properties dialog box.

- C02D for BAP

- C02B for BACP

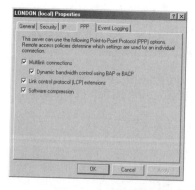

Figure 12.9 Setting PPP options for a remote access policy

▶ **Follow these steps to enable or disable BAP/BACP on a server-wide basis:**

1. In Routing and Remote Access Manager, right-click the server on which you want to enable BAP/BACP, and then click Properties.

2. In the PPP tab, select the Dynamic Bandwidth Control Using BAP Or BACP check box.

BAP policies are enforced through profile settings or Remote Access Policies. Remote Access Policies are accessed from Routing and Remote Access Manager or from IAS Manager.

BAP Additional Phone Numbers

The server can provide the client with additional telephone numbers to dial if extra bandwidth is needed. Using this option, the client only needs to know one telephone number but can still bring up extra lines as needed, as illustrated in Figure 12.10.

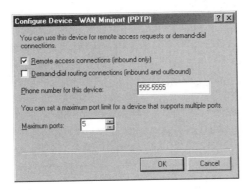

Figure 12.10 BAP additional telephone numbers

1. From the Routing and Remote Access Manager, go to Ports, go to Properties, select a port, and then click Configure.

2. Enter the telephone number of other modems to be used for Multilink.

Lesson Summary

In this lesson, you configured Routing and Remote Access for inbound connections, locked it down with RAPs, added remote access profiles for security, and controlled access with BAP.

Lesson 3: Supporting Virtual Private Networks

A virtual private network (VPN) is defined as the logical channel that allows the sending of data between two computers across an internetwork in a manner that mimics the properties of a dedicated private network. In this lesson, you will learn about VPNs in a routed environment and with the Internet.

After this lesson, you will be able to

- Describe the function of a VPN

- Describe a VPN in a routed environment

- Describe a VPN server with the Internet

Estimated lesson time: 20 minutes

Implementing a VPN

A VPN allows you to send data between two computers across an internetwork in a manner that mimics the properties of a dedicated private network (see Figure 12.11). For example, VPNs allow users working at home or on the road to connect securely to a remote corporate server using the routing infrastructure provided by a public internetwork such as the Internet. From the user's perspective, the VPN is a point-to-point connection between the user's computer and a corporate server. The nature of the intermediate internetwork (hereafter referred to as the transit internetwork) is irrelevant because it appears as if the data is being sent over a dedicated private link.

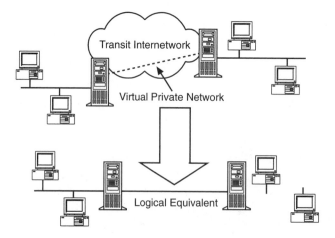

Figure 12.11 Virtual private network diagram

VPN technology also allows a corporation to connect with its branch offices or with other companies over a public internetwork (such as the Internet) while maintaining secure communications. The VPN connection across the Internet logically operates as a dedicated wide area network (WAN) link.

In both of these cases, the secure connection across the transit internetwork appears to the user as a virtual network interface providing private network communication over a public internetwork, hence the term virtual private network.

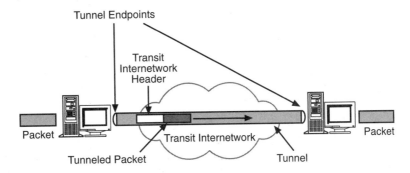

Figure 12.12 A VPN tunnel

Tunneling Basics

Tunneling, also known as encapsulation, is a method of using an internetwork infrastructure to transfer a payload (see Figure 12.12). The payload may be the frames (or packets) of another protocol. Instead of sending the frame as produced by the originating node, the frame is encapsulated with an additional header. The additional header provides routing information so that the encapsulated payload can traverse the intermediate internetwork. The encapsulated packets are then routed between tunnel endpoints over the transit internetwork. Once the encapsulated frames reach their destination on the transit internetwork, the frame is de-encapsulated and forwarded to its final destination.

This entire process (the encapsulation and transmission of packets) is known as tunneling. The logical path through which the encapsulated packets travel through the transit internetwork is called a tunnel.

Types of Tunneling

Tunneling can be achieved in one of the following ways:

- **Point-to-Point Tunneling Protocol (PPTP).** PPTP allows IP, Internetwork Packet Exchange (IPX), or NetBIOS Enhanced User Interface (NetBEUI) traffic to be encrypted and then encapsulated in an IP header to be sent across a corporate IP internetwork or public internetworks like the Internet.

- **Layer Two Tunneling Protocol (L2TP).** L2TP allows IP traffic to be encrypted and then sent over any medium that supports point-to-point datagram delivery, such as IP, frame relay, or Asynchronous Transfer Mode (ATM).

- **IP Security (IPSec) Tunnel mode.** IPSec Tunnel mode allows IP payloads to be encrypted and then encapsulated in an IP header to be sent across a corporate IP internetwork or public internetworks like the Internet.

- **IP-in-IP tunneling.** IP-in-IP tunneling encapsulates an existing IP datagram with an additional IP header. This allows a packet to traverse a network with disjointed capabilities or policies. A popular use of IP-in-IP tunneling is for forwarding multicast traffic through portions of the Internet that do not support multicast routing.

Integrating VPN in a Routed Environment

In some corporate internetworks (see Figure 12.13), the data of a department (such as the Human Resources department) is so sensitive that the department's LAN is physically disconnected from the rest of the corporate internetwork. Although this protects the department's data, it creates information accessibility problems for those users not physically connected to the separate LAN.

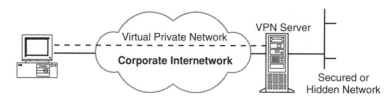

Figure 12.13 Corporate internetwork

VPNs allow the department's LAN to be physically connected to the corporate internetwork but separated by a VPN server. Note that the VPN server does not act as a router between the corporate internetwork and the department LAN. Users on the corporate internetwork having the appropriate credentials (based on a need-to-know policy within the company) can establish a VPN with the VPN server and gain access to the protected resources of the department. Additionally, all communication across the VPN can be encrypted for data confidentiality. For those users not having proper credentials, the department LAN is essentially hidden from view.

Integrating VPN Servers with the Internet

VPN allows users to use their ISP to securely connect to corporate server instead of making toll (or toll-free) calls to the corporate office. Using the connection to the local ISP, a VPN is created between the dial-up user and the corporate VPN server across the Internet (see Figure 12.14).

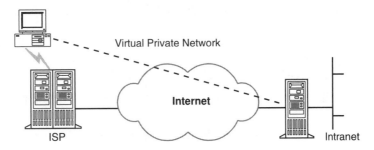

Figure 12.14 Remote Access over the Internet

To connect a network over the Internet (see Figure 12.15), you have two options:

- **Branch office using dedicated lines.** Rather than using conventional methods such as frame relay, both the branch office and the corporate hub routers are connected to the Internet using a local dedicated circuit and local ISP. Utilizing the local ISP connections, a VPN is created between the branch office router and corporate hub router across the Internet.

- **Branch office using a dial-up line.** Rather than having a router at the branch office make a long-distance call (or toll-free call) to a corporate or outsourced NAS, the router at the branch office calls its local ISP. From the connection to the local ISP, a VPN is created between the branch office router and the corporate hub router across the Internet.

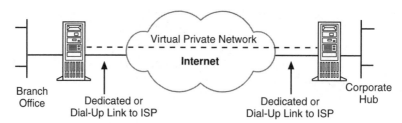

Figure 12.15 VPN over the Internet

Note In both cases, the users are not charged based on the distance between the offices because only local physical links are being used.

For VPN connections to be reliably available, the corporate hub router acting as a VPN server must be connected to a local ISP using a dedicated line. The VPN server must be listening 24 hours a day for incoming VPN traffic. Although this is possible with a dial-up connection, it is less reliable because dynamically assigned IP addresses are commonly used and the connection may not be persistent.

Practice: Creating VPN Interfaces

In this practice, you will create VPN interfaces on each router.

Exercise 1: Creating a Router Interface

1. From the Routing and Remote Access Manager, right-click Routing Interfaces and choose New Demand-Dial Interface, and then click Next.

2. Name the interface the name of the remote router you will be connecting to.

3. On the Connection Type page, select Connect Using Virtual Private Network (VPN), and then click Next.

4. On the VPN Type page, select L2TP, and then click Next.

5. Enter the IP address of the router you will be connecting to, and then click Next.

6. On the Protocols And Security page, check Route IP Packet On This Interface, and Add A User Account So A Remote Router Can Dial In, and then click Next.

   The Dial-In Credentials dialog box appears. This is the user name the remote router will be dialing in with. The name is grayed because it is the name of the interface you are creating.

7. Click Next.

8. Enter the local router name in the Dial-Out Credentials dialog box. This is the user name this router will use when connecting to the remote router. This user name will match the name of a demand-dial interface on the remote router. Leave Domain and Password blank, and then click Next.

9. Click Finish.

10. Repeat steps 1 to 9 on the other router.

Note When creating a router-to-router tunnel over a public network, filters should be set on the external router interfaces to allow only the tunneled traffic.

Once the router interfaces are created for both routers, you need to exchange the routes using Auto Static Update.

11. From the Routing and Remote Access Manager, go to IP Routing, General.

12. Right-click the demand-dial interface and choose Update Routes.

13. Repeat steps 11 and 12 on the other router.

14. To view the routes received during the Auto Static Update, from the Routing and Remote Access Manager, go to IP Routing, Static Routes.

    The routes should appear in the dialog box.

15. To test the tunnel, from Router 1, ping the IP address of Router 2.

    The demand-dial tunnel should be initiated and the ping should succeed.

Lesson Summary

A VPN is created when you send data between two computers across an internetwork in a manner that mimics the properties of a dedicated private network. In this lesson, you learned about VPNs in a routed environment and with the Internet.

Lesson 4: Supporting Multilink Connections

Multilink was first introduced in Windows NT 4.0 Remote Access Service. It enables multiple physical links to be combined into one logical link. Typically, two or more ISDN lines or modem links are bundled together for greater bandwidth. In this lesson, you learn about Multilink connections.

After this lesson, you will be able to

- Explain Multilink connections

Estimated lesson time: 10 minutes

Point-to-Point Protocol

The PPP was designed to send data across dial-up or dedicated point-to-point connections. PPP encapsulates IP, IPX, and NetBEUI packets within PPP frames, and then transmits the PPP-encapsulated packets across a point-to-point link. PPP can be used between routers over dedicated links or by a Remote Access Service client and server over dial-up links. PPP is made up of the following three main components, whose functions are described in the following list.

- **Encapsulation.** This allows the multiplexing of multiple transport protocols over the same link.

- **LCP.** PPP defines an extensible LCP for establishing, configuring, and testing the Data-Link connection. LCP provides the handshake for encapsulation format, packet size, bringing up or dropping the link, and authentication. Some examples of authentication protocols include PAP, CHAP, and EAP.

- **Network Control Protocol.** Network Control Protocols (NCPs) provide specific configuration needs for their respective transport protocols. For example, IPCP is the IP Control Protocol.

Note More information can be found on PPP and Multilink in RFC 1661: The Point-to-Point Protocol, and RFC 1990: PPP Multilink.

Multilink PPP

Multilink was first introduced in Windows NT 4.0 Remote Access Service. It enables multiple physical links to be combined into one logical link. Typically, two or more ISDN lines or modem links are bundled together for greater bandwidth. Support for Multilink is implemented through:

- **A new LCP option.** The ability to support Multilink is negotiated during PPP's LCP phase.

- **A new PPP network protocol.** A new PPP network protocol was created called MP (Multilink PPP). MP appears to PPP as a normal PPP payload. MP will resequence and recombine packets before handing them off to the actual transport protocol such as TCP/IP.

MP is encapsulated in PPP Data-link layer frames with the 003D hex protocol field. This information may be useful when reading PPP logs.

Lesson Summary

Multilink was first introduced in Windows NT 4.0 Remote Access Service. It allows the combining of multiple physical links into one logical link. Typically, two or more ISDN lines or modem links are bundled together for greater bandwidth.

Lesson 5: Using Routing and Remote Access with DHCP

When a Routing and Remote Access address pool is configured to use DHCP, no DHCP packets go over the wire to the Routing and Remote Access clients. In this lesson, you learn how Routing and Remote Access handles DHCP.

After this lesson, you will be able to

- Explain Routing and Remote Access and DHCP
- Describe how to implement the DHCP relay agent

Estimated lesson time: 10 minutes

Routing and Remote Access and DHCP

When a Routing and Remote Access address pool is configured to use DHCP, no DHCP packets go over the wire to the Routing and Remote Access clients. Routing and Remote Access uses DHCP to lease addresses in blocks of 10, and stores them in the registry. The network information center (NIC) used to lease these DHCP addresses is configurable in the user interface if two or more NICs are in the server. In earlier versions of Windows, the remote access server would renew and maintain these DHCP addresses indefinitely. In Windows 2000, the DHCP leases are released when Routing and Remote Access is shut down.

The number of addresses that Routing and Remote Access will lease at a time is configurable in the registry under \System\CurrentControlSet\Services\ RemoteAccess\Parameters\Ip\InitialAddressPoolSize. The value in this key is the number of DHCP leases Routing and Remote Access will initially reserve. These addresses are stored in the registry and are given to Routing and Remote Access clients. When the initial pool is used up, another block of this size is leased.

DHCP Relay Agent

The DHCP relay agent can now be used over Routing and Remote Access. The Routing and Remote Access client receives an IP address from the Routing and Remote Access server, but may use DHCPINFORM packets to obtain Windows Internet Name Service (WINS) and Domain Name System (DNS) addresses, domain name, or other DHCP options. DHCPINFORM messages are used to obtain option information without getting an IP address.

Note Sending the domain name using DHCPINFORM is of particular importance because PPP does configure this information.

DNS and WINS addresses received using DHCPINFORM override addresses obtained from the Routing and Remote Access server.

Practice: Configuring the DHCP Relay Agent to Work over Routing and Remote Access

Exercise 1: Configuring a DHCP Relay Agent

1. In the Routing and Remote Access Manager, right-click General under IP Routing, and select New Routing Protocol.

2. Choose DHCP Relay Agent, and then click OK.

3. Highlight DHCP Relay Agent, and then right-click Properties.

   The DHCP Relay Agent Properties dialog box appears, allowing you to configure the IP addresses of any DHCP server.

4. Click OK to close the DHCP Relay Agent Properties dialog box.

5. Right-click the DHCP Relay Agent and choose New Interface.

6. Select Internal (Internal represents the virtual interface connected to all Routing and Remote Access clients), and then click OK.

7. Click OK to close the DHCP Relay Agent Internal Properties dialog box.

Lesson Summary

When a Routing and Remote Access address pool is configured to use DHCP, no DHCP packets will go over the wire to the Routing and Remote Access clients. In this lesson, you learned how Routing and Remote Access handles DHCP and DHCP relay agents.

Lesson 6: Managing and Monitoring Remote Access

Managing and monitoring a remote access server can be done with several tools. In this lesson, you learn about remote access logging, accounting, Netsh, Network Monitor, and various resource kit utilities.

After this lesson, you will be able to

- Explain remote access logging
- Describe accounting
- Explain Netsh
- Understand Network Monitor's role in remote access
- List several resource kit utilities to monitor remote access

Estimated lesson time: 30 minutes

Logging User Authentication and Accounting Requests

Internet Authentication Service (IAS) can create log files based on the authentication and accounting requests received from the Network Access Servers (NASs) by collecting these packets in a centralized location. Setting up and using such log files to track authentication information—such as each accept, reject, and automatic account lockout—can help simplify administration of your service. You can set up and use logs to track accounting information—such as logon and logoff records—to help maintain records for billing purposes (see Figure 12.16).

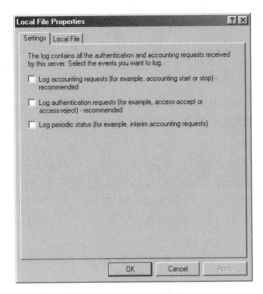

Figure 12.16 Remote Access logging

When you set up logging, you can specify the following:

- The requests to be logged
- The file format for the logs
- The frequency with which new logs are started
- The location where the logs are to be maintained

You can also select the types of requests received by the IAS server that are to be logged.

Accounting requests include the following:

- Accounting-on requests, which are sent by the NAS to indicate that the NAS is online and ready to accept connections
- Accounting-off requests, which are sent by the NAS to indicate that the NAS is going offline
- Accounting-start requests, which are sent by the NAS (after the user is accepted by the IAS server) to indicate the start of a user session
- Accounting-stop requests, which are sent by the NAS to indicate the end of a user session

Authentication requests include the following:

- Authentication requests, which are sent by the NAS on behalf of the connecting user. These entries in the log contain only incoming attributes.

- Authentication accepts and rejects, which are sent by IAS to the NAS to indicate whether the user should be accepted or rejected. These entries contain only outgoing attributes.

- Periodic status, to obtain interim accounting requests sent by some NASs during sessions.

- Accounting-interim requests, which are sent periodically by the NAS during a user session (if the acct-interim-interval attribute is configured in the remote access profile on the IAS server to support periodic requests).

Initially, it is recommended that you select the first two options and refine your logging methods after you determine which data best matches your needs.

When you set up your servers, specify whether new logs are started daily, weekly, monthly, or when the log reaches a specific size. You can also specify that a single log is maintained continually (regardless of file size), but this is not recommended. The file naming convention for logs is determined by the log period you select. Because changing this option can result in overwriting of existing logs, you should copy logs to a separate file before changing the log period. By default, the log files are located in the %systemroot%\System32\ LogFiles folder, but you have the option of specifying a different location.

Log File Records

Attributes are recorded in Unicode Translation Format-8 (UTF-8) encoding in a comma-delimited format. The format of the records in a log file depends on the file format.

- In IAS-formatted log files, each record starts with a fixed-format header, which consists of the NAS IP address, user name, record date, record time, service name, and computer name, which is followed by attribute-value pairs.

- In database-import log files, each record contains attribute values in a consistent sequence, starting with the computer name and are followed by the service name, record date, and record time. An NAS may not use all of the attributes specified in the database-import log format, but the comma-delimited location for each of these predefined attributes is maintained, even for attributes that have no value specified in a record.

Accounting

Routing and Remote Access can be configured to log accounting information in the following locations:

- Locally stored log files when configured for Windows accounting. The information logged and where it is stored are configured from the properties of the Remote Access Logging folder in the Routing and Remote Access snap-in.

- At a RADIUS server when configured for RADIUS accounting. If the RADIUS server is an IAS server, the log files are stored on the IAS server. The information logged and where it is stored are configured from the properties of the Remote Access Logging folder in the Internet Authentication Service snap-in.

Configuration of the Routing and Remote Access accounting provider is done from the Security tab from the properties of a remote access router in the Routing and Remote Access snap-in, as shown in Figure 12.17, or by using the Netsh tool.

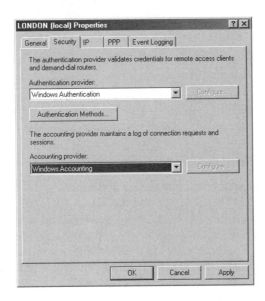

Figure 12.17 Remote Access accounting

Netsh Command-Line Tool

Netsh is a command-line and scripting tool for Windows 2000 networking components for local or remote computers. Netsh is supplied with Windows 2000. Netsh allows you to save a configuration script in a text file for archival purposes or for configuring other servers.

Netsh is a shell that can support multiple Windows 2000 components through the addition of Netsh helper dynamic-link libraries (DLLs). A Netsh helper DLL extends Netsh functionality by providing additional commands to monitor or configure a specific Windows 2000 networking component. Each Netsh helper DLL provides a context (a group of commands for a specific networking component). Within each context, subcontexts can exist. For example, within the routing context, the subcontexts IP and IPX exist to group IP routing and IPX routing commands together.

For Routing and Remote Access, Netsh has the following contexts:

- **ras.** Use commands in the ras context to configure remote access configuration.

- **aaaa.** Use commands in the aaaa context to configure the AAAA component used by both Routing and Remote Access and IAS.

- **routing.** Use commands in the routing context to configure IP and IPX routing.

- **interface.** Use commands in the interface context to configure demand-dial interfaces.

Network Monitor

Network Monitor enables you to detect and troubleshoot problems on LANs and on WANs, including Routing and Remote Access links. With Network Monitor you can identify network traffic patterns and network problems. For example, you can locate client-to-server connection problems, find a computer that makes a disproportionate number of work requests, capture frames (packets) directly from the network, display and filter the captured frames, and identify unauthorized users on your network.

Resource Kit Utilities

The following are Resource Kit utilities that make the job of managing and monitoring Routing and Remote Access easier.

RASLIST.EXE

The RASLIST.EXE command-line tool displays Routing and Remote Access server announcements from a network. Raslist listens for Routing and Remote Access server announcements on all active network cards in the computer from which it is run. Its output shows which card received the announcement. Raslist is a monitoring tool. It may take a few seconds for the data to begin to appear; data continues to appear until the tool is closed.

RASSRVMON.EXE

By using the RASSRVMON.EXE tool, you can monitor the remote access server activities on your server in greater detail than the standard Windows tools allow. Rassrvmon provides the following monitoring information:

- Server information, such as the time of first call to server, time of most recent call to server, total calls, total bytes passed through server, peak connection count, total connect time, currently connected users, and their connection information.

- Per Port information, which is the time of first call to port, time of most recent call to port, total connections to this port since server started, total bytes passed on this port, total errors on this port, and current port status.

- Summary information, such as statistics kept for each unique user/computer combination since the start of the monitoring, which include total connect time, total bytes transmitted, connection count, average connect time, and total error count.

- Individual connection information, which includes per-connection statistics for each connection: user name/computer name, IP address, connection establishment time, duration, bytes transmitted, error count, and line speed.

To allow for more flexibility, alerts can be set up to run a program of your choice. This gives you the flexibility to send mail, a page, a network popup, or any other action you can automate with an executable file name or a batch script.

RASUSERS.EXE

RASUSERS.EXE lets you list for a domain or a server all user accounts that have been granted permission to dial in to the network via Routing and Remote Access, a feature of Windows 2000 that implements remote access functionality.

TRACEENABLE.EXE

TRACEENABLE.EXE is a graphical user interface–based tool that enables tracing and displays current tracing options. Windows 2000 Routing and Remote Access has an extensive tracing capability that you can use to troubleshoot complex network problems. Tracing records internal component variables, function calls, and interactions. Separate Routing and Remote Access components can be independently enabled to log tracing information to files (file tracing). You must enable the tracing function by changing settings in the Windows 2000 registry using TRACEENABLE.EXE.

Using TRACEENABLE.EXE

As each tracing item is selected in the combo box, the values are displayed. Make your changes, and then click Set. This writes your changes to the registry. To get console tracing, you must turn it on for the component and turn it on with the master check box at the top of the Trace Enable window. For example, you would follow these steps to generate a log file for PPP:

1. Select PPP from the drop-down list.
2. Click Enable File Tracing.
3. Click Set.

    Tracing is now enabled for this component. In most cases the log file is created in %windir%\tracing.

Lesson Summary

Managing and monitoring a remote access server is done with several tools. In this lesson, you learned about remote access logging, accounting, Netsh, Network Monitor, and various resource kit utilities.

Lesson 7: Implementing Network Security

As you plan your network, you should implement security technologies that are appropriate for your organization. Addressing these issues early in your Windows 2000 deployment planning ensures that security cannot be breached and that you are ready to provide secure networking facilities when needed. In this lesson, you learn how to implement security on your network.

After this lesson, you will be able to

- Describe sections of a network security plan
- Identify network security risks
- Describe Windows 2000 security features
- Describe how to secure a connection between your network and the Internet

Estimated lesson time: 35 minutes

Planning for Network Security

Even if you are confident that you have implemented a secure network environment, it is important for you to review your security strategies considering the capabilities of Windows 2000. Some of the new network security technologies in Windows 2000 might cause you to rework your security plan. As you develop your network security plan, you should

- Assess your network security risks
- Determine your server size and placement requirements
- Prepare your staff
- Create and publish security policies and procedures
- Use a formal methodology to create a deployment plan for your security technologies
- Identify your user groups and their specific needs and security risks

Assessing Network Security Risks

Although the ability to share and obtain information is very beneficial, it also presents numerous security risks, which are described in Table 12.1.

Table 12.1 Network Security Risks

Security risk	Description
Identity interception	The intruder discovers the user name and password of a valid user. This can occur by a variety of methods, both social and technical.
Masquerade	An unauthorized user pretends to be a valid user. For example, a user assumes the Internet Protocol (IP) address of a trusted system and uses it to gain the access rights that are granted to the impersonated device or system.
Replay attack	The intruder records a network exchange between a user and a server and plays it back at a later time to impersonate the user.
Data interception	If data is moved across the network as plaintext, unauthorized persons can monitor and capture the data.
Manipulation	The intruder causes network data to be modified or corrupted. Unencrypted network financial transactions are vulnerable to manipulation. Viruses can corrupt network data.
Repudiation	Network-based business and financial transactions are compromised if the recipient of the transaction cannot be certain who sent the message.
Macro viruses	Application-specific viruses exploit the macro language of sophisticated documents and spreadsheets.
Denial of service	The intruder floods a server with requests that consume system resources and either crash the server or prevent useful work from being done. Crashing the server sometimes provides opportunities to penetrate the system.
Malicious mobile code	This term refers to malicious code running as an autoexecuted ActiveX control or Java Applet uploaded from the Internet on a Web server.
Misuse of privileges	An administrator of a computing system knowingly or mistakenly uses full privileges over the operating system to obtain private data.
Trojan horse	This is a general term for a malicious program that masquerades as a desirable and harmless utility.
Social engineering attack	Sometimes breaking into a network is as simple as calling new employees, telling them you are from the IT department, and asking them to verify their password for your records.

Competitors could attempt to gain access to proprietary product information, or unauthorized users could attempt to maliciously modify Web pages or overload computers so that they are unusable. Additionally, employees might access confidential information. It is important to prevent these types of security risks to ensure that your company's business functions proceed undisturbed.

Network Authentication

Authentication is the process of identifying users who attempt to connect to a network. Users who are authenticated on the network can utilize network resources based on their access permissions. To provide authentication to network users, you establish user accounts. This is critical for security management. Without authentication, resources such as files are accessible to unauthorized users.

Network Security Plan

To make sure that only the appropriate people have access to resources and data, you should plan your network security strategies well. This also provides you with accountability because you can track how network resources are used. Figure 12.18 illustrates the primary steps for determining your network security strategies.

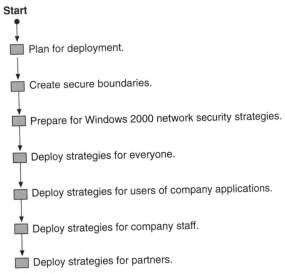

Start

☐ Plan for deployment.

☐ Create secure boundaries.

☐ Prepare for Windows 2000 network security strategies.

☐ Deploy strategies for everyone.

☐ Deploy strategies for users of company applications.

☐ Deploy strategies for company staff.

☐ Deploy strategies for partners.

Figure 12.18 Primary steps for determining network security strategies

Preparing Your Staff

Security technologies need to be deployed and managed by very capable and trustworthy people. They must integrate the entire network and network security infrastructure so that you can eliminate or minimize weaknesses. As the environment and requirements change, they must continually maintain the integrity of the network security infrastructure.

A critical factor for ensuring the success of your network security staff is to be sure they are well trained and kept up to date as technologies change. The staff needs to take time to learn Windows 2000, particularly its network security technologies. They also need to have opportunities to reinforce their training by experimentation and practical application. Windows 2000 security features are described in Table 12.2.

Table 12.2 Windows 2000 Security Features

Feature	Description
Security templates	Allows administrators to set various global and local security settings, including security-sensitive registry values; access controls on files and the registry; and security on system services.
Kerberos authentication	The primary security protocol for access within or across Windows 2000 domains. Provides mutual authentication of clients and servers and supports delegation and authorization through proxy mechanisms.
Public key infrastructure (PKI)	You can use integrated PKI for strong security in multiple Windows 2000 Internet and enterprise services, including extranet-based communications.
Smart card infrastructure	Windows 2000 includes a standard model for connecting smart card readers and cards with computers and device-independent application programming interfaces to enable applications that are smart card-aware.
IP Security Protocol (IPSec) management	IPSec supports network-level authentication, data integrity, and encryption to secure intranet, extranet, and Internet Web communications.
NT file system (NTFS) encryption	Public key–based NTFS can be enabled on a per-file or per-directory basis.

Although security technologies can be very effective, security itself combines those technologies with good business and social practices. No matter how advanced and well implemented the technology is, it is only as good as the methods used in employing and managing it.

Planning Distributed Network Security

Distributed network security involves the coordination of many security functions on a computer network to implement an overall security policy. Distributed security enables users to log on to appropriate computer systems and allows them to find and use the information they need. Much of the information on computer networks is available for anyone to read, but only a small group of people is allowed to update it. If the information is sensitive or private, only authorized individuals or groups are allowed to read the files. Protection and privacy of information transferred over public telephone networks, the Internet, and even segments of internal company networks are also a concern.

A typical security plan includes sections like those shown in Table 12.3. However, you should remember that your network security deployment plan could contain additional sections. The following are suggested as a minimum.

Table 12.3 Network Security Plan Sections

Section in the plan	Description
Security risks	Enumerates the types of security hazards that affect your enterprise.
Security strategies	Describes the general security strategies necessary to meet the risks.
PKI policies	Includes your plans for deploying certification authorities for internal and external security features.
Security group descriptions	Includes descriptions of security groups and their relationship to one another. This section maps group policies to security groups.
Group Policy	Includes how you configure security Group Policy settings, such as network password policies.
Network logon and authentication strategies	Includes authentication strategies for logging on to the network and for using remote access and smart card to log on.

continues

Table 12.3 Network Security Plan Sections *(continued)*

Section in the plan	Description
Information security strategies	Includes how you implement information security solutions, such as secure e-mail and secure Web communications.
Administrative policies	Includes policies for delegation of administrative tasks and monitoring of audit logs to detect suspicious activity.

Additionally, your organization might need more than one security plan. The amount of plans you have depends on the scope of your deployment. An international organization might need separate plans for each of its major subdivisions or locations, whereas a regional organization might need only one plan. Organizations with distinct policies for different user groups might need a network security plan for each group.

Testing Your Security Plans

You should always test and revise your network security plans by using test labs that represent the computing environments for your organization. In addition, you should conduct pilot programs to further test and refine your network security plans.

Internet Connection Issues

Today, most organizations want their computer infrastructure connected to the Internet because it provides valuable services to their staff and customers. A connection to the Internet allows your organization's staff to use e-mail to communicate with people around the world and to obtain information and files from a vast number of sources. It also allows your customers to obtain information and services from your organization at any time. In addition, your organization's staff can use company resources from home, hotels, or anywhere else they might be, and partners can use special facilities to allow them to work more effectively with your company. However, the services made available through Internet connection can be misused, which makes it necessary to employ network security strategies.

Implementing a Firewall

To secure your organization's network for access to and from the Internet, you need to put a firewall between the two, as illustrated in Figure 12.19. The firewall provides connectivity to the Internet for company staff while minimizing the risks that connectivity introduces. At the same time, it prevents access to computers on your network from the Internet, except for those computers authorized to have such access.

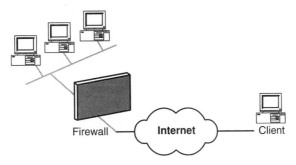

Figure 12.19 Firewall

A firewall employs packet filtering to allow or disallow the flow of very specific types of network traffic. IP packet filtering provides a way for you to define precisely what IP traffic is allowed to cross the firewall. IP packet filtering is important when you connect private intranets to public networks like the Internet. Many firewalls are also capable of detecting and defending against complex attacks.

Firewalls often act as proxy servers or routers because they forward traffic between a private network and a public network. The firewall or proxy server software examines all network packets on each interface to determine their intended address. If they meet specified criteria, the packets are forwarded to the recipient on the other network interface. The firewall may simply route packets, or it may act as a proxy server and translate the IP addresses on the private network.

Microsoft Proxy Server

Microsoft Proxy Server provides both proxy server and some firewall functions. Proxy Server runs on Windows 2000, and both need to be configured properly to provide full network security. If you have a version of Proxy Server earlier than 2.0 with Service Pack 1, you need to upgrade it for Windows 2000 compatibility when you upgrade the server to Windows 2000.

In many cases, the volume of traffic between a company network and the Internet is more than one proxy server can handle. In these situations, you can use multiple proxy servers; the traffic is coordinated among them automatically. For users on both the Internet and intranet sides, there appears to be only one proxy server.

Note Procedures for using Microsoft Proxy Server are included with the product. For more information about Microsoft Proxy Server and for details about Microsoft security technologies, go to the Web Resources page at *http://www.microsoft.com/windows2000/reskit/webresources*.

When you have a proxy server in place, complete with monitoring facilities and properly prepared staff, you can connect your network to an external network. You need only to be confident that the services you have authorized are available, and the risk for misuse is almost nonexistent. This environment requires diligent monitoring and maintenance, but you will also be ready to consider providing other secure networking services.

Lesson Summary

You should plan security strategies to make sure that only the appropriate people have access to resources and data on your network. In addition, you should implement security technologies that are appropriate for your organization. Always test and revise your network security plans by testing them in simulated environments that represent the computing environments for your organization. You can implement a firewall to secure your organization's network for access to and from the Internet. Microsoft Proxy Server provides both proxy server and firewall functions running with Windows 2000 Server.

Lesson 8: Configuring Routing and Remote Access Security

Remote access enables clients to connect to your network from a remote location through various hardware devices including network interface cards and modems. Once clients obtain a remote access connection, they can use network resources such as files in the same way as they would use a client computer directly connected to your LAN. In this lesson, you learn how to configure security for remote access on your network.

After this lesson, you will be able to

- Create a remote access policy
- Configure remote access security
- Configure encryption protocols
- Configure authentication protocols
- Configure and troubleshoot network protocol security

Estimated lesson time: 60 minutes

Overview of Remote Access

Routing and Remote Access is the service that lets remote users connect to your local network by telephone. Remote access provides an opportunity for intruders to access your network; therefore, Windows 2000 provides multiple security features to permit authorized access while limiting opportunities for mischief. When a client dials a remote access server on your network, the client is granted access to the network if the following are true:

- The request matches one of the remote access policies defined for the server.
- The user's account is enabled for remote access.
- Client/server authentication succeeds.

After the client has been identified and authorized, access to the network can be limited to specific servers, subnets, and protocol types, depending on the remote access profile of the client. Otherwise, all services typically available to a user connected to a LAN (including file and print sharing, Web server access, and messaging) are enabled by means of the remote access connection.

Configuring Protocols for Security

Consider that someone can intercept a user name and password while a user is attempting to log on to the Routing and Remote Access server using techniques similar to a wiretap. To prevent this, Routing and Remote Access can use a secure user authentication method, which includes the following:

- **Challenge Handshake Authentication Protocol (CHAP).** CHAP is designed to address the concern of passing passwords in plaintext. CHAP is the most common dial-up authentication protocol used. Because the algorithm for calculating CHAP responses is well known, it is very important that passwords be carefully chosen and that they are sufficiently long. CHAP passwords that are common words or names are vulnerable to dictionary attacks if they can be discovered by comparing responses to the CHAP challenge with every entry in a dictionary. Passwords that are not sufficiently long can be discovered by persistence by comparing the CHAP response to sequential trials until a match to the user's response is found.

- **Microsoft Challenge Handshake Authentication Protocol (MS-CHAP).** MS-CHAP is a variant of CHAP that does not require a plaintext version of the password on the authenticating server. MS-CHAP passwords are stored more securely at the server but have the same vulnerabilities to dictionary and brute force attacks as CHAP. In MS-CHAP the challenge response is calculated with a Message Digest 4 (MD4)-hashed version of the password and the network access server (NAS) challenge. This enables authentication over the Internet to a Windows 2000 domain controller (or a Windows NT 4.0 domain controller on which the update has not been installed).

- **Password Authentication Protocol (PAP).** PAP passes a password as a string from the user's computer to the NAS device. When the NAS forwards the password, it is encrypted using the RADIUS shared secret as an encryption key. PAP is the most flexible protocol because passing a plaintext password to the authentication server enables that server to compare the password with nearly any storage format. For example, UNIX passwords are stored as one-way encrypted strings that cannot be decrypted. PAP passwords can be compared to these strings by reproducing the encryption method. Because it uses a plaintext version of the password, PAP has a number of security vulnerabilities. Although the RADIUS protocol encrypts the password, it is transmitted as plaintext across the dial-up connection.

- **Shiva Password Authentication Protocol (SPAP).** SPAP is a reversible encryption mechanism employed by Shiva remote access servers. A Windows 2000 remote access client can use SPAP to authenticate itself to a Shiva remote access server. A remote access client running Windows 32-bit operating systems can use SPAP to authenticate itself to a Windows 2000 remote access server. SPAP is more secure than PAP but less secure than CHAP or MS-CHAP. SPAP offers no protection against remote server impersonation.

  Like PAP, SPAP is a simple exchange of messages. First, the remote access client sends an SPAP Authenticate-Request message to the remote access server containing the remote access client's user name and encrypted password. Next, the remote access server decrypts the password, checks the user name and password, and sends back either an SPAP Authenticate-Ack message when the user's credentials are correct, or an SPAP Authenticate-Nak message with a reason why the user's credentials were not correct.

- **Extensible Authentication Protocol (EAP).** EAP is an extension to PPP that allows for arbitrary authentication mechanisms to be employed for the validation of a PPP connection. With PPP authentication protocols such as MS-CHAP and SPAP, a specific authentication mechanism is chosen during the link establishment phase. Then, during the connection authentication phase, the negotiated authentication protocol is used to validate the connection. The authentication protocol itself is a fixed series of messages sent in a specific order. Architecturally, EAP is designed to allow authentication plug-in modules at both the client and server ends of a connection. By installing an EAP-type library file on both the remote access client and the remote access server, a new EAP type can be supported. This presents vendors with the opportunity to supply a new authentication scheme at any time. EAP provides the highest flexibility in authentication uniqueness and variations.

Practice: Using Security Protocols for a Virtual Private Network Connection

For a VPN to be secure, you need to use an appropriate security protocol. In this practice, you will configure a VPN to use the CHAP Authentication method.

Exercise 1: Enabling your Virtual Private Network (VPN) Server to use the CHAP Authentication Method

1. Click Start, point to Programs, point to Administrative Tools, and then click Routing And Remote Access.

2. Right-click the server name for which you want to enable authentication protocols, and then click Properties.

   The Server Properties dialog box appears.

3. In the Security tab, click Authentication Methods.

   The Authentication Methods dialog box appears.

4. In the Authentication Methods dialog box, select Encrypted Authentication, as illustrated in Figure 12.20, and then click OK.

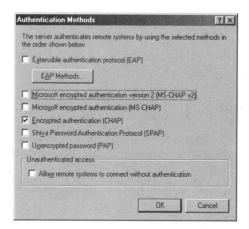

Figure 12.20 Using the CHAP authentication method

5. Click OK to close the Server Properties dialog box.

Creating Remote Access Policies

Routing and Remote Access and IAS both use remote access policies to determine whether to accept or reject connection attempts. In both cases, the remote access policies are stored locally. Policy is now dictated on a per-call basis.

With remote access policies, you can grant or deny authorization by time of day or day of the week, by the Windows 2000 group to which the remote access user belongs, by the type of connection being requested (dial-up networking or VPN connection), and so forth.

Local versus Centralized Policy Management

Because remote access policies are stored locally on either a remote access server or an IAS server, in order to centrally manage a single set of remote access policies for multiple remote access or VPN servers, you must do the following:

1. Install the Windows 2000 IAS as a RADIUS server on a computer.

2. Configure IAS with RADIUS clients that correspond to each of the Windows 2000 remote access or VPN servers.

3. On the IAS server, create the central set of policies that all Windows 2000 remote access servers are using.

4. Configure each of the Windows 2000 remote access servers as a RADIUS client to the IAS server.

After you configure a Windows 2000 remote access server as a RADIUS client to an IAS server, the local remote access policies stored on the remote access server are no longer used. Centralized management of remote access policies is also used when you have remote access servers that are running Windows NT 4.0 with the Routing and Remote Access Service (RRAS). You can configure the server that is running Windows NT 4.0 with RRAS as a RADIUS client to an IAS server. You cannot configure a remote access server that is running Windows NT 4.0 without RRAS to take advantage of centralized remote access policies.

Using Encryption Protocols

You can use data encryption to protect the data that is sent between the remote access client and the remote access server. Data encryption is important for financial institutions, law-enforcement and government agencies, and corporations that require secure data transfer. For installations where data confidentiality is required, the network administrator can set the remote access server to require encrypted communications. Users who connect to that server must encrypt their data, or the connection attempt is denied.

For VPN connections, you protect your data by encrypting it between the ends of the VPN. You should always use data encryption for VPN connections when private data is sent across a public network such as the Internet, where there is always a risk of unauthorized interception.

For dial-up networking connections, you can protect your data by encrypting it on the communications link between the remote access client and the remote access server. You should use data encryption when there is a risk of unauthorized interception of transmissions on the communications link between the remote access client and the remote access server. There are two forms of encryption available for demand-dial connections: Microsoft Point-to-Point Encryption (MPPE) and IP Security (IPSec).

- **MPPE.** All PPP connections, including Point-to-Point Tunneling Protocol (PPTP) but not including Layer 2 Tunneling Protocol (L2TP), can use MPPE. MPPE uses the Rivest-Shamir-Adleman (RSA) Cipher 4 (RC4) stream cipher and is only used when either the EAP-Transport Layer Security (TLS) or MS-CHAP (version 1 or version 2) authentication methods are used. MPPE can use 40-bit, 56-bit, or 128-bit encryption keys. The 40-bit key is designed for backwards compatibility and international use. The 56-bit key is designed for international use and adheres to United States encryption export laws. The 128-bit key is designed for North American use. By default, the highest key strength supported by the calling router and answering router is negotiated during the connection establishment process. If the answering router requires a higher key strength than is supported by the calling router, the connection attempt is rejected.

  Note For dial-up networking connections, Windows 2000 uses MPPE.

- **IPSec.** For demand-dial connections using L2TP over IPSec, encryption is determined by the establishment of the IPSec security association (SA). The available encryption algorithms include Data Encryption Standard (DES) with a 56-bit key, and triple DES (3DES), which uses three 56-bit keys and is designed for high-security environments. The initial encryption keys are derived from the IPSec authentication process.

For VPN connections, Windows 2000 uses MPPE with the PPTP, and IPSec encryption with the L2TP.

▶ **Follow these steps to configure encryption for a dial-up connection:**

1. Click Start, point to Programs, point to Administrative Tools, and then click Routing And Remote Access.

2. Under the server name, click Remote Access Policies.

3. In the details pane, right-click the remote access policy you want to configure, and then click Properties.

4. Click Edit Profile.

5. In the Encryption tab, illustrated in Figure 12.21, specify settings as needed, and then click OK.

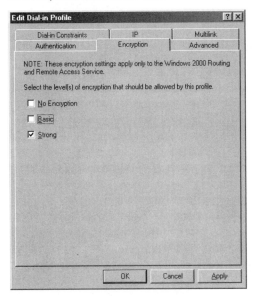

Figure 12.21 Setting the level of encryption

6. Click OK to close the Policy Properties dialog box.

Lesson Summary

Remote access enables clients to connect to your network from a remote location using various hardware devices, including network interface cards and modems. Once a client obtains a remote access connection, he or she can use network resources, such as files, just as when the client computer is directly connected to the LAN. In Windows 2000 you create remote access policies and then configure them for security. You can set the level of encryption and dial-up permissions for remote access.

Lesson 9: Windows 2000 Remote Access Administration Tools

Windows 2000 has tools and technologies to simplify administration of computers in your network. Terminal Services provides access to Windows 2000 and the latest Windows-based applications for client computers. It also allows system administrators to remotely administer network resources. In addition, Windows 2000 provides the Simple Network Management Protocol (SNMP), which allows you to monitor and communicate status information from SNMP agents to network management software. In this lesson, you learn how to use Terminal Services and SNMP to better manage and monitor your network.

After this lesson, you will be able to

- Configure Terminal Server for remote administration
- Install and configure the SNMP service
- Describe how the Windows 2000 SNMP service works

Estimated lesson time: 25 minutes

Windows 2000 Administration Capabilities

With Windows 2000, you can administer computers and services on your network either locally or remotely. Remote administration means using one computer to connect to another computer on a network for management purposes. Windows 2000 allows you to perform administration tasks for all computers on a network centrally, rather than at each computer's physical location. You can either use third-party management systems or use some of the tools and methods that Windows 2000 provides for remote administration.

Terminal Services

When you enable Terminal Services on a Windows 2000 Server, you either select Remote Administration or Application Server mode, as illustrated in Figure 12.22.

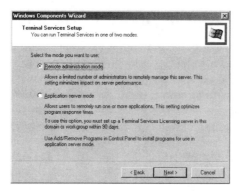

Figure 12.22 Selecting a mode for Terminal Services

Application Server mode allows you to deploy and manage applications from a central location. You can deploy a Windows 2000 interface as well as applications to computers that cannot run Windows 2000. Because Terminal Services is integrated into the Windows 2000 server products, you can run your applications on the server, and provide the user interface to clients that cannot run Windows 2000, such as Windows 3.11 or Windows CE computers connected to a terminal server.

Terminal Services also offers a Remote Administration mode that allows you to access, manage, and troubleshoot clients. Remote Administration mode allows you to remotely administer Windows 2000 servers over any TCP/IP connection, including remote access, Ethernet, the Internet, wireless, WAN, or a VPN. You can install Terminal Services from the Windows Components dialog box of the Add/Remove Programs applet in Control Panel, as illustrated in Figure 12.23.

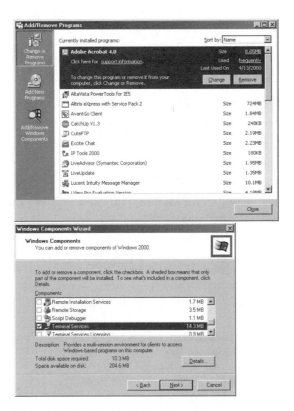

Figure 12.23 Terminal Services option

Using Terminal Server

Although a Remote Desktop Protocol (RDP) connection is configured automatically when Terminal Services is installed, you can use another procedure to make a new connection. Only one RDP connection can be configured for each network adapter in a Terminal server; however, you can configure additional connections using RDP if you install a network adapter for each connection on your computer.

▶ **Follow these steps to install a network adapter:**

1. Click Start, point to Programs, point to Administrative Tools, and then click Terminal Services Configuration.

2. Right-click the Connections tab, and then click Create New Connection.

   The Terminal Services Connection wizard appears.

3. In the first dialog of the wizard, you select a connection type, such as Microsoft RDP 5.0.

4. In the second dialog of the wizard, you set the encryption level to either Low, Medium, or High. You can also select standard Windows authentication.

5. In the third dialog of the wizard, you can set remote control options and set the level of control.

6. In the fourth dialog of the wizard, you select the connection name, transport type, and an optional comment.

7. In the fifth dialog of the wizard, you can select one or all network adapters for the transport type, and set the number of connections.

8. Click Finish to close the wizard.

Terminal Services allows a maximum of two concurrent Remote Administration connections that do not require licenses. A negligible amount of disk space, memory, and configuration for Terminal Services clients is required.

▶ **Follow these steps to allow a Terminal Server client computer to log on to a Windows 2000 Terminal Server:**

1. Click Start, point to Programs, point to Administrative Tools, and then click Computer Management.

2. To expand the branches, click the plus symbol (+) next to System Tools, click the plus symbol (+) next to Local Users And Groups, and then click the plus symbol (+) next to Users.

3. Double-click the user that you would like to enable to log on as a Windows NT Terminal Server client.

4. On the Terminal Services Profile tab, click the Allow Logon To Terminal Server check box, as illustrated in Figure 12.24, and then click OK.

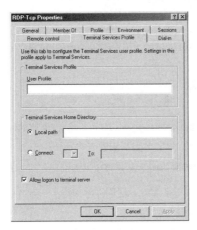

Figure 12.24 Allowing logon to the terminal server

5. Close Computer Management.

6. Click Start, point to Programs, point to Administrative Tools, and then click Terminal Services Configuration.

7. Open the Connections folder, and then click Rdp-Tcp.

8. On the Actions menu, click Properties.

9. On the Permissions tab, add the users or groups that you want to have permissions to this Windows NT Terminal Server.

10. Click OK to close the connection's Properties dialog box.

11. Close Terminal Services Configuration.

Simple Network Management Protocol (SNMP)

Simple Network Management Protocol (SNMP) is a network-management protocol frequently used in TCP/IP networks to monitor and manage computers and other devices (such as printers) connected to the network. SNMP can be installed and used on any computer running Windows 2000 and TCP/IP or IPX/SPX.

▶ **Follow these steps to install the SNMP service:**

1. Click Start, point to Settings, click Control Panel, double-click Add/ Remove Programs, and then click Add/Remove Windows Components.

    The Windows Component wizard appears.

2. In Components, click Management And Monitoring Tools, and then click Details.

    The Management And Monitoring Tools dialog box appears.

3. Select the Simple Network Management Protocol check box, and click OK.

4. In the Windows Component wizard, click Next.

    The Windows Component wizard installs SNMP.

5. Click Finish to close the Windows Component wizard.

Management Systems and Agents

SNMP is comprised of management systems and agents. A management system is any computer running SNMP management software. Although Windows 2000 does not include a management system, many third-party products such as Sun Net Manager or HP Open View are available. A management system requests information from an agent.

As illustrated in Figure 12.25, an agent is any computer running SNMP agent software, such as a Windows 2000–based computer, router, or hub. The Microsoft SNMP service is SNMP agent software. The primary function of an agent is to perform operations that a management system calls for.

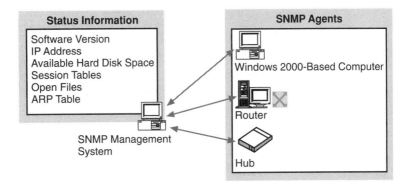

Figure 12.25 SNMP agents

The SNMP agent component also allows a Windows 2000 computer to be administered remotely. The only operation initiated by an agent is called a *trap*. A trap is a message sent by an agent to a management system indicating that an event has occurred on the host running the agent. As illustrated in Figure 12.26, the SNMP management software application does not have to run on the same computer as the SNMP agents.

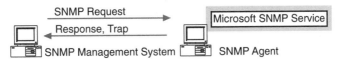

Figure 12.26 SNMP management system and agent

Benefits of SNMP

If you have installed a DHCP server, Internet Information Server, or WINS server software on a Windows 2000–based computer on the network, you can monitor these services by using an SNMP manager program. In addition, you can use Performance Monitor to examine TCP/IP-related performance counters. When you install the SNMP service, TCP/IP performance counters become available in System Monitor. The TCP/IP objects that are added include ICMP, TCP, IP, UDP, DHCP, WINS, FTP, Network Interface, and Internet Information Server. As illustrated in Figure 12.27, Performance Monitor counts

- Active TCP connections
- UDP datagrams received per second
- ICMP messages per second
- Total network interface bytes per second

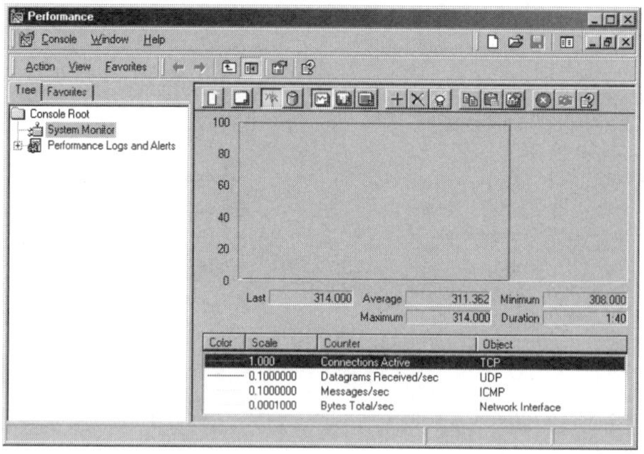

Figure 12.27 Monitoring TCP/IP objects with System Monitor

Lesson Summary

Windows 2000 provides two tools that can be used to remotely administer your system. These tools are Terminal Services and SNMP.

Terminal Services offers a Remote Administration mode that allows you to access, manage, and troubleshoot clients. Remote Administration mode allows you to remotely administer Windows 2000 servers over any TCP/IP connection.

SNMP is a network-management protocol widely used in TCP/IP networks. It can be used to communicate between a management program run by an administrator and the network-management agent running on a host or gateway. You can also use SNMP to monitor and control remote hosts and gateways on an internetwork. The Windows 2000 SNMP service allows a Windows 2000 computer to be monitored remotely. The SNMP service can handle requests from one or more hosts, and it can also report network-management information to one or more hosts, in discrete blocks of data called traps. When you install the SNMP service, TCP/IP performance counters become available in System Monitor.

Review

The following questions will help you determine whether you have learned enough to move on to the next chapter. If you have difficulty answering these questions, please go back and review the material in this chapter before beginning the next chapter. See Appendix A, "Questions and Answers," for the answers to these questions.

1. What is a VPN?

2. Demand-dial filters can screen traffic based on what fields of a packet?

3. Is the following statement true or false? When setting dial-in user permissions (Allow Access, Deny Access) through the User Property page, RAPs are not used.

4. Is the following statement true or false? DHCP packets are never sent over Routing and Remote Access links.

5. What is the function of BAP?

6. What are some potential security risks you should identify in your security plan?

7. What is authentication and how can you implement it?

8. What are some security features of Windows 2000?

9. How can you secure a connection between your network and the Internet?

10. What are some remote access protocols you can implement for security?

11. Name two forms of encryption available for demand-dial connections.

C H A P T E R   1 3

Managing Microsoft Windows Internet Name Service (WINS)

About This Chapter

Although Microsoft Windows Internet Name Service (WINS) servers are not needed in a network consisting entirely of Microsoft Windows 2000–based computers, they are crucial in most Transmission Control Protocol/Internet Protocol (TCP/IP) networks containing computers based on the older architectures of Windows NT 4.0, Windows 98, or Windows 95. In this chapter, you learn how to implement WINS on your network.

Before You Begin

To complete this chapter, you must have

- Two computers (Server01 and Server02) with Windows 2000 Server installed and configured with TCP/IP

Lesson 1: Introducing WINS

WINS provides a distributed database for registering and querying dynamic mappings of NetBIOS names for computers and groups used on your network. WINS maps NetBIOS names to IP addresses and was designed to solve the problems arising from NetBIOS name resolution in routed environments. WINS is the best choice for NetBIOS name resolution in routed networks that use NetBIOS over TCP/IP.

After this lesson, you will be able to

- Describe the relationship between NetBIOS and TCP/IP
- Describe the advantage of using WINS
- Describe a new Windows 2000 feature relating to NetBIOS

Estimated lesson time: 15 minutes

Name Resolution with NetBIOS

This section explains NetBIOS name resolution concepts and methods to help you better understand WINS functionality. This is useful because previous versions of Windows, such as Windows NT 4.0 and some Windows-based applications, use NetBIOS names to identify network resources.

Overview of NetBIOS

NetBIOS was developed for IBM in 1983 by Sytek Corporation to enable applications to communicate over a network. As illustrated in Figure 13.1, NetBIOS defines two entities:

- A session-level interface
- A session management/data transport protocol

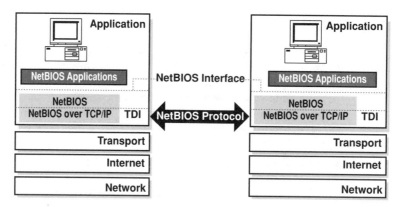

Figure 13.1 NetBIOS communication over TCP/IP

The NetBIOS interface is a presentation-layer application programming interface (API) for user applications to submit network input/output (I/O) and control directives to underlying network protocols. An application program that uses the NetBIOS interface API for network communication can be run on any protocol that supports the NetBIOS interface. This is implemented by the session layer software, such as NetBIOS Frame Protocol (NBFP) or NetBIOS over TCP/IP (NetBT), to perform the network I/O required to accommodate the NetBIOS interface command set.

NetBIOS provides commands and support for the following services:

- Network name registration and verification
- Session establishment and termination
- Reliable connection-oriented session data transfer
- Unreliable connectionless datagram data transfer
- Support protocol (driver) and adapter monitoring and management

NetBIOS Names

A NetBIOS name is a unique 16-byte address used to identify a NetBIOS resource on the network. This name is either a unique (exclusive) or group (nonexclusive) name. Unique names are typically used to send network communications to a specific process on a computer. Group names are used to send information to multiple computers at one time. An example of a process that uses a NetBIOS name is the File and Printer Sharing for Microsoft Networks service on a computer running Windows 2000. When your computer starts up, this service registers a unique NetBIOS name based on the name of your computer. The exact name used by the service is the 15-character computer name plus a 16th character of 0x20. If the computer name is not 15 characters long, it is padded with spaces up to 15 characters.

NetBIOS name resolution is the process of mapping a computer's NetBIOS name to an IP address. A computer's NetBIOS name must be resolved to an IP address before the IP address can be resolved to a hardware address. Microsoft TCP/IP uses several methods to resolve NetBIOS names; however, the exact mechanism by which NetBIOS names are resolved to IP addresses depends on the NetBIOS node type that is configured for the node. Request for Comments (RFC) 1001, "Protocol Standard for a NetBIOS Service on a TCP/UDP Transport: Concepts and Methods," defines the NetBIOS node types, as listed in Table 13.1.

Table 13.1   NetBIOS Node Types

Node type	Description
B-node (broadcast)	B-node uses broadcast NetBIOS name queries for name registration and resolution. B-node has two major problems: (1) Broadcasts disturb every node on the network. (2) Routers typically do not forward broadcasts, so only NetBIOS names on the local network can be resolved.
P-node (peer-to-peer)	P-node uses a NetBIOS name server, such as a WINS server, to resolve NetBIOS names. P-node does not use broadcasts; instead, it queries the name server directly.
M-node (mixed)	M-node is a combination of B-node and P-node. By default, an M-node functions as a B-node. If an M-node is unable to resolve a name by broadcast, it queries a NetBIOS name server using P-node.
H-node (hybrid)	H-node is a combination of P-node and B-node. By default, an H-node functions as a P-node. If an H-node is unable to resolve a name through the NetBIOS name server, it uses a broadcast to resolve the name.

Computers running Windows 2000 are B-node by default and become H-node when they are configured with a WINS server. Windows 2000 can also use a local database file called LMHOSTS to resolve remote NetBIOS names. The LMHOSTS file is stored in the %systemroot%\System32\Drivers\Etc folder. A sample LMHOSTS file (LMHOSTS.SAM) is included in this directory.

The LMHOSTS File

The LMHOSTS file is a static ASCII file used to resolve NetBIOS names to IP addresses of remote computers running Windows NT and other NetBIOS-based hosts.

Figure 13.2 shows an example of the LMHOSTS file.

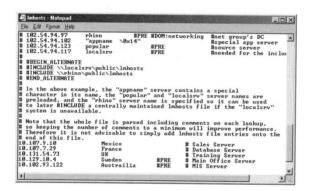

Figure 13.2 The LMHOSTS file

Predefined Keywords

An LMHOSTS file also contains predefined keywords that are prefixed with a #. If you use this LMHOSTS file on an older NetBT system such as LAN Manager, these directives are ignored as comments because they begin with a number sign (#). Table 13.2 lists the possible LMHOSTS keywords.

Table 13.2   LMHOSTS Keywords

Predefined keyword	Description
#PRE	Defines which entries should be initially preloaded as permanent entries in the name cache. Preloaded entries reduce network broadcasts, because names are resolved from cache rather than from broadcast or by parsing the LMHOSTS file. Entries with a #PRE tag are loaded automatically at initialization or manually by typing **nbtstat –R** at a command prompt.
#DOM:[*domain_name*]	Facilitates domain activity, such as logon validation over a router, account synchronization, and browsing.
#NOFNR	Avoids using NetBIOS-directed name queries for older LAN Manager UNIX systems.

Predefined keyword	Description
#INCLUDE	Loads and searches NetBIOS entries in a separate file from the default LMHOSTS file. Typically, an #INCLUDE file is a centrally located shared LMHOST file.
#BEGIN_ALTERNATE #END_ALTERNATE	Defines a redundant list of alternate locations for LMHOSTS files. The recommended way to #INCLUDE remote files is using a universal naming convention (UNC) path to ensure access to the file. Of course, the UNC names must exist in the LMHOSTS file with a proper IP address to NetBIOS name translation.
#MH	Adds multiple entries for a multihomed computer.

WINS Overview

WINS eliminates the need for broadcasts to resolve computer names to IP addresses and provides a dynamic database that maintains mappings of computer names to IP addresses. WINS is an enhanced NetBIOS name server (NBNS) designed by Microsoft to eliminate broadcast traffic associated with the B-node implementation of NetBT. It is used to register NetBIOS computer names and resolve them to IP addresses for both local and remote hosts.

There are several advantages of using WINS. The primary advantage is that client requests for computer name resolution are sent directly to a WINS server. If the WINS server can resolve the name, it sends the IP address directly to the client. As a result, a broadcast is not needed and network traffic is reduced. However, if the WINS server is unavailable, the WINS client can still use a broadcast in an attempt to resolve the name. Another advantage of using WINS is that the WINS database is updated dynamically, so it is always current. This eliminates the need for an LMHOSTS file. In addition, WINS provides network and interdomain browsing capabilities.

Before two NetBIOS-based hosts can communicate, the destination NetBIOS name must be resolved to an IP address. This is necessary because TCP/IP requires an IP address rather than a NetBIOS computer name to communicate. As illustrated in Figure 13.3, resolution uses the following process:

1. In a WINS environment, each time a WINS client starts, it registers its NetBIOS name/IP address mapping with a configured WINS server.

2. When a WINS client initiates a command to communicate with another host, the name query request is sent directly to the WINS server instead of being broadcast on the local network.

3. If the WINS server finds a NetBIOS name/IP address mapping for the destination host in this database, it returns the destination host's IP address to the WINS client. Because the WINS database obtains NetBIOS name/IP address mappings dynamically, it is always current.

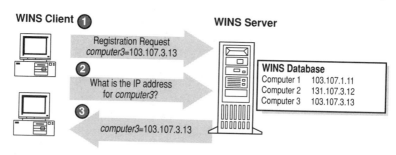

Figure 13.3 Name resolution with WINS

WINS and Windows 2000

Prior to Windows 2000, all MS-DOS and Windows-based operating systems required the NetBIOS naming interface to support network capabilities. With the release of Windows 2000, support for the NetBIOS naming interface is no longer required for networking computers because you can disable NetBT for each network connection. This feature is intended for computers that only use Domain Name System (DNS) name registration and resolution techniques and communicate by using the Client for Microsoft Networks and the File and Print Sharing for Microsoft Networks components with other computers where NetBT is disabled. Examples of disabling NetBT include computers in specialized or secured roles for your network, such as an edge proxy server or bastion host in a firewall environment, where NetBT support is not required or desired.

Another example is an environment consisting of host computers and programs that support the use of the DNS that could be built to run using Windows 2000 and other operating systems not requiring NetBIOS names, such as some versions of UNIX. However, most networks still need to integrate existing operating systems that require NetBIOS network names with computers running Windows 2000. For this reason, Microsoft has continued to provide default support for NetBIOS names with Windows 2000 to ease interoperability with legacy operating systems that require their use. This support is provided mainly in two ways:

- By default, all computers running Windows 2000 that use TCP/IP are enabled to provide client-side support for registering and resolving NetBIOS names.

    This support is provided through NetBT and can, if desired, be manually disabled.

- Windows 2000 Server continues to provide server-side support through WINS. WINS can be used to effectively manage NetBT-based networks.

Lesson Summary

Some applications and previous versions of Windows use NetBIOS names to identify network resources. WINS is an enhanced NBNS designed by Microsoft to eliminate broadcast traffic associated with the B-node implementation of NetBT. There are several advantages to using WINS. The primary advantage is that broadcast traffic is reduced because requests for name resolution are sent directly to the WINS server.

Lesson 2: The WINS Resolution Process

WINS uses standard methods of name registration, name renewal, and name release. This lesson introduces the different phases used to resolve a NetBIOS name to an IP address using WINS.

After this lesson, you will be able to

- Describe WINS name registration, renewal, release, query, and response

Estimated lesson time: 25 minutes

Resolving NetBIOS Names with WINS

When a client needs to contact another host on the network, it first contacts the WINS server to resolve the IP address using mapping information from the database of the server. The relational database engine of the WINS server accesses an indexed sequential access method (ISAM) database. The ISAM database is a replicated database that contains NetBIOS computer names and IP address mappings. For a WINS client to log on to the network, it must register its computer name and IP address with the WINS server. This creates an entry in the WINS database for every NetBIOS service running on the client. Because these entries are updated each time a WINS-enabled client logs on to the network, information stored in the WINS server database remains accurate.

The process WINS uses to resolve and maintain NetBIOS names is similar to the B-node implementation. The method used to renew a name is unique to NetBIOS node types that use a NetBIOS name server. WINS is an extension of RFCs 1001 and 1002. Figure 13.4 shows the process of resolving a NetBIOS name.

Name Registration

Each WINS client is configured with the IP address of a primary WINS server and optionally, a secondary WINS server. When a client starts, it registers its NetBIOS name and IP address with the configured WINS server. The WINS server stores the client's NetBIOS name/IP address mapping in its database.

Name Renewal

All NetBIOS names are registered on a temporary basis, which means that the same name can be used later by a different host if the original owner stops using it.

Name Release

Each WINS client is responsible for maintaining the lease on its registered name. When the name will no longer be used, for example when the computer is shut down, the WINS client sends a message to the WINS server to release it.

Name Query and Name Resolution

After a WINS client has registered its NetBIOS name and IP address with a WINS server, it can communicate with other hosts by obtaining the IP address of other NetBIOS-based computers from a WINS server. All WINS communications are done using directed datagrams over UDP port 137 (NBNS).

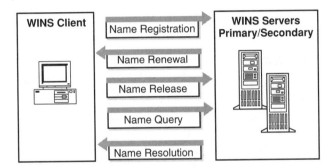

Figure 13.4 Name resolution between clients and a WINS server

Name Registration

Unlike the B-node implementation of NetBT, which broadcasts its name registration, WINS clients register their NetBIOS names with WINS servers.

When a WINS client initializes, it registers its NetBIOS name by sending a name registration request directly to the configured WINS server. NetBIOS names are registered when services or applications (such as the Workstation, Server, and Messenger), start.

If the WINS server is available and the name is not already registered by another WINS client, a successful registration message is returned to the client. This message contains the amount of time the NetBIOS name is registered to the client, specified as the Time to Live (TTL). Figure 13.5 shows the name registration process.

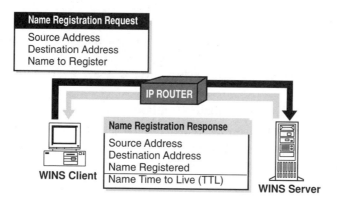

Figure 13.5 Name registration process

When a Duplicate Name Is Found

If there is a duplicate name registered in the WINS database, the WINS server sends a challenge to the currently registered owner of the name. The challenge is sent as a name query request. The WINS server sends the challenge three times at 500-millisecond intervals.

If the registered computer is a multihomed computer, the WINS server tries each IP address it has for the computer until it receives a response or until all of the IP addresses have been tried.

If the current registered owner responds successfully to the WINS server, the WINS server sends a negative name registration response to the WINS client that is attempting to register the name. If the current registered owner does not respond to the WINS server, the WINS server sends a successful name registration response to the WINS client that is attempting to register the name.

When the WINS Server Is Unavailable

A WINS client makes three attempts to find the primary WINS server. If it fails after the third attempt, the name registration request is sent to the secondary WINS server, if configured. If neither server is available, the WINS client may initiate a broadcast to register its name.

Name Renewal

To continue using the same NetBIOS name, a client must renew its registration before it expires. If a client does not renew the registration, the WINS server removes the record for that client from the WINS database.

Name Refresh Request

WINS clients must renew their name registrations before the renewal interval expires. The renewal interval determines how long the server stores the name registration as an active record in the WINS database. When a WINS client renews its name registration, it sends a name refresh request to the WINS server. The name refresh request includes the IP address and the NetBIOS name that the client seeks to refresh. The WINS server responds to the name refresh request with a name refresh response that includes a new renewal interval for the name. When a WINS client refreshes its name, it performs the following steps:

1. When a client has consumed half of its renewal interval, it sends a name refresh request to the primary WINS server.

2. If its name is not refreshed by the primary WINS server, the WINS client tries to refresh again in 10 minutes and continues to try the primary WINS server repeatedly every 10 minutes for a total of 1 hour. The WINS client, after trying to refresh its name registration with the primary WINS server for 1 hour, stops trying and attempts to refresh its name with the secondary WINS server.

3. If it is not refreshed by the secondary WINS server, the WINS client tries to refresh its name again using the secondary WINS server in 10 minutes and continues to try every 10 minutes for a total of 1 hour. The WINS client, after trying to refresh on the secondary WINS server for 1 hour, stops trying and tries to refresh using the primary WINS server. This process of trying the primary WINS server and then the secondary WINS server continues until the renewal interval is consumed or the WINS client has its name refreshed.

4. If the WINS client succeeds in refreshing its name, the renewal interval is reset on the WINS server.

5. If the WINS client fails to register during the renewal interval on either the primary or secondary WINS server, the name is released.

Figure 13.6 shows how a WINS client renews its lease to use the same NetBIOS name.

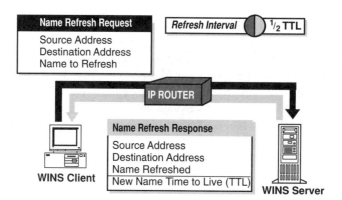

Figure 13.6 Renewing a lease using the same NetBIOS name

When a WINS server receives the name refresh request, it sends the client a name refresh response with a new TTL.

Name Release

When a WINS client is properly shut down, it sends a name release request directly to the WINS server for each registered name. The name release request includes the client's IP address and the NetBIOS name to be removed from the WINS database. This allows the name to be available for another client, as illustrated in Figure 13.7.

When the WINS server receives the name release request, it checks its database for the specified name. If the WINS server encounters a database error or if a different IP address maps the registered name, it sends a negative name release to the WINS client. Otherwise, the WINS server sends a positive name release and designates the specified name as inactive in its database. The name release response contains the released NetBIOS name and a TTL value of zero.

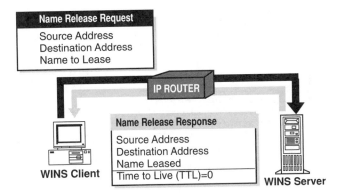

Figure 13.7 Name release request

Name Query and Name Response

A common method of resolving NetBIOS names to IP addresses is with an NBNS, such as WINS. When a WINS client is configured, by default, the H-node type of NetBT is used. The NBNS is always checked for a NetBIOS name/IP address mapping before initiating a broadcast. The following steps and illustration in Figure 13.8 demonstrate the process:

1. When a user initiates a Windows NT command, such as net use, the NetBIOS name cache is checked for the NetBIOS name/IP address mapping of the destination host.

2. If the name is not resolved from cache, a name query request is sent directly to the client's primary WINS server.

   If the primary WINS server is unavailable, the client resends the request two more times before switching to the secondary WINS server.

   When either WINS server resolves the name, a success message with the IP address for the requested NetBIOS name is sent to the source host.

3. If no WINS server can resolve the name, a name query response is sent back to the WINS client with the message "Requested name does not exist," and broadcast is implemented.

   If the name is not resolved from cache by a WINS server or broadcast, the name may still be resolved by parsing the LMHOSTS or Hosts file, or by using DNS.

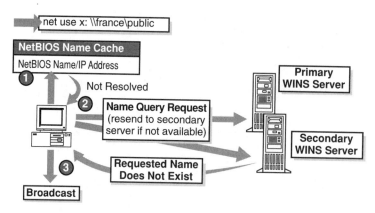

Figure 13.8 NetBIOS name server checked for NetBIOS name/IP address mapping

Lesson Summary

WINS uses standard name registration, name renewal, and name release methods. To continue using the same NetBIOS name, a client must renew its lease before it expires. When a WINS client is shut down, it notifies the WINS server that it no longer needs its NetBIOS name.

Lesson 3: Implementing WINS

For networks with servers running Windows 2000 Server and all other computers running Windows 2000 Professional, NetBIOS is no longer required for TCP/IP-based networking. Because of this change, WINS is needed for most networks but might not be required in some instances. In this lesson, you learn how to implement WINS on your network.

After this lesson, you will be able to

- Install and configure a WINS server
- Install and configure a WINS client
- Troubleshoot WINS clients and servers
- Manage and monitor WINS

Estimated lesson time: 40 minutes

When to Use WINS

When deciding whether you need to use WINS, you should first consider the following questions:

- **Do I have any existing computers or applications on my network that require the use of NetBIOS names?** All networked computers that run under any previously released Microsoft operating system, such as versions of MS-DOS, Windows, or Windows NT, require NetBIOS name support. Windows 2000 is the first Microsoft operating system that no longer requires NetBIOS naming. Therefore, NetBIOS names can still be required on your network to provide basic file and print services and support for many legacy applications used.

- **Are all computers on my network configured and able to support the use of another type of network naming, such as DNS?** Network naming is still a vital service for locating computers and resources throughout your network, even when NetBIOS names are not required. Before you decide to eliminate WINS or NetBIOS name support, be sure that all computers and programs on your network are able to function using another naming service, such as DNS.

- **Is my network a single subnet or routed with multiple subnets?** If your entire network is a small local area network (LAN) that occupies one physical network segment and has less than 50 clients, you can probably do without a WINS server.

Considerations for WINS Servers

Before you implement WINS in an internetwork, consider the number of WINS servers you will need. Only one WINS server is required for an internetwork because requests for name resolution are directed datagrams that can be routed. Two WINS servers ensure a backup system for fault tolerance. If one server becomes unavailable, the second server can be used to resolve names. You should also consider the following WINS server recommendations:

- There is no built-in limit to the number of WINS requests that can be handled by a WINS server, but typically it can handle 1500 name registrations and about 4500 name queries per minute.

- A conservative recommendation is one WINS server and a backup server for every 10,000 WINS clients.

- Computers with multiple processors have demonstrated performance improvements of approximately 25 percent for each additional processor, as a separate WINS thread is started for each processor.

- If logging of database changes is turned off (through WINS Manager), name registrations are much faster, but if a crash occurs, there is a risk of losing the last few updates.

WINS Requirements

Before you install WINS, you should determine that your server and clients meet the configuration requirements. The WINS service must be configured on at least one computer within the TCP/IP internetwork running Windows NT Server or Windows 2000 Server (it does not have to be a domain controller). The server must have an IP address, subnet mask, default gateway, and other TCP/IP parameters. These parameters can be assigned by a DHCP server, but statically assigned parameters are recommended.

A WINS client can be a computer running any of the following supported operating systems:

- Windows 2000
- Windows NT 3.5 and later
- Windows 95 or Windows 98
- Windows for Workgroups 3.11 running Microsoft TCP/IP-32
- Microsoft Network Client 3.0 for MS-DOS
- LAN Manager 2.2c for MS-DOS

The client must have an IP address of a WINS server configured for a primary WINS server or for primary and secondary WINS servers.

▶ **Follow these steps to install WINS on a Windows 2000–based server:**

1. In Control Panel, double-click Add/Remove Programs.

2. Click Add/Remove Windows Components.

   The Windows Component wizard opens.

3. On the Windows Components page, under Components, click Networking Services, and then click Details.

   The Networking Services dialog box appears.

4. Select the Windows Internet Name Service (WINS) check box, click OK, and then click Next.

Using Static Mappings

Mapped name-to-address entries can be added to WINS in either of two ways:

- Dynamically, by WINS-enabled clients directly contacting a WINS server to register, release, or renew their NetBIOS names in the server database

- Manually, by an administrator using the WINS console or command-line tools to add or delete statically mapped entries in the server database

Static entries are only useful when you need to add a name-to-address mapping to the server database for a computer that does not directly use WINS. For example, in some networks, servers running other operating systems cannot register a NetBIOS name directly with a WINS server. Although these names might be added to and resolved from an LMHOSTS file or by querying a DNS server, you might consider using a static WINS mapping instead.

▶ **Follow these steps to configure a static mapping:**

1. Click Start, point to Programs, point to Administrative Tools, and then click WINS.

2. In the WINS console, click Active Registrations under your WINS server.

3. On the Action menu, click New Static Mapping.

   The New Static Mapping dialog box appears, as illustrated in Figure 13.9.

Figure 13.9 The Add Static Mapping dialog box

4. In Computer Name, type the NetBIOS name of the computer.

5. In NetBIOS Scope (optional), you can type a NetBIOS scope identifier, if one is used, for the computer. Otherwise, leave this field blank.

6. In Type, click one of the supported types to indicate whether this entry is a Unique, Group, Domain Name, Internet, or Multihomed type entry, as detailed in Table 13.3.

7. In IP Address, type the address for the computer.

8. Click Apply to add the static mapping entry to the database.

   You can also add additional static mapping entries, see table 13.3. Click Apply each time you complete an entry, and then click Cancel to close when you finish adding static mapping entries.

9. Click OK to close the Add Static Mapping dialog box.

Table 13.3   Static WINS Mapping Types

Type option	Description
Unique	A unique name maps to a single IP address.
Group	Also referred to as a "Normal" group. When adding an entry to a group by using WINS Manager, you must enter the computer name and IP address. However, the IP addresses of individual members of a group are not stored in the WINS database. Because the member addresses are not stored, there is no limit to the number of members that can be added to a group. Broadcast name packets are used to communicate with group members.
Domain Name	A NetBIOS name-to-address mapping that has 0x1C as the 16th byte. A domain group stores up to a maximum of 25 addresses for members. For registrations after the 25th address, WINS overwrites a replica address or, if none is present, it overwrites the oldest registration.
Internet Group	Internet groups are user-defined groups that enable you to group resources, such as printers, for easy reference and browsing. An Internet group can store up to a maximum of 25 addresses for members. A dynamic member, however, does not replace a static member added by using WINS Manager or importing the LMHOSTS file.
Multihomed	A unique name that can have more than one address. This is used for multihomed computers. Each multihomed group name can contain a maximum of 25 addresses. For registrations after the 25th address, WINS overwrites a replica address or, if none is present, it overwrites the oldest registration.

Practice: Configuring a WINS Client

If a computer is a DHCP client, you can configure the DHCP server to provide DHCP clients with WINS configuration information. However, you can also manually configure WINS clients. If you manually configure WINS client computers with IP addresses of one or more WINS servers, those values take precedence over the same parameters that a DHCP server provides.

Exercise 1: Configuring a WINS Client with the IP Address of One or More WINS Servers

1. Open Network And Dial-Up Connections.

2. Right-click Local Area Connection, and then click Properties.

   The Local Area Connection Properties dialog box appears.

3. Select the Internet Protocol (TCP/IP) Properties entry in the list, and then click Properties.

   The Internet Protocol (TCP/IP) Properties dialog box appears.

4. Click Advanced and select the WINS Address tab, as illustrated in Figure 13.10.

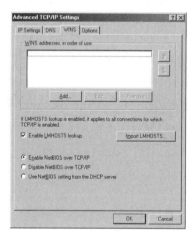

Figure 13.10 The WINS service on a Windows 2000 client

5. Click Add, type the IP address of your WINS server in the TCP/IP WINS Server dialog box, and then click Add.

The TCP/IP WINS Server dialog box closes and the WINS server you entered will be added to the list in the Advanced TCP/IP Settings dialog box.

6. Click OK to close the Advanced TCP/IP Settings dialog box.

7. Click OK to close the Internet Protocol (TCP/IP) Properties dialog box.

8. Click OK to close the Local Area Connection Properties dialog box.

Troubleshooting WINS

The following conditions can indicate basic problems with WINS:

- The administrator cannot connect to a WINS server using the WINS console.
- TCP/IP NetBIOS Helper service on the WINS client is down and cannot be restarted.
- WINS service is not running and cannot be restarted.

The first action you should take to resolve WINS problems is to verify that the appropriate services are running. You can do this at both the WINS server and WINS client.

▶ **Follow these steps to verify running services:**

1. Verify that the WINS service is running on the server.

2. Verify that the Workstation service, the Server service, and the TCP/IP NetBIOS Helper service are started on the clients.

If services do not start properly, you can use the Computer Management administrative tool to check the status column of the services, and then try to start them manually. If the service cannot be started, use Event Viewer to check the system event log and determine the cause of failure.

Note For WINS clients, "Started" should appear in the status column for TCP/IP NetBIOS Helper service. For WINS servers, "Started" should appear in the status column for Windows Internet Name Service (WINS).

The most common WINS client problem is failed name resolution. When name resolution fails at a client, first answer the following questions to identify the source of the problem:

- **Is the client computer able to use WINS, and is it correctly configured?**
  First, check that the client is configured to use both TCP/IP and WINS. Client configuration of WINS-related settings can be done manually by an administrator setting the TCP/IP configuration of the client or it can be done dynamically by a DHCP server providing the client its TCP/IP configuration. In most cases, computers running earlier versions of Microsoft operating systems are already able to use WINS once TCP/IP is installed and configured at the client. For Windows 2000, administrators can optionally disable NetBT for each client. If you disable NetBT, WINS cannot be used at the client.

  Note If the WINS server does not respond to a direct ping, the source of the problem is likely to be a network connectivity problem between the client and the WINS server.

- **Was the name that failed to resolve a NetBIOS or DNS name?**
  NetBIOS names are 15 characters or less and not structured like DNS names, which are generally longer and use periods to delimit each domain level within a name. For example, the short NetBIOS name PRINT-SRV1 and the longer DNS name print-srv1.example.microsoft.com might both refer to the same resource computer running Windows 2000 (a network print server) configured to use either name. If the short name was used at the client in the previous example, Windows 2000 would first involve NetBIOS name services, such as WINS or NetBT broadcasts, in its initial attempts to resolve the name. If a longer DNS name (or a name that uses periods) was involved in the failure, DNS is more likely the cause of the failed name resolution.

The most common WINS server problem is the inability to resolve names for clients. When a server fails to resolve a name for its clients, the failure most often is discovered by clients in one of two ways:

- The server sends a negative query response back to the client, such as an error message indicating "Name not found."

- The server sends a positive response back to the client, but the information contained in the response is incorrect.

If you determine that a WINS-related problem does not originate at the client, answer the following question to further troubleshoot the source of the problem at the WINS server of the client:

- **Is the WINS server able to service the client?** At the WINS server for the client that cannot locate a name, use Event Viewer or the WINS management console to see if WINS is currently running. If WINS is running on the server, search for the name previously requested by the client to see if it is in the WINS server database.

If the WINS server is failing or registering database corruption errors, you can use WINS database recovery techniques to help restore WINS operations. You can back up the WINS database by using the WINS administrative console. First, you specify a backup directory for the database, and then WINS executes database backups. The backup is performed every 3 hours by default. If your WINS database becomes corrupted, you can easily restore it. The easiest way to restore a local server database is to replicate data back from a replication partner. If the corruption is limited to a certain number of records, you can repair them by forcing replication of uncorrupted WINS records. This removes the affected records from other WINS servers. If changes are replicated among WINS servers quickly, the best way to restore a local WINS server database is to use a replication partner, provided that the WINS data is mostly up to date on the replication partner.

Managing and Monitoring WINS

The WINS console is fully integrated with the Microsoft Management Console (MMC) which provides the user with a powerful and more user-friendly tool you can customize for your efficiency. Because all server administrative utilities included for your use in Windows 2000 Server are part of MMC, new MMC-based utilities are easier to use, as they operate more predictably and follow a common design. In addition, several useful WINS features from earlier versions of Windows NT Server that were only configurable through the registry are now more directly usable. These include the ability to block records by a specific owner or WINS replication partner (formerly known as Persona Non Grata) or the ability to allow override of static mappings (formerly known as Migrate On/Off). In this lesson, you learn how to manage and monitor WINS through the WINS console.

Viewing WINS Server Statistics

You should view WINS server statistics periodically to monitor performance. By default, statistics automatically refresh every 10 minutes. You can also disable this feature by clearing the Automatically Update Statistics Every check box.

▶ **Follow these steps to open the WINS Server Statistics dialog box:**

1. Click Start, point to Programs, point to Administrative Tools, and then click WINS.

2. In the console tree, click the applicable WINS server.

3. On the Action menu, click Display Server Statistics.

4. To update the display while viewing WINS statistics, click Refresh.

Lesson Summary

To implement WINS, both the server and client require configuration. Configuring a static mapping for non-WINS clients allows WINS clients on remote networks to communicate with them. When troubleshooting WINS, the first thing you should do is verify that the appropriate services are running.

Lesson 4: Configuring WINS Replication

All WINS servers on an internetwork can be configured to fully replicate database entries with other WINS servers. This ensures that a name registered with one WINS server is eventually replicated to all other WINS servers. This lesson explains how WINS database entries are replicated to other WINS servers.

After this lesson, you will be able to

- Add a replication partner
- Perform WINS database replication

Estimated lesson time: 20 minutes

Replication Overview

Database replication occurs whenever the database changes, including when a name is released. Replicating databases enables a WINS server to resolve NetBIOS names of hosts registered with another WINS server. For example, if a host on Subnet 1 is registered with a WINS server on the same subnet but wants to communicate with a host on Subnet 2 and that host is registered with a different WINS server, the NetBIOS name cannot be resolved unless the two WINS servers have replicated their databases with each other.

To replicate database entries, each WINS server must be configured as either a pull or a push partner with at least one other WINS server. A push partner is a WINS server that sends a message to its pull partners notifying them when its WINS database has changed. When a WINS server's pull partners respond to the message with a replication request, the WINS server sends a copy of its new database entries (replicas) to its pull partners.

A pull partner is a WINS server that requests new database entries (replicas) from its push partners. This is done by requesting entries with a higher version number than the last entries it received during the last replication.

Note WINS servers replicate only new entries in their database. The entire WINS database is not replicated each time replication occurs.

Configuring a WINS Server as a Push or Pull Partner

Determining whether to configure a WINS server as a pull partner or push partner depends on your network environment. Remember the following rules when configuring WINS server replication:

- You must configure a push partner when servers are connected by fast links, because push replication occurs when the configured number of updated WINS database entries is reached.

- You must configure a pull partner between sites, especially across slow links, because pull replication can be configured to occur at specific intervals.

- You must configure each server to be both a push and pull partner to replicate database entries between them.

Note You configure a WINS server as a push or pull partner with the WINS administration tool.

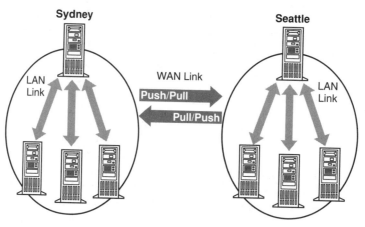

Figure 13.11 Push and pull partner configuration

When you apply these rules to the environment depicted in Figure 13.11, you must configure the server in the following manner.

- In both Sydney and Seattle, all WINS servers at each site push their new database entries to a single server at their site.

- The servers that receive the push replication are configured for pull replication between each other because the network link between Sydney and Seattle is relatively slow. Replication should occur when the link is the least used, such as late at night.

Configuring Database Replication

Database replication requires that you configure at least one push partner and one pull partner. There are four methods of starting the replication of the WINS database:

1. At system startup. Once a replication partner is configured, by default, WINS automatically pulls database entries each time WINS is started. The WINS server can also be configured to push on system startup.

2. At a configured interval, such as every 5 hours.

3. When a WINS server has reached a configured threshold for the number of registrations and changes to the WINS database. When the threshold (the update count setting) is reached, the WINS server notifies all of its pull partners, which will then request the new entries.

4. By forcing replication in the WINS administrative console, as illustrated in Figure 13.12.

Figure 13.12 Forcing WINS database replication

Practice: Performing WINS Database Replication

In this practice, you configure your WINS server to perform database replication with another WINS server.

Note To complete this practice you first need to configure your second computer (Server02) as a WINS server.

Exercise 1: Configuring WINS Replication Partners

In this exercise, you configure your second computer (Server02, a WINS server) as a replication partner.

1. Open the WINS administrative console.

2. Right-click the Replication Partners folder under your WINS server, and then click New Replication Partner.

   The New Replication Partners dialog box appears.

3. In the WINS Server box, type an IP address of a partner WINS server, and then click OK.

   The Replication Partners dialog box appears with your IP address added to the list of WINS servers, as illustrated in Figure 13.13.

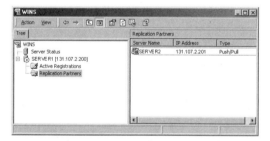

Figure 13.13 Replication partners listed in the WINS administrative console

4. Right-click the replication partner that you just added in the right pane, and then click Properties.

   The Server Properties dialog box appears.

5. Click the Advanced tab.

6. In the Replication Partner Type drop-down list box, select Pull.

7. The replication interval is set for 30 minutes.

8. Click OK.

Exercise 2: Forcing Replication

In this exercise, you force WINS to replicate the WINS database with the WINS server.

1. Right-click on the Replication Partners folder.

2. From the Context menu, click Replicate Now.

   A dialog box appears asking you if you are sure you want to start replication.

3. Click Yes.

   A message box appears indicating the replication request has been queued.

4. Click OK.

Planning How Many WINS Servers to Use

On a smaller network, a single WINS server can adequately service up to 10,000 clients for NetBIOS name resolution requests. To provide additional fault tolerance, you can configure a second computer running Windows 2000 Server as a backup WINS server for clients. If you use only two WINS servers, you can easily set them up as replication partners of each other. For simple replication between two servers, one server should be set as a pull partner and the other as a push partner. Replication can be either manual or automatic, which you can configure by selecting the Enable Automatic Partner Configuration check box in the Advanced tab of the Replication Partner Properties dialog box.

A larger network sometimes requires more WINS servers for several reasons, including, most importantly, the number of client connections per server. The number of users that each WINS server can support varies with usage patterns, data storage, and the processing capabilities of the WINS server computer. Some enterprise network environments require more robust hardware to handle WINS activity, so you might benefit from upgrading the server computer. When planning your servers, remember that each WINS server can simultaneously handle hundreds of registrations and queries per second. Any number of WINS servers can be specified for fault tolerance purposes. However, you should avoid deploying large numbers of WINS servers unless they are definitely necessary. By limiting the number of WINS servers on your network, you minimize traffic that results from replication, provide more effective NetBIOS name resolution, and reduce administrative requirements.

WINS Automatic Replication Partners

If your network supports multicasting, the WINS server can be configured to automatically find other WINS servers on the network by multicasting to the IP address 224.0.1.24. This multicasting occurs by default every 40 minutes. Any WINS servers found on the network are automatically configured as push and pull replication partners, with pull replication set to occur every 2 hours. If network routers do not support multicasting, the WINS server will find only other WINS servers on its subnet. Automatic WINS server partnerships are turned off by default. To manually disable this feature, use the Registry Editor to set UseSelfFndPnrs to 0 and McastIntvl to a large value.

Backing Up the WINS Database

The WINS console provides backup tools so that you can back up and restore the WINS database. When WINS backs up the server database, it creates a \Wins_bak\New folder under the backup folder you have specified as the Default backup path in Server Properties. Actual backups of the WINS database (WINS.MDB) are stored in this folder. By default, the backup path is the root folder on your system partition, such as C:\ After you specify a backup folder for the database, WINS performs complete database backups every three hours using the specified folder. WINS can also be configured to back up the database automatically when the service is stopped or the server computer is shut down.

▶ **Follow these steps to back up the WINS database:**

1. Click Start, point to Programs, point to Administrative Tools, and then click WINS.

2. In the console tree, click the applicable WINS server.

3. On the Action menu, click Backup Database.

4. When prompted to confirm, click Yes.

5. After backup is completed, click OK.

Important Do not specify a network drive as the backup location. In addition, if you change the WINS backup or database path in server properties, perform new backups to ensure successful future restorations of the WINS database. This is the only way for the active WINS database to be backed up, because the database is locked open while the WINS server is running.

Lesson Summary

All of the WINS servers on a given network can be configured to communicate with each other so that a name registered with one WINS server eventually will be known by all WINS servers. A pull partner requests WINS new database entries. A push partner sends a message to its pull partners notifying them that its WINS database has changed.

Review

Answering the following questions will reinforce key information presented
in this chapter. If you are unable to answer a question, review the appropriate
lesson and then try the question again. Answers to the questions can be found
in Appendix A, "Questions and Answers."

1. What are three benefits of WINS?

2. What two methods can be used to enable WINS on a client computer?

3. How many WINS servers are required in an intranet of 12 subnets?

4. What types of names are stored in the WINS database?

C H A P T E R   1 4

Managing Network Address Translation (NAT)

About This Chapter

Network address translation (NAT) is a protocol that allows a network with private addresses to access information on the Internet through an Internet Protocol (IP) translation process. In this chapter, you learn how to configure your home network or small office network to share a single connection to the Internet with NAT.

Before You Begin

To complete the lessons in this chapter, you must have

- Read and complete the exercises in Chapter 11, "Managing DHCP"

Lesson 1: Introducing NAT

NAT enables private IP addresses to be translated into public IP addresses for access to and from the Internet. This keeps traffic from passing directly to the internal network while saving the small office or home office user the time and expense of getting and maintaining a public address range. This lesson provides an overview of NAT.

After this lesson, you will be able to

- Describe the purpose of NAT
- Identify the components of NAT
- Describe how NAT works

Estimated lesson time: 45 minutes

Network Address Translation

NAT allows computers on a small network, such as a small office or home office, to share a single Internet connection with only a single public IP address. The computer on which NAT is installed can act as a network address translator, a simplified Dynamic Host Configuration Protocol (DHCP) server, a Domain Name System (DNS) proxy, and a Windows Internet Name Service (WINS) proxy. NAT allows host computers to share one or more publicly registered IP addresses, helping to conserve public address space.

Understanding Network Address Translation

With NAT in Windows 2000, you can configure your home network or small office network to share a single connection to the Internet. NAT consists of the following components:

- **Translation component.** The Windows 2000 router on which NAT is enabled, hereafter called the NAT computer, acts as a network address translator that translates the IP addresses and Transmission Control Protocol/User Datagram Protocol (TCP/UDP) port numbers of packets that are forwarded between the private network and the Internet.

- **Addressing component.** The NAT computer provides IP address configuration information to the other computers on the home network. The addressing component is a simplified DHCP server that allocates an IP address, a subnet mask, a default gateway, and the IP address of a DNS server. You must configure computers on the home network as DHCP clients to receive the IP configuration automatically. The default TCP/IP configuration for computers running Windows 2000, Windows NT, Windows 95, and Windows 98 is as a DHCP client.

- **Name resolution component.** The NAT computer becomes the DNS server for the other computers on the home network. The NAT computer receives name resolution requests and forwards them to the Internet-based DNS server for which it is configured and returns the responses to the home network computer.

Routed and Translated Internet Connections

There are two types of connections to the Internet: routed and translated. When planning for a routed connection, you need a range of IP addresses from your Internet service provider (ISP) to use on the internal portion of your network. Your ISP should also give you the IP address of the DNS server you need to use. You can either statically configure the IP address configuration of each computer or use a DHCP server.

The Windows 2000 router needs to be configured with a network adapter for the internal network (10 or 100 BaseT Ethernet, for example). It also needs to be configured with an Internet connection such as an analog or Integrated Services Digital Network (ISDN) modem, an xDSL modem, a cable modem, or a fractional T1 line.

The translated method, or NAT, gives you a more secure network because the addresses of your private network are completely hidden from the Internet. The connection-shared computer, which uses NAT, does all of the translation of Internet addresses to your private network, and vice versa. However, be aware that the NAT computer cannot translate all payloads. This is because some applications use IP addresses in fields other than the standard TCP/IP header fields.

The following protocols do not work with NAT:

- Kerberos protocol
- IP Security Protocol (IPSec)

The DHCP allocator functionality in NAT enables all DHCP clients in the network to automatically obtain an IP address, a subnet mask, a default gateway, and a DNS server address from the NAT computer. If you have any non-DHCP computers on the network, statically configure their IP address configuration.

To keep resource costs to a minimum on a small network, only one server running Windows 2000 is needed. Depending on whether you are running a translated or routed connection, this single server can suffice for NAT, Automatic Private IP Addressing (APIPA), Routing and Remote Access, and DHCP.

Public and Private Addresses

If your intranet is not connected to the Internet, any IP addressing can be deployed. If direct (routed) or indirect (proxy or translator) connectivity to the Internet is desired, there are two types of addresses you can use: public addresses and private addresses.

Public Addresses

Public addresses are assigned by the Internet Network Information Center (InterNIC) and consist of class-based network IDs or blocks of Classless Inter-Domain Routing (CIDR)-based addresses (called CIDR blocks) that are guaranteed to be globally unique to the Internet. When the public addresses are assigned, routes are programmed into the routers of the Internet so that traffic to the assigned public addresses can reach its location. Traffic to destination public addresses is reachable on the Internet.

Private Addresses

Each IP node requires an IP address that is globally unique to the IP internetwork. In the case of the Internet, each IP node on a network connected to the Internet requires an IP address that is globally unique to the Internet. As the Internet has grown, organizations connecting to the Internet have required a public address for each node on their intranets. This requirement has placed a huge demand on the pool of available public addresses.

When analyzing the addressing needs of organizations, the designers of the Internet noted that for many organizations, most of the hosts on the organization's intranet did not require direct connectivity to Internet hosts. Those hosts that did require a specific set of Internet services, such as World Wide Web access and e-mail, typically accessed the Internet services through application-layer gateways such as proxy servers and e-mail servers. The result was that most organizations only required a small number of public addresses for those nodes (such as proxies, routers, firewalls, and translators) that were directly connected to the Internet.

For the hosts within the organization that do not require direct access to the Internet, IP addresses that do not duplicate already assigned public addresses are required. To solve this addressing problem, the Internet designers reserved a portion of the IP address space and named this space the private address space. Private IP addresses are never assigned as public addresses. Because the public and private address spaces do not overlap, private addresses never duplicate public addresses. The following private IP address ranges are specified by Internet Request for Comments (RFC) 1918:

- **10.0.0.0 through 10.255.255.255.** The 10.0.0.0 private network is a class A network ID that allows the following range of valid IP addresses: 10.0.0.1 to 10.255.255.254. The 10.0.0.0 private network has 24 host bits that can be used for any subnetting scheme within the private organization.

- **172.16.0.0 through 172.31.255.255.** The 172.16.0.0 private network can be interpreted either as a block of 16 class B network IDs or as a 20-bit assignable address space (20 host bits) that can be used for any subnetting scheme within the private organization. The 172.16.0.0 private network allows the following range of valid IP addresses: 172.16.0.1 to 172.31.255.254.

- **192.168.0.0 through 192.168.255.255.** The 192.168.0.0/16 private network can be interpreted either as a block of 256 class C network IDs or as a 16-bit assignable address space (16 host bits) that can be used for any subnetting scheme within the private organization. The 192.168.0.0 private network allows the following range of valid IP addresses: 192.168.0.1 to 192.168.255.254.

Private addresses are not reachable on the Internet. Therefore, Internet traffic from a host that has a private address must either send its requests to an application-layer gateway (such as a proxy server), which has a valid public address, or have its private address translated into a valid public address by a network address translator before it is sent on the Internet.

How NAT Works

A network address translator is an IP router defined in RFC 1631 that can translate IP addresses and TCP/UDP port numbers of packets as they are being forwarded. Consider a small business network with multiple computers connecting to the Internet. A small business would normally have to obtain an ISP-allocated public IP address for each computer on its network. With NAT, however, the small business can use private addressing (as described in RFC 1597) and have the NAT map its private addresses to a single or to multiple public IP addresses as allocated by its ISP. For example, if a small business is using the 10.0.0.0 private network for its intranet and has been granted the public IP address of 198.200.200.1 by its ISP, the NAT maps (using static or dynamic mappings) all private IP addresses being used on network 10.0.0.0 to the public IP address of 198.200.200.1.

Static and Dynamic Address Mapping

NAT can use either static or dynamic mapping. A static mapping is configured so that traffic is always mapped a specific way. You could map all traffic to and from a specific private network location to a specific Internet location. For instance, to set up a Web server on a computer on your private network, you create a static mapping that maps [Public IP Address, TCP Port 80] to [Private IP Address, TCP Port 80].

Dynamic mappings are created when users on the private network initiate traffic with Internet locations. The NAT service automatically adds these mappings to its mapping table and refreshes them with each use. Dynamic mappings that are not refreshed are removed from the NAT mapping table after a configurable amount of time. For TCP connections, the default time out is 24 hours. For UDP traffic, the default time out is 1 minute.

Proper Translation of Header Fields

By default, NAT translates IP addresses and TCP/UDP ports. These modifications to the IP datagram require the modification and recalculation of the following fields in the IP, TCP, and UDP headers:

- Source IP address
- TCP, UDP, and IP checksum
- Source port

If the IP address and port information is only in the IP and TCP/UDP headers—for example, with Hypertext Transfer Protocol (HTTP) or World Wide Web traffic—the application protocol can be translated transparently. There are applications and protocols, however, that carry IP or port addressing information within their headers. File Transfer Protocol (FTP), for example, stores the dotted-decimal representation of IP addresses in the FTP header for the FTP port command. If the NAT does not properly translate the IP address, connectivity problems can occur. Additionally, in the case of FTP, because the IP address is stored in dotted-decimal format, the translated IP address in the FTP header can be a different size. Therefore, the NAT must also modify TCP sequence numbers to ensure that no data is lost.

NAT Editors

In the case where the NAT component must also translate and adjust the payload beyond the IP, TCP, and UDP headers, a NAT editor is required. A NAT editor is an installable component that can properly modify otherwise nontranslatable payloads so that they can be forwarded across a NAT. Windows 2000 includes built-in NAT editors for the following protocols:

- FTP
- Internet Control Message Protocol (ICMP)
- Point-to-Point Tunneling Protocol (PPTP)
- NetBIOS over TCP/IP

Additionally, the NAT routing protocol includes proxy software for the following protocols:

- H.323
- Direct Play
- Lightweight Directory Access Protocol (LDAP)-based Internet Locator Service (ILS) registration
- Remote procedure call

Note IPSec traffic is not translatable.

An example of NAT

If a small business is using the 192.168.0.0 private network ID for its intranet and has been granted the public address of w1.x1.y1.z1 by its ISP, NAT maps all private addresses on 192.168.0.0 to the IP address of w1.x1.y1.z1. If multiple private addresses are mapped to a single public address, NAT uses dynamically chosen TCP and UDP ports to distinguish one intranet location from another. Figure 14.1 shows an example of using NAT to transparently connect an intranet to the Internet.

Note The use of w1.x1.y1.z1 and w2.x2.y2.z2 is intended to represent valid public IP addresses as allocated by InterNIC or an ISP.

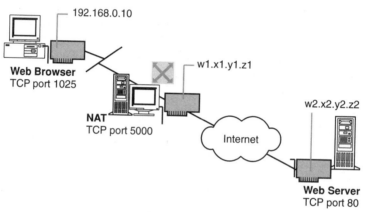

Figure 14.1 Using NAT to connect an intranet transparently to the Internet

NAT Processes in Windows 2000 Routing and Remote Access

For Windows 2000 Routing and Remote Access, the NAT component can be enabled by adding NAT as a routing protocol in the Routing and Remote Access snap-in.

Note NAT services are also available with the Internet Connection Sharing feature available from the Network And Dial-Up Connections folder, as explained in Lesson 2. Internet Connection Sharing performs the same function as the NAT routing protocol in Routing and Remote Access but it allows very little configuration flexibility. For information about configuring Internet Connection Sharing and why you would choose Internet Connection Sharing over the NAT routing protocol of Routing and Remote Access, see Windows 2000 Server Help.

Installed with the NAT routing protocol are a series of NAT editors. NAT consults the editors when the payload of the packet being translated matches one of the installed editors. The editors modify the payload and return the result to the NAT component. NAT interacts with the TCP/IP protocol in two important ways:

- To support dynamic port mappings, the NAT component requests unique TCP and UDP port numbers from the TCP/IP protocol stack when needed.

- To allow packets being sent between the private network and the Internet to first be passed to the NAT component for translation.

Figure 14.2 shows the NAT components and their relation to TCP/IP and other router components.

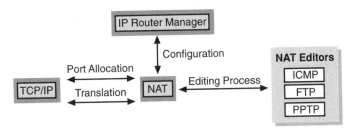

Figure 14.2 NAT components

Outbound Internet Traffic

For traffic from the private network that is outbound on the Internet interface, NAT first assesses whether or not an address/port mapping, whether static or dynamic, already exists for the packet. If not, a dynamic mapping is created. The NAT creates a mapping depending on whether there are single or multiple public IP addresses available.

- If a single public IP address is available, the NAT requests a new unique TCP or UDP port for the public IP address and uses that as the mapped port.

- If multiple public IP addresses are available, the NAT performs private-IP-address-to-public-IP-address mapping. For these mappings, the ports are not translated. When the last public IP address is needed, the NAT switches to performing address and port mapping, as it would in the case of the single public IP address.

After mapping, the NAT checks for editors and invokes one if necessary. After editing, the NAT modifies the IP and TCP or UDP headers and forwards the packet using the Internet interface. Figure 14.3 shows NAT processing for outbound Internet traffic.

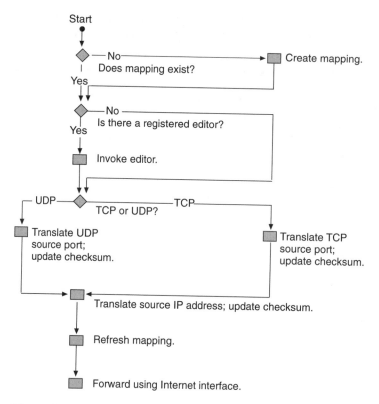

Start

— No — Does mapping exist? → Create mapping.

Yes

— No — Is there a registered editor?

Yes

Invoke editor.

UDP — TCP or UDP? — TCP

Translate UDP source port; update checksum.

Translate TCP source port; update checksum.

Translate source IP address; update checksum.

Refresh mapping.

Forward using Internet interface.

Figure 14.3 NAT processing of outbound Internet traffic

Inbound Internet Traffic

For traffic from the private network that is inbound on the Internet interface, the NAT first assesses whether an address/port mapping (whether static or dynamic) exists for the packet. If a mapping does not exist for the packet, it is silently discarded by the NAT.

This behavior protects the private network from malicious users on the Internet. The only way that Internet traffic is forwarded to the private network is either in response to traffic initiated by a private network user that created a dynamic mapping or because a static mapping exists so that Internet users can access specific resources on the private network.

After mapping, the NAT checks for editors and invokes one if necessary. After editing, the NAT modifies the TCP, UDP, and IP headers and forwards the frame using the private network interface. Figure 14.4 shows NAT processing for inbound Internet traffic.

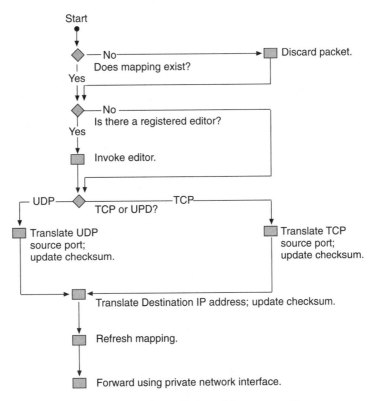

Figure 14.4 NAT processing of inbound Internet traffic

Additional NAT Routing Protocol Components

To help simplify the configuration of small networks connecting to the Internet, the NAT routing protocol for Windows 2000 also includes a DHCP allocator and a DNS proxy.

DHCP Allocator

The DHCP allocator component provides IP address configuration information to the other computers on the network. The DHCP allocator is a simplified DHCP server that allocates an IP address, a subnet mask, a default gateway, and the IP address of a DNS server. You must configure computers on the DHCP network as DHCP clients to receive the IP configuration automatically. The default TCP/IP configuration for Windows 2000, Windows NT, Windows 95, and Windows 98 computers is as a DHCP client.

Table 14.1 lists the DHCP options in the DHCPOFFER and DHCPACK messages issued by the DHCP allocator during the DHCP lease configuration process. You cannot modify these options or configure additional DHCP options.

Table 14.1   DHCP Lease Configuration Options

Option number	Option value	Description
1	255.255.0.0	Subnet mask
3	IP address of private interface	Router (default gateway)
6	IP address of private interface	DNS server (only issued if DNS proxy is enabled)
58 (0x3A)	5 minutes	Renewal time
59 (0x3B)	5 days	Rebinding time
51	7 days	IP address lease time
15 (0x0F)	Primary domain name of NAT computer	DNS domain

The DHCP allocator only supports a single scope of IP addresses as configured from the Address Assignment tab in the Properties Of The Network Address Translation (NAT) Routing Protocol dialog box in the Routing and Remote Access snap-in. The DHCP allocator does not support multiple scopes, superscopes, or multicast scopes. If you need this functionality, you should install a DHCP server and disable the DHCP allocator component of the NAT routing protocol.

DNS Proxy

The DNS proxy component acts as a DNS server to the computers on the network. DNS queries sent by a computer to the NAT server are forwarded to the DNS server. Responses to DNS queries computers receive via the NAT server are re-sent to the original small office or home office computer.

Lesson Summary

NAT enables private IP addresses to be translated into public IP addresses for traffic to and from the Internet. This keeps the internal network secure from the Internet, while saving the user the time and expense of acquiring and maintaining a public address range. A small business would normally have to obtain an ISP-allocated public IP address for each computer on its network. With the NAT, however, the small business can use private addressing and have the NAT map its private addresses to a single or to multiple public IP addresses as allocated by its ISP.

Lesson 2: Installing Internet Connection Sharing

Internet Connection Sharing (ICS) is a feature of Network and Dial-Up Connections that allows you to use Windows 2000 to connect your home network or small office network to the Internet. For example, you might have a home network that connects to the Internet by using a dial-up connection. In this lesson, you learn how to install ICS in Windows 2000.

After this lesson, you will be able to

- Enable the ICS feature of Windows 2000
- Configure Internet options for ICS

Estimated lesson time: 35 minutes

Internet Connection Sharing

ICS is a simple package consisting of DHCP, NAT, and DNS. You can use ICS to easily connect your entire network to the Internet. Because ICS provides a translated connection, all computers on a network can access Internet resources such as e-mail, Web sites, and FTP sites. ICS provides the following:

- Ease of configuration
- Single public IP address
- Fixed address range for hosts
- DNS proxy for name resolution
- Automatic IP addressing

ICS provides many more features than just address translation. Microsoft has added many features to make the configuration of Internet connections as simple as possible. ICS can be fully configured and administered from the Routing and Remote Access Manager. For a simple home network, a Connection Sharing wizard can also be launched from Control Panel Connections. The wizard does not allow configuration of any options but can get a home network up on the Internet in minutes. What simplifies the configuration is automatic addressing and automatic name resolution through the DHCP allocator, DNS proxy, and WINS proxy components. Each of these components provides a simplified configuration over the full version of DHCP, DNS, and WINS servers.

By enabling ICS on the computer that uses the dial-up connection, you are providing NAT, addressing, and name resolution services for all computers on your home network. After ICS is enabled and users verify their networking and Internet options, home network or small office network users can use applications such as Microsoft Internet Explorer and Microsoft Outlook Express as if they were directly connected to the ISP. The ICS computer then dials the ISP and creates the connection so that the user can reach the specified Web address or resource. To use the ICS feature, users on your home office or small office network must configure TCP/IP on their local area connection to obtain an IP address automatically.

Enabling Internet Connection Sharing

Before you enable ICS, consider the following:

- You should not use the ICS feature in a network with other Windows 2000 Server domain controllers, DNS servers, gateways, DHCP servers, or systems configured for static IP.

- When you enable ICS, the network adapter connected to the home or small office network is given a new IP address configuration. Existing TCP/IP connections on the ICS computer are lost and must be reestablished.

- To use the ICS feature, users on your home office or small office network must configure TCP/IP on their local area connection to obtain an IP address automatically.

- If the ICS computer is using ISDN or a modem to connect to the Internet, you must select the Enable On-Demand Dialing check box.

▶   **Follow these steps to enable ICS on a network connection:**

1. Click Start, point to Settings, and then click Network And Dial-Up Connections.

2. Right-click the dial-up, virtual private network (VPN), or the incoming connection you want to share, and then click Properties.

3. In the Sharing tab, select the Enable Internet Connection Sharing For This Connection check box.

4. If you want this connection to dial automatically when another computer on your home network attempts to access external resources, select the Enable On-Demand Dialing check box.

Installing Connection Sharing

Connection Sharing is configured from within the Routing and Remote Access Manager.

▶ **Follow these steps to install Connection Sharing:**

1. In the Routing and Remote Access Manager, open the IP Routing folder and right-click on General.

2. Click New Routing Protocol, as illustrated in Figure 14.5.

   The Select Routing Protocol dialog box appears.

3. In the Select Routing Protocol dialog box, click Connection Sharing.

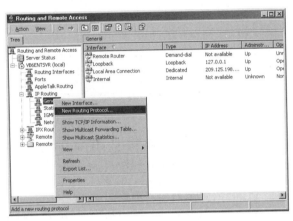

Figure 14.5 Routing and Remote Access Manager IP Routing menu

Configuring Internet Options for Internet Connection Sharing

If you have not previously established an Internet connection, you should do so.

▶ **Follow these steps to establish an Internet connection:**

1. Open Internet Explorer.

2. Click I Want To Set Up My Internet Connection Manually or I Want To Connect Through A Local Area Network (LAN), and then click Next.

3. Click I Connect Through A Local Area Network (LAN), and then click Next.

4. Clear the Automatic Discovery Of Proxy Server [Recommended] check box, and then click Next.

5. If you want to set up an Internet mail account now, and know your connection information, click Yes, and provide the e-mail account information for which the wizard prompts you. If you do not want to set up an Internet mail account, click No, click Next, and then click Finish.

If you have previously established an Internet connection, you are prompted to complete the following steps.

▶   **Follow these steps to configure Internet options for ICS:**

1. From the Tools menu, click Internet Options.

2. In the Connections tab, click Never Dial A Connection, and then click LAN Settings.

3. In Automatic Configuration, clear the Automatically Detect Settings and Use Automatic Configuration Script check boxes.

4. In Proxy Server, clear the Use A Proxy Server check box.

Internet Connection Sharing and NAT

To connect a small office or home office network to the Internet, you can use either a routed or translated connection. For a routed connection, the computer running Windows 2000 Server acts as an IP router that forwards packets between the internal network and the public Internet. Although conceptually simple, a routed connection requires knowledge of IP addressing and routing. However, routed connections enable all IP traffic between internal hosts and the public Internet. For more information, see the Small Office/Home Office (SOHO) Network to the Internet Help topic.

For a translated connection, the computer running Windows 2000 Server acts as a network address translator. Translated connections that use computers running Windows 2000 Server require less knowledge of IP addressing and routing and provide a simplified configuration for hosts and the Windows 2000 router. However, translated connections may not allow all IP traffic between SOHO hosts and Internet hosts.

In Windows 2000 Server, you can configure a translated connection to the Internet by using either the ICS feature of Network and Dial-Up Connections or the NAT routing protocol provided with Routing and Remote Access. Both ICS and NAT provide translation, addressing, and name resolution services to SOHO hosts.

As described in the previous section, ICS is designed to provide a single step of configuration (a single check box) on the computer running Windows 2000 to provide a translated connection to the Internet for all of the hosts on the network. However, once enabled, ICS does not allow further configuration beyond the configuration of applications and services. For example, ICS is designed for a single IP address obtained from an ISP and does not allow you to change the range of IP addresses allocated to hosts.

As you learned in Lesson 1, the NAT routing protocol is designed to provide maximum flexibility in the configuration of the computer running Windows 2000 Server to provide a translated connection to the Internet. NAT requires additional configuration steps; however, each step of the configuration is customizable. The NAT protocol allows for the use of ranges of IP addresses from the ISP and the configuration of the range of internal IP addresses allocated to hosts.

Table 14.2 summarizes the features and capabilities of ICS and NAT.

Table 14.2   ICS and NAT Features

ICS	NAT
Single check box configuration	Manual configuration
Single public IP address	Multiple public IP addresses
Fixed address range for internal hosts	Configurable address range for internal hosts
Single internal interface	Multiple internal interfaces

ICS and NAT are features of Windows 2000 Server that are designed to connect SOHO networks to the Internet. ICS and NAT are not designed to do the following:

- Directly connect separate private networks together
- Connect networks within an intranet
- Directly connect branch office networks to a corporate network
- Connect branch office networks to a corporate network over the Internet

Troubleshooting Connection Sharing (NAT)

Answer the following questions to troubleshoot configuration problems with Connection Sharing (NAT):

- **Are all of your interfaces (public and private) added to the Connection Sharing (NAT) routing protocol?** You must add both public (Internet) and private (small office or home office) interfaces to the Connection Sharing (NAT) routing protocol.

- **Is translation enabled on the Internet (external) interface?** You need to verify that the interface on the Windows router that connects to the Internet is configured for translation. The Enable Translation Across This Interface option in the General tab of the Properties Of The Internet Interface dialog box should be selected.

- **Is Connection Sharing enabled on the private (internal) interface?** You need to verify that the interface on the Windows router that connects to the internal network is configured for Connection Sharing. The Allow Clients On This Interface To Access Any Shared Networks option in the General tab of the Properties Of The Home Network Interface dialog box should be selected.

- **Is TCP/UDP port translation enabled?** If you only have a single public IP address, you need to verify that the Translate TCP/UDP Headers check box in the General tab of the Properties Of The External Interface dialog box is selected.

- **Is your range of public addresses set correctly?** If you have multiple public IP addresses, you need to verify that they are properly entered in the Address Pool tab of the Properties Of The Internet Interface dialog box. If your address pool includes an IP address that was not allocated to you by your ISP, inbound Internet traffic that is mapped to that IP address may be routed by the ISP to another location.

- **Is the protocol being used by a program translatable?** If you have some programs that do not seem to work through the NAT, you can try running them from the NAT computer. If they work from the NAT computer and not from a computer on the private network, the payload of the program may not be translatable. You can check the protocol being used by the program against the list of supported NAT editors.

- **Is Connection Sharing addressing enabled on the home office network?** If static addresses are not configured on the private network, verify that Connection Sharing addressing is enabled on the interfaces corresponding to the private network. To verify, click Interfaces in the Addressing tab of the Properties Of The Connection Sharing Object dialog box.

Lesson Summary

ICS is a feature of Network and Dial-Up Connections that allows you to use Windows 2000 to connect your home network or small office network to the Internet. ICS can be fully configured and administered from the Routing and Remote Access Manager. By enabling ICS on the computer that uses the dial-up connection, you are providing NAT, addressing, and name resolution services for all computers on your home network.

Lesson 3: Installing and Configuring NAT

The main function of NAT is to conserve limited IP address space. A secondary benefit of NAT is providing network connectivity without the need to understand IP routing or IP routing protocols. The NAT can be used without the knowledge or cooperation of an ISP. Contacting the ISP for the addition of static routes is not required. In this lesson, you learn how to install and configure NAT.

After this lesson, you will be able to

- Describe some design issues you should consider before implementing NAT
- Enable NAT addressing
- Configure interface IP address ranges
- Configure interface special ports
- Configure NAT network applications

Estimated lesson time: 20 minutes

Network Address Translation Design Considerations

A common use for NAT is Internet connectivity from a home or small network. To prevent problems, there are certain design issues you should consider before you implement NAT. For example, when using a NAT, private addresses are normally used on the internal network. As described in Lesson 1, private addresses are intended for internal networks, meaning those not directly connected to the Internet. It is recommended that you use these addresses instead of picking addresses at random to avoid potentially duplicating IP address assignment. Additionally, you should consider routing instead of a NAT because routing is fast and efficient, and IP was designed to be routed. However, routing requires valid IP addresses and considerable knowledge to be implemented.

IP Addressing Issues

You should use the following IP addresses from the InterNIC private IP network IDs: 10.0.0.0 with a subnet mask of 255.0.0.0, 172.16.0.0 with a subnet mask of 255.240.0.0, and 192.168.0.0 with a subnet mask of 255.255.0.0. By default, NAT uses the private network ID 192.168.0.0 with the subnet mask of 255.255.255.0 for the private network.

If you are using public IP networks that have not been allocated by the InterNIC or your ISP, you may be using the IP network ID of another organization on the Internet. This is known as illegal or overlapping IP addressing. If you are using overlapping public addresses, you cannot reach the Internet resources of the overlapping addresses. For example, if you use 1.0.0.0 with the subnet mask of 255.0.0.0, you cannot reach any Internet resources of the organization that is using the 1.0.0.0 network. You can also exclude specific IP addresses from the configured range. Excluded addresses are not allocated to private network hosts.

▶ **Follow these steps to configure the NAT server:**

1. Install and enable Routing and Remote Access.

   In the Routing And Remote Access Server Setup wizard, choose the options for ICS and to set up a router with the NAT routing protocol. After the wizard is finished, all of the configuration for NAT is complete. You do not need to complete steps 2 through 8. If you have already enabled Routing and Remote Access, complete steps 2 through 8, as needed.

2. Configure the IP address of the home network interface.

3. For the IP address of the LAN adapter that connects to the home network, you need to configure the following:

   - IP address: 192.168.0.1

   - Subnet mask: 255.255.255.0

   - No default gateway

Note The IP address in the preceding configuration for the home network interface is based on the default address range of 192.168.0.0 with a subnet mask of 255.255.255.0, which is configured for the addressing component of NAT. If you change this default address range, you should change the IP address of the private interface for the NAT computer to be the first IP address in the configured range. Using the first IP address in the range is a recommended practice, not a requirement of the NAT components.

---

4. Enable routing on your dial-up port.

   If your connection to the Internet is a permanent connection that appears in Windows 2000 as a LAN interface (such as DDS, T-Carrier, frame relay, permanent ISDN, xDSL, or cable modem), or if you are connecting your computer running Windows 2000 to another router before the connection to the Internet, and the LAN interface is configured with an IP address, subnet mask, and default gateway either statically or through DHCP, skip this step and proceed to step 6.

5. Create a demand-dial interface to connect to your ISP.

   You must create a demand-dial interface that is enabled for IP routing and uses your dial-up equipment and the credentials that you use to dial your ISP.

6. Create a default static route that uses the Internet interface.

   For a default static route, you need to select the demand-dial interface (for dial-up connections) or LAN interface (for permanent or intermediate router connections) that is used to connect to the Internet. The destination is 0.0.0.0 and the network mask is 0.0.0.0. For a demand-dial interface, the gateway IP address is not configurable.

7. Add the NAT routing protocol.

   Instructions for adding the NAT routing protocol are described in the next procedure.

8. Add your Internet and home network interfaces to the NAT routing protocol.

9. Enable NAT addressing and name resolution.

▶ **Follow these steps to add NAT as a routing protocol:**

1. Click Start, point to Programs, point to Administrative Tools, and then click Routing And Remote Access.

2. In the console tree, click General under Routing And Remote Access\Server Name\IP Routing.

3. Right-click General, and then click New Routing Protocol.

4. In the Select Routing Protocol dialog box, click Network Address Translation, and then click OK.

▶ **Follow these steps to enable NAT addressing:**

1. Click Start, point to Programs, point to Administrative Tools, and then click Routing And Remote Access.

2. In the console tree, click NAT.

3. Right-click NAT, and then click Properties.

4. In the Address Assignment tab, select the Automatically Assign IP Addresses By Using DHCP check box.

5. If applicable, in IP Address And Mask, configure the range of IP addresses to allocate to DHCP clients on the private network.

6. If applicable, click Exclude, configure the addresses to exclude from allocation to DHCP clients on the private network, and then click OK.

Single or Multiple Public Addresses

If you are using a single public IP address allocated by your ISP, no other IP address configuration is necessary. If you are using multiple IP addresses allocated by your ISP, you must configure the NAT interface with your range of public IP addresses. For the range of IP addresses given to you by your ISP, you must determine whether the range of public IP addresses can be expressed by using an IP address and a mask.

If you are allocated a number of addresses that have a power of 2 (2, 4, 8, 16, and so on), you can express the range by using a single IP address and mask. For example, if you are given the four public IP addresses 200.100.100.212, 200.100.100.213, 200.100.100.214, and 200.100.100.215 by your ISP, you can express these four addresses as 200.100.100.212 with a mask of 255.255.255.252. If your IP addresses are not expressible as an IP address and a subnet mask, you can enter them as a range or series of ranges by indicating the starting and ending IP addresses.

▶ **Follow these steps to configure interface IP address ranges:**

1. Click Start, point to Programs, point to Administrative Tools, and then click Routing And Remote Access.

2. In the console tree, click NAT.

3. In the details pane, right-click the interface you want to configure, and then click Properties.

4. In the Address Pool tab, click Add.

   If you are using a range of IP addresses that can be expressed with an IP address and a subnet mask, in Start Address, type the starting IP address, and in Mask, type the subnet mask. However, if you are using a range of IP addresses that cannot be expressed with an IP address and a subnet mask, in Start Address, type the starting IP address, and in End Address, type the ending IP address.

Allowing Inbound Connections

Normal NAT usage from a home or small business allows outbound connections from the private network to the public network. Programs such as Web browsers that run from the private network create connections to Internet resources. The return traffic from the Internet can cross the NAT because the connection was initiated from the private network. To allow Internet users to access resources on your private network, you must do the following:

- Configure a static IP address configuration on the resource server including IP address (from the range of IP addresses allocated by the NAT computer), subnet mask (from the range of IP addresses allocated by the NAT computer), default gateway (the private IP address of the NAT computer), and DNS server (the private IP address of the NAT computer).

- Exclude the IP address being used by the resource computer from the range of IP addresses being allocated by the NAT computer.

- Configure a special port. A special port is a static mapping of a public address and port number to a private address and port number. A special port maps an inbound connection from an Internet user to a specific address on your private network. By using a special port, you can create a Web server on your private network that is accessible from the Internet.

▶ **Follow these steps to configure interface special ports:**

1. Click Start, point to Programs, point to Administrative Tools, and then click Routing And Remote Access.

2. In the details pane, right-click the interface you want to configure, and then click Properties.

3. In the Special Ports tab, in Protocol, click either TCP or UDP, and then click Add.

4. In Incoming Port, type the port number of the incoming public traffic.

5. If a range of public IP addresses is configured, click On This Address Pool Entry, and then type the public IP address of the incoming public traffic.

6. In Outgoing Port, type the port number of the private network resource.

7. In Private Address, type the private address of the private network resource.

Configuring Applications and Services

You may need to configure applications and services to work properly across the Internet. For example, if users on your small office or home office network want to play the Diablo game with other users on the Internet, NAT must be configured for the Diablo application.

▶ **Follow these steps to configure NAT network applications:**

1. Click Start, point to Programs, point to Administrative Tools, and then click Routing And Remote Access.

2. In the console tree, click NAT.

3. Right-click NAT, and then click Properties.

4. In the Translation tab, click Applications.

5. To add a network application, in the Applications dialog box, click Add.

6. In the Add Application dialog box, type the settings for the network application, and then click OK.

Note You can also edit or remove an existing NAT network application by clicking Edit or Remove in the Applications dialog box.

Virtual Private Network Connections from a Translated Network

To access a private intranet using a VPN connection from a translated network, you can use the PPTP and create a VPN connection from a host on the internal network to the VPN server within the second private intranet. The NAT routing protocol has a NAT editor for PPTP traffic. Layer 2 Tunneling Protocol (L2TP) over IPSec connections do not work across the NAT server.

Virtual Private Networks and NATs

Not all traffic can by translated by the NAT. Some applications may have embedded IP addresses (not in the IP header) or may be encrypted. For these applications one can tunnel through the NAT using PPTP. PPTP does require an editor, which has been implemented in the NAT. Only the IP and Generic Routing Encapsulation (GRE) headers are edited or translated. The original IP datagram is not affected. This allows for encryption or otherwise unsupported applications to go through the NAT.

The source of the PPTP packets are translated to a NAT address. The encapsulated IP packet will have a source address assigned by the PPTP server. When the packet is beyond the PPTP server, the encapsulation is removed and the source address will be the one assigned by the PPTP server. If the PPTP server is using a pool of valid Internet addresses, the client now has a valid address and can go anywhere on the Internet. Any application will work, as the original IP datagram is not translated. Only the encapsulation or wrapper is translated by the NAT.

Note L2TP does not require a NAT editor. However, L2TP with IPSec cannot be translated by the NAT. There cannot be a NAT editor for IPSec.

This method of NAT bypass is only useful if there is a PPTP server to tunnel to. This will be good for branch offices or home users tunneling to a corporate network, as illustrated in Figure 14.6.

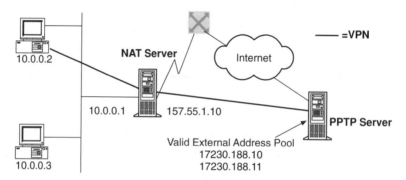

Figure 14.6 Implementing a VPN through a NAT server

Lesson Summary

When using a NAT, private addresses are normally used on the internal network. It is recommended that you use these addresses on a private network instead of picking addresses at random because they are potentially duplicate addresses not valid on the Internet. To prevent problems, you should identify design issues before you implement NAT. Normal NAT usage from a home or small business allows outbound connections from the private network to the public network. You may need to configure applications and services to work properly across the Internet. In addition, remember that not all traffic can be translated by the NAT because some applications may have embedded IP addresses or may be encrypted. For these applications, you can tunnel through the NAT using PPTP.

Review

Answering the following questions will reinforce key information presented in this chapter. If you are unable to answer a question, review the appropriate lesson and then try the question again. Answers to the questions can be found in Appendix A, "Questions and Answers."

1. What is the purpose of NAT?

2. What are the components of NAT?

3. If a small business is using the 10.0.0.0 private network for its intranet and has been granted the public IP address of 198.200.200.1 by its ISP, to what public IP address does NAT map all private IP addresses being used on network 10.0.0.0?

4. What must you do to allow Internet users to access resources on your private network?

C H A P T E R   1 5

Managing Microsoft Certificate Services

About This Chapter

Certificates are fundamental elements of the Microsoft Public Key Infrastructure (PKI). Certificates enable users to use smart card logon, send encrypted e-mail, and sign electronic documents. Certificates are issued, managed, renewed, and revoked by certificate authorities. In this chapter, you learn how to install and configure certificates.

Before You Begin

To complete this chapter, you must have

- Installed Microsoft Windows 2000 Server
- Installed Active Directory directory service
- Installed Domain Name System (DNS)

Lesson 1: Introducing Certificates

In this lesson, you learn about digital certificates and Microsoft Windows 2000 Certificate Services. Certificates are a very important part of Microsoft's PKI. You also learn about certificate authorities (CAs) supported by Windows 2000 Certificate Services.

After this lesson, you will be able to

- Define a certificate
- Explain the components of a certificate
- Describe the use of certificates
- Explain the difference between enterprise and standalone CAs

Estimated lesson time: 25 minutes

Overview of Certificates

A certificate (digital certificate, public key certificate) is a digital document that attests to the binding of a public key to an entity. The main purpose of a certificate is to generate confidence that the public key contained in the certificate actually belongs to the entity named in the certificate. As illustrated in Figure 15.1, certificates play a fundamental role in the Microsoft PKI.

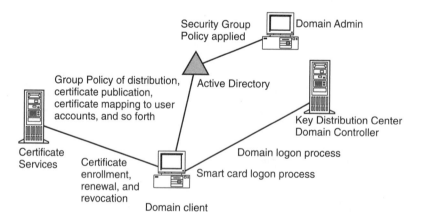

Figure 15.1 Certificate Services integrated with Active Directory directory service and distributed security services

A certificate may consist of a public key signed by a trusted entity. However, the most widely used structure and syntax for digital certificates is defined by the International Telecommunications Union (ITU) in ITU-T Recommendation X.509. Figure 15.2 illustrates a certificate that can be used to validate the sender of an e-mail message.

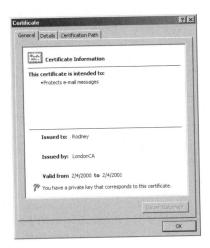

Figure 15.2 Sample certificate

An X.509 certificate contains information that identifies the user and provides information about the organization that issued the certificate. The information provided includes the serial number, validity period, issuer name, issuer signature, and subject (or user) name. The subject can be an individual, a business, a school, or some other organization, including a CA.

How Certificates Are Created

Certificates are issued by a CA, which can be any trusted service or entity willing to verify and validate the identities of those to whom it issues certificates, and the association of those identities with specific keys. Companies may issue certificates to employees, schools may issue certificates to students, and so on. Of course, a CA's public key must be trustworthy or the certificates it issues will not be trusted. Because anyone can become a CA, certificates are only as trustworthy as the authority that issues the underlying keys. The following six steps describe the process of requesting and issuing a certificate.

1. **Generating a key pair.** The applicant generates a public and private key pair or is assigned a key pair by some authority in his or her organization.

2. **Collecting required information.** The applicant collects whatever information the CA requires to issue a certificate. The information could include the applicant's e-mail address, birth certificate, fingerprints, and notarized documents—whatever the CA needs to be certain that the applicant is who he or she claims to be. CAs with stringent identification requirements produce certificates with high assurance. That is, their certificates generate a high level of confidence. CAs themselves are said to be of high, medium, or low assurance.

3. **Requesting the certificate.** The applicant sends a certificate request, which consists of his or her public key and the additional required information, to the CA. The certificate request may be encrypted using the CA's public key. Many requests are made using e-mail, but requests can also be sent by postal or courier service, for example, when the certificate request itself must be notarized.

4. **Verifying the information.** The CA applies whatever policy rules it requires to verify that the applicant should receive a certificate. As with identification requirements, a CA's verification policy and procedures influence the amount of confidence generated by the certificates it issues.

5. **Creating the certificate.** The CA creates and signs a digital document containing the applicant's public key and other appropriate information. The signature of the CA authenticates the binding of the subject's name to the subject's public key. The signed document is the certificate.

6. **Sending or posting the certificate.** The CA sends the certificate to the applicant or posts the certificate in a directory as appropriate.

How Certificates Are Used

Certificates are used to generate confidence in the legitimacy of specific public keys. A certificate must be signed with the issuer's private key; otherwise, it is not a certificate. Therefore, the issuer's signature can be verified using the issuer's public key. If an entity trusts the issuer, the entity can also have confidence that the public key contained in the certificate belongs to the subject named in the certificate.

Enterprise and Standalone CAs

Certificate Services includes two policy modules that permit two classes of CAs: enterprise CAs and standalone CAs. Within these two classes, there can be two types of CAs: a root CA or a subordinate CA. The policy modules define the actions that a CA can take when it receives a certificate request, and can be modified if necessary.

CAs are usually organized in a hierarchy in which the most trusted CA is at the top. The Windows 2000 PKI assumes a hierarchical CA model. There may be multiple disjointed hierarchies; there is no requirement that all CAs share a common top-level parent.

Enterprise CAs

In an enterprise, the enterprise root CA is the most trusted CA. There can be more than one enterprise root CA in a Windows 2000 domain, but there can be only one enterprise root CA in any given hierarchy. All other CAs in the hierarchy are enterprise-subordinate CAs.

An organization should install an enterprise CA if it will be issuing certificates to users or computers within the organization. It is not necessary to install a CA in every domain in the organization. For example, users in a child domain can use a CA in a parent domain. Enterprise CAs have a special policy module that enforces how certificates are processed and issued. The policy information used by these modules is stored centrally in Windows 2000 Active Directory directory service.

Note Active Directory and a DNS server must be running prior to installing an enterprise CA.

Standalone CAs

An organization that will be issuing certificates to users or computers outside the organization should install a standalone CA. There can be many standalone CAs, but there can be only one standalone CA per hierarchy. All other CAs in a hierarchy are either standalone subordinate CAs or enterprise subordinate CAs.

A standalone CA has a relatively simple default policy module and does not store any information remotely. Therefore, a standalone CA does not need to have Microsoft Windows 2000 Active Directory available.

Types of CAs

The setup requirements for the four types of CAs available from Certificate Services are described in the following sections.

Enterprise Root CA

An enterprise root CA is the root of an organization's CA hierarchy. An organization should set up an enterprise root CA if the CA will be issuing certificates to users and computers within the organization. In large organizations, the enterprise root CA is used only to issue certificates to subordinate CAs. The subordinate CAs issue certificates to users and computers.

The enterprise root CA requires the following:

- Windows 2000 Domain Name System (DNS) service
- Windows 2000 Active Directory directory service
- Administrative privileges on all servers

Enterprise Subordinate CA

An enterprise subordinate CA is a CA that issues certificates within an organization but is not the most trusted CA in that organization; it is subordinate to another CA in the hierarchy.

The enterprise subordinate CA has the following requirements:

- It must be associated with a CA that will process the subordinate CA's certificate requests. This could be an external commercial CA or a standalone CA.
- It must use Windows 2000 DNS Service.
- It must use Windows 2000 Active Directory directory service.
- It must have administrative privileges on all servers.

Standalone Root CA

A standalone root CA is the root of a CA trust hierarchy. The standalone root CA requires administrative privileges on the local server. An organization should install a standalone root CA if the CA will be issuing certificates outside of the organization's enterprise network, and the CA needs to be the root CA. A root CA typically only issues certificates to subordinate CAs.

Standalone Subordinate CA

A standalone subordinate CA is a CA that operates as a solitary certificate server or exists in a CA trust hierarchy. An organization should set up a standalone subordinate CA when it will be issuing certificates to entities outside the organization.

The standalone subordinate CA has the following requirements:

- It must be associated with a CA that will process the subordinate CA's certificate requests. This could be an external commercial CA.

- It has administrative privileges on the local server.

    Certificate enrollment is the process used for obtaining a digital certificate.

Lesson Summary

In this lesson, you learned that certificates are fundamental elements of the Microsoft PKI. Certificates enable users to use smart card logon, send encrypted e-mail, sign electronic documents, and so forth. Certificates are issued, managed, renewed, and revoked by CAs. In this lesson, you also learned how to install and configure certificates.

Lesson 2: Installing and Configuring Certificate Authority

In this lesson, you explore certificates in more detail by learning how to install and protect your CA. Next, you are introduced to various ways to enroll certificates.

After this lesson, you will be able to

- Explain how to use Certificate Authority Manager
- Explain how to install a CA
- Explain how to protect a CA
- Describe the certificate enrollment process

Estimated lesson time: 35 minutes

Deploying a CA

CAs will be installed during the upcoming practice, "Installing a Standalone Subordinate CA." The Certificate Services Installation wizard walks the administrator through the installation process. This section discusses key elements that should be considered before beginning the installation process.

- **Establishing a Windows 2000 domain.** If an enterprise CA is to be deployed, establish a domain before installing Certificate Services.

- **Active Directory integration.** Information concerning enterprise CAs is written into a CA object in Active Directory during installation. This provides information to domain clients about available CAs and the types of certificates they will issue.

- **Selecting the host server.** The root CA can run on any Windows 2000 Server platform, including a domain controller. Factors such as physical security requirements, expected loading, and connectivity requirements should be considered in making this decision.

- **Naming.** CA names are bound into their certificates and hence cannot change. Renaming a computer running Certificate Services is not supported. Consider factors such as organizational naming conventions and future requirements to distinguish among issuing CAs. The CA name (or common name) is critical because it is used to identify the CA object created in Active Directory for an enterprise CA.

- **Key generation.** The CA's public-private key pair will be generated during the installation process and is unique to this CA.

- **CA certificate.** For a root CA, the installation process will automatically generate a self-signed CA certificate using the CA's public-private key pair. For a child CA, the administrator has the option to generate a certificate request that may be submitted to an intermediate or root CA.

- **Issuing policy.** The enterprise CA setup automatically installs and configures the default enterprise policy module for the CA. The standalone CA setup automatically installs and configures the default standalone policy module. Custom policy modules can be substituted if necessary.

After a root CA has been established, it is possible to install intermediate or issuing CAs subordinate to this root CA. The only significant difference in the installation policy is that a certificate request is generated for submission to a root or intermediate CA. This request may be routed automatically to online CAs located by means of Active Directory, or it may be routed manually in an offline scenario. In either case, the resultant certificate must be installed at the CA before it can begin operation.

The enterprise CA trust model may or may not correspond to the Windows 2000 domain trust model. A direct mapping between CA trust relationships and domain trust relationships is not required. There is nothing that prevents a single CA from servicing entities in multiple domains or even entities outside the domain boundary. Similarly, a given domain may have multiple enterprise CAs.

Protecting a CA

CAs are highly valued resources, and it is often desirable to provide them with a high degree of protection. Specific actions that should be considered include:

- **Physical protection.** Because CAs represent highly trusted entities within an enterprise, they should be protected from tampering. This requirement is dependent on the inherent value of the certification made by the CA. For example, if the certificates provided by a server are used to provide security to users accessing their online bank accounts, physical protection of the server would be a good idea. Physical isolation of the CA server in a facility accessible only to security administrators can dramatically reduce the possibility of such physical attacks.

- **Key management.** The CA's private key provides the basis for trust in the certification process and should be secured from tampering. Cryptographic hardware modules (accessible to Certificate Services through a CryptoAPI Cryptographic Service Provider [CSP]) can provide tamper-resistant key storage and isolate the cryptographic operations from other software running on the server. This significantly reduces the likelihood of a CA key being compromised.

- **Restoration.** Loss of a CA—due to hardware failure, for example—can create a number of administrative and operational problems and prevent revocation of existing certificates. Certificate Services supports backup of a CA instance so it can be restored at a later time. This is an important part of the overall CA management process.

Certificate Enrollment

The process of obtaining a digital certificate is called certificate enrollment. The Windows 2000 PKI supports certificate enrollment to the Microsoft enterprise CA, standalone CA, or third-party CAs. Enrollment support is implemented in a transport-independent manner and is based on use of industry-standard public-key cryptography standards (PKCS) #10 certificate request messages and PKCS #7 responses containing the resulting certificate or certificate chain. At the time of this writing, certificates supporting RSA keys and signatures, digital signature algorithm (DSA) keys and signatures, and Diffie-Hellman keys are supported.

Multiple Enrollment Methods

The PKI supports multiple enrollment methods, including Web-based enrollment, an enrollment wizard, and policy-driven auto-enrollment that occurs as part of a user's logon processing. Microsoft plans to develop the certificate enrollment process in a manner consistent with the Certificate Request Syntax (CRS) draft currently in the Internet Engineering Task Force (IETF) Public-Key Infrastructure X.509 (PKIX) working group.

Web-Based Enrollment

The Web-based enrollment process begins with a client submitting a certificate request and ends with the installation of the certificate in the client application. Certificate Services includes a Hypertext Transfer Protocol (HTTP) enrollment control with forms, illustrated in Figure 15.3, for custom certificate enrollment and renewal applications for Microsoft Certificate Services. The enrollment control and its forms are accessed through the Certificate Services Enrollment page, which is available from the Certificate Services Administrative Tools Web page, located at *http://<server_name>/certsrv/default.asp*. You can customize the Microsoft Certificate Services Web pages to modify user options or provide links to online help, support, or user instructions.

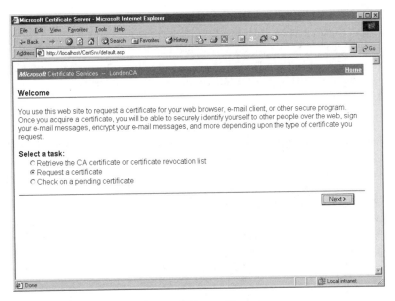

Figure 15.3 Certificate Server Web enrollment

Client Certificate Enrollment

Certificate Services supports client certificate enrollment using Internet Explorer version 3.0 or later. To obtain a client certificate with these browsers, the user opens the client authentication page and submits identification information. After Certificate Services creates the client certificate, it is returned to the browser, which installs the certificate on the client.

Automated Enrollment

The automated enrollment process is controlled by two key elements: certificate types and auto-enrollment objects. These are integrated with the Group Policy object and may be defined on a site, domain, organizational unit (OU), computer, or user basis.

Certificate types provide a template for a certificate and associate it with a common name for ease of administration. The template defines elements such as naming requirements, validity period, allowable CSPs for private key generation, algorithms, and extensions that should be incorporated into the certificate. The certificate types are logically separated into machine and user types and applied to the policy objects accordingly. Once defined, these certificate types are available for use with the auto-enrollment objects and Certificate Enrollment wizard.

This mechanism is not a replacement for the enterprise CA issuing policy, but is integrated with it. The CA service receives a set of certificate types as part of its policy object. These are used by the Enterprise Policy Module to define the types of certificates the CA is allowed to issue. The CA rejects requests for certificates that fail to match these criteria.

The auto-enrollment object defines policy for certificates that an entity in the domain should have. This can be applied on a machine and user basis. The types of certificates are incorporated by reference to the certificate type objects and may be any defined type. The auto-enrollment object provides sufficient information to determine whether an entity has the required certificates and enrolls those certificates with an enterprise CA if they are missing. Auto-enrollment objects also define policy on certificate renewal. This policy can be set by an administrator to occur in advance of certificate expiration, which supports long-term operation without direct user action. The auto-enrollment objects are processed, and any required actions taken, whenever policy is refreshed (logon time, Group Policy object refresh, and so on).

Practice: Installing a Standalone Subordinate CA

In this practice, you will install a standalone subordinate CA and then request a certificate to use from the local authority that you setup.

Exercise 1: Installing a Standalone Subordinate CA

In this exercise, you install and configure the standalone subordinate CA.

1. From Control Panel, select Add/Remove Programs.
2. Click Add/Remove Windows Components.
3. Check the box next to Certificate Services, and then click Next.
4. Select Standalone Root CA, and then click Next.
5. Fill in the CA identifying information.

    For CA name, type **ComputernameCA** and then click Next.
6. Use the default data storage locations, and then click Next.
7. During the CA installation process, you may need to click OK to stop the World Wide Web Publishing Service, and you need to give the location of the Windows 2000 installation files (specifically Certsrv.*).
8. Click Finish.
9. Close the Add/Remove Programs window.

Exercise 2: Requesting a Certificate from the Local CA

Now that the CA is installed, you can request a certificate.

1. Run Certificate Authority Manager.

   Notice that the service is started (indicated by a check mark), as illustrated in Figure 15.4.

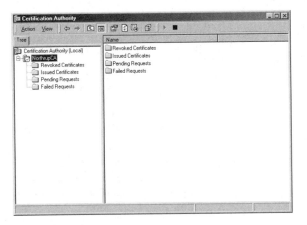

Figure 15.4 Certificate Authority Manager

2. Run Internet Explorer and connect to *http://<your_server>/certsrv/ default.asp.*

3. Request a Web browser certificate. The request will be pending.

4. Close Internet Explorer.

5. Open Certificate Authority and select the Pending Requests folder. Right-click your request and choose Issue from the All Tasks menu.

   In the left pane select the Issued Certificates folder, and notice that your request has been issued.

6. Run Internet Explorer, connect to *http://<your_server>/certsrv/ default.asp*, check on the Pending Certificate Request, and then install the certificate.

7. From the Tools menu, click Internet Options, Content, and then Certificates.

8. Under Certificates, highlight your certificate, and then click View. Notice that the certificate was issued by your computer, and close all windows.

Cryptographic Key Storage

Within the Microsoft PKI, cryptographic keys and associated certificates are stored and managed by the CryptoAPI subsystem. Keys are managed by CSPs and certificates are managed by the CryptoAPI certificate stores. The certificate stores are repositories for certificates, along with associated properties. By convention, the PKI defines five standard certificate stores, described in Table 15.1.

Table 15.1   Standard PKI Certificate Stores

Store	Description
MY	This store is used to hold a user's or computer's certificates, for which the associated private key is available.
CA	This store is used to hold issuing or intermediate CA certificates to use in building certificate verification chains.
TRUST	This store is used to hold certificate trust lists. These are an alternate mechanism for allowing an administrator to specify a collection of trusted CAs. An advantage of this type of store is that it is digitally signed and may be transmitted over nonsecure links.
ROOT	This store holds only self-signed CA certificates for trusted root CAs.
UserDS	This store provides a logical view of a certificate repository stored in Active Directory (for example, in the userCertificate property of the User object). Its purpose is to simplify access to these external repositories.

These are logical stores that can present a consistent, systemwide view of the available certificates that may reside on multiple physical stores (hard disk, smart cards, and so on). By using these services, applications can share certificates and are assured of consistent operation under administrative policy. The certificate management functions support decoding of X.509 v3 certificates and provide enumeration functions to assist in locating a specific certificate.

To simplify application development, the MY store maintains certificate properties that indicate the CSP and key-set name for the associated private key. Once an application has selected a certificate to use, it can use this information to obtain a CSP context for the correct private key.

Certificate Renewal

Certificate renewal is conceptually similar to enrollment, but takes advantage of the trust relationship inherent in an existing certificate. Renewal assumes the requesting entity wants a new certificate with the same attributes as an existing, valid certificate, but with extended validity dates. A renewal may use the existing public key or a new public key.

Renewal is of advantage primarily to the CA. A renewal request can presumably be processed more efficiently because the existing certificate attributes do not need to be verified again. Renewal is currently supported in the Windows 2000 PKI for automatically enrolled certificates. For other mechanisms, a renewal is treated as a new enrollment request.

Industry-standard message protocols for certificate renewal are not yet defined, but are included in the IETF PKIX CRS draft. Once these standards are ratified, Microsoft plans to implement the associated message formats.

Certificate and Key Recovery

Public-key pairs and certificates tend to have high value. If they are lost due to system failure, their replacement may be time-consuming and result in monetary loss. To address this issue, the Windows 2000 PKI supports enable you to back up and restore both certificates and associated key pairs through the certificate management administrative tools.

When exporting a certificate using the Certificate Manager, the user must specify whether to also export the associated key pair. If this option is selected, the information is exported as an encrypted (based on a user-supplied password) PKCS #12 message. This may later be imported to the system, or to another system, to restore the certificate and keys.

This operation assumes that the key pair is exportable by the CSP. This is true for the Microsoft Base Cryptographic Provider if the exportable flag was set at key generation time. Third-party CSPs may or may not support private key export. For example, smart card CSPs do not generally support this operation. For software CSPs with nonexportable keys, the alternative is to maintain a complete system-image backup, including all registry information.

Roaming

Roaming in the context of this discussion means the ability to use the same public key–based applications on different computers within the enterprise's Windows 2000 environment. The principal requirement is to make users' cryptographic keys and certificates available wherever they log on. The Windows 2000 PKI supports this in two ways.

First, if the Microsoft Base Cryptographic Providers are used, roaming keys and certificates are supported by the roaming profile mechanism. This is transparent to the user once roaming profiles are enabled. It is unlikely that this functionality will be supported by third-party CSPs, as they will generally use a different method of preserving key data, often on hardware devices.

Hardware token devices, such as smart cards, support roaming, provided they incorporate a physical certificate store. The smart card CSPs that ship with the Windows 2000 platform support this functionality. Roaming support is accomplished by moving the hardware token with the user.

Revocation

Certificates tend to be long-lived credentials. There are a number of reasons these credentials may become untrustworthy prior to their expiration. Those reasons include the following:

- Compromise, or suspected compromise, of an entity's private key
- Fraud in obtaining the certificate
- Change in status

PK-based functionality assumes distributed verification in which there is no need for direct communication with a central trusted entity that vouches for these credentials. This creates a need for revocation information that can be distributed to individuals attempting to verify certificates.

The application determines if and when revocation information is required. To support a variety of operational scenarios, the Windows 2000 PKI incorporates support of industry-standard certificate revocation lists (CRLs). Enterprise CAs support certificate revocation and CRL publication to Active Directory under administrative control. Domain clients can fetch this information, caching it locally, to use when verifying certificates. This same mechanism supports CRLs published by commercial CAs or third-party certificate server products, provided the published CRLs are accessible to clients over the network.

Trust

Certificate verification is of primary concern to clients using PK-based applications. If a given end-entity certificate can be shown to "chain" to a known trusted root CA, and if the intended certificate usage is consistent with the application context, it is considered valid. If either of these conditions is not true, it is considered invalid.

Within the PKI, users may make trust decisions that affect only themselves. They do this by installing or deleting trusted root CAs and by configuring associated usage restrictions by using the certificate management administrative tools. Within the enterprise, this is expected to be the exception rather than the rule. It is expected that these trust relationships will be established as part of the enterprise policy. Trust relationships established by policy are automatically propagated to Windows 2000 client computers.

Trusted CA Roots

Trust in root CAs may be set by policy to establish trust relationships used by domain clients in verifying PK certificates. The set of trusted CAs is configured using the Group Policy editor. It can be configured on a per-computer basis and will apply to all users of that computer.

In addition to establishing a root CA as trusted, the administrator can set usage properties associated with the CA. If specified, these restrict the purposes for which the CA-issued certificates are valid. Restrictions are specified based on object identifiers as defined for ExtendedKeyUsage extensions in the IETF PKIX Part 1 draft. Currently, these restrictions can be applied to the usage of any combination of the following:

- Server authentication
- Client authentication
- Code signing
- E-mail
- IP Security Protocol (IPSec) end system
- IPSec tunnel
- IPSec user
- Time stamping
- Microsoft Encrypted File System

Lesson Summary

In this lesson, you learned how to install and protect your CA. CAs are highly valued resources and it is important to protect them. You also learned various ways to provide enrollment of certificates. To obtain a client certificate, the user opens the client authentication page and submits identification information. Then, Certificate Services creates the client certificate that is returned to the browser and installed on the client.

Lesson 3: Managing Certificates

Once you start issuing certificates, or clients request that you issue them, management of certificates becomes an important issue. In this lesson, you learn how to manage certificates, revoke a certificate, and implement an Encrypting File System (EFS) recovery policy.

After this lesson, you will be able to

- Describe the steps to revoke a certificate
- Describe how to issue an EFS recovery policy

Estimated lesson time: 30 minutes

Revoked Certificates

When a certificate is marked as revoked, it is moved to the Revoked Certificates folder. The revoked certificate appears on the CRL the next time it is published. Certificates revoked with the reason code Certificate Hold can be unrevoked, left on Certificate Hold until they expire, or have their revocation reason code changed. This is the only reason code that allows you to change the status of a revoked certificate. It is useful if the status of the certificate is questionable, and is meant to provide some flexibility to the CA administrator.

Issued Certificates

In the details pane, examine the certificate request by noting the values for requester name, requester e-mail address, and any other fields that you consider critical information for issuing the certificate.

Pending Requests

In the details pane, examine the certificate request by noting the values for requester name, requester e-mail address, and any other fields that you consider critical information for issuing the certificate.

Failed Requests

Failed certificate requests should only occur when a member of the Cert Publishers or Administrators groups denies a certificate request.

How a Certificate Is Issued

When a certificate is presented to an entity as a means of identifying the certificate holder (the subject of the certificate), it is useful only if the entity receiving the certificate trusts the issuing CA. Certificates are issued under the following processes:

- **Key generation.** The individual or applicant requesting certification generates key pairs of public and private keys. The exception to this is personal digital certificates, in which case the CA generates the public and private keys and sends them to the end user.

- **Matching of policy information.** The applicant packages up the additional information necessary for the CA to issue the certificate (for example, proof of identity, tax ID number, e-mail address, and so on). The precise definition of this information is up to the CA.

- **Sending of public keys and information.** The applicant sends the public keys and information (often encrypted using the CA's public key) to the CA.

- **Verification of information.** The CA applies whatever policy rules it might require to verify that the applicant should receive a certificate.

- **Certificate creation.** The CA creates a digital document with the appropriate information (public keys, expiration date, and other data) and signs it using the CA's private key.

- **Sending or posting of certificate.** The CA may send the certificate to the applicant or post it publicly. The certificate is loaded onto the individual's system.

Certificate Revocation

Certificate authorities publish CRLs containing certificates that have been revoked by the CA. The certificate holder's private key may become compromised, or false information may be used to apply for the certificate. CRLs provide a way of withdrawing a certificate after it has been issued. CRLs are made available for downloading or online viewing by client applications.

To verify a certificate, all that is necessary is the public key of the CA and a check against the revocation list published by that CA. Certificates and CAs reduce the public-key distribution problem of verifying and trusting one (or more) public keys per individual. Instead, only the CA's public key must be trusted and verified, and then that can be relied on to allow verification of other certificates.

Practice: Revoking a Certificate

In this practice, you will revoke the certificate you obtained when completing the Practice in Lesson 2.

Exercise 1: Revoking the Certificate from Lesson 2

1. Open the Certificate Authority Manager.

2. Right-click your request under Issued Certificates, point to All Tasks, and then click Revoke Certificate.

3. When prompted for a reason code, select Cease Of Operation. Click Yes.

4. In the left pane, click Revoked Certificates.

   Notice your request has been revoked, as illustrated in Figure 15.5.

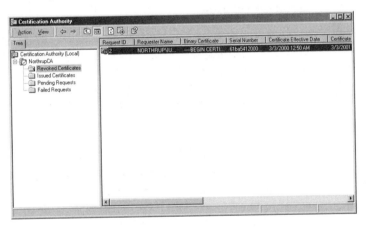

Figure 15.5 Certificate Authority revoked certificates

EFS Recovery Policy

Data recovery is available for the EFS as a part of the overall security policy for the system. For example, if you should ever lose your file encryption certificate and associated private key (through disk failure or any other reason), data recovery is available through the person who is the designated recovery agent. Or, in a business environment, an organization can recover data encrypted by an employee after the employee leaves.

EFS recovery policy specifies the data recovery agent accounts that are used within the scope of the policy. EFS requires an encrypted data recovery agent policy before it can be used, and it uses a default recovery agent account (the Administrator) if none has been chosen. In a domain, only members of the Domain Admins group can designate another account as the recovery agent account. In a small business or home environment where there are no domains, the computer's local Administrator account is the default recovery agent account. Only the Administrator account can change local recovery policy for a computer.

A recovery agent account is used to restore data for all computers covered by the policy. If a user's private key is lost, a file protected by that key can be backed up, and the backup sent by means of secure e-mail to a recovery agent administrator. The administrator restores the backup copy, opens it to read the file, copies the file in plaintext, and returns the plaintext file to the user using secure e-mail again.

As an alternative, the administrator can go to the computer that has the encrypted file, import his or her recovery agent certificate and private key, and perform the recovery there. However, this might not be safe and is not recommended because of the sensitivity of the recovery key—the administrator cannot afford to leave the recovery key on another computer.

Practice: Changing a Recovery Policy

In this practice, you change the recovery policy for the local computer. Before changing the recovery policy in any way, you should first back up the recovery keys to a floppy disk. In a domain, a default recovery policy is implemented for the domain when the first domain controller is set up. The domain administrator is issued the self-signed certificate, which designates the domain administrator as the recovery agent. To change the default recovery policy for a domain, log on to the first domain controller as an administrator.

Note To complete this practice, you must have the appropriate permissions to request the certificate and the CA must be configured to issue this type of certificate.

Exercise 1: Changing the Recovery Policy for the Local Computer

1. Click Start, click Run, type **mmc /a** and then click OK.

2. On the Console menu, click Add/Remove Snap-In, and then click Add.

3. Under Snap-In, click Group Policy, and then click Add.

4. Under Group Policy Object, make sure that Local Computer is displayed, click Finish, click Close, and then click OK.

5. In Navigate Local Computer Policy\Computer Configuration\Windows Settings\Security Settings\Public Key Policies, right-click Encrypted Data Recovery Agents, and then click one of the following options:

   - The Add command designates a user as an additional recovery agent using the Add Recovery Agent wizard.

   - The Delete Policy command deletes this EFS policy and every recovery agent. The effect of deleting the EFS policy and every recovery agent is that users will not be able to encrypt files on this computer. The computer issues a default self-signed certificate that designates the local administrator as the default recovery agent. If you delete this certificate without another policy in place, the computer has an empty recovery policy. An empty recovery policy means that no one is a recovery agent. This turns EFS off, thereby not allowing users to encrypt files on this computer.

6. To make changes to the File Recovery certificate, start by selecting Encrypted Data Recovery Agents in the left pane, as shown in Figure 15.6. Right-click the certificate in the right pane, and then click Properties. For example, you can give the certificate a friendly name and enter a text description.

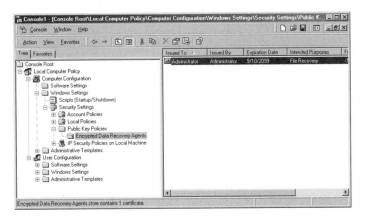

Figure 15.6 Group Policy for EFS recovery

Lesson Summary

You can manage certificates using the Certificate Authority snap-in for the Microsoft Management Console (MMC). Certificates revoked with the reason code Certificate Hold can be unrevoked. They can also be left on Certificate Hold until they expire or have their revocation reason code changed. Data recovery is available for the EFS as a part of the overall security policy for the system.

Review

Answering the following questions will reinforce key information presented in this chapter. If you are unable to answer a question, review the appropriate lesson and then try the question again. Answers to the questions can be found in Appendix A, "Questions and Answers."

1. What are certificates, and what is their purpose?

2. What is a certificate authority (CA), and what does it do?

3. What are the four types of Microsoft certificate authorities?

4. Name one reason for a certificate revocation.

5. What are the five PKI standard certificate stores?

PART 3

Active Directory Directory Service

Part 3 contains most of the information that relates to the Windows 2000 Active Directory portion of the 70-240 exam. This includes installing and configuring, managing network protocols, configuring desktops, and maintaining security. The chapters in this part primarily use Windows 2000 Server during the various hands-on practices and exercises. However, much of the information presented here is also applicable to Windows 2000 Professional.

Active Directory is the directory service included in Windows 2000 Server. It stores information about objects on a network and makes this information available to users and network administrators. Active Directory gives network users access to permitted resources anywhere on the network using a single logon process. It provides network administrators with an intuitive hierarchical view of the network and a single point of administration for all network objects.

CHAPTER 16

Introduction to Active Directory Directory Service

About This Chapter

A directory service is used to uniquely identify users and resources on a network. Active Directory directory service in Microsoft Windows 2000 is a significant enhancement over the directory services provided in previous versions of Windows. Active Directory provides a single point of network management, allowing you to add, remove, and relocate users and resources easily. This chapter introduces you to Active Directory and the administration tasks and administrative tools used to manage the service.

The primary Active Directory administration tasks are configuring and administering Active Directory, administering users and groups, securing network resources, administering the desktop computing environment, securing Active Directory, managing Active Directory performance, and installing Windows 2000 remotely. The primary Windows 2000 Active Directory administration tools are the Active Directory administrative tools, Microsoft Management Console (MMC) snap-ins (available in the Administrative Tools Start group), and the Task Scheduler (available in Control Panel).

Before You Begin

To complete this chapter, you must have

- Installed Windows 2000 Server on a computer (Server01)

    See Chapter 8, "Installing Microsoft Windows 2000" for more details.

- Experience logging on and off Windows 2000

Lesson 1: Active Directory Overview

Active Directory provides a method for designing a directory structure that meets the specfic needs of various types of organizations. This lesson introduces the use of objects in Active Directory and the function of each of its components.

After this lesson, you will be able to

- Explain the purpose of object attributes and the schema in Active Directory
- Identify the components of Active Directory
- Describe the function of Active Directory components

Estimated lesson time: 30 minutes

Active Directory Objects

Active Directory stores information about network resources, as well as all the services that make the information available and useful. The resources stored in the directory, such as user data, printers, servers, databases, groups, computers, and security policies, are known as *objects*.

An object is a distinct named set of attributes that represents a network resource. Object *attributes* are characteristics of objects in the directory. For example, the attributes of a user account might include the user's first and last names, department, and e-mail address (see Figure 16.1).

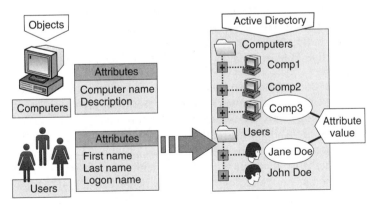

Figure 16.1 Active Directory objects and attributes

In Active Directory, you can organize objects into *classes*, which are logical groupings of objects. Examples of object classes are those representing user accounts, groups, computers, domains, or organizational units (OUs).

Note Some objects, known as *containers*, can contain other objects. For example, a domain is a container object that can contain information about users, computers, and other objects.

The Active Directory schema defines objects that can be stored in Active Directory.

Active Directory Schema

The Active Directory schema is the list that defines the kinds of objects and the types of information about those objects that can be stored in Active Directory. The definitions are themselves stored as objects so that Active Directory can manage the schema objects with the same object management operations used for managing the rest of the objects in Active Directory.

There are two types of definitions in the schema: *attributes* and *classes*. Attributes and classes are also referred to as *schema objects* or *metadata*.

Attributes are defined separately from classes. Each attribute is defined only once and can be used in multiple classes. For example, the Description attribute is used in many classes, but is defined once in the schema, assuring consistency.

Classes, also referred to as *object classes,* describe the possible Active Directory objects that can be created. Each class is a collection of attributes. When you create an object, the attributes store the information that describes the object. The User class, for example, is composed of many attributes, including Network Address, Home Directory, and so on. Every object in Active Directory is an instance of an object class.

A set of basic classes and attributes is included in Active Directory. Experienced developers and network administrators may dynamically extend the schema by defining new classes and attributes for existing classes. For example, if you need to provide information about users not currently defined in the schema, you must extend the schema for the Users class. However, extending the schema is an advanced operation with possible serious consequences. Because a schema cannot be deleted but only deactivated, and a schema is automatically replicated, you must plan and prepare before extending the schema.

Active Directory Components

Active Directory uses components to build a directory structure that meets the needs of your organization. The logical structures of your organization are represented by the following Active Directory components: domains, organizational units, trees, and forests. The physical structure of your organization is represented by the following Active Directory components: sites (physical subnets) and domain controllers. Active Directory completely separates the logical structure from the physical structure of your organization.

Logical Structures

In Active Directory, you organize resources in a logical structure that mirrors the logical structure of your organization. Grouping resources logically enables you to find a resource by its name rather than by its physical location. Because you group resources logically, Active Directory makes the network's physical structure transparent to users. Figure 16.2 illustrates the relationship of the Active Directory components.

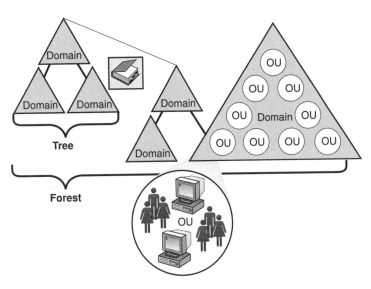

Figure 16.2 Resources organized in a logical hierarchical structure

Domains

The core unit of logical structure in Active Directory is the domain, which can store millions of objects. Objects stored in a domain are those considered "interesting" to the network. "Interesting" objects are items the networked community members need to do their jobs: printers, documents, e-mail addresses, databases, users, distributed components, and other resources. All network objects exist within a domain, and each domain stores information only about the objects it contains. Active Directory is made up of one or more domains. A domain can span more than one physical location.

Grouping objects into one or more domains allows your network to reflect your company's organization. Domains share these characteristics:

- All network objects exist within a domain, and each domain stores information only about the objects that it contains. Theoretically, a domain directory can contain up to 10 million objects, but one million objects per domain is a more practical number.

- A domain is a security boundary. Access control lists (ACLs) control access to domain objects. ACLs contain the permissions associated with objects that control which users can gain access to an object and what type of access users can gain to the objects. In Windows 2000, objects include files, folders, shares, printers, and other Active Directory objects. All security policies and settings—such as administrative rights, security policies, and ACLs—do not cross from one domain to another. The domain administrator has absolute rights to set policies only within that domain.

Organizational Units

An OU is a container used to organize objects within a domain into logical administrative groups that mirror your organization's functional or business structure. An OU can contain objects such as user accounts, groups, computers, printers, applications, file shares, and other OUs from the same domain. The OU hierarchy within a domain is independent of the OU hierarchy structure of other domains—each domain can implement its own OU hierarchy.

OUs can provide a means for handling administrative tasks, as they are the smallest grouping to which you can delegate administrative authority. Using OUs provide you with a way to delegate administration of users and resources.

In Figure 16.3, the domain.com domain for a particular organization contains three OUs: US, ORDERS, and DISP. In the summer months, the number of orders taken for shipping at the company increases, and management has requested the addition of a subadministrator for the Orders department. The subadministrator must only have the capability to create user accounts and provide users with access to Orders department files and shared printers. Rather than creating another domain, the request can be met by assigning the subadministrator the appropriate permissions within the ORDERS OU.

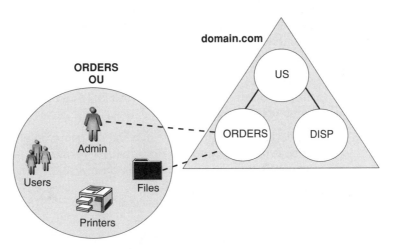

Figure 16.3 Using an organizational unit to handle administrative tasks

If the subadministrator is later required to create user accounts in the US, ORDERS, and DISP OUs, the appropriate permissions could be granted separately within each OU. However, a more efficient method would be to assign permissions once in the US OU and allow them to be inherited by the ORDERS and DISP OUs. By default, all child objects (ORDERS and DISP) within Active Directory inherit permissions from their parents (US). Granting permissions at a higher level and using inheritance capabilities can reduce administrative tasks.

Trees

A *tree* is a grouping or hierarchical arrangement of one or more Windows 2000 domains that you create by adding one or more child domains to an existing parent domain. Domains in a tree share a contiguous namespace and a hierarchical naming structure. Namespaces are covered in detail in Lesson 2 of this chapter. Trees share the following characteristics:

- Following Domain Name System (DNS) standards, the domain name of a child domain is the relative name of that child domain appended with the name of the parent domain. In Figure 16.4, microsoft.com is the parent domain and us.microsoft.com and uk.microsoft.com are its child domains. The child domain of uk.microsoft.com is sls.uk.microsoft.com.

- All domains within a single tree share a common schema, which is a formal definition of all object types that you can store in an Active Directory deployment.

- All domains within a single tree share a common *global catalog*, which is the central repository of information about objects in a tree. The global catalog is covered in detail in Lesson 2 of this chapter.

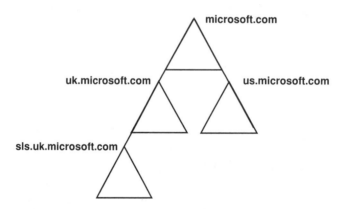

Figure 16.4 A domain tree

By creating a hierarchy of domains in a tree, you can retain security and allow for administration within an OU or within a single domain of a tree. Permissions can flow down the tree when permissions are granted to the user on an OU basis. This tree structure easily accommodates organizational changes.

Forests

A *forest* is a grouping or hierarchical arrangement of one or more separate, completely independent domain trees. Forests have the following characteristics:

- All trees in a forest share a common schema.
- Trees in a forest have different naming structures, according to their domains.
- All domains in a forest share a common global catalog.
- Domains in a forest operate independently, but the forest enables communication across the entire organization.
- Implicit two-way transitive trusts exist between domains and domain trees.

In Figure 16.5, the trees microsoft.com and msn.com form a forest. The namespace is contiguous only within each tree.

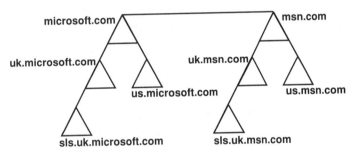

Figure 16.5 A forest of trees

Physical Structure

The physical components of Active Directory are sites and domain controllers. You use these components to develop a directory structure that mirrors the physical structure of your organization.

Sites

A *site* is a combination of one or more Internet Protocol (IP) subnets connected by a highly reliable and fast link to localize as much network traffic as possible. Typically, a site has the same boundaries as a local area network (LAN). When you group subnets on your network, you should combine only those subnets that have fast, cheap, and reliable network connections with one another. "Fast" network connections are at least 512 kilobits per second (Kbps). An available bandwidth of 128 Kbps and higher is sufficient.

With Active Directory, sites are not part of the namespace. When you browse the logical namespace, you see computers and users grouped into domains and OUs, not sites. Sites contain only computer objects and connection objects used to configure replication between sites.

Note A single domain can span multiple geographical sites, and a single site can include user accounts and computers belonging to multiple domains.

Domain Controllers

A domain controller is a computer running Windows 2000 Server that stores a replica of the domain directory (local domain database). Because a domain can contain one or more domain controllers, all domain controllers in a domain have a complete replica of the domain's portion of the directory.

The following list describes the functions of domain controllers:

- Each domain controller stores a complete copy of all Active Directory information for that domain, manages changes to that information, and replicates those changes to other domain controllers in the same domain.

- Domain controllers in a domain automatically replicate all objects in the domain to each other. When you perform an action that causes an update to Active Directory, you are actually making the change at one of the domain controllers. That domain controller then replicates the change to all other domain controllers within the domain. You can control replication of traffic between domain controllers in the network by specifying how often replication occurs and the amount of data that Windows 2000 replicates at one time.

- Domain controllers immediately replicate certain important updates, such as the disabling of a user account.

- Active Directory uses *multimaster replication*, in which no one domain controller is the master domain controller. Instead, all domain controllers within a domain are peers, and each domain controller contains a copy of the directory database that can be written to. Domain controllers may hold different information for short periods of time until all domain controllers have synchronized changes to Active Directory.

- Having more than one domain controller in a domain provides fault tolerance. If one domain controller is offline, another domain controller can provide all required functions, such as recording changes to Active Directory.

- Domain controllers manage all aspects of users' domain interaction, such as locating Active Directory objects and validating user logon attempts.

Lesson Summary

In this lesson you learned that an object is a distinct named set of attributes that represents a network resource in Active Directory. Objects' attributes describe the characteristics of a specific resource in the directory. In Active Directory, you can organize objects in classes, which are logical groupings of objects. You also learned that the Active Directory schema contains a formal definition of the contents and structure of Active Directory, including all attributes and object classes.

You also learned that Active Directory offers you a method for designing a directory structure to meet the needs of your organization's business structure and operations. Active Directory completely separates the logical structure of the domain hierarchy from the physical structure.

In Active Directory, grouping resources logically enables you to find a resource by its name rather than by its physical location. The core unit of logical structure in Active Directory is the domain, which stores information only about the objects that it contains. An OU is a container used to organize objects within a domain into logical administrative groups. A tree is a grouping or hierarchical arrangement of one or more Windows 2000 domains that share a contiguous namespace. A forest is a grouping or hierarchical arrangement of one or more trees.

The physical structure of Active Directory is based on sites and domain controllers. A site is a combination of one or more IP subnets connected by a high-speed link. A domain controller is a computer running Windows 2000 Server that stores a replica of the domain directory.

Lesson 2: Understanding Active Directory Concepts

There are several new concepts introduced with Active Directory, including the global catalog, replication, trust relationships, DNS namespaces, and naming conventions. It is important that you understand the meaning of these concepts as applied to Active Directory.

After this lesson, you will be able to

- Explain the purpose of the global catalog in Active Directory
- Explain Active Directory replication
- Explain the security relationships between domains in a tree (trusts)
- Describe the DNS namespace used by Active Directory
- Describe the naming conventions used by Active Directory

Estimated lesson time: 20 minutes

Global Catalog

The global catalog is the central repository of information about objects in a tree or forest, as shown in Figure 16.6. By default, a global catalog is created automatically on the initial domain controller in the forest, known as the *global catalog server.* The global catalog server stores a full replica of all object attributes in the directory for its host domain and a partial replica for all object attributes contained in the directory of every domain in the forest. The partial replica stores attributes that are most frequently used in search operations (such as a user's first and last names, logon name, and so on). Object attributes replicated to the global catalog inherit the same permissions as in source domains, ensuring that data in the global catalog is secure.

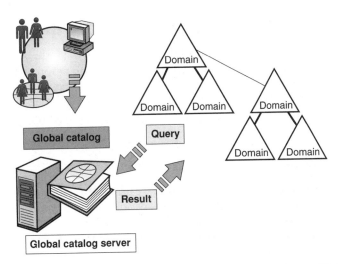

Figure 16.6 The global catalog is the central repository of information

The global catalog performs two key directory roles:

- It enables network logon by providing universal group membership information to a domain controller when a logon process is initiated.

- It enables finding directory information regardless of which domain in the forest actually contains the data.

When a user logs on to the network, the global catalog provides universal group membership information for the account to the domain controller processing the user logon information. If there is only one domain controller in the domain, the domain controller and the global catalog are the same server. If there are multiple domain controllers in the network, the global catalog is the domain controller configured as such. If a global catalog is not available when a user initiates a network logon process, the user is only able to log on to the local computer.

Important If a user is a member of the Domain Admins group, he or she is able to log on to the network even when the global catalog is not available.

The global catalog is designed to respond to user and programmatic queries about objects anywhere in the domain tree or forest with maximum speed and minimum network traffic. Because a single global catalog contains information about all objects in all domains in the forest, a query about an object can be resolved by a global catalog in the domain in which the query is initiated. Thus, finding information in the directory does not produce unnecessary query traffic across domain boundaries.

You can optionally configure any domain controller or designate additional domain controllers as global catalog servers. When considering which domain controllers to designate as global catalog servers, base your decision on the ability of your network structure to handle replication and query traffic. You should note, though, that the availability of additional servers can provide quicker responses to user inquiries, as well as redundancy. It is recommended that every major site in your enterprise have at least one global catalog server.

Replication

Users and services should be able to access directory information at any time from any computer in the domain tree or forest. Replication ensures that changes to a domain controller are reflected in all domain controllers within a domain. Directory information is replicated to domain controllers both within and among sites.

What Information Is Replicated

The information stored in the directory is partitioned into three categories. Each of these information categories is referred to as a *directory partition*. These directory partitions are the units of replication. The following information is contained in each directory:

- **Schema information.** This directory partition defines which objects can be created in the directory and what attributes those objects can have. This information is common to all domains in the domain tree or forest.

- **Configuration information.** This directory partition describes the logical structure of your configuration, and contains information such as domain structure or replication topology. This information is common to all domains in the domain tree or forest.

- **Domain data.** This directory partition describes all of the objects in a domain. This data is domain-specific and is not distributed to any other domains. For the purpose of finding information throughout the domain tree or forest, a subset of the properties for all objects in all domains is stored in the global catalog.

Schema and configuration information is replicated to all domain controllers in the domain tree or forest. All of the domain data for a particular domain is replicated to every domain controller in that domain. All of the objects in every domain, and a subset of the properties of all objects in a forest, are replicated to the global catalog.

A domain controller stores and replicates the following:

- The schema information for the domain tree or forest.

- The configuration information for all domains in the domain tree or forest.

- All directory objects and properties for its domain. This data is replicated to any additional domain controllers in the domain. For the purpose of finding information, a subset of the properties of all objects in the domain is replicated to the global catalog.

A global catalog stores and replicates the following:

- The schema information for a forest.

- The configuration information for all domains in a forest.

- A subset of the properties for all directory objects in the forest (replicated between global catalog servers only).

- All directory objects and all their properties for the domain in which the global catalog is located.

Caution Extensions to schema can have disastrous effects on large networks due to the network traffic generated by a full synchronization of all of the domain data.

How Replication Works

Active Directory replicates information within a site more frequently than across sites, balancing the need for up-to-date directory information with the limitations imposed by available network bandwidth.

Replication Within a Site

Within a site, Active Directory automatically generates a topology for replication among domain controllers in the same domain using a ring structure. The topology defines the path for directory updates to flow from one domain controller to another until all domain controllers receive the directory updates (see Figure 16.7).

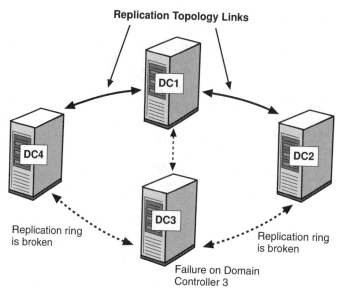

Figure 16.7 Replication topology

The ring structure ensures that there are at least two replication paths from one domain controller to another; if one domain controller is down temporarily, replication still continues to all other domain controllers.

Active Directory periodically analyzes the replication topology within a site to ensure that it is still efficient. If you add or remove a domain controller from the network or a site, Active Directory reconfigures the topology to reflect the change.

Replication Between Sites

To ensure replication between sites, you must customize how Active Directory replicates information using site links to represent network connections. Active Directory uses the network connection information to generate connection objects that provide efficient replication and fault tolerance.

You provide information about the replication protocol used, cost of a site link, times when the link is available for use, and how often the link should be used. Active Directory uses this information to determine which site link is used to replicate information. Customizing replication schedules so replication occurs during specific times, such as when network traffic is light, will make replication more efficient.

Note When operating in Native mode, Windows 2000 domain controllers do not replicate with pre–Windows 2000 domain controllers.

Trust Relationships

A *trust relationship* is a link between two domains in which the trusting domain honors the logon authentication of the trusted domain. Active Directory supports two forms of trust relationships:

- **Implicit two-way transitive trust.** This is a relationship between parent and child domains within a tree and between the top-level domains in a forest. This is the default trust relationship for Windows 2000; trust relationships among domains in a tree are established and maintained implicitly (automatically). Transitive trust is a feature of the Kerberos authentication protocol, which provides the distributed authentication and authorization in Windows 2000.

  For example, in Figure 16.8 a Kerberos transitive trust simply means that if Domain A trusts Domain B, and Domain B trusts Domain C, then Domain A trusts Domain C. As a result, a domain joining a tree immediately has trust relationships established with every domain in the tree. These trust relationships make all objects in the domains of the tree available to all other domains in the tree.

  Transitive trust between domains eliminates the management of interdomain trust accounts. Domains that are members of the same tree automatically participate in a transitive, bidirectional trust relationship with the parent domain. As a result, users in one domain can access resources to which they have been granted permission in all other domains in a tree.

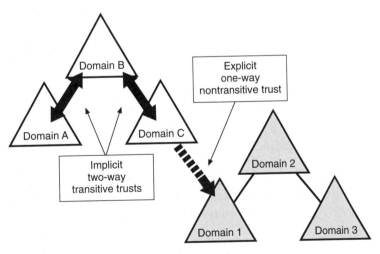

Figure 16.8 Active Directory supports two types of trust relationships

- **Explicit one-way nontransitive trust.** This is a relationship between domains that are not part of the same tree. A nontransitive trust is bounded by the two domains in the trust relationship and does not flow to any other domains in the forest. In most cases, you must explicitly (manually) create nontransitive trusts. For example, in Figure 16.8, a one-way, nontransitive trust is shown where Domain C trusts Domain 1, so users in Domain 1 can access resources in Domain C. Explicit one-way nontransitive trusts are the only form of trust possible with the following domains:

  - A Windows 2000 domain and a Windows NT domain

  - A Windows 2000 domain in one forest and a Windows 2000 domain in another forest

  - A Windows 2000 domain and an MIT Kerberos V5 realm, allowing a client in a Kerberos realm to authenticate to an Active Directory domain in order to access network resources in that domain

DNS Namespace

Active Directory, like all directory services, is primarily a namespace. A *namespace* is any bounded area in which a name can be resolved. *Name resolution* is the process of translating a name into some object or information that the name represents. The Active Directory namespace is based on the DNS naming scheme, which allows for interoperability with Internet technologies. Private networks use DNS extensively to resolve computer names and to locate computers within their local networks and the Internet. DNS provides the following benefits:

- DNS names are user-friendly, which means they are easier to remember than Internet Protocol (IP) addresses.

- DNS names remain more constant than IP addresses. An IP address for a server can change, but the server name remains the same.

- DNS allows users to connect to local servers using the same naming convention as used on the Internet.

Note For more information on DNS, see RFCs 1034 and 1035. To read the text of these Requests for Comment (RFCs), use your Web browser to search for **RFC 1034** and **RFC 1035**.

Because Active Directory uses DNS as its domain naming and location service, Windows 2000 domain names are also DNS names. Windows 2000 Server uses Dynamic DNS (DDNS), which enables clients with dynamically assigned addresses to register directly with a server running the DNS service and update the DNS table dynamically. DDNS eliminates the need for other Internet naming services, such as Windows Internet Name Service (WINS), in a homogeneous environment.

Important For Active Directory and associated client software to function correctly, you must have installed and configured the DNS service.

Name Servers

A DNS name server stores the zone database file. Name servers can store data for one zone or multiple zones. A name server is said to have authority for the domain namespace that the zone encompasses.

One name server contains the master zone database file, referred to as the *primary zone database file,* for the specified zone. As a result, there must be at least one name server for a zone. Changes to a zone, such as adding domains or hosts, are performed on the server that contains the primary zone database file.

Multiple name servers act as a backup to the name server containing the primary zone database file. Multiple name servers provide the following advantages:

- They perform zone transfers. The additional name servers obtain a copy of the zone database file from the name server that contains the primary database zone file. This is called a *zone transfer.* These name servers periodically query the name server containing the primary zone database file for updated zone data.

- They provide redundancy. If the name server containing the primary zone database file fails, the additional name servers can provide service.

- They improve access speed for remote locations. If there are a number of clients in remote locations, use additional name servers to reduce query traffic across slow wide area network (WAN) links.

- They reduce the load on the name server containing the primary zone database file.

Naming Conventions

Every object in Active Directory is identified by a name. Active Directory uses a variety of naming conventions: distinguished names (DNs), relative distinguished names (RDNs), globally unique identifiers (GUIDs), and user principal names (UPNs).

Distinguished Name

Every object in Active Directory has a distinguished name (DN) that uniquely identifies an object and contains sufficient information for a client to retrieve the object from the directory. The DN includes the name of the domain that holds the object as well as the complete path through the container hierarchy to the object.

For example, the following DN identifies the Firstname Lastname user object in the microsoft.com domain (where *Firstname* and *Lastname* represent the actual first and last name of a user account):

```
/DC=COM/DC=microsoft/OU=dev/CN=Users/CN=Firstname Lastname
```

Table 16.1 describes the attributes in the example.

Table 16.1   Distinguished Name Attributes

Attribute	Description
DC	Domain Component Name
OU	Organizational Unit Name
CN	Common Name

DNs must be unique. Active Directory does not allow duplicate DNs.

Note For more information on distinguished names, see RFC 1779. To read the text of this RFC, use your Web browser to search for **RFC 1779**.

Relative Distinguished Name

Active Directory supports querying by attributes, so you can locate an object even if the exact DN is unknown or has changed. The relative distinguished name (RDN) of an object is the part of the name that is an attribute of the object itself. In the preceding example, the RDN of the *Firstname Lastname* user object is Firstname Lastname. The RDN of the parent object is Users.

You can have duplicate RDNs for Active Directory objects, but you cannot have two objects with the same RDN in the same OU. For example, if a user account is named Jane Doe, you cannot have another user account called Jane Doe in the same OU. However, objects with duplicate RDN names can exist in separate OUs because they have different DNs (see Figure 16.9).

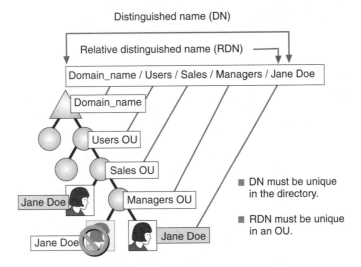

Figure 16.9 Distinguished names and relative distinguished names

Globally Unique Identifier

A globally unique identifier (GUID) is a 128-bit number that is guaranteed to be unique. GUIDs are assigned to objects when the objects are created. The GUID never changes, even if you move or rename the object. Applications can store the GUID of an object and use the GUID to retrieve that object regardless of its current DN.

In earlier versions of Windows NT, domain resources were associated to a security identifier (SID) that was generated within the domain. This meant that the SID was only guaranteed to be unique within the domain. A GUID is unique across all domains, meaning that you can move objects from domain to domain and they will still have a unique identifier.

User Principal Name

User accounts have a "friendly" name, the user principal name (UPN). The UPN is composed of a "shorthand" name for the user account and the DNS name of the tree where the user account object resides. For example, *Firstname Lastname* (substitute the first and last names of the actual user) in the microsoft.com tree might have a UPN of FirstnameL@microsoft.com (using the full first name and the first letter of the last name).

Lesson Summary

In this lesson you learned about several new concepts introduced with Active Directory, including the global catalog, replication, trust relationships, DNS namespaces, and naming conventions.

You learned that the global catalog is a service and a physical storage location that contains a replica of selected attributes for every object in Active Directory. You can use the global catalog to locate objects anywhere in the network without replication of all domain information between domain controllers.

Active Directory includes replication to ensure that changes to a domain controller are reflected in all domain controllers within a domain. Within a site, Active Directory automatically generates a ring topology for replication among domain controllers in the same domain. Between sites, you must customize how Active Directory replicates information using site links to specify how your sites are connected.

A trust relationship is a link between two domains in which the trusting domain honors the logon authentication of the trusted domain. Active Directory supports two forms of trust relationships: implicit two-way transitive trusts and explicit one-way nontransitive trusts.

In this lesson you also learned that Active Directory uses DNS as its domain naming and location service; therefore, Windows 2000 domain names are also DNS names. Windows 2000 Server uses DDNS, so clients with dynamically assigned addresses can register directly with a server running the DNS service and dynamically update the DNS table. There are contiguous namespaces and disjointed namespaces.

Finally, you learned about the naming conventions employed by Active Directory: DNs, RDNs, GUIDs, and UPNs.

Lesson 3: Active Directory Administration

There are several standard administration tasks involved with managing Active Directory. To perform these tasks, you use powerful and flexible Active Directory administrative tools that are included with Windows 2000 Server. These tools simplify directory service administration. You can use the standard consoles or you can use the MMC to create custom consoles that focus on individual management tasks. This lesson introduces the tasks and the Active Directory administrative tools and explains how they are perfomed using the MMC.

After this lesson, you will be able to

- Describe the tasks required for Windows 2000 Active Directory administration
- Describe the function of the Active Directory Users and Computers administrative console
- Describe the function of the Active Directory Sites and Services administrative console
- Describe the function of the Active Directory Domains and Trusts administrative console
- Describe the function and components of MMC, including console trees, details panes, snap-ins, extensions, and console modes

Estimated lesson time: 25 minutes

Windows 2000 Active Directory Administration Tasks

Administering Windows 2000 Active Directory involves both configuration and day-to-day maintenance tasks. Administrative tasks can be grouped into the six categories, as described in Table 16.2.

Table 16.2   Active Directory Administration Tasks

Administrative category	Specific tasks
Configuring Active Directory	Plan, deploy, manage, monitor, optimize, and troubleshoot Active Directory, including the domain structure, organizational unit (OU) structure, and site structure. Determine an efficient site topology.
Administering users and groups	Plan, create, and maintain user and group accounts to ensure that each user can log on to the network and gain access to necessary resources.
Securing network resources	Administer, monitor, and troubleshoot authentication services. Plan, implement, and enforce a security policy to ensure protection of data and shared network resources, including folders, files, and printers.
Administering Active Directory	Manage the location and control of Active Directory objects. Plan and implement Active Directory backup and restore operations.
Administering the desktop computing environment	Deploy, install, and configure the desktop computing environment using group policy.
Securing Active Directory	Administer, monitor, and troubleshoot a security configuration. Plan and implement a policy to audit network events so that you can find security breaches.
Managing Active Directory performance	Monitor, maintain, and troubleshoot domain controller performance and Active Directory components using performance monitoring and diagnostic tools.
Installing Windows 2000 remotely	Use Remote Installation Services to deploy Windows 2000 remotely.

Active Directory Administrative Tools

The Active Directory administrative tools are installed automatically on computers configured as Windows 2000 domain controllers. The administrative tools are also available with the optional Administrative Tools package. This package can be installed on other versions of Windows 2000 to allow you to administer Active Directory from a computer that is not a domain controller. The following Active Directory standard administrative tools are available on the Administrative Tools menu of all Windows 2000 domain controllers:

- Active Directory Domains and Trusts console
- Active Directory Sites and Services console
- Active Directory Users and Computers console

Active Directory Domains and Trusts Console

The Active Directory Domains and Trusts console helps you manage trust relationships between domains. These domains can be Windows 2000 domains in the same forest, Windows 2000 domains in different forests, pre–Windows 2000 domains, and even Kerberos V5 realms.

Using Active Directory Domains and Trusts, you can do the following:

- Provide interoperability with other domains (such as pre–Windows 2000 domains or domains in other Windows 2000 forests) by managing explicit domain trusts
- Change the mode of operation of a Windows 2000 domain from Mixed mode to Native mode
- Add and remove alternate UPN suffixes used to create user logon names
- Transfer the domain naming operations master role from one domain controller to another
- Provide information about domain management

Active Directory Sites and Services Console

You provide information about the physical structure of your network by publishing sites to Active Directory using the Active Directory Sites and Services console. Active Directory uses this information to determine how to replicate directory information and handle service requests.

Active Directory Users and Computers Console

The Active Directory Users and Computers console allows you to add, modify, delete, and organize Windows 2000 user accounts, computer accounts, security and distribution groups, and published resources in your organization's directory. It also allows you to manage domain controllers and OUs.

Other Active Directory Administrative Tools

In addition to the Active Directory consoles provided on the Administrative Tools menu, there are several other tools provided for administering Active Directory.

Active Directory Schema Snap-In

The Active Directory Schema snap-in allows you to view and modify Active Directory schema. This snap-in is not available by default on the Administrative Tools menu. You must install it, and all of the Windows 2000 administration tools, using Add/Remove Programs in the Control Panel. Do not use the ADMINPAK.MSI file on the Windows 2000 Server CD-ROM to perform these operations.

▶   **Follow these steps to install the Active Directory Schema snap-in:**

1. Log on as an Administrator.

2. Click Start, point to Settings, and then click Control Panel.

3. Double-click Add/Remove Programs.

4. On the Add/Remove Programs dialog box, click Change Or Remove Programs, click Windows 2000 Administration Tools, and then click Change.

5. On the Welcome To The Windows 2000 Administration Tools Setup Wizard page, click Next.

6. On the Setup Options page, click Install All Of The Administrative Tools, and then click Next.

7. The wizard installs the Windows 2000 Administration Tools. When it finishes, click Finish.

8. Close the Add/Remove Programs dialog box, and then close the Control Panel.

9. Click Start, and then click Run.

10. In the Open box, type **mmc** and then click OK.

11. On the Console menu, click Add/Remove Snap-In.

12. In the Add/Remove Snap-In dialog box, click Add.

13. In the Add Standalone Snap-In dialog box, in the Snap-In column, double-click Active Directory Schema, click Close, and then click OK.

14. To save this console, from the Console menu, click Save.

Important Modifying the Active Directory schema is an advanced operation that is best performed by experienced programmers or system administrators. For detailed information about modifying the Active Directory schema, see the *Microsoft Active Directory Programmer's Guide*.

Active Directory Support Tools

Several additional tools that can be used to configure, manage, and debug Active Directory are available in the Windows 2000 Support Tools. The Windows 2000 Support Tools are included on the Windows 2000 CD-ROM in the \Support\Tools folder. These tools are intended for use by Microsoft support personnel and experienced users.

To use Active Directory support tools you must first install the Windows 2000 Support Tools on your computer.

▶ **Follow these steps to install the Windows 2000 Support Tools:**

1. Start Windows 2000. You must log on as a member of the Administrator group to install these tools.

2. Insert the Windows 2000 CD into your CD-ROM drive.

3. When the Microsoft Windows 2000 CD screen appears, click Browse This CD.

4. Browse to the \Support\Tools directory.

5. Click SETUP.EXE.

6. Follow the instructions that appear on your screen.

The Setup program installs all Windows 2000 Support Tools files onto your hard disk and requires a maximum of 18.2 megabytes (MB) of free space.

Setup creates a Windows 2000 Support Tools folder within the Programs folder on the Start menu. For detailed information about individual tools, click the Tools Help menu item. Graphical User Interface (GUI) tools can be selected from the Tools menu.

Setup also adds the \Program Files\Resource Kit directory (or the directory name you choose for installing the tools) to your computer's Path statement.

Table 16.3 describes the support tools that pertain to Active Directory.

Table 16.3   Active Directory Support Tools

Tool	Used to
ACLDIAG.EXE: ACL Diagnostics[1]	Determine whether a user has been granted or denied access to an Active Directory object. It can also be used to reset access control lists to their default state.
ADSI Edit[3]	View all objects in the directory (including schema and configuration naming contexts), modify objects, and set access control lists on objects.
DFSUTIL.EXE: Distributed File System Utility[1]	Manage all aspects of distributed file system (Dfs), check the configuration concurrency of Dfs servers, and display the Dfs topology.
DNSCMD.EXE: DNS Server Troubleshooting Tool[1]	Check dynamic registration of DNS resource records including secure DNS update. Is also used to deregister resource records.
DSACLS.EXE[1]	View or modify the access control lists of objects in Active Directory.
DSASTAT.EXE: Active Directory Diagnostic Tool[1]	Compare naming contexts on domain controllers and detect differences.
LDP.EXE: Active Directory Administration Tool[2]	Allow Lightweight Directory Access Protocol (LDAP) operations to be performed against Active Directory.
MOVETREE.EXE: Active Directory Object Manager[1]	Move Active Directory objects such as OUs and users between domains in a single forest.
NETDOM.EXE: Windows 2000 Domain Manager[1]	Manage Windows 2000 domains and trust relationships.
NLTEST.EXE[1]	Provide a list of primary domain controllers, force a shutdown, provide information about trusts and replication.

Tool	Used to
REPADMIN.EXE: Replication Diagnostics Tool[1]	Check replication consistency between replication partners, monitor replication status, display replication metadata, force replication events and knowledge consistency checker recalculation.
REPLMON.EXE: Active Directory Replication Monitor[2]	Graphically display replication topology, monitor replication status (including policies), force replication events and knowledge consistency checker recalculation.
SDCHECK.EXE: Security Descriptor Check Utility[1]	Check ACL propagation and replication for specified objects in the directory. This tool enables an administrator to determine if ACLs are being inherited correctly and if ACL changes are being replicated from one domain controller to another.
SIDwalker: Security Administration Tools	Manage access control policies on Windows 2000 and Windows NT systems. SIDwalker consists of three separate programs: SHOWACCS.EXE[1] and SIDWALK.EXE[1] for examining and changing access control entries, and Security Migration Editor[3] for editing mapping between old and new security IDs (SIDs).

[1] command-line tool
[2] graphical user interface tool
[3] Microsoft Management Console snap-in

For more information about Active Directory support tools, see the *Microsoft Windows Server 2000 Resource Kit*.

Active Directory Service Interfaces

Active Directory Service Interfaces (ADSI) provides a simple, powerful, object-oriented interface to Active Directory. ADSI makes it easy for programmers and administrators to create programs utilizing directory services by using high-level tools such as Microsoft Visual Basic, Java, C, or Visual C++ as well as ActiveX Scripting Languages, such as VBScript, JScript, or PerlScript, without having to worry about the underlying differences between the different namespaces. ADSI is a fully programmable automation object for use by administrators.

ADSI enables you to build or buy programs that give you a single point of access to multiple directories in your network environment, whether those directories are based on LDAP or another protocol.

Microsoft Management Console

The MMC is a tool used to create, save, and open collections of administrative tools, which are called *consoles*. When you access the Active Directory administrative tools, you are accessing the MMC for that tool. The Active Directory Domains and Trusts, Active Directory Sites and Services, and Active Directory Users and Computers administrative tools are each a console. The console does not provide management functions itself, but is the program that hosts management applications called *snap-ins*. You use snap-ins to perform one or more administrative tasks.

There are two types of MMCs: preconfigured and custom. Preconfigured MMCs contain commonly used snap-ins, and they appear on the Administrative Tools menu. You create custom MMCs to perform a unique set of administrative tasks. You can use both preconfigured and custom MMCs for remote administration.

Preconfigured MMCs

Preconfigured MMCs contain snap-ins that you use to perform the most common administrative tasks. Windows 2000 installs a number of preconfigured MMCs during installation. Preconfigured MMCs have the following characteristics:

- They contain one or more snap-ins that provide the functionality to perform a related set of administrative tasks.

- They function in User mode. Because preconfigured MMCs are in User mode, you cannot modify them, save them, or add additional snap-ins. However, when you create custom consoles, you can add as many preconfigured consoles as you want as snap-ins to your custom console.

- They vary, depending on the operating system that the computer is running and the installed Windows 2000 components. Windows 2000 Server and Windows 2000 Professional have different preconfigured MMCs.

- They might be added by Windows 2000 when you install additional components. Optional Windows 2000 components might include additional preconfigured MMCs that Windows 2000 adds when you install a component. For example, when you install the DNS service, Windows 2000 also installs the DNS console.

Table 16.4 lists the typical preconfigured MMCs in Windows 2000 and their function.

Table 16.4   Preconfigured MMCs

Preconfigured MMC	Function
Active Directory Domains and Trusts [1,2]	Manages the trust relationships between domains
Active Directory Sites and Services [1,2]	Creates sites to manage the replication of Active Directory information
Active Directory Users and Computers [1,2]	Manages users, computers, security groups, and other objects in Active Directory
Component Services	Configures and manages COM+ applications
Computer Management	Manages disks and provides access to other tools to manage local and remote computers
Configure Your Server [1]	Sets up and configures Windows services for your network
Data Sources (ODBC)	Adds, removes, and configures Open Database Connectivity (ODBC) data sources and drivers
DHCP [1,2]	Used to configure and manage the Dynamic Host Configuration Protocol (DHCP) service
Distributed File System (DFS) [1]	Creates and manages DFSs that connect shared folders from different computers
DNS [1,2]	Manages the DNS service, which translates DNS computer names to IP addresses
Domain Controller Security Policy [1,2]	Used to view and modify security policy for the Domain Controllers OU
Domain Security Policy [1,2]	Used to view and modify security policy for the domain, such as user rights and audit policies
Event Viewer	Displays monitoring and troubleshooting messages from Windows and other programs
Internet Services Manager [1]	Manages Internet Information Services (IIS), the Web server for Internet and intranet Web sites
Licensing [1]	Manages client access licensing for a server product
Local Security Policy [3]	Used to view and modify local security policy, such as user rights and audit policies

continues

Table 16.4   Preconfigured MMCs *(continued)*

Preconfigured MMC	Function
Performance	Displays graphs of system performance and configures data logs and alerts
Routing and Remote Access [1]	Used to configure and manage the Routing and Remote Access service
Server Extensions Administrator [1]	Used to administer Microsoft FrontPage Server Extensions and FrontPage extended webs
Services	Starts and stops services
Telnet Server Administration [1]	Used to view and modify telnet server settings and connections

[1] MMC not available on Windows 2000 Professional.
[2] MMC not available on Windows 2000 Server standalone server.
[3] MMC not available on Windows 2000 Server domain controller.

Custom MMCs

You can use many of the preconfigured MMCs for administrative tasks. However, there will be times when you need to create your own custom MMCs. Although you can't modify preconfigured consoles, you can combine multiple preconfigured snap-ins with third-party snap-ins that perform related tasks to create custom MMCs. You can then do the following:

- Save the custom MMCs to use again.

- Distribute the custom MMCs to other administrators.

- Use the custom MMCs from any computer to centralize and unify administrative tasks.

Creating custom MMCs allows you to meet your administrative requirements by combining snap-ins that you use to perform common administrative tasks. By creating a custom MMC, you do not have to switch between different programs or different preconfigured MMCs because all of the snap-ins that you need to perform your job are located in the custom MMC.

Consoles are saved as files and have an .msc extension. All the settings for the snap-ins contained in the console are saved and restored when the file is opened, even if the console file is opened on a different computer or network.

Console Tree and Details Pane

Every MMC has a console tree. A *console tree* displays the hierarchical organization of the snap-ins contained with the MMC. As you can see in Figure 16.10, this MMC contains the Device Manager on the local computer and the Disk Defragmenter snap-ins.

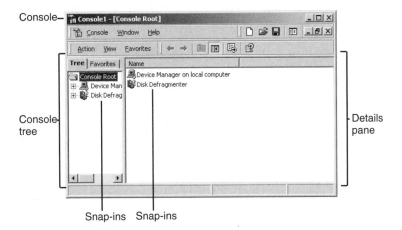

Figure 16.10 A sample MMC

The console tree organizes snap-ins that are part of the MMC. This allows you to easily locate a specific snap-in. Items that you add to the console tree appear under the console root. The *details pane* lists the contents of the active snap-in.

Every MMC contains the Action menu and the View menu. The choices on these menus are context-sensitive, depending on the current selection in the console tree.

Snap-Ins

Snap-ins are applications that are designed to work in an MMC. Use snap-ins to perform administrative tasks. There are two types of snap-ins: standalone snap-ins and extension snap-ins.

Standalone Snap-Ins

Standalone snap-ins are usually referred to simply as *snap-ins*. Use standalone snap-ins to perform Windows 2000 administrative tasks. Each snap-in provides one function or a related set of functions. Windows 2000 Server comes with standard snap-ins. Windows 2000 Professional includes a smaller set of standard snap-ins.

Extension Snap-Ins

Extension snap-ins are usually referred to simply as *extensions*. They are snap-ins that provide additional administrative functionality to another snap-in. The following are characteristics of extensions:

- Extensions are designed to work with one or more standalone snap-ins, based on the function of the standalone snap-in. For example, the Software Installation extension is available in the Group Policy snap-in; however, it is not available in the Disk Defragmenter snap-in, because Software Installation does not relate to the administrative task of disk defragmentation.

- When you add an extension, Windows 2000 displays only extensions that are compatible with the standalone snap-in. Windows 2000 places the extensions into the appropriate location within the standalone snap-in.

- When you add a snap-in to a console, MMC adds all available extensions by default. You can remove any extension from the snap-in.

- You can add an extension to multiple snap-ins.

Figure 16.11 demonstrates the concept of snap-ins and extensions. A toolbox (an MMC) holds a drill (a snap-in). You can use a drill with its standard drill bit, and you can perform additional functions with different drill bits (extensions).

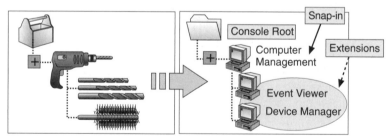

- Snap-ins are administrative tools.
- Extensions provide additional functionality to snap-ins.
  - Extensions are preassigned to snap-ins.
  - Multiple snap-ins may use the same extensions.

Figure 16.11 Snap-ins and extensions

Some standalone snap-ins, such as the Computer Management snap-in, can use extensions that provide additional functionality. However, some snap-ins, like Event Viewer, can act as a snap-in or an extension.

Console Options

Use console options to determine how each MMC operates by selecting the appropriate console mode. The console mode determines the MMC functionality for the person who is using a saved MMC. The two available console modes are Author mode and User mode.

Author Mode

When you save an MMC in Author mode, you enable full access to all MMC functionality, which includes modifying the MMC. Save the MMC using Author mode to allow those using it to do the following:

- Add or remove snap-ins
- Create new windows
- View all portions of the console tree
- Save MMCs

Note By default, all new MMCs are saved in Author mode.

User Mode

Usually, if you plan to distribute an MMC to other administrators, you save the MMC in User mode. When you set an MMC to User mode, users cannot add snap-ins to, remove snap-ins from, or save the MMC.

There are three types of User modes that allow different levels of access and functionality. Table 16.5 describes when to use each User mode.

Table 16.5   MMC Console User Modes

User mode	Use when
Full Access	You want to allow users to navigate between snap-ins, open new windows, and gain access to all portions of the console tree.
Limited Access, Multiple Windows	You do not want to allow users to open new windows or gain access to a portion of the console tree. You want to allow users to view multiple windows in the console.
Limited Access, Single Window	You do not want to allow users to open new windows or gain access to a portion of the console tree. You want to allow users to view only one window in the console.

Lesson Summary

In this lesson you learned about Active Directory administration tasks, which include configuring Active Directory, administering users and groups, securing network resources, administering Active Directory, administering the desktop computing environment, securing Active Directory, managing Active Directory performance, and installing Windows 2000 remotely.

You also learned about the Active Directory administrative tools you can use to accomplish these tasks. The Active Directory Domains and Trusts console manages the trust relationships between domains. The Active Directory Sites and Services console creates sites to manage the replication of Active Directory information. The Active Directory Users and Computers console manages users, computers, security groups, and other objects in Active Directory.

The MMC is a tool used to create, save, and open collections of administrative tools, called consoles. MMCs hold one or more management applications, called snap-ins, which you use to perform administrative tasks. Preconfigured MMCs contain commonly used snap-ins, and they appear on the Administrative Tools menu. You create custom MMCs to perform a unique set of administrative tasks. You can use both preconfigured and custom MMCs for remote administration.

You learned that every MMC has a console tree. The console tree displays the hierarchical organization of the snap-ins that are contained within that MMC. This allows you to locate a specific snap-in easily. The details pane lists the contents of the active snap-in. You also learned that there are two types of snap-ins: standalone snap-ins and extension snap-ins.

Finally, in this lesson you learned about console options. You use console options to determine how each MMC operates by selecting the appropriate console mode. The two available console modes are Author mode and User mode. When you save an MMC in Author mode, you enable full access to all MMC functionality, which includes modifying the MMC. When you set an MMC to User mode, users cannot add snap-ins to, remove snap-ins from, or save the MMC.

Review

The following questions will help you determine whether you have learned enough to move on to the next chapter. If you have difficulty answering these questions, please go back and review the material in this chapter before beginning the next chapter. See Appendix A, "Questions and Answers," for the answers to these questions.

1. What is the Active Directory schema?

2. What is the purpose of an organizational unit (OU)?

3. What are sites and domains and how are they different?

4. What is the difference between implicit two-way transitive trusts and explicit one-way nontransitive trusts?

5. What are the functions of the Active Directory Domains and Trusts, the Active Directory Sites and Services, and the Active Directory Users and Computers consoles?

6. When and why would you use an extension?

CHAPTER 17

Installing and Configuring Active Directory Directory Service

About This Chapter

The success of your Microsoft Windows 2000 implementation depends on your plan for implementing and configuring Active Directory directory service. This chapter assists you in planning your Active Directory implementation. It walks you through the steps of installing Active Directory using the Active Directory Installation Wizard, shows you how to implement an organizational unit (OU) structure, and presents procedures for setting OU properties. The chapter then introduces you to configuring site settings and inter-site replication after Active Directory is installed. This chapter also discusses the tasks necessary for configuring server settings.

Before You Begin

To complete this chapter, you must have

- Installed Microsoft Windows 2000 Server on a computer (Server01)

  See Chapter 8, "Installing Microsoft Windows 2000" for more details.

- Knowledge about the difference between a workgroup and a domain

- Knowledge about the difference between a domain controller and a member server

- Experience using the Microsoft Management Console (MMC)

Lesson 1: Installing Active Directory

This lesson presents information on installing and removing Active Directory including using the Active Directory Installation Wizard. The lesson also discusses the database and shared system volume that Active Directory creates during installation and setting up Domain Name System (DNS) for Active Directory. Finally, the lesson discusses domain modes.

After this lesson, you will be able to

- Install Active Directory
- Remove Active Directory from a domain controller

Estimated lesson time: 25 minutes

The Active Directory Installation Wizard

The Active Directory Installation Wizard can perform the following tasks:

- Add a domain controller to an existing domain
- Create the first domain controller of a new domain
- Create a new child domain
- Create a new domain tree
- Install a DNS server
- Create the database and database log files
- Create the shared system volume
- Remove Active Directory services from a domain controller

To launch the Active Directory Installation Wizard, run Configure Your Server on the Administrative Tools menu of the Start menu, or run DCPROMO from the command prompt. These two methods run the Active Directory Installation Wizard on a standalone server and help you through the process of installing Active Directory on the computer and creating a new domain controller.

As you install Active Directory, you can choose whether to add the new domain controller to an existing domain or create the first domain controller for a new domain.

Adding a Domain Controller to an Existing Domain

If you choose to add a domain controller to an existing domain, you create a peer domain controller. You create peer domain controllers for redundancy and to reduce the load on the existing domain controllers.

Creating the First Domain Controller for a New Domain

If you choose to create the first domain controller for a new domain, you create a new domain. You create domains on your network to partition your information, which enables you to scale Active Directory to meet the needs of your organization. When you create a new domain, you can create a new child domain or a new tree. Table 17.1 describes creating a new child domain and creating a new domain tree.

Table 17.1   Creating New Domains

Creating a new domain	Description
New child domain	When you create a child domain, the new domain is a child domain in an existing domain.
New domain tree	When you create a new tree, the new domain is not part of an existing domain. You can create a new tree in an existing forest, or you can create a new forest.

Configuring DNS for Active Directory

Active Directory uses DNS as its location service, enabling computers to find the location of domain controllers. To find a domain controller in a particular domain, a client queries DNS for resource records that provide the names and Internet Protocol (IP) addresses of the Lightweight Directory Access Protocol (LDAP) servers for the domain. LDAP is the protocol used to query and update Active Directory, and all domain controllers run the LDAP service. You cannot install Active Directory without having DNS on your network, because Active Directory uses DNS as its location service. However, you can install DNS separately without Active Directory.

You can configure your Windows 2000 DNS server automatically using the Active Directory Installation Wizard. Unless you are using a DNS server other than Windows 2000 or you want to perform a special configuration, you do not need to manually configure DNS to support Active Directory. However, if you want to set up a configuration other than the default configuration that the Active Directory Installation Wizard sets up, you can manually configure DNS using the DNS console.

The Database and Shared System Volume

Installing Active Directory creates the database and database log files, as well as the shared system volume. Table 17.2 describes these files.

Table 17.2   Types of Files Created by Installing Active Directory directory services

Type of file created	Description
Database and database log files	The database is the directory for the new domain. The default location for the database and database log files is *systemroot*\NTDS, where *systemroot* is the Windows 2000 directory. For best performance, place the database and the log file on separate hard disks.
Shared system volume	The shared system volume is a folder structure that exists on all Windows 2000 domain controllers. It stores scripts and some of the group policy objects for both the current domain and the enterprise. The default location for the shared system volume is *systemroot*\SYSVOL. The shared system volume must be located on a partition or volume formatted with Microsoft Windows NT file system (NTFS) 5.0.

Replication of the shared system volume occurs on the same schedule as replication of Active Directory. As a result, you may not notice file replication to or from the newly created system volume until two replication periods have elapsed (typically, 10 minutes). This is because the first file replication period updates the configuration of other system volumes so that they are aware of the newly created system volume.

Domain Modes

There are two domain modes: Mixed mode and Native mode.

Mixed Mode

When you first install or upgrade a domain controller to Windows 2000 Server, the domain controller is set to run in *Mixed mode*. Mixed mode allows the domain controller to interact with any domain controllers in the domain that are running previous versions of Windows NT.

Native Mode

When all the domain controllers in the domain run Windows 2000 Server, and you do not plan to add any more pre–Windows 2000 domain controllers to the domain, you can switch the domain from mixed mode to *Native mode*.

During the conversion from Mixed mode to Native mode, the following changes take place:

- Support for pre–Windows 2000 replication ceases. Because pre–Windows 2000 replication is gone, you can no longer have any domain controllers in your domain that are not running Windows 2000 Server.

- You can no longer add new pre–Windows 2000 domain controllers to the domain.

- The server that served as the primary domain controller (PDC) during migration is no longer the domain master, and all domain controllers begin acting as peers.

Note The change from Mixed mode to Native mode is one way only; you cannot change from Native mode to Mixed mode.

▶ **Follow these steps to change the domain mode to Native mode:**

1. Click Start, point to Programs, point to Administrative Tools, and then click Active Directory Users And Computers.

2. Right-click the domain and then click Properties.

3. On the General tab, click Change Mode.

4. In the Active Directory message box, click Yes, and then click OK.

5. Restart your computer.

Removing Active Directory Services from a Domain Controller

Running DCPROMO from the Run dialog box on an existing domain controller allows you to remove Active Directory from the domain controller, thus demoting it to a member server. If the domain controller is the last domain controller in the domain, it becomes a standalone server. If you remove Active Directory from all domain controllers in a domain, you also delete the directory database for the domain, and the domain no longer exists. Computers joined to this domain can no longer log on to the domain or use domain services.

▶ **Follow these steps to remove Active Directory from a domain controller:**

1. Log on as Administrator.

2. Click Start, click Run, and then type **dcpromo** in the Open box and click OK.

   The Active Directory Installation Wizard appears.

3. Click Next on the Welcome To The Active Directory Installation Wizard page.

4. If the server is the last domain controller in the domain, select the check box, and then click Next.

5. Enter a user name and password with Enterprise Administrator privileges for the domain, and then click Next.

6. Enter and confirm the password to be assigned to the server Administrator account, and then click Next.

7. Click Next on the Summary page.

8. Click Finish to complete the removal of Active Directory from the computer.

Practice: Installing Active Directory

In this practice you install Active Directory on your standalone server, which makes the server a domain controller of a new domain. In Exercise 1 you use the DCPROMO program and Active Directory Installation Wizard to install Active Directory. In Exercise 2 you view the domain you have created. In Exercise 3 you are introduced to the Active Directory Users and Computers console. In Exercise 4 you confirm that the DNS service is working.

Exercise 1: Promoting a Standalone Server to a Domain Controller

In this exercise, you run DCPROMO to install the Active Directory service on your standalone server, making it a domain controller in a new domain, in a new tree, and in a new forest.

1. Restart your computer and log on as Administrator.

2. If the Windows 2000 Configure Your Server page opens, close it because the DCPROMO program will be used instead to accomplish the tasks in this practice.

3. Click Start and then click Run.

   The Run dialog box appears.

4. Type **dcpromo** in the Open box and click OK.

   The Active Directory Installation Wizard appears.

5. Click Next.

   The Domain Controller Type page appears.

6. Select Domain Controller For A New Domain, and then click Next.

   The Create Tree Or Child Domain page appears.

7. Ensure that Create A New Domain Tree is selected, and then click Next.

   The Create Or Join Forest page appears.

8. Select Create A New Forest Of Domain Trees, and then click Next.

   The New Domain Name page appears.

9. In the Full DNS Name For New Domain box, type **microsoft.com** and click Next.

   (If you are not using microsoft.com as your DNS domain name, type the name you are using for your DNS domain name.)

   After a few moments, the NetBIOS Domain Name page appears.

10. Ensure that MICROSOFT (or a shortened form of the DNS name you have chosen) appears in the Domain NetBIOS Name box, and then click Next.

   The Database and Log Locations page appears.

11. Ensure that *systemroot*\NTDS is the location of both the database and the log and click Next. (If you did not install Windows 2000 in the WINNT directory, both locations should default to the NTDS folder in the folder where you installed Windows 2000.)

   The Shared System Volume page appears.

12. Ensure that the SYSVOL folder location is *systemroot*\SYSVOL. (If you did not install Windows 2000 in the WINNT directory, the SYSVOL location should default to a SYSVOL folder in the folder where you installed Windows 2000.)

   What is the one SYSVOL location requirement?

   What is the function of SYSVOL?

13. Click Next to accept *systemroot*\SYSVOL (or the path where you installed Windows 2000) as the path for SYSVOL.

   The Active Directory Installation Wizard message box appears, reminding you to install and configure a DNS server. Click OK. The Configure DNS page appears.

14. Select Yes, Install And Configure DNS On This Computer, and then click Next.

   The Permissions page appears.

15. Unless your network administrator tells you to do otherwise, select Permissions Compatible Only With Windows 2000 Servers, and then click Next.

   The Directory Services Restore Mode Administrator Password page appears.

16. Type the password you want to assign to this server's Administrator account in the event the computer is started in Directory Services Restore mode, and then click Next.

   The Summary page appears, listing the options that you selected.

17. Review the contents of the Summary page, and then click Next.

   The Configuring Active Directory progress indicator appears as the Active Directory service is installed on the server. This process takes several minutes, during which you are prompted to place the Windows 2000 Server CD-ROM into your CD-ROM drive.

18. When the Completing The Active Directory Installation Wizard page appears, click Finish, and then click Restart Now.

Exercise 2: Viewing Your Domain using My Network Places

In this exercise, you view your domain to verify Active Directory installation.

1. Log on as Administrator.

2. If the Windows 2000 Configure Your Server page appears, close it.

3. Double-click My Network Places.

   The My Network Places window appears.

   What selections do you see?

4. Double-click Entire Network, and then double-click Microsoft Windows Network.

   What do you see?

5. Close the Microsoft Windows Network window.

Exercise 3: Viewing a Domain Using the Active Directory Users And Computers Console

In this exercise, you use the Active Directory Users And Computers console to view your domain.

1. Click Start, point to Programs, point to Administrative Tools, and then click Active Directory Users And Computers.

   Windows 2000 displays the Active Directory Users And Computers console.

2. In the console tree, double-click microsoft.com (or the name of your domain).

   What selections are listed under microsoft?

3. In the console tree, click Domain Controllers.

   Notice that SERVER01 appears in the details pane. If you did not use SERVER01 as your server name, the DNS name of your server appears in the details pane.

4. Close the Active Directory Users And Computers console.

Exercise 4: Testing Your DNS Server

In this exercise, you confirm that your DNS service is working.

1. Click Start, point to Programs, point to Administrative Tools, and then click DNS.

2. The DNS console appears. In the DNS console tree, right-click SERVER01 (or the name of your server), and then click Properties.

   The SERVER01 Properties dialog box appears. (If you did not use SERVER01 as your server name, the dialog box reflects your server name.)

3. Click the Monitoring tab.

4. Under Select A Test Type, select the A Simple Query Against This DNS Server check box and the A Recursive Query To Other DNS Servers check box, and then click Test Now.

On the SERVER01 Properties dialog box, under Test Results, you should see PASS in the Simple Query and Recursive Query columns.

5. Click OK.

6. Close the DNS console.

Lesson Summary

In this lesson you learned about installing Active Directory, including running Windows 2000 Configure Your Server to start the Active Directory Installation Wizard. You can also go to a command prompt and type DCPROMO to launch the Active Directory Installation Wizard. You can use the Active Directory Installation Wizard to add a domain controller to an existing domain, to create the first domain controller of a new domain, to create a new child domain, and to create a new domain tree. You also learned how the Active Directory Installation Wizard can be used to remove Active Directory from a domain controller.

In this lesson you also learned about the Active Directory database, which is the directory for the new domain, and the database log files. The default location for the database and database log files is *systemroot*\NTDS. You also learned about the shared system volume that Active Directory creates during installation. The shared system volume is a folder structure that exists on all Windows 2000 domain controllers. It stores scripts and some of the group policy objects for both the current domain and the enterprise. The default location for the shared system volume is *systemroot*\SYSVOL.

You learned how Active Directory uses DNS as its location service, enabling computers to find the location of domain controllers. You cannot install Active Directory without having DNS on your network, because Active Directory uses DNS as its location service. You can configure your Windows 2000 DNS server automatically by using the Active Directory Installation wizard. Unless you are using a DNS server other than Windows 2000 or you want to perform a special configuration, you do not need to configure DNS manually to support Active Directory.

You also learned about Mixed and Native domain modes. Mixed mode allows compatibility with previous versions of Windows NT. Native mode is only used when all domain controllers in the domain are running Windows 2000 Server.

In the practice portion of this lesson, you used the Active Directory Installation wizard to install Active Directory on your computer, to promote your computer to a domain controller, and to create a domain. You then viewed your domain using My Network Places and the Active Directory Users And Computers console. Finally, you used the DNS console to confirm that your DNS service is working.

Lesson 2: Operations Master Roles

Operations master roles are special roles assigned to one or more domain controllers in an Active Directory domain. The domain controllers that are assigned these roles perform single-master replication. This lesson introduces you to operations master roles and the tasks involved with master role assignments.

After this lesson, you will be able to

- Describe the forest-wide operations master roles
- Describe the domain-wide operations master roles
- Plan operations master locations
- View operations master role assignments
- Transfer operations master role assignments

Estimated lesson time: 15 minutes

Operations Master Roles

Active Directory supports multimaster replication of the Active Directory database between all domain controllers in the domain. However, some changes are impractical to perform in multimaster fashion, so one or more domain controllers can be assigned to perform single-master operations, or operations that are not permitted to occur at different places in a network at the same time. This is called an operations master role. Operations master roles are assigned to domain controllers to perform single-master operations.

In any Active Directory forest, five operations master roles must be assigned to one or more domain controllers. Some roles must appear in every forest. Other roles must appear in every domain in the forest. You can change the assignment of operations master roles after setup, but in most cases this is not necessary. You must be aware of operations master roles assigned to a domain controller if problems develop on the domain controller or if you plan to take it out of service.

Forest-Wide Operations Master Roles

Every Active Directory forest must have the following roles:

- Schema master
- Domain naming master

These roles must be unique in the forest. This means that throughout the entire forest there can be only one schema master and one domain naming master.

Schema Master Role

The schema master domain controller controls all updates and modifications to the schema. To update the schema of a forest, you must have access to the schema master. At any time, there can be only one schema master in the entire forest.

Domain Naming Master Role

The domain controller holding the domain naming master role controls the addition or removal of domains in the forest. There can be only one domain naming master in the entire forest at any time.

Domain-Wide Operations Master Roles

Every domain in the forest must have the following roles:

- Relative identifier (ID) master
- PDC emulator
- Infrastructure master

These roles must be unique in each domain. This means that each domain in the forest can have only one relative ID master, PDC emulator, and infrastructure master.

Relative ID Master Role

The relative ID master allocates sequences of relative IDs to each of the various domain controllers in its domain. At any time, there can be only one domain controller acting as the relative ID master in each domain in the forest.

Whenever a domain controller creates a user, group, or computer object, it assigns the object a unique security ID (SID). The SID consists of a domain SID (which is the same for all SIDs created in the domain), and a relative ID that is unique for each SID created in the domain.

To move an object between domains (using MOVETREE.EXE: Active Directory Object Manager), you must initiate the move on the domain controller acting as the relative ID master of the domain that currently contains the object.

PDC Emulator Role

If the domain contains computers operating without Windows 2000 client software or if it contains Windows NT backup domain controllers (BDCs), the PDC emulator acts as a Windows NT PDC. It processes password changes from clients and replicates updates to the BDCs. At any time, there can be only one domain controller acting as the PDC emulator in each domain in the forest.

Even after all systems are upgraded to Windows 2000, and the Windows 2000 domain is operating in Native mode, the PDC emulator receives preferential replication of password changes performed by other domain controllers in the domain. If a password was recently changed, that change takes time to replicate to every domain controller in the domain. If a logon authentication fails at another domain controller due to a bad password, that domain controller forwards the authentication request to the PDC emulator before rejecting the logon attempt.

Infrastructure Master Role

The infrastructure master is responsible for updating the group-to-user references whenever the members of groups are renamed or changed. At any time, there can be only one domain controller acting as the infrastructure master in each domain.

When you rename or move a member of a group (and that member resides in a different domain from the group), the group may temporarily appear not to contain that member. The infrastructure master of the group's domain is responsible for updating the group so it knows the new name or location of the member. The infrastructure master distributes the update via multimaster replication.

There is no compromise to security during the time between the member rename and the group update. Only an administrator looking at that particular group membership would notice the temporary inconsistency.

Planning Operations Master Locations

In a small Active Directory forest with only one domain and one domain controller, that domain controller is assigned all the operations master roles. When you create the first domain in a new forest, all of the operations master roles are automatically assigned to the first domain controller in that domain.

When you create a new child domain or the root domain of a new domain tree in an existing forest, the first domain controller in the new domain is automatically assigned the following roles:

- Relative ID master
- PDC emulator
- Infrastructure master

Because there can be only one schema master and one domain naming master in the forest, these roles remain in the first domain created in the forest.

Figure 17.1 shows how the operations master roles are distributed throughout a forest by default.

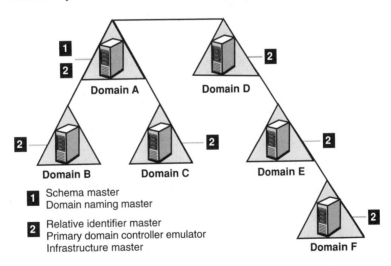

Figure 17.1 Operations master role default distribution in a forest

In Figure 17.1, Domain A was the first domain created in the forest (also called the forest root domain). It holds both of the forest-wide operations master roles. The first domain controller in each of the other domains is assigned the three domain-specific roles.

The default operations master locations work well for a forest deployed on a few domain controllers in a single site. In a forest with more domain controllers, or in a forest that spans multiple sites, you might want to transfer the default operations master role assignments to other domain controllers in the domain or forest.

Planning the Operations Master Role Assignments by Domain

If a domain has only one domain controller, that domain controller holds all of the domain roles. Otherwise, choose two well-connected domain controllers that are direct replication partners. Make one of the domain controllers the operations master domain controller. Make the other the *standby* operations master domain controller. The standby operations master domain controller is used in case of failure of the operations master domain controller.

In typical domains, you assign both the relative ID master and PDC emulator roles to the operations master domain controller. In a very large domain, you can reduce the peak load on the PDC emulator by placing these roles on separate domain controllers, both of which are direct replication partners of the standby operations master domain controller. Keep the two roles together unless the load on the operations master domain controller justifies separating the roles.

Unless there is only one domain controller in the domain, the infrastructure master role should not be assigned to the domain controller that is hosting the global catalog. However, you should assign the infrastructure master role to any domain controller that is well connected to a global catalog (from any domain) in the same site. If the operations master domain controller meets these requirements, use it unless the load justifies the extra management burden of separating the roles.

If the infrastructure master and global catalog are on the same domain controller, the infrastructure master will not function. The infrastructure master will never find data that is out of date, so it will never replicate any changes to the other domain controllers in the domain. If all the domain controllers in a domain are also hosting the global catalog, all of the domain controllers will have the current data and it does not matter which domain controller holds the infrastructure master role.

Planning the Operations Master Roles for the Forest

Once you have planned all of the domain roles for each domain, consider the forest roles. The schema master and the domain naming master roles should always be assigned to the same domain controller. For best performance, assign them to a domain controller that is well connected to the computers used by the administrator or group responsible for schema updates and the creation of new domains. The load of these operations master roles is very light, so, to simplify management, place these roles on the operations master domain controller of one of the domains in the forest.

Planning for Growth

Normally, as your forest grows, you will not need to change the locations of the various operations master roles. But when you are planning to decommission a domain controller, change the global catalog status of a domain controller, or reduce the connectivity of parts of your network, you should review your plan and revise the operations master role assignments, as necessary.

Identifying Operations Master Role Assignments

Before you can revise operations master role assignments, you need to view the current operations master role assignments for your domain.

▶   **Follow these steps to identify the relative ID master, the PDC emulator, or the infrastructure master role assignments:**

1. Open the Active Directory Users and Computers console.

2. In the console tree, right-click the Active Directory Users And Computers node, and then click Operations Masters.

3. In the Operations Master dialog box, do one of the following:

   - Click the RID tab. The name of the relative ID master appears in the Operations Master box.

   - Click the PDC tab. The name of the PDC emulator appears in the Operations Master box.

   - Click the Infrastructure tab. The name of the infrastructure master appears in the Operations Master box.

4. Click Cancel to close the Operations Master dialog box.

▶   **Follow these steps to identify the domain naming master role assignment:**

1. Open the Active Directory Domains And Trusts console.

2. In the console tree, right-click the Active Directory Domains And Trusts node, and then click Operations Master.

   In the Change Operations Master dialog box, the name of the current domain naming master appears in the Domain Naming Operations Master box.

3. Click Close to close the Change Operations Master dialog box.

▶   **Follow these steps to identify the schema master role assignment:**

1. Open the Active Directory Schema snap-in.

   Note The Active Directory Schema snap-in must be installed with the Windows 2000 Administration Tools using Add/Remove Programs in the Control Panel.

2. In the console tree, right-click Active Directory Schema, and then click Operations Master.

3. In the Change Schema Master dialog box, the name of the current schema master appears in the Current Operations Master box.

Transferring Operations Master Role Assignments

Transferring an operations master role assignment means moving it from one domain controller to another, with the cooperation of the original role holder. Depending upon the operations master role to be transferred, you perform the role transfer using one of the three Active Directory consoles.

▶   **Follow these steps to transfer the relative ID master, the PDC emulator, or the infrastructure master role assignments:**

1. Open the Active Directory Users And Computers console.

2. In the console tree, right-click the Domain node that will become the new relative ID master, PDC emulator, or infrastructure master, and then click Connect To Domain.

3. In the Connect To Domain dialog box, type the domain name or click Browse to select the domain from the list, and then click OK.

4. In the console tree, right-click the Active Directory Users And Computers node, and then click Operations Masters.

5. In the Operations Master dialog box, do one of the following:

   - Click the RID tab, and then click Change.

   - Click the PDC tab, and then click Change.

   - Click the Infrastructure tab, and then click Change.

6. Click OK to close the Operations Master dialog box.

▶ **Follow these steps to transfer the domain naming master role assignment:**

1. Open the Active Directory Domains And Trusts console.

2. In the Console tree, right-click the Domain Controller node that will become the new domain naming master, and then click Connect To Domain.

3. In the Connect To Domain dialog box, type the domain name or click Browse to select the domain from the list, and then click OK.

4. In the console tree, right-click the Active Directory Domains And Trusts node, and then click Operations Master.

5. In the Change Operations Master dialog box, click Change.

6. Click OK to close the Change Operations Master dialog box.

▶ **To transfer the schema master role assignment**

1. Open the Active Directory Schema snap-in.

   Note The Active Directory Schema snap-in must be installed with the Windows 2000 Administration Tools Using Add/Remove Programs in the Control Panel.

2. In the console tree, right-click Active Directory Schema, and then click Change Domain Controller.

3. In the Change Domain Controller dialog box, click one of the following:

   - Any DC. This lets Active Directory select the new schema operations master.

   - Specify Name. Then type the name of the new schema master to specify the new schema operations master.

4. Click OK.

5. In the console tree, right-click Active Directory Schema, and then click Operations Master.

6. In the Change Schema Master dialog box, click Change.

7. Click OK to close the Change Schema Master dialog box.

Responding to Operations Master Failures

Some of the operations master roles are crucial to the operation of your network. Others can be unavailable for quite some time before their absence becomes a problem. Generally, you will notice that a single master operations role holder is unavailable when you try to perform some function controlled by the particular operations master.

If an operations master is not available due to computer failure or network problems, you can *seize* the operations master role. This is also referred to as forcing the transfer of the operations master role.

Before forcing the transfer, first determine the cause and expected duration of the computer or network failure. If the cause is a networking problem or a server failure that will be resolved soon, wait for the role holder to become available again. If the domain controller that currently holds the role has failed, you must determine if it can be recovered and brought back online.

In general, seizing an operations master role is a drastic step that should be considered only if the current operations master will never again be available. The decision depends upon the role and how long the particular role holder will be unavailable. The impact of various role holder failures is discussed in the following sections.

Important A domain controller whose schema, domain naming, or relative ID master role has been seized must *never* be brought back online without the drives being reformatted and Windows 2000 reloaded first.

Schema Master Failure

Temporary loss of the schema operations master is not visible to network users. It will not be visible to network administrators either, unless they are trying to modify the schema or install an application that modifies the schema during installation.

If the schema master will be unavailable for an unacceptable length of time, you can seize the role to the standby operations master. However, seizing this role is a step that you should take only when the failure of the schema master is permanent.

Domain Naming Master Failure

Temporary loss of the domain naming master is not visible to network users. It will not be visible to network administrators either, unless they are trying to add a domain to the forest or remove a domain from the forest.

If the domain naming master will be unavailable for an unacceptable length of time, you can seize the role to the standby operations master. However, seizing this role is a step that you should take only when the failure of the domain naming master is permanent.

Relative ID Master Failure

Temporary loss of the relative ID operations master is not visible to network users. It will not be visible to network administrators either, unless they are creating objects and the domain in which they are creating the objects runs out of relative IDs.

If the relative ID master will be unavailable for an unacceptable length of time, you can seize the role to the operations master. However, seizing this role is a step that you should take only when the failure of the relative ID master is permanent.

PDC Emulator Failure

The loss of the PDC emulator affects network users. Therefore, when the PDC emulator is not available, you may need to immediately seize the role.

If the current PDC emulator master will be unavailable for an unacceptable length of time and its domain has clients without Windows 2000 client software, or if it contains Windows NT backup domain controllers, seize the PDC emulator master role to the standby operations master. When the original PDC emulator master is returned to service, you can return the role to the original domain controller.

Infrastructure Master Failure

Temporary loss of the infrastructure master is not visible to network users. It will not be visible to network administrators either, unless they have recently moved or renamed a large number of accounts.

If the infrastructure master will be unavailable for an unacceptable length of time, you can seize the role to a domain controller that is not a global catalog but is well connected to a global catalog (from any domain), ideally in the same site as the current global catalog. When the original infrastructure master is returned to service, you can transfer the role back to the original domain controller.

Lesson Summary

In this lesson you learned about the two forest-wide operations master roles, the schema master, and the domain naming master. You also learned about the three domain-wide operations master roles, the relative ID master, the PDC emulator, and the infrastructure master.

You learned the default operations master locations and some strategies for planning locations. You also learned how to view operations master role assignments and how to transfer operations master role assignments if necessary.

Lesson 3: Implementing an Organizational Unit Structure

You should create OUs that mirror your organization's functional or business structure. Each domain can implement its own OU hierarchy. If your enterprise contains several domains, you can create OU structures within each domain that are independent of the structures in the other domains. This lesson walks you through the steps for creating an OU structure.

After this lesson, you will be able to

- Create OUs

Estimated lesson time: 10 minutes

Creating OUs

Use the Active Directory Users and Computers console to create OUs. When you create an OU, it is always created on the first available domain controller that is contacted by the MMC, and then the OU is replicated to all domain controllers.

▶ **Follow these steps to create OUs:**

1. Log on as Administrator.

2. Click Start, point to Programs, point to Administrative Tools, and then click Active Directory Users And Computers.

3. Click the location where you want to create this OU, either a domain (such as microsoft.com) or another OU.

4. On the Action menu, point to New, and then click Organizational Unit.

5. In the New Object-Organizational Unit dialog box, in the Name box, type the name of the new OU, and then click OK.

Setting OU Properties

A set of default properties is associated with each OU that you create. These properties are equivalent to object attributes.

You can use the properties that you define for an OU to search for OUs in the directory.

The tabs in the Organizational Unit Properties dialog box contain information about each OU. The tabs are General, Managed By, and Group Policy. For example, if all the properties on the General tab are complete, as shown in Figure 17.2, you can locate the OU using the OU description or another field.

Figure 17.2 General tab of the OU properties dialog box

Table 17.3 describes the tabs in the Organizational Unit Properties dialog box.

Table 17.3   Tabs on the Organizational Unit Properties Dialog Box

Tab	Description
General	Documents the OU's description, street address, city, state or province, zip or postal code, and country or region
Managed By	Documents the OU manager's name, office location, street address, city, state or province, country or region, telephone number, and fax number
Group Policy	Documents the OU's group policy links

▶ **Follow these steps to set OU properties:**

1. Click Start, point to Programs, point to Administrative Tools, and then click Active Directory Users And Computers.

2. Expand the domain.

3. Right-click the appropriate OU, and then click Properties.

4. Click the appropriate tab for the OU properties that you want to enter or change, and then enter values for each property.

Practice: Creating an OU

In this practice, you create part of the organizational structure of a domain by creating three OUs.

Exercise 1: Create an OU

Complete this exercise on Server01.

1. Log on as Administrator.

2. Click Start, point to Programs, point to Administrative Tools, and then click Active Directory Users And Computers.

   Windows 2000 displays the Active Directory Users And Computers console.

3. Expand the microsoft.com domain (or the domain you set up).

   The OUs appear as folders with a directory book icon under the domain. Plain folders are specialized containers.

   What are the default OUs in your domain?

   To ensure that you are creating a new OU in the correct location, you must first select the location where you want to create this OU.

4. In the console tree, click your domain (such as microsoft.com).

5. On the Action menu, point to New, and then click Organizational Unit.

   The New Object-Organizational Unit dialog box appears. Notice that the only required information is the name of the OU. The dialog box indicates the location where the object will be created. This should be your domain.

6. In the Name box, type **Sales** and then click OK.

   Active Directory Users And Computers displays the newly created Sales OU in addition to the default OUs in your domain.

7. In the console tree, click the Sales OU.

8. On the Action menu, point to New, and then click Organizational Unit.

   The New Object-Organizational Unit dialog box appears.

9. In the name box, type **Trucks** and then click OK.

   Active Directory Users And Computers displays the newly created Trucks OU under the Sales OU in addition to the default OUs in your domain.

10. Under the Sales OU, create another OU called Autos.

Active Directory Users And Computers displays the newly created Autos OU under the Sales OU in addition to the Trucks OU and the default OUs in your domain (see Figure 17.3).

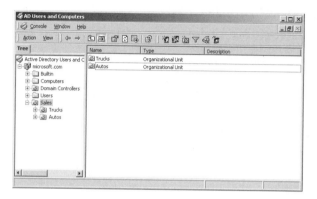

Figure 17.3 An OU structure

Lesson Summary

In this lesson you learned that you use the Active Directory Users And Computers console to create a new OU. When you create an OU, it is always created on the first available domain controller that is contacted by MMC, and then replicated to all domain controllers.

You also learned that there is a set of default properties associated with each OU that you create. You learned that these properties are equivalent to object attributes, so you can use these properties to search for OUs in the directory.

Lesson 4: Configuring Site Settings

Once Active Directory is installed, you need to configure your sites. This lesson walks you through the steps for configuring site settings, including creating a site, associating a subnet with a site, connecting a site using site links, and selecting a site license server.

After this lesson, you will be able to

- Configure site settings

Estimated lesson time: 20 minutes

Configuring Site Settings

To configure site settings you must complete the following tasks:

1. Create a site

2. Associate a subnet with the site

3. Connect the site using site links

4. Select a site license server

Sites

Sites define sets of domain controllers that are well connected in terms of speed and cost. Domain controllers in the same site replicate on the basis of notification. That is, when a domain controller has changes, it notifies its replication partners. The notified partner then requests the changes and replication takes place. Because there is no concern about replication speed or cost, replication within sites occurs as needed rather than as scheduled. Replication between sites occurs according to a schedule; you can use the schedule to determine the most beneficial time for replication to occur on the basis of network traffic and cost. A site is the equivalent of a set of one or more IP subnets.

When you install Active Directory on the first domain controller in the site, an object named Default-First-Site-Name is created in the Sites container. It is necessary to install the first domain controller into this site. Subsequent domain controllers are either installed into the site of the source domain controller (assuming the IP address maps to the site) or into existing site. When your first domain controller has been installed, you can rename Default-First-Site-Name to the name you want to use for the site.

When you install Active Directory on subsequent servers, if alternate sites have been defined in Active Directory and the IP address of the installation computer matches an existing subnet in a defined site, the domain controller is added to that site. Otherwise, it is added to the site of the source domain controller.

▶ **Follow these steps to create a new site:**

1. Click Start, point to Programs, point to Administrative Tools, and then click Active Directory Sites And Services.

2. Right-click the Sites folder, and then click New Site.

3. In the New Object-Site dialog box, shown in Figure 17.4, type the name of the new site in the Name box. Select a site link object, and then click OK.

Figure 17.4 New Object-Site dialog box

4. On the Active Directory message box, click OK.

▶ **Follow these steps to rename a site:**

1. Click Start, point to Programs, point to Administrative Tools, and then click Active Directory Sites And Services.

2. Click on the Sites folder.

3. Click the site you want to rename twice, slowly, or right-click the site you want to rename, and then click Rename.

4. Type the new site name over the existing site name. Click in an empty part of the console tree.

Subnets

Computers on Transmission Control Protocol/Internet Protocol (TCP/IP) networks are assigned to sites based on their location in a subnet or a set of subnets. Subnets group computers in a way that identifies their feasible physical proximity on the network. Subnet information is used to find a domain controller in the same site as the computer that is authenticated during logon, and it is used during Active Directory replication to determine the best routes between domain controllers.

▶ **Follow these steps to create a subnet:**

1. Click Start, point to Programs, point to Administrative Tools, and then click Active Directory Sites And Services.

2. Double-click the Sites folder.

3. Right-click the Subnets folder, and click New Subnet.

4. In the New Object-Subnet dialog box, shown in Figure 17.5, type the subnet address in the Address box. In the Mask box type the subnet mask that describes the range of addresses included in this site's subnet. Choose a site to associate this subnet with, and then click OK.

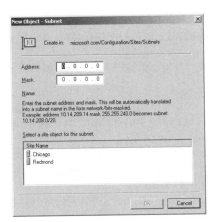

Figure 17.5 New Object-Subnet dialog box

▶ **Follow these steps to associate an existing subnet with a site:**

1. Click Start, point to Programs, point to Administrative Tools, and then click Active Directory Sites And Services.

2. Open the Subnets folder, right-click the subnet, and then click Properties.

3. In the Properties dialog box for the subnet, shown in Figure 17.6, select a site with which to associate this subnet from the choices available in the Site list, and then click OK.

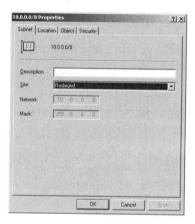

Figure 17.6 Properties dialog box for a subnet

Site Links

For replication to occur between two sites, a link must be established between the sites. Site links are not generated automatically and must be created in Active Directory Sites And Services. Unless a site link is in place, connections cannot be made between computers in the two sites and replication between the sites cannot take place. Each site link contains the schedule that determines when replication can occur between the sites that it connects. The Active Directory Sites And Services console guarantees that every site is placed in at least one site link. A site link can contain more than two sites, in which case all the sites are equally well connected.

When you install Active Directory on the first domain controller in the site, the Active Directory Installation Wizard automatically creates an object named DEFAULTIPSITELINK in the IP container. It is necessary to create this site link for the first default site, also created by the Active Directory Installation Wizard. Subsequent site links are created separately. When your first domain controller has been installed, you can change the DEFAULTIPSITELINK to the name you want to use for the site link.

Replication Protocols

Directory information can be exchanged over site links using different network protocols such as IP or Simple Mail Transfer Protocol (SMTP):

- **IP replication** uses remote procedure calls (RPCs) for replication over site links (inter-site) and within a site (intra-site). By default, inter-site IP replication does adhere to replication schedules, although you may configure Active Directory to ignore schedules. IP replication does not require a certification authority (CA).

- **SMTP replication** is only used for replication over site links (inter-site), and not for replication within a site (intra-site). Because SMTP is asynchronous, it typically ignores all schedules.

If you choose to use SMTP over site links, you must install and configure a certification authority (CA). The CA signs SMTP messages that are exchanged between domain controllers, ensuring the authenticity of directory updates.

▶ **Follow these steps to create a site link:**

1. Click Start, point to Programs, point to Administrative Tools, and then click Active Directory Sites And Services.

2. Open the Inter-Site Transports folder and right-click on either the IP or SMTP folder, depending on which protocol you want the site to use. Select New Site Link.

Caution If you create a site link that uses SMTP, you must have an Enterprise CA available and SMTP must be installed on all domain controllers that will use the site link.

3. In the New Object-Site Link dialog box, shown in Figure 17.7, type the name to be given to the site link in the Name field.

Figure 17.7 New Object-Site Link dialog box

4. Click two or more sites to connect, and then click Add.

5. Click OK.

▶ **Follow these steps to add a site to an existing site link:**

1. Click Start, point to Programs, point to Administrative Tools, and then click Active Directory Sites And Services.

2. Open the Inter-Site Transports folder and either the IP or SMTP folder, and right-click on the site link to which you want to add the site. Click Properties.

3. In the Properties dialog box for the site link, in the Sites Not In This Site Link box in the General Tab, click the site you want to add to this site link, and then click Add.

4. Click OK.

Site Licensing

An administrator can ensure an organization's legal compliance with Microsoft BackOffice software license agreements by monitoring license purchases, deletions, and usage. This licensing information is collected on a server by the License Logging service in Windows 2000 Server.

The License Logging service on each server in a site replicates this licensing information to a centralized database on a server called the site license server for the site. A site administrator or administrator for the site license server can then use the Licensing utility in Administrative Tools to view the licensing history for the entire site stored on the site license server.

The default site license server is the first domain controller created for the site, but the site license server does not have to be a domain controller. For optimal performance, however, the site license server and domain controller should be in the same site. In a large organization with multiple sites, licensing information for each site is collected separately by the site license server in each site.

▶ **Follow these steps to select a site license server:**

1. Click Start, point to Programs, point to Administrative Tools, and then click Active Directory Sites And Services.

2. Click on the site for which you want to assign a site license server.

3. In the details pane, right-click Licensing Site Settings, and then click Properties.

4. In the Licensing Site Settings Properties dialog box, click Change in the Licensing Computer box.

5. In the Select Computer dialog box, select the computer you want to designate as the site license server, and then click OK.

6. In the Licensing Site Settings Properties dialog box, click OK.

▶ **Follow these steps to view licensing for a site:**

1. Click Start, point to Programs, point to Administrative Tools, and click Licensing.

2. On the License menu, choose Select Domain to connect to the site license server for the domain.

3. In the Select Domain dialog box, enter the name of the site license server in the Domain box, and then click OK.

Practice: Configuring a Site

In this practice you configure a site. To configure a site you must first create a site. You must then associate a subnet with the site and connect the site using site links. Finally, you must select a site license server.

Exercise 1: Rename an Exisiting Site

In this exercise, you will rename the default site name to Redmond. This will give you a site to link to in a later exercise.

1. Click Start, point to Programs, point to Administrative Tools, and then click Active Directory Sites And Services.

   The Active Directory Sites And Services console appears.

2. Click on the Sites folder.

   What objects appear in the details pane?

3. Right-click the Default-First-Site-Name site, and then click Rename.

4. Type the new site name, **Redmond**, over Default-First-Site-Name. Click in an empty part of the console tree.

   The Default-First-Site-Name site has been renamed Redmond.

Exercise 2: Create a New Site

In this exercise, you will create a new site. This site will be configured in the following exercises.

1. Right-click the Sites folder, and then click New Site.

   The New Object-Site dialog box appears.

2. In the Name box, type **Chicago**. Select DEFAULTIPSITELINK for the Chicago site's site link, and then click OK.

The Active Directory message box appears reminding you that to finish configuring the site Chicago you must:

- Ensure that the site is linked to other sites with site links as appropriate.

- Add subnets for the site to the subnets container.

- Install one or more domain controllers in the site or move existing domain controllers into the site.

- Select the licensing for the site.

3. Click OK.

Exercise 3: Create a Subnet

In this exercise, you create a subnet for the new Chicago site.

1. Double-click the Sites folder.

2. Right-click the Subnets folder, and click New Subnet.

The New Object-Subnet dialog box appears.

3. In the Address box, type **10.10.1.1** for the subnet address. In the Mask box type **255.0.0.0** for the subnet mask that describes the range of addresses included in this site's subnet. Choose the Chicago site to associate to this subnet, and then click OK.

The 10.0.0.0/8 subnet is created and the Chicago site is associated to the subnet.

Exercise 4: Associate an Existing Subnet with a Site

In this exercise, you associate an existing subnet with the existing Redmond site.

1. Open the Subnets folder, right-click the 10.0.0.0/8 subnet, and then click Properties.

The Properties dialog box for the 10.0.0.0/8 subnet appears with the Subnet tab chosen.

2. In the Sites list, select the Redmond site to associate to this subnet, and then click OK.

Exercise 5: Create a Site Link

In this exercise, you link the Redmond and Chicago sites.

1. Open the Inter-Site Transports folder and click the IP folder.

   What object appears in the details pane?

2. Right-click the IP folder, and then select New Site Link.

   The New Object-Site Link dialog box appears.

3. In the Name box, type **Redmond to Chicago**.

4. Ensure that the Chicago and Redmond sites are in the Sites In This Site Link box, and then click OK.

Exercise 6: Select a Site License Server

Before you can use a link, you need to select the appropriate site license server. In this exercise, you select the license server for the Chicago site.

1. Click on the Chicago site.

2. In the details pane, right-click Licensing Site Settings, and then click Properties.

   The Licensing Site Settings Properties dialog box appears.

3. In the Licensing Computer box, click Change.

   The Select Computer dialog box appears.

4. Select the SERVER01 (or the name you selected for your computer), and then click OK.

   You return to the Licensing Site Settings Properties dialog box. The computer is SERVER01 and the domain is microsoft.com (or the computer and domain you selected) for the site license server in the Licensing Computer box.

5. Click OK.

6. Close Active Directory Sites and Services.

7. To verify that the license is valid, Click Start, point to Programs, point to Administrative Tools, and then click Licensing.

   The MICROSOFT.COM-Licensing utility appears. You can view licensing information using the Products View tab.

Lesson Summary

In this lesson you learned how to configure sites. After you create a site, you must add subnets for the site to the subnets container, ensure that the site is linked to other sites with site links as appropriate, and select the licensing for the site. Subnets group computers in a way that identifies their physical proximity on the network. Site links contain the cost and schedule for replication traffic and allow replication to occur between two sites.

You also learned how the License Logging service on each server in a site replicates this licensing information to a centralized database on a server called the site license server for the site. A site administrator or administrator for the site license server can then use the Licensing utility in Administrative Tools to view the licensing history for the entire site stored on the site license server.

In the practice portion of this lesson you created a site, associated a subnet with the site, connected a site using site links, and selected a site license server.

Lesson 5: Configuring Inter-Site Replication

Network connections are represented by site links. By creating site links and configuring their cost, replication frequency, and replication availability, you provide the directory service with information about how to use these connections to replicate directory data. You can improve site link connectivity by linking overlapping existing site links together into site link bridges, or you can bridge all site links and maximize connectivity. You can also designate a server, known as a bridgehead server, to serve as a contact point for the exchange of directory information between sites. This lesson explains how to configure inter-site replication.

After this lesson, you will be able to

- Configure inter-site replication

Estimated lesson time: 25 minutes

Configuring Inter-Site Replication

To configure inter-site replication you must complete the following tasks:

1. Create site links (see Lesson 4)
2. Configure site link attributes
3. Create site link bridges
4. Configure connection objects (optional)
5. Designate a preferred bridgehead server (optional)

Site Link Attributes

You should provide information about site link cost, replication frequency, and replication availability for all site links as part of the process of configuring inter-site replication.

Site Link Cost

You configure site link cost to assign a value for the cost of each available connection used for inter-site replication. If you have multiple redundant network connections, establish site links for each connection, and then assign costs to these site links that reflect their relative bandwidth. For example, if you have a high-speed T1 line and a dial-up network connection in case the

T1 line is unavailable, configure a lower cost for the T1 line and a higher cost for the dial-up network connection. Active Directory always chooses the connection on a per-cost basis, so the cheaper connection is used as long as it is available.

▶ **Follow these steps to configure site link cost:**

1. Click Start, point to Programs, point to Administrative Tools, and then click Active Directory Sites And Services.

2. Open the Inter-Site Transports folder and either the IP or SMTP folder, and right-click on the site link for which you want to configure site link cost. Click Properties.

3. On the Properties dialog box for the site link, shown in Figure 17.8, enter a value for the cost of replication in the Cost box. The default cost is 100; the lower the value, the higher the priority. For example, the cost of a T1 link might be 100, while the cost of a dial-up link might be 120.

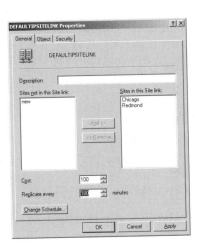

Figure 17.8 Properties dialog box for a site link

4. Click OK.

Replication Frequency

Configure site link replication frequency for site links by providing an integer value that tells Active Directory how many minutes it should wait before using a connection to check for replication updates. The replication interval must be at least 15 and no more than 10,080 minutes (equal to one week). A site link must be available for any replication to occur, so if a site link is scheduled as unavailable when the number of minutes between replication updates has passed, no replication will occur.

▶ **Follow these steps to configure site link replication frequency:**

1. Click Start, point to Programs, point to Administrative Tools, and then click Active Directory Sites And Services.

2. Open the Inter-Site Transports folder and either the IP or SMTP folder, and right-click on the site link for which you want to configure site replication frequency. Click Properties.

3. On the Properties dialog box for the site link, enter the number of minutes between replications in the Replicate Every box. The default time is 180; the value is processed as the nearest multiple of 15, ranging from a minimum of 15 to a maximum of 10,080 minutes (one week).

4. Click OK.

Replication Availability

Configure site link replication availability to determine when a site link will be available for replication. Because SMTP is asynchronous, it typically ignores all schedules. Therefore, do not configure site link replication availability on SMTP site links unless

- The site links use scheduled connections.

- The SMTP queue is not on a schedule.

- Information is being exchanged directly from one server to another and not through intermediaries as is the case, for example, on a network backbone.

▶   **Follow these steps to configure site link replication availability:**

1. Click Start, point to Programs, point to Administrative Tools, and then click Active Directory Sites And Services.

2. Open the Inter-Site Transports folder and either the IP or SMTP folder, and right-click on the site link for which you want to configure site link replication availability. Click Properties.

3. In the Properties dialog box for the site link, click Change Schedule.

4. On the Schedule For dialog box for the site link, shown in Figure 17.9, select the block of time when this connection is or is not available to replicate directory information, and then click OK.

5. In the Properties dialog box for the site link, click OK.

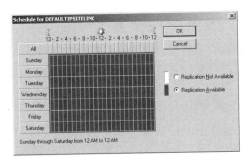

Figure 17.9 Schedule for dialog box for a site link

Note This following procedure has no effect if you have enabled Ignore Schedules on the Properties dialog box for the inter-site transport.

▶   **Follow these steps to ignore schedules for an inter-site transport:**

1. Click Start, point to Programs, point to Administrative Tools, and then click Active Directory Sites And Services.

2. Open the Inter-Site Transports folder and right-click either the IP or SMTP folder, and then click Properties.

3. In the IP or SMTP Properties dialog box, on the General tab, click the Ignore Schedules check box.

4. Click OK.

Site Link Bridges

When more than two sites are linked for replication and use the same transport, by default, all the site links are "bridged" in terms of cost, assuming that the site links have common sites. When site links are bridged, they are *transitive*. That is, all site links for a specific transport implicitly belong to a single site link bridge for that transport. So in the common case of a fully routed IP network (where all sites can communicate with each other via IP), you do not have to configure any site link bridges. If your IP network is not fully routed, you can turn off the transitive site link feature for the IP transport, in which case all IP site links are considered intransitive and you configure site link bridges. A site link bridge is the equivalent of a disjoint network; all site links within the bridge can route transitively, but they do not route outside of the bridge.

▶ **Follow these steps to create a site link bridge:**

1. Click Start, point to Programs, point to Administrative Tools, and then click Active Directory Sites And Services.

2. Open the Inter-Site Transports folder and right-click either the IP or SMTP folder, and then click New Site Link Bridge.

3. In the New Object-Site Link Bridge dialog box, shown in Figure 17.10, type a name for the site link bridge in the Name box.

Figure 17.10 New Object-Site Link Bridge dialog box

4. Click two or more sites to connect, and then click Add.

5. Click OK.

Note The following procedure is redundant and has no effect if you have enabled Bridge All Site Links on the Properties dialog box for the inter-site transport.

▶ **Follow these steps to bridge all site links for an inter-site transport:**

1. Click Start, point to Programs, point to Administrative Tools, and then click Active Directory Sites And Services.

2. Open the Inter-Site Transports folder and right-click either the IP or SMTP folder, and then click Properties.

3. In the IP or SMTP Properties dialog box, on the General tab, click the Bridge All Site Links check box.

4. Click OK.

Manually Configuring Connections

Active Directory automatically creates and deletes connections under normal conditions. Although you can manually add or configure connections or force replication over a particular connection, normally you should allow replication to be automatically optimized based on information you provide to Active Directory Sites And Services about your deployment. Only create connections manually if you are certain the connection is required, and you want the connection to persist until it is manually removed.

▶ **Follow these steps to manually configure connections:**

1. Click Start, point to Programs, point to Administrative Tools, and then click Active Directory Sites And Services.

2. Double-click the site that contains the domain controller for which you want to manually add or configure a connection.

3. Open the Servers folder, open the domain controller, right-click NTDS Settings, and then click New Active Directory Connection.

4. In the Find Domain Controllers dialog box, click the domain controller that you want to include in the connection object, and then click OK.

5. In the New Object-Connection dialog box, type a name for the new Connection object in the Name field, and then click OK.

▶ **Follow these steps to force replication over a connection:**

1. Click Start, point to Programs, point to Administrative Tools, and then click Active Directory Sites And Services.

2. Double-click the site that contains the connection over which you want to replicate directory information.

3. Open the Servers folder, select the domain controller, and then open NTDS Settings.

4. Right-click the connection over which you want to replicate directory information, and click Replicate Now (see Figure 17.11).

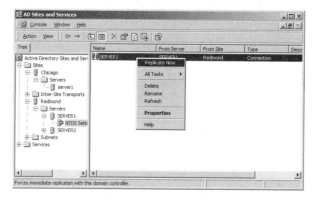

Figure 17.11 Forcing replication over a connection

Designating a Preferred Bridgehead Server

Ordinarily, all domain controllers are used to exchange information between sites, but you can further control replication behavior by specifying a bridgehead server for inter-site replicated information. Establishing a bridgehead server provides some ranking or criteria for choosing which domain controller should be preferred as the recipient for inter-site replication. This bridgehead server subsequently distributes the directory information via intra-site replication.

Bridgehead servers are the contact point for exchange of directory information between sites. You can specify a preferred bridgehead server if you have a computer with appropriate bandwidth to transmit and receive information. If there is typically a high level of directory information exchange, a computer with more bandwidth can ensure the information exchanges are handled promptly. Matching the demands of your Active Directory deployment with a domain controller with the capacity to handle those demands enables efficient updates of directory information.

You can specify multiple preferred bridgehead servers, but only one will be the active preferred bridgehead server at any time at a single site. If the active preferred bridgehead server fails, Active Directory selects another preferred bridgehead server to be the active preferred bridgehead server from the set you designate. If no active preferred bridgehead server is available and there are no other preferred bridgehead servers available for Active Directory to select, it selects another domain controller in the site to be the preferred bridgehead server. This can be a problem if the domain controller Active Directory selects does not have the bandwidth to efficiently handle the increased requirements posed by being a preferred bridgehead server.

You must specify a preferred bridgehead server if your deployment uses a firewall to protect a site. Establish your firewall proxy server as the preferred bridgehead server, making it the contact point for exchanging information with servers outside the firewall. If you do not do this, directory information may not be successfully exchanged.

Establishing a preferred bridgehead server designates that server as the preeminent server for information exchange over the protocol for which the site link is established. Other domain controllers could still exchange directory information if a need arises, but under normal conditions, the bridgehead server is used as the first choice to receive and send all directory traffic.

▶ **Follow these steps to designate a preferred bridgehead server:**

1. Click Start, point to Programs, point to Administrative Tools, and then click Active Directory Sites And Services.

2. In the Active Directory Sites And Services console tree, right-click the domain controller that you want to make a bridgehead server, and then click Properties.

3. On the Properties dialog box for the domain controller, in the Transports Available For Inter-Site Data Transfer box, click the inter-site transport or transports for which this computer will be a preferred bridgehead server, and then click Add.

4. Click OK.

Practice: Configuring Inter-Site Replication

In this practice you configure site link cost, replication availability, and replication frequency. You then configure a site link bridge.

Exercise 1: Configure Site Link

Since Active Directory uses cost to determine which connection to use, you need to assign a cost to each site link. In this exercise you assign an arbitrary cost to the Redmond to Chicago site link.

1. Click Start, point to Programs, point to Administrative Tools, and then click Active Directory Sites And Services.

   The Active Directory Sites And Services console appears.

2. Open the Inter-Site Transports folder and the IP folder, and right-click the Redmond To Chicago site link you configured in the Lesson 5. Click Properties.

   The Redmond To Chicago Properties dialog box appears.

3. In the Cost box, type **20** for the cost of replication.

Exercise 2: Configure Site Link Replication Frequency

In this exercise, you specify how long Active Directory waits before using a this connection to check for replication updates.

1. In the Replicate Every box, type **120** for the number of minutes between replications.

Exercise 3: Configure Site Link Replication Availability

In this exercise, you will configure the Redmond To Chicago site link to be available 8:00 am to 9:00 am and 4:00 pm to 5:00 pm, Monday through Friday.

1. Click Change Schedule.

   The Schedule For Redmond To Chicago dialog box appears.

2. Make the connection available at all times except Monday through Friday from 8 A.M. to 9 A.M. and from 4 P.M. to 5 P.M., and then click OK.

3. On the Redmond To Chicago Properties dialog box, click OK.

Exercise 4: Create a Site Link Bridge

In this exercise, you create a bridge between the Redmond To Chicago site link and the DEFAULTIPSITELINK.

1. Open the Inter-Site Transports folder, right-click the IP folder, and then click New Site Link Bridge.

   The New Object-Site Link Bridge dialog box appears.

2. In the Name box, type **Redmond to Chicago Bridge**.

3. Ensure that the DEFAULTIPSITELINK and Redmond to Chicago site links are in the Site Links In This Site Link Bridge box, and then click OK.

Lesson Summary

In this lesson you learned that you should provide information about site link cost, replication frequency, and replication availability for all site links as part of the process of configuring inter-site replication. Active Directory always chooses the connection on a per-cost basis, so the cheaper connection will be used as long as it is available. You can improve site link connectivity by linking overlapping existing site links together into site link bridges, or you can bridge all site links and maximize connectivity. You also learned that you can designate a domain controller as a bridgehead server to specify which domain controller should be preferred as the recipient for inter-site replication.

In the practice portion of this lesson you configured site link cost, replication availability, and replication frequency. You then configured a site link bridge.

Lesson 6: Troubleshooting Replication

This lesson describes problems you may encounter that relate to replication. Most problems involving poor directory information can be remedied with Active Directory Sites And Services. Problems with directory information might mean that:

- New directory information is not distributed in a timely fashion
- Service requests are not handled in a timely fashion

This lesson also describes how to check replication topology.

After this lesson, you will be able to

- Troubleshoot replication

Estimated lesson time: 5 minutes

Troubleshooting Replication

Ineffective replication can result in declining Active Directory performance, which might include new users not being recognized. Ineffective replication or request handling primarily results in out-of-date directory information or unavailable domain controllers. Each problem or cause has one or more possible solutions. Replication troubleshooting scenarios are discussed in Table 17.4.

Table 17.4   Replication Troubleshooting Scenarios

Symptom: Replication of directory information has stopped

Cause	Solution
The sites containing the clients and domain controllers are not connected by site links to domain controllers in other sites in the network. This results in a failure of directory information to be exchanged between sites.	Create a site link from the current site to a site that is connected to the rest of the sites in the network.

Symptom: Replication has slowed but not stopped

Cause	Solution
Although all sites are connected by site links, your inter-site replication structure is not as complete as it might be. Directory information is replicated to all domain controllers if they are all connected by site links, but this is not optimal. If there are site links but no site link bridges, changes made to domain controllers may take an unacceptably long time to be distributed to other domain controllers that are not closely linked.	Make sure Active Directory has been configured properly. To span the multiple site links that need more efficient replication, consider creating a site link bridge or consider bridging all site links.

Symptom: Replication has slowed but not stopped

Cause	Solution
The current network resources are insufficient to handle the amount of replication traffic. This can affect services unrelated to Active Directory, because the exchange of directory information is consuming an inordinate amount of network resources.	Increase the proportion of available network resources relative to directory traffic. Decrease the frequency of the replication schedule. Configure site link costs. To achieve network connections with more bandwidth, create site links or site link bridges.
Directory information changed at domain controllers in one site is not being updated in domain controllers in other sites in a timely fashion because inter-site replication is scheduled too infrequently.	Increase the frequency of replication. If the replication is occurring over a site link bridge, check which site link is restricting replication. Increase the time range during which replication can occur or the frequency of replication within the time frame for that site link.
Clients are having to request authentication, information, and services from a domain controller with a low-bandwidth connection. This may result in clients receiving a slow response for authentication, directory information, or other services.	Check if there is a site that will better serve the client's subnet. If a client who is experiencing poor service is isolated from domain controllers, consider creating another site with its own domain controller that will include the client. Install a connection with more bandwidth.

Checking Replication Topology

Active Directory runs a process that considers the cost of inter-site connections, checks if any previously available domain controllers are no longer available, checks if new domain controllers have been added, and then uses this information to add or remove connection objects to create an efficient replication topology. This process does not affect manually created connection objects.

▶   **Follow these steps to check the replication topology:**

1. Click Start, point to Programs, point to Administrative Tools, and then click Active Directory Sites And Services.

2. In the Active Directory Sites And Services console tree, double-click the server that you want to use to check replication topology.

3. Right-click NTDS Settings, point to All Tasks, and then click Check Replication Topology.

Lesson Summary

In this lesson you examined some replication problems you may encounter and possible solutions to these problems.

Lesson 7: Maintaining Server Settings

To meet changing business needs, you may need to update server settings for a site. This lesson examines some tasks for updating server settings to meet the changing needs of your organization. The tasks include creating a server object in a site, moving a server object between sites, enabling or disabling a global catalog, and removing an inoperative server object from a site.

After this lesson, you will be able to

▪Maintain server settings for a site

Estimated lesson time: 10 minutes

Maintaining Server Settings

As a site changes and grows based on business needs, you may find it necessary to meet these changing needs by updating server settings for the site. The tasks you may need to perform to maintain server settings are

- Creating a server object in a site
- Moving a server object between sites
- Enabling or disabling a global catalog
- Removing an inoperative server object from a site

Creating a Server Object in a Site

This procedure can be used to create member servers and domain controllers in a site. Creating a server object is not the same as installing a domain controller using the Active Directory Installation Wizard.

▶ **Follow these steps to create a server object in a site:**

1. Click Start, point to Programs, point to Administrative Tools, and then click Active Directory Sites And Services.

2. In the Active Directory Sites And Services console tree, double-click the site that you want to contain the new domain controller server object.

3. Right-click the Servers folder, point to New, and then click Server.

4. On the New Object-Server dialog box, enter the name for the new server object in the Name box, and then click OK.

Moving Server Objects Between Sites

▶ **The following procedure can be used to move member servers and domain controllers between sites.**

1. Click Start, point to Programs, point to Administrative Tools, and then click Active Directory Sites And Services.

2. In the Active Directory Sites And Services console tree, right-click the server object that you want to move to a different site, and then click Move.

3. In the Move Server dialog box, click the site to which you want to move the server object, and then click OK.

Enabling or Disabling a Global Catalog

Clients must have access to a global catalog to log on, so you should have at least one global catalog in every site to receive the benefits of containing network traffic provided by using sites.

▶ **Follow these steps to enable or disable a global catalog:**

1. Click Start, point to Programs, point to Administrative Tools, and then click Active Directory Sites And Services.

2. In the Active Directory Sites And Services console tree, double-click the domain controller hosting the global catalog.

3. Right-click NTDS Settings, and then click Properties.

4. Do one of the following:

   - To enable a global catalog, select the Global Catalog check box, and then click OK.

   - To disable a global catalog, clear the Global Catalog check box, and then click OK.

Removing an Inoperative Server Object from a Site

Use the following procedure only if you want to permanently remove a server object from a site. If you plan to reactivate the server, delete the NTDS Settings object for the server, rather than the server object itself. When you bring the server back online, Active Directory automatically creates a new NTDS Settings object, inserting the server into the replication topology as appropriate.

▶ **Follow these steps to remove an inoperative server object from a site:**

1. Click Start, point to Programs, point to Administrative Tools, and then click Active Directory Sites And Services.

2. In the Acive Directory Sites And Services console tree, right-click the server object to be removed, and then click Delete.

3. On the Active Directory message box, click Yes.

Lesson Summary

In this lesson you learned the various tasks to perform to maintain and update server settings as the needs of your organization change. The tasks included: creating a server object in a site, moving a server object between sites, enabling or disabling a global catalog, and removing an inoperative server object from a site.

Review

The following questions will help you determine whether you have learned enough to move on to the next chapter. If you have difficulty answering these questions, please go back and review the material in this chapter before beginning the next chapter. See Appendix A, "Questions and Answers," for the answers to these questions.

1. What are some reasons for creating more than one domain?

2. Your company has an external Internet namespace reserved with a DNS registration authority. As you plan the Active Directory implementation for your company, you decide to recommend extending the namespace for the internal network. What benefits does this option provide?

3. In what two ways does your site configuration affect Windows 2000?

4. What is the shared system volume, what purpose does it serve, where is it located, and what is its name?

5. What is the purpose of the operations master roles?

6. What administrative tool is used to create OUs?

7. What four tasks must be completed to configure a site?

8. What two site configuration objects does the Active Directory Installation wizard create automatically?

9. Which replication protocol uses RPCs for replication over site links (inter-site) and within a site (intra-site)?

10. What three tasks must be completed to configure inter-site replication?

11. What is the difference between replication frequency and replication availability?

12. What is the function of a bridgehead server?

C H A P T E R   1 8

Managing Domain Name System for Active Directory Directory Service

About This Chapter

For Microsoft Windows 2000 Server, the Domain Name System (DNS) service has been carefully integrated into the design and implementation of Active Directory directory services. When deploying Active Directory and Windows 2000 Server together you should keep in mind the following points.

- DNS name resolution is needed to locate Windows 2000 domain controllers. The Netlogon service uses DNS server support for the service (SRV) resource record to provide registration of domain controllers in your DNS domain namespace.

- Active Directory can be used to store, integrate, and replicate zones.

In Chapter 10, "Managing Domain Name System" you learned about DNS name resolution and how to configure Microsoft Windows 2000 Server for DNS. This chapter explores the benefits of using Active Directory–integrated zones and provides practice in configuring zones. Finally, this chapter discusses zone replication and transfer and provides information on troubleshooting an Active Directory DNS configuration.

Before You Begin

To complete this chapter, you must have

- Installed Windows 2000 Server onto Server01

- Completed Chapter 10, "Managing Domain Name System"

- Installed Active Directory on Server01

- Experience using Microsoft Management Console snap-ins (MMCs)

Lesson 1: Zones and Active Directory Directory Service

The DNS service allows a DNS namespace to be divided up into zones that store name information about one or more DNS domains. The zone becomes the authoritative source for information about each DNS domain name included in a zone. This lesson introduces you to DNS zones and how they are configured.

After this lesson, you will be able to

- Identify zone types
- List the benefits of Active Directory–integrated zones
- Explain zone delegation
- Configure zones

Estimated lesson time: 30 minutes

Zones

The DNS service provides the option of dividing up the namespace into one or more zones, which can then be stored, distributed, and replicated to other DNS servers. The DNS namespace represents the logical structure of your network resources, and DNS zones provide physical storage for these resources.

Zone Planning

When deciding whether or not to divide your DNS namespace to make additional zones, your answers to the following questions will help you determine whether or not to use additional zones:

- Is there a need to delegate management of part of your DNS namespace to another location or department within your organization?
- Is there a need to divide one large zone into smaller zones for distributing traffic loads among multiple servers, improve DNS name resolution performance, or create a more fault-tolerant DNS environment?
- Is there a need to extend the namespace by adding numerous subdomains at once, such as to accommodate the opening of a new branch or site?

If you can answer "yes" to one of these questions, it may be useful to add or restructure your namespace into additional zones. When choosing how to structure zones, you should use a plan that meets the needs of your organization.

There are two zone lookup types: forward lookup zones and reverse lookup zones.

Forward Lookup Zones

A *forward lookup zone* enables forward lookup queries. On name servers, you must configure at least one forward lookup zone for the DNS service to work. When you install Active Directory using the Active Directory Installation wizard and allow the wizard to install and configure your DNS server, the wizard automatically creates a forward lookup zone based on the DNS name you specified for the server.

Zone Type

There are three types of zones that you can configure:

- **Active Directory–integrated.** An Active Directory–integrated zone is the master copy of a new zone. The zone uses Active Directory to store and replicate zone files.

- **Standard primary.** A standard primary zone is the master copy of a new zone stored in a standard text file. You administer and maintain a primary zone on the computer on which you create the zone.

- **Standard secondary.** A standard secondary zone is a replica of an existing zone. Secondary zones are read-only and are stored in standard text files. A primary zone must be configured to create a secondary zone. When creating a secondary zone, you must specify the DNS server, called the master server, that will transfer zone information to the name server containing the standard secondary zone. You create a secondary zone to provide redundancy and to reduce the load on the name server containing the primary zone database file.

Benefits of Active Directory–Integrated Zones

For networks deploying DNS to support Active Directory, directory-integrated primary zones are strongly recommended and provide multimaster update and enhanced security, automatic zone replication and synchronization, simplified planning, and faster directory replication.

- Multimaster update and enhanced security based on the capabilities of Active Directory.

  In a standard zone storage model, DNS updates are conducted based on a single-master update model. In this model, a single authoritative DNS server for a zone is designated as the primary source for the zone. This server maintains the master copy of the zone in a local file. With this model, the primary server for the zone represents a single fixed point of failure. If this server is not available, update requests from DNS clients are not processed for the zone.

  With directory-integrated storage, dynamic updates to DNS are conducted based on a multimaster update model. In this model, any authoritative DNS server (such as a domain controller running the DNS service) is designated as a primary source for the zone. Because the master copy of the zone is maintained in the Active Directory database, which is fully replicated to all domain controllers, the zone can be updated by the DNS service at any domain controller in the domain. With the multimaster update model of Active Directory, any of the primary servers for the directory-integrated zone can process requests from DNS clients to update the zone as long as a domain controller is available and reachable on the network.

  Also, when using directory-integrated zones, you can use access control list (ACL) editing to provide granulated access to either the zone or a specified resource record in the zone. For example, an ACL for a specific domain name in the zone can be restricted so that dynamic updates are only allowed for specified DNS clients or to authorize only a secure group such as domain administrators with permissions for updating zone or record properties for it. This security feature is not available with standard primary zones.

- Zones are replicated and synchronized to new domain controllers automatically whenever a new zone is added to an Active Directory domain.

  Although DNS service can be selectively removed from a domain controller, directory-integrated zones are already stored at each domain controller, so zone storage and management are not additional resources. Also, the methods used to synchronize directory-stored information offer performance improvement over standard zone update methods, which can potentially require transfer of the entire zone.

- By integrating storage of your DNS namespace in Active Directory, you simplify planning and administration for both DNS and Active Directory.

  When namespaces are stored and replicated separately (for example, one for DNS storage and replication and another for Active Directory), an additional administrative complexity is added to planning and designing your network and allowing for its eventual growth. By integrating DNS storage, you can unify managing of storage and replication for both DNS and Active Directory information as a single administrative entity.

- Directory replication is faster and more efficient than standard DNS replication.

  Because Active Directory replication processing is performed on a per-property basis, only relevant changes are propagated. This allows less data to be used and submitted in updates for directory-stored zones.

Zone Name

Typically, a zone is named after the highest domain in the hierarchy that the zone encompasses—that is, the root domain for the zone. For example, for a zone that encompasses both microsoft.com and sales.microsoft.com, the zone name would be microsoft.com.

Zone File

For the standard primary forward lookup zone type you must specify a zone file. The zone file is the zone database file name, which defaults to the zone name with a .dns extension. For example, if your zone name is microsoft.com, the default zone database file name is MICROSOFT.COM.DNS.

When migrating a zone from another server, you can import the existing zone file. You must place the existing file in the *systemroot*\System32\DNS directory on the target computer before creating the new zone, where systemroot indicates the Windows 2000 installation folder, typically C:\Winnt.

Master DNS Servers

For the standard secondary forward lookup zone type you must specify the DNS server(s) from which you want to copy the zone. You must enter the Internet Protocol (IP) address of one or more DNS servers.

Reverse Lookup Zones

A *reverse lookup zone* enables reverse lookup queries. Reverse lookup zones are not required by DNS servers in order to provide functionality. However, a reverse lookup zone is required to run troubleshooting tools, such as NSLOOKUP, and to record a name instead of an IP address in Internet Information Services (IIS) log files.

Resource Records

Resource records are entries in the zone database file that associate DNS domain names to related data for a given network resource, such as an IP address. There are many different types of resource records. When a zone is created, DNS automatically adds two resource records: the Start of Authority (SOA) and the Name Server (NS) records. Table 18.1 describes these resource record types, along with the other frequently used resource records.

Table 18.1   Frequently Used Resource Record Types

Resource record type	Description
Host (A)	Lists the host name-to-IP-address mappings for a forward lookup zone.
Alias (CNAME)	Creates an alias, or alternate name, for the specified host name. You can use a Canonical Name (CNAME) record to use more than one name to point to a single IP address. For example, you can host a File Transfer Protocol (FTP) server, such as *ftp.microsoft.com,* and a Web server, such as *www.microsoft.com*, on the same computer.
Host Information (HINFO)	Identifies the central processing unit (CPU) and operating system used by the host. Use this record as a low-cost resource-tracking tool.
Mail Exchanger (MX)	Identifies which mail exchanger to contact for a specified domain and in what order to use each mail host.
Name Server (NS)	Lists the name servers that are assigned to a particular domain.
Pointer (PTR)	Points to another part of the domain namespace. For example, in a reverse lookup zone, it lists the IP-address-to-name mapping.

continues

Table 18.1   Frequently Used Resource Record Types *(continued)*

Resource record type	Description
Service (SRV)	Identifies which servers are hosting a particular service. For example, if a client needs to find a server to validate logon requests, the client can send a query to the DNS server to obtain a list of domain controllers and their associated IP addresses.
Start of Authority (SOA)	Identifies which name server is the authoritative source of information for data within this domain. The first record in the zone database file must be the SOA record.

Note For more information on resource records, use your Web browser to search for **RFC 1035**, **RFC 1183**, **RFC 1886**, and **RFC 2052** to retrieve the contents of these Requests for Comment (RFCs).

▶   **Follow these steps to view a resource record:**

1. In the DNS console tree, click the zone for which you want to view a resource record.

2. In the details pane, click the record you want to view.

3. On the Action menu, click Properties.

4. On the Properties dialog box, view the properties specific to the record you selected.

5. When you have finished viewing the record, click OK.

To add a resource record, right-click the zone to which you want to add the record, and then select the type of record that you want to add, for example New Host or New Mail Exchanger.

Delegating Zones

A zone starts as a storage database for a single DNS domain name. If other domains are added below the domain used to create the zone, these domains can either be part of the same zone or part of another zone. Once a subdomain is added, it can then be

- Managed and included as part of the original zone records
- Delegated away to another zone created to support the subdomain

For example, Figure 18.1 shows the microsoft.com domain, which contains domain names for Microsoft. When the microsoft.com domain is first created at a single server, it is configured as a single zone for all of the Microsoft DNS namespace. If, however, the microsoft.com domain needs to use subdomains, those subdomains must be included in the zone or delegated away to another zone. In Figure 18.1, the *example* subdomain was added to the microsoft.com domain. The example.microsoft.com zone was created to support the example.microsoft.com subdomain.

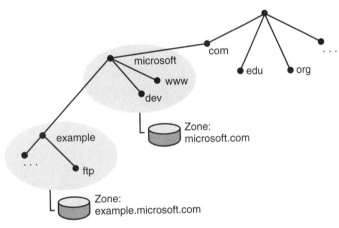

Figure 18.1 Delegating a new subdomain to a new zone

When you delegate zones within a namespace, you must also create SOA resource records to point to the authoritative DNS server for the new zone. This is necessary both to transfer authority and to provide correct referral to other DNS servers and clients of the new servers being made authoritative for the new zone. The New Delegation wizard is available to assist in delegation of zones.

Note All domains (or subdomains) that appear as part of the applicable zone delegation must be created in the current zone prior to performing delegation.

Lesson Summary

In this lesson you learned that the DNS service provides the option of dividing up the namespace into one or more zones, which can then be stored, distributed, and replicated to other DNS servers. The DNS namespace represents the logical structure of your network resources, and DNS zones provide physical storage for these resources.

You also learned how to configure forward and reverse lookup zones and that directory-integrated primary zones are strongly recommended and provide the following benefits: multimaster update and enhanced security, automatic zone replication when new domain controllers are added, simplified administration with integrated namespace storage, and faster replication.

Finally, you learned how to add resource records and delegate zones when new subdomains are added.

Lesson 2: Zone Replication and Transfer

This lesson introduces zone replication and transfer. *Zone transfer* is the process by which DNS servers interact to maintain and synchronize authoritative name data.

After this lesson, you will be able to

- Explain the purpose of zone transfers
- Configure zone transfers

Estimated lesson time: 10 minutes

Zone Replication and Zone Transfers

Because of the important role that zones play in DNS, it is intended that they be available from more than one DNS server on the network to provide availability and fault tolerance when resolving name queries. Otherwise, if a single server is used and that server is not responding, queries for names in the zone can fail. For additional servers to host a zone, zone transfers are required to replicate and synchronize all copies of the zone used at each server configured to host the zone.

When structuring your zones, there are several good reasons to use additional DNS servers for zone replication:

- Added DNS servers provide zone redundancy, enabling DNS names in the zone to be resolved for clients if a primary server for the zone stops responding.

- Added DNS servers can be placed to reduce DNS network traffic. For example, adding a DNS server to the opposing side of a low-speed wide area network (WAN) link can be useful in managing and reducing network traffic.

- Additional secondary servers can be used to reduce loads on a primary server for a zone.

When a new DNS server is added to the network and is configured as a new secondary server for an existing zone, it performs a full zone transfer (AXFR) to obtain and replicate a full copy of resource records for the zone. For earlier DNS server implementations, this same method of full transfer for a zone is also used when the zone requires updating after changes are made to the zone. For Windows 2000 Server, the DNS service supports incremental zone transfer (IXFR), a revised DNS zone transfer process for intermediate changes.

Incremental Zone Transfers

IXFR is described in RFC 1995 as an additional DNS standard for replicating DNS zones. IXFRs provide a more efficient method of propagating zone changes and updates.

In earlier DNS implementations, any request for an update of zone data required a full transfer of the entire zone database using an AXFR query. With incremental transfer, an IXFR query is used instead. IXFR allows the secondary server to pull only those zone changes it needs to synchronize its copy of the zone with its source, either a primary or secondary copy of the zone maintained by another DNS server.

With IXFR zone transfers, differences between the source and replicated versions of the zone are first determined. If the zones are identified to be the same version—as indicated by the serial number field in the SOA resource record of each zone—no transfer is made.

If the serial number for the zone at the source is greater than at the requesting secondary server, a transfer is made of only those changes to resource records for each incremental version of the zone. For an IXFR query to succeed and changes to be sent, the source DNS server for the zone must keep a history of incremental zone changes to use when answering these queries. The incremental transfer process requires substantially less traffic on a network, and zone transfers are completed much faster.

Example of a Zone Transfer

In addition to a manual initiation, a zone transfer occurs during any of the following scenarios:

- When starting the DNS service on the secondary server for a zone
- When the refresh interval time expires for the zone
- When changes are made to the primary zone and a notify list is configured

Zone transfers are always initiated by the secondary server for a zone and sent to the DNS server configured as its source for the zone. This DNS server can be any other DNS server that loads the zone, either a primary or another secondary server. When the source server receives the request for the zone, it can reply with either a partial or full transfer of the zone.

As shown in Figure 18.2, zone transfers between servers follow an ordered process. This process varies depending on whether a zone has been previously replicated or if initial replication of a new zone is being performed.

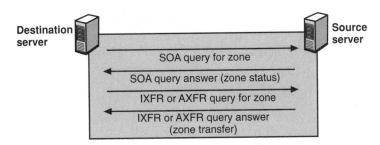

Figure 18.2 Zone transfer process

In this example, the following sequence of steps is performed for a requesting secondary server—the destination server—for a zone and its source server, another DNS server that hosts the zone.

1. During new configuration, the destination server sends an initial (AXFR) transfer request for the zone to the DNS server configured as its source for the zone.

2. The source server responds and fully transfers the zone to the destination server.

   The zone is delivered to the server requesting the transfer with its version established by use of a serial number field in the properties for the SOA resource record. The SOA record also contains a stated refresh interval in seconds (by default, 15 minutes) to indicate when the destination server should next request renewal of the zone with the source server.

3. When the refresh interval expires, the destination server requests renewal of the zone from the source server with an SOA query.

4. The source server answers the query for its SOA record.

   This response contains the serial number for the zone in its current state at the source server.

5. The destination server checks the serial number of the SOA record in the response and determines how to renew the zone.

   If the value of the serial number in the SOA response is equal to its current local serial number, it concludes the zone is the same at both servers and a zone transfer is not needed. The destination server then renews the zone by resetting its refresh interval based on the value of this field in the SOA response from its source server.

   If the value of the serial number in the SOA response is higher than its current local serial number, it concludes that the zone has been updated and a transfer is needed.

6. If the destination server concludes the zone has changed, it sends an IXFR query to the source server containing its current local value for the serial number in the SOA record for the zone.

7. The source server responds with either an incremental or full transfer of the zone.

   If the source server supports incremental transfer by maintaining a history of recent and incremental zone changes for modified resource records, it can answer with an incremental (IXFR) transfer of the zone.

   If the source server does not support incremental transfer or does not have a history of zone changes, it can, alternatively, answer with a full (AXFR) transfer of the zone instead.

Note Incremental zone transfer through IXFR query is supported in Windows 2000 Server. For earlier versions of the DNS service running in Windows NT Server 4.0, and for many other DNS server implementations, incremental zone transfer is not available and only full-zone (AXFR) queries and transfers are used to replicate zones.

Zone Transfer Security

The DNS console permits you to specify the servers allowed to participate in zone transfers. This can help prevent an undesired attempt by an unknown or unapproved DNS server to pull, or request, zone updates.

▶ **Follow these steps to specify servers allowed to participate in zone transfers:**

1. Click Start, point to Programs, point to Administrative Tools, and then click DNS.

2. In the DNS console tree, right-click the zone for which you want to set up zone transfers, and then click Properties.

3. Select the Zone Transfers tab (see Figure 18.3).

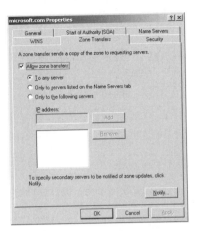

Figure 18.3 The Zone Transfers tab

4. Specify the servers for which you want to allow zone transfers, and then click OK.

DNS Notification

The DNS service supports DNS notification, which is an updated revision to the DNS standard specification (RFC 1996). DNS notification implements a push mechanism for notifying a select set of secondary servers for a zone when a zone is updated. The notified servers can then initiate the zone transfer process and pull changes from the notifying server to update the zone.

Use DNS notification only to notify DNS servers that are operating as secondary servers for a zone. For replication of directory-integrated zones, DNS notification is not needed. This is because any DNS servers that load a zone from Active Directory automatically poll the directory approximately once every 15 minutes (depending on the SOA refresh interval setting) to update and refresh the zone. In these cases, configuring a notification list can actually degrade system performance by causing unnecessary additional transfer requests for the updated zone.

▶ **Follow these steps to specify servers to be notified:**

1. Click Start, point to Programs, point to Administrative Tools, and then click DNS.

2. In the DNS console tree, right-click the zone for which you want to set up zone transfers, and then click Properties.

3. Select the Zone Transfers tab, and then click Notify.

4. In the Notify dialog box (see Figure 18.4), specify the secondary servers to be notified when the zone changes, and then click OK.

Figure 18.4 The Notify dialog box

The DNS Notify Process

The following is a brief summary of the typical DNS Notify process:

1. The local zone on a DNS server acting as a source for the zone to other servers is updated. When the zone is updated at the source, the serial number field in the SOA record also updates, indicating a new local version of the zone.

2. The source server sends a notify message to other servers specified on the Notify screen.

3. All secondary servers that receive the notification message can then respond by initiating a zone transfer request back to the notifying server. The normal zone transfer process can then continue as described in the previous section.

Lesson Summary

In this lesson you learned how zone transfers are required to replicate and synchronize all copies of the zone used at each server configured to host the zone. For earlier DNS server implementations, when a new DNS server is added to the network and is configured as a new secondary server for an existing zone, it performs a full initial transfer of the zone to obtain and replicate a full copy of resource records for the zone. For Windows 2000 Server, the DNS service supports incremental zone transfer, a revised, more efficient DNS zone transfer process for intermediate changes.

You also learned how the DNS console permits you to specify the servers allowed to participate in zone transfers. Finally, you learned how DNS notification implements a push mechanism for notifying a select set of secondary servers for a zone when a zone is updated. The notified servers can then initiate the zone transfer process and pull changes from the notifying server to update the zone. The DNS console allows you to specify the secondary servers for notification; for replication of directory-integrated zones, DNS notification is not needed.

Lesson 3: Monitoring and Troubleshooting DNS for Active Directory Directory Service

This lesson explains the monitoring options available for DNS servers. It also describes problems you may encounter that relate to configuring DNS for Active Directory and possible solutions to these problems.

After this lesson, you will be able to

- Monitor DNS server
- Troubleshoot DNS configuration for Active Directory

Estimated lesson time: 10 minutes

Monitoring DNS Servers

Windows 2000 Server includes options for monitoring DNS servers:

- Default logging of DNS server event messages to the DNS server log
- Additional debug options for trace logging to a text file on the DNS server computer

DNS Server Event Logging

For Windows 2000 Server, DNS server event messages are kept separate from events raised by other applications and services in the DNS server log, which can be viewed using Event Viewer. The DNS server log contains basic predetermined events logged by the DNS server service, such as when the DNS server starts and stops.

You can also use Event Viewer to view and monitor client-related DNS events. These events appear in the system log and are written by the DNS client service at any computers running Windows 2000 (all versions).

Debug Options

The DNS console allows you to set additional logging options to create a temporary trace log as a text-based file of DNS server activity. The file created and used for this feature, DNS.LOG, is stored in the *systemroot*\System32\DNS folder. For Windows 2000 DNS servers, the debug logging options described in Table 18.2 are supported for use.

Table 18.2   DNS Server Debug Logging Options

Logging option	Description
Query	Logs queries received by the DNS server service from clients
Notify	Logs notification messages received by the DNS server service from other servers
Update	Logs dynamic updates received by the DNS server service from other computers
Questions	Logs the contents of the question section for each DNS query message processed by the DNS server service
Answers	Logs the contents of the answer section for each DNS query message processed by the DNS server service
Send	Logs the number of DNS query messages sent by the DNS server service
Receive	Logs the number of DNS query messages received by the DNS server service
UDP	Logs the number of DNS requests received by the DNS server service over a UDP port
TCP	Logs the number of DNS requests received by the DNS server service over a TCP port
Full Packets	Logs the number of full packets written and sent by the DNS server service
Write Through	Logs the number of packets written through by the DNS server service and back to the zone

By default, all debug logging options are disabled. When selectively enabled, the DNS server service can perform additional trace-level logging of selected types of events or messages for general troubleshooting and debugging of the server.

Debug logging can be resource-intensive, affecting overall server performance and consuming disk space. Therefore, it should only be used temporarily when more detailed information about server performance is needed.

▶   **Follow these steps to set DNS Server debug options:**

1. In the DNS console tree, right-click the name server, and then click Properties.

2. On the Logging tab, select the debug options you want to log, and then click OK.

DNS Troubleshooting Scenarios

Table 18.3 describes some zone problems you may encounter and possible solutions to these problems.

Table 18.3   Troubleshooting Scenarios for Zone Problems

Symptom: A problem related to zone transfers

Cause	Solution
The DNS server service is stopped or the zone is paused.	Verify that the master (source) and secondary (destination) DNS servers involved in completing transfer of the zone are both started and that the zone is not paused at either server.
The DNS servers used during a transfer do not have network connectivity with each other.	Eliminate the possibility of a basic network connectivity problem between the two servers. Using the Ping command, ping each DNS server by its IP address from its remote counterpart. Both ping tests should succeed. If not, investigate and resolve intermediate network connectivity issues.
The serial number is the same at both the source and destination servers. Because the value is the same at both servers, there is no zone transfer between the servers.	Using the DNS console, perform the following tasks: On the Start of Authority (SOA) tab, increase the value of the serial number for the zone at the master server (source) to a number greater than the value at the applicable secondary server (destination). Initiate zone transfer at the secondary server.
The master server (source) and its targeted secondary server (destination) are having interoperability-related problems.	Investigate possible causes for any problems related to interoperability between Windows 2000 DNS servers and other DNS servers running different implementations, such as an older version of the Berkeley Internet Name Domain (BIND) distribution.
The zone has resource records or other data that cannot be interpreted by the DNS server.	Verify that the zone does not contain incompatible data, such as unsupported resource record types or data errors. Also, verify that the server has not been configured in advance to prevent loading a zone when bad data is found and investigate its method for checking names. These settings can be configured using the DNS console.
Authoritative zone data is incorrect.	If a zone transfer continues to fail, ensure that the zone does not contain nonstandard data. To determine if erroneous zone data is a likely source for a failed zone transfer, look in the DNS server event log for messages.

Symptom: Zone delegation appears to be broken

Cause	Solution
Zone delegations are not configured correctly.	Review how zone delegations are used and revise your zone configurations as needed.

Table 18.4 describes some problems you may encounter with dynamic updates and possible solutions to these problems.

Table 18.4   Troubleshooting Scenarios for Dynamic Updates

Symptom: The client is not performing dynamic updates

Cause	Solution
The client (or its Dynamic Host Configuration Protocol [DHCP] server) does not support the use of the DNS dynamic update protocol.	Verify that your clients or servers support the DNS dynamic update protocol using the options for dynamic update support provided in Windows 2000. In order for client computers to be registered and updated dynamically with a DNS server, either, you must have installed or upgraded client computers to Windows 2000 or you must have installed and be using a Windows 2000 DHCP server on your network to lease client computers.
The client was not able to register and update with the DNS server because of missing or incomplete DNS configuration.	Verify that the client is fully and correctly configured for DNS, and update its configuration as needed. To update the DNS configuration for a client, either configure a primary DNS suffix at the client computer for static TCP/IP clients or configure a connection-specific DNS suffix for use at one of the installed network connections at the client computer.
The DNS client attempted to update its information with the DNS server but failed because of a problem related to the server.	If a client can reach its preferred and alternate DNS servers as configured, it is likely that the cause of its failed updates can be found elsewhere. At Windows 2000 client computers, use Event Viewer to check the System log for any event messages that explain why attempts by the client to dynamically update its host (A) or pointer (PTR) resource records failed.
The DNS server does not support dynamic updates.	Verify that the DNS server used by the client can support the DNS dynamic update protocol, as described in RFC 2136. For Windows DNS servers, only Windows 2000 DNS servers support dynamic updates. The DNS server provided with Windows NT Server 4.0 does not.
The DNS server supports dynamic updates but is not configured to accept them.	Verify that the primary zone where clients require updates is configured to allow dynamic updates. For Windows 2000 DNS servers, the default for a new primary zone is to not accept dynamic updates. At the DNS server that loads the applicable primary zone, modify zone properties to allow updates.
The zone database is not available.	Verify that the zone exists. Verify that the zone is available for update. For a standard primary zone, verify that the zone file exists at the server and that the zone is not paused. Secondary zones do not support dynamic updates. For Active Directory–integrated zones, verify that the DNS server is running as a domain controller and has access to the Active Directory database where zone data is stored.

Lesson Summary

In this lesson you learned about the monitoring options available for DNS servers. You also examined some DNS configuration problems you may encounter and possible solutions to these problems.

Review

The following questions will help you determine whether you have learned enough to move on to the next chapter. If you have difficulty answering these questions, please go back and review the material in this chapter before beginning the next chapter. See Appendix A, "Questions and Answers," for the answers to these questions.

1. What are the advantages of using the Active Directory–integrated zone type?

2. What is the purpose of the source of authority (SOA) resource record?

3. What must be done when you delegate zones within a namespace?

4. Why is an incremental zone transfer (IXFR) query more efficient than a full-zone transfer (AXFR) query?

C H A P T E R   1 9

Managing Active Directory Components

About This Chapter

Managing Active Directory directory services goes beyond setup and configuration. It entails locating objects, assigning permissions to objects, publishing resources, moving objects within and between domains, delegating administrative control to organizational units (OUs), backing up and restoring, troubleshooting, monitoring performance, and diagnosing Active Directory issues. This chapter provides details on Active Directory administrative tasks, including how to use performance monitoring tools, diagnostic tools, and shared folder monitoring help you to manage Active Directory performance.

Before You Begin

As an experienced Windows NT Server 4.0 professional, you should already have many of the skills needed to manage Active Directory. These include:

- Setting up users and groups
- Securing network resources
- Administering shared folders
- Configuring a domain controller

To complete this chapter, you must also have

- Installed Windows 2000 Server on a computer (Server01)

  See Chapter 8, "Installing Microsoft Windows 2000," for more details.
- Experience logging on and off Microsoft Windows 2000
- Knowledge about the Active Directory naming conventions
- Obtained the knowledge and skills necessary to set up MMCs
- Installed Active Directory using the exercises in Chapter 17, "Installing and Configuring Active Directory"

Lesson 1: Locating Active Directory Objects

Active Directory stores information about objects on the network. Each object is a distinct, named set of attributes that represents a specific network entity. Active Directory is designed to provide information to queries about directory objects from both users and programs. In this lesson, you learn how to use Find (located in the Active Directory Users And Computers console) to locate Active Directory objects.

After this lesson, you will be able to

- Identify the types of Active Directory objects
- Use Find to locate any type of Active Directory object

Estimated lesson time: 15 minutes

Understanding Common Active Directory Objects

Adding new resources to your network creates new Active Directory objects that represent these resources. You should be familiar with some of the common Active Directory objects. Table 19.1 describes the contents of the most common object types that you can add to Active Directory.

Table 19.1   Common Object Types and Their Contents

Object type	Contents
User account	This is the information that allows a user to log on to Windows 2000, such as the user logon name. This information also has many optional fields including First Name, Last Name, Display Name, Telephone Number, E-Mail, and Home.
Contact	This is information about a person with a connection to the organization. This information also has many optional fields including Telephone Number, E-mail, Address, and Home Page.
Group	This is a collection of user accounts, groups, or computers that you can create and use to simplify administration.

continues

Table 19.1   Common Object Types and Their Contents *(continued)*

Object type	Contents
Shared folder	This is a pointer to the shared folder on a computer. A *pointer* contains the address of certain data, rather than the data itself. Shared folders and printers exist in the registry of a computer. When you publish a shared folder in Active Directory, you create an object that contains a pointer to the shared folder.
Printer	This is a pointer to a printer on a computer. You must manually publish a printer on a computer that is not in Active Directory. Microsoft Windows 2000 automatically adds printers that you create on domain computers to Active Directory.
Computer	This is the information about a computer that is a member of the domain.
Domain controllers	This is the information about a domain controller including an optional description, its Domain Name System (DNS) name, its pre–Windows 2000 name, the version of the operating system loaded on the domain controller, the location, and who is responsible for managing the domain controller.
Organizational Unit (OU)	This contains other objects, including other OUs. It is used to organize Active Directory objects.

Using Find

To locate Active Directory objects, open the Active Directory Users And Computers console located in the Administrative Tools folder. Then right-click a domain or a container in the console tree and click Find. The Find dialog box provides options that allow you to search the global catalog to locate Active Directory objects (see Figure 19.1). The Find dialog box helps you create a Lightweight Directory Access Protocol (LDAP) query that will be executed against the directory or a specific OU. The global catalog contains a partial replica of the Entire Directory, so it stores information about every object in a domain tree or forest. Because the global catalog contains information about every object, a user can find information regardless of which domain in the tree or forest contains the data. Active Directory automatically generates the contents of the global catalog from the domains that make up the directory.

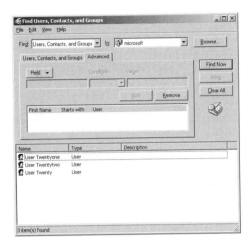

Figure 19.1 Using the Find dialog box to locate objects

Table 19.2 describes the options in the Find dialog box.

Table 19.2   Options in the Find Dialog Box

Element	Description
Find	A list of object types for which you can search, including users, contacts, and groups; computers; printers; shared folders; OUs; and custom search. Custom search builds the LDAP query or allows you to enter your own LDAP query based on parameters you enter. For example, the LDAP query OU=*er* (entered in the Advanced tab) searches for OU names containing "er" in the middle and returns the Domain Controllers OU.
In	A list of locations in which you can search, including the entire Active Directory, a specific domain, or an OU.
Browse	A button that allows you to select the path of your search.
Advanced	The context-sensitive tab in which you define the search criteria to locate the object that you need. This tab provides an array of choices when you choose to find users, contacts, and groups; computers; printers; shared folders; or OUs. When you choose custom search, the Advanced tab makes you type in the query manually or create a search through the use of the most common available attributes that are organized by object type on the Custom Search tab. The Custom Search tab provides the same elements that are otherwise found on the Advanced tab.

continues

Table 19.2   Options in the Find Dialog Box *(continued)*

Element	Description
Field	A context-sensitive list of the attributes for which you can search on the object type that you select; located in the Advanced tab.
Condition	A context-sensitive list of the methods available to further define the search for an attribute; located in the Advanced tab.
Value	A box that allows you to enter the value for the condition of the field (attribute) that you are using to search the Directory; located in the Advanced tab. You can search for an object by using an attribute of the object only if you enter a value for the attribute. For example, if you are looking for users whose first name starts with the letter R, you select First Name in the field list, select Starts With in the condition list, and type R in the Value box.
Search Criteria	A box that lists each search criteria that you have defined; located in the Advanced tab. To define a search criterion, you use the Field list, Condition list, and Value box, and then click Add. To remove search criteria, select the criteria, and then click Remove. You can add or remove search criteria to narrow or widen your search.
Find Now	A button used to begin a search after search criteria are defined.
Stop	A button used to stop a search. Items found up to the point of stopping the search are displayed.
Clear All	A button used to clear the specified search criteria.
Results	A box that opens at the bottom of the Find window and displays the results of your search after you click Find Now.

Practice: Searching Active Directory

In this practice, you search Active Directory for objects based on search criteria that you provide. First you create user accounts for the practice. Next you find a user's account based on his or her primary phone number. Finally you find a printer that is able to staple the pages it prints.

Important You need to have a local printer installed on your computer. However, you do *not* need a printing device connected to the computer. If you do not have a local printer installed, create one now. Remember that *printing device* refers to the physical machine that prints and that *local printer* refers to the software that Windows 2000 needs to send data to the printing device.

Exercise 1: Create User Accounts in a Domain

Before you can search for an object, you need to create user accounts that contain the search objects. In this exercise, you create user accounts that are used throughout this practice.

1. Log on to your domain as Administrator, and then open the Active Directory Users And Computers console.

2. In the console tree, click Users.

3. On the Action menu, point to New, and then click User.

   Notice that the New Object-User dialog box shows that the new user account is being created in the Users folder of your domain.

4. Create the user accounts shown in the following table.

   User Accounts for Practice

First Name	Last Name	User Logon Name	Password	Change Password
User	Twenty	User20	Password	Default setting
User	Twentyone	User21	Password	Default setting
User	Twentytwo	User22	Password	Default setting

   Make each user a member of the Print Operators group or another group with the right to log on locally to a domain controller.

5. Edit the properties of the User20 account that you created, and in the General tab of the Properties dialog box, in the Telephone Number box, type **555-1234**.

Exercise 2: Find User Accounts in the Domain

In this exercise, you find a specific user account based on the account's phone number.

1. In the console tree, right-click the name of your domain, and then click Find.

   Windows 2000 displays the Find dialog box.

   In the Find dialog box, what object type can you select for a search?

2. Ensure that Users, Contacts, And Groups is selected in the Find box, and then click Find Now. What do you see?

Notice how Windows 2000 can find objects, such as user accounts, regardless of their location.

3. In the Find Users, Contacts, And Groups dialog box, click Clear All, and then click OK to acknowledge that you want to clear the search results.

4. In the In list, select your domain.

5. Click the Advanced tab.

6. Click Field, point to User, and then scroll down and click Telephone Number.

   Notice that Windows 2000 fills in Starts With in the Condition list.

7. In the Value box, type **555**, and then click Add.

8. Click Find Now.

   In the Find Users, Contacts, And Groups dialog box, Windows 2000 displays the User20 account for which you typed the telephone number 555-1234.

9. Close the Find Users, Contacts, And Groups dialog box.

Exercise 3: View Printers in Active Directory Users and Computers

In this exercise, you need to find a printer that can staple the pages it prints.

1. On the View menu, click Users, Groups, And Computers As Containers.

   By default, Active Directory Users And Computers does not show printers. You have to change the view options.

2. In the console tree, expand Domain Controllers to view your computer.

   Active Directory Users And Computers displays your computer in the console tree. Notice that you can expand the computer because it is now shown as a container.

3. In the console tree, click the name of your computer.

   Active Directory Users And Computers displays all printers on your computer as objects that are associated with your computer.

4. To view the properties of a printer, double-click on the name of the printer.

5. On the Properties dialog box for the printer, click the Staple check box to identify the printer as one that can staple, and then click OK.

6. Minimize Active Directory Users And Computers.

7. Click Start, point to Search, and then click For Printers.

8. In the Find Printers dialog box, click the Features tab.

9. Click the Can Staple check box.

10. In the In list, select your domain, and then click Find Now.

    Windows 2000 displays the printer that you modified in the list of printers that are capable of stapling.

11. Close the Find Printers dialog box.

Lesson Summary

In this lesson, you learned that common Active Directory objects include user accounts, contacts, groups, shared folders, printers, computers, domain controllers, and OUs. You learned to locate objects by starting the Active Directory Users And Computers console, right-clicking an object within a domain in the console tree, and clicking Find. The Find dialog box provides fields that allow you to search for Active Directory objects.

In the practice portion of this lesson, you searched Active Directory for objects based on search criteria you specified.

Lesson 2: Controlling Access to Active Directory Objects

Windows 2000 uses an object-based security model to implement access control for all Active Directory objects. This security model is similar to the one that Windows 2000 uses to implement Microsoft Windows NT file system (NTFS) security. Every Active Directory object has a security descriptor that defines who has the permissions to gain access to the object and what type of access is allowed. Windows 2000 uses these security descriptors to control access to objects. This lesson explains how to set permissions for Active Directory objects.

After this lesson, you will be able to

- Set permissions on Active Directory objects to control user access

Estimated lesson time: 20 minutes

Understanding Active Directory Permissions

Active Directory permissions provide security for resources by allowing you to control who can gain access to individual objects or object attributes and the type of access that you will allow.

Active Directory Security

Use Active Directory permissions to determine who has the permissions to gain access to the object and what type of access is allowed. An administrator or the object owner must assign permissions to the object before users can gain access to the object. Windows 2000 stores a list of user access permissions, called the access control list (ACL), for every Active Directory object. The ACL for an object lists who can access the object and the specific actions that each user can perform on the object.

You can use permissions to assign administrative privileges to a specific user or group for an OU, a hierarchy of OUs, or a single object, without assigning administrative permissions for controlling other Active Directory objects.

Object Permissions

The object type determines which permissions you can select. Permissions vary for different object types. For example, you can assign the Reset Password permission for a user object but not for a printer object.

A user can be a member of multiple groups, each with different permissions that provide different levels of access to objects. When you assign a permission to a user for access to an object and that user is a member of a group to which you assigned a different permission, the user's effective permissions are the combination of the user and group permissions. For example, if a user alone has Read permission for an object and is a member of a group with Write permission, the user's effective permission for the object is Read and Write.

You can allow or deny permissions. Denied permissions take precedence over any permissions that you otherwise allow for user accounts and groups. If you deny a user permission to gain access to an object, the user will not have that permission, even if you allow the permission for a group of which the user is a member. You should deny permissions only when it is absolutely necessary to deny permission to a specific user who is a member of a group with allowed permissions.

Note Always ensure that all objects have at least one user with the Full Control permission. Failure to do so might result in some objects being inaccessible to the person using the Active Directory Users And Computers console, even an administrator, unless object ownership is changed.

Standard Permissions and Special Permissions

You can set standard permissions and special permissions on objects. Standard permissions are the most frequently assigned permissions and are composed of special permissions. Special permissions provide you with a finer degree of control for assigning access to objects.

For example, the standard Write permission is composed of the Write All Properties, Add/Remove Self As Member, and Read special permissions.

Table 19.3 lists standard object permissions that are available for most objects (most object types also have special permissions) and the type of access that each standard permission allows.

Table 19.3   Standard Object Permissions and Type of Access Allowed

Object permission	Allows the user to
Full Control	Change permissions and take ownership and perform the tasks that are allowed by all other standard permissions
Read	View objects and object attributes, the object owner, and Active Directory permissions
Write	Change object attributes
Create All Child Objects	Add any type of child object to an OU
Delete All Child Objects	Remove any type of object from an OU

Assigning Active Directory Permissions

You can use the Active Directory Users And Computers console to set standard permissions for objects and attributes of objects. You use the Security tab of the Properties dialog box for the object to assign permissions (see Figure 19.2). The Properties dialog box is different for each object type.

Important You must select Advanced Features on the View menu to access the Security tab and assign standard permissions for an object.

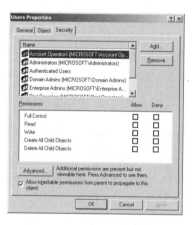

Figure 19.2 Setting Active Directory permissions

If the check boxes under Permissions are shaded, the object has inherited permissions from the parent object. To prevent an object from inheriting permissions from a parent folder, clear the Allow Inheritable Permissions From Parent To Propagate To This Object check box.

▶ **Follow these steps to assign standard permissions for an object:**

1. In Active Directory Users And Computers, on the View menu, ensure that Advanced Features is selected.

2. Select an object, click Properties on the Action menu, and then click the Security tab in the Properties dialog box for the object.

3. To assign standard permissions:

   ▪ To add a new permission, click Add, click the user account or group to which you want to assign permissions, click Add, and then click OK.

   ▪ To change an existing permission, click the user account or group.

4. Under Permissions, select the Allow check box or the Deny check box for each permission you want to add or remove.

Standard permissions are sufficient for most administrative tasks. However, you might need to view the special permissions that constitute a standard permission. Occasionally the Security tab displays a user or a group where none of the standard permissions is allowed or denied; in such a case, the user or group has been given special permissions that are accessible through the Advanced button.

▶ **Follow these steps to view special permissions:**

1. In the Security tab in the Properties dialog box for the object, click Advanced.

2. In the Access Control Settings For dialog box for the object (an example is shown in Figure 19.3), in the Permissions tab, click the entry that you want to view in the Permission Entries list, and then click View/Edit.

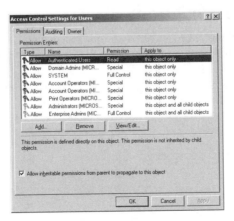

Figure 19.3 Access Control Settings For Users dialog box

3. In the Permission Entry For dialog box (see Figure 19.4) for the object, view the special permissions on the appropriate tab.

Use the Object tab to view special object permissions assigned to the user or group, or use the Properties tab to view user or group read and write access to specific object properties.

Note Avoid assigning permissions for specific properties of objects because this can complicate system administration. Errors can result, such as Active Directory objects not being visible, which prevents users from completing tasks.

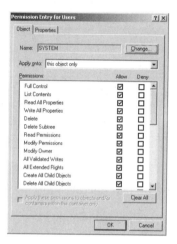

Figure 19.4 Permission Entry For Users dialog box

Using Permissions Inheritance

Permissions inheritance for Active Directory objects, which is similar to file and folder permissions inheritance, minimizes the number of times that you need to assign permissions for objects. When you assign permissions, you can apply the permissions to child objects, which propagates the permissions to all of the child objects for a parent object, as shown in Figure 19.5. To indicate that permissions are inherited, the check boxes for inherited permissions are shown as shaded.

- Permissions flow down to child objects.

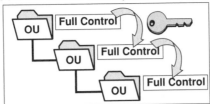

- Preventing inheritance stops the flow of permissions.

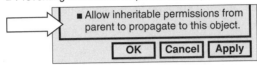

Figure 19.5 Inheriting permissions and blocking inheritance

For example, you can assign Full Control permission to a group for an OU that contains printers and then propagate this permission to all child objects. The result is that all group members can administer all printers in the OU.

You can specify that permissions for a given object are propagated to all child objects. You can also prevent permissions inheritance. When you copy previously inherited permissions, you start with exactly the same permissions that the object currently inherits from its parent object. However, any permissions for the parent object that you modify after blocking inheritance no longer apply. When you remove previously inherited permissions, Windows 2000 removes existing permissions and assigns no additional permissions to the object. You have to assign any permissions you want for the object.

Preventing Permissions Inheritance

You can prevent permissions inheritance so that a child object does not inherit permissions from its parent object by clearing the Allow Inheritable Permissions From Parent To Propagate To This Object check box. When you prevent inheritance, only the permissions that you explicitly assign to the object apply. You use the Security tab in the Properties dialog box to prevent permissions inheritance.

When you prevent permissions inheritance, Windows 2000 allows you to

- Copy previously inherited permissions to the object. The new explicit permissions for the object are a copy of the permissions that it previously inherited from its parent object. Then, according to your needs, you can make any necessary changes to the permissions.

- Remove previously inherited permissions from the object. Windows 2000 removes any previously inherited permissions. No permissions exist for the object. You can then assign any permissions for the object, according to your needs.

Practice: Controlling Access to Active Directory Objects

In this practice, you create an OU with two users and review the default security settings on Active Directory components.

Caution In the following exercise, you should not change any security settings in Active Directory. Making changes could result in losing access to portions of Active Directory.

Exercise 1: Create an OU Containing Two User Accounts

In this exercise, you create a new organizational unit and add two user accounts to this OU.

1. Log on to your domain as Administrator, and then open Active Directory Users and Computers.

2. In the console tree, click on the name of your domain.

3. On the Action menu, point to New, and then click Organizational Unit.

4. In the New Object-Organizational Unit dialog box, in the Name box, type **security1** and then click OK.

5. In the Security1 OU, create a user account that has the First Name field and the User Logon Name field set to Assistant1. Type **password** as the password and accept the defaults for all other options.

6. In the same OU, create another user account that has the First Name field and the User Logon Name set to Secretary1. Type **password** as the password and accept the defaults for all other options.

7. Grant both users membership in the Print Operators group or another group with the right to log on locally to the domain controller.

Exercise 2: View Default Active Directory Permissions for an OU

Before you assign permissions, you should determine what, if any, permissions the users may have as a result of belonging to any groups. In this exercise you view and then record the default Active Directory permissions.

1. On the View menu, enable Advanced Features.

   Enabling the viewing of advanced features allows you to review and configure Active Directory permissions.

2. In the console tree, right-click Security1, and then click Properties.

3. Click the Security tab.

4. In the following table, list the groups that have permissions for the Security1 OU. You will need to refer to these permissions in Lesson 5.

Groups that Have Permissions for the Security1 OU

User account or group	Assigned permissions

How can you tell if any of the default permissions are inherited from the domain, which is the parent object?

Exercise 3: View Special Permissions for an OU

Again, before assigning permissions, you should determine what permissions have already been assigned to the users. In this exercise, you will view any special permissions that have been assigned to the users or groups.

1. In the Security1 Properties dialog box, in the Security tab, click Advanced.

   The Access Control Settings For Security1 dialog box appears.

2. To view special permissions for Account Operators, in the Permission Entries box, click each entry for Account Operators, and then click View/Edit.

   The Permission Entry For Security1 dialog box appears.

   What object permissions are assigned to Account Operators? What can Account Operators do in this OU? (Hint: Check each permission entry for Account Operators in the Permission Entries box in the Access Control Settings For Security1 dialog box.)

   Do any objects within this OU inherit the permissions assigned to the Account Operators group? Why or why not?

3. Close all open dialog boxes, but do not close Active Directory Users and Computers.

Exercise 4: View the Default Active Directory Permissions for a User Object

In this exercise, you will view and record any default Active Directory permissions assigned to a user object.

1. In the Active Directory Users And Computers console tree, click Security1.

2. In the details pane, right-click Secretary1, and then click Properties.

3. Click the Security tab.

4. In the following table, list the groups that have permissions for the Secretary1 user account. You will need to refer to these permissions in Lesson 5. If the dialog box indicates that special permissions are present for a group, do not list the special permissions to which you can gain access through the Advanced button.

Permissions for the Secretary1 User Account

Group	Assigned permissions

Are the standard permissions for a user object the same as those for an OU object? Why or why not?

Are any of the standard permissions inherited from Security1, the parent object? How can you tell?

What do the permissions of the Account Operators group allow its members to do with the user object?

5. Close all programs and log off Windows 2000.

Lesson Summary

In this lesson, you learned that every Active Directory object has a security descriptor that defines who has permission to gain access to the object and what type of access is allowed. An administrator or the object owner must assign permissions to an object before users can gain access to it. Windows 2000 stores a list of user access permissions, called the ACL, for every Active Directory object.

You also learned how to set standard permissions and special permissions on objects. The standard permissions are Full Control, Write, Read, Create All Child Objects, and Delete All Child Objects. Special permissions provide you with a finer degree of control over assigning access to objects. Permissions inheritance in Active Directory minimizes the number of times that you need to assign permissions for objects. When you assign permissions, you can apply the permissions to child objects, which propagates the permissions inheritance for a given parent object. You also learned how to block permissions inheritance.

In the practice portion of this lesson, you created an OU with two users and reviewed the default security settings on Active Directory components.

Lesson 3: Publishing Resources in Active Directory Directory Service

As an administrator, you need to be able to provide secure and selective publication of network resources to network users and make it easy for users to find information. Active Directory stores this information for rapid retrieval and integrates Windows 2000 security mechanisms to control access. This lesson explains how to publish resources in Active Directory.

After this lesson, you will be able to

- Publish shared folders
- Publish printers
- Publish network services

Estimated lesson time: 10 minutes

Publishing Resources in Active Directory

Resources that can be published in the directory include objects such as users, computers, printers, folders, files, and network services.

Publishing Users and Computers

User and computer accounts are added to the directory using the Active Directory Users And Computers console. Information about the accounts that is useful for other network users is published automatically. Other information, such as account security information, is made available only to certain administrator groups.

Publishing Shared Resources

Publishing information about shared resources such as printers, folders, and files makes it easy for users to find these resources on the network. Windows 2000 network printers are automatically published in the directory when installed. Information about Windows NT printers and shared folders can be published in the directory using the Active Directory Users And Computers console.

▶ **Follow these steps to publish a shared folder:**

1. Click Start, point to Programs, point to Administrative Tools, and then click Active Directory Users And Computers.

2. In the console tree, double-click the Domain node.

3. Right-click the container in which you want to add the shared folder, point to New, and click Shared Folder.

4. In the New Object-Shared Folder dialog box, type the name of the folder in the Name box.

5. In the Network Path box, type the universal naming convention (UNC) name (\\server\share\) that you want to publish in the directory, and then click OK.

The shared folder appears in the directory in the container you selected.

▶ **Follow these steps to publish a Windows NT printer:**

Note The Windows NT printer must be installed before publishing in Active Directory. To install a Windows NT printer, click Start, point to Settings, and then click Printers.

1. Click Start, point to Programs, point to Administrative Tools, and then click Active Directory Users And Computers.

2. In the console tree, double-click the Domain node.

3. In the console tree, right-click the container where you want to publish the printer, point to New, and then click Printer.

In the New Object-Printer dialog box, type the UNC name that you want to publish in the directory in the Network Path Of The Pre–Windows 2000 Print Share box, and then click OK.

The Windows NT printer appears in the directory in the folder you selected.

Publishing Network Services

Network–enabled services, such as Certificate Services, can be published in the directory so administrators can find and administer them using the Active Directory Sites And Services console. By publishing a service, rather than computers or servers, administrators can focus on managing the service regardless of which computer is providing the service or where the computer is located. Additional services or applications can be published in the directory using Active Directory programming interfaces.

The following sections describe some types of service information that may be useful to publish to the directory. The qualities that make a service appropriate for publishing may be better understood by understanding how Active Directory uses services.

Categories of Service Information

Binding and configuration information are the two types of information frequently published using Active Directory.

- Binding information allows clients to connect to services that do not have well-known bindings and that conform to a service-centric model. By publishing the bindings for these kinds of services, Windows 2000 can automatically establish connections with services. Machine-centric services are typically handled on a service-by-service basis and should not be published to the directory.

- Configuration information can be common across client applications. Publishing this information allows you to distribute current configuration information for these applications to all clients in the domain. The configuration information is accessed by client applications as needed. This eases the process of configuring applications for users and gives you more control over application behaviors.

Characteristics of Service Information

Service information that you publish to the directory is most effective if it has the following characteristics:

- **Useful to many clients.** Information that is useful to a small set of clients or that is useful only in certain areas of the network should not be published. If not widely used, this information wastes network resources, since it is published to every domain controller in the domain.

- **Relatively stable and unchanging.** Although there may be exceptions to this rule, it generally makes sense to publish only service information that changes less frequently than every two replication intervals. For intra-site replication, the maximum replication period is 15 minutes, and for inter-site replication, the maximum replication period is configured based on the replication interval of the site link used for the replication. Object properties that change more frequently create excessive demands on network resources. Property values may be out of date until updates are published, which can take as long as the maximum replication period. Consequently, having properties out of date for that period of time must not create unacceptable conditions. For example, some network services select a valid Transmission Control Protocol (TCP) port for use each time they are started. After selecting the port, the service updates Active Directory with this information, which is stored as the service connection point. Clients access the service connection point when they want to use the service, but if the new service connection point has not been replicated when the client requests it, the client receives an outdated port, rendering the service temporarily inaccessible.

- **Well-defined, reasonable properties.** Information that is of a consistent form is easier for services to use. The information should be relatively small in size.

Example of Service Publication

The following sequence of steps is an example of service publication using Active Directory Sites and Services.

▶ **Follow these steps to set security permissions and delegate control of certificate templates:**

1. Log on to the system as an Administrator.

2. Click Start, point to Programs, point to Administrative Tools, and then click Active Directory Sites And Services.

3. In the console tree, click Active Directory Sites And Services.

4. On the View menu, click Show Services node.

5. In the console tree, click Active Directory Sites And Services, click Services, click Public Key Services, and click Certificate Templates.

6. For each certificate template for which you want to set security permissions, double-click the certificate template in the details pane to open properties.

7. On the Properties dialog box for the certificate template, click the Security tab and set the security permissions accordingly.

8. Click OK.

These changes apply only to certificate templates in the current domain.

Lesson Summary

In this lesson, you learned how to publish shared folders, printers, and network services in Active Directory.

Lesson 4: Moving Active Directory Objects

You move objects from one location to another when organizational or administrative functions change—for example, when an employee moves from one department to another. This lesson shows you how to move Active Directory objects within and between domains.

After this lesson, you will be able to

- Move objects within a domain

- Move objects between domains

- Move workstations or member servers between domains

- Move domain controllers between sites

Estimated lesson time: 20 minutes

Moving Objects

In the logical environment, you can move objects within and between domains in Active Directory. In the physical environment, you can move domain controllers between sites.

Moving Objects Within a Domain

To reduce administrative overhead, you can move objects with identical security requirements into an OU or container within a domain. You can then assign access permissions to the OU or container and all objects in it.

▶   **Follow these steps to move objects within a domain:**

1. In Active Directory Users And Computers, select the object to move, and then from the Action menu, click Move.

2. In the Move dialog box (see Figure 19.6), select the OU or container to which you want the object to move, and then click OK.

The following conditions apply when you move objects between OUs or containers:

- Permissions that are assigned directly to objects remain the same.

- The objects inherit permissions from the new OU or container. Any permissions that were previously inherited from the old OU or container no longer affect the objects.

- You can move multiple objects at the same time.

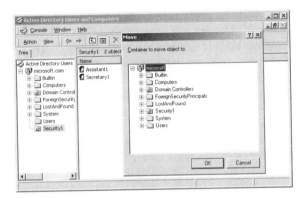

Figure 19.6 The Move dialog box

Note To simplify assignment of permissions for printers, move printers on different print servers that require identical permissions to the same OU or container. Printers are located in the Computer object for the print server. To view a printer, click View, and then click Users, Groups, And Computers As Containers.

Moving Objects Between Domains

To support domain consolidation or organizational restructuring operations, Windows 2000 allows you to move objects between domains. The MOVETREE command-line utility is used to move Active Directory objects such as OUs, users, and groups between domains in a single forest, with some exceptions. This tool is available in Windows 2000 Support Tools. The Windows 2000 Support Tools are included on the Windows 2000 CD-ROM in the \SUPPORT\TOOLS folder.

The procedure for moving an object (whether it be a leaf object or the root object) involves taking an existing object and moving it below an existing parent. The distinguished name of the moved object reflects its new position in the hierarchy. The object's globally unique identifier (GUID) is unchanged by a move or rename.

As users and groups are migrated from one domain to another, they are given a new security identifier (SID). To preserve the security credentials of an account when it is moved from one domain to another, Windows 2000 supports SIDHistory, a security attribute available only in Windows 2000 Native mode. As users and groups are moved from one domain to another, to reduce the administrative overhead of resetting ACLs and ownership of resources, the old SID is added to the SIDHistory attribute for the new object. Whenever users log on, any SIDs present in their SIDHistory, or any SIDs present in the SIDHistory of a group of which the users are members, are added to their access token, and they are given permissions and ownership to any resources that they previously had.

MOVETREE allows an OU to be moved to another domain, keeping all of the linked group policy objects (GPOs) in the old domain intact. The GPO link is moved and continues to work, although clients receive their group policy settings from the GPOs located in the old domain.

Supported MOVETREE Operations

The following operations are supported with the MOVETREE utility:

- Move an object or a nonempty container to a different domain. Valid only within the same forest.

- Move Domain Local and Global groups *between* domains without members and *within* domains with members. Valid only within the same forest.

- Move Universal groups with members *within* and *between* domains. Valid only within the same forest.

Unsupported MOVETREE Operations

Some objects and information are not moved. Objects that are not moved are classified as *orphaned objects* and are placed in an "orphan" container in the LostAndFound container in the source domain. The LostAndFound container is visible in the Active Directory Users And Computers console in Advanced View. The orphan container is named using the GUID of the parent container being moved and it contains the objects that were selected for the MOVETREE operation. Specifically, objects and information that cannot be moved by using the MOVETREE utility are:

- Local and Domain Global groups that contain members. Universal group memberships remain intact so that security is not compromised.

- The domain join information for computer objects. The MOVETREE utility can move a computer object from one domain to another, along with its subordinate objects. However, the MOVETREE utility does not disjoin a computer from its source domain and rejoin it to the target domain. For this reason, the NETDOM utility is recommended to move computer objects.

- Associated object data. This includes group policies, user profiles, logon scripts, users' personal data, encrypted files, smart cards, and public key certificates. Group policies would need to be applied to the users, groups, or computers. New smart cards and certificates would need to be issued from the Certificate Authority (CA) in the new domain. Use additional scripts or management tools, such as the Remote Administration Scripts, in conjunction with MOVETREE, to perform these additional steps.

- System objects. Those objects identified by the objectClass being marked as systemOnly.

- Objects in the configuration or schema naming contexts.

- Objects in the special containers in the domain. Objects in the Builtin, ForeignSecurityPrincipals, System, and LostAndFound containers.

- Domain controllers or any object whose parent is a domain controller.

- Any object with the same name as an object that already exists in the target domain.

MOVETREE may fail due to some of the following error conditions:

- The source domain controller cannot transfer the relative ID master role owner.

- The source object is locked due to another operation in progress. For example, if another user is currently creating child objects under the source object that is selected for the move operation.

- Either the source or destination domain has invalid credentials.

- The destination knows the source object is deleted but the source does not. For example, the source object has been deleted on a different domain controller, but due to replication latency the source domain controller has not yet received the deletion event.

- There is a failure at the destination domain controller. For example, if the destination domain controller's disk is full.

- The source and destination have a schema mismatch.

Moving Users

Moving users between domains is supported with the following restrictions:

- If the user object contains any objects, the move operation fails. The user object must be a leaf object.

- If a security accounts manager (SAM) constraint is met, the move operation fails. SAM constraints include when the user's *samAccountName* already exists in the destination domain, or if the user's password length does not meet the password restrictions in the target domain.

- If the user object belongs to a Global group from the source domain, its membership is voided and the move operation fails. This is because a Global group can only have a member in the same domain, thereby preventing movement of any member of a Global group.

However, there is one exception: If the user object belongs to the Domain Users group (without belonging to any other Global groups) and the Domain Users group is this user object's Primary group, the move operation succeeds. It succeeds because when a user object is created, the system automatically places it into the Domain Users group and assigns the Domain Users group as its Primary group.

Moving Groups

Like users, groups can be moved between domains, with similar restrictions:

- If the group object contains any object, the move operation fails.

- If its membership and its reverse memberships do not fulfill the requirements of its type, the operation fails.

- If the group's *samAccountName* exists on the destination domain, the move operation fails.

Moving Objects Between Domains Using MOVETREE

Before using the MOVETREE utility, verify that you have the necessary privileges to perform this operation. For example, make sure that you are authorized to move and create objects in both the source and destination domains. The MOVETREE utility can be used from the command line and can be called from a batch file to script user and group creation.

▶ **Follow these steps to move objects between domains using MOVETREE:**

1. Open a command prompt and type **movetree {/start | /startnocheck | /continue | /check} /s** *SrcDSA* **/d** *DstDSA* **/sdn** *SrcDN* **/ddn** *DstDN* **[/u [***Domain***\]***Username* **/p** *Password***] [/verbose] [{/? | /help}]**

   where:

   - **/start** initiates a MOVETREE operation. This command includes a /check operation by default. To start a MOVETREE operation with no check, use /startnocheck.

   - **/continue** continues the execution of a previously paused or failed MOVETREE operation.

   - **/check** performs a test run of the MOVETREE operation, checking the whole tree without moving any objects.

   - **/s** *SrcDSA* is the source server's fully qualified primary DNS name.

   - **/d** *DstDSA* is the destination server's fully qualified primary DNS name.

   - **/sdn** *SrcDN* is the distinguished name of the leaf, container, or subtree you are moving from the source domain.

   - **/ddn** *DstDN* is the distinguished name of the leaf, container, or subtree you are moving to the destination domain.

- **/u [*Domain*]*Username* /p *Password*** runs MOVETREE under the credentials of a valid *Username* and *Password*. Optionally, a *Domain* can be specified as well. If these optional arguments are not provided, MOVETREE uses the credentials of the currently logged-on user.

- **/verbose** runs MOVETREE in Verbose mode, which displays more details about the operation as it runs (optional).

- **/?** or **/help** displays syntax information.

MOVETREE Command Example

In the Marketing domain, there is a server called Server1 and an OU called Promotions. In the Sales domain, there is a server called Server2. The desired operation is to move the Promotions OU from Marketing to Sales and rename the new OU Sales Promotions. The MOVETREE command performs a test run, and then, if no errors are encountered, performs the move operation.

```
movetree /start /s Server1.Marketing.Reskit.Com /d
Server2.Sales.Reskit.com /sdn
OU=Promotions,DC=Marketing,DC=Reskit,DC=Com /ddn OU=Sales
Promotions,DC=Sales,DC=Reskit,DC=Com
```

MOVETREE Log Files

The following log files are created after the MOVETREE operation. They are located in the directory where you performed the MOVETREE operation.

- **MOVETREE.ERR** lists any errors encountered during the MOVETREE operation.

- **MOVETREE.LOG** lists statistical results of the MOVETREE operation.

- **MOVETREE.CHK** lists any potential errors or conflicts detected during the move operation's precheck phase (or test phase).

Moving Workstations or Member Servers Between Domains

You can use NETDOM Windows 2000 Domain Manager support tool to move a workstation or member server from one domain to another. This tool is available in the Windows 2000 Support Tools. The Windows 2000 Support Tools are included on the Windows 2000 CD-ROM in the \Support\Tools folder.

▶ **Follow these steps to move a workstation or member server from one domain to another:**

1. Open a command prompt and type **netdom move /D:***domain* [/**OU:***ou_path*] [/**Ud:***User* /**Pd:**{*password*|*}] [/**Uo:***User* / **Po:**{*password*|*}] [/**Reboot:**[*time_in_seconds*]]

   where:

   - /*domain* is the domain that the workstation or member server should belong to after the operation is completed.

   - /**OU:***ou_path* is the name of a destination OU in /D:*domain*.

   - /**Ud:***User* is the user account used to make the connection with the domain specified by the /D argument. If this option is not specified, the current user account is used.

   - /**Pd:**{*password*|*} is the password of the user account specified with /Ud. If *, then the password is prompted for.

   - /**Uo:***User* is the user account used to make the connection with the object on which the action is to be performed. If this option is not specified, the current user account is used.

   - /**Po:**{*password*|*} is the password of the user account specified with /Uo. If the value used is *, the password is prompted for.

   - /**Reboot:**[*time_in_seconds*] specifies that the computer being moved should be shut down and automatically rebooted after the operation has completed. If the number of seconds is not specified, a default value of 20 seconds is used.

NETDOM Command Example

To move a workstation named mywksta from its current domain into the mydomain domain, you would type the following command:

```
netdom move /d:mydomain mywksta /ud:mydomain\admin
/pd:password
```

If the destination is a Windows 2000 domain, the SIDHistory for the workstation is updated, retaining the security permissions that the computer account had previously.

Moving Domain Controllers Between Sites

In general, you can install a domain controller into a site that has existing domain controllers. The exception to this rule is the first domain controller installed, which automatically creates the Default-First-Site-Name site. You cannot create a first domain controller in any site but Default-First-Site-Name, but you can create a domain controller in a site that has a previously existing domain controller and then move it to another site. Therefore, after the first domain controller has been installed, creating Default-First-Site-Name, you can create other domain controllers in this site and then move them to alternative sites.

The following procedure may also be used to move member servers between sites.

▶ **Follow these steps to move a domain controller between sites:**

1. In Active Directory Sites And Services, select the domain controller that you want to move to a different site, and then click Move on the Action menu.

2. In the Move Server dialog box (see Figure 19.7), select the site to which you want to move the domain controller, and then click OK.

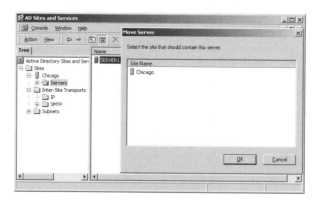

Figure 19.7 The Move Server dialog box

Practice: Moving Objects Within a Domain

In this practice you move three user accounts from one OU to another. You also attempt to log on using a different account.

Exercise 1: Move Objects Within the Domain

In this exercise, you will move user accounts from one OU to another.

1. Log on to your domain as Administrator, and then open Active Directory Users And Computers.

2. In the console tree, click Users.

3. Select all three user accounts (User20, User21, and User22) that you created in Lesson 1 of this chapter by clicking one of the user accounts, press Ctrl, and then click the remaining two user accounts.

4. On the Action menu, click Move.

5. In the Move dialog box, to select the new location for the user accounts, expand your domain, click Security1 (the OU you set up in Lesson 2), and then click OK.

   Notice that the user accounts that you moved no longer appear in the Users container.

6. To verify that the user accounts were moved to the correct location, in the console tree, click Security1.

   Notice that the user accounts that you moved are now located in the Security1 OU.

7. Close the Active Directory Users And Computers console.

Exercise 2: Log On as a User in a Nonstandard OU

In this exercise, you will attempt to log on to one of the accounts you just moved to a new OU.

1. Log on to your domain by using the User21 account.

   Did Windows 2000 require you to specify the OU in which your user account is located as part of the logon process? Why or why not?

2. Log off Windows 2000.

Lesson Summary

In this lesson, you learned how to move objects within domains in Active Directory using the Move dialog box. You learned how to move objects between domains using the MOVETREE command-line utility. You learned how to move workstations or member servers between domains using the NETDOM command-line utility. You also learned how to move domain controllers between sites using the Move Server dialog box.

In the practice portion of this lesson, you used Active Directory Users and Computers to select the object to move within a domain, and you used the Move dialog box to select the location to which you want to move the object.

Lesson 5: Delegating Administrative Control of Active Directory Objects

In this lesson you learn that you can delegate administrative control of objects to individuals so that they can perform administrative tasks on the objects. You also learn how to use the Delegation Of Control wizard to delegate control of objects and the guidelines for delegating control.

After this lesson, you will be able to

- Delegate administrative control of OUs and objects

Estimated lesson time: 20 minutes

Guidelines for Delegating Control

You delegate administrative control of objects by assigning permissions to the object to allow users or groups of users to administer the objects. An administrator can delegate the following types of control:

- Assign a user the permissions to change properties on a particular container.

- Assign a user the permissions to create, modify, or delete objects of a specific type in a specific OU or container.

- Assign a user the permissions to modify specific properties on objects of a specific type in a specific OU or container.

Because tracking permissions at the OU or container level is easier than tracking permissions on objects or object attributes, the most common method of delegating administrative control is to assign permissions at the OU or container level. Assigning permissions at the OU or container level allows you to delegate administrative control for the objects that are contained in the OU or container. Use the Delegation Of Control wizard to assign permissions at the OU or container level.

For example, you can delegate administrative control by assigning Full Control for an OU to the appropriate manager, giving them control only within his or her area of responsibility. By delegating control of the OU to the manager, you can decentralize administrative operations and issues. This reduces your administration time and costs by distributing administrative control closer to its point of service.

To help you delegate administrative control, you may want to follow these suggestions:

- Assign control at the OU or container level whenever possible. Assigning control at the OU or container level allows for easier tracking of permission assignments. Tracking permission assignments becomes more complex for objects and object attributes.

- Use the Delegation Of Control wizard. The wizard assigns permissions only at the OU or container level. The wizard simplifies the process of assigning object permissions by stepping you through the process.

- Track the delegation of permission assignments. Tracking assignments allows you to maintain records to easily review security settings.

- Follow business requirements. Follow any guidelines that your organization has in place for delegating control.

Delegation Of Control Wizard

The Delegation Of Control wizard steps you through the process of assigning permissions at the OU or container level. More specialized permissions must be manually assigned.

In Active Directory Users And Computers, click the OU or container for which you want to delegate control, and then on the Action menu, click Delegate Control to start the wizard.

Table 19.4 describes the Delegation Of Control wizard options.

Table 19.4   Delegation Of Control Wizard Options

Option	Description
Users Or Groups	Allows you to select the user accounts or groups to which you want to delegate control.
Tasks To Delegate	Allows you to select common tasks from a list or create custom tasks to delegate.
Active Directory Object Type (available only when custom tasks are selected in "Tasks To Delegate")	Allows you to select the scope of the tasks you want to delegate, either This Folder, Existing Objects In This Folder, and Creation Of New Objects In This Folder or Only The Following Objects In This Folder.

Option	Description
Permissions (available only when custom tasks are selected in "Tasks To Delegate")	Select one of the following permissions to delegate:
	General—the most commonly assigned permissions that are available for the object
	Property-Specific—the permissions that you can assign to the attributes of the object
	Creation/Deletion Of Specific Child Objects—the permissions to create and delete child objects.

Guidelines for Administering Active Directory

The following are best practices for administering Active Directory:

- In larger organizations, coordinate your Active Directory structure with other administrators. You can move objects later, but this might create extra work.

- When you create Active Directory objects, such as user accounts, complete all attributes that are important to your organization. Completing the attributes gives you more flexibility when you search for objects.

- Use deny permissions sparingly. If you assign permissions correctly, you should not need to deny permissions. In most cases, denied permissions indicate mistakes that were made in assigning group membership.

- Always ensure that at least one user has Full Control for each Active Directory object. Failure to do so might result in objects being inaccessible.

- Ensure that delegated users take responsibility and can be held accountable. You gain nothing if you delegate administrative control without ensuring future accountability. As an administrator, you are ultimately responsible for all of the administrative changes that are made. If the users to whom you delegate responsibility are not performing the administrative tasks, you will need to assume responsibility for their failure.

- Provide training for users who have control of objects. Ensure that the users to whom you delegate responsibility understand their responsibilities and know how to perform the administrative tasks.

Practice: Delegating Administrative Control in Active Directory

In this practice you delegate to a user control over objects in an OU. Refer to the tables that you completed in Lesson 2 to answer the questions in this practice.

Exercise 1: Test Current Permissions

In this exercise, you will determine what permissions currently exist.

1. Log on to your domain as Assistant1, and type **password** as the password.

2. Start Active Directory Users And Computers.

3. In the console tree, expand your domain, and then click Security1.

   What user objects are visible in the Security1 OU?

   Which permissions allow you to see these objects? (Hint: Refer to your answers in Lesson 2.)

   For the user account with the logon name Secretary1, change the logon hours. Were you successful? Why or why not?

   For the Assistant1 user account, under which you are currently logged on, change the logon hours. Were you successful? Why or why not?

4. Close Active Directory Users And Computers and log off Windows 2000.

Exercise 2: Use the Delegation Of Control Wizard to Assign Active Directory Permissions

In this exercise, you delegate the control of Active Directory permissions for the OU to user Assistant1.

1. Log on to your domain as Administrator and open Active Directory Users and Computers.

2. In the console tree, expand your domain.

3. Click Security1, and then on the Action menu, click Delegate Control.

4. In the Delegation Of Control wizard, click Next.

   The Delegation Of Control wizard displays the Users Or Groups page.

   Notice that the wizard does not display any user accounts or groups. You will add a user account to which to delegate control.

5. Click Add.

   The Select Users, Computers, Or Groups dialog box appears.

6. Select Assistant1, click Add, and then click OK.

7. Click Next.

   The Delegation Of Control wizard displays the Tasks To Delegate page. Here you can choose to delegate common tasks from a list or create custom tasks to delegate.

8. For this exercise, confirm that Delegate The Following Common Tasks is selected, click the Create, Delete, And Manage User Accounts check box, and then click Next.

   The Delegation Of Control wizard displays the Completing The Delegation Of Control Wizard page.

9. Review the Summary page.

   - If all choices reflect the delegation of control on all objects for Assistant1, click Finish.

   - To make changes, click Back.

10. Close Active Directory Users And Computers and log off Windows 2000.

Exercise 3: Test Delegated Permissions

In this exercise, you test to confirm that Assistant1 has the permissions you delegated in the prior exercise.

1. Log on to your domain as Assistant1, and type **password** as your password.
2. Open Active Directory Users And Computers.
3. In the console tree, expand your domain, and then click Security1.
4. Attempt to change the logon hours for the user accounts in the Security1 OU.

   Were you successful? Why or why not?

5. Attempt to change the logon hours for a user account in the Users container.

   Were you successful? Why or why not?

6. Close Active Directory Users And Computers and log off Windows 2000.

Lesson Summary

In this lesson, you learned that you can delegate administrative control of objects to individuals so that they can perform administrative tasks on the objects. Assigning permissions at the OU or container level allows you to delegate administrative control for the objects that are contained in the OU or container. You learned how to use the Delegation Of Control wizard to delegate control of objects and the guidelines for delegating control. In the practice portion of this lesson, you used the Delegation Of Control wizard to delegate to a user control over objects in an OU.

Lesson 6: Active Directory Performance Monitoring Tools

Monitoring Active Directory performance is an important part of maintaining and administering your Microsoft Windows 2000 installation. You use Active Directory performance data to

- Understand Active Directory performance and the corresponding effect on your system's resources
- Observe changes and trends in performance and resource usage so you can plan for future upgrades
- Test configuration changes or other tuning efforts by monitoring the results
- Diagnose problems and target components or processes for optimization

This lesson introduces you to the Active Directory performance monitoring tools and guides you through the steps required to set up Active Directory performance monitoring.

After this lesson, you will be able to

- Describe the purpose of the Event Viewer console
- Use the Event Viewer console to view event logs
- Describe the components of the Performance console
- Describe the purpose of the System Monitor
- Use the System Monitor to monitor performance counters
- Describe the purpose of counter logs, trace logs, and alerts
- Use Performance Logs and Alerts to create counter logs, trace logs, and alerts

Estimated lesson time: 50 minutes

Performance Monitoring Tools

Windows 2000 provides several tools for monitoring Active Directory performance. On the Administrative Tools menu, the Event Viewer console allows you to view log files and error messages sent by applications. The Performance console provides a graphical way to view performance of Active Directory according to measurements, or counters, that you select. The Performance console also provides a means to log activity or send alerts according to those measurements and view the logs either printed or online.

The Event Viewer Console

Windows 2000 provides the Event Viewer console as a way to monitor Windows-wide events such as application, system, and security events, and service-specific events such as directory service events. These events are recorded in event logs. For example, if you need detailed information about when directory partitions are being replicated, you would study the File Replication Service log in the Event Viewer.

Also, if you experience problems with Active Directory, it is recommended that the directory service event logs be the *first* item that you use to investigate the causes of the problem. By using information from the event log, you can better understand the sequence and types of events that led up to a particular performance problem.

Event Viewer can be used to view, locate, filter, and archive information contained in Windows 2000 security logs and to configure security logs. The procedures for each of these tasks are similar for the event logs used to monitor Active Directory performance. These logs are described in Table 19.5.

Table 19.5   Event Logs for Monitoring Active Directory Performance

Log	Description
Application	Contains errors, warnings, or information generated by applications, such as a database server or an e-mail program. The application developer presets which events to record.
Directory Service	Contains errors, warnings, and information generated by Active Directory (see Figure 19.8).
File Replication Service	Contains errors, warnings, and information generated by the File Replication service.
System	Contains errors, warnings, and information generated by Windows 2000. Windows 2000 presets which events to record.

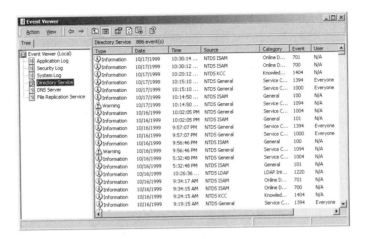

Figure 19.8 The Directory Service log

The Performance Console

The Performance console allows you to monitor conditions within local and remote computers anywhere in your network and to summarize performance at selected intervals. The Performance console can use various counters for monitoring real-time resource usage. It can log results into a file so that you can view and diagnose historical performance problems. With appropriate permissions, it can monitor resource usage of other computers that run server services on the network. The Performance console can also be used for collecting baseline performance data and then configured to send alerts to the Event Log or other locations about exceptions to the baseline.

The Performance console contains two snap-ins: System Monitor (an ActiveX control) and Performance Logs And Alerts.

System Monitor

With System Monitor, you can measure Active Directory performance on your own computer or other computers on a network. You can perform the following tasks:

- Collect and view real-time performance data on a local computer or from several remote computers

- View data collected either currently or previously recorded in a counter log

- Present data in a printable graph, histogram, or report view

- Incorporate System Monitor functionality into Microsoft Word or other applications in the Microsoft Office suite by means of Automation

- Create Hypertext Markup Language (HTML) pages from performance views

- Create reusable monitoring configurations that can be installed on other computers using the Microsoft Management Console (MMC)

A sample System Monitor is shown in Figure 19.9.

You can define the Active Directory data you want to collect in the following ways:

- **Type of data.** To select the data to be collected, you specify performance objects and performance counters.

- **Source of data.** System Monitor can collect data from your local computer or from other computers on the network where you have permission. (By default, administrative permission associated with the task is required.) In addition, you can include real-time data or data collected previously using counter logs.

- **Sampling parameters.** System Monitor supports manual, on-demand sampling or automatic sampling based on a time interval you specify. When viewing logged data, you can also choose starting and stopping times so that you can view data spanning a specific time range.

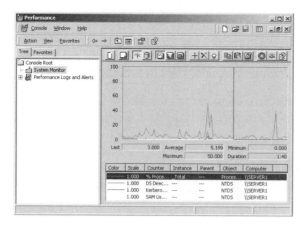

Figure 19.9 A sample System Monitor

In addition to options for defining data content, you have considerable flexibility in designing the appearance of your System Monitor views:

- **Type of display.** System Monitor supports chart, histogram, and report views.

- **Display characteristics.** For any of the three display types, you can define the characteristics, colors, and fonts for the display.

Defining Data for Monitoring

To begin monitoring data, you specify performance objects and performance counters. A *performance object* is a logical connection of counters that is associated with a resource or service that can be monitored. For the purposes of monitoring Active Directory, you monitor the activity of the NTDS (NT Directory Service) performance object. By using System Monitor, you can track the activity of performance objects through the use of counters. *Performance counters* refer to the multitude of conditions that can apply to a performance object. For example, if you need to find out the number of connected LDAP client sessions, you can select the LDAP Client Sessions counter under the NTDS performance object and then view the current activity by using System Monitor.

The NTDS Performance Object Counters

The NTDS performance object contains many performance counters that provide statistics about Active Directory performance. After determining the statistics you want to monitor, you must find the matching performance counters.

Performance counters can provide some baseline analysis information for capacity and performance planning. Typically, counters that are suited for capacity planning contain the word "total" in their name. These counters fall into three types: statistic counters, ratio counters, and accumulative counters. *Statistic counters* show totals per second. An example is DRA (Directory Replication Agent) Inbound Properties Total/Sec, which is the total number of object properties received from inbound replication partners. *Ratio counters* show percentage of total. An example is DS (Directory Service) % Writes From LDAP, which is the percentage of directory writes coming from LDAP query. *Accumulative counters* show totals since Active Directory was last started. An example is DRA Inbound Bytes Total Since Boot, which is the total number of bytes replicated in, the sum of the number of uncompressed bytes (never compressed) and the number of compressed bytes (after compression).

Each counter has its own guidelines and limits. The counters in Table 19.6 are of special interest for the reasons described.

Table 19.6   Important Active Directory System Monitor Counters on the NTDS Performance Object

Counter	Description
DRA Inbound Bytes Compressed (Between Sites, After Compression)/Sec	The compressed size (in bytes) of inbound compressed replication data (size after compression, from Directory System Agents [DSAs] in other sites).
DRA Inbound Bytes Compressed (Between Sites, Before Compression)/Sec	The original size (in bytes) of inbound compressed replication data (size before compression, from DSAs in other sites).
DRA Inbound Bytes Not Compressed (Within Site)/Sec	The number of bytes received through inbound replication that were not compressed at the source—that is, from other DSAs in the same site.
DRA Inbound Bytes Total/Sec	The total number of bytes received through replication, per second. It is the sum of the number of uncompressed bytes (never compressed) and the number of compressed bytes (after compression).
DRA Inbound Full Sync Objects Remaining	The number of objects remaining until the full synchronization process is completed, or set.
DRA Inbound Objects/Sec	The number of objects received, per second, from replication partners through inbound replication.
DRA Inbound Objects Applied/Sec	The rate, per second, at which replication updates are received from replication partners and applied by the local directory service. This count excludes changes that are received but not applied (for example, when the change is already present). This indicates how much replication update activity is occurring on the server as a result of changes generated on other servers.
DRA Inbound Objects Filtered/Sec	The number of objects received per second from inbound replication partners that contained no updates that needed to be applied.
DRA Inbound Object Updates Remaining in Packet	The number of object updates received in the current directory replication update packet that have not yet been applied to the local server. This tells you whether the monitored server is receiving changes but taking a long time applying them to the database.
DRA Inbound Properties Applied/Sec	The number of properties that are applied through inbound replication as a result of reconciliation logic.

Counter	Description
DRA Inbound Properties Filtered/Sec	The number of property changes that are already known received during the replication.
DRA Inbound Properties Total/Sec	The total number of object properties received per second from inbound replication partners.
DRA Inbound Values (DNs Only)/Sec	The number of object property values received from inbound replication partners that are Distinguished Names (DNs), per second. This includes objects that reference other objects. Distinguished Names values, such as group or distribution list memberships, are more expensive to apply than other kinds of values because group or distribution list objects can include hundreds and thousands of members and therefore are much bigger than a simple object with only one or two attributes. This counter might explain why inbound changes are slow to be applied to the database.
DRA Inbound Values Total/Sec	The total number of object property values received from inbound replication partners per second. Each inbound object has one or more properties, and each property has zero or more values. Zero values indicate property removal.
DRA Outbound Bytes Compressed (Between Sites, After Compression)/Sec	The compressed size (in bytes) of outbound compressed replication data, after compression, from DSAs in other sites.
DRA Outbound Bytes Compressed (Between Sites, Before Compression)/Sec	The original size (in bytes) of outbound compressed replication data, before compression, from DSAs in other sites.
DRA Outbound Bytes Not Compressed (Within Site)/Sec	The number of bytes replicated out that were not compressed, that is, from DSAs in the same site.
DRA Outbound Bytes Total/Sec	The total number of bytes replicated out per second. The sum of the number of uncompressed bytes (never compressed) and the number of compressed bytes (after compression).
DRA Outbound Objects/Sec	The number of objects replicated out per second.
DRA Outbound Objects Filtered/Sec	The number of objects acknowledged by outbound replication that required no updates. They also represent objects that the outbound partner did not already have.

continues

Table 19.6 **Important Active Directory System Monitor Counters on the NTDS Performance Object** *(continued)*

Counter	Description
DRA Outbound Properties/Sec	The number of properties replicated out per second. This tells you whether a source server is returning objects or not.
DRA Outbound Values (DNs Only)/Sec	The number of object property values containing DNs sent to outbound replication partners. DN values, such as group or distribution list memberships, are more expensive to read than other kinds of values because group or distribution list objects can include hundreds and thousands of members and therefore are much bigger than a simple object with only one or two attributes.
DRA Outbound Values Total/Sec	The number of object property values sent to outbound replication partners per second.
DRA Pending Replication Synchronizations	The number of directory synchronizations that are queued for this server but not yet processed. This helps in determining replication backlog; the larger the number, the larger the backlog.
DRA Sync Requests Made	The number of synchronization requests made to replication partners.
DS Directory Reads/Sec	The number of directory reads per second.
DS Directory Writes/Sec	The number of directory writes per second.
DS Security Descriptor Suboperations/Sec	The number of Security Descriptor Propagation suboperations per second. One Security Descriptor Propagation operation is made up of many suboperations. A suboperation roughly corresponds to an object the propagation causes the propagator to examine.
DS Security Descriptor Propagations Events	The number of Security Descriptor Propagation events that are queued but not yet processed.
DS Threads in Use	The current number of threads in use by the directory service (different than the number of threads in the directory service process). Threads in Use is the number of threads currently servicing client application programming interface (API) calls and can be used to indicate whether additional processors can be of benefit.

Counter	Description
Kerberos Authentications/Sec	The number of times per second that clients use a ticket to this domain controller to authenticate this domain controller.
LDAP Bind Time	The time (in milliseconds) taken for the last successful LDAP binding.
LDAP Client Sessions LDAP Searches/Sec	The number of connected LDAP client sessions. The number of search operations per second performed by LDAP clients.
LDAP Successful Binds/Sec	The number of successful LDAP binds per second.
NTLM Authentications	The number of NT LAN Manager (NTLM) authentications per second serviced by this domain controller.
XDS Client Sessions	The number of connected Extended Directory Service (XDS) client sessions. This indicates the number of connections from other Windows NT services and the Windows NT Administrator program.

Monitoring Performance Counters

You can select the performance counters to monitor and then view them graphically in the System Monitor as a chart, histogram, or log file data display.

▶ **Follow these steps to monitor Active Directory performance counters:**

1. From the Start menu, select Programs, point to Administrative Tools, and then click Performance.

2. Right-click the System Monitor details pane and click Add Counters.

3. In the Add Counters dialog box (see Figure 19.10):

   - To monitor any computer on which the monitoring console is run, click Use Local Computer Counters.

   - To monitor a specific computer, regardless of where the monitoring console is run, click Select Counters From Computer and select a computer name from the list (the name of the local computer is selected by default).

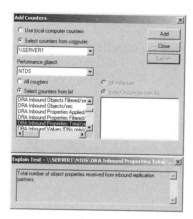

Figure 19.10 The Add Counters dialog box

4. In the Performance Object list, select the NTDS performance object.

Note For a description of a particular counter (see Figure 19.10), click the name of the counter from the list, and then click Explain.

---

5. Select the counters to monitor.

- To monitor all counters for the NTDS performance object, click All Counters.

   Note Because there are many counters, monitoring all counters affects processing time and is not a practical solution.

- To monitor only selected counters, click Select Counters From List and select the counters you want to monitor. You can select multiple counters by clicking on a counter and holding the Ctrl key.

6. Click Add.

7. When you are finished adding counters, click Close.

   The counters that you selected appear in the lower part of the screen; each counter is represented by its own color. Choose either the chart, histogram, or report display view by clicking the appropriate toolbar button.

Note When creating a System Monitor snap-in for export, make sure to select Use Local Computer Counters on the Select Counters dialog box. Otherwise, System Monitor obtains data from the computer named in the text box, regardless of where the snap-in is installed.

Performance Logs and Alerts

The Performance Logs And Alerts snap-in enables you to create counter logs, trace logs, and system alerts automatically from local or remote computers.

Counter Logs

Counter logs, which are similar to System Monitor, support the definition of performance objects and performance counters and setting sampling intervals for monitoring data about hardware resources and system services. Counter logs collect performance counter data in a comma-separated or tab-separated format for easy import to spreadsheet or database programs. You can view logged counter data using System Monitor or export the data to a file for analysis and report generation.

Trace Logs

Using the default system data provider or another nonsystem provider, trace logs record data when certain activities such as a disk I/O operation or a page fault occur. When the event occurs, the provider sends the data to the Performance Logs and Alerts service. This differs from the operation of counter logs; when counter logs are in use, the service obtains data from the system when the update interval has elapsed, rather than waiting for a specific event.

Active Directory nonsystem providers include those for NetLogon, the Kerberos protocol, SAM, and Windows NT Active Directory Service. These providers generate trace log files containing messages that may be used to track the operations performed.

A parsing tool is required to interpret the trace log output. Developers can create such a tool using APIs provided on the Microsoft Developer Web site (*http://msdn.microsoft.com/*).

Logging Options

For both counter and trace logs you can

- Define start and stop times, filenames, file types, file sizes, and other parameters for automatic log generation and manage multiple logging sessions from a single console window.

- Start and stop logging either manually on demand or automatically based on a user-defined schedule.

- Configure additional settings for automatic logging, such as automatic file renaming, and set parameters for stopping and starting a log based on the elapsed time or the file size.

- Define a program that runs when a log is stopped.

- View logs during collection as well as after collection has stopped. Because logging runs as a service, data collection occurs regardless of whether any user is logged on to the computer being monitored.

Counter and Trace Logging Requirements

To create or modify a log, you must have Full Control permission for the following registry key, which controls the Performance Logs and Alerts service:

HKEY_LOCAL_MACHINE\SYSTEM\CurrentControlSet\Services\ SysmonLog\Log Queries

Administrators usually have this permission by default. Administrators can grant permission to users by using the Security menu in REGEDT32.EXE.

To run the Performance Logs and Alerts service (which runs in the background when you configure a log), you must have permission to start or otherwise configure services on the system. Administrators have this right by default and can grant it to users by using group policy. To log data on a remote computer, the Performance Logs and Alerts service must run under an account that has access to the remote system.

Creating a Counter Log

To create a counter log, you first define the counters you want to log and then set log file and scheduling parameters.

▶ **Follow these steps to create a counter log:**

1. From the Start menu, select Programs, point to Administrative Tools, and then click Performance.

2. Double-click Performance Logs And Alerts, and then click Counter Logs.

   Any existing logs will be listed in the details pane. A green icon indicates that a log is running; a red icon indicates that a log has been stopped.

3. Right-click a blank area of the details pane, and then click New Log Settings.

4. In the New Log Settings dialog box, in the Name box, type the name of the log, and then click OK.

5. In the General tab of the counter log's dialog box, type the name of the path and filename of the log file in the Current Log File Name box, and then click Add.

6. In the Select Counters dialog box, choose the computer for which you want to log counters.

   - To log counters from the computer on which the Performance Logs and Alerts service will run, click Use Local Computer Counters.

   - To log counters from a specific computer regardless of where the service is run, click Select Counters From Computer and select the name of the computer you want to monitor from the list.

7. In the Performance Object list, select an object to log.

8. Select the counters you want to log from the list, and then click Add.

9. Click Close when you have finished selecting counters to log.

10. In the Log Files tab of the counter log's dialog box, configure the options shown in Figure 19.11 and described in Table 19.7.

Table 19.7   Options on the Log Files Tab

Option	Description
Location	The name of the folder where you want the log file created, or click Browse to search for the folder.
File Name	A partial or base name for the log file. You can use File Name in conjunction with End File Names With if appropriate. Appears on the details pane.
End File Names With	The suffix style you want from the list. Distinguish between individual log files with the same log filename that are in a group of logs that have been automatically generated.
Start Numbering At	The start number for automatic file numbering, when you select nnnnnn as the End File Names With.

continues

Table 19.7   Options on the Log Files Tab *(continued)*

Option	Description
Log File Type	The format you want for this log file. Text File—CSV, defines a comma-delimited log file (with a .csv extension). Use this format to export the log data to a spreadsheet program. Text File—TSV defines a tab-delimited log file (with a .tsv extension). Use this format to export the log data to a spreadsheet program. Binary File defines a sequential, binary-format log file (with a .blg extension). Use this file format if you want to be able to record data instances that are intermittent—that is, stopping and resuming after the log has begun running. Nonbinary file formats cannot accommodate instances that are not persistent throughout the duration of the log. Binary Circular File defines a circular, binary-format log file (with a .blg extension). Use this file format to record data continuously to the same log file, overwriting previous records with new data.
Comment	A comment or description for the log file. Appears in the details pane.
Log File Size	Maximum Limit - data is continuously collected in a log file until it reaches limits set by disk quotas or the operating system. Limit Of - the maximum size (in kilobytes, up to two gigabytes) of the log file. Select this option if you want to do circular logging.

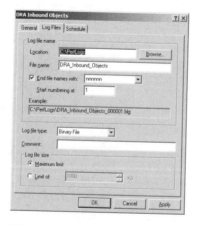

Figure 19.11 The Log Files tab of a counter log's dialog box

11. In the Schedule tab of the counter log's dialog box, configure the options shown in Figure 19.12 and described in Table 19.8.

Table 19.8   Options on the Schedule Tab

Option	Description
Start Log	Manually - logging starts manually. At - logging starts according to the time and date parameters you set.
Stop Log	Manually - logging stops manually. After - logging stops after the time you specify. At - logging stops at the time and date parameters you set. When The Log File Is Full - logging stops when the log file reaches a maximum size.
When A Log File Closes	Start A New Log File - logging resumes in a new file after logging stops for the current log file. Run This Command - a command you specify is run when a log file closes.

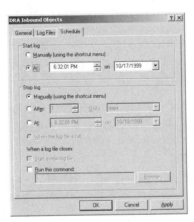

Figure 19.12 The Schedule tab of a counter log's dialog box

12. Click OK.

Note When creating a Performance Logs and Alerts snap-in for export, make sure to select Use Local Computer Counters on the Select Counters dialog box. Otherwise, counter logs will obtain data from the computer named in the text box, regardless of where the snap-in is installed.

Creating a Trace Log

To create a trace log, you first define how you want events logged and then set log file and scheduling parameters.

▶ **Follow these steps to create a trace log:**

1. From the Start menu, select Programs, point to Administrative Tools, and then click Performance.

2. Double-click Performance Logs And Alerts, and then click Trace Logs.

   Any existing logs will be listed in the details pane. A green icon indicates that a log is running; a red icon indicates that a log has been stopped.

3. Right-click a blank area of the details pane, and then click New Log Settings.

4. In the New Log Settings dialog box, in the Name box, type the name of the log, and then click OK.

   In the General tab of the trace log's Properties dialog box, the name of the path and filename of the log file is shown in the Current Log File Name box. By default, the log file is created in the PerfLogs folder in the root directory, and a sequence number is appended to the filename you entered and the sequential trace file type with the .etl extension.

5. Select which events you want logged.

   - Select Events Logged By System Provider for the default provider (the Windows kernel trace provider) to monitor processes, threads, and other activity. To define events for logging, click the check boxes as appropriate. This can create some performance overhead for the system.

   - Select Nonsystem Providers to select the trace data providers you want—for example, if you have written your own providers. Use the Add or Remove buttons to select or remove nonsystem providers.

   For a list of the installed providers and their status (enabled or not), click Provider Status.

   Note You can have only one trace log that uses the system provider running at a time. In addition, you cannot concurrently run multiple trace logs from the same nonsystem provider. If the system trace provider is enabled, nonsystem providers cannot be enabled, and vice versa. However, you can enable multiple nonsystem providers simultaneously.

   ---

6. In the Log Files tab of the trace log's Properties dialog box, configure the options as you do for counter logs, except for the options shown in Table 19.9.

Table 19.9   Trace Log–Specific Options in the Log Files Tab

Option	Description
Log File Type	The format you want for this log file: Circular Trace File - defines a circular trace log file (with an .etl extension). Use this file format to record data continuously to the same log file, overwriting previous records with new data. Sequential Trace File defines a sequential trace log file (with an .etl extension) that collects data until it reaches a user-defined limit and then closes and starts a new file.
Log File Size	Maximum Limit - data is continuously collected in a log file until it reaches limits set by disk quotas or the operating system. Limit Of - the maximum size (in megabytes) of the log file. Select this option if you want to do circular logging.

7. In the Schedule tab of the trace log's Properties dialog box, configure the options as shown for counter logs.

8. Click OK.

Note Trace logging of file details and page faults can generate an extremely large amount of data. It is recommended that you limit trace logging using the file details and page fault options to a maximum of 2 hours.

Alerts

Alerts, which are similar to System Monitor and counter logs, support the use of performance objects and performance counters and setting sampling intervals for monitoring data about hardware resources and system services. Using this data, you can create an alert for a counter, which logs an entry in the application event log, sends a network message to a computer, starts a performance data log, or runs a program when the selected counter's value exceeds or falls below a specified setting.

You can start or stop an alert scan either manually on demand or automatically based on a user-defined schedule.

Creating an Alert

To create an alert, you first define the counters you want to monitor for the alert and then set alert triggering and scheduling parameters.

▶ **Follow these steps to create an alert:**

1. From the Start menu, select Programs, point to Administrative Tools, and then click Performance.

2. Double-click Performance Logs And Alerts, and then click Alerts.

   Any existing alerts will be listed in the details pane. A green icon indicates that the alerts are running; a red icon indicates alerts have been stopped.

3. Right-click a blank area of the details pane and click New Alert Settings.

4. In the New Alert Settings dialog box, in the Name box, type the name of the alert, and then click OK.

5. In the Comment box on the alert's dialog box, type a comment to describe the alert as needed, and then click Add.

6. In the Select Counters dialog box, choose the computer for which you want to create an alert.

   - To create an alert on the computer on which the Performance Logs and Alerts service will run, click Use Local Computer Counters.

   - To create an alert on a specific computer regardless of where the service is run, click Select Counters From Computer and specify the name of the computer.

7. In the Performance Object list, select an object to monitor.

8. Select the counters you want to monitor, and then click Add.

9. Click Close when you have finished selecting counters to monitor for the alert.

10. In the Alert When The Value Is list, specify Under or Over, and in the Limit box, specify the value that triggers the alert.

11. In the Sample Data Every section, specify the amount and the unit of measure for the update interval.

12. In the Action tab of the alert's dialog box, select when an alert is triggered as shown in Figure 19.13 and described in the following table.

Options on the Action Tab

Option	Description
Log An Entry In The Application Event Log	Creates an entry visible in Event Viewer
Send A Network Message To	Triggers the messenger service to send a message to the specified computer
Start Performance Data Log	Runs a specified counter log when an alert occurs
Run This Program	Triggers the service to create a process and run a specified program when an alert occurs
Command Line Arguments	Triggers the service to copy specified command-line arguments when the Run This Program option is used

13. In the Schedule tab of the alert's dialog box, configure the options as shown for counter logs.

14. Click OK.

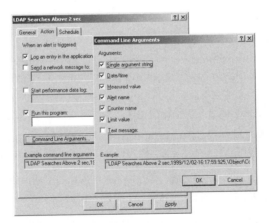

Figure 19.13 The Action tab of an alert's dialog box and the Command Line Arguments dialog box

Practice: Using System Monitor

In this practice, you monitor specified performance counters using System Monitor. Then you use Performance Logs and Alerts to create a counter log and an alert for the LDAP Searches/Sec counter.

Exercise 1: Monitoring Performance Counters

In this exercise, you select performance counters to monitor and then view them graphically in the System Monitor as a chart, histogram, or log file data display.

1. From the Start menu, select Programs, point to Administrative Tools, and then click Performance.

2. In the console tree, click System Monitor.

3. Right-click the System Monitor details pane and click Add Counters.

4. Click Select Counters From Computer and ensure that the name of the local computer is selected.

5. In the Performance Object list, select the NTDS performance object.

6. Click Select Counters From List and select the DRA Pending Replication Synchronizations counter to monitor, and then click Add.

7. Select the LDAP Searches/Sec counter to monitor, and then click Add.

8. Click Close.

   The counters that you selected appear in the lower part of the screen; each counter is represented by its own color. Choose either the chart, histogram, or report display view by clicking the appropriate toolbar button.

Exercise 2: Creating a Counter Log

In this exercise, you create a counter log by first defining the counters you want to log and then setting log file and scheduling parameters.

1. From the Start menu, select Programs, point to Administrative Tools, and then click Performance.

2. Double-click Performance Logs And Alerts, and then click Counter Logs.

3. Right-click a blank area of the details pane, and then click New Log Settings.

4. In the New Log Settings dialog box, in the Name box, type **LDAP Searches Per Sec** and click OK.

5. In the General tab of the LDAP Searches Per Sec dialog box, ensure that the default name of the path and filename of the log file in the Current Log File Name box is showing, and then click Add.

6. In the Select Counters dialog box, click Select Counters From Computer and ensure that the name of the local computer is selected.

7. In the Performance Object list, select the NTDS performance object to log.

8. Select the LDAP Searches/Sec counter to log, click Add, and then click Close.

9. In the Log Files tab, set the following options:

   - Location: C:\PerfLogs (where C:\ is the name of your system drive)

   - File Name: LDAP_Searches_Per_Sec

   - End File Names With: nnnnnn

   - Start Numbering At: 1

   - Log File Type: Text File—CSV

   - Log File Size: Maximum Limit

10. In the Schedule tab, set the following options:

   - Start Log At: a time 3 minutes from now

   - Stop Log After: 2 minutes

11. Click OK.

12. When the log starts in 3 minutes, open Active Directory Users And Computers, open and close various OUs and objects, and then close Active Directory Users And Computers.

13. When the log has stopped, you can view the contents of the counter log by opening the file \PERFLOGS\ LDAP_SEARCHES_PER_SEC_000001.CSV using a spreadsheet program such as Microsoft Excel.

Exercise 3: Creating an Alert

In this exercise, you create an alert by first defining the counters you want to monitor for the alert and then setting alert triggering and scheduling parameters.

1. From the Start menu, select Programs, point to Administrative Tools, and then click Performance.

2. Double-click Performance Logs And Alerts, and then click Alerts.

3. Right-click a blank area of the details pane and click New Alert Settings.

4. In the New Alert Settings dialog box, in the Name box, type **LDAP Searches Above 5 Sec** and click OK.

5. In the Comment box on the alert's dialog box, type **Alerts when LDAP Searches are more than 5 per second** and click Add.

6. In the Select Counters dialog box, click Select Counters From Computer and ensure that the name of the local computer is selected.

7. In the Performance Object list, click the NTDS performance object to monitor.

8. Select the LDAP Searches/Sec counter to monitor, click Add, and then click Close.

9. In the Alert When The Value Is box, specify Over, and in Limit, specify 5.

10. In the Sample Data Every section, specify the interval of 3 seconds.

11. In the Action tab, select the Log An Entry In The Application Event Log check box.

12. In the Schedule tab, set the following options:

    - Start Scan At: a time 3 minutes from now

    - Stop Scan After: 2 minutes

13. Click OK.

14. When the log starts in 3 minutes, open Active Directory Users And Computers, open and close various OUs and objects, and then close Active Directory Users And Computers.

15. When the log has stopped, you can view the alerts in the Application Log in Event Viewer. View the alert information by double-clicking the log entries.

Lesson Summary

In this lesson, you learned about the Active Directory performance monitoring tools, the Event Viewer console, and the Performance console.

The Event Viewer console is a tool to monitor events such as application or system errors or the successful starting of a service. If you experience problems with Active Directory, it is recommended that the directory service event logs be the first item that you use to investigate the causes of the problem.

The Performance console allows you to monitor conditions within local and remote computers anywhere in your network and to summarize performance at selected intervals. The Performance console contains two snap-ins: System Monitor (an ActiveX control) and Performance Logs And Alerts. With System Monitor, you can measure Active Directory performance on your own computer or other computers on a network. The Performance Logs And Alerts snap-in enables you to create counter logs, trace logs, and system alerts automatically from local or remote computers.

In the practice portion of this lesson, you monitored specified performance counters using System Monitor. Then you used Performance Logs And Alerts to create a counter log and an alert for the LDAP Searches/Sec counter.

Lesson 7: Active Directory Support Tools

Some of the Windows 2000 Support Tools included on the Windows 2000 CD-ROM can help you monitor, maintain, and troubleshoot Active Directory. This lesson introduces you to the Windows 2000 Support Tools used to support Active Directory.

After this lesson, you will be able to

- Install the Windows 2000 Support Tools

- Identify the Windows 2000 Support Tools used to support Active Directory

Estimated lesson time: 10 minutes

Active Directory Support Tools

The Windows 2000 Support Tools included on the Windows 2000 CD-ROM are intended for use by Microsoft support personnel and experienced users to assist in diagnosing and resolving computer problems.

The following tools are available for support of Active Directory:

- LDP.EXE: Active Directory Administration Tool

- REPLMON.EXE: Active Directory Replication Monitor

- REPADMIN.EXE: Replication Diagnostics Tool*

- DSASTAT.EXE: Active Directory Diagnostic Tool*

- SDCHECK.EXE: Security Descriptor Check Utility*

- NLTEST.EXE*

- ACLDIAG.EXE: ACL Diagnostics*

- DSACLS.EXE*

*Command-prompt-only tools

LDP.EXE: Active Directory Administration Tool

The Active Directory Administration Tool allows users to perform LDAP operations, such as connect, bind, search, modify, add, and delete, against any LDAP-compatible directory, such as Active Directory. LDAP is an Internet-standard wire protocol used by Active Directory. The Active Directory Administration Tool is a graphical tool located on the Tools menu within Windows 2000 Support Tools.

In troubleshooting, the Administration Tool can be used by administrators to view objects stored in Active Directory along with their metadata, such as security descriptors and replication metadata.

REPLMON.EXE: Active Directory Replication Monitor

The Active Directory Replication Monitor tool enables administrators to view the low-level status of Active Directory replication, force synchronization between domain controllers, view the topology in a graphical format, and monitor the status and performance of domain controller replication using a graphical interface. The Active Directory Replication Monitor is a graphical tool located on the Tools menu within Windows 2000 Support Tools.

Active Directory Replication Monitor Features

Some of the key features of the Active Directory Replication Monitor are

- **Graphical displays.** Replication Monitor displays whether or not the monitored server is a global catalog server, automatically discovers the directory partitions that the monitored server hosts, graphically displays this breakdown, and shows the replication partners that are used for inbound replication for each directory partition. Replication Monitor distinguishes between direct replication partners, transitive replication partners, bridgehead servers, and servers removed from the network in the user interface. Failures from a specific replication partner are indicated by a change in the icon used for the partner.

- **Replication status history.** The history of replication status per directory partition, per replication partner is recorded, generating a granular history of what occurred between two domain controllers. This history can be viewed through Replication Monitor's user interface or can be viewed offline or remotely through a text editor.

- **Property pages.** For direct replication partners, a series of property pages displays the following for each partner: the name of the domain controller, its GUID, the directory partition that it replicates to the monitored server, the transport used (remote procedure call [RPC] or Simple Mail Transfer Protocol [SMTP] and distinguishes between intra- and inter-site when RPC is used), the time of the last successful and attempted replication events, update sequence number (USN) values, and any special properties of the connection between the two servers.

- **Status report generation.** Administrators can generate a status report for the monitored server that includes a listing of the directory partitions for the server, the status of each replication partner (direct and transitive) for each directory partition, detail on which domain controllers the monitored server notifies when changes have been recorded, the status of any group policy objects (GPOs), the domain controllers that hold the Flexible Single Master Operations (FSMO) roles, a snapshot of the performance counters on the computer, and the registry configuration of the server (including parameters for the Knowledge Consistency Checker [KCC], Active Directory, Jet database, and LDAP). Additionally, the administrator can also choose to record (in the same report) the enterprise configuration, which includes each site, site link, site link bridge, subnet, and domain controller (regardless of domain) and the properties of each type of object just mentioned. For example, for the domain controller properties, this records the GUID that makes up the DNS record that is used in replication, the location of the computer account in Active Directory, the inter-site mail address (if it exists), the host name of the computer, and any special flags for the server (whether or not it is a global catalog server). This can be extremely helpful when trouble-shooting an Active Directory replication problem.

- **Server wizard.** With Server wizard, administrators can either browse for the server to monitor or explicitly enter it. The administrator can also create an .ini file, which predefines the names of the servers to monitor, which is then loaded by Replication Monitor to populate the user interface.

- **Graphical site topology.** Replication Monitor displays a graphical view of the intra-site topology and, by using the context menu for a given domain controller in the view, allows the administrator to quickly display the properties of the server and any intra- and inter-site connections that exist for that server.

- **Properties display.** Administrators can display the properties for the monitored server including the server name, the DNS host name of the computer, the location of the computer account in Active Directory, preferred bridgehead status, any special flags for the server (for example, if it is the Primary Domain Controller [PDC] Emulator for its domain or not), which computers it believes to hold the FSMO roles, the replication connections (Replication Monitor differentiates between administrator and automatically generated connection objects) and the reasons they were created, and the IP configuration of the monitored server.

- **Statistics and replication state polling.** In Automatic Update mode, Replication Monitor polls the server at an administrator-defined interval to get the current statistics and replication state. This feature generates a history of changes for each monitored server and its replication partners and allows the administrator to see topology changes as they occur for each monitored server. In this mode, Replication Monitor also monitors the count of failed replication attempts for each replication partner. If the failure count meets or exceeds an administrator-defined value, it can write to the event log and send an e-mail notification to the administrator.

- **Replication triggering.** Administrators can trigger replication on a server with a specific replication partner, with all other domain controllers in the site, or all other domain controllers intra- and inter-site.

- **KCC triggering.** Administrators can trigger the Knowledge Consistency Checker (KCC) on the monitored server to recalculate the replication topology.

- **Display nonreplicated changes.** Administrators can display, on demand, Active Directory changes that have not yet replicated from a given replication partner.

REPADMIN.EXE: Replication Diagnostics Tool

REPADMIN.EXE is a command-line tool that assists administrators in diagnosing replication problems between Windows 2000 domain controllers.

During normal operation, the KCC automatically manages the replication topology for each naming context held on domain controllers.

REPADMIN.EXE allows the administrator to view the replication topology as seen from the perspective of each domain controller. In addition, REPADMIN.EXE can be used to manually create the replication topology (although in normal practice this should not be necessary), to force replication events between domain controllers, and to view both the replication metadata and up-to-dateness vectors.

Note During the normal course of operations, there is no need to manually create the replication topology. Incorrect use of this tool may adversely impact the replication topology. The major use of this tool is to monitor replication so problems such as offline servers or unavailable local area network (LAN)/wide area network (WAN) connections can be identified.

DSASTAT.EXE: Active Directory Diagnostic Tool

DSASTAT.EXE is a command-line tool that compares and detects differences between naming contexts on domain controllers.

DSASTAT.EXE can be used to compare two directory trees across replicas within the same domain or, in the case of a global catalog, across different domains. The tool retrieves capacity statistics, such as MB per server, objects per server, and MB per object class, and performs comparisons of attributes of replicated objects.

The user specifies the targeted domain controllers and additional operational parameters from the command line or from an initialization file. DSASTAT.EXE determines if domain controllers in a domain have a consistent and accurate image of their own domain. In the case of global catalogs, DSASTAT.EXE checks to see if the global catalog has a consistent image with domain controllers in other domains. As a complement to the replication monitoring tools, REPADMIN.EXE and REPLMON.EXE, DSASTAT.EXE can be used to ensure that domain controllers are up to date with one another.

SDCHECK.EXE: Security Descriptor Check Utility

SDCHECK.EXE is a command-line tool that displays the security descriptor for any object stored in the Active Directory. The security descriptor contains the ACLs defining the permissions that users have on objects stored in the Active Directory.

To enable administrators to determine the effective access controls on an object, SDCHECK.EXE also displays the object hierarchy and any ACLs that are inherited by the object from its parent.

As changes are made to the ACLs of an object or its parent, they are propagated automatically by the Active Directory. SDCHECK.EXE displays the security descriptor propagation metadata so that administrators can monitor these changes with respect to propagation of inherited ACLs as well as replication of ACLs from other domain controllers.

As a compliment to the replication monitoring tools, REPADMIN.EXE, REPLMON.EXE, and SDCHECK.EXE can be used to ensure that domain controllers are up to date with one another.

NLTEST.EXE

NLTEST.EXE is a command-line tool that helps perform network administrative tasks such as the following:

- Testing trust relationships and the state of a domain controller replication in a Windows domain

- Querying and checking on the status of trust

- Forcing a shutdown

- Getting a list of PDCs

- Forcing a user account database into sync on Microsoft Windows NT Server 4.0 or earlier domain controllers (Windows 2000 domain controllers use a completely different mechanism for maintaining user accounts.)

NLTEST.EXE runs only on x86-based computers.

ACLDIAG.EXE: ACL Diagnostics

ACLDIAG.EXE is a command-line tool that helps diagnose and troubleshoot problems with permissions on Active Directory objects. It reads security attributes from ACLs and outputs information in either readable or tab-delimited format. The latter can be uploaded into a text file for searches on particular permissions, users, or groups, or into a spreadsheet or database for reporting. The tool also provides some simple cleanup functionality.

With ACLDIAG.EXE, you can

- Compare the ACL on a directory services object to the permissions defined in the schema defaults
- Check or fix standard delegations performed using templates from the Delegation Of Control wizard in the Active Directory Users And Computers console
- Get effective permissions granted to a specific user or group or to all users and groups that show up in the ACL

ACLDIAG.EXE displays only the permissions of objects the user has the right to view. Because GPOs are virtual objects that have no distinguished name, this tool cannot be used on them.

For general-purpose ACL reporting and setting from the command prompt, you can also use DSACLS.EXE, another Windows 2000 Support tool.

DSACLS.EXE

DSACLS.EXE is a command-line tool that facilitates management of ACLs for directory services. DSACLS.EXE enables you to query and manipulate security attributes on Active Directory objects. It is the command-line equivalent of the Security page on various Active Directory snap-in tools.

Along with ACLDIAG.EXE, another Windows 2000 Support tool, DSACLS.EXE provides security configuration and diagnosis functionality on Active Directory objects from the command prompt.

Lesson Summary

In this lesson, you were introduced to the Windows 2000 Support Tools that support Active Directory.

Lesson 8: Monitoring Access to Shared Folders

Windows 2000 includes the Shared Folders snap-in so that you can easily monitor access to network resources and send administrative messages to users. You monitor access to network resources to assess and manage current usage on network servers.

After this lesson, you will be able to

- Identify the tool included with Windows 2000 to monitor access to network resources and to send administrative messages

- Identify who can monitor access to network resources

- Determine the shared folders on a computer

- Monitor shared folders

- Monitor open files

- Disconnect users from one or all open files

Estimated lesson time: 20 minutes

Why Monitor Network Resources?

Some of the reasons it is important to assess and manage network resources are the following:

- **Maintenance.** You should determine which users are currently using a resource so that you can notify them before making the resource temporarily or permanently unavailable.

- **Security.** You should monitor user access to resources that are confidential or need to be secure to verify that only authorized users are accessing them.

- **Planning.** You should determine which resources are being used and how much they are being used so that you can plan for future system growth.

Microsoft Windows 2000 includes the Shared Folders snap-in so that you can easily monitor access to network resources and send administrative messages to users. The Shared Folders snap-in is preconfigured in the Computer Management console, allowing you to monitor resources on the local computer. If you add the Shared Folders snap-in to an MMC, you can specify whether you want to monitor the resources on the local computer or a remote computer.

Network Resource Monitoring Requirements

Not all users can monitor access to network resources. Table 19.10 lists the group membership requirements for monitoring access to network resources.

Table 19.10   Groups that Can Access Network Resources

A member of these groups	Can monitor
Administrators or Server Operators for the domain	All computers in the domain
Administrators or Power Users for a member server, stand-alone server, or computer running Microsoft Windows 2000 Professional	That computer

Monitoring Access to Shared Folders

You use the Shares folder in the Shared Folders snap-in to view a list of all shared folders on the computer and to determine how many users have a connection to each folder. In Figure 19.14, the Shares folder has been selected in the Computer Management console tree and all the shared folders on that computer are shown in the details pane.

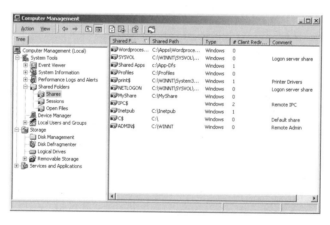

Figure 19.14 The Shares folder of the Shared Folders snap-in

Table 19.11 explains the information provided in the details pane shown in Figure 19.14.

Table 19.11   Fields in the Details Pane for the Shares Folder

Column name	Description
Shared Folder	The name of the shared folders on the computer.
Shared Path	The path to the shared folder.
Type	The operating system that must be running on a computer so that it can be used to gain access to the shared folder.
# Client Redirections	The number of clients who have made a remote connection to the shared folder.
Comment	Descriptive text about the folder. This comment was provided when the folder was shared.

Note   Windows 2000 does not update the list of shared folders, open files, and user sessions automatically. To update these lists, on the Action menu, click Refresh.

Determining How Many Users Can Access a Shared Folder Concurrently

You can use the Shared Folders snap-in to determine the maximum number of users that are permitted to gain access to a folder. In the Shared Folders details pane, click the shared folder for which you want to determine the maximum number of concurrent users that can access the folder. On the Action menu, click Properties, and the Properties dialog box for the shared folder appears. The General tab shows you the user limit.

You can also use the Shared Folders snap-in to determine if the maximum number of users that are permitted to gain access to a folder has been reached. This is an easy way to troubleshoot connectivity problems. If a user cannot connect to a share, determine the number of connections to the share and the maximum connections allowed. If the maximum number of connections has already been made, the user cannot connect to the shared resource.

Modifying Shared Folder Properties

You can modify existing shared folders, including shared folder permissions, from the Shares folder. To change a shared folder's properties, click the shared folder, and then on the Action menu, click Properties. The General tab of the Properties dialog box shows you the share name, the path to the shared folder, and any comment that has been entered. The General tab also allows you to view and set a user limit for accessing the shared folder. The Security tab allows you to view and change the shared folders permissions.

Monitoring Open Files

Use the Open Files folder in the Shared Folders snap-in to view a list of open files that are located in shared folders and the users who have a current connection to each file (see Figure 19.15). You can use this information when you need to contact users to notify them that you are shutting down the system. Additionally, you can determine which users have a current connection and should be contacted when another user is trying to gain access to a file that is in use.

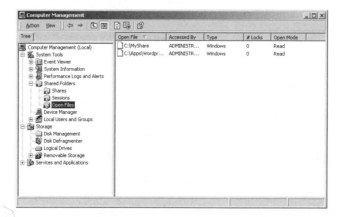

Figure 19.15 The Open Files folder of the Shared Folders snap-in

Table 19.12 describes the information that is available in the Open Files folder.

Table 19.12   Information Available in the Open Files Folder

Column name	Description
Open File	The name of the open files on the computer.
Accessed By	The logon name of the user who has the file open.
Type	The operating system running on the computer where the user is logged on.
# Locks	The number of locks on the file. Programs can request the operating system to lock a file to gain exclusive access and prevent other programs from making changes to the file.
Open Mode	The type of access that the user's application requested when it opened the file, such as Read or Write.

Disconnecting Users from Open Files

You can disconnect users from one open file or from all open files. If you make changes to NTFS permissions for a file that is currently opened by a user, the new permissions will not affect the user until he or she closes and then attempts to reopen the file.

You can force these changes to take place immediately by doing either of the following:

- Disconnecting all users from all open files. To disconnect all users from all open files, in the Shared Folders snap-in console tree, click Open Files, and then on the Action menu, click Disconnect All Open Files.

- Disconnecting all users from one open file. To disconnect users from one open file, in the Shared Folders snap-in console tree, click Open Files. In the details pane select the open file, and then on the Action menu, click Close Open File.

Caution Disconnecting users from open files can result in data loss.

Sending Console Messages

To avoid data loss, you can send a message to some or all users who have an active session with the shared folders that you are managing.

▶ **Follow these steps to send a console message to a connected user:**

1. Click the Shared Folders snap-in, click the Action menu, select All Tasks, and then click Send Console Message.

2. In the Send Console Message dialog box, type the message you want to send to users in the Message box.

3. Select the computer name that will receive the message in the Recipients box, and then click Send.

   If a user is logged on to more than one computer, only the computer that has its name in the recipient list will receive the message.

   If any recipients do not successfully receive the message, you are returned to the Send Console Message dialog box. Recipients that did not successfully receive the message are the only computer names remaining in the list. You should check to see if the computer names are valid or if the computers are unavailable.

Practice: Managing Shared Folders

In this practice, you use the Shared Folders snap-in to view the shared folders and open files on your server. Then you disconnect all users from all open files.

Exercise 1: View the Shared Folders on Your Computer

In this exercise, you will determine which folders on your computer are shared.

1. Click Start, point to Programs, point to Administrative Tools, and then click Computer Management.

2. In the console tree of Computer Management, expand System Tools, and then expand Shared Folders.

3. In the console tree, click Shares under Shared Folders.

   Notice that the details pane shows a list of the existing Shared Folders on your computer.

Exercise 2: View the Open Files on Your Computer

In this exercise, you will determine which shared files on your computer are currently being used by someone else.

1. In the console tree, click Open Files under Shared Folders.

   If you are working on a computer that is not connected to a network, there will not be any open files because the open files only show connections from a remote computer to a share on your computer.

Exercise 3: Disconnect All Users from Open Files on Your Computer

In this exercise, you will disconnect anyone currently using a shared file on your computer.

1. In the console tree, select Open Files under Shared Folders, and then click Disconnect All Open Files on the Action menu.

   If you are not on a network, there will not be any open files to disconnect.

2. Close Computer Management.

Lesson Summary

In this lesson, you learned that Windows 2000 includes the Shared Folders snap-in so that you can monitor access to network resources. You can monitor resources on the local computer or on a remote computer. To monitor resources on a remote computer, you specify the computer on which you want to monitor resources when you add the Shared Folders snap-in to the MMC.

You also learned that you use the Shares folder in the Shared Folders snap-in to view a list of all shared folders on the computer and to determine how many users have a connection to each folder. The General tab of the Properties page for a shared folder shows you the user limit, or maximum number of users that can concurrently connect to that share. You use the Open Files folder in the Shared Folders snap-in to view a list of open files that are located in shared folders and the users who have a current connection to each file.

In the practice portion of this lesson, you viewed the shared folders, opened files on your server, and disconnected all users from all open files.

Review

The following questions will help you determine whether you have learned enough to move on to the next chapter. If you have difficulty answering these questions, please go back and review the material in this chapter before beginning the next chapter. See Appendix A, "Questions and Answers," for the answers to these questions.

1. How does the global catalog help users locate Active Directory objects?

2. You want to allow the manager of the Sales department to create, modify, and delete only user accounts for sales personnel. How can you accomplish this?

3. What happens to the permissions of an object when you move it from one OU to another OU?

4. The Delegation Of Control wizard allows you to set administrative control at what level?

5. When backing up Active Directory, what type of data must you specify to be backed up? What is included in this data type?

6. When you restart the computer in Directory Services Restore Mode, what logon must you use? Why?

7. If you experience problems with Active Directory, what item should you investigate first?

8. What is the difference between a performance object and a performance counter?

9. What is the difference between a counter log and a trace log?

10. What actions can be triggered by an alert?

11. What does the Active Directory Replication Monitor support tool allow an administrator to do, and how is this tool accessed?

12. If you want to find out which files are open in a shared folder and the users who have a current connection to those files, what action should you take?

13. What four tasks must be completed to configure a site?

14. What two site configuration objects does the Active Directory Installation wizard create automatically?

15. Which replication protocol uses RPCs for replication over site links (inter-site) and within a site (intra-site)?

16. What three tasks must be completed to configure inter-site replication?

C H A P T E R   2 0

Managing Desktop Configurations Using Group Policy and Remote Installation Services

About This Chapter

Maintaining consistent desktop configurations is one method of reducing the total cost of ownership (TCO) of computer systems. Consistent configurations make those systems easier to update, maintain, and troubleshoot. With Active Directory directory service installed, there are a couple of methods (listed below) you can use to maintain desktop configurations:

- Group Policy
- Remote Installation Services (RIS)

Administrators can use Group Policy to manage desktop configurations for groups of computers and users. Group Policy is very flexible and includes options for registry–based policy settings, security settings, application management, scripts, computer startup and shutdown, logon and logoff, and folder redirection. Microsoft Windows 2000 Server includes hundreds of Group Policy settings you can configure.

You can use RIS to set up new client computers remotely without the need to physically visit each client workstation. Specifically, you can install an operating system (OS) on a remote boot–enabled client computer by connecting the computer to the network, starting the client computer, and logging on with a valid user account.

This chapter explains the use of both group policies and RIS.

Before You Begin

As an experienced Windows NT 4.0 professional, you should already have many of the skills needed to manage Active Directory. These include:

- Setting up users and groups
- Securing network resources

To complete this chapter, you must also have

- Installed Windows 2000 Server on a computer (Server01)

  See Chapter 8, "Installing Microsoft Windows 2000" for more details.

- Configured the computer (Server01) as a domain controller in a domain
- Experience logging on and off Microsoft Windows 2000
- Knowledge about the Active Directory naming conventions

- Obtained the knowledge and skills necessary to set up Microsoft Management Console snap-ins (MMCs)

- Installed Active Directory using the exercises in Chapter 17, "Installing and Configuring Active Directory Directory Service"

- Completed the exercises and obtained the knowledge and skills covered in Chapter 19, "Managing Active Directory Components"

Lesson 1: Implementing Group Policy

You can use Group Policy to establish configuration settings for your organization. This lesson guides you through the steps of implementing a group policy using the Group Policy tab and the Group Policy snap-in. You also learn how to modify a group policy.

After this lesson, you will be able to

- Implement a group policy
- Modify a group policy

Estimated lesson time: 60 minutes

Implementing Group Policy

The tasks for implementing Group Policy are

1. Creating a group policy object (GPO)
2. Creating a console for the GPO
3. Delegating administrative control of the GPO
4. Specifying Group Policy settings for the GPO
5. Disabling unused Group Policy settings
6. Indicating any GPO processing exceptions
7. Filtering the scope of the GPO
8. Linking the GPO to a site, domain, or organizational unit (OU)

Creating a GPO

The first step in implementing a group policy is to create a GPO. Recall that a GPO is a collection of Group Policy settings.

▶ **Follow these steps to create a GPO:**

1. Determine the type of GPO you want to create.

- To create a GPO linked to a domain or an OU, open Active Directory Users And Computers.

- To create a GPO linked to a site, open Active Directory Sites And Services.

2. Right-click the site, domain, or OU for which you want to create a GPO, click Properties, and select the Group Policy tab (see Figure 20.1).

3. Click New, and then type the name you would like to use for this GPO.

   By default, the new GPO is linked to the site, domain, or OU that was selected in the MMC when it was created and its settings apply to that site, domain, or OU.

4. Click Close.

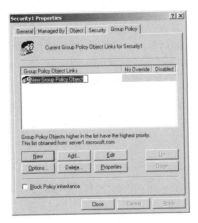

Figure 20.1 Group Policy tab

Creating a GPO Console

After you create a GPO, you should add the Group Policy snap-in to an MMC and create a standalone GPO console. After saving the console, you can open it whenever necessary from the Administrative Tools menu.

Delegating Administrative Control of a GPO

After you create a GPO, it is important to determine which groups of administrators have access permissions to the GPO. The default permissions on GPOs are shown in Table 20.1.

Table 20.1   Default GPO Permissions

Security group	Default settings
Authenticated Users	Read, Apply Group Policy, Special Permissions
CREATOR OWNER	Special Permissions

continues

Table 20.1   Default GPO Permissions *(continued)*

Security group	Default settings
Domain Administrators	Read, Write, Create All Child Objects, Delete All Child Objects, Special Permissions
Enterprise Administrators	Read, Write, Create All Child Objects, Delete All Child Objects, Special Permissions
SYSTEM	Read, Write, Create All Child Objects, Delete All Child Objects, Special Permissions

By default, the Default Domain Policy GPO cannot be deleted by any administrator. This prevents the accidental deletion of this GPO, which contains important required settings for the domain.

If you are working with a GPO from a pre-built console, such as the Active Directory Users And Computers, the Delegation Of Control wizard is not available for use in delegating administrative control of a GPO; it only controls security of an object.

▶   **Follow these steps to delegate administrative control of a GPO:**

1. Access the Group Policy snap-in for the GPO.

2. Right-click the Root node of the console and click Properties.

3. Click the Security tab (see Figure 20.2), and then click the security group for which you want to allow or deny administrative access to the GPO.

   If you need to change the list of security groups for which you want to allow or deny administrative access to the GPO, you can add or remove security groups using Add and Remove.

4. To provide administrative control of all aspects of the GPO, set the Read permission to Allow and set the Write permission to Allow.

   A user or administrator who has Read access but does not have Write access to a GPO cannot use the Group Policy snap-in to see the settings that it contains. All extensions to the Group Policy snap-in require Write access to open a GPO.

5. Click OK.

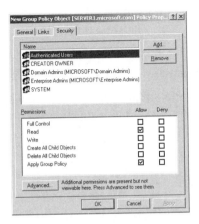

Figure 20.2 GPO Properties Security tab

Specifying Group Policy Settings

After you create a GPO and determine the administrators who have access permissions to the GPO, you can specify the Group Policy settings.

▶ **Follow these steps to specify Group Policy settings for a GPO:**

1. Access the Group Policy snap-in for the GPO (see Figure 20.3).

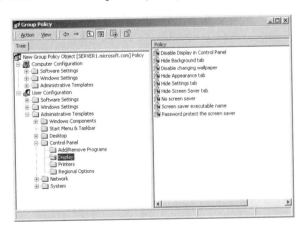

Figure 20.3 Group Policy snap-in

2. In the console tree, expand the item that represents the particular policy you want to set.

   For example, in Figure 20.3, User Configuration, Administrative Templates, and Control Panel were expanded, and then Display was expanded.

3. In the details pane, right-click the policy that you want to set, and then click Properties. In Figure 20.4, the Hide Screen Saver Tab policy was selected in the details pane.

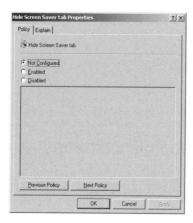

Figure 20.4 Hide Screen Saver Tab Properties dialog box

4. Click Enabled to apply the policy to users or computers that are subject to this GPO, and then click OK.

   Not Configured indicates that no change will be made to the registry regarding this setting. Disabled indicates that the registry will indicate that the policy does not apply to users or computers that are subject to this GPO.

Disabling Unused Group Policy Settings

If, under the Computer Configuration or User Configuration node of the console, a GPO has only settings that are Not Configured, you can avoid processing those settings by disabling the node. This expedites startup and logon for those users and computers subject to the GPO.

▶ **Follow these steps to disable the Computer Configuration or User Configuration settings for a GPO:**

1. Access the Group Policy snap-in for the GPO.

2. Right-click the Root node of the console and click Properties.

3. In the General tab in the Properties dialog box:

   ▪ To disable the Computer Configuration settings, click the Disable Computer Configuration Settings check box.

   ▪ To disable the User Configuration settings, click the Disable User Configuration Settings check box.

4. Click OK.

Indicating GPO Processing Exceptions

GPOs are processed according to the Active Directory hierarchy: first the local GPO, then the site GPOs, domain GPOs, and finally the OU GPOs. However, you can change the default order of processing Group Policy settings. You do so by modifying the order of GPOs for an object, specifying the Block Policy Inheritance option, specifying the No Override option, or enabling the Loopback setting.

▶ **Follow these steps to modify the order of GPOs for an object:**

1. Open Active Directory Users And Computers to set the order of GPOs for a domain or OU, or open Active Directory Sites And Services to modify the order of GPOs for a site.

2. In the console tree, right-click the site, domain, or OU for which you want to modify the GPO order, click Properties, and then click the Group Policy tab.

3. In the Group Policy Object Links list, select the GPO and click the Up button (as shown in Figure 20.5) or the Down button to change the priority for a GPO for this site, domain, or OU. Windows 2000 processes GPOs from the top of the list to the bottom of the list.

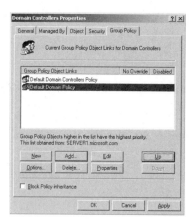

Figure 20.5 Modifying the order of GPOs

▶ **Follow these steps to specify the Block Policy Inheritance option:**

1. Open Active Directory Users And Computers to specify the Block Policy Inheritance option for a domain or OU, or open Active Directory Sites And Services to specify the Block Policy Inheritance option for a site.

2. In the console tree, right-click the site, domain, or OU for which you want to specify the Block Policy Inheritance option, click Properties, and then click the Group Policy tab.

3. Select the Block Policy Inheritance check box to specify that all GPOs linked to higher level sites, domains, or OUs should be blocked from linking to this site, domain, or OU. You cannot block GPOs that use the No Override option.

▶ **Follow these steps to specify the No Override option:**

1. Open Active Directory Users And Computers to specify the No Override option for a domain or OU, or open Active Directory Sites And Services to specify the No Override option for a site.

2. In the console, right-click the site, domain, or OU to which the GPO is linked, click Properties, and then click the Group Policy tab.

3. Select the GPO, click Options, select the No Override check box in the Options dialog box (see Figure 20.6) to specify that other GPOs should be prevented from overriding settings in this GPO, and then click OK.

Figure 20.6 Options dialog box

▶ **Follow these steps to enable the Loopback setting:**

1. Access the Group Policy snap-in for the GPO.

2. In the console tree, expand Computer Configuration, Administrative Templates, System, and Group Policy.

3. In the details pane, double-click User Group Policy Loopback Processing Mode.

4. In the User Group Policy Loopback Processing Mode Properties dialog box, click Enabled.

5. Select one of the following modes in the Mode list:

   - **Replace.** Use this to replace the GPO list for the user with the GPO list already obtained for the computer at computer startup.

   - **Merge.** Use this to append the GPO list obtained for the user at logon with the GPO list already obtained for the computer at computer startup.

6. Click OK.

Filtering GPO Scope

The policies in a GPO apply only to users who have Read and Apply Group Policy permissions for that GPO. You can filter the scope of a GPO by creating security groups and then assigning Read and Apply Group Policy permissions to the selected groups. Thus, you can prevent a policy from applying to a specific group by denying that group Read and Apply Group Policy permissions to the GPO.

► **Follow these steps to filter the scope of a GPO:**

1. Access the Group Policy snap-in for the GPO.

2. Right-click the Root node of the console, and then click Properties.

3. Click the Security tab (see Figure 20.7), and then click the security group through which to filter this GPO.

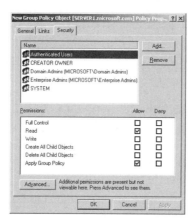

Figure 20.7 Security tab of the GPO properties dialog box

If you need to change the list of security groups through which to filter this GPO, you can add or remove security groups using Add and Remove.

4. Set the permissions as shown in Table 20.2, and then click OK.

Table 20.2   Permissions for GPO Scopes

GPO scope	Set these permissions	Result
Members of this security group should have this GPO applied to them.	Set Apply Group Policy (AGP) to Allow. Set Read to Allow.	This GPO applies to members of this security group unless they are members of at least one other security group that has AGP set to Deny, or Read set to Deny, or both.
Members of this security group are exempt from this GPO.	Set AGP to Deny. Set Read to Deny.	This GPO never applies to members of this security group regardless of the permissions those members have in other security groups.
Membership in this security group is irrelevant to whether the GPO should be applied.	Set AGP to neither Allow nor Deny. Set Read to neither Allow nor Deny.	This GPO applies to members of this security group only if they have both AGP and Read set to Allow as members of at least one other security group. They also must not have AGP or Read set to Deny as members of any other security group.

Linking a GPO

By default, a new GPO is linked to the site, domain, or OU that was selected in the MMC when it was created. Therefore, its settings apply to that site, domain, or OU. Use the Group Policy tab for the site, domain, or OU properties to link a GPO to additional sites, domains, or OUs.

▶ **Follow these steps to link a GPO to a site, domain, or OU:**

1. Open Active Directory Users And Computers to link a GPO to a domain or OU, or open Active Directory Sites And Services to link a GPO to a site.

2. In the console, right-click the site, domain, or OU to which the GPO should be linked.

3. Click Properties, and then click the Group Policy tab.

4. If the GPO already appears in the Group Policy Object Links list, then click Cancel. If the GPO does not appear in the Group Policy Object Links list, then click Add.

5. In the Add A Group Policy Object Link dialog box (see Figure 20.8), click the All tab, click the desired GPO, and then click OK.

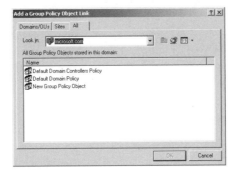

Figure 20.8 Add A Group Policy Object Link dialog box

6. In the Properties dialog box for the site, domain, or OU, click OK.

Modifying Group Policy

The following is the sequence of tasks used to modify Group Policy:

1. Removing a GPO link

2. Deleting a GPO

3. Editing a GPO and GPO settings

Removing a GPO Link

Removing a GPO link simply unlinks the GPO from the specified site, domain, or OU. The GPO remains in Active Directory until it is deleted.

▶ **Follow these steps to remove a GPO link:**

1. Open Active Directory Users And Computers to unlink a GPO from a domain or OU, or open Active Directory Sites And Services to unlink a GPO from a site.

2. In the console, right-click the site, domain, or OU from which the GPO should be unlinked.

3. Click Properties, and then click the Group Policy tab.

4. In the Group Policy tab, select the GPO that you want to unlink, and then click Delete.

5. In the Delete dialog box, click Remove The Link From The List.

   The GPO remains in Active Directory but is no longer linked.

Deleting a GPO

If you delete a GPO, it is removed from Active Directory, and any sites, domains, or OUs to which it is linked will no longer be affected by it. You may wish to take the less drastic step of removing the GPO link, which disassociates the GPO from its OU but leaves the GPO intact in Active Directory.

▶ **Follow these steps to delete a GPO:**

1. Open Active Directory Users And Computers to delete a GPO from a domain or OU, or open Active Directory Sites And Services to delete a GPO from a site.

2. In the console, right-click the site, domain, or OU from which the GPO should be deleted.

3. Click Properties, and then click the Group Policy tab.

4. In the Group Policy tab, select the GPO that you want to delete, and then click Delete.

5. In the Delete dialog box, click Remove The Link And Delete The Group Policy Object Permanently, and then click OK.

   The GPO is removed from Active Directory.

Editing a GPO and GPO Settings

To edit a GPO or its settings, follow the procedures outlined earlier in this lesson for creating a GPO and for specifying Group Policy settings.

Practice: Implementing a Group Policy

In this practice, you implement a Group Policy for your domain. In Exercises 1 through 8, you create a GPO, create a GPO console, delegate administrative control of the GPO, specify Group Policy settings for the GPO, disable unused Group Policy settings, indicate a GPO processing exception, filter the scope of the GPO, and link the GPO to an additional OU. In Exercise 9, you test the Group Policy.

Exercise 1: Creating a GPO

In this exercise, you create a GPO at the OU level.

1. Log on to the domain as Administrator.

2. Click Start, point to Programs, point to Administrative Tools, and then click Active Directory Users And Computers.

3. Double-click microsoft.com (or the name of the domain you have created).

4. Create a new OU called Dispatch.

5. Right-click the Dispatch OU, click Properties, and then select the Group Policy tab.

6. Click New, and then type **DispatchPolicy** to name this GPO.

7. Click Close.

Exercise 2: Creating a GPO Console

In this exercise, you create a console for the DispatchPolicy GPO. After saving it, you can open it whenever necessary from the Administrative Tools menu.

1. Click Start, and then point to Run.

   The Run dialog box appears.

2. Type **mmc** in the Open box, and then click OK.

   A new MMC appears.

3. From the Console menu, click Add/Remove Snap-In.

   The Add/Remove Snap-In dialog box appears.

4. Click Add.

   The Add Standalone Snap-In dialog box appears.

5. Select Group Policy, and then click Add.

   The Select Group Policy Object page appears.

6. Click Browse to find the DispatchPolicy GPO.

   The Browse For A Group Policy Object dialog box appears.

7. Click the All tab, click the DispatchPolicy GPO, and then click OK.

   The Select Group Policy Object page appears with DispatchPolicy in the Group Policy Object box.

8. Click Finish, and then click Close on the Add Standalone Snap-In dialog box.

9. Click OK on the Add/Remove Snap-In dialog box.

10. On the Console menu, click Save As.

    The Save As dialog box appears.

11. Type **DispatchPolicy GPO** in the File Name box, and then click Save.

    The DispatchPolicy GPO is now available on the Administrative Tools menu.

Exercise 3: Delegating Administrative Control of a GPO

In this exercise you delegate administrative control for the DispatchPolicy GPO to the Administrators group.

1. Access the DispatchPolicy GPO console.

2. Right-click the Root node of the console, DispatchPolicy [server1.microsoft.com] Policy, click Properties, and then click the Security tab.

   The DispatchPolicy [server1.microsoft.com] Policy Properties dialog box appears.

3. Add the Administrators group using the Add button.

4. To provide administrative control of all aspects of the GPO to the Administrators group, set Read, Write, Create All Child Objects, and Delete All Child Objects to Allow for the group.

5. Click OK.

Exercise 4: Specifying Group Policy Settings

In this exercise, you specify some Group Policy settings for the DispatchPolicy GPO.

1. In the DispatchPolicy GPO console, in the console tree, expand the Root node of the console.

2. Click User Configuration, and then click Administrative Templates.

3. In the console tree, click Start Menu & Task Bar.

   What appears in the details pane?

4. In the details pane, double-click Remove Search Menu From Start Menu.

   The Remove Search Menu From Start Menu Properties dialog box appears.

5. Click Enabled, and then click OK.

   How can you tell at a glance that this setting is enabled?

6. Repeat Steps 4 and 5 to enable the Remove Run Menu From Start Menu policy (still under User Configuration).

7. In the console tree, double-click System, and then click Logon/Logoff.

   The policies available for this category appear in the details pane.

8. In the details pane, enable the Disable Lock Computer policy and click OK.

Exercise 5: Disabling Unused Group Policy Settings

In this exercise, you disable the Computer Configuration node of the console, as this node contains only settings that are not configured. This expedites startup for those users and computers subject to the GPO.

1. On the DispatchPolicy GPO console, right-click the Root node of the console, and then click Properties.

    The DispatchPolicy [server1.microsoft.com] Policy Properties dialog box appears.

2. In the General tab, click Disable Computer Configuration Settings.

    The Confirm Disable message box appears, asking you to confirm that you want to disable the Computer Configuration settings.

3. Click Yes, and then click OK.

Exercise 6: Indicating GPO Processing Exceptions

In this exercise, you set the No Override option to prevent other GPOs from overriding the policies set in the DispatchPolicy GPO.

1. Click Start, point to Programs, point to Administrative Tools, and then click Active Directory Users And Computers.

2. Right-click the Dispatch OU, and then click Properties.

    The Dispatch Properties dialog box appears.

3. Click the Group Policy tab, click the DispatchPolicy GPO, and then click Options.

    The DispatchPolicy Options dialog box appears.

4. Select the No Override check box, and then click OK.

5. In the Dispatch Properties dialog box, click OK.

Exercise 7: Filtering GPO Scope

In this exercise, you prevent a policy from applying to the Sales security group by denying that group Read permission to the GPO. You created the Sales group and its members in Chapter 7, "Managing Security."

1. In the DispatchPolicy GPO console, right-click the Root node of the console, and then click Properties.

   The DispatchPolicy [server1.microsoft.com] Policy Properties dialog box appears.

2. Click the Security tab, and then click the Sales security group. Add the Sales group using the Add button.

3. For the Sales group, set Apply Group Policy to Deny and set Read to Deny, and then click OK.

   The Security message box appears, asking you to confirm that you want to prevent the DispatchPolicy from applying to the Sales group.

4. Click Yes.

Exercise 8: Linking a GPO

By default, the DispatchPolicy GPO is linked and its settings apply to the Dispatch OU. In this exercise, you link the DispatchPolicy GPO to the Security1 OU you created in Chapter 19, "Managing Active Directory Components."

1. Click Start, point to Programs, point to Administrative Tools, and then click Active Directory Users And Computers.

2. Right-click the Security1 OU, and then click Properties.

   The Security1 Properties dialog box appears.

3. Click the Group Policy tab, and then click Add.

   The Add A Group Policy Object Link dialog box appears.

4. Click the All tab, click the DispatchPolicy GPO, and then click OK.

5. In the Security1 Properties dialog box, click OK.

Exercise 9: Testing a GPO

In this exercise, you view the effects of the Group Policy implemented in the previous exercises.

1. Log on as Assistant1, a member of the Security1 OU.

2. Press Ctrl+Alt+Delete.

   The Windows Security dialog box appears.

   Are you able to lock the workstation? Why?

3. Click Cancel, and then click Start.

   Does the Search command appear on the Start menu?

   Does the Run command appear on the Start menu?

4. Log off as Assistant1, and then log on as Administrator.

5. Make Assistant1 a member of the Sales security group.

6. Log off as Administrator, and then log on as Assistant1.

7. Press Ctrl+Alt+Delete.

   Are you able to lock the workstation? Why?

8. Log off the computer.

Lesson Summary

In this lesson, you learned the tasks involved with implementing Group Policy. The tasks are creating a GPO; creating a GPO console; delegating administrative control of the GPO; specifying Group Policy settings for the GPO; disabling unused Group Policy settings; indicating GPO processing exceptions; filtering the scope of the GPO; and linking the GPO to a site, domain, or OU.

In the practice portion of this lesson, you implemented a Group Policy for your domain. You created a GPO, created a console for the GPO, delegated administrative control of the GPO, specified Group Policy settings for the GPO, disabled unused Group Policy settings, set the No Override option for the GPO, filtered the scope of the GPO, and linked the GPO to an additional OU. Finally, you tested the effects of the GPO.

Lesson 2: Managing Software Using Group Policy

The Software Installation extension, a software management feature of Windows 2000, is the administrator's primary tool for managing software within an organization. Managing software using Software Installation provides your users with immediate access to the software they need to perform their jobs and ensures that users have an easy and consistent experience when working with software throughout its life cycle. Users no longer need to look for a network share, use a CD-ROM, or install, fix, and upgrade software themselves. This lesson walks you through the steps for implementing Software Installation.

After this lesson, you will be able to

- Deploy software using Group Policy
- Configure deployment options
- Maintain software using Group Policy

Estimated lesson time: 75 minutes

Software Management Tools

Three tools are provided with Windows 2000 Server for software installation and maintenance. Table 20.3 describes these tools.

Table 20.3   Windows 2000 Software Installation and Maintenance Tools

Tool	Role
The Software Installation extension of the Group Policy snap-in	Used by administrators to manage software
Windows Installer	Installs software packaged in Windows Installer files
Add/Remove Programs in Control Panel	Used by users to manage software on their own computers

The Software Installation Extension

The Software Installation extension is the administrator's primary tool for managing software within an organization. Software Installation works in conjunction with Group Policy and Active Directory, establishing a Group Policy–based software management system that allows you to centrally manage the following tasks:

- Initial deployment of software.

- Mandatory and nonmandatory upgrades, patches, and quick fixes for software. You can update a version of the software or replace it. You can even upgrade the OS using service packs.

- Removal of software.

Using Software Installation, you can centrally manage the installation of software on a client computer by assigning applications to users or computers or by publishing applications for users. *Assign* required or mandatory software to users or to computers. *Publish* software that users might find useful to perform their jobs.

Assigning Applications

When you assign an application to a user, the application is advertised to the user the next time he or she logs on to a workstation. The application advertisement follows the user regardless of which physical computer he or she actually uses. This application is installed the first time the user activates the application on the computer, either by selecting the application on the Start menu or by activating a document associated with the application.

When you assign an application to the computer, the application is advertised and the installation is performed when it is safe to do so. Typically this happens when the computer starts up so that there are no competing processes on the computer.

Publishing Applications

When you publish the application to users, the application does not appear installed on the users' computers. No shortcuts are visible on the desktop or Start menu, and no changes are made to the local registry on the users' computers. Instead, published applications store their advertisement attributes in Active Directory. Then, information such as the application's name and file associations is exposed to the users in the Active Directory container. The application is then available for the user to install using Add/Remove Programs in Control Panel or by clicking a file associated with the application (such as an .xls file for Microsoft Excel).

How Software Installation Works

The Software Installation extension uses Windows Installer technology to systematically maintain software. Windows Installer is a service that allows the OS to manage the installation process. Windows Installer is composed of three key parts:

- An OS service that performs the installation, modification, and removal of the software in accordance with the information in the Windows Installer package

- The Windows Installer package, a database containing information that describes the installed state of the application

- An application programming interface (API) that allows applications to interact with Windows Installer to install or remove additional features of the application after the initial installation is complete

Because Software Installation takes advantage of Windows Installer, users can take advantage of self-repairing applications. Windows Installer notes when a program file is missing and immediately reinstalls the damaged or missing files, thereby fixing the application.

The Windows Installer package is a file that contains explicit instructions on the installation and removal of specific applications. The developer who produces the application provides the Windows Installer package .msi file and ships it with the application. If a Windows Installer package does not come with an application, you might need to create a Windows Installer package, or repackage the application, using a third-party tool.

You can only deploy software using the Software Installation extension if the file type fits one of the following categories:

- Native Windows Installer package (.msi) files are developed as a part of the application and take full advantage of the Windows Installer.

- Repackaged application (.msi) files allow you to repackage applications that do not have a native Windows Installer package in much the same way that you repackage software today to customize installations.

- An existing setup program—an application (.zap) file—installs an application by using its original SETUP.EXE program.

In addition, you can make modifications to customize the installation of a Windows Installer package at the time of assignment or publication. Modifications are saved with the .mst file extension.

Other files you may encounter during Software Installation are

- Patch (.msp) files, which are used for bug fixes, service packs, and similar files
- Application assignment scripts (.aas files), which contain instructions associated with the assignment or publication of a package

Customizing Windows Installer Packages

You can customize Windows Installer applications by using *modifications*, also called *transforms*. The Windows Installer package format provides for customization by allowing you to "transform" the original package using authoring and repackaging tools. Some applications also provide wizards or templates that permit a user to create modifications.

For example, Microsoft Office 2000 supplies a Customization wizard that builds modifications. Using the Microsoft Office 2000 Customization wizard, you can create a modification that allows you to manage the configuration of Microsoft Office 2000 that is deployed to users. A modification might be designed to accommodate Microsoft Word as a key feature, installing it during the first installation. Less popular features, such as revision support or document translators, could be installed on first usage, and other features, such as clip art, might not be installed at all. You might have another modification that provides all of the features of Word and does not install Microsoft PowerPoint. The exact mix of which features to install and when to install them varies based on the audience for the application and how they use the software.

Implementing Software Installation

The following is the sequences of tasks used to implement software installation:

1. Planning and preparing the software installation
2. Setting up a software distribution point
3. Specifying software installation defaults
4. Deploying software applications
5. Setting automatic installation options
6. Setting up application categories
7. Setting software application properties
8. Maintaining software applications

Planning and Preparing a Software Installation

When planning a software installation, you should do the following:

- Review your organization's software requirements on the basis of your overall organizational structure within Active Directory and your available GPOs.

- Determine how you want to deploy your applications.

- Create a pilot to test how you want to assign or publish software to users or computers.

- Prepare your software using a format that allows you to manage it based on what your organization requires, and test all of the Windows Installer packages or repackaged software.

Table 20.4 describes strategies and considerations for implementing a software installation. Some of these strategies might seem contradictory, but select the strategies that meet your business goals.

Table 20.4   Strategies and Considerations for Implementing Software Installation

Strategy	Considerations
Create OUs based on software management needs.	Allows you to target applications to the appropriate set of users. Group Policy security settings are not required to target the appropriate set of users.
Deploy software close to the root in the Active Directory tree.	Makes it easy to provide all users in an organization with access to an application. This reduces administration because you can deploy a single GPO rather than having to re-create that object in multiple containers deep in the Active Directory tree.
Deploy multiple applications with a single GPO.	Reduces administration overhead by allowing you to create and manage a single GPO rather than multiple GPOs. The logon process is faster because a single GPO deploying 10 applications processes faster than 10 GPOs each deploying one application. This is appropriate in organizations where users share the same core set of applications.
Publish or assign one application only once in the same GPO or in a series of GPOs that might apply to a single user or computer.	Makes it easier to determine which instance of the application applies to the user or computer.

Software licenses are required for software written by independent software vendors and distributed using software distribution points (SDPs). It is your responsibility to match the number of users who can access software to the number of licenses you have on hand. It is also your responsibility to verify that you are working within the guidelines provided by each independent software vendor with the software.

Gather the package formats for the software and perform any necessary modifications to the packages.

Setting Up an SDP

After you have planned and prepared for software management, the next step is to copy the software to one or more SDPs, network locations from which people are able to get the software that they need.

▶ **Follow these steps to set up an SDP:**

1. Create the folders for the software on the file server that will be the SDP and make the folders network shares.

2. Replicate the software to the SDPs by placing or copying the software, packages, modifications, all necessary files, and components to a distri-bution share(s). Place all software (the package and all related installa-tion files) in a separate folder on the SDP.

3. Set the appropriate permissions on the folders so that only administrators can change the files (Read and Write) and users can only read the files from the SDP folders and shares. Use Group Policy to manage the software within the appropriate GPO.

Note Some software supports special commands to facilitate the creation of an SDP. For example, Microsoft Office 2000 should be prepared by running SETUP /A from a command prompt. This allows you to enter the software key once for all users, and the network share (SDP) location to copy the files to. Other software might have other ways to expand any compressed files from the distribution media and transfer the files to the appropriate location.

Specifying Software Installation Defaults

A GPO can contain several settings that affect how an application is installed, managed, and removed. You can globally define the default settings for the new packages within the GPO in the General tab of the Software Installation Properties dialog box. Some of these settings can be changed later by editing the package properties in the Software Installation extension.

▶ **Follow these steps to specify software installation defaults:**

1. Open the Group Policy snap-in, and then in Computer Or User Configuration, open Software Settings.

2. Right-click the Software Installation node, and then click Properties.

3. In the General tab of the Software Installation Properties dialog box (see Figure 20.9), type the path to the default SDP for packages (.msi files) in the Default Package Location box.

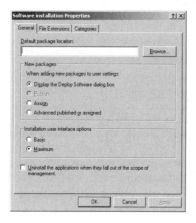

Figure 20.9 General tab of the Software Installation Properties dialog box

4. In the New Packages section, select one of the following:

- **Display The Deploy Software Dialog Box.** Choose this to specify that when you add a new package, the Deploy Software dialog box will display, allowing you to assign, publish, or configure package properties.

- **Publish.** Choose this to specify that when you add a new package, by default you want it published with standard package properties. Packages can only be published to users, not computers. If this is an installation under the Computer Configuration node of the Group Policy snap-in, the Publish choice appears dimmed.

- **Assign.** Choose this to specify that when you add a new package by default, you want it assigned with standard package properties. Packages can be assigned to users and computers.

- **Advanced Published Or Assigned.** Choose this to specify that when you add a new package, the Configure Package Properties form should appear.

5. In the Installation User Interface Options section, select one of the following:

- **Basic.** Choose this to provide only a basic display of the install process.

- **Maximum.** Choose this to provide all installation messages and screens during the package installation.

6. Check the Uninstall The Applications When They Fall Out Of The Scope Of Management check box to specify that the package should be removed when the GPO no longer applies to users or computers.

7. Click OK.

Deploying Software Applications

Given that software can be either assigned or published and may be targeted to users or computers, you can establish a workable combination to meet your software management goals. Table 20.5 details the different approaches to software deployment.

Table 20.5   Software Deployment Approaches

	Publish (user only)	Assign (user)	Assign (computer)
After deployment, the software is available for installation after	The next logon	The next logon	The next time the computer starts
Typically the user installs the software from	Add/Remove Programs in Control Panel	Start menu or Desktop shortcut	The software is already installed (the software automatically installs when the computer reboots)
If the software is not installed, and the user opens a file associated with the software, does the software install?	Yes (if auto-install is turned on)	Yes	Does not apply; the software is already installed
Can the user remove the software using Add/Remove Programs in Control Panel?	Yes, and the user can choose to install it again from Add/Remove Programs in Control Panel	Yes, and the software is available for installation again from the typical install points	No. Only the local administrator can remove the software; a user can run a repair on the software
Supported installation files are	Windows Installer packages, .zap files	Windows Installer packages	Windows Installer packages

Modifications, or .mst files, are customizations applied to Windows Installer packages. A modification must be applied at the time of assignment or publication, not at the time of installation.

Assigning Applications

Assign an application when you want everyone to have the application on his or her computer. An application can be published to both computers and users.

▶ **Follow these steps to assign applications:**

1. Open the Group Policy snap-in, and then, in Computer Or User Configuration, open Software Settings.

2. Right-click the Software Installation node, click New, and click Package.

   The File Name list in the Open dialog box shows those Windows Installer packages located at the SDP you specified as the default. If the Windows Installer package is located on a different network share, you can browse to find the SDP for the package.

3. In the File Name list in the Open dialog box, select the Windows Installer package to be assigned, and then click Open.

4. In the Deploy Software dialog box (see Figure 20.10), click Assigned, and then click OK. If this is an application under the Computer Configuration node of the Group Policy snap-in, the Published choice appears dimmed, because packages can only be assigned to computers, not published.

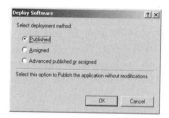

Figure 20.10 Deploy Software dialog box

Publishing Applications

Publish an application when you want the application to be available to people managed by the GPO, should they want the application. With published applications, it is up to each person to decide whether or not to install the published application. An application can only be published to users.

▶   **Follow these steps to publish applications:**

1. Open the Group Policy snap-in. In User Configuration, open Software Settings.

2. Right-click the Software Installation node, click New, and then click Package.

   The File Name list in the Open dialog box shows those packages located at the SDP you specified as the default. If the Windows Installer package is located on a different network share, you can browse to find the SDP for the package.

3. In the File Name list in the Open dialog box, select the Windows Installer package to be published, and then click Open.

4. In the Deploy Software dialog box (see Figure 20.10), click Published, and then click OK.

   The application is available for users to install either by using Add/ Remove Programs in Control Panel or by opening a file with a file name extension that you have associated with the application.

Deploying Applications with Modifications

Modifications are associated with the Windows Installer package at deployment time rather than when the Windows Installer is actually using the package to install or modify the application. Modifications (.mst files) are applied to Windows Installer packages (which have the .msi extension) in an order specified by the administrator. This order must be determined before the application is assigned or published.

▶   **Follow these steps to add or remove modifications for applications:**

1. Open the Group Policy snap-in. In Computer Or User Configuration, open Software Settings.

2. Right-click the Software Installation node, click New, and then click Package.

3. In the File Name list in the Open dialog box, select the Windows Installer package to be published, and then click Open.

4. In the Deploy Software dialog box, click Advanced Published Or Assigned, and then click OK.

5. In the Properties dialog box for the package, click the Modifications tab (see Figure 20.11).

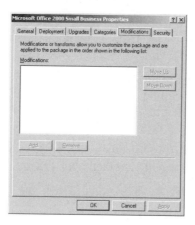

Figure 20.11 Modifications tab of the Properties dialog box

- To add modifications, click Add. In the Open dialog box, browse to find the modification file (.mst), and then click Open. You can add multiple modifications.

- To remove modifications, click the modification you want to remove, and then click Remove. Repeat until each unwanted modification has been removed.

- To set the order of modifications, select a modification and then click Move Up or Move Down. Modifications are applied according to the order specified in the list.

6. Make sure that the modifications are configured exactly the way you want them, and then click OK.

Important Do not click OK until you have finished configuring the modifications. When you click OK, the package is assigned or published immediately. If the modifications are not properly configured, you will have to uninstall the package or upgrade the package with a correctly configured version.

Setting Automatic Installation Options

To determine which application users install when they select a file, you can select a file extension and configure a priority for installing applications associated with the file extension using the File Extensions tab in the Software Installation Properties dialog box. The first application listed is the application installed in association with the file extension.

For example, if you use a GPO to deploy both Microsoft Word 2000 and Microsoft FrontPage 2000, both of these applications can edit HyperText Markup Language (HTML) documents, files with the .htm extension. To configure the file extension priority so that users who are managed by this GPO always install Microsoft FrontPage, set FrontPage as the application with the highest priority for the .htm extension. When users managed by this GPO who have installed neither Microsoft Word 2000 nor Microsoft FrontPage 2000 receive an .htm file (by e-mail or other means) and they double-click on the .htm file, Software Installation installs FrontPage 2000 and opens the .htm file for editing. Without Software Installation, the user would see the Open With dialog box and be asked to select the best alternative from the software already present on his or her computer.

File extension associations are managed on a per-GPO basis. Changing the priority order in a GPO affects only those users who have that GPO applied to them.

▶   **Follow these steps to set automatic installation options based on file name extension:**

1. Open the Group Policy snap-in. In Computer Or User Configuration, open Software Settings.

2. Right-click the Software Installation node, and then click Properties.

3. In the File Extensions tab of the Software Installation Properties dialog box (see Figure 20.12), select the file extension for which you want to specify an automatic software installation from the Select File Extension list.

4. In the Application Precedence list box, move the application with the highest precedence by default to the top of the list using the Up or Down buttons. The application at the top of the list is automatically installed if a document with the selected file name extension is invoked before the application has been installed.

5. Click OK.

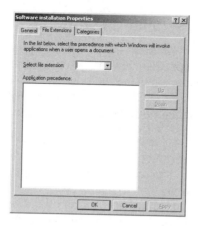

Figure 20.12 File Extensions tab of the Software Installation Properties dialog box

Setting Up Application Categories

You can organize assigned and published applications into logical categories to make it easier for users to locate the appropriate application from within Add/Remove Programs in Control Panel. Windows 2000 does not ship with any predefined categories.

The categories that you establish are per domain, not per GPO. You only need to define them once for the whole domain.

▶ **Follow these steps to set up categories for applications to be managed:**

1. Open the Group Policy snap-in. In Computer Or User Configuration, open Software Settings.

2. Right-click the Software Installation node, and then click Properties.

3. In the Categories tab of the Software Installation Properties dialog box (see Figure 20.13), click Add.

4. In the Enter New Category dialog box, type the name of the application category in the Category box and click OK.

5. On the Software Installation Properties dialog box, click OK.

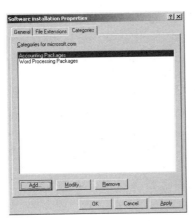

Figure 20.13 Categories tab of the Software Installation Properties dialog box

Setting Software Application Properties

You can fine-tune each application by editing installation options, specifying application categories to be used, and setting permissions for the software installation.

Editing Installation Options for Applications

Although you may have globally defined the default settings for new packages within the GPO in the General tab of the Software Installation Properties dialog box, some of these same settings can be changed later by editing the package properties. Installation options affect how an application is installed, managed, and removed.

▶ **Follow these steps to edit installation options for applications:**

1. Open the Group Policy snap-in. In Computer Or User Configuration, open Software Settings.

2. Click the Software Installation node.

3. In the details pane, right-click the application for which you want to edit installation options, and then click Properties.

4. In the Deployment tab of the Properties dialog box for the application (see Figure 20.14), select one of the following in the Deployment Type area:

- **Published** to allow users in the selected site, domain, or OU to install the application using either Add/Remove Programs in Control Panel or the application installation by file activation.

- **Assigned** to allow users in the selected site, domain, or OU to receive this application the next time they log on (for assignment to users) or when the computer restarts (for assignment to computers).

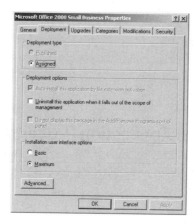

Figure 20.14 Deployment tab of the Properties dialog box

5. In the Deployment Options area, select one of the following:

- **Auto-Install This Application By File Extension Activation.** Choose this to use the application precedence for the file name extension as determined in the File Extensions tab of the Software Installation Properties dialog box. If this is an application under the Computer Configuration node of the Group Policy snap-in, the check box appears dimmed and selected, because by default the application is installed automatically.

- **Uninstall This Application When It Falls Out Of The Scope Of Management.** Choose this to remove the application at logon (for users) or startup (for computers) if they move to a site, domain, or OU for which the application is not deployed.

- **Do Not Display This Package In The Add/Remove Programs Control Panel.** Choose this to specify that this package should not be displayed in Add/Remove Programs in Control Panel.

6. In the Installation User Interface Options area, select one of the following:

   - **Basic.** Choose this to provide only a basic display to users during the install process.

   - **Maximum.** Choose this to provide all installation messages and screens to users during the package installation.

7. Click Advanced to display the Advanced Deployment Options dialog box. In the Advanced Deployment Options area, select either of the following check boxes:

   - **Ignore Language When Deploying This Package.** Choose this to specify whether to deploy the package even if it is in a different language.

   - **Remove Previous Installs Of This Product From (Users/Computers) If Product Was Not Installed By Group Policy–based Software Installation.** Choose this to specify whether to remove previous installs of this product from users or computers if product was not installed by Group Policy–based Software Installation.

8. Click OK.

9. On the Properties dialog box, click OK.

Specifying Application Categories

You must associate applications with existing categories. Categories you set generally pertain to published applications only, as assigned applications do not appear in Add/Remove Programs in Control Panel. The application appears in the selected categories in Add/Remove Programs, which the user can use to install the application.

▶ **Follow these steps to specify application categories for Add/Remove Programs in Control Panel:**

1. Open the Group Policy snap-in. In Computer Or User Configuration, open Software Settings.

2. Click the Software Installation node.

3. In the details pane, right-click the application for which you want to specify application categories, and then click Properties.

4. In the Categories tab of the Properties dialog box for the application (see Figure 20.15), click the category you want to specify from the Available Categories list, and then click Select.

5. Repeat Step 4 to specify additional categories. Click OK when you finish selecting categories.

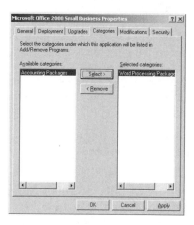

Figure 20.15 Categories tab of the Properties dialog box

Setting Permissions for Software Installation

Permissions set for software installation pertain only to the application installation.

▶ **Follow these steps to set permissions for software installation:**

1. Open the Group Policy snap-in. In Computer Or User Configuration, open Software Settings.

2. Click the Software Installation node.

3. In the details pane, right-click the application for which you want to specify software installation permissions, and then click Properties.

4. In the Security tab of the application's Properties dialog box, click the security group on which to set permissions.

   Administrators who manage the application installation should have the Full Control permission set to Allow. Users who use the software assigned or published by the application should have the Read permission set to Allow.

5. Click OK.

Maintaining Software Applications

After the deployment of software applications it may be necessary to upgrade or remove them at some point in the software life cycle.

Upgrading Applications

Several events in the life cycle of the software can trigger an upgrade, including the following:

- The original developer of the software releases a new version with new and improved features.
- The organization chooses to use a different vendor's application.

Upgrades typically involve major changes to the software and normally have new version numbers. Usually a substantial number of files change for an upgrade. You can use the Software Installation extension to establish the procedure to upgrade an existing application to the current release.

▶   **Follow these steps to upgrade applications:**

1. Open the Group Policy snap-in. In Computer Or User Configuration, open Software Settings.

2. Click the Software Installation node.

3. In the details pane, right-click the Windows Installer package that will function as the upgrade (not the package to be upgraded), and then click Properties. You will have previously assigned or published this package.

4. In the Upgrades tab of the application's Properties dialog box, click Add to create or add to the list of packages that are to be upgraded by the current package.

5. In the Add Upgrade Package dialog box (see Figure 20.16), specify either Current Group Policy Object or A Specific GPO as the source of the package to be upgraded. In the latter case, click Browse, click the GPO you want, and then in the Browse For A Group Policy Object dialog box, click OK.

Figure 20.16 Add Upgrade Package dialog box

A list of all the other packages assigned to be published within the selected GPO appears under the heading Package To Upgrade. Depending on the GPO, this list may have zero or more entries.

6. Click the package to upgrade.

7. Click either Uninstall The Existing Package, Then Install The Upgrade Package, or Package Can Upgrade Over The Existing Package. Click OK. Typically, the uninstall option is used to replace an application with a completely different one (perhaps from a different vendor). The upgrade option is used to install a newer version of the same product while retaining the user's application preferences, document type associations, and so on.

8. On the Upgrades tab in the Properties dialog box, enable the Required Upgrade For Existing Packages check box if you want the upgrade to be mandatory, and then click OK.

If this is an upgrade under the Computer Configuration node of the Group Policy snap-in, the check box appears dimmed and selected, because packages can only be assigned to computers, not published.

Removing Applications

At some point, users may no longer require an application, so you may need to remove it. For example, the following two issues can be resolved by using the removal choices set within the Software Installation extension:

- **A version of a software application is no longer supported.** Administrators can remove the software version from Software Installation without forcing the (physical) removal of the software from the computers of users who are still using the software. Users can continue to use the software until they remove it themselves. No user is able to install the software version (from the Start menu, from Add/Remove Programs in Control Panel, or by document invocation).

- **A software application is no longer used.** Administrators can force the removal of the software. The software is automatically deleted from a computer, either the next time the computer is turned on (when the software is assigned to the computer) or the next time the user logs on (when the software is assigned to the user). Users cannot install or run the software.

Note When you originally deploy the software, if you want the application to be removed when a GPO no longer applies, select the Uninstall This Application When It Falls Out Of The Scope of Management option.

▶ **Follow these steps to remove applications:**

1. Open the Group Policy snap-in. In Computer Or User Configuration, open Software Settings.

2. Click the Software Installation node.

3. In the details pane, right-click the application you want to remove, click All Tasks, and then click Remove.

4. In the Remove Software Dialog box, select one of the following removal options:

   - **Immediately Uninstall The Software From Users And Computers.** Select this option to specify that the application be removed the next time a user logs on or restarts the computer.

   - **Allow Users To Continue To Use The Software, But Prevent New Installations.** Select this option to specify that users can continue to use the application if they have already installed it. If they remove the application or have never installed it, they will not be able to install it.

5. Click OK.

Lesson Summary

In this lesson you learned how the Software Installation extension helps you specify how applications are installed and maintained in your organization. You can centrally manage the installation of software on a client computer by assigning applications to users or computers or by publishing applications for users. *Assign* required or mandatory software to users or to computers. *Publish* software that users might find useful to perform their jobs.

The Software Installation extension uses Windows Installer technology to systematically maintain software. The Windows Installer package is a file that contains explicit instructions for installing and removing specific applications.

You also learned the tasks used for implementing software installation: planning and preparing; setting up an SDP; specifying software installation defaults; deploying software applications; setting automatic installation options; setting up application categories; setting software application properties; and maintaining software applications.

Lesson 3: Managing Special Folders Using Group Policy

Microsoft Windows 2000 allows you to redirect the folders containing a user's profile to a location on the network using the Folder Redirection extension in the Group Policy snap-in. This lesson introduces special folder redirection and walks you through the steps for setting up folder redirection using Group Policy.

After this lesson, you will be able to

- Redirect special folders

Estimated lesson time: 15 minutes

Folder Redirection

You use the Folder Redirection extension to the Group Policy snap-in to redirect certain Windows 2000 special folders to network locations. Special folders such as My Documents and My Pictures are located in C:\Documents and Settings (where C:\ is the name of your system drive).

Windows 2000 allows the following special folders to be redirected:

- Application Data
- Desktop
- My Documents
- My Pictures
- Start Menu

The Folder Redirection extension is located under User Configuration, Windows Settings in the Group Policy snap-in.

Advantages of Redirecting the My Documents Folder

The following benefits pertain to redirecting any folder, but redirecting My Documents can be particularly advantageous because this folder tends to become large over time.

- Even if a user logs on to various computers on the network, his or her documents are always available.

- When roaming user profiles are used, only the network path to the My Documents folder is part of the roaming user profile, not the My Documents folder itself. Therefore, its contents do not have to be copied back and forth between the client computer and the server each time the user logs on or off, and the process of logging on or off can be much faster than it was in Windows NT 4.0.

- Data stored on a shared network server can be backed up as part of routine system administration. This is safer because it requires no action on the part of the user.

- The system administrator can use Group Policy to set disk quotas, limiting the amount of space taken up by users' special folders.

- Data specific to a user can be redirected to a different hard disk on the user's local computer from the hard disk holding the OS files. This makes the user's data safer if the OS needs to be reinstalled.

Default Special Folder Locations

The default locations for special folders that have not been redirected depend on the OS that was in place previously (see Table 20.6).

Table 20.6   Default Locations for Special Folders

Operating system	Location of special folders
Windows 2000 new installation (no previous OS), Windows 2000 upgrade of Windows 95, or Windows 98 with user profiles disabled	C:\Documents and Settings (where C:\ is the name of your system drive); for example, C:\Documents and Settings
Windows 2000 upgrade of Windows NT 4.0 or Windows NT 3.51	*systemroot*\Profiles; for example, C:\WinNT\Profiles
Windows 2000 upgrade of Windows 95 or Windows 98 with user profiles enabled	*systemroot*\Profiles; for example, C:\Windows\System\Profiles

Setting Up Folder Redirection

There are two ways to set up folder redirection:

- Redirect special folders to a location according to security group membership.

- Redirect special folders to one location for everyone in the site, domain, or OU.

In addition, you can also direct the My Pictures folder to follow the redirection of the My Documents folder (to remain as its subfolder whenever My Documents is redirected, as it does by default).

Note The default (My Pictures following My Documents) is recommended unless you have a specific reason (such as file share scalability) for separating My Pictures from My Documents. If they are separated, a shortcut takes the place of the My Pictures folder in My Documents.

▶   **Follow these steps to redirect special folders to a location according to security group membership:**

1. Open a GPO linked to the site, domain, or OU containing the users whose special folders you want to redirect to a network location.

2. In User Configuration, open Windows Settings, and then double-click the Folder Redirection node to show the folder you want to redirect.

3. Right-click the folder you want (such as Desktop, My Documents, and so on), and then click Properties.

4. In the Target tab in the Properties dialog box for the folder (see Figure 20.17), in the Setting list, select Advanced-Specify Locations For Various User Groups, and then click Add.

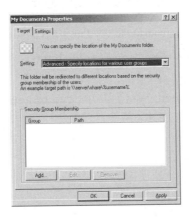

Figure 20.17 Target tab in the Properties dialog box

5. In the Specify Group And Location dialog box (see Figure 20.18), in the Security Group Membership box, click Browse.

Figure 20.18 Specify Group And Location dialog box

6. In the Select Group dialog box, click the security group for which you want to redirect the folder, and then click OK.

7. In the Specify Group And Location dialog box, in the Target Folder Location box, click Browse.

8. On the Browse For Folder dialog box, select the redirect location you want for this security group, and then click OK.

   If you enter a drive letter, such as D:\, this must represent a valid path on the user's local computer. It is recommended that you enter a full universal naming convention (UNC) path.

   If you want each user in the specified security group to have his or her own subfolder at this location, you can incorporate %username% into the UNC path, such as *server**share*\%username%. Including %username% in the path is recommended. For example, SecUser, member of the Users security group could have My Documents redirected to \\server1\share\secuser\My Documents when using \\server1\share\%username%\My Documents.

9. In the Specify Group And Location dialog box, click OK.

10. If you want to redirect folders for members of other security groups, repeat Steps 4 through 9 until all the groups have been entered.

11. In the Properties dialog box for the folder, click the Settings tab (see Figure 20.19), and then set each of the following options (the default setting is recommended):

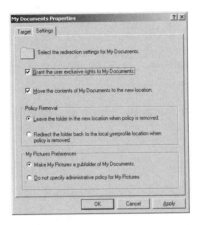

Figure 20.19 Settings tab of the Properties dialog box

- **Grant The User Exclusive Rights To (the special folder type).** Use this option to allow the user and the local system full rights to the folder, and no one else, not even administrators, has any rights. If this setting is disabled, no changes are made to the permissions on the folder. The permissions that apply by default remain in effect. This option is enabled by default.

- **Move The Contents Of (the user's current special folder) To The New Location.** Use this option to redirect the contents of the folder to the new location. This option is enabled by default.

12. Choose one of the following options in the Policy Removal area (the default setting is recommended):

- **Leave The Folder In The New Location When Policy Is Removed.** Use this option to leave the folder it its new location even though the GPO no longer applies. This option is enabled by default.

- **Redirect The Folder Back To The Local User Profile Location When Policy Is Removed.** Use this option to move the folder back to its local user profile location when the GPO no longer applies.

Important See the section on Policy Removal Considerations for details on selecting a policy removal option.

---

13. Available for the My Documents folder only, choose one of the following options in the My Pictures Preferences area:

- **Make My Pictures A Subfolder Of My Documents** to redirect My Pictures automatically to remain a subfolder of My Documents.

- **Do Not Specify Administrative Policy For My Pictures** to remove My Pictures as a subfolder of My Documents and have the user profile determine the location of My Pictures.

Note You can also specify if you want the My Pictures folder to follow the My Documents folder by setting the folder redirection properties for My Pictures.

14. Click OK.

▶ **Follow these steps to redirect special folders to one location for everyone in the site, domain, or OU:**

1. Open a GPO linked to the site, domain, or OU containing the users whose special folders you want to redirect to a network location.

2. In User Configuration, open Windows Settings, and then double-click the Folder Redirection node to show the folder you want to redirect.

3. Right-click the folder you want (such as Desktop, My Documents, and so on), and then click Properties.

4. In the Target tab in the Properties dialog box for the folder (see Figure 20.17), in the Setting list, select Basic-Redirect Everyone's Folder To The Same Location, and then click Browse.

5. On the Browse For Folder dialog box, select the redirect location you want for this GPO.

   If you enter a drive letter, such as D:\, this must represent a valid path on the user's local computer. It is recommended that you enter a full UNC path.

   If you want each user in the site, domain, or organizational unit to have his or her own subfolder at this location, you can incorporate %username% into the UNC path, such as *server**share*\\%username%. Including %username% in the path is recommended. For example, SecUser, member of the Users security group could have My Documents redirected to \\server1\share\secuser\My Documents when using \\server1\share\%username%\My Documents.

6. In the Browse For Folder dialog box, click OK.

7. In the Properties dialog box for the folder, click the Settings tab (see Figure 20.19), and then set each of the following options (the default setting is recommended):

   - **Grant The User Exclusive Rights To (the special folder type).** Use this option to allow the user and the local system full rights to the folder, and no one else, not even administrators, has any rights. If this setting is disabled, no changes are made to the permissions on the folder. The permissions that apply by default remain in effect. This option is enabled by default.

   - **Move The Contents Of (the user's current special folder) To The New Location.** Use this option to redirect the contents of the folder to the new location. This option is enabled by default.

8. Choose one of the following options in the Policy Removal area (the default setting is recommended):

   - **Leave The Folder In The New Location When Policy Is Removed.** Use this option to leave the folder it its new location even though the GPO no longer applies. This option is enabled by default.

   - **Redirect The Folder Back To The Local User Profile Location When Policy Is Removed.** Use this option to move the folder back to its local user profile location when the GPO no longer applies.

Important See the section on Policy Removal Considerations for details on selecting a policy removal option.

---

9. Choose one of the following options in the My Pictures Preferences area:

   - **Make My Pictures A Subfolder Of My Documents.** Use this option to redirect My Pictures automatically to remain a subfolder of My Documents.

   - **Do Not Specify Administrative Policy For My Pictures.** Use this option to remove My Pictures as a subfolder of My Documents and have the user profile determine the location of My Pictures.

Note You can also specify if you want the My Pictures folder to follow the My Documents folder by setting the folder redirection properties for My Pictures. This is described in the next procedure.

---

10. Click OK.

▶ **Follow these steps to direct the My Pictures folder to follow the redirection of the My Documents folder:**

1. Open a GPO linked to the site, domain, or OU containing the users whose My Pictures folders you want to direct.

2. In User Configuration, open Windows Settings, and then double-click the Folder Redirection node.

3. Right-click My Pictures (a folder located in My Documents), and then click Properties.

4. In the My Pictures Properties dialog box, in the Setting list, select Follow The My Documents Folder, and then click OK.

Policy Removal Considerations

Table 20.7 summarizes what happens to redirected folders and their contents when the Group Policy object no longer applies.

Table 20.7   Policy Removal Considerations

When the Move The Contents Of (special folder type) To The New Location Setting is	And the policy removal option is	Results when policy is removed are
Enabled	Redirect The Folder Back To The User Profile Location When Policy Is Removed	The special folder returns to its user profile location. The contents are copied, not moved, back to the user profile location. The contents are not deleted from the redirected location. The user continues to have access to the contents, but only on the local computer.
Disabled	Redirect The Folder Back To The User Profile Location When Policy Is Removed	The special folder returns to its user profile location. The contents are not copied or moved to the user profile location. *Caution:* If the contents of a folder are not copied to the user profile location, the user can no longer see them.
Either Enabled or Disabled	Leave The Folder In The New Location When Policy Is Removed	The special folder remains at its redirected location. The contents remain at the redirected location. The user continues to have access to the contents at the redirected folder.

Lesson Summary

In this lesson, you learned how to redirect the folders containing a user's profile to a location on the network. Windows 2000 allows the following special folders to be redirected: Application Data, Desktop, My Documents, My Pictures, and Start Menu. You also learned that the Folder Redirection extension in the Group Policy snap-in is used to redirect special folders. Folder redirection can be set up to redirect special folders to a location according to security group membership or to redirect special folders to one location for everyone in the site, domain, or OU.

Lesson 4: Troubleshooting Group Policy

This lesson describes problems you may encounter that relate to Group Policy. It also describes some best practices you should employ to keep Group Policy troubleshooting activities to a minimum.

After this lesson, you will be able to

- Troubleshoot Group Policy
- Employ best practices for Group Policy

Estimated lesson time: 10 minutes

Troubleshooting Group Policy

An important part of troubleshooting Group Policy problems is to consider dependencies between components. For example, Software Installation relies on Group Policy, and Group Policy relies on Active Directory directory service. Active Directory relies on proper configuration of network services. When trying to fix problems that appear in one component, it is generally helpful to check whether components, services, and resources on which it relies are working correctly. Event logs are useful for tracking down problems caused by this type of hierarchical dependency.

Table 20.8 describes scenarios in which there are problems that might occur with Group Policy snap-in.

Table 20.8   Group Policy Snap-In Problems and Solutions

Symptom: The user cannot open a GPO even though he or she has Read access to it

Cause	Solution
An administrator must have both Read permission and Write permission for the GPO to open it in the Group Policy snap-in.	Be a member of a security group with Read and Write permission for the GPO. For example, a domain administrator can manage nonlocal GPOs. An administrator for a computer can edit the local GPO on that computer.

Symptom: When the user tries to edit a GPO, the "Failed To Open The Group Policy Object" message appears

Cause	Solution
A networking problem, specifically a problem with the Domain Name System (DNS) configuration.	Make sure DNS is working properly.

Table 20.9 describes scenarios where Group Policy settings are not taking effect.

Table 20.9   Group Policy Settings Problems and Solutions

Symptom: Group Policy is not being applied to users and computers in a security group that contains those users and computers, even though a GPO is linked to an OU containing that security group

Cause	Solution
This is correct behavior. Group Policy affects only users and computers contained in sites, domains, and OUs. GPOs are not applied to security groups.	Link GPOs to sites, domains, and OUs only. Keep in mind that the location of a security group in Active Directory is unrelated to whether Group Policy applies to the users and computers in that security group.

Symptom: Group Policy is not affecting users and computers in a site, domain, or OU

Cause	Solution
Group Policy settings can be prevented, intentionally or inadvertently, from taking effect on users and computers in several ways. A GPO can be disabled from affecting users, computers, or both. It also needs to be linked either directly to an OU containing the users and computers or linked to a parent domain or OU so that the Group Policy settings apply through inheritance. When multiple GPOs apply, they are processed in this order: local, site, domain, OU. By default, settings applied later have precedence. In addition, Group Policy can be blocked at the level of any OU, or enforced through a setting of No Override applied to a particular GPO link. Finally, the user or computer must belong to one or more security groups with appropriate permissions set.	Make sure that the intended policy is not being blocked. Make sure no policy set at a higher level of Active Directory has been set to No Override. If Block Policy Inheritance and No Override are both used, keep in mind that No Override takes precedence. Verify that the user or computer is not a member of any security group for which the Accelerated Graphics Port (AGP) permission is set to Deny. Verify that the user or computer is a member of at least one security group for which the AGP permission is set to Allow. Verify that the user or computer is a member of at least one security group for which the Read permission is set to Allow.

continues

Table 20.9   Group Policy Settings Problems and Solutions *(continued)*

Symptom: Group Policy is not affecting users and computers in an Active Directory container

Cause	Solution
GPOs cannot be linked to Active Directory containers other than sites, domains, and OUs.	Link a GPO to an OU that is a parent to the Active Directory container. Then, by default, those settings are applied to the users and computers in the container through inheritance.

Symptom: Group Policy is not taking effect on the local computer

Cause	Solution
Local policies are the weakest. Any nonlocal GPO can overwrite them.	Check to see what GPOs are being applied through Active Directory and if those GPOs have settings that are in conflict with the local settings.

Table 20.10 describes scenarios in which there are problems using the Software Installation extension.

Table 20.10   Software Installation Extension Problems and Solutions

Symptom: Published applications do not appear in Add/Remove Programs in Control Panel

Cause	Solution
Several causes are possible: Group Policy was not applied; Active Directory cannot be accessed; user does not have any published applications in the GPOs that apply to him or her; client is running Terminal Server.	Investigate each possibility. Note that Software Installation is not supported for Terminal Server clients.

Symptom: Document activation of a published application does not cause the application to install

Cause	Solution
The administrator did not set auto-install.	Ensure that Auto-Install This Application By File Extension Activation is checked in the Deployment tab in the application's properties sheet.

Symptom: The user receives an error message such as "The Feature You Are Trying To Install Cannot Be Found In The Source Directory"

Cause	Solution
There are Network or permissions problems.	Make sure the network is working correctly. Ensure that the user has Read and AGP permission for the GPO. Ensure that the user has Read permission for the SDP. Ensure that the user has Read permission for the application.

Symptom: After removal of an application, the shortcuts for the application still appear on the user's desktop

Cause	Solution
The user has created shortcuts and Windows Installer has no knowledge of them.	The user must remove the shortcuts manually.

Symptom: The user receives an error message such as "Another Installation Is Already In Progress"

Cause	Solution
An uninstallation might be taking place in the background with no user interface presented, or the user might have inadvertently triggered two installations simultaneously (which is not supported).	The user can try again later.

Symptom: The user opens an already installed application, and the Windows Installer starts

Cause	Solution
An application might be undergoing automatic repair, or a user-required feature is being added.	No action is required.

Symptom: The user receives error messages such as "Active Directory Will Not Allow The Package To Be Deployed" or "Cannot Prepare Package For Deployment"

Cause	Solution
The package might be corrupted or there might be a networking problem.	Investigate and take appropriate action.

Group Policy Best Practices

The following best practices should minimize your need to troubleshoot Group Policy.

General Group Policy Practices

- **Disable unused parts of a GPO.** If a GPO only has settings, under the User Configuration or Computer Configuration node of the console, that are Not Configured, you can avoid processing those settings by disabling the node. This expedites startup and logon for those users and computers subject to the GPO.

- **Use the Block Policy Inheritance and No Override features sparingly.** Routine use of these features makes it difficult to troubleshoot Group Policy.

- **Minimize the number of GPOs associated with users or computers in domains or OUs.** The more GPOs applied to a user, the longer it takes to start up and log on.

- **Filter policy based on security group membership.** Users who do not have permissions directing that a particular GPO be applied to them can avoid the associated logon delay because the GPO will not be processed for those users.

- **Use loopback only when necessary.** Use loopback only if you need the desktop configuration to be the same regardless of who logs on.

- **Avoid cross-domain GPO assignments.** The processing of GPOs will slow logon and startup if Group Policy is obtained from another domain.

Software Installation Practices

- **Specify application categories for your organization.** Using categories makes it easier for users to find an application in Add/Remove Programs in Control Panel. For example, you could define categories such as Sales Applications, Accounting Applications, and so on.

- **Make sure Windows Installer packages include modifications before they are published or assigned.** Remember that modifications are applied to packages at the time of assignment or publication. In practical terms, this means that you should make sure the Modifications tab of the package Properties dialog box is set up as you intend before you click OK. If you neglect to do this, and assign or publish a modified package before you have completely configured it, you can either remove the software and republish or reassign it or upgrade the software with a completely modified version.

- **Assign or publish just once per GPO.** A Windows Installer package should be assigned or published no more than once in the same GPO. For example, if you assign Microsoft Office to the computers affected by a GPO, do not assign or publish it to users affected by the GPO.

- **Take advantage of authoring tools.** Developers familiar with the files, registry entries, and other requirements for an application to work properly can author native Windows Installer packages using tools available from various software vendors.

- **Repackage existing software.** You can use commercially available tools to create Windows Installer packages for software that does not include natively authored .msi files. These tools work by comparing a computer's state before and after installation. For best results, install the software onto a computer free of other application software (perform a clean installation).

- **Use SMS and Dfs.** Microsoft Systems Management Server (SMS) and the Windows 2000 Distributed File System (Dfs) are helpful in managing the SDPs (the network shares from which users install their managed software).

- **Assign or publish close to the root in the Active Directory hierarchy.** Because Group Policy settings apply by default to child Active Directory containers, it is efficient to assign or publish by linking a GPO to a parent OU or domain. Use security descriptors (such as Access Control Entries [ACEs]) on the GPO for finer control over who receives the software.

- **Use Software Installation properties for widely scoped control.** This spares administrative keystrokes when assigning or publishing a large number of packages with similar properties in a single GPO—for example, when all the software is published and it all comes from the same SDP.

- **Use Windows Installer package properties for fine control.** Use the package properties for assigning or publishing a single package.

Folder Redirection Practices

- **Incorporate %username% into fully qualified UNC paths.** This allows users to have their own folders. For example, the user could specify *server**share*\%username%\My Documents and the username would be included in the path.

- **Have My Pictures follow My Documents.** This is advisable unless there is a compelling reason not to, such as file share scalability.

- **Consider effects of policy removal.** Keep in mind the behavior your Folder Redirection policies will have upon policy removal, as described in "Policy Removal Considerations."

- **Accept defaults.** In general, accept the default Folder Redirection settings.

Lesson Summary

In this lesson you examined some Group Policy problems that you may encounter and possible solutions. You also learned some best practices for handling Group Policy.

Lesson 5: Remote Installation Services Overview

RIS was discussed briefly in Chapter 1, "Installing Windows 2000 Professional." This lesson and the lessons that follow provide a more detailed look at RIS.

This lesson starts with an overview of the RIS architecture and components and the Microsoft Windows 2000 services that are required to take advantage of the Remote OS Installation feature. This lesson also describes the client components and services that are required to implement Remote OS Installation in your organization.

After this lesson, you will be able to

- Identify the services and components that make up the Remote OS Installation feature
- Explain how the Remote OS Installation process works
- Identify RIS server and client requirements
- Identify network cards supported by RIS boot disk

Estimated lesson time: 20 minutes

Remote OS Installation Overview

Figure 20.20 illustrates the services and components that make up the Remote OS Installation feature.

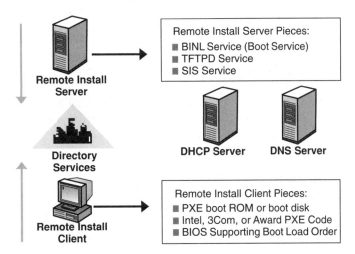

Figure 20.20 Remote OS Installation

Remote OS Installation uses some of the existing services that may already be deployed and in use within your organization and adds some services that you may or may not be familiar with. Remote OS Installation requires Active Directory, an updated Dynamic Host Configuration Protocol (DHCP) server, and a compliant version of DNS.

Remote Install Server Components

When RIS is installed, these additional services are added to the server:

- **Boot Information Negotiation Layer (BINL).** The BINL service is added during the RIS installation process and provides overall management of the RIS environment. The BINL service is responsible for answering client computer network service requests, querying Active Directory on behalf of the client computer, and ensuring that the correct policy and configuration settings are applied to the client computer during the OS installation. The BINL service makes sure the client is passed the correct files and, in the case of a client that already has a corresponding computer account within the Active Directory service (prestaged), makes sure it is serviced by the correct RIS server. If the client computer has not been prestaged, BINL creates the client computer account object within Active Directory.

- **Trivial File Transfer Protocol Daemon (TFTPD).** This server-side TFTP service is responsible for hosting specific file download requests made by the client computer. The TFTPD service is used to download the Client Installation wizard (CIW) and all client dialog boxes contained within the Client Installation wizard for a given session.

- **Single Instance Store (SIS).** SIS is the service responsible for reducing disk space requirements on the volumes used for storing RIS installation images. When you install RIS as an optional component, you are prompted for a drive and directory where you would like to install RIS, known as the RIS volume. The SIS service attaches itself to the RIS volume and looks for any duplicate files that are placed on that volume. If duplicate files are found, SIS creates a link to the duplicates, thus reducing the disk space required.

Remote Install Client Components

There are two types of remote boot–enabled client computers:

- Computers with Pre-Boot eXecution Environment (PXE) DHCP–based remote boot ROMS

- Computers with network cards supported by the RIS Boot Disk

PXE Remote Boot Technology

Remote OS Installation uses the new PXE DHCP–based remote boot technology to initiate the installation of an OS from a remote source to a client hard disk. The remote source—a server that supports RIS—provides the network equivalent of a CD-ROM-based installation of Windows 2000 Professional or a preconfigured Remote Installation Preparation (RIPrep) desktop image. The Windows 2000 Professional OS is currently the only installation option supported by RIS.

- **CD-based installation.** The CD-ROM-based option is similar to setting up a workstation directly from the Windows 2000 Professional CD-ROM; however, the source files reside across the network on available RIS servers.

- **RIPrep image format.** The RIPrep imaging option allows a network administrator to clone a standard corporate desktop configuration, complete with OS configurations, desktop customizations, and locally installed applications. After first installing and configuring the Windows 2000 Professional OS, its services, and any standard applications on a computer, the network administrator runs a wizard that prepares the installation image and replicates it to an available RIS server on the network for installation on other clients.

Once the images have been posted on the RIS server(s), end users equipped with PXE–based remote boot–enabled client computers can request to install those images from any available RIS server on the network. The fact that the user can install the OS without administrator assistance means the administrator is free to complete other tasks requiring his or her attention, thus saving both the time and expense normally associated with OS installations.

How the PXE Remote Boot Technology Works

PXE is a new form of remote boot technology. PXE provides companies with the ability to use their existing Transmission Control Protocol/Internet Protocol (TCP/IP) network infrastructure with DHCP to discover RIS servers on the network. Net PC/PC98–compliant systems can take advantage of the remote boot technology included in the Windows 2000 OS. Net PC/PC98 refers to the annual guide for hardware developers co-authored by Microsoft with Intel, including contributions from Compaq and other industry hardware manufacturers. PC98 is intended to provide standards for hardware development that advance the PC platform and enable Microsoft to include advanced features, like RIS, in the Windows platform.

Figure 20.21 describes the step-by-step process the PXE remote-boot ROM goes through during every network service boot request.

When a PXE–enabled client computer is turned on, the PXE–based ROM requests an IP address from a DHCP server using the normal DHCP discovery process. As part of the initial DHCP discover request, the client computer identifies itself as being PXE–enabled, which indicates to the RIS servers on the network that it is looking to be serviced. Any available RIS server on the network can respond by providing the client with its IP address and the name of a boot file the client should request if that client wants service from that server. When the client computer responds to the server indicating that it wants service, the DHCP service sends a message granting service. The client must also request service from the BINL service, which then passes the bootstrap file to the client and ensures that prestaged clients are serviced by the correct RIS server.

After the network bootstrap program is sent to the client by the BINL service, the client-side experience will be different, depending on the remote installation server vendor that is responding to the client request for service. The following sections detail the implementation of Remote OS Installation that is included in the Windows 2000 Server OS.

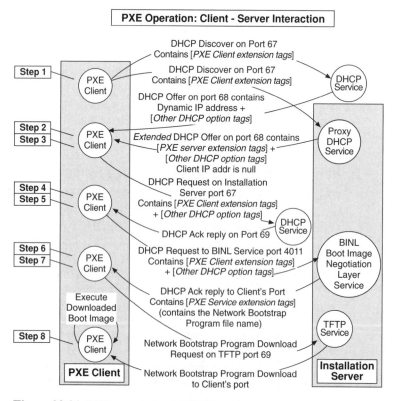

Figure 20.21 PXE remote boot ROM boot process

The RIS Boot Disk

For computers that do not contain a PXE–based remote-boot ROM, Windows 2000 provides the administrator with a tool to create a remote boot disk for use with RIS. The RIS remote boot disk can be used with a variety of Peripheral Component Interconnect (PCI)–based network adapter cards. Using the RIS boot disk eliminates the need to retrofit existing client computers with new network cards that contain a PXE–based remote-boot ROM to take advantage of the Remote OS Installation feature. The RIS boot disk simulates the PXE remote boot sequence and supports frequently used network cards.

How the Remote OS Installation Process Works

A graphical representation of how the Remote OS Installation process works is shown in Figure 20.22. The process is the same for both the PXE remote-boot ROM and the RIS boot disk boot processes. Each step of the process is then discussed in detail.

The process of contacting an RIS server and selecting an OS image is accomplished in a few steps. The following steps are the sequence of events that take place when a PXE–enabled client computer starts on the network and is serviced by an RIS server.

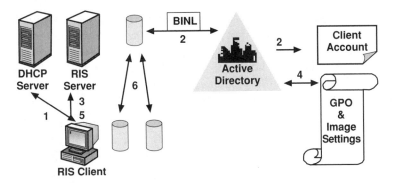

Figure 20.22 RIS architecture

The Remote OS Installation Process

1. An RIS client connected to the network starts. During the power up, the computer initiates a network service request. As part of the network service request, a DHCP discover packet is sent to the network requesting an IP address from the closest DHCP server, the IP address of an available RIS server. As part of that request, the client sends its globally unique identifier (GUID). The GUID is present in client computers that are PC98– or Net PC–compliant and is found in the system basic input/output system (BIOS) of the computer. The DHCP server responds to the request by providing an IP address to the client. Any available RIS server can respond with its IP address and the name of the boot file the client should request if the client selects that RIS server for service. The user is prompted to press the F12 key to initiate service from that RIS server.

2. The RIS server (using the BINL service) must check in Active Directory for the existence of a prestaged client computer account that matches this client computer. BINL checks for the existence of a client computer by querying Active Directory for a client computer that matches the GUID sent in Step 1.

3. Once the RIS server has checked for the existence of a client computer account, the Client Installation wizard is downloaded to the client computer. It prompts the user to log on to the network.

4. Once the user logs on, the RIS server checks Active Directory for a corresponding user account, verifying the password. RIS then checks the RIS-specific Group Policy settings to find out which installation options the user should have access to. RIS also checks to see which OS images the specific user should be offered. The Client Installation wizard makes those options available to the client (see Figure 20.23).

5. If the user is only allowed a single installation option and OS choice, he or she is not prompted to select anything. If the user has more than one installation option and OS image available to him or her for installation, the list of images is displayed for selection. The Client Installation wizard warns the user that the installation will reformat his or her hard disk and previously stored information will be deleted, and then prompts the user to start the Remote OS Installation.

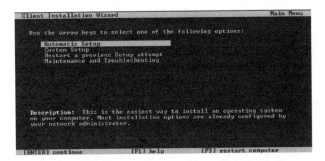

Figure 20.23 Client Installation wizard installation options

Note To configure the setup options displayed to users in the Client Installation wizard, see Lesson 6, "Implementing RIS," for more information.

---

6. Once the user confirms the installation settings on the summary screen, the OS installation begins. At this point, if a client computer account was not present in Active Directory, the BINL service creates the client computer account, thus automatically providing a name for the computer. The OS is installed locally as an unattended installation, which means the end user is not offered any installation choices during the OS installation phase.

Important Because the Client Installation wizard is running in a preboot execution environment, there is no support for extended characters in either the text displayed or the input fields (user name, password, domain, or any custom input parameters). Careful consideration should be taken before creating user or domain names that contain extended characters because they will be not be usable with RIS.

The Remote OS Installation process is straightforward from an end user perspective. The administrator can guide the user through a successful OS installation by predetermining the installation options, if any, an end user has access to. The administrator can also restrict the OS image or images a user has access to, thus ensuring the correct OS installation type is offered to the user for a successful installation.

RIS Server and Client Requirements

This following are RIS server hardware requirements:

- Pentium or Pentium II 166 MHz (200 MHz or faster processor recommended)
- 64 megabytes (MB) of RAM (96 to 128 MB if additional services such as Active Directory, DHCP, and DNS are installed)
- 2 gigabyte (GB) minimum hard disk or partition dedicated to the RIS directory tree. RIS requires a significant amount of disk space.
- 10 or 100 megabits per second (mbps) network adapter card (100 mbps preferred)

Important A separate partition from the system's boot partition is required to install the RIS. RIS cannot be installed on the same drive as the system volume. The volume you choose to install RIS onto must be formatted with the NTFS.

Server Software Requirements

The following services can be installed either on individual servers or on the same server and must be active and available:

- DNS
- DHCP
- Active Directory

Client Hardware Requirements

This following are RIS client hardware requirements:

- Pentium 166 MHz or faster processor Net PC client computer
- 32 MB RAM minimum (64 MB recommended)
- 800 MB hard disk drive
- Supported PCI Plug and Play network adapter card
- PXE–based remote-boot ROM version .99c or later (optional)

Network Cards Supported by RIS Boot Disk

The RIS boot disk supports the following network card models. You can also run the RBFG utility at the command prompt, and then select Adapter List to see a list of supported network cards.

3Com Network Adapters

- 3C900 (Combo and TP0)
- 3C900B (Combo, FL, TPC, TP0)
- 3C905 (T4 and TX)
- 3C905B (Combo, TX, FX)
- 3C905C (TX)

AMD Network Adapters

- AMD PCNet and Fast PCNet

Compaq Network Adapters

- Netflex 100 (NetIntelligent II)
- Netflex 110 (NetIntelligent III)
- Netflex 3

Digital Equipment Corp (DEC) Network Adapters

- DE 450
- DE 500

Hewlett-Packard Network Adapters

- HP Deskdirect 10/100 TX

Intel Corporation Network Adapters

- Intel Pro 10+
- Intel Pro 100+
- Intel Pro 100B (including the E100 series)

SMC Network Adapters

- SMC 8432
- SMC 9332
- SMC 9432

Note The RIS boot disk generator only supports PCI–based network cards. Industry Standard Architecture (ISA), Extended Industry Standard Architecture (EISA), and token ring cards are not supported.

Lesson Summary

In this lesson you learned about RIS architecture and the Windows 2000 services that are required to take advantage of the Remote OS Installation feature. You also learned about the server and client components and services that are required to implement Remote OS Installation.

Lesson 6: Implementing RIS

This section discusses the tasks necessary to implement RIS, including setting up and configuring RIS, creating an RIPrep image, creating an RIS boot disk, and verifying an RIS configuration.

After this lesson, you will be able to

- Set up RIS
- Configure RIS
- Create an RIPrep image
- Create an RIS boot disk
- Verify an RIS configuration

Estimated lesson time: 30 minutes

Implementing RIS

To implement RIS, you must complete the following tasks:

- Set up RIS
- Configure RIS
- Create an RIPrep image
- Create an RIS boot disk (optional)
- Verify the RIS configuration

Setting Up RIS

RIS requires a two-stage setup process: adding the RIS component and installing RIS.

Important Refer to the "RIS Server and Client Requirements" section in Lesson 6, "Implementing RIS," before attempting to set up RIS.

Adding the RIS Component

The first stage of RIS setup is adding RIS as an optional component. This stage copies the files required for installation to the hard disk drive on the server. You can add the RIS component during Windows 2000 Server installation or after the server installation by using Add/Remove Programs.

▶ **Follow these steps to add the RIS component:**

1. Access the Windows Components wizard in one of the following ways:

   ▪ During Windows 2000 Server installation.

   ▪ Click Start, point to Settings, point to Control Panel, open Add/Remove Programs, and then click Add/Remove Windows Components.

2. In the Windows Components Wizard dialog box, shown in Figure 20.24, select the Remote Installation Services check box, and then click Next.

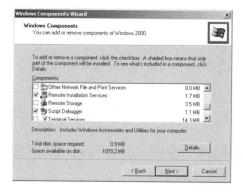

Figure 20.24 Windows Components Wizard dialog box

3. Insert the Windows 2000 Server CD-ROM when prompted.

4. On the Completing The Windows Components Wizard page, click Finish.

5. In the System Settings Change message box, click Yes to restart the server before installing RIS.

Installing RIS

The second stage of RIS setup occurs when RIS is installed. This stage installs RIS on the server.

▶ **Follow these steps to install RIS:**

1. Click Start, point to Programs, point to Administrative Tools, and then click Configure Your Server.

2. In the Configure Your Server dialog box, click Finish Setup.

3. In the Add/Remove Programs dialog box, in the Configure Remote Installation Services box, click Configure to start the Remote Installation Services Setup wizard.

4. In the Welcome To The Remote Installation Services Setup Wizard dialog box, click Next.

5. Continue through the prompts provided by the Remote Installation Services Setup wizard, including:

   - A location on the server where the RIS folder will be created

   - Whether the RIS server should begin servicing client computers immediately after completing setup

   - The location of the Windows 2000 Professional CD-ROM or a location on the network that contains the installation files

   - A location on the server where image installation files will be copied

   - A friendly description and associated help text that describes the OS image to users of the Client Installation wizard

After the Remote Installation Services Setup wizard completes, depending on the settings chosen, the RIS server either begins servicing client computers or pauses while you set RIS configuration options. The next section describes the configuration options available to an RIS administrator.

Configuring RIS

By default, an RIS server is not configured to begin servicing client computers immediately after the installation of RIS is completed. To configure RIS, you must complete the following tasks:

- Authorize RIS servers

- Set RIS server properties

- Set RIS client installation options

- Set RIPrep image permissions

Authorizing RIS Servers

By specifying the RIS servers allowed to run on your network, you can prevent unauthorized (often referred to as *rogue*) RIS servers, ensuring that only RIS servers authorized by administrators can service clients. If an attempt is made to start an unauthorized RIS server on the network, it will be automatically shut down and thus unable to service client computers. An RIS server must be authorized before it can service client computers.

▶ **Follow these steps to authorize RIS servers:**

1. Click Start, point to Programs, point to Administrative Tools, and then click DHCP.

2. In the DHCP console tree, click the DHCP node.

3. On the Action menu, click Manage Authorized Servers.

4. In the Manage Authorized Servers dialog box, click Authorize.

5. In the Authorize DHCP Server dialog box, type the name or IP address of the RIS server to be authorized, and then click OK.

6. In the DHCP message box, click Yes.

7. In the Manage Authorized Servers dialog box, select the computer, and then click OK.

   The authorized RIS server is now listed under the DHCP node.

Setting RIS Server Properties

By setting properties on individual RIS servers, you control how the server supplies RIS to clients requesting service.

▶ **Follow these steps to set RIS server properties:**

1. Click Start, point to Programs, point to Administrative Tools, and then click Active Directory Users And Computers.

2. In the console tree, click the folder that contains the computer whose configuration you want to verify, such as Computers or Domain Controllers.

3. In the details pane, right-click the applicable RIS server, and then click Properties.

4. In the Properties dialog box for the server, click the Remote Install tab.

5. In the Remote Install tab (see Figure 20.25) of the Properties dialog box, set the options described in Table 20.11.

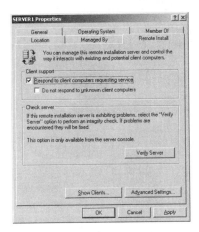

Figure 20.25 Remote Install tab

Table 20.11   Options on the Remote Install Tab of the Properties Dialog Box

Configuration option	Description
Respond To Client Computers Requesting Service	The RIS server responds to all clients requesting service.
Do Not Respond To Unknown Client Computers	The RIS server does not respond to unknown client computers. This option is available only if the Respond To Client Computers Requesting Service check box is checked.

6. In the Remote Install tab, click Advanced Settings.

7. In the Remote Installation Services Properties dialog box for the server, in the New Clients tab (see Figure 20.26), set the options described in Table 20.12.

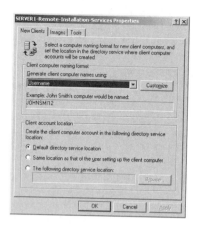

Figure 20.26 New Clients tab on the Remote Installation Services Properties dialog box

Table 20.12   Options on the New Clients Tab of the Remote Installation Services Dialog Box

Configuration option	Description
Generate Client Computer Names Using	When the client computer name is automatically generated, this option determines how the name is formatted. It provides flexibility in naming new client computers during OS installation without the need for end user or administrator involvement.
Customize	This option accesses the Computer Account Generation dialog box on which you can create a custom naming format for the client computer.
Client Account Location	This option specifies one of three directory service locations of the client computer account. Default Directory Service Location specifies that the computer account object for the client computer be created in the Active Directory location where all computer accounts are created by default during the domain join operation. Same Location As That Of The User Setting Up The Client Computer specifies that the client computer account object be created within the same Active Directory container as the user setting up the machine. Use The Following Directory Service Location allows the administrator to set a specific Active Directory container where all client computer account objects installing from this server are created. It is assumed that most administrators will select this option and specify a specific container for all remote installation client computer account objects to be created in.

8. In the Remote Installation Services Properties dialog box for the server, in the Images tab (see Figure 20.27), view the images installed on the RIS server. Click Add and follow the directions in the wizard to install additional images on the RIS server. See Lesson 7, "Administering RIS," for details.

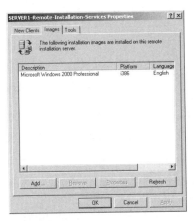

Figure 20.27 Images tab on the Remote Installation Services Properties dialog box

9. In the Remote Installation Services Properties dialog box for the server, in the Tools tab (see Figure 20.28), view the maintenance and trouble-shooting tools installed on the RIS server.

10. In the Remote Installation Services Properties dialog box, click OK.

11. In the Properties dialog box for the server, click OK.

Administrators wishing to remotely manage their servers from computers running Windows 2000 Professional can access the administrative tools by installing the Windows 2000 Administration Tools package located on the Windows 2000 Server CD-ROM.

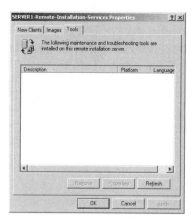

Figure 20.28 Tools tab on the Remote Installation Services Properties dialog box

Note When using Windows 2000 Administration Tools on a system other than the RIS server, the administrator cannot add additional OS images or verify the integrity of the RIS server. All other configuration options are available.

Setting RIS Client Installation Options

By setting the RIS client installation options, you can control the options presented to different groups of users during the Client Installation wizard. There are four client installation options (see Figure 20.23) that can appear on the Client Installation wizard:

- Automatic Setup

- Custom Setup

- Restart A Previous Setup Attempt

- Maintenance And Troubleshooting

Automatic Setup

The Automatic Setup option is the client installation option that all users of the Remote OS Installation feature have access to by default. The Automatic Setup option allows you to restrict the OS installation options so that the user simply logs on and the OS installation starts automatically. The user is not prompted during the OS install, which avoids calls to help desk professionals for assistance and saves the organization additional expenses in support costs.

While restricting installation options, you can still allow users to choose the OS for installation. Remote OS Installation allows you to provide a friendly description and associated help text that describes the OS options so that an end user can choose the most appropriate OS.

By preselecting the Remote OS Installation configuration options, you predefine the automatic machine naming format and the location within Active Directory where client computer accounts will be created.

Custom Setup

The Custom Setup option is very similar to the Automatic Setup option, but it also allows you to set up a computer for another person within the organization. This option can be used to fully preinstall a client computer or to prestage the client computer by creating a corresponding computer account within the Active Directory service.

The Custom Setup option lets you override the automatic computer naming and location where the computer account is created within Active Directory. By default, the RIS server will generate a computer name based on a format defined by the Remote OS Installation administrator. You can also define where client computer account objects (CAOs) will be created in the Active Directory service during the installation. By default, the automatic computer naming policy is set to create computer names based on the person who logs on to the Client Installation wizard.

Restart A Previous Setup Attempt

The Restart A Previous Setup Attempt option is provided in the event that the installation of the OS fails for any reason. The Client Installation wizard can be customized to ask a series of questions about the specific OS being installed. When restarting a failed OS setup attempt, the end user is not asked these questions again. Rather, Setup already has this information and simply restarts the file copy operation and completes the OS installation.

Maintenance And Troubleshooting

The Maintenance And Troubleshooting option provides access to third-party hardware and software vendor tools. These tools range from system BIOS flash updates and memory virus scanners to a wide range of computer diagnostic tools that check for hardware-related problems. These tools are available before installing and starting the OS on the client computer.

If the option to display the Maintenance And Troubleshooting menu is enabled, user access to individual tool images is controlled in the same way as OS options, by setting specific end user permissions on the individual answer file (.sif) for that tool. For example, you can allow end users access to only one computer diagnostic tool while providing help desk professionals with access to the entire suite of diagnostic tools. When the user calls a help desk professional for assistance, the professional can guide him or her through the diagnostic tool to get the information necessary to diagnose the problem. If the help desk staff must visit the end user for further investigation, they simply log on to the Client Installation wizard and, based on their credentials, they can access the tools they need to resolve the problem.

▶   **Follow these steps to set client installation options:**

1. Click Start, point to Programs, point to Administrative Tools, and then click Active Directory Users And Computers.

2. In the console tree, right-click the applicable OU, such as Computers or Domain Controllers, click Properties, and then click the Group Policy tab.

3. In the Properties dialog box for the Group Policy, click the Group PolicyGPO, and then click Edit to start Group Policy.

4. In the Group Policy console tree, click User Configuration, open Windows Settings, and then click Remote Installation Services.

5. Double-click the Choice Options object.

    In the Choice Options Properties dialog box (see Figure 20.29), the following installation options affect how the Client Installation wizard appears to users:

    - Automatic Setup

    - Custom Setup

    - Restart Setup

    - Tools

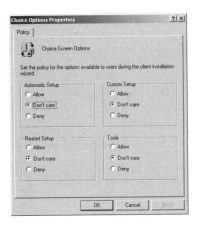

Figure 20.29 Choice Options Properties dialog box

6. Click one of the following Group Policy options for each installation option:

   - **Allow.** Use this policy option to offer the installation option to users to which this policy applies.

   - **Don't Care.** Use this policy option to accept the policy settings of the parent container. For example, if the administrator for the entire domain has set Group Policy that is specific to RIS, and the administrator of this container has chosen the Don't Care option, the policy that is set on the domain is applied to all users that are affected by that policy. Don't Care is the default setting.

   - **Deny.** Use this policy option to deny the users that are affected by this policy access to the installation option.

7. In the Choice Options Properties dialog box, click OK.

8. Close the Group Policy snap-in, and then, in the Properties dialog box for the Group Policy, click OK.

Note Because the changes that you make to RIS policy take effect only when the policy is propagated (applied) to your computer, do one of the following to initiate policy propagation:

   - Type **secedit /refreshpolicy user_policy** at the command prompt, and then press Enter.

   - Restart your computer.

   - Wait for automatic policy propagation, which occurs at regular, configurable intervals. By default, policy propagation occurs every 8 hours.

Setting RIPrep Image Permissions

By specifying which users or groups of users should have access to the RIPrep OS images available on the RIS server, you can guide users through the selection of the unattended OS installation appropriate for their role within the company. By default, when an OS image is added to an RIS server, the image is available to all users serviced by that RIS server.

▶   **Follow these steps to set RIPrep image permissions:**

1. Click Start, point to Programs, point to Accessories, and then click Windows Explorer.

2. In the \RemoteInstall\Setup*applicable_language*\Images\ *applicable_image_name*\i386\templates folder (or the location on the server where you chose to copy image installation files), right-click the appropriate .sif file, and then click Properties.

3. In the Properties dialog box for the file, click the Security tab.

4. Set the appropriate permissions to allow users access to images, and click OK.

Note To reduce the work involved in maintaining the security applied to images, where possible, set the security on the Templates folder of the image rather than the individual .sif files. Grant or restrict access to groups rather than individual users.

Create an RIPrep Image

To build and maintain standard desktops, many organizations use disk imaging or cloning software that allows you to configure a client computer exactly as you want it, and then make a copy of that image for installation on client computers on the network. Remote OS Installation supports creation and installation of standard desktop images using RIPrep images.

Before you can create an RIPrep image, you must complete the following tasks:

- Create the source computer
- Configure the workstation

Creating the Source Computer

To create the source computer, use the Remote OS Installation feature to remotely install the base Windows 2000 Professional OS. Once the OS is installed, you can install applications or application suites, including in-house line of business (LOB) applications. Then configure the workstation to adhere to company policies. For example, you may choose to define specific screen colors, set the background bitmap to a company-based logo, remove any games installed by the base OS, and set Internet Explorer proxy settings.

Configuring the Workstation

When creating RIPrep images, it is important to understand the relationship of user profiles, the changes made to an RIPrep source computer, and the desired result for users that log on to computers that are installed using the RIPrep image. Applications that carry the "Certified for Windows" logo properly separate user-specific and computer-specific configuration settings and data, and can therefore be installed computer-wide so that they are available to all users of the system. Such applications would also then be available to all users of systems later installed with the resulting RIPrep image. Non-Windows 2000–compliant applications may perform and/or rely on per-user configurations that are specific to the profile of the user actually installing the application prior to running RIPrep (typically a local administrator), rather than to all users of the system. Such configurations remain specific to that user, which may result in the application or configuration setting not being available or not functioning properly for users of computers installed with the RIPrep image. In addition, some nonapplication configuration changes, such as the wallpaper specified for the user desktop, are by default applied only to the current user's profile and will not be applied to users of systems installed with the RIPrep image.

You must thoroughly test any applications or configuration settings desired for use in an RIPrep image to ensure they will work properly with your organization's implementation of user profiles. To test, make the change as one user (typically a local administrator of the computer), log off, and log on as a user account that is representative of your organization. If the changes you made are applied to the second user, the changes will also apply to users that log on to systems installed with an RIPrep image that contains the same change. To complete the test, create an RIPrep image, restore it to a different computer, and log on as a different representative user. Verify that the changes are applied and fully functional.

Some configuration settings can be copied directly from the profile they were applied to (the local administrator in the preceding example), the All Users profile, such as the desktop wallpaper, some Start menu options, and short-cuts. However, all such changes must be tested carefully to verify that their functionality is not broken by the manual adjustments.

Creating an RIPrep Image

When the workstation is configured exactly to specifications, you are ready to create an RIPrep image.

▶ **Follow these steps to create an RIPrep image:**

1. On the client workstation, click Start, click Run, and then type the UNC path of the RIPrep utility in the Open box and click OK. For example: *Server**Share*\RemoteInstall\Admin\i386\RIPREP.EXE

2. In the Welcome To The Remote Installation Preparation Wizard dialog box, click Next.

3. Continue through the prompts provided by the Remote Installation Preparation wizard, including the following:

   ▪ **Server Name.** The name of the server to which this installation image will be copied. By default this is the server on which you are running the Remote Installation Preparation wizard.

   ▪ **Folder Name.** The name of the folder on the RIS server to which this installation image will be copied.

   ▪ **Friendly Description And Help Text.** A friendly description and associated help text that describes the OS image to users of the Client Installation wizard.

4. Stop all programs or services on the source computer before proceeding. Review the list of programs or services that are currently running on the source computer, close any running applications, and then click Next.

5. Review the settings summary, and then click Next.

6. Review the information from Completing The Remote Installation Preparation Wizard and click Next to replicate the source computer installation image onto the RIS server.

Note If the source computer contains a 1 GB disk drive and the destination computer contains a 2 GB disk drive, by default RIS formats the destination computer's drive as a 2 GB partition in the same file system format as the source computer used to create the image.

After the initial image questions have been answered, the wizard configures the workstation to a generic state, removing anything unique to the client installation such as the computer's unique security identifier (SID), computer name, and any registry settings unique to that system. Once the preparation phase is complete, the image is automatically replicated to the RIS server provided. After the image is replicated to the RIS server, it is added to the list of available OS installation choices displayed within the Client Installation wizard. At this point, any remote boot–enabled or compatible client computers that use the PXE–based remote boot technology can install the image.

7. The source computer shuts down when the image replication process is complete. The abbreviated Setup program automatically runs when you restart the source computer. Complete the setup process to use this client computer to create another installation image.

RIPrep Requirements

- The destination computer (the computer that installs the image posted to the RIS server) is not required to contain hardware identical to that of the source computer that was used to create the image. RIPrep uses the Plug and Play support in the computer running Windows 2000 Professional to detect differences between the source and the destination computers' hardware during image installation. However, the hardware abstraction layer (HAL) drivers must be the same between the source computer and all destination computers that later install the image (for example, they both must be Advanced Configuration and Power Interface (ACPI)–based or both must be non-ACPI-based). In most cases, workstations do not require the unique HAL drivers that servers require.

- The destination computer's disk capacity must be equal to or larger than that of the source computer.

- All copies of Microsoft software made or installed using RIS must be properly licensed. All copies of other software made or installed using RIS must be properly licensed, and it is the licensee's obligation to ensure that it is licensed to make any such copies.

RIPrep Limitations

- RIPrep currently supports replicating a single disk-single partition (C partition only) Windows 2000 Professional installation to an available RIS server. This means that the OS and all of the applications that make up the standard installation must reside on the C partition prior to running the Remote Installation Preparation wizard.

- The Remote Installation Preparation wizard currently allows source image replication only to available RIS servers. Source replication to alternate drives or media types is not supported.

- Replication of encrypted files is not supported.

- Changes made in the source computer's registry before running the Remote Installation Preparation wizard are not maintained in the installation image.

- Modifications to replicated installation images are not supported.

Installation Image Sources

When you use the Remote Installation Preparation wizard to create an installation image of a client computer that was originally installed using a retail version (rather than a Select or original equipment manufacturer [OEM] version) of Windows 2000 Professional, the RIS unattended setup answer file (RIPREP.SIF) must be modified to include the product identification number (PID). The PID is a unique identification number specific to each copy of Windows 2000 Professional used to identify the OS installation and track the number of copies installed throughout an organization.

Note If the PID is not entered in the RIPREP.SIF file, the installation process stops and the user is prompted for the PID information during the installation of that RIPrep image.

▶ **Follow these steps to include the PID in the RIPREP.SIF file:**

1. Open the RIPREP.SIF file located at \RemoteInstall\Setup*applicable_ language*\Images*applicable_image_name*\i386\Templates\RIPREP.SIF.

2. Type **ProductID = "*xxxxx-xxx-xxxxxxx-xxxxx*"** (including the dashes and quotation marks, where *x* is the PID of the retail version of Windows 2000 Professional) into the [UserData] section of the RIPREP.SIF file.

The PID for each client installation is randomly generated using the PID entered in the RIPREP.SIF file.

When the source computer OS is installed from the Select or OEM version of the Windows 2000 Professional CD, the PID does not need to be modified in the RIPREP.SIF file.

Creating an RIS Boot Disk

You must create a boot disk to support existing client computers that do not have a PXE–based remote boot–enabled ROM but do have a supported network adapter. The RIS boot disk works like the PXE boot process. First you turn on the computer, booting from the RIS boot disk. Then you immediately press F12 to initiate a network service boot, and the Client Installation wizard is downloaded and starts. Once the Client Installation wizard starts, the rest of the RIS process is identical regardless of whether the client was booted using a PXE boot ROM or the RIS remote boot disk.

▶   **Follow these steps to create an RIS boot disk:**

1. Click Start, click Run, and then type the UNC path of the RBFG utility in the Open box and click OK. For example: *server**share*\RemoteInstall\ Admin\i386\RBFG.EXE

2. Insert a formatted disk into the disk drive.

3. In the Windows 2000 Remote Boot Disk Generator dialog box (see Figure 20.30), click the appropriate destination drive option (either Drive A or Drive B), and then click Create Disk.

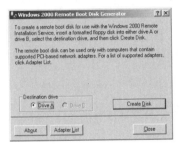

Figure 20.30 Windows 2000 Remote Boot Disk Generator dialog box

4. Click Close when the disk is ready, and then remove the disk from the disk drive.

Note You can use the boot disk only with computers that contain supported PCI–based network adapters. To view the list of supported network adapters, click Adapter List in the Windows 2000 Remote Boot Disk Generator dialog box.

Verifying an RIS Configuration

RIS enables you to check the integrity of the RIS–enabled server. You can verify an RIS configuration if you suspect that the server is failing, if you are currently seeing inconsistent behavior, or if you need to restore an RIS volume from backup. The Check Server wizard checks whether all of the settings, services, and configuration options are correctly set and functioning.

▶   **Follow these steps to verify an RIS configuration:**

1. Click Start, point to Programs, point to Administrative Tools, and then click Active Directory Users And Computers.

2. In the console tree, click the folder that contains the computer whose configuration you want to verify, such as Computers or Domain Controllers.

3. In the details pane, right-click the applicable RIS server, and then click Properties.

4. In the Properties dialog box for the server, in the Remote Install tab, click Verify Server to start the Check Server wizard.

5. On the Welcome To The Check Server Wizard page, click Next.

6. Read the summary on the Remote Installation Services Verification Complete page, and then click Finish.

Note If you are verifying the server configuration because you need to restore an RIS volume from backup, you must verify the server configuration before you restore the volume.

Lesson Summary

In this lesson you learned about the tasks necessary to implement RIS, including setting up and configuring RIS, creating an RIPrep image, creating an RIS boot disk, and verifying an RIS configuration.

Lesson 7: Administering RIS

This lesson discusses the tasks necessary to administer RIS, including managing client installation images, managing RIS client computers, and managing RIS security.

After this lesson, you will be able to

- Manage RIS client installation images
- Manage RIS client computers
- Manage RIS security

Estimated lesson time: 20 minutes

Managing RIS

Managing RIS includes the following tasks:

- Managing RIS client installation images
- Managing RIS client computers
- Managing RIS security

Managing RIS Client Installation Images

Managing RIS client installation images includes the following tasks:

- Adding new client OS installation images
- Associating unattended setup answer files

▶   **Follow these steps to add a new client OS installation image:**

1. Click Start, point to Programs, point to Administrative Tools, and then click Active Directory Users And Computers.

2. In the console tree, right-click the applicable RIS server, and then click Properties.

3. In the Properties dialog box for the server, click the Remote Install tab, and then click Advanced Settings.

4. In the Remote Installation Services Properties dialog box, click the Images tab.

5. Click Add to start the Add wizard.

6. On the New Answer File Or Installation Image page, click Add A New Installation Image, and then click Next to start the Add Installation Image wizard.

7. On the Welcome To The Add Installation Image Wizard page, click Next.

8. On the Installation Source Files Location page, type the location of the Windows 2000 Professional installation image, and then click Next. The location can be either a CD-ROM or network share.

9. On the Windows Installation Image Folder Name page, type a name for the Windows installation image, and then click Next.

10. On the Friendly Description And Help Text page, enter the friendly description and help text for the installation image, and then click Next.

11. If a previous set of Client Installation wizard screens exists, the Previous Client Installation Screens Found page appears. Select the Client Installation wizard screen you want to use for this image, and then click Next.

12. On the Review Settings page, review the installation summary, and then click Finish.

    The Remote Installation Setup wizard completes the addition of the new client installation image.

▶ **Follow these steps to associate unattended setup answer files:**

1. Click Start, point to Programs, point to Administrative Tools, and then click Active Directory Users And Computers.

2. In the console tree, right-click the applicable RIS server, and then click Properties.

3. In the Properties dialog box for the server, click the Remote Install tab, and then click Advanced Settings.

4. In the Remote Installation Services Properties dialog box, click the Images tab.

5. Click Add to start the Add wizard.

6. On the New Answer File Or Installation Image page, click Associate A New Answer File To An Existing Image, and then click Next.

7. On the Unattended Setup Answer File Source page, click the source that contains the unattended setup file you want to copy:

   - Windows Image Sample Files
   - Another Remote Installation Server
   - An Alternate Location

8. Click Next.

9. On the Select An Installation Image page, select the installation image the answer file will be associated with, and then click Next.

10. On the Select A Sample Answer File page, select a sample unattended setup answer file, and then click Next.

11. On the Friendly Description And Help Text page, enter the friendly description and help text for the installation image, and then click Next.

12. On the Review Settings page, review the settings summary, and then click Finish.

Managing RIS Client Computers

Managing RIS client computers includes the following tasks:

- Prestaging RIS client computers
- Finding RIS client computers

Prestaging RIS Client Computers

Prestaging an RIS client computer is the process of creating a valid client CAO within Active Directory. By prestaging the client computer account in Active Directory, you can configure the RIS servers to respond only to prestaged client computers. This ensures that only those client computers that have been prestaged as authorized users are allowed to install an OS from the RIS server. Prestaging can save time and money by reducing, and in some cases eliminating, the need to fully preinstall the computer.

When you prestage a client computer, you can define a specific computer name and optionally specify the RIS server to service the computer. This information is used to identify and route the client computers during the network service boot request. Make sure you set the appropriate access permissions for users of the prestaged client computer. When prestaging a client computer into a domain with multiple domain controllers, the replication delay of the client CAO information can cause a client computer to be serviced by another RIS server.

▶ **Follow these steps to prestage a client computer:**

1. Click Start, point to Programs, point to Administrative Tools, and then click Active Directory Users And Computers.

2. In the console tree, right-click the applicable OU that will contain the new client computer, click New, and then click Computer.

3. In the New Object-Computer dialog box (see Figure 20.31), type the client computer name, authorize domain join permissions for the user or security group containing the user that will receive the physical computer this computer account represents, and then click Next.

Figure 20.31 New Object-Computer dialog box

4. In the Managed dialog box (see Figure 20.32), click This Is A Managed Computer, type the client computer GUID into the text entry field, and then click Next. See "Locating the GUID for Client Computers" later in this lesson for details.

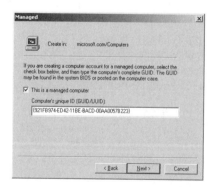

Figure 20.32 Managed dialog box

5. In the Host Server dialog box (see Figure 20.33), click one of the following options to determine which server will support this client computer:

- **Any Available Remote Installation Server.** Selecting this option indicates this client computer can be serviced by any RIS server.

- **The Following Remote Installation Server.** Selecting this option allows you to designate a specific server.

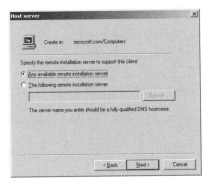

Figure 20.33 Host Server dialog box

You can use the options in the Host Server dialog box to manually set clients across the available RIS servers within your organization and to segment the network traffic, if you know the physical location of the specific RIS server and where this computer will be delivered. For example, if an RIS server is located on the fifth floor of your building and you are delivering these computers to users on that floor, you could choose to assign this computer to the RIS server on the fifth floor.

6. Click Next.

7. Review the settings on the New Object-Computer dialog box, and then click Finish.

Finding RIS Client Computers

You can search Active Directory for RIS client computer accounts using their computer name or GUID. The Show Clients feature searches for all client computers that are prestaged for this RIS server. The search process can include the entire Active Directory structure or be limited to a specific domain. The search process returns a list of the client computers and displays them by their computer name and GUID.

The Show Clients search process uses a wildcard search attribute appended to the current RIS server computer name. For example, if the RIS server is named RISsvr1, the Show Clients feature will use RISsvr1* for the server name. When you use the Show Clients feature in multiple RIS server environments, the search result might contain client computers from multiple servers. For example, if you have multiple RIS servers with computer names such as RISsvr1, RISsvr10, and RISsvr100, the search will return, from each of the servers, client computers that begin with the same computer name.

Locating the GUID for Client Computers

The computer's GUID appears on the following:

- The label on the side of the computer case
- The label inside the computer case
- The BIOS of the client computer

The manufacturer supplies the computer's GUID. The GUID must be in the form {*dddddddd-dddd-dddd-dddd-dddddddddddd*}, where *d* is a hexadecimal text digit. For example, it could be eight hexadecimal text digits, followed by four, then four, then four, then twelve, as in the following: {921FB974-ED42-11BE-BACD-00AA0057B223}

Valid entries for the client GUID are restricted to the following digits and characters:

    0 1 2 3 4 5 6 7 8 9 a b c d e f - A B C D E F

Dashes are optional and spaces are ignored. Brackets { } must be included.

▶   **Follow these steps to find RIS client computers:**

1. Click Start, point to Programs, point to Administrative Tools, and then click Active Directory Users And Computers.

2. In the console tree, right-click the applicable RIS server, and then click Properties.

3. In the Properties dialog box for the server, click the Remote Install tab.

4. In the Remote Install dialog box, click Show Clients.

5. In the Find Remote Installation Clients dialog box (see Figure 20.34), in the GUID box, enter the client computer's GUID, and then click Find Now.

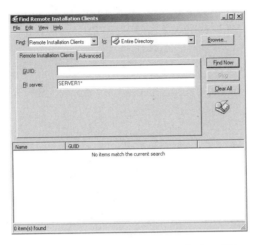

Figure 20.34 Find Remote Installation Clients dialog box

Note You can limit the client computer search to a specific RIS server by entering the server name in the RI Server box.

---

6. The RIS client computers appear in the Name and GUID columns in the lower portion of the Find Remote Installation Clients dialog box.

7. Close the Find Remote Installation Clients dialog box.

8. Close the Properties dialog box for the server.

Managing RIS Security

Managing RIS security includes the following tasks:

- Setting permissions for creating prestaged and user-created computer accounts
- Setting permissions for joining computers created in the Computers container and OUs to the domain

Setting Permissions for Creating Computer Accounts

To create new computer accounts in Active Directory, users need to have permissions and rights assigned to them. You must determine which users will be creating new client computer accounts and modify the users' rights and privileges accordingly.

▶ **Follow these steps to set permissions for creating prestaged computer accounts:**

1. Click Start, point to Programs, point to Administrative Tools, and then click Active Directory Users And Computers.

2. On the View menu, enable Users, Groups And Computers As Containers and Advanced Features.

3. In the console tree, right-click the applicable client computer account, and then click Properties.

4. In the Properties dialog box, click the Security tab, and then click Add.

5. In the Select Users, Computers, Or Groups dialog box, select the user or group from the list, click Add, and then click OK.

6. In the Properties dialog box, click the user or group you have added.

7. In the Permissions box, click the Read, Write, Change Password, and Reset Password permissions, and then click OK.

   If a group is allowed to have these permissions, remember to add users to that group.

   For client computer accounts that are prestaged in another Active Directory folder location, expand the Active Directory Users And Computers console and select the appropriate client computer account.

▶ **Follow these steps to set permissions for creating user-created computer accounts:**

1. Click Start, point to Programs, point to Administrative Tools, and then click Active Directory Users And Computers.

2. In the console tree, right-click the applicable domain, and then click Delegate Control to start the Delegation Of Control wizard.

3. On the Welcome To The Delegation Of Control Wizard page, click Next.

4. On the Users Or Groups page, click Add.

5. In the Select Users, Computers, Or Groups dialog box, click the user account or security group (preferred) containing the users you are setting permissions for, click Add, and then click OK.

6. On the Users Or Groups page, click Next.

7. On the Tasks To Delegate page, click Delegate The Following Common Tasks, click Join A Computer To The Domain, and then click Next.

8. Review the delegation of control summary information, and then click Finish.

Setting Permissions for Joining Computer Accounts to a Domain

To join new computer accounts to the domain, users need to have permissions and rights assigned to them. You must determine which users will be joining new client computer accounts to a domain and modify the users' rights and privileges accordingly.

▶ **Follow these steps to set permissions for joining computer accounts created in the Computers container to the domain:**

1. Click Start, point to Programs, point to Administrative Tools, and then click Active Directory Users And Computers.

2. In the console tree, right-click the applicable domain, and then click Delegate Control to start the Delegation Of Control wizard.

3. On the Welcome To The Delegation Of Control Wizard page, click Next.

4. On the Users Or Groups page, click Add.

5. In the Select Users, Computers, Or Groups dialog box, click the user account or security group (preferred) containing the users that will be joining client computers to the domain, click Add, and then click OK.

6. On the Users Or Groups page, click Next.

7. On the Tasks To Delegate page, click Delegate The Following Common Tasks, click Join A Computer To The Domain, and then click Next.

8. Review the delegation of control summary information, and then click Finish.

▶ **Follow these steps to set permissions for joining computer accounts created in OUs to the domain:**

1. Click Start, point to Programs, point to Administrative Tools, and then click Active Directory Users And Computers.

2. In the console tree, right-click the applicable OU, and then click Properties.

3. In the Properties dialog box for the OU, in the Group Policy tab, click the GPO in the Group Policy Object Links box, and then click Edit.

4. In the Group Policy snap-in, open Computer Configuration, click Windows Settings, click Security Settings, click Local Policies, and then click User Rights Assignment.

5. Double-click Add Workstations To Domain.

6. In the Security Policy Setting dialog box, click Add.

7. In the Add User Or Group dialog box, type or use the Browse button to enter the names of the user accounts or security groups (preferred) containing the users who will be adding client computers to the domain in the User And Group Names box, and then click OK.

8. In the Security Policy Setting dialog box, click OK.

9. Close the Group Policy snap-in.

10. In the Properties dialog box for the OU, click OK.

Note Because the changes that you make to RIS policy take effect only when the policy is propagated (applied) to your computer, do one of the following to initiate policy propagation:

- Type **secedit /refreshpolicy machine_policy** at the command prompt, and then press Enter.

- Restart your computer.

- Wait for automatic policy propagation, which occurs at regular, configurable intervals. By default, policy propagation occurs every 8 hours.

Lesson Summary

In this lesson, you learned about the tasks necessary to administer RIS, including managing RIS client installation images, managing RIS client computers, and managing RIS security.

Lesson 8: RIS Frequently Asked Questions and Troubleshooting

This lesson provides answers to frequently asked RIS questions. It also describes some RIS problems you may encounter and possible solutions.

After this lesson, you will be able to

- Troubleshoot RIS

Estimated lesson time: 15 minutes

Frequently Asked RIS Questions

This following are frequently asked RIS questions and answers to those questions.

Question 1: How can I tell if I have the correct PXE ROM version?

Answer: When the Net PC or client computer containing a remote-boot ROM starts, the version of the PXE ROM appears on the screen. RIS supports version .99c or greater PXE ROMs. You may be required to obtain a newer version of the PXE-based ROM code from your OEM if you have problems with the existing ROM version installed on a client computer.

Question 2: How can I tell if the client computer has received an IP address and has contacted the RIS server?

Answer: When the client computer boots, you will see the PXE boot ROM begin to load and initialize. The following remote-boot ROM load sequence occurs with most PC98 and Net PCs, PXE ROM–based computers, and the computers using the RIS boot disk.

Remote Boot ROM Load Sequence

Step 1: The client computer displays the message "DHCP," which indicates that the client is requesting an IP address from the DHCP server. This can also mean that the client has obtained an IP address from DHCP and is awaiting a response from the RIS server. To verify that the client is receiving an IP address, check the IP leases that have been granted on your DHCP server.

Troubleshooting: If the client does not receive the message, an IP address might not have been received or the BINL server might not be responding. Consider the following:

- Is the DHCP server available and has the service started? DHCP and RIS servers must be authorized in Active Directory for their services to start. Make sure the service has started and that other clients that are not remote boot–enabled are receiving IP addresses on this segment.

- Does the DHCP server have a defined IP address scope and has it been activated?

- Is there a router between the client and the DHCP server that is not allowing DHCP packets through?

- Are there any error messages in the event log under the system log for DHCP?

- Can other client computers—that is, those that are not remote boot–enabled clients—receive an IP address on this network segment?

Step 2: When the client receives an IP address from the DHCP server, the message may change to "BINL." This indicates that the client successfully leased an IP address and is now waiting to contact the RIS server. The client will eventually time out and post the error message "No Bootfile received from DHCP, BINL, or Bootp."

Troubleshooting: If the client does not receive the BINL message, this indicates the client is not receiving a response from the RIS server. Consider the following:

- Is the RIS server available and has the RIS started? RIS servers must be authorized to start on the network. Use the DHCP console to authorize both DHCP and RIS servers within Active Directory.

- Are other remote boot–enabled clients receiving the Client Installation wizard? If so, this client computer either is not supported or is having remote boot ROM-related problems. Check the version of the PXE ROM on the client computer. Also, check Active Directory to see whether the administrator has prestaged this client computer to an RIS server that is offline or unavailable to the client computer.

- Is a router between the client and the RIS server not allowing the DHCP–based requests or responses through? The RIS server communicates by way of the DHCP packet type during the initial service request and response sequence. You may need to configure the router to forward the DHCP packets.

- Are there any error messages in the event log under the system or application logs specific to RIS (BINLSVC), DNS, or Active Directory?

Step 3: The client then changes to TFTP or prompts the user to press F12. This indicates that the client has contacted the RIS server and is waiting to receive the first image file—the Client Installation wizard. You might not see the BINL and TFTP message on some machines because this sequence can complete very quickly.

Troubleshooting: If the client machine does not get a response from the RIS server, the client will time out and send an error message saying that it did not receive a file from DHCP, BINL, or TFTP. In this case, the RIS server did not answer the client computer. Do the following:

1. Stop and restart the BINLSVC service by clicking Start and pointing to Run.

2. In the Run dialog box, type **Net Stop BINLSVC Net Start BINLSVC** in the text field, and then click OK.

3. Unless you have prestaged the client computer in Active Directory prior to starting the client computer, check the RIS server properties to make sure the Respond To Client Computers Requesting Service check box is selected and that the Do Not Respond To Unknown Client Computers check box is cleared.

4. Check the event log in Event Viewer to make sure no errors relating to DHCP, DNS, RIS (BINLSVC), or Active Directory exist.

Step 4: At this point, the client should have downloaded and displayed the Client Installation wizard Welcome screen.

Question 3: Is the pre-boot portion of the PXE–based remote boot-ROM secure?

Answer: No. The entire boot ROM sequence and OS installation or replication process is not secure with regard to packet-type encryption, client/server spoofing, or wire sniffer–based mechanisms. As such, use caution when using RIS on your corporate network. Make sure you allow only authorized RIS servers on your network and that you control the number of administrators allowed to install and configure RIS servers.

Question 4: Does RIS preserve the file attributes and security settings defined on the source computer when using the RIPrep image feature?

Answer: Yes. The file attributes and security settings that are defined on the source computer are preserved on the destination computer that installs that image. However, the RIPrep feature does not support the encrypted file system if enabled and used on the source client computer.

Question 5: How do I replicate all of the OS installation images currently located on one RIS server to other RIS servers on the network for consistency across all client installations?

Answer: Currently the RIS feature does not provide a mechanism for replication of OS images from one RIS server to another, but there are several mechanisms you can use to solve this problem. Use the strong replication features of the Systems Management Server product, which provides for scheduled replication, compression, and slow-link features. You can also use other vendor solutions for OS image replication. Make sure the replication mechanism you choose supports maintaining the file attributes and security settings of the source images.

Question 6: Can I have an RIS server and another vendor remote boot server on the network at the same time? If so, what are the implications?

Answer: Yes, you can have multiple vendor remote boot/installation (RB/RI) servers on one physical network. It is important to understand that currently the remote boot PXE ROM code does not know the difference between vendors' RB/RI servers. As such, when a remote boot–enabled client computer starts and requests the IP address of an RB/RI server, all of the available servers will respond to that client; thus, the client has no way to ensure it is serviced by a specific RB/RI server.

RIS enables you to prestage client computers into Active Directory and determine which RIS server will service a client computer. By configuring the RIS server to answer only known client computers (prestaged), you are assured that the correct RIS server will service the client.

Not all other RB/RI vendors have implemented the ability to ignore service requests. You might need to isolate the specific vendors' servers on the network so that these vendors' RB/RI servers do not answer clients.

Question 7: Can I add more network adapters to the RIS boot disk?

Answer: No. The RBFG.EXE utility cannot be modified with regard to the number of supported network adapters for this release of RIS. Microsoft will be adding network card adapters over time and will make the updated RBFG.EXE utility available through normal distribution channels such as the World Wide Web, Windows updates, and future service or feature pack updates.

Question 8: Can I use the Active Directory object attributes to create a naming format for use with the RIS automatic computer-naming feature?

Answer: No. The existing attributes supported with the automatic computer naming feature use Active Directory. However, not all of the Active Directory object attributes are currently supported.

Troubleshooting RIS

Table 20.13 describes some RIS problems you may encounter and possible solutions.

Table 20.13   Troubleshooting Scenarios for RIS

Symptom: Command settings are not being processed during the unattended installation

Cause	Solution
When using the "OemPreinstall = yes" setting in an .sif file, the correct directory information is required.	Change the directory information to \RemoteInstall\Setup*applicable_language*\ Images*applicable_image_name*\oem.

Symptom: Language choice options are not displayed during the Client Installation wizard session

Cause	Solution
By default, RIS uses the WELCOME.OSC file to manage the client installation image choices. For multiple language installation image options, you need to replace the default WELCOME.OSC file with the MULTILNG.OSC file.	The Client Installation wizard uses the WELCOME.OSC file located in the \RemoteInstall\OSChooser folder to manage client installation image choices. When you remove the WELCOME.OSC file and rename the MULTILNG.OSC file to WELCOME.OSC, the Client Installation wizard also offers a menu of multiple language choices to the user. You can edit the WELCOME.OSC file to create custom language options.

Symptom: The client computer is prestaged to an RIS server but is being serviced by a different server

Cause	Solution
When you prestage a client computer into a domain with multiple domain controllers, the replication delay of the CAO information can cause a client computer to be serviced by another RIS server.	You can wait for the computer account information to be propagated during the next scheduled replication session or modify the replication frequency between your domain controllers.

continues

Table 20.13   Troubleshooting Scenarios for RIS *(continued)*

Symptom: Following the restoration of a backup of an RIS volume, RIS no longer functions properly

Cause	Solution
Backup restored the volume without an SIS directory.	Verify the configuration of the RIS volume and then restore the volume again.

Lesson Summary

In this lesson, you reviewed frequently asked RIS questions and answers. You also examined some RIS problems you may encounter and possible solutions to these problems.

Review

The following questions will help you determine whether you have learned enough to move on to the next chapter. If you have difficulty answering these questions, please go back and review the material in this chapter before beginning the next chapter. See Appendix A, "Questions and Answers," for the answers to these questions.

1. In what order is Group Policy implemented through the Active Directory structure?

2. Name the tasks for implementing Group Policy.

3. What is the difference between Block Policy Inheritance and No Override?

4. What is the difference between assigning software and publishing software?

5. What folders can be redirected?

6. What is RIS? What types of remote booting are supported by RIS?

7. What does PXE remote boot technology provide?

8. What is the RIS boot disk?

9. What is an RIPrep image?

10. What is the Client Installation wizard?

C H A P T E R   2 1

Managing Active Directory Security Solutions

About This Chapter

Security settings define the security-relevant behavior of Windows 2000. Through the use of group policy objects (GPOs) in Active Directory, administrators can centrally apply the security levels required to protect enterprise systems. Local GPOs can also be used to apply security to nonenterprise and workgroup systems. This chapter provides details on using security settings to configure a system's security.

Before You Begin

To complete this chapter, you must have

- Installed Windows 2000 Server on a computer (Server01)

  See Chapter 8, "Installing Microsoft Windows 2000," for more details.

- Configured the computer (Server01) as a domain controller in a domain

- The ability to manage and configure groups by using group policies (as explained in Chapter 19, "Managing Active Directory Components")

Lesson 1: Security Configuration Overview

You use the Security Settings extension in the Group Policy snap-in to define security configurations for computers and groups. This lesson introduces the security configuration settings.

After this lesson, you will be able to

- Recognize security configuration settings in a GPO

Estimated lesson time: 10 minutes

Security Configuration Settings

A *security configuration* consists of security settings applied to each security area supported by Microsoft Windows 2000. You use the Security Settings extension in the Group Policy snap-in to configure the following security areas for a nonlocal GPO:

- Account policies
- Local policies
- Event log
- Restricted groups
- System services
- Registry
- File system
- Public key policies
- Internet Protocol (IP) security policies

Account Policies

Account policies apply to user accounts. This security area contains attributes for the following policies.

- **Password Policy.** For domain or local user accounts. Determines settings for passwords such as enforcement and lifetimes.

- **Account Lockout Policy.** For domain or local user accounts. Determines when and for whom an account will be locked out of the system.

- **Kerberos Policy.** For domain user accounts. Determines Kerberos-related settings, such as ticket lifetimes and enforcement.

Important Account policies should not be configured for organizational units (OUs) that do not contain any computers, as OUs that contain only users will always receive account policy from the domain.

When setting account policies in Active Directory, keep in mind that Windows 2000 only allows one domain account policy: the account policy applied to the root domain of the domain tree. The domain account policy becomes the default account policy of any Windows 2000 workstation or server that is a member of the domain. The only exception to this rule is when another account policy is defined for an organizational unit (OU). The account policy settings for the OU affect the local policy on any computers contained in the OU, as is the case with a Domain Controllers OU.

Local Policies

These policies pertain to the security settings on the computer used by an application or user. Local policies are based on the computer you are logged on to and the rights you have on that particular computer. This security area contains attributes for the following policies:

- **Audit Policy.** Determines which security events are logged into the security log on the computer (successful attempts, failed attempts, or both). (The security log is a part of the Event Viewer console.)

- **User Rights Assignment.** Determines which users or groups have logon or task privileges on the computer.

- **Security Options.** Enables or disables security settings for the computer, such as digital signing of data, Administrator and Guest account names, floppy drive and CD-ROM access, driver installation, and logon prompts.

Local policies, by definition, are local to a computer. When these settings are imported to a GPO in Active Directory, they affect the local security settings of any computer accounts to which that GPO is applied.

Event Log

The event log security area defines attributes related to the Application, Security, and System event logs. These attributes are maximum log size, access rights for each log, and retention settings and methods (see Figure 21.1).

Event log size and log wrapping should be defined to match your business and security requirements. To take advantage of group policy settings, you may consider implementing these event log settings at the site, domain, or OU level.

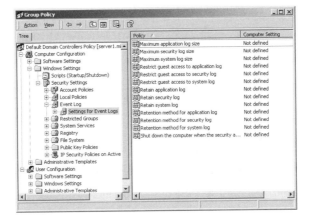

Figure 21.1 Event log settings

Restricted Groups

The Restricted Groups security area provides an important new security feature that acts as a governor for group membership. Restricted Groups automatically provides security memberships for default Windows 2000 groups that have predefined capabilities, such as Administrators, Power Users, Print Operators, Server Operators, and Domain Admins. You can later add any groups that you consider sensitive or privileged to the Restricted Groups security list.

For example, the Power Users group is automatically part of Restricted Groups, since it is a default Windows 2000 group. Assume it contains two users: Alice and Bob. Using the Active Directory Users And Computers console, Bob adds Charles to the group to cover for him while he is on vacation. However, no one remembers to remove Charles from the group when Bob comes back from vacation. In actual deployments, over time, these situations can add up, resulting in extra members in various groups who should no longer have these rights. Configuring security through Restricted Groups can prevent this situation. Because only Alice and Bob are listed in the Restricted Groups node for Power Users, when group policy settings are applied, Charles is removed from the group automatically.

Configuring Restricted Groups ensures that group memberships are set as specified. Groups and users not specified in Restricted Groups are removed from the specific group. In addition, the reverse membership configuration option ensures that each Restricted Group is a member of only those groups specified in the Member Of column. For these reasons, Restricted Groups should be used primarily to configure membership of local groups on workstation or member servers.

System Services

The system services area is used to configure security and startup settings for services running on a computer.

The Security properties for the service determine what user or group accounts have permission to read/write/delete/execute, as well as inheritance settings, auditing, and ownership permission.

The startup settings are

- **Automatic.** Starts a service automatically at system start time.
- **Manual.** Starts a service only if manually started.
- **Disabled.** The service is disabled so it cannot be started.

If you choose to set system service startup to Automatic, perform adequate testing to verify that the services can start without user intervention. You should track the system services used on a computer. For performance optimization, set unnecessary or unused services to Manual.

Registry and File System Areas

The registry area is used to configure security on registry keys. The file system area is used to configure security on specific file paths. You can edit the Security properties of the registry key or file path defining what user or group accounts have permission to read/write/delete/execute, as well as inheritance settings, auditing, and ownership permission.

Public Key Policies

The public key policies area is used to configure encrypted data recovery agents, domain roots, and trusted certificate authorities.

IP Security Policies

The IP security policies area is used to configure network Internet Protocol (IP) security.

Lesson Summary

In this lesson, you were introduced to the security configuration settings in a nonlocal GPO. This included security settings for account policies and local policies and configuring event logs. The lesson also introduced the use of restricted groups and explained the use of system services and the registry area when configuring for security. The lesson ended with explanations of the uses of public key and IP Security policies.

Lesson 2: Auditing

In this lesson, you learn about Windows 2000 auditing, which is a tool for maintaining network security. Auditing allows you to track user activities and system-wide events. You learn about audit policies and what you need to consider before you set one up. You also learn how to set up auditing on resources.

After this lesson, you will be able to

- Describe the purpose of auditing
- Plan an audit strategy and determine which events to audit
- Set up an audit policy
- Set up auditing on files and folders
- Set up auditing on Active Directory objects
- Set up auditing on printers

Estimated lesson time: 60 minutes

Understanding Auditing

Auditing in Microsoft Windows 2000 is the process of tracking both user activities and Windows 2000 activities, which are called *events,* on a computer. Through auditing, you can specify which events are written to the security log. For example, the security log can maintain a record of valid and invalid logon attempts and events relating to creating, opening, or deleting files or other objects. An audit entry in the security log contains the following information:

- The action that was performed
- The user who performed the action
- The success or failure of the event and when the event occurred

Using an Audit Policy

An *audit policy* defines the categories of events that Windows 2000 records in the security log on each computer. The security log allows you to track the events that you specify.

Windows 2000 writes events to the security log on the computer where the event occurs. For example, any time someone tries to log on to the domain using a domain user account and the logon attempt fails, Windows 2000 writes an event to the security log on the domain controller. The event is recorded on the domain controller rather than on the computer at which the logon attempt was made because it is the domain controller that attempted to and could not authenticate the logon attempt.

You can set up an audit policy for a computer to do the following:

- Track the success and failure of events, such as logon attempts by users, an attempt by a particular user to read a specific file, changes to a user account or to group memberships, and changes to your security settings
- Eliminate or minimize the risk of unauthorized use of resources

You use Event Viewer to view events that Windows 2000 has recorded in the security log. You can also archive log files to track trends over time—for example, to determine the use of printers or files or to verify attempts at unauthorized use of resources.

Audit Policy Guidelines

When you plan an audit policy, you must determine on which computers to set up auditing. Auditing is turned off by default. As you are determining which computers to audit, you must also plan the events to audit on each computer. Windows 2000 records audited events on each computer separately.

After you have determined the events to audit, you must determine whether to audit the success of events, failure of events, or both. Tracking successful events can tell you how often Windows 2000 or users gain access to specific files, printers, or other objects. You can use this information for resource planning. Tracking failed events can alert you to possible security breaches. For example, if you notice several failed logon attempts by a certain user account, especially if these attempts are occurring outside normal business hours, you can assume that an unauthorized person is attempting to break into your system.

Other guidelines in determining your audit policy include the following:

- **Determine if you need to track trends of system usage.** If so, plan to archive event logs. Archiving these logs allows you to view how usage changes over time and to plan to increase system resources before they become a problem.
- **Review security logs frequently.** You should set a schedule and regularly review security logs because configuring auditing alone does not alert you to security breaches.

- **Define an audit policy that is useful and manageable.** Always audit sensitive and confidential data. Audit only those events that provide you with meaningful information about your network environment. This minimizes use of server resources and makes essential information easier to locate. Auditing too many types of events can create excess overhead for Windows 2000.

- **Audit resource access by the Everyone group instead of the Users group.** This ensures that you audit anyone who can connect to the network, not just the users for whom you create user accounts in the domain. You should also audit resource access failures by the Everyone group.

- **Audit all administrative tasks by the administrative groups.** This ensures that you audit any additions or changes made by administrators.

Configuring Auditing

You implement an audit policy based on the role of the computer in the Windows 2000 network. Auditing is configured differently for the following types of computers running Windows 2000:

- For member or standalone servers, or computers running Windows 2000 Professional, an audit policy is set for each individual computer. To audit events that occur on a local computer, you configure a local group policy for that computer, which applies to that computer only.

- For domain controllers, an audit policy is set for all domain controllers in the domain. To audit events that occur on domain controllers, you configure the audit policy in a nonlocal GPO for the domain, which applies to all domain controllers and is accessible through the Domain Controllers OU.

The event categories on a domain controller are identical to those on a computer that is not a domain controller.

Auditing Requirements

The requirements to set up and administer auditing are as follows:

- You must have the Manage Auditing And Security Log user right for the computer where you want to configure an audit policy or review an audit log. By default, Windows 2000 grants these rights to the Administrators group.

- The files and folders to be audited must be on NT file system (NTFS) volumes.

Setting Up Auditing

Setting up auditing is a two-part process:

1. **Set the audit policy.** The audit policy enables auditing of objects but does not activate auditing of specific objects.

2. **Enable auditing of specific resources.** You specify the specific events to audit for files, folders, printers, and Active Directory objects. Windows 2000 then tracks and logs the specified events.

Setting Up an Audit Policy

The first step in implementing an audit GPO is selecting the categories of events that Windows 2000 audits. For each event category that you can audit, the configuration settings indicate whether to track successful or failed attempts. You set audit policies in the Group Policy snap-in. The security log is limited in size. Select the events to be audited carefully and consider the amount of disk space you are willing to devote to the security log. Table 21.1 describes the event categories that Windows 2000 can audit.

Table 21.1   Types of Events Audited by Windows 2000

Event category	Description
Account logon	A domain controller received a request to validate a user account.
Account management	An administrator created, changed, or deleted a user account or group. A user account was renamed, disabled, or enabled, or a password was set or changed.
Directory service access	A user gained access to an Active Directory object. You must configure specific Active Directory objects for auditing to log this type of event.
Logon events	A user logged on or logged off, or a user made or canceled a network connection to the computer.
Object access	A user gained access to a file, folder, or printer. You must configure specific files, folders, or printers for auditing. Directory service access is auditing a user's access to specific Active Directory objects. Object access is auditing a user's access to files, folders, and printers.
Policy change	A change was made to the user security options, user rights, or audit policies.

Event category	Description
Privilege use	A user exercised a right, such as changing the system time (this does not include rights that are related to logging on and logging off).
Process tracking	A program performed an action. This information is generally useful only for programmers who want to track details of program execution.
System events	A user restarted or shut down the computer, or an event occurred that affects Windows 2000 security or the security log (for example, the audit log is full and Windows 2000 discards entries).

▶ **Follow these steps to set an audit policy for a domain controller:**

1. Open Active Directory Users And Computers.

2. In the console tree, right-click Domain Controllers, and then click Properties.

3. In the Group Policy tab, click the policy in which you want set the audit policy, and then click Edit.

4. In the Group Policy snap-in, in the console tree, click Computer Configuration, double-click Windows Settings, double-click Security Settings, double-click Local Policies, and then double-click Audit Policy.

   The console displays the current audit policy settings in the details pane, as shown in Figure 21.2.

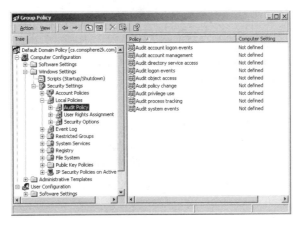

Figure 21.2 Custom console showing events that Windows 2000 can audit

5. In the details pane, right-click the event category you want to audit, and then click Security.

6. In the Template Security Policy Setting dialog box (see Figure 21.3), click Define These Policy Settings In The Template, and then click one or both:

   - **Success.** This audits successful attempts for the event category

   - **Failure.** This audits failed attempts for the event category

7. Click OK.

8. Because the changes that you make to your computer's audit policy take effect only when the policy is propagated (applied) to your computer, do one of the following to initiate policy propagation:

   - Type **secedit /refreshpolicy machine_policy** at the command prompt, and then press Enter.

   - Restart your computer.

   - Wait for automatic policy propagation, which occurs at regular, configurable intervals. By default, policy propagation occurs every 8 hours.

Figure 21.3 The Template Security Policy Setting dialog box

▶ **Follow these steps to set an audit policy on a computer that does not participate in a domain:**

1. Click Start, point to Programs, point to Administrative Tools, and then click Local Security Policy.

2. In Local Security Settings, in the console tree, double-click Local Policies, and then double-click Audit Policy.

3. In the details pane, right-click the event category you want to audit, and then click Security.

4. In the Local Security Policy Setting dialog box (see Figure 21.4), click one or both of the following check boxes:

  - **Success.** This audits successful attempts for the event category

  - **Failure.** This audits failed attempts for the event category

The Effective Policy Setting box shows the security setting value currently enforced on the system. If an audit policy has already been set at the domain level or the OU level, it overrides the local audit policy.

5. Click OK.

6. Because the changes that you make to your computer's audit policy take effect only when the policy is propagated (applied) to your computer, do one of the following to initiate policy propagation:

  - Type **secedit /refreshpolicy machine_policy** at the command prompt, and then press Enter.

  - Restart your computer.

  - Wait for automatic policy propagation, which occurs at regular, configurable intervals. By default, policy propagation occurs every 8 hours.

Figure 21.4 The Local Security Policy Setting dialog box

▶ **Follow these steps to set an audit policy on a member server or workstation:**

1. Create an OU for the remote computer(s) and add the desired machine account(s) to the OU.

2. Using Active Directory Users and Computers, as described in the steps outlined earlier to set an audit policy for a domain controller, create an audit policy to enable security auditing.

Note Security auditing for workstations, member servers, and domain controllers can be enabled remotely only by domain and enterprise administrators.

Auditing Access to Files and Folders

If security breaches are an issue for your organization, you can set up auditing for files and folders on NTFS partitions. To audit user access to files and folders, you must first set the Audit Object Access event category, which includes files and folders, in the audit policy.

Once you have set Audit Object Access in your audit policy, you enable auditing for specific files and folders and specify which types of access to audit (by users or groups).

▶ **Follow these steps to set up auditing for specific files and folders:**

1. In Windows Explorer, right-click the file or folder you want to audit, and then click Properties.

2. In the Security tab in the Properties dialog box for a file or folder, click Advanced.

3. In the Access Control Settings For dialog box for the file or folder, in the Auditing tab, click Add, select the users and groups for whom you want to audit file and folder access, and then click OK.

4. In the Auditing Entry For dialog box for the file or folder (see Figure 21.5), select the Successful check box, the Failed check box, or both check boxes for the events that you want to audit.

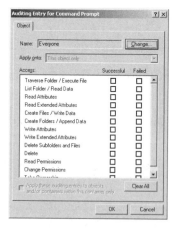

Figure 21.5 The Auditing Entry For dialog box for the Command Prompt file

Table 21.2 describes the events that can be audited for files and folders and explains what action triggers the event to occur.

Table 21.2   User Events and What Triggers Them

Event	User activity that triggers the event
Traverse Folder/Execute File	Moving through folders to reach other files or folders, even if the user has no permissions to traversed folders (folders only) or running program files (files only)
List Folder/Read Data	Viewing filenames and subfolder names within a folder (folders only) or viewing data in files (files only)
Read Attributes and Read Extended Attributes	Displaying the attributes of a file or folder
Create Files/Write Data	Creating files within a folder (folders only) or changing the contents of a file (files only)
Create Folders/Append Data	Creating folders within a folder (folders only) or making changes to the end of the file but not changing, deleting, or overwriting existing data (files only)
Write Attributes and Write Extended Attributes	Changing attributes of a file or folder
Delete Subfolders And Files	Deleting a file or subfolder in a folder
Delete	Deleting a file or folder
Read Permissions	Viewing permissions or the file owner for a file or folder
Change Permissions	Changing permissions for a file or folder
Take Ownership	Taking ownership of a file or folder

5. In the Apply Onto list (available only for folders), specify where objects are audited. By default, this box is set to This Folder, Subfolders And Files, so any auditing changes that you make to a parent folder also apply to all child folders and all files in the parent and child folders. Where objects are audited depends on the selection in the Apply Onto list and whether the Apply These Auditing Entries To Objects And/Or Containers Within This Container Only check box is selected, as shown in Table 21.3.

Table 21.3   Results When the Apply These Auditing Entries To Objects And/Or Containers Within This Container Only Check Box Is Cleared

Apply onto	Audits current folder	Audits subfolders in the current folder	Audits files in the current folder	Audits all subsequent folders	Audits files in all subsequent subfolders
This folder only	X				
This folder, subfolders, and files	X	X	X	X	X
This folder and subfolders	X	X		X	
This folder and files	X		X		X
Subfolders and files only		X	X	X	X
Subfolders only		X		X	
Files only			X		X

When the Apply These Auditing Entries To Objects And/Or Containers Within This Container Only check box is selected, auditing is applied to the selection in the Apply Onto box and all applicable child objects within the tree.

6. Click OK to return to the Access Control Settings For dialog box for the file or folder.

7. To prevent changes that are made to a parent folder from applying to the currently selected file or folder, clear the Allow Inheritable Auditing Entries From Parent To Propagate To This Object check box.

   If the check boxes under Access are shaded in the Auditing Entry For dialog box for the file or folder, or if the Remove button is unavailable in the Access Control Settings For dialog box for the file or folder, auditing has been inherited from the parent folder.

8. Click OK.

Auditing Access to Active Directory Objects

As with auditing file and folder access, to audit Active Directory object access, you must configure an audit policy and then set auditing for specific objects, such as users, computers, OUs, or groups, by specifying which types of access and access by which users to audit. You audit Active Directory objects to track access to Active Directory objects, such as changing the properties on a user account. To enable auditing of user access to Active Directory objects, set the Audit Directory Service Access event category in the audit policy.

▶ **Follow these steps to set up auditing for specific Active Directory objects:**

1. In Active Directory Users And Computers, click View, and then click Advanced Features.

2. Select the object that you want to audit, click Properties on the Action menu, click the Security tab, and then click the Advanced button.

3. In the Access Control Settings For dialog box for the object, in the Auditing tab, click Add, select the users or groups for whom you want to audit file and folder access, and then click OK.

4. In the Auditing Entry For dialog box for the object (see Figure 21.6), select the Successful check box, the Failed check box, or both check boxes for the events that you want to audit.

   Table 21.4 describes some of the audit events for Active Directory objects and explains what action triggers the event.

Table 21.4   Some Active Directory Object Events and What Trigger Them

Event	User activity that triggers the event
Full Control	Performing any type of access to the audited object
List Contents	Viewing the objects within the audited object
Read All Properties	Viewing any attribute of the audited object
Write All Properties	Changing any attribute of the audited object
Create All Child Objects	Creating any object within the audited object
Delete All Child Objects	Deleting any object within the audited object
Read Permissions	Viewing the permissions for the audited object
Modify Permissions	Changing the permissions for the audited object
Modify Owner	Taking ownership of the audited object

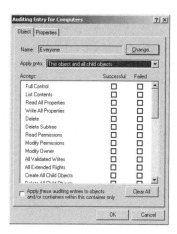

Figure 21.6 The Auditing Entry For dialog box for the Computers folder

5. In the Apply Onto list, specify where objects are audited. By default, this box is set to This Object And All Child Objects, so any auditing changes that you make to a parent object also apply to all child objects. Where objects are audited depends on the selection in the Apply Onto list and whether the Apply These Auditing Entries To Objects And/Or Containers Within This Container Only check box is selected. These two features are only enabled for objects that act as containers.

6. Click OK to return to the Access Control Settings For dialog box for the object.

7. To prevent changes that are made to a parent folder from applying to the currently selected file or folder, clear the Allow Inheritable Auditing Entries From Parent To Propagate To This Object check box.

   If the check boxes under Access are shaded in the Auditing Entry For dialog box for the object, or if the Remove button is unavailable in the Access Control Settings For dialog box for the object, auditing has been inherited from the parent folder.

8. Click OK.

Auditing Access to Printers

Audit access to printers to track access to sensitive printers. To audit access to printers, set the Audit Object Access event category in your audit policy, which includes printers. Then, enable auditing for specific printers and specify which types of access and access by which users to audit. After you select the printer, use the same steps that you use to set up auditing on files and folders.

▶ **Follow these steps to set up auditing on a printer:**

1. Click Start, point to Settings, and then click Printers.

2. In the Printers system folder, right-click the printer you want to audit, and then click Properties.

3. In the Properties dialog box for the printer, click the Security tab, and then click Advanced.

4. In the Access Control Settings For dialog box for the printer, in the Auditing tab, click Add, select the appropriate users or groups for whom you want to audit printer access, click Add, and then click OK.

5. In the Auditing Entry For dialog box for the printer (see Figure 21.7), select the Successful check box, the Failed check box, or both check boxes for the events that you want to audit.

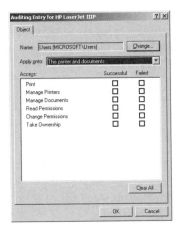

Figure 21.7 The Auditing Entry For dialog box for a printer

Table 21.5 lists audit events for printers and explains what action triggers the event to occur.

Table 21.5   Printer Events and What Triggers Them

Event	User activity that triggers the event
Print	Printing a file
Manage Printers	Changing printer settings, pausing a printer, sharing a printer, or removing a printer

continues

Table 21.5   Printer Events and What Triggers Them *(continued)*

Event	User activity that triggers the event
Manage Documents	Changing job settings; pausing, restarting, moving, or deleting documents; sharing a printer; or changing printer properties
Read Permissions	Viewing printer permissions
Change Permissions	Changing printer permissions
Take Ownership	Taking printer ownership

6. In the Apply Onto list, select where the auditing setting applies.

7. Click OK in the appropriate dialog boxes to exit.

Auditing Practices

Table 21.6 lists various events that you should audit as well as the specific security threat that the audit event monitors.

Table 21.6   Recommended Audit Events

Audit event	Potential threat
Failure audit for logon/logoff.	Random password hack
Success audit for logon/logoff.	Stolen password break-in
Success audit for user rights, user and group management, security change policies, restart, shutdown, and system events.	Misuse of privileges
Success and failure audit for file-access and object-access events. File Manager success and failure audit of Read/Write access by suspect users or groups for the sensitive files.	Improper access to sensitive files
Success and failure audit for file-access printers and object-access events. Print Manager success and failure audit of print access by suspect users or groups for the printers.	Improper access to printers
Success and failure write access auditing for program files (.exe and .dll extensions). Success and failure auditing for process tracking. Run suspect programs; examine security log for unexpected attempts to modify program files or create unexpected processes. Run only when actively monitoring the system log.	Virus outbreak

Practice: Auditing Resources and Events

In this practice, you plan a domain audit policy. You then set up an audit policy for a domain controller by enabling auditing of certain events. You set up auditing of a file, a printer, and an Active Directory object.

Exercise 1: Planning a Domain Audit Policy

In this exercise, you plan an audit policy for your server. You need to determine the following:

- Which types of events to audit
- Whether to audit the success or failure of an event, or both

Use the following criteria to make your decisions:

- Record unsuccessful attempts to gain access to the network.
- Record unauthorized access to the files that make up the Customer database.
- For billing purposes, track color printer usage.
- Track whenever someone tries to tamper with the server hardware.
- Keep a record of actions that an administrator performs to track unauthorized changes.
- Track backup procedures to prevent data theft.
- Track unauthorized access to sensitive Active Directory objects.

Record your decisions to audit successful events, failed events, or both for the actions listed in the following table.

Audit Policy Plan for Exercise 1

Action to audit	Successful	Failed
Account logon events		
Account management		
Directory service access		
Logon events		
Object access		
Policy change		
Privilege use		
Process tracking		
System events		

Exercise 2: Setting Up an Audit Policy

In this exercise you enable auditing for selected event categories.

1. Open Active Directory Users And Computers.

2. In the console tree, right-click Domain Controllers, and then click Properties.

3. In the Properties dialog box, in the Group Policy tab, select the Default Domain Controllers Policy group policy, and then click Edit.

4. In the Group Policy snap-in, in the console tree, click Computer Configuration, double-click Windows Settings, double-click Security Settings, double-click Local Policies, and then double-click Audit Policy.

5. To set the audit policy, in the details pane, double-click each event category, and then select either Success or Failure as listed in the following table.

Audit Policy Settings for Exercise 2

Event category	Success	Failure
Account logon events		
Account management	X	
Directory service access		X
Logon events		X
Object access	X	X
Policy change	X	
Privilege use	X	
Process tracking		
System events	X	X

6. Close the Group Policy snap-in.

7. Close the Domain Controllers Properties dialog box.

8. Start a command prompt.

9. At the command prompt, type **secedit /refreshpolicy machine_policy**, then press Enter.

   The policy changes take effect in a few moments.

10. Close the command prompt.

Exercise 3: Setting Up Auditing of Files

In this exercise, you set up auditing for a file.

▶ **To set up auditing of files**

1. In Windows Explorer, locate a file such as a simple text file.

2. Right-click the filename, and then click Properties.

3. In the Properties dialog box, click the Security tab, and then click Advanced.

4. In the Access Control Settings For dialog box for the text file, click the Auditing tab.

5. Click Add.

6. In the Select User, Computer, Or Group dialog box, double-click Everyone in the list of user accounts and groups.

7. In the Auditing Entry For dialog box for the text file, select the Successful check box and the Failed check box for each of the following events:

   - Create Files/Write Data

   - Delete

   - Change Permissions

   - Take Ownership

8. Click OK.

   Windows 2000 displays the Everyone group in the Access Control Settings For dialog box for the text file.

9. Click OK to apply your changes.

▶ **To change file permissions**

1. In the Properties dialog box, on the Security tab, add the Everyone group.

2. Change the NTFS permissions for the Everyone group to only the Read permission for the file, and clear the Allow Inheritable Permissions From Parent To Propagate To This Object check box.

   The Security message box appears asking you to confirm that you want to clear the Allow Inheritable Permissions From Parent To Propagate To This Object check box.

3. On the Security message box, click Remove, and then click OK.

   Any other permissions are removed.

4. Click OK to close the Properties dialog box, and then close Windows Explorer.

Exercise 4: Setting Up Auditing of a Printer

In this exercise, you set up auditing of a printer.

Important To complete this exercise, you need to have a local printer installed on your computer. However, you do *not* need a printing device connected to the computer. If you do not have a local printer installed, create one now. Remember that *printing device* refers to the physical machine that prints and that *local printer* refers to the software that Windows 2000 needs to send data to the printing device.

---

1. Click Start, point to Settings, and then click Printers.

2. In the Printers system folder, right-click a printer associated with your computer, and then click Properties.

3. Click the Security tab, and then click Advanced.

4. In the Access Control Settings For dialog box for the printer, click the Auditing tab, and then click Add.

5. In the Select User, Computer, Or Group dialog box, double-click Everyone in the list box.

6. In the Auditing Entry For dialog box for the printer, select the Successful check box for all types of access.

7. Click OK.

   Windows 2000 displays the Everyone group in the Access Control Settings For dialog box for the printer.

8. In the Access Control Settings For dialog box for the printer, click OK to apply your changes.

9. Click OK to close the printer Properties dialog box.

10. Close the Printers system folder.

Exercise 5: Setting Up Auditing of an Active Directory Object

In this exercise, you set up auditing of an Active Directory object.

1. Start Active Directory Users And Computers.

2. On the View menu, click Advanced Features.

3. In the console tree, click your domain.

4. In the details pane, click Users, and then on the Action menu, click Properties.

5. In the Users Properties dialog box, click the Security tab, and then click Advanced.

6. In the Access Control Settings For Users dialog box, click the Auditing tab, and then double-click Everyone.

    The Auditing Entry For Users dialog box appears.

    Review the default audit settings for object access by members of the Everyone group. How do the audited types of access differ from the types of access that are not audited?

7. Click OK three times to close the Auditing Entry For Users, the Access Control Settings For Users, and the Users Properties dialog boxes.

    On which computer or computers does Windows 2000 record log entries for Active Directory access? Will you be able to review them?

8. Close Active Directory Users And Computers.

Lesson Summary

In this lesson, you learned how to set up an audit policy. The first step in implementing an audit policy is selecting the event categories that Windows 2000 audits. For each event that you can audit, the configuration settings indicate whether to track successful or failed attempts.

For member or standalone servers, or computers running Windows 2000 Professional, an audit policy is set for each individual computer. To audit events that occur on a local computer, you configure a local group policy for that computer, which applies to that computer only.

For domain controllers, an audit policy is set for all domain controllers in the domain. To audit events that occur on domain controllers, you configure a nonlocal group policy for the domain, which applies to all domain controllers.

In the practice portion of this lesson, you planned a domain audit policy; set up an audit policy for a domain controller; and set up auditing of a file, a printer, and an Active Directory object.

Lesson 3: Using Security Logs

The security log contains information on security events that are specified in the audit policy. To view the security log, you use the Event Viewer console. Event Viewer also allows you to find specific events within log files, filter the events shown in log files, and archive security log files.

After this lesson, you will be able to

- View a log
- Locate events in a log
- Filter events in a log
- Configure the size of audit logs
- Archive security logs

Estimated lesson time: 25 minutes

Understanding Windows 2000 Logs

You use the Event Viewer console to view information contained in Windows 2000 logs. By default, there are three logs available to view in Event Viewer. These logs are described in Table 21.7.

Table 21.7   Logs Maintained by Windows 2000

Log	Description
Application log	Contains errors, warnings, or information generated by programs such as a database program or an e-mail program. The program developer presets which events to record.
Security log	Contains information about the success or failure of audited events. The events that Windows 2000 records are a result of your audit policy.
System log	Contains errors, warnings, and information generated by Windows 2000. Windows 2000 presets which events to record.

Application and system logs can be viewed by all users. Security logs are accessible only to system administrators. By default, security logging is turned off. To enable security logging, you must use group policy at the appropriate level to set up an audit policy.

Note If additional services are installed, they might add their own event log. For example, the Domain Name System (DNS) Service logs events that this service generates in the DNS server log.

Viewing Security Logs

The security log contains information about events that are monitored by an audit policy, such as failed and successful logon attempts.

▶   **Follow these steps to view the security log:**

1. Click Start, point to Programs, point to Administrative Tools, and then click Event Viewer.

2. In the console tree, select Security Log.

   In the details pane, Event Viewer displays a list of log entries and summary information for each item, as shown in Figure 21.8.

   Successful events appear with a key icon and unsuccessful events appear with a lock icon. Other important information includes the date and time that the event occurred, the category of the event, and the user who generated the event.

   The category indicates the event category, such as object access, account management, directory service access, or logon events.

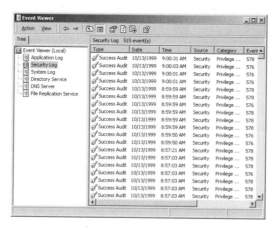

Figure 21.8 Event Viewer displaying a sample security log

3. To view additional information for any event, double-click the event.

Windows 2000 records events in the security log on the computer at which the event occurred. You can view these events from any computer as long as you have administrative privileges for the computer where the events occurred.

▶ **Follow these steps to view the security log on a remote computer:**

1. Ensure that security auditing has been enabled on a remote machine. (See Lesson 2, "Auditing," for details.)

2. Click Start, point to Programs, point to Administrative Tools, and then click Event Viewer.

3. Right-click the Event Viewer (Local) node and select Connect To Another Computer.

4. In the Select Computer dialog box, click Another Computer and type the network name, IP address, or DNS address for the computer for which Event Viewer will display a security log. You can also browse for the computer name.

5. Click OK.

Locating Events

When you first start Event Viewer, it automatically displays all events that are recorded in the security log. You can search for specific events by using the Find command.

▶ **Follow these steps to find events:**

1. Start Event Viewer, click the security log, and then click Find on the View menu.

2. On the Find In dialog box for the security log, configure the options shown in Figure 21.9 and described in Table 21.8.

Table 21.8   Options on the Find In Dialog Box

Option	Description
Event Types	Check boxes that indicate the types of events to find. In the security log, you can only find audit events because others are not recorded.
Event Source	A list that indicates the software or component driver that logged the event.
Category	A list that indicates the event category, such as a logon or logoff attempt or a system event.

continues

Table 21.8   Options on the Find In Dialog Box *(continued)*

Option	Description
Event ID	An event number to identify the event. This number helps product support representatives track events.
User	A user logon name.
Computer	A computer name.
Description	Text that is in the description of the event.
Search Direction	The direction in which to search the log (up or down).
Find Next	Finds and selects the next occurrence defined by the Find settings.

Figure 21.9 The Find In dialog box for a security log

Filtering Events

An event log can contain a lot of information that may not be of use in specific circumstances. For example, if you want to see an attempt to write to a text file without the necessary permissions, you might have to dig through hundreds of non-related events before finding what you want. To show specific events that appear in the security log, you can reduce the number of events to display by using the Filter command.

▶   **Follow these steps to filter events:**

1. Start Event Viewer, click the security log, and then click Filter on the View menu.

2. In the Security Log Properties dialog box, in the Filter tab, configure the options shown in Figure 21.10 and described in Table 21.9.

Table 21.9   Options on the Filter Tab of the Security Log Properties Dialog Box

Option	Description
Event Types	Check boxes that indicate the types of events to filter. In the security log, you can only filter using audit events because others are not recorded.
Event Source	A list that indicates the software or component driver that logged the event.
Category	A list that indicates the type of event, such as a logon or logoff attempt or a system event.
Event ID	An event number to identify the event. This number helps product support representatives track events.
User	A user logon name.
Computer	A computer name.
From	The beginning of the range of events that you want to filter. In the list under From, select First Event to see events starting with the first event in the log. Select Events On to see events that occurred starting at a specific time and date.
To	The end of the range of events that you want to filter. In the list under To, select Last Event to see events ending with the last event in the log. Select Events On to see events that occurred ending at a specific time and date.

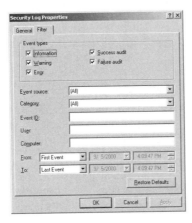

Figure 21.10 The Filter tab of the Security Log Properties dialog box

Configuring Security Logs

Security logging begins when you set an audit policy for the domain controller or local computer. Logging stops when the security log becomes full and cannot overwrite itself, either because it has been set for manual clearing or because the first event in the log is not old enough. When security logging stops, an error may be written to the application log. You can avoid a full security log by logging only key events. You can configure the properties of each individual audit log.

▶ **Follow these steps to configure the settings for security logs:**

1. Open Event Viewer.

2. Right-click the security log in the console tree, and then click Properties.

3. In the Security Log Properties dialog box, in the General tab, configure the options shown in Figure 21.11 and described in Table 21.10.

Table 21.10   Options on the General Tab of the Security Log Properties Dialog Box

Option	Description
Display Name	The name of the log view. You can change the name to distinguish different views of the same log on one computer or to distinguish logs on different computers.
Log Name	The name and location of the log file.
Maximum Log Size	The size of each log, which can be from 64 KB to 4,194,240 KB (4 GB). The default size is 512 KB.
Overwrite Events As Needed	Specifies whether all new events will be written to the log, even when the log is full. When the log is full, each new event replaces the oldest event. Use this option with caution; it can be used to hide undesirable events.
Overwrite Events Older Than X Days	Specifies the number of days (1 to 365) that a log file is retained before it is overwritten. New events will not be added if the maximum log size is reached and there are no events older than this period.
Do Not Overwrite Events (Clear Log Manually)	Specifies whether existing events will be retained when the log is full. If the maximum log size is reached, new events are discarded. This option requires you to manually clear the log.
Using A Low Speed Connection	Specifies whether the log file is located on another computer and whether your computer is connected to it by a low-speed device, such as a modem.

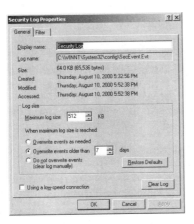

Figure 21.11 The General tab of the Security Log Properties dialog box

When the log is full and no more events can be logged, you can free the log by manually clearing it. Clearing the log erases all events permanently. Reducing the amount of time you keep an event also frees the log if it allows the next record to be overwritten.

▶ **Follow these steps to manually clear the security log:**

1. Open Event Viewer.

2. Right-click the security log in the console tree, and then click Clear All Events.

3. On the Event Viewer message box

   ▪ Click Yes to archive the log before clearing

   ▪ Click No to permanently discard the current event records and start recording new events

4. If you clicked Yes, in the Save As dialog box, in the File Name list, type a name to use for the log file to be archived.

5. In the Save As Type list, click a file format, and then click Save.

Archiving Security Logs

Archiving security logs allows you to maintain a history of security-related events. Many organizations have policies on keeping archive logs for a specified period to track security-related information over time. When you archive a log file, the entire log is saved, regardless of filtering options.

▶ **Follow these steps to archive a security log:**

1. Open Event Viewer.

2. Right-click the security log in the console tree, and then click Save Log File As.

3. In the Save As dialog box, in the File Name list, type a name to use for the log file to be archived.

4. In the Save As Type list, click a file format, and then click Save.

If you archive a log in log-file format, you can reopen it in Event Viewer. Logs saved as event log files (*.evt) retain the binary data for each event recorded. If you archive a log in text or comma-delimited format (*.txt and *.csv, respectively), you can reopen the log in other programs such as word processing or spreadsheet programs. Logs saved in text or comma-delimited format do not retain the binary data.

▶ **Follow these steps to view an archived security log:**

1. Open Event Viewer.

2. Right-click the security log in the console tree, and then click Open Log File.

3. In the Open dialog box, click the file you want to open. You may need to search for the drive or folder that contains the document.

4. In the Log Type list, select Security for the type of log to be opened.

5. In the Display Name box, enter the name of the file as you want it to appear in the console tree, and then click Open.

To remove an archived log file from your system, delete the file in Windows Explorer.

Practice: Using the Security Log

In this practice, you view the security log file and configure Event Viewer to overwrite events when the log file is filled. You then clear and archive a security log file.

Important Before attempting the exercises in this practice, you must first complete all exercises in Lesson 2.

Exercise 1: Viewing the Security Log

In this exercise, you view the security log for your computer. Then, you use Event Viewer to filter events and to search for potential security breaches.

1. Click Start, click Programs, click Administrative Tools, and then click Event Viewer.

2. In the console tree, click the security log and view the contents. As you scroll through the log, double-click a couple of events to view a description.

Exercise 2: Managing the Security Log

In this exercise, you configure Event Viewer to overwrite events when the log file gets full.

1. Right-click the security log in the console tree, and then click Properties.

2. In the Security Log Properties dialog box, click Overwrite Events As Needed.

3. In the Maximum Log Size box, change the maximum log size to 2048 KB, and then click OK.

   Windows 2000 now allows the log to grow to 2048 KB and will over-write older events with new events as necessary.

Exercise 3: Clearing and Archiving the Security Log

In this exercise, you clear the security log, archive a security log, and view the archived security log.

1. Open Event Viewer.

2. Right-click the security log in the console tree, and then click Clear All Events.

3. In the Event Viewer message box, click Yes to archive the log before clearing.

4. In the Save As dialog box, in the File Name list, type **archive** to name the log file to be archived.

5. In the Save As Type list, ensure that the Event Log (*.evt) file type is selected, and then click Save.

6. To view the archived security log, right-click the security log in the console tree, and then click Open Log File.

7. On the Open dialog box, click the ARCHIVE.EVT file (or the name of the file you archived).

8. In the Log Type list, select Security for the type of log to be opened.

9. In the Display Name box, ensure that Saved Security Log appears, and then click Open.

   The Saved Security Log appears in Event Viewer. You cannot click Refresh or Clear All Events to update the display or to clear an archived log.

10. Close Event Viewer.

Lesson Summary

In this lesson, you learned about the Windows 2000 security log. You learned how to use Event Viewer to view the contents of the Windows 2000 security logs, to locate and display specific events in security logs, to configure log size, and to archive security logs.

In the practice portion of this lesson, you viewed the security log file and configured Event Viewer to overwrite events when the log file is filled. You then cleared and archived a security log file.

Lesson 4: User Rights

Although access to Windows 2000 objects such as files, folders, and printers is controlled by permissions, user rights grant other privileges and logon rights to users and groups in your computing environment.

After this lesson, you will be able to

- Explain the purpose of user rights
- Explain the purpose of privileges and logon rights
- Assign user rights to users and groups

Estimated lesson time: 10 minutes

User Rights

Administrators can assign specific rights to group accounts or to individual user accounts. These rights authorize users to perform specific actions, such as logging on to a system interactively or backing up files and directories. *User rights* are different from permissions because user rights apply to user accounts, and permissions are attached to objects. Additionally, because user rights are part of a GPO, user rights can be overridden depending on the GPO affecting the user.

User rights define capabilities at the local level. Although user rights can apply to individual user accounts, user rights are best administered on a group account basis. This ensures that a user logging on as a member of a group automatically inherits the rights associated with that group. By assigning user rights to groups rather than individual users, you simplify the task of user account administration. When users in a group all require the same user rights, you can assign the set of user rights once to the group rather than repeatedly assigning the same set of user rights to each individual user account.

User rights that are assigned to a group are applied to all members of the group while they remain members. If a user is a member of multiple groups, the user's rights are cumulative, which means that the user has more than one set of rights. The only time that rights assigned to one group might conflict with those assigned to another is in the case of certain logon rights. In general, however, user rights assigned to one group do not conflict with the rights assigned to another group. To remove rights from a user, the administrator simply removes the user from the group. In this case, the user no longer has the rights assigned to that group.

There are two types of user rights: privileges and logon rights.

Privileges

Privileges specify allowable user actions on the network. Table 21.11 describes the privileges that can be assigned to a user.

Table 21.11   Privileges

Privilege	Description
Act As Part Of The Operating System	Allows a process to authenticate as any user and therefore gain access to the same resources as any user. Only low-level authentication services should require this privilege. The potential access is not limited to what is associated with the user by default, because the calling process may request that arbitrary additional accesses be put in the access token. Of even more concern is that the calling process can build an anonymous token that can provide any and all accesses. Additionally, this token does not provide a primary identity for tracking events in the audit log. Processes that require this privilege should use the LocalSystem account, which already includes this privilege, rather than using a separate user account with this privilege specially assigned.
Add Workstations To Domain	Allows the user to add a computer to a specific domain. The user specifies the domain through an administrative user interface on the computer being added, creating an object in the Computer container of Active Directory. The behavior of this privilege is duplicated in Windows 2000 by another access control mechanism (permissions attached to the Computer container or OU).
Back Up Files And Directories	Allows the user to circumvent file and directory permissions to back up the system. Specifically, the privilege is similar to granting the following permissions on all files and folders on the local computer: Traverse Folder/Execute File, List Folder/Read Data, Read Attributes, Read Extended Attributes, and Read Permissions. See also the Restore Files And Directories privilege.
Bypass Traverse Checking	Allows the user to pass through directories to which the user otherwise has no access, while navigating an object path in any Windows file system or in the registry. This privilege does not allow the user to list the contents of a directory, only to traverse directories.
Change The System Time	Allows the user to set the time for the internal clock of the computer.
Create A Pagefile	Allows the user to create and change the size of a pagefile by specifying a paging file size for a given drive in the System Properties Performance Options.

Privilege	Description
Create A Token Object	Allows a process to create a token that it can then use to get access to any local resources when the process uses NtCreate-Token() or other token-creation application programming interfaces (APIs). It is recommended that processes requiring this privilege use the LocalSystem account, which already includes this privilege, rather than using a separate user account with this privilege specially assigned.
Create Permanent Shared Objects	Allows a process to create a directory object in the Windows 2000 object manager. This privilege is useful to Kernel-mode components that plan to extend the Windows 2000 object namespace. Because components running in Kernel mode already have this privilege assigned to them, it is not necessary to specifically assign this privilege.
Debug Programs	Allows the user to attach a debugger to any process, providing powerful access to sensitive and critical system operating components.
Enable Computer And User Accounts To Be Trusted For Delegation	Allows the user to set the Trusted For Delegation setting on a user or computer object. The user or object that is granted this privilege must have write access to the account control flags on the user or computer object. A server process either running on a computer that is trusted for delegation or run by a user that is trusted for delegation can access resources on another computer. This uses a client's delegated credentials, as long as the client account does not have the Account Cannot Be Delegated account control flag set. Misuse of this privilege or of the Trusted For Delegation settings could make the network vulnerable to sophisticated attacks using Trojan horse programs that impersonate incoming clients and use their credentials to gain access to network resources.
Force Shutdown From A Remote System	Allows a user to shut down a computer from a remote location on the network. See also the Shut Down The System privilege.
Generate Security Audits	Allows a process to make entries in the security log for object access auditing. The process can also generate other security audits. The security log is used to trace unauthorized system access. See also the Manage Auditing And Security Log privilege.
Increase Quotas	Allows a process with write property access to another process to increase the processor quota assigned to that other process. This privilege is useful for system tuning, but can be abused, as in a denial-of-service attack.
Increase Scheduling Priority	Allows a process with write property access to another process to increase the execution priority of that other process. A user with this privilege can change the scheduling priority of a process through the Task Manager user interface.

continues

Table 21.11   Privileges *(continued)*

Privilege	Description
Load And Unload Device Drivers	Allows a user to install and uninstall Plug and Play device drivers. Device drivers that are not Plug and Play are not affected by this privilege and can only be installed by administrators. Because device drivers run as trusted (highly-privileged) programs, this privilege could be misused to install hostile programs and give these programs destructive access to resources.
Lock Pages In Memory	Allows a process to keep data in physical memory, preventing the system from paging the data to virtual memory on disk. Exercising this privilege could significantly affect system performance. This privilege is obsolete and is therefore never checked.
Manage Auditing And Security Log	Allows a user to specify object access auditing options for individual resources such as files, Active Directory objects, and registry keys. Object access auditing is not actually performed unless you have enabled it in the computer-wide audit policy settings under Group Policy or under Group Policy defined in Active Directory; this privilege does not grant access to the computer-wide audit policy. A user with this privilege can also view and clear the security log from the Event Viewer.
Modify Firmware Environment Values	Allows modification of the system environment variables, either by a user through the System Properties or by a process.
Profile Single Process	Allows a user to use Windows NT and Windows 2000 performance-monitoring tools to monitor the performance of nonsystem processes.
Profile System Performance	Allows a user to use Windows NT and Windows 2000 performance-monitoring tools to monitor the performance of system processes.
Remove Computer From Docking Station	Allows a user to undock a computer using the Windows 2000 user interface.
Replace A Process Level Token	Allows a process to replace the default token associated with a subprocess that has been started.
Restore Files And Directories	Allows a user to circumvent file and directory permissions when restoring backed up files and directories and to set any valid security principal as the owner of an object. See also the Back Up Files And Directories privilege.
Shut Down The System	Allows a user to shut down the local computer.
Synchronize Directory Service Data	Allows a process to provide directory synchronization services; relevant only on domain controllers. By default, this privilege is assigned to the Administrator and LocalSystem accounts on domain controllers.
Take Ownership Of Files Or Other Objects	Allows a user to take ownership of any securable object in the system, including Active Directory objects, files and folders, printers, registry keys, processes, and threads.

Some of these privileges can override permissions set on an object. For example, a user logged on to a domain account as a member of the Backup Operators group has the right to perform backup operations for all domain servers. However, this requires that users have the ability to read all files on those servers, even files on which their owners have set permissions that explicitly deny access to all users, including members of the Backup Operators group. A user right, in this case the right to perform a backup, takes precedence over all file and directory permissions.

Logon Rights

Logon rights specify the ways in which a user can log on to a system. Table 21.12 describes the logon rights that can be assigned to a user.

Table 21.12   Logon Rights

Logon right	Description
Access This Computer From The Network	Allows a user to connect to the computer over the network. By default, this privilege is granted to Administrators, Everyone, and Power Users.
Deny Access To This Computer From The Network	Prohibits a user or group from connecting to the computer from the network. By default, no one is denied this right.
Deny Logon As A Batch Job	Prohibits a user or group from logging on through a batch-queue facility. By default, no one is denied this right.
Deny Logon As A Service	Prohibits a user or group from logging on as a service. By default, no one is denied this right.
Deny Logon Locally	Prohibits a user or group from logging on locally. By default, no one is denied this right.
Log On As A Batch Job	Allows a user to log on using a batch-queue facility. By default, this privilege is granted to Administrators.
Log On As A Service	Allows a security principal to log on as a service, as a way of establishing a security context. The LocalSystem account always retains the right to log on as a service. Any service that runs under a separate account must be granted this right. By default, this right is not granted to anyone.
Log On Locally	Allows a user to log on at the computer's keyboard. By default, this right is granted to Administrators, Account Operators, Backup Operators, Print Operators, and Server Operators.

The special user account LocalSystem has almost all privileges and logon rights assigned to it because all processes that are running as part of the operating system are associated with this account, and these processes require a complete set of user rights.

Assigning User Rights

To ease the task of user account administration, you should assign user rights primarily to group accounts rather than to individual user accounts. When you assign privileges to a group account, users are automatically assigned those privileges when they become members of that group.

▶ **Follow these steps to assign user rights:**

1. Access the Group Policy snap-in for a GPO.

2. In the Group Policy snap-in, click Computer Configuration, double-click Windows Settings, double-click Security Settings, double-click Local Policies, and then double-click User Rights Assignment.

3. In the details pane, right-click the user right that you want to set, and then click Security.

4. In the Templates Security Policy Setting dialog box (see Figure 21.12), click the Define These Policy Settings check box, and then click Add.

Figure 21.12 The Template Security Policy Setting dialog box

5. In the Add User Or Group dialog box, add the users and/or groups you want to be affected by this user right, and then click OK.

6. Click OK twice when you have finished adding users and/or groups.

   A list of users and/or groups appears in the Computer Setting column in the details pane.

Lesson Summary

In this lesson, you learned how user rights grant specific privileges and logon rights to users and groups in your computing environment. Privileges specify allowable user actions on the network. Logon rights specify the ways in which a user can log on to a system. To ease the task of user account administration, you should assign user rights primarily to group accounts, rather than to individual user accounts. User rights are assigned using the Group Policy snap-in.

Lesson 5: Using Security Templates

Windows 2000 provides a centralized method of defining security using security templates. This lesson explains how to use security templates.

After this lesson, you will be able to

- Explain the purpose of security templates
- Explain the purpose of the predefined security templates
- Manage security templates

Estimated lesson time: 25 minutes

Security Templates Overview

A *security template* is a physical representation of a security configuration, a single file where a group of security settings is stored. Locating all security settings in one place streamlines security administration. Each template is saved as a text-based .inf file. This allows you to copy, paste, import, or export some or all of the template attributes. With the exceptions of IP security and public key policies, all security attributes can be contained in a security template.

Security Template Uses

You can import (apply) a security template file to a local or nonlocal GPO. Any computer or user accounts in the site, domain, or OU to which the GPO is applied receive the security template settings. Importing a security template to a GPO eases domain administration by configuring security for multiple computers at once.

The security settings in the local GPO are the initial settings applied to a computer. You can export the local security settings to a security template file to preserve initial system security settings. This enables the restoration of the initial security settings at any later point.

Predefined Security Templates

Windows 2000 includes a set of predefined security templates, each based on the role of a computer and common security scenarios: from security settings for low-security domain clients to highly secure domain controllers. These templates can be used as provided, they can be modified, or they can serve as a basis for creating custom security templates. Do not apply predefined security templates to production systems without testing to ensure that the right level of application functionality is maintained for your network and system architecture.

The following are the predefined security templates:

- Default domain controller security settings (BASICDC.INF)
- Default server security settings (BASICSV.INF)
- Default workstation security settings (BASICWK.INF)
- Compatible workstation or server security settings (COMPATWS.INF)
- Default security settings updated for domain controllers (DC SECURITY.INF)
- Highly secure domain controller security settings (HISECDC.INF)
- Highly secure workstation or server security settings (HISECWS.INF)
- Removes the Terminal Server User security identifier (SID) from Windows 2000 server (NOTSSID.INF)
- Optional Component File Security for server (OCFILESS.INF)
- Optional Component File Security for workstation (OCFILESW.INF)
- Secure domain controller security settings (SECUREDC.INF)
- Secure workstation or server security settings (SECUREWS.INF)
- Out of the box default security settings (SETUP SECURITY.INF)

By default, these templates are stored in the *systemroot*\Security\Templates folder.

Security Levels

The predefined security templates are designed to cover the following common requirements for security:

- **Basic (BASIC*.INF).** The basic configuration templates are provided as a means to reverse the application of a different security configuration. The basic configurations apply the Windows 2000 default security settings to all security areas except those pertaining to user rights. These are not modified in the basic templates because application setup programs commonly modify user rights to enable successful use of the application. It is not the intent of the basic configuration files to undo such modifications.

- **Compatible (COMPAT*.INF).** By default, Windows 2000 security is configured such that members of the local users group have ideal security settings and members of the local Power Users group have security settings that are compatible with Windows NT 4.0 users. This default configuration enables development of applications to a standard definition of a secure Windows environment, while still allowing existing applications to run successfully under the less secure Power User configuration. By default, all users that are authenticated by Windows 2000 are members of the Power Users group. This may be too unsecured for some environments, where it would be preferable to have users, by default, only be members of the Users group, and decrease the security on the Users group to the level where the applications run successfully. The compatible templates are designed for such environments. By lowering the security levels on specific files, folders, and registry keys that are commonly accessed by applications, the compatible templates allow most applications to run successfully. In addition, as it is assumed that the administrator applying the compatible template does not want users to be Power Users, all members of the Power Users group are removed.

- **Secure (SECURE*.INF).** The secure templates implement recommended security settings for all security areas except files, folders, and registry keys. These are not modified because file system and registry permissions are configured securely by default.

- **Highly Secure (HISEC*.INF).** The highly secure templates define security settings for Windows 2000 network communications. The security areas are set to require maximum protection for network traffic and protocols used between computers running Windows 2000. As a result, such computers configured with a highly secure template can only communicate with other Windows 2000 computers. They will not be able to communicate with computers running Windows 95, Windows 98, or Windows NT.

Managing Security Templates

The following is the sequence of tasks required for managing security templates:

1. Accessing the Security Templates console

2. Customizing a predefined security template

3. Defining a new security template

4. Importing a security template to a local and nonlocal GPO

5. Exporting security settings to a security template

Accessing the Security Templates Console

The Security Templates console is the main tool for managing security templates.

▶ **Follow these steps to access the Security Templates console:**

1. Decide whether to add the Security Templates console to an existing console or create a new console.

   - To create a new console, click Start, click Run, type **mmc** and then click OK.

   - To add the Security Templates console to an existing console, open the console, and proceed to Step 2.

2. On the Console menu, click Add/Remove Snap-In, and then click Add.

3. In the Add Standalone Snap-In dialog box, select Security Templates, click Add, click Close, and then click OK.

4. On the Console menu, click Save.

5. Enter the name to assign to this console and click Save.

   The console appears on the Administrative Tools menu.

Customizing a Predefined Security Template

Customizing a predefined security template allows you to save the predefined template as a new template (to preserve the original predefined template) and then make edits to security settings to create a new template.

▶ **Follow these steps to customize a predefined security template:**

1. In the Security Templates console (see Figure 21.13), double-click Security Templates.

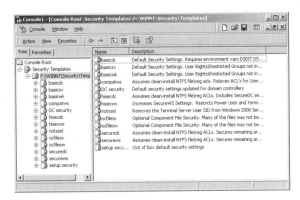

Figure 21.13 The Security Templates console

2. Double-click the default path folder (*systemroot*\Security\Templates), right-click the predefined template you want to modify, and then click Save As.

3. In the Save As dialog box, in the File Name box, specify a filename for the new security template, and then click Save.

4. In the console tree, right-click the new security template, and then select Set Description.

5. In the Security Template Description dialog box, type a description for the new security template, and then click OK.

6. In the console tree, double-click the new security template to display the security policies, and double-click the security policy you want to modify (such as Account Policies).

7. Click the security policy you want to customize (such as Password Policy), and then double-click the security setting to modify (such as Minimum Password Length).

8. On the Template Security Policy Setting dialog box, click the Define This Policy Setting In The Template check box to allow configuration, and then configure the security setting.

9. Click OK.

10. Configure other security settings as needed.

11. Close the Security Templates console.

12. In the Save Security Templates dialog box, click Yes to save the new security template file.

Defining a New Security Template

You can define a new security template and then modify the default settings to meet your requirements.

▶ **Follow these steps to define a new security template:**

1. In the Security Templates console, double-click Security Templates.

2. Right-click the template path folder where you want to store the new template and click New Template.

3. In the dialog box for the templates folder, type the name and description for your new security template, and then click OK.

4. In the console tree, right-click the new security template, and then select Set Description.

5. In the Security Template Description dialog box, type a description for the new security template, and then click OK.

6. In the console tree, double-click the new security template to display the security policies, and double-click the security policy you want to define (such as Account Policies).

7. Click the security policy you want to define (such as Password Policy), and then double-click the security setting to define (such as Minimum Password Length).

8. In the Template Security Policy Setting dialog box, click the Define This Policy Setting In The Template check box to allow configuration, and then configure the security setting.

9. Click OK.

10. Configure other security settings as needed.

11. Close the Security Templates console.

12. In the Save Security Templates dialog box, click Yes to save the new security template file.

Importing a Security Template to a GPO

You can import a security template to local or nonlocal GPOs. Importing security templates makes administration easier because security is configured in one step for multiple objects.

▶   **Follow these steps to import a security template to a local and nonlocal GPO:**

1. In a console from which you manage local or nonlocal group policy settings, click the GPO to which you want to import the security template.

2. In the console tree, right-click Security Settings, and then click Import Policy.

3. In the Import Policy From dialog box (see Figure 21.14), click the security template you want to import, and then click Open.

Figure 21.14 The Import Policy From dialog box

4. Because the security settings are applied when the group policy is propagated (applied) to your computer, do one of the following to initiate policy propagation:

   - Type **secedit /refreshpolicy machine_policy** at the command prompt, and then press Enter.

   - Restart your computer.

   - Wait for automatic policy propagation, which occurs at regular, configurable intervals. By default, policy propagation occurs every 8 hours.

Exporting Security Settings to a Security Template

You can export both local and effective security settings to a security template. By exporting the local settings to a security template, you can preserve initial system settings. Because the local GPO is overridden by domain-based GPOs, the local security settings are available for restoration later, if necessary. By exporting the effective security settings to a security template, you can then import the settings into a security database (discussed in the next lesson), overlay new templates, and analyze potential conflicts.

▶ **Follow these steps to export security settings to a security template:**

   1. Click Start, point to Programs, point to Administrative Tools, and then click Local Security Policy.

   2. In the console tree, right-click Security Settings, click Export Policy, and select Local Policy or Effective Policy.

   3. In the Export Policy To dialog box (see Figure 21.15), type the name of the security template to which you want to export security settings, and then click Save.

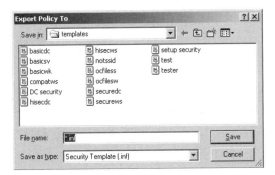

Figure 21.15 The Export Policy To dialog box

Practice: Managing Security Templates

In this practice, you access the Security Templates console and customize a predefined security template.

Exercise 1: Accessing the Security Templates Console

In this exercise, you access the Security Templates console, the main tool for managing security templates.

1. Click Start, click Run, type **mmc** and then click OK.

2. On the Console menu, click Add/Remove Snap-In, and then click Add.

3. In the Add Standalone Snap-In dialog box, select Security Templates, click Add, click Close, and then click OK.

4. On the Console menu, click Save.

5. In the File Name list, type **Security Templates** to name this console, and then click Save. The console appears on the Administrative Tools menu.

Exercise 2: Customizing a Predefined Security Template

In this exercise, you customize a predefined security template by saving the predefined template as a new template (to preserve the original predefined template) and then making edits to security settings to create a new template.

1. In the Security Templates console, double-click Security Templates.

2. Double-click the default path folder (*systemroot*\Security\Templates), right-click the Basicdc template, and then click Save As.

3. In the Save As dialog box, in the File Name box, type **new template** and then click Save.

4. In the console tree, right-click New Template, and then select Set Description.

5. In the Security Template Description dialog box, type the description **New domain controller template** and then click OK.

6. In the console tree, double-click the new security template to display the security policies.

7. Double-click Account Policies, click Password Policy, and then double-click Minimum Password Length.

8. In the Template Security Policy Setting dialog box, click the Define This Policy Setting In The Template check box to allow configuration, and then set the password to be at least 10 characters.

9. Click OK.

10. Close the Security Templates console and save the console settings.

11. In the Save Security Templates dialog box, click Yes to save the NEW TEMPLATE.INF security template file.

Lesson Summary

In this lesson, you learned that a security template is a physical representation of a security configuration, a single file where a group of security settings is stored. Locating all security settings in one place streamlines security administration.

You learned that the tasks for managing security templates are accessing the Security Templates console, customizing a predefined security template, defining a new security template, importing a security template to a local and nonlocal GPO, and exporting security settings to a security template.

In the practice portion of this lesson, you accessed the Security Templates console, which is the main tool used to manage security templates, and customized a predefined security template.

Lesson 6: Security Configuration and Analysis

Security Configuration and Analysis is a tool that enables you to configure security, analyze security, view results, and resolve any discrepancies revealed by analysis. This tool is located on the Security Configuration and Analysis console. This lesson shows you how to use the Security Configuration and Analysis console.

After this lesson, you will be able to

- Explain how the Security Configuration and Analysis console works
- Use the Security Configuration and Analysis console to perform security configuration and analysis tasks

Estimated lesson time: 25 minutes

How the Security Configuration and Analysis Console Works

The Security Configuration and Analysis console uses a database to perform configuration and analysis functions. The security configuration and analysis database is a computer-specific data store. The database architecture allows the use of personal databases, security template import and export, and the combination of multiple security templates into one composite security template that can be used for analysis or configuration. New security templates can be incrementally added to the database to create a composite security template; overwriting a template is also an option. You can also create personal databases for storing your own customized security templates.

Security Configuration

The Security Configuration and Analysis console can be used to configure local system security. By using personal databases, you can import security templates created with the Security Templates console and apply these templates to the GPO for the local computer. This immediately configures the system security with the levels specified in the template.

Security Analysis

The state of the operating system and applications on a computer is dynamic. For example, security levels may occasionally be required to change temporarily in order to enable immediate resolution of an administration or network issue. After this security requirement is finished, the temporary change may not be reversed. This means that a computer may no longer meet the requirements for enterprise security.

The Security Configuration and Analysis console allows administrators to perform a quick security analysis. In the analysis, recommendations are presented alongside current system settings, and icons or remarks are used to highlight any areas where the current settings do not match the proposed level of security. Security Configuration and Analysis also offers the ability to resolve any discrepancies revealed by analysis.

Regular analysis enables an administrator to track and ensure an adequate level of security on each computer as part of an enterprise risk management program. Analysis is highly specified and information about all system aspects related to security is provided in the results. This enables an administrator to tune the security levels, and most importantly, to detect any security flaws that may occur in the system over time.

Using Security Configuration and Analysis

The following is the sequence of tasks required to use Security Configuration and Analysis:

1. Accessing the Security Configuration and Analysis console

2. Setting a working security database

3. Importing a security template into a security database

4. Analyzing system security

5. Viewing security analysis results

6. Configuring system security

7. Exporting security database settings to a security template

Accessing the Security Configuration and Analysis Console

The Security Configuration and Analysis console is the main tool for using the Security Configuration and Analysis tool.

▶ **Follow these steps to access the Security Configuration and Analysis console:**

1. Do one of the following:

   - To add the Security Configuration and Analysis console to a new console, click Start, click Run, type **mmc** and then click OK.

   - To add the Security Configuration and Analysis console to an existing console, go directly to Step 2.

2. On the Console menu, click Add/Remove Snap-In, and then click Add.

3. In the Add Standalone Snap-In dialog box, select Security Configuration And Analysis and click Add.

4. Click Close, and then click OK.

5. On the Console menu, click Save.

6. Enter the name to assign to this console and click Save.

   The console appears on the Administrative Tools menu.

Setting a Working Security Database

The Security Configuration and Analysis console uses a database to perform configuration and analysis functions. Before you can configure or analyze security, you must determine the working security database to use.

▶ **Follow these steps to set a working security database:**

1. In the Security Configuration and Analysis console (see Figure 21.16), right-click Security Configuration And Analysis.

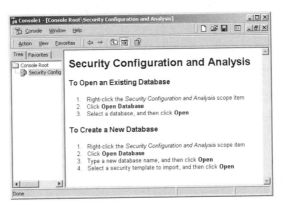

Figure 21.16 The Security Configuration and Analysis console

2. Click Open Database.

3. In the Open Database dialog box, choose an existing personal database or type a filename to create a new personal database, and then click Open.

   - If you chose an existing personal database, this database is now the working security database.

   - If you created a new personal database, the Import Template dialog box appears.

4. Select the security template to load into the security database, and then click Open.

   This database is now the working security database.

Importing a Security Template into a Security Database

In Lesson 5, "Using Security Templates," you learned to import a security template directly into a GPO. In this lesson, you import a security template into the security database used in the Security Configuration and Analysis console.

You can merge several different templates into one composite template, which can then can be used for analysis or configuration of a system, by importing each template into a working database. The database merges the various templates to create one composite template, resolving conflicts in order of import; the last one imported takes precedence when there is contention. Only if you chose to overwrite will they not be merged into a composite template (stored configuration). Once the templates are imported to the selected database, you can analyze or configure the system.

▶ **Follow these steps to import a security template into a security database:**

1. In the Security Configuration and Analysis console, right-click Security Configuration And Analysis.

2. Open or create a working security database.

3. Select Import Template.

4. Select a security template file, and then click Open.

5. Repeat the previous step for each template you want to merge with previous templates into the database.

Note If you want to replace the template rather than merge it into the stored template, click the Clear This Database Before Importing check box in the Import Template dialog box.

Analyzing System Security

Security Configuration and Analysis performs security analysis by comparing the current state of system security against a security template that you have imported to a personal database. This template is the database configuration, and it is the template that contains your preferred or recommended security settings for that system.

Security Configuration and Analysis queries the system's security settings for all security areas in the database configuration. Values found are compared to the database configuration. If the current system settings match the database configuration settings, they are assumed to be correct. If not, the policies in question are displayed as potential problems that need investigation.

▶ **Follow these steps to analyze system security:**

1. In the Security Configuration and Analysis console, set a working database (if one is not currently set).

2. Right-click Security Configuration And Analysis, and then click Analyze Computer Now.

3. In the Perform Analysis dialog box, verify the path for the log file location, and then click OK.

   The different security areas are displayed as they are analyzed. Once this is complete, you can check the log file or review the results.

   Note To check the log file, right-click Security Configuration And Analysis, and then click View Log File.

Viewing Security Analysis Results

The Security Configuration and Analysis console displays the analysis results organized by security area with visual flags to indicate problems. For each security policy in the security area, the current database and computer configuration settings are displayed.

▶ **Follow these steps to view security analysis results:**

1. In the Security Configuration and Analysis console, click Security Configuration And Analysis.

2. Double-click a security policies node (such as Account Policies), and then click the security area (such as Password Policy) for which you want to view results.

3. In the details pane (see Figure 21.17), the Policy column indicates the policy name for the analysis results, the Database Setting column indicates the security value in your template, and the Computer Setting column indicates the current security level in the system.

   - A red X indicates a difference from the database configuration.

   - A green check mark indicates consistency with the database configuration.

   - No icon indicates that the security policy was not included in your template and therefore not analyzed.

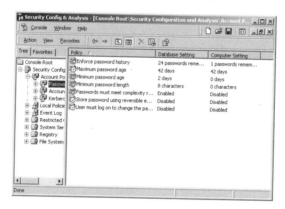

Figure 21.17 Analysis results for Password Policy

Configuring System Security

Security Configuration and Analysis enables you to resolve any discrepancies revealed by analysis, including the following:

- Accepting or changing some or all of the values flagged or not included in the configuration if you determine the local system security levels are valid due to the context (role) of a particular computer

- Configuring the system to the original database configuration values if you determine the system is not in compliance with valid security levels

- Importing a more appropriate template, for the role of a particular computer, into the database as the new database configuration and applying it to the system

You can repeat the import process and load multiple templates. The database merges the various templates to create one composite template, resolving conflicts in order of import; the last one imported takes precedence when there is contention. Once the templates are imported to the database, you can choose Configure System Now to apply the stored template (database configuration) to the system.

Important These changes are made to the stored template in the database, not to the security template file. The security template file is only modified if you either return to Security Templates and edit that template or export the stored configuration to the same template file.

Using the Security Configuration and Analysis console is not recommended when you are analyzing security for domain-based clients, as you would have to go to each client individually. In this case, you should return to the Security Templates console, modify the template, and reapply it to the appropriate GPO.

▶ **Follow these steps to configure system security:**

1. In the Security Configuration and Analysis console, set a working database (if one is not currently set).

2. Right-click Security Configuration And Analysis, and then click Configure Computer Now.

3. In the Configure System dialog box, click OK to use the default analysis log or enter a filename and valid path.

   The different security areas are displayed as they are configured. Once this is complete, you can check the log file or analyze system security and view the results.

▶ **Follow these steps to edit the database security configuration:**

1. In the Security Configuration and Analysis console, click Security Configuration And Analysis.

2. Double-click a security policies node (such as Account Policies), and then click a security area (such as Password Policy).

3. In the details pane, double-click the security attribute you want to edit.

4. Click the Define This Policy In The Database check box to allow editing.

5. Enter a new value for the security policy, and then click OK.

6. Repeat the previous four steps for each security policy you want to edit.

▶ **Follow these steps to view security configuration results:**

1. In the console from which you manage group policy, double-click the GPO.

2. In the console tree, click Security Settings.

3. Double-click a security policy node (such as Account Policies), and then click a security area (such as Password Policy).

4. Double-click the security attribute you want to view (such as Minimum Password Length).

Exporting Security Templates

The export feature provides the ability to save a security database configuration as a new template file that can be imported into other databases, used as is to analyze or configure a system, or even redefined with the Security Templates console.

▶ **To export security database settings to a security template:**

1. In the Security Configuration and Analysis console, right-click Security Configuration And Analysis.

2. If you have created a composite security template by importing multiple templates into one database and you want to save the composite template as a separate template file, click Export Template.

3. In the Export Template To dialog box, type a valid filename in the File Name box, type a path to where your template should be saved in the Save In list, and select the type of file you want to save in the Save As Type list, and then click Save.

Practice: Using Security Configuration and Analysis

In this practice, you access the Security Configuration and Analysis console, set a working security database, analyze system security, and then view the results.

Exercise 1: Accessing the Security Configuration and Analysis Console

In this exercise, you access the Security Configuration and Analysis console, the main tool for using the Security Configuration and Analysis tool.

1. Click Run, type **mmc** and then click OK.

2. On the Console menu, click Add/Remove Snap-In, and then click Add.

3. In the Add Standalone Snap-In dialog box, select Security Configuration And Analysis, and then click Add.

4. Click Close, and then click OK.

5. On the Console menu, click Save.

6. In the File Name box, type **security config & analysis** to name this console and click Save.

   The console appears on the Administrative Tools menu.

Exercise 2: Setting a Working Security Database

In this exercise, you determine the working security database to use.

1. In the Security Configuration and Analysis console, right-click Security Configuration And Analysis.

2. Click Open Database.

3. In the Open Database dialog box, in the File Name box, type **new** for the new personal database file name, and then click Open.

4. In the Import Template dialog box, select the Securedc security template to load into the security database, and then click Open.

   The *new* database is now the working security database, and it contains the *Securedc* security template.

Exercise 3: Analyzing System Security

In this exercise, you analyze system security, comparing the settings in the security template *Securedc* with the security settings currently running on your system.

1. Right-click Security Configuration And Analysis, and then click Analyze Computer Now.

2. In the Perform Analysis dialog box, verify the path for the log file location, and then click OK.

   The different security areas are displayed as they are analyzed.

Exercise 4: Viewing Security Analysis Results

In this exercise, you view the security analysis results.

1. In the Security Configuration and Analysis console, click Security Configuration And Analysis.

2. Double-click the Account Policies node, and then click the Password Policy security area.

   In the details pane, what is indicated in the Policy column? In the Database Setting column? In the Computer Setting column?

   In the Policy column, what does the red X indicate? What does the green check mark indicate?

Lesson Summary

In this lesson, you learned how the Security Configuration and Analysis console uses a database to perform configuration and analysis functions.

You learned that when you configure system security using the Security Configuration and Analysis console, changes are made to the stored template in the database, not to the security template file. The security template file is only modified if you either return to Security Templates and edit that template or export the stored configuration to the same template file.

You also learned that Security Configuration and Analysis performs security analysis by comparing the current state of system security against a security template that you have imported to a personal database. This template is the database configuration, and it is the template that contains your preferred or recommended security settings for that system.

In the practice portion of this lesson, you accessed the Security Configuration and Analysis console, set a working security database, analyzed system security, and then viewed the results.

Lesson 7: Troubleshooting a Security Configuration

This lesson describes problems you may encounter that relate to security configuration and presents solutions to those problems.

After this lesson, you will be able to

- Troubleshoot a security configuration

Estimated lesson time: 5 minutes

Troubleshooting a Security Configuration

Table 21.13 describes scenarios in which there are problems using a security configuration and presents solutions to those problems.

Table 21.13   Security Configuration Troubleshooting Scenarios

Symptom: Received error message: Event message: Event ID 1202, Event source: scecli, Warning (0x%x) occurs to apply security policies

Cause	Solution
Group policy was not refreshed after changes were made.	Trigger another application of group policy settings or local policy refresh by using the Secedit command-line tool to refresh security settings.

Symptom: Received error message: Failed to open the Group Policy Object

Cause	Solution
The most likely causes for this error are network-related.	Check the DNS configuration for the following: Make sure that there are no stale entries in the DNS database. Resolve local DNS servers and Internet service provider (ISP) DNS server entries. For example, the DNS settings for a local LAN network adapter points to two DNS servers: the local DNS server (possibly the same computer) and the DNS server of an ISP. If you try to ping your domain, a message may indicate that this is an unknown host. Even with correct local DNS entries, the ISP DNS server cannot identify your domain, so there is a difference in their databases. To resolve this error, remove the second and add the ISP DNS server *IPAddress* to the forwarders in the local DNS server.

continues

Table 21.13   Security Configuration Troubleshooting Scenarios *(continued)*

Symptom: Modified security settings are not taking effect

Cause	Solution
Any policies configured locally may be overridden by like policies specified in the domain. If your setting shows up in local policy but not in effective policy, it implies that there is a policy from the domain that is overriding your setting. Also, as group policy changes are applied periodically, it is likely that the policy changes made in the directory have not yet been refreshed in your computer.	Manually do a policy refresh by typing **secedit /refreshpolicy machine_policy** at the command line.

Symptom: Policies do not migrate from Windows NT 4.0 to Windows 2000

Cause	Solution
Windows NT 4.0 policies cannot be migrated to Windows 2000. In Windows NT 4.0, system policies were stored in one .pol file with group information embedded; no method is available to translate that information to the Windows 2000 Active Directory structure. Groups are handled very differently in Windows 2000.	Windows NT 4.0 clients accessing a Windows 2000 Server computer and Windows 2000 Professional clients accessing a Windows NT 4.0 Server computer will use the Netlogon share (the Windows NT 4.0 model). With Windows 2000 Server, when a Windows NT 4.0 client is upgraded to Windows 2000, it gets only Active Directory–based group policy settings and not Windows NT 4.0–style policies. Although Windows NT 4.0–style policies may be enabled (using a group policy setting) if the administrator chooses to do so, this practice is strongly discouraged. Windows NT 4.0–style policies are applied only during the logon process. This means that both computer and user settings are processed. This is not optimal behavior for the following reasons. The Windows NT 4.0–style computer settings override the group policy settings that have already been applied to the computer during startup. During the group policy settings refresh cycle, the group policy settings change any conflicting settings back. This creates an indeterminate state. Windows NT 4.0–style policies result in persistent settings in the registry (tattooing). Note also that Terminal Server cannot allow computer settings to be set based on a user logon.

Lesson Summary

In this lesson, you examined some security problems that you may encounter and possible solutions.

Review

The following questions are intended to reinforce key information presented in the chapter. If you are unable to answer a question, review the appropriate lesson and then try the question again. Answers to the questions can be found in Appendix A, "Questions and Answers."

1. On which computer do you set an audit policy to audit a folder that is located on a member server that belongs to a domain?

2. What is the difference between what the audit policy settings track for directory service access and object access?

3. When you view a security log, how do you determine if an event failed or was successful?

4. How are user rights different from permissions?

5. What is a security template and why is it useful?

6. Where does the Security Configuration and Analysis console store information for performing configuration and analysis functions?

PART 4

Microsoft Windows 2000 Server

Part 4 contains information that relates to the Windows 2000 Server portion of the 70-240 exam. A lot of the objectives for this portion of the exam are the same as objectives from the Windows 2000 Professional portion of the exam, but the information from the Windows 2000 Professional section is not repeated here (except where necessary for content and presentation flow). This part concentrates on the unique aspects of Windows 2000 Server with minimal repetitive information. The following chapters primarily use Windows 2000 Server during the various hands-on practices and exercises.

The unique features of Windows 2000 Server (over that of Windows 2000 Professional) discussed here include Internet services, the distributed file system (Dfs) and File Replication Service (FRS). This part also discusses monitoring and managing the network, in addition to securing the system. The chapter on security includes a discussion on public key technologies, the Kerberos protocol, and the various tools used to configure and manage Windows 2000 security.

C H A P T E R   2 2

Managing Microsoft Windows 2000 Terminal Services

About This Chapter

Microsoft Windows 2000 Terminal Services allows client computers to access Windows 2000 and the latest Windows applications from a central server. This shared method of using the operating system and applications means that client computers can be smaller and less expensive than those used with previous operating systems.

This chapter describes Terminal Services, what tools are included with the feature, and how to install Terminal Services. An important aspect of Terminal Services is managing the appropriate software licensing. The chapter explains the various Terminal Services licensing components. The chapter ends with a discussion on deploying Terminal Services to client computers.

Before You Begin

To complete this chapter, you must have

- Installed Windows 2000 Server on both computers (Server01 and Server02)

  See Chapter 8, "Installing Microsoft Windows 2000," for more details.

- An installed and configured modem in Server01 (The installation of Windows 2000 Server may have automatically detected your modem. If not, use the Add/Remove Hardware application in Control Panel to install the software to support your modem.)

Lesson 1: Introducing Terminal Services

Terminal Services provides access to Windows 2000 and the latest Windows–based applications for client computers. It also provides access to your desktop and installed applications anywhere, from any supported client. Terminal Services is a built-in feature of Windows 2000 that allows IT managers and system administrators to increase flexibility in application deployment, control computer management costs, and remotely administer network resources.

After this lesson, you will be able to

- Describe Terminal Services
- Explain the advantages of remote administration for Terminal Services
- Describe the uses of Application Server

Estimated lesson time: 5 minutes

Overview of Terminal Services

Terminal Services running on a Windows 2000 server enables all client application execution, data processing, and data storage to occur on the server. It provides remote access to a server desktop through terminal emulation software. The terminal emulation software can run on a number of client hardware devices, such as a personal computer, a Windows CE–based Handheld PC (H/PC), or a terminal.

With Terminal Services, the terminal emulation software sends keystrokes and mouse movements to the server. Terminal Services does all the data manipulation locally and passes back the display. This approach allows remote control of servers and centralized application management, which minimizes network bandwidth requirements between the server and client.

Users can gain access to Terminal Services over any Transmission Control Protocol/Internet Protocol (TCP/IP) connection including Remote Access, Ethernet, the Internet, wireless, wide area network (WAN), or virtual private network (VPN). The user experience is limited only by the slowest link in the connection, and the security of the link is governed by the TCP/IP deployment in the data center.

Terminal Services provides remote administration of network resources, a uniform experience to users in branch offices in remote locations, or a graphical interface to line of business applications on text-based computers.

Terminal Services is a built-in feature of Windows 2000. You can enable Terminal Services in one of two modes: Remote Administration and Application Server.

Remote Administration

Remote Administration gives system administrators a powerful method for remotely administering every computer running Windows 2000 Server over any TCP/IP connection. You can administer file and print sharing, edit the registry from another computer on the network, or perform any task as if you were sitting at the console. You can use Remote Administration mode to manage servers not normally compatible with the Application Server mode of Terminal Services, such as servers running the Cluster service.

Remote Administration mode installs only the remote access components of Terminal Services. It does not install application-sharing components. This means that you can use Remote Administration with very little overhead on mission-critical servers. Terminal Services allows a maximum of two concurrent Remote Administration connections. No additional licensing is required for those connections, and you do not need a license server.

Application Server

In Application Server mode, you can deploy and manage applications from a central location, saving administrators development and deployment time as well as the time and effort required for maintenance and upgrade. After an application is deployed in Terminal Services, many clients can connect—through a Remote Access connection, LAN, or WAN, and from many different types of clients.

You can install applications directly at the Terminal server, or you can use remote installation. For example, you can use Group Policy and Active Directory service to publish Windows Installer application packages to a Terminal server or a group of Terminal servers. Applications can be installed only by an Administrator on a per-server basis and only if the appropriate Group Policy setting is enabled.

Client licensing is required when deploying a Terminal server as an application server. Each client computer, regardless of what protocol it uses to connect to Terminal server, must have the Terminal Services Client Access License as well as the Windows 2000 Client Access License.

Lesson Summary

Terminal Services running on a Windows 2000 server enables all client application execution, data processing, and data storage to take place on the server. It provides remote access to a server desktop through terminal emulation software.

You can enable Terminal Services in one of two modes: Remote Administration and Application Server. Remote Administration gives system administrators a powerful method for remotely administering each Windows 2000 server over any TCP/IP connection. In Application Server mode, you can deploy and manage applications from a central location, saving administrators development and deployment time as well as the time and effort required for maintenance and upgrade.

Lesson 2: Terminal Services Tools and Installation

To help you install Terminal Services for Windows 2000, additional administration tools are added to the Administrative Tools folder. These include Terminal Services Client Creator, Terminal Services Manager, Terminal Services Configuration, and Terminal Services Licensing.

After this lesson, you will be able to

- Describe the uses of the following Terminal Services administration tools:
  - Terminal Services Client Creator
  - Terminal Services Manager
  - Terminal Services Configuration
  - Terminal Services Licensing
- Install Terminal Services with the appropriate administration tools

Estimated lesson time: 30 minutes

Note Terminal Services Licensing is installed only if Application Server mode is selected or if Adminpak.msi is installed.

Terminal Services Client Creator

Use this tool to create floppy disks for installing the Terminal Services Client software on Windows for Workgroups, Windows 95, Windows 98, and Windows NT platforms.

Terminal Services Manager

With this tool, you can manage all Windows 2000 servers running Terminal Services. Administrators can view current users, servers, and processes. Additionally, administrators can send messages to specific users, use the Remote Control feature, and terminate processes. Figure 22.1 shows the Terminal Services Manager console running inside a terminal services session.

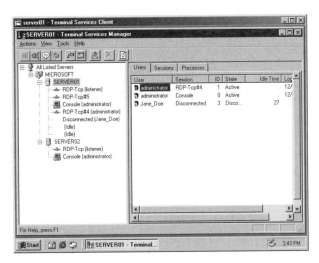

Figure 22.1 Using Terminal Services Manager to manage Terminal Services running on Server01

Terminal Services Configuration

This tool allows you to manage your Remote Desktop Protocol (RDP) configuration. Modifying options in this tool are global, unless you choose to inherit information from the same options located in the user configuration. Available options include setting connection encryption, logon settings, time-outs, initial programs run on successful logon, remote control options, Windows printer mapping, LPT port mapping, clipboard mapping, and applying these options to a specific LAN adapter.

Terminal Services Licensing

With this tool, you store and track Windows 2000 Terminal Services client access licenses. It can be installed either during installation of Terminal Services or later. When a client logs on to Terminal Services, Terminal Services validates the client license. If a client does not have a license or requires a replacement license, Terminal Services requests one from the license server. The license server provides a license from its pool of available licenses, and Terminal Services passes the license to the client. If there are no available licenses, the license server grants a temporary license for the client. After it is granted, each client license is associated with a particular computer or terminal.

Practice: Installing Terminal Services and Running Remote Administration

In this practice, you install Terminal Services to run in Remote Administration mode on Server01. You then run a remote administration session from Server02.

Exercise 1: Installing Terminal Services

Make sure that the Windows 2000 Server installation CD-ROM is inserted in the CD-ROM drive on Server01.

1. Log on to Server01 as Administrator with a password of *password*.
2. Click the Start menu, point to Settings, and then click Control Panel.
3. In Control Panel, double-click Add/Remove Programs.

    The Add/Remove Programs dialog box appears.

4. In the left frame, click Add/Remove Windows Components.

    After a few moments, the Windows Components wizard appears.

5. Scroll down and select the Terminal Services check box, and then click Next.

    The Terminal Services Setup screen appears.

6. Read the information on this screen, verify that the Remote Administration Mode radio button is selected, and then click Next.

    The Configuring Components screen appears as Windows 2000 configures and installs components. After a few minutes, the Completing The Windows Components Wizard screen appears.

7. Click Finish.

    The Add/Remove Programs dialog box appears.

8. Click Close, and then close Control Panel.

    A System Setting Change message box appears, informing you that you must restart the computer before the settings can take effect.

9. Click Yes to restart the computer.
10. After Server01 restarts, logon as Administrator.
11. In the Open text box, type **server01\c$\Program Files\terminal services client** and then click OK.
12. Log off Server01.
13. From Server02, log on to Server01 as Administrator with a password of *password*. Make sure you are logging on to the MICROSOFT domain.

14. Click the Start menu, and then click Run.

    The Run dialog box appears.

15. In the Open text box, type **\\server01\c$\Program Files\terminal services client** and then click OK.

    The Terminal Services Client window appears.

16. Double-click the Conman icon.

    Client Connection Manager appears.

17. Click the first toolbar icon.

    The Client Connection Manager wizard starts.

18. Click Next.

    The Create A Connection screen appears.

19. In the Connection Name text box, type **Server01 Remote Administration**.

20. In the Server name or IP Address text box, type **Server01** and click Next.

    The Automatic Logon screen appears.

21. Click the Logon Automatically With This Information check box.

22. In the User Name text box, type **administrator**.

23. In the Password text box, type **password**.

24. In the Domain text box, type **microsoft** and then click Next.

    The Screen options screen appears.

25. Select a resolution that the monitor on Server02 can support. If you don't know what resolution it supports, choose the 640 x 480 radio button.

26. Click Next.

    The Connection Properties screen appears.

27. Click the Enable Data Compression and Cache Bitmaps check boxes and click Next.

    The Starting A Program screen appears.

28. Click Next.

    The Icon And Program Group screen appears.

29. Click Next.

    The Completing The Client Connection Manager Wizard screen appears.

30. Click Finish.

    The Client Connection Manager appears with the new connection you created.

31. Double-click the Server01 Remote Administration icon.

    A Connecting box appears. A terminal window then opens, whose title bar is SERVER01 – Terminal Services Client (Server01 Remote Administration).

32. In the Log On To Windows dialog box, type **password** and then click OK.

    You are now able to remotely administer Server01 from Server02. Notice that on the Server01 monitor, the computer is not logged on but you are logged on to Server01 from Server02.

33. Close the SERVER01 – Terminal Services Client (Server01 Remote Administration) terminal window appearing on Server02.

    A Disconnect Windows Session message box appears stating that you are about to disconnect from Server01 but that you can return to this session later and continue to run programs started in this terminal session.

34. Click OK.

35. Close the Client Connection Manager and close the Terminal Services Client window.

Lesson Summary

In this lesson, you learned that when you install Terminal Services for Windows 2000, additional administration tools are added to the Administrative Tools folder. These include Terminal Services Client Creator, Terminal Services Manager, Terminal Services Configuration, and Terminal Services Licensing.

In the practice for this lesson, you installed Terminal Services to run in Remote Administration mode, and then practiced remote administration on your second computer.

Lesson 3: Terminal Services Licensing Components

Terminal Services has its own method for licensing clients that log on to Terminal servers. This method is separate from the licensing method for Windows 2000 Server clients. Terminal Services licensing includes four components: the Microsoft Clearinghouse, a license server, a Terminal server, and client licenses.

After this lesson, you will be able to

- Explain the use of the following components of Terminal Services licensing:

  □ Microsoft Clearinghouse

  □ License Server

  □ Terminal Server

  □ Client License

- Administer a license server

Estimated lesson time: 45 minutes

Microsoft Clearinghouse

The Microsoft Clearinghouse is the database that Microsoft maintains to activate license servers and to issue client license key packs to the license servers that request them. The Clearinghouse stores information about all activated license servers and client license key packs that have been issued. You can access the Clearinghouse through the Licensing wizard in the Terminal Services Licensing snap-in.

License Server

A license server stores all Terminal Services client licenses that have been installed for a Terminal server and tracks the licenses that have been issued to client computers or terminals. A Terminal server must be able to connect to an activated license server before clients can be issued licenses. One activated license server can serve multiple Terminal servers.

Terminal Server

A Terminal server is the computer on which Terminal Services is enabled and running. It provides clients access to Windows–based applications running entirely on the server and supports multiple client sessions on the server. When clients log on to a Terminal server, the server validates the client license. If a client does not have a license, the Terminal server requests one for the client from the license server.

Client Licenses

Each client computer or terminal that connects to a Terminal server must have a valid client license. The client license is stored locally and presented to the Terminal server each time the client connects to the server. The server validates the license and then allows the client to connect.

Administering the License Server

Deploying Terminal Services license server includes setting up the license server, enabling the server, activating the server, and installing the licenses.

Setting Up a License Server

A license server is required by Terminal Services when running in Application Server mode. The Terminal Services Licensing service is a low-impact service that stores the client licenses that have been issued for a Terminal server and tracks the licenses that have been issued to client computers or terminals.

The license server must be activated through the Microsoft Clearinghouse and loaded with Client Access Licenses for distribution from the Clearinghouse. The license server is accessed by the Terminal servers only to issue a new license and need only be administered to obtain licenses from the Clearinghouse.

Enabling a License Server

You can enable the Terminal Services Licensing service on your computer when you run Windows 2000 Server Setup. In a production environment, it is recommended that you enable Terminal Services on a member server or standalone server, and that you install the license server on a different computer. Terminal Services is resource intensive.

There are two types of license servers: a domain license server and an enterprise license server. Before installing the license server, consider which of the following two types of license servers you require:

- **Domain license server.** This is an appropriate choice if you want to maintain a separate license server for each domain. If you have workgroups or Windows NT 4.0 domains, a domain license server is the only type that you can install. Terminal servers can access domain license servers only if they are in the same domain as the license server. By default, a license server is installed as a domain license server.

- **Enterprise license server.** This license server can serve Terminal servers in any domain within a site, but the domain must be a Windows 2000 domain. It can serve only Terminal servers in the same site. This type of license server is appropriate if you have many domains. Enterprise license servers can only be installed by using Add/Remove Programs. They cannot be installed during Windows 2000 setup.

When deciding where on your physical network to deploy your license server, consider how a Terminal server discovers and communicates with a license server. Upon enabling Terminal Services, the Terminal server begins polling the domain and Active Directory service looking for a license server. (In a workgroup environment, the Terminal server broadcasts to all the servers in the workgroup on the same subnet.)

Note In Windows 2000 domains, the domain license server must be installed on a domain controller. In workgroups or Windows NT 4.0 domains, the domain license server can be installed on any server. If you are planning to eventually migrate from a Workgroup or Windows NT 4.0 domain to a Windows 2000 domain, you might want to install the license server on a computer that can be promoted to a Windows 2000 domain controller.

To activate the license server quickly and to access the Microsoft Clearinghouse through the Internet, install the server on a computer that has Internet access.

You must enable a Windows 2000 license server within 90 days of enabling Windows 2000 Terminal Services. If you have not enabled the license service when this period ends, your Windows 2000 Terminal Services will fail to operate.

Activating a License Server

A license server must be activated in order to identify the server and allow it to issue client licenses to your Terminal servers. You can activate a license server by using the Licensing wizard.

There are four ways to get the required information to Microsoft to activate your license server:

- Internet
- Web–based
- Fax
- Telephone

If the computer running the Terminal Services Licensing snap-in is connected to the Internet, the Internet activation method is the quickest and easiest method. The Licensing wizard directs you to the secure Microsoft site where license servers are activated. When you activate the license server, Microsoft provides the server with a digital certificate that validates server ownership and identity. Using this certificate, a license server can make subsequent transactions with Microsoft and receive client access licenses for your Terminal servers.

If your license server does not have Internet connectivity but you do have the ability to access the Web from a browser on another computer, you can activate your license server using the Web–based activation method. The Licensing wizard directs you to the secure Microsoft Web site to obtain a certificate for the license server.

Alternate methods for activating a license server include faxing your information to or calling the Customer Support Center (CSC) nearest you. The Licensing wizard also guides you through these steps. You can locate the appropriate telephone or fax number to call by using the Licensing wizard. If you use the fax activation method, your confirmed request is returned by fax from Microsoft. If you use the telephone activation method, your request is completed with a customer service representative over the telephone.

You are required to activate a license server only once. While waiting to complete the activation process, your license server can issue temporary licenses for clients that allow them to use Terminal servers for up to 90 days.

The digital certificate that uniquely identifies your license server is stored in the form of a License Server ID. Place a copy of this number in a safe location. To view this number after your license server has been activated, highlight the license server and select Properties from the View menu. Set your communication method to World Wide Web, and click OK. Then select Install Licenses from the Action menu and click Next. The License Server ID is listed in the center of the Licensing Wizard screen.

Installing Licenses

Terminal Services licenses must be installed on your license server in order for the Internet Connector setting to be enabled or for non-Windows 2000 clients to permanently access a Windows 2000 Terminal server. To obtain Windows 2000 Terminal Services Client Access licenses or Internet Connector licenses, purchase them through your standard software procurement method. After you purchase them, you can then install the licenses using the Licensing wizard.

After you have installed your licenses, your license server can begin deploying the licenses. Clients with 90-day temporary licenses will have their licenses upgraded to a Terminal Services Client Access license the next time they log on (unless the number of client access licenses installed has exceeded the number of outstanding temporary licenses).

Practice: Installing Terminal Services Licensing

In this practice, you install Terminal Services Licensing on Server01 to serve the license requirements of Application Server mode.

Exercise 1: Installing Terminal Services Licensing

Make sure that the Windows 2000 Server installation CD-ROM is inserted in the CD-ROM drive on Server01.

Note In a production environment, it is advisable to install licensing services on a computer that is not also running Terminal Services in Application Server mode.

---

1. Log on to Server01 as Administrator with a password of *password*.

2. Click the Start menu, point to Settings, and then click Control Panel.

3. In Control Panel, double-click Add/Remove Programs.

   The Add/Remove Programs dialog box appears.

4. In the left frame, click Add/Remove Windows Components.

   After a few moments, the Windows Components wizard appears.

5. Scroll down and select the Terminal Services Licensing check box, and then click Next.

   The Terminal Services Setup screen appears.

6. Select the Application Server Mode radio button, and then click Next.

   The Terminal Services Setup screen appears and informs you that Windows 2000 Administrative Tools may not work properly after the installation of Terminal services in Application Server mode.

7. Click Next.

   The Terminal Services Licensing Setup screen appears.

8. Click the Your Entire Enterprise radio button.

   Notice that the license server database is stored in C:\WINNT\System32\LServer.

9. Click Next.

   The Configuring Components screen appears as Windows 2000 configures and installs components. After a few minutes, the Completing The Windows Components Wizard screen appears.

10. Click Finish.

    The Add/Remove Programs dialog box appears.

11. Click Close, and then close Control Panel.

    A System Setting Change message box appears, informing you that you must restart the computer before the settings can take effect.

12. Click Yes to restart the computer.

13. Log on to Server01 as Administrator with a password of *password*.

14. Click the Start menu, point to Programs, point to Administrative Tools, and then click Terminal Services Licensing.

    The Terminal Services Licensing snap-in appears and the Terminal Services Licensing Manager status box appears as Terminal Services are located. Once Server01 is found, it appears in the details pane with a status of Not Activated.

15. In the details pane, click SERVER01.

16. Click the Action menu, and then click Activate Server.

    The Licensing wizard appears.

17. Click Next.

    The Connection Method screen appears.

18. In the Connection Method drop-down list box, select Telephone, and then click Next.

    The Country/Region Selection screen appears.

19. Select a country, and then click Next.

20. Without entering a license server ID, click Next.

    A Licensing Wizard message box appears explaining that the license server ID entered is not valid or was not entered.

21. Click OK.

22. On the License Server Activation screen, click Cancel.

23. Close the Terminal Services Licensing snap-in.

    The Terminal Services Licensing component is installed and you will be able to use Terminal Services in Application Server mode for 90 days. Before 90 days have passed, you must activate the server using the Terminal Services Licensing snap-in and information provided to you by Microsoft.

Lesson Summary

Terminal Services licensing includes four components: the Microsoft Clearinghouse, a license server, a Terminal server, and client licenses. Deploying a Terminal Services license server includes setting up the license server, enabling the server, activating the license server, and installing the licenses.

Lesson 4: Deploying Terminal Services to Client Computers

Client computers or terminals connect to a Terminal server using a small client program installed on disk or in firmware. The choice of which client platform to use depends on the current installed base and individual user need. At a minimum, ensure that every client computer or terminal that you expect to connect to a Terminal server is physically capable of hosting the client software and connecting over the network. This lesson walks you through the various procedures used to deploy Terminal Services to Client computers.

After this lesson, you will be able to

- Optimize Terminal Services deployment to client computers
- Determine the best method to upgrade existing terminal services
- Install and configure applications

Estimated lesson time: 45 minutes

Preparing to Deploy Terminal Services

Windows–based client computers connecting to Terminal Services should have at least a 386 microprocessor running at 33 MHz (though a 486/66 is recommended), a 16-bit VGA video card, and the Microsoft TCP/IP stack. The Terminal Services client runs on Windows for Workgroups 3.11, Windows 95, Windows 98, Windows NT 3.51 or later, and Windows 2000.

The Terminal Services client takes up only about 500 KB of disk space and typically uses approximately 4 MB of RAM when running. If client bitmap caching is enabled, another 10 MB of disk space might be used. For best performance, a computer running the Terminal Services client should have a total of 8 MB of physical RAM or more under Windows for Workgroups 3.11 or Windows 95, 24 MB or more for Windows 98, and 32 MB or more for Windows 2000.

Note A Terminal Services client for Windows CE devices can be found on the Windows 2000 Server installation CD-ROM in the \Valueadd\msft\mgmt\ mstsc_hpc folder.

The RDP client software is installed by default as a subcomponent of Terminal Services. The various clients are installed in the directory %systemroot%\ system32\clients\tsclient.

There are two ways to deploy the client:

- Create a file share to do the installation over the network.

- Select Terminal Services Client Creator from the Administrative Tools menu and make a client image that can be installed with a floppy disk.

Note The Terminal Services client requires TCP/IP to connect to the server, but Terminal Services itself can use IPX to gain access to Novell servers if necessary.

Client Configurations

You can optimize Terminal Services by following these recommendations:

- Disable the Active Desktop.

- Disable smooth scrolling.

- Minimize the use of graphics and animation, including animated graphics, screen savers, blinking cursors, and the animated Microsoft Office Assistant. Place shortcuts on the desktop and keep the Programs submenu as flat as possible. Avoid using bitmaps in wallpaper; in Display Properties, set Wallpaper to None on the Background tab and select a single color from the Appearance tab.

- Enable file sharing on client computers and share drives with easily identifiable names like "drivec." Be aware of the security implications involved.

- Avoid the use of MS-DOS or Win16 (16-bit) applications where possible.

- Configure the Terminal server to return the user's logon name rather than the computer name to applications that make use of a NetBIOS function that calls for the computer name.

- Train users to use Terminal Services hot key sequences. There are a few important differences in the hot key sequences used in a Terminal Services client session than in a Windows 2000 session.

Upgrading to Terminal Services

The approach you take to upgrade to Terminal Services depends upon your existing Terminal Services setup.

WinFrame with or without MetaFrame

There is no direct upgrade path from WinFrame to Terminal Services. In this case you first have to upgrade to Microsoft Terminal Server 4.0 and then upgrade to Windows 2000.

Terminal Server 4.0 without MetaFrame

With Terminal Server 4.0 installed, there is a direct upgrade path to Terminal Services. When you install Windows 2000, the server recognizes the Terminal Server 4.0 edition, automatically performs the upgrade, and automatically enables Terminal Services in Application Server mode. Note that you might need to reinstall existing applications if you enable Terminal Services in Application Server mode.

Terminal Server 4.0 with MetaFrame

Upgrading from Terminal Services 4.0 with MetaFrame is similar to upgrading from Terminal Server 4.0, but first you need to upgrade to the MetaFrame version for Windows 2000. After MetaFrame is upgraded, you can follow the same procedure for upgrading from Terminal Server 4.0 without MetaFrame.

Windows NT without Terminal Services

When you install Windows 2000, select Terminal Services in Remote Administration or Application mode to enable Terminal Services.

Installing and Configuring Applications

A Windows 2000 server that is configured to run Terminal Services in Application Server mode provides multiple concurrent user connections to any number of applications.

It is recommended that applications be added or removed by using the Add/Remove Programs function under Control Panel. This process automatically manages the Terminal Services installation requirements. It is also possible to install the application directly by putting the server into Install mode.

To put the Terminal Server in Install mode, type **change user /install**. After the software installation is complete, type **change user /execute** to return the Terminal Server to Execute mode.

The change user commands are not necessary when using Add/Remove Programs because Add/Remove Programs takes care of this process in the background. Add/Remove Programs is preferred because there is always the possibility of error or omission when using the command lines. If an application is installed without using Add/Remove Programs and without using the command line to set the Install mode, the application should be removed and reinstalled.

Only administrators are allowed to install applications on a Terminal Services application server.

Deploying Applications through Group Policy

Deploying applications through Active Directory and Group Policy by using Windows Installer is a very flexible application deployment method. It allows applications to be installed and managed in a number of different ways. The following are the three main ways applications can be deployed using Windows Installer:

- A user installs them on a local computer.
- The system administrator assigns them from the domain controller to a user or a computer.
- The system administrator publishes from the domain controller for a user.

Before an application can be installed using Windows Installer, an .MSI installation package must be available for the application.

Deploying Applications from a Domain Controller

To deploy an application from a domain controller, a system administrator needs to assign an .MSI–based application to a computer. Application servers cannot assign or publish applications to users.

Transform files are required if the original application installation package did not install all of the necessary components of the application to the local disk. Transform files allow you to select what, if anything, needs to be installed during the installation.

A system administrator can also install an application from a remote session or the console of an application server. A typical installation is initiated by using the following command:

```
Msiexec/I ApplicationName.MSI
TRANSFORMS=TransformFileName.MST ALLUSERS=1
```

The installation of an application in a multi-user environment is quite different from an installation to an individual user. Application server software installation must not jeopardize the system that is running, and the installation must be configured to allow concurrent users. For these reasons, only administrators can install applications, and users are not able to install anything.

It is the responsibility of the system administrator to decide which applications are needed and to ensure that applications are locally installed and available before allowing remote user connections.

Practice: Installing and Configuring Terminal Services and Terminal Services Licensing

In this practice you install Windows 2000 Terminal Services and then run remote administration from Server02 to Server01. Next, you install Terminal Services Licensing and then establish a terminal session from Server02 to Server01.

Exercise 1: Preparing an Application for Terminal Services Application Mode Operation

In this exercise, you uninstall the Windows 2000 Administration Tools and then reinstall them to ensure that they run properly from a terminal session. Make sure that the Windows 2000 Server installation CD-ROM is inserted in the CD-ROM drive on Server01 and that you are logged on as Administrator on Server01.

1. On Server01, click the Start menu, point to Settings, and then click Control Panel.

2. In Control Panel, double-click Add/Remove Programs.

   The Add/Remove Programs dialog box appears.

3. In the Currently Installed Programs box, click Windows 2000 Administrative Tools, and then click the Remove button.

   The Add/Remove Programs message box appears, asking if you want to remove the Windows 2000 Administrative Tools from your computer.

4. Click Yes.

   A Windows Installer status box appears and then the Windows 2000 Administrative Tools status box appears as the tools are removed.

   The Add/Remove Programs dialog box no longer contains the Windows 2000 Administrative Tools.

5. In the left frame, click Add New Programs.

6. From the main window, click CD or Floppy.

   The Install Program From Floppy Disk Or CD-ROM screen appears.

7. Click Next.

The Run Installation Program screen appears.

8. In the Open text box, type **<cd-rom>:\i386\adminpak.msi** where *<cd-rom>* is the drive letter of your CD-ROM drive.

9. Click Next.

The Windows Installer status box appears and then the Windows 2000 Administrative Tools Installation status box appears. After a few moments, the Windows 2000 Administrative Tools Setup wizard appears.

10. Click Next.

The Installation Progress screen appears as installation proceeds.

After a few minutes, the Completing The Windows 2000 Administrative Tools Setup wizard appears.

11. Click Finish.

The After Installation screen appears.

12. Click Next.

The Finish Admin Install screen appears.

13. Read the text on this screen, and then click Finish.

The Add/Remove Programs dialog box appears.

14. Click the Close button.

15. Close Control Panel.

Exercise 2: Connecting to Terminal Services in Application Mode and Running Terminal Services Tools

In this exercise, you install the Terminal Services client on Server02 and then run a terminal screen from Server02 to Server01. Inside the terminal session running on Server02, you monitor the session using tools installed on Server01. Server01 and Server02 should be logged on as Administrator to the MICROSOFT domain.

1. On Server01, click the Start menu, and then click Run.

The Run dialog box appears.

2. In the Open text box, type **C:\winnt\system32\clients** and then click OK.

The Clients window appears.

3. Click the Tsclient folder.

4. Click the File menu, and then click Sharing.

   The Tsclient Properties dialog box appears with the Sharing tab active.

5. Click the Share This Folder radio button.

   Tsclient appears in the Share Name text box.

6. Click OK.

7. Close the Clients window.

8. On Server02, click the Start menu, and then click Run.

   The Run dialog box appears.

9. In the Open text box, type **\\server01\tsclient** and then click OK.

   The Tsclient On Server01 window appears.

10. Double-click the Win32 folder.

11. Double-click the Disks folder.

12. Double-click the Disk1 folder.

13. Double-click the Setup icon.

    The Terminal Services Client Setup screen appears.

14. Click Continue.

    The Name And Organization Information dialog box appears.

15. Type your name, and then click OK.

    The Confirm Name And Organization Information message box appears.

16. Click OK.

    A License Agreement message box appears.

17. Click the I Agree button.

    The Terminal Services Client Setup dialog box appears.

    Notice that the client software is installed below the Program Files folder.

18. Click the large button to install the Terminal Services Client software.

    The Terminal Services Client Setup message box appears asking if you want this installation routine to apply to all users of this computer.

19. Click Yes.

    The installation progresses and then the Terminal Service Client Setup message box appears stating that the installation was successful.

20. Click OK.

21. Close the Disk1 window.

22. On Server02, click the Start menu, point to Programs, point to Terminal Services Client, and then click the Terminal Services Client icon.

    The Terminal Services Client dialog box appears.

23. In the Server drop-down list box, type **Server01**.

24. Leave the Screen area at 640 x 480, verify that the Enable Disk Compression check box is selected, and select the Cache Bitmaps To Disk check box.

25. Click the Connect button.

    The Server01 – Terminal Services Client window appears.

26. In the Log On To Windows dialog box, type **Jane_Doe.** In the Password field, type **student** and then click OK.

    Notice that the Jane_Doe personal profile appears which is indicated by the custom color scheme.

27. From within the terminal session, click the Start menu, point to Programs, point to Administrative Tools, and then click Terminal Services Manager.

    The SERVER01 – Terminal Services Manager snap-in starts inside of the terminal session.

28. In the console tree, click SERVER01.

29. In the details pane, click Jane_Doe.

30. Click the Actions menu, and then click Status.

    Status information about the Jane_Doe session appears.

31. Click the Close button.

32. Click the Actions menu, and then click Send Message.

    The Send Message dialog box appears.

33. In the top Message title box, type **Message from the Administrator** and in the bottom Message box, type **Terminal Services will be shutting down for maintenance in a few minutes. Please close your session.**

34. Click OK.

    A message box from the Administrator appears in the terminal session.

35. Click OK.

36. Close the SERVER01 – Terminal Services Manager snap-in, and then close the SERVER01 – Terminal Services Client window.

    The Disconnect Windows Session message box appears.

37. Read the message, and then click OK.

38. Shut down Server02 and Server01.

Lesson Summary

In this lesson, you learned that every client computer or terminal that you expect to connect to a Terminal server must be physically capable of hosting the client software and connecting over the network. A Windows 2000 server that is configured to run Terminal Services in Application Server mode provides multiple concurrent user connections to any number of applications. You can deploy applications through Active Directory and Group Policy or from a domain controller.

Review

The following questions will help you determine whether you have learned enough to move on to the next chapter. If you have difficulty answering these questions, please go back and review the material in this chapter before beginning the next chapter. See Appendix A, "Questions and Answers," for the answers to these questions.

1. If Terminal Services is not licensed, what features of Terminal Services will work and for how long?

C H A P T E R   2 3

Internet Services

About This Chapter

Microsoft Windows 2000 Server supports a number of services that extend the functionality of the Windows 2000 operating system to help it interoperate with the Internet. This chapter focuses on several of these services, including Internet Information Services (IIS), Web site management, and Telnet services. The chapter also provides the information necessary to implement each of these services into a Windows 2000 environment and administer that service once it is implemented.

Before You Begin

To complete this chapter, you must have

- Installed Windows 2000 Server on two computers (Server01 and Server02)

  See Chapter 8, "Installing Microsoft Windows 2000," for more details.

Lesson 1: Exploring Microsoft Internet Information Services 5.0 Features

Windows 2000 Server includes an updated version of IIS (version 5.0). IIS runs as an enterprise service within Windows 2000 and uses other services provided by Windows 2000, such as security and Active Directory directory service. IIS 5.0 improves the Web server's reliability, performance, management, security, and application services. Many of these improvements result from the way IIS 5.0 incorporates new operating system features in Windows 2000. This lesson provides an overview of IIS 5.0 and explains how to install IIS and configure a Web environment.

After this lesson, you will be able to

- Install IIS 5.0 and configure a Web environment

Estimated lesson time: 60 minutes

Introduction to Microsoft IIS 5.0

While IIS 4.0 focused on security, administration, programmability, and support for Internet standards, IIS 5.0 builds on these capabilities to deliver the type of Web sites required in an increasingly intranet- and Internet-centric business environment. In particular, IIS 5.0 has been improved in the following four areas: reliability and performance, management, security, and application environment.

Reliability and Performance

IIS 5.0 performs better and is more reliable than previous versions for a number of reasons. Internally, the speed of the IIS 5.0 engine has been increased through coding refinements. The new Reliable Restart feature lets system administrators quickly restart the server. Beyond these inherent capabilities, this version also introduces features you can use to improve the speed and reliability of Web sites.

One of the more significant improvements in IIS 5.0 is the addition of application protection through support for pooled, out-of-process applications. To better control resource consumption, new throttling features (based on the new job object feature of Windows 2000) make it easier for administrators to allocate the amount of central processing unit (CPU) bandwidth available to processes, as well as the amount of network bandwidth available to sites. In addition, the new Socket Pooling feature allows multiple sites sharing a port also to share a set of sockets.

Application Protection

Most operating systems view a process as a unit of work in a system. Services and applications are processes that run in memory areas allocated by the operating system to each process. In IIS 5.0, application protection refers to the way in which the operating system guards each application process from other processes in memory. In earlier versions of IIS, all Internet Server application programming interface (ISAPI) applications (including Active Server Pages [ASP] technology) shared the resources and memory of the IIS server process. Although this provided fast performance, unstable components could cause the IIS server to hang or crash, which made it more difficult to develop and debug new components. In addition, in-process components could not be unloaded unless the server was restarted—which meant that modifying existing components would affect all sites that shared the same IIS server, whether they were directly affected by the upgrade or not.

As a first step toward addressing these issues, IIS 4.0 allowed applications to run either in the same IIS server process (Inetinfo.exe) or out-of-process, that is in a process separate from the IIS server process. The DLLHost.exe acts as a surrogate application to the IIS server process to manage each out-of-process application. Out-of-process applications are run separately from one another, which is memory intensive and less efficient than running in-process. In IIS 5.0, there is a third option: applications can be run in a pooled process separate from the IIS server process. This approach allows related applications to be run together without adversely affecting the IIS server process. These three options provide varying levels of protection, each of which impacts performance. Greater isolation comes at the cost of slower performance.

Reliable Restart

In the event of a system failure, it is clearly important to be able to get IIS back to an operational state as quickly as possible. In the past, rebooting was an acceptable, although not optimal, way to restart IIS. To reliably restart IIS, an administrator needed to start up four separate services after every stoppage and was required to have specialized knowledge, such as which services to start and in what order. To avoid this, Windows 2000 includes IIS Reliable Restart, which is a faster, easier, more flexible one-step restart process.

Socket Pooling

IIS 5.0 increases performance by also being able to optimize access to your Web site. A socket is a protocol identifier for a particular node on a network. The socket consists of a node address and a port number that identifies the service. For example, port 80 on an Internet node represents the World Wide Web HTTP service on a Web server.

In IIS 4.0, each Web site is bound to a different IP address, which means that each site has its own socket that is not shared with sites bound to other IP addresses. Each socket is created when the site starts, and consumes significant nonpaged random access memory (RAM). This memory consumption limits the number of sites bound to IP addresses that can be created on a single machine.

For IIS 5.0, this process has been modified so that sites bound to different IP addresses but sharing the same port number can share the same set of sockets. The end result is that more sites can be bound to an IP address on the same computer than in IIS 4.0. In IIS 5.0, these shared sockets are used flexibly among all of the started sites, thus reducing resource consumption.

Multisite Hosting

To improve the scalability of IIS, Windows 2000 Server supports the capability of hosting multiple Web sites on a single server. This can save the time and money for a company that wants to host different sites for different departments, or for an ISP hosting multiple sites for different customers.

The key to hosting multiple sites on a single server is being able to distinguish between them. This can be done in several ways, each using the Web site's identification. Each Web site has a unique, three-part identity it uses to receive and to respond to requests: a port number, an IP address, and a host header name. With IIS 5.0, companies can host multiple Web sites on a single server by using one of three techniques: assigning different ports, assigning different IP addresses, or assigning different host header names. Each Web site can share two out of three unique characteristics and still be identified as a unique site.

Note IIS 4.0 also allows you to host multiple Web sites on a single server.

Process Throttling

If you run multiple Web sites that primarily use Hypertext Markup Language (HTML) pages on one computer, or if you have other applications running on the same computer as your Web server, you can limit how much processor time a Web site's applications are permitted to use. This can help ensure that processor time is available to other Web sites or applications unrelated to IIS.

Bandwidth Throttling

If the network or Internet connection used by your Web server is also used by other services such as e-mail or news, you may want to limit the bandwidth used by your Web server in order to free up bandwidth for other services. *Bandwidth Throttling* is an improved feature in IIS 5.0 that allows administrators to regulate the amount of server bandwidth each site uses by throttling the available bandwidth for the net card. For example, this allows an ISP to guarantee a predetermined amount of bandwidth to each site.

Note IIS 4.0 allows you to throttle bandwidth on a per–Web site basis.

Management

A core design goal for IIS 5.0 was to make the Web server easier for managers to use. For example, some administrators found IIS 4.0 difficult to install. With IIS 5.0, the installation process is built right into Windows 2000 Server Setup. In addition, to make it easier to configure security settings, there are three new security wizards. This release also includes improved command-line administration scripts as well as additional built-in management scripts.

Setup and Upgrade Integration

The setup process for IIS 5.0 is integrated with Windows 2000 Server setup, and IIS 5.0 installs by default as a Windows component of Windows 2000 Server. In the Windows Components wizard, it is listed as Internet Information Services (IIS). During operating system setup, a wizard helps you either to install a new copy of IIS 5.0 or to upgrade an older version.

IIS creates a default Web site, an Administration Web site, and a Default SMTP Virtual Server when you install Windows 2000 Server. You can add or remove IIS or select additional components, such as the Network News Transfer Protocol (NNTP) Service, by using the Add/Remove Programs application in Control Panel. Then from Add/Remove Programs, start the Windows Components wizard, and then click the Details button of the IIS component.

Centralized Administration

IIS 5.0 is managed by using the Internet Information Services snap-in (Figure 23.1), which is integrated with other administrative functions of Windows 2000. (In previous releases, this tool was called Internet Service Manager.) You can access the Internet Information Services snap-in through the Internet Information Services snap-in, which is located in the Administrative Tools program group. The Internet Information Services snap-in is also located in the Computer Management snap-in under Services and Applications.

Figure 23.1 Internet Information Services snap-in

The browser–based administrative tool, Internet Services Manager (HTML), is no longer available in the Administrative Tools program group, but it is still available to let you remotely administer IIS over an Hypertext Transfer Protocol (HTTP) or HTTPS (secure HTTP) connection, depending on how you have the Administration Web site configured for security. You can run Internet Services Manager (HTML) by selecting the Administration Web Site node in the console tree of the Internet Information Services snap-in and then clicking Browse from the Action menu. Or you can access it directly by specifying the server name, the TCP port number assigned to the site, and the administration Web site address as shown in the Address field in Figure 23.2.

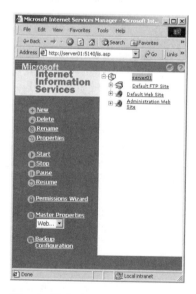

Figure 23.2 Administering IIS on Server01 from a remote computer

Note The TCP port number assigned to the administration site is randomly selected and is between 2,000 and 9,999. View the Administration Web Site Properties dialog box under the Web Site tab to determine or change the port number assigned to the site.

Browsers other than Microsoft Internet Explorer can be used to access the administration Web site, but basic authentication must be enabled if the browser does not support NT LAN Manager (NTLM) authentication and you don't want to enable anonymous access. In addition, you can use Terminal Services to remotely administer IIS by using the Internet Information Services snap-in.

Delegated Administration

To help distribute the workload of administrative tasks, administrators can add administration accounts to the Operators group. Members of the Operators group have limited administration privileges on Web sites. For example, an Internet Service Provider (ISP) that hosts sites for a number of different companies can assign delegates from each company as the operators for each company's Web site. Operators can administer properties that affect only their respective sites. They do not have access to properties that affect IIS, the Windows server computer hosting IIS, or the network. This lets an IT or ISP administrator who hosts multiple Web sites on a single server delegate the day-to-day management of the Web site without giving up total administrative control.

Process Accounting

Process Accounting (sometimes referred to as CPU Usage Logging, CPU Accounting, or Job Object Accounting) is a new feature in IIS 5.0 that lets administrators monitor and log how Web sites use CPU resources on the server. Process Accounting adds fields to the W3C Extended log file to record information about how Web sites use CPU resources on the server. ISPs can use this information to determine which sites are using disproportionately high CPU resources or that may have malfunctioning scripts or Common Gateway Interface (CGI) processes. IT managers can use this information to charge back the cost of hosting a Web site or application to the appropriate division within a company or to determine how to adjust process throttling to control resource utilization.

To enable process accounting on a site using the Internet Information Services snap-in, open the site's property page and from the properties of the W3C Extended Log File Format, choose the Extended Properties tab. In the Internet Service Manager (HTML), follow the same navigation and then choose the Extended Properties link. Figure 23.3 shows the Extended Logging Properties dialog box and the Extended Logging Options Web page.

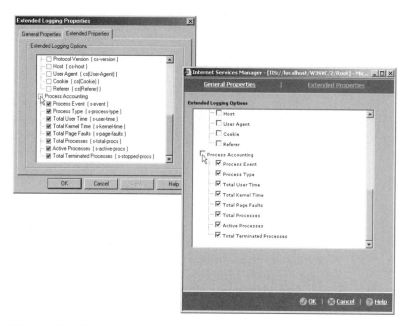

Figure 23.3 Enabling process accounting through the Extended Logging Properties dialog box or through the Extended Logging Options Web page

Improved Command-Line Administration Scripts

IIS 5.0 ships with scripts that can be executed from the command line to automate the management of common Web server tasks. These scripts are located in the \Inetpub\Scripts folder. Administration scripts automate some of the most common administrative tasks. You can use them to create and control Web sites, applications, directories, and more. Administrators can also create custom scripts that automate the management of IIS. Windows Script Host (WSH) is used to run the .vbs administration scripts included in IIS 5.0.

Backing Up and Restoring IIS

The Internet Information Services snap-in includes options that allow you to back up and restore your IIS configuration so that you can save the IIS 5.0 metabase settings to make it easy to return to a safe, known state. By using this method, you can back up and restore your Web server configuration, but not your content files or those settings that remain in the registry.

To back up and restore your Web server configuration, select the IIS computer in Internet Information Services snap-in, and then select the Backup/Restore Configuration option from the Action menu. The Configuration Backup/

Restore dialog box that appears (Figure 23.4) allows you to create a backup, restore a backup, or delete a backup that has already been created.

Figure 23.4 Accessing the Configuration Backup/Restore dialog box for Server01

Custom Error Messages

When a user attempts to connect to a Web site and an HTTP error occurs, a generic message is sent back to the client browser with a brief description of what happened during the attempt to establish a connection. With IIS 5.0, as with IIS 4.0, you can send other, more informative error messages to clients that encounter an ASP or HTML error on your site. You can use the custom error messages that IIS 5.0 provides or create you own.

In IIS 5.0, the custom error messages are stored in %systemroot%\Help\ iisHelp\common folder. In IIS 4.0, custom error messages are stored in the %systemroot%\Help\common folder. The prefix of the custom error message file is the name of the error, and the extension is .htm. If the error message contains a period, such as error 403.3, the corresponding custom message file name contains a hyphen, for example, 403-3.htm.

Support for FrontPage Server Extensions

Windows 2000 Server allows administrators to use FrontPage Web authoring and management features to deploy and manage Web sites. With FrontPage Server Extensions, administrators can view and manage a Web site in a graphical interface. In addition, authors can create, edit, and post Web pages to IIS remotely. The FrontPage Server Extensions snap-in allows you to administer the FrontPage Server Extensions and FrontPage–extended Web sites.

Unlike previous versions of IIS, FrontPage Web is enabled by default. You can access the FrontPage Extensions snap-in from the Server Extensions Administrator Microsoft Management Console (MMC) or from the Internet Information Services snap-in. The following two setup features in the FrontPage Server Extensions snap-in are important for initially configuring and checking the extensions:

- **Configuring an existing Web server to use the server extensions.** Once a Web site is configured to use server extensions, Web applications that depend on server extensions, like FrontPage, can operate against the Web site.

- **Checking server extension security.** This feature allows you to check the security of any Web site or a single Web site running Server Extensions.

In the Internet Information Services snap-in, configuring an existing Web server for server extensions is accomplished by selecting a Web site and then, from the Action menu, pointing to New and clicking the Server Extensions Web option. To check server extension security of all Web sites, choose Internet Information Services in the console tree, and then from the Action menu, point to All Tasks and click Check Server Extensions. To check server extensions on a single site, select the site from the console tree, and follow the same navigation procedure as you did to check all sites.

Web Distributed Authoring and Versioning

The Web is a great medium for publishing documents, but until now it hasn't been easy for organizations to use the Internet to let users collaborate on documents. That's because while it is easy to read documents stored on a Web site, it has not been easy for users to make changes to those documents. To address this need, IIS 5.0 has added full support for Web Distributed Authoring and Versioning (WebDAV).

By setting up a WebDAV directory on your Web server, you can let users share documents over the Internet or an intranet. WebDAV in IIS 5.0 takes advantage of the security and file access features provided by Windows 2000, so you can lock and unlock resources to let multiple people read a file, while only one person at a time can modify the file. WebDAV is discussed in more detail in Lesson 2, "Administering a Web Environment."

Distributed File System

IIS 5.0 makes use of the Windows 2000 distributed file system (Dfs). Dfs is a means for uniting files on different computers into a single namespace. Dfs lets system administrators build a single, hierarchical view of multiple file servers and file server shares on the network, making it easier for users to access and manage files that are physically distributed across a network. With Dfs, you can make files that are distributed across multiple servers appear to users as if they reside in one place on the network. Users no longer need to know and specify the actual physical location of files in order to access them.

HTTP Compression

HTTP compression allows faster transmission of pages between a Web server and compression-enabled clients. This is useful in situations where bandwidth is limited. Depending on the content you're hosting, your storage space, and the connection speed of your typical Web site visitor, HTTP compression can provide faster transmission of pages between your Web server and compression-enabled browsers.

In the Internet Information Services snap-in, HTTP Compression is enabled from the master properties of the Internet Information Services node. On the Internet Information Services Properties dialog box, click the Edit button for the WWW Service and then choose the Service tab (Figure 23.5).

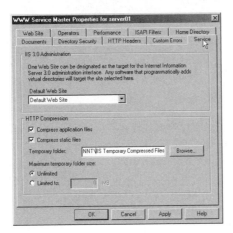

Figure 23.5 WWW Service Master Properties for Server01 as seen from the Internet Information Services snap-in

From the Internet Information Service (HTML) home page, click the Service option under Master Properties. View the service properties and configure compression (Figure 23.6).

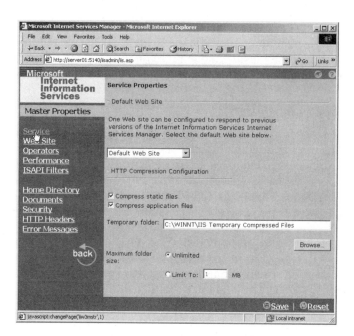

Figure 23.6 WWW Service Master Properties for Server01 as seen from Internet Services Manager (HTML) page

FTP and FTP Restart

The File Transfer Protocol (FTP) service, an industry-standard protocol used to publish information to a Web server, is integrated into Windows 2000 Server. In IIS 5.0, the FTP Restart protocol is also supported by Windows 2000 Server. It provides a faster and smoother way to download information from the Internet. If an interruption occurs during data transfer from an FTP site, the download can continue where it left off, without the entire file having to be downloaded again.

Note This feature is available only to FTP clients that support the FTP restart function. The FTP client initiates the REST command to connect and continue a failed download.

Security

Security features, which are an important area of improvement in IIS 5.0, take advantage of the Internet-standard security features that are fully integrated with Windows 2000.

Security Standards

The security protocols supported in IIS 5.0 are described in the following table.

Table 23.1   Security Standards

Security	Protocol description
Fortezza	Support for the U.S. government security standard called Fortezza is new in IIS 5.0. Fortezza satisfies the Defense Message System security architecture with a cryptographic mechanism that provides message confidentiality, integrity, authentication, non-repudiation, and access control to messages, components, and systems. These features are implemented both with server and browser software and with PC-Card card hardware.
Secure Sockets Layer (SSL) 3.0	SSL security protocols are used widely by Internet browsers and servers for authentication, message integrity, and confidentiality. You can configure your Web server's SSL security features to verify the integrity of your content, verify the identity of users, and encrypt network transmissions. SSL relies upon certificates. Microsoft Certificate Services can be used to issue certificates.
Transport Layer Security (TLS)	TLS is based on SSL. It provides for cryptographic user authentication and provides a way for independent programmers to write TLS-enabled code that can exchange crypto graphic information with another process without a programmer needing to be familiar with another programmer's code. In addition, TLS is intended to provide a framework that can be used by new public key and bulk encryption methods as they emerge. TLS also focuses on improving performance by reducing network traffic and providing an optional session caching scheme that can reduce the number of connections that need to be established from scratch.
PKCS #7	This protocol describes the format of encrypted data such as digital signatures or digital envelopes. Both of these are involved in the certificate features of IIS.
PKCS #10	This protocol describes the format of requests for certificates that are submitted to certification authorities.

continues

Table 23.1 Security Standards *(continued)*

Security	Protocol description
Basic Authentication	Basic Authentication is a part of the HTTP 1.0 specification. It sends passwords over networks in Base64-encoded format. The Basic Authentication method is a widely used, industry-standard method for collecting user name and password information. The advantage of Basic Authentication is that it is part of the HTTP specification, and is supported by most browsers. The disadvantage is that Web browsers using Basic Authentication transmit passwords in an unencrypted form. By monitoring communications on your network, someone could easily intercept and decipher these passwords by using publicly available tools. Therefore, Basic Authentication is not recommended unless you are confident that the connection between the user and your Web server is secure, with a direct cable connection, a dedicated line, or a secure intranet.
Digest authentication	A new feature of IIS 5.0, Digest Authentication, offers the same features as Basic Authentication but involves a different method for transmitting the authentication credentials. The authentication credentials pass through a one-way process, often referred to as *hashing*. The result of this process is called a *hash*, or *message digest*, and the original text cannot be deciphered from the hash. The server generates additional information that is added to the password before hashing so no one can capture the password hash and use it to impersonate the true client. This is a shared secret password methodology. This a clear advantage over Basic Authentication, in which the password can be intercepted and used by an unauthorized person. Digest Authentication is structured to be usable across proxy servers and other firewall applications and is available to WebDAV. Because Digest Authentication is a new HTTP 1.1 feature, not all browsers support it. If a non-compliant browser makes a request on a server that requires Digest Authentication, the server will reject the request and send the client an error message. Digest Authentication is supported only for Windows 2000 domains, and Internet Explorer version 5 or later is one of the few browsers that supports this feature.
Integrated Windows Authentication	This authentication method provides NTLM (Windows NT Challenge/Response) authentication for older versions of Internet Explorer 3.0 that use it to cryptographically authenticate with IIS. Integrated Windows Authentication also provides Web sites and new versions of Internet Explorer with Kerberos v5 authentication. Integrated Windows Authentication is only used if Anonymous access is disabled or denied as a result of NTFS permissions restrictions. Integrated Windows Authentication is not supported over Proxy server connections.

Security Mechanisms

IIS 5.0 uses five basic security mechanisms: authentication, certificates, access control, encryption, and auditing.

Authentication

Authentication allows you to confirm the identity of anyone requesting access to your Web sites. IIS supports the following types of authentication for HTTP and FTP services:

- Anonymous FTP and HTTP authentication

- Basic FTP and HTTP authentication

- Anonymous FTP and HTTP authentication

- Digest authentication for Windows 2000 Domains and browsers supporting this HTTP 1.1 authentication method

- Integrated Windows authentication (HTTP only)

Certificates

To complete the authentication process, you need a mechanism for verifying user identities. Certificates are digital identification documents that allow both servers and clients to authenticate each other. They are required for the server and client's browser to set up an SSL connection over which encrypted information can be sent. Server certificates usually contain information about your company and the organization that issued the certificate. Client certificates usually contain identifying information about the user and the organization that issued the certificate.

Access Control

After verifying the identity of a user, you'll want to control their access to resources on your server. IIS 5.0 uses two layers of access control: Web permissions and NTFS permissions. Web permissions apply to all HTTP clients and define access to server resources. NTFS permissions define what level of access individual user accounts have to folders and files on the server.

Encryption

Once you've controlled access to information, you need to protect that information as it passes over the Internet. Encryption scrambles the information before it is sent, and decryption unscrambles it after it is received. You can let users exchange private information, such as credit card numbers or phone numbers, with your server in a secure way by using encryption The foundation for this encryption is the SSL 3.0 protocol and the emerging

Transport Layer Security (TLS) 1.0 protocol, which provides a secure way of establishing an encrypted communication link with users. SSL confirms the authenticity of your Web site and, optionally, the identity of users accessing restricted Web sites.

Auditing

The last step to ensuring security is to regularly monitor your site's usage. Administrators can use security auditing techniques to monitor a broad range of user and Web server security activity. Auditing consists of creating auditing policies for directory and file access or server events and monitoring the security logs to detect any access attempts by unauthorized persons.

Security Wizards

To make it simpler to establish and maintain security settings, IIS 5.0 includes three new security task wizards: the Web Server Certificate wizard, the Permissions wizard, and the Certificate Trust Lists wizard.

The Certificate wizard simplifies certificate administration tasks, such as creating certificate requests and managing the certificate life cycle. The Web Server Certificate wizard is started from the Server Certificate button on the properties of a Web site in the Internet Information Services snap-in.

Figure 23.7 Starting the Web Server Certificate wizard on the Properties page of the Administration Web site

---

Note Using Internet Information Services (HTML) to create a Web server certificate is similar to using the Internet Information Services snap-in; however, there is no HTML-based wizard to walk you through the configuration process.

SSL security is an increasingly common requirement for Web sites that provide e-commerce and access to sensitive business information. The new wizard makes it easy to set up SSL-enabled Web sites on a Windows 2000 Server computer. In addition, this wizard makes it easier to establish and maintain SSL encryption and client certificate authentication.

The Permissions wizard walks administrators through the tasks of setting up permissions and authenticated access on an IIS Web site, making it much easier to set up and manage a Web site that requires authenticated access to its content.

The Permissions wizard is started from the Internet Information Services snap-in. Select either a Web site or FTP site. From the Action menu, point to All Tasks and then click Permissions wizard. Figure 23.8 shows the Permissions Wizard screen started from the Internet Information Services snap-in.

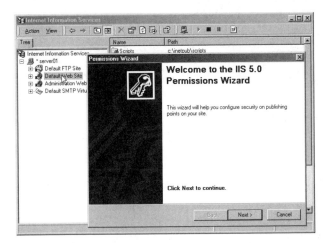

Figure 23.8 Permissions Wizard screen for the Default Web site

The Permissions wizard can also be started from Internet Services Manager (HTML) by selecting a Web or FTP site from the home page and then clicking the Permissions Wizard link in the left frame of the home page, as shown in Figure 23.9.

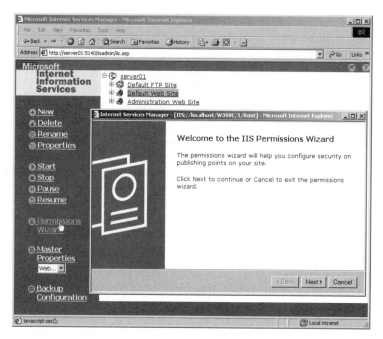

Figure 23.9 HTML-based Permissions Wizard screen for the Default Web site

The Permissions wizard provides two top-level options:

- Inherited security settings applied to the parent site or virtual directory
- Security settings based on a template

Two templates are available for configuring security: the Public Web Site template and the Secure Web Site template. The Public Web Site template applies security settings that are cross-browser compatible and provide access to the site regardless of whether the user has a Windows 2000 account for the network being accessed. The Secure Web Site template applies security settings that only users with Windows 2000 user accounts can access.

The Certificate Trust List wizard allows administrators to configure certificate trust lists (CTLs). A *CTL* is a list of trusted certification authorities (CAs) for a particular directory. CTLs are especially useful for ISPs that have several Web sites on their server and who need to have a different list of approved CAs for each site. CTLs are available only at the Web site level and are not available for FTP sites.

After a Server Certificate is configured for the site, the Certificate Trust List wizard is run from the properties of a Web site in the Internet Information Services snap-in. On the Directory Security tab of the Properties dialog box, click the Edit button under Secure Communications to display the Secure Communications dialog box. From this dialog box, select the Enable Certificate Trust List check box and then click New. The Certificate Trust List wizard appears (Figure 23.10).

Figure 23.10 Navigating to the Certificate Trust List wizard after enabling CTL

You can also enable and configure CTL from the Internet Service Manager (HTML), but there is no corresponding HTML-based wizard. Also, you cannot edit the certificates through the HTML interface, but you can edit the certificates from the Internet Information Services snap-in.

Application Environment

IIS 5.0 includes performance enhancements that make it easier to develop Web-enabled applications. The ASP technology within IIS, combined with the data access and component services within Windows 2000 Server, provide a well-rounded application environment.

With this release, enhanced flow control and error handling, Windows Script Host Components, and other improvements make ASP easier to use for script writers and Web application developers. In addition, features such as scriptless ASP, ASP self-tuning, and performance-enhanced objects, as well as improvements within the Windows 2000 operating system, can increase the speed of ASP applications.

ASP is a server-side scripting environment that you can use to create and run dynamic, interactive Web server applications. With ASP, you can combine HTML pages, script commands, and Component Object Model (COM) components to create interactive Web pages or Web-based applications that are easy to deploy and modify. There are a number of new ASP features in IIS 5.0, such as new flow control capabilities and error handling features that make it easier to write and control the behavior of Web applications. Other new features, such as scriptless ASP processing, improve the performance of ASP pages.

Component Services

IIS 5.0 and the Component Services (COM+) included in Windows 2000 Server work together to form a basic architecture for building Web applications. In IIS version 4.0, Microsoft Transaction Server (MTS) provided transaction support. In IIS 5.0 and Windows 2000, Component Services provides all the transaction support of MTS, in addition to a number of other component development and deployment features. IIS uses the functionality provided by Component Services to perform the following tasks:

- Isolate applications into distinct processes

- Manage communication between Component Object Model (COM) components (including the ASP built-in objects)

- Coordinate transaction processing for transactional ASP applications

Active Directory Directory Service

Active Directory directory service in Windows 2000 Server is used to store and manage information about networked resources. By providing a centralized store for essential information, Active Directory simplifies network management, makes it easier for users to find resources, and makes it easier for developers to write applications.

Microsoft Active Directory Service Interfaces (ADSI) is a COM-based directory service model that allows client applications that are ADSI-compliant to access a wide variety of distinct directory protocols, including Active Directory, LDAP, and NDS, while using a single, standard set of interfaces. ADSI shields the client application from the implementation and operational details of the underlying data store or protocol.

IIS stores most Internet site configuration information in the IIS metabase. IIS exposes a low-level DCOM interface that allows applications to gain access to and manipulate the metabase. To make it easy to access the metabase, IIS also includes an ADSI provider that provides most of the functionality provided by the DCOM interface, and exposes it to any ADSI-compliant client applications.

Installing IIS 5.0

Internet Information Services 5.0 is a component of the Windows 2000 operating system. Installation and removal of IIS is accomplished in one of three ways: when installing or upgrading Windows 2000, by using the Add/Remove Programs utility in Control Panel, or by using an unattended.txt file during an unattended installation.

When performing a clean installation of Windows 2000 Server, IIS is installed by default. You can remove IIS or select IIS components to be added or removed by using the Add/Remove Programs utility.

When you upgrade from a previous version of Windows 95, Windows 98, or Windows NT to Windows 2000, Setup attempts to detect previous versions of IIS, Peer Web Services, or Personal Web Server. If one of these programs is detected, IIS 5.0 is installed. You cannot prevent an upgrade to IIS 5.0 if a previous version of IIS, Peer Web Services, or Personal Web Server is detected. However, IIS 5.0 will not be installed if these existing services are not detected.

When installing IIS 5.0, either as an upgrade or as a clean install, Setup verifies that the TCP/IP protocol suite is installed. If Setup does not find TCP/IP installed, it automatically installs the protocol suite and configures it to use DHCP.

During the IIS installation, the Default Web site, Administration Web site, Default SMTP Virtual Server, and Default FTP site are created. Managing the Web sites and the FTP site are discussed in more detail in Lesson 2, "Administering a Web Environment."

Note The Default SMTP Virtual Server is beyond the scope of this training kit. SMTP provides e-mail message delivery support to intranet- and Internet-enabled applications.

Setting Up a Web Environment

Whether your site is on an intranet or the Internet, the principles of providing content are the same. You place your Web files in folders on your server so that users can establish an HTTP connection and view your files with a Web browser. But beyond simply storing files on your server, you must manage how your site is deployed and, more importantly, how your site evolves.

Getting Started

You should set up your Web site by indicating which folders contain the documents that you want to publish. The Web server cannot publish documents that are not within these specified folders. So, the first step in deploying a Web site should be to determine how you want your files organized. You then use the Internet Information Services snap-in or the Internet Services Manager (HTML) interface to identify which folders (called directories in the snap-in and HTML interface) are part of the site.

If you want to get started right away without having to create a special folder structure, and your files are all located on the same hard disk of the computer running IIS, you can publish your documents immediately by copying your Web files into the default home folder. Intranet users can then access these files by using any of the following URLs:

- *http://<computer_name/file_name>*
- *http://<FQDN/file_name>*
- *http://<IP_address/file_name>*

Where *computer_name*, *FQDN*, and *IP_address* identify the Web server.

Note In the following section, the words *folder* and *folders* are replaced by the words *directory* and *directories* because the latter are used in the IIS interface.

Defining Home Directories

Each Web site and FTP site must have one home directory. The home directory is the central location for your published pages. It contains a home page (typically named index.htm, index.html, default.asp, default.htm, or default.html) that welcomes Web browser users and contains links to other pages in your site. More than one default document can be specified for a single site. IIS displays the first default document it finds. The home directory is mapped to your site's domain name or to your server name. For example, if your site's Internet domain name is www.microsoft.com and your home directory is C:\Website\Microsoft, browsers use the URL *http://www.microsoft.com* to access files in your home directory. On an intranet, if your server name is AcctServer, browsers can use the URL *http://acctserver* to access files in your home directory.

A default home directory is created when you install IIS and when you create a new Web site. If you are setting up both a Web site and an FTP site on the same computer, you must specify a different home directory for each service (WWW and FTP). The default home directory for the WWW service is \InetPub\Wwwroot. The default home directory for the FTP service is \InetPub\Ftproot. You can choose a different directory as your home directory.

You can use the Internet Information Services snap-in to change the home directory. Select a Web site or FTP site and open its Properties dialog box. Click the Home Directory tab, and then specify where your home directory is located (Figure 23.11).

Figure 23.11 Home Directory tab of the Default Web Site Properties dialog box

If you select a directory on a network share, you may need to type a user name and password to access the resource. It is recommend that you use the IUSR_*computername* account. If you use an account that has administration permissions on the server, clients can gain access to server operations. This seriously jeopardizes the security of your network.

Notice that the home directory can reside on the computer running IIS, on a share, or can be redirected to a URL hosted by another Web site. The share option provides transparent support for Dfs.

Creating Virtual Directories

You can create a virtual directory to publish from a directory not contained within your home directory. A virtual directory is one that is not contained in the home directory but appears to client browsers as though it were.

A virtual directory has an alias, a name that Web browsers use to access that directory. Because an alias is usually shorter than the path name of the directory, it is more convenient for users to type. An alias also is more secure; users do not know where your files are physically located on the server and cannot use that information to modify your files. Aliases also make it easier for you to move directories in your site. Rather than change the URL for the directory, you can simply change the mapping between the alias and the physical location of the directory.

For a simple Web site, you may not need to add virtual directories. You can instead place all of your files in the site's home directory. If you have a complex site or want to specify different URLs for different parts of your site, you can add virtual directories as needed.

The Internet Information Services snap-in or the Internet Services Manger (HTML) allows you to create a virtual directory. In the Internet Information Services snap-in, select the Web site or FTP site to which you want to add a virtual directory. From the Action menu, click New and then click Virtual Directory. The Virtual Directory Creation wizard walks you through the process of creating a virtual directory (Figure 23.12).

Figure 23.12 Creating a virtual directory for the Default Web site using the Virtual Directory Creation wizard

In Internet Services Manager (HTML), the same link used to create a new site is also used to publish your content to a virtual directory or a directory. After selecting a site in Internet Services Manager (HTML) and clicking New link in the left frame, the IIS New Site wizard appears. On the next screen in the wizard, you select the Virtual Directory radio button to publish a new virtual directory.

Reroute Requests with Redirects

When a browser requests a page on your Web site, the Web server locates the page identified by the URL and returns it to the browser. When you move a page on your Web site, you can't always correct all of the links that refer to the old URL of the page. To make sure that browsers can find the page at the new URL, you instruct the Web server to give the browser the new URL. The browser uses the new URL to request the page again. This process is called *redirecting a browser request* or *redirecting to another URL*. Redirecting a request for a page is similar to using a forwarding address with a postal service. The forwarding address ensures that letters and packages addressed to your original residence are delivered to your new residence.

Redirecting a URL is useful when you are updating your Web site and want to make a portion of the site temporarily unavailable, or when you have changed the name of a virtual directory and want links to files in the original virtual directory to access the same files in the new virtual directory.

You can use the Internet Information Services snap-in to redirect requests to a Web site, a virtual directory, or another directory. Select the Web site, virtual directory, or directory and open its Properties dialog box. For a Web site, use the Home Directory tab; for a virtual directory, use the Virtual Directory tab; for a directory, use the Directory tab. Select the A Redirection To A URL option, and type the URL of the destination in the Redirect To text box.

Other Tools

It is often useful to dynamically alter Web content after the content has been requested but before it is returned to the browser. IIS includes two features that provide this functionality: server-side includes (SSI) and the ASP scripting environment.

Using SSI, you can carry out a whole host of Web site management activities from adding dynamic time-stamping to running a special shell command each time a file is requested. SSI commands, called *directives*, are added to Web pages at design time. When a page is requested, the Web server parses out all the directives it finds in a Web page and then executes them. A commonly used SSI directive inserts, or includes the contents of a file into a Web page. For example, if you are required to continually update a Web page advertisement, you could use SSI to include the advertisement's HTML source into the Web page. To update the advertisement, you need only modify the file containing advertisement's HTML source. You do not have to know a scripting language to use SSI; simply follow the correct directive syntax.

ASP is a server-side scripting environment that you can use to dynamically alter Web content. Although ASP is primarily designed for Web application development, it has many features that can be used to make Web sites easier to manage. For example, with ASP you can track users visiting a Web site, or you can customize Web content based on browser capabilities. However, unlike SSI, ASP requires you to use a scripting language such as VBScript or JScript.

Using ASP to Manage Web Site Content

Windows 2000 includes Microsoft ASP, a server-side scripting environment that you can use to automate and centralize many of your Web site management tasks.

Scripting

A *script* is a series of instructions and commands that you can use to programmatically alter the content of your Web pages. If you have ever visited an online store that enabled you to search for items and check product availability, then undoubtedly you have encountered some type of script.

There are two kinds of scripting: client-side and server-side. Client-side scripts run on the Web browser and are embedded in a Web page between HTML <SCRIPT> and </SCRIPT> tags. If you view the HTML source for a highly dynamic Web page, you will most likely discover a client-side script.

Server-side scripts run exclusively on the Web server and are most often used to modify Web pages before they are delivered to the browser. Server-side scripts can instruct the Web server to perform an action such as process user input or log how often a user visits your Web site. You can think of server-side scripts as affecting how the Web server assembles a Web page before it's sent to the browser. Server-side scripts can greatly facilitate your management of Web content by processing data and automatically updating Web pages.

ASP Overview

Just as you might write a custom macro to automate repetitive spreadsheet or word processing tasks, you can create a server-side script to automatically perform difficult or repetitious Web management tasks. Imagine that you need to update a Web site consisting of several dozen pages containing identical formatting information (bylines, company logos, copyright information, and so on). Normally, such work is time consuming and requires that you update (and test) each page manually. However, you can use ASP to automate such work.

ASP is a powerful, server-side scripting environment that you can use to write scripts with only a standard text editor, such as Notepad. For example, using ASP you could create a central file that contains information common to all of the pages of a Web site. While designing the Web site, you could add a one-line script command to each page that inserts the contents of the central file. Whenever you need to update your site's navigation menu, for example, you need only update the central file; changes would automatically appear the next time a user reloads and views the Web content.

ASP uses *delimiters* to differentiate script commands from regular text and HTML. Specifically, <% and %> delimiters enclose script commands that are to be executed by the server, as opposed to < and > delimiters used by HTML to denote tags that are to be parsed by a Web browser.

The following example script illustrates how ASP works:

```
<%
author = "Max"
department = "Quality Assurance"
%>

This page was updated <B>today</B>, by <%= author %> from
the <%= department %> Department.
```

When viewed in a Web browser, a page containing this script appears as follows:

```
This page was updated today, by Max from the Quality Assur-
ance Department.
```

However, a user viewing the source for this page from a Web browser would see only the following text and HTML:

```
This page was updated <B>today</B>, by Max from the Quality
Assurance Department.
```

The script runs on the server (that is, commands within the <% and %> delimiters are executed on the server) and returns only HTML to a user's browser.

At a minimum, all ASP files must have an .ASP extension and contain script commands written in a scripting language such as Microsoft Visual Basic Scripting Edition (VBScript) or Microsoft JScript. If you are new to scripting and need to learn the fundamentals, visit the Microsoft Windows Script Technologies Web site at *http://msdn.microsoft.com/scripting/*.

Practice: Accessing the Administration Web Site

In this practice, you use the Internet Information Services snap-in to configure the Administration Web site. You configure access to this sensitive area of the Web server. You then run Internet Service Manager (HTML) to test access capability to the site. Complete this practice on Server01.

Exercise 1: Configuring the Administration Web Site with the Internet Information Services Snap-in

In this exercise, you use the Internet Informations Services snap-in to configure the Administration Web site.

1. Log on to Server01 as Administrator with a password of *password*.

2. Click the Start button, point to Programs, point to Administrative Tools, and then click Internet Services Manager.

   The Internet Information Services snap-in appears.

3. In the console tree, expand * server01.

   Four containers appears under * server01: Default FTP site, Default Web site, Administration Web site, and Default SMTP Virtual Server.

4. In the console tree, expand Administration Web site.

   Notice that two virtual directories, IISAdmin and IISHelp, appear.

5. In the console tree, click on Administration Web site.

6. Click the Action menu, and then click Properties.

   The Administration Web Site Properties dialog box appears.

7. With the Web Site tab active, record the TCP Port value appearing in the TCP Port text box.

   This random value between 2000–9999 is referred to in this exercise as a variable with a name of *tcp_port*.

8. Under the Enable Logging check box, verify that W3C Extended Log File Format is selected, and then click the Properties button.

   The Extended Logging Properties dialog box appears. Notice that the log file is stored in the %WinDir%\System32\LogFiles, which is equivalent to %SystemRoot%\System32\LogFiles.

9. Click the Extended Properties tab.

10. Scroll down to the bottom of the Extended Logging Options box and then select the Process Accounting check box.

11. Click OK to close the Extended Logging Properties dialog box.

    The Administration Web Site Properties dialog box appears.

12. Click the Directory Security tab.

13. In the Anonymous Access And Authentication Control region of the screen, click the Edit button.

    The Authentication Methods dialog box appears.

    Notice that Anonymous access is not available to the Administration Web site, Basic authentication is not enabled, and that Integrated Windows authentication is enabled.

    This configuration means that a browser client connecting to the Administration Web site must be able to authenticate using either secure NTLM or Kerberos authentication. The type of Integrated Windows authentication method used is browser dependent.

14. Select the Digest Authentication For Windows Domain Servers check box.

    An IIS WWW Configuration message box appears and explains that only Windows 2000 domain accounts can be used and that passwords will be stored as encrypted clear text.

15. Click Yes.

    This provides additional security in your Windows 2000 domain. You will only be using Windows 2000 domain user accounts to access the Administration Web site.

16. Click OK to close the Authentication Methods dialog box.

    The Administration Web Site Properties dialog box appears.

17. In the IP Address And Domain Name Restrictions region of the screen, click the Edit button.

    The IP Address and Domain Name Restrictions dialog box appears.

    Notice that the Denied Access radio button is selected and that only the local loopback address, 127.0.0.1 is granted access to this area.

18. Click the Granted Access radio button so that you can access the Administration Web site from any computer in your training network.

    For additional security, consider adding specific IP addresses, a scope of IP addresses, or computers within a specific domain that can access the Administration Web site. This last option is resource intensive and not recommended for most implementations of IIS 5.0.

19. Click OK.

20. Click OK to close the Administration Web Site Properties dialog box.

    The Inheritance Overrides dialog box appears and explains that the Child node, IISAdmin, defines the value of "Authentication Methods." You will override the currently configured value in favor of the value you configured for the Administration Web Site node.

21. In the Child Nodes box, click IISAdmin and then click OK.

The Inheritance Overrides dialog box appears again for the IISHelp Child node.

22. Click IISHelp and click OK.

23. Close Internet Information Services snap-in.

Exercise 2: Accessing the Administration Web Site from Internet Service Manager (HTML)

In this exercise, you attempt to access the Administration Web site with the new settings you configured in the previous exercise.

Note The *tcp_port* variable in this exercise must be replaced with the value you obtained from the previous exercise.

---

1. On Server01, click the Start button and then click Run.

The Run dialog box appears.

2. In the Open text box, type **http://server01:<tcp_port>** and then click OK.

Internet Explorer starts and a Microsoft Internet Explorer text box appears and explains that you are not running a secure connection for Web-based administration.

This means that while authentication information between the browser and the Administration Web site is secure, data transmission after the connection is established is not secure.

3. Click OK.

Internet Explorer shows the Internet Services Manager (HTML) interface.

4. Explore the three Web sites appearing in the main window of the interface. Use the links in the left frame to explore the features discussed in this lesson.

5. Close Internet Explorer.

Exercise 3: Configuring SSL Access to the Administration Web Site

In this exercise, you apply the SSL protocol to the Administration Web site to establish secure communications when operating on this site. To do this, you issue your own server certificate using Server01 and Certificate Services.

Note You should have installed Certificate Services when completing Chapter 15, "Managing Certificate Services." If you did not, you need to install these services before attempting this exercise.

---

1. On Server01, open Internet Services Manager.

   The Internet Information Services snap-in appears.

2. In the console tree, expand * server01.

3. Click on the Administration Web site.

4. Click the Action menu, and then click Properties.

   The Administration Web Site Properties dialog box appears.

5. Click the Directory Security tab.

6. In the Secure Communications region of the screen, click Server Certificate.

   The Welcome to the Web Server Certificate wizard appears.

7. Read the information on this screen, and then click Next.

   The IIS Certificate wizard appears.

8. Confirm that the Create A New Certificate radio button is selected, and then click Next.

   The Delayed or Immediate Request screen appears.

9. Click the Send The Request Immediately To An Online Certification Authority radio button, and then click Next.

   The Name and Security Settings screen appears.

   Notice that the default name given to this certificate is Administration Web site and that the bit length is set to 512 bits.

10. Click Next.

    The Organization Information screen appears.

11. In the Organization drop-down list box, type **Microsoft Corporation** and in the Organizational Unit drop-down list box, type **Microsoft Press**.

12. Click Next.

    The Your Site's Common Name screen appears.

13. In the Common Name text box, type **server01.microsoft.com**. and then click next.

    The Geographical Information screen appears.

14. Do not change the value in the Country/Region drop-down list box.

15. In the State/Province drop-down list box, type **Washington** and in the City/Locality drop-down list box, type **Redmond**.

16. Click Next.

The Choose A Certification Authority screen appears and server01.microsoft.com\Enterprise CA appears in the Certification Authorities drop-down list box.

17. Click Next.

The Certificate Request Submission screen appears.

18. Read through the summary information on this screen and then click Next.

After a few moments, the Completing the Web Server Certificate Wizard screen appears.

19. Click Finish.

The Administration Web Site Properties dialog box appears. Notice that under the Secure Communications region of the screen, the View Certificate and Edit buttons are now available.

20. In the Secure Communications region of the screen, click the Edit button.

The Secure Communications dialog box appears.

21. Click the Require Secure Channel (SSL) check box.

22. Verify that the Ignore Client Certificates radio button is selected, and then Click OK.

The Administration Web Site Properties dialog box appears.

23. Click the Web Site tab.

24. In the SSL Port field, type **5000**.

25. Click OK.

26. Close the Internet Information Services snap-in.

Exercise 4: Testing Access to the Secured Administration Web Site

In this exercise, you test access to the Administration Web site now that a server certificate and SSL has been configured for the site.

1. On Server01, click the Start button, and then click Run.

The Run dialog box appears.

2. In the Open text box, type **http://server01:<tcp_port>** and then click OK.

The *tcp_port* variable in this exercise must be replaced with the value you obtained in Exercise 1.

Internet Explorer starts and a message appears, explaining that the page must be viewed over a secure channel.

3. In the Internet Explorer Address drop-down list box, type **https://server01.microsoft.com:5000** and then click Go. The 5000 value is the *SSL_port* value you typed on the Web Site tab.

   A Security Alert message box appears stating that you are about to view information over a secure connection.

4. Click the In The Future Do Not Show This Warning check box and then click OK.

   The Enter Network Password dialog box appears.

5. In the User Name text box, type **Administrator**, in the Password text box, type **password**, and in the Domain text box, type **microsoft**.

6. Select the Save This Password In Your Password List check box, and then click OK.

   The Internet Services Manager (HTML) interface appears. Notice that there is a lock icon on the bottom right corner of the status bar.

7. Place the mouse pointer on top of the lock icon.

   Notice that a tip states: "SSL secured (56 Bit)." 128-bit encryption is available from the Secure Communications dialog box for the properties of the site. In the previous exercise, you configured SSL for the connection but you did not require 128-bit encryption.

8. Double-click the lock icon.

   The Certificate dialog box appears.

9. Review the information under the tabs of the Certificate dialog box.

   From the Certificate dialog box you can run the Certificate Import wizard to copy certificate information from the local computer to a certificate store.

10. Click OK.

11. Close the Internet Services Manager (HTML) interface.

Lesson Summary

In this lesson, you learned that IIS 5.0 introduces improvements in reliability and performance, management, security, and application environment. IIS also introduces features you can use to improve the speed and reliability of Web sites, such as the addition of application protection through support for pooled, out-of-process applications. In addition, IIS 5.0 makes the Web server easier for managers to use. For example, the installation process is built right into Windows 2000 Server Setup. And, to make it easier to configure security settings, there are three new security wizards. Security features are an important area of improvement in IIS 5.0, which takes advantage of the Internet-standard security features that are fully integrated with Windows 2000. IIS 5.0 also adds performance enhancements to make it easier to debug and deploy Web–enabled applications.

You also learned that installation and removal of IIS is accomplished in one of three ways: when installing or upgrading Windows 2000, by using the Add/Remove Programs utility in Control Panel, or by using an unattended.txt file during an unattended installation. When IIS is installed, a Default Web site, Administration Web site and Default SMTP Virtual Server are created. You should set up your Web site by indicating which directories contain the documents that you want to publish. Each Web or FTP site must have one home directory. To publish from any directory not contained within your home directory, you can create a virtual directory. Windows 2000 includes Microsoft ASP, a server-side scripting environment that you can use to automate and centralize many of your Web site management tasks.

Lesson 2: Administering a Web Environment

When IIS is installed, a default Web site is created, allowing you to quickly and easily implement a Web environment. However, you can modify that Web environment to meet your specific needs. In addition, you can implement Web Distributed Authoring and Versioning (WebDAV), which allows you to share documents over the Internet or an intranet. This lesson covers several aspects of administering a Web environment: Web site management, FTP site management, and WebDAV publishing. Administering Web and FTP sites is very similar and, as a result, are discussed together. This is followed by a discussion of WebDAV publishing.

After this lesson, you will be able to

- Administer Web and FTP sites
- Manage WebDAV publishing

Estimated lesson time: 35 minutes

Administering Web and FTP Sites

Originally, each domain name, such as www.microsoft.com, represented an individual computer. With IIS 5.0, multiple Web sites or FTP sites can be hosted simultaneously on a single computer running Windows 2000 Server. Each Web site can host one or more domain names. Because each site mimics the appearance of an individual computer, sites are sometimes referred to as *virtual servers*.

Web Sites and FTP Sites

Whether your system is on an intranet or the Internet, you can create multiple Web sites and FTP sites on a single computer running Windows 2000 in one of three ways:

- Append port numbers to the IP address
- Use multiple IP addresses, each having its own network adapter card
- Assign multiple domain names and IP addresses to one network adapter card by using host header names

The example in Figure 23.13 illustrates an intranet scenario where the system administrator has installed Windows 2000 Server with IIS on the company's server, resulting in one default Web site: *http://CompanyServer*. The system administrator then creates two additional Web sites, one for each of two departments: Marketing and Human Resources.

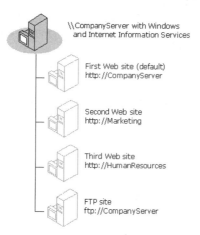

Figure 23.13 An intranet with multiple Web sites

Though hosted on the same computer, CompanyServer, Marketing, and HumanResources each appears to be a unique Web site. These departmental sites have the same security options as they would if they existed on separate computers because each site has its own access and administration permission settings. In addition, the administrative tasks can be distributed to members of each department.

Note When creating a very large number of sites, be sure to consider computer hardware and network limitations and upgrade these resources as necessary.

Properties and Inheritance of Properties on Sites

Properties are values that can be set on your Web site. For example, you can use the Internet Information Services snap-in to change the TCP port assigned to the default Web site from the default value of 80 to another port number. Properties for a site are displayed in the Properties dialog box (Figure 23.14) for that site and stored in a database called the metabase.

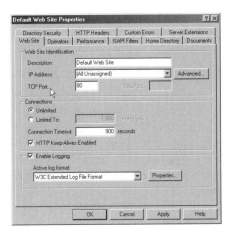

Figure 23.14 Properties dialog box for the default Web site

During the installation of IIS, default values were assigned to the various properties. You can use the default settings in IIS, or you can customize these settings to suit your Web publishing needs. You may be able to provide additional value, better performance, and improved security by making adjustments to the default settings.

Note In the first Practice in this chapter, "Accessing the Administration Web Site," you adjusted the properties of the Administration Web site to increase security to this sensitive area.

Properties can be set on the site level, directory level, or on the file level. Settings on higher levels (such as the site level) are automatically used, or inherited, by the lower levels (such as the directory level) but can still be edited individually at the lower level as well. Once a property has been changed on an individual site, directory, or file, later changes to the master defaults do not automatically override the individual setting. Instead, you receive a warning message asking whether you want to change the individual site, directory, or file setting to match the new defaults.

Some properties have a value that takes the form of a list. For instance, the value of the default document can be a list of documents to be loaded when users do not specify a file in a URL. Custom error messages, TCP/IP access control, script mappings, and Multipurpose Internet Mail Extensions (MIME) mappings are other examples of properties stored in a list format. Although these lists have multiple entries, IIS treats the entire list as a single property. If you edit a list on a directory and then make a global change on the site level, the list at the directory level is completely replaced with the new list from the site level; the lists are not merged. Also, properties with list values display their lists only at the master level, or on a site or directory that has been changed from the default value. List values are not displayed if they are the inherited defaults.

Master properties, server extensions, bandwidth throttling, and MIME mapping for a site's services are viewed from the properties of a Computer node appearing in the Internet Information Services snap-in or in the Internet Services Manager (HTML) interface. Figure 23.15 shows the WWW Service master properties accessed from the first Edit button appearing in the Properties screen of a Computer node.

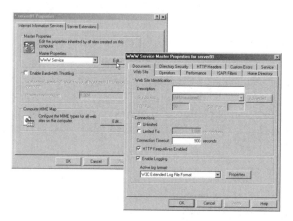

Figure 23.15 WWW Service Master Properties for Server01

On the Internet Services Manager (HTML) interface there is a Master Properties link and drop-down list box on the left frame of the home page (Figure 23.15).

ISAPI filters are displayed in a list format, but they are not treated as a list. If you add filters at the site level, the new filters are merged with the list of filters from the master level. If two filters have the same priority setting, the filter from the master level is loaded before the filter from the site level. Installed ISAPI filters and their priority are viewed from the ISAPI Filters tab contained in the WWW Service Master Properties, and on the properties page of each Web site.

If the default property values need to be modified and you are creating several Web or FTP sites, you can edit the default values so that each site you create inherits your custom values.

Operators Group

Operators are a special group of users who have limited administrative privileges on individual Web sites. Members of the Operators group can administer properties that affect only their respective sites. They do not have access to properties that affect IIS, the Windows server computer hosting IIS, or the network.

For example, an ISP who hosts sites for a number of different companies can assign delegates from each company as the operators for each company's Web site. This method of distributed server administration has the following advantages:

- Each member of the Operators group can act as the site administrator and can change or reconfigure the Web site as necessary. For example, the operator can set Web site access permissions, enable logging, change the default document or footer, set content expiration, and enable content ratings features.

- The Web site operator is not permitted to change the identification of Web sites, configure the anonymous user name or password, throttle bandwidth, create virtual directories or change their paths, or change application isolation.

- Because members of the Operators group have more limited privileges than Web site administrators, they are unable to remotely browse the file system and therefore cannot set properties on directories and files, unless a universal naming convention (UNC) path is used.

Administering Sites Remotely

Because it may not always be convenient to perform administrative tasks on the computer running IIS, two remote administration options are available. If you are connecting to your server over the Internet or through a proxy server, you can use the browser-based Internet Services Manager (HTML) to change properties on your site. If you are on an intranet, you can use either the Internet Services Manager (HTML) or the Internet Information Services snap-in. Although Internet Services Manager (HTML) offers many of the same features as the snap-in, property changes that require coordination with Windows utilities, such as certificate mapping, cannot be made with Internet Services Manager (HTML).

Note In previous releases the Internet Information Services snap-in was called the Internet Services Manager. The Internet Information Services snap-in appears on the Administrative Tools menu as Internet Services Manager.

Internet Services Manager (HTML) uses a Web site listed as Administration Web site to access IIS properties. When IIS is installed, a port number between 2,000 and 9,999 is randomly selected and assigned to this Web site. The site responds to Web browser requests for all domain names installed on the computer, provided the port number is appended to the address. If Basic authentication is used, the administrator is asked for a user name and password when the site is reached. Only members of the Administrators group and Operators group can use the site.

Note Although the HTML version of Internet Services Manager (HTML) has much of the same functionality of the Internet Information Services snap-in, the HTML version is designed along the lines of a Web page. Accessing context menus on interface objects is not supported. Many of the familiar toolbar buttons or tab headings are displayed as links in the left frame. Because of these differences, instructions in the documentation may not always precisely describe the steps performed in Internet Services Manager (HTML).

You can also use Terminal Services over a network connection (such as local area network [LAN], Point-to-Point Tunneling Protocol [PPTP], or dial-up) to remotely administer IIS. Terminal Services does not require you to install Microsoft Management Console (MMC) or the Internet Information Services snap-in on the remote computer.

The IIS 5.0 online documentation is available for you to use when you are performing remote administration tasks. To reach the documentation, start the Administration Web site and then click the book icon in the top right corner of the home page. This link opens a new window to the following URL *http://<servername>/iishelp/iis/misc/default.asp*, where *<servername>* is an identifying name (IP address, computer name, or fully qualified domain name [FQDN]) of the computer running IIS.

The IIS documentation search function is dependent on the Indexing Service. The Indexing Service is installed in Windows 2000 Server by default but is set to manual startup. The Indexing Service is configured from the Computer Management snap-in under the Services and Applications node. So that the IIS 5.0 documentation is indexed for searches, add the physical path to the iisHelp folder to the Web Directories folder for the Indexing Service. After configuring the Indexing Service, startup can be set to Automatic by using the Services snap-in.

Note The Indexing Service can be processor intensive, particularly if a significant amount of material must be indexed. Consider running Indexing Service functions on a computer with enough resources to accommodate this function.

FTP Restart

FTP Restart addresses the problem of losing a network connection while downloading files. Clients that support FTP Restart need only re-establish their FTP connection, and the file transfer automatically picks up where it left off.

Note The IIS 5.0 implementation of FTP Restart is not enabled when using FTP to download wildcard requests (MGET), uploading files to a server (PUT), or downloading files larger than 4 gigabytes.

Managing Sites

The process of managing sites includes a number of tasks, such as starting and stopping sites, adding sites, naming sites, and restarting IIS.

Starting and Stopping Sites

By default, sites start automatically when your computer restarts. Stopping a site stops Internet services and unloads Internet services from your computer's memory. Pausing a site prevents Internet services from accepting new connections but does not affect requests that are already being processed. Starting a site restarts or resumes Internet services.

To start, stop, or pause a site, use the Internet Information Services snap-in. Select the site you want to start, stop, or pause, and then click the Start Item, Stop Item, or Pause Item button on the toolbar.

Note If a site stops unexpectedly, the Internet Information Services snap-in may not correctly indicate the state of the server. Before restarting, click Stop, and then click Start to restart the site.

Adding Sites

You can add new sites to a computer by launching the Web Site Creation wizard, the FTP Site Creation wizard, or the SMTP Virtual Server wizard in the Internet Information Services snap-in. Select the computer or a site, click the Action menu, click New, and then click Web Site, FTP Site, or SMTP Virtual Server to launch the corresponding wizard.

Note The SMTP Virtual Server wizard is beyond the scope of this training kit and is therefore not explained any further.

Follow the on-screen directions to assign identification information to your new site. You must provide the port address and the home directory path. If you are adding additional sites to a single IP address by using host headers, you must assign a host header name.

Note The All Unassigned option in the Enter The IP Address To Use For This Web Site drop-down list of the Web Site Creation wizard (or in the IP Address drop-down list in the FTP Site Creation wizard) refers to IP addresses that are assigned to a computer but not assigned to a specific site. The default Web site uses all of the IP addresses that are not assigned to other sites. Only one site can be set to use unassigned IP addresses.

Naming Web Sites

Each Web site (virtual server) has a descriptive name and can support one or more host header names. Host header names make it possible to host multiple domain names on one computer. Not all browsers support the use of host header names. Internet Explorer 3.0, Netscape Navigator 2.0, and later versions of both browsers support the use of host header names; earlier versions of the browsers do not.

If a visitor attempts to connect to your site with an older browser that does not support host headers, the visitor is directed to the default Web site assigned to that IP address (if a default site is enabled), which may not necessarily be the site requested. Also, if a request from any browser is received for a site that is currently stopped, the visitor receives the default Web site instead. For this reason, carefully consider what the default Web site displays. Typically, ISPs display their own home page as the default, and not one of their customers' Web sites. This prevents requests for a stopped site from reaching the wrong site. Additionally, the default site can include a script that supports the use of host header names for older browsers.

You can use the Internet Information Services snap-in to name a site. Select the Web site and open its Properties dialog box. On the Web Site tab, type a descriptive name for the site in the Description box (Figure 23.14).

Stop, Start, Restart, or Reboot in IIS

In IIS 5.0, you can stop, start, or reset (restart option) all of your Internet Services or reboot the server from within the Internet Information Services snap-in. The stop, start, and restart functions make it less likely that you will need to reboot the server when applications misbehave or become unavailable.

The restart function conveniently stops and starts Internet Services, effectively resetting the service. To restart IIS, select the Computer node in the console tree, click the Action menu, and then select Restart IIS. Figure 23.16 shows the resulting Stop/Start/Reboot dialog box.

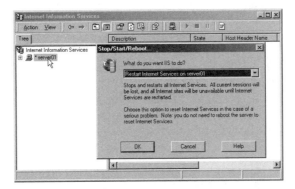

Figure 23.16 Restarting Internet Services on Server01

The drop-down list box shown in Figure 23.16 also contains start and stop IIS options and the Reboot Server option.

Important Restarting stops all Drwtsn32.exe, Mtx.exe, and Dllhost.exe processes in order to restart Internet services. You cannot stop or start IIS or reboot the server by using browser-based Internet Services Manager (HTML). However, both the snap-in and the HTML interface can be used to individually start, stop, pause, and resume individual sites.

You should use the Internet Information Services snap-in to restart Internet services, not the Services snap-in in Computer Management. Because several Internet services run in one process, Internet services shut down and restart differently from other Windows services.

Backing Up and Restoring IIS

You can back up your IIS configuration so that it is easy to return to a previous state. The steps to restore a configuration differ depending upon whether you removed and reinstalled IIS.

You can use the Internet Information Services snap-in to back up your IIS configuration. Select the Computer node in the console tree, click the Action menu, and then select Backup/Restore Configuration.

This backup method provides a way to restore only your IIS settings, not your content files. Also, this method will not work if you reinstall your operating system, and Backup files cannot be used to restore an IIS configuration on other Windows 2000 computers.

Note You can back up IIS using the Internet Services Manager (HTML) interface, but you must use the Internet Information Services snap-in to restore your configuration. The Backup Configuration link appears in the left pane of the Internet Services Manager (HTML) interface (Figure 23.2).

To restore your IIS configuration in the Internet Information Services snap-in, select the Computer node in the console tree, click the Action menu, and then click Backup/Restore Configuration. Select a backup file and click the Restore button. When asked whether to restore your configuration settings, click Yes.

Managing WebDAV Publishing

WebDAV extends the HTTP/1.1 protocol to allow clients to publish, lock, and manage resources on the Web. WebDAV is integrated into IIS and allows clients to do the following:

- Manipulate resources in a WebDAV publishing directory on your server. For example, with this feature, users with the appropriate permissions can copy and move files around in a WebDAV directory.

- Modify properties associated with certain resources. For example, a user can write to and retrieve a file's property information.

- Lock and unlock resources so that multiple users can read a file concurrently, but only one person at a time can modify the file.

- Search the content and properties of files in a WebDAV directory.

Setting up a WebDAV publishing directory on your server is as straightforward as setting up a virtual directory. Once you have set up your publishing directory, users with the appropriate permissions can publish documents to the server and manipulate files in the directory.

WebDAV Clients

You can access a WebDAV publishing directory through one of the Microsoft products described in the following list, or through any other client that supports the industry-standard WebDAV protocol.

- Windows 2000 connects to a WebDAV server through the Add Network Place wizard and displays the contents of a WebDAV directory as if it were part of the same file system on your local computer. Once connected, you can drag and drop files, retrieve and modify file properties, and do many other file-system tasks.

  For example, if you create a virtual directory named WebDAV under the Default Web site on server01.microsoft.com, you can access it from the following address: *http://server01.microsoft.com/webdav/*.

- Internet Explorer 5.0 connects to a WebDAV directory and lets you do the same file-system tasks as you can through Windows 2000.

  Make sure to enable the Directory Browsing permission in the properties of the virtual directory in order to access the virtual directory using Internet Explorer 5.0.

- Office 2000 creates, publishes, edits, and saves documents directly into a WebDAV directory through any application in Office 2000.

Searching in WebDAV

Once connected to a WebDAV directory, you can quickly search the files on that directory for content as well as properties. For example, you can search for all files that contain the word table or for all files written by a user named Fred.

Integrated Security

Because WebDAV is integrated with Windows 2000 and IIS 5.0, it borrows the security features offered by both. These features include the IIS permissions specified in the Internet Information Services snap-in and the discretionary access control lists (DACLs) in the NTFS file system.

Because clients with proper permissions can write to a WebDAV directory, it is vital that you can control who is accessing your directory at all times. To help control access, IIS 5.0 has reinforced Integrated Windows authentication by building in support for the Kerberos 5 authentication protocol. By selecting Integrated Windows authentication, you can make sure that only clients with permission can access and write to the WebDAV directory on your intranet.

In addition, IIS 5.0 introduces a new type of authentication called Digest authentication. This type of authentication was created for Windows domain servers and offers tighter security for passwords and for transmitting information across the Internet.

Creating a Publishing Directory

To set up a publishing directory, create a physical directory below Inetpub. For example, if you call the directory WebDAV, the path to this directory might be C:\Inetpub\WebDAV.

You can actually put this directory anywhere, except under the Wwwroot directory. (Wwwroot is an exception because its default DACLs are different from those on other directories).

In the Internet Information Services snap-in, create a new Web site or use an existing site and then create a virtual directory beneath it. Type **WebDAV**, or any other convenient name, as the alias for this virtual directory, and link it to the physical directory you just created. Grant Read, Write, and Browsing access permissions for the virtual directory.

You are granting users the right to publish documents on this virtual directory and to see a list of the files in it. Although not recommended for security reasons, you can grant the same access to your entire Web site and allow clients to publish to your entire Web server.

Note Granting Write access does not enable clients to modify ASP or any other script-mapped files. To allow these files to be modified, you must grant Write permission and Script source access after creating the virtual directory.

Once you finish setting up a WebDAV virtual directory, you can allow clients to publish to it.

Managing WebDAV Security

To protect your server and its content, you must coordinate three different aspects of security into an integrated whole: authenticating clients, controlling access, and denying service.

Authenticating Clients

IIS 5.0 offers the following levels of client authentication:

- **Anonymous.** Anonymous access grants anyone access to the directory, and therefore, you should turn it off for a WebDAV directory. Without controlling who has access, your directory could be vandalized by unknown clients.

- **Basic.** Basic authentication sends passwords over the connection in clear text. Because clear text can easily be intercepted and read, you should turn on Basic authentication only if you encrypt data through SSL.

- **Integrated Windows.** Integrated Windows authentication works best when you are setting up a WebDAV directory on an intranet.

- **Digest.** Digest authentication is the best choice for publishing information on a server over the Internet and through firewalls.

The best way to configure a WebDAV directory depends on the kind of publishing you want to do. When you create a virtual directory through IIS 5.0, Anonymous and Integrated Windows authentication are both turned on. Although this default configuration works well for clients connecting to your server, reading content on a Web page, and running scripts, it does not work well with clients publishing to a directory and manipulating files in that directory.

Controlling Access

You can control access to your WebDAV directory by coordinating IIS 5.0 and Windows 2000 permissions.

Setting Up Web Permissions

How you configure Web permissions is based on the purpose of the material you are publishing. These purposes may include the ability to do the following:

- **Read, Write, Directory Browsing enabled.** Turning on these permissions lets clients see a list of resources, modify them (except for those resources without Write permission), publish their own resources, and manipulate files.

- **Write enabled, Read and Directory Browsing disabled.** If you want clients to publish private information on the directory, but do not want others to see what has been published, set Write permission, but do not set Read or Directory browsing permission. This configuration works well if clients are submitting ballots or performance reviews. Note that disabling Directory Browsing permission denies access to browser clients attempting to access the WebDAV directory.

- **Read and Write enabled, Directory Browsing disabled.** Set this configuration if you want to rely on obscuring file names as a security method. However, be aware that "security by obscurity" is a low-level precautionary method, because a vandal could easily guess file names by trial and error.

- **Index This Resource enabled.** Be sure to enable Indexing Service if you plan to let clients search directory resources.

Controlling Access with DACLs

When setting up a WebDAV publishing directory on an NTFS file system drive, Windows 2000 Server gives everyone Full Control by default. Change this level of permission so that everyone has Read permission only. Then grant Write permission to certain individuals or groups.

Protecting Script Code

If you have script files in your publishing directory that you do not want to expose to clients, you can easily deny access to these files by making sure Script source access is not granted. Scripts include files with extensions that appear in the Applications Mapping list. All other executable files will be treated as static HTML files, including files with .exe extensions, unless Scripts and Executables is enabled for the directory.

To prevent .exe files from being downloaded and treated as if they were HTML files, select the Scripts And Executables option from the Execute Permissions drop-down list, which is located on the Virtual Directory tab of the publishing directory's Properties dialog box (Figure 23.17).

Figure 23.17 Selecting the Scripts and Executables option from the Execute Permissions drop-down list box

This level of permission makes all executable files subject to the Script source access setting. In other words, if Script source access is selected, clients with Read permission can see all executables, and clients with Write permission can edit them as well as run them. This configuration is a security risk because programs can then be published to the directory and run against the site.

With the following permissions, clients can write to an executable file that does not appear in the Application Mapping:

- Write permission
- Execute Permissions set to Scripts only

With the following permissions, clients can also write to an executable file:

- Script source access granted
- Execute Permissions set to Scripts and Executables

Denying Service

Dragging and dropping extremely large files into a WebDAV directory can take up a large amount of disk space. To limit the amount of space that can be used, consider setting quotas on disk usage.

Publishing and Managing Files

Users can connect to a WebDAV publishing directory, publish documents by dragging them from their computers to the publishing directory, and manipulate files in the directory.

Note Even if users connect from behind a firewall, they can still publish on a WebDAV directory if they have the correct permissions and if the firewall is configured to allow publishing.

From a Windows 2000 computer, you can connect to a WebDAV publishing directory on another server through My Network Places.

You can also connect to a WebDAV directory through Internet Explorer 5.0 on the Windows 2000, Windows NT 4.0, Windows 98, or Windows 95 operating systems. Once connected, you can manipulate files and publish to that directory just as you could after connecting through Windows 2000. In addition you can create, publish, or save documents in a WebDAV directory through any Office 2000 application.

Lesson Summary

In this lesson, you learned that Multiple Web site or FTP sites can be hosted simultaneously on a single computer running Windows 2000 Server. This gives the appearance of being several computers. Each Web site can host one or more domain names. Managing sites includes a number of tasks, such as starting and stopping sites, adding sites, naming sites, and restarting IIS.

You also learned that you can back up your IIS configuration so that it is easy to return to a previous state, and you can administer IIS remotely. WebDAV extends the HTTP/1.1 protocol to allow clients to publish, lock, and manage resources on the Web. Once connected to a WebDAV directory, you can quickly search the files on that directory for content as well as properties. You can place a WebDAV directory anywhere you want, except under the Wwwroot directory. You can protect your server and content by coordinating different aspects of security (authenticating clients, controlling access, and denying service) into an integrated whole. Once you have created a WebDAV publishing directory, you can configure your directory to allow users to search for content and file properties. From Windows 2000, you can connect to a WebDAV publishing directory on another server. You can connect to a WebDAV directory through Internet Explorer 5.0 on the Windows 2000, Windows NT 4.0, Windows 98, or Windows 95 operating systems.

Lesson 3: Configuring and Running Telnet Services

In Windows 2000, Telnet provides user support for the Telnet protocol, a part of the TCP/IP suite. Telnet is a remote access protocol that you can use to log on to a remote computer, network device, or private TCP/IP network. Telnet Server and Telnet Client work together to allow users to communicate with a remote computer. In Windows 2000, Telnet Server is installed as a service, simply named Telnet. The Telnet Server allows users of a Telnet client to log on to the computer running the Telnet Server and run character-mode applications on that computer. The Telnet Server acts as a gateway through which computers running the Telnet client can communicate with each other. The Telnet client allows users to connect to a remote computer and interact with that computer through a terminal window.

After this lesson, you will be able to

- Set up the Windows 2000 Telnet Server to allow a computer running the Telnet client to access it
- Use the Telnet Client to connect to the Telnet service

Estimated lesson time: 25 minutes

Telnet Server

Windows 2000 Telnet Server allows users of a Telnet client to connect to the computer running the Telnet Server and use command-line commands on the computer as if they were sitting in front of it. Telnet clients can connect to a server, log on to that server, and run character-mode applications. The Telnet Server also acts as a gateway for Telnet clients to communicate with each other. A computer running the Telnet Server can support a maximum of 63 Telnet client computers at any given time.

Telnet Server Connection Licensing

Two Telnet Server connection licenses are provided with each installation of Windows 2000 Server. This limits Telnet service to two connecting Telnet clients at a time. If you need additional licenses, use Telnet Server from the Windows Services for UNIX add-on pack.

Telnet Authentication

You can use your local Windows 2000 user name and password or domain account information to access the Telnet server. The security scheme is integrated into Windows 2000 security. If you do not use the NTLM authentication option, the user name and password are sent to the Telnet server as plaintext.

If you are using NTLM authentication, the client uses the Windows 2000 security context for authentication and the user is not prompted for a user name and password. The user name and password are encrypted.

Note If the User Must Change Password At Next Logon option is set for a user, the user cannot log on to the Telnet service when NTLM authentication is used. The user must log on to the server directly and change the password, and then log on through the Telnet client.

Starting and Stopping Telnet Server

In a Windows 2000 Server default installation, the Telnet service is set to manual startup. You can use the Services snap-in or the Computer Management snap-in to start, stop, or configure the Telnet service for automatic startup. Figure 23.18 shows the Telnet Properties dialog box for the Telnet service.

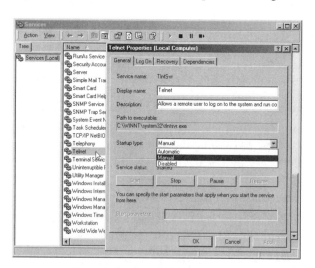

Figure 23.18 Telnet Properties page showing the Startup type options for this server service

In the Computer Management snap-in, Telnet is a service located under the Services and Applications node. Select Services from the console tree, and then select Telnet from the list of services in the details pane.

You can also start or stop the Telnet service from a command prompt. To start Telnet Server, type **net start tlntsvr** or **net start telnet** at the command prompt, and then press Enter. To stop Telnet Server, type **net stop tlntsvr** or **net stop telnet** at the command prompt, and then press Enter.

Telnet Server Admin Utility

You can use the Telnet Server Admin utility to start, stop, or get information about Telnet Server. You can also use it to get a list of current users, terminate a user's session, or change Telnet Server registry settings.

Caution Incorrectly editing the registry may severely damage your system. Before making changes to the registry, it is strongly recommended that you back up any valuable data on the computer.

To open the Telnet Server Admin utility, click the Telnet Administration Tool in the Administrative Tools program group or click Start, click Run, type **tlntadmn** and then click OK. If you cannot open the Telnet Server Admin utility, you may need to install the Administration Tools pack (Adminpak.msi).

Table 23.2 lists the Telnet Server Administration utility options.

Table 23.2   Options for the Telnet Server Administration Utility

Option	Name	Description
0	Quit this application	Ends the Telnet Server Admin utility session.
1	List the current users	Gives a list of the current users, including the user name, domain, remote computer address, session ID, and log time.
2	Terminate a user session	Terminates a selected user's session.
3	Display/change	Provides a list of registry settings that you can change. See Table 23.3.
4	Start the service	Starts the Telnet Server service.
5	Stop the service	Stops the Telnet Server service.

Registry changes made using the Telnet Server Admin utility modify settings stored in the following registry key on the Telnet server computer: HKEY_LOCAL_MACHINE\SOFTWARE\Microsoft\TelnetServer\1.0. This registration location is shown in Figure 23.19.

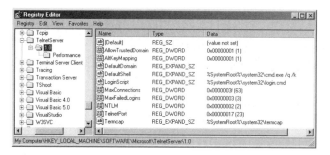

Figure 23.19 Telnet Server registry settings that can be modified by using the Telnet Server Admin utility

Table 23.3 lists the Telnet Server registry settings that you can change.

Table 23.3   Telnet Server Registry Settings

Option	Name	Description	Default value
0	Exit this menu	Exits this menu and returns to the original Telnet Server Administration utility options.	N/A
1	AllowTrustedDomain	Changes the current value of the trusted domain.	1
2	AltKeyMapping	Changes the current value.	1
3	DefaultDomain	Sets the default domain name.	. (A period means the current domain of the Telnet server.)
4	DefaultShell	Displays the path location for the shell installation.	%systemroot%\System32\Cmd.exe /q /k. The /q switch disables echo and the /k switch carries out a command but does not close the command window.
5	LogonScript	Displays the path location and name for the Telnet service global client login script file. By default, this file maps the Telnet client to their home directory if one is specified in the user's profile.	%systemroot%\System32\login.cmd

Option	Name	Description	Default value
6	MaxFailedLogins	Displays the maximum number of failed attempts to log on before a connection is terminated.	3
7	NTLM	Displays the current number of allowed NTLM authenticated logons.	2
8	TelnetPort	Displays the default Telnet Server port.	23

Note The Termcap registry setting specifies the location of the Termcap (Terminal Capabilities) file, which is used by a number of terminal client utilities to determine how to move the cursor during a terminal session.

When you change the default domain account, the setting takes effect only after the Telnet service is restarted. You must be logged on as a member of the Administrators group to use the Telnet Server Administration utility.

Troubleshooting

Table 23.4 provides information about a few common problems you might encounter when running Telnet Server.

Table 23.4   Common Telnet Server Problems

Error message	Cause	Solution
Invalid input	The entered value was not acceptable.	Review the range of the optional values and re-type your choice.
Failed to open the registry key	The Telnet server must be running to open a registry key. This error indicates that it is not currently running.	Start Telnet service.
Failed to query the registry value	The Telnet server must be running to query a registry value. This error indicates that it is not currently running.	Start Telnet service.

Telnet Client

You can use Microsoft Telnet Client to connect to a remote computer running the Telnet service or other Telnet server software. Once you have made this connection, you can communicate with the Telnet server. The type of session you conduct depends on how the Telnet software is configured. Communication, games, system administration, and local logon simulations are some typical uses of Telnet.

The Telnet client uses the Telnet protocol, part of the TCP/IP suite of protocols, to connect to a remote computer over a network. The Telnet client software allows a computer to connect to a remote server. You can use the Telnet client provided with Windows 2000 to connect to a remote computer, log on to the remote computer, and interact with it as if you were sitting in front of it.

Users of previous versions of Microsoft Telnet Client may notice a few changes in the version included with Windows 2000. The most obvious change is that Telnet Client is now a command-line application rather than a Windows application. As a command-line application, Telnet Client will seem very familiar to users of UNIX-based Telnet clients.

An important new feature found in Telnet Client is NTLM authentication support. Using this feature, a computer using Telnet Client can log on to a Windows 2000 computer running the Telnet service by using NTLM authentication.

Note Telnet session logging is not supported in Microsoft Telnet Client.

Using Telnet

To open Telnet, click Start, click Run, and then type **telnet**. You can also type **telnet** at the command prompt. To use Telnet, you must have the TCP/IP protocol installed and configured on your computer and you must have a user account established on a remote host.

To display help for Telnet, type **help** at the Microsoft Telnet command prompt. To connect to a site, type **connect** *<computer_name>* where *<computer_name>* is the IP address or host name of the computer running the Telnet service.

Practice: Configuring and Connecting to the Telnet Service

In this practice, you configure the Telnet service to start on Server01. You then connect to the Telnet service from Server01 and verify the connection. Complete this practice from Server01.

Note If you are running Server02, you may complete Exercise 2 from Server02.

Exercise 1: Enabling and Configuring the Telnet Service

In this exercise, you configure the Telnet service for automatic startup and then start the Telnet service.

1. Log on to Server01 as Administrator with a password of *password*.

2. Click the Start button, point to Programs, point to Administrative Tools, and then click Services.

   The Services console appears.

3. In the details pane, scroll down and double-click Telnet.

   The Telnet Properties (Local Computer) dialog box appears.

4. Change the Startup Type drop-down list box from Manual to Automatic.

5. Under Service status, click the Start button.

   A Service Control status box appears briefly as the Telnet service starts.

6. Click OK to close the Telnet Properties (Local Computer) dialog box.

7. Close the Services console.

Exercise 2: Using the Microsoft Telnet Client

In this exercise, you connect to the Telnet service from the Microsoft Telnet Client. You may complete this procedure on either Server01 or Server02. Completing the procedure from Server02 provides remote access to Server01. However, for the purpose of training, running these commands from Server01 is adequate. If you complete this procedure from Server02, log on as Administrator before starting.

1. Click the Start button, and then click Run.

   The Run dialog box appears.

2. In the Open text box, type **telnet** and then click OK.

   The Microsoft Telnet command prompt appears.

3. Type **help** or **?** to see a list of available commands.

   A list of supported commands appears.

4. Type **open server01**.

   A Welcome to Microsoft Telnet Server message appears.

Note You can use abbreviations for the commands you type. For example, **o server01** is equivalent to **open server01**.

---

5. Any commands that you can run from the command line on Server01 can be run from the Telnet shell.

6. Leave the Telnet session active while you complete the next exercise.

Exercise 3: Running the Telnet Server Administration Tool

In this exercise, you monitor the Telnet service for Telnet client connections and then disconnect the connected Telnet client using the Telnet Server Administrator.

1. Click the Start button, and then click Run.

   The Run dialog box appears.

2. In the Open text box, type **tlntadmn** and then click OK.

   The Telnet Server Admin utility command window appears.

3. Type **1** to list the current users.

   Statistics on the administrator user appear.

4. Type **2** to terminate a user session.

   A message appears instructing you to type a user's session ID to terminate.

5. Type **1**. This is the session ID of the connected user.

   A list of command options reappears.

6. Return to the Microsoft Telnet client window on Server01 or Server02.

   Notice that the connection with the host was lost.

7. Press any key to continue.

   You are returned to the Microsoft Telnet Client command window.

8. Type **q** or **quit** to close the Microsoft Telnet Client command window.

9. Return to the Telnet Server Administrator command window.

10. Type **0** to close the Telnet Server Administrator.

Lesson Summary

In this lesson, you learned that the Telnet service and a Telnet client work together to allow users to communicate with a remote computer. The Windows 2000 Telnet service allows users of the Microsoft Telnet Client to connect remotely to the computer and use command-line applications on the computer as if they were sitting in front of it. You can use the Services snap-in, the Computer Management snap-in, or the command prompt to start or stop the Telnet service. In addition, you can use the Telnet Server Admin utility to start, stop, or get information about the Telnet service. You can also use it to get a list of current users, terminate a user's session, or change Telnet service registry settings. Telnet Client allows you to connect to a remote computer running Telnet server software. NTLM authentication is supported when a Telnet Client connects to the Telnet service. Telnet provides user support for the Telnet protocol, a remote access protocol you can use to log on to a remote computer, network device, or private network.

Review

The following questions are intended to reinforce key information presented in this chapter. If you are unable to answer a question, review the appropriate lesson and then try the question again. Answers to the questions can be found in Appendix A, "Questions and Answers."

1. You are accessing the IIS 5.0 documentation from Internet Services Manager (HTML). All of the documentation appears and you are able to access information via the Index tab. Under the Index tab, you find the phrase Process Accounting. However, when you perform a search on this phrase, the Web browser reports that your search phrase cannot be found. What is the most likely reason that this is happening?

2. You have created a virtual directory for the purpose of Web Distributed Authoring and Versioning (WebDAV) publishing. The home directory of the Web site is accessible from Internet Explorer 5.0, but when you attempt to access the virtual directory for WebDAV publishing, access is denied. Name two reasons why this may happen and how you can solve this access problem.

3. Why is it important that the Microsoft Telnet Client and the Microsoft Telnet service support NT LAN Manager (NTLM) authentication?

C H A P T E R   2 4

Advanced File Systems

About This Chapter

This chapter introduces you to the distributed file system (Dfs) and the File Replication Service (FRS). Dfs allows system administrators to make it easier for users to access and manage files that are physically distributed across a network. With Dfs, you can make files distributed across multiple servers appear to users as if they reside in one place on the network. Users no longer need to know and specify the actual physical location of files in order to access them. Dfs uses FRS to automatically synchronize content between assigned replicas. The Microsoft Active Directory Sites And Services snap-in uses FRS to replicate topology and global catalog information across domain controllers.

Before You Begin

To complete the lessons in this chapter, you must have

- Installed Windows 2000 Server on two computers (Server01 and Server02)

  See Chapter 8, "Installing Microsoft Windows 2000" for more details.

- Installed Active Directory using the exercises in Chapter 17, "Installing and Configuring Active Directory Directory Service"

- Completed the exercises and obtained the knowledge and skills covered in Chapter 19, "Managing Active Directory Components"

Lesson 1: Distributed File System

Dfs for Windows 2000 Server provides users with convenient access to shared folders that are distributed throughout a network. A single Dfs shared folder serves as an access point to other shared folders in the network.

After this lesson, you will be able to

- Configure a standalone Dfs root
- Configure a Dfs link
- Configure a fault-tolerant Dfs root

Estimated lesson time: 35 minutes

Dfs Overview

Dfs is a single, logical, hierarchical file system. It organizes shared folders on different computers in a network to provide a logical tree structure for file system resources. Figure 24.1 shows how Dfs can organize resources that reside on different components of a network.

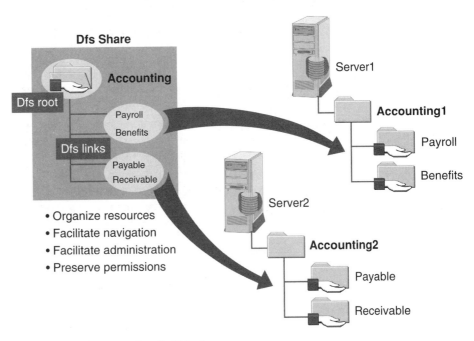

Figure 24.1 An example of a Dfs share

Because the Dfs tree is a single point of reference, users can easily gain access to network resources regardless of the actual location of the underlying resources. As Figure 24.1 demonstrates, accounting file system resources from multiple servers are organized in one logical Dfs root named Accounting.

A user who navigates a Dfs-managed shared folder does not need to know the name of the server on which the folder is shared. This simplifies network access because users no longer need to locate the server on which a specific resource resides. After connecting to a Dfs root, users can browse and gain access to all resources below the root, regardless of the location of the server on which the resource resides. In the example above, users needing access to accounting file resources would be able to find them in this one location.

A Dfs share uses a tree structure containing a root and Dfs links. To create a Dfs share, you must first create a Dfs root. Each Dfs root can have multiple Dfs links beneath it, each of which points to a shared folder on the network. The Dfs links of the Dfs root represent shared folders (*<computer_name>\ <share_name>*) that can be physically located on different file servers.

The Table 24.1 describes the advantages of using Dfs.

Table 24.1   Dfs Advantages

Function	Advantages
Network administration	Dfs simplifies network administration. If a server fails, you can move a Dfs link from one server to another without users being aware of the change. All that is required to move a Dfs link is to modify the Dfs folder to refer to the new server location of the shared folders. Users continue to use the same Dfs path for the Dfs link.
Namespace	Clients access file resources by using a single namespace (the Dfs root), as opposed to mapping logical drive letters throughout the enterprise.
Memory overhead	Windows 2000 and Windows NT 4.0 clients use no additional memory because Dfs support is integrated with the Microsoft client redirector for both Windows 2000 and Windows NT 4.0. The Dfs Service for Microsoft Network Client must be installed on top of the Windows 95– and Windows 98–based Microsoft client redirector for the Windows 32-bit client to access a Dfs share. Without this service installed, Windows 95 and Windows 98 clients can access standard shares that are Dfs links of a Dfs root share.

Function	Advantages
Server replacement	Administrators can replace file servers without affecting the namespace used by network clients simply by updating the path for the new server in the Distributed File System snap-in.
Load balancing and fault tolerance	Dfs provides a level of load balancing and fault tolerance since clients randomly select a physical server to connect to from the list of alternates returned by the Dfs server.
Extensibility	The Dfs namespace can be extended at any time to incorporate additional disk space or new business requirements.
Network permissions	Dfs preserves network permissions. No additional permissions or security are required because Dfs volumes use existing Windows 2000 file and directory permissions. Access compatibility lists (ACLs) on Windows 2000 fault-tolerant replicas are replicated.
Client caching	Dfs clients cache frequently used network resources without experiencing delays locating servers. The first access to a new area of the Dfs tree incurs a slight performance loss (analogous to performing a Net Use command). Caching this data eliminates any performance penalty for subsequent accesses until the client is rebooted or the cache expires.
Internet services integration	Dfs works with IIS. Links made to other pages stored in Dfs Information do not have to be updated if the initial page is physically moved from one server to another, provided an administrator reconfigures Dfs accordingly. If the server hosting an Internet page is removed and the page is republished elsewhere, the links on that page do not have to be reconfigured.

Limits of Dfs

Table 24.2 details the limitations of Dfs.

Table 24.2   Dfs Limitations

Description	Limit
Maximum number of characters per file path	260
Maximum number of alternates per volume	32
Maximum number of Dfs roots per server	1
Maximum number of Dfs roots per domain	Unlimited
Maximum number of volumes hosted in a domain or enterprise	Limited by system resources. Six thousand have been successfully tested in standalone roots.

Types of Dfs Roots

The Dfs service is automatically installed with the installation of Windows 2000 Server. The service can be paused, stopped, and started but not removed from the operating system.

Two types of Dfs roots can be configured on Windows 2000 servers: standalone Dfs roots and domain Dfs roots (sometimes called fault-tolerant Dfs roots).

Standalone Dfs Roots

The following characteristics are common to standalone Dfs roots:

- Standalone Dfs information is stored in the local registry.

- A standalone Dfs root permits a single level of Dfs links.

- When using the Distributed File System snap-in to connect to existing standalone Dfs roots, all servers known to the browse list are retrieved since there is no unique NetBIOS name registered by Dfs–enabled servers.

- Standalone Dfs roots can be located on all supported file systems, although locating resources on NTFS formatted partitions is recommended.

- Standalone Dfs roots offer no replication or backup; consequently, the Dfs root represents a single point of failure. You can create a replica from a standalone Dfs root; however, file replication services are not available.

Domain Dfs Roots

The following characteristics are common to Dfs fault-tolerant roots:

- In a domain Dfs root, multiple servers hand out referrals for the Dfs namespace. Fault-tolerant Dfs roots use Active Directory to store Dfs tree topology and remove the root as a single point of failure.

- A fault-tolerant Dfs root is stored in Active Directory and replicated to every participating Dfs root server. Changes to a Dfs tree are automatically synchronized with Active Directory. This ensures that you can always restore a Dfs tree topology if the Dfs root is offline for any reason. You can also implement fault tolerance at the file and content levels by assigning alternate resources to a Dfs volume. Any Branch node on the Dfs tree can be serviced by a set of replicated resources. If a client connection to one alternate resource fails for any reason, the Dfs client attempts to connect to another. The Dfs client cycles through the alternates until an available one is found.

- Fault-tolerant roots must be located on NTFS version 5.0 formatted partitions.

- The list of domains and servers is populated by querying the global catalog for all fault-tolerant Dfs roots (ObjectClass = ftDfs).

- Dfs replication topology uses the existing Active Directory replication topology.

Configuring Dfs

Windows 2000 allows you to configure standalone Dfs roots, Dfs links, and domain Dfs roots.

Configuring a Standalone Dfs Root

Standalone Dfs stores the Dfs topology on a single computer. This type of Dfs provides no fault tolerance if the computer that stores the Dfs topology or any of the shared folders that Dfs uses fails.

A standalone Dfs root is physically located on the server to which users initially connect. The first step in setting up standalone Dfs is to create the Dfs root.

To create a standalone Dfs root, use the Distributed File System snap-in to start the New Dfs Root wizard. Figure 24.2 shows the Select The Dfs Root Type screen with the Create A Standalone Dfs Root radio button selected.

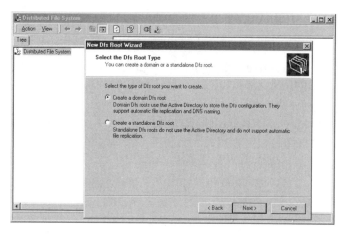

Figure 24.2 Creating a standalone Dfs root from the Distributed File System snap-in

Table 24.3 describes the screens within the wizard and what actions you can take to configure the new Dfs root.

Table 24.3   Dfs Root Wizard Actions

Screen	Actions
Select The Dfs Root Type	Select the Create A Standalone Dfs Root option (Figure 24.2).
Specify The Host Server For The Dfs Root	Enter the initial connection point for all resources in the Dfs tree. You can create a Dfs root on any computer running Windows 2000 Server.
Specify The Dfs Share	Enter a shared folder to host the Dfs root. You can choose an existing shared folder or create a new share.
Name The Dfs Root	Enter a descriptive name in the Comment text box for the Dfs root.
Completing The New Root Wizard	Review the settings for the Host Server, Root Share, and Root Name text boxes. Click Back if you need to make changes, or click Finish to complete the setup process.

Configuring a Domain Dfs Root

Domain Dfs writes the Dfs topology to the Active Directory store. This type of Dfs allows Dfs links to point to multiple identical shared folders (also called replicas) for fault tolerance. In addition, it supports Domain Name System (DNS), multiple levels of child volumes, and file replication.

To create a fault-tolerant Dfs root, use the Distributed File System tool to start the New Dfs Root wizard.

Configuring New Dfs Links

Users can browse folders under a Dfs root without knowing where the referenced resources are physically located. After you create a Dfs root, you can create Dfs links (also known as Child nodes).

To create a Dfs link, open the Distributed File System snap-in, and click the Dfs root to which you will attach a Dfs link. On the Action menu, click New Dfs Link. The Create A New Dfs Link dialog box appears, as shown in Figure 24.3.

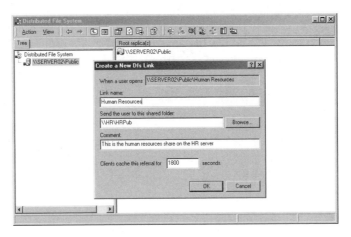

Figure 24.3 Creating a New Dfs Link off a public Dfs root for a human resources share

Table 24.4 describes the options in the dialog box.

Table 24.4 Create A New Dfs Link Dialog Box Options

Option	Description
Link Name	The name below the Dfs root that users will see when they connect to Dfs.
Send The User To This Shared Folder	The UNC name for the actual location of the shared folder the Dfs link refers to. Note that the Dfs host server must be able to access any shared folders referred to in a Dfs link.
Comment	Additional information (optional) to help keep track of the shared folder (for example, the actual name of the shared folder).
Clients Cache This Dfs Referral For X Seconds	Length of time for which clients cache a referral to a Dfs link. After the referral time expires, a client queries the Dfs server about the location of the Dfs link, even if the client has previously established a connection with the Dfs link.

The Dfs link appears below the Dfs root volume in the Distributed File System tool and appears to a Dfs–enabled client as a folder below the Dfs root. Figure 24.4 shows the appearance of a Dfs root named \\Server02\Public and a Dfs link on another server.

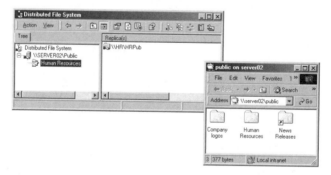

Figure 24.4 A Dfs root and a Dfs link as they appear in the Distributed File System snap-in and how they appear on a Dfs–enabled client

Practice: Creating a Dfs Root and Dfs Link

In this practice, you configure shares, create a standalone Dfs root, and then create Dfs links.

Exercise 1: Creating Directories and Shares

In this exercise, you create or use existing folders and create shares for the folders. You can use any method you prefer to create folders and shares or follow the steps in this exercise.

1. Log on to Server01 as Administrator with a password of *password*.

2. Open My Computer on the desktop.

   The My Computer window appears.

3. Open Local Disk (H:).

4. From the File menu, select New, and then select Folder.

   A folder named New Folder appears in the Local Disk (H:) window, and the blinking cursor appears inside the New Folder box.

5. Rename the folder "Public."

6. Select the Public folder, and from the File menu, choose Sharing.

   The Public Properties dialog box appears.

7. Select the Share This Folder radio button, and in the Comment text box, type **Dfs root share**.

8. Click OK.

   The Public folder appears with a hand underneath the folder.

9. Repeat steps 2 to 8 to create the folders and shares listed in the following table, using default permissions.

   Be aware that in some cases, the folders will be created on drive letters other than H:, and in one case, a share will be created on Server02 to a folder that already exists.

Computer name	Drive	Folder	Share name	Purpose/Comment
Server02	C:	\Inetpub\wwwroot	internal	Internal Web content
Server01	H:	\Press	Press	Current press releases
Server01	C:	\Inetpub\ftproot	ftproot	FTP root directory mapped partition
Server01	I:	\dev\TechDocs	TechDocs	Technical documents area
Server01	C:	\Public\Press	PressRepl	Current press releases replica

Exercise 2: Creating a Standalone Dfs Root on Server01

In this exercise, you create a standalone Dfs root to host the shares created in Exercise 1.

1. Click the Start button, point to Programs, point to Administrative Tools, and then click Distributed File System.

   The Distributed File System snap-in appears.

2. Read the message displayed in the right pane.

3. On the Action menu, click New Dfs Root.

   The New Dfs Root wizard appears.

4. Read the information on the Welcome To The New Dfs Root Wizard, and then click Next.

5. On the Select The Dfs Root Type screen, notice that there are two types of Dfs you can create:

   - A domain Dfs root that writes the Dfs tree topology to the Active Directory store and supports DNS and file replication

   - A standalone Dfs root that does not use Active Directory and does not support automatic file replication

   Because you have not configured a domain controller at this point in your training, you will create a standalone Dfs root.

6. Select the Create A Standalone Dfs Root radio button, and then click Next.

7. On the Specify The Host Server For The Dfs Root screen, confirm that SERVER01 is displayed, and then click Next.

   On the Specify The Dfs Root Share screen, specify a share you created in Exercise 1.

   Notice that you can use an existing share for the Dfs root, or the wizard can create a new shared folder for you.

8. Verify that the Use An Existing Share radio button is selected, and then from the drop-down menu, select Public.

9. Click Next.

10. In the Comment text box appearing on the Name The Dfs Root screen, type **Public access share** and then click Next.

11. Review the settings appearing on the Completing The New Dfs Root Wizard screen, and then click Finish.

12. The Distributed File System snap-in appears and the Dfs root is configured on SERVER01 to Public.

Exercise 3: Creating Dfs Links

In the following exercise, you create Dfs links below the \\SERVER01\Public Dfs root.

1. In the left pane of the Distributed File System snap-in, select \\SERVER01\Public.

2. Click on the Action menu, and notice that New Root Replica and Replication Policy are not available.

3. Click New Dfs Link.

   The Create A New Dfs Link dialog box appears.

4. In the Link Name text box, type **intranet**.

5. Click Browse.

   The Browse For Folder window appears.

6. Expand the + sign to the left of Computers Near Me.

7. Expand the + sign to the left of Server02, and then click internal and click OK.

   The Send The User To This Shared Folder text box contains \\Server02\internal.

8. In the Comment text box, type **Internal Web content** and click OK.

9. Always begin this step by clicking on \\SERVER01\Public in the Distributed File System snap-in, and then repeat steps 3–8 to create new Dfs links using information in the following table:

Link Name	Send The User To This Shared Folder	Comment
news	\\Server01\Press	Current Press Releases
ftp	\\Server01\ftproot	FTP Root Directory
tech	\\Server01\TechDocs	Technical Documents Area

Note Rather than browsing for a share, you can enter the server and share name using standard UNC syntax.

Exercise 4: Creating a Dfs Replica

In the following exercise, you create a replica of the News Dfs link. This Dfs link points to the H:\Press folder shared as Press, and the replica is stored on C:\Public\Press folder, which is shared as PressRepl.

Note Because you created a standalone Dfs link, files must be manually copied or synchronized between the two folders. File replication services are not available for replicas created on a standalone Dfs link.

---

1. Select the News link in the left pane of the Distributed File System snap-in.

2. On the Action menu, click New Replica.

   The Add A New Replica dialog box appears.

3. In the Send The User To This Shared Folder text box, type **\\SERVER01\PressRepl**. Notice that no replication policy can be configured for this replica.

4. Click OK.

   In the right pane, both the \\SERVER01\Press and \\SERVER01\PressRepl shares appear.

Exercise 5: Accessing the Dfs on Server01

In this exercise, you use the batch file provided with this training kit to copy files to Dfs links created in Exercises 1 to 3. After the files are copied, you access the files through Windows Explorer.

Important The batch file included with this training kit will work properly only if both servers are running, the shares are created exactly as specified in this practice, and the Administrator account password is *password* on both computers.

---

1. Insert the Windows 2000 Server Training Supplemental CD-ROM into the CD-ROM drive in Server01.

2. Open the CD-ROM drive from My Computer.

3. Open the \chapt24\ex1 folder.

4. Click on the ex1copy.bat file, and from the File menu, click Open.

   A command window opens as files are copied to the Dfs links, and then the command window closes.

   Complete all of the remaining steps in this exercise from Server02.

5. To access the standalone Dfs root on Server01 from Server02, open My Network Places, and then open Computers Near Me.

   The Computers Near Me window appears showing all computers in the workgroup.

6. Click on Server01, and from the File menu, click Open.

   All shares and the Dfs root (Public) appear along with other objects on Server01. Notice that the Public folder appears like any share on Server01.

7. Click on the Public folder, and from the File menu, click Open.

   The four Dfs links created in Exercise 3 appear.

8. Open each folder and verify that the following files are present.

Folder	File(s)
ftp	dirmap.htm, dirmap.txt
intranet	Q240126 - Best Practices for Using Sysprep with NTFS Volumes.htm
news	press.wri
tech	Dfsnew.doc, RFS 1777.txt

Note that the intranet folder will contain additional files since this folder points to a directory created during the installation of Windows 2000 Server.

Which folder represents a location on a server other than Server01?

Which folder represents a mounted drive to a previously empty folder?

Earlier in this exercise, you created a replica of the Press Dfs link. The name of that replica is \\SERVER01\PressRepl. This Dfs link is a shared folder by the name of PressRepl and is located in C:\Public\Press. If you examine the contents of this directory, you will notice that it is empty. However, when you view the News Dfs link, you will notice that there is a file named Press.wri. Why is the PressRepl Dfs replica empty?

Tip You can use the Distributed File System snap-in to check the status of the Dfs links and to open a window to the contents of the link.

Lesson Summary

Dfs provides a convenient way for users to access shared folders that are distributed throughout a network. A single Dfs shared folder, called a Dfs root, serves as an access point to other shared folders in the network, called Dfs links. Dfs organizes shared folders on different computers in a network into a single, logical, hierarchical file system. Dfs facilitates network navigation and administration while preserving network permissions. Two types of Dfs roots can be configured on Windows 2000 servers: standalone Dfs roots and domain Dfs roots. Standalone Dfs stores the Dfs topology on a single computer. This type of Dfs provides no fault tolerance if the computer that stores the Dfs topology or any of the shared folders that Dfs uses fails. Domain Dfs writes the Dfs topology to the Active Directory store. This type of Dfs allows Dfs links to point to multiple identical shared folders and supports file replication for fault tolerance. In addition, it supports DNS and multiple levels of Dfs links. Dfs uses the FRS to replicate data in domain Dfs roots and domain Dfs links. When changes are made to a Dfs link that is part of a domain Dfs root, the changes are automatically replicated to other replica members.

Lesson 2: File Replication Service

FRS is the file replication service in Windows 2000 Server. It is used to copy and maintain files on multiple servers simultaneously and to replicate the Windows 2000 system volume (SYSVOL) on all domain controllers. In addition, it can be configured to replicate data for domain Dfs roots.

After this lesson, you will be able to

- Describe what data can be replicated by FRS
- Configure replication for domain Dfs roots
- Describe the replication process in the Active Directory and FRS

Estimated lesson time: 25 minutes

FRS Replication

FRS is installed automatically on all Windows 2000 servers. It is configured to start automatically on all domain controllers and manually on all standalone and member servers. Although Active Directory replication and the FRS are independent of each other, they share common replication topology, terminology, and methodology. In fact, the Active Directory store uses FRS to synchronize the directory among all domain controllers.

Each Windows 2000 domain has one or more servers that serve as domain controllers. Each domain controller stores a complete copy of the Active Directory store for its domain and is involved in managing changes and updates to the directory.

Within a site, Active Directory automatically generates a ring topology for replication among domain controllers in the same domain. The topology defines the path for directory updates to flow from one domain controller to another until all domain controllers receive the directory updates.

The ring structure ensures that there are at least two replication paths from one domain controller to another; if one domain controller is down temporarily, replication still continues to all other domain controllers.

Active Directory uses multimaster replication, in which no one domain controller is the master; instead, all domain controllers within a domain are equivalent.

Active Directory periodically analyzes the replication topology within a site to ensure that it is still efficient. If you add or remove a domain controller from the network or a site, Active Directory reconfigures the topology to reflect the change.

Sites and Replication

A site is made up of one or more IP subnets that identify a group of well-connected computers. Only those subnets that share fast and reliable network connections of at least 512 kilobits per second (Kbps) should be combined.

Domain structure and site structure are maintained separately in Active Directory. A single domain can include multiple sites, and a single site can include multiple domains or parts of multiple domains, as shown in Figure 24.5.

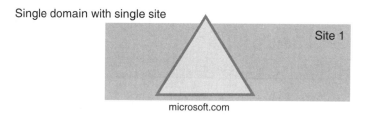

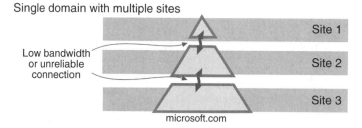

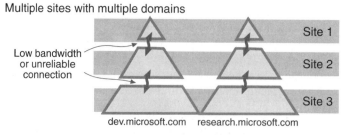

Figure 24.5 A single domain with a single site, a single domain with multiple sites, and multiple sites with multiple domains

There are two types of replication: intra-site replication and inter-site replication.

Intra-Site Replication

Intra-site replication has the following characteristics:

- It occurs between domain controllers within a site.
- Replicated data is not compressed.
- The default replication interval is 5 minutes.
- Replication is *trigger-based,* that is, a notification is sent when certain criteria are met, and then the data is pulled from the server.

Inter-Site Replication

Inter-site replication has the following characteristics:

- It occurs between domain controllers in different sites.
- You can specify the time when inter-site replication should occur. The default replication interval is 3 hours.
- You can specify the network transport used.
- It is compressed, regardless of the transport used.
- Compression reduces the data on the network by 88 to 90 percent.

One disadvantage of inter-site replication is that it is not configured automatically; it must be configured by an administrator.

Knowledge Consistency Checker

Within a site, a process called the Knowledge Consistency Checker (KCC) generates a ring topology for replication among domain controllers in the same domain. The generated topology defines paths for directory updates to flow from one domain controller to another until all domain controllers have received the directory updates.

This ring structure guarantees that there are at least two replication paths from one domain controller to another, ensuring that if one domain controller is temporarily down, replication continues to all other domain controllers. In addition, the ring structure is created such that an update takes, at most, three "hops" from the domain controller where it originates to any other domain controller in the site.

The KCC periodically analyzes the replication topology within a site to ensure that the replication topology is efficient. If a domain controller is added or removed from the network or a site, the KCC reconfigures the topology to reflect the change.

Note Administrators can make modifications to the replication topology, including changing the schedule for inter-site replication, to meet the requirements of an organization.

Unique Sequence Numbers

When a directory object is updated at a domain controller, either through a change that a user or administrator makes or by replication from another domain controller, the domain controller assigns the change a unique sequence number (USN). Each domain controller maintains its own USNs and applies USNs incrementally to each directory change made at the domain controller.

When the domain controller writes the change into the directory, it also writes the USN of the change with the property.

Each domain controller maintains a table of the USNs that it receives from every other domain controller in the domain, and the table lists the highest USN that is received from each domain controller. Each domain controller then periodically notifies the other domain controllers in the domain that it has received changes and sends its current USN. Each domain controller that receives this message checks its USN table for the last USN that it received from the sending domain controller. If there are changes and the domain controller has not received them, it requests that only the changes be sent.

Using USNs eliminates the need for precise timestamps for changes and for time to be synchronized precisely among domain controllers within a domain. However, timestamps are still applied to directory changes for tie breaking.

Using USNs also simplifies recovery after a failure. When a domain controller is running again after a failure, it restarts replication by asking each of the other domain controllers for changed USNs greater than the last USN in the table for that domain controller. Because the table is updated automatically as the change is applied, interrupted replication cycles pick up exactly where they left off, with no loss or duplication of updates.

Implementing FRS

Implementation of FRS consists of several phases: replicating SYSVOL, replicating domain Dfs roots, and configuring FRS for inter-site replication.

Replicating SYSVOL

Changes to the %systemroot%\SYSVOL directory on any domain controller are automatically replicated to the other domain controllers within the site. The replication topology and process is separate from but identical to Active Directory replication. When an administrator adds, removes, or modifies the contents of %systemroot%\SYSVOL folder on any domain controller, those changes are replicated to the other domain controllers within the site automatically.

The default folder structure is as follows:

- %systemroot%\SYSVOL\Sysvol*domain_name*\Policies

- %systemroot%\SYSVOL\Sysvol*domain_name*\Scripts

Any files and folders added to %systemroot%\SYSVOL\Sysvol*domain_name* are automatically replicated.

Replicating Dfs Fault-tolerant Roots

Dfs uses FRS to replicate data in domain Dfs links. When changes are made to a domain Dfs link that is part of a domain Dfs root, the changes are automatically replicated to other replica members.

Dfs and file replication support the following features:

- Multimaster replication replicates modified files and modified ACLs when a file is closed.

- Files can be modified on any replica member.

- Only Windows 2000 NTFS volumes have the potential to replicate. Other shares can be published as alternates, but no replication occurs.

- Replication is journal based.

- Replication is Remote Procedure Call (RPC) based.

- FRS topology follows Active Directory replication topology.

The process of Dfs replication consists of the following steps:

1. A file changes. This is noted when a user closes a file.

2. NTFS makes an entry in the NTFS Change Log.

3. FRS monitors the NTFS journal for changes to Dfs links.

4. FRS makes an entry into its own journal.

5. FRS generates a staging file of the file change.

6. FRS holds on to changes until scheduled to replicate.

7. The destination pulls the staging file and applies the new files.

Adding Replica Dfs Root Servers

Each Dfs root or link can reference a replicated set of shared resources. Dfs clients automatically select the nearest replica based on site topology information.

To add Dfs replica servers to a Dfs domain root or link, right-click the Dfs root in the Distributed File System Manager tool, click New, and then click Root Replica. Enter the UNC path for the replica server and share.

Enabling Dfs Replication

Dfs replication is disabled by default. To enable replication, right-click the Dfs root or Dfs link in the Distributed File System snap-in, and then select Replication Policy. Highlight every server in the replica set that you want to participate in FRS replication, and click the Enable button. Servers that do not participate in replication must be synchronized manually.

Configuring FRS for Inter-Site Replication

You can configure inter-site replication by using the Active Directory Sites And Services snap-in. To configure the FRS settings, you must create a new site link for the inter-site transport protocol listed in the console tree. Once you've created the site link, right-click the site link object and click Properties. The Properties dialog box opens. You can now configure the inter-site replication as necessary.

Lesson Summary

FRS is the automatic file replication service in Windows 2000 Server. It copies and maintains files on multiple servers. There are two types of replication: intra-site replication and inter-site replication. Sites are defined as one or more subnets that identify a group of well-connected computers. Within a site, the KCC process automatically generates a ring topology for replication among domain controllers in the same domain. Implementing FRS consists of several phases, including replicating SYSVOL, replicating domain Dfs roots, and configuring FRS.

Review

The following questions are intended to reinforce key information presented in this chapter. If you are unable to answer a question, review the appropriate lesson and then try the question again. Answers to the questions can be found in Appendix A, "Questions and Answers."

1. How does a mounted drive to an empty folder differ from a Dfs root?

2. In the Practice "Creating a Dfs Root and Dfs Link," you were asked to notice that New Root Replica and Replication Policy were not available options in the Distributed File System snap-in. Explain why these options are not available.

3. How is the Knowledge Consistency Checker (KCC) involved in maintaining Active Directory store synchronization between domain controllers?

4. What data does the FRS replicate?

C H A P T E R   2 5

Disaster Planning and Recovery

About This Chapter

Two of the top requirements for a business operating system are high reliability and availability. In the context of an operating system, *reliability* refers to how consistently a server runs applications and services, while *availability* refers to the amount of time a system can be used. Reliability is increased by reducing the potential causes of system failure. Availability is increased by addressing the causes of downtime. In other words, reliable and available systems resist failure and are easy to restart after they have been shut down. This chapter focuses on planning on preventing a disaster and implementing disaster protection. In addition, the chapter reviews several approaches to disaster recovery to assist you should your system fail.

Before You Begin

To complete this chapter, you must have

- Installed Windows 2000 Server on a computer (Server01)

  See Chapter 8, "Installing Microsoft Windows 2000" for more details.

- Server01 configured as a domain controller

Lesson 1: Implementing Disaster Protection

A *computer disaster* is any event that renders a computer unable to start. This can include the destruction of the master boot record stored on a system device, the deletion of one or more operating system files, destruction of a computer's physical system device, or destruction of the computer itself. The term *disaster protection* refers to any effort to prevent computer disasters and minimize downtime in the event of system failure. You can achieve a level of disaster protection by configuring an uninterruptible power supply (UPS) and implementing fault-tolerant disk configurations.

After this lesson, you will be able to

- Configure a UPS to provide power if a local power source fails

- Implement disk fault tolerance

Estimated lesson time: 40 minutes

Configuring an Uninterruptible Power Supply

Disaster recovery is the restoration of a computer so that you can log on and access system resources after a computer disaster has occurred. One common type of computer disaster is the loss of local power, which can result in damaged or lost data on a server or client computer. While companies usually protect servers against this type of disaster, you might also consider providing protection for client computers against power loss, depending on the reliability of your local power supply.

An *uninterruptible power supply* provides power if the local power fails and usually is rated to provide a specific amount of power for a specific period of time. In general, a UPS should provide power long enough for you to shut down a computer in an orderly way by quitting processes and closing sessions.

Note Before purchasing a UPS for use with Windows 2000, determine whether the proposed device is on the Windows 2000 Hardware Compatibility List (HCL).

Configuring Options for the UPS Service

Use the UPS tab of the Power Options Properties dialog box to configure the UPS service. You can access this dialog box by selecting Power Options in Control Panel. To configure the UPS service, you must specify the following information:

- The COM port to which the UPS device is connected
- The conditions that trigger the UPS device to send a signal, such as a power failure, low battery power, and remote shutdown by the UPS device
- The time interval for maintaining battery power, recharging the battery, and sending warning messages after power failure

Note The configuration options for the UPS service can vary depending on the specific UPS device attached to your computer. For details about possible settings, see the manufacturer's documentation included with the UPS device.

Testing a UPS Configuration

After you have configured the UPS service for your computer, test the configuration to ensure that your computer is protected from power failures. You can simulate a power failure by disconnecting the main power supply to the UPS device. During the test, the computer and peripherals connected to the UPS device should remain operational, messages should display, and events should be logged.

Note You should not use a production computer to test the UPS configuration. You should use a spare computer or test computer. If you use a production computer, you could lose some of the data on the computer and possibly have to reinstall Windows 2000. Remember, when a computer suddenly stops, data can be lost or corrupted. The reason for having a UPS is to allow a graceful shutdown of the computers rather than an abrupt stop.

In addition, you should wait until the UPS battery reaches a low level to verify that an orderly shutdown occurs. Then, restore the main power source to the UPS device and check the event log to ensure that all actions were logged and there were no errors.

Note Some UPS manufacturers provide their own UPS software to take advantage of the unique features of their UPS devices.

Implementing Disk Fault Tolerance

Fault tolerance is the ability of a computer or operating system to respond to a catastrophic event, such as a power outage or hardware failure, so that no data is lost and that work in progress is not corrupted. Fully fault-tolerant systems using fault-tolerant disk arrays prevent the loss of data.

Although the data is available and current in a fault-tolerant system, you should still make backups to protect the information on hard disks from erroneous deletions, fire, theft, or other disasters. Disk fault tolerance is not an alternative to a backup strategy with offsite storage, which is the best insurance for recovering lost or damaged data.

If you experience the loss of a hard disk due to mechanical or electrical failure and have not implemented fault tolerance, your only option for recovering the data on the failed drive is to replace the hard disk and restore your data from a backup. However, the loss of access to the data while you replace the hard disk and restore your data can translate into lost time and money.

RAID Implementations

To maintain access to data during the loss of a single hard disk, Windows 2000 Server provides a software implementation of a fault tolerance technology known as redundant array of independent disks (RAID). RAID provides fault tolerance by implementing data redundancy. With data redundancy, a computer writes data to more than one disk, which protects the data in the event of a single hard disk failure.

You can implement RAID fault tolerance as either a software or hardware solution.

Software Implementations of RAID

Windows 2000 Server supports two software implementations of RAID: mirrored volumes (RAID 1) and striped volumes with parity (RAID 5), otherwise known as RAID-5 volumes. However, you can create new RAID volumes only on Windows 2000 dynamic disks.

With software implementations of RAID, there is no fault tolerance following a failure until the fault is repaired. If a second fault occurs before the data lost from the first fault is regenerated, you can recover the data only by restoring it from a backup.

Note When you upgrade Windows NT 4.0 to Windows 2000, any existing mirror sets or stripe sets with parity are retained. Windows 2000 provides limited support for these fault tolerance sets, allowing you to manage and delete them.

Hardware Implementations of RAID

In a hardware solution, the disk controller interface handles the creation and regeneration of redundant information. Some hardware vendors implement RAID data protection directly in their hardware, as with disk array controller cards. Because these methods are vendor specific and bypass the fault tolerance software drivers of the operating system, they offer performance improvements over software implementations of RAID. In addition, hardware implementations of RAID usually include extra features, such as additional fault-tolerant RAID configurations, hot swapping of failed hard disks, hot sparing for online failover, and dedicated cache memory for improved performance.

Note The level of RAID supported in a hardware implementation depends on the hardware manufacturer.

Consider the following when deciding whether to use a software or hardware implementation of RAID:

- Hardware fault tolerance is more expensive than software fault tolerance.

- Hardware fault tolerance generally provides faster disk I/O than software fault tolerance.

- Hardware fault tolerance solutions might limit equipment options to a single vendor.

- Hardware fault tolerance solutions might implement hot swapping of hard disks to allow for replacement of a failed hard disk without shutting down the computer and hot sparing so that a failed disk is automatically replaced by an online spare.

Mirrored Volumes

A mirrored volume uses the Windows 2000 Server fault tolerance driver (Ftdisk.sys) to write the same data to a volume on each of two physical disks simultaneously, as shown in Figure 25.1. Each volume is considered a member of the mirrored volume. Implementing a mirrored volume helps to ensure the survival of data in the event that one member of the mirrored volume fails.

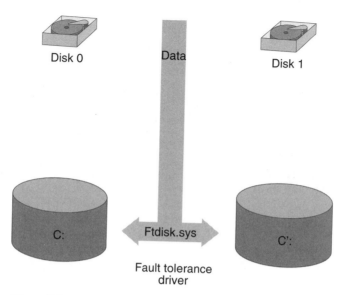

Figure 25.1 Mirrored volume

A mirrored volume can contain any partition, including the boot or system partition; however, both disks in a mirrored volume must be Windows 2000 dynamic disks.

Mirrored volumes can be striped across multiple disks. This configuration is often referred to as RAID 10, RAID 1 mirroring, and RAID 0 striping. Unlike RAID 0, RAID 10 is a fault-tolerant RAID configuration because each disk in the stripe is also mirrored. RAID 10 improves disk input/output (I/O) by performing read and write operations across the stripe.

Performance on Mirrored Volumes

Mirrored volumes can enhance read performance because the fault tolerance driver reads from both members of the volume at once. There can be a slight decrease in write performance because the fault tolerance driver must write to both members. When one member of a mirrored volume fails, performance returns to normal because the fault tolerance driver works with only a single partition.

Because disk space usage is only 50 percent (two members for one set of data), mirrored volumes can be expensive.

Caution Deleting a mirrored volume deletes all the information stored on that volume.

Disk Duplexing

If the same disk controller controls both physical disks in a mirrored volume and the disk controller fails, neither member of the mirrored volume is accessible. You can install a second controller in the computer so that each disk in the mirrored volume has its own controller. This arrangement, called *disk duplexing*, can protect the mirrored volume against both controller failure and hard disk failure. Some hardware implementations of disk duplexing use two or more channels on a single disk controller card.

Disk duplexing reduces bus traffic and potentially improves read performance. Disk duplexing is a hardware enhancement to a Windows 2000 mirrored volume and requires no additional software configuration.

RAID-5 Volumes

Windows 2000 Server also supports fault tolerance through striped volumes with parity (RAID 5). *Parity* is a mathematical method of determining the number of odd and even bits in a number or series of numbers, which can be used to reconstruct data if one number in a sequence of numbers is lost.

In a RAID-5 volume, Windows 2000 achieves fault tolerance by adding a parity-information stripe to each disk partition in the volume, as shown in Figure 25.2. If a single disk fails, Windows 2000 can use the data and parity information on the remaining disks to reconstruct the data that was on the failed disk.

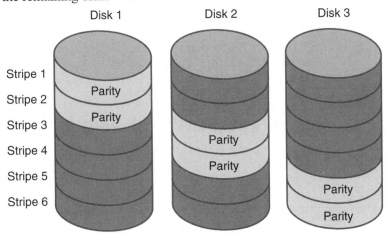

Figure 25.2 RAID-5 parity-information stripes

Because of the parity calculation, write operations on a RAID-5 volume are slower than on a mirrored volume. However, RAID-5 volumes provide better read performance than mirrored volumes, especially with multiple controllers, because data is distributed among multiple drives. If a disk fails, however, the read performance on a RAID-5 volume slows while Windows 2000 Server reconstructs the data for the failed disk by using parity information.

RAID-5 volumes have a cost advantage over mirrored volumes because disk usage is optimized. The more disks you have in the RAID-5 volume, the less the cost of the redundant data stripe. Table 25.1 shows how the amount of space required for the data stripe decreases with the addition of 2-gigabyte (GB) disks to the RAID-5 volume.

Table 25.1   Data Stripe Size vs. Disk Size

Number of disks	Disk space used	Available disk space	Redundancy
3	6 GB	4 GB	33 percent
4	8 GB	6 GB	25 percent
5	10 GB	8 GB	20 percent

There are some restrictions that RAID-5 volumes implement in software. First, RAID-5 volumes involve a minimum of three drives and a maximum of 32 drives. Second, a software-level RAID-5 volume cannot contain the boot or system partition.

The Windows 2000 operating system is not aware of RAID implementations in hardware. Therefore, the restrictions that apply to software-level RAID do not apply to hardware-level RAID configurations.

Mirrored Volumes versus RAID-5 Volumes

Mirrored volumes and RAID-5 volumes provide different levels of fault tolerance. Deciding which option to implement depends on the level of protection you require and the cost of hardware. The major differences between mirrored volumes (RAID 1) and RAID-5 volumes are performance and cost. Table 25.2 describes some differences between software-level RAID 1 and RAID 5.

Table 25.2   Differences Between RAID 1 and RAID 5

Mirrored volumes RAID 1	Striped volumes with parity RAID 5
Supports FAT and NTFS	Supports FAT and NTFS
Can protect system or boot partition	Cannot protect system or boot partition
Requires 2 hard disks	Requires a minimum of 3 hard disks and allows a maximum of 32 hard disks
Has a higher cost per megabyte	Has a lower cost per megabyte
50 percent utilization	33 percent minimum utilization
Has good write performance	Has moderate write performance
Has good read performance	Has excellent read performance
Uses less system memory	Requires more system memory

Generally, mirrored volumes offer read and write performance comparable to that of single disks. RAID-5 volumes offer better read performance than mirrored volumes, especially with multiple controllers, because data is distributed among multiple drives. However, the need to calculate parity information requires more computer memory, which can slow write performance.

Mirroring uses only 50 percent of the available disk space, so it is more expensive in cost per megabyte (MB) than disks without mirroring. RAID 5 uses 33 percent of the available disk space for parity information when you use the minimum number of hard disks (three). With RAID 5, disk utilization improves as you increase the number of hard disks.

Implementing RAID Systems

The software-level fault tolerance features of Windows 2000 Server are available only on Windows 2000 dynamic disks. In Windows 2000 Server, you create software-level mirrored and RAID-5 volumes by using the Create Volume wizard in the Computer Management snap-in.

To create a volume by using the Create Volume wizard, access the Disk Management folder in the Computer Management snap-in. When you select the Disk Management folder, the details pane of the Computer Management window displays a text view of the physical disks in your computer and a graphical view (Figure 25.3).

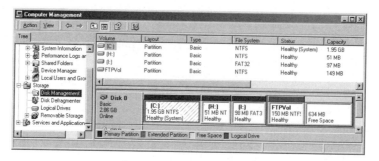

Figure 25.3 Disk Management folder of the Computer Management snap-in

In the details pane, select an area of unallocated space. Then, from the Action menu, point to All Tasks and click Create Volume. Follow the steps in the Create Volume wizard to create a volume.

Note Windows 2000 Advanced Server and Windows 2000 Data Center support server clustering for an even higher level of fault tolerance. Clustering is beyond the scope of this training kit.

Lesson Summary

In this lesson, you learned that you can achieve a level of disaster protection by configuring a UPS and by implementing disk fault tolerance. A UPS provides power in case the local power fails. In general, a UPS should provide power long enough to warn users connected to the server of the failure and to then perform an orderly shut down. You can configure the UPS service on the UPS tab of the Power Options Properties dialog box. After you have configured the UPS service for your computer, you should test the configuration to ensure that your computer is protected from power failures.

You also learned that in addition to UPS for power protection, fault-tolerant RAID provides an additional level of data protection. You can use fault-tolerant RAID configurations to implement disk fault tolerance as either a software or hardware solution. A software-level mirrored volume uses the Windows 2000 Server fault tolerance driver (Ftdisk.sys) to write the same data to a volume on each of two physical disks simultaneously. Windows 2000 Server also supports fault tolerance through software-level striped volumes with parity (RAID 5). In a RAID-5 volume, Windows 2000 achieves fault tolerance by adding a parity-information stripe to each disk partition in the volume. Generally, mirrored volumes offer read and write performance comparable to that of single disks. RAID-5 volumes offer better read performance than mirrored volumes. RAID implementations benefit from using multiple controllers (disk duplexing) because disk I/O is distributed among multiple data channels to increase performance and fault tolerance. You create software-level mirrored and RAID-5 volumes by using the Create Volume wizard in the Computer Management snap-in.

Lesson 2: Recovering from a Disaster

Reliability and availability are in part affected by your system's ability to recover from a disaster. Disaster recovery allows you to restore a computer so that you can log on and access system resources after a computer disaster has occurred. This lesson provides information on repairing a Windows 2000 installation, restoring data, and recovering a RAID-5 or mirrored volume.

After this lesson, you will be able to

- Use Safe mode, the Recovery Console, and the Emergency Repair Disk (ERD) to repair a Windows 2000 installation
- Restore data that has been backed up
- Recover a RAID-5 or RAID-1 volume

Estimated lesson time: 60 minutes

Repairing the Windows 2000 Installation

Windows 2000 has several features that allow you to repair a system that does not start or load Windows 2000. These features are useful if some of your system files become corrupted or are accidentally erased, or if you have installed software or device drivers that cause your system to not work properly. Windows 2000 includes three methods that allow you to repair a system: Safe mode, the Recovery Console, and the Emergency Repair Disk (ERD).

Note You can also reinstall Windows 2000 over a damaged Windows 2000 system or install Windows 2000 into a separate folder. This may be time consuming, but it is useful if the emergency repair process does not solve your problem. If you reinstall Windows 2000, you might lose changes that have been made to your system, such as service pack upgrades.

Safe Mode

Safe mode lets you start your system with a minimal set of device drivers and services. For example, if newly installed device drivers or software are preventing your computer from starting, you might be able to start you computer in Safe mode and then remove the software or device drivers from your system. Safe mode does not work in all circumstances, especially if your system files are corrupted or missing or your hard disk is damaged or has failed.

In Safe mode, Windows 2000 uses default settings (Video Graphics Adapter [VGA] monitor, Microsoft mouse driver, and the minimum device drivers required to start Windows). If a symptom does not reappear when you start in Safe mode, you can eliminate the default settings and minimum device drivers as possible causes of the problem.

You can choose one of the following options when you start Safe mode:

- **Safe Mode.** This option starts Windows 2000 and uses only basic files and drivers (mouse, except serial mice; monitor; keyboard; mass storage; base video; default system services; and no network connections). If your computer does not start successfully by using Safe mode, you might need to use the ERD to repair your system.

- **Safe Mode With Networking.** This option starts Windows 2000 with only basic files and drivers, plus network connections.

- **Safe Mode With Command Prompt.** This option starts Windows 2000 with only basic files and drivers. After a user logs on, the command prompt is displayed instead of the Windows desktop, Start menu, and Taskbar.

- **Enable Boot Logging.** This option starts Windows 2000 while logging all the installed drivers and services that were loaded (or not loaded) by the system to a file. This file is called ntbtlog.txt and is located in the %systemroot% directory. Safe mode, Safe mode with Networking, and Safe mode with Command Prompt add to the boot log a list of all the drivers and services that are loaded. The boot log is useful in determining the exact cause of system startup problems.

- **Enable VGA Mode.** This option starts Windows 2000 with the basic VGA driver. This mode is useful when you have installed a new driver for your video card that is causing Windows 2000 to not start properly. The basic video driver is always used when you start Windows 2000 in Safe mode (either Safe mode, Safe mode with Networking, or Safe mode with Command Prompt).

- **Last Known Good Configuration.** This option starts Windows 2000 with the registry information that Windows saved at the last shutdown. Use this option only in cases of incorrect configuration. Last Known Good Configuration does not solve problems caused by corrupted, incompatible, or missing drivers or files. Also, any changes made since the last successful startup will be lost.

- **Directory Service Restore Mode.** This option is used to restore the SYSVOL directory and Active Directory service on a domain controller. It is available only on domain controllers.

- **Debugging Mode.** This option starts Windows 2000 while sending debug information through a serial cable to another computer. This is an important mode for software developers.

If you are using or have used Remote Install Services to install Windows 2000 on your computer, you might see additional options related to restoring or recovering your system through Remote Install Services.

To start Windows 2000 in Safe mode, restart your computer. Press F8 when you see the message Please Select The Operating System To Start. Use the arrow keys to highlight the appropriate Safe mode option, and then press Enter.

Safe mode helps you diagnose problems. If a symptom does not reappear when you start in Safe mode, you can eliminate the default settings and minimum device drivers as possible causes. If a newly added device or a changed driver is causing problems, you can use Safe mode to remove the device or reverse the change.

Recovery Console

The Recovery Console is a text-mode command interpreter that is separate from the Windows 2000 command prompt and allows the system administrator to gain access to the hard disk of a computer running Windows 2000, regardless of the file system (NTFS or FAT) used, for basic troubleshooting and system maintenance. Since starting Windows 2000 is not a prerequisite for using the Recovery Console, it can help you recover when your Windows 2000–based computer does not start properly or at all.

The Recovery Console allows you to obtain limited access to NTFS, FAT16, and FAT32 volumes without starting the graphical interface. The Recovery Console allows administrators and Microsoft Product Support Services technicians to start and stop services and repair the system in a very precise manner. It can also be used to repair the master boot record and boot sector and to format volumes. The Recovery Console prevents unauthorized access to volumes by requiring the user to enter the system administrator password.

Starting the Recovery Console

To start the Recovery Console, start the computer from the Windows 2000 installation CD-ROM or the Windows 2000 Setup floppy disks. If you do not have Setup floppy disks and your computer cannot start from the Windows 2000 installation CD-ROM, use another computer and the Makeboot.exe or Makebt32.exe utility to create the Setup floppy disks.

If the Recovery Console was installed on the local hard disk, it can also be accessed from the Windows 2000 startup menu. However, if the master boot record or the system volume boot sector has been damaged, you need to start the computer by using either the Windows 2000 Setup floppy disks or the Windows 2000 installation CD-ROM to access the Recovery Console.

To add the Recovery Console to existing installations of Windows 2000, on the Start menu, click Run, and then type *<cdrom>***:\I386\Winnt32.exe / cmdcons** where *<cdrom>* is the drive letter of the CD-ROM drive.

The installation of the Recovery Console requires approximately 7 MB of disk space on the system partition.

Important You cannot preinstall the Recovery Console on a computer that contains a mirrored volume. First break the mirror, and then install the Recovery Console. After the Recovery Console is installed, you can reestablish the mirrored volume.

If the Recovery Console is not installed, run Windows 2000 Setup. Press Enter at the Setup Notification screen. Press R to repair a Windows 2000 installation, and then press C to use the Recovery Console.

Certain installations and configurations can affect how you use the Recovery Console:

- If there is more than one installation of Windows 2000 or Windows NT 4.0 or earlier, they are shown in the Recovery Console Startup menu.

- Mirrored volumes appear twice in the Recovery Console Startup menu, but each entry has the same drive letter, so they are actually the same drive.

- Changes made with the Recovery Console to mirrored volumes are mirrored.

To access the disk by using the Recovery Console, press the number key representing the Windows 2000 installation that you want to repair, and then press Enter. The Recovery Console prompts you for the administrator password. If you press Enter without typing a number, the Recovery Console exits and restarts the computer.

Note To use the Recovery Console, you must know the password for the local Administrator account. If you do not have the correct password, Recovery Console does not allow access to the computer. If an incorrect password is entered three times, the Recovery Console quits and restarts the computer. However, you can use either the Group Policy snap-in or the Security Configuration And Analysis snap-in to enable automatic administrative logon. This setting is contained in the Security Options node, and the value name is Recovery Console: Allow Automatic Administrative Logon.

Once the password has been validated, you have full access to the Recovery Console but limited access to the hard disk. You can access the following partitions and folders on your computer:

- %systemroot% and subfolders of the Windows 2000 installation in which you are currently logged on

- The root of all partitions, including %systemdrive%, the CD-ROM, and floppy drive with some restrictions (Floppy drive restrictions are outlined later in this lesson.)

Note With the Set command enabled, you can copy files to removable media, disable the file copy prompt, use wild cards with the Copy command, and access all paths on the system. The Set command is an optional Recovery Console command that can be enabled by using either the Group Policy snap-in or the Security Configuration And Analysis snap-in.

The Recovery Console prevents access to other folders such as Program Files or Documents And Settings, as well as to folders containing other installations of Windows 2000. However, you can use the logon command to access an alternate installation. Alternatively, you can gain access to other installation folders by restarting the Recovery Console, choosing the number representing that installation, and then entering the administrator password for that installation.

You cannot copy a file from the local hard disk to a floppy disk, but you can copy a file from a floppy disk or a CD-ROM to any hard disk, and from a hard disk to another hard disk. However, with the Set command enabled, you can copy files to a floppy disk. The Recovery Console displays an Access Is Denied error message when it detects invalid commands.

Important The Set command makes use of Recovery Console environment variables to enable disk write access to floppy disks as well as to enable other options. To enable the user to modify the restricted default Recovery Console environment variables, a policy setting must be made.

The Recovery Console buffers previously entered commands and makes them available to the user with the up and down arrow keys. To edit a previously entered command, use Backspace to move the cursor to the point of the edit and retype the remainder of the command. At any point, you can quit the Recovery Console and restart the computer by typing **exit** at the command prompt.

Note that the Recovery Console might not map disk volumes with the same drive letters they have in Windows 2000. If you are having trouble copying files from one location to another, use the Map command from the Recovery Console to make sure that the drive mappings for both the source and the target locations are correct.

Tip You can use the Help command to list the commands supported by the Recovery Console. In addition, the /? switch works with every Recovery Console command to display a Help screen that includes a description of the command, its syntax, a definition of its parameters, and other useful information.

Emergency Repair Disk

If your system does not start and using Safe mode or the Recovery Console has not helped, you can try using the ERD. Backup includes a wizard to help you create an ERD. If a system failure occurs, first start the system by using the Windows 2000 installation CD-ROM or the Windows 2000 Setup floppy disks, which can be created by running Makeboot.exe or Makebt32.exe from the Bootdisk folder of the Windows 2000 installation CD-ROM. In Text mode, type **r** to enter recovery options and type **r** again to enter Emergency Repair. Then use the ERD to restore core system files. Note that you cannot repair all disk problems by using the ERD.

Make sure to create an ERD when your computer is functioning well so that you are prepared if you need to repair system files. You can use the ERD to fix problems that might be preventing you from starting your computer. This includes problems with your registry, system files, partition boot sector, and startup environment. However, the ERD does not back up data or programs and is not a replacement for regular system backups.

The Windows 2000 ERD, unlike the ERD used with Windows NT, does not contain a copy of the registry files. The backup registry files are in the folder %systemroot%\Repair as they are in Windows NT. However, these files are from the original installation of Windows 2000. In the event of a problem, they can be used to return your computer to a usable state.

When you back up system state data, a copy of your registry files is placed in the folder %systemroot%\Repair\Regback. If your registry files become corrupted or are accidentally erased, use the files in this folder to repair your registry without performing a full restore of the system state data. This method is recommended for advanced users only and can also be accomplished by using the Recovery Console commands.

Creating the Emergency Repair Disk

When the ERD is created, the files described in Table 25.3 are copied from %systemroot%\Repair to a floppy disk.

Table 25.3   Files Copied to ERD Floppy Disk

File name	Contents
Autoexec.nt	A copy of %systemroot%\System32\Autoexec.nt, which is used to initialize the MS-DOS environment.
Config.nt	A copy of %systemroot%\System32\Config.nt, which is used to initialize the MS-DOS environment.
Setup.log	A log of which files were installed and of Cyclic Redundancy Check (CRC) information for use during the emergency repair process. This file has the read-only, system, and hidden attributes, and it is not visible unless you have configured My Computer to show all files or used the dir /a, dir /as or dir /ah command-line commands.

Create the ERD after Windows 2000 is installed. Re-create the ERD after each service pack, system date, or updated driver is installed. Be sure to make a copy of your current ERD and store it in a secure location, perhaps off site.

Emergency Repair Process

If you have prepared an ERD, you can use it to help repair system files after starting the computer by using either the Windows 2000 installation CD-ROM or the Windows 2000 Setup floppy disks. However, the Windows 2000 installation CD-ROM is required for replacing any damaged files.

The ERD must include current configuration information. Make sure that you have an ERD for each installation of Windows 2000 on your computer, and never use an ERD from another computer.

When you start the emergency repair process, you will be asked to choose one of the following options:

- **Manual Repair.** To choose from a list of repair options, press M. It is recommended that only advanced users or administrators choose this option. You can use it to repair system files, boot sector problems, and startup environment problems.

- **Fast Repair.** To perform all repair options, press F. This is the easier option to use and does not require user input. If you choose this option, the emergency recovery process attempts to repair problems related to system files, the boot sector on your system disk, and your startup environment (if your computer has more than one operating system installed). This option also checks and repairs the registry files by loading and unloading each registry key. If a key is not successfully checked, it is automatically copied from the repair directory to the folder %systemroot%\System32\Config.

If you select Manual Repair, the registry files are not checked. If you select Fast Repair and the folder %systemroot%\Repair is accessible, the registry files are checked. If the folder %systemroot%\Repair is inaccessible (for example, due to file system corruption), the registry files are not checked.

Manual Repair allows you to select from the following three options:

- **Inspect Startup Environment.** Inspect Startup Environment verifies that the Windows 2000 files in the system partition are correct. If any of the files needed to start Windows 2000 are missing or corrupted, Repair replaces them from the Windows 2000 installation CD-ROM. These include Ntldr and Ntdetect.com. If Boot.ini is missing, it is re-created.

- **Verify Windows 2000 System Files.** Verify Windows 2000 System Files uses a checksum to verify that each installed file is good and matches the file that was installed from the Windows 2000 installation CD-ROM. If the recovery process determines that a file on the disk does not match what was installed, it displays a message that identifies the file and asks if you want to replace it. The emergency repair process also verifies that startup files, such as Ntldr and Ntoskrnl.exe, are present and valid.

- **Inspect Boot Sector.** Inspect Boot Sector verifies that the boot sector on the system partition still references Ntldr. The Emergency Repair Process can only replace the boot sector for the system partition on the first hard disk. The Emergency Repair Process can also repair the boot sector for the system partition on the startup disk.

Note If the boot sector is infected with a virus, boot the computer using an antivirus boot diskette. Instruct the antivirus program to inspect and cure the boot sector. An antivirus program for inspecting the boot sector is included on the Windows 2000 Server Installation CD-ROM in the \3RDPARTY\CA_ANTIV folder. This program might not be included on the Windows 2000 Server installation CD-ROM included with this training kit.

If the Emergency Repair Process Does Not Fix Your System

If you have performed the emergency repair process and the computer still does not operate normally, you can perform an in-place upgrade over the existing installation. This is a last resort before reinstalling the operating system. However, note that the time required to perform an upgrade is similar to the time it takes to reinstall the operating system.

Note If you perform an in-place upgrade of your Windows 2000 existing installation, you might lose some customized settings of your system files.

Restoring Data

Restoring corrupt or lost data is critical for all corporations and is the goal of all backup jobs. To ensure that you can successfully restore data, you should follow certain guidelines, such as keeping thorough documentation on all of your backup jobs. In addition, you must select the backup sets, files, and folders to restore. You can also specify additional settings based on your restore requirements. Windows Backup provides a Restore wizard to help you restore data, or you can restore data without using the wizard.

Preparing to Restore Data

When critical data is lost, you need to restore the data quickly. Use the following guidelines to prepare for restoring data:

- Base your restore strategy on the backup type you used for the backup. If time is critical when you are restoring data, your restore strategy must ensure that the backup types you choose for backups expedite the restore process. For example, use normal and differential backups so that you need to restore only the last normal backup and the last differential backup.

- Perform a trial restore periodically to verify that Windows Backup is backing up your files correctly. A trial restore can uncover hardware problems that do not show up with backup file verifications. Restore the data to an alternate location, and then compare the restored data to the data on the original hard disk.

- Keep documentation for each backup job. Create and print a detailed Backup log for each backup job. A detailed backup log contains a record of all files and folders that were backed up. By using the Backup log, you can quickly locate which piece of media contains the files you need to restore without having to load the catalogs. A *catalog* is an index of the files and folders from a backup job that Windows 2000 automatically creates and stores with the backup job on the computer running Windows Backup.

- Keep a record of multiple backup jobs in a calendar format that shows the days on which you perform the backup jobs. For each job, note the backup type and identify the storage used, such as a tape number or removable disk name. Then, if you need to restore data, you can easily review several weeks' worth of backup jobs to select which type to use.

Selecting Backup Sets, Files, and Folders to Restore

The first step in restoring data is to select the data to restore. You can select individual files and folders, an entire backup job, or a backup set. A *backup set* is a collection of files or folders from one volume that you back up during a backup job. If you back up two volumes on a hard disk during a backup job, the job has two backup sets. You can select the data to restore in the catalog.

To restore data, use the Restore wizard, which you access through Windows Backup. After you run the wizard, the initial settings for the restore process are displayed in the Completing The Restore Wizard screen. At this time, you can perform one of the following actions:

- Finish the restore process by clicking the Finish button. If you choose to finish the restore job, the Restore wizard requests verification for the source of the restore media and then performs the restore. During the restore process, the Restore wizard displays status information about the restore.

- Specify advanced restore options by clicking the Advanced button.

Specifying Advanced Restore Settings

The advanced settings in the Restore wizard vary, depending on the types of backup media from which you are restoring. After you have finished the Restore wizard, Windows Backup does the following:

- Prompts you to verify your selection of the source media to use to restore data. After the verification, Windows Backup starts the restore process.

- Displays status information about the restore process. As with a backup process, you can choose to view the report (restore log) of the restore. It contains information about the restore, such as the number of files that have been restored and the duration of the restore process.

Table 25.4 describes the advanced restore options.

Table 25.4   Advanced Restore Options

Option	Description
Restore Files To	The target location for the data you are restoring. You can choose from the following options:
	Original Location. Replaces corrupted or lost data.
	Alternate Location. Restores an older version of a file or does a practice restore.
	Single Folder. Consolidates the files from a tree structure into a single folder. For example, use this option if you want copies of specific files but do not want to restore the hierarchical structure of the files. If you select either an alternate location or a single folder, you must provide the path.
When Restoring A File That Is Already On My Computer	You can choose from the following options:
	Do Not Replace The File On My Disk (Recommended). Prevents accidental overwriting of existing data. This option is the default.
	Replace The File On My Disk Only If The File On Disk Is Older Than The Backup Copy. Verifies that the most recent copy exists on the computer.
	Always Replace The File On My Computer. Windows Backup does not provide a confirmation message if it encounters a duplicate file name during the restore operation.
Advanced Restore Options	The options for whether or not to restore security or special system files. You can choose from the following options:
	Restore Security. Applies the original permissions to files you are restoring to an NTFS volume. Security settings include access permissions, audit entries, and ownership. This option is available only if you have backed up data from an NTFS volume and are restoring to an NTFS volume.
	Restore Removable Storage Database. Restores the configuration database for Removable Storage Management (RSM) devices and the media pool settings. The database is located in %systemroot%\system32\remotestorage.

Option	Description
	Restore Junction Points, And Restore File And Folder Data Under Junction Points To The Original Location. Restores junction points on your hard disk as well as the data the junction points refer to. If you have any mounted drives and you want to restore the data that mounted drives point to, you should select this check box. If you do not select this check box, the junction point is restored but the data your junction point refers to might not be accessible.

Practice: Restoring Data

In this practice, you delete the Inetpub folder and then run a restore routine to restore the Inetpub folder. Complete this practice on Server01.

Note Before you start this exercise, you need to use the Backup wizard (see Lesson 2, "Backing Up Data," of Chapter 6, "Monitoring and Optimizing System Performance," if you need to review backup procedures) and backup the system state (the Active Directory store, Boot files, Registry settings, COM+ Class Registration database, SYSVOL folder and Certificate Services database) to a file called backup1.bkf.

Exercise 1: Deleting Critical Data

In this exercise, you intentionally delete Boot.ini on Server01. Typically, deleting critical files is an accident or a result of hardware failure.

1. Double-click My Computer, and then double-click Local Disk (C:).

   The Local Disk (C:) window appears.

2. Maximize the window.

3. Click the Tools menu, and then click Folder Options.

   The Folder Options dialog box appears.

4. Click the View tab.

5. Clear the Hide Protected Operating System Files (Recommended) check box.

   A Warning message box appears stating that you are about to show critical hidden and system files.

6. Click Yes.

    The Folder Options dialog box appears.

7. Click OK.

    More files appear in the Local Disk (C:) window.

8. Click once on Boot.ini.

9. Click the File menu, and then click Delete.

    A Confirm File Delete message box appears asking if you are sure you want to delete this critical file.

10. Click Yes.

    The Boot.ini file is now gone. While you could recover it from the Recycle Bin, you will use the restore program in the next exercise to recover the file that was backed up before you began this exercise.

11. Keep the Local Disk (C:) window maximized; it will be used in the next exercise.

Exercise 2: Restoring Critical Data

In this exercise, you recover Boot.ini on Server01 from a backup set.

1. In the Local Disk (C:) window, double-click Backup1.bkf.

    The Backup - [Untitled] dialog box appears.

2. Click the Restore Wizard button.

    The Welcome To The Restore Wizard screen appears.

3. Click Next.

    The What To Restore screen appears, prompting you to select the backup media from which you wish to restore files.

    Notice that the only media from which you can restore is a file and the backup files are listed according to the media label specified.

4. Under the What To Restore box, expand the first backup job you created when you began Exercise 1.

    Notice that drive C appears as the first folder in the backup file. Windows Backup creates a separate backup set for each volume backed up. All folders and files backed up from a single volume appear under the drive letter for the volume.

5. Expand drive C.

   The Backup File Name dialog box appears with C:\ Backup1.bkf in the Catalog Backup File text box.

   If C:\Backup2.bkf appears, change the name to C:\Backup1.bkf.

6. Click OK.

7. When you are returned to the What To Restore screen, click on C:.

   Boot.ini appears in the Name column.

8. In the Name column, click the Boot.ini check box, and then click Next.

   The Completing The Restore Wizard screen appears, prompting you to start the restore operation and use the default restore settings.

9. Click the Advanced button.

   The Where To Restore screen appears, prompting you for a target location to restore files.

10. Click the drop-down list box to review the restore location options.

11. Verify that Original Location is selected, and click Next.

12. The How To Restore screen appears, prompting you to specify how to process duplicate files during the restore job.

13. Verify that the Do Not Replace The File On My Disk (Recommended) radio button is selected, and then click Next.

14. The Advanced Restore Options screen appears, prompting you to select security options for the restore job.

15. Verify that the Restore Security check box is selected, clear the Restore Junction Points, Not The Folders And File Data They Reference check box, and then click Next.

    The Completing The Restore Wizard screen appears, displaying a summary of the restore options you selected.

16. Click Finish to begin the restore process.

    Windows Backup displays the Enter Backup File Name dialog box, prompting you to supply or verify the name of the backup file that contains the folders and files to be restored.

17. Verify that C:\Backup1.bkf appears in the Restore From Backup File text box, and then click OK.

    The Selection Information dialog box appears.

    The Restore Progress dialog box appears, providing the status of the restore operation, statistics on estimated and actual amount of data being processed, the time that has elapsed, and the estimated time that remains for the restore operation.

18. When the Restore Progress dialog box indicates that the restore is complete, click the Report button.

    Notepad starts and displays the report. Notice that the details about the restore operation are appended to the Backup log. This provides a centralized location from which to view all status information for this backup and restore operation.

19. Examine the report, and then close Notepad.

20. In the Restore Progress dialog box, click Close.

    The Backup [Untitled] dialog box appears with the Welcome tab active.

21. Close the Backup [Untitled] dialog box.

    The Local Disk (C:) window appears.

22. Notice that Boot.ini has been restored.

23. Close the Local Disk (C:) window.

Recovering a Mirrored or RAID-5 Volume

This section provides information about recovering from a mirrored volume failure and repairing a RAID-5 volume.

Recovering from a Mirrored Volume Failure

In a mirrored volume, the computer saves data to each member simultaneously. If one member fails, the functional member continues to operate.

To replace the failed member, you must first "remove" the failed disk from the mirrored volume. Using the Computer Management snap-in, you can isolate the working member as a separate volume. Then you can replace the failed disk with a functional disk.

To re-create the mirrored volume after replacing the failed disk, click the working partition in the Computer Management window, and then click Add Mirror. The computer then presents the option to mirror this partition to the replacement disk.

In Figure 25.4, drive D on disk 0 is mirrored on disk 1. Drive D on disk 1 is the secondary member of the mirrored volume.

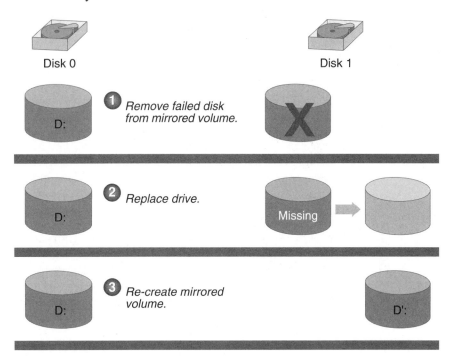

Figure 25.4 Replacing a failed disk in a mirrored volume

In the event of the failure of the primary member of a mirrored volume, including the boot partition, use a boot disk to start the computer and access the functioning member. The Boot.ini file on the boot disk must include the Advanced RISC Computing (ARC) path pointing to the mirrored partition. It is recommended that you create and test a boot disk immediately after implementing a mirrored volume.

Note Replacing a failed member is not the only reason to remove a mirrored volume. You might also remove one member of a mirrored volume to reclaim the disk space for other purposes.

Repairing a RAID-5 Volume

If a member of a RAID-5 volume fails, the computer continues to operate with access to all data. However, as data is requested, the Windows 2000 Server fault tolerance driver uses the data and parity bits on the remaining members to regenerate the missing data in RAM. During this regeneration, computer performance decreases.

To restore the computer's level of performance, you can replace the failed drive and then repair the RAID-5 volume. The fault tolerance driver reads the parity information from the parity information stripes on the remaining members, and then re-creates the data contained on the missing member. When complete, the fault tolerance driver writes the data to the new member.

Lesson Summary

In this lesson, you learned that disaster recovery allows you to restore a computer so that you can log on and access system resources after a computer disaster has occurred. Windows 2000 includes three methods that allow you to repair a system: Safe mode, the Recovery Console, and the ERD. Safe mode lets you start your system with a minimal set of device drivers and services. The Recovery Console is a text-mode command interpreter that is separate from the Windows 2000 command prompt and allows the system administrator to gain access to the hard disk of a computer running Windows 2000. The ERD allows you to restore core system files.

You also learned that in addition to repairing a system, you should be able to restore data. Windows Backup provides a Restore wizard to help you restore data, or you can restore data without using the wizard. Also, if you have set up your system with disk fault tolerance, you can recover from a mirrored volume failure or repair a RAID-5 volume.

Review

The following questions will help you determine whether you have learned enough to move on to the next chapter. If you have difficulty answering these questions, please go back and review the material in this chapter before beginning the next chapter. See Appendix A, "Questions and Answers," for the answers to these questions.

1. You have configured a computer to boot Windows 2000 Server as the default operating system, and Windows NT 4.0 Server as the optional operating system. After modifying the attributes of files on %systemdrive% and deleting some of the files, the computer does not display Windows NT 4.0 Server as an operating system to start. Windows 2000 Server starts up properly. The problem is caused because you deleted a file. What is the name of the file, and what can you do to recover from this error?

2. Why would the Use Hardware Compression, If Available check box be unavailable in the Backup wizard?

3. How can you test the configuration of the uninterruptible power supply (UPS) service on a computer?

C H A P T E R   2 6

Microsoft Windows 2000 Server Network Management and Monitoring

About This Chapter

Microsoft Windows 2000 Server includes tools that help you manage and monitor your network effectively and efficiently. Simple Network Management Protocol (SNMP) allows you to monitor and communicate the status of the network. Network Monitor allows you to view network activity and detect problems on a network. Both of these tools and their uses are discussed in this chapter.

Before You Begin

To complete this chapter, you must have

- Installed Windows 2000 Server on a computer (Server01)

  See Chapter 8, "Installing Microsoft Windows 2000," for more details.

- Server01 configured as a domain controller

Lesson 1: Simple Network Management Protocol Service

To meet the challenges of designing an effective network management platform for heterogeneous TCP/IP–based networks, the SNMP was defined in 1988 and approved as an Internet standard in 1990 by the Internet Activities Board (IAB). SNMP allows you to monitor and communicate status information from SNMP agents to a network management station (NMS). This lesson provides the background and conceptual material necessary to understand and implement SNMP within the context of Windows 2000.

After this lesson, you will be able to

- Define SNMP Communities
- Install and configure SNMP Service
- Troubleshoot SNMP Service

Estimated lesson time: 35 minutes

Overview of SNMP

SNMP is a network management standard widely used with Transmission Control Protocol/Internet Protocol (TCP/IP) networks and, more recently, with Internetwork Packet Exchange (IPX) networks. SNMP provides a method of managing network nodes (servers, workstations, routers, bridges, and hubs) from a centrally located NMS.

To perform its management services, SNMP uses a distributed architecture of management systems and agents, as shown in Figure 26.1. The centrally located host, which is running network management software, is referred to as an NMS, or an SNMP manager. Managed network nodes are referred to as SNMP agents.

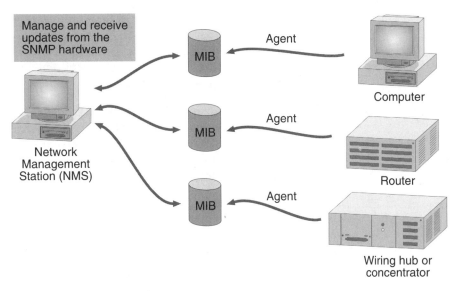

Figure 26.1 Distributed architecture used by SNMP

The agent reports hardware status and configuration information to a database called a Management Information Base (MIB). The MIB defines the hardware and software information in the host that should be collected by the SNMP agent. The SNMP agent communicates with the NMS to provide device-monitoring functions.

Network management is critical for resource management and auditing. SNMP can be used in several ways:

- **To configure remote devices.** You can configure information so that it can be sent to each networked host from the NMS.

- **To monitor network performance.** You can track the speed of processing and network throughput and collect information about the success of data transmissions.

- **To detect network faults or inappropriate access.** You can configure trigger alarms on network devices that alert you to the occurrence of specific events. When an alarm is triggered, the device forwards an event message via a trap to the NMS. The following are common types of events for which an alarm can be configured:

  - Shutdown or restart of a device

  - Detection of a link failure on a router

  - Inappropriate access to a network node

- **To audit network usage.** You can monitor overall network usage to identify user or group access or types of usage for network devices or services. This information can be used to generate direct billing of individual or group accounts or to justify current network costs or planned expenditures.

The Windows 2000 implementation of the SNMP agent is a 32-bit service that supports computers running TCP/IP and IPX protocols. Windows 2000 implements SNMP versions 1 and 2C. These versions are based on industry standards that define how network management information is structured, stored, and communicated between agents and management systems for TCP/IP–based networks.

To use the information that the Windows 2000 SNMP service provides, you must have at least one NMS. The Windows 2000 SNMP service provides only the SNMP agent; it does not include SNMP management software. You can use a third-party SNMP management software application on the host to act as the management system.

Note A number of software manufacturers design network management systems to run on UNIX or Windows NT and Windows 2000 operating systems.

Management Systems and Agents

The NMS does not have to run on the same computer as the SNMP agents. The NMS can request the following information from SNMP agents:

- Network protocol identification and statistics
- Dynamic identification of devices attached to the network (a process referred to as discovery)
- Hardware and software configuration data
- Device performance and usage statistics
- Device error and event messages
- Program and application usage statistics

The management system can also send a configuration request to the agent that requests the agent to change a local parameter; however, this is a rare occurrence because most client parameters have read-only access.

SNMP agents provide SNMP managers with information about activities that occur at the Internet Protocol (IP) network layer and respond to management system requests for information. Any computer running SNMP agent software, such as the Windows 2000 SNMP service, is an SNMP agent. The agent service can be configured to determine what statistics are to be tracked and what management systems are authorized to request information.

In general, agents do not originate messages; they only respond to messages. The exception is an alarm message triggered by a specific event. An alarm message is known as a *trap message*. A *trap* is an alarm-triggering event on an agent computer, such as a system reboot or illegal access. Traps and trap messages provide a rudimentary form of security by notifying the management system whenever such an event occurs.

Management Information Base

A Management Information Base (MIB) is a container of objects. Each object represents a particular type of information. This collection of objects contains information required by a management system. For example, one MIB object can represent the number of active sessions on an agent; another can represent the amount of available hard drive space on the agent. All the information a management system might request from an agent is stored in various MIBs.

An MIB defines the following values for each object it contains:

- Name and identifier.
- Defined data type.
- A textual description of the object.
- An index method used for complex data-type objects (usually described as a multidimensional array or as tabular data). Complex data refers to such items as the list of network interfaces configured into the system, the routing table, or the Address Resolution Protocol (ARP) table.
- Read/write permissions.

Each object in an MIB has a unique identifier that contains the following information:

- Type (counter, string, gauge, or address)
- Access level (read or read/write)
- Size restriction
- Range information

The Windows 2000 SNMP service supports the Internet MIB II; LAN Manager MIB II; Host Resources MIB; and Microsoft proprietary MIBs, such as the WINS, DHCP, and IIS MIBs.

SNMP Messages

Both agents and management systems use SNMP messages to inspect and communicate information about managed objects. SNMP messages are sent via the User Datagram Protocol (UDP). IP is used to route messages between the management system and host. By default, UDP port 161 is used to listen for SNMP messages and port 162 is used to listen for SNMP traps.

When an NMS sends requests to a network device, the agent program on the device receives the requests and retrieves the requested information from the MIBs. The agent sends the requested information back to the initiating NMS. An SNMP agent sends information when a trap event occurs or when it responds to a request for information from a management system.

The management system and agent programs use the following types of messages:

- **GET.** This is the basic SNMP request message. Sent by an NMS, it requests information about a single MIB entry on an agent—for example, the amount of free disk space.

- **GET-NEXT.** This is an extended type of request message that can be used to browse the entire hierarchy of management objects. When it processes a GET-NEXT request for a particular object, the agent returns the identity and value of the object that logically follows the previous information that was sent. The GET-NEXT request is useful mostly for dynamic tables, such as an internal IP route table.

- **SET.** This is a message that can be used to send and assign an updated MIB value to the agent when write access is permitted.

- **GET-BULK.** This is a request that the data transferred by the agent be as large as possible within the given restraints of message size. This minimizes the number of protocol exchanges required to retrieve a large amount of management information.

- **NOTIFY.** This is an unsolicited message sent by an agent to a management system when the agent detects a certain type of event. It is also called a trap message. For example, a trap message might be sent when a system restart occurs. The NMS that receives the trap message is referred to as the trap destination.

Figure 26.2 is an example of how management systems and agents communicate information.

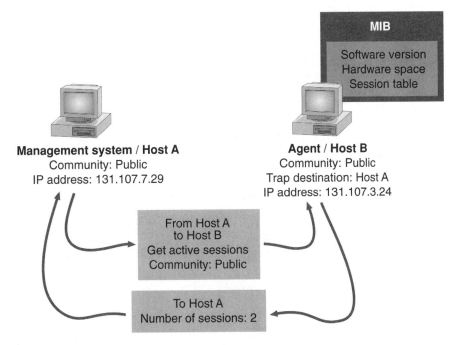

Figure 26.2 SNMP manager and agent interaction

The following is the seqence of steps in the communication process:

1. A management system forms an SNMP message that contains an information request (GET), the name of the community to which the management system belongs, and the destination of the message—the agent's IP
   address (131.107.3.24).

2. The SNMP message is sent to the agent.

3. The agent receives the packet and decodes it. The community name
   (Public) is verified as acceptable.

4. The SNMP service calls the appropriate subagent to retrieve the session
   information requested from the MIB.

5. The SNMP takes the session information from the subagent and forms a
   return SNMP message that contains the number of active sessions and
   the destination—the management system's IP address (131.107.7.29).

6. The SNMP message is sent to the management system.

Defining SNMP Communities

You can assign groups of hosts to SNMP communities for limited security checking of agents and management systems or for administration. Communities are identified by community names that you assign. A host can belong to multiple communities at the same time, but an agent does not accept a request from a management system outside its list of acceptable community names.

You can define communities logically to take advantage of the basic authentication service provided by SNMP. Figure 26.3 shows an example of two communities, Public and Public 2:

- Agent 1 can send traps and other messages to Manager 2 because they are both members of the Public 2 community.

- Agent 2, Agent 3, and Agent 4 can send traps and messages to Manager 1 because they are all members, by default, of the Public community.

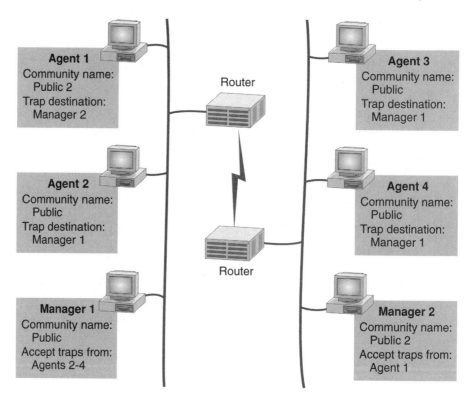

Figure 26.3 Example of two communities: Public and Public 2

Community names are managed by configuring SNMP security properties, which are described later in this lesson.

Note There is no relationship between community names and domain or workgroup names. Community names represent a shared password for groups of network hosts, and they should be selected and changed as you would change any password. Deciding which hosts belong to the same community is generally determined by physical proximity.

Installing and Configuring the SNMP Service

The SNMP agent is not installed by default on Windows 2000 Server. It is installed from the Control Panel Add/Remove Windows Programs application. From the Add/Remove Programs window, choose Add/Remove Windows Components, and from the Windows Components wizard that appears, choose Management And Monitoring Tools. The Management And Monitoring Tools item contains Simple Network Management Protocol, which is the SNMP agent. This agent is listed as SNMP Service after it is installed.

Once the SNMP service is installed, you can configure the SNMP services through the Services node of the Computer Management snap-in or through the Services snap-in in the Administrative Tools program group. In the Services node, select SNMP Service from the details pane, and then select Properties from the Action menu. The SNMP Service Properties dialog box appears, as shown in Figure 26.4.

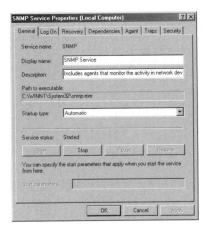

Figure 26.4 SNMP Service Properties dialog box

> **Note** The SNMP Trap Service is also installed when SNMP is installed. The trap service passes traps from a local or remote computer to a trap destination, typically an NMS, running on the local computer.

SNMP Service Properties

You can use the General, Log On, and Recovery tabs in the SNMP Service Properties dialog box to configure how the SNMP service starts, logs on to the system, and recovers from an abnormal program termination of the service or operating system. Other services listed in the Computer Management snap-in contain these four tabs for service configuration. The General tab allows you to start or stop the service. You can also specify a display name, description, startup type, and start parameters. Another tab called the Dependencies tab provides a list of those services (if any) that depend on the SNMP service and those that the SNMP service depends on. By default, the SNMP service depends on Event Log.

Windows 2000 SNMP Agent Properties

The SNMP agent provides the related management system with information on activities that occur at the IP network layer. The SNMP service sends agent information in response to an SNMP request or in an SNMP trap message.

You can configure the agent properties on the Agent tab of the SNMP Service Properties dialog box. The Agent tab lists the services you can select. These services are described in Table 26.1.

Table 26.1   SNMP Agent Services

Agent service	Conditions for selecting this service
Physical	The computer manages physical devices, such as a hard disk partition.
Applications	The computer uses any applications that send data via TCP/IP. This service should always be enabled.
Datalink and subnetwork	The computer manages a bridge.
Internet	The computer is an IP gateway (router).
End-to-end	The computer is an IP host. This service should always be enabled.

The Agent tab also allows you to configure the name of the person to contact, such as the network administrator, and the location of the contact person. An NMS might require this information when communicating with the SNMP agent.

Trap Properties

SNMP traps can be used for limited security checking. When configured for an agent, the SNMP service generates trap messages whenever specific events occur. These messages are sent to a trap destination, typically an NMS. For example, an agent can be configured to initiate an authentication trap if a request for information is sent by an unrecognized management system. Trap messages can also be generated for events such as host system startup or shutdown.

You can configure trap destinations on the Traps tab of the SNMP Service Properties dialog box. Trap destinations consist of the computer name or the IP or IPX address of the management system. The trap destination must be a network–enabled host running SNMP management software. Trap destinations can be configured by a user, but the events (such as a system reboot) that generate a trap message are internally defined by the SNMP agent.

Security Properties

You can configure SNMP security on the Security tab of the SNMP Service Properties dialog box. The following list describes the options you can configure on the Security tab.

- **Send authentication traps.** When an SNMP agent receives a request that does not contain a valid community name or the host sending the message is not on the list of acceptable hosts, the agent can send an authentication trap message to one or more trap destinations (management systems). The trap message indicates that the SNMP request failed authentication. This is a default setting.

- **Accepted community names.** The SNMP service requires the configuration of at least one default community name. The name Public is generally used as the community name because it is universally accepted in all SNMP implementations. You can delete or change the default community name or add multiple community names. The Public SNMP community name is not secure because it is so widely used. Therefore, consider removing this name. If the SNMP agent receives a request from a community that is not on the list, it generates an authentication trap. If no community names are defined, the SNMP agent denies all incoming SNMP requests.

- **Community rights.** You can select permission levels that determine how an agent processes SNMP requests from the various communities. For example, you can configure the permissions level to block the SNMP agent from processing any request from a specific community.

- **Accept SNMP packets from any host.** In this context, the source host and list of acceptable hosts refer to the source SNMP management system and the list of other acceptable management systems. When this option is enabled, no SNMP packets are rejected on the basis of the name or address of the source host or on the basis of the list of acceptable hosts. This option is enabled by default.

- **Only accept SNMP packets from these hosts.** This option provides limited security. When the option is enabled, only SNMP packets received from the hosts on a list of allowed hosts are accepted. The SNMP agent rejects messages from other hosts and sends an authentication trap. Limiting access only to hosts on a list provides a higher level of security than limiting access to specific communities because a community name can encompass a large group of hosts.

Troubleshooting SNMP

This section contains methods for determining the cause of SNMP-related communication problems. Run normal workloads during your testing to gain realistic feedback.

Event Viewer

SNMP error handling has been improved in Windows 2000. Manual configuration of SNMP error-logging parameters has been replaced with improved error handling that is integrated with Event Viewer. Use Event Viewer if you suspect a problem with the SNMP service.

Windows Internet Naming Service

When querying WINS server MIBs, you might need to increase the SNMP time-out period on the SNMP management system. For example, if some WINS queries work and others time out, increase the time-out period.

IPX Addresses

If you enter an IPX address as a trap destination when installing SNMP service, you might receive an Error 3 error message when you restart your computer. This occurs when the IPX address has been entered incorrectly—by using a comma or hyphen to separate a network number from a media access control (MAC) address. For example, SNMP management software might normally accept an address like 00008022,0002C0-F7AABD. However, the Windows 2000 SNMP service does not recognize an address with a comma or hyphen between the network number and MAC address.

The address used for an IPX trap destination must follow the IETF defined 8.12 format for the network number and MAC address: *xxxxxxxx.yyyyyyyyyyyy*, where *xxxxxxxx* is the network number and *yyyyyyyyyyyy* is the MAC address.

SNMP Service Files

Table 26.2 contains a list of the SNMP-associated files provided as part of the SNMP service. Refer to this table for troubleshooting assistance.

Table 26.2   Files Associated with SNMP

File	Description
Wsnmp32.dll, Mgmtapi.dll	Windows 2000–based SNMP manager APIs. These APIs listen for manager requests and send the requests to SNMP agents and receive responses from them.
*.dll	Extension agent dynamic-link libraries (DLLs) such as Inetmib1.dll for IIS, and Dhcpmib.dll for Dynamic Host Configuration Protocol (DHCP). These extension agents support the proprietary MIBs for these products.
Mib.bin	Installed with the SNMP service and used by the Management API (Mgmtapi.dll). The file maps text-based object names to numerical OID object identifiers.
Snmp.exe	SNMP agent service; a master (proxy) agent. This program accepts manager program requests and forwards the requests to the appropriate extension-subagent DLL for processing.
Snmptrap.exe	A background process. The program receives SNMP traps from the SNMP agent and forwards them to the SNMP Management API on the management console. The program starts only when the SNMP manager API receives a manager request for traps.

Figure 26.5 shows how the various SNMP files work together to communicate to and from an NMS.

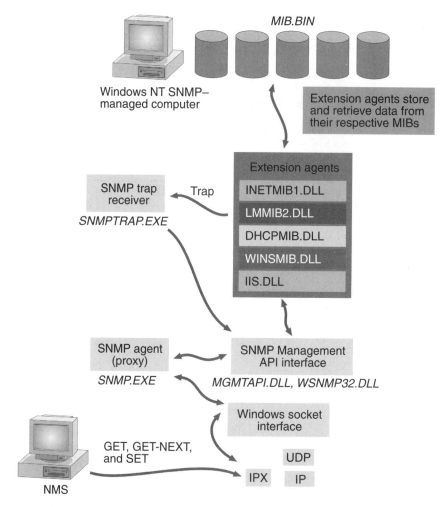

Figure 26.5 Communication to and from the SNMP service

Lesson Summary

In this lesson, you learned that SNMP is a network management standard that provides a method of managing network devices such as servers, workstations, routers, bridges, and hubs from a centrally located host. To perform its management services, SNMP uses a distributed architecture of management systems and agents. The SNMP management system, commonly known as an NMS, can request the information from managed computers (SNMP agents). SNMP agents provide the NMS with information about activities that occur at the IP network layer and respond to management system requests for information. SNMP uses an MIB as a container for objects; each container represents a particular type of information. Both agents and NMS use SNMP messages to inspect and communicate information about managed objects.

You also learned that you can assign groups of hosts to SNMP communities for limited security checking of agents and NMS or for administration. Communities are identified by community names that you assign. For additional security, you can specify the IP address or host name of network management system(s) in which the SNMP agent should communicate.

The lesson ended with a discussion on configuring the SNMP service through the Services node of the Computer Management snap-in or through the Services snap-in in the Administrative Tools program group. The SNMP Service Properties dialog box allows you to configure the various properties of the SNMP service.

Lesson 2: Network Monitor

Unlike System Monitor, which is used to monitor anything from hardware to software, Network Monitor focuses exclusively on network activity. Network Monitor allows you to view network activity and detect problems on a network. For example, you can use Network Monitor to diagnose hardware and software problems when two or more computers cannot communicate. You can also copy a log of network activity into a file and then send the file to a professional network analyst or support organization. Network application developers can use Network Monitor to monitor and debug network applications as they are developed.

After this lesson, you will be able to

- Use Network Monitor to capture and display network frames

Estimated lesson time: 35 minutes

Overview of Network Monitor

Network Monitor tracks network throughput in terms of captured network traffic. Network Monitor monitors traffic only on the local network segment. To monitor remote traffic, you must use the version of Network Monitor that ships with Microsoft Systems Management Server (SMS) version 1.2 or 2.0.

Network Monitor monitors the network data stream, which consists of all information transferred over a network at any given time. Before transmission, this information is divided by the network software into smaller pieces, called frames or packets. Each frame contains the following information:

- The source address of the computer that sent the message
- The destination address of the computer that received the frame
- Headers from each protocol used to send the frame
- The data or a portion of the information being sent
- A trailer that usually contains a CRC to verify frame integrity

The process by which Network Monitor copies frames is referred to as *capturing*. You can use Network Monitor to capture all local network traffic or you can single out a subset of frames to be captured. You can also make a capture respond to events on your network. For example, you can make the network start an executable file when Network Monitor detects a particular set of conditions on the network. This is similar to the system Alerts feature in the Performance Logs And Alerts snap-in.

After you have captured data, you can view it in the Network Monitor user interface. Network Monitor does much of the data analysis for you by translating the raw capture data into its logical frame structure.

For security, Windows 2000 Network Monitor captures only those frames, including broadcast and multicast frames, sent to or from the local computer. Network Monitor also displays overall network segment statistics for broadcast frames, multicast frames, network use, total bytes received per second, and total frames received per second.

To help protect your network from unauthorized use of Network Monitor installations, Network Monitor detects other installations of Network Monitor that are running on the local segment of your network. Network Monitor also detects all instances of the Network Monitor driver being used remotely (by either Network Monitor from SMS or the Network Segment object in System Monitor) to capture data on your network.

When Network Monitor detects other Network Monitor installations running on the network, it displays the following information:

- The name of the computer
- The name of the user logged on at the computer
- The state of Network Monitor on the remote computer (running, capturing, or transmitting)
- The adapter address of the remote computer
- The version number of Network Monitor on the remote computer

In some instances, your network architecture might prevent one installation of Network Monitor from detecting another. For example, if an installation is separated from yours by a router that does not forward multicasts, your installation cannot detect that installation.

Network Monitor uses a network driver interface specification (NDIS) feature to copy all frames it detects to its capture buffer, a resizable storage area in memory. The default size is 1 MB; however, you can adjust the size manually as needed. The buffer is a memory-mapped file and occupies disk space.

Note Because Network Monitor uses the Local-only mode of NDIS instead of Promiscuous mode (in which the network adapter passes on all frames sent on the network), you can use Network Monitor even if your network adapter does not support Promiscuous mode. Networking performance is not affected when you use an NDIS driver to capture frames. (Putting the network adapter in Promiscuous mode can add 30 percent or more to the load on the CPU.)

Installing Network Monitor Tools

Network Monitor Tools include both the Network Monitor console and the Network Monitor driver. These tools are not installed by default on Windows 2000 Server. You can install them from the Control Panel Add/Remove Windows Programs application. From the Add/Remove Programs window, choose Add/Remove Windows Components, and from the Windows Components wizard that appears, choose Management And Monitoring Tools. The Management And Monitoring Tools item contains Network Monitor Tools. Once installed, the Network Monitor console appears in the Administrative Tools program group and Network Monitor Driver is listed in the Local Area Connection Properties dialog box.

Capturing Frame Data

To capture frame data, Network Monitor and the Network Monitor driver must be installed on your computer running Windows 2000. The Network Monitor driver (also called the Network Monitor agent) enables Network Monitor to receive frames from a network adapter and allows the Network Monitor provided with SMS to capture and display frames from a remote computer, including those with a dial-up network connection. When the user of a computer running SMS Network Monitor connects remotely to a computer on which the Network Monitor driver has been installed, and that user initiates a capture, network statistics are captured locally on the computer running the network monitor driver and the data from the capture is viewed from the managing computer.

Note Network Monitor drivers for other Windows operating systems other than Windows 2000 are provided with SMS. When you install Network Monitor on a computer running Windows 2000, the Network Monitor driver is automatically installed.

To capture data, open Network Monitor and select Start from the Capture menu. As frames are captured from the network, statistics about the frames are displayed in the Network Monitor Capture window, as shown in Figure 26.6.

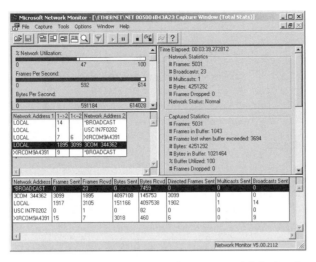

Figure 26.6 Capture window of the Network Monitor interface

Network Monitor displays session statistics from the first 100 unique network sessions it detects. To reset statistics and see information on the next 100 network sessions detected, select Clear Statistics from the Capture menu.

Using Capture Filters

A capture filter functions like a database query. You can use it to specify the types of network information you want to monitor. For example, to see only a specific subset of computers or protocols, you can create an address database, use the database to add addresses to your filter, and then save the filter to a file. By filtering frames, you save both buffer resources and time. Later, if necessary, you can load the capture filter file and use the filter again.

To design a capture filter, specify decision statements in the Capture Filter dialog box (Figure 26.7).

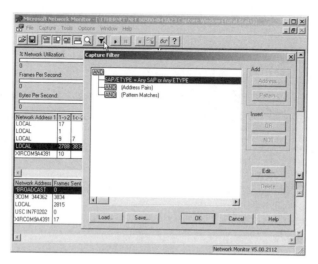

Figure 26.7 Capture Filter dialog box

To open the Capture Filter dialog box, select Filter from the Capture menu, click the funnel toolbar icon (Figure 26.7), or press F8. The dialog box displays the filter's decision tree, which is a graphical representation of a filter's logic. When you include or exclude information from your capture specifications, the decision tree reflects these specifications.

Filtering by Protocol

To capture frames that use a specific protocol, specify the protocol on the SAP/ETYPE= line of the capture filter. For example, to capture only IP frames, disable all protocols and then enable IP ETYPE 0x800 and IP SAP 0x6. By default, all the protocols that Network Monitor supports are enabled.

Filtering by Address

To capture frames from specific computers on your network, specify one or more address pairs in a capture filter. You can monitor up to four specific address pairs simultaneously.

An address pair consists of the following:

- The addresses of the two computers between which you want to monitor traffic

- Arrows that specify the traffic direction you want to monitor

- The INCLUDE or EXCLUDE keyword, indicating how Network Monitor should respond to a frame that meets a filter's specifications

Regardless of the sequence in which statements appear in the Capture Filter dialog box, EXCLUDE statements are evaluated first. Therefore, if a frame meets the criteria specified in an EXCLUDE statement in a filter containing both an EXCLUDE statement and an INCLUDE statement, that frame is discarded. Network Monitor does not test that frame by INCLUDE statements to see if it also meets that criterion.

Filtering by Data Pattern

By specifying a pattern match in a capture filter, you can do the following:

- Limit a capture to only those frames containing a specific pattern of ASCII or hexadecimal data

- Specify how many bytes (offsets) into the frame the pattern must occur

When you filter based on a pattern match at a specific point in the data, you must specify where the pattern occurs in the frame (how many bytes from the beginning or end). If your network medium uses variable-sized frames, specify to begin counting in for a pattern match from the end of the topology header.

Displaying Captured Data

To simplify data analysis, Network Monitor interprets raw data collected during the capture and displays it in the Capture window. To display captured information in the Capture window, click Stop And View on the Capture menu while the capture is running. You can also display the Capture window by opening a file with the .cap extension. If you have stopped a capture, you can view the data in the Capture window by selecting Display Captured Data from the Capture menu, clicking the glasses toolbar icon, or pressing F12.

Figure 26.8 shows the key elements in the Capture window.

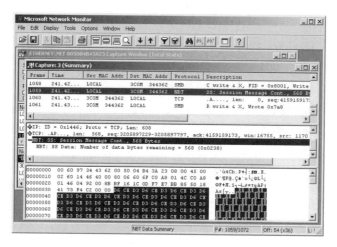

Figure 26.8 Capture window in Network Monitor

Using Display Filters

You can use a display filter to determine which frames to display. Like a capture filter, a display filter functions like a database query, allowing you to single out specific types of information. But because a display filter operates on data that has already been captured, it does not affect the contents of the Network Monitor capture buffer.

You can filter a frame using the following information:

- The source or destination address of the frame
- The protocols used to send the frame
- The properties and values contained in the frame (A property is a data field within a protocol header. A protocol's properties indicate the purpose of the protocol.)

The capture window must have the focus in Network Monitor for the Display Filter dialog box to appear. Figure 26.9 shows the Display Filter dialog box, which is accessed from the Display menu, by pressing F8, or by clicking the funnel toolbar icon.

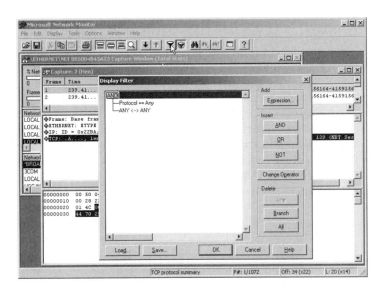

Figure 26.9 Display Filter dialog box

To design a display filter, specify decision statements in the Display Filter dialog box. Information in the Display Filter dialog box is in the form of a decision tree, which is a graphical representation of a filter's logic. When you modify display filter specifications, the decision tree reflects these modifications. You must click OK to save the specified decision statement and add it to the decision tree before adding another decision statement.

Although capture filters are limited to four address filter expressions, display filters are not. With display filters, you can also use AND, OR, and NOT logic. When you display captured data, all available information about the captured frames appears in the Frame Viewer window. To display only those frames sent by a specific protocol, edit the Protocol line in the Display Filter dialog box.

Protocol properties are information that defines a protocol's purpose. Because the purpose of protocols varies, properties differ from one protocol to another. Suppose, for example, that you have captured a large number of frames that use the Server Message Block (SMB) protocol but you want to examine only those frames in which the SMB protocol was used to create a directory on your computer. In this instance, you can single out frames where the SMB command property is equal to the Make Directory command.

When you display captured data, all addresses from which information was captured appear in the Frame Viewer window. To display only those frames originating from a specific computer, edit the ANY < – > ANY line in the Display Filter dialog box.

Network Monitor Performance Issues

Network Monitor creates a memory-mapped file for its capture buffer. For best results, make sure you create a capture buffer large enough to accommodate the traffic you need.

In addition, although you cannot adjust the frame size, you can store only part of the frame, thereby reducing the amount of wasted capture buffer space. For example, if you are interested only in the data in the frame header, set the frame size (in bytes) to the size of the header frame. Network Monitor discards the frame data as it stores frames in the capture buffer, thereby using less capture buffer space.

Running Network Monitor in the background is a way to reduce the amount of system resources necessary to operate the program. To run Network Monitor in the background, choose Dedicated Capture Mode from the Capture menu. This is one strategy to reduce resource use if network packets are being dropped rather than captured.

Lesson Summary

In this lesson, you learned that Network Monitor allows you to view and detect problems on networks. It tracks network throughput in terms of captured network traffic. Network Monitor monitors the network data stream on the local segment, which consists of all information transferred over the network segment at any given time. To capture frame data, Network Monitor and the Network Monitor driver must be installed on your Windows 2000 computer. The Network Monitor driver enables Network Monitor to receive frames from a network adapter. A capture filter functions like a database query. You can use it to specify the types of network information you want to monitor. To simplify data analysis, Network Monitor interprets raw data collected during the capture and displays it in the Frame Viewer window. You can use a display filter to specify what information you want to view in the Frame Viewer window. Like a capture filter, a display filter functions like a database query, allowing you to single out specific types of information.

Review

The following questions will help you determine whether you have learned enough to move on to the next chapter. If you have difficulty answering these questions, please go back and review the material in this chapter before beginning the next chapter. See Appendix A, "Questions and Answers," for the answers to these questions.

1. You want to filter out all network traffic except for traffic between two computers, and you also want to locate specific data within the packets. Which Network Monitor filter features should you specify?

2. You goal is to make sure that only two network management stations in your organization are able to communicate with the Simple Network Management Protocol (SNMP) agents. What measures can you take when configuring the SNMP service to enhance security?

C H A P T E R   2 7

Microsoft Windows 2000 Security

About This Chapter

Microsoft Windows 2000 introduces a comprehensive public key infrastructure (PKI) to the Windows platform. PKI extends the Windows–based public key (PK) cryptographic services introduced over the past few years, providing an integrated set of services and administrative tools for creating, deploying, and managing PK–based applications. This chapter describes the Windows 2000 PKI, discusses the primary public key technologies that are supported by Windows 2000, and provides an overview of the Kerberos and IPSec protocols in Windows 2000. Finally, the chapter introduces you to Windows 2000 security configuration tools and to auditing, a tool you can use to maintain network security.

Note Windows 2000 security is a sophisticated and comprehensive set of services. Although this chapter introduces you to Windows 2000 security, it cannot address it in depth. You should refer to Windows 2000 Help and the Microsoft Web site (*http://www.microsoft.com*) to supplement the material in this chapter.

Before You Begin

To complete the lessons in this chapter, you must have

- Installed Windows 2000 Server on a computer (Server01)

  See Chapter 8, "Installing Microsoft Windows 2000" for more details.

- Server01 configured as a domain controller

Lesson 1: Public Key Infrastructure

Public key cryptography is a critical technology for e-commerce, intranets, extranets, and other Web-enabled applications. However, to take advantage of the benefits of public key cryptography, a supporting infrastructure is needed. The Windows 2000 operating system includes a native PKI that is designed from the ground up to take full advantage of the Windows 2000 security architecture. This lesson provides an overview of the Windows 2000 PKI and includes discussions about security properties, cryptography, certificates, and Microsoft Certificate Services.

After this lesson, you will be able to

- Describe the fundamental concepts of public key cryptography and the Windows 2000 implementation of PKI

- Process certificate requests and add certificate authorities (CAs)

- Install Certificate Services

Estimated lesson time: 35 minutes

Security Properties

Computer security includes everything from the physical computing environment to the software environment. In a software environment, security should provide four functions: authentication, integrity, confidentiality, and anti-replay.

Authentication

Authentication is the process of reliably determining the genuine identity of the communicating computer (host) or user. Authentication is based on cryptography; it ensures that an attacker eavesdropping on the network cannot gain the information needed to impersonate a valid user or entity. It allows a communicating entity to prove its identity to another entity before unprotected data is sent across the network. Without strong authentication, any data and the host it is sent from is suspect.

Integrity

Integrity is the correctness of data as it was originally sent. Integrity services protect data from unauthorized modification in transit. Without data integrity, any data and the host it is sent from is suspect.

Confidentiality

Confidentiality ensures that data is disclosed only to intended recipients.

Anti-Replay

Anti-replay, also called *replay prevention,* ensures that datagrams are not retransmitted. Each datagram sent is unique. This uniqueness prevents attacks in which a message is intercepted, stored, and re-used later to attempt illegal access to information.

Cryptography

Cryptography is a set of mathematical techniques for encrypting and decrypting data so it can be transmitted securely and not be interpreted by unauthorized parties. Cryptography uses keys in conjunction with algorithms to secure data. A *key* is a value used to encrypt or decrypt information. Even if the algorithm is publicly known, security is not compromised because the data cannot be read without the key. For example, the algorithm of a combination lock is common knowledge: the dials are moved in a specific order to open the lock. However, the key to the lock—the numbers of the combination code—is secret and known only to the person with the combination. In other words, the key provides the security, not the algorithm. The algorithm provides the infrastructure in which the key is applied. Security systems can be based on public key or secret key cryptography, which are described later in this lesson.

There are a number of well-known cryptographic algorithms, each supporting different security operations. Table 27.1 describes several well-known cryptographic algorithms.

Table 27.1   Cryptographic Algorithms

Algorithm	Description
Rivest-Shamir-Adleman (RSA)	A general purpose algorithm that can support digital signatures, distributed authentication, secret key agreement via public key, and bulk data encryption without prior shared secrets.
Digital Signature Standard (DSA)	A public key algorithm used for producing digital signatures.
Diffie-Hellman	A public key cryptography algorithm that allows two communicating entities to agree on a shared key without requiring encryption during the key generation.
Hash Message Authentication Code (HMAC)	A secret key algorithm that provides integrity, authentication, and anti-replay. HMAC uses hash functions combined with a secret key. A *hash*, also known as a message digest, is used to create and verify a digital signature.
HMAC-Message Digest function (MD5)	A hash function that produces a 128-bit value known as a 5 digital signature. This signature is used for authentication, integrity, and anti-replay.
HMAC-Secure Hash Algorithm (SHA)	A hash function that produces a 160-bit digital signature and that is used for authentication, integrity, and anti-replay.
Data Encryption Standard-Cipher Chaining (DES-CBC)	A secret key algorithm used for confidentiality. A random number is generated and used with the secret key to encrypt data.

Public Key Cryptography

Public key cryptography is an asymmetric scheme that uses a pair of keys for encryption. It is called asymmetric because it uses two encryption keys that are mathematically related. These related keys are called the public and private key pair. To use public key encryption, an object (such as a user) must generate a public and private key pair. The object has only one private key (its own) but may obtain multiple public keys that pair to other private keys. Objects obtain public keys in one of two ways:

- The owner of the private key sends the receiver the matching public key.

- The receiver obtains the key from a directory service such as Active Directory service or Domain Name System (DNS).

A public and private key pair are typically used for two purposes: data encryption and digital message signing.

Data Encryption. Data encryption provides confidentiality by ensuring that only the intended recipient is able to decrypt and view the original data. When secure data must be transmitted, the sender obtains the recipient's public key. The sender then uses the recipient's public key to encrypt data and send it. When the recipient receives the data, the recipient uses his or her own private key to decrypt the data. Encryption is only secure if the sender uses the recipient's public key for encryption. If a sender uses his or her private key to encrypt data, anyone can capture the data and decrypt it by obtaining the sender's public key.

Digital Message Signing. Digital signing provides authentication and integrity but does not provide confidentiality. Digital signing allows a recipient to be certain of the identity of the sender and verifies the content has not been modified during transit. This is to prevent the originator of a message from attempting to send a message under the guise of another identity.

When a sender signs a message, a message digest is created. A message digest is a representation of the message and is similar to a Cyclic Redundancy Check (CRC). The sender uses his or her private key to encrypt the message digest. When the recipient receives the message, the recipient obtains the sender's public key to decrypt the message digest. The recipient then creates a message digest from the message and compares the message digest to the decrypted message digest. If the message digests match, integrity is guaranteed (Figure 27.1).

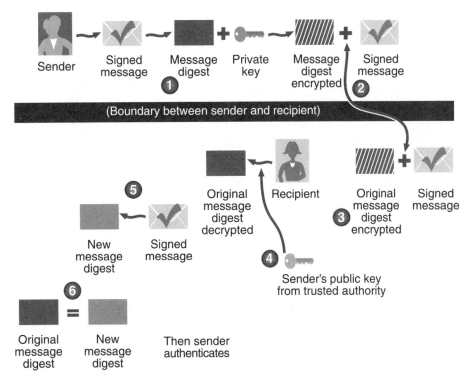

Figure 27.1 Using a signed message, message digest and the PKI to verify authenticity of sender

Authentication is provided through the key pair. Since the message digest was encrypted by using the sender's private key (and only the sender's public key decrypts the message digest), the recipient can be certain that the message came from the owner of the key pair. The recipient, however, must have a mechanism for ensuring that the key pair belongs to the intended sender and not someone impersonating the sender. This is done through a certificate issued by a trusted third party, which confirms the identity of the owner of the public key. The trusted third party is known as a Certificate Authority (CA), which will be discussed later in the lesson.

Secret Keys

A *secret key* (also known as *shared secret* or *shared secret key*) is used in much the same way as a public key; however, there is only one key that provides security. Secret keys are generally used only for a particular session or for a short period of time before being discarded. Secret keys have an advantage over public keys because of their temporary status. If, for example, an unauthorized person became aware of the key, that person may be able to gain access to a session. However, the unauthorized person would not be able to impersonate either the user or computer outside of the session, and would not have access to other resources with the secret key.

In order to get the shared secret key to both parties, there must exist a mechanism for doing so without compromising security. If the key was sent over the network, an eavesdropper (someone using a network-monitoring tool to capture packets on the network) would have easy access to the key.

Secret Key Exchange

A common solution to providing the secret key to both parties is using public keys. Public keys make it possible to encrypt the secret key as it is sent across the network. Public keys ensure confidentiality, authentication, and integrity; therefore, security is not compromised when a secret key is sent.

For example, if Bruce wants to send data to Max by using a secret key, Bruce and Max each generate half of the secret key. Bruce obtains Max's public key to encrypt his half of the secret key and send it to Max. Likewise, Max obtains Bruce's public key to encrypt his half of the secret key and sends it to Bruce. Bruce and Max then combine the halves of the secret key to generate the shared secret key to be used for encrypting the data to be sent (Figure 27.2). This secret key negotiation and the use of the secret key to encrypt the data provide authenticity, integrity, and confidentiality.

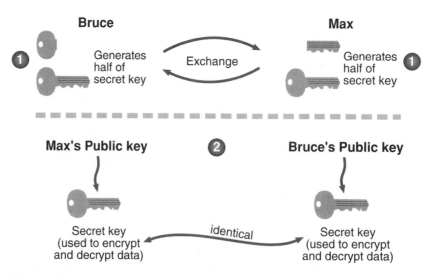

Figure 27.2 Secret key exchange where two users (Bruce and Max) each generate half of a secret key to create a shared secret key

Data Encryption

In order to provide confidentiality, the data must be encrypted by using the shared secret key. Because there is only one key known to both the sender and the receiver, encryption is a straightforward process. The sender encrypts the data with the shared secret key, and the receiver decrypts it with the shared secret key. Since no other entity on the network has knowledge of the secret key, the data is safe from attack. The sender and the receiver generally discard shared secret keys once the session has been terminated.

Certificates

Public key encryption assumes that the identity of the key pair owner is established beyond doubt. A *digital certificate*, also referred to simply as a *certificate*, is a set of data that completely identifies an entity. A trusted CA issues certificates after the authority has verified the entity's identity. The CA provides a trusted third party for both communicating parties.

For example, if Tucker wants to send authenticated data to Max, Tucker sends his public key to Max. A trusted CA certifies Tucker's public key, thus certifying Tucker's identity. Because Max trusts the CA, he trusts Tucker.

This process is similar to that of a notary public. A person signs a document in front of a notary public and provides proof of identity. The notary public is a trusted entity so that anyone examining the document can be sure that the signature is authentic. Likewise, when the sender of a message signs the message with a private key, the recipient of the message can use the sender's public key, signed by a trusted CA, to verify that the sender is legitimate. Since the trusted CA certifies the public key, the recipient can be sure that the sender is the assumed sender. A trusted CA may be a third-party provider of certificates such as VeriSign or Certificate Services.

A user can, for example, obtain a digital certificate for use with e-mail. The digital certificate includes the public key and information about the user. When the user sends e-mail, the e-mail includes a digital signature that uses the private key. The recipient obtains the public key and determines whether or not the sender of the mail message is the assumed sender. A private key is never sent to the recipient.

X.509

The term *X.509* refers to the International Telecommunication Union-Telecommunication (ITU-T) standard for certificate syntax and format. The Windows 2000 certificate–based processes use the X.509 standard. Because it is possible to use certificates for different applications (for example, secure e-mail, file system encryption), each certificate has different information contained within it. However, certificates should, at a minimum, contain the following attributes:

- Version
- Serial number
- Signature algorithm ID
- Issuer name
- Validity period
- Subject (user) name
- Subject public key information
- Issuer unique identifier
- Subject unique identifier
- Extensions
- Signature on the above fields

Certificate Revocation Lists

Certificates, like most real-world forms of identification, can expire and become invalid. The CA can also revoke them for other reasons. In order to handle the existence of invalid certificates, the CA maintains a certificate revocation list (CRL). The CRL is available to network users to determine the validity of any given certificate.

CA Hierarchy

Rather than having one trusted CA provide authentication for the entire Internet or intranet, it is possible to have CAs certify other CAs. This hierarchical structure, called a chain, allows users to trust a single CA rather than having to trust all CAs. This chaining of CAs provides several benefits:

- **Flexibility.** It is easy to move, revoke, or chain CA's without affecting other parts of the organization.
- **Distributed Administration.** Administrators can be responsible for their own sites.
- **Security Policies.** Security policies can be different at each CA site.

The CA at the top of the chain is referred to as the root CA. CAs below the root are referred to as intermediate, subordinate, or issuing CAs.

Certificate Services

Certificate Services enables an organization to manage the issuance, renewal, and revocation of digital certificates without having to rely on external certificate authorities. In addition, Certificate Services allows an organization to fully control the policies associated with issuing, managing, and revoking certificates, as well as the format and contents of the certificates themselves. In addition, Certificate Services logs all transactions, enabling the administrator to track, audit, and manage certificate requests.

Certificate Services Features

Microsoft Certificate Services has a number of features that make it valuable to organizations that do not choose to rely upon external certificate authorities and who require a flexible tool that can be adapted to the needs of their organization.

Policy Independence. In order to obtain a certificate, requesters must meet certain criteria. This criteria is defined in certificate policies. For example, one policy may grant commercial certificates only if applicants present their identification in person. Another policy may grant credentials based on e-mail requests.

Policies are implemented in policy components that can be written in Java, Visual Basic, or Microsoft C/C++. The default policy for Certificate Services allows users to request certificates through a Hypertext Markup Language (HTML) page.

Transport Independence. Certificate Services can request and distribute certificates through any transport mechanism. That is, it can accept certificate requests from an applicant and post certificates to the applicant through Hypertext Transfer Protocol (HTTP), remote procedure call (RPC), disk file, or custom transport.

Adherence to Standards. Certificate Services can perform the following services:

- Accept standard Public Key Cryptography Standards (PKCS) #10 requests
- Support PKCS #7 cryptographically signed data
- Issue X.509 version 1.0 and 3.0 certificates

Support for additional certificate formats can be added to Certificate Services. Certificate Services includes a Lightweight Directory Access Protocol (LDAP) component so that Certificate Services can integrate with the Active Directory service.

Key Management. The security of a certification system depends on the protection of private keys. The design of Certificate Services ensures that individuals cannot access private key information without authorization. Certificate Services relies on Microsoft CryptoAPI to provide key management functionality and other cryptographic capabilities for building a secure store, with certificates kept in a certificate store.

Certificate Services Architecture

Certificate Services' architectural elements include the server engine that handles certificate requests and other modules that perform tasks by communicating with the server engine. Figure 27.3 illustrates how the components communicate with the server engine.

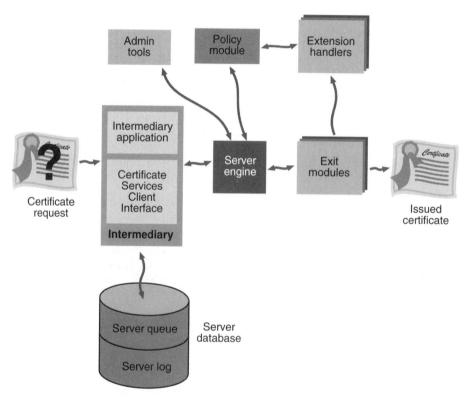

Figure 27.3 Server engine and other components of Certificate Services

Server Engine

The server engine is the core component of Certificate Services. The engine acts as a broker for all requests it receives from the entry modules, driving the flow of information between components during the processing of a request and generation of a certificate. At each processing stage, the engine interacts with the various modules to ensure appropriate action is taken based on the state of the request.

Intermediary

The intermediary is the architectural component that receives new certificate requests from clients and submits them to the server engine. The intermediary is composed of two parts: the intermediary application that performs actions on behalf of clients and the Certificate Services Client Interface that handles communications between the intermediary application and the server engine.

Intermediary applications can be written to handle certificate requests from different types of clients, across multiple transports, or according to policy-specific criteria. Microsoft Internet Information Services (IIS) is an intermediary application that provides support for clients over Hypertext Transfer Protocol (http). Intermediaries can also check on the status of a previously submitted request and obtain the Certificate Services' configuration information.

Server Database

Certificate Services includes a server database that maintains status information and a log of all issued certificates and certificate revocation lists (CRLs). The database is composed of two parts: the server log and the server queue.

Server Log

The server log stores all certificates and CRLs issued by the server so that administrators can track, audit, and archive server activity. In addition, the server log is used by the server engine to store pending revocations before publishing them in the CRL. The server log also stores recent certificate requests for a configurable period in case a problem is encountered when a certificate is issued.

Server Queue

The server queue maintains status information (receipt, parsing, authorization, signing, and dispatch) as the server processes a certificate request.

Policy Module

The policy module contains the set of rules governing issuance, renewal, and revocation of certificates. All requests received by the server engine are passed to the policy module for validation. Policy modules are also used to parse any supplemental information provided within a request and set properties on the certificate accordingly.

Extension Handlers

Extension handlers work in tandem with the policy module to set custom extensions on a certificate. Each extension handler acts as a template for the custom extensions that should appear in a certificate. The policy module must load the appropriate extension handler when it is needed.

Exit Modules

Exit modules publish completed certificates and CRLs through any number of transports or protocols. By default, the server notifies each exit module installed on the server whenever a certificate or CRL is published.

Certificate Services provides a Component Object Model (COM) interface for writing custom exit modules for different transports and protocols or for custom delivery options. For example, an LDAP exit module might be used to publish only client certificates in a directory service and not server certificates. In this case, the exit module can use the COM interface to determine the type of certificate that the server is issuing and filter out any that are not client certificates.

Processing Certificate Requests

Certificate Services provides services for processing certificate requests and issuing digital certificates (Figure 27.4).

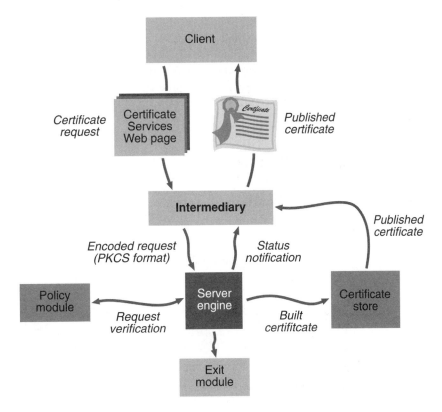

Figure 27.4 Processing certificate requests

Certificate Services performs the following steps when processing a certificate request:

1. The certificate request is sent by the client to an intermediary application. The intermediary application formats it into a PKCS #10 format request and submits it to the server engine.

2. The server engine calls the policy module, which queries request properties, decides whether or not the request is authorized, and sets optional certificate properties.

3. If the request is approved, the server engine takes the request and builds a complete certificate.

4. The server engine stores the completed certificate in the certificate store and notifies the intermediary application of the request status. If the exit module has so requested, the server engine notifies it of a certificate issuance event. This allows the exit module to perform further operations, such as publishing the certificate to a directory service.

5. The intermediary gets the published certificate from the certificate store and passes it back to the client.

Enrolling Certificates

The process of obtaining a digital certificate is called *certificate enrollment*. This process begins with a client submitting a certificate request and ends with the installation of the issued certificate in the client application.

The enrollment control and its forms are accessed through the Certificate Services Enrollment Page (see Figure 27.5). This page is available from the Certificate Services Web page at *http://server_name/certsrv/*.

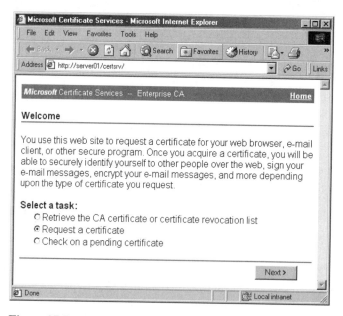

Figure 27.5 Enrollment control form for Server01 configured as an Enterprise CA

Certificate Authority Certificates

In the process of issuing a digital certificate, the CA validates the identity of the individual requesting the certificate and then signs the certificate with its own private key.

A client application, such as Microsoft Internet Explorer, checks the CA signature before accepting a certificate. If the CA signature is not valid or comes from an unknown source, Internet Explorer warns the user by displaying a security message and may prevent the user from accepting the certificate.

Note If Internet Explorer is set to the low security level, it will not warn the user of invalid certificates. This setting is appropriate for highly trusted intranet environments and is inappropriate for Internet access.

In addition to the server and client authentication certificates issued by Certificate Services, there are certificates that identify CAs.

The CA certificate is a signature certificate that contains a public key used to verify digital signatures. It identifies the CA that issues authentication certificates to the servers and clients that request these certificates. Clients use the CA certificate of the CA issuing the server certificate to validate the server certificate. Servers use the CA certificate of the CA issuing the client certificate to validate the client certificate.

A self-signed CA certificate is also called a root certificate because it is the certificate for the root CA. The root CA must sign its own CA certificate because by definition there is no higher certifying authority to sign its CA certificate.

Distribution and Installation of CA Certificates

CA certificates are not requested and issued in the same manner as server and client authentication certificates. Server and client authentication certificates are unique for each requesting server and client, and are not shared—they must be generated and issued by a CA upon demand. In contrast, the CA certificate does not require issuance upon demand. Instead, it is created once and then made readily available to all servers or clients who request certificates from the CA.

A commonly used technique for distributing CA certificates is to place them in a location known and accessible to anyone who requests certificates from the CA.

Installing Certificate Services

You can install Certificate Services by using the Add/Remove Programs utility in Control Panel or optionally during the installation of Windows 2000 Server. Administrators familiar with creating CAs can choose a custom setup by using the advanced options available when installing Certificate Services. Those unfamiliar with creating CAs can select the default settings.

Certificate Authority Type

The CA type allows selection of how the CA will be utilized in a CA hierarchy and whether or not the CA will rely upon Active Directory service. The following certificate authority types are available:

- **Enterprise Root CA.** This CA becomes the root CA for the hierarchy and requires Active Directory service.

- **Enterprise Subordinate CA.** This CA becomes a subordinate CA to an Enterprise Root CA. It requires Active Directory service. It requests a certificate from the Enterprise Root CA.

- **Standalone Root CA.** This CA becomes the root CA for the hierarchy but does not require Active Directory service.

- **Standalone Subordinate CA.** This CA becomes a subordinate CA to a Standalone Root CA. It does not require Active Directory service. It requests a certificate from the Standalone Root CA.

When installing the Certificate Services as an Enterprise CA, Certificate Services copies the certificates into Active Directory service. Security support providers such as the Kerberos protocol can query Active Directory service to get the certificate, which contains the public key.

CA Information

You must supply information about the initial CA that is created when you install Certificate Services. This information includes the CA name and other necessary information. None of this information can be changed after the CA setup is complete.

Advanced Configuration

The advanced configuration contains options for the type of cryptography algorithms to be used for the CA that you are creating. The advanced configuration options include the name of the cryptographic provider, the hash algorithm, the option to use existing public keys and private keys, and the key length.

Administering Certificate Services

The main tool used to administer Certificate Services is the Certification Authority snap-in (Figure 27.6).

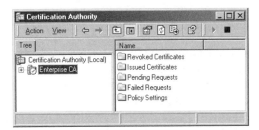

Figure 27.6 Certification Authority snap-in for an Enterprise CA

The Certification Authority snap-in allows you to perform a variety of administrative tasks:

- Start or stop the Certificate services
- Set security permissions and delegate control of a CA
- View a CA certificate
- Back up a CA
- Restore a CA from a backup copy
- Renew a root CA
- Renew a subordinate CA
- Manage certificate revocation
- Manage certificate requests
- Manage certificate templates
- Change policy settings
- Map certificate to user accounts
- Modify the Policy Module or Exit Module

You can use the Certification Authority snap-in to administer a certification authority on the local computer or on another computer. The snap-in is installed when Certificate Services are installed or when installing the Administration Pack (Adminpak.msi).

Certutil.exe is a command-line utility used for administering certificate services. Running certutil without any command-line switches displays summary information about the local certificate authority. Certutil is used to dump and display CA configuration information, configure Certificate Services, back up and restore CA components, and verify certificates, key pairs, and certificate chains.

If you need to set security for the CA Web pages, you should use the Internet Information Services snap-in. Expand the Default Web Site from the console tree and then select CertSrv. From the Action menu, select Properties. On the Directory Security tab, under Anonymous access and authentication control, click Edit. In the Authentication Methods dialog box, configure the security settings for the CA Web pages.

Practice: Installing and Configuring Certificate Services

In this practice you install an Enterprise Root CA and use this CA to issue, install, and revoke certificates. Note that the secure way to configure Certification Services is to create a root CA that only issues certificates to subordinate CA types. The subordinate CA types then issue certificates for specific purposes such as application services and authentication. Using a root CA for this purpose is not secure because if the root CA security is breached, all certificates issued are compromised. However, for the purpose of learning how to install and configure certificate services, a root CA can be used.

Exercise 1: Installing Certificate Services and Configuring the Certificate Authority

In this exercise, you install Certificate Services on Server01. Server01 acts as an Enterprise Root CA.

1. Log on to Server01 as Administrator with a password of *password*.

2. Click Start, point to Settings, and then click Control Panel.

   Control Panel appears.

3. Double-click the Add/Remove Programs application.

   The Add/Remove Programs window appears.

4. In the left pane, click the Add/Remove Windows components icon.

   The Windows Components wizard appears.

5. Click the Certificate Services check box.

   A Microsoft Certificate Services message box appears stating that once Certificate Services is installed, the computer cannot be renamed and it cannot join or be removed from a domain.

6. Click Yes.

7. On the Windows Components screen, click Details.

   The Certificate Services window appears.

   Notice that Certificate Services subcomponents include both the service used to create a certificate authority and a Web enrollment form for submitting requests and retrieving certificates from the computer running as a CA.

8. Click OK.

9. On the Windows Components screen, click Next.

   The Certification Authority Type screen appears.

10. Select each radio button and read the text appearing in the Description box.

    Notice that the Enterprise CA types can only be used if Active Directory service is running. The standalone CA types run independently of Active Directory service. Thus, they can be used in the presence or absence of Active Directory service. If Active Directory service is present, the standalone CA types will use it. Subordinate CA types are dependent on the presence of a CA higher up in the CA hierarchy.

11. Click the Enterprise Root CA radio button and click the Advanced Options check box.

12. Click Next.

    The Public And Private Key Pair screen appears.

    Notice that there are a number of Cryptographic Service Providers (CSPs), each with one or more associated hash algorithms used to generate key pairs. From this screen you can also specify the key length or use existing keys installed on the computer, import keys, and view certificates.

13. In the CSP list box, verify that Microsoft Base Cryptographic Provider v1.0 is selected. In the Hash Algorithm list box, verify that the SHA-1 hash algorithm is selected. In the Key Length drop-down list box, verify that Default is selected. Click Next.

    The CA Identifying Information screen appears.

14. Type the information in the table into the text boxes on the CA Identifying Information screen.

Label	Value to type
CA name	Enterprise CA
Organization	Microsoft Corporation
Organizational unit	Microsoft Press
City	Redmond
State or province	Washington
E-mail	ca-mp@microsoft.com
CA description	Root CA for self-study training only

Notice that this certificate is configured to be valid for two years.

15. Click Next.

The Data Storage Location screen appears.

Notice that the certificate database and log file folder, CertLog, is stored on the boot partition. If disk capacity on the boot partition is limited, consider specifying another secure partition for the certificate database and log folder.

The Store configuration information in a shared folder is not necessary if Active Directory service is running and the computer operating as the certificate authority is a member of a domain. Configuration information about the CA is automatically published to the Active Directory store.

16. Click Next.

A Microsoft Certificate Services message box appears stating that Internet Information Services is running on the computer and warning you that it must be stopped in order for you to be able to continue.

17. Click OK.

The Configuring Components screen appears as the software is installed and configured, and then the Completing The Windows Components Wizard screen appears.

18. Click Finish and then on the Add/Remove Programs window, click Close.

19. Close Control Panel.

Exercise 2: Running Certificate Services

In this exercise you generate, install, and revoke a certificate on Server01. You will use the Certificate Enrollment URL and the Certification Authority snap-in to complete this exercise.

1. Open Certification Authority from the Administrative Tools program group.

   The Certification Authority snap-in appears.

2. In the console tree, expand the Enterprise CA node.

3. In the console tree, select the Issued Certificates folder and then minimize the Certification Authority snap-in.

4. Click the Start menu and then choose run.

   The Run dialog box appears.

5. In the Open text box, type **http://server01/certsrv** and then click OK.

   The Internet Connection wizard appears.

6. Click the I Want To Setup My Internet Connection Manually, or I Want To Connect Through A Local Area Network (LAN) radio button.

7. Click Next.

   The Setting Up Your Internet Connection screen appears.

8. Click the I Connect Through A Local Area Network (LAN) radio button.

9. Click Next.

   The Local Area Network Internet Configuration screen appears.

10. Clear the Automatic Discovery Of Proxy Server (Recommended) check box.

11. Click Next.

    The Set Up Your Internet Mail Account screen appears.

12. Click the No radio button, and then click Next.

    The Completing The Internet Connection wizard appears.

13. Click Finish.

    Internet Explorer appears and displays the certificate services enrollment page.

14. Read the information on this page and then verify that the Request A Certificate radio button is selected.

15. Click Next.

   The Choose Request Type page appears and the User Certificate Request radio button is selected.

16. Click Next.

   The User Certificate – Identifying Information page appears.

17. Click More Options.

   Notice that the CSP selected was the CSP type you specified during installation of Certificate Services.

18. Click Submit.

   The Certificate Issued page appears.

19. Minimize Internet Explorer and restore the Certification Authority snap-in.

   The Certification Authority snap-in appears, and one certificate is listed in the details pane. If you don't see the certificate request, press F5 to refresh the details pane.

20. Double-click the certificate appearing in the details pane.

   The Certificate dialog box appears with three tabs.

21. Click the Details tab.

22. In the top box below the Show drop-down list box, click Issuer.

   Notice that the information appearing in the bottom box is the information you typed into the CA Identifying Information screen.

23. Click OK.

24. Minimize the Certification Authority snap-in and restore Internet Explorer.

25. Click the Install This Certificate hyperlink.

   The Certificate Installed page appears stating that you have successfully installed a certificate.

26. Close Internet Explorer.

27. Restore the Certification Authority snap-in and select the certificate in the details pane.

28. Click the Action Menu, point to All Tasks and then click Revoke Certificate.

   The Certificate Revocation dialog box appears.

29. In the Reason Code drop-down list box choose Key Compromise, and then click Yes.

30. In the console tree, click the Revoked Certificates folder.

    The revoked certificate appears in the details pane.

31. Click the Action menu, point to All Tasks and then click Publish.

    The Certificate Revocation List dialog box appears stating that the previous list is still valid.

32. Click Yes.

33. Close the Certification Authority snap-in.

34. Click the Start menu, and then click Run.

    The URL to the Certsrv directory appears.

35. Click OK.

    Internet Explorer appears and displays the certificate services enrollment page.

36. Click the Retrieve The CA Certificate Or Certificate Revocation List radio button, and then click next.

37. Click the Download Latest Certificate Revocation List hyperlink.

    The File Download dialog box appears.

38. Click the Open This File From Its Current Location radio button, and then click OK.

    The Certificate Revocation List dialog box appears.

39. Click the Revocation List tab.

40. In the Revoked Certificates box, click the item that appears.

    In the Revocation entry box, the Serial number of the revoked certificate, the date of revocation, and the reason for revocation appear.

41. Click OK.

42. Close Internet Explorer.

Lesson Summary

Windows 2000 includes a native PKI that is designed to take full advantage of the Windows 2000 security architecture. Public key cryptography is an asymmetric scheme that uses a pair of keys for encryption. To use public key encryption, a user must generate a public and private key pair. Public key encryption uses digital certificates to completely identify the key pair owner. The Windows 2000 certificate–based processes use the X.509 standard. Certificate Services enables an organization to manage the issuance, renewal, and revocation of digital certificates without having to rely on external CAs. Certificate Services supports policy independence, transport independence, adherence to standards, and key management. Certificate Services architectural elements include the server engine that handles certificate requests and other modules that perform tasks by communicating with the server engine. Certificate Services provides services for processing certificate requests and issuing digital certificates. You can install Certificate Services by using the Add/Remove Programs utility in Control Panel or optionally during Windows 2000 Server installation. The tools used to administer Certificate Services once it is installed are the Certification Authority snap-in, the Certutil utility, and the Certificate Services enrollment Web page.

Lesson 2: Public Key Technologies

Windows 2000 extends security by supporting a number of technologies that are based on public key security, including the Secure Channel authentication package, smart cards, Authenticode, the Encrypting File System (EFS), and Internet Protocol Security (IPSec). This lesson reviews each of these technologies and explains how they fit into the PKI framework.

After this lesson, you will be able to

- Describe the primary public key–based components of Windows 2000 security

Estimated lesson time: 35 minutes

Secure Channel Authentication Package

In Windows 2000, a Secure Channel (SChannel) authentication package is located below the Security Support Provider Interface (SSPI) as shown in Figure 27.7.

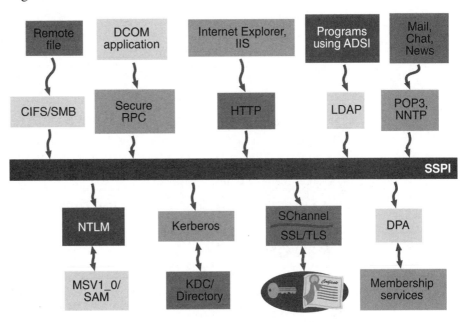

Figure 27.7 Authentication Services architecture in Windows 2000

The SChannel authentication package implements the Secure Sockets Layer (SSL) 3.0 protocol and the Transport Layer Security (TLS) 1.0 protocol. SSL and TLS are flexible security protocols that can be layered on top of other transport protocols. They rely on PK-based authentication technology and use PK–based key negotiation to generate a unique encryption key for each client/server session. They are most commonly associated with Web–based applications and the HTTP protocol (referred to as HTTPS).

The TLS protocol is based on the SSL 3.0 protocol and moves forward as the Internet Engineering Task Force (IETF) standard. The differences between TLS 1.0 and SSL 3.0 are not significant, but they are enough that TLS 1.0 and SSL 3.0 cannot interoperate. TLS 1.0, however, does have a negotiation mechanism whereby TLS can back down to and use SSL 3.0. Therefore, a client that supports only SSL 3.0 can still communicate with a server that supports TLS 1.0.

Both the SSL and TLS protocols provide secure data communication through data encryption and decryption, client authentication, and optional server authentication. Both are typically used to send and receive private communication across the Internet by using public key cryptography as its authentication method.

The SSL/TLS protocol is implemented by an SChannel provider (such as IIS, Proxy Server, and Exchange), and by client applications that transit the Internet (such as Internet Explorer and Microsoft Outlook e-mail clients). Applications request the services of SSL and TLS through the SSPI API.

The benefits of SSL and TLS include the following:

- Authentication that assures the client that data is sent to the correct server and that the server is secure

- Encryption that assures that nothing other than the secure target server can read the data

- Data integrity that assures that the transferred data has not been altered

Smart Cards

Smart cards, which are the size of credit cards, can be used to store a user's public key, private key, and certificate. Smart cards are a secure way to protect and control a user's keys, instead of storing them on a computer. A user's keys and certificates move with the user. Security-critical computations are performed by the smart card, instead of exposing a user's private key to the computer. In addition, smart cards enhance software-only solutions, such as logon and secure e-mail.

To use a smart card, a computer must have a smart card reader. A smart card is an ISO 7816–compatible device that contains an embedded microprocessor, an RSA or equivalent cryptography coprocessor, and local storage. The local storage includes the following:

- 6 to 24 KB ROM for the smart card operating system and applications

- 128 to 512 bytes of RAM for run-time data

- 1 to 16 KB EEPROM for user data

Smart Card Logon

Windows 2000 introduces PK–based smart card logon as an alternative to passwords for domain authentication. This relies on a PC/SC Workgroup-compliant smart card infrastructure, first introduced for Windows NT and Windows 95 in December 1997, and RSA–capable smart cards with supporting CryptoAPI CSPs. The authentication process makes use of the PKINIT protocol to integrate PK–based authentication with the Windows 2000 Kerberos protocol access-control system.

During operation, the system recognizes a smart card insertion event as an alternative to the standard Ctrl+Alt+Del secure attention sequence to initiate a logon. The user is then prompted for the smart card PIN code, which controls access to operations with the private key stored on the smart card. In this system, the smart card also contains a copy of the user's certificate (issued by an enterprise CA). This allows the user to roam within the domain.

Authenticode

The growing use of the Internet has led to an increased reliance on downloaded active content, such as Windows–based applications, ActiveX controls, and Java applets. The result has been a heightened concern for the safety of such downloads, since they often occur as a side effect of Web scripts without any·specific user notification. In response to these concerns, Microsoft introduced Authenticode digital signature technology in 1996 and introduced significant enhancements of it in 1997.

Authenticode technology, a security feature in Microsoft Internet Explorer, assures accountability and authenticity for software components on the Internet. Authenticode verifies that the software hasn't been tampered with and identifies the publisher of the software. Users can decide on a case-by-case basis what code to download, based on their experience with and trust in a software publisher. By signing their code, developers can build an increasingly trusting relationship with their users.

Authenticode technology allows software publishers to digitally sign any form of active content, including multiple-file archives. These signatures may be used to verify both the publishers of the content and the content integrity at download time. This verification infrastructure scales to the worldwide base of users of Windows by relying on a hierarchical CA structure in which a small number of commercial CAs issue software-publishing certificates. For enterprise needs, the Windows 2000 PKI allows you to issue Authenticode certificates to internal developers or contractors and allows any employee to verify the origin and integrity of downloaded applications.

Encrypting File System

EFS is an extension to the NTFS file system that provides strong data protection and encryption for files and folders. The encryption technology is based on use of public keys and runs as an integrated system service, making it easy to manage, difficult to attack, and transparent to the user. This is particularly useful for securing data on computers that may be vulnerable to theft, such as mobile computers.

The encrypting user's public key is used in the encryption process, ensuring data privacy. Decryption is denied to any user without the corresponding private key. A special recovery key is also generated for each encrypted file. This key is for emergency use by a qualified administrator in the event that an employee leaves or a private key is lost.

Encryption and decryption are done transparently during the input/output (I/O) process. EFS imposes no discernible performance penalty during the encryption/decryption process.

EFS also supports encryption and decryption of files stored on remote NTFS volumes. However, EFS addresses only the encryption and decryption of stored data. Although encrypted files can be exported, data is transferred over the network in a clear (unencrypted) format by default. Windows 2000 provides network protocols such as SSL, TLS, and IPSec to encrypt data during transfer over the network.

Data Protection

EFS uses a combination of the user's public and private keys as well as a randomly generated file-encryption key (FEK). The FEK is a 128-bit key for North America and a 40-bit key for international releases. Windows 2000 uses the Data Encryption Standard X (DESX) algorithm to encrypt files.

Data Recovery

The Encrypted Data Recovery Policy (EDRP) is used to specify who can recover data in case a user's private key is lost. An EDRP is automatically generated on standalone computers to minimize administration. Computers that are members of a domain receive the EDRP from the domain policy. For security, recovery is limited to the encrypted data; it is not possible to recover the users' keys.

Encrypted Backup and Restoration

Because members of the Backup Operators group do not have the keys necessary for decryption, encrypted data is read and stored in the backup as an opaque stream of data.

Fault Tolerance

Encryption and decryption are sensitive operations because failure could result in data loss. Therefore, EFS makes all operations automatic. If an operation cannot be completed, it is completely undone. For example, if a computer loses power during an encryption operation, EFS undoes the operation on restart so that the file is in a consistent state.

Once a file is encrypted, the processes of encryption and decryption are automatic and transparent to users and applications whenever the file is used. It is possible to perform encryption one file at a time or one folder at a time.

You can encrypt a file or folder in Windows Explorer and from the command prompt.

Note It is not possible to use NTFS compression and encryption on the same file. Compression and encryption are mutually exclusive.

Encrypting File System Encryption

EFS encrypts, decrypts, and recovers files. Figure 27.8 provides an overview of the encryption process. The numbered steps shown in the illustration are described below.

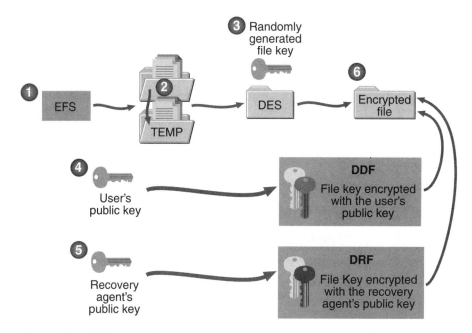

Figure 27.8 EFS encryption process

When a user encrypts a file in EFS, the following process occurs:

1. The EFS service opens the file for exclusive access.

2. All data streams in the file are copied to a temporary file.

3. A file key is randomly generated and used to encrypt the file according to the DES encryption scheme.

4. A Data Decryption Field (DDF) is created that contains the file key, which is encrypted with the user's public key.

5. A Data Recovery Field (DRF) is created that contains the file key, this time encrypted with the recovery agent's public key. The recovery agent's public key is obtained from the EDRP.

6. The EFS server writes the encrypted data, along with the DDF and DRF, back to the file.

EFS Decryption

The decryption process uses the DDF, created during encryption, to decrypt a file. Figure 27.9 provides an overview of the decryption process. The numbered steps shown in the illustration are described below.

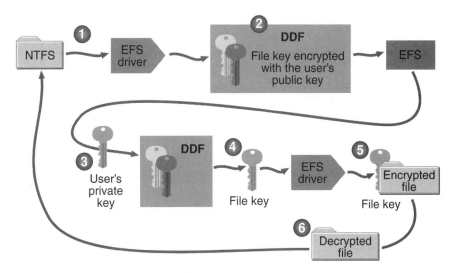

Figure 27.9 EFS decryption process

When a file is decrypted in EFS, the following sequence of steps takes place:

1. When an application accesses an encrypted file, NTFS recognizes the file as encrypted and sends a request to the EFS driver.

2. The EFS driver retrieves the DDF and passes it to the EFS service.

3. The EFS service decrypts the DDF with the user's private key to obtain the file key.

4. The EFS service passes the file key back to the EFS driver.

5. The EFS driver uses the file key to decrypt the file.

6. The EFS driver returns the decrypted data to NTFS, which then completes the file request, and sends the data to the requesting application.

EFS Recovery

The EFS recovery is much the same as the decryption process. Figure 27.10 provides an overview of the recovery process. The numbered steps shown in the illustration are described below.

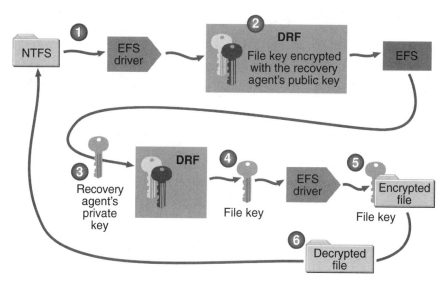

Figure 27.10 EFS recovery process

When a file is recovered in EFS, the following process takes place:

1. NTFS sends a request to the EFS driver.

2. The EFS driver retrieves the DRF and passes it to the EFS service.

3. The EFS service recovers the DRF by using the recovery agent's private key to obtain the file key.

4. The EFS service passes the file key back to the EFS driver.

5. The EFS driver uses the file key to recover the file.

6. The EFS driver returns the recovered data to NTFS, which then completes the file request, and sends the data to the requesting application.

Cipher Command-Line Utility

The cipher command-line utility allows you to encrypt and decrypt files from a command prompt. The command uses the following syntax:

```
cipher [/e| /d] [/s:dir] [/a][/i] [/f] [/q] [/h] [/k]
[pathname [...]]
```

If no parameters are used, the cipher command displays the encryption state of the current folder and any files it contains. Spaces must be put in between multiple parameters. Table 27.2 provides a description of each parameter.

Table 27.2   Cipher Command Parameters

Parameter	Description
/e	Encrypts the specified folders. Folders are marked so that files added to the folder later will be encrypted.
/d	Decrypts the specified folders. Folders are marked so that files added to the folder later will not be encrypted.
/s:dir	Performs the selected operation on folders in the specified folder and all subfolders.
/a	Performs the selected operation on files with the specified names. If there is no matching file, this parameter is ignored.
/i	Continues performing the specified operation even after errors have occurred. By default, cipher stops when an error is encountered.
/f	Forces the encryption or decryption of all specified objects. By default, files that have already been encrypted or decrypted are skipped.
/q	Reports only the most essential information.
/h	Displays files with hidden or system attributes. By default, these files are not encrypted or decrypted.
/k	Creates a new file encryption certificate on the computer where CIPHER is run. This switch causes all other switches to be ignored. Therefore, run /k exclusive of the other switches.
pathname	Specifies a pattern, file, or folder. You can use multiple filenames and wildcards.

Examples

To encrypt the C:\My Documents directory, type **cipher /e "My Documents"** at the C: command prompt.

To encrypt all files on the C: drive with the word "test" in the filename, type **cipher /e /s *test*** at the C: command prompt.

Practice: Configuring and Using File Encryption

In this practice you configure a data recovery policy in the domain, and then encrypt a folder. Complete this practice on Server01.

Exercise 1: Configuring a Data Recovery Policy for the Domain

Recovery policy is configured by default when the first domain controller is installed. As a result, a self-signed certificate assigns the domain administrator as the recovery agent. In this exercise, you manually add the administrator as the recovery agent before using EFS.

1. Log on to Server01 as Administrator with a password of *password*.

2. Click Run, verify that the URL for the Certificate Services enrollment page (*http://server01/certsrv/*) appears, and then click OK.

   Internet Explorer appears and it is displaying the Certificate Services enrollment page.

3. Verify that the Request A Certificate radio button is selected and then click Next.

   The Choose Request Type page appears.

4. Click the Advanced Request radio button, and then click Next.

   The Advanced Certificate Requests page appears.

5. Verify that the Submit A Certificate Request To This CA Using A Form radio button is selected, and then click Next.

   The Advanced Certificate Requests form page appears.

6. From the Certificate Template drop-down list box select EFS Recovery Agent.

7. Click Submit.

   The Certificate Issued page appears.

8. Click the Install This Certificate hyperlink.

   A Certificate Installed page appears.

9. Close Internet Explorer.

   Note You can complete all of the preceding steps in this exercise from the Group Policy snap-in. In step 19 of this exercise, you choose Create rather than Add. The Create option creates the certificate and then allows you to assign the certificate to the group policy.

10. Open the Active Directory Users And Computers snap-in from the Administrative Tools group.

11. Expand the console tree and then select the Microsoft.com node.

12. Click the Action menu and then click Properties.

13. The microsoft.com Properties dialog box appears.

14. Click the Group Policy tab and then click Edit.

    The Group Policy snap-in appears.

15. Under the Computer Configuration node, expand the Windows Settings container.

16. Under the Windows Settings container, expand the Security Settings node.

17. Under the Security Settings node, expand the Public Key Policies container.

18. Under the Public Key Policies container, expand the Encrypted Data Recovery Agents container.

19. Click the Action menu, and then click Add.

    The Add Recovery Agent wizard appears.

20. Click Next.

    The Select Recovery Agents screen appears.

21. Read the Select Recovery Agents screen and then click Browse Directory.

    The Find Users, Contacts, And Groups dialog box appears.

22. Click Find Now.

23. In the list of Users And Groups, double-click Administrator.

    The Select Recover Agents screen appears.

24. Click Next.

    The Completing The Add Recovery Agent wizard appears.

25. Click Finish.

    Administrator appears in the details pane of the Group Policy snap-in.

26. Click the entry in the details pane.

27. Click the Action menu and then click Properties.

   The Administrator Properties dialog box appears.

   Notice that all purposes are enabled for this certificate. The only purpose currently available for this certificate is File Recovery.

28. Click OK.

29. Close the Group Policy snap-in.

   The microsoft.com Properties dialog box appears.

30. Click OK.

   The Active Directory Users And Computers snap-in appears.

31. Click the View menu and then click Advanced Features.

32. In the console tree, click the Users container.

33. In the details pane, click Administrator.

34. Click the Action menu, and then click Properties.

   The Administrator Properties dialog box appears.

35. Click the Published Certificates tab.

   The list of X.509 certificates published to this user account appears.

   Notice that two certificates were published to the Administrator account and were issued by the Administrator account. The certificate listed as File Recovery under the Intended Purpose column is used to recover files encrypted with EFS if the original private key is lost or otherwise invalid.

36. Click OK.

37. Close the Active Directory Users And Computers snap-in.

Exercise 2: Encrypting a Folder using EFS

In this exercise, you encrypt a folder using the Windows Explorer on Server01.

1. On the desktop, double-click My Computer.

   The My Computer window appears.

2. Double-click the Local Disk (C:) drive.

   The Local Disk (C:) window appears.

3. Double-click the Document And Settings folder.

   The Document And Settings window appears.

4. Double-click the Administrator folder.

   The Administrator window appears.

5. Click once on the My Documents folder.

6. Click the File menu and then click Properties.

   The My Documents Properties dialog box appears.

7. Click the Advanced button.

   The Advanced Attributes dialog box appears.

8. Click the Encrypt Contents To Secure Data check box, and then click OK.

   The My Documents Properties dialog box appears.

9. Click OK.

   The Confirm Attribute Changes dialog box appears.

10. Click the Apply Changes To This Folder, Subfolders And Files radio button.

11. Click OK.

    The My Documents Properties dialog box appears, and then the Applying Attributes status message box appears. When the operation has completed, the My Documents Properties dialog box closes.

12. The Administrator window appears.

    Notice that the Attributes for the selected My Documents folder is Encrypted.

13. Close the Administrator window.

Internet Protocol Security

Chapter 9, "Managing Network Protocols," introduced IPSec. This chapter continues with the discussion of IPSec, providing more details about how IPSec is used to support public key security.

IPSec in Windows 2000 is designed to protect sensitive data on a TCP/IP network. IPSec is useful when the network between two communicating computers is not secure. It provides confidentiality, integrity, and authentication of IP traffic for each packet traversing the network.

When using IPSec, the two computers communicating over the network first agree on the highest common security policy; then each handles the IP Security at its respective end. Before sending data across the network, the computer initiating communication transparently encrypts the data by using IP Security. The destination computer transparently decrypts the data before passing it to the destination process. Because the data is passed down to and encrypted at the IP protocol level, separate security packages are not required for each protocol in the TCP/IP suite.

Using IPSec to encrypt all IP network traffic ensures that any TCP/IP-based communication is secure from network eavesdropping. Any routers or switches that are in the path between the communicating computers can simply forward the encrypted IP packets.

Note To ensure full compatibility with previous versions of Windows, a computer running Windows 2000 configured for IPSec sends the data without encryption to pre–Windows 2000 computers.

IPSec Policies

With Windows 2000 IPSec, you can create policies that define the type and level of security to be used during network communication.

Negotiation Policies

Negotiation policies determine the security services used during network communication. The security protocol chosen for negotiation policies is the basis for the security services. For example, if the IP Authentication Header protocol is chosen, integrity, authentication, and anti-replay services are provided—but not confidentiality.

It is possible to set multiple security methods for each negotiation policy. If the first method is not acceptable for the security association, the service continues through an ordered list until it finds a policy it can use to establish the association. If the negotiation is not successful, the communication is established without IPSec.

IP Filters

IP filters direct actions based on the destination of an IP packet, what IP protocol is in effect, and the related ports that the protocol uses. Each IP packet is checked against the IP filter, and if a match is found, the properties of the associated security policy are used to send the communication. Filters need to be configured for both incoming and outgoing traffic.

Security Policies

Security policies are used to configure IPSec attributes. These policies are made up of associated negotiation policies and IP filters, and are associated with domain controller policies. Security policies define the type and level of security to use for any given IP network communication. An IP security policy can be assigned to the default domain policy, the default local policy, or a customized domain policy.

A computer logging on to a domain automatically obtains the properties of the default domain and local policies, including the IPSec policy assigned to the domain policy.

IPSec Components

The Windows 2000 installation process installs the services, protocols, and drivers necessary for IPSec:

- IPSec Policy Agent service
- Internet Security Association and Key Management Protocol (ISAKMP)
- Oakley Key Management protocol
- IPSec driver

The ISAKMP and Oakly Key Management protocols are collectively referred to as IKE protocols.

IPSec Policy Agent Service

During system initialization, the IPSec Policy Agent service retrieves IPSec polices from the Active Directory service. The IPSec Policy Agent service passes the policy information to the IPSec network driver and the IKE protocols. The IPSec Policy Agent service does not store policies locally; instead, it must retrieve them from the Active Directory store. The IPSec Policy Agent service also starts both the IKE protocols and the IPSec driver.

ISAKMP/Oakley (IKE) Protocols

Using the information in the IPSec policy, the IKE protocols negotiate and establish a Security Association (SA) between computers. The Kerberos protocol service authenticates the identities of the communicating computers. Finally, the IKE protocols send the SA and key information to the IPSec driver.

IPSec Driver

This driver examines all IP packets for a match with an IP filter. If a match is found, the IPSec driver holds the packets in a queue while the IKE protocols generate the necessary SA and key to secure the packet. After the IPSec driver receives the information from the IKE protocols, the driver encrypts the IP packets and sends them to the destination computer.

Example of IPSec Communication

In this example, User 1 on Computer A is sending data to User 2 on Computer B. IP Security has been implemented for both computers. Figure 27.11 provides an overview of the IPSec communication process. The numbered steps shown in the illustration are described on the following page.

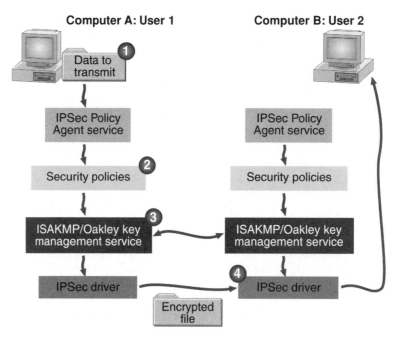

Figure 27.11 An example of the IPSec communication process

At the user level, the process of securing the IP packets is transparent and works as follows:

1. User 1 launches an application that communicates on the network by using TCP/IP to send data to User 2. The security policies assigned to Computer A and Computer B determine the level of security for the network communication.

2. The IPSec Policy Agent service retrieves the policies and passes them to the IKE protocols and IPSec driver.

3. The IKE protocols on each computer use the negotiation policies associated with the assigned security policy to establish the key and a common negotiation method, or SA. The results of the policy negotiation are passed between the two computers to the IPSec driver, which uses the key to encrypt the data.

4. Finally, the IPSec driver sends the encrypted data to Computer B. The IPSec driver on Computer B decrypts the data and passes it on to the receiving application.

Lesson Summary

Windows 2000 extends security by supporting a number of technologies that are based on public key security, including the SChannel authentication package, smart cards, Authenticode, the EFS, and IPSec. The SChannel authentication package implements SSL 3.0 and the TLS 1.0. SSL and TLS are flexible security protocols that can be layered on top of other transport protocols. Smart cards are credit-card-sized devices that can be used to store a user's public key, private key, and certificate. Smart cards are a secure way to protect and control a user's keys instead of storing them on a computer. Authenticode technology allows software publishers to digitally sign any form of active content, including multiple-file archives. These signatures can be used to verify both the publishers of the content and the content integrity at download time. EFS is an extension to the NTFS file system that provides strong data protection and encryption for files and folders. The encryption technology is based on the use of public keys and runs as an integrated system service. IPSec in Windows 2000 is designed to protect sensitive data on a TCP/IP network. IPSec is useful when the network between two communicating computers is not secure. It provides confidentiality, integrity, and authentication of IP traffic per packet.

Lesson 3: The Kerberos Protocol in Windows 2000

A standard process within computer security is to include a function that requires users to prove that they are who they claim to be. This affirmation of identity is accomplished when the user supplies the correct password for the user account. For example, when User1 attempts to connect to a server to access a file, the server must be sure that it is really User1 sending the request. Traditionally, the server assumes that it is User1 because the correct password was supplied when the connection was established. Stronger security is accomplished by having a trusted third party verify the identity of the user. This is a core function of the Kerberos authentication protocol.

After this lesson, you will be able to

- Describe the Kerberos protocol and how it works in Windows 2000

Estimated lesson time: 35 minutes

Overview of the Kerberos Protocol

The Kerberos protocol is the default authentication provider in Windows 2000 and the primary security protocol. It allows users to use a single logon to access all resources. The Kerberos protocol verifies both the identity of the user and the integrity of the session data. This is accomplished by having a Kerberos protocol service installed on each domain controller and a Kerberos client installed on all computers running Windows 2000.

Note The Active Directory client for Windows 95 and Windows 98 allows users to log on by using the Kerberos v5 authentication protocol.

When the Kerberos authentication protocol is used, a trusted Kerberos service on a server verifies the user's identity. Before connecting to the server the user requests a ticket from the Kerberos service, called the Kerberos Key Distribution Center service, to confirm the user's identity. The user then sends this ticket to the target server. Because the server trusts the Kerberos service to vouch for user identities, the server accepts the ticket as proof of the authenticity of the user.

When using the Kerberos authentication protocol, users can no longer log on and then access resources simply by providing a valid user ID and the correct password. Instead of trusting the source, the resource must contact the Kerberos service to obtain a ticket that vouches for the user. The Kerberos service operates as a trusted third party to generate session keys and grant tickets for specific client/server sessions.

When the Kerberos service issues a ticket, it contains the following components:

- Session key
- Name of the user to whom the session key was issued
- Expiration period of the ticket
- Any additional data fields or settings that may be required

The expiration period of a ticket is defined by the domain policy. If a ticket expires during an active session, the Kerberos service notifies the client and the server to refresh the ticket. The Kerberos service then generates a new session key and the session is resumed.

Kerberos Protocol Terms

To better understand the Kerberos protocol, you should review the following terms used to describe the various components of the Kerberos protocol.

Principal

A *principal* is a uniquely named user, client, or server that participates in a network communication.

Realm

A *realm* is an authentication boundary, which can be compared to a Windows 2000 domain. Each organization wishing to run a Kerberos server establishes its own realm. A Windows 2000 domain is a Kerberos realm but is named domain to maintain naming conventions established previously for Windows NT.

Secret Key

A *secret key* is an encryption key that is shared by a client or a server and a trusted third party to encrypt the information that is to be moved between them. In the case of the Kerberos protocol, the trusted third party is the Kerberos service. In the case of a principal, the secret key is typically based upon a hash or encryption of the principal's password. Secret keys are never transmitted on the network; only the encrypted information is transmitted.

Session Key

The *session key* is a temporary encryption key used between two principals, with a lifetime limited to the duration of a single login session. The session key is exchanged between the communication partners and is therefore known as a shared secret. The session key is always sent encrypted.

Authenticator

An *authenticator* is a record that is used to verify that a request actually originated from the principal. An authenticator contains information that verifies the identity of the sender and the time the request was initiated. This information is encrypted with the shared session key that is known only by the communicating principals. An authenticator is typically sent along with a ticket to allow the receiver to verify that the intended client recently initiated a request.

Key Distribution Center

The key distribution center (KDC) provides two functions: acting as the authentication server (AS) and the ticket granting service (TGS). The TGS distributes tickets to clients that wish to connect to services on the network. However, before a client can use the TGS to obtain tickets, it must first obtain a special ticket (the ticket granting ticket [TGT]) from the AS.

Privilege Attribute Certificate

The privilege attribute certificate (PAC) is a structure that contains the user's security ID (SID).

Tickets

In a basic Kerberos protocol exchange, the client contacts the TGS and requests a ticket for the target server before contacting the target server. A *ticket* is a record that allows a client to authenticate itself to a server; it is simply a certificate issued by the Kerberos service. The ticket is encrypted so that only the target server is able to decrypt and read it. Tickets contain the identity of the requesting client, the timestamp, the servers session key, the lifetime of the ticket, and other information (such as the PAC) that helps verify the identity of the client to the target server. Tickets are reusable within their life span, which is usually 8 hours.

Ticket Granting Tickets

One method for using the Kerberos protocol is to simply request a ticket for each target server from the TGS portion of the Kerberos service whenever the user wants to access the specified target server. Using this method, the response from the request would contain a session key and other information that is encrypted with the user's secret key. This method results in a component of the user's secret key being exposed on the network every time a new ticket request is made.

In Windows 2000, the Kerberos protocol protects the secret key by initially authenticating the user and then requesting a ticket granting ticket (TGT). A TGT is a request for a ticket and a random session key to be used with the TGS portion of the Kerberos service. After obtaining the ticket, the user can contact a service at any time; the requested ticket does not come from the AS, but from the TGS. The reply is encrypted not with the user's secret key, but with the session key that the AS provided for use with the TGS.

Features of the Kerberos Protocol

The Kerberos protocol has several advantages over traditional challenge/response authentication systems.

Mature Open Standard

The Windows 2000 implementation of the Kerberos protocol complies with RFC 1510 and RFC 1964. It can interoperate with other implementations of the Kerberos protocol that also comply with the RFCs. Therefore, Kerberos protocol clients on other platforms, such as UNIX, can be authenticated by Windows 2000. In some cases, however, implementation-dependent values do not exist or are unavailable. In the absence of required data, the Windows 2000 Kerberos service attempts to match the principal name in the ticket either to a Windows 2000 user account or to a default account created for this purpose.

Faster Connection Authentication

When using the Kerberos protocol, servers do not need to do pass-through authentication. A server running Windows 2000 can verify the client credentials by using the client-supplied ticket, without having to query the Kerberos service. This is because the client will have already obtained a Kerberos protocol ticket from a domain controller, which the server can then use to build the client's access token. Since the server is required to do less work when establishing a connection, it can more easily accommodate a large number of simultaneous connection requests.

Mutual Authentication

The Kerberos protocol provides mutual authentication of both the client and server. The Windows NTLM authentication protocol provides only client authentication, and it assumes that all servers are trusted. It does not verify the identity of the server that a client connects to. The assumption that all servers can be trusted is no longer valid. Mutual authentication of both client and server is an important foundation for secure networks.

Delegation of Authentication

Delegation of authentication allows a user to connect to an application server, which in turn can connect to one or more additional servers on the client's behalf, by using the client's credentials.

Transitive Trusts

Authentication credentials issued by one Kerberos service are accepted by all Kerberos services within the domain.

Kerberos Authentication Process

The Kerberos authentication process involves the client computer negotiating exchanges between the target server and the KDC. Figure 27.12 provides an overview of the authentication process. The numbered steps shown in the illustration are described below.

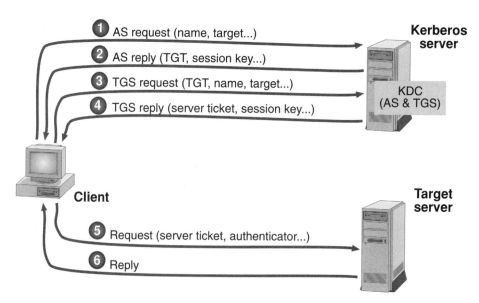

Figure 27.12 Kerberos authentication process

The Kerberos authentication process works as follows:

1. The client sends an initial AS request to the AS portion of the Kerberos service. The AS includes the client's principal name and the principal name of the target server for which it is requesting a ticket.

2. The Kerberos service generates an AS reply and sends it to the client. The reply contains the following:

   - A TGT for the TGS portion of the Kerberos service. The TGT is encrypted with the TGS secret key. The TGT contains the user's SID. By encrypting the TGT with the TGS secret key, the client is unable to change the SID properties.

   - A session key for exchanges with the TGS portion of the Kerberos service. The session key is encrypted with the client's secret key. The client's secret key is a computation of the client's password. It is similar to the session key used in NTLM challenge/response. The encryption here makes it difficult for someone to steal the session key.

3. The client generates and sends a TGS request that contains the client's and target server's principal names, realms, and the TGT that identifies the client.

4. The TGS portion of the Kerberos service generates and sends a TGS reply to the client. This reply contains a ticket for the target server. The ticket is encrypted with the server's secret key. The server's secret key is a computation of the password generated when the server joined the domain. The reply also includes other information, including the session key.

5. The client extracts the session key for the target server and generates a request for the server. This request contains the target server and an authenticator encrypted with the session key. The client sends this request to the target server by using an established transport path.

6. The target server decrypts the ticket by using its secret key to obtain the session key. The server then uses the session key to decrypt the authenticator to verify the client. If the client has requested mutual authentication, the target server generates a reply encrypted with the session key and sends it to the client. Mutual authentication not only authenticates the client to the target server, but also authenticates the target server to the client.

Note The AS and TGS exchanges with the Kerberos service operate over UDP port 88. The exchanges between the client and target server are dependent on the protocol in use between the two principals.

Kerberos Protocol Delegation

Occasionally, it is necessary for an application server to connect to another server on behalf of a client. Like impersonation, delegation is used to ensure that proper security permissions are applied against the application server's request.

The Kerberos authentication protocol supports delegated authentication. This type of authentication is used when a client transaction involves multiple servers. In this case, each of the verifying servers obtains another ticket and authenticates the ticket to the requested server on behalf of the client. There is no restriction on the number of consecutive servers that can delegate authentication. This is different from impersonation, in that the server accesses remote resources on the behalf of the client instead of local resources.

Figure 27.13 provides an overview of the Kerberos protocol delegation process. The numbered steps in the diagram are described below.

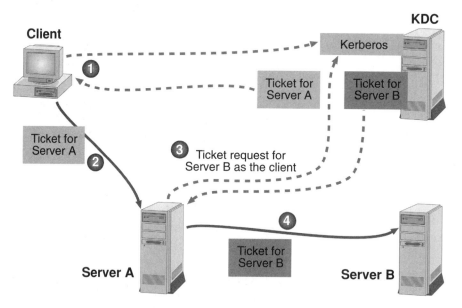

Figure 27.13 Kerberos protocol delegation process

The following steps describe the access of resources involving two servers:

1. The client requests and receives a ticket for target Server A from the Kerberos service.

2. The client sends the ticket directly to Server A.

3. Server A sends a request, impersonating the client, to the Kerberos service for a ticket for target Server B. The Kerberos service responds with a ticket that allows the client to access Server B.

4. Server A can send the ticket to Server B, accessing Server B as the client.

Kerberos Protocol Logon Processes

The addition of the Kerberos protocol as an authentication package in Windows 2000 affects various aspects of the logon process. However, the portions of the logon process that run before an authentication package becomes involved remain unchanged in Windows 2000.

Local Interactive Logon

When a local interactive logon occurs, the user logs on with a user account that exists on the local computer rather than with a domain user account. Figure 27.14 provides an overview of the local interactive logon process in Windows 2000. The numbered steps in the diagram are described below.

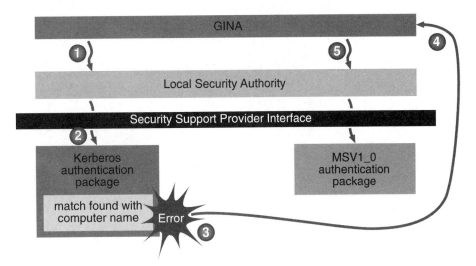

Figure 27.14 Local interactive logon process

For local user accounts, the following takes place in Windows 2000:

1. When the Graphical Identification and Authentication (GINA) DLL receives the logon request, it forwards the request to the Local Service Authority (LSA). This request specifies the Kerberos protocol as the authentication package to use because this is the default package in Windows 2000.

2. LSA processes the request and sends it to the Kerberos authentication package.

3. When the Kerberos protocol receives the logon request. The Kerberos protocol returns an error because it is used only when authenticating logon requests for domain user accounts, not local user accounts.

4. LSA receives the error and returns an error to the GINA.

5. The GINA resubmits the logon request to LSA specifying the "MSV1_0" authentication package. The logon process then takes place as it would for a local interactive logon under Windows NT 4.0.

Domain Interactive Logon

The exchange that occurs when a user logs on to Windows 2000 with a domain user account is similar to the basic Kerberos protocol exchange. Figure 27.15 provides an overview of this logon process. The number steps in the diagram are described below.

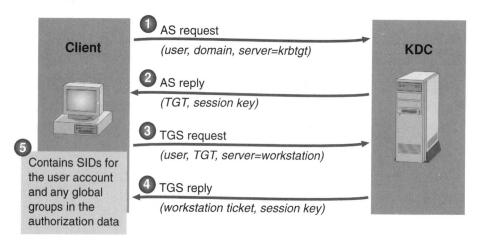

Figure 27.15 Domain interactive logon process

The following are the steps in the domain interactive logon process:

1. When the logon request reaches the LSA, it passes the request to the Kerberos authentication package. The client sends an initial AS request to the Kerberos service, providing the user name and domain name. This is a request for authentication and a TGT. The request is made by using the principal name of krbtgt@<*domain_name*>, where <*domain_name*> is the name of the domain in which the user account is located. The first domain controller in the domain automatically generates the krbtgt@<*domain_name*> account.

2. The Kerberos service generates an AS reply containing a TGT (encrypted with the Kerberos secret key) and a session key for the TGS exchanges (encrypted with the client's secret key). This response is sent back to the client. The authorization data portion of the TGT contains the SID for the user account and SIDs for any global groups to which the user belongs. The SIDs are returned to the LSA for inclusion in the user's access token. The SIDs are copied by the Kerberos service from the TGT into subsequent tickets obtained from the Kerberos service.

3. The client generates and sends a TGS request containing the client's principal name and realm, the TGT to identify the client, and the local workstation name as the target server. This is done to request access to the local computer for the user.

4. The Kerberos service generates and sends a TGS reply. This reply contains a ticket for the workstation and other information, including the session key (encrypted by using the session key from the TGT). Also included in the authorization data portion of the TGS reply are the SIDs for the user account and any global groups copied by the Kerberos service from the original TGT.

5. The Kerberos authentication package returns the list of SIDs to the LSA.

Windows 2000 services use the Kernel Mode SSPI to perform authentication. Instead of communicating directly with the Kerberos authentication package, both services access the Kerberos protocol through an authentication package built into LSA. This authentication package is called the Negotiate package.

During startup, both the Server and Workstation services initialize their interface with the Negotiate package in LSA by using SSPI. During this process, the server service obtains a credential handle for its default credentials.

The network communication occurs in two segments: protocol negotiation and session setup. Before a user can establish a session with the server, the client computer and the server must agree on the security protocol to use by determining which version of security they both support. Once the client has been authenticated and has a ticket, it can establish a session with the server.

Kerberos Protocol Public Key Support

Windows 2000 extends the functionality of the Kerberos protocol to allow it to interact with the Active Directory service. Windows 2000 includes extensions to the Kerberos v5 authentication protocol to support public key–based authentication. The public key extensions allow clients to request an initial TGT by using a private key. The Kerberos service verifies such a request by using the user's public key that is obtained from the user's X.509 certificate published to the Active Directory store. In order to obtain a ticket, the user's X.509 certificate must be stored in their user object. If the Kerberos service finds the certificate, the Kerberos service issues a ticket for the client and the standard Kerberos authentication procedure is followed thereafter. This replaces the secret key that is known only to the principal and the KDC. Smart cards, for example, use public key extensions provided by the Kerberos protocol.

Lesson Summary

The Kerberos protocol is the default authentication provider in Windows 2000 and the primary security protocol. To better understand the Kerberos protocol, you should be familiar with the terms common to the Kerberos protocol, including principal, realm, secret key, session key, authenticator, KDC, AS, TGS, PAC, ticket, and TGT. The Kerberos authentication process involves the client computer negotiating exchanges between the target server and the KDC. The Kerberos authentication protocol supports delegated authentication. When a local interactive logon occurs, the user logs on with a user account that exists on the local computer rather than with a domain user account. The exchange that occurs when a user logs on to Windows 2000 with a domain user account is similar to the basic Kerberos protocol exchange. Windows 2000 services use the Kernel Mode SSPI to perform authentication. In addition, Windows 2000 extends the functionality of the Kerberos protocol to allow it to interact with Active Directory service. Windows 2000 includes extensions to the Kerberos v5 authentication protocol to support public key–based authentication.

Lesson 4: Security Configuration Tools

Windows 2000 provides a set of security configuration tools that are designed to reduce the costs associated with security configuration and analysis of Windows 2000 networks. These tools are the Microsoft Management Console (MMC) snap-ins that allow you to configure Windows 2000 security settings and perform periodic analyses of the system to ensure that the configuration remains intact or to make necessary changes over time. Security settings include security policies (account and local policies), access control (services, files, and the registry), event logs, group membership (restricted groups), IPSec security policies, and public key policies. The security configuration tools include three snap-ins: the Security Configuration And Analysis snap-in, the Security Templates snap-in, and the Group Policy snap-in.

After this lesson, you will be able to

- Understand how the security configuration tools are used to configure security settings and analyze system security in your Windows 2000 network

Estimated lesson time: 30 minutes

Security Configuration And Analysis Snap-In

The Security Configuration And Analysis snap-in allows you to configure and analyze local system security.

Security Configuration

The Security Configuration And Analysis snap-in can also be used to directly configure local system security. You can import security templates created with the Security Templates snap-in and apply these templates to the group policy object (GPO) for the local computer. This immediately configures the system security with the levels specified in the template.

Security Analysis

The state of the operating system and applications on a computer is dynamic. For example, security levels may be required to change temporarily to enable immediate resolution of an administration or network issue; this change can often go unreversed. This means that a computer may no longer meet the requirements for enterprise security.

Regular analysis enables an administrator to track and ensure an adequate level of security on each computer as part of an enterprise risk management program. Analysis is highly specified; information about all system aspects related to security is provided in the results. This enables an administrator to tune the security levels and, most importantly, to detect any security flaws that may occur in the system over time.

The Security Configuration And Analysis snap-in enables quick review of security analysis results. Recommendations are presented along with current system settings, and icons or remarks are used to highlight any areas where current settings do not match the proposed level of security. The Security Configuration And Analysis snap-in also allows you to resolve any discrepancies revealed by analysis.

If frequent analysis of a large number of computers is required, as in a domain-based infrastructure, the Secedit command-line tool may be used as a method of batch analysis. However, analysis results still must be viewed by using the Security Configuration And Analysis snap-in. For more information about the Secedit utility, see Windows 2000 Help.

Using the Security Configuration And Analysis Snap-In

The Security Configuration And Analysis snap-in (Figure 27.16) reviews and analyzes your system security settings and recommends modifications to the current system settings. Administrators can use the snap-in to adjust the security policy and detect security flaws that arise in the system.

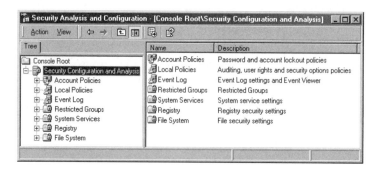

Figure 27.16 Security Configuration And Analysis snap-in

The Security Configuration And Analysis snap-in allows you to perform a variety of tasks. They are:

- Set a working database
- Import a security template
- Analyze system security
- Review security analysis results
- Configure system security
- Edit the base security configuration
- Export a security template

For details about how to perform each of these tasks, see Windows 2000 Help.

Security Templates Snap-In

A security template is a physical representation of a security configuration; it is a file where a group of security settings may be stored. Windows 2000 includes a set of security templates. Each template is based on the role of a computer. The templates range from security settings for low security domain clients to highly secure domain controllers. They can be used as provided, be modified, or serve as a basis for creating custom security templates.

Using the Security Templates Snap-In

The Security Templates snap-in (Figure 27.17) is a tool for creating and assigning security templates for one or more computers.

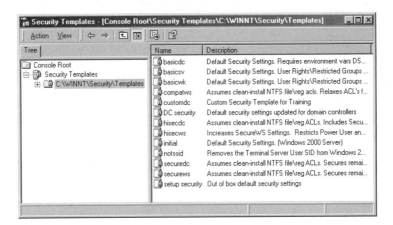

Figure 27.17 Security Templates snap-in

A security template is a physical file representation of a security configuration, and can be applied to a local computer or imported to a GPO in the Active Directory service. When you import a security template to a GPO, Group Policy processes the template and makes the corresponding changes to the members of that GPO, which may be users or computers.

The Security Templates snap-in allows you to perform a variety of tasks:

- Customize a predefined security template
- Define a security template
- Delete a security template
- Refresh the security template list
- Set a description for a security template

Practice: Creating and Using the Security Analysis And Configuration Snap-In

In this practice you create a custom snap-in containing the Security Analysis And Configuration snap-in and the Security Templates snap-in. Next, you customize a template and open a new database using the custom template. You then analyze the security settings of Server01 against the template and apply the template's configuration to the security settings of Server01. Complete this practice on Server01.

Exercise 1: Creating a Security Analysis And Configuration Snap-in

You run the MMC and add the Security Analysis And Configuration snap-in. MMC version 1.2, which is included with Windows 2000, allows you to add multiple snap-ins to an existing console. For the purpose of clarity, in this practice you create a new console rather than adding to an existing console running other snap-ins.

1. Log on to Server01 as Administrator with a password of *password*.
2. Click Start and then click Run.

   The Run dialog box appears.
3. In the Open text box, type **mmc** and then click OK.

   An empty MMC console named Console1 opens.
4. Click the Console menu and then click Add/Remove Snap-in.

   The Add/Remove Snap-in dialog box appears.

5. Click the Add button.

    The Add Standalone snap-in window appears.

6. Scroll down and click Security Configuration And Analysis and then click the Add button.

7. Click Close.

    The Add/Remove Snap-in dialog box appears.

8. Click OK.

9. Click the Console menu and then click Save.

    The Save As dialog box appears.

10. In the File Name text box, type **Security** and then click Save.

Exercise 2: Adding and Configuring Security using the Security Template Snap-in to the Security Console

Before analyzing Server01 and applying new security settings, you install the Security Template snap-in to the Security console.

1. Click the Console menu, and then choose Add/Remove snap-in.

    The Add/Remove Snap-in dialog box appears.

2. Click the Add button.

    The Add Standalone Snap-in window appears.

3. Scroll down and click Security Templates, and then click the Add button.

4. Click Close.

    The Add/Remove Snap-in dialog box appears.

5. Click OK.

6. Click the Console menu and then click Save.

7. Expand the Security Templates node then expand the C:\WINNT\Security\Templates folder.

    All of the defined templates appear in the console tree and in the details pane.

8. Expand the Securedc.

    This is an incremental security template usually used after a basic security template is applied. For the purpose of this exercise, this template is sufficient.

9. Expand the Account Policies node, and then click Password Policy.

   Password policy settings appear in the details pane.

10. In the details pane, double-click Minimum Password Length.

    The Template Security Policy Setting dialog box appears.

11. In the Password Must Be At Least box, change the value to 5 characters and then click OK.

12. In the console tree, click Securedc.

13. Click the Action menu, and then click Save As.

    The Save As window appears.

14. In the File Name text box, type **customdc** and then click Save.

15. In the console tree, click Customdc.

16. Click the Action menu and click Set Description.

    The Security Template Description box appears.

17. In the Description box, type **Custom Security Template for Training** and click OK.

18. In the console tree, click the C:\WINNT\Security\Templates folder.

    Notice in the details pane that customdc now has a description associated with it.

19. Read the other template descriptions to familiarize yourself with the templates included with Windows 2000 Server.

Exercise 3: Creating a New Security Database

In this exercise you create a new security database.

1. In the console tree, click Security Configuration And Analysis and read the text in the details pane.

2. Click the Action menu, and then click Open Database.

   The Open Database dialog box appears.

3. In the File Name text box, type **training** and then click Open.

   The Import Template dialog box appears.

4. Click Customdc.inf, and then click Open.

   This is the custom template you created in the Exercise 2.

Exercise 4: Analyzing Current Security Settings

In this exercise you analyze the current settings of Server01 against the custom template you created in Exercise 2.

1. In the console tree, verify that the Security Configuration And Analysis node is selected.

2. Click the Action menu and then click Analyze Computer Now.

   The Perform Analysis dialog box appears and shows the path and name of the error log as C:\Documents and Settings\Administrator\Local Settings\Temp\training.log.

3. Click OK.

   The Analyzing System Security status box appears as various aspects of Server01's security configuration are checked against the template.

4. When the analysis is complete, expand the Security Configuration And Analysis node.

5. Expand the Account Policies node, and then click the Password Policy node.

   In the details pane, both template settings and the computer's settings are displayed for each policy. Discrepancies appear with a red circle with a white "X" in the center. Consistencies appear with a white circle and a green check mark in the center. If there is no flag or check mark, the security setting is not specified in the template.

6. In the console tree, click the Security Configuration And Analysis node.

7. Click the Action menu and then click Configure Computer Now.

   The Configure System dialog box appears.

8. Click OK.

9. Click the Action menu and then click Analyze Computer Now.

   The Perform Analysis dialog box appears.

10. Click OK.

11. Review the policy settings to verify that the Database Settings column is equivalent to the Computer Setting column.

12. Close the Security snap-in.

    The Microsoft Management Console message box appears.

13. Click Yes.

14. If a Save Security Templates window appears, click Yes.

Group Policy Snap-In

Security settings define the security-relevant behavior of the system. Through the use of GPOs in Active Directory service, administrators can centrally apply the security levels required to protect enterprise systems.

When determining settings for a GPO that contains multiple computers, the organizational and functional character of that given site, domain, or organizational unit (OU) must be considered. For example, the security levels necessary for an OU containing computers in a sales department would be very different from that for an OU containing finance department computers.

The Group Policy snap-in allows you to configure security centrally in the Active Directory store. A Security Settings folder is located on the Computer Configuration node and the User Configuration node. The security settings allow Group Policy administrators to set policies that can restrict user access to files and folders, set how many incorrect passwords a user can enter before the user is locked out, and control user rights, such as which users are able to log on at a domain server.

Lesson Summary

Windows 2000 provides a set of security configuration tools that allow you to configure Windows 2000 security settings and perform periodic analyses of the system to ensure that the configuration remains intact or to make necessary changes over time. The Security Configuration And Analysis snap-in allows you to configure and analyze local system security. It reviews and analyzes your system security settings and recommends modifications to the current system settings. The Security Templates snap-in allows you to create and assign security templates for one or more computers. The Group Policy snap-in allows you to configure security centrally in the Active Directory store.

Lesson 5: Microsoft Windows 2000 Auditing

In this lesson, you learn about Windows 2000 auditing, which is a tool for maintaining network security. Auditing allows you to track user activities and system-wide events. In addition, you learn about audit policies and what you need to consider before you set up a policy. You also learn how to set up auditing on resources and how to maintain security logs.

After this lesson, you will be able to

- Plan an audit strategy and determine which events to audit
- Set up auditing on Active Directory service objects and on files, folders, and printers
- Use Event Viewer to view a log and locate events

Estimated lesson time: 45 minutes

Overview of Windows 2000 Auditing

Auditing in Microsoft Windows 2000 is the process of tracking both user activities and Windows 2000 activities, called events, on a computer. Through auditing, you can specify that Windows 2000 writes a record of an event to the security log. The security log maintains a record of valid and invalid logon attempts and events related to creating, opening, or deleting files or other objects. An audit entry in the security log contains the following information:

- The action that was performed
- The user who performed the action
- The success or failure of the event and when the event occurred

Using an Audit Policy

An audit policy defines the types of security events that Windows 2000 records in the security log on each computer. The security log allows you to track the events that you specify.

Windows 2000 writes events to the security log on the computer on which the event occurs. For example, you can configure auditing so that any time someone tries to log on to the domain by using a domain user account and the logon attempt fails, Windows 2000 writes an event to the security log on the domain controller. The event is recorded on the domain controller rather than on the computer at which the logon attempt was made, because it is the domain controller that attempted to and could not authenticate the logon attempt.

You can set up an audit policy for a computer to do the following:

- Track the success and failure of events, such as logon attempts by users, an attempt by a particular user to read a specific file, changes to a user account or to group memberships, and changes to your security settings

- Eliminate or minimize the risk of unauthorized use of resources

You can use Event Viewer to view events that Windows 2000 has recorded in the security log. You can also archive log files to track trends over time—for example, to determine the use of printers or files or to verify attempts at unauthorized use of resources.

Planning an Audit Policy

When you plan an audit policy, you must determine the computers on which to set up auditing. Auditing is turned off by default. As you are determining which computers to audit, you must also plan what to audit on each computer. Windows 2000 records audited events on each computer separately.

The types of events that you can audit include the following:

- Access to files and folders

- Users logging on and off

- Shutting down and restarting a computer running Windows 2000 Server

- Changes to user accounts and groups

- Attempts to make changes to Active Directory objects

After you have determined the types of events to audit, you must determine whether to audit the success and/or failure of events. Tracking successful events can tell you how often Windows 2000 users or services gain access to specific files, printers, or other objects. You can use this information for resource planning. Tracking failed events can alert you to possible security breaches. For example, if you notice a lot of failed logon attempts by a certain user account, especially if these attempts are occurring outside normal business hours, an unauthorized person might be attempting to break into your system.

Consider the following guidelines in determining your audit policy:

- Determine if you need to track trends of system usage. If so, plan to archive event logs. Archiving these logs allows you to view how usage changes over time and allows you to plan to increase system resources before they become a problem.

- Review security logs frequently. You should set a schedule and regularly review security logs because configuring auditing alone does not alert you to security breaches.

- Define an audit policy that is useful and manageable. Always audit sensitive and confidential data. Audit only those events that provide you with meaningful information about your network environment. This minimizes usage of server resources and makes essential information easier to locate. Auditing too many types of events can create excess overhead for Windows 2000.

- Audit resource access by the Everyone group instead of the Users group. This ensures that you audit anyone who can connect to the network, not just the users for whom you create user accounts in the domain.

Implementing an Audit Policy

Auditing is a powerful tool for tracking events that occur on computers in your organization. To implement auditing, you must consider auditing requirements and set the audit policy. After you set an audit policy on a computer, you can implement auditing on files, folders, printers, and Active Directory objects.

Configuring Auditing

You can implement an audit policy based on the role of the computer in the Windows 2000 network. Auditing is configured differently for the following types of computers running Windows 2000:

- For member or standalone servers or computers running Windows 2000 Professional, an audit policy is set for each individual computer. For example, to audit user access to a file on a member server, you set the audit policy on that computer.

- For domain controllers, an audit policy is set for all domain controllers in the domain. To audit events that occur on domain controllers, such as changes to Active Directory objects, you configure a group policy for the domain, which applies to all domain controllers.

Note The types of events that you can audit on a domain controller are identical to those you can audit on a computer that is not a domain controller. The procedure is similar as well, but you use a group policy for the domain to control auditing for domain controllers.

Auditing Requirements

The requirements to set up and administer auditing are as follows:

- You must have the Manage Auditing And Security Log permission for the computer where you want to configure an audit policy or review an audit log. Windows 2000 grants these rights to the Administrators group by default.

- The files and folders to be audited must be on NTFS volumes.

Setting Up Auditing

Setting up auditing is a two-part process:

1. Setting the audit policy. The audit policy enables auditing of objects but does not activate auditing of specific objects.

2. Enabling auditing of specific resources. You identify the specific events to audit for files, folders, printers, and Active Directory objects. Windows 2000 then tracks and logs the specified events.

Setting an Audit Policy

The first step in implementing an audit policy is selecting the types of events that Windows 2000 audits. For each event that you can audit, the configuration settings indicate whether to track successful or failed attempts. You can set audit policies by using the Group Policy snap-in.

Table 27.3 describes the types of events that Windows 2000 can audit.

Table 27.3   Events That Can Be Audited by Windows 2000

Event	Description
Account logon events	A domain controller received a request to validate a user account.
Account management	An administrator created, changed, or deleted a user account or group. A user account was renamed, disabled, or enabled, or a password was set or changed.
Directory service access	A user gained access to an Active Directory object. You must configure specific Active Directory objects for auditing to log this type of event.
Logon events	A user logged on or logged off, or a user made or canceled a network connection to the computer.
Object access	A user gained access to a file, folder, or printer. You must configure specific files, folders, or printers for auditing. Directory service access is auditing a user's access to specific Active Directory objects. Object access is auditing a user's access to files, folders, and printers.
Policy change	A change was made to the user security options, user rights, or audit policies.
Privilege use	A user exercised a right, such as changing the system time. (This does not include rights that are related to logging on and logging off.)
Process tracking	A program performed an action. This information is generally useful only for programmers who want to track details of program execution.
System	A user restarted or shut down the computer, or an event occurred that affects Windows 2000 security or the security log. (For example, the audit log is full and Windows 2000 discards entries.)

To set an audit policy on a computer that is not a domain controller, create a custom MMC and add the Group Policy snap-in. In the console tree, select Audit Policy from the Computer Configuration node, as shown in Figure 27.18. The console displays the current audit policy settings in the details pane.

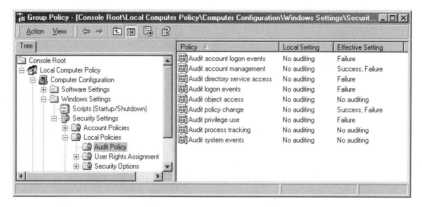

Figure 27.18 Group Policy snap-in with the Audit Policy folder selected

Changes that you make to your computer's audit policy take effect when one of the following events occurs:

- Policy propagation is initiated by typing **secedit /refreshpolicy machine_policy** at the command prompt and then pressing Enter.

- Your computer is restarted. Windows 2000 applies changes that you made to your audit policy the next time your computer is restarted.

- Policy propagation occurs. Policy propagation is a process that applies policy settings, including audit policy settings, to your computer. Automatic policy propagation occurs at regular, configurable intervals. By default, policy propagation occurs every 8 hours.

Auditing Access to Files and Folders

If security breaches are an issue for your organization, you can set up auditing for files and folders on NTFS partitions. To audit user access to files and folders, you must first enable the Audit object access policy, which includes files and folders.

Once you have set your audit policy to audit object access, you enable auditing for specific files and folders and specify which types of access, by which users or groups, to audit. To enable auditing for a specific file or folder, open the Properties dialog box for that file or folder, select the Security tab, and then click Advanced. Select the Auditing tab and configure auditing for the selected file or folder.

Auditing Access to Active Directory Objects

To audit Active Directory object access, you must configure an audit policy and then set auditing for specific objects, such as users, computers, OUs, or groups by specifying which types of access and access by which users to audit.

To enable auditing of access to Active Directory objects, enable the Audit directory services access policy in the Group Policy snap-in.

To enable auditing for specific Active Directory objects, open the Active Directory Users And Computers snap-in and select Advanced Features from the View menu. Open the Properties dialog box for the object that you want to audit. On the Security tab, click Advanced. Select the Auditing tab and configure auditing for that object.

Auditing Access to Printers

You can audit access to printers in order to track access to sensitive printers. To audit access to printers, enable the Audit Object Access policy, which includes printers. Then enable auditing for specific printers, and specify which types of access and access by which users to audit. After you select the printer, you use the same steps that you use to set up auditing on files and folders.

To set up auditing on a printer, open the Properties dialog box for the printer that you want to audit. On the Security tab, click Advanced. Select the Auditing tab and configure auditing for the printer.

Using Event Viewer

You can use Event Viewer to perform a variety of tasks, including viewing the audit logs that are generated as a result of setting audit policies and auditing events. You can also use Event Viewer to view the contents of security log files and find specific events within log files.

Windows 2000 Logs

You can use Event Viewer to view information contained in Windows 2000 logs. By default there are three logs available to view in Event Viewer. These logs are described in Table 27.4.

Table 27.4   Logs Viewable with Event Viewer

Log	Description
Application log	Contains errors, warnings, or information generated by programs, such as a database program or an e-mail program. The program developer presets which events to record.
Security log	Contains information about the success or failure of audited events. The events that Windows 2000 records are a result of your audit policy.
System log	Contains errors, warnings, and information generated by Windows 2000. Windows 2000 presets which events to record.

Note If additional services are installed, they might add their own event log. For example, the DNS service logs DNS events in the DNS Server log.

Viewing the Security Log

The Security log contains information about events that are monitored by an audit policy, such as failed and successful logon attempts. You can view the Security log in the Event Viewer snap-in, as shown in Figure 27-19.

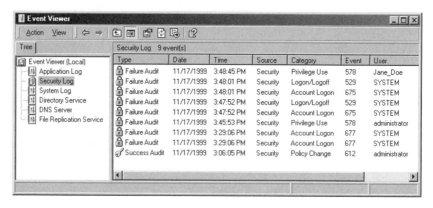

Figure 27.19 Event Viewer snap-in with the Security Log selected

In the details pane, Event Viewer displays a list of log entries and summary information for each item.

Successful events appear with a key icon, and unsuccessful events appear with a lock icon. Other important information includes the date and time that the event occurred, the category of the event, and the user who generated the event. The category indicates the type of event, such as object access, account management, directory service access, or logon events.

Windows 2000 records events in the Security log on the computer at which the event occurred. You can view these events from any computer as long as you have administrative privileges for the computer where the events occurred. To view the Security log on a remote computer, point Event Viewer to a remote computer when you add this snap-in to a console.

Locating Events

When you first start Event Viewer, it automatically displays all events that are recorded in the selected log. To change what appears in the log, you can locate selected events by using the Filter command. You can also search for specific events by using the Find command. To filter or find events, start Event Viewer and then click Filter or click Find on the View menu.

Managing Audit Logs

You can track trends in Windows 2000 by archiving event logs and comparing logs from different periods. Viewing trends helps you determine resource use and plan for growth. If unauthorized use of resources is a concern, you can also use logs to determine patterns of usage. Windows 2000 allows you to control the size of the logs and to specify the action that Windows 2000 takes when a log becomes full.

You can configure the properties of each individual audit log. To configure the settings for logs, select the log in Event Viewer, and then display the Properties dialog box for the log.

Use the Properties dialog box for each type of audit log to control the size of each log, which can be from 64 KB to 4,194,240 KB (4 GB). The default size is 512 KB. You can also use the log properties to control the action that Windows 2000 takes when the log fills up.

Tip Use the Security Configuration And Analysis snap-in to configure settings for Event Viewer.

Archiving Logs

Archiving security logs allows you to maintain a history of security-related events. Many companies have policies on keeping archive logs for a specified period to track security-related information over time. If you want to save the log file, clear all events, or open a log file, select the log from the Event Viewer console tree, and then select the appropriate option from the Action menu.

Lesson Summary

Auditing in Windows 2000 is the process of tracking both user activities and Windows 2000 activities, called events, on a computer. Through auditing, you can specify that Windows 2000 writes a record of an event to the Security log. An audit policy defines the types of security events that Windows 2000 records in the Security log on each computer. The Security log allows you to track the events that you specify. When you plan an audit policy you must determine on which computers to set up auditing. As you are determining which computers to audit, you must also plan what to audit on each computer. To implement auditing, you need to consider auditing requirements and set the audit policy. After you set an audit policy on a computer, you can implement auditing on files, folders, printers, and Active Directory objects. You can use Event Viewer to view the audit logs that are generated as a result of setting the audit policy and auditing events. You can also use Event Viewer to view the contents of Security log files and find specific events within log files.

Review

The following questions are intended to reinforce key information presented in this chapter. If you are unable to answer a question, review the appropriate lesson and then try the question again. Answers to the questions can be found in Appendix A, "Questions and Answers."

1. Which key is associated with the creation of digital signatures, the public key or the private key? Explain your answer.

2. What security credential(s) are in use if you are supporting client computers running Windows 2000 and Windows NT that authenticate to servers running Windows 2000 Server and Windows NT Server?

3. How can a security template be used to facilitate configuration and analysis of security settings?

4. Where is the Certificate Services Enrollment page and what is its purpose?

5. What steps must you follow to enable auditing of specific file objects on domain controllers in a domain where Group Policy is enabled?

APPENDIX A

Questions and Answers

Introduction

Review

1. What is the primary difference between Windows 2000 Professional and Windows 2000 Server?

   Windows 2000 Professional is optimized for use alone as a desktop operating system, as a networked computer in a peer-to-peer workgroup environment, or as a workstation in a Windows 2000 Server domain environment. Windows 2000 Server is optimized for use as a file, print, and application server, as well as a Web-server platform.

2. What is the major difference between a workgroup and a domain?

   The major difference between a workgroup and a domain is where the user account information resides for user logon authentication. For a workgroup, user account information resides in the local security database on each computer in the workgroup. For the domain, the user account information resides in the Active Directory database.

3. Which of the integral subsystems is responsible for running Active Directory?

   The Security subsystem.

4. What is the purpose of the Active Directory service?

Active Directory is the directory service included in Windows 2000 Server. It stores information about objects on a network and makes this information available to users and network administrators. Active Directory gives network users access to permitted resources anywhere on the network using a single logon process. It provides network administrators with an intuitive hierarchical view of the network and a single point of administration for all network objects.

5. What happens when a user logs on to a domain?

Windows 2000 sends the logon information to a domain controller, which compares it to the user's information in the directory. If the information matches, the domain controller authenticates the user and issues an access token for the user.

6. How would you use the Windows 2000 Security dialog box?

The Windows 2000 Security dialog box provides easy access to important security options, including the ability to lock a computer, change a password, stop programs that are not responding, log off a computer, and shut down the computer. You can also determine the domains to which you are logged on and the user account that you used to log on.

Chapter 1

Review

1. How do you install the Windows 2000 deployment tools, such as the Setup Manager wizard and the System Preparation tool?

To install the Windows 2000 deployment tools, display the contents of the Deploy.cab file, which is located in the Support\Tools folder on the Windows 2000 CD-ROM. Select all the files you want to extract, right-click a selected file, and then select Extract from the menu. You will be prompted for a destination and the location and name of a folder for the extracted files.

2. Which five resources must you have to use Remote Installation Services to install Windows 2000 Professional?

You must have Windows 2000 Server with RIS installed, a DNS server available on the network, a DHCP server available on the network, a Windows 2000 domain to provide Active Directory directory service, and client computers that meet the Net PC specification or have a boot floppy to connect to the RIS server.

3. What utility is provided in Windows 2000 to create boot floppies and how do you access it?

   Windows 2000 ships with the Windows 2000 Remote Boot Disk Generator, rbfg.exe, which is used to create boot disks. It is found on the RIS server in the folder where the Windows 2000 Professional installation files are stored. The path is RemoteInst\Admin\i386\rbfg.exe.

4. You are planning on installing 45 computers with Windows 2000 Professional. You have determined that these 45 computers have seven different network adapter cards. How do you determine whether these seven different types of network adapter cards are supported by the boot floppies you created?

   The boot floppies created using Rbfg only support the PCI-based network adapters listed in the Adapter List. Start Rbfg.exe and then click the Adapter List button to see the list of supported adapters.

5. You have a portable computer running Windows 95 and you want to upgrade it to Windows 2000. The computer has 16 MB of RAM, and this can be upgraded to 24 MB. Can you upgrade this computer to Windows 2000? If not, how would you make it so this computer was able to access Active Directory directory service?

   No, Windows 2000 Professional requires at least 64 MB of memory. You can install the Directory Service Client for Windows 95 or 98. The laptop would then be able to access Active Directory directory service.

6. Name at least two problems the System Preparation tool resolves when creating and copying a master disk image to other computers.

   The System Preparation tool adds a system service to the master image that will create a unique local domain security ID (SID) the first time the computer to which the master image is copied is started.

   The System Preparation tool adds a Mini-Setup wizard to the master disk image that runs the first time the computer to which the master image is copied is started. It guides the user through entering the user-specific information such as the end-user license agreement, the Product ID, user name, company name, and time zone selection.

   The System Preparation tool causes the master image to force the computer on which the master image is copied to run a full Plug and Play device detection. Hence peripherals, such as the network adapter, the video adapter, and sound cards on the computer on which the disk image was copied need not be identical to the ones on the computer on which the image was generated.

7. Your company has decided to install Windows 2000 Professional on all new computers that are purchased for desktop users. What should you do before you purchase new computers to ensure that Windows 2000 can be installed and run without difficulty?

   Verify that the hardware components meet the minimum requirements for Windows 2000. Also, verify that all of the hardware components that are installed in the new computers are listed on the Windows 2000 HCL. If a component is not listed, contact the manufacturer to verify that a Windows 2000 driver is available.

8. You are attempting to install Windows 2000 Professional from a CD-ROM. However, you have discovered that your computer doesn't support booting from the CD-ROM drive. How can you install Windows 2000?

   Start the computer by using the Setup boot disks. When prompted, insert the Windows 2000 Professional CD-ROM, and then continue setup.

9. You are installing Windows 2000 Server on a computer that will be a client in an existing Windows 2000 domain. You want to add the computer to the domain during installation. What information do you need, and which computers must be available on the network before you run the Setup program?

   You need the DNS domain name of the domain that you are joining. You must also make sure that a computer account for the client exists in the domain, or you must have the user name and password of a user account in the domain with the authority to create computer accounts in the domain. A server running the DNS service and a domain controller in the domain you are joining must be available on the network.

10. You are using a CD-ROM to install Windows 2000 Professional on a computer that was previously running another operating system. How should you configure the hard disk to simplify the installation process?

    Use a disk partitioning tool to remove any existing partitions, and then create and format a new partition for the Windows 2000 installation.

11. You are installing Windows 2000 Professional over the network. Before you install to a client computer, what must you do?

    Locate the path to the shared installation files on the distribution server. Create a 500-MB FAT partition on the target computer (1 GB recommended). Create a client disk with a network client so that you can connect from the computer, without an operating system, to the distribution server.

Chapter 2

▶ Page 101

12. Click Computer Management (Local), and then click the Extensions tab.

The MMC displays a list of available extensions for the Computer Management snap-in.

What option determines which extensions MMC displays in the Available Extensions list in this dialog box?

The available extensions depend on which snap-in you select.

▶ Page 124

8. Change the working directory to the root directory of drive C (if necessary) or to the root directory of the drive where you mounted your volume, type **dir**, and then press Enter.

How much free space does the Dir command report?

Answer will vary.

Why is there a difference between the free space reported for drive C and the free space reported for C:\Mount?

If you mounted your volume on a drive other than drive C, replace C with the appropriate drive letter.

▶ Page 132

1. On the Quota tab of the Local Disk (C:) Properties dialog box, click the Quota Entries button.

Windows 2000 displays the Quota Entries For Local Disk (C:) window.

Are any user accounts listed? Why or why not?

Yes. The accounts listed are those that have logged on and gained access to drive C.

5. Click OK.

Windows 2000 displays the Add New Quota Entry dialog box.

What are the default settings for the user you just set a quota limit for?

Limit disk space to 10 MB and Set the warning level to 6 MB. These are the default settings that are selected for drive C.

▶ Page 133

5. Copy the i386 folder from your CD-ROM to the User5 folder.

Windows 2000 Professional begins copying files from the i386 folder on the CD-ROM to a new i386 folder in the User5 folder on drive C. After copying several files, however, Windows 2000 displays the Error Copying File Or Folder dialog box, indicating that there isn't enough room on the disk.

Why did you get this error message?

You have exceeded your quota limit and since the Deny Disk Space To Users Exceeding Quota Limit check box is selected, once you exceed your quota limit, you can't use more disk space.

▶ Page 145

4. In the details pane, double-click Hardware Resources, and then double-click IRQs.

Are there any IRQs being shared?

Answer will vary.

Review

1. What should you do if you can't see any output on the secondary display?

   If you can't see any output on the secondary display, try the following:

   - **Activate the device in the Display Properties dialog box.**

   - **Confirm that you chose the correct video driver.**

   - **Restart the computer and check its status in Device Manager.**

   - **Switch the order of the display adapters on the motherboard.**

2. You have configured recovery options on a computer running Windows 2000 Professional to write debugging information to a file if a system failure occurs. You notice, however, that the file isn't being created. What could be causing this problem?

   The problem could be one or more of the following:

   - **The paging file size could be set to less than the amount of physical RAM in your system.**

   - **The paging file might not be located on your system partition.**

   - **You might not have enough free space to create the Memory.dmp file.**

3. You installed a new network interface card (NIC) in your computer, but it doesn't seem to be working. Describe how you would troubleshoot this problem.

   You would do the following to troubleshoot the problem:

   - **Check Device Manager to determine whether Windows 2000 properly detected the network card.**

   - **If the card isn't listed in Device Manager, run the Add/Remove Hardware wizard to have Windows 2000 detect the new card. If the card is listed in Device Manager but the icon representing the new card contains either an exclamation mark or a stop sign, view the properties of the card for further details. You might need to reinstall the drivers for the card, or the card might be causing a resource conflict.**

4. You install a new 10-GB disk drive that you want to divide into five equal 2-GB sections. What are your options?

   You can leave the disk as a basic disk and then create a combination of primary partitions (up to three) and logical drives in an extended partition; or, you can upgrade the disk to a dynamic disk and create five 2-GB simple volumes.

5. You are trying to create a striped volume on your Windows NT Server to improve performance. You confirm that you have enough unallocated disk space on two disks in your computer, but when you right-click an area of unallocated space on a disk, a dialog box appears indicating that your only option is to create a partition. What is the problem and how would you resolve it?

   You can create striped volumes only on dynamic disks. The fact that you are presented with the option to create a partition rather than a volume indicates that the disk you are trying to use is a basic disk. You will need to upgrade all of the disks that you want to use in your striped volume to dynamic disks before you stripe them.

6. You add a new disk to your computer and attempt to extend an existing volume to include the unallocated space on the new disk, but the option to extend the volume isn't available. What is the problem and how would you resolve it?

   The existing volume is not formatted with Microsoft Windows 2000 File System (NTFS). You can extend only NTFS volumes. You should back up any data on the existing volume, convert it to NTFS, and then extend the volume.

7. You dual boot your computer with Windows 98 and Windows 2000 Professional. You upgrade a second drive—which you are using to archive files—from basic storage to dynamic storage. The next time you try to access your archived files from Windows 98, you are unable to read the files. Why?

   Only Windows 2000 can read dynamic storage.

8. You are the administrator for a computer running Windows 2000 Professional. You want to restrict users to 25 MB of available storage space. How do you configure the volumes on the computer?

   Format all volumes with NTFS and enable disk quotas for all of the volumes. Specify a limit of 25 MB and select the Deny Disk Space To Users Exceeding Quota Limit check box.

9. The Sales department archives old sales data on a network computer running Windows 2000 Professional. Several other departments share the server. You have begun to receive complaints from users in other departments that the server has little remaining disk space. What can you do to alleviate the problem?

   Compress the folders that the Sales department uses to store archive data.

10. A friend of yours just installed Windows 2000 Professional on his home computer. He called you to help him configure Advanced Power Management (APM), and when you told him to double-click Power Options in Control Panel and click on the APM tab, he told you he did not have an APM tab. What is the most likely reason there is no APM tab?

    The most likely reason there is no APM is that his computer does not have an APM-based BIOS installed. When Windows 2000 does not detect an APM-based BIOS, Setup does not install APM and there is no APM tab in the Power Options Properties dialog box.

11. Many commercial airlines require you to turn off portable computers during certain portions of a flight. Does placing your computer in Hibernate mode comply with these airline regulations? Why or why not?

    No. Hibernate mode makes your computer appear to be turned off, but it is not. You must shut down your computer to comply with these airline regulations.

12. Your boss has started to manually assign resource settings to all devices, including Plug and Play devices, and wants you to finish the job. What should you do?

Explain to your boss that it is not a good idea to manually change or assign resource settings for Plug and Play devices. Windows 2000 arbitrates resources, but if you manually assign them, then Windows 2000 will not be able to arbitrate the assigned resources if requested by another Plug and Play device.

13. You receive a call at the Help desk from a user who is trying to configure her fax settings, and she tells you that she does not have an Advanced Options tab. What could the problem be?

For the Advanced Options tab to be displayed, the user must be logged on as Administrator or have administrator privileges.

Chapter 3

▶ Page 188

1. In the first example, the Data folder is shared. The Sales group has the shared folder Read permission for the Data folder and the NTFS Full Control permission for the Sales subfolder.

What are the Sales group's effective permissions for the Sales subfolder when they gain access to the Sales subfolder by making a connection to the Data shared folder?

The Sales group has the Read permission for the Sales subfolder because when shared folder permissions are combined with NTFS permissions, the more restrictive permission applies.

2. In the second example, the Users folder contains user home folders. Each user home folder contains data that is accessible only to the user for whom the folder is named. The Users folder has been shared, and the Users group has the shared folder Full Control permission for the Users folder. User1 and User2 have the NTFS Full Control permission for only their home folder and no NTFS permissions for other folders. These users are all members of the Users group.

What permissions does User1 have when he or she accesses the User1 subfolder by making a connection to the Users shared folder? What are User1's permissions for the User2 subfolder?

User1 has the Full Control permission for the User1 subfolder because both the shared folder permission and the NTFS permission allow Full Control. User1 can't access the User2 subfolder because she or he has no NTFS permissions to gain access to it.

▶ Page 231

3. Which user is specified in the Notify box? Why?

The Notify box currently displays the user Administrator because Administrator printed the document.

1. In the Readme.txt Document Properties dialog box, on the General tab, notice the default priority.

What is the current priority? Is it the lowest or highest priority?

The current priority is the default of 1, which is the lowest priority.

Review

1. A print server can connect to two different types of print devices. What are these two types of print devices, and what are the differences?

The two types are local and network-interface print devices. A local print device is connected directly to a physical port of the print server. A network-interface print device is connected to the print server through the network. Also, a network-interface print device requires a network interface card.

2. You have added and shared a printer. What must you do to set up client computers running Windows 2000 so that users can print, and why?

You (or the user) must make a connection to the printer from the client computer. When you make a connection to the printer from the client computer, Windows 2000 automatically copies the printer driver to the client computer.

3. What advantages does connecting to a printer by using http://*server_name*/printers provide for users?

It allows a user to make a connection to a printer without having to use the Add Printer wizard. It makes a connection to a Web site, which displays all of the printers for which the user has permission. The Web site also provides information on the printers to help the user make the correct selection. Also, a Web designer can customize this Web page, for example displaying a floor plan that shows the location of print devices, which makes it easier for users to choose a print device.

4. Why would you connect multiple printers to one print device?

To set priorities between the printers so that users can send critical documents to the printer with the highest priority. These documents will always print before documents that are sent from printers with lower priorities.

5. Why would you create a printer pool?

   To speed up printing. Users can print to one printer that has several print devices so that documents do not wait in the print queue. It also simplifies administration; it's easier to manage one printer for several print devices than it is to manage one printer for each print device.

6. Which printer permission does a user need to change the priority on another user's document?

   The Manage Documents permission.

7. In an environment where many users print to the same print device, how can you help reduce the likelihood of users picking up the wrong documents?

   Create a separator page that identifies and separates printed documents.

8. Can you redirect a single document?

   No. You can change the configuration of the print server only to send documents to another printer or print device, which redirects all documents on that printer.

9. A user needs to print a large document. How can the user print the job after hours, without being present while the document prints?

   You can control print jobs by setting the printing time. You set the printing time for a document on the General tab of the Properties dialog box for the document. To open the Properties dialog box for a document, select the document in the printer's window, click the Document menu, and then click Properties. Click Only From in the Schedule section of the Properties dialog box, and then set the Only From hour to the earliest time you want the document to begin printing after regular business hours. Set the To time to a couple of hours before normal business hours start. To set the printing time for a document, you must be the owner of the document or have the Manage Documents permission for the appropriate printer.

10. What are the advantages of using a Web browser to administer printing?

    You can administer any printer on a Windows 2000 print server on the intranet by using any computer running a Web browser, regardless of whether the computer is running Windows 2000 or has the correct printer driver installed. Additionally, a Web browser provides a summary page and reports real-time print device status, and you can customize the interface.

11. What is the default permission when a volume is formatted with NTFS? Who has access to the volume?

    The default permission is Full Control. The Everyone group has access to the volume.

12. If a user has Write permission for a folder and is also a member of a group with Read permission for the folder, what are the user's effective permissions for the folder?

    The user has both Read permission and Write permission for the folder because NTFS permissions are cumulative.

13. If you assign the Modify permission to a user account for a folder and the Read permission for a file, and then you copy the file to that folder, which permission does the user have for the file?

    The user can modify the file because the file inherits the Modify permission from the folder.

14. What happens to permissions that are assigned to a file when the file is moved from one folder to another folder on the same NTFS volume? What happens when the file is moved to a folder on another NTFS volume?

    When the file is moved from one folder to another folder on the same NTFS volume, the file retains its permissions. When the file is moved to a folder on a different NTFS volume, the file inherits the permissions of the destination folder.

15. If an employee leaves the company, what must you do to transfer ownership of his or her files and folders to another employee?

    You must be logged on as Administrator to take ownership of the employee's folders and files. Assign the Take Ownership special access permission to another employee to allow that employee to take ownership of the folders and files. Notify the employee to whom you assigned Take Ownership to take ownership of the folders and files.

16. What three details should you check when a user can't gain access to a resource?

    Check the permissions that are assigned to the user account and to groups in which the user is a member.

    Check whether the user account, or a group of which the user is a member, has been denied permission for the file or folder.

    Check whether the folder or file has been copied to any other file or folder or moved to another volume. If it has, the permissions will have changed.

17. The Sales department archives existing sales data on a network computer running Windows 2000 Professional. Several other departments share the server. You have begun to receive complaints from users in other departments that the server has little remaining disk space. What can you do to alleviate the problem?

Compress the folders that the Sales department uses to store archive data.

18. When a folder is shared on a FAT volume, what does a user with the Full Control shared folder permissions for the folder have access to?

All folders and files in the shared folder.

19. What are the shared folder permissions?

Full Control, Change, and Read.

20. By default, what are the permissions that are assigned to a shared folder?

The Everyone group is assigned the Full Control permission.

21. When a folder is shared on an NTFS volume, what does a user with the Full Control shared folder permissions for the folder have access to?

Only the folder, but not necessarily any of the folder's contents. The user would also need NTFS permissions for each file and subfolder in the shared folder to gain access to those files and subfolders.

22. When you share a public folder, why should you use centralized data folders?

When you use centralized data folders you can back up data easily.

23. What is the best way to secure files and folders that you share on NTFS partitions?

Put the files that you want to share in a shared folder and keep the default shared folder permission (the Everyone group with the Full Control permission for the shared folder). Assign NTFS permissions to users and groups to control access to all contents in the shared folder or to individual files.

Chapter 4

Review

1. What information is required to create a local user account?

   A user name.

2. What are built-in user accounts and what are they used for?

   Windows 2000 automatically creates accounts called built-in accounts. Two commonly used built-in accounts are Administrator and Guest. You use the built-in Administrator account to manage the overall computer network (for example, creating and modifying user accounts and groups, and setting account properties on user accounts). You use the built-in Guest account to give occasional users the ability to log on and gain access to resources.

Chapter 5

▶ Page 289

6. To verify that the IP address is working and configured for your adapter, type **ping 127.0.0.1** and then press Enter.

   What happens?

   Four "Reply from 127.0.0.l" messages should appear.

7. If you have a computer that you are using to test connectivity, type **ping** *ip_address* (where *ip_address* is the IP address of the computer you are using to test connectivity), and then press Enter. If you don't have a computer to test connectivity, skip this step and proceed to step 7.

   What happens?

   Four "Reply from *ip_address*" messages should appear.

▶ Page 290

4. Click Obtain An IP Address Automatically.

   Which IP address settings will the DHCP Service configure for your computer?

   IP address and subnet mask.

▶ Page 291

2. At the command prompt, type **ipconfig /renew** and then press Enter.

There will be a pause while Windows 2000 attempts to locate a DHCP server on the network.

What message appears, and what does it indicate?

DHCP Server Unreachable.

Your computer was not assigned an address from a DHCP server because there wasn't one available.

2. Pressing Spacebar as necessary, record the current TCP/IP settings for your local area connection in the following table.

Setting	Value
IP address	**Answer will vary.**
Subnet mask	**Answer will vary.**
Default gateway	**Answer will vary.**

Is this the same IP address that was assigned to your computer in Exercise 3? Why or why not?

No, the IP address isn't the same as the one assigned in Exercise 3. In this exercise, the Automatic Private IP Addressing feature of Windows 2000 assigned the IP address because a DHCP server wasn't available. In Exercise 3, the DHCP Service assigned an IP address.

▶ Page 292

5. If you have a computer to test TCP/IP connectivity with your computer, type **ping** *ip_address* (where *ip_address* is the IP address of the computer that you are using to test connectivity), and then press Enter. If you don't have a computer to test connectivity, skip this step and proceed to Exercise 5.

Were you successful? Why or why not?

Answers will vary. If you don't have a computer that you can use to test your computer's connectivity, you can't do this exercise.

- **No, because the computer you are using to test your computer's connectivity is configured with a static IP address in another network and no default gateway is configured on your computer.**

- **Yes, because the computer you are using to test your computer's connectivity is also configured with an IP address assigned by Automatic Private IP Addressing. Further, it is on the same subnet so a default gateway is unnecessary.**

Review

1. Your computer running Windows 2000 Client for Microsoft Networks was configured manually for TCP/IP. You can connect to any host on your own subnet, but you can't connect to or even ping any host on a remote subnet. What is the likely cause of the problem and how would you fix it?

   The default gateway might be missing or incorrect. You specify the default gateway in the Internet Protocol (TCP/IP) Properties dialog box (under Network And Dial-Up Connections in My Network Places). Other possibilities are that the default gateway is offline or that the subnet mask is incorrect.

2. While you're using the Network Connection wizard, you must configure two new settings regarding sharing the connection. Describe the difference between these two settings.

   The settings are whether you want to allow others that use the computer to use the connection (access to the connection) and whether you want to allow other computers to access resources through this port (sharing the connection once it is established).

3. What is callback and when might you want to enable it?

   The callback feature causes the remote server to disconnect and call back the client attempting to access the remote server. By using callback, you can have the bill for the telephone call charged to your telephone number rather than to the telephone number of the user who called in. You can also use callback to increase security by specifying the callback number. Even if an unauthorized user calls in, the system calls back at the number you specified, not the number of the unauthorized user.

Chapter 6

▶ Page 346

2. Restart the computer.

   What error do you receive when attempting to restart the computer?

   NTLDR is missing. Press Ctrl+Alt+Del to restart.

Review

1. What benefits do you gain by Microsoft digitally signing all system files?

   Windows 2000 drivers and operating system files are digitally signed by Microsoft to ensure the files have not been tampered with. Some applications overwrite existing operating files as part of their installation process. These files may cause system errors that are difficult to troubleshoot. Device Manager allows you to look at the Driver tab and verify that the digital signer of the installed driver is correct. This can save you many frustrating hours of trying to resolve problems caused by a file that replaced one or more original operating system drivers.

2. What are three tools/utilities Microsoft has provided to help you make sure the files on your system have the correct digital signature?

   Windows 2000 provides Device Manager, which allows you to verify that the digital signer of the installed driver is correct. Windows 2000 also provides two utilities to verify the digital signatures. The first utility is the File Signature Verification utility (sigverif). Windows 2000 also provides System File Checker (SFC), a command-line utility that you can use to check the digital signature of files.

3. You need to schedule a maintenance utility to automatically run once a week on your computer, which is running Windows 2000 Professional. How do you accomplish this?

   Use Task Scheduler to schedule the necessary maintenance utilities to run at specific times.

4. You need to create a custom console for an administrator who needs to use only the Computer Management and Active Directory Manager snap-ins. The administrator

   a. Must not be able to add any additional snap-ins.

   b. Needs full access to all snap-ins.

   c. Must be able to navigate between snap-ins.

   Which console mode would you use to configure the custom console?

   User mode, Full Access.

5. A user calls the help desk in a panic. She spent 15 hours editing a proposal as an offline file at her house. Over the weekend, her boss came into the office and spent about 4 hours editing the same proposal. She needs to synchronize the files, but she doesn't want to lose her edits or those made by her boss. What can she do?

If both her cached offline copy of the file and the network copy of the file are edited, she should rename her version of the file so that both copies will exist on her hard disk and on the network. She can then compare the two and edit her version, adding any edits made by her boss.

6. You install a new device driver for a SCSI adapter in your computer. When you restart the computer, however, Windows 2000 stops responding after the kernel load phase. How can you get Windows 2000 to restart successfully?

Select the Last Known Good Configuration option to use the LastKnownGood configuration control to start Windows 2000 because it doesn't contain any reference to the new, and possibly faulty, driver.

Chapter 7

▶ Page 372

1. Use the Group Policy snap-in to configure the following Account Policies settings:

   - A user should have at least five different passwords before he or she accesses a previously used password.

   - After changing a password, a user must wait 24 hours before he or she can change it again.

   - A user should change his or her password every three weeks.

   Which settings did you use for each of the three listed items?

   Set Enforce Password History to 5 so that a user must have at least five different passwords before he or she can access a previously used password.

   Set Minimum Password Age to one day so that a user must wait 24 hours before he or she can change it again.

   Set Maximum Password Age to 21 days so that a user must change his/her password every three weeks.

2. Change your password to *waters.*

   Were you successful? Why or why not?

   You were successful because the minimum password length is set to 6, and the password *waters* contains six characters.

▶ Page 373

3. Change your password to *papers*.

Were you successful? Why or why not?

You weren't successful because you must wait 24 hours (one day) before you can change your password a second time. A Change Password dialog box appeared indicating that you can't change the password at this time.

5. Use Account Lockout Policy settings to do the following:

- Lock out a user account after four failed logon attempts.

- Lock out user accounts until the administrator unlocks the user account.

Which Account Lockout Policy settings did you use for each of the two conditions?

Set Account Lockout Threshold to 4 to lock out a user account after four failed logon attempts. When you set one of the three Account Lockout Policy options and the other two options have not been set, a dialog box appears indicating that the other two options will be set to default values.

Set Account Lockout Duration to 0 to have locked accounts remain locked until the administrator unlocks them.

▶ Page 381

2. Start Windows Explorer and open the file File1.txt in the Secret folder.

What happens?

A Notepad dialog box appears indicating that Access Is Denied.

Review

1. Why should you use groups?

Use groups to simplify administration by granting rights and assigning permissions once to the group rather than multiple times to each individual member.

2. How do you create a local group?

Start the Computer Management snap-in and expand Local Users And Groups. Right-click Groups, and then click New Group. Fill in the appropriate fields and then click Create.

3. Are there any consequences to deleting a group?

When you delete a group, the unique identifier that the system uses to represent the group is lost. Even if you create a second group with the same name, the group will not have the same identifier, so you must grant the group any permissions or rights that it once had, and you must reassign membership to users who need to be a member of that group.

4. What's the difference between built-in local groups and local groups?

You create local groups and assign the appropriate permissions to them. You can customize local groups to meet your specific needs.

Windows 2000 Professional comes with precreated built-in local groups. You can't create built-in local groups. Built-in local groups give rights to perform system tasks on a single computer, such as backing up and restoring files, changing the system time, and administering system resources.

5. What two tasks must you perform to audit access to a file?

Set the audit policy for object access and configure the file for the type of access to audit.

6. Who can set up auditing for a computer?

By default, only members of the Administrators group can set up and administer auditing. You can also give other users the Manage Auditing and Security log user right, which is required to configure an audit policy and review audit logs.

7. Why would you want to force users to change passwords?

Forcing users to change passwords regularly decreases the chances of an unauthorized person breaking into your computer. If a user account and password combination for your computer falls into unauthorized hands, forcing users to change their passwords regularly makes it more likely that the user account and password combination will fail, providing more security to the computer.

8. Why would you want to control the length of the passwords used on your computers?

Longer passwords are more difficult to figure out because there are more characters to discover. In general, you want to do what you can to make it difficult to get unauthorized access to your computers.

9. Why would you want to lock out a user account?

If a user forgets his or her password, he or she can ask the administrator to reset the password. If someone repeatedly enters an incorrect password, the person is probably trying to gain unauthorized access to your computer. Setting a limit on the number of failed logon attempts and locking out any user account that exceeds this number makes it more difficult for someone to gain unauthorized access to your computers.

10. Why would you want to force users to press Ctrl+Alt+Del before they can log on to your computers?

To increase security on your computers, you can force users to press Ctrl+Alt+Del before they can log on. This key combination is recognized only by Windows and ensures that only Windows is receiving the password and not a Trojan horse program waiting to capture your password.

11. How do you prevent the last user name from being displayed in the Windows Security or Log On To Windows dialog box?

To prevent the last user name from being displayed in the Windows Security or Log On To Windows dialog box, click the Local Policies node in the console tree of the Local Security Settings window, and then click Security Options. In the details pane, right-click Do Not Display Last User Name In Logon Screen, click Security, and then enable this feature.

Chapter 8

▶ Page 469

4. What folder appears directly under the win2000dist folder that does not appear in the i386 folder?

OEM

16. What is the purpose of the UDF file?

The UDF file allows each automated setup to be customized with the unique settings contained in the file. To start an unattended setup, the UniqueID contained in the UDF file is specified on the command line. During setup the unique data in the UDF file is merged into the answer file.

Review

1. If you are installing Microsoft Windows NT in a dual-boot configuration on the same computer, which file system should you choose? Why?

   The best choice is FAT. Although both Windows 2000 and Windows NT support NTFS, Windows 2000 supports advanced features provided by NTFS 5.0. For example, file encryption is supported in NTFS 5.0, but previous versions of NTFS did not support file encryption. Therefore, when Windows NT is running on a dual-boot computer, it will not be able to read encrypted files created in Windows 2000.

2. Which licensing mode should you select if users in your organization require frequent access to multiple servers? Why?

   Per Seat licensing is the best choice for this environment. A Per Seat license is more expensive per client computer than Per Server licensing but becomes much less expensive when many client computers access several servers. If Per Server licensing is used in this environment, each server must be individually licensed for client computer access.

3. You are installing Windows 2000 Server on a computer that will be a member server in an existing Windows 2000 domain. You want to add the computer to the domain during installation. What information do you need, and what computers must be available on the network, before you run the Setup program?

   You need the DNS domain name of the domain that you are joining. You must also make sure that a computer account for the member server exists in the domain or you must have the user name and password of a user account in the domain with the authority to create computer accounts in the domain. A server running the DNS service and a domain controller in the domain you are joining must be available on the network. If dynamic IP addressing is configured during setup, a server supporting DHCP must be available to assign an address to the computer.

4. You are using a CD-ROM to install Windows 2000 Server on a computer that was previously running another operating system. There is not enough space on the hard disk to run both operating systems, so you have decided to repartition the hard disk and install a clean copy of Windows 2000 Server. Name two methods for repartitioning the hard disk.

1. Use a disk partitioning tool like MS-DOS fdisk to remove any existing partitions, and then create and format a new partition for the Windows 2000 installation.

2. Start the computer by booting from the Windows 2000 Server Setup disk. During the Text-mode portion of installation, you can delete the partition and then create and format a new one. Continue the installation of Windows 2000 Server to the new partition.

5. You are installing Windows 2000 over the network. Before you install to a client computer, what must you do?

Locate the path to the shared installation files on the distribution server. Create a 671-MB FAT partition on the target computer (2 GB recommended). Create a client disk with a network client so that you can connect from the computer, without an operating system, to the distribution server.

6. A client is running Windows NT 3.5 Server and is interested in upgrading to Windows 2000. From the list of choices, choose all possible upgrade paths:

   a. Upgrade to Windows NT 3.51 Workstation and then to Windows 2000 Server.

   b. Upgrade to Windows NT 4.0 Server and then to Windows 2000 Server.

   c. Upgrade directly to Windows 2000 Server.

   d. Run Convert.exe to modify any NTFS partitions for file system compatibility with Windows 2000, and then upgrade to Windows 2000 Server.

   e. Upgrade to Windows NT 3.51 Server and then to Windows 2000 Server.

b and e

Answer a is wrong because Windows NT Workstation (3.5*x* or 4.0) cannot be upgraded to Windows 2000 Server.

Answer c is wrong because Windows NT 3.5 cannot be directly upgraded to Windows 2000 Server.

Answer d is wrong because the Windows 2000 Setup process automatically upgrades NTFS to NTFS version 5.0.

7. In your current network environment, user disk space utilization has been a major issue. Describe three services in Windows 2000 Server to help you manage this issue.

   Answer 1: Disk quotas in NTFS version 5.0 allow you to control per-user disk space usage by disk.

   Answer 2: Disk compression allows you to compress data at the disk, directory, or file level. Disk compression does not affect a user's allocated quota. Quotas are calculated based on the uncompressed file size.

   Answer 3: Remote Storage Services provides an extension to disk space by making removable media accessible for file storage. Infrequently used data is automatically archived to removable media. Archived data is still easily accessible to the user; however, data retrieval is slower than with unarchived data.

8. What is the purpose of using the /tempdrive: or /t: installation switches with Winnt32.exe or Winnt.exe, respectively?

   The Winnt32.exe /tempdrive: switch and the Winnt.exe /t: switch copy the Windows 2000 Server installation files to the drive specified with the switch. For example, Winn32.exe /tempdrive:d copies all Windows 2000 installation files to the D: partition. Using this switch also tells Setup which partition should be the boot partition for the installation of Windows 2000 Server.

9. You are asked to develop a strategy for rapidly installing Windows 2000 Server for one of your clients. You have assessed their environment and have determined that the following three sets of computers require Windows 2000 Server:

   - There are 30 unidentical computer configurations currently running Windows NT Server 4.0 that need to be upgraded to Windows 2000 Server.

   - There are 20 identical computers that need a new installation of Windows 2000 Server.

   - Remote sites will run a clean installation of Windows 2000 Server. You want to make sure that they install a standard image of Windows 2000 Server that is consistent with your local configuration of the operating system. You will provide them with hard disks that they will install in their servers.

   What are the steps for your installation strategy?

   For the 30 computers that need to be upgraded, build an answer file and a distribution share using Setup Manager. Further customize the answer file with a text editor. Use a product such as SMS to auto-

mate the distribution of operating system upgrades. If SMS is not available, run winnt32 with the /unattend switch and the other switches described in Lesson 1 that are designed to automate the installation process.

For the 20 identical computers, set up one computer with the operating system and all applications that you need to replicate on all other computers. Copy sysprep.exe, sysprepcl.exe, and sysprep.inf (answer file format) into the $OEM\$1\Sysprep folder. Make sure the [GuiRunOnce] section of the answer file calls sysprep.exe with the -quiet switch to continue the setup without any user interaction. Create an image with a third-party image utility, and copy this image to each of the 20 identical computers. Upon reboot, Mini-Setup will run using information in sysprep.inf to complete the setup.

For the remote sites, use /Syspart to prepare the disks for the second half of the installation. Ship the disks to the remote sites and instruct the local administrators to install them in their servers as the bootable drive, usually by setting the SCSI ID to 0 or 7, depending on the SCSI hardware.

You can also use the bootable CD-ROM method. If you use this method, include a floppy disk containing the winnt.sif file to automate Setup.

10. What is the purpose of the OEM folder and the subfolders created beneath it by Setup Manager?

The oem folder contains the optional cmdlines.txt file and subfolders for original equipment manufacturer (OEM) files and other files needed to complete or customize automated installation. Folders below oem hold all files that are not part of a standard installation of Windows 2000 Server. These folders map to specific partitions and directories on the computer running an unattended installation. The folders below OEM and their purposes are as follows:

$$	Copies files from this distribution folder location to $windir$ or $systemroot$. For a standard installation of Windows 2000 Server, these variables map to C:\Winnt. There are other folders below this one too, such as Help for OEM help files and System32 for files that must be copied to the System32 directory.
$1	Copies files from this distribution folder location to the root of the system drive. This location is equivalent to the %systemdrive% variable. In a typical installation of Windows 2000 Server, this variable maps to the C:\ root. The $1 folder contains a drivers folder for third-party driver installation.

Drive letter   **Folders named after a specific drive letter map to the drive letter on the local computer. For example, if you need to copy files to the E: drive during setup, create an E folder and place files or folders in this folder.**

Text mode   **Contains any special HALs or mass storage device drivers required for installing and running Windows 2000 Server.**

11. How does Cmdlines.txt differ from [GuiRunOnce]?

Cmdlines.txt runs commands before a user is logged on and in the context of the system account. Any command line or installation that can occur without a user logon can complete using Cmdlines.txt. [GuiRunOnce], a section in the answer file, runs in the context of a user account and after the user logs on for the first time. This is an ideal place to run user specific scripts, such as scripts that add printers or scripts that automatically configure a user's e-mail configuration.

12. How does Syspart differ from Sysprep?

Syspart is a switch of Winnt32.exe. This switch completes the Pre-Copy phase of Windows 2000 Server Setup. After it is complete, the disk used for the Pre-Copy phase can be installed in another computer. Upon booting from this disk, the Text-mode phase of setup continues. Syspart is ideal for dissimilar systems that require a faster setup procedure than is provided by running Windows 2000 Setup manually. Syspart can be further automated by calling an answer file as well as Syspart from the Winnt32 command line.

Sysprep prepares a computer for imaging. After the operating system and applications are installed on a computer, Sysprep is run to prepare it for imaging. Next, an imaging utility is used to create an image of the prepared disk. The image is downloaded to identical or nearly identical computers, and Sysprep Mini-Setup continues to complete the installation. The Mini-Setup process can be further automated with a Sysprep.inf file.

Chapter 9

▶ Page 547   10. What is the purpose of the default response rule?

The default response rule enables negotiation with computers requesting IPSec. A default response rule is added to each new policy you create, but it is not automatically activated. A default response rule can be used for any computer that does not require security, but must be able to appropriately respond when another computer requests secured communications. It can also be used as a template for defining custom rules.

Review

1. What is the purpose of a subnet mask?

   A mask is a portion of the IP address that enables IP to distinguish the network ID from the host ID.

2. What is the minimum number of areas in an OSPF internetwork?

   An OSPF internetwork always has at least one area called the backbone, whether or not it is subdivided into areas.

3. What is the NWLink Auto Detect feature?

   The Windows 2000 NWLink Auto Detect feature detects the frame type and network number that are configured on NetWare server(s) on the same network. NWLink Auto Detect is the recommended option for configuring both the network number and the frame type. If the Auto Detect feature selects an inappropriate frame type and network number for a particular adapter, you can manually reset an NWLink frame type or network number for that given adapter.

4. By what standards group is IPSec defined?

   IPsec is defined by the Internet Engineering Task Force (IETF) IP Security working group.

5. Define the difference between secret- and public-key cryptography.

   Secret key cryptography uses a single preshared key. Public key cryptography uses a key pair, one for encrypting data and verifying digital signatures and the second for decrypting data and creating digital signatures.

6. What functionality does ISAKMP/Oakley provide?

   ISAKMP/Oakley establishes a secure channel between two computers for communication and establishes an SA.

7. What are rules comprised of?

   Rules are comprised of IP filters, negotiation policies, authentication methods, IP tunneling attributes, and adapter types.

8. What is an IP filter used for?

   IP filters are used to check datagrams for a match against each filter specification. This allows for filtering based on the source and destination address, DNS name, protocol, or protocol ports.

9. How do System Monitor and Network Monitor allow you to monitor security on your network?

   System Monitor is used to monitor anything from hardware to software, and can also monitor security events such as Errors Access Permissions, Errors Granted Access, Errors Logon, and IIS Security. Network Monitor focuses exclusively on network activity to allow you to understand the traffic and behavior of your network components. If you install the full version available from Systems Management Server, you can capture and view every packet on the network.

10. How is Event Viewer used to monitor security?

   Although you can use Event Viewer to gather information about hardware and software problems, it can also be used to monitor Windows 2000 security events such as valid and invalid logon attempts. The security log can also contain events related to resource use, such as creating, opening, or deleting files or other objects.

11. How do you enable remote access logging in Windows 2000?

   You can enable event logging in the Event Logging tab on the properties of a remote access server in Routing and Remote Access.

Chapter 10

Review

1. Describe the differences between primary, secondary, and master name servers.

   A primary name server has zone information in locally maintained zone files. A secondary name server must download the zone information, they do not maintain a local file. A master name server is the source of the downloads for a secondary name server (which could be a primary or secondary name server).

2. Describe the difference between a domain and a zone.

   A domain is a branch of the DNS name space. A zone is a portion of a domain. A zone exists as a separate file on the disk storing resource records.

3. Describe the difference between recursive and iterative queries.

   In a recursive query, the client instructs the DNS server to respond with either the requested information or an error that the information was not found.

   In an iterative query, the DNS server responds with the best answer it has. If the information is not available, the typical answer is a referral to another name server that can help resolve the request.

4. List the files required for a Windows 2000 DNS implementation.

   Database file, cache file, and reverse lookup file.

5. Describe the purpose of the boot file.

   The boot file is used in the Berkeley Internet Name Daemon implementation to start up and configure the DNS server.

6. How many zones can a single DNS server host?

   A single DNS server can be configured to host zero, one, or multiple zones.

7. What benefits do DNS clients obtain from the dynamic update feature of Windows 2000?

   Dynamic update enables DNS client computers to register and dynamically update their resource records with a DNS server whenever changes occur. This reduces the need for manual administration of zone records, especially for clients that frequently move or change locations and use DHCP to obtain an IP address.

8. Name one benefit and one disadvantage of a caching-only server.

   The benefit provided by caching-only servers is that they do not generate zone transfer network traffic because they do not contain any zones. A disadvantage of a caching-only server is that when the server is initially started, it has no cached information and must build up this information over time as it services requests.

9. List and describe three DNS performance counters.

- **Dynamic update and secure dynamic update counters are used to measure registration and update activity generated by dynamic clients**

- **Memory usage counters are used to measure system memory usage and memory allocation patterns created by operating the server computer as a Windows 2000 DNS server**

- **Recursive lookup counters are used to measure queries and responses when the DNS Server service uses recursion to look up and fully resolve DNS names on behalf of requesting clients**

Chapter 11

Review

1. What is DHCP?

   Dynamic Host Configuration Protocol is a TCP/IP service protocol thatsimplifies the administrative management of IP address configuration by automating address configuration for network clients.

2. Describe the integration of DHCP with DNS.

   A DHCP server can enable dynamic updates in the DNS name space for any DHCP clients that support these updates. Scope clients can then use DNS with dynamic updates to update their computer name-to-IP address mapping information whenever changes occur to their DHCP-assigned address.

3. What is a DHCP client?

   The term client is used to describe a networked computer that requests and uses the DHCP services offered by a DHCP server.

4. What is IP autoconfiguration in Windows 2000?

   IP Autoconfiguration is the ability of Windows 2000–based clients to automatically configure an IP address and subnet mask if a DHCP server is unavailable at system start time.

5. Why is it important to plan an implementation of DHCP for a network?

   Many networks use WINS or DNS (or possibly both) for registering dynamic name-to-address mappings. To provide name resolution services, you must plan for interoperability of DHCP with these services. Most network administrators implementing DHCP also plan a strategy for implementing DNS and WINS servers.

6. What tool do you use to manage DHCP servers in Windows 2000?

The primary tool that you use to manage DHCP servers is DHCP Manager, which is a Microsoft Management Console (MMC) component that is added to the Administrative Tools menu when you install the DHCP service.

7. What is the source of most DHCP-related problems?

Most DHCP-related problems are identified as a client IP configuration failure. These failures are most often discovered by clients in one of the following ways:

- **The client might be configured to use an IP address not provided by the server.**

- **The server sends a negative response back to the client, and the client displays an error message or popup indicating that a DHCP server could not be found.**

The server leases the client an address but the client appears to have other network configuration–based problems, such as the inability to register or resolve DNS or NetBIOS names, or to perceive other computers beyond its subnet.

Chapter 12

Review

1. What is a VPN?

A VPN is a simulated point-to-point connection using encapsulation. This connection can span any underlying network, including the Internet. Security or some form of encryption is usually required to get the "private" part of the definition.

2. Demand-dial filters can screen traffic based on what fields of a packet?

Source and destination IP address, IP protocol identifier, source and destination ports, ICMP type, and ICMP code.

3. Is the following statement true or false? When setting dial-in user permissions (Allow Access, Deny Access) through the User Property page, RAPs are not used.

False. In the user interface it appears that RAP is not used. In actuality, the dial-in user settings work in conjunction with RAP.

4. Is the following statement true or false? DHCP packets are never sent over Routing and Remote Access links.

   False. Routing and Remote Access clients do not use DHCP to get an address, but may use DHCPINFORM packets to get other configuration options. The DHCP relay agent must be installed and using the "internal" interface for this to work.

5. What is the function of BAP?

   To bring up or drop modem or ISDN links as needed for bandwidth on demand.

6. What are some potential security risks you should identify in your security plan?

   It could be possible for competitors to gain access to proprietary product information, or unauthorized users could attempt to maliciously modify Web pages or overload computers so that they are unusable.

7. What is authentication and how can you implement it?

   Authentication is the process of identifying users who attempt to connect to a network. When users are authenticated on your network, they can utilize network resources based on their access permissions. To provide authentication to network users, you establish user accounts.

8. What are some security features of Windows 2000?

   - **Security templates**
   - **Kerberos authentication**
   - **Public key infrastructure (PKI)**
   - **IPSec management**
   - **NT file system encryption**

9. How can you secure a connection between your network and the Internet?

   To secure your organization's network for access to and from the Internet, you can put a firewall between the two networks. The firewall provides connectivity for network users to the Internet while minimizing the risks that connectivity introduces. It also prevents access to computers on your network from the Internet, except for those computers authorized to have such access.

10. What are some remote access protocols you can implement for security?

    - **Challenge Handshake Authentication Protocol (CHAP)**
    - **Microsoft Challenge Handshake Authentication Protocol (MS-CHAP)**
    - **Password Authentication Protocol (PAP)**
    - **Shiva Password Authentication Protocol (SPAP)**
    - **Extensible Authentication Protocol (EAP)**

11. Name two forms of encryption available for demand-dial connections.

    Microsoft Point-to-Point Encryption (MPPE) and Internet Protocol Security (IPSec).

Chapter 13

Review

1. What are three benefits of WINS?

    - **Automatic name registration and resolution of NetBIOS names**
    - **Provides internetwork and interdomain browsing**
    - **Eliminates the need for a local LMHOSTS file**

2. What two methods can be used to enable WINS on a client computer?

    Manual and automatic with DHCP.

3. How many WINS servers are required in an intranet of 12 subnets?

    Only one is required. It is recommended to have multiple servers for redundancy.

4. What types of names are stored in the WINS database?

    NetBIOS unique and group names.

Chapter 14

Review

1. What is the purpose of NAT?

   NAT allows computers on a small network, such as a home office, to share a single Internet connection.

2. What are the components of NAT?

   The translation component is the router on which NAT is enabled. The addressing component provides IP address configuration information to the other computers on the home network. The name resolution component becomes the DNS server for the other computers on the home network. When name resolution requests are received by the NAT computer, it forwards the name resolution requests to the Internet-based DNS server for which it is configured and returns the responses to the home network computer.

3. If a small business is using the 10.0.0.0 private network for its intranet and has been granted the public IP address of 198.200.200.1 by its ISP, to what public IP address does NAT map all private IP addresses being used on network 10.0.0.0?

   The NAT maps (using static or dynamic mappings) all private IP addresses being used on network 10.0.0.0 to the public IP address of 198.200.200.1.

4. What must you do to allow Internet users to access resources on your private network?

   You must configure a static IP address configuration on the resource server including IP address, subnet mask, default gateway, and DNS server. You should exclude the IP address being used by the resource computer from the range of IP addresses being allocated by the NAT computer. Next, you configure a special port, which is a static mapping of a public address and port number to a private address and port number.

Chapter 15

Review

1. What are certificates, and what is their purpose?

   A certificate (digital certificate, public-key certificate) is a digital document that attests to the binding of a public key to an entity. The main purpose of a certificate is to generate confidence that the public key contained in the certificate actually belongs to the entity named in the certificate.

2. What is a certificate authority (CA), and what does it do?

   Certificates are issued by a CA, which can be any trusted service or entity willing to vouch for the identities of those to whom it issues certificates, and the association of those identities with specific keys.

3. What are the four types of Microsoft certificate authorities?

   Enterprise root CA, enterprise subordinate CA, standalone root CA, and standalone subordinate CA.

4. Name one reason for a certificate revocation.

   - **Compromise, or suspected compromise, of an entity's private key**

   - **Fraud in obtaining the certificate**

   - **Change in status**

5. What are the five PKI standard certificate stores?

   MY, CA, TRUST, ROOT, and UserDS.

Chapter 16

Review

1. What is the Active Directory schema?

   The schema contains a formal definition of the contents and structure of Active Directory, including all attributes, classes, and class properties.

2. What is the purpose of an organizational unit (OU)?

An OU is a container used to organize objects within a domain into logical administrative groups that mirror your organization's functional or business structure. An OU can contain objects such as user accounts, contacts, groups, computers, printers, applications, file shares, and other OUs from the same domain.

3. What are sites and domains and how are they different?

A site is a combination of one or more IP subnets that should be connected by a high-speed link. A domain is a logical grouping of servers and other network resources organized under a single name. A site is a component of Active Directory's physical structure, whereas a domain is a component of the logical structure.

4. What is the difference between implicit two-way transitive trusts and explicit one-way nontransitive trusts?

An implicit two-way transitive trust is a trust between domains that are part of the Windows 2000 scalable namespace, for example, between parent and child domains within a tree and between the top-level domains in a forest. These trust relationships make all objects in all the domains of the tree available to all other domains in the tree.

An explicit one-way nontransitive trust is a relationship between domains that are not part of the same tree. One-way trusts support connections to existing pre-Windows 2000 domains to allow the configuration of trust relationships with domains in other trees.

5. What are the functions of the Active Directory Domains and Trusts, the Active Directory Sites and Services, and the Active Directory Users and Computers consoles?

The Active Directory Domains and Trusts console manages the trust relationships between domains. The Active Directory Sites and Services console creates sites to manage the replication of Active Directory information. The Active Directory Users and Computers console manages users, computers, security groups, and other objects in Active Directory.

6. When and why would you use an extension?

You would use an extension when specific snap-ins need additional functionality. Extensions are snap-ins that provide additional administrative functionality to another snap-in. A standalone snap-in provides one function or a related set of functions.

Chapter 17

▶ Page 847

12. Ensure that the Sysvol folder location is *systemroot*\SYSVOL. (If you did not install Windows 2000 in the WINNT directory, the Sysvol location should default to a SYSVOL folder in the folder where you installed Windows 2000.)

What is the one Sysvol location requirement?

Sysvol must be located on a Windows 2000 partition that is formatted as NTFS 5.0.

What is the function of Sysvol?

Sysvol is a system volume hosted on all Windows 2000 domain controllers. It stores scripts and part of the group policy objects for both the current domain and the enterprise. *systemroot*\SYSVOL\SYSVOL stores domain public files.

▶ Page 848

3. Double-click My Network Places.

The My Network Places window appears.

What selections do you see?

Add Network Place and Entire Network.

4. Double-click Entire Network, and then double-click Microsoft Windows Network.

What do you see?

Your domain set up in the previous exercise, microsoft.com. Answer may vary depending on your domain name.

▶ Page 849

2. In the console tree, double-click microsoft.com (or the name of your domain).

What selections are listed under microsoft.com?

Builtin, Computers, Domain Controllers, and Users.

▶ Page 865

3. Expand the microsoft.com domain (or the domain you set up).

The OUs appear as folders with a directory book icon under the domain. Plain folders are specialized containers.

What are the default OUs in your domain?

Domain Controllers. The Builtin, Computers, and Users folders are container objects.

▶ Page 874

2. Click on the Sites folder.

What objects appear in the details pane?

Default-First-Site-Name (the default site created by the Active Directory Installation Wizard), the Inter-Site Transports container, and the Subnets container.

▶ Page 876

1. Open the Inter-Site Transports folder and click the IP folder.

What object appears in the details pane?

DEFAULTIPSITELINK, the default site link created by the Active Directory Installation Wizard.

Review

1. What are some reasons for creating more than one domain?

Some reasons for creating more than one domain are to allow for decentralized network administration, control replication, allow for different password requirements between organizations, manage massive numbers of objects, allow for different Internet domain names, allow for international requirements, and to meet internal political requirements.

2. Your company has an external Internet namespace reserved with a DNS registration authority. As you plan the Active Directory implementation for your company, you decide to recommend extending the namespace for the internal network. What benefits does this option provide?

Extending an existing namespace provides consistent tree names for internal and external resources, making it easier for users to locate, refer, and use resources. In addition, this plan allows your company to use the same logon and user account names for internal and external resources. Finally, you do not have to reserve an additional DNS namespace.

3. In what two ways does your site configuration affect Windows 2000?

Your site configuration affects workstation logon and authentication. When a user logs on, Windows 2000 will try to find a domain controller in the same site as the user's computer to service the user's logon request and subsequent requests for network information.

Your site configuration also affects directory replication. You can configure the schedule and path for replication of a domain's directory differently for intersite replication, as opposed to replication within a site. Generally, you should set replication between sites to be less frequent than replication within a site.

4. What is the shared system volume, what purpose does it serve, where is it located, and what is its name?

The shared system volume is a folder structure that exists on all Windows 2000 domain controllers. It stores scripts and some of the group policy objects for both the current domain and the enterprise. The default location and name for the shared system volume is *systemroot*\SYSVOL. The shared system volume must be located on a partition or volume formatted with NTFS 5.0.

5. What is the purpose of the operations master roles?

Because some changes are impractical to perform in multimaster fashion, one or more domain controllers can be assigned to perform operations that are single-master (not permitted to occur at different places in a network at the same time). Operations master roles are assigned to domain controllers to perform single-master operations.

6. What administrative tool is used to create OUs?

The Active Directory Users and Computers console are used to create OUs.

7. What four tasks must be completed to configure a site?

You must create a site, associate a subnet with the site, connect the site using site links, and select a licensing computer for the site.

8. What two site configuration objects does the Active Directory Installation wizard create automatically?

The Active Directory Installation Wizard automatically creates an object named Default-First-Site-Name in the Sites container and an object named DEFAULTIPSITELINK in the IP container.

9. Which replication protocol uses RPCs for replication over site links (inter-site) and within a site (intra-site)?

IP replication protocol.

10. What three tasks must be completed to configure inter-site replication?

Create site links, configure site link attributes (such as site link cost, replication frequency, and replication availability), and create site link bridges.

11. What is the difference between replication frequency and replication availability?

Replication frequency is the duration between replications on a site link. Replication availability is when a site link is available to replicate directory information.

12. What is the function of a bridgehead server?

A bridgehead server provides some ranking or criteria for choosing which domain controller should be preferred as the recipient for inter-site replication. The bridgehead server then distributes the directory information via inter-site replication.

Chapter 18

Review

1. What are the advantages of using the Active Directory–integrated zone type?

   Multimaster update and enhanced security are based on the capabilities of Active Directory. Zones are replicated and synchronized to new domain controllers automatically whenever a new zone is added to an Active Directory domain. By integrating storage of your DNS namespace in Active Directory, you simplify planning and administration for both DNS and Active Directory. Directory replication is faster and more efficient than with standard DNS replication.

2. What is the purpose of the source of authority (SOA) resource record?

   The SOA resource record identifies which name server is the authoritative source of information for data within this domain. The first record in the zone database file must be the SOA record. The SOA resource record also stores properties such as version information and timings that affect zone renewal or expiration. These properties affect how often transfers of the zone are done between servers authoritative for the zone.

3. What must be done when you delegate zones within a namespace?

   When you delegate zones within a namespace, you must also create SOA resource records to point to the authoritative DNS server for the new zone. This is necessary both to transfer authority and to provide correct referral to other DNS servers and clients of the new servers being made authoritative for the new zone.

4. Why is an incremental zone transfer (IXFR) query more efficient than a full zone transfer (AXFR) query?

   An IXFR query allows the secondary server to pull only those zone changes it needs to synchronize its copy of the zone with its source, either a primary or secondary copy of the zone maintained by another DNS server. An AXFR query provides a full transfer of the entire zone database.

Chapter 19

▶ Page 927   1. In the console tree, right-click on the name of your domain, and then click Find.

Windows 2000 displays the Find dialog box.

In the Find dialog box, what object type can you select for a search?

Users, Contacts, and Groups; Computers; Printers; Shared Folders; Organizational Units; Custom Search, and Remote Installation Clients (if Remote Installation Services [RIS] is installed).

▶ Page 928   2. Ensure that Users, Contacts, And Groups is selected in the Find box, and then click Find Now. What do you see?

The list of users and groups in the domain.

▶ Page 937   4. In the following table, list the groups that have permissions for the Security1 OU. You will need to refer to these permissions in Lesson 5.

Groups that Have Permissions for the Security1 OU

User Account or Group	Assigned Permissions
Account Operators	Advanced permissions
Administrators	Inherits the Read, Write, and Create All Child Objects permissions and also has advanced permissions
Authenticated Users	Read
Domain Admins	Full Control
Enterprise Admins	Inherits Full Control
Pre–Windows 2000 Compatible Access	Advanced permissions
Print Operators	Advanced permissions
SYSTEM	Full Control

How can you tell if any of the default permissions are inherited from the domain, which is the parent object?

The permissions that are assigned to Administrators are inherited from the parent object. The check boxes for inherited permissions are shown as shaded.

▶ Page 938

2. To view special permissions for Account Operators, in the Permission Entries box, click each entry for Account Operators, and then click View/Edit.

The Permission Entry For Security1 dialog box appears.

What object permissions are assigned to Account Operators? What can Account Operators do in this OU? (Hint: Check each permission entry for Account Operators in the Permission Entries box in the Access Control Settings For Security1 dialog box.)

The permissions that are assigned to Account Operators are Create User Objects, Delete User Objects, Create Group Objects, Delete Group Objects, Create Computer Objects, and Delete Computer Objects. Account operators can only create and delete user accounts, groups, and computers.

Do any objects within this OU inherit the permissions assigned to the Account Operators group? Why or why not?

No. Objects within this OU do not inherit these permissions. The Apply To column in the Permission Entries list in the Access Control Settings For Security1 dialog box shows that permissions granted to Account Operators are applied to This Object Only.

▶ Page 939

4. In the following table, list the groups that have permissions for the Secretary1 user account. You will need to refer to these permissions in Lesson 5. If the dialog box indicates that special permissions are present for a group, do not list the special permissions to which you can gain access through the Advanced button.

Permissions for the Secretary1 User Account

Group	Assigned Permissions
Account Operators	Full Control
Administrators	Inherits all permissions, except the Full Control and Delete All Child Objects permissions, and also has advanced permissions
Authenticated Users	Read permission for General, Personal, Public, and Web Information
Cert Publishers	Advanced
Domain Admins	Full Control
Enterprise Admins	Inherits Full Control
Everyone	Change Password

Group	Assigned Permissions
Pre–Windows 2000 Compatible Access	Inherits Read, Read Phone and Mail Options, Read General Information, Read Group Membership, Read Personal, Public, Remote Access, Logon, and Web Information, and Read Account Restrictions
RAS and IAS Servers	Read permission for Group Membership, Remote Access Information, Account Restrictions, and Logon Information
SELF	Read, Change Password, Receive As, Send As; Read permission for Phone and Mail Options, General Information, Group Membership, Personal Information, Public Information, Remote Access Information, Account Restrictions, Logon Information, and Web Information; Write permission for Phone and Mail Options, Personal Information, and Web Information
SYSTEM	Full Control

Are the standard permissions for a user object the same as those for an OU object? Why or why not?

No. Standard permissions for each type of object are different. The reason for the differences is that different object types are used for different tasks, and therefore the security needs for each object type differ.

Are any of the standard permissions inherited from Security1, the parent object? How can you tell?

Only the standard permissions that are assigned to Administrators, and Enterprise Admins are inherited from the parent object. The check boxes for inherited permissions are shown as shaded.

What do the permissions of the Account Operators group allow its members to do with the user object?

Account Operators have Full Control. A member of the group can make any changes to a user object, including deleting it.

▶ Page 955   1. Log on to your domain by using the User21 account.

Did Windows 2000 require you to specify the OU in which your user account is located as part of the logon process? Why or why not?

No. Windows 2000 automatically locates the user object in Active Directory, independent of its exact location.

▶ Page 960

3. In the console tree, expand your domain, and then click Security1.

What user objects are visible in the Security1 OU?

The Secretary1 and Assistant1 user accounts, also User20, User 21, and User22.

Which permissions allow you to see these objects? (Hint: Refer to your answers in Lesson 2.)

The Assistant1 user account automatically belongs to the Authenticated Users built-in group, which has Read permission for the OU.

For the user account with the logon name Secretary1, change the logon hours. Were you successful? Why or why not?

No. The Assistant1 user account does not have Write permission for the Secretary1 object.

For the Assistant1 user account, under which you are currently logged on, change the logon hours. Were you successful? Why or why not?

No. The Assistant1 user account does not have Write permission for the Assistant 1 object.

▶ Page 962

4. Attempt to change the logon hours for the Assistant1 and Secretary1 user accounts in the Security1 OU.

Were you successful? Why or why not?

Yes. The Assistant1 user account has been assigned Full Control permission for all user objects in the OU. This includes the permission to change the logon hours.

5. Attempt to change the logon hours for a user account in the Users container.

Were you successful? Why or why not?

No. The Assistant1 user account has not been assigned any permissions for the Users container.

Review

1. How does the global catalog help users locate Active Directory objects?

The global catalog contains a partial replica of the entire directory, so it stores information about every object in a domain tree or forest. Because the global catalog contains information about every object, a user can find information regardless of which domain in the tree or forest contains the data. Active Directory automatically generates the contents of the global catalog from the domains that make up the directory.

2. You want to allow the manager of the Sales department to create, modify, and delete only user accounts for sales personnel. How can you accomplish this?

Place all of the sales personnel user accounts in an OU, and then delegate control of the OU to the manager of the Sales department.

3. What happens to the permissions of an object when you move it from one OU to another OU?

Permissions assigned directly to the object remain the same. The object also inherits permissions from the new OU. Any permissions previously inherited from the old OU no longer affect the object.

4. The Delegation Of Control wizard allows you to set administrative control at what level?

OU or container.

5. When backing up Active Directory, what type of data must you specify to be backed up? What is included in this data type?

You must indicate that you need to back up System State data. For Windows 2000 Server operating systems, the System State data comprises the registry, COM+ Class Registration database, system boot files, and the Certificate Services database (if the server is a certificate server). If the server is a domain controller, Active Directory and the SYSVOL directory are also contained in the System State data.

6. When you restart the computer in Directory Services Restore Mode, what logon must you use? Why?

When you restart the computer in Directory Services Restore Mode, you must log on as an Administrator by using a valid Security Accounts Manager (SAM) account name and password, *not* the Active Directory Administrator's name and password. This is because Active Directory is offline, and account verification cannot occur. Rather, the SAM accounts database is used to control access to Active Directory while it is offline. You specified this password when you set up Active Directory.

7. If you experience problems with Active Directory, what item should you investigate first?

You should examine the directory service event logs in Event Viewer.

8. What is the difference between a performance object and a performance counter?

A performance object is a logical connection of performance counters associated with a resource or service that can be monitored. A performance counter is a condition that applies to a performance object.

9. What is the difference between a counter log and a trace log?

Counter logs collect performance counter data for a specified interval. Trace logs record data collected by the operating system provider or one or more nonsystem providers when certain activities such as a disk I/O operation or a page fault occur. When counter logs are in use, the Performance Logs and Alerts service obtains data from the system when the update interval has elapsed, rather than waiting for a specific event, as for trace logs.

10. What actions can be triggered by an alert?

Alerts can log an entry in the application event log, send a network message to a computer, start a performance data log, or run a program when the alert counter's value exceeds or falls below a specified setting.

11. What does the Active Directory Replication Monitor support tool allow an administrator to do, and how is this tool accessed?

The Active Directory Replication Monitor tool enables administrators to view the low-level status of Active Directory replication, force synchronization between domain controllers, view the topology in a graphical format, and monitor the status and performance of domain controller replication through a graphical interface. The Active Directory Replication Monitor is a graphical tool accessed on the Tools menu within Windows 2000 Support Tools.

12. If you want to find out which files are open in a shared folder and the users who have a current connection to those files, what action should you take?

Click Start, point to Programs, point to Administrative Tools, and then click Computer Management. In the console tree of Computer Management, expand System Tools, and then expand Shared Folders. In the console tree, click Open Files under Shared Folders.

13. What four tasks must be completed to configure a site?

Create a site, associate a subnet with the site, connect the site using site links, and select a licensing computer for the site.

14. What two site configuration objects does the Active Directory Installation wizard create automatically?

    The Active Directory Installation wizard automatically creates an object named Default-First-Site-Name in the Sites container and an object named DEFAULTIPSITELINK in the IP container.

15. Which replication protocol uses RPCs for replication over site links (inter-site) and within a site (intra-site)?

    IP replication protocol.

16. What three tasks must be completed to configure inter-site replication?

    Create site links, configure site link attributes (such as site link cost, replication frequency, and replication availability), and create site link bridges.

Chapter 20

▶ Page 1019

3. In the console tree, click Start Menu & Task Bar.

    What appears in the details pane?

    The policies available for the Start Menu & Task Bar category appear in the details pane.

5. Click Enabled, and then click OK.

    How can you tell at a glance that this setting is enabled?

    The setting is listed as enabled in the details pane.

▶ Page 1022

2. Press Ctrl+Alt+Delete.

    The Windows Security dialog box appears.

    Are you able to lock the workstation? Why?

    No, the Lock Computer option is not available. Assistant1 is unable to lock the workstation because the DispatchPolicy GPO was linked to the Security1 OU in Exercise 8.

3. Click Cancel, and then click Start.

    Does the Search command appear on the Start menu?

    No.

    Does the Run command appear on the Start menu?

    No.

7. Press Ctrl+Alt+Delete.

Are you able to lock the workstation? Why?

Yes, the Lock Computer option is available. Assistant1 is able to lock the computer because the Sales group was filtered from the DispatchPolicy GPO scope in Exercise 7.

Review

1. In what order is Group Policy implemented through the Active Directory structure?

    Group Policy is implemented in the following order: site, domain, and then OU.

2. Name the tasks for implementing Group Policy.

    The tasks for implementing Group Policy are creating a GPO; creating a snap-in for the GPO; delegating administrative control of the GPO; specifying Group Policy settings for the GPO; disabling unused Group Policy settings; indicating any GPO processing exceptions; filtering the scope of the GPO; and linking the GPO to a site, domain, or OU.

3. What is the difference between Block Policy Inheritance and No Override?

    Block Policy Inheritance is applied directly to the site, domain, or OU. It is not applied to GPOs, nor is it applied to GPO links. Thus Block Policy Inheritance deflects *all* Group Policy settings that reach the site, domain, or OU from above (by way of linkage to parents in the Active Directory hierarchy) no matter what GPOs those settings originate from. GPO links set to No Override are always applied and cannot be blocked using the Block Policy Inheritance option.

    Any GPO linked to a site, domain, or OU (not the local GPO) can be set to No Override with respect to that site, domain, or OU so that none of its policy settings can be overwritten. When more than one GPO has been set to No Override, the one highest in the Active Directory hierarchy (or higher in the hierarchy specified by the administrator at each fixed level in Active Directory) takes precedence. No Override is applied to the GPO link.

4. What is the difference between assigning software and publishing software?

You assign a software application when you want everyone to have the application on his or her computer. An application can be published to both computers and users.

You publish a software application when you want the application to be available to people managed by the GPO, should the person want the application. With published applications it is up to each person to decide whether or not to install the published application. An application can only be published to users.

5. What folders can be redirected?

Application Data, Desktop, My Documents, My Pictures, and Start Menu.

6. What is RIS? What types of remote booting are supported by RIS?

Remote Installation Services (RIS) are software services that allow an administrator to set up new client computers remotely without having to visit each client. The target clients must support remote booting. There are two types of remote boot–enabled client computers: Computers with Pre-Boot eXecution Environment (PXE) Dynamic Host Configuration Protocol (DHCP)–-based remote boot ROMS and computers with network cards supported by the RIS Boot Disk.

7. What does PXE remote boot technology provide?

Pre-Boot eXecution Environment (PXE) is a new form of remote boot technology that has been created within the computing industry. PXE provides companies with the ability to use their existing TCP/IP network infrastructure with DHCP to discover RIS servers on the network. Net PC/PC98-compliant systems can take advantage of the remote boot technology included in the Windows 2000 OS. Net PC/PC98 refers to the annual guide for hardware developers co-authored by Microsoft with Intel, including contributions from Compaq and other industry hardware manufacturers. PC98 is intended to provide standards for hardware development that advance the PC platform and enable Microsoft to include advanced features, like RIS, in the Windows platform.

8. What is the RIS boot disk?

For computers that do not contain a PXE-based remote boot ROM, Windows 2000 provides the administrator with a tool to create a remote boot disk for use with RIS. The RIS remote boot disk can be used with a variety of PCI-based network adapter cards. Using the RIS boot disk eliminates the need to retrofit existing client computers with new network cards that contain a PXE-based remote boot ROM to take advantage of the Remote OS Installation feature. The RIS boot disk simulates the PXE remote boot sequence and supports frequently used network cards.

9. What is an RIPrep image?

The Remote Installation Preparation (RIPrep) image is a clone of a standard corporate desktop configuration, complete with operating system configurations, desktop customizations, and locally installed applications. After first installing and configuring the Windows 2000 Professional OS, its services, and any standard applications on a computer, the network administrator runs a wizard that prepares the installation image and replicates it to an available RIS server on the network for installation on other clients.

10. What is the Client Installation wizard?

Users of a remote boot–enabled client use the Client Installation wizard to select installation options, OSs, and maintenance and troubleshooting tools. The wizard prompts the user for his or her user name, password, and domain name. After the user's credentials have been validated, the wizard displays the installation options that are available for the user. After the user selects an option, the selected OS installation image is copied to the client computer's local hard disk.

Chapter 21

▶ Page 1127   Record your decisions to audit successful events, failed events, or both for the actions listed in Table 21.7.

Answers may vary. Possible answers include the following:

Account logon events: Failed (for network access attempts)

Account management: Successful (for administrator actions) Directory service access: Failed (for unauthorized access)

Logon events: Failed (for network access attempts)

Object access: Successful (for printer use) and Failed (for unauthorized access)

Policy change: Successful (for administrator actions)

Privilege use: Successful (for administrator actions and backup procedures) Process tracking: Nothing (useful primarily for developers)

System events: Successful and Failed (for attempts to breach the server)

▶ Page 1131

6. In the Access Control Settings For Users dialog box, click the Auditing tab, and then double-click Everyone.

The Auditing Entry For Users dialog box appears.

Review the default audit settings for object access by members of the Everyone group. How do the audited types of access differ from the types of access that are not audited?

All types of access that result in a change of the object are audited; types of access that do not result in a change of the object are not audited.

7. Click OK three times to close the Auditing Entry For Users, the Access Control Settings For Users, and the Users Properties dialog boxes.

On which computer or computers does Windows 2000 record log entries for Active Directory access? Will you be able to review them?

Windows 2000 records auditing events for Active Directory access at domain controllers, at the organizational unit (OU) level. Because you configured auditing for a domain controller, you will be able to view auditing events for Active Directory access. If you had configured auditing for the Local Computer, or the Default Domain Policy, you would not be able to view auditing events for Active Directory access.

▶ Page 1168

2. Double-click the Account Policies node, and then click the Password Policy security area.

In the details pane, what is indicated in the Policy column? In the Database Setting column? In the Computer Setting column?

The Policy column indicates the policy name for the analysis results. The Database Setting column indicates the security value in your template. The Computer Setting column indicates the current security level in the system.

In the Policy column, what does the red X indicate? What does the green check mark indicate?

A red X indicates a difference in the data from the database configuration. A green check mark indicates consistency with data in the database configuration.

Review

1. On which computer do you set an audit policy to audit a folder that is located on a member server that belongs to a domain?

   You set the audit policy on the member server; the audit policy must be set on the computer where the folder is located.

2. What is the difference between what the audit policy settings track for directory service access and object access?

   Directory service access tracks whether a user gained access to an Active Directory object. Object access tracks whether a user gained access to a file, folder, or printer.

3. When you view a security log, how do you determine if an event failed or was successful?

   Successful events appear with a key icon. Unsuccessful events appear with a lock icon.

4. How are user rights different from permissions?

   User rights are different from permissions because user rights apply to user accounts and permissions are attached to objects.

5. What is a security template and why is it useful?

   A security template is a physical representation of a security configuration, a single file where a group of security settings is stored. Locating all security settings in one place streamlines security administration.

6. Where does the Security Configuration and Analysis console store information for performing configuration and analysis functions?

   The Security Configuration and Analysis console uses a database to perform configuration and analysis functions.

Chapter 22

1. If Terminal Services is not licensed, what features of Terminal Services will work and for how long?

   Remote Administration mode allows for two remote control sessions with the computer running Terminal Services. No Terminal Service client license is necessary for this function. In Application Server mode, a Terminal Service client license is required for each session. The Terminal Service continues to function for 90 days without Terminal Service client licenses installed on the Terminal Services License server.

Chapter 23

▶ Page 1230
7. With the Web Site tab active, record the TCP Port value appearing in the TCP Port text box.

Port value will vary but should be between 2000-9999.

Review

1. You are accessing the IIS 5.0 documentation from Internet Services Manager (HTML). All of the documentation appears and you are able to access information via the Index tab. Under the Index tab, you find the phrase Process Accounting. However, when you perform a search on this phrase, the Web browser reports that your search phrase cannot be found. What is the most likely reason that this is happening?

The indexing service has been started because the Web browser did not report the inability to perform a search. Because the phrase was not found it could be that you have not configured the Indexing Service to catalog the iisHelp folder or the Indexing Service has not completed the task of indexing this folder's contents.

2. You have created a virtual directory for the purpose of Web Distributed Authoring and Versioning (WebDAV) publishing. The home directory of the Web site is accessible from Internet Explorer 5.0, but when you attempt to access the virtual directory for WebDAV publishing, access is denied. Name two reasons why this may happen and how you can solve this access problem.

WebDAV security is managed by the file system and Internet Services. Therefore, access could be denied because the physical directory for WebDAV has an access compatibility list (ACL) that does not allow the browser client to access the folder. If access is allowed at the file system level, verify that Read, Write, and Directory Browsing on the WebDAV virtual directory is enabled. For Active Server Pages (**ASP**) **support also make sure to enable Script source access.**

3. Why is it important that the Microsoft Telnet Client and the Microsoft Telnet service support NT LAN Manager (NTLM)authentication?

NTLM authentication protects authentication information from being transmitted across a network from the Telnet client to the Telnet server. A user is authenticated in the context of the current logon. If authentication is necessary, NTLM challenge/response authentication protects logon information. This is an important security feature of Windows 2000 Telnet.

Chapter 24

Review

1. How does a mounted drive to an empty folder differ from a Dfs root?

   A mounted drive to an empty folder allows for folder redirection. When you store files in a folder that points to a mounted partition, the files are redirected to the partition. This feature provides limited resource consolidation. A Dfs root provides a central point where disparate resources are consolidated through Dfs links. These links are then presented to the users as a single share containing folders. This feature provides robust resource consolidation.

2. In the Practice "Creating a Dfs Root and Dfs Link," you were asked to notice that New Root Replica and Replication Policy were not available options in the Distributed File System snap-in. Explain why these options are not available.

   New Root Replica and Replication Policy are available only for domain Dfs roots. In the practice a standalone Dfs root was config-ured. A new root replica makes it possible to replicate the Dfs root to other servers on the network. This feature provides fault tolerance and load balancing. If a server hosting the Dfs root fails, users access the Dfs root from the other replicas. If all servers replicating the Dfs root are available, they will load balance user requests. Replication policy allows you to configure the settings for replicating the Dfs root and Dfs shares below it.

3. How is the Knowledge Consistency Checker (KCC) involved in maintain-ing Active Directory store synchronization between domain controllers?

   KCC creates a ring topology for intra-domain replication. This topology provides a path for Active Directory store updates to flow from one domain controller to the next. It also provides two replica-tion paths, a path on either side of the ring to continue replication even if the ring structure is temporarily broken.

4. What data does the FRS replicate?

   System Volume data and domain Dfs roots and Dfs links configured for replication.

Chapter 25

Review

1. You have configured a computer to boot Windows 2000 Server as the default operating system, and Windows NT 4.0 Server as the optional operating system. After modifying the attributes of files on %systemdrive% and deleting some of the files, the computer does not display Windows NT 4.0 Server as an operating system to start. Windows 2000 Server starts up properly. The problem is caused because you deleted a file. What is the name of the file, and what can you do to recover from this error?

   You deleted the Boot.ini file. Boot.ini allows for multiboot. If this file is missing, the default operating system starts. To recover this file, run the Emergency Repair Disk (ERD), choose Manual Repair, and then choose Inspect Startup Environment.

2. Why would the Use Hardware Compression, If Available check box be unavailable in the Backup wizard?

   This option is available only if an installed tape device and its driver supports hardware compression.

3. How can you test the configuration of the uninterruptible power supply (UPS) service on a computer?

   You can simulate a power failure by disconnecting the main power supply to the UPS device. During the test, the computer and peripherals connected to the UPS device should remain operational, messages should display, and events should continue to be logged.

   In addition, you should wait until the UPS battery reaches a low level to verify that a graceful shutdown occurs. Then restore the main power to the UPS device and check the event log to ensure that all actions were logged and there were no errors.

   Note that this procedure requires a UPS that communicates with the computer through a Component Object Model (COM) port or a proprietary interface provided with the UPS.

Chapter 26

Review

1. You want to filter out all network traffic except for traffic between two computers, and you also want to locate specific data within the packets. Which Network Monitor filter features should you specify?

    Filter for Address Pairs, where you specify the media access control (MAC) address of each computer, and Pattern Matches, where you filter for specific patterns in Hex or ASCII contained in the frames.

2. You goal is to make sure that only two network management stations in your organization are able to communicate with the Simple Network Management Protocol (SNMP) agents. What measures can you take when configuring the SNMP service to enhance security?

    Using the Security tab of the SNMP Service Properties dialog box, make the following configuration changes:

    - **Specify a unique community name and remove the Public community name.**

    - **Adjust the community rights settings so that the network management station (NMS) can complete the functions you want to enable. If you aren't sure of the community rights you need, configure this for READ ONLY and adjust it by NMS to SNMP service testing.**

    - **Select the Accept SNMP Packets From These Hosts radio button, and then specify the host name, Internet Protocol (IP), or Internetwork Packet Exchange (IPX) address of the two network management stations.**

    - **If you will be sending traps to an NMS, make sure to specify the Trap destination(s) under the Traps tab.**

Chapter 27

Review

1. Which key is associated with the creation of digital signatures, the public key or the private key? Explain your answer.

    Private keys are associated with the creation of digital signatures. You use a private key to transform data in such a way that users are able to verify that only you could have created the encrypted data. Decrypting the data is achieved through the application of the public key. However, only the private key is used to create the digital signature.

2. What security credential(s) are in use if you are supporting client computers running Windows 2000 and Windows NT that authenticate to servers running Windows 2000 Server and Windows NT Server?

Windows NT client computers will authenticate to both Windows 2000 and Windows NT Servers using NT LAN Manager (NTLM) credentials (Windows NT domain name, username, and encrypted password). Windows 2000 client computers authenticate to the computers running Windows 2000 Server using Kerberos authentication (domain name, username, Kerberos-encrypted password), and they authenticate to the computers running Windows NT Server using NTLM authentication.

3. How can a security template be used to facilitate configuration and analysis of security settings?

A template can be applied to a security configuration database created by the Security Analysis and Configuration snap-in. After the database is created, the current settings of the computer can be compared to the settings dictated by the policy. After reviewing discrepancies between policy and computer security settings, the same snap-in can be used to configure the computer's security settings to the template's settings.

4. Where is the Certificate Services Enrollment page and what is its purpose?

The Certificate Services Enrollment page is a Web page that allows for the easy creation and monitoring of certificate requests, and for the retrieval of CRLs and certificates.

5. What steps must you follow to enable auditing of specific file objects on domain controllers in a domain where Group Policy is enabled?

Use Active Directory Users And Computers to open a group policy (typically the Default Domain group policy object [GPO] or the Default Domain controller Policy GPO). Navigate to the Audit Policy node below the Windows Settings – Security Settings – Local Policies node. In the details pane, double-click Audit Object Access and enable success or failure attempts as appropriate. Using Windows Explorer, navigate to the specific file or folder that you need to access. Access the properties of the file or folder object, click the Security tab, then click the Advanced button. From the Access Control Settings dialog box, select View/Edit to modify the audit policy of a selected user or group or add a new user or group to audit. Be cautious about how much file object auditing you configure. This feature can be processor intensive if it is configured improperly.

Glossary

A

access control entry (ACE)   One of the entries on the access control list (ACL) that controls user account or group access to a resource. The entry must allow the type of access that is requested (for example, Read access) for the user to gain access. If no ACE exists in the ACL, the user can't gain access to the resource or folder on an NTFS partition.

access control list (ACL)   The mechanisms for limiting access to certain items of information or certain controls based on users' identity and their membership in various predefined groups. Access control is typically used by system administrators for controlling user access to network resources such as servers, directories, and files, and is typically implemented by granting permissions to users and groups for access to specific objects.

access token   The user's identification for the computers in the domain or for that local computer. The access token contains the user's security settings, including the user's security ID (SID).

Account   *See* user account.

account lockout   A Microsoft Windows 2000 security feature that locks a user account if a number of failed logon attempts takes place within a specified amount of time, based on security policy lockout settings. Locked accounts cannot log on.

account policy   Controls how passwords must be used by all user accounts in a domain or on an individual computer.

Active Directory Domains and Trusts console   An administrative tool that allows you to manage trust relationships between domains. These domains can be Microsoft Windows 2000 domains in the same forest, Windows 2000 domains in different forests, pre–Windows 2000 domains, and even Kerberos v5 realms.

Active Directory schema   A description of the object classes and attributes stored in Active Directory directory service. For each object class, the schema defines the attributes an object class must have, the additional attributes it may have, and the object class that can be its parent. The Active Directory schema can be updated dynamically by creating or modifying the schema objects stored in Active Directory. Like every object in Active Directory, schema objects have an access control list (ACL), so only authorized users may alter the schema.

Active Directory Schema console   An administrative tool that allows you to view and modify Active Directory schema. You must install the Active Directory Schema console from the Microsoft Windows 2000 Administration tools on the Windows 2000 Server CD-ROM.

Active Directory directory service   The directory service included with Microsoft Windows 2000 Server. It stores information about objects on a network and makes this information available to users and network administrators. Active Directory allows users to use a single logon process to access permitted resources anywhere on the network. Active Directory provides network administrators with an intuitive hierarchical view of the network and a single point of administration for all network objects.

Active Directory Service Interfaces (ADSI) A directory service model and a set of Component Object Model (COM) interfaces. ASDI enables Microsoft Windows 95, Windows 98, Windows NT, and Windows 2000 applications to access several network directory services, including Active Directory.

Active Directory Sites and Services console An administrative tool that contains information about the physical structure of your network. Active Directory uses this information to determine how to replicate directory information and handle service requests.

Active Directory Support Tools   Additional administrative tools that can be used to configure, manage, and debug Active Directory; included in Microsoft Windows 2000 Support Tools. The Windows 2000 Support Tools are included on the Windows 2000 CD-ROM in the \Support\Tools folder. These tools are intended for use by Microsoft support personnel and experienced users to assist in diagnosing and resolving computer problems.

Active Directory Users and Computers console An administrative tool designed to perform day-to-day Active Directory administration tasks. These tasks include creating, deleting, modifying, moving, and setting permissions on objects stored in the directory. These objects include organizational units, users, contacts, groups, computers, printers, and shared file objects.

Advanced Configuration and Power Interface (ACPI)   An open industry specification that defines power management for a wide range of mobile, desktop, and server computers and peripherals. ACPI is the foundation for the OnNow industry initiative that allows system manufacturers to deliver computers that start at the touch of a keyboard. ACPI design is essential to take full advantage of power management and Plug and Play in Windows 2000.

application assignment   A process that uses Software Installation (an extension of Group Policy) to assign programs to groups of users. The programs appear to be installed and available on the users' desktops when they log on. You assign programs to a particular group policy object (GPO), which in turn is associated with a selected directory object (site, domain, or organizational unit). When you assign programs, they are advertised to every user managed by the GPO. Advertising the program installs only enough information about the program to make program shortcuts appear on the Start menu and the necessary file associations appear in the registry. When users managed by the GPO log on to a computer running Microsoft Windows 2000, the program appears on their Start menu. When users select the program from the Start menu for the first time, the program is installed. You can also install advertised programs by clicking a document managed by the program (either by file extension or by COM-based activation).

asymmetric digital subscriber line (ADSL)
A modem technology that converts existing twisted-pair telephone lines into access paths for multimedia and high-speed data communications. These new connections can transmit more than 8 Mbps to the subscriber and up to 1 Mbps from the subscriber. ADSL is recognized as a physical layer transmission protocol for unshielded twisted-pair media.

Asynchronous Transfer Mode (ATM)   A high-speed, connection-oriented protocol used to transport multiple types of traffic across a network. ATM packages data in a 53-byte, fixed-length cell that can be switched quickly between logical connections on a network.

audit policy   A policy that determines the security events to be reported to the network administrator.

auditing   The process that tracks the activities of users by recording selected types of events in the Security log of a server or a workstation.

authentication   The process by which the system validates the user's logon information. A user's name and password are compared against an authorized list. If the system detects a match, access is granted to the extent specified in the permissions list for that user. When a user logs on to an account on a

computer running Microsoft Windows 2000 Professional, the authentication is performed by the workstation. When a user logs on to an account on a Windows 2000 Server domain, any server in that domain may perform authentication.

Author mode   A console mode that enables full access to all Microsoft Management Console (MMC) functionality, including adding or removing snap-ins, creating new windows, viewing all portions of the console tree, and saving MMCs.

authoritative restore   A type of restore operation on a Microsoft Windows 2000 domain controller in which the objects in the restored directory are treated as authoritative, replacing (through replication) all existing copies of those objects. Authoritative restore is applicable only to replicated System State data such as Active Directory data and File Replication service data. You must use the NTDSUTIL.EXE utility to perform an authoritative restore.

B

backup domain controller (BDC)   In Microsoft Windows NT Server 4.0 or earlier, a computer running Windows NT Server that receives a copy of the domain's directory database (which contains all account and security policy information for the domain). The copy is synchronized periodically and automatically with the master copy on the primary domain controller (PDC). BDCs also authenticate user logon information and can be promoted to function as PDCs as needed. Multiple BDCs can exist in a domain. Windows NT 3.51 and 4.0 BDCs can participate in a Microsoft Windows 2000 domain when the domain is configured in Mixed mode.

backup job A single process of backing up data.

backup set A collection of files, folders, and other data that have been backed up and stored in a file or on one or more tapes.

backup types The method which determines which data is backed up and how it is backed up. There are five backup types: copy, daily, differential, incremental, and normal.

Bandwidth Allocation Protocol (BAP) A Point-to-Point Protocol (PPP) control protocol that helps provide bandwidth on demand. BAP dynamically controls the use of multi-linked lines and is an efficient mechanism for controlling connection costs while dynamically providing optimum bandwidth.

boot files The system files needed to start Microsoft Windows 2000. For Intel–based computers, this includes NTLDR and NTDETECT.COM. For Compaq Alpha–based systems, this is OSLOADER.EXE.

Boot Information Negotiation Layer (BINL) A service that runs on the Microsoft Windows 2000 Server and acts on client boot requests.

boot logging A process in which a computer that is starting (booting) creates a log file that records the loading of each device and service. In Microsoft Windows 2000, this log file is called NTBTLOG.TXT and is saved in the *systemroot* directory.

boot partition The partition that contains the Microsoft Windows 2000 operating system and its support files. The boot partition can be, but does not have to be, the same as the system partition.

boot volume The volume that contains the Microsoft Windows 2000 operating system and its support files. The boot volume can be, but does not have to be, the same as the system volume.

built-in groups The default groups provided with Microsoft Windows 2000 Professional and Windows 2000 Server. Built-in groups have been granted useful collections of rights and built-in abilities. In most cases, built-in groups provide all the capabilities needed by a particular user.

built-in user account Default data that is used to perform administrative tasks or to gain access to network resources.

C

CA *See* certificate authority (CA).

callback A Microsoft Windows 2000 feature that you can set to cause the remote server to disconnect and call back the client attempting to access the remote server. This reduces the client's phone bill by having the call charged to the remote server's phone number. The callback feature can also improve security by calling back the phone number that you specified.

certificate A collection of data used for authentication and secure exchange of information on nonsecured networks, such as the Internet. A certificate securely binds a public key to the entity that holds the corresponding private key. Certificates are digitally signed by the issuing CA and can be managed for a user, computer, or service. The most widely accepted format for certificates is defined by ITU-T X.509 international standards.

certificate authority (CA)   An entity responsible for establishing the authenticity of public keys belonging to users or other CAs. Activities of a CA may include binding public keys to distinguished names through signed certificates, managing certificate serial numbers, and revoking certificates.

certificate services   Software services that provide authentication support, including secure e-mail, Web-based authentication, and smart card authentication. These services contrast with Internet Authentication Services (IAS), which provide authentication for dial-in users.

child domain   For Domain Name System (DNS), domains located in the namespace tree directly beneath another domain name (the parent domain). For example, example.microsoft.com would be a child domain of the parent domain, microsoft.com. A child domain is also called a subdomain.

child object   An object that resides in another object. For example, a file is a child object that resides in a folder, which is the parent object.

Client Installation wizard   In Remote Installation Services (RIS), the Client Installation wizard makes installation options available to the client.

common groups   Groups that appear in the program list on the Start menu for all users who log on to the computer. Only administrators can create or change common groups.

computer account   An account that is created by a domain administrator and uniquely identifies the computer on the domain. The Microsoft Windows 2000 computer account matches the name of the computer joining the domain.

console   A collection of administrative tools.

console mode   The technique used to determine the Microsoft Management Console (MMC) functionality for the person who is using a saved MMC. The two available console modes are Author mode and User mode.

console tree   The left pane in a Microsoft Management Console (MMC) that displays the items contained in the console. By default it is the left pane of a console window, but it can be hidden. The items in the console tree and their hierarchical organization determine the capabilities of a console.

D

data store (the database file NTDS.DIT)
The directory database.

default groups   Groups that have a predetermined set of user rights or group membership. Microsoft Windows 2000 has four categories of default groups: predefined, built-in, built-in local, and special identity.

default user profile   The profile that serves as a basis for all user profiles. Every user profile begins as a copy of the default user profile, which is stored on each computer running Microsoft Windows 2000 Professional or Windows 2000 Server.

details pane   The pane in the Microsoft Management Console (MMC) that displays the details for the selected item in the console tree. The details can be a list of items or they can be administrative properties, services, and events that are acted on by a console or snap-in.

Dfs link   A link from a distributed file system (Dfs) root to one or more shared files, another Dfs root, or a domain-based volume.

Dfs replication   The process of copying data from a data store or file system to multiple computers to synchronize the data. Active Directory directory services provides multimaster replication of the directory between domain controllers within a given domain. The replicas of the directory on each domain controller are writeable. This allows updates to be applied to any replica of a given domain. The replication service automatically copies the changes from a given replica to all other replicas.

Dfs root   A container for files and Dfs links.

DHCP   *See* Dynamic Host Configuration Protocol (DHCP).

DHCP client   Any network-enabled device that supports the ability to communicate with a Dynamic Host Configuration Protocol (DHCP) server for the purpose of obtaining dynamic leased Internet Protocol (IP) configuration and related optional parameters information.

DHCP scope   A range of Internet Protocol (IP) addresses that are available to be leased or assigned to Dynamic Host Configuration Protocol (DHCP) clients by the DHCP service.

DHCP server   In Microsoft Windows 2000 Server, a computer running the Microsoft Dynamic Host Configuration Protocol (DHCP) service that offers dynamic configuration of Internet Protocol (IP) addresses and related information to DHCP-enabled clients.

differential backup   A backup method that copies files created or changed since the last normal (or incremental) backup. It does not mark files as having been backed up.

digital signature   A means for originators of a message, file, or other digitally encoded information to bind their identity to the information. The process of signing informa-tion entails transforming the information, as well as some secret information held by the sender, into a tag called a *signature*.

digital video disc (DVD)   Also known as a digital versatile disc, an optical storage medium with higher capacity and bandwidth than a compact disc. A DVD can hold a full-length film with up to 133 minutes of high-quality video (in MPEG-2 format) and audio.

direct memory access (DMA)   Memory access that doesn't involve the microprocessor, frequently employed for data transfer directly between memory and an "intelligent" periph-eral device such as a disk drive.

direct memory access (DMA) channel   A channel for direct memory access that doesn't involve the microprocessor, providing data transfer directly between memory and a disk drive.

directory   An information source (for example, a telephone directory) that contains information about people, computer files, or other objects. In a file system, a directory stores information about files. In a distributed computing environ-ment (such as a Microsoft Windows 2000 domain), the directory stores information about objects such as printers, fax servers, applica-tions, databases, and other users.

directory database   The physical storage for each replica of Active Directory. Directory database is also called the *data store*.

directory service   Provides the methods for storing directory data and making this data available to network users and administrators. For example, Active Directory stores informa-tion about user accounts, such as names, passwords, phone numbers, and so on, and enables other authorized users on the same network to access this information.

Directory Services Restore mode   A special safe mode that allows you to restore the System State data on a domain controller. When your computer is started in this mode you can restore the SYSVOL directory and Active Directory database. You can only restore System State data on a local computer. You cannot restore the System State data on a remote computer.

Directory System Agent (DSA)   A software construct that builds a hierarchy from the parent-child relationships stored in the directory. Provides application programming interfaces (APIs) for directory access calls.

Discretionary Access Control List (DACL) A list that represents part of an object's security descriptor that allows or denies permissions to specific users and groups.

disk duplexing   *See* disk mirroring.

disk duplicating   *See* disk mirroring.

diskless computers   Computers that have neither a floppy disk nor a hard disk. Diskless computers depend on special ROM to provide users with an interface through which they can log on to the network.

disk mirroring   A technique, also known as disk duplicating, in which all or part of a hard disk is duplicated onto one or more hard disks, each of which ideally is attached to its own controller. With disk mirroring, any change made to the original disk is simultaneously made to the other disk or disks. Disk mirroring is used in situations in which a backup copy of current data must be maintained at all times. *See also* disk striping.

disk striping   A technique that divides data into 64 K blocks and spreads it equally in a fixed rate and order among all disks in an array. Disk striping doesn't provide any fault tolerance because there is no data redundancy. If any partition in the set fails, all data is lost. *See also* disk mirroring.

distinguished name (DN)   A name that uniquely identifies an object by using the relative name for the object, plus the names of container objects and domains that contain the object. The distinguished name identifies the object as well as its location in a tree. Every object in Active Directory has a distinguished name. A typical distinguished name might be: CN=MyName,CN=Users,DC=Microsoft, DC=Com. This identifies the MyName user object in the microsoft.com domain.

distributed file system (Dfs)   A service used to build a logical structure of file shares from separate computers and presented to users and administrators in a single directory tree.

distribution server   A server that stores the distribution folder structure, which contains the files needed to install a product—for example, Microsoft Windows 2000.

DNS name server   In the Domain Name System (DNS) client/server model, the server containing information about a portion of the DNS database that makes computer names available to client resolvers querying for name resolution across the Internet.

domain   In Microsoft Windows 2000 and Active Directory, a collection of computers defined by the administrator of a Windows 2000 Server network that share a common directory database. A domain has a unique name and provides access to the centralized user accounts and group accounts maintained by the domain administrator. Each domain has its own security policies and security relationships with other domains and represents a single security boundary of a Windows 2000 computer network. Active Directory is made up of one or more domains, each of which can span more than one physical location. For Domain Name System (DNS), a domain is any tree or subtree within the DNS namespace. Although the names for DNS domains often correspond to Active Directory domains, DNS domains should not be confused with Windows 2000 and Active Directory networking domains.

domain controller   In a Microsoft Windows 2000 Server domain, a computer running Windows 2000 Server that manages user access to a network, which includes logging on, authentication, and access to the directory and shared resources.

domain local group   A security or distribution group that can contain universal groups, global groups, and accounts from any domain in the domain tree or forest. A domain local group can also contain other domain local groups from its own domain. Rights and permissions can be assigned only at the domain containing the group.

domain model   A grouping of one or more domains with administration and communication links between them that is arranged for the purpose of user and resource management.

domain name   In Microsoft Windows 2000 and Active Directory, the name given by an administrator to a collection of networked computers that share a common directory. For Domain Name System (DNS), domain names are specific node names in the DNS namespace tree. DNS domain names use singular node names joined together by periods (.) that indicate each node level in the namespace.

Domain Name System (DNS)   A static, hierarchical name service for Transmission Control Protocol/Internet Protocol (TCP/IP) hosts. The network administrator configures the DNS with a list of host names and Internet Protocol (IP) addresses, allowing users of workstations configured to query the DNS to specify remote systems by host names rather than IP addresses. DNS domains should not be confused with Microsoft Windows 2000 networking domains.

domain namespace   The database structure used by the Domain Name System (DNS).

domain naming master   The domain controller assigned to control the addition or removal of domains in the forest. At any time, there can be only one domain naming master in the forest.

domain user account   A database that allows a user to log on to the domain to gain access to network resources.

Dynamic DNS (DDNS)   Enables clients with dynamically assigned addresses to register directly with a server running the Domain Name System (DNS) service and update the DNS table dynamically. DDNS eliminates the need for other Internet naming services, such as Windows Internet Name Service (WINS), in a homogeneous environment.

Dynamic Host Configuration Protocol (DHCP)   A Transmission Control Protocol/Internet Protocol (TCP/IP) service protocol that offers dynamic leased configuration of host IP addresses and distributes other configuration parameters to eligible network clients. DHCP provides safe, reliable, and simple TCP/IP network configuration, prevents address conflicts, and helps conserve the use of client Internet Protocol (IP) addresses on the network. DHCP uses a client/server model where the DHCP server maintains centralized management of IP addresses that are used on the network. DHCP-supporting clients can then request and obtain lease of an IP address from a DHCP server as part of their network boot process.

dynamic-link library   An operating system feature that allows executable routines (generally serving a specific function or set of functions) to be stored separately as files with .dll extensions. These routines are loaded only when needed by the program that calls them.

dynamic volume   A logical volume that is created using Disk Management. Dynamic volume types include simple, spanned, striped, mirrored, and RAID-5. You must create dynamic volumes on dynamic disks.

E

effective permissions   The sum of the NTFS permissions assigned to the user account and to all of the groups to which the user belongs. If a user has Read permission for a folder and is a member of a group with Write permission for the same folder, the user has both Read and Write permission for the folder.

EFS   *See* encrypting file system (EFS).

encrypting file system (EFS)   Microsoft Windows 2000 file system that enables users to encrypt files and folders on an NTFS volume to keep them safe from intruders who have physical access to the disk.

encryption   The process of making information indecipherable to protect it from unauthorized viewing or use, especially during transmission or when the data is stored on a transportable magnetic medium. A key is required to decode the information.

environment subsystems   One of the components of the Microsoft Windows 2000 User mode; emulate different operating systems by presenting the application programming interfaces (APIs) that the applications expect to be available. The environment subsystems accept the API calls made by the application, convert the API calls into a format understood by Windows 2000, and then pass the converted API to the Executive Services for processing.

Event Log service   A service that records events in the system, security, and application logs. The Event Log service is located in Event Viewer.

event logging   The Microsoft Windows 2000 process of recording an audit entry in the audit trail whenever certain events occur, such as services starting and stopping or users logging on and off and accessing resources. You can use Event Viewer to review AppleTalk network integration (formerly Services for Macintosh) events as well as Windows 2000 events.

Event Viewer   Maintains logs about application, security, and system events on your computer.

Everyone group   In Microsoft Windows NT, includes all local and remote users who have connected to the computer, including those who connect as guests. You cannot control who becomes a member of the Everyone group; however, you can assign permissions and rights.

explicit one-way nontransitive trust   A type of trust relationship in which only one of the two domains trusts the other domain. For example, Domain A trusts Domain B and Domain B does not trust Domain A. All one-way trusts are nontransitive.

extended partition   A portion of a basic disk that can contain logical drives. Use an extended partition if you want to have more than four volumes on your basic disk. Only one of the four partitions allowed per physical disk can be an extended partition, and no primary partition needs to be present to create an extended partition. Extended partitions can be created only on basic disks.

Extensible Authentication Protocol (EAP)
An extension to the Point-to-Point Protocol (PPP) that works with Dial-Up, Point-to-Point Tunneling Protocol (PPTP), and Layer Two Tunneling Protocol (L2TP) clients. EAP allows for an arbitrary authentication mechanism to validate a dial-in connection. The exact authentication method to be used is negotiated by the dial-in client and the remote access server.

Extensible Storage Engine (ESE)   The Active Directory database engine. ESE (ESENT.DLL) is an improved version of the Jet database that is used in Microsoft Exchange Server versions 4.*x* and 5.5. It implements a transacted database system, which means that it uses log files to ensure that committed transactions are safe.

extension snap-ins   Usually referred to simply as *extensions*. They are snap-ins that provide additional administrative functionality to other snap-ins.

F

file replication service (FRS)   A service used by the Microsoft distributed file system (Dfs) to automatically synchronize content between assigned replicas, and by Active Directory Sites and Services to replicate topological and global catalog information across domain controllers.

file sharing   The ability of a computer running Microsoft Windows 2000 to share parts (or all) of its local file system(s) with remote computers.

folder redirection   An extension within group policy that allows you to redirect the following Microsoft Windows 2000 special folders to network locations: Application Data, Desktop, My Documents, My Pictures, and Start Menu.

forest   A collection of one or more Microsoft Windows 2000 domains that share a common schema, configuration, and global catalog, and are linked with two-way transitive trusts.

forward lookup   In Domain Name System (DNS), a query process in which the friendly DNS domain name of a host computer is searched to find its Internet Protocol (IP) address.

full zone transfer (AXFR)   The standard query type supported by all Domain Name System (DNS) servers to update and synchronize zone data when the zone has been changed. When a DNS query is made using AXFR as the specified query type, the entire zone is transferred as the response.

fully qualified domain name (FQDN)   A Domain Name System (DNS) domain name that has been stated unambiguously so as to indicate with absolute certainty its location in the domain namespace tree. Fully qualified domain names differ from relative names in that they are typically stated with a trailing period (.), for example, host.example.microsoft.com, to qualify their position to the root of the namespace.

G

global account   For Microsoft Windows 2000 Server, a normal user account in a user's domain. Most user accounts are global accounts. If there are multiple domains in the network, it is best if each user in the network has only one user account in only one domain, and each user's access to other domains is accomplished through the establishment of domain trust relationships.

global catalog   A domain controller that contains a partial replica of every domain in Active Directory. A global catalog holds a replica of every object in Active Directory, but with a limited number of each object's attributes. The global catalog stores those attributes most frequently used in search operations (such as a user's first name and last name) and those attributes required to locate a full replica of the object. The Active Directory replication system builds the global catalog automatically. The attributes replicated into the global catalog include a base set defined by Microsoft. Administrators can specify additional properties to meet the needs of their installation.

global catalog server   A Microsoft Windows 2000 domain controller that holds a copy of the global catalog for the forest.

global group   For Microsoft Windows 2000 Server, a group that can be granted rights and permissions and can become a member of local groups in its own domain, the member servers and workstations thereof, and trusting domains. A global group can contain user accounts only from its own domain. Global groups provide a way to create sets of users from inside the domain, and can be used for access to resources both in and out of the domain. Global groups cannot be created or

maintained on computers running Microsoft Windows 2000 Professional. However, for Windows 2000 Professional computers that participate in a domain, domain global groups can be granted rights and permissions at those workstations and can become members of local groups at those workstations.

globally unique identifier (GUID)   A 128-bit number that is guaranteed to be unique. GUIDs are assigned to objects when the objects are created. The GUID never changes, even if you move or rename the object. Applications can store the GUID of an object and use the GUID to retrieve that object regardless of its current distinguished name.

group memberships   The groups to which a user account belongs. Permissions and rights granted to a group are also provided to its members. In most cases, the actions a user can perform in Microsoft Windows 2000 are determined by the group memberships of the user account that has been logged on to.

group policy   The Microsoft Windows 2000 Microsoft Management Console (MMC) snap-in used to specify the behavior of users' desktops. A group policy object (GPO), which an administrator creates using the Group Policy snap-in, is the mechanism for configuring desktop settings.

Group Policy object (GPO)   A collection of group policy settings. GPOs are essentially the documents created by the Group Policy snap-in. GPOs are stored at the domain level and they affect users and computers contained in sites, domains, and organizational units. In addition, each Microsoft Windows 2000 computer has exactly one group of settings stored locally, called the *local GPO*.

group scopes   Allow you to use groups in different ways to assign permissions. The scope of a group determines where in the network you are able to use the group to assign permissions to the group. The three group scopes are global, domain local, and universal.

guest account   A built-in account used to log on to a computer running Microsoft Windows 2000 when a user does not have an account on the computer or domain or in any of the domains trusted by the computer's domain.

H

Hardware Compatibility List (HCL)   A list of the devices supported by Microsoft Windows 2000. The latest version of the HCL can be downloaded from the Hardware Compatibility List Web page at *http://www.microsoft.com/hwtest/hcl/*.

HCL   *See* Hardware Compatibility List (HCL).

home directory   Specified in Active Directory Users And Computers or Local Users And Groups, a folder that is accessible to the user and can contain files and programs for that user. A home directory can be assigned to an individual user or can be shared by many users. Some programs use the home directory as the default folder for the Open and Save As dialog boxes. Other programs use My Documents.

host name   The name of a device on a network. For a device on a Microsoft Windows NT or Windows 2000 network, this can be the same as the computer name, but it may not be. The host name must be in the Hosts file, or it must be known by a Domain Name System (DNS) server, for that host to be found by another computer attempting to communicate with it.

I

implicit two-way transitive trust   A type of trust relationship in which both of the domains in the relationship trust each other. In a two-way trust relationship, each domain has established a one-way trust with the other domain. For example, Domain A trusts Domain B and Domain B trusts Domain A. Two-way trusts can be transitive or non-transitive. All two-way trusts between Microsoft Windows 2000 domains in the same domain tree or forest are transitive.

incremental zone transfer (IXFR)   An alternate query type that can be used by some Domain Name System (DNS) servers to update and synchronize zone data when a zone is changed. When IXFR is supported between DNS servers, servers can keep track of and transfer only those incremental resource record changes between each version of the zone.

infrastructure master   The domain controller assigned to update group-to-user references whenever group memberships are changed, and to replicate these changes to any other domain controllers in the domain. At any time, there can be only one infrastructure master in a particular domain.

initial master   A shared folder whose existing files and folders are replicated to other shared folders when replication is initially configured. After replication is complete, there is no initial master, as any of the replicas can accept changes and propagate them to the other replicas. The initial master then becomes another replica.

IntelliMirror   A set of powerful features native to Microsoft Windows 2000 for desktop change and configuration management technology. IntelliMirror combines the advantages of centralized computing with the performance and flexibility of distributed computing.

Internet Information Services (IIS)   Software services that support Web site creation, configuration, and management, along with other Internet functions. Microsoft Internet Information Services include Network News Transfer Protocol (NNTP), File Transfer Protocol (FTP), and Simple Mail Transfer Protocol (SMTP).

Internet Protocol Security (IPSec)   A framework of open standards for ensuring secure private communications over IP networks by using cryptographic security services.

IPSec   *See* Internet Protocol Security (IPSec).

K

Kerberos v5 protocol   An Internet standard security protocol for handling authentication of user or system identity. With Kerberos v5 protocol, passwords that are sent across network lines are encrypted, not sent as plaintext. Kerberos v5 also includes other security features.

kernel mode   Provides direct access to memory and executes in an isolated memory area. Kernel mode consists of four components: Microsoft Windows 2000 Executive, Device Drivers, the Microkernel, and the Hardware Abstraction Layer (HAL).

key   In database management, an identifier for a record or group of records in a data file. Most often, the key is defined as the contents of a single field, called the key field in some database management programs and the index field in others. Keys are maintained in tables and are indexed to speed record retrieval. Keys also refer to code that deciphers encrypted data.

L

Layer 2 Tunneling Protocol (L2TP)   An industry-standard Internet tunneling protocol. Unlike Point-to-Point Tunneling Protocol (PPTP), L2TP does not require Internet Protocol (IP) connectivity between the client workstation and the server. L2TP requires only that the tunnel medium provide packet-oriented point-to-point connectivity. The protocol can be used over media such as Asynchronous Transfer Mode (ATM), Frame Relay, and X.25. L2TP provides the same functionality as PPTP. Based on Layer 2 Forwarding (L2F) and PPTP specifications, L2TP allows clients to set up tunnels across intervening networks.

Lightweight Directory Access Protocol (LDAP) The primary access protocol for Active Directory. LDAP version 3 is defined by a set of Proposed Standard documents in Internet Engineering Task Force (IETF) Request for Comments (RFC) 2251.

local group   For computers running Microsoft Windows 2000 Professional and member servers, a group that can be granted permissions and rights from its own computer and (if the computer participates in a domain) user accounts and global groups both from its own domain and from trusted domains.

local group policy object   One group policy object (GPO) stored on each computer whether or not the computer is part of an Active Directory environment or a networked environment. Local GPO settings can be overridden by nonlocal GPOs and are the least influential if the computer is in an Active Directory environment. In a non-networked environment (or in a networked environment lacking a Microsoft Windows 2000 domain controller), the local GPO's settings are more important because they are not overridden by nonlocal GPOs.

local user   The user at the computer.

local user account   For Microsoft Windows 2000 Server, a user account provided in a domain for a user whose global account is not in a trusted domain. A local account is not required where trust relationships exist between domains.

local user profile   A user profile that is created automatically on the computer the first time a user logs on to a computer running Microsoft Windows 2000 Professional or Windows 2000 Server.

M

mandatory user profile   A user profile that is not updated when the user logs off. It is downloaded to the user's desktop each time the user logs on and is created by an administrator and assigned to one or more users to create consistent or job-specific user profiles. Only members of the Administrators group can change profiles.

master server   An authoritative Domain Name System (DNS) server for a zone. Master servers can vary and are one of two types (either primary or secondary masters), depending on how the server obtains its zone data.

Microsoft Management Console (MMC)
A framework for hosting administrative tools called *consoles*. A console may contain tools, folders or other containers, World Wide Web pages, and other administrative items. These items are displayed in the left pane of the console, called a *console tree*. A console has one or more windows that can provide views of the console tree. The main MMC window provides commands and tools for authoring consoles. The authoring features of MMC and the console tree itself may be hidden when a console is in User mode.

mixed mode   The default domain mode setting on Microsoft Windows 2000 domain controllers. Mixed mode allows Windows NT and Windows 2000 backup domain controllers to coexist in a domain. Mixed mode does not support the universal and nested group enhancements of Windows 2000. The domain mode setting can be changed to Windows 2000 native mode when all Windows NT domain controllers are removed from a domain.

mounted drive   A drive attached to an empty folder on an NTFS volume. Mounted drives function the same as any other drive, but are assigned a label or name instead of a drive letter. The mounted drive's name is resolved to a full file system path instead of just a drive letter. Members of the Administrators group can use Disk Management to create mounted drives or reassign drive letters.

multimaster replication   A replication model in which any domain controller accepts and replicates directory changes to any other domain controller. This differs from other replication models in which one computer stores the single modifiable copy of the directory and other computers store backup copies.

N

namespace   A set of unique names for resources or items used in a shared computing environment. For Microsoft Management Console (MMC), the namespace is represented by the console tree, which displays all of the snap-ins and resources that are accessible to a console. For Domain Name System (DNS), namespace is the vertical or hierarchical structure of the domain name tree.

native mode   The condition in which all domain controllers in the domain have been upgraded to Microsoft Windows 2000 and an administrator has enabled native mode operation (through Active Directory Users And Computers).

nonauthoritative restore   A restore of a backup copy of a Microsoft Windows 2000 domain controller in which the objects in the restored directory are not treated as authoritative. The restored objects are updated with changes held in other replicas of the restored domain.

noncontainer object   An object that cannot logically contain other objects. For example, a file is a noncontainer object.

nonlocal group policy object   A group policy object (GPO) linked to Active Directory objects (sites, domains, or organizational units) that can be applied to either users or computers. To use nonlocal GPOs, you must have a Microsoft Windows 2000 domain controller installed. Following the properties of Active Directory, nonlocal GPOs are applied hierarchically from the least restrictive group (site) to the most restrictive group (organizational unit) and are cumulative.

nontransitive trust   *See* explicit one-way nontransitive trust.

O

Open Shortest Path First (OSPF)   A routing protocol for IP networks, such as the Internet, that allows a router to calculate the shortest path to each node for sending messages.

operations master roles   A domain controller that has been assigned one or more special roles in an Active Directory domain. The domain controllers assigned these roles perform operations that are single master (not permitted to occur at different places on the network at the same time). Examples of these operations include resource identifier allocation, schema modification, primary domain controller (PDC) election, and certain infrastructure changes. The domain controller that controls the particular operation owns the operations master role for that operation. The ownership of these operations master roles can be transferred to other domain controllers.

organizational unit (OU)   An Active Directory container object used within domains. OUs are logical containers into which you can place users, groups, computers, and other OUs. It can contain objects only from its parent domain. An OU is the smallest scope to which you can apply a group policy or delegate authority.

owner   In Microsoft Windows 2000, the person who controls how permissions are set on objects and can grant permissions to others.

P

parent domain   For Domain Name System (DNS), a domain that is located in the namespace tree directly above other derivative domain names (child domains). For example, microsoft.com would be the parent domain for example.microsoft.com, a child domain.

paging file   A special file on one or more of the hard disks of a computer running Microsoft Windows 2000. Windows 2000 uses virtual memory to store some of the program code and other information in RAM and to temporarily store some of the program code and other information on the computer's hard disks. This increases the amount of available memory on the computer.

partition boot sector   A portion of a hard disk partition that contains information about the disk's file system and a short machine language program that loads the Windows operating system.

permissions inheritance   A mechanism that allows a given access control entry (ACE) to be copied from the container where it was applied to all children of the container. Inheritance can be combined with delegation to grant administrative rights to a whole subtree of the directory in a single update operation.

point-to-point configuration   Dedicated circuits that are also known as private, or leased, lines. They are the most popular wide area network (WAN) communication circuits in use today. The carrier guarantees full-duplex bandwidth by setting up a permanent link from each endpoint, using bridges and routers to connect LANs through the circuits. *See also* Point-to-Point Protocol (PPP), Point-to-Point Tunneling Protocol (PPTP).

Point-to-Point Protocol (PPP)   A data-link protocol for transmitting TCP/IP packets over dial-up telephone connections, such as between a computer and the Internet. PPP was developed by the Internet Engineering Task Force (IETF) in 1991.

Point-to-Point Tunneling Protocol (PPTP)   Networking technology that supports multiprotocol virtual private networks (VPNs), enabling remote users to access corporate networks securely across the Internet or other networks by dialing into an Internet Service Provider (ISP) or by connecting directly to the Internet. The PPTP tunnels, or encapsulates, Internet Protocol (IP), Internetwork Packet Exchange (IPX), or NetBEUI traffic inside of IP packets. This means that users can remotely run applications that are dependent on particular network protocols.

policy   The mechanism by which desktop settings are configured automatically, as defined by the administrator. Depending on context, this can refer to Microsoft Windows 2000 Group Policy, Windows NT 4.0 system policy, or a specific setting in a Group Policy object (GPO).

Portable Operating System Interface for UNIX (POSIX)   An Institute of Electrical and Electronics Engineers (IEEE) standard that defines a set of operating system services. Programs that adhere to the POSIX standard can be easily ported from one system to another. POSIX was based on UNIX system services, but was created in a way that allows it to be implemented by other operating systems.

POSIX   *See* Portable Operating System Interface for UNIX (POSIX).

PPP   *See* Point-to-Point Protocol (PPP).

PPTP   *See* Point-to-Point Tunneling Protocol (PPTP).

primary domain controller (PDC)   In a Microsoft Windows NT Server 4.0 or earlier domain, the computer running Windows NT Server that authenticates domain logons and maintains the directory database for a domain. The PDC tracks changes made to accounts of all computers on a domain. It is the only computer to receive these changes directly. A domain has only one PDC. In Microsoft Windows 2000, one of the domain controllers in each domain is identified as the PDC for compatibility with Windows NT 4.0 and earlier versions of Windows NT.

primary master   An authoritative Domain Name System (DNS) server for a zone that can be used as a point of update for the zone. Only primary masters can be updated directly to process zone updates, which include adding, removing, or modifying resource records that are stored as zone data. Primary masters are also used as the first sources for replicating the zone to other DNS servers.

primary partition   A volume you create using unallocated space on a basic disk. Microsoft Windows 2000 and other operating systems can start from a primary partition. You can create up to four primary partitions on a basic disk, or three primary partitions and an extended partition. Primary partitions can be created only on basic disks and cannot be subpartitioned.

primary zone database file   The master zone database file. Changes to a zone, such as adding domains or hosts, are performed on the server that contains the primary zone database file.

print device   The hardware device that produces printed documents.

printer   The software interface between the operating system and the print device. The printer defines where a document will go to reach the print device, when it will go, and how various other aspects of the printing process will be handled.

Q

Quality of Service (QoS)   A set of quality assurance standards and mechanisms for data transmission that is implemented in Microsoft Windows 2000.

R

redundant array of independent disks (RAID) A standardization of fault-tolerant options in five levels. The levels offer various combinations of performance, reliability, and cost. Formerly known as redundant array of inexpensive disks.

Remote Access Server   Any Microsoft Windows 2000–based computer configured to accept remote access connections.

Remote Authentication Dial-In User Service (RADIUS)   A security authentication protocol widely used by Internet Service Providers (ISPs). RADIUS provides authentication and accounting services for distributed dial-up networking.

Remote Installation Services (RIS)   Software services that allow an administrator to set up new client computers remotely, without having to visit each client. The target clients must support remote booting.

roaming user profile   A server-based user profile that is downloaded to the local computer when a user logs on, and is updated both locally and on the server when the user logs off. A roaming user profile is available from the server when logging on to any computer running Microsoft Windows 2000 Professional or Windows 2000 Server. When logging on, the user can use the local user profile if it is more current than the copy on the server.

S

schema　A database description to the database management system that contains a formal definition of the contents and structure of Active Directory, including all attributes, classes, and class properties. For each object class, the schema defines which attributes an instance of the class must have, which additional attributes it can have, and which object class can be a parent of the current object class.

schema master　The domain controller assigned to control all updates to the schema within a forest. At any time, there can be only one schema master in the forest.

security group　Used to assign permissions to gain access to resources. Programs that are designed to search Active Directory can also use security groups for nonsecurity-related purposes, such as retrieving user information for use in a Web application. A security group also has all the capabilities of a distribution group. Microsoft Windows 2000 uses only security groups.

security identifier (SID)　A unique number that identifies user, group, and computer accounts. Every account on your network is issued a unique SID when the account is first created. Internal processes in Microsoft Windows 2000 refer to an account's SID rather than the account's user or group name. If you create an account, delete it, and then create an account with the same user name, the new account will not have the rights or permissions previously granted to the old account because the accounts have different SID numbers.

security template　A physical representation of a security configuration; a single file where a group of security settings is stored. Locating all security settings in one place eases security administration. Each template is saved as a text-based .inf file. This allows you to copy, paste, import, or export some or all of the template attributes.

shared resource　Any device, data, or program that is used by more than one other device or program. For Microsoft Windows 2000, shared resources refer to any resource that is made available to network users, such as folders, files, printers, and named pipes. A shared resource can also refer to a resource on a server that is available to network users.

snap-in　A type of tool you can add to a console supported by Microsoft Management Console (MMC). A standalone snap-in can be added by itself; an extension snap-in can only be added to extend the function of another snap-in.

software distribution point　In Software Installation, a network location from which users are able to get the software that they need.

Software Installation　An extension within Group Policy that is the administrator's primary tool for managing software within an organization. Software Installation works in conjunction with group policy and Active Directory directory service, establishing a Group Policy–based software management system that allows you to centrally manage the initial deployment of software, mandatory and nonmandatory upgrades, patches, quick fixes, and the removal of software.

Start-of-Authority (SOA) resource record
A record that indicates the starting point or original point of authority for information stored in a zone. The SOA resource record is the first resource record created when adding a new zone. It also contains several parameters used by other computers that use Domain Name System (DNS) to determine how long they will use information for the zone and how often updates are required.

system partition The partition that contains the hardware-specific files needed to load Microsoft Windows 2000 (for example, NTLDR, OSLOADER, BOOT.INI, NTDETECT.COM). The system partition can be, but does not have to be, the same as the boot partition.

systemroot The path and folder name where the Microsoft Windows 2000 system files are located. Typically, this is C:\Winnt, although you can designate a different drive or folder when you install Windows 2000. You can use the value %systemroot% to replace the actual location of the folder that contains the Windows 2000 system files. To identify your systemroot folder, click Start, click Run, and then type **%systemroot%**.

system volume The volume that contains the hardware-specific files needed to load Microsoft Windows 2000. The system volume can be, but does not have to be, the same volume as the boot volume.

SYSVOL A shared directory that stores the server copy of the domain's public files, which are replicated among all domain controllers in the domain.

T

Task Manager A Microsoft Windows 2000 utility that provides information about programs and processes running on the computer. Using Task Manager, you can end or run programs, end processes, and display a dynamic overview of your computer's performance.

Task Scheduler A tool used to schedule programs and batch files to run once, at regular intervals, or at specific times.

Terminal services Software services that allow client applications to be run on a server so that client computers can function as terminals rather than as independent systems. The server provides a multisession environment and runs the Microsoft Windows–based programs being used on the clients.

total cost of ownership (TCO) The total amount of money and time associated with purchasing computer hardware and software and deploying, configuring, and maintaining the hardware and software. TCO includes hardware and software updates, training, maintenance, administration, and technical support.

tree A set of Microsoft Windows 2000 domains connected together via a two-way transitive trust, sharing a common schema, configuration, and global catalog. The domains must form a contiguous hierarchical namespace such that if microsoft.com is the root of the tree, example.microsoft.com is a child of microsoft.com, another.example.microsoft.com is a child of example.microsoft.com, and so on.

trust relationship A logical relationship established between domains to allow pass-through authentication, in which a trusting domain honors the logon authentications of a trusted domain. User accounts and global groups defined in a trusted domain can be given rights and permissions in a trusting domain, even though the user accounts or groups do not exist in the trusting domain's directory.

tunnel A logical connection over which data is encapsulated. Typically, both encapsulation and encryption are performed and the tunnel is a private, secure link between a remote user or host and a private network.

U

universal group   A security or distribution group that can be used anywhere in the domain tree or forest. A universal group can have members from any Microsoft Windows 2000 domain in the domain tree or forest. It can also include other universal groups, global groups, and accounts from any domain in the domain tree or forest. Rights and permissions must be assigned on a per-domain basis, but can be assigned at any domain in the domain tree or forest. Universal groups can be members of domain local groups and other universal groups but cannot be members of global groups. Universal groups appear in the global catalog and should contain primarily global groups.

universal naming convention (UNC) name
The full Microsoft Windows 2000 name of a resource on a network. It conforms to the *servername**sharename* syntax, where servername is the name of the server and sharename is the name of the shared resource. UNC names of directories or files can also include the directory path under the share name, with the following syntax: *servername*\ *sharename**directory**filename*.

user account   A record that consists of all the information that defines a user to Microsoft Windows 2000. This includes the user name and password required for the user to log on, the groups in which the user account has membership, and the rights and permissions the user has for using the computer and network and accessing their resources. For Windows 2000 Professional and member servers, user accounts are managed with the Local Users and Groups console. For Windows 2000 Server domain controllers, user accounts are managed with the Active Directory Users And Computers console.

user groups   Groups of users who meet online or in person to discuss installation, administration, and other network challenges for the purpose of sharing and drawing on each other's expertise in developing ideas and solutions.

user mode   A console mode that does not enable full access to all Microsoft Management Console (MMC) functionality. There are three types of User modes that allow different levels of access and functionality: Full Access; Limited Access, Multiple Windows; and Limited Access, Single Window.

user name   A unique name identifying a user account to Microsoft Windows 2000. An account's user name must be unique among the other group names and user names within its own domain or workgroup.

user principal name (UPN)   This consists of a user account name (sometimes referred to as the *user logon name*) and a domain name identifying the domain in which the user account is located. This is the standard usage for logging on to a Microsoft Windows 2000 domain. The format is: user@domain.com (as for an e-mail address).

user profile   A profile that defines the Microsoft Windows 2000 environment that is loaded by the system when a user logs on. It includes all the user-specific settings of a user's Windows 2000 environment, such as program items, screen colors, network connections, printer connections, mouse settings, and window size and position.

user rights   Tasks a user is permitted to perform on a computer system or domain, such as backing up files and folders, adding or deleting users in a workstation or domain, and shutting down a computer system. Rights can be granted to groups or to user accounts, but are best reserved for use by groups. User rights are set in group policy.

user rights policy Security settings that manage the assignment of rights to groups and user accounts.

V

virtual private network (VPN) The extension of a private network that encompasses encapsulated, encrypted, and authenticated links across shared or public networks. VPN connections can provide remote access and routed connections to private networks over the Internet.

volume A portion of a physical disk that functions as though it were a physically separate disk. In My Computer and Microsoft Windows Explorer, volumes appear as local disks such as C: or D:.

volume set A partition consisting of disk space on one or more physical disks that was created with Microsoft Windows NT 4.0 or earlier. You can delete volume sets only with Windows 2000. To create new volumes that span multiple disks, use spanned volumes on dynamic disks.

W

Windows 2000 Advanced Server A powerful departmental and application server that provides rich network operations system (NOS) and Internet services. Advanced Server supports large physical memories, clustering, and load balancing.

Windows 2000 Datacenter Server The most powerful and functional server operating system in the Microsoft Windows 2000 family. It is optimized for large data warehouses, econometric analysis, large-scale simulations in science and engineering, and server consolidation projects.

Windows 2000 Executive A component that performs most of the input/output (I/O) and object management, including security. It does not perform screen and keyboard I/O; the Microsoft Win32 subsystem performs these functions. The Microsoft Windows 2000 Executive contains the Windows 2000 kernel mode components.

Windows 2000 Professional A high-performance, secure network client computer and corporate desktop operating system that includes the best features of Microsoft Windows 98, significantly extending the manageability, reliability, security, and performance of Windows NT Workstation 4.0. Microsoft Windows 2000 Professional can be used alone as a desktop operating system, networked in a peer-to-peer workgroup environment, or used as a workstation in a Windows 2000 Server domain environment.

Windows 2000 Server A file, print, and applications server, as well as a Web server platform that contains all of the features of Microsoft Windows 2000 Professional plus many new server-specific functions. This product is ideal for small- to medium-sized enterprise application deployments, Web servers, workgroups, and branch offices.

Windows Installer An applications that installs software packaged in Microsoft Windows Installer files.

workgroup A simple grouping of computers, intended only to help users find such things as printers and shared folders within that group. Workgroups in Windows 2000 do not offer the centralized user accounts and authentication offered by domains.

Z

zone   In a Domain Name System (DNS) database, a subtree of the DNS database that is administered as a single separate entity, a DNS server. This administrative unit can consist of a single domain or a domain with subdomains. A DNS zone administrator sets up one or more name servers for the zone.

zone database file   The file where name-to-IP-address mappings for a zone are stored.

zone transfer   The process by which Domain Name System (DNS) servers interact to maintain and synchronize authoritative name data. When a DNS server is configured as a secondary master for a zone, it periodically queries another DNS server configured as its source for the zone. If the version of the zone kept by the source is different, the secondary master server pulls zone data from its source DNS server to synchronize zone data.

Index